Great Events from History

The 19th Century

1801-1900

Great Events from History

The 19th Century

1801-1900

Volume 3
1864-1890

Editor
John Powell
Oklahoma Baptist University

Salem Press
Pasadena, California Hackensack, New Jersey

Cover photos (pictured clockwise, from top left): Rodin's *The Thinker* (The Granger Collection, New York); Immigrants on ship, 1887 (The Granger Collection, New York); Shaka Zulu (The Granger Collection, New York); Hokusai print (The Granger Collection, New York); Eiffel Tower (PhotoDisc); Mexican flag (The Granger Collection, New York)

∞ The paper used in these volumes conforms to the American National Standard for Permanence of Paper for Printed Library Materials, Z39.48-1992 (R1997).

Some of the essays in this work originally appeared in the following Salem Press sets: *Chronology of European History: 15,000 B.C. to 1997* (1997, edited by John Powell; associate editors, E. G. Weltin, José M. Sánchez, Thomas P. Neill, and Edward P. Keleher); *Great Events from History: North American Series, Revised Edition* (1997, edited by Frank N. Magill); *Great Events from History II: Science and Technology* (1991, edited by Frank N. Magill); *Great Events from History II: Human Rights* (1992, edited by Frank N. Magill); *Great Events from History II: Arts and Culture* (1993, edited by Frank N. Magill); and *Great Events from History II: Business and Commerce* (1994, edited by Frank N. Magill). New material has been added.

Library of Congress Cataloging-in-Publication Data

Great events from history. The 19th century, 1801-1900 / editor, John Powell.
p. cm.
Some of the essays in this work appeared in various other Salem Press sets.
Includes bibliographical references and index.
ISBN-13: 978-1-58765-297-4 (set : alk. paper)
ISBN-10: 1-58765-297-8 (set : alk. paper)
ISBN-13: 978-1-58765-300-1 (v. 3 : alk. paper)
ISBN-10: 1-58765-300-1 (v. 3 : alk. paper)
[etc.]
1. Nineteenth century. I. Powell, John, 1954- II. Title: 19th century, 1801-1900. III. Title: Nineteenth century, 1801-1900.
D358.G74 2006
909.81—dc22

2006019789

First Printing

PRINTED IN THE UNITED STATES OF AMERICA

Contents

1860's *(continued)*

1870's

1880's

1890's

Keyword List of Contents

Abdelkader Leads Algeria Against France (1832-1847) . . . 508
Abdicates, Hawaii's Last Monarch (Jan. 24, 1895) . . . 1797
Abel and Takamine Isolate Adrenaline (1897-1901) . . . 1869
Abolish Suttee in India, British (Dec. 4, 1829) . . . 428
Abolished Throughout the British Empire, Slavery Is (Aug. 28, 1833) . . . 533
Abu Simbel, Burckhardt Discovers Egypt's (Mar. 22, 1812) . . . 163
Academy Is Established, U.S. Military (Mar. 16, 1802) . . . 35
Acquires Oregon Territory, United States (June 15, 1846) . . . 718
Acquires the Cape Colony, Britain (Aug. 13, 1814) . . . 213
Act, Arthur Signs the Chinese Exclusion (May 9, 1882) . . . 1558
Act, British North America (July 1, 1867) . . . 1219
Act, British Parliament Passes Municipal Corporations (Sept. 9, 1835) . . . 575
Act, British Parliament Passes the Factory (1833) . . . 525
Act, British Parliament Passes the Matrimonial Causes (Aug. 28, 1857) . . . 952
Act, Canada's Indian (1876) . . . 1437
Act, Congress Passes Dingley Tariff (July 24, 1897) . . . 1880
Act, Congress Passes Indian Removal (May 28, 1830) . . . 460
Act, Congress Passes the Kansas-Nebraska (May 30, 1854) . . . 891
Act, Grant Signs Indian Appropriation (Mar. 3, 1871) . . . 1355
Act, Harrison Signs the Sherman Antitrust (July 20, 1890) . . . 1712
Act, Interstate Commerce (Feb. 4, 1887) . . . 1655
Act, Lincoln Signs the Homestead (May 20, 1862) . . . 1064
Act, Lincoln Signs the Morrill Land Grant (July 2, 1862) . . . 1066
Act Erodes Indian Tribal Unity, General Allotment (Feb. 8, 1887) . . . 1657
Act Fosters Canadian Settlement, Dominion Lands (1872) . . . 1369
Act of 1820, Congress Passes Land (Apr. 24, 1820) . . . 328
Act of 1832, British Parliament Passes the Reform (June 4, 1832) . . . 514
Act of 1841, Congress Passes Preemption (Sept. 4, 1841) . . . 653
Act of 1866, Civil Rights (Apr. 9, 1866) . . . 1175
Act of 1867, British Parliament Passes the Reform (Aug., 1867) . . . 1222
Act of 1884, British Parliament Passes the Franchise (Dec. 6, 1884) . . . 1627
Act Reforms the Federal Civil Service, Pendleton (Jan. 16, 1883) . . . 1577
Acts, British Parliament Passes the Six (Dec. 11-30, 1819) . . . 305
Acts, British Parliament Repeals the Combination (1824) . . . 365
Acts, Congress Passes the National Bank (Feb. 25, 1863-June 3, 1864) . . . 1093
Adams-Onís Treaty Gives the United States Florida (Feb. 22, 1819) . . . 293
Addams Opens Chicago's Hull-House (Sept. 18, 1889) . . . 1692
Administration, Scandals Rock the Grant (Sept. 24, 1869-1877) . . . 1296
Adopts a New Constitution, Japan (Feb. 11, 1889) . . . 1683
Adopts Gas Lighting, Britain (1802) . . . 29
Adrenaline, Abel and Takamine Isolate (1897-1901) . . . 1869
Adrianople, Treaty of (Sept. 24, 1829) . . . 426
Advance Proslavery Arguments, Southerners (c. 1830-1865) . . . 442
Advances His Theory of Positivism, Comte (1851-1854) . . . 833
Advances the Cellular Theory of Immunity, Metchnikoff (1882-1901) . . . 1545
Adventures of Huckleberry Finn, Twain Publishes (Dec., 1884-Feb., 1885) . . . 1624
Advocates Artificial Fertilizers, Liebig (1840) . . . 638
Aesthetic Movement Arises (1870's) . . . 1310
Affair, Dreyfus (October, 1894-July, 1906) . . . 1788

Afghan War, First (1839-1842) 617
Africa, Berlin Conference Lays Groundwork for the Partition of (Nov. 15, 1884-Feb. 26, 1885) 1619
Africa, Exploration of East (1848-1889). 756
Africa, Exploration of North (1822-1874) 345
Africa, Exploration of West (May 4, 1805-1830) 80
Africa's Congo Basin, Exploration of (1873-1880) 1382
Africa's Great Trek Begins, South (1835) 563
African American University Opens, First (Jan. 1, 1857) 936
African Methodist Episcopal Church Is Founded (Apr. 9, 1816). 257
African Resistance in Rhodesia, British Subdue (October, 1893-October, 1897) 1763
African Slaves, Congress Bans Importation of (Mar. 2, 1807) 103
African War, South (Oct. 11, 1899-May 31, 1902) 1932
Afternoon of a Faun Premieres, Debussy's *Prelude to the* (Dec. 22, 1894) 1791
Age, Beethoven's *Eroica* Symphony Introduces the Romantic (Apr. 7, 1805) 78
Age, *La Sylphide* Inaugurates Romantic Ballet's Golden (Mar. 12, 1832). 511
Age of Flamenco Begins, Golden (c. 1869) . . . 1282
Air Brake, Westinghouse Patents His (Apr., 1869) 1287
Akron Woman's Rights Convention (May 28-29, 1851) 843
Alaska to the United States, Russia Sells (Mar. 30, 1867) 1213
Algeria, France Conquers (June 14-July 5, 1830) 464
Algeria Against France, Abdelkader Leads (1832-1847). 508
Alliance, Bakunin Founds the Social Democratic (1868) 1235
Alliance, Franco-Russian (Jan. 4, 1894) 1776
Alliance Is Formed, Triple (May 20, 1882). . . . 1561
Allotment Act Erodes Indian Tribal Unity, General (Feb. 8, 1887) 1657
Amalgamates Kimberley Diamondfields, Rhodes (Mar. 13, 1888) 1674
Amendment, Suffragists Protest the Fourteenth (May 10, 1866) 1181
Amendment Is Ratified, Fourteenth (July 9, 1868) 1261
Amendment Is Ratified, Thirteenth (Dec. 6, 1865). 1167
Amendment Is Ratified, Twelfth (Sept. 25, 1804) 69
America, Establishment of the Confederate States of (Feb. 8, 1861) 1022
America, Professional Theaters Spread Throughout (c. 1801-1850) 14
America, Tocqueville Visits (May, 1831-Feb., 1832) 493
America Wins the First America's Cup Race (Aug. 22, 1851). 846
American Anti-Slavery Society Is Founded (Dec., 1833). 542
American Bible Society Is Founded (May 8, 1816) 260
American Buffalo Slaughter, Great (c. 1871-1883) 1343
American Circus, Barnum Creates the First Modern (Apr. 10, 1871). 1360
American Congress, First Pan- (October, 1889-Apr., 1890) 1695
American Dictionary of English, Webster Publishes the First (Nov., 1828) 418
American Era of "Old" Immigration (1840's-1850's) 631
American Federation of Labor Is Founded (Dec. 8, 1886) 1652
American Fur Company Is Chartered (Apr. 6, 1808) 119
American Library Association Is Founded (Oct. 4-6, 1876) 1467
American Literature, Irving's *Sketch Book* Transforms (1819-1820) 288
American Literature Flourishes, Brahmin School of (1880's). 1520
American Migration Begins, Westward (c. 1815-1830) 221
American Renaissance in Literature (c. 1830's-1860's) 435
American Southwest, Pike Explores the (July 15, 1806-July 1, 1807) 90
American War, Spanish- (Apr. 24-Dec. 10, 1898) 1903
American West, Frémont Explores the (May, 1842-1854) 660
American West, Powell Publishes His Report on the (1879) 1504
American Whig Party, Clay Begins (Apr. 14, 1834) 551

America's "New" Immigration Era Begins (1892) 1730
America's Cup Race, *America* Wins the First (Aug. 22, 1851) 846
Amerika Shipping Line Begins, Hamburg- (1847) 740
Amistad Slave Revolt (July 2, 1839) 622
Ampère Reveals Magnetism's Relationship to Electricity (Nov. 6, 1820) 334
Amsterdam, First Birth Control Clinic Opens in (1882) 1542
Analysis of Logic, Boole Publishes *The Mathematical* (1847) 737
Ancient Troy, Schliemann Excavates (Apr., 1870-1873) 1321
Andersen Publishes His First Fairy Tales (May 8, 1835) 570
Andrew Johnson, Impeachment of (Feb. 24-May 26, 1868) 1245
Anesthesia Is Demonstrated, Safe Surgical (Oct. 16, 1846) 735
Anglo-Sikh War, Second (Apr., 1848-Mar., 1849) 779
Announces Closing of the Frontier, U.S. Census Bureau (1890) 1705
Announces His Discovery of the Tuberculosis Bacillus, Koch (Mar. 24, 1882) 1550
Antarctic, Europeans Explore the (1820-early 1840's) 317
Anthony Is Tried for Voting (June 17-18, 1873) 1404
Anti-Irish Riots Erupt in Philadelphia (May 6-July 5, 1844) 681
Anti-Japanese Yellow Peril Campaign Begins (May 4, 1892) 1742
Antiobscenity Law, Congress Passes the Comstock (Mar. 3, 1873) 1394
Antiquities, Stephens Begins Uncovering Mayan (Nov., 1839) 628
Antiseptic Procedures, Semmelweis Develops (May, 1847) 745
Antiseptic Surgery, Lister Publishes His Theory on (1867) 1204
Anti-Slavery Society Is Founded, American (Dec., 1833) 542
Anti-Socialist Law, Germany Passes (Oct. 19, 1878) 1499
Antitoxin, Behring Discovers the Diphtheria (Dec. 11, 1890) 1715
Antitrust Act, Harrison Signs the Sherman (July 20, 1890) 1712
Apache and Navajo War (Apr. 30, 1860-1865) 1005
Apache Wars (Feb. 6, 1861-Sept. 4, 1886) 1019
Appears on U.S. Coins, "In God We Trust" (Apr. 22, 1864) 1119
Appears to Bernadette Soubirous, Virgin Mary (Feb. 11-July 16, 1858) 958
Appomattox and Assassination of Lincoln, Surrender at (Apr. 9 and 14, 1865) 1146
Appropriation Act, Grant Signs Indian (Mar. 3, 1871) 1355
Arabia, Exploration of (1814-1879) 199
Arabic Literary Renaissance (19th cent.) 1
Arc Lamp, Davy Develops the (c. 1801-1810) . . . 11
Archaeopteryx Lithographica Is Discovered (1861) 1014
Arguments, Southerners Advance Proslavery (c. 1830-1865) 442
Arises, Aesthetic Movement (1870's) 1310
Arises, China's Self-Strengthening Movement (1860's) 995
Arises in New England, Transcendental Movement (1836) 581
Armenians, Ottomans Attempt to Exterminate (1894-1896) 1773
Army, Booth Establishes the Salvation (July, 1865) 1155
Army Besieges Paris, Prussian (Sept. 20, 1870-Jan. 28, 1871) 1331
Arnold Reforms Rugby School (1828-1842) . . . 406
Aroostook War (1838-1839) 600
Art Movement, Courbet Establishes Realist (1855) 911
Art Opens, Metropolitan Museum of (Feb. 20, 1872) 1372
Art Theater Is Founded, Moscow (Oct. 14, 1898) 1910
Arthur," Tennyson Publishes "Morte d' (1842) 655
Arthur Signs the Chinese Exclusion Act (May 9, 1882) 1558
Articulates "Open Door" Policy Toward China, Hay (Sept. 6, 1899-July 3, 1900) 1928
Articulates the Monroe Doctrine, President Monroe (Dec. 2, 1823) 361
Articulation of Quantum Theory (Dec. 14, 1900) 1980

Artificial Fertilizers, Liebig Advocates (1840) . . . 638
Arts and Crafts Movement, New Guilds Promote the (1884) . . . 1597
Ashanti War, Second British- (Jan. 22, 1873-Feb. 13, 1874) . . . 1389
Ashburton Treaty Settles Maine's Canadian Border, Webster- (Aug. 9, 1842) . . . 666
Asia, Przhevalsky Explores Central (1871-1885) . . . 1346
"Aspirin" Is Registered as a Trade Name (Jan. 23, 1897) . . . 1875
Assassination of Lincoln, Surrender at Appomattox and (Apr. 9 and 14, 1865) . . . 1146
Assassinations, London's Cato Street Conspirators Plot (Feb. 23, 1820) . . . 323
Association Forms, San Francisco's Chinese Six Companies (Nov. 12, 1882) . . . 1569
Association Is Founded, American Library (Oct. 4-6, 1876) . . . 1467
Associations Begin Forming, Woman Suffrage (May, 1869) . . . 1290
Associations Unite, Women's Rights (Feb. 17-18, 1890) . . . 1709
Assyrian Ruins, Layard Explores and Excavates (1839-1847) . . . 619
Asteroid Is Discovered, First (Jan. 1, 1801) . . . 17
Astorian Expeditions Explore the Pacific Northwest Coast (Sept. 8, 1810-May, 1812) . . . 134
At the Moulin Rouge, Toulouse-Lautrec Paints (1892-1895) . . . 1734
Atlanta Compromise Speech, Washington's (Sept. 18, 1895) . . . 1811
Atlantic, *Savannah* Is the First Steamship to Cross the (May 22-June 20, 1819) . . . 303
Atomic Theory of Matter, Dalton Formulates the (1803-1808) . . . 43
Attempt to Exterminate Armenians, Ottomans (1894-1896) . . . 1773
Attempts to Reach the North Pole, Nansen (1893-1896) . . . 1754
Ausgleich, Austrian (May 29, 1867) . . . 1216
Austerlitz, Battle of (Dec. 2, 1805) . . . 86
Australia, Flinders Explores (Dec. 6, 1801-Aug., 1803) . . . 26
Australia, Is Founded, Melbourne, (Aug. 16, 1835) . . . 573
Australia, Last Convicts Land in Western (1868) . . . 1238
Austria and Prussia's Seven Weeks' War (June 15-Aug. 23, 1866) . . . 1190
Austrian Ausgleich (May 29, 1867) . . . 1216
Automatic Dial Telephone System, Strowger Patents (Mar. 11, 1891) . . . 1724
Automobile, Benz Patents the First Practical (Jan. 29, 1886) . . . 1640

Babbage Designs a Mechanical Calculator (1819-1833) . . . 291
Bacillus, Koch Announces His Discovery of the Tuberculosis (Mar. 24, 1882) . . . 1550
Bahāʾīism Takes Form (1863) . . . 1078
Bakunin Founds the Social Democratic Alliance (1868) . . . 1235
Balaklava, Battle of (Oct. 25, 1854) . . . 900
Ballet's Golden Age, *La Sylphide* Inaugurates Romantic (Mar. 12, 1832) . . . 511
Baltimore and Ohio Railroad Opens (Jan. 7, 1830) . . . 447
Bank Acts, Congress Passes the National (Feb. 25, 1863-June 3, 1864) . . . 1093
Bank of the United States, Jackson Vetoes Rechartering of the (July 10, 1832) . . . 518
Bank of the United States Is Chartered, Second (Apr., 1816) . . . 255
Bans Importation of African Slaves, Congress (Mar. 2, 1807) . . . 103
Barbed Wire, Glidden Patents (Nov. 24, 1874) . . . 1416
Barber of Seville Debuts, Rossini's *The* (Feb. 20, 1816) . . . 252
Barbizon School of Landscape Painting Flourishes (c. 1830-1870) . . . 445
Barcelona's Templo Expiatorio de la Sagrada Família, Gaudí Begins (Nov. 3, 1883) . . . 1592
Barnum Creates the First Modern American Circus (Apr. 10, 1871) . . . 1360
Baseball Begins, Modern (c. 1845) . . . 693
Baseball's First Professional Club Forms (1869) . . . 1276
Basin, Exploration of Africa's Congo (1873-1880) . . . 1382
Basketball, Naismith Invents (1891) . . . 1721
Basuto War (1865-1868) . . . 1141
Battle of Austerlitz (Dec. 2, 1805) . . . 86
Battle of Balaklava (Oct. 25, 1854) . . . 900
Battle of Borodino (Sept. 7, 1812) . . . 176
Battle of Bull Run, First (July 21, 1861) . . . 1045
Battle of Chapultepec (Sept. 12-13, 1847) . . . 751

Battle of Könniggrätz (July 3, 1866) 1193
Battle of Leipzig (Oct. 16-19, 1813) 191
Battle of New Orleans (Jan. 8, 1815) 227
Battle of Palo Alto (May 8, 1846) 707
Battle of Salamanca (July 22, 1812) 173
Battle of Sedan (Sept. 1, 1870) 1328
Battle of Solferino (June 24, 1859). 976
Battle of Tel el Kebir (Sept. 13, 1882) 1566
Battle of the Little Bighorn (June 25, 1876) . . . 1454
Battle of the *Monitor* and the *Virginia* (Mar. 9, 1862) 1061
Battle of the Thames (Oct. 5, 1813) 188
Battle of Tippecanoe (Nov. 7, 1811) 157
Battle of Trafalgar (Oct. 21, 1805) 83
Battle of Waterloo (June 18, 1815). 243
Battles of Gettysburg, Vicksburg, and Chattanooga (July 1-Nov. 25, 1863) 1102
Battles of Isandlwana and Rorke's Drift (Jan. 22-23, 1879) 1507
Bay Rebellion, Morant (Oct. 7-12, 1865). 1161
Beethoven's *Eroica* Symphony Introduces the Romantic Age (Apr. 7, 1805) 78
Beethoven's Ninth Symphony, First Performance of (May 7, 1824) 380
Begin Forming, Woman Suffrage Associations (May, 1869) 1290
Begin Immigrating to California, Chinese (1849). 793
Begin Migration to Utah, Mormons (Feb. 4, 1846) 703
Begin Modernization of Korean Government, Kabo Reforms (July 8, 1894-Jan. 1, 1896) 1782
Begin Ravaging Easter Island, Slave Traders (Nov., 1862). 1076
Begin Settling Western Canada, Immigrant Farmers (1896) 1831
Begins, America's "New" Immigration Era (1892) 1730
Begins, Anti-Japanese Yellow Peril Campaign (May 4, 1892) 1742
Begins, California Gold Rush (Jan. 24, 1848) . . . 763
Begins, Clipper Ship Era (c. 1845). 690
Begins, Commercial Oil Drilling (Aug. 27, 1859) 985
Begins, Fraser River Gold Rush (Mar. 23, 1858) 960
Begins, Golden Age of Flamenco (c. 1869) . . . 1282
Begins, Hamburg-Amerika Shipping Line (1847). 740
Begins, Klondike Gold Rush (Aug. 17, 1896) 1857
Begins, Modern Baseball (c. 1845) 693
Begins, Naturalist Movement (c. 1865). 1138
Begins, Oxford Movement (July 14, 1833) 530
Begins, Panic of 1837 (Mar. 17, 1837). 591
Begins, Pre-Raphaelite Brotherhood (Fall, 1848) 790
Begins, Scramble for Chinese Concessions (Nov. 14, 1897) 1888
Begins, Second Riel Rebellion (Mar. 19, 1885) 1633
Begins, South Africa's Great Trek (1835) 563
Begins, Westward American Migration (c. 1815-1830) 221
Begins American Whig Party, Clay (Apr. 14, 1834) 551
Begins Barcelona's Templo Expiatorio de la Sagrada Família, Gaudí (Nov. 3, 1883) 1592
Begins Colonizing Tasmania, Great Britain (Sept. 7, 1803) 55
Begins Developing Germ Theory and Microbiology, Pasteur (1857) 933
Begins London Exile, Mazzini (Jan. 12, 1837) 589
Begins Publication, *Cherokee Phoenix* (Feb. 21, 1828) 408
Begins Publishing *The Liberator*, Garrison (Jan. 1, 1831) 487
Begins Trigonometrical Survey of India, Lambton (Apr. 10, 1802) 40
Begins Uncovering Mayan Antiquities, Stephens (Nov., 1839) 628
Begins Violent Eruption, Tambora Volcano (Apr. 5, 1815). 234
Behring Discovers the Diphtheria Antitoxin (Dec. 11, 1890) 1715
Beijerinck Discovers Viruses (1898) 1892
Belgian Revolution (Aug. 25, 1830-May 21, 1833) 474
Bell Demonstrates the Telephone (June 25, 1876) 1457
Benz Patents the First Practical Automobile (Jan. 29, 1886). 1640
Bequeaths Funds for the Nobel Prizes, Nobel (Nov. 27, 1895) 1817
Berlin, Congress of (June 13-July 13, 1878) 1492

Berlin Conference Lays Groundwork for the Partition of Africa (Nov. 15, 1884-Feb. 26, 1885) . . . 1619
Bernadette Soubirous, Virgin Mary Appears to (Feb. 11-July 16, 1858) . . . 958
Besieges Paris, Prussian Army (Sept. 20, 1870-Jan. 28, 1871) . . . 1331
Bessemer Patents Improved Steel-Processing Method (1855) . . . 909
Bible and Tract Society Is Founded, Watch Tower (1870-1871) . . . 1316
Bible Society Is Founded, American (May 8, 1816) . . . 260
Bible Society Is Founded, British and Foreign (1804) . . . 57
Biedermeier Furniture Style Becomes Popular (c. 1815-1848) . . . 225
Bighorn, Battle of the Little (June 25, 1876) . . . 1454
Bill, Indian Legislative Council Enacts the Ilbert (Jan. 25, 1884) . . . 1606
Biogeography, Wallace's Expeditions Give Rise to (1854-1862) . . . 885
Birth Control Clinic Opens in Amsterdam, First (1882) . . . 1542
Birth of the Ku Klux Klan (1866) . . . 1169
Birth of the Penny Press (Sept. 3, 1833) . . . 536
Birth of the People's Party (July 4-5, 1892) . . . 1745
Birth of the Republican Party (July 6, 1854) . . . 894
Bismarck Becomes Prussia's Minister-President (Sept. 24, 1862) . . . 1073
Bismarck Introduces Social Security Programs in Germany (1881-1889) . . . 1534
Bizet's *Carmen* Premieres in Paris (Mar. 3, 1875) . . . 1420
Bjerknes Founds Scientific Weather Forecasting (July, 1897-July, 1904) . . . 1877
Black Code, Mississippi Enacts First Post-Civil War (Nov. 24, 1865) . . . 1164
Black Codes, Ohio Enacts the First (Jan., 1804) . . . 62
Black Voters, Mississippi Constitution Disfranchises (1890) . . . 1702
Blair Patents His First Seed Planter (Oct. 14, 1834) . . . 557
Blanc Publishes *The Organization of Labour* (1839) . . . 610
Bleak House, Dickens Publishes (Mar., 1852-Sept., 1853) . . . 855
Bleeding Kansas (May, 1856-Aug., 1858) . . . 919
Bloody Island Massacre, California's (May 6, 1850) . . . 820
Boer War, First (Dec. 16, 1880-Mar. 6, 1881) . . . 1531
Bolívar's Military Campaigns (Mar., 1813-Dec. 9, 1824) . . . 181
Bonaparte Becomes Emperor of France, Louis Napoleon (Dec. 2, 1852) . . . 861
Bonaparte Is Crowned Napoleon I (Dec. 2, 1804) . . . 72
Boole Publishes *The Mathematical Analysis of Logic* (1847) . . . 737
Booth Establishes the Salvation Army (July, 1865) . . . 1155
Border, Gadsden Purchase Completes the U.S.-Mexican (Dec. 31, 1853) . . . 882
Border, Webster-Ashburton Treaty Settles Maine's Canadian (Aug. 9, 1842) . . . 666
Borodino, Battle of (Sept. 7, 1812) . . . 176
Boulanger Crisis, French Right Wing Revives During (Jan., 1886-1889) . . . 1638
Bourbon Dynasty Is Restored, France's (Apr. 11, 1814-July 29, 1830) . . . 210
Bowdler Publishes *The Family Shakespeare* (1807) . . . 93
Boxer Rebellion (May, 1900-Sept. 7, 1901) . . . 1961
"Boycott," Irish Tenant Farmers Stage First (Sept.-Nov., 1880) . . . 1528
Brahmin School of American Literature Flourishes (1880's) . . . 1520
Brake, Westinghouse Patents His Air (Apr., 1869) . . . 1287
Brazil Becomes Independent (Sept. 7, 1822) . . . 348
Brethren, First Meetings of the Plymouth (c. 1826-1827) . . . 398
Bridge Opens, Brooklyn (May 24, 1883) . . . 1580
Britain, Fashoda Incident Pits France vs. (July 10-Nov. 3, 1898) . . . 1908
Britain, Gladstone Becomes Prime Minister of (Dec. 3, 1868-Feb. 20, 1874) . . . 1274
Britain, Treaty of Washington Settles U.S. Claims vs. (May 8, 1871) . . . 1363
Britain Acquires the Cape Colony (Aug. 13, 1814) . . . 213
Britain Adopts Gas Lighting (1802) . . . 29
Britain Begins Colonizing Tasmania, Great (Sept. 7, 1803) . . . 55
Britain Establishes Penny Postage, Great (Jan. 10, 1840) . . . 641

Britain Occupies the Falkland Islands, Great (Jan., 1833) 527
Britain Strengthens Its Royal Navy, Great (1889). 1680
Britain Withdraws from the Concert of Europe, Great (Oct. 20-30, 1822) 350
Britain's First Trades Union Congress Forms, Great (June 2, 1868). 1255
British Abolish Suttee in India (Dec. 4, 1829) . . . 428
British-Ashanti War, Second (Jan. 22, 1873-Feb. 13, 1874) 1389
British Canada, Rebellions Rock (Oct. 23-Dec. 16, 1837) 595
British Empire, Slavery Is Abolished Throughout the (Aug. 28, 1833) 533
British Expedition to Ethiopia (Apr., 1868) . . . 1250
British Houses of Parliament Are Rebuilt (Apr. 27, 1840-Feb., 1852) 643
British Labour Party Is Formed (Feb. 27, 1900) 1954
British North America Act (July 1, 1867) 1219
British Parliament, Rothschild Is First Jewish Member of (July 26, 1858) 966
British Parliament Passes Municipal Corporations Act (Sept. 9, 1835). 575
British Parliament Passes New Poor Law (Aug. 14, 1834). 554
British Parliament Passes the Factory Act (1833). 525
British Parliament Passes the Franchise Act of 1884 (Dec. 6, 1884) 1627
British Parliament Passes the Matrimonial Causes Act (Aug. 28, 1857) 952
British Parliament Passes the Reform Act of 1832 (June 4, 1832). 514
British Parliament Passes the Reform Act of 1867 (Aug., 1867). 1222
British Parliament Passes the Six Acts (Dec. 11-30, 1819) 305
British Parliament Repeals the Combination Acts (1824) 365
British Parliament Repeals the Corn Laws (June 15, 1846) 715
British Politics, Irish Home Rule Debate Dominates (June, 1886-Sept. 9, 1893) 1645
British Subdue African Resistance in Rhodesia (October, 1893-October, 1897) 1763
Brooklyn Bridge Opens (May 24, 1883) 1580
Brooks Brothers Introduces Button-Down Shirts (1896). 1828
Brotherhood Begins, Pre-Raphaelite (Fall, 1848) 790
Brothers Grimm Publish Fairy Tales (1812-1815) 160
Brothers Introduces Button-Down Shirts, Brooks (1896) 1828
Brownie Cameras, Kodak Introduces (Feb., 1900). 1950
Brown's Raid on Harpers Ferry (Oct. 16-18, 1859) 988
Brunel Launches the SS *Great Eastern* (Jan. 31, 1858) 955
Buckland Presents the First Public Dinosaur Description (Feb. 20, 1824) 374
Buffalo Slaughter, Great American (c. 1871-1883). 1343
Building Opens, New Library of Congress (Nov. 1, 1897). 1886
Built, First U.S. Petroleum Refinery Is (1850). 807
Built, World's First Skyscraper Is (1883-1885) 1575
Bulgarian Revolt Against the Ottoman Empire (May, 1876) 1445
Bull Run, First Battle of (July 21, 1861) 1045
Burckhardt Discovers Egypt's Abu Simbel (Mar. 22, 1812). 163
Bureau, Congress Creates the Freedmen's (Mar. 3, 1865) 1143
Bureau Announces Closing of the Frontier, U.S. Census (1890) 1705
Burlesque and Vaudeville, Rise of (1850's-1880's) 803
Burlingame Treaty (July 28, 1868) 1264
Burr's Conspiracy (Mar., 1805-Sept. 1, 1807) . . . 75
Burton Enters Mecca in Disguise (Sept. 12, 1853) 873
Business, Ward Launches a Mail-Order (Aug., 1872). 1378
Button-Down Shirts, Brooks Brothers Introduces (1896) 1828

Cabin, Stowe Publishes *Uncle Tom's* (1852) . . . 852
Cable Is Completed, First Transatlantic (July 27, 1866). 1196
Calculator, Babbage Designs a Mechanical (1819-1833). 291
California, Chinese Begin Immigrating to (1849). 793

California and the Southwest, United States Occupies (June 30, 1846-Jan. 13, 1847) 722
California Gold Rush Begins (Jan. 24, 1848) . . . 763
Californians Form Native Sons of the Golden State, Chinese (May 10, 1895) 1806
California's Bloody Island Massacre (May 6, 1850) 820
Calligraphy Emerges, China's Stele School of (1820's). 307
Cameras, Kodak Introduces Brownie (Feb., 1900) 1950
Campaign Begins, Anti-Japanese Yellow Peril (May 4, 1892) 1742
Campaigns, Bolívar's Military (Mar., 1813-Dec. 9, 1824) 181
Campaigns, San Martín's Military (Jan. 18, 1817-July 28, 1821) 273
Canada, Immigrant Farmers Begin Settling Western (1896) 1831
Canada, Irish Immigration to (1829-1836). 423
Canada, Rebellions Rock British (Oct. 23-Dec. 16, 1837) 595
Canada, Ukrainian Mennonites Begin Settling in (1873). 1380
Canada Forms the North-West Mounted Police (May 23, 1873) 1401
Canada Is Established, Supreme Court of (1875) 1418
Canada Is Founded, National Council of Women of (Oct. 27, 1893) 1768
Canada Unite, Upper and Lower (Feb. 10, 1841) 650
Canada's Grand Trunk Railway Is Incorporated (Nov. 10, 1852). 858
Canada's Indian Act (1876). 1437
Canada's Mackenzie Era (Nov. 5, 1873-Oct. 9, 1878). 1407
Canada's Prime Minister, Macdonald Returns as (Sept., 1878) 1496
Canada's Responsible Government, First Test of (Apr. 25, 1849) 797
Canadian Border, Webster-Ashburton Treaty Settles Maine's (Aug. 9, 1842) 666
Canadian Prime Minister, Laurier Becomes the First French (July 11, 1896). 1854
Canadian Settlement, Dominion Lands Act Fosters (1872) 1369
Canal Opens, Erie (Oct. 26, 1825) 391
Canal Opens, Germany's Kiel (June 20, 1895) 1808
Canal Opens, Suez (Nov. 17, 1869) 1301
Cape Colony, Britain Acquires the (Aug. 13, 1814) 213
Carlist Wars Unsettle Spain (Sept. 29, 1833-1849) 539
Carlyle Publishes *Past and Present* (1843) 669
Carmen Premieres in Paris, Bizet's (Mar. 3, 1875) 1420
Carolinas, Sherman Marches Through Georgia and the (Nov. 15, 1864-Apr. 18, 1865) 1127
Carrie, Dreiser Publishes *Sister* (Nov. 8, 1900) 1976
Cart War, Texas's (August-Dec., 1857) 950
Cases, Cherokee (Mar. 18, 1831, and Mar. 3, 1832) 491
Cases, Civil Rights (Oct. 15, 1883). 1586
Catholic, Newman Becomes a Roman (Oct. 9, 1845) 700
Catholic Church in Germany, Kulturkampf Against the (1871-1877) 1340
Catholic Emancipation, Roman (May 9, 1828-Apr. 13, 1829) 414
Cato Street Conspirators Plot Assassinations, London's (Feb. 23, 1820). 323
Cell Theory, Schwann and Virchow Develop (1838-1839). 602
Cellular Theory of Immunity, Metchnikoff Advances the (1882-1901) 1545
Celluloid Film, Goodwin Develops (May, 1887) 1663
Census Bureau Announces Closing of the Frontier, U.S. (1890) 1705
Centennial Exposition, Philadelphia Hosts the (May 10-Nov. 10, 1876). 1451
Central Asia, Przhevalsky Explores (1871-1885) 1346
Cereal Industry, Kellogg's Corn Flakes Launch the Dry (1894-1895) 1770
Champlain and St. Lawrence Railroad Opens (July 21, 1836) 587
Chapultepec, Battle of (Sept. 12-13, 1847) 751
Charles X, July Revolution Deposes (July 29, 1830) 470
Charter Oath, Promulgation of Japan's (Apr. 6, 1868) 1253
Chartered, American Fur Company Is (Apr. 6, 1808). 119
Chartered, Second Bank of the United States Is (Apr., 1816). 255

Chartist Movement (May 8, 1838-Apr. 10, 1848) 605
Chattanooga, Battles of Gettysburg, Vicksburg, and (July 1-Nov. 25, 1863) 1102
Cherokee Cases (Mar. 18, 1831, and Mar. 3, 1832) 491
Cherokee Phoenix Begins Publication (Feb. 21, 1828) 408
Chicago Fire, Great (Oct. 8-10, 1871) 1366
Chicago World's Fair (May 1-Oct. 30, 1893) 1757
Chicago's Hull-House, Addams Opens (Sept. 18, 1889) 1692
Children Opens, New York Infirmary for Indigent Women and (May 12, 1857) 947
China, Hay Articulates "Open Door" Policy Toward (Sept. 6, 1899-July 3, 1900) 1928
China, Muslim Rebellions in (Winter, 1855-Jan. 2, 1878) 917
China's Self-Strengthening Movement Arises (1860's) 995
China's Stele School of Calligraphy Emerges (1820's) 307
China's Taiping Rebellion (Jan. 11, 1851-late summer, 1864) 836
Chinese Begin Immigrating to California (1849) 793
Chinese Californians Form Native Sons of the Golden State (May 10, 1895) 1806
Chinese Concessions Begins, Scramble for (Nov. 14, 1897) 1888
Chinese Exclusion Act, Arthur Signs the (May 9, 1882) 1558
Chinese Six Companies Association Forms, San Francisco's (Nov. 12, 1882) 1569
Chisholm Trail Opens (1867) 1201
Christian Science Movement, Eddy Establishes the (Oct. 30, 1875) 1431
Church, Smith Founds the Mormon (Apr. 6, 1830) 457
Church in Germany, Kulturkampf Against the Catholic (1871-1877) 1340
Church Is Founded, African Methodist Episcopal (Apr. 9, 1816) 257
Church Is Founded, Unitarian (May, 1819) 299
Circulation War, Hearst-Pulitzer (1895-1898) 1794
Circus, Barnum Creates the First Modern American (Apr. 10, 1871) 1360
Civil Rights Act of 1866 (Apr. 9, 1866) 1175
Civil Rights Cases (Oct. 15, 1883) 1586
Civil Service, Pendleton Act Reforms the Federal (Jan. 16, 1883) 1577
Civil War, Díaz Drives Mexico into (1871-1876) 1338
Civil War, U.S. (Apr. 12, 1861-Apr. 9, 1865) 1036
Civil War Black Code, Mississippi Enacts First Post- (Nov. 24, 1865) 1164
Civilization, Evans Discovers Crete's Minoan (Mar. 23, 1900) 1956
Cixi's Coup Preserves Qing Dynasty Power (Nov. 1-2, 1861) 1055
Claims vs. Britain, Treaty of Washington Settles U.S. (May 8, 1871) 1363
Clark Expedition, Lewis and (May 14, 1804-Sept. 23, 1806) 65
Clausius Formulates the Second Law of Thermodynamics (1850-1865) 813
Clay Begins American Whig Party (Apr. 14, 1834) 551
Clermont, Maiden Voyage of the (Aug. 17, 1807) 111
Clinic Opens in Amsterdam, First Birth Control (1882) 1542
Clipper Ship Era Begins (c. 1845) 690
Closing of the Frontier, U.S. Census Bureau Announces (1890) 1705
Club Forms, Baseball's First Professional (1869) 1276
Coast, Astorian Expeditions Explore the Pacific Northwest (Sept. 8, 1810-May, 1812) 134
Cobbett Founds the *Political Register* (Jan., 1802) 32
Coca-Cola, Pemberton Introduces (May 8, 1886) 1643
Cockney School, Rise of the (Dec., 1816) 263
Code, Mississippi Enacts First Post-Civil War Black (Nov. 24, 1865) 1164
Codes, Ohio Enacts the First Black (Jan., 1804) 62
Coins, "In God We Trust" Appears on U.S. (Apr. 22, 1864) 1119
College Opens, Oberlin (Dec. 3, 1833) 546
College Opens, Vassar (Sept. 26, 1865) 1158
Colonizing Tasmania, Great Britain Begins (Sept. 7, 1803) 55
Colored People Is Founded, National Council of (July 6, 1853) 870

Colt Patents the Revolver (Feb. 25, 1836) 584
Combination Acts, British Parliament Repeals the (1824) 365
Commerce Act, Interstate (Feb. 4, 1887) 1655
Commercial Oil Drilling Begins (Aug. 27, 1859) 985
Commercial Projection of Motion Pictures, First (Dec. 28, 1895) 1820
Commonwealth v. Hunt (Mar., 1842) 658
Commune, Paris (Mar. 18-May 28, 1871) 1358
Communist Manifesto, Marx and Engels Publish *The* (Feb., 1848) 767
Communitarian Experiments at New Harmony (Spring, 1814-1830) 206
Company Is Chartered, American Fur (Apr. 6, 1808) 119
Company Is Incorporated, Standard Oil (Jan. 10, 1870). 1318
Completed, First Transatlantic Cable Is (July 27, 1866). 1196
Completed, First Transcontinental Railroad Is (May 10, 1869) 1293
Completed, Transcontinental Telegraph Is (Oct. 24, 1861) 1048
Completes the First Flying Dirigible, Zeppelin (July 2, 1900) 1969
Completes *The Tokaido Fifty-Three Stations*, Hiroshige (1831-1834) 484
Completes the U.S.-Mexican Border, Gadsden Purchase (Dec. 31, 1853). 882
Compromise, Missouri (Mar. 3, 1820). 325
Compromise of 1850 (Jan. 29-Sept. 20, 1850). . . 816
Compromise Speech, Washington's Atlanta (Sept. 18, 1895) 1811
Comstock Antiobscenity Law, Congress Passes the (Mar. 3, 1873) 1394
Comte Advances His Theory of Positivism (1851-1854). 833
Conan Doyle Introduces Sherlock Holmes (Dec., 1887) 1666
Concert of Europe, Great Britain Withdraws from the (Oct. 20-30, 1822) 350
Concessions Begins, Scramble for Chinese (Nov. 14, 1897) 1888
Concessions to Irish Nationalists, Kilmainham Treaty Makes (May 2, 1882) 1556
Confederate General to Surrender, Watie Is Last (June 23, 1865). 1153
Confederate States of America, Establishment of the (Feb. 8, 1861). 1022
Confederation Is Formed, North German (1866-1867) 1173
Confederation Is Formed, Swiss (Sept. 12, 1848) 787
Conference, First Hague Peace (May 18-July, 1899) 1926
Conference Lays Groundwork for the Partition of Africa, Berlin (Nov. 15, 1884-Feb. 26, 1885). 1619
Confronts the Nian Rebellion, Qing Dynasty (1853-1868). 864
Congo Basin, Exploration of Africa's (1873-1880) 1382
Congress, First Pan-American (October, 1889-Apr., 1890) 1695
Congress Bans Importation of African Slaves (Mar. 2, 1807) 103
Congress Building Opens, New Library of (Nov. 1, 1897). 1886
Congress Creates the Freedmen's Bureau (Mar. 3, 1865) 1143
Congress Enacts the Page Law (Mar. 3, 1875) 1423
Congress Is Founded, Indian National (1885) 1630
Congress of Berlin (June 13-July 13, 1878) . . . 1492
Congress of Vienna (Sept. 15, 1814-June 11, 1815) 216
Congress Passes Dingley Tariff Act (July 24, 1897) 1880
Congress Passes Indian Removal Act (May 28, 1830) 460
Congress Passes Land Act of 1820 (Apr. 24, 1820) 328
Congress Passes Preemption Act of 1841 (Sept. 4, 1841) 653
Congress Passes the Comstock Antiobscenity Law (Mar. 3, 1873) 1394
Congress Passes the Kansas-Nebraska Act (May 30, 1854) 891
Congress Passes the National Bank Acts (Feb. 25, 1863-June 3, 1864) 1093
Conquers Algeria, France (June 14-July 5, 1830) 464
Conspiracy, Burr's (Mar., 1805-Sept. 1, 1807) . . . 75
Conspirators Plot Assassinations, London's Cato Street (Feb. 23, 1820). 323
Constitution, Japan Adopts a New (Feb. 11, 1889) 1683

Constitution Disfranchises Black Voters, Mississippi (1890) 1702
Constitution of 1876, Spanish (1876) 1440
Construction of the National Road (1811-1840) 146
Controversy, Nullification (Nov. 24, 1832-Jan. 21, 1833) 521
Convention, Akron Woman's Rights (May 28-29, 1851) 843
Convention, Hartford (Dec. 15, 1814-Jan. 5, 1815) 219
Convention, Seneca Falls (July 19-20, 1848) 784
Converts Magnetic Force into Electricity, Faraday (October, 1831) 502
Convicts Land in Western Australia, Last (1868) 1238
Corn Flakes Launch the Dry Cereal Industry, Kellogg's (1894-1895) 1770
Corn Laws, British Parliament Repeals the (June 15, 1846) 715
Coronation, Queen Victoria's (June 28, 1838) 608
Corporations Act, British Parliament Passes Municipal (Sept. 9, 1835) 575
Costumbrismo Movement (c. 1820-1860) 320
Council Enacts the Ilbert Bill, Indian Legislative (Jan. 25, 1884) 1606
Council of Colored People Is Founded, National (July 6, 1853) 870
Council of Women of Canada Is Founded, National (Oct. 27, 1893) 1768
Coup Preserves Qing Dynasty Power, Cixi's (Nov. 1-2, 1861) 1055
Courbet Establishes Realist Art Movement (1855) 911
Court of Canada Is Established, Supreme (1875) 1418
Crafts Movement, New Guilds Promote the Arts and (1884) 1597
Created, U.S. Department of Education Is (Mar. 2, 1867) 1210
Creates the First Modern American Circus, Barnum (Apr. 10, 1871) 1360
Creates the Freedmen's Bureau, Congress (Mar. 3, 1865) 1143
Creek Massacre, Sand (Nov. 29, 1864) 1130
Creek Treaty, Medicine Lodge (Oct. 21, 1867) 1228
Creek War (July 27, 1813-Aug. 9, 1814) 185
Crete's Minoan Civilization, Evans Discovers (Mar. 23, 1900) 1956
"Crime of 1873" (Feb. 12, 1873) 1392
Crimea, Nightingale Takes Charge of Nursing in the (Nov. 4, 1854) 903
Crimean War (Oct. 4, 1853-Mar. 30, 1856) 876
Crisis, French Right Wing Revives During Boulanger (Jan., 1886-1889) 1638
Cro-Magnon Remains, Lartet Discovers the First (Mar., 1868) 1247
Cross the Atlantic, *Savannah* Is the First Steamship to (May 22-June 20, 1819) 303
Crowned Napoleon I, Bonaparte Is (Dec. 2, 1804) 72
Crushes Polish Rebellion, Russia (Jan. 22-Sept., 1863) 1090
Cuban War of Independence (Feb. 24, 1895-1898) 1802
Cuba's Ten Years' War (Oct. 10, 1868-Feb. 10, 1878) 1269
Cup Race, *America* Wins the First America's (Aug. 22, 1851) 846
Customs Union, German States Join to Form (Jan. 1, 1834) 549
Cycle, First Performance of Wagner's Ring (Aug. 13-17, 1876) 1464
Cylinder Phonograph, Edison Patents the (Dec. 24, 1877) 1484

Daguerre and Niépce Invent Daguerreotype Photography (1839) 613
Daguerreotype Photography, Daguerre and Niépce Invent (1839) 613
Dahomey-French Wars (Nov., 1889-Jan., 1894) 1697
Dalton Formulates the Atomic Theory of Matter (1803-1808) 43
Dance, Joplin Popularizes Ragtime Music and (1899) 1917
Danish-Prussian War (Feb. 1-Oct. 30, 1864) 1117
Darlington Railway Opens, Stockton and (September 27, 1825) 388
D'Arthur," Tennyson Publishes "Morte (1842) 655
Darwin Publishes *On the Origin of Species* (Nov. 24, 1859) 991
Darwin Publishes *The Descent of Man* (1871) 1334
Darwinism, Spencer Introduces Principles of Social (1862) 1058

Das Kapital, Marx Publishes (1867) 1207
Davy Develops the Arc Lamp (c. 1801-1810). . . . 11
Debate Dominates British Politics, Irish Home Rule (June, 1886-Sept. 9, 1893) 1645
Debate Slavery and Westward Expansion, Webster and Hayne (Jan. 19-27, 1830). 451
Debates, Lincoln-Douglas (June 16-Oct. 15, 1858) 963
Debussy's *Prelude to the Afternoon of a Faun* Premieres (Dec. 22, 1894). 1791
Debuts, Rossini's *The Barber of Seville* (Feb. 20, 1816) 252
Debuts, Wagner's *Flying Dutchman* (Jan. 2, 1843) 672
Decadent Movement Flourishes (c. 1884-1924). 1600
Decembrist Revolt (Dec. 26, 1825) 395
Declaration of the Rights of Women (July 4, 1876) 1460
Decrees Papal Infallibility Dogma, Vatican I (Dec. 8, 1869-Oct. 20, 1870) 1307
Decrees the Immaculate Conception Dogma, Pius IX (Dec. 8, 1854) 906
Dedicated, Eiffel Tower Is (Mar. 31, 1889) . . . 1686
Dedicated, Statue of Liberty Is (Oct. 28, 1886) 1649
Defines "Eugenics," Galton (1883). 1572
Delacroix Paints *Liberty Leading the People* (October-Dec., 1830) 476
Democratic Alliance, Bakunin Founds the Social (1868) 1235
Democratic Labor Party Is Formed, Russian Social- (Mar., 1898). 1895
Demonstrated, Safe Surgical Anesthesia Is (Oct. 16, 1846) 735
Demonstrates the Incandescent Lamp, Edison (Oct. 21, 1879) 1517
Demonstrates the Telephone, Bell (June 25, 1876) 1457
Department of Education Is Created, U.S. (Mar. 2, 1867). 1210
Department Store Opens in Paris, First Modern (1869) 1279
Deposes Charles X, July Revolution (July 29, 1830) 470
Depot Opens, Ellis Island Immigration (Jan. 1, 1892) 1737
Descent of Man, Darwin Publishes *The* (1871) 1334
Description, Buckland Presents the First Public Dinosaur (Feb. 20, 1824) 374
Design Firm, Morris Founds (1861) 1016
Designs a Mechanical Calculator, Babbage (1819-1833). 291
Destroy Industrial Machines, Luddites (Mar. 11, 1811-1816) 151
Develop Cell Theory, Schwann and Virchow (1838-1839). 602
Developing Germ Theory and Microbiology, Pasteur Begins (1857) 933
Development of Working-Class Libraries (19th cent.) 3
Develops Antiseptic Procedures, Semmelweis (May, 1847). 745
Develops Celluloid Film, Goodwin (May, 1887) 1663
Develops New Integration Theory, Lebesgue (1900) 1941
Develops Systematic History, Ranke (1824). . . . 371
Develops the Arc Lamp, Davy (c. 1801-1810) . . . 11
Develops the Periodic Table of Elements, Mendeleyev (1869-1871) 1284
Develops the Theory of Mitosis, Roux (1880's) 1523
Dial Telephone System, Strowger Patents Automatic (Mar. 11, 1891) 1724
Diamondfields, Rhodes Amalgamates Kimberley (Mar. 13, 1888) 1674
Díaz Drives Mexico into Civil War (1871-1876) 1338
Dickens Publishes *Bleak House* (Mar., 1852-Sept., 1853). 855
Dictionary of English, Webster Publishes the First American (Nov., 1828) 418
Diesel Engine, Diesel Patents the (Feb., 1892) 1740
Diesel Patents the Diesel Engine (Feb., 1892) 1740
Dingley Tariff Act, Congress Passes (July 24, 1897) 1880
Dinosaur Description, Buckland Presents the First Public (Feb. 20, 1824). 374
Diphtheria Antitoxin, Behring Discovers the (Dec. 11, 1890) 1715
Dirigible, Zeppelin Completes the First Flying (July 2, 1900) 1969
Discovered, *Archaeopteryx Lithographica* Is (1861) 1014
Discovered, First Asteroid Is (Jan. 1, 1801). 17

Discovered, Stratosphere and Troposphere Are (Apr., 1898-1903) 1900
Discovered in New South Wales, Gold Is (1851) 828
Discovered in the Transvaal, Gold Is (June 21, 1884) 1612
Discovers Crete's Minoan Civilization, Evans (Mar. 23, 1900) 1956
Discovers Egypt's Abu Simbel, Burckhardt (Mar. 22, 1812) 163
Discovers the Diphtheria Antitoxin, Behring (Dec. 11, 1890) 1715
Discovers the First Cro-Magnon Remains, Lartet (Mar., 1868) 1247
Discovers Viruses, Beijerinck (1898) 1892
Discovers X Rays, Röntgen (Nov. 9, 1895) . . . 1814
Discovery of the Tuberculosis Bacillus, Koch Announces His (Mar. 24, 1882) 1550
Disfranchises Black Voters, Mississippi Constitution (1890) 1702
Disguise, Burton Enters Mecca in (Sept. 12, 1853) 873
Docks at Mobile, Last Slave Ship (July, 1859) 979
Doctrine, President Monroe Articulates the Monroe (Dec. 2, 1823) 361
Dogma, Pius IX Decrees the Immaculate Conception (Dec. 8, 1854) 906
Dogma, Vatican I Decrees Papal Infallibility (Dec. 8, 1869-Oct. 20, 1870) 1307
Doll's House Introduces Modern Realistic Drama, *A* (1879) 1501
Dolores, Hidalgo Issues El Grito de (Sept. 16, 1810) 138
Dominates British Politics, Irish Home Rule Debate (June, 1886-Sept. 9, 1893) 1645
Dominion Lands Act Fosters Canadian Settlement (1872) 1369
Dorr Rebellion, Rhode Island's (May 18, 1842) 664
Dos de Mayo Insurrection in Spain (May 2, 1808) 122
Dostoevski Is Exiled to Siberia (Dec., 1849) . . . 800
Douglas Debates, Lincoln- (June 16-Oct. 15, 1858) 963
Douglass Launches *The North Star* (Dec. 3, 1847) 753
Doyle Introduces Sherlock Holmes, Conan (Dec., 1887) 1666
Draft Law, Union Enacts the First National (Mar. 3, 1863) 1095
Drama, *A Doll's House* Introduces Modern Realistic (1879) 1501
Dreams, Freud Publishes *The Interpretation of* (1900) 1938
Dred Scott v. Sandford (Mar. 6, 1857) 938
Dreiser Publishes *Sister Carrie* (Nov. 8, 1900) 1976
Dreyfus Affair (October, 1894-July, 1906) 1788
Drilling Begins, Commercial Oil (Aug. 27, 1859) 985
Dry Cereal Industry, Kellogg's Corn Flakes Launch the (1894-1895) 1770
Dunlop Patents the Pneumatic Tire (Dec. 7, 1888) 1677
Dutchman Debuts, Wagner's *Flying* (Jan. 2, 1843) 672
Dynamite, Nobel Patents (October, 1867) 1226
Dynasty, Greece Unifies Under the Glücksburg (1863-1913) 1081
Dynasty Confronts the Nian Rebellion, Qing (1853-1868) 864
Dynasty Is Restored, France's Bourbon (Apr. 11, 1814-July 29, 1830) 210
Dynasty Power, Cixi's Coup Preserves Qing (Nov. 1-2, 1861) 1055

East Africa, Exploration of (1848-1889) 756
Easter Island, Slave Traders Begin Ravaging (Nov., 1862) 1076
Economic Principles, Ricardo Identifies Seven Key (1817) 267
Economist, Wilson Launches *The* (Sept. 2, 1843) 678
Eddy Establishes the Christian Science Movement (Oct. 30, 1875) 1431
Edison Demonstrates the Incandescent Lamp (Oct. 21, 1879) 1517
Edison Patents the Cylinder Phonograph (Dec. 24, 1877) 1484
Education Is Created, U.S. Department of (Mar. 2, 1867) 1210
Egypt Fights the Wahhābīs (1811-1818) 143
Egyptian Wars, Turko- (1832-1841) 505
Egypt's Abu Simbel, Burckhardt Discovers (Mar. 22, 1812) 163
Eiffel Tower Is Dedicated (Mar. 31, 1889) 1686
1812, War of (June 18, 1812-Dec. 24, 1814) . . . 166

1820, Congress Passes Land Act of (Apr. 24, 1820) 328
1824, Paris Salon of (1824) 368
1824, U.S. Election of (Dec. 1, 1824-Feb. 9, 1825) 383
1828, U.S. Election of (Dec. 3, 1828) 421
1832, British Parliament Passes the Reform Act of (June 4, 1832) 514
1837 Begins, Panic of (Mar. 17, 1837). 591
1840, U.S. Election of (Dec. 2, 1840) 646
1848, Italian Revolution of (Jan. 12, 1848-Aug. 28, 1849) 760
1848, Paris Revolution of (Feb. 22-June, 1848) 773
1848, Prussian Revolution of (Mar. 3-Nov. 3, 1848) 776
1850, Compromise of (Jan. 29-Sept. 20, 1850) 816
1867, British Parliament Passes the Reform Act of (Aug., 1867) 1222
1868, Spanish Revolution of (Sept. 30, 1868) 1266
1873," "Crime of (Feb. 12, 1873). 1392
1876, Spanish Constitution of (1876). 1440
1884, U.S. Election of (Nov. 4, 1884) 1615
El Grito de Dolores, Hidalgo Issues (Sept. 16, 1810) 138
Elected President, McKinley Is (Nov. 3, 1896) 1860
Elected U.S. President, Lincoln Is (Nov. 6, 1860) 1010
Election of 1824, U.S. (Dec. 1, 1824-Feb. 9, 1825) 383
Election of 1828, U.S. (Dec. 3, 1828) 421
Election of 1840, U.S. (Dec. 2, 1840) 646
Election of 1884, U.S. (Nov. 4, 1884) 1615
Electricity, Ampère Reveals Magnetism's Relationship to (Nov. 6, 1820) 334
Electricity, Faraday Converts Magnetic Force into (October, 1831) 502
Elects Jefferson President, House of Representatives (Feb. 17, 1801) 20
Elements, Mendeleyev Develops the Periodic Table of (1869-1871) 1284
Elevator, Otis Installs the First Passenger (Mar. 23, 1857). 942
Elgin Ships Parthenon Marbles to England (1803-1812) 46
Ellis Island Immigration Depot Opens (Jan. 1, 1892) 1737
Ellis Publishes *Sexual Inversion* (1897) 1867
Emancipation, Roman Catholic (May 9, 1828-Apr. 13, 1829) 414
Emancipation of Russian Serfs (Mar. 3, 1861) 1026
Emancipation Proclamation, Lincoln Issues the (Jan. 1, 1863) 1084
Emergence of the Primitives (1801) 9
Emerges, China's Stele School of Calligraphy (1820's). 307
Emperor of France, Louis Napoleon Bonaparte Becomes (Dec. 2, 1852) 861
Emperors' League Is Formed, Three (May 6-Oct. 22, 1873). 1398
Empire, Bulgarian Revolt Against the Ottoman (May, 1876). 1445
Empire, German States Unite Within German (Jan. 18, 1871). 1349
Empire, Greeks Fight for Independence from the Ottoman (Mar. 7, 1821-Sept. 29, 1829) 336
Empire, Slavery Is Abolished Throughout the British (Aug. 28, 1833). 533
Enacts First Post-Civil War Black Code, Mississippi (Nov. 24, 1865). 1164
Enacts the First Black Codes, Ohio (Jan., 1804). 62
Enacts the First National Draft Law, Union (Mar. 3, 1863). 1095
Enacts the Ilbert Bill, Indian Legislative Council (Jan. 25, 1884). 1606
Enacts the Page Law, Congress (Mar. 3, 1875) 1423
Encyclical on Labor, Papal (May 15, 1891) . . . 1727
Ends Mexican War, Treaty of Guadalupe Hidalgo (Feb. 2, 1848) 770
Engels Publish *The Communist Manifesto*, Marx and (Feb., 1848) 767
Engine, Diesel Patents the Diesel (Feb., 1892) 1740
Engine, Lenoir Patents the Internal Combustion (1860). 998
Engine, Otto Invents a Practical Internal Combustion (May, 1876) 1449
Engine, Trevithick Patents the High-Pressure Steam (Mar. 24, 1802). 38
England, Elgin Ships Parthenon Marbles to (1803-1812) 46
England's Poet Laureate, Tennyson Becomes (Nov. 5, 1850) 825

English, Webster Publishes the First American Dictionary of (Nov., 1828) 418
Enters Mecca in Disguise, Burton (Sept. 12, 1853) 873
Episcopal Church Is Founded, African Methodist (Apr. 9, 1816) 257
Era, Canada's Mackenzie (Nov. 5, 1873-Oct. 9, 1878) 1407
Era Begins, America's "New" Immigration (1892) 1730
Era Begins, Clipper Ship (c. 1845). 690
Era of "Old" Immigration, American (1840's-1850's) 631
Erie Canal Opens (Oct. 26, 1825) 391
Erodes Indian Tribal Unity, General Allotment Act (Feb. 8, 1887). 1657
Eroica Symphony Introduces the Romantic Age, Beethoven's (Apr. 7, 1805) 78
Errors, Pius IX Issues the Syllabus of (Dec. 8, 1864). 1133
Erupt in Philadelphia, Anti-Irish Riots (May 6-July 5, 1844) 681
Eruption, Tambora Volcano Begins Violent (Apr. 5, 1815). 234
Erupts, Krakatoa Volcano (Aug. 27, 1883). . . . 1583
Essen, Krupp Works Open at (Sept. 20, 1811). . . 154
Established, Supreme Court of Canada Is (1875) 1418
Established, Third French Republic Is (Feb. 13, 1871-1875) 1353
Established, U.S. Military Academy Is (Mar. 16, 1802) 35
Establishes Malaria's Transmission Vector, Ross (Aug. 20, 1897) 1883
Establishes Penny Postage, Great Britain (Jan. 10, 1840) 641
Establishes Realist Art Movement, Courbet (1855). 911
Establishes the Christian Science Movement, Eddy (Oct. 30, 1875) 1431
Establishes the Salvation Army, Booth (July, 1865). 1155
Establishment of Independent U.S. Treasury (Aug. 1, 1846) 726
Establishment of the Confederate States of America (Feb. 8, 1861) 1022
Ethiopia, British Expedition to (Apr., 1868) 1250
Ethiopia Repels Italian Invasion (Mar. 1, 1896) 1842
"Eugenics," Galton Defines (1883). 1572
Europe, Great Britain Withdraws from the Concert of (Oct. 20-30, 1822) 350
Europeans Explore the Antarctic (1820-early 1840's) 317
Evans Discovers Crete's Minoan Civilization (Mar. 23, 1900) 1956
Examined, Strauss Publishes *The Life of Jesus Critically* (1835-1836) 566
Excavates Ancient Troy, Schliemann (Apr., 1870-1873) 1321
Excavates Assyrian Ruins, Layard Explores and (1839-1847) 619
Exclusion Act, Arthur Signs the Chinese (May 9, 1882) 1558
Exhibition, First Impressionist (Apr. 15, 1874) 1410
Exhibits *The Thinker*, Rodin (1888) 1669
Exile, Mazzini Begins London (Jan. 12, 1837) 589
Exiled to Siberia, Dostoevski Is (Dec., 1849) . . . 800
Expands into Korea, Japan (1870's) 1313
Expansion, Webster and Hayne Debate Slavery and Westward (Jan. 19-27, 1830) . . . 451
Expansion, Zulu (c. 1817-1828) 270
Expedites Transcontinental Mail, Pony Express (Apr. 3, 1860-Oct. 26, 1861). 1001
Expedition, Lewis and Clark (May 14, 1804-Sept. 23, 1806). 65
Expedition to Ethiopia, British (Apr., 1868) . . . 1250
Expeditions Explore the Pacific Northwest Coast, Astorian (Sept. 8, 1810-May, 1812) 134
Expeditions Give Rise to Biogeography, Wallace's (1854-1862) 885
Expelled from Russia, Naples, and Spain, Jesuits Are (1820) 315
Experiments at New Harmony, Communitarian (Spring, 1814-1830) 206
Exploration of Africa's Congo Basin (1873-1880) 1382
Exploration of Arabia (1814-1879) 199
Exploration of East Africa (1848-1889) 756
Exploration of North Africa (1822-1874) 345
Exploration of West Africa (May 4, 1805-1830). 80
Explore the Antarctic, Europeans (1820-early 1840's) 317
Explore the Pacific Northwest Coast, Astorian Expeditions (Sept. 8, 1810-May, 1812) 134

Explores and Excavates Assyrian Ruins, Layard (1839-1847) 619
Explores Australia, Flinders (Dec. 6, 1801-Aug., 1803) 26
Explores Central Asia, Przhevalsky (1871-1885) 1346
Explores the American Southwest, Pike (July 15, 1806-July 1, 1807) 90
Explores the American West, Frémont (May, 1842-1854) 660
Explores the Far West, Jedediah Smith (1822-1831) 342
Exposition, Philadelphia Hosts the Centennial (May 10-Nov. 10, 1876) 1451
Exterminate Armenians, Ottomans Attempt to (1894-1896) 1773

Fabian Society Is Founded (Jan., 1884). 1603
Factory Act, British Parliament Passes the (1833). 525
Fair, Chicago World's (May 1-Oct. 30, 1893) 1757
Fair, London Hosts the First World's (May 1-Oct. 15, 1851). 840
Fairy Tales, Andersen Publishes His First (May 8, 1835). 570
Fairy Tales, Brothers Grimm Publish (1812-1815) 160
Falkland Islands, Great Britain Occupies the (Jan., 1833) 527
Falls, First U.S. Hydroelectric Plant Opens at Niagara (Nov. 16, 1896) 1863
Falls, Livingstone Sees the Victoria (Nov. 17, 1853) 879
Family Shakespeare, Bowdler Publishes *The* (1807) 93
Famine, Great Irish (1845-1854). 696
Far West, Jedediah Smith Explores the (1822-1831) 342
Faraday Converts Magnetic Force into Electricity (October, 1831) 502
Farmers Begin Settling Western Canada, Immigrant (1896) 1831
Farmers Stage First "Boycott," Irish Tenant (Sept.-Nov., 1880). 1528
Fashoda Incident Pits France vs. Britain (July 10-Nov. 3, 1898) 1908
Faun Premieres, Debussy's *Prelude to the Afternoon of a* (Dec. 22, 1894) 1791
Federal Civil Service, Pendleton Act Reforms the (Jan. 16, 1883). 1577
Federation of Labor Is Founded, American (Dec. 8, 1886) 1652
Female Seminary Is Founded, Hartford (May, 1823) 356
Female Seminary Opens, Mount Holyoke (Nov. 8, 1837) 597
Fenian Risings for Irish Independence (June, 1866-1871) 1184
Ferguson, Plessy v. (May 18, 1896) 1848
Fertilizers, Liebig Advocates Artificial (1840). 638
Fetterman Massacre (Dec. 21, 1866) 1199
Fever, Suppression of Yellow (June, 1900-1904) 1966
Fifty-Three Stations, Hiroshige Completes *The Tokaido* (1831-1834). 484
Fight for Independence from the Ottoman Empire, Greeks (Mar. 7, 1821-Sept. 29, 1829) 336
Fights the Wahhābīs, Egypt (1811-1818) 143
Film, Goodwin Develops Celluloid (May, 1887) 1663
Finney Lectures on "Revivals of Religion" (1835). 560
Fire, Great Chicago (Oct. 8-10, 1871) 1366
Firm, Morris Founds Design (1861) 1016
First Afghan War (1839-1842). 617
First African American University Opens (Jan. 1, 1857) 936
First American Dictionary of English, Webster Publishes the (Nov., 1828) 418
First America's Cup Race, *America* Wins the (Aug. 22, 1851). 846
First Asteroid Is Discovered (Jan. 1, 1801) 17
First Battle of Bull Run (July 21, 1861) 1045
First Birth Control Clinic Opens in Amsterdam (1882) 1542
First Black Codes, Ohio Enacts the (Jan., 1804). 62
First Boer War (Dec. 16, 1880-Mar. 6, 1881) 1531
First "Boycott," Irish Tenant Farmers Stage (Sept.-Nov., 1880). 1528
First Commercial Projection of Motion Pictures (Dec. 28, 1895). 1820
First Cro-Magnon Remains, Lartet Discovers the (Mar., 1868) 1247

First Fairy Tales, Andersen Publishes His (May 8, 1835). 570
First Flying Dirigible, Zeppelin Completes the (July 2, 1900) 1969
First French Canadian Prime Minister, Laurier Becomes the (July 11, 1896) 1854
First Hague Peace Conference (May 18-July, 1899). 1926
First Impressionist Exhibition (Apr. 15, 1874) 1410
First International Is Founded (Sept. 28, 1864). 1124
First Jewish Member of British Parliament, Rothschild Is (July 26, 1858) 966
First Labour Member, Hardie Becomes Parliament's (Aug. 3, 1892). 1748
First Meetings of the Plymouth Brethren (c. 1826-1827) 398
First Minstrel Shows (Feb. 6, 1843) 675
First Modern American Circus, Barnum Creates the (Apr. 10, 1871) 1360
First Modern Department Store Opens in Paris (1869) 1279
First National Draft Law, Union Enacts the (Mar. 3, 1863). 1095
First Opium War (Sept., 1839-Aug. 29, 1842). . . 625
First Pan-American Congress (October, 1889-Apr., 1890) 1695
First Passenger Elevator, Otis Installs the (Mar. 23, 1857). 942
First Performance of Beethoven's Ninth Symphony (May 7, 1824) 380
First Performance of Wagner's Ring Cycle (Aug. 13-17, 1876) 1464
First Polish Rebellion (Nov. 29, 1830-Aug. 15, 1831) 479
First Post-Civil War Black Code, Mississippi Enacts (Nov. 24, 1865) 1164
First Practical Automobile, Benz Patents the (Jan. 29, 1886). 1640
First Professional Club Forms, Baseball's (1869) 1276
First Public Dinosaur Description, Buckland Presents the (Feb. 20, 1824) 374
First Riel Rebellion (Oct. 11, 1869-July 15, 1870) 1299
First Seed Planter, Blair Patents His (Oct. 14, 1834) 557
First Skyscraper Is Built, World's (1883-1885) 1575
First Steamship to Cross the Atlantic, *Savannah* Is the (May 22-June 20, 1819) 303
First Telegraph Message, Morse Sends (May 24, 1844) 684
First Test of Canada's Responsible Government (Apr. 25, 1849) 797
First Trades Union Congress Forms, Great Britain's (June 2, 1868) 1255
First Transatlantic Cable Is Completed (July 27, 1866). 1196
First Transcontinental Railroad Is Completed (May 10, 1869) 1293
First Underground Railroad Opens in London (Jan. 10, 1863). 1087
First U.S. Hydroelectric Plant Opens at Niagara Falls (Nov. 16, 1896) 1863
First U.S. National Park, Yellowstone Becomes the (Mar. 1, 1872) 1375
First U.S. Petroleum Refinery Is Built (1850) . . . 807
First World's Fair, London Hosts the (May 1-Oct. 15, 1851). 840
Flamenco Begins, Golden Age of (c. 1869) . . . 1282
Flaubert Publishes *Madame Bovary* (Oct. 1-Dec. 15, 1856) 926
Fletcher v. Peck (Mar. 16, 1810). 131
Flinders Explores Australia (Dec. 6, 1801-Aug., 1803) 26
Flood, Johnstown (May 31, 1889) 1689
Florida, Adams-Onís Treaty Gives the United States (Feb. 22, 1819) 293
Flourishes, Barbizon School of Landscape Painting (c. 1830-1870). 445
Flourishes, Brahmin School of American Literature (1880's) 1520
Flourishes, Decadent Movement (c. 1884-1924) 1600
Flourishes, Underground Railroad (c. 1850-1860) 809
Flying Dirigible, Zeppelin Completes the First (July 2, 1900) 1969
Flying Dutchman Debuts, Wagner's (Jan. 2, 1843) 672
Force into Electricity, Faraday Converts Magnetic (October, 1831) 502
Forecasting, Bjerknes Founds Scientific Weather (July, 1897-July, 1904) 1877
Foreign Bible Society Is Founded, British and (1804) 57
Form, Bahāʾīism Takes (1863) 1078

Form Customs Union, German States Join to (Jan. 1, 1834) 549
Form Native Sons of the Golden State, Chinese Californians (May 10, 1895) 1806
Formed, British Labour Party Is (Feb. 27, 1900) 1954
Formed, National Grange Is (Dec. 4, 1867) . . . 1231
Formed, North German Confederation Is (1866-1867). 1173
Formed, Russian Social-Democratic Labor Party Is (Mar., 1898) 1895
Formed, Swiss Confederation Is (Sept. 12, 1848) 787
Formed, Three Emperors' League Is (May 6-Oct. 22, 1873) 1398
Formed, Triple Alliance Is (May 20, 1882). . . . 1561
Former Samurai Rise in Satsuma Rebellion (Jan.-Sept. 24, 1877) 1469
Forming, Woman Suffrage Associations Begin (May, 1869) 1290
Forms, Baseball's First Professional Club (1869) 1276
Forms, Great Britain's First Trades Union Congress (June 2, 1868). 1255
Forms, San Francisco's Chinese Six Companies Association (Nov. 12, 1882) . . . 1569
Forms the North-West Mounted Police, Canada (May 23, 1873) 1401
Formulates the Atomic Theory of Matter, Dalton (1803-1808) 43
Formulates the Second Law of Thermodynamics, Clausius (1850-1865). 813
Fosters Canadian Settlement, Dominion Lands Act (1872). 1369
Found in Germany, Neanderthal Skull Is (Aug., 1856) 923
Foundations of Geometry, Hilbert Publishes *The* (1899). 1913
Founded, African Methodist Episcopal Church Is (Apr. 9, 1816) 257
Founded, American Anti-Slavery Society Is (Dec., 1833). 542
Founded, American Bible Society Is (May 8, 1816). 260
Founded, American Federation of Labor Is (Dec. 8, 1886) 1652
Founded, American Library Association Is (Oct. 4-6, 1876) 1467
Founded, British and Foreign Bible Society Is (1804) 57
Founded, Fabian Society Is (Jan., 1884) 1603
Founded, First International Is (Sept. 28, 1864). 1124
Founded, Hartford Female Seminary Is (May, 1823) 356
Founded, Indian National Congress Is (1885) 1630
Founded, Melbourne, Australia, Is (Aug. 16, 1835) 573
Founded, Modern *New York Times* Is (Sept. 18, 1851). 849
Founded, Moscow Art Theater Is (Oct. 14, 1898) 1910
Founded, National Council of Colored People Is (July 6, 1853) 870
Founded, National Council of Women of Canada Is (Oct. 27, 1893) 1768
Founded, Smithsonian Institution Is (Aug. 10, 1846) 729
Founded, Theosophical Society Is (Sept., 1875) 1429
Founded, Unitarian Church Is (May, 1819) 299
Founded, Watch Tower Bible and Tract Society Is (1870-1871) 1316
Founding of McGill University (1813). 179
Founds Design Firm, Morris (1861) 1016
Founds Prophetstown, Tenskwatawa (Apr., 1808) 116
Founds Scientific Weather Forecasting, Bjerknes (July, 1897-July, 1904) 1877
Founds the Mormon Church, Smith (Apr. 6, 1830) 457
Founds the *Political Register*, Cobbett (Jan., 1802). 32
Founds the Social Democratic Alliance, Bakunin (1868) 1235
Founds the Zionist Movement, Herzl (Feb., 1896-Aug., 1897). 1836
Founds Young Italy, Mazzini (1831). 482
Fourteenth Amendment, Suffragists Protest the (May 10, 1866) 1181
Fourteenth Amendment Is Ratified (July 9, 1868) 1261
France, Abdelkader Leads Algeria Against (1832-1847). 508
France, Louis Napoleon Bonaparte Becomes Emperor of (Dec. 2, 1852) 861
France and Spain Invade Vietnam (Aug., 1858) 968

France Conquers Algeria (June 14-July 5, 1830) 464
France Occupies Mexico (Oct. 31, 1861-June 19, 1867). 1051
France vs. Britain, Fashoda Incident Pits (July 10-Nov. 3, 1898) 1908
France's Bourbon Dynasty Is Restored (Apr. 11, 1814-July 29, 1830) 210
Franchise Act of 1884, British Parliament Passes the (Dec. 6, 1884) 1627
Francis Joseph I Meet at Villafranca, Napoleon III and (July 11, 1859). 982
Franco-Prussian War (July 19, 1870-Jan. 28, 1871) 1325
Franco-Russian Alliance (Jan. 4, 1894). 1776
Fraser River Gold Rush Begins (Mar. 23, 1858) 960
Fraunhofer Invents the Spectroscope (1814). . . . 194
Free Public School Movement (1820's-1830's) 310
Freedmen's Bureau, Congress Creates the (Mar. 3, 1865). 1143
Frémont Explores the American West (May, 1842-1854) 660
French Indochina War (Apr., 1882-1885) 1553
French Republic Is Established, Third (Feb. 13, 1871-1875) 1353
French Right Wing Revives During Boulanger Crisis (Jan., 1886-1889). 1638
French Wars, Dahomey- (Nov., 1889-Jan., 1894). 1697
Freud Publishes *The Interpretation of Dreams* (1900) 1938
Frontier, U.S. Census Bureau Announces Closing of the (1890) 1705
Fugitive Slave Law, Second (Sept. 18, 1850) . . . 822
Fuji, Hokusai Produces *Thirty-Six Views of Mount* (1823-1831). 353
Funds for the Nobel Prizes, Nobel Bequeaths (Nov. 27, 1895) 1817
Fur Company Is Chartered, American (Apr. 6, 1808) 119
Furniture Style Becomes Popular, Biedermeier (c. 1815-1848) 225

Gadsden Purchase Completes the U.S.-Mexican Border (Dec. 31, 1853) 882
Galloping Horse, Muybridge Photographs a (1878) 1487
Galton Defines "Eugenics" (1883) 1572
Galveston Hurricane (Sept. 8, 1900) 1972
Games Are Inaugurated, Modern Olympic (Apr. 6, 1896) 1845
Garibaldi's Redshirts Land in Sicily (May-July, 1860). 1008
Garrison Begins Publishing *The Liberator* (Jan. 1, 1831) 487
Gas Lighting, Britain Adopts (1802) 29
Gaudí Begins Barcelona's Templo Expiatorio de la Sagrada Família (Nov. 3, 1883) 1592
General Allotment Act Erodes Indian Tribal Unity (Feb. 8, 1887). 1657
General Electric Opens Research Laboratory (Dec. 15, 1900) 1983
General to Surrender, Watie Is Last Confederate (June 23, 1865) 1153
Geology, Lyell Publishes *Principles of* (July, 1830) 467
Geometry, Hilbert Publishes *The Foundations of* (1899). 1913
Georgia and the Carolinas, Sherman Marches Through (Nov. 15, 1864-Apr. 18, 1865) . . . 1127
Germ Theory and Microbiology, Pasteur Begins Developing (1857) 933
German Confederation, Organization of the (June 8-9, 1815) 239
German Confederation Is Formed, North (1866-1867) 1173
German Empire, German States Unite Within (Jan. 18, 1871). 1349
German States Join to Form Customs Union (Jan. 1, 1834) 549
German States Unite Within German Empire (Jan. 18, 1871). 1349
Germany, Bismarck Introduces Social Security Programs in (1881-1889) 1534
Germany, Kulturkampf Against the Catholic Church in (1871-1877) 1340
Germany, Neanderthal Skull Is Found in (Aug., 1856) 923
Germany Movement, Young (1826-1842). 400
Germany Passes Anti-Socialist Law (Oct. 19, 1878) 1499
Germany's Kiel Canal Opens (June 20, 1895) 1808
Gettysburg, Vicksburg, and Chattanooga, Battles of (July 1-Nov. 25, 1863) 1102
Ghent Takes Effect, Treaty of (Feb. 17, 1815). . . 230
Giant Moas, Scientists Study Remains of (1830's-1840's). 432

Gibbons v. Ogden (Mar. 2, 1824) 376
Gives the United States Florida, Adams-Onís Treaty (Feb. 22, 1819) 293
Gives Women the Vote, Wyoming (Dec., 1869) 1304
Gladstone Becomes Prime Minister of Britain (Dec. 3, 1868-Feb. 20, 1874) 1274
Glidden Patents Barbed Wire (Nov. 24, 1874) 1416
Glücksburg Dynasty, Greece Unifies Under the (1863-1913) 1081
God We Trust" Appears on U.S. Coins, "In (Apr. 22, 1864) 1119
Gold Is Discovered in New South Wales (1851). 828
Gold Is Discovered in the Transvaal (June 21, 1884) 1612
Gold Rush Begins, California (Jan. 24, 1848) . . . 763
Gold Rush Begins, Fraser River (Mar. 23, 1858) 960
Gold Rush Begins, Klondike (Aug. 17, 1896) 1857
Golden Age, *La Sylphide* Inaugurates Romantic Ballet's (Mar. 12, 1832) 511
Golden Age of Flamenco Begins (c. 1869). . . . 1282
Golden State, Chinese Californians Form Native Sons of the (May 10, 1895) 1806
Goodwin Develops Celluloid Film (May, 1887) 1663
Goodyear Patents Vulcanized Rubber (June 15, 1844) 687
Government, First Test of Canada's Responsible (Apr. 25, 1849) 797
Government, Kabo Reforms Begin Modernization of Korean (July 8, 1894-Jan. 1, 1896). 1782
Goya Paints *Third of May 1808: Execution of the Citizens of Madrid* (Mar., 1814) 203
Grand Trunk Railway Is Incorporated, Canada's (Nov. 10, 1852) 858
Grange Is Formed, National (Dec. 4, 1867) . . . 1231
Grant Administration, Scandals Rock the (Sept. 24, 1869-1877) 1296
Grant Signs Indian Appropriation Act (Mar. 3, 1871) 1355
Great American Buffalo Slaughter (c. 1871-1883) 1343
Great Britain Begins Colonizing Tasmania (Sept. 7, 1803) 55
Great Britain Establishes Penny Postage (Jan. 10, 1840) 641
Great Britain Occupies the Falkland Islands (Jan., 1833) 527
Great Britain Strengthens Its Royal Navy (1889) 1680
Great Britain Withdraws from the Concert of Europe (Oct. 20-30, 1822) 350
Great Britain's First Trades Union Congress Forms (June 2, 1868) 1255
Great Chicago Fire (Oct. 8-10, 1871). 1366
Great Eastern, Brunel Launches the SS (Jan. 31, 1858) 955
Great Irish Famine (1845-1854) 696
Great Java War (1825-1830) 386
Great Sioux War (Aug. 17, 1862-Dec. 28, 1863) 1070
Great Trek Begins, South Africa's (1835) 563
Greco-Turkish War (Jan. 21-May 20, 1897) . . . 1872
Greece Unifies Under the Glücksburg Dynasty (1863-1913) 1081
Greeks Fight for Independence from the Ottoman Empire (Mar. 7, 1821-Sept. 29, 1829) 336
Grimm Publish Fairy Tales, Brothers (1812-1815) 160
Grito de Dolores, Hidalgo Issues El (Sept. 16, 1810) 138
Ground Is Broken for the Washington Monument (July 4, 1848). 781
Guadalupe Hidalgo Ends Mexican War, Treaty of (Feb. 2, 1848) 770
Guilds Promote the Arts and Crafts Movement, New (1884) 1597
Gun, Maxim Patents His Machine (1884) 1594

Hague Peace Conference, First (May 18-July, 1899). 1926
Hamburg-Amerika Shipping Line Begins (1847). 740
Happersett, Minor v. (Mar. 9, 1875) 1426
Hardie Becomes Parliament's First Labour Member (Aug. 3, 1892) 1748
Harpers Ferry, Brown's Raid on (Oct. 16-18, 1859) 988
Harrison Signs the Sherman Antitrust Act (July 20, 1890) 1712
Hartford Convention (Dec. 15, 1814-Jan. 5, 1815) 219

Hartford Female Seminary Is Founded (May, 1823) 356
Hawaii's Last Monarch Abdicates (Jan. 24, 1895) 1797
Hay Articulates "Open Door" Policy Toward China (Sept. 6, 1899-July 3, 1900) 1928
Hayes Becomes President (Mar. 5, 1877) 1472
Hayne Debate Slavery and Westward Expansion, Webster and (Jan. 19-27, 1830) 451
Hearst-Pulitzer Circulation War (1895-1898) 1794
Hegel Publishes *The Phenomenology of Spirit* (Apr., 1807). 106
Hereditary Theory, Rediscovery of Mendel's (1899-1900) 1920
Heredity, Mendel Proposes Laws of (1865) . . . 1135
Hernani Incites Rioting, Hugo's (Mar. 3, 1830) 454
Herzl Founds the Zionist Movement (Feb., 1896-Aug., 1897). 1836
Hidalgo Ends Mexican War, Treaty of Guadalupe (Feb. 2, 1848). 770
Hidalgo Issues El Grito de Dolores (Sept. 16, 1810) 138
High-Pressure Steam Engine, Trevithick Patents the (Mar. 24, 1802) 38
Hilbert Publishes *The Foundations of Geometry* (1899) 1913
Hill Launches Housing Reform in London (1864) 1114
Hiroshige Completes *The Tokaido Fifty-Three Stations* (1831-1834) 484
History, Ranke Develops Systematic (1824). . . . 371
Hokusai Produces *Thirty-Six Views of Mount Fuji* (1823-1831) 353
Holmes, Conan Doyle Introduces Sherlock (Dec., 1887) 1666
Holyoke Female Seminary Opens, Mount (Nov. 8, 1837) 597
Home Rule Debate Dominates British Politics, Irish (June, 1886-Sept. 9, 1893). 1645
Homestead Act, Lincoln Signs the (May 20, 1862) 1064
Horse, Muybridge Photographs a Galloping (1878) 1487
Hosts the Centennial Exposition, Philadelphia (May 10-Nov. 10, 1876) 1451
Hosts the First World's Fair, London (May 1-Oct. 15, 1851). 840
House Introduces Modern Realistic Drama, *A Doll's* (1879) 1501
House of Representatives Elects Jefferson President (Feb. 17, 1801) 20
Houses of Parliament Are Rebuilt, British (Apr. 27, 1840-Feb., 1852) 643
Housing Reform in London, Hill Launches (1864) 1114
Howe Patents His Sewing Machine (Sept. 10, 1846) 732
Huckleberry Finn, Twain Publishes *Adventures of* (Dec., 1884-Feb., 1885) 1624
Hugo's *Hernani* Incites Rioting (Mar. 3, 1830) 454
Hull-House, Addams Opens Chicago's (Sept. 18, 1889) 1692
Hunt, Commonwealth v. (Mar., 1842) 658
Hurricane, Galveston (Sept. 8, 1900) 1972
Hydroelectric Plant Opens at Niagara Falls, First U.S. (Nov. 16, 1896). 1863

Ilbert Bill, Indian Legislative Council Enacts the (Jan. 25, 1884). 1606
Immaculate Conception Dogma, Pius IX Decrees the (Dec. 8, 1854) 906
Immigrant Farmers Begin Settling Western Canada (1896). 1831
Immigrating to California, Chinese Begin (1849). 793
Immigration, American Era of "Old" (1840's-1850's) 631
Immigration Depot Opens, Ellis Island (Jan. 1, 1892) 1737
Immigration Era Begins, America's "New" (1892) 1730
Immigration to Canada, Irish (1829-1836). 423
Immunity, Metchnikoff Advances the Cellular Theory of (1882-1901) 1545
Impeachment of Andrew Johnson (Feb. 24-May 26, 1868). 1245
Importation of African Slaves, Congress Bans (Mar. 2, 1807) 103
Impressionist Exhibition, First (Apr. 15, 1874) 1410
Impressionist Movement Begins, Post- (Late 1870's) 1434
Improved Steel-Processing Method, Bessemer Patents (1855) 909
"In God We Trust" Appears on U.S. Coins (Apr. 22, 1864) 1119

Inaugurated, Modern Olympic Games Are (Apr. 6, 1896) 1845
Inaugurated President, Lincoln Is (Mar. 4, 1861) 1028
Inaugurates Romantic Ballet's Golden Age, *La Sylphide* (Mar. 12, 1832) 511
Incandescent Lamp, Edison Demonstrates the (Oct. 21, 1879) 1517
Incident Pits France vs. Britain, Fashoda (July 10-Nov. 3, 1898) 1908
Incites Rioting, Hugo's *Hernani* (Mar. 3, 1830) 454
Incorporated, Canada's Grand Trunk Railway Is (Nov. 10, 1852) 858
Incorporated, Standard Oil Company Is (Jan. 10, 1870) 1318
Independence, Cuban War of (Feb. 24, 1895-1898) 1802
Independence, Fenian Risings for Irish (June, 1866-1871) 1184
Independence, Liberia Proclaims Its (July 26, 1847) 748
Independence, Mexican War of (Sept. 16, 1810-Sept. 28, 1821) 140
Independence from the Ottoman Empire, Greeks Fight for (Mar. 7, 1821-Sept. 29, 1829) 336
Independent, Brazil Becomes (Sept. 7, 1822) 348
Independent U.S. Treasury, Establishment of (Aug. 1, 1846) 726
India, British Abolish Suttee in (Dec. 4, 1829) 428
India, Lambton Begins Trigonometrical Survey of (Apr. 10, 1802) 40
Indian Act, Canada's (1876) 1437
Indian Appropriation Act, Grant Signs (Mar. 3, 1871) 1355
Indian Legislative Council Enacts the Ilbert Bill (Jan. 25, 1884) 1606
Indian National Congress Is Founded (1885) 1630
Indian Removal Act, Congress Passes (May 28, 1830) 460
Indian Tribal Unity, General Allotment Act Erodes (Feb. 8, 1887) 1657
Indigent Women and Children Opens, New York Infirmary for (May 12, 1857) 947
Indochina War, French (Apr., 1882-1885) 1553
Industrial Machines, Luddites Destroy (Mar. 11, 1811-1816) 151
Industry, Kellogg's Corn Flakes Launch the Dry Cereal (1894-1895) 1770
Infallibility Dogma, Vatican I Decrees Papal (Dec. 8, 1869-Oct. 20, 1870) 1307
Infirmary for Indigent Women and Children Opens, New York (May 12, 1857) 947
Installs the First Passenger Elevator, Otis (Mar. 23, 1857) 942
Institution Is Founded, Smithsonian (Aug. 10, 1846) 729
Insurrection, Philippine (Feb. 4, 1899-July 4, 1902) 1922
Insurrection, Turner Launches Slave (Aug. 21, 1831) 499
Insurrection in Spain, Dos de Mayo (May 2, 1808) 122
Integration Theory, Lebesgue Develops New (1900) 1941
Internal Combustion Engine, Lenoir Patents the (1860) 998
Internal Combustion Engine, Otto Invents a Practical (May, 1876) 1449
International Is Founded, First (Sept. 28, 1864) 1124
International Red Cross Is Launched (Aug. 22, 1864) 1122
Interpretation of Dreams, Freud Publishes *The* (1900) 1938
Interstate Commerce Act (Feb. 4, 1887) 1655
Introduces Brownie Cameras, Kodak (Feb., 1900) 1950
Introduces Button-Down Shirts, Brooks Brothers (1896) 1828
Introduces Coca-Cola, Pemberton (May 8, 1886) 1643
Introduces Modern Realistic Drama, *A Doll's House* (1879) 1501
Introduces Principles of Social Darwinism, Spencer (1862) 1058
Introduces Sherlock Holmes, Conan Doyle (Dec., 1887) 1666
Introduces Social Security Programs in Germany, Bismarck (1881-1889) 1534
Introduces *The Lancet*, Wakley (Oct. 5, 1823) 358
Introduces the Romantic Age, Beethoven's *Eroica* Symphony (Apr. 7, 1805) 78
Invade Vietnam, France and Spain (Aug., 1858) 968
Invades Nicaragua, Walker (June 16, 1855-May 1, 1857) 914

Invades Russia, Napoleon (June 23-Dec. 14, 1812) 170
Invasion, Ethiopia Repels Italian (Mar. 1, 1896) 1842
Invent Daguerreotype Photography, Daguerre and Niépce (1839) 613
Invents a Practical Internal Combustion Engine, Otto (May, 1876) 1449
Invents Basketball, Naismith (1891) 1721
Invents the Inverted Pendulum Seismograph, Wiechert (1900) 1944
Invents the Reaper, McCormick (Summer, 1831) 496
Invents the Spectroscope, Fraunhofer (1814) . . . 194
Invents the Stethoscope, Laënnec (1816) 250
Inverted Pendulum Seismograph, Wiechert Invents the (1900) 1944
Irish Famine, Great (1845-1854). 696
Irish Home Rule Debate Dominates British Politics (June, 1886-Sept. 9, 1893) 1645
Irish Immigration to Canada (1829-1836) 423
Irish Independence, Fenian Risings for (June, 1866-1871) 1184
Irish Melodies, Moore Publishes (1807-1834) . . . 96
Irish Nationalists, Kilmainham Treaty Makes Concessions to (May 2, 1882). 1556
Irish Riots Erupt in Philadelphia, Anti- (May 6-July 5, 1844) 681
Irish Tenant Farmers Stage First "Boycott" (Sept.-Nov., 1880) 1528
Irving Manages London's Lyceum Theatre (1878-1899) 1490
Irving's *Sketch Book* Transforms American Literature (1819-1820) 288
Isandlwana and Rorke's Drift, Battles of (Jan. 22-23, 1879) 1507
Island, Slave Traders Begin Ravaging Easter (Nov., 1862). 1076
Island, Stevenson Publishes *Treasure* (July, 1881-1883) 1537
Island Immigration Depot Opens, Ellis (Jan. 1, 1892) 1737
Islands, Great Britain Occupies the Falkland (Jan., 1833) 527
Isolate Adrenaline, Abel and Takamine (1897-1901) 1869
Issues El Grito de Dolores, Hidalgo (Sept. 16, 1810) 138
Issues the Emancipation Proclamation, Lincoln (Jan. 1, 1863) 1084
Issues the Syllabus of Errors, Pius IX (Dec. 8, 1864). 1133
Italian Invasion, Ethiopia Repels (Mar. 1, 1896) 1842
Italian Revolution of 1848 (Jan. 12, 1848-Aug. 28, 1849) 760
Italy, Mazzini Founds Young (1831). 482
Italy Is Proclaimed a Kingdom (Mar. 17, 1861) 1032

Jackson Vetoes Rechartering of the Bank of the United States (July 10, 1832). 518
Jameson Raid (Dec. 29, 1895-Jan. 2, 1896) . . . 1824
Janissary Revolt, Ottomans Suppress the (1808-1826). 114
Japan Adopts a New Constitution (Feb. 11, 1889) 1683
Japan Expands into Korea (1870's). 1313
Japan to Western Trade, Perry Opens (Mar. 31, 1854) 888
Japanese Rule, Korean Military Mutinies Against (July 23, 1882-Jan. 9, 1885) 1563
Japanese War, Sino- (Aug. 1, 1894-Apr. 17, 1895) 1784
Japanese Yellow Peril Campaign Begins, Anti- (May 4, 1892) 1742
Japan's Charter Oath, Promulgation of (Apr. 6, 1868) 1253
Japan's Meiji Restoration (Jan. 3, 1868) 1242
Java War, Great (1825-1830) 386
Jedediah Smith Explores the Far West (1822-1831). 342
Jefferson President, House of Representatives Elects (Feb. 17, 1801) 20
Jesuits Are Expelled from Russia, Naples, and Spain (1820) 315
Jesus Critically Examined, Strauss Publishes *The Life of* (1835-1836) 566
Jewish Member of British Parliament, Rothschild Is First (July 26, 1858) 966
Johnson, Impeachment of Andrew (Feb. 24-May 26, 1868). 1245
Johnstown Flood (May 31, 1889). 1689
Join to Form Customs Union, German States (Jan. 1, 1834) 549
Joplin Popularizes Ragtime Music and Dance (1899) 1917
Journalism, Rise of Yellow (1880's-1890's) . . . 1526
July Revolution Deposes Charles X (July 29, 1830) 470

Kabo Reforms Begin Modernization of Korean Government (July 8, 1894-Jan. 1, 1896) . . . 1782
Kansas, Bleeding (May, 1856-Aug., 1858) 919
Kansas-Nebraska Act, Congress Passes the (May 30, 1854) 891
Kapital, Marx Publishes *Das* (1867) 1207
Kellogg's Corn Flakes Launch the Dry Cereal Industry (1894-1895) 1770
Key Economic Principles, Ricardo Identifies Seven (1817) 267
Khartoum, Siege of (Mar. 13, 1884-Jan. 26, 1885) 1609
Kiel Canal Opens, Germany's (June 20, 1895) 1808
Kilmainham Treaty Makes Concessions to Irish Nationalists (May 2, 1882) 1556
Kimberley Diamondfields, Rhodes Amalgamates (Mar. 13, 1888) 1674
Kingdom, Italy Is Proclaimed a (Mar. 17, 1861) 1032
Klondike Gold Rush Begins (Aug. 17, 1896). . . 1857
Klux Klan, Birth of the Ku (1866) 1169
Knickerbocker School, Rise of the (1807-1850) 99
Koch Announces His Discovery of the Tuberculosis Bacillus (Mar. 24, 1882) 1550
Kodak Introduces Brownie Cameras (Feb., 1900) 1950
Könniggrätz, Battle of (July 3, 1866) 1193
Korea, Japan Expands into (1870's) 1313
Korean Government, Kabo Reforms Begin Modernization of (July 8, 1894-Jan. 1, 1896) 1782
Korean Military Mutinies Against Japanese Rule (July 23, 1882-Jan. 9, 1885). 1563
Krakatoa Volcano Erupts (Aug. 27, 1883) 1583
Krupp Works Open at Essen (Sept. 20, 1811) . . . 154
Ku Klux Klan, Birth of the (1866) 1169
Kulturkampf Against the Catholic Church in Germany (1871-1877). 1340

La Sylphide Inaugurates Romantic Ballet's Golden Age (Mar. 12, 1832) 511
Labor, Papal Encyclical on (May 15, 1891) . . . 1727
Labor Is Founded, American Federation of (Dec. 8, 1886) 1652
Labor Party Is Formed, Russian Social-Democratic (Mar., 1898) 1895
Laboratory, General Electric Opens Research (Dec. 15, 1900) 1983
Labour, Blanc Publishes *The Organization of* (1839). 610
Labour Member, Hardie Becomes Parliament's First (Aug. 3, 1892) 1748
Labour Party Is Formed, British (Feb. 27, 1900) 1954
Laënnec Invents the Stethoscope (1816). 250
Lamarck Publishes *Zoological Philosophy* (1809). 128
Lambton Begins Trigonometrical Survey of India (Apr. 10, 1802). 40
Lamp, Davy Develops the Arc (c. 1801-1810) . . . 11
Lamp, Edison Demonstrates the Incandescent (Oct. 21, 1879) 1517
Lancet, Wakley Introduces *The* (Oct. 5, 1823). . . 358
Land Act of 1820, Congress Passes (Apr. 24, 1820) 328
Land Grant Act, Lincoln Signs the Morrill (July 2, 1862) 1066
Land in Sicily, Garibaldi's Redshirts (May-July, 1860). 1008
Land in Western Australia, Last Convicts (1868) 1238
Lands Act Fosters Canadian Settlement, Dominion (1872) 1369
Landscape Painting Flourishes, Barbizon School of (c. 1830-1870) 445
Lartet Discovers the First Cro-Magnon Remains (Mar., 1868) 1247
Last Confederate General to Surrender, Watie Is (June 23, 1865) 1153
Last Convicts Land in Western Australia (1868) 1238
Last Monarch Abdicates, Hawaii's (Jan. 24, 1895) 1797
Last Slave Ship Docks at Mobile (July, 1859). . . 979
Launch the Dry Cereal Industry, Kellogg's Corn Flakes (1894-1895) 1770
Launched, International Red Cross Is (Aug. 22, 1864). 1122
Launches a Mail-Order Business, Ward (Aug., 1872) 1378
Launches Housing Reform in London, Hill (1864) 1114
Launches Slave Insurrection, Turner (Aug. 21, 1831) 499
Launches *The Economist*, Wilson (Sept. 2, 1843) 678
Launches *The North Star*, Douglass (Dec. 3, 1847) 753

Launches the SS *Great Eastern*, Brunel (Jan. 31, 1858) 955
Laureate, Tennyson Becomes England's Poet (Nov. 5, 1850) 825
Laurier Becomes the First French Canadian Prime Minister (July 11, 1896) 1854
Law, British Parliament Passes New Poor (Aug. 14, 1834). 554
Law, Congress Enacts the Page (Mar. 3, 1875) 1423
Law, Congress Passes the Comstock Antiobscenity (Mar. 3, 1873) 1394
Law, Germany Passes Anti-Socialist (Oct. 19, 1878) 1499
Law, Second Fugitive Slave (Sept. 18, 1850) . . . 822
Law, Union Enacts the First National Draft (Mar. 3, 1863). 1095
Law of Thermodynamics, Clausius Formulates the Second (1850-1865) 813
Laws of Heredity, Mendel Proposes (1865) . . . 1135
Layard Explores and Excavates Assyrian Ruins (1839-1847). 619
Leading the People, Delacroix Paints *Liberty* (October-Dec., 1830). 476
Leads Algeria Against France, Abdelkader (1832-1847). 508
League Is Formed, Three Emperors' (May 6-Oct. 22, 1873). 1398
Lebesgue Develops New Integration Theory (1900) 1941
Lectures on "Revivals of Religion," Finney (1835). 560
Legislative Council Enacts the Ilbert Bill, Indian (Jan. 25, 1884). 1606
Leipzig, Battle of (Oct. 16-19, 1813) 191
Lenoir Patents the Internal Combustion Engine (1860). 998
Lewis and Clark Expedition (May 14, 1804-Sept. 23, 1806). 65
Liberator, Garrison Begins Publishing *The* (Jan. 1, 1831) 487
Liberia Proclaims Its Independence (July 26, 1847) 748
Liberty, Mill Publishes *On* (1859) 971
Liberty Is Dedicated, Statue of (Oct. 28, 1886) 1649
Liberty Leading the People, Delacroix Paints (October-Dec., 1830) 476
Libraries, Development of Working-Class (19th cent.) 3
Library Association Is Founded, American (Oct. 4-6, 1876) 1467
Library of Congress Building Opens, New (Nov. 1, 1897). 1886
Liebig Advocates Artificial Fertilizers (1840) . . . 638
Life of Jesus Critically Examined, Strauss Publishes *The* (1835-1836) 566
Lighting, Britain Adopts Gas (1802) 29
Lincoln, Surrender at Appomattox and Assassination of (Apr. 9 and 14, 1865) 1146
Lincoln-Douglas Debates (June 16-Oct. 15, 1858) 963
Lincoln Is Elected U.S. President (Nov. 6, 1860) 1010
Lincoln Is Inaugurated President (Mar. 4, 1861) 1028
Lincoln Issues the Emancipation Proclamation (Jan. 1, 1863) 1084
Lincoln Signs the Homestead Act (May 20, 1862) 1064
Lincoln Signs the Morrill Land Grant Act (July 2, 1862) 1066
Lister Publishes His Theory on Antiseptic Surgery (1867) 1204
Literary Renaissance, Arabic (19th cent.) 1
Literature, American Renaissance in (c. 1830's-1860's) 435
Literature, Irving's *Sketch Book* Transforms American (1819-1820) 288
Literature Flourishes, Brahmin School of American (1880's) 1520
Lithographica Is Discovered, *Archaeopteryx* (1861) 1014
Little Bighorn, Battle of the (June 25, 1876) . . . 1454
Livingstone Sees the Victoria Falls (Nov. 17, 1853) 879
Lodge Creek Treaty, Medicine (Oct. 21, 1867) 1228
Logic, Boole Publishes *The Mathematical Analysis of* (1847) 737
London, First Underground Railroad Opens in (Jan. 10, 1863). 1087
London, Hill Launches Housing Reform in (1864) 1114
London Exile, Mazzini Begins (Jan. 12, 1837) 589
London Hosts the First World's Fair (May 1-Oct. 15, 1851). 840
London's Cato Street Conspirators Plot Assassinations (Feb. 23, 1820) 323

London's Lyceum Theatre, Irving Manages (1878-1899) 1490
London's Savoy Theatre Opens (Oct. 10, 1881) 1539
Long Walk of the Navajos (Aug., 1863-Sept., 1866) 1105
Louis Napoleon Bonaparte Becomes Emperor of France (Dec. 2, 1852) 861
Louisiana Purchase (May 9, 1803) 51
Lower Canada Unite, Upper and (Feb. 10, 1841) 650
Luddites Destroy Industrial Machines (Mar. 11, 1811-1816) 151
Lyceum Theatre, Irving Manages London's (1878-1899) 1490
Lyell Publishes *Principles of Geology* (July, 1830) 467

McCormick Invents the Reaper (Summer, 1831) 496
McCulloch v. Maryland (Mar. 6, 1819) 296
Macdonald Returns as Canada's Prime Minister (Sept., 1878). 1496
McGill University, Founding of (1813) 179
Machine, Howe Patents His Sewing (Sept. 10, 1846) 732
Machine Gun, Maxim Patents His (1884) 1594
Machines, Luddites Destroy Industrial (Mar. 11, 1811-1816) 151
Mackenzie Era, Canada's (Nov. 5, 1873-Oct. 9, 1878) 1407
McKinley Is Elected President (Nov. 3, 1896) 1860
Madame Bovary, Flaubert Publishes (Oct. 1-Dec. 15, 1856) 926
Madison, Madison v. (Feb. 24, 1803) 49
Mafeking, Siege of (Oct. 13, 1899-May 17, 1900) 1935
Magnetic Force into Electricity, Faraday Converts (October, 1831). 502
Magnetism's Relationship to Electricity, Ampère Reveals (Nov. 6, 1820) 334
Maiden Voyage of the *Clermont* (Aug. 17, 1807) 111
Mail, Pony Express Expedites Transcontinental (Apr. 3, 1860-Oct. 26, 1861) 1001
Mail-Order Business, Ward Launches a (Aug., 1872) 1378
Maine's Canadian Border, Webster-Ashburton Treaty Settles (Aug. 9, 1842). 666
Malaria's Transmission Vector, Ross Establishes (Aug. 20, 1897). 1883
Mamlūks Massacred, Muḥammad ʿAlī Has the (Mar. 1, 1811). 149
Man, Darwin Publishes *The Descent of* (1871) 1334
Manages London's Lyceum Theatre, Irving (1878-1899) 1490
Manifesto, Marx and Engels Publish *The Communist* (Feb., 1848) 767
Maratha War, Third (Nov. 5, 1817-June 3, 1818) 276
Marbles to England, Elgin Ships Parthenon (1803-1812) 46
Marbury v. Madison (Feb. 24, 1803) 49
Marches Through Georgia and the Carolinas, Sherman (Nov. 15, 1864-Apr. 18, 1865) . . . 1127
Marconi Patents the Wireless Telegraph (June, 1896) 1851
Marx and Engels Publish *The Communist Manifesto* (Feb., 1848) 767
Marx Publishes *Das Kapital* (1867) 1207
Mary Appears to Bernadette Soubirous, Virgin (Feb. 11-July 16, 1858). 958
Maryland, McCulloch v. (Mar. 6, 1819) 296
Massacre, California's Bloody Island (May 6, 1850) 820
Massacre, Fetterman (Dec. 21, 1866). 1199
Massacre, Sand Creek (Nov. 29, 1864). 1130
Massacre, Washita River (Nov. 27, 1868) 1271
Massacre, Wounded Knee (Dec. 29, 1890). . . . 1718
Massacred, Muḥammad ʿAlī Has the Mamlūks (Mar. 1, 1811). 149
Mathematical Analysis of Logic, Boole Publishes *The* (1847) 737
Matrimonial Causes Act, British Parliament Passes the (Aug. 28, 1857) 952
Matter, Dalton Formulates the Atomic Theory of (1803-1808). 43
Maxim Patents His Machine Gun (1884). 1594
Mayan Antiquities, Stephens Begins Uncovering (Nov., 1839). 628
Mayo Insurrection in Spain, Dos de (May 2, 1808) 122
Mazzini Begins London Exile (Jan. 12, 1837). . . 589
Mazzini Founds Young Italy (1831) 482
Mecca in Disguise, Burton Enters (Sept. 12, 1853) 873
Mechanical Calculator, Babbage Designs a (1819-1833). 291

Medicine Lodge Creek Treaty (Oct. 21, 1867) 1228
Meet at Villafranca, Napoleon III and Francis Joseph I (July 11, 1859) 982
Meetings of the Plymouth Brethren, First (c. 1826-1827) 398
Meiji Restoration, Japan's (Jan. 3, 1868) 1242
Melbourne, Australia, Is Founded (Aug. 16, 1835) 573
Melodies, Moore Publishes *Irish* (1807-1834) . . . 96
Melville Publishes *Moby Dick* (1851) 830
Member of British Parliament, Rothschild Is First Jewish (July 26, 1858) 966
Memphis and New Orleans Race Riots (May and July, 1866) 1178
Mendel Proposes Laws of Heredity (1865). . . . 1135
Mendeleyev Develops the Periodic Table of Elements (1869-1871). 1284
Mendel's Hereditary Theory, Rediscovery of (1899-1900) 1920
Mennonites Begin Settling in Canada, Ukrainian (1873) 1380
Message, Morse Sends First Telegraph (May 24, 1844) 684
Metabolism, Saussure Publishes His Research on Plant (1804). 59
Metchnikoff Advances the Cellular Theory of Immunity (1882-1901) 1545
Method, Bessemer Patents Improved Steel-Processing (1855). 909
Methodist Episcopal Church Is Founded, African (Apr. 9, 1816) 257
Metropolitan Museum of Art Opens (Feb. 20, 1872) 1372
Metropolitan Opera House Opens in New York (Oct. 22, 1883) 1589
Mexican Border, Gadsden Purchase Completes the U.S.- (Dec. 31, 1853). 882
Mexican War (May 13, 1846-Feb. 2, 1848) 710
Mexican War, Treaty of Guadalupe Hidalgo Ends (Feb. 2, 1848). 770
Mexican War of Independence (Sept. 16, 1810-Sept. 28, 1821) 140
Mexico, France Occupies (Oct. 31, 1861-June 19, 1867). 1051
Mexico into Civil War, Díaz Drives (1871-1876) 1338
Microbiology, Pasteur Begins Developing Germ Theory and (1857) 933
Migration Begins, Westward American (c. 1815-1830) 221
Migration to Utah, Mormons Begin (Feb. 4, 1846) 703
Miguelite Wars, Portugal's (1828-1834). 403
Military Academy Is Established, U.S. (Mar. 16, 1802). 35
Military Campaigns, Bolívar's (Mar., 1813-Dec. 9, 1824) 181
Military Campaigns, San Martín's (Jan. 18, 1817-July 28, 1821) 273
Military Mutinies Against Japanese Rule, Korean (July 23, 1882-Jan. 9, 1885) 1563
Mill Publishes *On Liberty* (1859) 971
Minister-President, Bismarck Becomes Prussia's (Sept. 24, 1862). 1073
Minoan Civilization, Evans Discovers Crete's (Mar. 23, 1900) 1956
Minor v. Happersett (Mar. 9, 1875). 1426
Minstrel Shows, First (Feb. 6, 1843). 675
Mississippi Constitution Disfranchises Black Voters (1890) 1702
Mississippi Enacts First Post-Civil War Black Code (Nov. 24, 1865) 1164
Missouri Compromise (Mar. 3, 1820) 325
Mitosis, Roux Develops the Theory of (1880's) 1523
Moas, Scientists Study Remains of Giant (1830's-1840's). 432
Mobile, Last Slave Ship Docks at (July, 1859) 979
Moby Dick, Melville Publishes (1851). 830
Modern American Circus, Barnum Creates the First (Apr. 10, 1871). 1360
Modern Baseball Begins (c. 1845). 693
Modern Department Store Opens in Paris, First (1869) 1279
Modern *New York Times* Is Founded (Sept. 18, 1851) 849
Modern Olympic Games Are Inaugurated (Apr. 6, 1896) 1845
Modern Realistic Drama, *A Doll's House* Introduces (1879) 1501
Modernization of Korean Government, Kabo Reforms Begin (July 8, 1894-Jan. 1, 1896). 1782
Monarch Abdicates, Hawaii's Last (Jan. 24, 1895) 1797
Monitor and the *Virginia*, Battle of the (Mar. 9, 1862) 1061

Monroe Articulates the Monroe Doctrine, President (Dec. 2, 1823) 361
Monroe Doctrine, President Monroe Articulates the (Dec. 2, 1823). 361
Monument, Ground Is Broken for the Washington (July 4, 1848) 781
Moore Publishes *Irish Melodies* (1807-1834). . . . 96
Morant Bay Rebellion (Oct. 7-12, 1865) 1161
Mormon Church, Smith Founds the (Apr. 6, 1830) 457
Mormons Begin Migration to Utah (Feb. 4, 1846) 703
Morrill Land Grant Act, Lincoln Signs the (July 2, 1862) 1066
Morris Founds Design Firm (1861). 1016
Morse Sends First Telegraph Message (May 24, 1844) 684
"Morte d'Arthur," Tennyson Publishes (1842). . . 655
Moscow Art Theater Is Founded (Oct. 14, 1898) 1910
Motion Pictures, First Commercial Projection of (Dec. 28, 1895). 1820
Moulin Rouge, Toulouse-Lautrec Paints *At the* (1892-1895) 1734
Mount Fuji, Hokusai Produces *Thirty-Six Views of* (1823-1831) 353
Mount Holyoke Female Seminary Opens (Nov. 8, 1837) 597
Mounted Police, Canada Forms the North-West (May 23, 1873) 1401
Movement, Chartist (May 8, 1838-Apr. 10, 1848) 605
Movement, *Costumbrismo* (c. 1820-1860). 320
Movement, Courbet Establishes Realist Art (1855). 911
Movement, Eddy Establishes the Christian Science (Oct. 30, 1875) 1431
Movement, Free Public School (1820's-1830's) 310
Movement, Herzl Founds the Zionist (Feb., 1896-Aug., 1897). 1836
Movement, New Guilds Promote the Arts and Crafts (1884) 1597
Movement, Rise of the Symbolist (1886). 1636
Movement, Russian Realist (1840's-1880's) . . . 635
Movement, Social Reform (1820's-1850's) 312
Movement, Young Germany (1826-1842). 400
Movement Arises, Aesthetic (1870's) 1310
Movement Arises, China's Self-Strengthening (1860's). 995
Movement Arises in New England, Transcendental (1836) 581
Movement Begins, Naturalist (c. 1865). 1138
Movement Begins, Oxford (July 14, 1833) 530
Movement Begins, Post-Impressionist (Late 1870's) 1434
Movement Flourishes, Decadent (c. 1884-1924) 1600
Muḥammad ʿAlī Has the Mamlūks Massacred (Mar. 1, 1811). 149
Munch Paints *The Scream* (1893). 1751
Municipal Corporations Act, British Parliament Passes (Sept. 9, 1835) 575
Museum of Art Opens, Metropolitan (Feb. 20, 1872) 1372
Music, Rise of Tin Pan Alley (1890's) 1700
Music and Dance, Joplin Popularizes Ragtime (1899) 1917
Muslim Rebellions in China (Winter, 1855-Jan. 2, 1878) 917
Mutinies Against Japanese Rule, Korean Military (July 23, 1882-Jan. 9, 1885) 1563
Mutiny Against British Rule, Sepoy (May 10, 1857-July 8, 1858) 944
Muybridge Photographs a Galloping Horse (1878) 1487

Naismith Invents Basketball (1891) 1721
Nansen Attempts to Reach the North Pole (1893-1896) 1754
Naples, and Spain, Jesuits Are Expelled from Russia, (1820) 315
Napoleon I, Bonaparte Is Crowned (Dec. 2, 1804). 72
Napoleon III and Francis Joseph I Meet at Villafranca (July 11, 1859) 982
Napoleon Bonaparte Becomes Emperor of France, Louis (Dec. 2, 1852) 861
Napoleon Invades Russia (June 23-Dec. 14, 1812) 170
National Bank Acts, Congress Passes the (Feb. 25, 1863-June 3, 1864) 1093
National Congress Is Founded, Indian (1885) 1630
National Council of Colored People Is Founded (July 6, 1853) 870
National Council of Women of Canada Is Founded (Oct. 27, 1893) 1768
National Draft Law, Union Enacts the First (Mar. 3, 1863). 1095

National Grange Is Formed (Dec. 4, 1867) 1231
National Park, Yellowstone Becomes the First U.S. (Mar. 1, 1872) 1375
National Road, Construction of the (1811-1840) 146
Nationalists, Kilmainham Treaty Makes Concessions to Irish (May 2, 1882) 1556
Native Sons of the Golden State, Chinese Californians Form (May 10, 1895) 1806
Naturalist Movement Begins (c. 1865) 1138
Navajo War, Apache and (Apr. 30, 1860-1865) 1005
Navajos, Long Walk of the (Aug., 1863-Sept., 1866) 1105
Navy, Great Britain Strengthens Its Royal (1889) 1680
Neanderthal Skull Is Found in Germany (Aug., 1856) 923
Neapolitan Revolution (July 2, 1820-Mar., 1821) 330
Nebraska Act, Congress Passes the Kansas-(May 30, 1854) 891
Nervous System, Ramón y Cajal Shows How Neurons Work in the (1888-1906) 1671
Neurons Work in the Nervous System, Ramón y Cajal Shows How (1888-1906) . . . 1671
New Constitution, Japan Adopts a (Feb. 11, 1889) 1683
New England, Transcendental Movement Arises in (1836) 581
New Guilds Promote the Arts and Crafts Movement (1884) 1597
New Harmony, Communitarian Experiments at (Spring, 1814-1830) 206
"New" Immigration Era Begins, America's (1892) 1730
New Integration Theory, Lebesgue Develops (1900) 1941
New Library of Congress Building Opens (Nov. 1, 1897) 1886
New Orleans, Battle of (Jan. 8, 1815) 227
New Orleans Race Riots, Memphis and (May and July, 1866) 1178
New Poor Law, British Parliament Passes (Aug. 14, 1834) 554
New South Wales, Gold Is Discovered in (1851) 828
New York, Metropolitan Opera House Opens in (Oct. 22, 1883) 1589
New York Infirmary for Indigent Women and Children Opens (May 12, 1857) 947
New York Times Is Founded, Modern (Sept. 18, 1851) 849
New Zealand Women Win Voting Rights (Sept. 19, 1893) 1761
Newman Becomes a Roman Catholic (Oct. 9, 1845) 700
Nez Perce War (June 15-Oct. 5, 1877) 1479
Niagara Falls, First U.S. Hydroelectric Plant Opens at (Nov. 16, 1896) 1863
Nian Rebellion, Qing Dynasty Confronts the (1853-1868) 864
Nicaragua, Walker Invades (June 16, 1855-May 1, 1857) 914
Niépce Invent Daguerreotype Photography, Daguerre and (1839) 613
Nightingale Takes Charge of Nursing in the Crimea (Nov. 4, 1854) 903
Ninth Symphony, First Performance of Beethoven's (May 7, 1824) 380
Nobel Bequeaths Funds for the Nobel Prizes (Nov. 27, 1895) 1817
Nobel Patents Dynamite (October, 1867) 1226
Nobel Prizes, Nobel Bequeaths Funds for the (Nov. 27, 1895) 1817
North Africa, Exploration of (1822-1874) 345
North America Act, British (July 1, 1867) 1219
North German Confederation Is Formed (1866-1867) 1173
North Pole, Nansen Attempts to Reach the (1893-1896) 1754
North Star, Douglass Launches *The* (Dec. 3, 1847) 753
Northwest Coast, Astorian Expeditions Explore the Pacific (Sept. 8, 1810-May, 1812) 134
North-West Mounted Police, Canada Forms the (May 23, 1873) 1401
Northwest Passage, Search for the (1818-1854) 282
Nullification Controversy (Nov. 24, 1832-Jan. 21, 1833) 521
Nursing in the Crimea, Nightingale Takes Charge of (Nov. 4, 1854) 903

Oath, Promulgation of Japan's Charter (Apr. 6, 1868) 1253
Oberlin College Opens (Dec. 3, 1833) 546
Occupies California and the Southwest, United States (June 30, 1846-Jan. 13, 1847) 722

Occupies Mexico, France (Oct. 31, 1861-June 19, 1867) . . . 1051
Occupies the Falkland Islands, Great Britain (Jan., 1833) . . . 527
Ogden, Gibbons v. (Mar. 2, 1824) . . . 376
Ohio Enacts the First Black Codes (Jan., 1804) . . . 62
Ohio Railroad Opens, Baltimore and (Jan. 7, 1830) . . . 447
Oil Company Is Incorporated, Standard (Jan. 10, 1870) . . . 1318
Oil Drilling Begins, Commercial (Aug. 27, 1859) . . . 985
Oil Trust Is Organized, Standard (Jan. 2, 1882) . . . 1547
"Old" Immigration, American Era of (1840's-1850's) . . . 631
Olympic Games Are Inaugurated, Modern (Apr. 6, 1896) . . . 1845
On Liberty, Mill Publishes (1859) . . . 971
On the Origin of Species, Darwin Publishes (Nov. 24, 1859) . . . 991
Onís Treaty Gives the United States Florida, Adams- (Feb. 22, 1819) . . . 293
Open at Essen, Krupp Works (Sept. 20, 1811) . . . 154
"Open Door" Policy Toward China, Hay Articulates (Sept. 6, 1899-July 3, 1900) . . . 1928
Opens, Baltimore and Ohio Railroad (Jan. 7, 1830) . . . 447
Opens, Brooklyn Bridge (May 24, 1883) . . . 1580
Opens, Champlain and St. Lawrence Railroad (July 21, 1836) . . . 587
Opens, Chisholm Trail (1867) . . . 1201
Opens, Ellis Island Immigration Depot (Jan. 1, 1892) . . . 1737
Opens, Erie Canal (Oct. 26, 1825) . . . 391
Opens, Germany's Kiel Canal (June 20, 1895) . . . 1808
Opens, London's Savoy Theatre (Oct. 10, 1881) . . . 1539
Opens, Metropolitan Museum of Art (Feb. 20, 1872) . . . 1372
Opens, Mount Holyoke Female Seminary (Nov. 8, 1837) . . . 597
Opens, New Library of Congress Building (Nov. 1, 1897) . . . 1886
Opens, New York Infirmary for Indigent Women and Children (May 12, 1857) . . . 947
Opens, Oberlin College (Dec. 3, 1833) . . . 546
Opens, Paris's Salon des Refusés (May 15, 1863) . . . 1099
Opens, Santa Fe Trail (Sept., 1821) . . . 339
Opens, Stockton and Darlington Railway (September 27, 1825) . . . 388
Opens, Suez Canal (Nov. 17, 1869) . . . 1301
Opens, Vassar College (Sept. 26, 1865) . . . 1158
Opens at Niagara Falls, First U.S. Hydroelectric Plant (Nov. 16, 1896) . . . 1863
Opens Chicago's Hull-House, Addams (Sept. 18, 1889) . . . 1692
Opens in Amsterdam, First Birth Control Clinic (1882) . . . 1542
Opens in London, First Underground Railroad (Jan. 10, 1863) . . . 1087
Opens in New York, Metropolitan Opera House (Oct. 22, 1883) . . . 1589
Opens in Paris, First Modern Department Store (1869) . . . 1279
Opens Japan to Western Trade, Perry (Mar. 31, 1854) . . . 888
Opens Research Laboratory, General Electric (Dec. 15, 1900) . . . 1983
Opera House Opens in New York, Metropolitan (Oct. 22, 1883) . . . 1589
Opium War, First (Sept., 1839-Aug. 29, 1842) . . . 625
Opium War, Second (Oct. 23, 1856-Nov. 6, 1860) . . . 930
Oregon Territory, United States Acquires (June 15, 1846) . . . 718
Organization of Labour, Blanc Publishes *The* (1839) . . . 610
Organization of the German Confederation (June 8-9, 1815) . . . 239
Organized, Standard Oil Trust Is (Jan. 2, 1882) . . . 1547
Origin of Species, Darwin Publishes *On the* (Nov. 24, 1859) . . . 991
Otis Installs the First Passenger Elevator (Mar. 23, 1857) . . . 942
Otto Invents a Practical Internal Combustion Engine (May, 1876) . . . 1449
Ottoman Empire, Bulgarian Revolt Against the (May, 1876) . . . 1445
Ottoman Empire, Greeks Fight for Independence from the (Mar. 7, 1821-Sept. 29, 1829) . . . 336
Ottomans Attempt to Exterminate Armenians (1894-1896) . . . 1773

Ottomans Suppress the Janissary Revolt (1808-1826) 114
Outlaws Slavery, Zanzibar (1873-1897) 1386
Oxford Movement Begins (July 14, 1833). 530

Pacific, War of the (Apr. 5, 1879-Oct. 20, 1883) 1514
Pacific Northwest Coast, Astorian Expeditions Explore the (Sept. 8, 1810-May, 1812). 134
Pacific Railroad Surveys (Mar. 2, 1853-1857). . . 867
Page Law, Congress Enacts the (Mar. 3, 1875) 1423
Painting Flourishes, Barbizon School of Landscape (c. 1830-1870) 445
Paints *At the Moulin Rouge*, Toulouse-Lautrec (1892-1895) 1734
Paints *Liberty Leading the People*, Delacroix (October-Dec., 1830) 476
Paints *The Scream*, Munch (1893) 1751
Paints *Third of May 1808: Execution of the Citizens of Madrid*, Goya (Mar., 1814). 203
Palo Alto, Battle of (May 8, 1846) 707
Pan-American Congress, First (October, 1889-Apr., 1890) 1695
Panic of 1837 Begins (Mar. 17, 1837) 591
Papal Encyclical on Labor (May 15, 1891). . . . 1727
Papal Infallibility Dogma, Vatican I Decrees (Dec. 8, 1869-Oct. 20, 1870) 1307
Paraguayan War (May 1, 1865-June 20, 1870). 1150
Paris, Bizet's *Carmen* Premieres in (Mar. 3, 1875) 1420
Paris, First Modern Department Store Opens in (1869). 1279
Paris, Prussian Army Besieges (Sept. 20, 1870-Jan. 28, 1871) 1331
Paris, Second Peace of (Nov. 20, 1815) 247
Paris Commune (Mar. 18-May 28, 1871). 1358
Paris Revolution of 1848 (Feb. 22-June, 1848) 773
Paris Salon of 1824 (1824). 368
Paris's Salon des Refusés Opens (May 15, 1863) 1099
Park, Yellowstone Becomes the First U.S. National (Mar. 1, 1872) 1375
Parliament, Rothschild Is First Jewish Member of British (July 26, 1858). 966
Parliament Are Rebuilt, British Houses of (Apr. 27, 1840-Feb., 1852) 643
Parliament Passes Municipal Corporations Act, British (Sept. 9, 1835) 575
Parliament Passes New Poor Law, British (Aug. 14, 1834). 554
Parliament Passes the Factory Act, British (1833). 525
Parliament Passes the Franchise Act of 1884, British (Dec. 6, 1884) 1627
Parliament Passes the Matrimonial Causes Act, British (Aug. 28, 1857) 952
Parliament Passes the Reform Act of 1832, British (June 4, 1832). 514
Parliament Passes the Reform Act of 1867, British (Aug., 1867) 1222
Parliament Passes the Six Acts, British (Dec. 11-30, 1819) 305
Parliament Repeals the Combination Acts, British (1824). 365
Parliament Repeals the Corn Laws, British (June 15, 1846) 715
Parliament's First Labour Member, Hardie Becomes (Aug. 3, 1892) 1748
Parthenon Marbles to England, Elgin Ships (1803-1812) 46
Partition of Africa, Berlin Conference Lays Groundwork for the (Nov. 15, 1884-Feb. 26, 1885). 1619
Party, Birth of the People's (July 4-5, 1892) . . . 1745
Party, Birth of the Republican (July 6, 1854) . . . 894
Party, Clay Begins American Whig (Apr. 14, 1834) 551
Party Is Formed, British Labour (Feb. 27, 1900) 1954
Party Is Formed, Russian Social-Democratic Labor (Mar., 1898) 1895
Passage, Search for the Northwest (1818-1854) 282
Passenger Elevator, Otis Installs the First (Mar. 23, 1857) 942
Passes Anti-Socialist Law, Germany (Oct. 19, 1878) 1499
Passes Dingley Tariff Act, Congress (July 24, 1897) 1880
Passes Indian Removal Act, Congress (May 28, 1830) 460
Passes Land Act of 1820, Congress (Apr. 24, 1820) 328
Passes Municipal Corporations Act, British Parliament (Sept. 9, 1835) 575

Passes New Poor Law, British Parliament (Aug. 14, 1834) 554
Passes Preemption Act of 1841, Congress (Sept. 4, 1841) 653
Passes the Comstock Antiobscenity Law, Congress (Mar. 3, 1873) 1394
Passes the Factory Act, British Parliament (1833) 525
Passes the Franchise Act of 1884, British Parliament (Dec. 6, 1884) 1627
Passes the Kansas-Nebraska Act, Congress (May 30, 1854) 891
Passes the Matrimonial Causes Act, British Parliament (Aug. 28, 1857) 952
Passes the National Bank Acts, Congress (Feb. 25, 1863-June 3, 1864) 1093
Passes the Reform Act of 1832, British Parliament (June 4, 1832) 514
Passes the Reform Act of 1867, British Parliament (Aug., 1867) 1222
Passes the Six Acts, British Parliament (Dec. 11-30, 1819) 305
Past and Present, Carlyle Publishes (1843) 669
Pasteur Begins Developing Germ Theory and Microbiology (1857) 933
Patents a Practical Typewriter, Sholes (June 23, 1868) 1258
Patents Automatic Dial Telephone System, Strowger (Mar. 11, 1891) 1724
Patents Barbed Wire, Glidden (Nov. 24, 1874) 1416
Patents Dynamite, Nobel (October, 1867) 1226
Patents His Air Brake, Westinghouse (Apr., 1869) 1287
Patents His First Seed Planter, Blair (Oct. 14, 1834) 557
Patents His Machine Gun, Maxim (1884) 1594
Patents His Sewing Machine, Howe (Sept. 10, 1846) 732
Patents Improved Steel-Processing Method, Bessemer (1855) 909
Patents the Cylinder Phonograph, Edison (Dec. 24, 1877) 1484
Patents the Diesel Engine, Diesel (Feb., 1892) 1740
Patents the First Practical Automobile, Benz (Jan. 29, 1886) 1640
Patents the High-Pressure Steam Engine, Trevithick (Mar. 24, 1802) 38
Patents the Internal Combustion Engine, Lenoir (1860) 998
Patents the Pneumatic Tire, Dunlop (Dec. 7, 1888) 1677
Patents the Revolver, Colt (Feb. 25, 1836) 584
Patents the Wireless Telegraph, Marconi (June, 1896) 1851
Patents Vulcanized Rubber, Goodyear (June 15, 1844) 687
Peace Conference, First Hague (May 18-July, 1899) 1926
Peace of Paris, Second (Nov. 20, 1815) 247
Peck, Fletcher v. (Mar. 16, 1810) 131
Pemberton Introduces Coca-Cola (May 8, 1886) 1643
Pendleton Act Reforms the Federal Civil Service (Jan. 16, 1883) 1577
Pendulum Seismograph, Wiechert Invents the Inverted (1900) 1944
Peninsular War in Spain (May 2, 1808-Nov., 1813) 125
Penny Postage, Great Britain Establishes (Jan. 10, 1840) 641
Penny Press, Birth of the (Sept. 3, 1833) 536
People, Delacroix Paints *Liberty Leading the* (October-Dec., 1830) 476
People Is Founded, National Council of Colored (July 6, 1853) 870
People's Party, Birth of the (July 4-5, 1892) . . . 1745
Performance of Beethoven's Ninth Symphony, First (May 7, 1824) 380
Performance of Wagner's Ring Cycle, First (Aug. 13-17, 1876) 1464
Periodic Table of Elements, Mendeleyev Develops the (1869-1871) 1284
Perry Opens Japan to Western Trade (Mar. 31, 1854) 888
Petroleum Refinery Is Built, First U.S. (1850) . . . 807
Phenomenology of Spirit, Hegel Publishes *The* (Apr., 1807) 106
Philadelphia, Anti-Irish Riots Erupt in (May 6-July 5, 1844) 681
Philadelphia Hosts the Centennial Exposition (May 10-Nov. 10, 1876) 1451
Philippine Insurrection (Feb. 4, 1899-July 4, 1902) 1922
Philosophy, Lamarck Publishes *Zoological* (1809) 128
Phoenix Begins Publication, *Cherokee* (Feb. 21, 1828) 408

Phonograph, Edison Patents the Cylinder (Dec. 24, 1877) 1484
Photographs a Galloping Horse, Muybridge (1878) 1487
Photography, Daguerre and Niépce Invent Daguerreotype (1839) 613
Pictures, First Commercial Projection of Motion (Dec. 28, 1895) 1820
Pike Explores the American Southwest (July 15, 1806-July 1, 1807) 90
Pius IX Decrees the Immaculate Conception Dogma (Dec. 8, 1854) 906
Pius IX Issues the Syllabus of Errors (Dec. 8, 1864). 1133
Plant Metabolism, Saussure Publishes His Research on (1804) 59
Plant Opens at Niagara Falls, First U.S. Hydroelectric (Nov. 16, 1896) 1863
Planter, Blair Patents His First Seed (Oct. 14, 1834) 557
Plessy v. Ferguson (May 18, 1896). 1848
Plot Assassinations, London's Cato Street Conspirators (Feb. 23, 1820) 323
Plymouth Brethren, First Meetings of the (c. 1826-1827) 398
Pneumatic Tire, Dunlop Patents the (Dec. 7, 1888) 1677
Poet Laureate, Tennyson Becomes England's (Nov. 5, 1850) 825
Pole, Nansen Attempts to Reach the North (1893-1896) 1754
Police, Canada Forms the North-West Mounted (May 23, 1873) 1401
Policy Toward China, Hay Articulates "Open Door" (Sept. 6, 1899-July 3, 1900). 1928
Polish Rebellion, First (Nov. 29, 1830-Aug. 15, 1831) 479
Polish Rebellion, Russia Crushes (Jan. 22-Sept., 1863) 1090
Political Register, Cobbett Founds the (Jan., 1802). 32
Politics, Irish Home Rule Debate Dominates British (June, 1886-Sept. 9, 1893) 1645
Pony Express Expedites Transcontinental Mail (Apr. 3, 1860-Oct. 26, 1861) 1001
Poor Law, British Parliament Passes New (Aug. 14, 1834). 554
Popular, Biedermeier Furniture Style Becomes (c. 1815-1848) 225
Popularizes Ragtime Music and Dance, Joplin (1899) 1917
Portugal's Miguelite Wars (1828-1834) 403
Positivism, Comte Advances His Theory of (1851-1854). 833
Post-Civil War Black Code, Mississippi Enacts First (Nov. 24, 1865) 1164
Post-Impressionist Movement Begins (Late 1870's) 1434
Postage, Great Britain Establishes Penny (Jan. 10, 1840) 641
Powell Publishes His Report on the American West (1879) 1504
Power, Cixi's Coup Preserves Qing Dynasty (Nov. 1-2, 1861). 1055
Practical Automobile, Benz Patents the First (Jan. 29, 1886). 1640
Practical Internal Combustion Engine, Otto Invents a (May, 1876). 1449
Practical Typewriter, Sholes Patents a (June 23, 1868) 1258
Preemption Act of 1841, Congress Passes (Sept. 4, 1841) 653
Prelude to the Afternoon of a Faun Premieres, Debussy's (Dec. 22, 1894) 1791
Premieres, Debussy's *Prelude to the Afternoon of a Faun* (Dec. 22, 1894). 1791
Premieres in Paris, Bizet's *Carmen* (Mar. 3, 1875) 1420
Premieres in Rome, Puccini's *Tosca* (Jan. 14, 1900) 1946
Pre-Raphaelite Brotherhood Begins (Fall, 1848) 790
Presents the First Public Dinosaur Description, Buckland (Feb. 20, 1824). 374
Preserves Qing Dynasty Power, Cixi's Coup (Nov. 1-2, 1861). 1055
President, Hayes Becomes (Mar. 5, 1877) 1472
President, House of Representatives Elects Jefferson (Feb. 17, 1801) 20
President, Lincoln Is Elected U.S. (Nov. 6, 1860) 1010
President, Lincoln Is Inaugurated (Mar. 4, 1861) 1028
President, McKinley Is Elected (Nov. 3, 1896) 1860
President Monroe Articulates the Monroe Doctrine (Dec. 2, 1823). 361
Press, Birth of the Penny (Sept. 3, 1833). 536

Prime Minister, Laurier Becomes the First French Canadian (July 11, 1896) 1854
Prime Minister, Macdonald Returns as Canada's (Sept., 1878) 1496
Prime Minister of Britain, Gladstone Becomes (Dec. 3, 1868-Feb. 20, 1874) 1274
Primitives, Emergence of the (1801) 9
Principles, Ricardo Identifies Seven Key Economic (1817) 267
Principles of Geology, Lyell Publishes (July, 1830) 467
Principles of Social Darwinism, Spencer Introduces (1862) 1058
Prizes, Nobel Bequeaths Funds for the Nobel (Nov. 27, 1895) 1817
Procedures, Semmelweis Develops Antiseptic (May, 1847). 745
Proclaimed a Kingdom, Italy Is (Mar. 17, 1861) 1032
Proclaims Its Independence, Liberia (July 26, 1847) 748
Proclamation, Lincoln Issues the Emancipation (Jan. 1, 1863) 1084
Professional Club Forms, Baseball's First (1869) 1276
Professional Theaters Spread Throughout America (c. 1801-1850) 14
Programs in Germany, Bismarck Introduces Social Security (1881-1889) 1534
Projection of Motion Pictures, First Commercial (Dec. 28, 1895) 1820
Promote the Arts and Crafts Movement, New Guilds (1884) 1597
Promulgation of Japan's Charter Oath (Apr. 6, 1868) 1253
Prophetstown, Tenskwatawa Founds (Apr., 1808) 116
Proposes Laws of Heredity, Mendel (1865) . . . 1135
Proslavery Arguments, Southerners Advance (c. 1830-1865) 442
Protest the Fourteenth Amendment, Suffragists (May 10, 1866) 1181
Prussian Army Besieges Paris (Sept. 20, 1870-Jan. 28, 1871) 1331
Prussian Revolution of 1848 (Mar. 3-Nov. 3, 1848) 776
Prussian War, Danish- (Feb. 1-Oct. 30, 1864). 1117
Prussian War, Franco- (July 19, 1870-Jan. 28, 1871) 1325
Prussia's Minister-President, Bismarck Becomes (Sept. 24, 1862) 1073
Prussia's Seven Weeks' War, Austria and (June 15-Aug. 23, 1866). 1190
Przhevalsky Explores Central Asia (1871-1885) 1346
Public Dinosaur Description, Buckland Presents the First (Feb. 20, 1824) 374
Public School Movement, Free (1820's-1830's) 310
Publication, *Cherokee Phoenix* Begins (Feb. 21, 1828) 408
Publish Fairy Tales, Brothers Grimm (1812-1815) 160
Publish *The Communist Manifesto*, Marx and Engels (Feb., 1848). 767
Publishes *Adventures of Huckleberry Finn*, Twain (Dec., 1884-Feb., 1885) 1624
Publishes *Bleak House*, Dickens (Mar., 1852-Sept., 1853). 855
Publishes *Das Kapital*, Marx (1867) 1207
Publishes His First Fairy Tales, Andersen (May 8, 1835). 570
Publishes His Report on the American West, Powell (1879) 1504
Publishes His Research on Plant Metabolism, Saussure (1804) 59
Publishes His Theory on Antiseptic Surgery, Lister (1867). 1204
Publishes *Irish Melodies*, Moore (1807-1834) . . . 96
Publishes *Madame Bovary*, Flaubert (Oct. 1-Dec. 15, 1856) 926
Publishes *Moby Dick*, Melville (1851). 830
Publishes "Morte d'Arthur," Tennyson (1842). 655
Publishes *On Liberty*, Mill (1859) 971
Publishes *On the Origin of Species*, Darwin (Nov. 24, 1859). 991
Publishes *Past and Present*, Carlyle (1843) 669
Publishes *Principles of Geology*, Lyell (July, 1830) 467
Publishes *Self-Help*, Smiles (1859) 974
Publishes *Sexual Inversion*, Ellis (1897) 1867
Publishes *Sister Carrie*, Dreiser (Nov. 8, 1900) 1976
Publishes *The Descent of Man*, Darwin (1871) 1334
Publishes *The Family Shakespeare*, Bowdler (1807) 93

Publishes the First American Dictionary of English, Webster (Nov., 1828) 418
Publishes *The Foundations of Geometry*, Hilbert (1899) 1913
Publishes *The Interpretation of Dreams*, Freud (1900) 1938
Publishes *The Life of Jesus Critically Examined*, Strauss (1835-1836) 566
Publishes *The Mathematical Analysis of Logic*, Boole (1847) 737
Publishes *The Organization of Labour*, Blanc (1839). 610
Publishes *The Phenomenology of Spirit*, Hegel (Apr., 1807). 106
Publishes *The World as Will and Idea*, Schopenhauer (1819). 285
Publishes *Treasure Island*, Stevenson (July, 1881-1883) 1537
Publishes *Uncle Tom's Cabin*, Stowe (1852) . . . 852
Publishes *Waverley*, Scott (1814) 196
Publishes *Zoological Philosophy*, Lamarck (1809). 128
Publishing *The Liberator*, Garrison Begins (Jan. 1, 1831) 487
Puccini's *Tosca* Premieres in Rome (Jan. 14, 1900) 1946
Pulitzer Circulation War, Hearst- (1895-1898) 1794
Pullman Strike (May 11-July 11, 1894). 1779
Purchase, Louisiana (May 9, 1803) 51
Purchase Completes the U.S.-Mexican Border, Gadsden (Dec. 31, 1853) 882

Qing Dynasty Confronts the Nian Rebellion (1853-1868). 864
Qing Dynasty Power, Cixi's Coup Preserves (Nov. 1-2, 1861). 1055
Quantum Theory, Articulation of (Dec. 14, 1900) 1980
Queen Victoria's Coronation (June 28, 1838) . . . 608

Race, *America* Wins the First America's Cup (Aug. 22, 1851). 846
Race Riots, Memphis and New Orleans (May and July, 1866) 1178
Ragtime Music and Dance, Joplin Popularizes (1899) 1917
Raid, Jameson (Dec. 29, 1895-Jan. 2, 1896) . . . 1824
Raid on Harpers Ferry, Brown's (Oct. 16-18, 1859) 988
Raids, Red River (June 1, 1815-Aug., 1817). . . . 236
Railroad Flourishes, Underground (c. 1850-1860) 809
Railroad Is Completed, First Transcontinental (May 10, 1869) 1293
Railroad Opens, Baltimore and Ohio (Jan. 7, 1830) 447
Railroad Opens, Champlain and St. Lawrence (July 21, 1836) 587
Railroad Opens in London, First Underground (Jan. 10, 1863). 1087
Railroad Surveys, Pacific (Mar. 2, 1853-1857) 867
Railway Is Incorporated, Canada's Grand Trunk (Nov. 10, 1852). 858
Railway Opens, Stockton and Darlington (September 27, 1825). 388
Ramón y Cajal Shows How Neurons Work in the Nervous System (1888-1906) 1671
Ranke Develops Systematic History (1824) 371
Raphaelite Brotherhood Begins, Pre- (Fall, 1848) 790
Ratified, Fourteenth Amendment Is (July 9, 1868) 1261
Ratified, Thirteenth Amendment Is (Dec. 6, 1865). 1167
Ratified, Twelfth Amendment Is (Sept. 25, 1804). 69
Ravaging Easter Island, Slave Traders Begin (Nov., 1862). 1076
Reach the North Pole, Nansen Attempts to (1893-1896) 1754
Realist Art Movement, Courbet Establishes (1855). 911
Realist Movement, Russian (1840's-1880's) . . . 635
Realistic Drama, *A Doll's House* Introduces Modern (1879) 1501
Reaper, McCormick Invents the (Summer, 1831) 496
Rebellion, Boxer (May, 1900-Sept. 7, 1901) . . . 1961
Rebellion, China's Taiping (Jan. 11, 1851-late summer, 1864) 836
Rebellion, First Polish (Nov. 29, 1830-Aug. 15, 1831) 479
Rebellion, First Riel (Oct. 11, 1869-July 15, 1870) 1299
Rebellion, Former Samurai Rise in Satsuma (Jan.-Sept. 24, 1877) 1469
Rebellion, Morant Bay (Oct. 7-12, 1865). 1161

Rebellion, Qing Dynasty Confronts the Nian (1853-1868). 864
Rebellion, Rhode Island's Dorr (May 18, 1842) 664
Rebellion, Russia Crushes Polish (Jan. 22-Sept., 1863) 1090
Rebellion, Taos (Jan. 19-Feb. 3, 1847). 743
Rebellion Begins, Second Riel (Mar. 19, 1885) 1633
Rebellions in China, Muslim (Winter, 1855-Jan. 2, 1878) 917
Rebellions Rock British Canada (Oct. 23-Dec. 16, 1837) 595
Rebuilt, British Houses of Parliament Are (Apr. 27, 1840-Feb., 1852) 643
Rechartering of the Bank of the United States, Jackson Vetoes (July 10, 1832). 518
Reconstruction of the South (Dec. 8, 1863-Apr. 24, 1877). 1109
Red Cloud's War (June 13, 1866-Nov. 6, 1868). 1187
Red Cross Is Launched, International (Aug. 22, 1864). 1122
Red River Raids (June 1, 1815-Aug., 1817) 236
Red River War (June 27, 1874-June 2, 1875) 1413
Rediscovery of Mendel's Hereditary Theory (1899-1900) 1920
Redshirts Land in Sicily, Garibaldi's (May-July, 1860) 1008
Refinery Is Built, First U.S. Petroleum (1850). . . 807
Reform Act of 1832, British Parliament Passes the (June 4, 1832). 514
Reform Act of 1867, British Parliament Passes the (Aug., 1867). 1222
Reform in London, Hill Launches Housing (1864) 1114
Reform Movement, Social (1820's-1850's) 312
Reforms Begin Modernization of Korean Government, Kabo (July 8, 1894-Jan. 1, 1896) 1782
Reforms Rugby School, Arnold (1828-1842) . . . 406
Reforms the Federal Civil Service, Pendleton Act (Jan. 16, 1883) 1577
Refusés Opens, Paris's Salon des (May 15, 1863) 1099
Registered as a Trade Name, "Aspirin" Is (Jan. 23, 1897). 1875
Relationship to Electricity, Ampère Reveals Magnetism's (Nov. 6, 1820) 334
Religion," Finney Lectures on "Revivals of (1835). 560
Remains, Lartet Discovers the First Cro-Magnon (Mar., 1868) 1247
Remains of Giant Moas, Scientists Study (1830's-1840's). 432
Removal Act, Congress Passes Indian (May 28, 1830) 460
Renaissance, Arabic Literary (19th cent.) 1
Renaissance in Literature, American (c. 1830's-1860's) 435
Repeals the Combination Acts, British Parliament (1824). 365
Repeals the Corn Laws, British Parliament (June 15, 1846) 715
Repels Italian Invasion, Ethiopia (Mar. 1, 1896) 1842
Report on the American West, Powell Publishes His (1879) 1504
Republic Is Established, Third French (Feb. 13, 1871-1875) 1353
Republican Party, Birth of the (July 6, 1854) . . . 894
Research on Plant Metabolism, Saussure Publishes His (1804). 59
Resistance in Rhodesia, British Subdue African (October, 1893-October, 1897) 1763
Responsible Government, First Test of Canada's (Apr. 25, 1849). 797
Restoration, Japan's Meiji (Jan. 3, 1868). 1242
Restored, France's Bourbon Dynasty Is (Apr. 11, 1814-July 29, 1830) 210
Returns as Canada's Prime Minister, Macdonald (Sept., 1878) 1496
"Revivals of Religion," Finney Lectures on (1835). 560
Revives During Boulanger Crisis, French Right Wing (Jan., 1886-1889) 1638
Revolt, *Amistad* Slave (July 2, 1839) 622
Revolt, Decembrist (Dec. 26, 1825) 395
Revolt, Ottomans Suppress the Janissary (1808-1826). 114
Revolt, Texas's Salinero (Sept. 10-Dec. 17, 1877) 1482
Revolt Against the Ottoman Empire, Bulgarian (May, 1876) 1445
Revolution, Belgian (Aug. 25, 1830-May 21, 1833) 474
Revolution, Neapolitan (July 2, 1820-Mar., 1821) 330

Revolution, Texas (Oct. 2, 1835-Apr. 21, 1836) 577
Revolution Deposes Charles X, July (July 29, 1830) 470
Revolution of 1848, Italian (Jan. 12, 1848-Aug. 28, 1849) 760
Revolution of 1848, Paris (Feb. 22-June, 1848) 773
Revolution of 1848, Prussian (Mar. 3-Nov. 3, 1848) 776
Revolution of 1868, Spanish (Sept. 30, 1868) 1266
Revolver, Colt Patents the (Feb. 25, 1836). 584
Rhode Island's Dorr Rebellion (May 18, 1842) 664
Rhodes Amalgamates Kimberley Diamondfields (Mar. 13, 1888) 1674
Rhodesia, British Subdue African Resistance in (October, 1893-October, 1897). 1763
Ricardo Identifies Seven Key Economic Principles (1817) 267
Riel Rebellion, First (Oct. 11, 1869-July 15, 1870) 1299
Riel Rebellion Begins, Second (Mar. 19, 1885) 1633
Right Wing Revives During Boulanger Crisis, French (Jan., 1886-1889) 1638
Rights, New Zealand Women Win Voting (Sept. 19, 1893) 1761
Rights Associations Unite, Women's (Feb. 17-18, 1890). 1709
Rights Convention, Akron Woman's (May 28-29, 1851) 843
Rights of Women, Declaration of the (July 4, 1876) 1460
Ring Cycle, First Performance of Wagner's (Aug. 13-17, 1876) 1464
Rioting, Hugo's *Hernani* Incites (Mar. 3, 1830) 454
Riots, Memphis and New Orleans Race (May and July, 1866) 1178
Riots Erupt in Philadelphia, Anti-Irish (May 6-July 5, 1844) 681
Rise in Satsuma Rebellion, Former Samurai (Jan.-Sept. 24, 1877) 1469
Rise of Burlesque and Vaudeville (1850's-1880's) 803
Rise of the Cockney School (Dec., 1816) 263
Rise of the Knickerbocker School (1807-1850). 99
Rise of the Symbolist Movement (1886) 1636
Rise of Tin Pan Alley Music (1890's) 1700
Rise of Yellow Journalism (1880's-1890's) . . . 1526
Risings for Irish Independence, Fenian (June, 1866-1871) 1184
River Gold Rush Begins, Fraser (Mar. 23, 1858) 960
River Massacre, Washita (Nov. 27, 1868) 1271
River Raids, Red (June 1, 1815-Aug., 1817). . . . 236
River War, Red (June 27, 1874-June 2, 1875) 1413
Road, Construction of the National (1811-1840) 146
Rock British Canada, Rebellions (Oct. 23-Dec. 16, 1837) 595
Rock the Grant Administration, Scandals (Sept. 24, 1869-1877). 1296
Rodin Exhibits *The Thinker* (1888). 1669
Roman Catholic, Newman Becomes a (Oct. 9, 1845) 700
Roman Catholic Emancipation (May 9, 1828-Apr. 13, 1829) 414
Romantic Age, Beethoven's *Eroica* Symphony Introduces the (Apr. 7, 1805) 78
Romantic Ballet's Golden Age, *La Sylphide* Inaugurates (Mar. 12, 1832) 511
Rome, Puccini's *Tosca* Premieres in (Jan. 14, 1900) 1946
Röntgen Discovers X Rays (Nov. 9, 1895). . . . 1814
Rorke's Drift, Battles of Isandlwana and (Jan. 22-23, 1879). 1507
Ross Establishes Malaria's Transmission Vector (Aug. 20, 1897) 1883
Rossini's *The Barber of Seville* Debuts (Feb. 20, 1816) 252
Rothschild Is First Jewish Member of British Parliament (July 26, 1858) 966
Roux Develops the Theory of Mitosis (1880's) 1523
Royal Navy, Great Britain Strengthens Its (1889) 1680
Rubber, Goodyear Patents Vulcanized (June 15, 1844) 687
Rugby School, Arnold Reforms (1828-1842) . . . 406
Ruins, Layard Explores and Excavates Assyrian (1839-1847). 619
Rule, Sepoy Mutiny Against British (May 10, 1857-July 8, 1858) 944
Russia, Napoleon Invades (June 23-Dec. 14, 1812) 170

Russia Crushes Polish Rebellion (Jan. 22-Sept., 1863) . . . 1090
Russia, Naples, and Spain, Jesuits Are Expelled from (1820) . . . 315
Russia Sells Alaska to the United States (Mar. 30, 1867) . . . 1213
Russian Alliance, Franco- (Jan. 4, 1894) . . . 1776
Russian Realist Movement (1840's-1880's) . . . 635
Russian Serfs, Emancipation of (Mar. 3, 1861) . . . 1026
Russian Social-Democratic Labor Party Is Formed (Mar., 1898) . . . 1895
Russo-Turkish War, Second (Apr. 26, 1828-Aug. 28, 1829) . . . 412
Russo-Turkish War, Third (Apr. 24, 1877-Jan. 31, 1878) . . . 1476

Safe Surgical Anesthesia Is Demonstrated (Oct. 16, 1846) . . . 735
Salamanca, Battle of (July 22, 1812) . . . 173
Salinero Revolt, Texas's (Sept. 10-Dec. 17, 1877) . . . 1482
Salon des Refusés Opens, Paris's (May 15, 1863) . . . 1099
Salon of 1824, Paris (1824) . . . 368
Salvation Army, Booth Establishes the (July, 1865) . . . 1155
Samurai Rise in Satsuma Rebellion, Former (Jan.-Sept. 24, 1877) . . . 1469
San Francisco's Chinese Six Companies Association Forms (Nov. 12, 1882) . . . 1569
San Martín's Military Campaigns (Jan. 18, 1817-July 28, 1821) . . . 273
Sand Creek Massacre (Nov. 29, 1864) . . . 1130
Sandford, Dred Scott v. (Mar. 6, 1857) . . . 938
Santa Fe Trail Opens (Sept., 1821) . . . 339
Satsuma Rebellion, Former Samurai Rise in (Jan.-Sept. 24, 1877) . . . 1469
Saussure Publishes His Research on Plant Metabolism (1804) . . . 59
Savannah Is the First Steamship to Cross the Atlantic (May 22-June 20, 1819) . . . 303
Savoy Theatre Opens, London's (Oct. 10, 1881) . . . 1539
Scandals Rock the Grant Administration (Sept. 24, 1869-1877) . . . 1296
Schliemann Excavates Ancient Troy (Apr., 1870-1873) . . . 1321
School, Arnold Reforms Rugby (1828-1842) . . . 406
School, Rise of the Cockney (Dec., 1816) . . . 263
School, Rise of the Knickerbocker (1807-1850) . . . 99
School Movement, Free Public (1820's-1830's) . . . 310
School of American Literature Flourishes, Brahmin (1880's) . . . 1520
School of Calligraphy Emerges, China's Stele (1820's) . . . 307
School of Landscape Painting Flourishes, Barbizon (c. 1830-1870) . . . 445
Schopenhauer Publishes *The World as Will and Idea* (1819) . . . 285
Schwann and Virchow Develop Cell Theory (1838-1839) . . . 602
Scientific Weather Forecasting, Bjerknes Founds (July, 1897-July, 1904) . . . 1877
Scientists Study Remains of Giant Moas (1830's-1840's) . . . 432
Scott Publishes *Waverley* (1814) . . . 196
Scramble for Chinese Concessions Begins (Nov. 14, 1897) . . . 1888
Scream, Munch Paints *The* (1893) . . . 1751
Search for the Northwest Passage (1818-1854) . . . 282
Second Anglo-Sikh War (Apr., 1848-Mar., 1849) . . . 779
Second Bank of the United States Is Chartered (Apr., 1816) . . . 255
Second British-Ashanti War (Jan. 22, 1873-Feb. 13, 1874) . . . 1389
Second Fugitive Slave Law (Sept. 18, 1850) . . . 822
Second Law of Thermodynamics, Clausius Formulates the (1850-1865) . . . 813
Second Opium War (Oct. 23, 1856-Nov. 6, 1860) . . . 930
Second Peace of Paris (Nov. 20, 1815) . . . 247
Second Riel Rebellion Begins (Mar. 19, 1885) . . . 1633
Second Russo-Turkish War (Apr. 26, 1828-Aug. 28, 1829) . . . 412
Sedan, Battle of (Sept. 1, 1870) . . . 1328
Seed Planter, Blair Patents His First (Oct. 14, 1834) . . . 557
Sees the Victoria Falls, Livingstone (Nov. 17, 1853) . . . 879
Seismograph, Wiechert Invents the Inverted Pendulum (1900) . . . 1944
Self-Help, Smiles Publishes (1859) . . . 974
Self-Strengthening Movement Arises, China's (1860's) . . . 995

Sells Alaska to the United States, Russia (Mar. 30, 1867) 1213
Seminary Is Founded, Hartford Female (May, 1823). 356
Seminary Opens, Mount Holyoke Female (Nov. 8, 1837) 597
Seminole Wars (Nov. 21, 1817-Mar. 27, 1858) 278
Semmelweis Develops Antiseptic Procedures (May, 1847). 745
Sends First Telegraph Message, Morse (May 24, 1844) 684
Seneca Falls Convention (July 19-20, 1848) 784
Sepoy Mutiny Against British Rule (May 10, 1857-July 8, 1858) 944
Serfs, Emancipation of Russian (Mar. 3, 1861) 1026
Settlement, Dominion Lands Act Fosters Canadian (1872). 1369
Settles Maine's Canadian Border, Webster-Ashburton Treaty (Aug. 9, 1842). 666
Settles U.S. Claims vs. Britain, Treaty of Washington (May 8, 1871) 1363
Settling in Canada, Ukrainian Mennonites Begin (1873) 1380
Settling Western Canada, Immigrant Farmers Begin (1896) 1831
Sevastopol, Siege of (Oct. 17, 1854-Sept. 11, 1855) 897
Seven Key Economic Principles, Ricardo Identifies (1817) 267
Seven Weeks' War, Austria and Prussia's (June 15-Aug. 23, 1866). 1190
Seville Debuts, Rossini's *The Barber of* (Feb. 20, 1816) 252
Sewing Machine, Howe Patents His (Sept. 10, 1846) 732
Sexual Inversion, Ellis Publishes (1897) 1867
Shakespeare, Bowdler Publishes *The Family* (1807) 93
Sherlock Holmes, Conan Doyle Introduces (Dec., 1887) 1666
Sherman Antitrust Act, Harrison Signs the (July 20, 1890) 1712
Sherman Marches Through Georgia and the Carolinas (Nov. 15, 1864-Apr. 18, 1865) . . . 1127
Ship Docks at Mobile, Last Slave (July, 1859) 979
Ship Era Begins, Clipper (c. 1845). 690
Shipping Line Begins, Hamburg-Amerika (1847). 740
Ships Parthenon Marbles to England, Elgin (1803-1812) 46
Shirts, Brooks Brothers Introduces Button-Down (1896) 1828
Sholes Patents a Practical Typewriter (June 23, 1868) 1258
Shows, First Minstrel (Feb. 6, 1843). 675
Siberia, Dostoevski Is Exiled to (Dec., 1849) 800
Sicily, Garibaldi's Redshirts Land in (May-July, 1860). 1008
Siege of Khartoum (Mar. 13, 1884-Jan. 26, 1885) 1609
Siege of Mafeking (Oct. 13, 1899-May 17, 1900) 1935
Siege of Sevastopol (Oct. 17, 1854-Sept. 11, 1855) 897
Signs Indian Appropriation Act, Grant (Mar. 3, 1871). 1355
Signs the Chinese Exclusion Act, Arthur (May 9, 1882) 1558
Signs the Homestead Act, Lincoln (May 20, 1862) 1064
Signs the Morrill Land Grant Act, Lincoln (July 2, 1862) 1066
Signs the Sherman Antitrust Act, Harrison (July 20, 1890) 1712
Sikh War, Second Anglo- (Apr., 1848-Mar., 1849) 779
Sino-Japanese War (Aug. 1, 1894-Apr. 17, 1895) 1784
Sioux War (1876-1877). 1442
Sioux War, Great (Aug. 17, 1862-Dec. 28, 1863) 1070
Sister Carrie, Dreiser Publishes (Nov. 8, 1900) 1976
Six Acts, British Parliament Passes the (Dec. 11-30, 1819) 305
Sketch Book Transforms American Literature, Irving's (1819-1820) 288
Skull Is Found in Germany, Neanderthal (Aug., 1856) 923
Skyscraper Is Built, World's First (1883-1885) 1575
Slaughter, Great American Buffalo (c. 1871-1883) 1343
Slave Insurrection, Turner Launches (Aug. 21, 1831). 499

Slave Law, Second Fugitive (Sept. 18, 1850) 822
Slave Revolt, *Amistad* (July 2, 1839) 622
Slave Ship Docks at Mobile, Last (July, 1859) 979
Slave Traders Begin Ravaging Easter Island (Nov., 1862). 1076
Slavery, Zanzibar Outlaws (1873-1897) 1386
Slavery and Westward Expansion, Webster and Hayne Debate (Jan. 19-27, 1830) 451
Slavery Is Abolished Throughout the British Empire (Aug. 28, 1833) 533
Slavery Society Is Founded, American Anti- (Dec., 1833). 542
Slaves, Congress Bans Importation of African (Mar. 2, 1807) 103
Smiles Publishes *Self-Help* (1859) 974
Smith Explores the Far West, Jedediah (1822-1831) 342
Smith Founds the Mormon Church (Apr. 6, 1830) 457
Smithsonian Institution Is Founded (Aug. 10, 1846) 729
Social Darwinism, Spencer Introduces Principles of (1862) 1058
Social Democratic Alliance, Bakunin Founds the (1868) 1235
Social-Democratic Labor Party Is Formed, Russian (Mar., 1898) 1895
Social Reform Movement (1820's-1850's) 312
Social Security Programs in Germany, Bismarck Introduces (1881-1889) 1534
Socialist Law, Germany Passes Anti- (Oct. 19, 1878) 1499
Society Is Founded, American Anti-Slavery (Dec., 1833). 542
Society Is Founded, American Bible (May 8, 1816) 260
Society Is Founded, British and Foreign Bible (1804) 57
Society Is Founded, Fabian (Jan., 1884) 1603
Society Is Founded, Theosophical (Sept., 1875) 1429
Solferino, Battle of (June 24, 1859) 976
Sons of the Golden State, Chinese Californians Form Native (May 10, 1895) 1806
Soubirous, Virgin Mary Appears to Bernadette (Feb. 11-July 16, 1858). 958
South, Reconstruction of the (Dec. 8, 1863-Apr. 24, 1877). 1109
South African War (Oct. 11, 1899-May 31, 1902) 1932
South Africa's Great Trek Begins (1835) 563
Southerners Advance Proslavery Arguments (c. 1830-1865) 442
Southwest, Pike Explores the American (July 15, 1806-July 1, 1807). 90
Southwest, United States Occupies California and the (June 30, 1846-Jan. 13, 1847) 722
Spain, Carlist Wars Unsettle (Sept. 29, 1833-1849) 539
Spain, Dos de Mayo Insurrection in (May 2, 1808) 122
Spain, Jesuits Are Expelled from Russia, Naples, and (1820) 315
Spain, Peninsular War in (May 2, 1808-Nov., 1813) 125
Spain Invade Vietnam, France and (Aug., 1858) 968
Spanish-American War (Apr. 24-Dec. 10, 1898) 1903
Spanish Constitution of 1876 (1876) 1440
Spanish Revolution of 1868 (Sept. 30, 1868). . . 1266
Species, Darwin Publishes *On the Origin of* (Nov. 24, 1859). 991
Spectroscope, Fraunhofer Invents the (1814) . . . 194
Speech, Washington's Atlanta Compromise (Sept. 18, 1895) 1811
Spencer Introduces Principles of Social Darwinism (1862). 1058
Spirit, Hegel Publishes *The Phenomenology of* (Apr., 1807). 106
Spread of the Waltz (19th cent.) 6
Spread Throughout America, Professional Theaters (c. 1801-1850) 14
St. Lawrence Railroad Opens, Champlain and (July 21, 1836) 587
St. Petersburg, Tchaikovsky's *Swan Lake* Is Staged in (Jan. 27, 1895) 1800
SS *Great Eastern*, Brunel Launches the (Jan. 31, 1858) 955
Stage First "Boycott," Irish Tenant Farmers (Sept.-Nov., 1880). 1528
Staged in St. Petersburg, Tchaikovsky's *Swan Lake* Is (Jan. 27, 1895) 1800
Standard Oil Company Is Incorporated (Jan. 10, 1870). 1318
Standard Oil Trust Is Organized (Jan. 2, 1882) 1547

States Join to Form Customs Union, German (Jan. 1, 1834) 549
States of America, Establishment of the Confederate (Feb. 8, 1861) 1022
States Unite Within German Empire, German (Jan. 18, 1871). 1349
Stations, Hiroshige Completes *The Tokaido Fifty-Three* (1831-1834) 484
Statue of Liberty Is Dedicated (Oct. 28, 1886) 1649
Steam Engine, Trevithick Patents the High-Pressure (Mar. 24, 1802). 38
Steel-Processing Method, Bessemer Patents Improved (1855) 909
Stele School of Calligraphy Emerges, China's (1820's). 307
Stephens Begins Uncovering Mayan Antiquities (Nov., 1839) 628
Stethoscope, Laënnec Invents the (1816) 250
Stevenson Publishes *Treasure Island* (July, 1881-1883) 1537
Stockton and Darlington Railway Opens (September 27, 1825). 388
Store Opens in Paris, First Modern Department (1869) 1279
Stowe Publishes *Uncle Tom's Cabin* (1852). . . . 852
Stratosphere and Troposphere Are Discovered (Apr., 1898-1903) 1900
Strauss Publishes *The Life of Jesus Critically Examined* (1835-1836) 566
Street Conspirators Plot Assassinations, London's Cato (Feb. 23, 1820). 323
Strengthens Its Royal Navy, Great Britain (1889) 1680
Strike, Pullman (May 11-July 11, 1894) 1779
Strowger Patents Automatic Dial Telephone System (Mar. 11, 1891) 1724
Study Remains of Giant Moas, Scientists (1830's-1840's). 432
Style Becomes Popular, Biedermeier Furniture (c. 1815-1848) 225
Subdue African Resistance in Rhodesia, British (October, 1893-October, 1897) 1763
Sudanese War (Mar., 1896-Nov., 1899) 1839
Suez Canal Opens (Nov. 17, 1869) 1301
Suffrage Associations Begin Forming, Woman (May, 1869) 1290
Suffragists Protest the Fourteenth Amendment (May 10, 1866) 1181
Suppress the Janissary Revolt, Ottomans (1808-1826). 114
Suppression of Yellow Fever (June, 1900-1904) 1966
Supreme Court of Canada Is Established (1875) 1418
Surgery, Lister Publishes His Theory on Antiseptic (1867) 1204
Surgical Anesthesia Is Demonstrated, Safe (Oct. 16, 1846) 735
Surrender, Watie Is Last Confederate General to (June 23, 1865) 1153
Surrender at Appomattox and Assassination of Lincoln (Apr. 9 and 14, 1865). 1146
Survey of India, Lambton Begins Trigonometrical (Apr. 10, 1802). 40
Surveys, Pacific Railroad (Mar. 2, 1853-1857) 867
Suttee in India, British Abolish (Dec. 4, 1829) 428
Swan Lake Is Staged in St. Petersburg, Tchaikovsky's (Jan. 27, 1895) 1800
Swiss Confederation Is Formed (Sept. 12, 1848) 787
Syllabus of Errors, Pius IX Issues the (Dec. 8, 1864). 1133
Sylphide Inaugurates Romantic Ballet's Golden Age, *La* (Mar. 12, 1832) 511
Symbolist Movement, Rise of the (1886). 1636
Symphony, First Performance of Beethoven's Ninth (May 7, 1824) 380
Symphony Introduces the Romantic Age, Beethoven's *Eroica* (Apr. 7, 1805) 78
Systematic History, Ranke Develops (1824). . . . 371

Table of Elements, Mendeleyev Develops the Periodic (1869-1871) 1284
Taiping Rebellion, China's (Jan. 11, 1851-late summer, 1864) 836
Takamine Isolate Adrenaline, Abel and (1897-1901) 1869
Tales, Andersen Publishes His First Fairy (May 8, 1835). 570
Tales, Brothers Grimm Publish Fairy (1812-1815) 160
Tambora Volcano Begins Violent Eruption (Apr. 5, 1815). 234
Taos Rebellion (Jan. 19-Feb. 3, 1847) 743
Tariff Act, Congress Passes Dingley (July 24, 1897) 1880

Tasmania, Great Britain Begins Colonizing (Sept. 7, 1803) 55
Tchaikovsky's *Swan Lake* Is Staged in St. Petersburg (Jan. 27, 1895) 1800
Tears, Trail of (1830-1842) 438
Tel el Kebir, Battle of (Sept. 13, 1882) 1566
Telegraph, Marconi Patents the Wireless (June, 1896) 1851
Telegraph Is Completed, Transcontinental (Oct. 24, 1861) 1048
Telegraph Message, Morse Sends First (May 24, 1844) 684
Telephone, Bell Demonstrates the (June 25, 1876) 1457
Telephone System, Strowger Patents Automatic Dial (Mar. 11, 1891). 1724
Templo Expiatorio de la Sagrada Família, Gaudí Begins Barcelona's (Nov. 3, 1883). 1592
Ten Years' War, Cuba's (Oct. 10, 1868-Feb. 10, 1878) 1269
Tenant Farmers Stage First "Boycott," Irish (Sept.-Nov., 1880). 1528
Tennyson Becomes England's Poet Laureate (Nov. 5, 1850) 825
Tennyson Publishes "Morte d'Arthur" (1842) . . . 655
Tenskwatawa Founds Prophetstown (Apr., 1808). 116
Test of Canada's Responsible Government, First (Apr. 25, 1849) 797
Texas Revolution (Oct. 2, 1835-Apr. 21, 1836) 577
Texas's Cart War (August-Dec., 1857) 950
Texas's Salinero Revolt (Sept. 10-Dec. 17, 1877) 1482
Thames, Battle of the (Oct. 5, 1813) 188
Theater Is Founded, Moscow Art (Oct. 14, 1898) 1910
Theaters Spread Throughout America, Professional (c. 1801-1850) 14
Theatre, Irving Manages London's Lyceum (1878-1899) 1490
Theatre Opens, London's Savoy (Oct. 10, 1881) 1539
Theory, Articulation of Quantum (Dec. 14, 1900) 1980
Theory, Lebesgue Develops New Integration (1900) 1941
Theory, Rediscovery of Mendel's Hereditary (1899-1900) 1920
Theory, Schwann and Virchow Develop Cell (1838-1839). 602
Theory and Microbiology, Pasteur Begins Developing Germ (1857) 933
Theory of Immunity, Metchnikoff Advances the Cellular (1882-1901) 1545
Theory of Matter, Dalton Formulates the Atomic (1803-1808) 43
Theory of Mitosis, Roux Develops the (1880's) 1523
Theory of Positivism, Comte Advances His (1851-1854). 833
Theory on Antiseptic Surgery, Lister Publishes His (1867) 1204
Theosophical Society Is Founded (Sept., 1875) 1429
Thermodynamics, Clausius Formulates the Second Law of (1850-1865) 813
Thinker, Rodin Exhibits *The* (1888) 1669
Third French Republic Is Established (Feb. 13, 1871-1875) 1353
Third Maratha War (Nov. 5, 1817-June 3, 1818) 276
Third of May 1808: Execution of the Citizens of Madrid, Goya Paints (Mar., 1814) 203
Third Russo-Turkish War (Apr. 24, 1877-Jan. 31, 1878) 1476
Thirteenth Amendment Is Ratified (Dec. 6, 1865). 1167
Thirty-Six Views of Mount Fuji, Hokusai Produces (1823-1831) 353
Three Emperors' League Is Formed (May 6-Oct. 22, 1873) 1398
Times Is Founded, Modern *New York* (Sept. 18, 1851) 849
Tin Pan Alley Music, Rise of (1890's) 1700
Tippecanoe, Battle of (Nov. 7, 1811) 157
Tire, Dunlop Patents the Pneumatic (Dec. 7, 1888) 1677
Tocqueville Visits America (May, 1831-Feb., 1832) 493
Tokaido Fifty-Three Stations, Hiroshige Completes *The* (1831-1834) 484
Tom's Cabin, Stowe Publishes *Uncle* (1852) . . . 852
Tosca Premieres in Rome, Puccini's (Jan. 14, 1900) 1946
Toulouse-Lautrec Paints *At the Moulin Rouge* (1892-1895) 1734
Tower Is Dedicated, Eiffel (Mar. 31, 1889) . . . 1686

Tract Society Is Founded, Watch Tower Bible and (1870-1871) . . . 1316
Trade, Perry Opens Japan to Western (Mar. 31, 1854) . . . 888
Trade Name, "Aspirin" Is Registered as a (Jan. 23, 1897) . . . 1875
Traders Begin Ravaging Easter Island, Slave (Nov., 1862) . . . 1076
Trades Union Congress Forms, Great Britain's First (June 2, 1868) . . . 1255
Trafalgar, Battle of (Oct. 21, 1805) . . . 83
Trail of Tears (1830-1842) . . . 438
Trail Opens, Chisholm (1867) . . . 1201
Trail Opens, Santa Fe (Sept., 1821) . . . 339
Transatlantic Cable Is Completed, First (July 27, 1866) . . . 1196
Transcendental Movement Arises in New England (1836) . . . 581
Transcontinental Mail, Pony Express Expedites (Apr. 3, 1860-Oct. 26, 1861) . . . 1001
Transcontinental Railroad Is Completed, First (May 10, 1869) . . . 1293
Transcontinental Telegraph Is Completed (Oct. 24, 1861) . . . 1048
Transforms American Literature, Irving's *Sketch Book* (1819-1820) . . . 288
Transmission Vector, Ross Establishes Malaria's (Aug. 20, 1897) . . . 1883
Transvaal, Gold Is Discovered in the (June 21, 1884) . . . 1612
Treasure Island, Stevenson Publishes (July, 1881-1883) . . . 1537
Treasury, Establishment of Independent U.S. (Aug. 1, 1846) . . . 726
Treaty, Burlingame (July 28, 1868) . . . 1264
Treaty, Medicine Lodge Creek (Oct. 21, 1867) . . . 1228
Treaty Gives the United States Florida, Adams-Onís (Feb. 22, 1819) . . . 293
Treaty Makes Concessions to Irish Nationalists, Kilmainham (May 2, 1882) . . . 1556
Treaty of Adrianople (Sept. 24, 1829) . . . 426
Treaty of Ghent Takes Effect (Feb. 17, 1815) . . . 230
Treaty of Guadalupe Hidalgo Ends Mexican War (Feb. 2, 1848) . . . 770
Treaty of Washington Settles U.S. Claims vs. Britain (May 8, 1871) . . . 1363
Treaty Settles Maine's Canadian Border, Webster-Ashburton (Aug. 9, 1842) . . . 666
Trek Begins, South Africa's Great (1835) . . . 563
Trevithick Patents the High-Pressure Steam Engine (Mar. 24, 1802) . . . 38
Tribal Unity, General Allotment Act Erodes Indian (Feb. 8, 1887) . . . 1657
Tried for Voting, Anthony Is (June 17-18, 1873) . . . 1404
Trigonometrical Survey of India, Lambton Begins (Apr. 10, 1802) . . . 40
Triple Alliance Is Formed (May 20, 1882) . . . 1561
Tripolitan War (Summer, 1801-Summer, 1805) . . . 23
Troposphere Are Discovered, Stratosphere and (Apr., 1898-1903) . . . 1900
Troy, Schliemann Excavates Ancient (Apr., 1870-1873) . . . 1321
Trust" Appears on U.S. Coins, "In God We (Apr. 22, 1864) . . . 1119
Trust Is Organized, Standard Oil (Jan. 2, 1882) . . . 1547
Tuberculosis Bacillus, Koch Announces His Discovery of the (Mar. 24, 1882) . . . 1550
Turkish War, Greco- (Jan. 21-May 20, 1897) . . . 1872
Turkish War, Second Russo- (Apr. 26, 1828-Aug. 28, 1829) . . . 412
Turkish War, Third Russo- (Apr. 24, 1877-Jan. 31, 1878) . . . 1476
Turko-Egyptian Wars (1832-1841) . . . 505
Turner Launches Slave Insurrection (Aug. 21, 1831) . . . 499
Twain Publishes *Adventures of Huckleberry Finn* (Dec., 1884-Feb., 1885) . . . 1624
Twelfth Amendment Is Ratified (Sept. 25, 1804) . . . 69
Typewriter, Sholes Patents a Practical (June 23, 1868) . . . 1258

Ukrainian Mennonites Begin Settling in Canada (1873) . . . 1380
Uncle Tom's Cabin, Stowe Publishes (1852) . . . 852
Uncovering Mayan Antiquities, Stephens Begins (Nov., 1839) . . . 628
Underground Railroad Flourishes (c. 1850-1860) . . . 809
Underground Railroad Opens in London, First (Jan. 10, 1863) . . . 1087
Unifies Under the Glücksburg Dynasty, Greece (1863-1913) . . . 1081
Union, German States Join to Form Customs (Jan. 1, 1834) . . . 549

Union Congress Forms, Great Britain's First Trades (June 2, 1868) 1255
Union Enacts the First National Draft Law (Mar. 3, 1863) 1095
Unitarian Church Is Founded (May, 1819). 299
Unite, Upper and Lower Canada (Feb. 10, 1841) 650
Unite, Women's Rights Associations (Feb. 17-18, 1890). 1709
Unite Within German Empire, German States (Jan. 18, 1871). 1349
United States, Jackson Vetoes Rechartering of the Bank of the (July 10, 1832). 518
United States, Russia Sells Alaska to the (Mar. 30, 1867) 1213
United States Acquires Oregon Territory (June 15, 1846) 718
United States Florida, Adams-Onís Treaty Gives the (Feb. 22, 1819). 293
United States Is Chartered, Second Bank of the (Apr., 1816). 255
United States Occupies California and the Southwest (June 30, 1846-Jan. 13, 1847) . . . 722
United States v. Wong Kim Ark (Mar. 28, 1898) 1897
Unity, General Allotment Act Erodes Indian Tribal (Feb. 8, 1887) 1657
University, Founding of McGill (1813) 179
University Opens, First African American (Jan. 1, 1857) 936
Unsettle Spain, Carlist Wars (Sept. 29, 1833-1849) 539
Upper and Lower Canada Unite (Feb. 10, 1841) 650
U.S. Census Bureau Announces Closing of the Frontier (1890) 1705
U.S. Civil War (Apr. 12, 1861-Apr. 9, 1865). . . 1036
U.S. Claims vs. Britain, Treaty of Washington Settles (May 8, 1871) 1363
U.S. Coins, "In God We Trust" Appears on (Apr. 22, 1864) 1119
U.S. Department of Education Is Created (Mar. 2, 1867) 1210
U.S. Election of 1824 (Dec. 1, 1824-Feb. 9, 1825) 383
U.S. Election of 1828 (Dec. 3, 1828) 421
U.S. Election of 1840 (Dec. 2, 1840) 646
U.S. Election of 1884 (Nov. 4, 1884). 1615
U.S. Hydroelectric Plant Opens at Niagara Falls, First (Nov. 16, 1896) 1863
U.S.-Mexican Border, Gadsden Purchase Completes the (Dec. 31, 1853) 882
U.S. Military Academy Is Established (Mar. 16, 1802) 35
U.S. National Park, Yellowstone Becomes the First (Mar. 1, 1872) 1375
U.S. Petroleum Refinery Is Built, First (1850). . . 807
U.S. President, Lincoln Is Elected (Nov. 6, 1860) 1010
U.S. Treasury, Establishment of Independent (Aug. 1, 1846) 726
Utah, Mormons Begin Migration to (Feb. 4, 1846) 703

Vassar College Opens (Sept. 26, 1865). 1158
Vatican I Decrees Papal Infallibility Dogma (Dec. 8, 1869-Oct. 20, 1870) 1307
Vaudeville, Rise of Burlesque and (1850's-1880's) 803
Vetoes Rechartering of the Bank of the United States, Jackson (July 10, 1832). 518
Vicksburg, and Chattanooga, Battles of Gettysburg, (July 1-Nov. 25, 1863) 1102
Victoria Falls, Livingstone Sees the (Nov. 17, 1853) 879
Victoria's Coronation, Queen (June 28, 1838) 608
Vienna, Congress of (Sept. 15, 1814-June 11, 1815) 216
Vietnam, France and Spain Invade (Aug., 1858) 968
Views of Mount Fuji, Hokusai Produces *Thirty-Six* (1823-1831) 353
Villafranca, Napoleon III and Francis Joseph I Meet at (July 11, 1859) 982
Violent Eruption, Tambora Volcano Begins (Apr. 5, 1815). 234
Virchow Develop Cell Theory, Schwann and (1838-1839). 602
Virgin Mary Appears to Bernadette Soubirous (Feb. 11-July 16, 1858). 958
Virginia, Battle of the *Monitor* and the (Mar. 9, 1862) 1061
Viruses, Beijerinck Discovers (1898). 1892
Visits America, Tocqueville (May, 1831-Feb., 1832) 493
Volcano Begins Violent Eruption, Tambora (Apr. 5, 1815). 234
Volcano Erupts, Krakatoa (Aug. 27, 1883). . . . 1583

Vote, Wyoming Gives Women the (Dec., 1869) 1304
Voters, Mississippi Constitution Disfranchises Black (1890). 1702
Voting, Anthony Is Tried for (June 17-18, 1873) 1404
Voting Rights, New Zealand Women Win (Sept. 19, 1893) 1761
Voyage of the *Clermont*, Maiden (Aug. 17, 1807) 111
Vulcanized Rubber, Goodyear Patents (June 15, 1844) 687

Wagner's *Flying Dutchman* Debuts (Jan. 2, 1843) 672
Wagner's Ring Cycle, First Performance of (Aug. 13-17, 1876) 1464
Wahhābīs, Egypt Fights the (1811-1818) 143
Wakley Introduces *The Lancet* (Oct. 5, 1823) . . . 358
Walk of the Navajos, Long (Aug., 1863-Sept., 1866) 1105
Walker Invades Nicaragua (June 16, 1855-May 1, 1857) 914
Wallace's Expeditions Give Rise to Biogeography (1854-1862). 885
Waltz, Spread of the (19th cent.) 6
War, Apache and Navajo (Apr. 30, 1860-1865) 1005
War, Aroostook (1838-1839). 600
War, Austria and Prussia's Seven Weeks' (June 15-Aug. 23, 1866). 1190
War, Basuto (1865-1868) 1141
War, Creek (July 27, 1813-Aug. 9, 1814) 185
War, Crimean (Oct. 4, 1853-Mar. 30, 1856). . . . 876
War, Cuba's Ten Years' (Oct. 10, 1868-Feb. 10, 1878) 1269
War, Danish-Prussian (Feb. 1-Oct. 30, 1864). . . 1117
War, Díaz Drives Mexico into Civil (1871-1876) 1338
War, First Afghan (1839-1842) 617
War, First Boer (Dec. 16, 1880-Mar. 6, 1881) 1531
War, First Opium (Sept., 1839-Aug. 29, 1 842). 625
War, Franco-Prussian (July 19, 1870-Jan. 28, 1871) 1325
War, French Indochina (Apr., 1882-1885) 1553
War, Great Java (1825-1830) 386
War, Great Sioux (Aug. 17, 1862-Dec. 28, 1863) 1070
War, Greco-Turkish (Jan. 21-May 20, 1897) . . . 1872
War, Hearst-Pulitzer Circulation (1895-1898) 1794
War, Mexican (May 13, 1846-Feb. 2, 1848). . . . 710
War, Nez Perce (June 15-Oct. 5, 1877). 1479
War, Paraguayan (May 1, 1865-June 20, 1870). 1150
War, Red Cloud's (June 13, 1866-Nov. 6, 1868). 1187
War, Red River (June 27, 1874-June 2, 1875) 1413
War, Second Anglo-Sikh (Apr., 1848-Mar., 1849) 779
War, Second British-Ashanti (Jan. 22, 1873-Feb. 13, 1874) 1389
War, Second Opium (Oct. 23, 1856-Nov. 6, 1860) 930
War, Second Russo-Turkish (Apr. 26, 1828-Aug. 28, 1829) 412
War, Sino-Japanese (Aug. 1, 1894-Apr. 17, 1895) 1784
War, Sioux (1876-1877) 1442
War, South African (Oct. 11, 1899-May 31, 1902) 1932
War, Spanish-American (Apr. 24-Dec. 10, 1898) 1903
War, Sudanese (Mar., 1896-Nov., 1899) 1839
War, Texas's Cart (August-Dec., 1857) 950
War, Third Maratha (Nov. 5, 1817-June 3, 1818) 276
War, Third Russo-Turkish (Apr. 24, 1877-Jan. 31, 1878) 1476
War, Treaty of Guadalupe Hidalgo Ends Mexican (Feb. 2, 1848). 770
War, Tripolitan (Summer, 1801-Summer, 1805). 23
War, U.S. Civil (Apr. 12, 1861-Apr. 9, 1865) 1036
War, Zulu (Jan. 22-Aug., 1879). 1511
War in Spain, Peninsular (May 2, 1808-Nov., 1813) 125
War of 1812 (June 18, 1812-Dec. 24, 1814). . . . 166
War of Independence, Cuban (Feb. 24, 1895-1898) 1802
War of Independence, Mexican (Sept. 16, 1810-Sept. 28, 1821) 140
War of the Pacific (Apr. 5, 1879-Oct. 20, 1883) 1514
Ward Launches a Mail-Order Business (Aug., 1872). 1378

Wars, Apache (Feb. 6, 1861-Sept. 4, 1886) 1019
Wars, Dahomey-French (Nov., 1889-Jan., 1894). 1697
Wars, Portugal's Miguelite (1828-1834) 403
Wars, Seminole (Nov. 21, 1817-Mar. 27, 1858) 278
Wars, Turko-Egyptian (1832-1841) 505
Wars Unsettle Spain, Carlist (Sept. 29, 1833-1849) 539
Washington Monument, Ground Is Broken for the (July 4, 1848) 781
Washington Settles U.S. Claims vs. Britain, Treaty of (May 8, 1871). 1363
Washington's Atlanta Compromise Speech (Sept. 18, 1895) 1811
Washita River Massacre (Nov. 27, 1868). 1271
Watch Tower Bible and Tract Society Is Founded (1870-1871) 1316
Waterloo, Battle of (June 18, 1815) 243
Watie Is Last Confederate General to Surrender (June 23, 1865). 1153
Waverley, Scott Publishes (1814) 196
We Trust" Appears on U.S. Coins, "In God (Apr. 22, 1864) 1119
Weather Forecasting, Bjerknes Founds Scientific (July, 1897-July, 1904). 1877
Webster and Hayne Debate Slavery and Westward Expansion (Jan. 19-27, 1830). . . . 451
Webster-Ashburton Treaty Settles Maine's Canadian Border (Aug. 9, 1842) 666
Webster Publishes the First American Dictionary of English (Nov., 1828) 418
West, Frémont Explores the American (May, 1842-1854) 660
West, Jedediah Smith Explores the Far (1822-1831) 342
West, Powell Publishes His Report on the American (1879) 1504
West Africa, Exploration of (May 4, 1805-1830). 80
Western Australia, Last Convicts Land in (1868) 1238
Western Canada, Immigrant Farmers Begin Settling (1896). 1831
Western Trade, Perry Opens Japan to (Mar. 31, 1854) 888
Westinghouse Patents His Air Brake (Apr., 1869) 1287
Westward American Migration Begins (c. 1815-1830) 221
Westward Expansion, Webster and Hayne Debate Slavery and (Jan. 19-27, 1830). 451
Whig Party, Clay Begins American (Apr. 14, 1834) 551
Wiechert Invents the Inverted Pendulum Seismograph (1900) 1944
Wilson Launches *The Economist* (Sept. 2, 1843) 678
Win Voting Rights, New Zealand Women (Sept. 19, 1893) 1761
Wins the First America's Cup Race, *America* (Aug. 22, 1851). 846
Wire, Glidden Patents Barbed (Nov. 24, 1874) 1416
Wireless Telegraph, Marconi Patents the (June, 1896) 1851
Withdraws from the Concert of Europe, Great Britain (Oct. 20-30, 1822) 350
Woman Suffrage Associations Begin Forming (May, 1869) 1290
Woman's Rights Convention, Akron (May 28-29, 1851) 843
Women, Declaration of the Rights of (July 4, 1876) 1460
Women and Children Opens, New York Infirmary for Indigent (May 12, 1857) 947
Women of Canada Is Founded, National Council of (Oct. 27, 1893) 1768
Women the Vote, Wyoming Gives (Dec., 1869) 1304
Women Win Voting Rights, New Zealand (Sept. 19, 1893) 1761
Women's Rights Associations Unite (Feb. 17-18, 1890). 1709
Wong Kim Ark, United States v. (Mar. 28, 1898) 1897
Work in the Nervous System, Ramón y Cajal Shows How Neurons (1888-1906) 1671
Working-Class Libraries, Development of (19th cent.) 3
Works Open at Essen, Krupp (Sept. 20, 1811). . . 154
World as Will and Idea, Schopenhauer Publishes *The* (1819) 285
World's Fair, Chicago (May 1-Oct. 30, 1893) 1757
World's Fair, London Hosts the First (May 1-Oct. 15, 1851). 840

World's First Skyscraper Is Built (1883-1885) 1575
Wounded Knee Massacre (Dec. 29, 1890) 1718
Wyoming Gives Women the Vote (Dec., 1869) 1304

X Rays, Röntgen Discovers (Nov. 9, 1895) 1814

Yellow Fever, Suppression of (June, 1900-1904) 1966
Yellow Journalism, Rise of (1880's-1890's) . . . 1526
Yellow Peril Campaign Begins, Anti-Japanese (May 4, 1892) 1742
Yellowstone Becomes the First U.S. National Park (Mar. 1, 1872) 1375
Young Germany Movement (1826-1842) 400
Young Italy, Mazzini Founds (1831). 482

Zanzibar Outlaws Slavery (1873-1897). 1386
Zeppelin Completes the First Flying Dirigible (July 2, 1900) 1969
Zionist Movement, Herzl Founds the (Feb., 1896-Aug., 1897). 1836
Zoological Philosophy, Lamarck Publishes (1809). 128
Zulu Expansion (c. 1817-1828) 270
Zulu War (Jan. 22-Aug., 1879) 1511

List of Maps, Tables, and Sidebars

The World in 1801

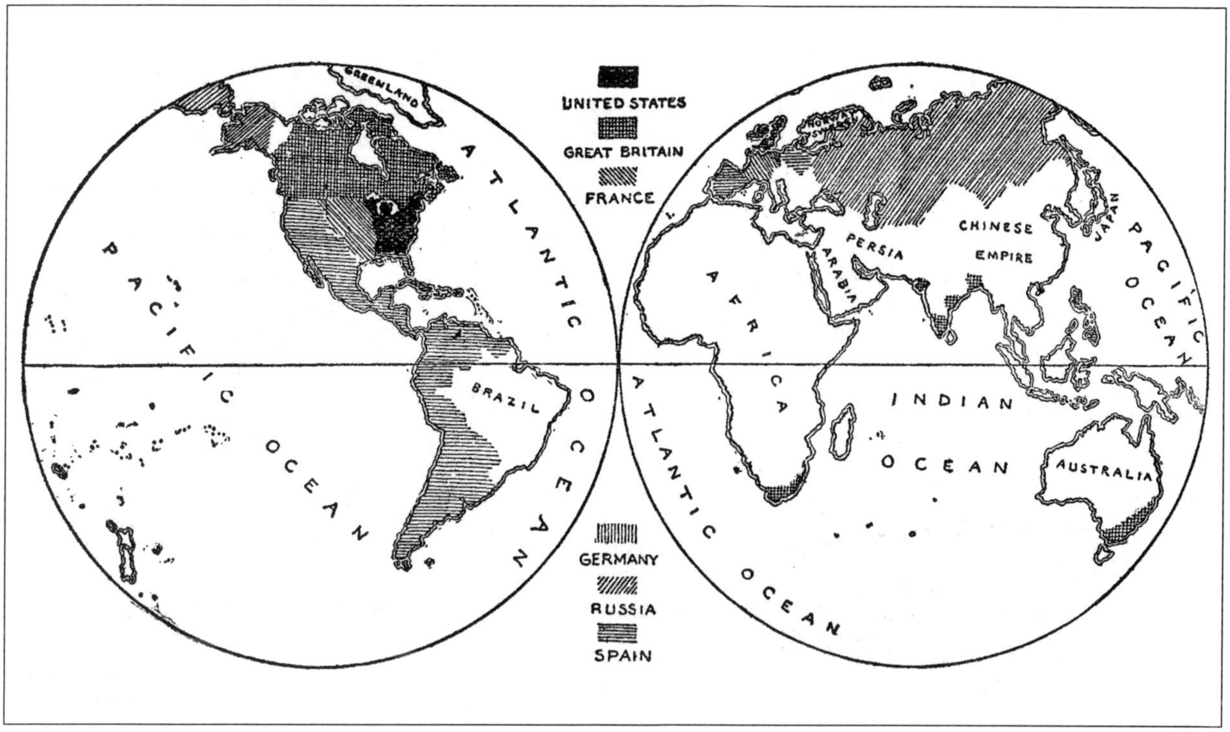

The World in 1900

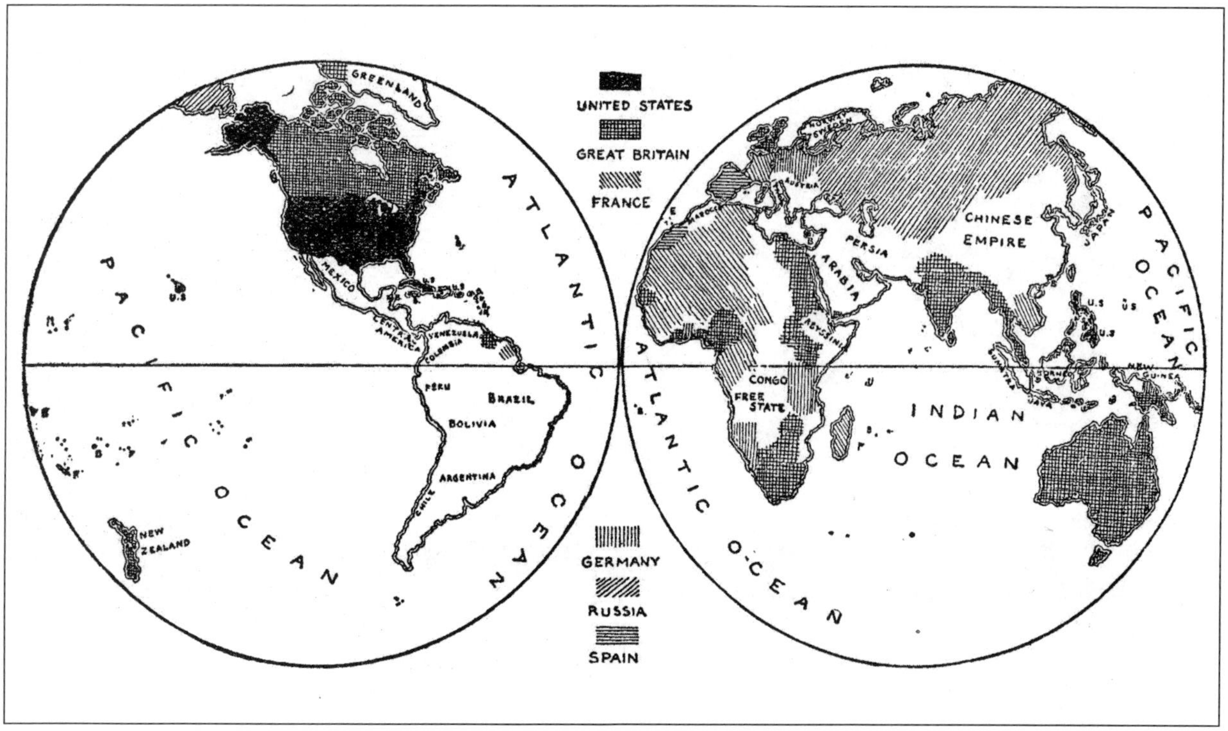

Africa at the End of the Nineteenth Century

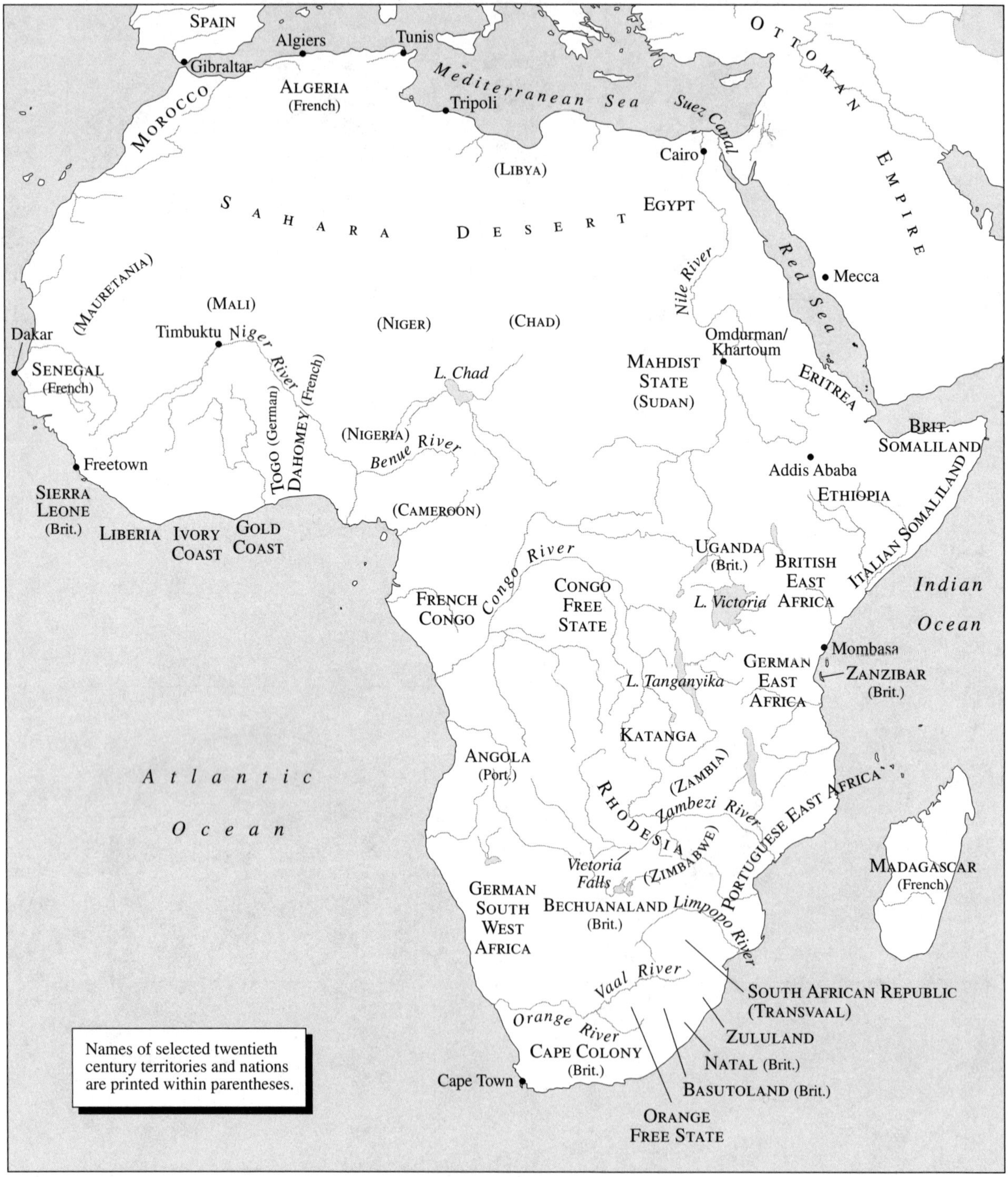

ASIA AND AUSTRALASIA AT THE END OF THE NINETEENTH CENTURY

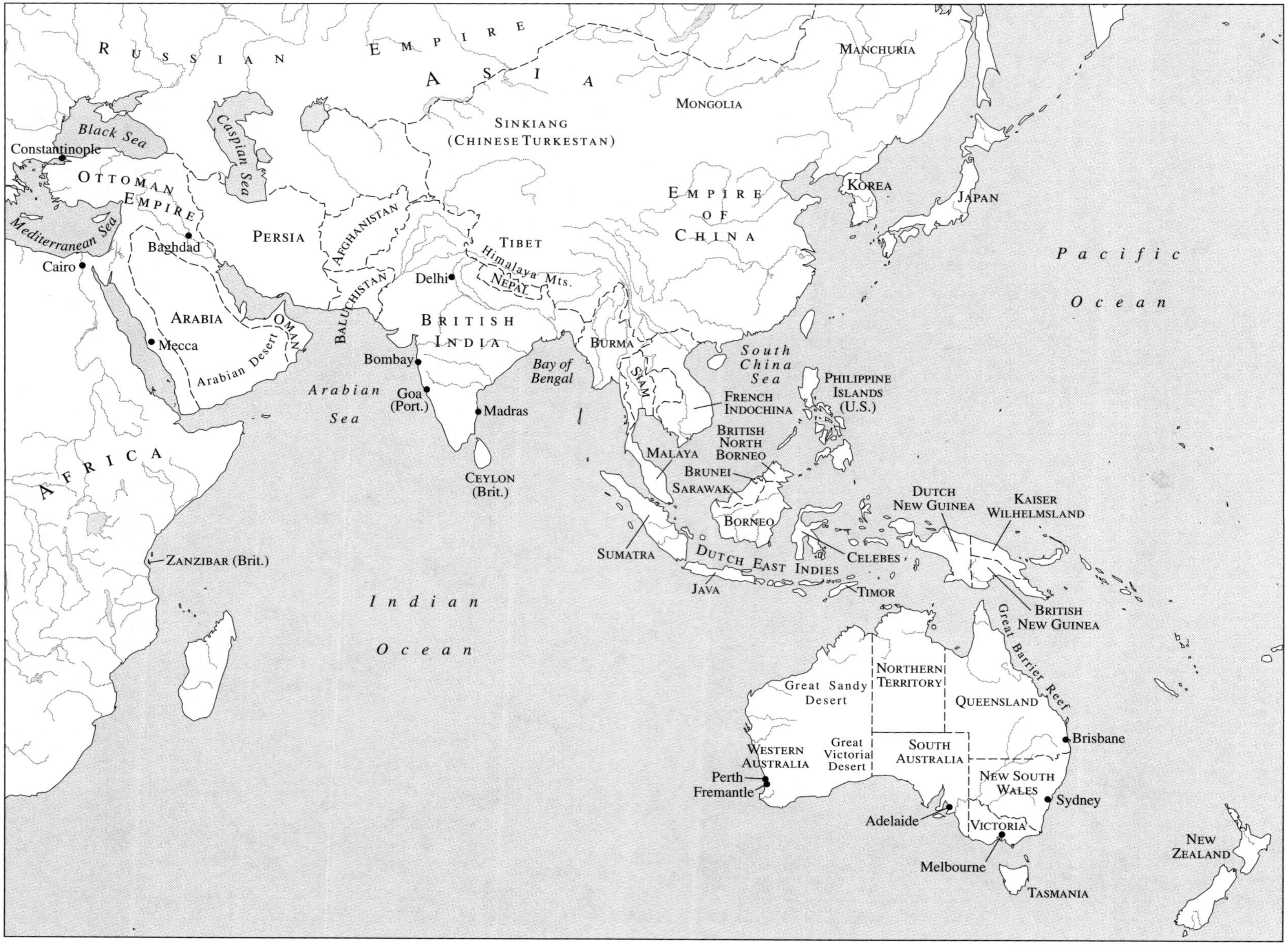

Europe at the End of the Nineteenth Century

North America at the End of the Nineteenth Century

South America at the End of the Nineteenth Century

Great Events from History

The 19th Century

1801-1900

December 8, 1864
Pius IX Issues the Syllabus of Errors

In his defense of a papacy under siege, Pope Pius IX proved unrelenting in his condemnation of secular ideas and values that he deemed dangerous to the spiritual mission of the Roman Catholic Church. The Syllabus of Errors, a list of such ideas and values that were to be avoided by Catholics, reflected the depth and breadth of the pope's alienation from modern secular society.

Locale: Rome (now in Italy)
Category: Religion and theology

Key Figures

Pius IX (Giovanni Maria Mastai-Ferretti; 1792-1878), Roman Catholic Pope, 1846-1878
Luigi Bilio (1826-1884), chief aide to Pius IX in composing the Syllabus of Errors
Félix-Antoine-Philibert Dupanloup (1802-1878), bishop of Orléans

Summary of Event

During the nineteenth century, many nationalists sought to replace the dominion of kings who ruled by divine right with constitutionally based national states united through common ties of geography, cultural traditions, and ethnic composition. Nationalists in Italy, however, faced a particularly formidable task. That land had not known unity since the collapse of the Western Roman Empire in the fifth century. By 1848, it was divided among four major powers, three of which were adamantly opposed to the trend toward national unity and democracy.

Foremost in opposition was the papacy in Rome. By the nineteenth century, popes for nearly eleven hundred years had held title to an aggregate of territories known as the Papal States. These lands encompassed some 118,000 square miles, straddling central Italy north of Rome. By splitting the Italian peninsula into two parts, north and south, this papal domain blocked any effective Italian unification. It was therefore a prime objective of the Italian nationalist movement to strip the Papal States from the papacy. A few wanted to abolish the papacy altogether.

The pope who had to confront this grave threat to papal power was a former Italian archbishop and cardinal who took the name Pius IX upon his election in 1846. At first, liberals and democrats found much to praise in Pius IX's progressive policies. Among other measures, he granted amnesty to more than one thousand political prisoners in the Papal States, relaxed restrictions on Jews in Rome, and even allowed a constitution to be drawn up for the Papal States.

Militant Italian nationalists wanted more, however. They demanded that the papacy declare war on the Austrian Empire, whose troops then occupied parts of northeastern Italy, including Venice. When the pope refused, insisting that he would never attack another Christian state, riots erupted in Rome, his prime minister was assassinated, and Pius himself was forced to flee in disguise to Naples. In Rome, the charismatic nationalist leader Giuseppe Mazzini proclaimed a ramshackle republic that was soon crushed by French troops, but by the time the French escorted Pius back to his city in 1850, his whole perspective had been transformed.

The pope's bitter experience with Mazzini's Roman republic would color the remaining twenty-eight years of his pontificate. Henceforth, Pius IX viewed with fear and loathing the modern culture of his day, above all, nationalism and secularism. In subsequent speeches and writings, the pope broadened his targets to include a wide range of modern intellectual, religious, and social currents that he regarded as potentially lethal to the Christian faith.

The papacy's plight in Rome became desperate in 1858, when the Austrian army in northeastern Italy that had long protected the Papal States was driven from the peninsula. The victorious coalition driving out the Austrians was led by the small northern Italian state of Piedmont-Sardinia, under its able prime minister Count Cavour. He had become the driving force toward the unification of all Italy.

With the Austrians gone, Cavour quickly seized the Papal States, and when the king of Naples was deposed in 1861, all Italian lands but Rome were in Cavour's hands. The same year, Cavour proclaimed the new nation and installed Victor Emmanuel II, the king of his own Piedmont-Sardinia, as the first king of Italy. Cavour became the prime minister of the new nation. Only a small garrison provided by Pius IX's last major ally, the French emperor Napoleon III, stood between the pope and his enemies.

It was against this background that Pius IX issued one of the most controversial documents in papal history. *Syllabus errorum* (Syllabus of Errors) was promulgated on December 8, 1864, as an appendix to the papal encyc-

Pope Pius IX. (R. S. Peale/J. A. Hill)

lical *Quanta cura* (with what great care), but the Syllabus of Errors would take on a life of its own. Believing the time to be ripe at last, the pope had appointed a senior papal official, Luigi Bilio, to help prepare a list of current ideas, practices, and tendencies considered heretical or otherwise inadmissible by the Church. The list was to be compiled from the pope's own oral and written pronouncements since the beginning of his pontificate.

The resulting Syllabus of Errors was composed of eighty propositions that identified modern political, religious, and intellectual phenomena deemed unacceptable by Rome. The language of the propositions was often scathing. For example, the pope regarded nationalism, socialism, democracy, and liberalism as deplorable substitute religions in direct rivalry with Christianity. Another proposition, one clearly related to contemporary events, asserted the papacy's absolute right to own and administer land, because such ownership was essential to the welfare and mission of the Church.

Other propositions of the Syllabus of Errors asserted that freedom of worship and of conscience could not be allowed, because true religion must tolerate no divergence. Rejected also were all forms of secular rationalism as found in modern science and philosophy, from which God was excluded. The sheer scope and harshness concentrated in this single document left many in Europe both stunned and deeply puzzled. Others were outraged. Most Roman Catholic liberals were dismayed but remained loyal. An immediate question was how binding the document was on the Roman Catholic community. Opinion on this question has never been settled by Catholic theologians. A larger question was whether the pope really intended to declare war, in effect, on the entire secular world.

In a Rome encircled by his enemies, the pope well recognized by 1864 how precarious his situation had become. He had suffered humiliation and huge losses at the hands of the new Italian state of Mazzini and Cavour. The Syllabus of Errors can be seen, in part, as a lashing out by Pius IX against his perceived tormentors. In fact, some of the Syllabus of Errors's bitterest attacks on political and intellectual trends related directly to the actions and beliefs of the contemporary Italian government and its leading politicians, Mazzini and Cavour. The document does not explicitly limit its target to Italy, however, nor does it provide for any exceptions to its blanket condemnations.

The French bishop Félix-Antoine-Philibert Dupanloup sought in an 1865 pamphlet to soften the impact of the Syllabus of Errors by construing it as a description of a perfect society, an ideal state of affairs that could never exist in this world. Dupanloup contended that in the real world of the nineteenth century, the forms of government, science, and religion excoriated in the Syllabus of Errors had in practice to be tolerated by the Church. Indeed, some good could come from the insights of secular politics, science, and philosophy, so long as God was not excluded from them. Thus, human reason could be greatly illuminated by the teachings of the faith as in the medieval philosophy of Thomas Aquinas. Dupanloup's rationale did not satisfy everyone, although, interestingly, Pius IX commended it as an acceptable interpretation.

SIGNIFICANCE

The Syllabus of Errors created a sensation across Europe. Previously scattered among diverse, sometimes obscure sources, the provocative papal opinions it expressed had a far greater impact when concentrated in a single publication. Despite ambitious attempts to place the Syllabus of Errors in its contemporary context and in a less baleful light, the curious document inevitably became ready fodder for critics of the Church. In general, the Syllabus of Errors can be seen as a last defiant declaration of a venerable papal monarchy come to grief in a secular world it no longer understood. While Pius IX could not prevent the triumph of nationalism, liberalism, and science across Europe, he would not cease trying.

Worse was still to come. In 1870, Pius IX convened the Vatican Council, which approved the doctrine of papal infallibility in certain matters of faith and morals. Immediately following the council's adjournment, Napoleon III was deposed by a victorious Prussian army. This caused a sudden evacuation of the French garrison defending Rome. The Italian nationalists swiftly seized the city and confined the pope to the tiny enclave of the Vatican. He never acknowledged the authority of the Italian state, nor would he ever leave the Vatican again.

Rome's fall in 1870 marked the end of an era. Over a very eventful and significant pontificate, still the longest in Church history, Pius IX did keep the papacy intact, despite his loss of the papal lands. He was the last priest-king of the Roman Catholic Church. In this age of transition, the Syllabus of Errors would stand as testimony to the iron determination of a pope to prevent further erosion of the Church's moral authority and to warn the faithful against seductive worldly attractions that could imperil their salvation.

—*Donald Sullivan*

FURTHER READING

Chadwick, Owen. *A History of the Popes, 1830-1914*. New York: Oxford University Press, 1998. Contains five chapters on Pius IX, including an excellent discussion of the context and significance of the Syllabus of Errors.

Coppa, Frank J. *The Modern Papacy Since 1789*. London: Longman, 1998. An addition to the already extensive scholarship on the Syllabus of Errors, reconsidering its place in nineteenth and twentieth century papal history.

Hales, E. E. Y. *Pio Nono: A Study in European Politics and Religion in the Nineteenth Century*. New York: P. J. Kennedy and Sons, 1954. Sympathetic but even-handed biography of Pius IX, including the Syllabus of Errors. Still the definitive life of Pius IX in English.

Pope Against Modern Errors: Sixteen Papal Documents. Rockford, Ill.: Tan Books, 1999. Contains the complete text of the encyclical letter *Quanta cura*, including the Syllabus of Errors.

SEE ALSO: 1835-1836: Strauss Publishes *The Life of Jesus Critically Examined*; Jan. 12, 1848-Aug. 28, 1849: Italian Revolution of 1848; Dec. 8, 1854: Pius IX Decrees the Immaculate Conception Dogma; Mar. 17, 1861: Italy Is Proclaimed a Kingdom; Dec. 8, 1869-Oct. 20, 1870: Vatican I Decrees Papal Infallibility Dogma; 1881-1889: Bismarck Introduces Social Security Programs in Germany; May 15, 1891: Papal Encyclical on Labor.

RELATED ARTICLES in *Great Lives from History: The Nineteenth Century, 1801-1900:* Count Cavour; Giuseppe Mazzini; Napoleon III; Pius IX.

1865
MENDEL PROPOSES LAWS OF HEREDITY

Gregor Mendel's experiments with pea plants refuted the then-accepted theory of "blending inheritance" and suggested instead that inheritance is particulate. Because he performed extensive cross-fertilizations and produced and examined numerous offspring, Mendel's laws of heredity constituted the first mathematically robust theory of inheritance.

LOCALE: Brno, Austria (now in Czech Republic)
CATEGORIES: Genetics; science and technology; mathematics

KEY FIGURES

Gregor Mendel (1822-1884), Austrian monk and scientist

Cyrill Franz Napp (1792-1867), Austrian abbot and plant breeder

SUMMARY OF EVENT

The understanding of heredity during the nineteenth century was at a crossroads. Since the days of Greek antiquity, there had been a debate over how offspring were formed. Hippocrates (c. 460-c. 370 B.C.E.) proposed that the seminal fluids of both the male and female contained a collection of particles from all over the body. When these fluids were brought together during copulation, they fused together and became the fetus. This theory is often called "pangenesis" and is the forerunner of the nineteenth century theory of blending inheritance.

Aristotle (384-322 B.C.E.) proposed an alternative model in which menstrual fluid in the female contained particles from throughout her body and semen from the man was the active principle that shaped these particles into a fetus. Later theories dispensed with particles entirely and proposed that the female contained miniature, preformed embryos in her ovaries and that semen from the male acted as nourishment for the developing fetus. A variation of this preformation theory held that the preformed embryo was in the sperm and the woman simply nourished it as it grew. Eventually, the recognition that offspring typically display a combination of traits from both parents removed support for preformation theories and led to an almost universal acceptance of pangenesis, and thus of blending inheritance.

The validity of blending inheritance was considered self-evident. Offspring, for the most part, contain a blending of traits from their parents. Breeders, though, had always been aware of exceptions called "sports." A sport possessed a new trait not seen in either parent. Rather than seeing this as a challenge to blending inheritance, they assumed the new trait to be a defect resulting from an error in the joining of parental particles. More careful, scientific breeding experiments revealed more troubling challenges to the theory of blending inheritance. Sometimes, when parents had differing traits, their offspring displayed the trait of one parent instead of a blending of the traits of both. Such results awaited an explanation at the time that Gregor Mendel began his experiments in 1856.

Mendel was a university-educated Augustinian novitiate at a monastery in Brno, Austria. Although he never successfully passed the teaching examinations, he had taught natural history and physics at the Oberrealschule in Brno for sixteen years. With this background and the support of his abbot, Cyrill Franz Napp, Mendel began conducting crossbreeding studies on garden peas (*Pisum sativum*). He was not the first plant breeder to study peas. Others had discovered that crossing certain pure-breeding varieties of peas resulted in offspring with just one form of a trait. No one, however, had yet offered an adequate explanation for this result.

Why did Mendel succeed where others had failed? The primary reason was probably his meticulous and careful experiments. During the seven years that he conducted these experiments, he produced and analyzed approximately twenty-eight thousand plants. This large number of experimental results allowed for more accurate mathematical calculations. He also crossbred plants over several generations, noting the frequency of a given trait in each generation. To make his data easier to manage, he focused on only seven traits that were consistently easy to differentiate. He was also lucky in that the genes for five of the seven traits he tracked are now known to reside on separate chromosomes and are therefore not linked. The remaining two traits have their genes on the same chromosome and are therefore linked, but they are so far apart that when a cross-fertilization in-

BATESON DEFENDS MENDEL

Gregor Mendel conducted his experiments with pea plants more than three decades before his theories were finally given a serious audience by the scientific community—and even then, detractors sought to bury the unknown monk's achievement. In his preface to Mendel's Principles of Heredity, *William Bateson stated why he felt compelled to defend the work of Gregor Mendel, whose work had laid the foundation for modern genetics.*

In the Study of Evolution progress had well-nigh stopped. . . . Such was our state when two years ago it was suddenly discovered that an unknown man, Gregor Johann Mendel, had, alone, and unheeded, broken off from the rest—in the moment that Darwin was at work—and cut a way through. . . .

In the world of knowledge we are accustomed to look for some strenuous effort to understand a new truth even in those who are indisposed to believe. It was therefore with a regret approaching to indignation that I read Professor [Raphael] Weldon's criticism. Were such a piece from the hand of a junior it might safely be neglected; but coming from Professor Weldon there was the danger—almost the certainty—that the small band of younger men who are thinking of research in this field would take it they had learnt the gist of Mendel, would imagine his teaching exposed by Professor Weldon, and look elsewhere for lines of work.

In evolutionary studies we have no Areopagus. With us it is not . . . that an open court is always sitting, composed of men themselves workers, keenly interested in every new thing, skilled and well versed in the facts. Where this is the case, doctrine is soon tried and the false trodden down. But in our sparse and apathetic community error mostly grows unheeded, choking truth. That fate must not befall Mendel now.

Source: William Bateson, *Mendel's Principles of Heredity: A Defence* (New York: Cambridge University Press, 1902).

volving both traits is done, they behave like unlinked genes. Had some of the genes been closely linked, Mendel might have been confused by the progeny ratios he observed.

Mendel's experiments yielded similar results for all seven of the traits he studied. For example, when he crossbred pea plants grown from round seeds with pea plants grown from wrinkled seeds, all of the resulting offspring produced pods with round seeds. When he allowed these plants to self-fertilize, both round-seeded plants and plants with wrinkled seeds resulted, and there were consistently three times as many round-seeded offspring as there were offspring with wrinkled seeds. These results were expressed by Mendel as a 3:1 ratio of round to wrinkled.

It was Mendel's interpretation of these results that proved revolutionary. He hypothesized that the inheritance of each trait was controlled by discrete particles that were contributed by each parent. The observable expression of a particular trait in a particular offspring (now known as its phenotype) was determined by which specific particles that offspring had inherited (now referred to as its genotype). When there were different particles, as, for example, in the case of seed shape, one of the particles would be dominant over the other. In the case of seed shape, the particle for round seeds was dominant over the particle for wrinkled seeds.

To account for the patterns he observed, Mendel concluded that the genotype of each plant cell comprised a specific pair of particles controlling the expression of each trait. The original, purebreeding parents had only one type of particle. Thus they contained either two round particles or two wrinkled particles. The first-generation offspring each possessed both one round and one wrinkled particle, but because the round particles were dominant, all first-generation offspring were of the round-seeded phenotype.

Mendel expanded upon this model to produce his law of segregation, which described how the hereditary particles were passed to offspring. Eggs and sperm (gametes) contained only one hereditary particle for each trait. The particles segregated during the formation of gametes, and when the egg and sperm joined together during fertilization, the normal condition of two particles per trait was restored in the offspring.

Mendel went on to perform dihybrid and trihybrid cross-fertilizations, that is, fertilizations crossbreeding two and three contrasting traits, respectively. One of Mendel's dihybrid crosses was between smooth-seeded, purple-flowered (smooth, purple) plants and wrinkle-seeded, white-flowered (wrinkled, white) plants. The first-generation offspring were all smooth, purple. Allowing these first-generation plants to self-fertilize produced four different phenotypes in the following ratio: 9:3:3:1 (smooth and purple: smooth and white: wrinkled and purple: wrinkled and white). Mendel noted that within the dihybrid ratio, each of the individual traits taken alone still formed a 3:1 ratio. The same observation held true for his trihybrid crosses.

Mendel generalized his conclusions from the dihybrid and trihybrid crosses and formulated his law of independent assortment. This law stated that the particles governing the expression of each trait followed the law of segregation and that each trait was expressed independently of all others. In other words, the pattern of inheritance for one trait had no effect on the inheritance of any other trait. It was in formulating this law that Mendel's luck in choosing traits controlled by unlinked genes is apparent.

Mendel presented his findings in 1865 at the meeting of the Society for Natural Sciences. They was published in *Verhandlungen des Naturforschenden vereines* (proceedings of the society for natural sciences) as *Versuche über Pflanzenhybriden* (1865; *Experiments in Plant Hybridization*, 1901). His paper was received with little fanfare, and it is likely that few in attendance actually understood what Mendel was proposing. It was rare at the time to use the type of mathematics and probability calculations that Mendel had in breeding studies, and his conclusions were dependent on understanding the math. Being published in the journal of a small, isolated scientific society meant that few others took notice either.

Mendel died in 1884, and his great discovery of the laws of segregation and independent assortment languished in obscurity, essentially forgotten. His paper was later independently "rediscovered" near the turn of the century by three different biologists: Erich Tschermak von Seysenegg, Carl Correns, and Hugo de Vries. They helped to popularize Mendel's model, which would form the basis for all modern genetics.

SIGNIFICANCE

Considering Mendel as the founder of genetics is entirely appropriate, given that his basic laws are still useful to geneticists in the twenty-first century. Although Mendel had no knowledge of the inner workings of cells and knew nothing of deoxyribonucleic acid (DNA) or chromosomes, his two laws are entirely consistent with the way genes behave. Consequently, many modern textbook accounts use the language of genes and chromosomes to describe Mendel's work and findings.

If Mendel's paper had received wider attention in his day, it is likely that the field of genetics would have expanded several decades earlier than it did. If Charles Darwin had read Mendel's paper, he might have realized that Mendel's model of inheritance provided the specific mechanism for natural selection that was missing from Darwin's own theory. Ironically, Darwin did own a copy of Mendel's paper, but he never read it. The pages were still uncut. It was left to later generations, then, to acknowledge Mendel's gift to science.

—*Bryan Ness*

FURTHER READING

Carlson, Elof Axel. *Mendel's Legacy: The Origin of Classical Genetics*. Woodbury, N.Y.: Cold Spring Harbor Laboratory Press, 2004. A history of classical genetics that shows how Mendel's research laid the primary groundwork for modern genetics.

Edelson, Edward. *Gregor Mendel: And the Roots of Genetics*. Oxford, England: Oxford University Press, 2001. Part of the Oxford Portraits in Science series, this basic introduction to Mendel explains how he developed his laws of genetics.

Henig, Robin Marantz. *The Monk in the Garden: The Lost and Found Genius of Gregor Mendel, the Father of Genetics*. New York: Mariner Books, 2001. A recent biography of Mendel that gives insights into the founder of genetics and discusses the "lost and found" nature of his discoveries.

Sturtevant, A. H. *History of Genetics*. Reprint. Woodbury, N.Y.: Cold Spring Harbor Laboratory Press, 2001. Classic text by a geneticist who was present for many of the genetic discoveries of the first half of the twentieth century. Provides a comprehensive history, beginning before Mendel, that places the Austrian monk's work in its larger scientific context.

Wood, Roger J., and Vitezslav Orel. *Genetic Prehistory in Selective Breeding: A Prelude to Mendel*. Oxford, England: Oxford University Press, 2001. Focuses on the developments in animal and plant breeding from 1700 to 1860; a good introduction to the ideas surrounding inheritance when Mendel began his work.

SEE ALSO: 1809: Lamarck Publishes *Zoological Philosophy*; 1838-1839: Schwann and Virchow Develop Cell Theory; 1854-1862: Wallace's Expeditions Give Rise to Biogeography; Nov. 24, 1859: Darwin Publishes *On the Origin of Species*; 1871: Darwin Publishes *The Descent of Man*; 1880's: Roux Develops the Theory of Mitosis; 1883: Galton Defines "Eugenics"; 1899-1900: Rediscovery of Mendel's Hereditary Theory.

RELATED ARTICLES in *Great Lives from History: The Nineteenth Century, 1801-1900:* Charles Darwin; Gregor Mendel.

c. 1865
NATURALIST MOVEMENT BEGINS

A literary movement whose practitioners describe reality as precisely as possible using descriptive methods deemed scientific, naturalism was inspired by French novelists. Although the term is often used synonymously with realism, which also aims at precise descriptions of all social strata but mostly the downtrodden, naturalism differs from realism by emphasizing that existence is entirely part of nature and not supernatural, metaphysical, or spiritual.

LOCALE: Paris, France
CATEGORY: Literature

KEY FIGURES

Émile Zola (1840-1902), author and main proponent of naturalism
Paul Alexis (1847-1901), Zola's first biographer
Hippolyte Taine (1828-1893), literary critic, philosopher, and historian
Honoré de Balzac (1799-1850),
Gustave Flaubert (1821-1880),
Jules de Goncourt (1830-1870), and
Edmond de Goncourt (1822-1896), French novelists
Henry Céard (1851-1924),
Léon Hennique (1850-1935),
Joris-Karl Huysmans (1848-1907), and
Guy de Maupassant (1850-1893), naturalist writers

SUMMARY OF EVENT

Naturalist thought emerged during the late 1860's in France with the novels of the brothers Edmond de Goncourt and Jules de Goncourt (*Germinie Lacerteux*, 1865; English translation, 1887) and of Émile Zola (*Thérèse Raquin*, 1867; English translation, 1881). Before the particular body of convictions that informed these early "naturalist" novels, a "naturalist" was understood to refer to someone working in the natural sciences. The term also had a philosophical meaning, referring to a doctrine that denied the existence of the metaphysical or supernatural and embraced the natural, material world. During the early nineteenth century "naturalism" acquired an aesthetic sense when French poet Charles Baudelaire used the term to refer (somewhat disparagingly) to a form of painting that sought to render nature faithfully.

Zola, considered the main proponent of naturalism at its beginnings, drew on these three earlier meanings of naturalism, and their application to literature, when he used the term in the 1860's in reference to the work of Hippolyte Taine, a literary critic, philosopher, and historian, whom Zola held in great esteem. Taine believed that the intellectual world was governed by the same types of laws as the material world, and that it was necessary to define these laws if one wished to understand the human spirit.

The development of naturalist thought also was greatly influenced by positivism, a scientific doctrine that held it was possible to explain life through reason and observation. This faith in scientific enquiry is the principal difference between naturalism and the realist movement that preceded it. Yet many realist novelists also provided models for Zola. Honoré de Balzac's monumental *La Comédie humaine* (1829-1848; *The Comedy of Human Life*, 1885-1893, 1896; also known as *The Human Comedy*) offered a comprehensive study of characters from a variety of different backgrounds. Gustave Flaubert's *Madame Bovary* (1857; English translation, 1886) shocked readers with its detached analysis of a woman's different states of mind and its detailed description of her death by poisoning. The Goncourt brother's novel *Germinie Lacerteux*, considered realist as well as naturalist by many, aimed to be an objective study of the breakdown of the Goncourt brothers' maid. Naturalism took the working classes as its subject and analyzed the contemporary world, inspired by discoveries and new methods in medicine.

In 1870, Zola began what was to be his most important literary project, a series of twenty novels known as *Les Rougon-Macquart* (1871-1893; *The Rougon-Macquart Novels*, 1885-1907). These novels investigate two branches of one family, the legitimate Rougons and the illegitimate Macquarts, living during the Second Em-

Émile Zola. (Library of Congress)

pire (1852-1871). By studying family histories, Zola was able to analyze one of his favorite subjects, the influence of heredity and environment on the shaping of character. Again, these objectives were informed by the scientific discourse of Zola's time. Zola had read Prosper Lucas's *Traité philosophique et physiologique de l'hérédité naturelle* (pb. 1850; philosophical and physiological treatise on natural heredity), which stressed the importance of heredity in the formation of human character and behavior.

Heredity and the impact of one's environment also were the subjects of Charles Darwin's *On the Origin of Species by Means of Natural Selection*, which had been published in 1859 but was translated into French only in 1865. Zola shared Darwin's view of the individual as a product of his or her environment. Because of this belief in the determining effects of heredity and environment, the fates of the characters in Zola's fiction are often presented as inevitable.

In 1880, midway through the writing of the *Rougon Macquart* series, Zola published an essay called *Le Roman expérimental* (*The Experimental Novel*, 1893), in which is found his most complete description of naturalism. This work was influenced by another contemporary scientific text, Claude Bernard's *Introduction à l'étude de la médecine expérimentale* (1865; *Introduction to the Study of Experimental Medicine*, 1927). In that text, Bernard tried to establish a method of scientific investigation for the then-new science of medicine. Zola responded to this by trying to adopt Bernard's methods and apply them to literature. Zola argued in *Le Roman expérimental* that if the scientific method could be used to explain the physical world then it also could be used to explain human passions and the intellect.

It is just prior to the publication of *Le Roman expérimental* that naturalism dates its beginnings as a literary movement. The movement is generally considered to have begun in 1877, when the young writers Paul Alexis, Henry Céard, Léon Hennique, Joris-Karl Huysmans, Octave Mirbeau, and Guy de Maupassant organized a dinner at the restaurant Trapp to honor Zola, Flaubert, and Edmond de Goncourt. Three years later, Zola and the same group of younger writers (with the exception of Mirbeau) published a collective anthology of their work called *Les Soirées de Médan* (1880), which has been read as a kind of manifesto of the group.

Although Zola seems to have felt that naturalism constituted a united movement because of the shared scientific method of its members, other literary naturalists tended to view his methods with more skepticism. The similarities one finds in naturalist fiction tend to be, rather, in the choice of subject matter. Because of the naturalist's interest in the physical world, subjects such as disease, madness, alcoholism, and sexual desire predominate over metaphysical themes such as morality, sin, or guilt.

Zola continued to write naturalist novels and plays until his death in 1902, but it has been argued that naturalism as a collective enterprise ended very shortly after its launch. After 1880, Zola retreated to his home in Médan to write many of the most remarkable novels comprising the *Rougon Macquart* series: *Pot-Bouille* (1882; *Piping Hot*, 1924), *Au bonheur des dames* (1883; *The Ladies Paradise*, 1883), *La Joie de vivre* (1884; *Life's Joys*, 1884), *Germinal* (1885; English translation, 1885), *L'Œuvre* (1886; *His Masterpiece*, 1886), and *La Terre* (1887; *The Soil*, 1888). During this time Huysmans and Maupassant began to have doubts about Zola's theories.

Another group of five young writers—Paul Bonnetain, J. H. Rosny, Lucien Descaves, Paul Margueritte, and Gustave Guiches), paralleling the group who wrote the *Soirées de Médan*, published the "Manifeste des cinq contre 'La Terre'" (1887; manifesto of the five against *La Terre*). Claiming to have previously admired Zola, this group declared that the subject of his novel *La Terre* was virtually scatological and that the master had descended to the pits of the unspeakable.

Despite these public statements of adherence or abhorrence, naturalist plays continued to be performed and naturalist texts continued to be written and published in France, in other European countries, and in North America until well into the twentieth century.

SIGNIFICANCE

By the early 1880's the influence of the naturalist movement had spread to Italy and was greatly influential in the development of verism (truthfulness and detail in literary and artistic depiction), based on the fiction of Giovanni Verga. Naturalism also moved into Spain, where elements can be seen in the novels of Emilia de Pardo Bazán and Benito Pérez Galdós.

German naturalists such as Karl Bleibtreu, Wilhelm Bölsche, and Arno Holz seemed to feel the attraction of the natural sciences to a greater extent even than did Zola. Naturalism was also expressed in American fiction by authors such as Hamlin Garland, Stephen Crane, Frank Norris, James Farrell, Jack London, and Theodore Dreiser.

The movement responded to an interest in subject matter that had not been deemed appropriate for literature: the real, the mundane, the working classes, the poor, and similar subjects. Naturalism testified to how critically scientific discourse played a role in the literature of the last half of the nineteenth and beginning of the twentieth century.

—*Margot Irvine*

FURTHER READING

Baguley, David. *Naturalist Fiction: The Entropic Vision*. New York: Cambridge University Press, 1990. The most important and comprehensive study of naturalism written in English.

Bloom, Harold, ed. *Emile Zola*. Philadelphia: Chelsea House, 2004. A collection of essays by a prolific literary critic dealing with Zola's fiction and with naturalism.

Goncourt, Edmond, and Jules de Goncourt. *Germinie Lacerteux*. Translated by Leonard Tancock. New York: Penguin Books, 1984. Part of the Penguin Classics series. A modern edition, with an introductory essay by the translator, of the Goncourt brothers' first naturalist novel.

Mesch, Rachel L. "The Sex of Science: Medicine, Naturalism, and Feminism in Lucie-Delarue-Mardrus's 'Marie, fille-mère.'" *Nineteenth-Century French Studies* 31 (2003): 324-340. Although naturalism is generally viewed as a movement dominated by male authors, this article describes a French woman's use of naturalism in her fiction.

Pagano, Tullio. *Experimental Fictions: From Emile Zola's Naturalism to Giovanni Verga's Verism*. London: Associated University Presses, 1999. A comparative study of naturalism in the works of Zola and verism in Verga's works.

Zola, Émile. *Therese Raquin*. Translated by Robin Buss. London: Penguin Books, 2004. A modern edition in the Penguin Classics series of what many consider Zola's first novel in the naturalist tradition. Includes an introduction by the translator.

SEE ALSO: c. 1820-1860: *Costumbrismo* Movement; May 8, 1835: Andersen Publishes His First Fairy Tales; 1840's-1880's: Russian Realist Movement; Fall, 1848: Pre-Raphaelite Brotherhood Begins; 1851-1854: Comte Advances His Theory of Positivism; 1855: Courbet Establishes Realist Art Movement; 1870's: Aesthetic Movement Arises; 1879: *A Doll's House* Introduces Modern Realistic Drama; 1880's: Brahmin School of American Literature Flourishes; c. 1884-1924: Decadent Movement Flourishes; 1886: Rise of the Symbolist Movement.

RELATED ARTICLES in *Great Lives from History: The Nineteenth Century, 1801-1900:* Honoré de Balzac; Charles Baudelaire; Claude Bernard; Stephen Crane; Charles Darwin; Gustave Flaubert; Thomas Hardy; Frederic Harrison; Henrik Ibsen; Guy de Maupassant; Stendhal; Hippolyte Taine; Émile Zola.

1865-1868
BASUTO WAR

After founding a kingdom in the Drakensberg Mountains, the Sotho people spent several decades resisting the incursions of their Afrikaner neighbors. When they were on the verge of being conquered, they looked to Great Britain for assistance. The British annexation of Sotho territory protected the Sotho from the Afrikaners and assured their fragile independence amid white expansion.

LOCALE: Lesotho; Orange Free State (now in South Africa)

CATEGORIES: Expansion and land acquisition; wars, uprisings, and civil unrest

KEY FIGURES

Moshoeshoe (c. 1786-1870), founder-king of the Sotho, r. 1820-1870

George Cathcart (1794-1854), governor of the Cape Colony, 1852-1854

Sir George Grey (1812-1898), governor of the Cape Colony, 1854-1861

Sir Philip Wodehouse (1811-1887), governor of the Cape Colony, 1862-1870

Johannes Hendricus Brand (1823-1888), president of the Orange Free State, 1864-1888

Henry Warden (1800-1856), British resident in the Orange River Sovereignty

SUMMARY OF EVENT

The Sotho Kingdom, which formed the basis of modern Lesotho, arose from the chaos of the Zulu expansion of the early nineteenth century. After establishing a secure defensive refuge in the Drakensberg Mountains at Thaba Bosiu, Moshoeshoe led his people to safety and organized a nation-state based on extensive marriage alliances and shrewd diplomacy. However, the arrival of Afrikaner (Boer) voortrekkers in the region between the Orange and Vaal Rivers during the Great Trek presented a new and dangerous challenge to the independence and stability of the Sotho, who were also known as Basotho (Basuto). The situation was made even more complicated with the imposition of the British into the area. For his part, Moshoeshoe endeavored to learn all that he could about the British and the Afrikaners, and invited French missionaries into his kingdom who could serve as intermediaries and advisers for Sotho diplomatic affairs.

The struggle over land between the Sotho and the Afrikaners moved the British to mediate in hopes of settling the dispute. In 1845, the British arranged an agreement among several African chiefs, including Moshoeshoe, that would permit Afrikaner settlers access to some lands while restricting them to others. The British provided supervision of the deal in the person of Major Henry Warden. However, Moshoeshoe could not attempt to control all the chiefs under him without weakening his own authority. Fearing revolt or even disintegration of his state, Moshoeshoe could only enforce the agreement in a limited manner. After further disputes arose, the British again intervened in 1848, when they occupied the Transorangia region and created the Orange River Sovereignty to govern the Afrikaner settlers.

While remaining in the region as the British resident, Warden attempted to fix a boundary between Afrikaner and Sotho territory. The Warden Line, as it was called, heavily favored the Afrikaners in territorial gains, but Moshoeshoe had little choice but to accept the concessions. Despite the separation, continued raiding by both sides forced Warden to act. Siding with the Afrikaners, Warden led an armed force against the Sotho, but was repelled. In 1852, the Cape Colony's governor, George Cathcart, led a new campaign to retaliate for Warden's defeat, but he was also turned back. Moshoeshoe diplomatically claimed he had been defeated and did not press his advantage. Moshoeshoe's tactful diplomacy, along with the increasing costs of maintaining peace in the interior, persuaded the British to withdraw and leave the Afrikaners and Sotho to resolve their differences themselves. The British made this decision official in the Convention of Bloemfontein in 1854.

Freed from British supervision, the Afrikaners expanded into Sotho territory, and both sides raided each other in blatant disregard of the Warden Line. The Afrikaners of the Orange Free State, as their domain was now called, requested British arbitration. This request was granted and in 1858 governor George Grey presided over the Treaty of Aliwal North. Although Moshoeshoe regained some Sotho territory through this treaty, he was well aware of his inability to control the territorial expansion of his people, whose numbers were rapidly increasing. Meanwhile, border disputes continued and the Afrikaners, with their superior firepower, became more difficult to repel. It was becoming obvious to Moshoeshoe, who was now in his seventies and concerned about rivalries among his sons for succession, that the Sotho could not prevail in a defensive war with the Afrikaners.

In 1865, a new war broke out and the Orange Free State, which had grown stronger and much more aggressive under its new president, Johannes Hendricus Brand, ravaged Sotho territory. Using the British humanitarian movement to his advantage, Moshoeshoe portrayed the Sotho as victims of Afrikaner aggression and made it clear that his intentions were only to save his people from Afrikaner tyranny. He petitioned the British to intervene, but they were at first reluctant to reverse the policy already set with the Convention of Bloemfontein. In 1866, Moshoeshoe was forced to sign the Treaty of Thaba Bosiu with the Orange Free State; under its terms, he ceded almost all arable Sotho land to the Orange Free State. Afterward, Afrikaner troops withdrew for a time, but the Sotho returned to their ceded lands, thereby prompting a new conflict. Moshoeshoe and the Sotho remained secure on their natural fortress at Thaba Bosiu, but the Afrikaners further devastated the region.

Moshoeshoe again appealed to the British for aid. He even considered allowing Great Britain's land-hungry Natal Colony to annex his territory to preserve it from Afrikaner occupation. The British government considered this option, as it would require little effort on their part. However, the new Cape governor, Sir Philip Wodehouse, not trusting Natal's ability to administer the annexed territory, feared annexation might result in the breakup of the Sotho Kingdom and create an even more unstable situation. Wodehouse tried to keep British colonists strictly neutral in the Basuto War, but the situation progressed beyond his power to control from afar. Moshoeshoe's desperate pleas for peace and denunciations of Afrikaner hostility began to be heard, though distantly.

In 1868, the British government finally approved the annexation of the Sotho land. However, Wodehouse altered the agreement to have the newly annexed territory administered from London as a protectorate, and not as an addition to the Natal province. Moshoeshoe, who himself only considered annexation to Natal out of desperation, quickly agreed to the conditions. The boundaries of the new protectorate of Basutoland made it cohesive, but it still lost the arable land held prior to 1865. The Second Treaty of Aliwal North sealed the agreement and confirmed British protection of the Sotho. For president Johannes Hendricus Brand and the Orange Free State, who had almost defeated the Sotho, the result sparked outrage. However, Wodehouse's threat to cut off the supply of firearms and ammunition through the Cape Colony persuaded Brand and the Afrikaners to accept the terms, thus ending the Basuto War.

SIGNIFICANCE

Moshoeshoe died two years later, in 1870, but he succeeded where so many other African leaders failed. Despite enormous odds, Moshoeshoe had maintained the independence of his people in the face of Zulu and Afrikaner expansion. The administration of Basutoland was later handed to the Cape Colony in 1871, and the British attempted to impose disarmament on the Sotho, but their resistance in what became known as the Gun War ensured the fragile independence of Basutoland.

Moshoeshoe founded a nation-state and further provided for its protection through skillful, diplomatic maneuvering. He understood the conflicts between the Afrikaners and British, and used that knowledge to formulate a clever plan of playing one off the other. By seeking British protection, Moshoeshoe created the basis for the modern state of Lesotho, which would eventually gain full independence from Britain in 1966. The Basuto War and its antecedents provided an excellent example of African statesmanship and fully demonstrated the effects of white expansion and rivalry on the native peoples of South Africa.

—Branden C. McCullough

FURTHER READING

Eldredge, Elizabeth. *A South African Kingdom: The Pursuit of Security in Nineteenth-Century Lesotho*. Reprint. Cambridge, England: Cambridge University Press, 2002. Discusses the expansion of the Afrikaners and the role of British colonialism from the perspective of the Sotho.

Knight, Ian. *Warrior Chiefs of Southern Africa: Shaka of the Zulu, Moshoeshoe of the Basotho, Mzilikazi of the Matabele, Maquomo of the Xhosa*. Durban, South Africa: Riverside Press, 1994. Compares the various models of leadership among the tribes of Africa, with special focus on Moshoeshoe's guidance and legacy.

MacKinnon, Aran. "Africans, Afrikaners, and the British in the Interior, 1830-1870." In *The Making of South Africa: Culture and Politics*. Upper Saddle River, N.J.: Pearson Prentice Hall, 2004. General work that details the prelude to the Afrikaner-Sotho conflict, the war itself, and its consequences clearly and concisely.

Thompson, Leonard. *Survival in Two Worlds: Moshoeshoe of Lesotho, 1786-1870*. Oxford, England: Clarendon Press, 1975. Classic biography by a distinguished historian of South Africa that provides insights into the difficulties of Moshoeshoe's reign and his agency in the politics of the war.

SEE ALSO: c. 1817-1828: Zulu Expansion; 1835: South Africa's Great Trek Begins; Jan. 22-23, 1879: Battles of Isandlwana and Rorke's Drift; Jan. 22-Aug., 1879: Zulu War; Dec. 16, 1880-Mar. 6, 1881: First Boer War.

RELATED ARTICLES in *Great Lives from History: The Nineteenth Century, 1801-1900:* Sir George Grey; Paul Kruger; Shaka.

March 3, 1865
CONGRESS CREATES THE FREEDMEN'S BUREAU

To assist the adjustment of African American slaves to freedom as the Civil War was coming to a close, the U.S. government established the Freedmen's Bureau but never provided it with the resources it needed to fulfill its mission properly.

ALSO KNOWN AS: U.S. Bureau of Refugees, Freedmen, and Abandoned Lands

LOCALE: Washington, D.C.

CATEGORIES: Civil rights and liberties; organizations and institutions; social issues and reform

KEY FIGURES

Oliver O. Howard (1830-1909), chief commissioner of the Freedmen's Bureau

Andrew Johnson (1808-1875), president of the United States, 1865-1869

Thaddeus Stevens (1792-1868), Pennsylvania congressman

SUMMARY OF EVENT

On March 3, 1865, shortly before the Civil War (1861-1865) ended, the U.S. Congress created the Freedmen's Bureau as a temporary agency within the War Department. Also known as the U.S. Bureau of Refugees, Freedmen, and Abandoned Lands, the new agency was administered by General Oliver O. Howard from 1865 until it was dismantled by Congress in 1872. The primary objective of the bureau was to help newly freed African American slaves to function as free men, women, and children. To achieve its goal, the bureau was expected to assume responsibility for all matters related to the newly freed slaves in the southern states.

The bureau faced enormous challenges because of the broad scope of his mission, its limited resources, political conflicts over Reconstruction policies, and a generally hostile environment. The work of the bureau was performed by General Howard and a network of assistant commissioners in various states, largely in the South. The Freedmen's Bureau attempted to address many of the needs of the newly freed slaves, including labor relations, education, landownership, medical care, food distribution, family reunification, legal protection, and legal services within the African American community.

The Freedmen's Bureau dealt with such labor-related issues as the transporting and relocating of refugees and newly freed persons for employment, contract and wage disputes, and harsh legislation enacted by some states. After the Civil War, many southern states passed laws known as black codes that required freed slaves to have lawful employment or businesses. Otherwise, they would be subject to fines and could be jailed for vagrancy. Sheriffs could hire them out to anyone who would pay their fines. Because of the desperate scarcity of jobs in the postwar South, state laws allowed former slave owners to maintain rigid control over newly freed slaves.

Another type of discriminatory law gave former owners of orphaned African Americans the right to hire them as apprentices instead of placing them with their relatives. This law also resulted in the continuation of virtually free labor for many white southerners. The Freedmen's Bureau has been criticized for the failure of its agents to negotiate labor contracts in the interest of the newly freed. The bureau was frequently accused of protecting the rights of the southern planters instead.

Obtaining education was an important goal for newly freed African Americans. They understood that literacy would enable them to enter into contracts and establish businesses on their own, and would aid them in legal matters. The Freedmen's Bureau provided some support by providing teachers, schools, and books and by coordinating volunteers. The bureau also made a contribution to the founding of black colleges and universities. Southern whites generally opposed educating African Americans because of their fear that education would make former slaves too independent and unwilling to work under the terms established by white employers. Southerners therefore sought to control the educational systems in their states. White planters used various methods to exert

Recently freed slaves in a temporary "freedman's village" in Virginia. (Corbis)

control: frequent changes in administrative personnel, the use of racial stereotypes regarding the intellectual inferiority of African Americans, and educational policy making based on paternalism and self-interest. Consequently, educational opportunities were significantly restricted for black youths.

Eager to acquire property, newly freed slaves demonstrated their desire to own their own land as individuals and formed associations to purchase large tracts of land. Their sense of family and community was the basis for their strong desire to own land. The Freedmen's Bureau was initially authorized to distribute land that had been confiscated from southern plantation owners during the Civil War. Specifically, on the sea islands of South Carolina, the bureau was mandated to lease or sell lands that had been confiscated. This land was to be distributed in parcels of forty acres.

The decision of Congress to authorize the distribution of land was based on a proposal made by Thaddeus Stevens, a Republican congressman from Pennsylvania. However, President Andrew Johnson acceded to pressure from the rebellious planters to return their lands. The plantation owners were pardoned, and their property rights were restored by the president. Consequently, all land that had been distributed to African Americans was returned to its previous owners. The dispossessed black people were then encouraged to sign contracts to work on the land that they had briefly owned. Many refused to comply with this arrangement. Others would not voluntarily leave the property they once owned. Those who refused to vacate were evicted.

A medical department was created within the Freedmen's Bureau to be a temporary service, to ensure that medical services were provided to African Americans until local governments assumed that responsibility. In spite of inadequate resources, the bureau founded forty-five hospitals in fourteen states. Among the common problems of the medical department were inadequately staffed hospitals, medical personnel with little control over health concerns, frequent personnel changes and hospital relocations, and lack of funds to purchase food for patients. Despite these problems, the bureau experienced some success in providing for the medical needs of black people. Although it could not meet the medical needs of many, it rendered medical services to large numbers of former slaves.

The Freedmen's Bureau also attempted to provide for the social welfare of the freed persons. The agency was noted for rationing food to refugees and former slaves; it assisted families in reuniting with members who had been sold or separated in other ways during the era of slavery.

Protecting the civil rights of the former slaves was a major task of the Freedmen's Bureau. Many Republican politicians believed that African Americans should have the same rights as white Americans. However, the black codes of many southern states severely restricted black civil rights. Exacting social and economic control over African Americans, these laws represented a new form of slavery. In cases in which state laws limited African American rights, the bureau attempted to invoke provisions of the 1866 federal Civil Rights Act, which offered African Americans the same legal protections and rights as whites to testify in courts, own property, enforce legal contracts, and sue. However, the bureau found it difficult to enforce the Civil Rights Act and to prosecute state officials who enforced discriminatory laws. A shortage of agents and a reluctance among bureau commissioners to challenge local officials contributed to the agency's limited success.

Finally, the Freedmen's Bureau also established tribunals to address minor legal disputes of African Americans within their own communities. In many instances, freed slaves were able to resolve their own problems. When they could not, they presented their legal concerns to bureau agents.

SIGNIFICANCE

The task assigned to the Freedmen's Bureau was monumental. The responsibilities of the bureau significantly exceeded the resources and authority granted to it by Congress. The bureau's ability to perform its varied tasks also was impeded by personnel shortages. President Johnson's Reconstruction policies represented another major challenge to the bureau, as they were not always supportive of the bureau's mandate and objectives. Myriad problems associated with the bureau meant that the newly freed men, women, and children were not able to receive the goods and services necessary to gain economic independence. Consequently, they developed extensive self-help networks to address their needs.

—*K. Sue Jewell*

FURTHER READING

Bankston, Carl L., III, ed. *African American History*. 3 vols. Pasadena, Calif.: Salem Press, 2005. Encyclopedic reference work on African American history that includes entries on the Freedmen's Bureau, black laws, and many related subjects.

Crouch, Barry A. *The Freedmen's Bureau and Black*

Texans. Austin: University of Texas Press, 1982. Discusses the Reconstruction era and the Freedmen's Bureau in the state of Texas. Explores how bureau agents performed their tasks in a hostile climate characterized by racial injustices and resistance to change.

Foster, Gaines M. "The Limitations of Federal Health Care for Freedmen, 1862-1868." In *The Freedmen's Bureau and Black Freedom*, edited by Donald G. Nieman. New York: Garland, 1994. Detailed discussion of the medical needs of African Americans following emancipation. Explores the various problems that adversely affected the bureau's ability to deliver medical services to African Americans.

Franklin, John Hope, and Alfred A. Moss, Jr. *From Slavery to Freedom: A History of African Americans*. 8th ed. Boston: McGraw-Hill, 2000. Focuses on the history of people of African descent brought to the United States as slaves. Examines the harsh social and economic conditions that have confronted African Americans and the strategies they used to survive in spite of these societal barriers.

Magdol, Edward. *A Right to the Land: Essays on the Freedmen's Community*. Westport, Conn.: Greenwood Press, 1977. Examines the problems confronting African Americans as freed men, women, and children during Reconstruction. Emphasizes the efforts that African Americans pursued to acquire land and their relentless quest for self-determination.

Rasmussen, R. Kent. *Farewell to Jim Crow: The Rise and Fall of Segregation in America*. New York: Facts On File, 1997. Written for young adults, this brief but comprehensive history of segregation in U.S. history examines the successes and failures of the Freedmen's Bureau.

Westwood, Howard C. "Getting Justice for the Freedmen." In *The Freedmen's Bureau and Black Freedom*, edited by Donald G. Nieman. New York: Garland, 1994. Explores how the Freedmen's Bureau's agents addressed the legal concerns of freed persons during the Reconstruction era.

SEE ALSO: Jan. 1, 1857: First African American University Opens; May 20, 1862: Lincoln Signs the Homestead Act; July 2, 1862: Lincoln Signs the Morrill Land Grant Act; Dec. 8, 1863-Apr. 24, 1877: Reconstruction of the South; Nov. 24, 1865: Mississippi Enacts First Post-Civil War Black Code; 1866: Birth of the Ku Klux Klan; Apr. 9, 1866: Civil Rights Act of 1866; May and July, 1866: Memphis and New Orleans Race Riots; July 9, 1868: Fourteenth Amendment Is Ratified; 1890: Mississippi Constitution Disfranchises Black Voters; Sept. 18, 1895: Washington's Atlanta Compromise Speech.

RELATED ARTICLES in *Great Lives from History: The Nineteenth Century, 1801-1900:* Samuel Gridley Howe; Andrew Johnson; Thaddeus Stevens.

April 9 and 14, 1865
SURRENDER AT APPOMATTOX AND ASSASSINATION OF LINCOLN

Five days after the South began capitulating to end the fighting of the Civil War, President Abraham Lincoln was shot by a Confederate sympathizer, leaving his successor to direct the course of postwar Reconstruction in the defeated South.

LOCALE: Appomattox Courthouse, Virginia; Washington, D.C.

CATEGORIES: Terrorism and political assassination; wars, uprisings, and civil unrest

KEY FIGURES

Ulysses S. Grant (1822-1885), chief commander of the victorious Union armies

Robert E. Lee (1807-1870), chief commander of the defeated Confederate armies

Abraham Lincoln (1809-1865), president of the United States, 1861-1865

John Wilkes Booth (1838-1865), professional actor and Southern sympathizer

Andrew Johnson (1808-1875), vice president and successor to Lincoln

William H. Seward (1801-1872), secretary of state

Edwin M. Stanton (1814-1869), secretary of war

SUMMARY OF EVENT

President Abraham Lincoln was the chief architect of the Union victory that ended the long U.S. Civil War. In March, 1864, he called General Ulysses S. Grant to the White House and placed him in overall command of the Union armies. Grant then embarked upon a vigorous campaign aimed at the Confederate capital at Richmond,

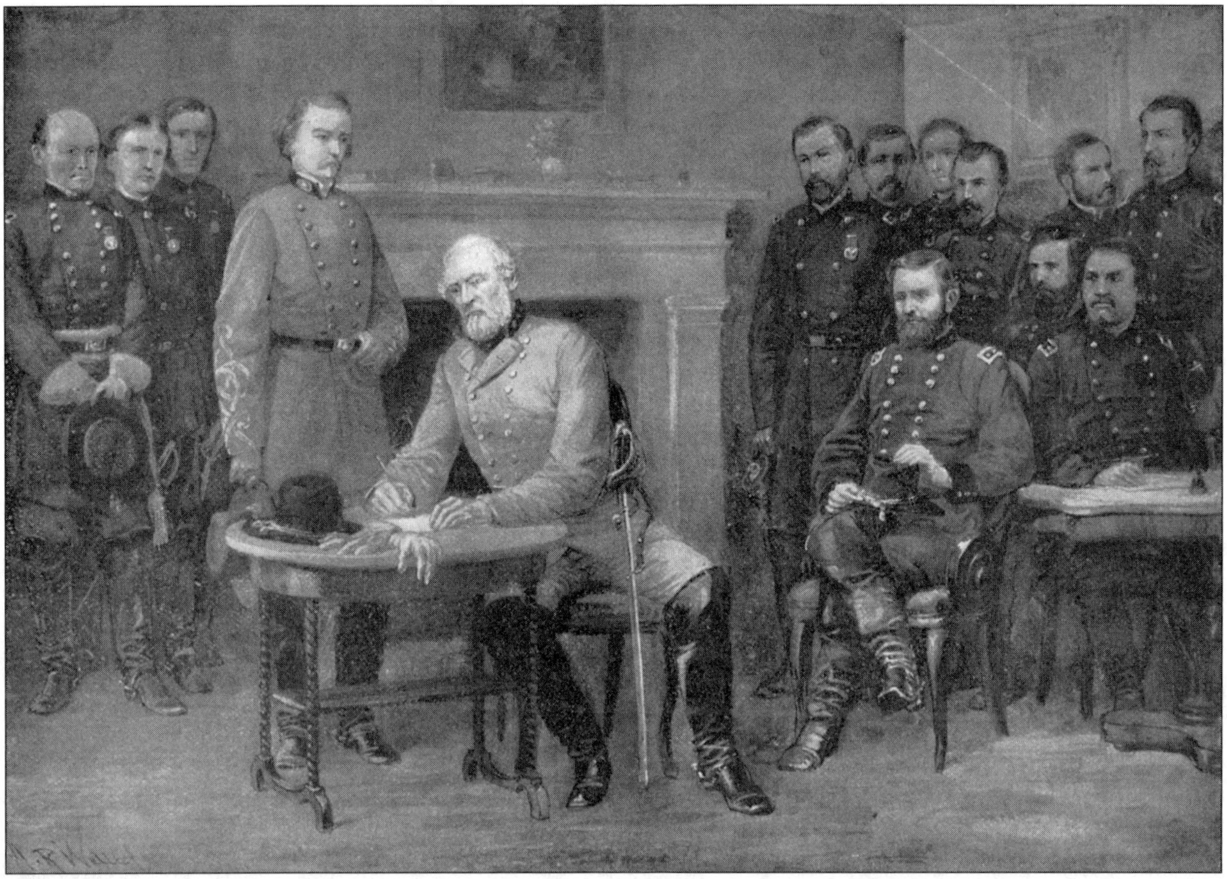

General Robert E. Lee signs the terms of surrender as Union general Ulysses S. Grant (seated at right) looks on. (The Co-Operative Publishing Company)

engaging General Robert E. Lee's Army of Northern Virginia in two important battles west of Fredricksburg, Virginia—Wilderness, May 5-7, and Spotsylvania, May 8-9, 1864. Grant suffered heavy casualties but pushed on to Cold Harbor (June 1-3). There, the Confederates repulsed his attack, which, had it been successful, would have led to the fall of Richmond. Grant then attempted to outflank Lee by crossing the James River and driving toward Petersburg, where he intended to cut vital rail connections. Lee was able to check Grant's advance short of Petersburg, however, and a nine-month stalemate ensued.

Meanwhile, General William T. Sherman had completed his destructive march from Atlanta to the sea at Savannah, Georgia. He then moved northward in a march that was to take him through South Carolina and North Carolina. All signs pointed to a Confederate defeat in 1865: The Union blockade was becoming increasingly effective; Great Britain no longer showed much sympathy for the Confederacy; the economy of the South was breaking down under the impact of the war; and Grant continued to receive troop replacements, whereas Lee's troops were becoming exhausted. A peace conference, which Confederate president Jefferson Davis had suggested, was held on February 3, 1865. Confederate vice president Alexander H. Stephens led the delegation from the South, while Lincoln spoke for the Union. Lincoln insisted upon the disbanding of the Confederate forces, but the Confederacy was not then willing to surrender.

In April, 1865, Grant was able to extend Lee's lines to the breaking point, and Lee was forced to evacuate the Confederate capital of Richmond as well as Petersburg. Lee's escape route lay to the west and south; he hoped to join forces with General Joe Johnston in North Carolina, but Grant's forces blocked his escape. Now convinced of the futility of continuing the war, Lee met Grant at the McLean house in Appomattox Courthouse, where he surrendered on April 9. Following the spirit of President

Lincoln's instructions, Grant agreed to release Lee's officers and men on parole. Lee's troops were allowed to keep their horses, mules, and sidearms and then return home.

In short order, the other scattered Confederate armies followed General Lee's lead and began the ordeal of surrender. The last significant group of men under arms, those under the command of General Joseph Johnston, began surrender negotiations with Sherman on April 17. The war had wrought a death toll far greater than anyone could have imagined four years earlier: 360,000 Union soldiers, 260,000 men from the South, and unknown numbers of civilians. The economic havoc would leave the South devastated for a century.

News of Lee's surrender reached Washington, D.C., on the same day that it took place, and it was received with great rejoicing. Lincoln made several extemporaneous speeches and delivered one prepared address during the course of the next several days in response to the demands of exuberant crowds. It was Lincoln's view that the South should be welcomed back as brothers to enable healing to begin. In this regard, he was strongly opposed by the Radical Republicans within Congress. It was their view that the South had started the war and should be made to pay for it. Whether Lincoln might have curbed their hatred, had he lived, remains an unanswered question for history.

At approximately 8:30 P.M. on April 14, President and Mrs. Lincoln, in company with Clara Harris and Major Henry R. Rathbone, entered Ford's Theater in Washington to see a performance of the play *Our American Cousin*. At about 10:15 P.M., John Wilkes Booth, a twenty-six-year-old actor who sympathized with the South, slipped into the president's box and fired one shot into the back of Lincoln's head. The president was mortally wounded and died the next morning at 7:22 A.M., without ever regaining consciousness. His body was taken back to Springfield, Illinois, on a circuitous seventeen-hundred-mile route that retraced the 1861 journey he made to Washington, D.C., for his first inauguration.

After shooting Lincoln, Booth jumped onto the stage, breaking a small bone in his leg as he landed. From

Contemporary depiction of Abraham Lincoln's assassination. Edwin Booth (right) entered Lincoln's theater box, fired a single bullet into his head, and then jumped down to the stage. (Library of Congress)

the stage he shouted the motto of Virginia, *Sic semper tyrannis* (thus ever to tyrants). In the confusion, he managed to evade capture in Washington, escaping over the bridge into Virginia. There, his broken leg was set by Dr. Samuel Mudd. It remains unclear whether Mudd was aware of the significance of his patient. Booth was eventually trapped in a tobacco shed near Port Royal, Virginia, on April 26. There he died, either by his own hand or from a shot fired by one of the soldiers attempting to arrest him.

The assassination of Lincoln was only one part of a major plot to murder the most important Union officials. Secretary of State William H. Seward and his sons, Frederick and Augustus, suffered knife wounds at the hands of Lewis Paine, a former Confederate soldier and devotee of Booth. George A. Atzerodt, an alcoholic, was assigned by Booth to kill Vice President Andrew Johnson, but he failed to make the attempt. Secretary of War Edwin Stanton took charge of the investigation and ordered the arrest of Paine, Atzerodt, David Herold, Edward Spangler, Samuel Arnold, Michael O'Laughlin, Samuel Mudd, and Mary E. Surratt, the owner of the boardinghouse in which the conspirators met. It is likely that Surratt knew nothing of Booth's plot. However, she and Dr. Mudd were caught up in the passion for revenge that followed Lincoln's murder.

The alleged conspirators were tried before a military commission whose jurisdiction in their cases was questionable. The trial lasted from May 10 to June 30, and all the defendants were found guilty. Atzerodt, Paine, Herold, and Surratt were hanged seven days after the trial ended, while Spangler, Arnold, Mudd, and O'Laughlin were sentenced to life imprisonment. Surratt's execution was almost certainly a miscarriage of justice that could not have been carried out if a few weeks or months had been allowed for passions to cool. By contrast, her son John escaped immediate capture and, when tried in 1867, was released after a jury failed to agree on a verdict.

SIGNIFICANCE

Those sentenced to life imprisonment were pardoned in 1869, with the exception of O'Laughlin, who died of yellow fever at the Dry Tortugas prison off Key West. Dr. Mudd was found guilty as an accessory after the fact, and also sentenced to life imprisonment. However, his heroic actions during the yellow fever epidemic resulted in a commutation of his sentence, and he also was freed in 1869. Mudd's descendants have continued to argue for his innocence. Former president of the Confederacy Jefferson Davis was taken prisoner soon after Lee's surrender. Although he was indicted for treason and imprisoned two years at Fort Monroe, he never came to trial.

The most important, and also the most enigmatic, consequence of Lincoln's assassination was the fact that the task of reconstructing the South after the war was left to his successor, Andrew Johnson. An entirely different kind of politician, Johnson quickly ran afoul of the Radical Republicans in Congress and nearly lost his presidency to impeachment. Meanwhile, Congress took control of Reconstruction and was inclined to punish the South for having caused the Civil War. If Lincoln had lived through his second term in office, Reconstruction would certainly have taken a different course, but it is impossible to know for certain what that course might have been.

—*Mark A. Plummer, updated by Richard Adler*

FURTHER READING

Bishop, Jim. *The Day Lincoln Was Shot*. New York: Harper & Row, 1955. Detailed and fascinating hour-by-hour account of the last day in Lincoln's life.

Bonekemper, Edward H., III. *A Victor, Not a Butcher: Ulysses S. Grant's Overlooked Military Genius*. Washington, D.C.: Regnery Publishing, 2004.

Donald, David Herbert. *Lincoln*. New York: Simon & Schuster, 1995. Highly readable biography that explores Lincoln's political motivations. The author portrays Lincoln as ambitious, often defeated, and tormented by a difficult marriage, yet having a remarkable capacity for growth and the ability to hold the nation together during the Civil War.

Gienapp, William E. *Abraham Lincoln and Civil War America: A Biography*. New York: Oxford University Press, 2002. Most of this biography covers Lincoln's years in the White House, which coincided with the Civil War years. The book describes his handling of the Civil War, depicting him as a shrewd politician and an extraordinary military commander.

McPherson, James M. *Battle Cry of Freedom*. New York: Oxford University Press, 1988. Arguably the finest one-volume account of the Civil War, which it places within the perspective of the mid-nineteenth century United States.

Marvel, William. *Lee's Last Retreat: The Flight to Appomattox*. Chapel Hill: University of North Carolina Press, 2002. Scholarly study of Robert E. Lee's last campaigns and the series of setbacks that led him to surrender to Grant.

Moore, Guy. *The Case of Mrs. Surratt*. Norman: University of Oklahoma Press, 1954. Discusses the role (or lack of it) played by Mrs. Mary Surratt, the innkeeper who was apparently innocently caught up in Lincoln's assassination.

Oates, Stephen B. *With Malice Toward None*. New York: Harper Perennial, 1994. Update of Oates's excellent 1977 biography of Lincoln.

Reck, W. Emerson. *A. Lincoln: His Last Twenty-four Hours*. Columbia: University of South Carolina Press, 1994. Another detailed account of Lincoln's last day.

Simpson, Brooks D. *The Reconstruction Presidents*. Lawrence: University Press of Kansas, 1998. Comparative study of the four U.S. presidents who were involved in Reconstruction policies: Abraham Lincoln, Andrew Johnson, Ulysses S. Grant, and Rutherford B. Hayes. Simpson concludes that Johnson, Lincoln's immediate successor, was an inflexible president, unable to overcome his racism and hatred.

SEE ALSO: Nov. 6, 1860: Lincoln Is Elected U.S. President; Mar. 4, 1861: Lincoln Is Inaugurated President; Apr. 12, 1861-Apr. 9, 1865: U.S. Civil War; July 21, 1861: First Battle of Bull Run; July 1-Nov. 25, 1863: Battles of Gettysburg, Vicksburg, and Chattanooga; Dec. 8, 1863-Apr. 24, 1877: Reconstruction of the South; Nov. 15, 1864-Apr. 18, 1865: Sherman Marches Through Georgia and the Carolinas; June 23, 1865: Watie Is Last Confederate General to Surrender; Feb. 24-May 26, 1868: Impeachment of Andrew Johnson.

RELATED ARTICLES in *Great Lives from History: The Nineteenth Century, 1801-1900:* Edwin Booth; Ulysses S. Grant; Andrew Johnson; Robert E. Lee; Abraham Lincoln; William H. Seward; Edwin M. Stanton.

May 1, 1865-June 20, 1870
PARAGUAYAN WAR

Also known as the War of the Triple Alliance, or López War, South America's bloodiest international conflict succeeded in establishing permanent boundaries for Argentina, Brazil, Paraguay, and Uruguay at the cost of overwhelming casualties among the Paraguayans.

ALSO KNOWN AS: War of the Triple Alliance; López War

LOCALE: Argentina; Brazil; Paraguay; Uruguay

CATEGORIES: Wars, uprisings, and civil unrest; diplomacy and international relations; expansion and land acquisition

KEY FIGURES

Francisco Solano López (1826-1870), dictator of Paraguay

Bartolomé Mitre (1821-1906), president of Argentina

Duque de Caxias (Luís Alves de Lima e Silva; 1803-1880), Brazilian military commander

Pedro II (1825-1891), emperor of Brazil, r. 1840-1889

Venancio Flores (1809-1868), president of Uruguay

Eliza Lynch (1835-1886), Irish mistress of Francisco Solano López

SUMMARY OF EVENT

As early as the sixteenth century, Spain and Portugal had vied over access to the Plata estuary, where the Paraná, Paraguay, and Uruguay Rivers empty into the Atlantic Ocean. This impressive river system provided access to the silver-mining regions of Spanish Peru, as well as to the interior of Portuguese Brazil. When the Spanish and Portuguese colonies achieved independence in the first decades of the nineteenth century, the question of which new nation would control the rivers had to be decided. In 1828, Brazil and Argentina averted war by creating the independent nation of Uruguay in the contested territory. As a result, Argentina would not totally dominate access to the Plata river system.

Meanwhile, the new nation of Paraguay emerged upriver, despite the antagonism of the Argentine dictator Juan Manuel de Rosas. By the end of the 1820's, the old Spanish viceroyalty of La Plata had been replaced by the countries of Argentina, Paraguay, and Uruguay. Independence did not, however, immediately result in stable rule. For decades, Argentina suffered from political conflicts between the region centered around the port of Buenos Aires and the interior provinces. The Brazilian Empire also experienced political turmoil, as several separatist regional rebellions occurred in 1830 and 1850. Contests for power in Uruguay often resulted in interference from the government of Brazil or Argentina. Paraguay, on the other hand, enjoyed stability under two dictators who promoted self-sufficiency for their people.

In the 1850's, the issue of boundaries in the region intensified. Brazilian cattle ranchers who had settled along the border of Uruguay ignored official boundaries and allowed their herds to roam freely. As Brazilians prospered along the Uruguayan border, the Paraguayan dictator became concerned that Brazil would become too involved in the affairs of that nation. Paraguayans had come to believe that the political equilibrium of the region depended on preserving the independence of Uruguay. Otherwise, Paraguay's access to the Paraná and Paraguay Rivers would depend solely on the good will of the Argentines in Buenos Aires.

The years leading up to the war witnessed significant political transitions in Argentina, Brazil, and Paraguay. In 1852, the Argentine dictator was deposed, creating an opportunity for constitutional government. In Brazil, the young emperor Pedro II finally succeeded in taming his internal regional conflicts. Still, the country was divided politically between conservatives and the more reform-oriented Liberal Party. Regional differences in the large empire remained pronounced. The Brazilian economy, built upon the export of coffee, sugar, and cotton, depended on the labor of African slaves. The toughest political question of the era had to do with the fate of the institution of slavery, especially after Abraham Lincoln issued the Emancipation Proclamation in the United States in 1863.

In Paraguay, Francisco Solano López, raised to inherit the presidency, came into his birthright upon the death of his father in 1862. In the 1850's, he had traveled across the Atlantic and witnessed European industrial and military superiority over Russia in the Crimean War. Determined to promote industrialization in Paraguay, he recruited European engineers and technicians to build an iron foundry and a railroad in his country. While in Paris, he met Eliza Lynch, a young Irishwoman, who became his mistress and returned with him to Paraguay. Although they never married, she bore him five children. Presiding over the social scene in Paraguay's capital city, Asunción, Lynch brought a new level of European sophistication to a nation whose inhabitants were primarily Guarani Indians.

In late 1864, Brazilian troops marched into Uruguay to support the presidential bid of Venancio Flores, who favored the interests of southern Brazilian ranchers. In protest, Francisco Solano López, now dictator of Paraguay, seized a Brazilian steamer carrying the president of the province of Mato Grosso to his new post. He commandeered the vessel and all that was on it. Shortly thereafter Paraguayan troops crossed into Mato Grosso. Realizing that a military campaign in this remote region of Brazil would not alter the situation in Uruguay, López requested permission from Argentina's president Bartolomé Mitre to send troops through the Argentine province of Corrientes on their way to guarantee the independence of Uruguay. Upon Mitre's refusal, Paraguay declared war on Argentina and sent in troops that occupied the town of Corrientes. On May 1, 1865, Argentina and Uruguay joined Brazil in the Triple Alliance to fight López.

Young men in Brazil rallied to the cause, joining the army as "Volunteers of the Fatherland." Paraguay, nonetheless, commanded the largest number of troops, and these soldiers fought tenaciously in what they viewed as a struggle to preserve national autonomy. Brazil and Argentina, however, were far larger countries and could endure more readily a protracted struggle.

For five years, armies of the Triple Alliance attempted to capture López. The climate and terrain in Paraguay were unforgiving. Many soldiers died of disease in the first few months of the war. As the number of casualties rose, enthusiasm for the war waned. Internal conflict in Argentina, exacerbated by the war, meant the Argentines could not spare many soldiers for the Paraguayan campaign. Brazilians, too, began to resist joining the army. To raise troops, Pedro agreed to enlist slaves who would be freed once the war ended. Although some Brazilians were concerned about relying on enslaved soldiers, army officers in their command praised their discipline and commitment to the cause of Brazil. Once they returned from the front, these military commanders became strong supporters of freeing all Brazilian slaves.

Brazilians lamented the fact that they were so woefully unprepared for war. A conflict they had believed would be over in months stretched into years. The number of casualties was staggering. Only in 1868 did the forces of the Triple Alliance take Asunción; even then, the war did not end, as López fled with his closest advisers and established a new capital. The duque de Caxias, the commander of Brazil's forces, retired in 1868, exhausted by the prolonged war. He returned to Rio de Janeiro quietly; there was no hero's welcome for the man who, for thirty years, had fought to preserve the integrity of the empire.

The emperor's son-in-law next took command of the Brazilian army. For more than a year, they chased López as he moved his forces deeper into the hinterland. By the time López was captured in 1870, his army consisted primarily of teenage boys. Although all sides suffered high casualties in the war, Paraguay was devastated by its defeat. Nonetheless, fears that Paraguayan territory would be divided between Argentina and Brazil were not realized. Paraguay lost some land to those two nations, but it preserved its independence. The war did, however, define national boundaries in the region. It also settled definitively the question of access to the Paraná, Paraguay, and Uruguay Rivers.

SIGNIFICANCE

The Paraguayan War, or the War of the Triple Alliance, had the greatest impact on the two countries that contributed the most troops to the cause: Paraguay and Brazil. The male population of Paraguay was devastated. The entire population declined by approximately 20 percent over the course of the war, but the number of men who died was far greater than that of women. Possibly as many as 70 percent of Paraguay's men perished between 1865 and 1870. It would not be easy to return that nation to normalcy. In fact, the political instability generated by the war shattered the fifty years of prosperity that Paraguay had enjoyed immediately after independence.

In Brazil, the end of the war ushered in a series of reforms. In 1871, the Brazilian parliament passed a law freeing all children born to slave women; complete abolition of slavery followed in 1888. During the war, the need for a more professional army had become abundantly clear. In the 1870's and 1880's, efforts to modernize recruitment and training of soldiers led to the creation of a much more efficient fighting force. From this newly professionalized group support for republican government grew, and in 1889 the Brazilian emperor was deposed by an army coup d'etat.

—*Joan E. Meznar*

FURTHER READING

Barman, Roderick J. *Citizen Emperor: Pedro II and the Making of Brazil, 1825-1891*. Stanford, Calif.: Stanford University Press, 1999. Includes an excellent chapter on the conduct of the Paraguayan War from the perspective of Brazilian politics.

Graham, Richard, ed. *A Century of Brazilian History Since 1865: Issues and Problems*. New York: Alfred A. Knopf, 1969. Includes three selections on the war, one each from the Brazilian, Paraguayan, and Argentine perspectives.

Kraay, Hendrick, and Thomas L. Whigham, eds. *I Die With My Country: Perspectives on the Paraguayan War, 1864-1870*. Lincoln: University of Nebraska Press, 2004. A carefully chosen collection of ten essays written by North American and South American scholars that portray the complexities of the war.

Leuchars, Chris. *To the Bitter End: Paraguay and the War of the Triple Alliance*. Westport, Conn.: Greenwood Press, 2002. A detailed, engagingly written account of the military campaigns of the Paraguayan War.

Whigham, Thomas L. *The Paraguayan War: Causes and Early Conduct*. Lincoln: University of Nebraska Press, 2002. The first of a proposed multivolume study; provides a comprehensive account of the background to the war, as well as the first years of conflict. Meticulously researched in all four of the countries involved.

SEE ALSO: Mar., 1813-Dec. 9, 1824: Bolívar's Military Campaigns; Jan. 18, 1817-July 28, 1821: San Martín's Military Campaigns; Sept. 7, 1822: Brazil Becomes Independent; Jan., 1833: Great Britain Occupies the Falkland Islands; Oct. 4, 1853-Mar. 30, 1856: Crimean War; Apr. 5, 1879-Oct. 20, 1883: War of the Pacific.

RELATED ARTICLES in *Great Lives from History: The Nineteenth Century, 1801-1900:* Abraham Lincoln; Pedro II.

June 23, 1865
WATIE IS LAST CONFEDERATE GENERAL TO SURRENDER

Among the thousands of Native Americans who fought in the Civil War, the Cherokee leader Stand Watie stood out—both as the only Native American to achieve the rank of brigadier and as the last Confederate general to surrender his forces after the war was declared over.

LOCALE: Indian Territory; southwestern Missouri; western Arkansas
CATEGORY: Wars, uprisings, and civil unrest

KEY FIGURES

Stand Watie (1806-1871), Cherokee leader who became a Confederate brigadier general
John Drew (1796-1865), Cherokee who commanded a regiment of full-blooded Cherokees
Jefferson Davis (1808-1889), president of the Confederate States of America
Ben McCulloch (1811-1862), Confederate Indian Territory commander
Albert Pike (1809-1891), Confederate commander in the Department of Indian Territory
John Ross (1790-1866), principal chief of the Cherokee Nation

SUMMARY OF EVENT

After the outbreak of the Civil War in April, 1861, both the Union and the Confederate governments looked toward Indian Territory for support from Native Americans. Most of the Indians in the territory were members of the so-called Five Civilized Tribes—Cherokee, Chickasaw, Choctaw, Creek, and Seminole. Many of them had connections with the federal government through various agencies, but many also had southern roots in the Carolinas, Alabama, Kentucky, Georgia, and Tennessee. Hence, their loyalties in the Civil War were divided.

In March, 1861, the new Confederate president, Jefferson Davis, commissioned Albert Pike to visit Indian Territory to seek treaties with the Five Civilized Tribes. Davis hoped that a strong Confederate force in Indian Territory would prevent Union sympathizers in Kansas from raiding Texas. Pike's visit with all the tribes in Indian Territory was largely successful. Shortly afterward, Confederate general Ben McCulloch raised two regiments from among the Indians. One was led by Colonel John Drew, a full-blooded Cherokee, and the other was commanded by Colonel Stand Watie, who was three-quarters Cherokee.

Drew and Watie were bitter enemies, and through much of the war, Confederate commanders on the western front had to keep their two Cherokee regiments separated as much as possible. Watie had been born in Georgia and was one of the signers of the New Echota Treaty (1835), by which the Cherokees sold their lands in Georgia to the U.S. government. He was also a prosperous Cherokee landowner and businessman, a brilliant warrior, and a member of an opposition faction within the Cherokee tribe. His signature on the new Echota Treaty put him at odds with the more dominant faction of the Cherokee Nation, led by John Ross.

Watie proved to be a great military leader, and even in the face of extreme hardships, especially during the winter months, he kept his regiment together and participated in numerous battles. He would eventually become the last major Confederate commander to surrender at the conclusion of the war.

Although the treaties that the Indians signed with the Confederacy promised that Indian regiments would not be required to fight outside Indian Territory, Watie's

Confederate general Stand Watie. (Library of Congress)

troops also were called to duty in Missouri and Arkansas. Over a four-year span, the old Cherokee warrior and his forces fought at Wilson's Creek, Newtonia, Bird Creek, Pea Ridge, Spavinaw, Fort Wayne, Fort Gibson, Honey Springs, Webber's Falls, Poison Spring, Massard Prairie, and Cabin Creek. Watie's abilities on the battlefield were widely recognized and greatly heralded by both his contemporaries and historians. His greatest skills were gaining and keeping the confidence of his troops and his wily guerrilla tactics. His regiment also fought the Second Battle at Newtonia in Southwest Missouri in 1864 without him.

The first Newtonia battle, fought in 1862, is of major historic significance, because it was the only Civil War battle in which American Indians fought on both sides. In most battles, Watie's Cherokees fought admirably. In a losing cause at the Battle of Pea Ridge in Arkansas, however, they and Drew's troops were accused of bad conduct because they were too easily routed and because they allegedly scalped some of the Union casualties. This act, when reported to the upper command of the Confederate army, created a great embarrassment among officers, most of whom had been trained at such prestigious military academies as West Point, where cadets were taught to be gentlemen as well as warriors. The loss at Pea Ridge was made even greater by the death of General McCulloch, who had organized and fought with the Cherokees from the beginning.

Despite the overwhelming support that Indians initially gave to the Confederacy in 1861, after the tide of war turned in favor of the Union, and the Confederacy could no long supply its forces on the frontier, disenchantment took hold of the leaders of the various tribes. In February, 1863, the Cherokee Council met on Cowskin Prairie in Indian Territory and voted to end its alliance with the Confederacy. However, Watie refused to accept the vote and vowed to continue his fight. This created an even deeper split within the Cherokee Nation.

Watie's forces and Cherokee civilians with attachments in the South remained loyal to Watie and even established a government that they claimed was the legitimate government of the Cherokee Nation. These Southern sympathizers elected Watie as the principal chief. The Cherokees who were now aligned with Union forces recognized John Ross as their chief, although he left Indian Territory and returned to his wife's family in Pennsylvania. At the time of this deepening split, about ten thousand Cherokees had Union sympathies, and about seven thousand supported the Confederacy. This Cherokee split actually created a civil war within a civil war.

On May 10, 1864, Watie was promoted to the rank of brigadier general. He was the only American Indian who attained that rank in the Civil War. During the remaining months of the conflict, Watie fought without reservations for the Confederacy. One of his most spectacular successes was the sinking of the steam-driven ferry *J. R. Williams* on the Arkansas River at Pleasant Bluff and making off with food and clothing for his Cherokee and Creek troopers, while breaking a major supply route for Union forces at Fort Gibson. Successful raids on Union supplies kept Watie's forces busy, well supplied, and inspired to stay in the fight. As the military situation for the Confederacy grew worse, Watie called all the Cherokee units to his camp on June 24, 1864. At that meeting, the Cherokee troops resolved unanimously to reenlist for the duration of the war, regardless of how long it lasted.

During the following September, Watie masterminded a plan to attack and steal a Union supply-wagon train worth one million dollars. This battle was fought at Cabin Creek in Indian Territory and is said to have been Watie's greatest success. His brilliance and bravery were not enough, however, as the Confederacy continued to lose battle after battle. On April 9, 1865, General Robert E. Lee surrendered for the Confederacy at Appomattox Courthouse in Virginia. General Watie fought on, hoping to win the battle for the West, but it was not to be. On June 23, 1865, he surrendered at Doakesville in Indian Territory. He was the last Confederate general to lay down his sword.

Significance

The contribution made by American Indians in the Civil War was enormous. Of the estimated 3,500 who fought for the Union, 1,018, or more than 28 percent, died while in service to their country. Census figures in the Cherokee Nation showed a population of 21,000 in 1860. By 1867, that number had dropped to 13,566. Approximately one-third of the nation had been lost, either in battle or to hunger and exposure, which were suffered by soldiers and civilians alike. After the war, Stand Watie became more involved in the political activities of the Cherokee Nation and in resettling his people in the aftermath of the conflict. On September 7, 1871, the great general became ill and was taken to his old home at Honey Creek, where he died on September 9.

—*Kay Hively*

Further Reading

Cunningham, Frank. *General Stand Watie's Confederate Indians*. 1959. Norman: University of Oklahoma

Press, 1998. A full account of Stand Watie's efforts during the Civil War and his political life within the Cherokee Nation that includes many photographs of that era.

Dale, Edward Everett, and Morris L. Wardell. *History of Oklahoma*. New York: Prentice-Hall, 1948. Contains a thorough chapter on the Civil War in Oklahoma by two Oklahoma historians.

Gaines, W. Craig. *The Confederate Cherokees: John Drew's Regiment of Mounted Rifles*. Baton Rouge: Louisiana State University Press, 1989. Concentrates on Colonel John Drew's regiment and contrasts it with Stand Watie's more successful regiment.

Josephy, Alvin M., Jr. *Civil War in the American West*. New York: Alfred A. Knopf, 1991. Study of the Civil War battles that were fought west of the Mississippi River by an expert in Native American history.

McLoughlin, William G. *After the Trail of Tears: The Cherokees' Struggle for Sovereignty, 1839-1880*. Chapel Hill: University of North Carolina Press, 1993. Examines the social, cultural, and political history of the Cherokee Nation in the forty years after the tribe was forced to resettle in Oklahoma. Describes Ross's leadership during this period.

Woodworth, S. E. *Jefferson Davis and His Generals: The Failure of Confederate Command in the West*. Lawrence: University Press of Kansas, 1990. Discusses Jefferson's top military men and their leadership on the western front during the Civil War.

SEE ALSO: 1830-1842: Trail of Tears; Feb. 6, 1861-Sept. 4, 1886: Apache Wars; Feb. 8, 1861: Establishment of the Confederate States of America; Apr. 12, 1861-Apr. 9, 1865: U.S. Civil War; Aug. 17, 1862-Dec. 28, 1863: Great Sioux War; Aug., 1863-Sept., 1866: Long Walk of the Navajos; Nov. 15, 1864-Apr. 18, 1865: Sherman Marches Through Georgia and the Carolinas; Nov. 29, 1864: Sand Creek Massacre; Apr. 9 and 14, 1865: Surrender at Appomattox and Assassination of Lincoln.

RELATED ARTICLES in *Great Lives from History: The Nineteenth Century, 1801-1900:* Jefferson Davis; John Ross.

July, 1865
BOOTH ESTABLISHES THE SALVATION ARMY

Evangelists William and Catherine Booth, who were part of a revivalist crusade at the Whitechapel Mission in London's East End, founded the evangelical Salvation Army to work for social reform and charity. The group's distinctive methods and uniforms, and its publicity, aroused considerable opposition from some corners and praise from others.

ALSO KNOWN AS: Christian Revival Association; Christian Mission
LOCALE: East End, London, England
CATEGORIES: Organizations and institutions; religion and theology; social issues and reform; women's issues

KEY FIGURES

William Booth (1829-1912), preacher, revivalist, social reformer, and cofounder of the Salvation Army
Catherine Mumford Booth (1829-1890), preacher, revivalist, social reformer, and cofounder of the Salvation Army
William Bramwell Booth (1856-1929), eldest child of the Booths who succeeded his father as general

SUMMARY OF EVENT

The future cofounder of the Salvation Army, William Booth, experienced a religious conversion at the age of fifteen in 1844 and became a Methodist preacher and street evangelist in London and other cities. He was licensed as a preacher in the Methodist New Connexion, functioning as a traveling evangelist, until he resigned from that organization in 1861 because of disagreement about evangelistic approaches. Cofounder Catherine Mumford Booth was from a Methodist background and, as a child, read the entire Bible several times; later she became involved in the temperance movement.

Booth and Mumford first met in 1852 and married in 1855, forming an extraordinary partnership as preachers, evangelists, and social reformers. The Booths were greatly influenced by American revivalists Charles Grandison Finney, James Caughey, and Phoebe Palmer, who had conducted successful evangelistic tours of the British Isles in the 1850's and 1860's, which featured a nondenominational approach based on advanced publicity and an emotional appeal to be converted. Booth had little theological training and adopted the "holiness" emphasis of Finney and Palmer, which called for "entire sanctification" after one's initial conversion. Mumford held advanced views about the role of women preachers; she overcame Booth's opposition and began preaching on her own in 1860 after defending Palmer's right to preach and evangelize. In many ways Mumford was a more effective preacher than her husband.

From 1861 to 1865, the Booths were traveling evangelists with four children, an uncertain income, an uncertain future, and uncertain of "God's call." During this period they developed some tactics that later became staples for the Salvation Army. By 1863 they had begun using converts to help evangelize. In February, 1865, Mumford accepted an invitation for speaking engagements in London, a move that would bring the Booths closer to Catherine's mother, who would be able to help care for the children. In July, William accepted an invitation from a group of men who published a magazine called *Revival* to begin preaching in the East End of London, an area notorious for its squalor and poverty. Out of his six-week speaking engagement he developed the Whitechapel Mission, which changed names several times before it decided on Salvation Army in 1878. Thus began Booth's permanent focus on evangelism and later social reform centered in London.

Booth's mission from 1865 to 1879 can be divided into three phases: 1865-1866, when Booth operated under London groups; 1867-1870, when Booth created a committee to help with financial matters; and 1870-1879, when Booth developed more structure as the army's general superintendent and membership increased and stabilized. By 1868 the organization had its own magazine, *East London Evangelist*, which was renamed the *Christian Mission* in 1870, and between seven thousand and fourteen thousand people attended services at the mission's main location and other sites in London. In 1869, Booth purchased the mission's soup kitchen and set up the Food for Millions shops, which served inexpensive soup and other meals.

William Booth around 1907. (Library of Congress)

Much of the Booths' success has been attributed to adapting to the structure of the working-class neighborhoods, street preaching, open-air meetings and meetings in music halls, door-to-door visitation, tract distribution, and using religious words set to the music of popular tunes. The Booths also employed many women. Furthermore, the Salvation Army was shunned by traditional denominations, which tended to frown on their work with the extremely poor. The Church of England was especially harsh in its criticism because it believed the Salvation Army was sending a simplistic message and because the Booths did not encourage converts to join denominational churches.

A major turning point came in 1878, when the organization adopted the Salvation Army as its name. Booth chose the name because he believed the organization was fighting a "war." Booth was selected general superintendent and had the power to appoint his successor, spend organizational funds, and publish an annual financial statement. Within the first year, Booth had an eleven-point doctrinal statement in place, which all Salvation Army workers had to sign. Workers had to agree to a literal understanding of the Bible and believe a number of points: the trinity and the humanity and divinity of Jesus Christ, the fall of Adam and Eve, Jesus' atonement for the entire world, salvation through repentance and regeneration, justification by faith, complete sanctification, personal and general resurrection, and heaven and hell. Theologically, these points did not differ much from American and English revivalists.

The Salvation Army published a new magazine, *The War Cry*, and developed its Hallelujah Band, ranks, and the distinctive uniforms. In 1880, it began to branch out, expanding from London to other English cities, continental Europe, the United States, Australia, and India, becoming a global organization with more than nine thousand corps members and almost sixteen thousand of-

"DARKEST ENGLAND"

William Booth published In Darkest England *shortly after the explorer Henry Morton Stanley published* In Darkest Africa *in 1890. Booth opens his own book with a long discussion of Africa's "darkness" and then compares England to Africa.*

. . . while brooding over the awful presentation of life as it exists in the vast African forest, it seemed to me only too vivid a picture of many parts of our own land. As there is a darkest Africa is there not also a darkest England? Civilisation, which can breed its own barbarians, does it not also breed its own pygmies? May we not find a parallel at our own doors, and discover within a stone's throw of our cathedrals and palaces similar horrors to those which Stanley has found existing in the great Equatorial forest?

The more the mind dwells upon the subject, the closer the analogy appears. The ivory raiders who brutally traffic in the unfortunate denizens of the forest glades, what are they but the publicans who flourish on the weakness of our poor? The two tribes of savages the human baboon and the handsome dwarf, who will not speak lest it impede him in his task, may be accepted as the two varieties who are continually present with us—the vicious, lazy lout, and the toiling slave. They, too, have lost all faith of life being other than it is and has been. As in Africa, it is all trees, trees, trees with no other world conceivable; so is it here—it is all vice and poverty and crime. To many the world is all slum, with the Workhouse as an intermediate purgatory before the grave. And just as Mr. Stanley's Zanzibaris lost faith, and could only be induced to plod on in brooding sullenness of dull despair, so the most of our social reformers, no matter how cheerily they may have started off, with forty pioneers swinging blithely their axes as they force their way in to the wood, soon become depressed and despairing. Who can battle against the ten thousand million trees? Who can hope to make headway against the innumerable adverse conditions which doom the dweller in Darkest England to eternal and immutable misery? . . .

An analogy is as good as a suggestion; it becomes wearisome when it is pressed too far. But before leaving it, think for a moment how close the parallel is, and how strange it is that so much interest should be excited by a narrative of human squalor and human heroism in a distant continent, while greater squalor and heroism not less magnificent may be observed at our very doors. . . .

Source: William Booth, *In Darkest England* (Chicago: C. H. Sergel, 1890), part 1, chapter 1.

ficers worldwide at the time of Booth's death.

All eight of the Booths' children were involved in the Salvation Army and all except a mentally challenged daughter held leadership positions. During the 1880's many army workers were harassed by the so-called Skeleton Army of local toughs, a group opposed to the Salvation Army's position against alcohol consumption and hired by owners of liquor shops and public houses. Also, Salvation Army workers suffered arrest at the hands of local authorities for violations of ordinances against public parades. Important milestones in the Salvation Army's social welfare programs include working to rehabilitate prostitutes (1881), working with drunks and criminals (1883), and campaigning against teenage prostitution (1885). The army appealed to the English government for funds for its activities in 1889.

Mumford died of cancer in October, 1890. Her influence on her husband and the Salvation Army was significant, especially in the area of equality for women. Shortly after Mumford's death, Booth published *In Darkest England and the Way Out* (1890), his call for major social reform. Influenced by previous studies of poverty in England and written with the help of other members of the Salvation Army and a crusading journalist, the book proposed an ambitious plan to end unemployment in England by transferring the unemployed to the country and teaching them to farm. Also, the plan was to settle some workers in England's colonies.

In a section on "city colonies," the book set out an ambitious social welfare assistance plan of homeless shelters, day-care centers, and missing persons bureaus. Booth also campaigned against the dangers of the matchmaking industry, which caused workers using yellow phosphorus to suffer from phossy jaw. In 1891 the Salvation Army opened its own matchmaking facility, using red phosphorus, which does not cause the disease; its workers were paid twice as much as the largest matchmaker in London.

In his later years, Booth traveled extensively in England and abroad and garnered many honors. Upon his death in 1912, he was succeeded by his oldest child, William Bramwell Booth, who served as general superintendent until 1929.

SIGNIFICANCE

Modern scholarship has questioned whether or not the Salvation Army was successful in its goal of reaching the residents of urban slums (or "heathens," as William Booth referred to them) with the Christian message.

Scholars have reached different conclusions on this point, but they have acknowledged the army's prominent role in social reform and women's empowerment.

The Salvation Army survived defections from some of Booth's children in 1896 and 1902, but despite internal squabbles within the Booth family, the Salvation Army became a well-known worldwide organization in the twentieth century. In fact, a poll conducted in 2005 placed it within the top ten "enduring institutions." The red donations kettle, a familiar sight to many American Christmas shoppers, was introduced in San Francisco during the early 1890's as part of an effort to collect funds for Christmas dinners for the poor; a century later the Salvation Army was the top fundraising charitable organization in the United States. According to Salvation Army statistics for 2002, it serves in 109 countries and uses 175 languages in the course of its work. In the wake of the deadly Asian tsunami of December 26, 2004, the Salvation Army was one of the charities at the forefront of relief efforts. The recipients of its charitable efforts would regard it as a success.

—*Mark C. Herman*

FURTHER READING

Christian History 9, issue 26, no. 2 (1990). The entire issue is devoted to articles on the Booths and the Salvation Army. Readable and geared toward the general reader.

Hattersley, Roy. *Blood and Fire: William and Catherine Booth and Their Salvation Army*. New York: Doubleday, 2000. A dual biography that emphasizes Catherine Booth's contributions to the formation and work of the Salvation Army.

Murdoch, Norman. *Origins of the Salvation Army*. Knoxville: University of Tennessee Press, 1994. A scholarly treatment that is especially strong on how American revivalists influenced the Booths.

Walker, Pamela J. *Pulling the Devil's Kingdom Down: The Salvation Army in Victorian Britain*. Berkeley: University of California Press, 2001. An analytical work with a strong emphasis on women's roles in the establishment and work of the Salvation Army.

Winston, Diane. *Red-Hot and Righteous: The Urban Religion of the Salvation Army*. Cambridge, Mass.: Harvard University Press, 1999. Although focusing on the Salvation Army in America, this work discusses the English background and presents the transatlantic context of the organization.

SEE ALSO: 1820's-1850's: Social Reform Movement; May 12, 1857: New York Infirmary for Indigent Women and Children Opens; 1864: Hill Launches Housing Reform in London; 1870-1871: Watch Tower Bible and Tract Society Is Founded; Sept. 18, 1889: Addams Opens Chicago's Hull-House.

RELATED ARTICLES in *Great Lives from History: The Nineteenth Century, 1801-1900:* Annie Besant; William Booth; Sir Thomas Fowell Buxton; Dorothea Dix; Dame Millicent Garrett Fawcett; Elizabeth Fry; Octavia Hill; Florence Nightingale; Henry Morton Stanley.

September 26, 1865
VASSAR COLLEGE OPENS

Vassar was not the first college for women in the United States, but when it opened, it was the first to offer a full liberal arts curriculum comparable to that of a good men's college.

LOCALE: Poughkeepsie, New York
CATEGORIES: Education; women's issues; organizations and institutions

KEY FIGURES

Milo Parker Jewett (1808-1882), first president of Vassar
John Howard Raymond (1814-1878), second president of Vassar
Matthew Vassar (1792-1868), brewer who founded the college
Maria Mitchell (1818-1889), famous astronomer who was the college's first woman professor

SUMMARY OF EVENT

When Vassar College opened its doors to students on September 26, 1865, a new era began in the higher education of women in the United States. Although many schools for women existed in 1865, and some called themselves colleges, none offered a full college course. Indeed, few women's schools offered more than high school educations, and the best existing institution,

Mount Holyoke Female Seminary, was then approximately equivalent to a modern junior college. Oberlin College, Antioch College, and some western state universities permitted women to take courses, but few women succeeded in meeting the requirements of a bachelor of arts degree. Vassar was unique in offering women an education as rigorous and complete as that offered in the best men's colleges. Its success set a new standard for women's education that other institutions would endeavor to match.

Self-made, self-educated, and proud of what he had achieved without formal education, Matthew Vassar was an unlikely person to found any kind of educational institution. Born in England, he had come to the United States in 1796 with his parents as a four-year-old child. His parents settled in Poughkeepsie, New York, where they operated a brewery. In 1811, Vassar opened his own brewery, and his thrift and shrewd investments soon multiplied his wealth. He married in 1813 but never had children. During a trip to Europe in 1845, he was impressed by Thomas Guy's Hospital in London, with its handsome building and monumental statue of the founder. He decided to leave money in his will to build a similar institution in Poughkeepsie.

Vassar showed no interest in higher education for women until after he discussed his hospital plans with Milo Parker Jewett, a Baptist minister who, in 1855, took over a school for girls in a building owned by Vassar. Jewett convinced Vassar that to build and endow "a college for young women which shall be to them what Yale and Harvard are to young men" would create a unique institution that would be a much more memorable monument to his name than any hospital. After some hesitation, Vassar decided to begin the college during his lifetime. In January, 1861, the New York State Legislature passed a charter creating the college, and when the board of trustees met for the first time the following month, Vassar gave them $408,000 to start building. The donation represented half of his estate, and the rest was to follow later. Jewett became the first president of the college, but a falling-out with Vassar led to his resignation in 1864.

During the four years that the campus was under construction, Vassar publicized his new institution widely; *Godey's Lady's Book* and *Harper's Weekly* spread the news across the nation. By September, 1865, the great Main Building—modeled after the Tuileries Palace, which Vassar had admired during his tour of France—was ready. Designed to house the entire college, the building contained apartments for president and faculty, rooms for students, classrooms, offices, a library, a large dining room, and an impressive chapel.

John Howard Raymond, who succeeded Jewett as president, organized a curriculum fully as rigorous as that of any existing college. When Vassar opened, 353 students between fifteen and twenty-four years of age arrived, but fewer than half were ready to undertake college-level work. Raymond had to establish a preparatory department to bring most of them up to grade. Not until 1886 would improvements in U.S. secondary education for women permit Vassar to eliminate its preparatory department.

Matthew Vassar had hoped to hire women as faculty, but except for Maria Mitchell, who was already world famous as an astronomer whose discovery of a comet had garnered her a gold medal from the king of Denmark, all the professors were men. Women filled the lower teaching ranks. To entice Mitchell to the college, Vassar built an observatory for her on the college grounds, where she chose to live with her father.

Vassar's publicity attracted the attention of critics as well as students. Opponents argued that women were mentally inferior to men and unable to meet male intellectual standards, that they would not be able to stand the physical strain of higher education and would develop

Maria Mitchell. (Library of Congress)

brain fever; and that should they manage to survive college, their children would be sickly, if they were able to have children at all. Vassar set out to deflect and disprove all criticism. To protect the health of students, courses in hygiene and physiology were required in the freshman year. A gymnasium with room for a riding school was one of the three original buildings, wide corridors provided room for exercise in winter, and three miles of walkways and riding paths could be used in better weather. To protect the morals of the students, Vassar required them to live under the direct supervision of resident teachers and follow rigid daily schedules. As alumnae began to succeed in various professions, the college trumpeted their achievements as proof of the ability of women to profit from a rigorous liberal arts education.

Other women's colleges followed Vassar's lead. When Wellesley opened in 1875, only thirty of its first 314 students were at college level, and the school opened a large preparatory program. Smith College, which opened during the same year, refused to start a preparatory department and attracted only fourteen students. By 1885, when Bryn Mawr opened, preparatory departments were no longer necessary, and Bryn Mawr was able to offer graduate degree programs from the start. Mount Holyoke Female Seminary added a college-level program and, in 1893, changed its name to Mount Holyoke College. State universities also responded to Vassar. The University of Wisconsin, which had shunted women into a separate college with more limited and more elementary courses than those available to men, abolished the separate college in 1871.

By the 1890's, the so-called Seven Sister women's colleges—Vassar, Wellesley, Smith, Mount Holyoke, Bryn Mawr, Radcliffe, and Barnard—were solidly established and able to hire better-educated and more distinguished faculty, many of them women. Gifts from wealthy donors paid for elaborate buildings. Financial aid for students, however, was limited, and students tended to come from upper-middle-class homes with parents who were professionals or businesspersons. The students came with the full support of their parents and often cited encouragement from fathers as the decisive factor in their decision to go to college.

Separatism, with women in control of all extracurricular life, fostered the development of a women's culture on campus and encouraged a belief in the special mission of educated women. In contrast to coeducational institutions, at which men dominated extracurricular activities, students at women's colleges controlled all student life, organizing meetings, politicking among classmates, and handling budgets. Students were prepared to fill leadership roles in national social and political reform movements. Graduates also contributed through volunteer work to school boards and other local institutions. Many graduates became teachers and school administrators; less frequently, they went into medicine, law, or business.

SIGNIFICANCE

By the 1920's, as the nation became more affluent, female student populations changed, showing less interest in reform or preparation for a profession than in enjoying the college experience. Coming from more socially elite and wealthier homes, many of these women had less interest in their studies and little reason to prepare to support themselves. Most planned to marry and raise families; few would try for professions.

During the 1960's, the whole concept of separate education for women came into question, and on women's college campuses the merits of separate education versus coeducation were debated. After lengthy discussion, Vassar turned down an invitation to merge with Yale University but, in 1969, decided to become coeducational on its own campus. Radcliffe merged totally into Harvard. The other five Sisters did not become coeducational, although the presence of men on campus became normal under exchange agreements with nearby men's colleges. Proponents of women's colleges insisted on the continuing value of institutions at which women dominated college life.

—Milton Berman

FURTHER READING

Albers, Henry, ed. *Maria Mitchell: A Life in Journals and Letters.* Clinton Corners, N.Y.: College Avenue Press, 2001. Biography of Vassar College's first woman professor by another former Vassar professor.

Bruno, Maryann, and Elizabeth A. Daniels. *Vassar College.* Charleston, S.C.: Arcadia, 2001. Well-illustrated history of Vassar, from its founding through the turn of the twenty-first century. Both authors are Vassar graduates and veteran college staff members.

Gordon, Lynn D. "Vassar College, 1865-1920: Women with Missions." In *Gender and Higher Education in the Progressive Era.* New Haven, Conn.: Yale University Press, 1990. Describes how students and women faculty transformed Matthew Vassar's institution.

Horowitz, Helen Lefkowitz. *Alma Mater: Design and Experience in the Women's Colleges from Their*

Nineteenth-Century Beginnings to the 1930's. 2d ed. Amherst: University of Massachusetts Press, 1993. Discusses how the designs chosen for buildings affected college operations and the life of students and faculty.

________. *Campus Life: Undergraduate Cultures from the End of the Eighteenth Century to the Present.* New York: Alfred A. Knopf, 1987. Discusses how student expectations about college life changed over the centuries. Chapter 4 deals with the experiences of women.

Kendall, Elaine. *"Peculiar Institutions": An Informal History of the Seven Sister Colleges.* New York: G. P. Putnam's Sons, 1976. Witty and anecdotal account of the origins and development of elite eastern women's colleges.

Newcomer, Mabel. *A Century of Higher Education for American Women.* New York: Harper & Bros., 1959. Despite its age, this is the standard history of college education for women; it offers invaluable details.

Taylor, James Monroe. *Before Vassar Opened: A Contribution to the History of the Higher Education of Women in America.* Boston: Houghton Mifflin, 1914. A scholarly history, by the fourth president of Vassar College, that is the source of all later accounts of the founding of Vassar.

Woody, Thomas. *A History of Women's Education in the United States.* New York: Science Press, 1929. Although dated in some of its interpretations, this book is the classic work on women's education in the United States.

SEE ALSO: 1813: Founding of McGill University; May, 1823: Hartford Female Seminary Is Founded; Dec. 3, 1833: Oberlin College Opens; Nov. 8, 1837: Mount Holyoke Female Seminary Opens; May 12, 1857: New York Infirmary for Indigent Women and Children Opens.

RELATED ARTICLES in *Great Lives from History: The Nineteenth Century, 1801-1900:* Catharine Beecher; Mary Lyon; Maria Mitchell; Alice Freeman Palmer; Ellen Swallow Richards.

October 7-12, 1865
MORANT BAY REBELLION

In the Morant Bay Rebellion, a group of Jamaicans rose up against their British colonizers, killing officials and burning property. Inspired by Baptist teachings as much as by colonial racist oppression, the rebellion represented an attempt to make the British deliver on their promises of emancipation, but it was quickly suppressed and in the end merely strengthened the status quo.

LOCALE: Jamaica
CATEGORY: Wars, uprisings, and civil unrest

KEY FIGURES

Paul Bogle (d. 1865), Jamaican Baptist preacher and rebel leader
George William Gordon (1820-1865), Jamaican assemblyman
Edward John Eyre (1815-1901), governor of Jamaica, 1864-1866
Baron von Ketelhodt (d. 1865), colonial Jamaican magistrate and planter
Victor Herschell (d. 1865), curate of Bath

SUMMARY OF EVENT

The British parliament's emancipation of slaves throughout the British Empire in 1833 did not end the exploitation and subjection of African Jamaicans by the British. Whites continued to dominate the island by restricting to themselves the privileges of full citizenship, such as voting and landholding. In 1865, the recognition of this persistent inequality—worsened by drought—was combined with Baptist religious fervor, resulting in an attempt to avenge British injustices. Accordingly, on Wednesday, October 11, 1865, Paul Bogle, a Baptist preacher of African descent, marched on the courthouse in Morant Bay with about three hundred supporters. They burned down the building and then killed local white officials and planters who had stood in their way.

On the next day, October 12, the rebels moved on to the nearby town of Bath, attacking manor houses en route until they met reinforcements from the colonial militia. The insurrection then ended almost as soon as it had begun, but Governor Edward John Eyre's subsequent, bloody overreaction, intended to repress any further dissent, ironically led to the abdication of the Jamaican planter class. The British crown then became the direct ruler of the island.

The eastern part of Jamaica had witnessed resistance against the British long before Bogle took up arms. Sugar and slavery required a constant influx of laborers, many of whom tried to flee to the mountainous interior if given a chance. Maroons, escaped slaves from the first generations, had fought to establish their own autonomous region there by 1739. Western areas of the island also witnessed rebellions against slavery during the eighteenth century, but it was not until the Baptist wars of 1831-1832 that a serious island-wide threat to British rule precipitated emancipation.

Ironically, the maroons who fought so early for their own freedom were used by the British to catch other fugitives and then to put down further revolts, including that in Morant Bay. They provided much needed support for the thin layer of white British residents on Jamaica, who were outnumbered by people of color by a ratio of nearly 30 to 1. By the early 1860's, it was the power of Baptist missionaries and the growing popularity of the African interpretation of the Baptist religion that continued to erode the hegemony of the planters, already weakened by emancipation and competition from other sugar producers.

E. B. Underhill, the secretary of the Baptist Missionary Society in England, unwittingly set the stage for the riot in Morant Bay and the repression that came on its heels. Following a visit to Jamaica in 1859-1860, Underhill became concerned about the freed peasantry's underemployment, lack of food, and lack of political power. He wrote a detailed report in January, 1865, to the secretary of state for the colonies, complaining about those issues. The secretary forwarded the letter to Governor Eyre, who then forwarded it to magistrates, planters, and clergy, hoping for a vigorous rebuttal of the allegations. Instead, someone leaked the letter to Jamaican newspapers, which, in turn, published it and generated a firestorm of debate.

Colonial officials responded predictably to the newspaper story. They denied that there was any problem and blamed blacks for their own poverty and despair. The missionaries were the only white constituent group to verify Underhill's view, and they sponsored a series of public meetings to agitate for reform. These meetings attracted a wide array of individuals not used to participating in politics, including middle-class mulatto professionals as well as hungry peasants and field laborers from the countryside.

The so-called Underhill meetings might have vented all of these groups' discontent without anyone resorting to violence had not African Jamaicans always viewed division among whites as a cue to attempt to overthrow their oppressors once and for all. Under the circumstances, an uprising was inevitable, but the setting for the rebellion when it came was seemingly unlikely. The parish of St. Thomas-in-the-East, which included Morant Bay, had seen little Baptist missionary outreach, because the planters there had actively discouraged such outreach. Underhill himself estimated that 80 percent of the parish was not Christian in any sense of the word. It was one of the last places to hold an Underhill meeting, which had to be conducted outside when the local magistrates declared that the courthouse would never be available for such a purpose. Most critical to the actual outbreak of disorder, however, were the born-again conversions of two leaders in the parish, Paul Bogle and George William Gordon.

Gordon laid the egg that Bogle hatched. Bogle was one of the peasant freeholders who were rich enough to qualify to vote and who had put Gordon, a mulatto planter, into the Jamaica Assembly in 1863. Gordon had become a Baptist just before he was elected and ordained Bogle as a lay preacher in the African Baptist tradition. Gordon had echoed the concerns of Underhill before the publication of the latter's letter. Encouraged by Gordon, Bogle had helped to organize the Underhill meeting at St. Thomas-in-the-East.

The St. Thomas-in-the-East meeting sent a delegation to Morant Bay, but the governor refused to meet with this delegation. Bogle was a member of the delegation, and after the governor's refusal to meet with him, the game plans of Bogle and Gordon seem to have diverged. Gordon wanted to continue peacefully to appeal their case up the governmental hierarchy, all the way to Queen Victoria. Bogle, however, wished to focus only on the colonial authorities, whom he was prepared to confront by any means necessary.

The Morant Bay Rebellion began on October 7, 1865, when the local court convicted Bogle's cousin, Lewis Miller, of trespassing, because he had allowed his horse to feed on the grounds of an estate that already was sublet to local peasants. This ruling did not go unchallenged; even before the guilty verdict, a crowd of around 150 peasants and laborers that included Paul Bogle had edged into the courthouse and was prepared to disrupt the otherwise routine proceedings. Even though Miller himself had pleaded guilty, Bogle insisted that the defendant would not pay the fine and would officially appeal his conviction. A confrontation ensued in which Bogle and others prevented a man accused by police of inciting a riot from being taken to jail.

Magistrates issued warrants for the arrest of Bogle, his brother, and other identified ringleaders of the impertinent crowd. When the police went to execute these warrants on October 10, another crowd beat the constables back and temporarily arrested the officers instead. The next day witnessed Bogle's march on the courthouse, which only turned violent when members of the colonial militia fired on the protestors, killing seven. The troops were badly outnumbered and quickly withdrew, leaving the vestrymen to have their fates decided by those they had mistreated. The courthouse was symbolically burned and the most oppressive of the white authorities—such as Baron von Ketelhodt, the chief magistrate, and the Reverend Victor Herschell, the curate of Bath—were killed. For about twenty-four hours, Bogle's group effectively ruled Morant Bay, until they left for nearby Bath and met the militia reinforcements directly.

Governor Eyre then overreacted. Worried that the rebellion might develop into another Haitian Rebellion or Sepoy Mutiny—both events in which European were killed by subject peoples—he instituted martial law in the entire county of Surrey, outside Kingston. Troops were allowed to shoot on sight any person of color whom they suspected of being subversive. While no exact number of those killed by the militia was kept, 354 people were executed after quick, perfunctory "trials," and an additional 85 people were recorded to have been shot or hanged without a trial. Paul Bogle was one of the latter: He was tracked down and murdered. George William Gordon, who knew nothing of the events of October 7 and October 11, was hanged after a show trial. Many others who had nothing to do with the melee at the courthouse, including women and children, were beaten and whipped, and nearly one thousand peasant homes in the vicinity were arbitrarily demolished.

Significance

The Morant Bay Rebellion was slightly successful, in that the planting class and its assembly, which had long oppressed African Jamaicans, was replaced by direct Crown rule of the colony. Governor Eyre's repression drew a mixed yet spirited response in Great Britain itself, with advocates for the working class seeing him as the devil incarnate. Indeed, agitation stemming in part from the Morant Bay Rebellion helped persuade Conservative prime minister Benjamin Disraeli to coopt any further working-class dissent by extending the franchise to workers with the Reform Bill of 1867.

Such gradualist paternalism also marked the change in leadership in Jamaica itself. In 1866, Governor Sir John Peter Grant began increasing slightly the land redistribution granted to squatters, as well as the funding of roads, schools, and other needed infrastructure. Blacks blamed Eyre for the bloodshed, but they absolved Queen Victoria and her family, who, by the end of the nineteenth century, were seen as the Great Emancipators. Ironically, in that sense, the Morant Bay Rebellion tended to strengthen the racial hierarchy on the island, at least until the late 1930's, by removing the planters and their assembly from power.

—Charles H. Ford

Further Reading

Bakan, Abigail B. *Ideology and Class Conflict in Jamaica: The Politics of Rebellion*. Quebec: McGill-Queens University Press, 1990. Within a Marxist framework, this book compares the Morant Bay Rebellion with the Baptist wars of 1831-1832 and the strikes of 1938-1939.

DeRose, Michelle. "'Is the Lan' I Want': Reconfiguring Metaphors and Redefining History in Andrew Salkey's Epic *Jamaica*." *Contemporary Literature* 39, no. 2 (Summer, 1998): 212-237. This cogent analysis of an epic poem from the 1970's testifies to the prominent status of the Morant Bay Rebellion in the making of Jamaican nationalism.

Heuman, Gad. *"The Killing Time": The Morant Bay Rebellion in Jamaica*. Knoxville: University of Tennessee Press, 1994. Provides the most accurate narrative of the rebellion and the subsequent repression it triggered.

Holt, Thomas C. *The Problem of Freedom: Race, Labor, and Politics in Jamaica and Britain, 1832-1938*. Baltimore: Johns Hopkins University Press, 1992. Places the Morant Bay Rebellion within the wider context of British imperialism from emancipation to Bustamente.

See also: Aug. 28, 1833: Slavery Is Abolished Throughout the British Empire; May 10, 1857-July 8, 1858: Sepoy Mutiny Against British Rule; Aug., 1867: British Parliament Passes the Reform Act of 1867.

Related articles in *Great Lives from History: The Nineteenth Century, 1801-1900:* Benjamin Disraeli; Queen Victoria.

November 24, 1865
MISSISSIPPI ENACTS FIRST POST-CIVIL WAR BLACK CODE

Fearing the consequences of the abolition of slavery after the Civil War, southern states began passing laws designed to limit the rights of newly freed African Americans.

ALSO KNOWN AS: Black laws
LOCALE: Southern United States
CATEGORIES: Civil rights and liberties; laws, acts, and legal history

KEY FIGURES

Benjamin G. Humphreys (1808-1882), governor of Mississippi, 1865-1868
Andrew Johnson (1808-1875), president of the United States, 1865-1869
Daniel E. Sickles (1819-1914), federal military commander in South Carolina
Alfred H. Terry (1827-1890), federal military commander in Virginia
Lyman Trumbull (1813-1896), Illinois senator who chaired the Senate Judiciary Committee

SUMMARY OF EVENT

The months immediately following the end of the U.S. Civil War (1861-1865) were a period of great uncertainty. The Union's wartime president, Abraham Lincoln, had been assassinated, and his successor, Andrew Johnson, was untested as a leader. Strong leadership could not be expected from Capitol Hill, either, as Congress had gone into a long recess. Within the defeated southern states, a host of questions required immediate answers. Foremost among these were questions relating to the new role of the recently freed slaves. Would they continue to furnish an economical and reliable labor force for southern cotton planters? Would they try to exact subtle or blatant revenge upon their former masters? Should lawmakers grant them the vote? Should the U.S. government give them land? Should the states pay the cost of their basic education? What legal rights would these five million African Americans enjoy in the postbellum South?

President Johnson developed a lenient plan for the postwar reconstruction of the South, one that called on the southern states quickly to reorganize their own governments. His only major demands of these new governments were that they agree that no state had the right to secede from the Union, and that they ratify the Thirteenth Amendment, which abolished slavery throughout the United States.

As reconstituted southern state legislatures began to meet, their exclusively white members were eager to pass laws that would answer some of the nagging questions about the future place of African Americans in southern society. Many legislators believed former slaves would not work unless forced to do so, and they feared the double specter of an economy without a labor supply and a huge mass of discontented black people who would live on charity or plunder. In earlier years, laws known as the slave codes had controlled the African American population. Some lawmakers now called for a renewal of the slave codes to control the freed black population.

Mississippi's legislature was the first to take up the question of African American rights. When it met in October, 1865, it quickly fell into arguments over what policies on racial matters should be enacted. Nearly half the legislators favored laws that would, in almost every way, return African Americans to the position they had occupied in the time of slavery. However, Governor Benjamin G. Humphreys intervened to urge lawmakers to ensure certain basic rights to the newly freed slaves. After Humphreys intervened, moderates in the Mississippi legislature had the upper hand and, on November 24, 1865, enacted a bill titled An Act to Confer Civil Rights on Freedmen.

As its title promised, Mississippi's new law did confer some rights on African Americans that they had not enjoyed as slaves. These rights included the right to sue and be sued, the right to swear out criminal complaints against others, the right to purchase or inherit land, the right to marry, and the right to draw up labor or other contracts. Although the title of the law mentions civil rights, the law was remarkable primarily for the rights that it *denied* to African Americans. While it gave African Americans the right to own land, it denied them the right to rent rural land, thereby helping to perpetuate the existence of a large class of landless agricultural workers who would have to work for low wages. The act recognized the right of African Americans to marry but also provided that interracial marriage would be punished by life imprisonment for both parties. The right to testify in court was eroded by certain provisions that said the right to testify applied neither to cases in which both parties in lawsuits or criminal cases were white, nor to criminal cases in which defendants were African Americans.

Most ominous was the provision in Mississippi's law that every black Mississippian sign a one-year labor contract by the first of each year and honor that contract. Should employees leave their employers before the end of the year, law-enforcement officers were empowered to return them forcibly to their places of employment. In a provision reminiscent of the old laws that forbade giving help to runaway slaves, this new law made it a crime to give food, clothing, or shelter to black workers who left their employers while still under contract. The punishment for helping runaways was up to two months in jail. Those who helped fugitives find work in states other than Mississippi could be sentenced for up to six months in jail. Once again, securing a stable labor supply for the state was at the forefront of lawmakers' goals.

After Mississippi passed this first post-Civil War black code, a flood of other laws soon followed in Mississippi and the other southern states. South Carolina's black codes forbade African Americans from working in any field other than agriculture unless they paid a prohibitively high fee. Black farmworkers in South Carolina were required by law to work from sunup to sundown and forbidden from leaving their employers' plantations without their employers' permission.

South Carolina and Mississippi both enacted severe vagrancy laws that called for the arrest of idle persons, drunkards, gamblers, wanderers, fighters, people who wasted their pay, circus hands, actors, and even jugglers. If these persons were African American, they were to be considered vagrants and fined up to one hundred dollars and imprisoned. If they could not pay their fines, their labor would be auctioned off to white employers, and their wages could be used to satisfy their fines.

Black codes varied from state to state, but their northern opponents said they all had the common goal of returning the freed slaves to a system equivalent to bondage. In some southern states, African Americans were prohibited from owning guns. In other states, they were forbidden to assemble in groups or subjected to evening curfews. President Johnson, himself a southerner, saw little objectionable in the black codes, but many northern politicians did. For example, General Daniel E. Sickles,

Contemporary Currier & Ives print of a cartoon commenting on the refusal of southern states to acknowledge the changed status of African Americans after the Civil War. As the white man is about to be swept over a cataract, he refuses to accept the help of a free black man, while President Ulysses S. Grant chides him.

who commanded federal troops occupying South Carolina, and General Alfred H. Terry, who commanded federal troops in Virginia, overturned all or parts of the black codes in their areas, pending action in Congress. In Washington, Senator Lyman Trumbull wrote the Civil Rights Act of 1866, which declared that all persons born in the United States were U.S. citizens, and that all U.S. citizens enjoyed equality before the law. Congress passed this measure over the veto of President Johnson. In 1868, the Fourteenth Amendment brought this same promise of equality before the law into the Constitution itself.

SIGNIFICANCE

The black codes were barely enforced. Overturned by the actions of occupying generals during Reconstruction, and later by the U.S. courts, which found them in conflict with the Fourteenth Amendment, they were important chiefly for fueling a conflict in Washington between Johnson's lenient Reconstruction plan and Congress's insistence that the basic rights of African Americans be protected. These codes are also important for their role in bringing about passage of the Fourteenth Amendment. Although African American rights generally were protected between 1866 and 1876, the southern states found many ways to draft laws that were color-blind on their face but that could be enforced in a racially biased way. After Reconstruction, few southern elected officials, and few officeholders nationwide, were interested in championing African American civil rights.

—Stephen Cresswell

FURTHER READING

Bankston, Carl L., III, ed. *African American History*. 3 vols. Pasadena, Calif.: Salem Press, 2005. Encyclopedic reference work on African American history that includes entries on the black codes, civil rights laws, and many related subjects.

Cohen, William. "Negro Involuntary Servitude in the South, 1865-1940: A Preliminary Analysis." *Journal of Southern History* 42 (February, 1976): 35-50. Discusses the larger picture of black labor and its lack of freedoms, linking the black codes to peonage and to the South's convict labor system.

Foner, Eric. *Reconstruction: America's Unfinished Revolution*. New York: Harper & Row, 1988. This massive volume is the basic history of Reconstruction; chapter 5 covers the black codes and related events.

Franklin, John Hope, and Alfred A. Moss, Jr. *From Slavery to Freedom: A History of African Americans*. 8th ed. Boston: McGraw-Hill, 2000. This standard history of the black experience in America examines the changes that former slaves went through in the decades following the Civil War.

Harris, William C. *Presidential Reconstruction in Mississippi*. Baton Rouge: Louisiana State University Press, 1967. Discusses the drafting of Mississippi's black codes, which are especially important because they were a model for other southern state legislatures.

Litwack, Leon F. *Been in the Storm So Long: The Aftermath of Slavery*. New York: Alfred A. Knopf, 1979. Tells the Reconstruction story as much through the eyes of the freed slaves as from the point of view of white government officials.

Rasmussen, R. Kent. *Farewell to Jim Crow: The Rise and Fall of Segregation in America*. New York: Facts On File, 1997. This brief but comprehensive history of segregation in U.S. history, which is written for young adults, examines the entire history of racially discriminatory legislation.

Wilson, Theodore B. *The Black Codes of the South*. Tuscaloosa: University of Alabama Press, 1965. The only book exclusively devoted to the black codes. Provides thoughtful analysis of the meaning of these laws in southern and African American history.

SEE ALSO: Jan., 1804: Ohio Enacts the First Black Codes; Dec. 8, 1863-Apr. 24, 1877: Reconstruction of the South; Mar. 3, 1865: Congress Creates the Freedmen's Bureau; 1866: Birth of the Ku Klux Klan; Apr. 9, 1866: Civil Rights Act of 1866; May and July, 1866: Memphis and New Orleans Race Riots; July 9, 1868: Fourteenth Amendment Is Ratified; Oct. 15, 1883: Civil Rights Cases; 1890: Mississippi Constitution Disfranchises Black Voters; May 18, 1896: *Plessy v. Ferguson*.

RELATED ARTICLES in *Great Lives from History: The Nineteenth Century, 1801-1900:* Andrew Johnson; Thaddeus Stevens.

December 6, 1865
THIRTEENTH AMENDMENT IS RATIFIED

This first of the three Civil War amendments brought a final and definitive end to slavery in the United States but did not by itself confer civil rights on former slaves.

LOCALE: Washington, D.C.
CATEGORIES: Human rights; laws, acts, and legal history; civil rights and liberties

KEY FIGURES

Frederick Douglass (1817?-1895), abolitionist and orator
William Lloyd Garrison (1805-1879), publisher of *The Liberator* and a founder of the American Anti-Slavery Society
Abraham Lincoln (1809-1865), president, 1861-1865
Andrew Johnson (1808-1875), vice president under Lincoln and president, 1865-1869
Robert Dale Owen (1801-1877), abolitionist whose writings influenced Lincoln

SUMMARY OF EVENT

The antislavery and abolition movements in the United States did not begin with the Civil War (1861-1865). As early as 1652, the state of Rhode Island passed antislavery legislation. In 1773, Benjamin Franklin and Dr. Benjamin Rush formed the first abolition society in America. In 1832, the New England Anti-Slavery Society was formed by newspaper editor William Lloyd Garrison, who also helped found the American Anti-Slavery Society in 1833. The Society of Friends, or Quakers, a religious group who settled early in the history of the United States, were also active in the antislavery movement. Their religion forbade the holding of slaves. Quakers primarily settled in the northern part of the country.

In 1807, federal legislation was passed outlawing the importation of slaves after January 1, 1808. However, that law did not end the use of slaves in the United States. The writers of the U.S. Constitution had not been able to resolve the issue of slavery in 1787 and had declared that the slave trade could end by 1808 or anytime later. Eventually, the inability of national leaders to resolve this issue would divide the nation. The Missouri Compromise of 1820 banned slavery in most of the western states and territories. This was overturned by the Supreme Court in 1857, in the infamous *Dred Scott* decision.

By the 1850's, the split between the slave and free states was well entrenched. In an attempt to appease pro- and antislavery proponents, Congress adopted five provisions in the Compromise of 1850. The most notable was the Second Fugitive Slave Law, passed in 1850. It provided for slaves who escaped from the South and were found in northern antislavery states to be returned to their owners. A great deal of violence erupted over this legislation, which led to the act's repeal on June 28, 1864. Meanwhile, the split between the North and the South eventually resulted in the Civil War.

The abolitionist movement had fought for decades for an end to slavery. Robert Dale Owen, an abolitionist and legislator, struggled for the emancipation of slaves and is thought to have influenced President Abraham Lincoln with his tract *Policy of Emancipation* (1863). Another radical opponent of slavery was Wendell Phillips, a noted speaker and a graduate of Harvard Law School. He believed that the U.S. Constitution supported slavery and therefore was owed no allegiance by abolitionists. Harriet Tubman was active in the Underground Railroad, which was successful in bringing many slaves into northern states that would not return them to their owners. John Brown adopted more violent means of expressing his abolitionist sentiment. He raided the federal arsenal at Harpers Ferry, Virginia, and encouraged a slave revolt. He was eventually hanged for his fanaticism. Frederick Douglass was an important abolitionist who played a significant role in the passage toward freedom for the slaves. A runaway slave, he spoke eloquently about the need to redress the wrongs created by slavery.

After the Civil War began in April, 1861, the abolitionist movement placed greater pressure on President Lincoln to issue an emancipation proclamation. Lincoln had focused a great deal of attention on the issue of slav-

> **THIRTEENTH AMENDMENT TO THE U.S. CONSTITUTION**
>
> SECTION 1. Neither slavery nor involuntary servitude, except as a punishment for crime whereof the party shall have been duly convicted, shall exist within the United States, or any place subject to their jurisdiction.
>
> SECTION 2. Congress shall have power to enforce this article by appropriate legislation.

ery during the famous Lincoln-Douglas debates. Lincoln finally issued his Emancipation Proclamation on September 22, 1862, well after the war started. His proclamation announced that in states that had seceded from the union, all slaves would be freed effective January 1, 1863. This proclamation did not actually free many slaves. It did not apply to slave states that were still part of the Union and was unenforceable in those states involved in the Confederacy. The major function of the Emancipation Proclamation was to announce to all that one of the Union's goals in the Civil War was to end slavery. Also, as Union troops occupied Confederate territories, they freed the slaves in the areas they controlled.

At the time that the war began, the African American population of the United States consisted of approximately 4.5 million people, 4 million of whom were slaves. White supremacy was the general ideology of both southerners and northerners. Slaves were denied such rights as the right to legal marriage, choice of residence, and education, and existed in perpetual servitude. Without significant changes in institutional structures, there was no hope of freedom.

The Thirteenth Amendment was one of three amendments known as the Civil War amendments. The combined purpose of these three amendments was to free the slaves and promote their participation in their country. The Thirteenth Amendment states that

> neither slavery nor involuntary servitude, except as a punishment for crime whereof the party shall have been duly convicted, shall exist within the United States, or any place subject to their jurisdiction.

One of the battles surrounding the Thirteenth Amendment in particular, and all the Civil War amendments in general, concerned the interpretation of the Tenth Amendment to the Constitution. Part of the Bill of Rights that was adopted in 1791, the Tenth Amendment states that no federal legislation can detract from the power of state government. Those who opposed the Thirteenth Amendment claimed that the right to allow slavery was not specifically denied in the Constitution and therefore fell within the authority of the state.

With the passage of the Thirteenth Amendment, the long fight to abolish slavery in the United States was over. The amendment was ratified on December 6, 1865, and officially announced on December 18, 1865. For some abolitionists, such as William Lloyd Garrison, the battle had been won: Slavery was ended. Others, however, saw the Thirteenth Amendment as only a beginning in the struggle for African American rights.

Frederick Douglass did not share Garrison's high hopes. He believed that slavery would not be fully abolished until the former slaves acquired the right to vote. The passage of the Civil Rights Act of 1866 did not provide this right. It was not until the passage of the Fourteenth Amendment, in 1868, that citizenship and the rights thereof were guaranteed to "all persons born or naturalized in the United States." Finally, in February, 1870, ratification of the Fifteenth Amendment expressly awarded former slaves the right to vote. Within weeks, the first African American in the U.S. Senate, Hiram R. Revels of Mississippi, took his seat.

SIGNIFICANCE

On April 15, 1865, President Lincoln died from wounds inflicted by an assassin. Vice President Andrew Johnson then became president and prepared to oversee Reconstruction of the nation. Johnson, however, was not highly supportive or sympathetic to the needs of the former slaves. He blocked every attempt to extend rights to former slaves. In fact, Johnson vetoed most of the civil rights legislation passed by Congress, only to have his vetoes overridden by Congress. Impeachment charges eventually ensued, and Johnson was spared by only a one-vote margin. At that point, Johnson withdrew from Reconstruction activities and allowed Congress to control the process.

One interesting note is the relationship between the woman suffrage movement and the abolition and black suffrage process. The decision over whether to support the call for the black vote divided the woman suffrage movement. Some believed that a gradual transition, in which first black men received the vote and then all women received the vote, would meet with greater success. Two such women were Lucy Stone and Julia Ward Howe. Others believed that suffrage was "all or nothing," and that women should not forsake their own cause in order to gain the vote for others. Susan B. Anthony and Elizabeth Cady Stanton were opposed to legislation that specifically referred to men and neglected suffrage for women. It was not until the passage of the Nineteenth Amendment in 1920 that women gained the long-sought suffrage.

Meanwhile, the major impact of the Thirteenth Amendment was to end American slavery forever. The Supreme Court subsequently ruled that the amendment might also provide grounds for congressional action against the "badges and incidents" of slavery. However, use of the amendment for that purpose has been relatively uncommon.

—*Sharon L. Larson*

FURTHER READING

Franklin, John Hope, and Alfred A. Moss, Jr. *From Slavery to Freedom: A History of African Americans*. 8th ed. Boston: McGraw-Hill, 2000. This standard history of the black experience in America details the changes undergone by African Americans during the movement toward abolition and after they achieved citizenship.

Lawson, Bill E., and Frank M. Kirkland. *Frederick Douglass: A Critical Reader*. Malden, Mass.: Blackwell, 1999. Collection of essays on the leading black abolitionist spokesperson of the nineteenth century.

Lewis, Thomas T., and Richard L. Wilson, eds. *Encyclopedia of the U.S. Supreme Court*. 3 vols. Pasadena, Calif.: Salem Press, 2001. Comprehensive reference work on the Supreme Court that contains substantial discussions of issues surrounding the U.S. Constitution and its amendments.

Owen, Robert Dale. *The Wrong of Slavery, the Right of Emancipation, and the Future of the African Race in the United States*. Philadelphia: J. B. Lippincott, 1864. Writings on the issue of slavery in the United States from an abolitionist of the slave era who is believed to have helped move Abraham Lincoln to issue the Emancipation Proclamation.

Stauffer, John. *The Black Hearts of Men: Radical Abolitionists and the Transformation of Race*. Cambridge, Mass.: Harvard University Press, 2002. Describes the interracial alliance of abolitionists Frederick Douglass, James McCune Smith, Gerrit Smith, and John Brown.

SEE ALSO: Mar. 2, 1807: Congress Bans Importation of African Slaves; c. 1830-1865: Southerners Advance Proslavery Arguments; Aug. 28, 1833: Slavery Is Abolished Throughout the British Empire; Dec., 1833: American Anti-Slavery Society Is Founded; Dec. 3, 1847: Douglass Launches *The North Star*; Apr. 12, 1861-Apr. 9, 1865: U.S. Civil War; Jan. 1, 1863: Lincoln Issues the Emancipation Proclamation; Dec. 8, 1863-Apr. 24, 1877: Reconstruction of the South; Apr. 9, 1866: Civil Rights Act of 1866; July 9, 1868: Fourteenth Amendment Is Ratified; Oct. 15, 1883: Civil Rights Cases; May 18, 1896: *Plessy v. Ferguson*.

RELATED ARTICLES in *Great Lives from History: The Nineteenth Century, 1801-1900:* Frederick Douglass; William Lloyd Garrison; Andrew Johnson; Abraham Lincoln.

1866
BIRTH OF THE KU KLUX KLAN

Formed by white southerners who were disaffected by the outcome of the Civil War and the liberation of African Americans, the original Ku Klux Klan was short lived. However, it left a legacy that would grow into an organization of institutionalized race hatred and survive into the twenty-first century.

LOCALE: Pulaski, Tennessee

CATEGORIES: Organizations and institutions; terrorism and political assassination

KEY FIGURES

Nathan Bedford Forrest (1821-1877), grand wizard of the first Klan

Edward Young Clarke (b. 1839), advertising man who promoted the Klan during the 1920's

Samuel Moffett Ralston (1857-1925), senator with Klan connections

Edward L. Jackson (1873-1954), governor of Indiana

William Joseph Simmons (1880-1945), preacher who founded the second Klan in 1915

D. C. Stephenson (1891-1966), grand dragon in Indiana

David E. Duke (b. 1950), klansman who ran for national office

SUMMARY OF EVENT

With the end of the Civil War (1861-1865) in the United States in 1865 and the emancipation of African American slaves in the South, tension arose between old-order southern whites and Radical Republicans of the North who were devoted to a strict plan of Reconstruction that required southern states to repeal their discriminatory laws and guarantee civil and voting rights to African Americans. Federal instruments for ensuring African American rights included the Freedmen's Bureau and the Union Leagues. In reaction to the activities of these organizations, white supremacist organizations sprouted in the years immediately following the Civil War. Such organizations included the Knights of the White Camelia, the White League, the Invisible Circle, the Pale Faces, and the Ku Klux Klan (KKK).

The Ku Klux Klan would eventually lend its name to a confederation of organizations spread throughout the United States, but it began on a small scale in 1866. It was started in Pulaski, Tennessee, as a fraternal order for white male Protestants who were linked by their opposition to Radical Reconstructionism and an agenda to promote white dominance in the South. The early Klan established many of the unusual rituals and violent activities for which the Ku Klux Klan would become notorious throughout its long history.

The early members of the Klan regarded the South as an "invisible empire," with "realms" consisting of the southern states. A "grand dragon" headed each realm, and the entire "empire" was led by Grand Wizard General Nathan Bedford Forrest. Leadership posts had titles such as "giant," "cyclops," "geni," "hydra," and "goblin." The original Klan also established the practice of members wearing white robes and pointed hoods that covered their faces. The practice arose from the belief that black people were so superstitious that they would be easily intimidated by the menacing, ghost-like appearance of their oppressors. The hooded costumes also allowed members to maintain anonymity during nighttime rides, when they harassed African Americans whom they considered to be "uppity Negroes" and anyone who defended them. Such offensive language remains a testament to the bigotry and racism deeply entrenched in white American society and fed upon by the Klan.

Thomas Nast cartoon published in Harper's Weekly *in 1874 vilifying the Ku Klux Klan as inflicting on former slaves a fate worse than slavery itself.* (Library of Congress)

The early Klan soon began perpetrating acts of violence, including whippings, house-burnings, kidnappings, and lynchings. In 1869, as Klan violence was escalating, Forrest disbanded the organization. On May 31, 1870, and on April 20, 1871, the U.S. Congress passed the Ku Klux Klan Acts, or Force Acts, designed to break up the white supremacist groups. Speaking in the Senate on March 18, 1871, for the second Force Act, John Sherman said of the Ku Klux Klan:

> They are secret, oath-bound; they murder, rob, plunder, whip, and scourge; and they commit these crimes, not upon the high and lofty, but upon the lowly, upon the poor, upon the feeble men and women who are utterly defenceless. . . . Where is there an organization against which humanity revolts more than it does against this?

The Ku Klux Klan Acts were passed, but parts of them were later ruled unconstitutional by the U.S. Supreme Court.

The original Klan was short lived, but it later resurfaced during times of racial tension, often in conjunction with periods marked by xenophobia and anti-immigrant paranoia. The first major resurgence of the Klan occurred in 1915. In November of that year, the new Ku Klux Klan was founded by preacher William Joseph Simmons on Stone Mountain, Georgia. Simmons proclaimed the new organization to be a "high-class, mystic, social, patriotic" society devoted to defending womanhood, white Protestant values, and "native-born, white, gentile Americans."

The image of the Klan as a protector of white virtue was reinforced by D. W. Griffith's popular 1915 film *Birth of a Nation*, which was based on the novel *The Clansman: An Historical Romance of the Ku Klux Klan* (1906) by Thomas F. Dixon, Jr. Griffith's film depicted lustful blacks assaulting white women, with hooded members of the Klan riding to the rescue. It was probably no coincidence the rise of the new Klan presaged the period of the Red Scare (1919-1920) and the Immigration Act of 1921, the first such legislation in the United States to establish immigration quotas on the basis of national origin.

The new Ku Klux Klan cloaked itself as a patriotic organization devoted to preserving traditional American values against enemies in the nation's midst. An upsurge of nationalist fervor swelled the ranks of the Klan, this time far beyond the borders of the South. White men and women both joined to ensure the survival of the white race. This second Klan adopted the rituals and regalia of its predecessor as well as the same antiblack ideology, to which it added anti-Roman Catholic, anti-Semitic, anti-immigrant, anti-birth-control, anti-Darwinist, and anti-Prohibition stances. Promoted by ad-man Edward Young Clarke, Klan membership reached approximately 100,000 by 1921. By some estimates, membership rose to more than 5 million during the 1920's, and the Klan rolls included some members of Congress.

Some Klan observers have argued that the power of the Klan was actually worse in the North than it was in the South. In 1924, an outspoken opponent of the Klan, journalist William Allen White, lost a bid for the governorship of Kansas to a Klan sympathizer. In Indiana, local grand dragon D. C. Stephenson, who was known to rule the statehouse, helped elect Samuel Moffett Ralston, a Klan member, to the Senate in 1922. Stephenson also influenced voters to elect Edward L. Jackson as governor in 1925. Jackson and Stephenson were later disgraced by investigations into their misuse of funds. Stephenson was also later convicted of second-degree murder after kidnapping and raping his secretary, who took poison to force him to get her to authorities.

Stephenson is only one example of the criminal personalities that typified Klan membership. The Klan has been credited with perpetrating more than five hundred hangings and burnings of African Americans. Klan victims were primarily men who broke the "racist codes" kept in secret by the Klan. In 1924, forty thousand Klansmen marched down Pennsylvania Avenue in Washington, D.C., sending a message to the federal government that there should be a white, Protestant United States. Eventually, however, the Klan's growing identification with brutal violence alienated many of its members, whose numbers are believed to have dropped to about thirty thousand by 1930.

Klan activities again increased shortly before U.S. entry into World War II in 1941, and membership rose toward the 100,000 mark. However, when the U.S. Congress assessed the organization more than one-half million dollars in back taxes in 1944, the Klan again dissolved itself to escape payment. Two years later, however, Atlanta physician Samuel Green united smaller Klan groups into the Association of Georgia Klans and was soon joined by other reincarnations, such as the Federated Ku Klux Klans, the Original Southern Klans, and the Knights of the Ku Klux Klan. These groups revived the old racist agenda and violent methods of previous Klans and during this period were responsible for hundreds of criminal acts. Of equal concern was the Klan's political influence: A governor of Texas was elected with the support of the Klan, and a senator from Maine was similarly elected. Even a Supreme Court justice, Hugo Black, revealed in 1937 that he had once been a member of the Ku Klux Klan.

During the 1940's, many states passed laws that revoked Klan charters, and many southern communities issued regulations against the wearing of Klan masks. The U.S. Justice Department placed the Klan on its list of subversive elements, and in 1952 the Federal Bureau of Investigation used the Lindbergh law (one of the 1934 Crime Control Acts) against the Klan. Another direct challenge to the principles of the Klan came during the 1960's with the rise of the Civil Rights movement and new federal civil rights legislation. Martin Luther King, Jr., prophesied early in the decade that it would be a "season of suffering." On September 15, 1963, a Klan bomb tore apart the Sixteenth Street Baptist Church in Birmingham, Alabama, killing four young children.

Despite the outrage of much of the nation, the violence continued, led by members of the Klan who made a mockery of the courts and the laws that they had broken. Less than a year after the Birmingham bombing, three civil rights workers were killed in Mississippi, including one African American and two whites from the North involved in voter registration drives. This infamous event was later documented in the 1988 motion picture *Mississippi Burning*. Such acts prompted President Lyndon B.

Johnson, in a televised speech in March, 1965, to denounce the Klan as he announced the arrest of four Klansmen for murder.

After the convictions of many of its members in the 1960's, the Ku Klux Klan became comparatively dormant, and its roster of members reflected low numbers. However, as it had done in previous periods of dormancy, the Klan refused to die. Busing for integration of public schools during the 1970's provoked Klan opposition in both the South and the North. In 1979, in Greensboro, North Carolina, Klan members killed several members of the Communist Party in a daylight battle on an open street. Since that time, Klan members have been known to patrol the Mexican border, armed with weapons and citizen-band radios, in efforts to drive illegal immigrants back to Mexico. The Klan has even been active in suburban California, at times driving out African Americans who attempted to move there. On the Gulf Coast, many boats fly the infamous AKIA flag, whose acronym stands for "A Klansman I Am," a term that dates back to the 1920's. Klan members try to discourage or run out Vietnamese fishers.

Notable Klan leaders active after 1970 include James Venable, for whom the Klan became little more than a hobby, and Bill Wilkinson, a former disciple of David Duke. Robert Shelton, long a grand dragon, helped elect two Alabama governors. David Duke, a Klan leader until the late 1980's, was elected a congressman from Louisiana, despite his well-publicized Klan associations. In 1991, Duke ran for governor of Louisiana and almost won. During the 1980's, the Klan stepped up its anti-Semitic activities, planning multiple bombings in Nashville. During the 1990's, Klan leaders trained their members and their children for what they believed was an imminent race war, and taught followers survival skills and weaponry at remote camps throughout the country.

Significance

Throughout its many generations, the Klan has maintained that it is a patriotic organization, interested in preserving the principles upon which the United States was originally based. However, the Klan's history of violence against African Americans, nonwhites in general, and Jews is the most anti-American sentiment conceivable in a republic founded on the principles of tolerance in service of "life, liberty, and the pursuit of happiness."

A major blow was struck against the Klan by the Klanwatch Project of the Southern Poverty Law Center, in Montgomery, Alabama, when, in 1984, attorney Morris Dees began pressing civil suits against several Klan members, effectively removing their personal assets, funds received from members, and even buildings owned by the Klan. Despite such setbacks, as late as 2005, the Ku Klux Klan continued to solicit new "Aryan" members and even maintained a Web site for this purpose. However, in contrast to the organization's traditional image, it now stressed a different message:

> The Imperial Klans of America Knights of the Ku Klux Klan are a legal and law abiding organization that will NOT tolerate illegal acts of any sort. If you take it upon yourself to violate the law, you do so on your own, If you commit an illegal act it will result in your membership with the IKA to be on suspension and you may be banished. We cannot and will not be responsible for any member committing any illegal acts.

—*The Editors*

Further Reading

Bridges, Tyler. *The Rise of David Duke*. Jackson: University Press of Mississippi, 1994. A thorough discussion of a dangerous member of the Klan in the 1990's.

Chalmers, David Mark. *Hooded Americanism: The History of the Ku Klux Klan*. 3d ed. Durham, N.C.: Duke University Press, 1987. Considered the bible of works about the Klan, this book has seen numerous editions and updatings.

Ezekiel, Raphael. *The Racist Mind: Portraits of American Neo-Nazis and Klansmen*. New York: Viking Press, 1995. Psychological insights into racism. Explores conditions of childhood, education, and other factors in an attempt to explain racist behavior.

MacLean, Nancy. *Behind the Mask of Chivalry: The Making of the Second Ku Klux Klan*. New York: Oxford University Press, 1995. Scholarly history of the Klan's twentieth century renaissance.

Quarles, Chester L. *The Ku Klux Klan and Related American Racialist and Antisemitic Organizations: A History and Analysis*. Jefferson, N.C.: McFarland, 1999. Study of the Klan in the broader context of white supremacist organizations.

Randel, William. *The Ku Klux Klan: A Century of Infamy*. Philadelphia: Chilton Books, 1965. An excellent history of origins and events, which also uses a moral perspective.

Stanton, Bill. *Klanwatch: Bringing the Ku Klux Klan to Justice*. New York: Weidenfeld, 1991. The former Klanwatch director explains new initiatives to disable the Klan, most of which have been effective.

Trelease, Allen W. *White Terror: The Ku Klux Klan Conspiracy and the Southern Reconstruction*. Baton Rouge: Louisiana State University Press, 1995. Scholarly study of the disruptive role of the Ku Klux Klan during post-Civil War Reconstruction.

Wade, Wyn Draig. *The Fiery Cross: The Ku Klux Klan in America*. New York: Simon & Schuster, 1987. Wade recounts the Klan's history and episodes of violence, revealing its legacy of race hatred.

See also: Dec. 8, 1863-Apr. 24, 1877: Reconstruction of the South; Mar. 3, 1865: Congress Creates the Freedmen's Bureau; Nov. 24, 1865: Mississippi Enacts First Post-Civil War Black Code; Apr. 9, 1866: Civil Rights Act of 1866; May and July, 1866: Memphis and New Orleans Race Riots; July 9, 1868: Fourteenth Amendment Is Ratified.

Related article in *Great Lives from History: The Nineteenth Century, 1801-1900:* Thaddeus Stevens.

1866-1867
North German Confederation Is Formed

In the wake of the Seven Weeks' War, the German states north of the Main River formed a confederation under the direction of Prussia. The confederation heralded a major step in the process of German unification, looking ahead to the creation of the German Empire in 1871.

Locale: Northern German states
Categories: Government and politics; expansion and land acquisition

Key Figures

Otto von Bismarck (1815-1898), minister-president of Prussia and later chancellor of the North German Federation

Napoleon III (Louis Napoleon Bonaparte; 1808-1873), emperor of the French, r. 1852-1870

William I (1797-1888), king of Prussia, r. 1861-1888, titular president of the North German Confederation, and later emperor of Germany, r. 1871-1888

Summary of Event

At the beginning of 1866, the German states were still organized as they had been at the Congress of Vienna of 1815, a loosely ordered group of sovereign states called the Germanic Confederation (*Deutsche Bund*). However, tension was building between the two major states of the Confederation, Austria and Prussia, and war broke out between them in June of 1866. Prussia, led by Minister-President Otto von Bismarck, quickly demonstrated its military superiority at the Battle of Königgrätz (also called Sadowa). The war ended in late July, earning it the name Seven Weeks' War, and a treaty was signed between the principals on August 23, 1866, the Peace of Prague.

Under the new arrangement, the Habsburg Dynasty of Austria agreed to withdraw its power from the rest of the German states and allow them to be organized by the Hohenzollern Dynasty of Prussia. The kingdom of Prussia itself annexed several formerly sovereign German states that had supported Austria in the Confederation, including Hanover, Hesse-Cassel, Nassau, and the free city of Frankfurt am Main. Prussia also annexed the Danish duchies of Schleswig and Holstein, where the Austro-Prussian conflict had begun. By 1867, all of the German states north of the Main River agreed to join Prussia in a new North German Confederation (*Norddeutsche Bund*). The three states south of the Main River, Baden, Württemberg, and Bavaria, remained separate as buffers between the Prussian-dominated north and Austria.

Bismarck's diplomatic and political maneuvering in founding the North German Confederation is generally conceded to have been brilliant, even by those who are critical of him. Internally, Bismarck manipulated nationalist and liberal political groups to bring them to his support. Many Germans of the middle classes had feared and hated him. His "blood and iron" policies, although authoritarian, had proven effective. Moreover, he supported the creation of a parliamentary body, the Reichstag, to be elected by universal equal male suffrage, a position considered relatively liberal for its day. Similarly, he brilliantly worked with King William I of Prussia, organizing the constitution to have William named "president" of the new confederation, a stepping stone to having him later crowned German emperor.

Externally, Bismarck offered a relatively generous peace to Austria in return for its cooperation in Prussia's unification plans for the rest of Germany. Dualistic tension between the Habsburgs of Austria and the Hohenzollerns of Prussia was nearly two centuries old. One of the major issues of the nineteenth century was whether Germany should be unified under the Habsburgs (including Austria) for a "Greater Germany," or under the Hohenzollerns (excluding Austria) for a "Smaller Germany." Bismarck's settlement encouraged Austria to accept Prussia's new role, and the two dynasties became close allies from 1866 through 1918. On the other hand, Bismarck effectively held the other powers, France, Great Britain, and Russia, aloof from the struggle.

Bismarck was particularly clever in manipulating Napoleon III. The French emperor was tantalized by Bismarck's suggestion that France might receive compensation in Luxembourg and the Rhineland as Prussia expanded, but Bismarck never allowed Napoleon to do so. Eventually, in 1870, Bismarck tricked Napoleon into declaring war on the North German Confederation, preparing the way for the German victories in the Franco-Prussian War (1870-1871). When faced with the French "threat," the three south German states of Baden, Württemberg, and Bavaria enthusiastically joined with the North German Confederation, bringing the confederation to its end with the formation of the German Empire in 1871.

Bismarck's plan for unity called for a much stronger union than the Germanic Confederation of 1815. Thus some historians have translated the German word *Bund* as "confederation" for the 1815 creation and as "federation" for the 1866 state. In the North German Confederation, King William I of Prussia held the executive authority as the "president." Acting through the chancellor he had appointed as the chief executive officer of the state (Bismarck), the king-president had authority over foreign affairs and the administration of the state; the king also had direct authority over the military forces of all the states when the country was at war.

There was a kind of upper house, the Federal Council (*Bundesrat*), which was superficially similar to the Diet of the old Germanic Confederation, being composed of representatives from the twenty-two states. Each state had representation based on its size, so Prussia easily dominated the Council. The lower house (Reichstag) was more-or-less freely elected, and it had significant legislative powers. However, Bismarck adjusted the constitution so that the Reichstag had few powers of the purse strings and therefore little influence over the executive branch of government. This constitutional system was transferred directly into the German Empire of 1871, merely changing the name of the "president" to "emperor."

SIGNIFICANCE

The constitution of the North German Confederation was much debated at the time, and it continued to show some signs of constitutional growth until its demise in the revolutions that closed World War I in 1918. It seems inaccurate and unfair, therefore, to dismiss it as "pseudo-constitutional absolutism," as some historians have done. Nevertheless, it was clearly designed by Bismarck as a means to preserve the power of the traditional elites in a newly national Germany. Although it lasted only four years, the North German Confederation was a major step in the development of the modern German state with all its faults, and those who created it bear significant responsibility for setting the constitutional agenda for twentieth century Germany.

—*Christopher J. Kauffman,*
updated by Gordon R. Mork

FURTHER READING

Craig, Gordon A. *The Politics of the Prussian Army, 1640-1945*. Oxford, England: Clarendon Press, 1955. Although dealing with a longer time period, the centerpiece of this book is the struggle of civil-military relations in Prussia during the Bismarck period.

Feuchtwanger, Edgar. *Bismarck*. London: Routledge, 2002. Concise biography, reassessing Bismarck's historical significance.

Friedjung, Heinrich. *The Struggle for Supremacy in Germany, 1859-1866*. New York: Russell & Russell, 1966. An interpretation of German unification from an Austrian point of view.

Gall, Lothar. Bismarck: *The White Revolutionary*. Translated by J. A. Underwood. 2 vols. Boston: Unwin Hyman, 1990. A political biography from a post-World War II West German historian.

Lerman, Katharine Anne. *Bismarck*. New York: Pearson Longman, 2004. One of the titles in the Profiles in Power series, this book focuses on Bismarck's exercise of power as a crucial means of understanding his personality and statecraft.

Medlicott, W. N. *Bismarck and Modern Germany*. London: English Universities Press, 1965. A standard British political biography of Bismarck providing a balanced treatment.

Plfanze, Otto. *Bismarck and the Development of Germany*. 3 vols. Princeton, N.J.: Princeton University Press, 1990. The major study of Bismarck and Bismarckian Germany in English. Volume 1, first published in 1963 and revised and republished in 1990, deals with the North German Confederation.

SEE ALSO: Jan. 1, 1834: German States Join to Form Customs Union; Mar. 3-Nov. 3, 1848: Prussian Revolution of 1848; Sept. 24, 1862: Bismarck Becomes Prussia's Minister-President; Feb. 1-Oct. 30, 1864: Danish-Prussian War; June 15-Aug. 23, 1866: Austria and Prussia's Seven Weeks' War; July 3, 1866: Battle of Könniggrätz; July 19, 1870-Jan. 28, 1871: Franco-Prussian War; Sept. 20, 1870-Jan. 28, 1871: Prussian Army Besieges Paris; 1871-1877: Kulturkampf Against the Catholic Church in Germany; Jan. 18, 1871: German States Unite Within German Empire; May 6-Oct. 22, 1873: Three Emperors' League Is Formed; Oct. 19, 1878: Germany Passes Anti-Socialist Law; May 20, 1882: Triple Alliance Is Formed.

RELATED ARTICLES in *Great Lives from History: The Nineteenth Century, 1801-1900:* Otto von Bismarck; Napoleon III.

April 9, 1866

CIVIL RIGHTS ACT OF 1866

After President Andrew Johnson vetoed the Civil Rights Act, Congress overrode his veto, and the new law joined the Thirteenth Amendment to the Constitution as the first federal legislation to enhance the rights of former slaves.

LOCALE: Washington, D.C.

CATEGORIES: Laws, acts, and legal history; civil rights and liberties; social issues and reform; government and politics

KEY FIGURES

Andrew Johnson (1808-1875), president of the United States, 1865-1869

Thaddeus Stevens (1792-1868), antislavery Republican congressman

Charles Sumner (1811-1874), Republican senator opposed to slavery

SUMMARY OF EVENT

At the end of the U.S. Civil War (1861-1865) lay the long road of Reconstruction. As early as 1863, President Abraham Lincoln had expressed a plan for Reconstruction after the Civil War. These plans required a loyalty oath and acceptance of emancipation from southern states desiring readmission to the union. It was not until after Lincoln's assassination that Reconstruction began in earnest.

Andrew Johnson, the seventeenth president of the United States, was vice president at the time of Lincoln's death in 1865. He inherited the problems of rebuilding the country after a lengthy civil war, which had ended in April, 1865. Johnson believed that the responsibility for developing Reconstruction policy should be handled by the president. Johnson's Reconstruction policy provided for a loyalty oath by citizens of states seeking readmission, revocation of the act of secession, abolition of slavery, and repudiation of the Confederate war debt. Several states—including Arkansas, Louisiana, and Tennessee—were readmitted in early 1865 without congressional approval. By the end of 1865, all states had been readmitted except Texas. This Reconstruction plan, however, failed to address the issues associated with the former slaves and their rights.

Congress believed that a debt was owed to the former slaves. In 1865, it created the Freedmen's Bureau as a temporary assistance program to address some of this debt. Food, medicine, schools, and land were made available to freedmen. Early in 1866, Congress passed a new Freedmen's Bureau Act and the first federal Civil Rights Act. Both were vetoed by President Johnson, because he feared that the legislation would extend to people of other races. He asked, "Was it sound to make all these colored peoples citizens?" Congress succeeded in quickly overturning these vetoes. J. W. Forney reported that the Senate, prodded by the abolitionist senator Charles Sumner, agreed to pass the vetoed legislation with a two-thirds majority on April 6, 1866. The House of Representatives, similarly led by Thaddeus Stevens, followed suit on April 9, 1866, the anniversary of the Confederacy's surrender.

During this same time, less positive events were affecting the free blacks. The year 1866 brought the founding of the Ku Klux Klan. African Americans were subjected to killings, beatings, and torture. This often occurred to keep them out of the political arena, which offered opportunities for power. Perhaps more detrimental to African Americans was the institutionalized racism of the black codes. Also known as black laws, black codes were legal enactments developed to regulate the actions and behaviors of freedmen in the South. These codes allowed legal marriage between African Americans, limited rights to testify in court, and limited rights to sue others.

The black codes also supervised the movements of African Americans in the South, restricted the assembly of unsupervised groups of black people, forbade intermarriage between people of color and whites, banned African Americans from carrying weapons, restricted African American children to apprenticeships that were nearly slavery, and forced black people into employment contracts that carried criminal penalties if abandoned. Violation of these codes often resulted in stiffer criminal punishment for African Americans than similar violations did for whites. Southern politicians reinstated by Andrew Johnson's Reconstruction policy were responsible for passage of these codes. It was in this environment that Congress found it necessary to develop legislation to combat the antiblack sentiment.

The Civil Rights Act of 1866 was the first federal law to protect the civil rights of African Americans. Section 1 of this provision established the right of citizenship to all persons born in the United States, without regard to previous servitude. As citizens, African Americans were granted the right to enter into and enforce contracts; inherit, lease, sell, hold, and convey property; give evidence in courts; benefit equally from all laws and ordinances; and be subject to punishments that were the same as given to whites for similar crimes.

Section 2 provided for misdemeanor penalties for anyone who deprived another of the rights afforded in section 1. Additional sections dealt with those who were granted the authority to prosecute and enforce this legislation. In order to ensure that this legislation would be enforced, Congress further established acts that were referred to as enforcement acts. Additionally, Congress drafted the Fourteenth Amendment to the Constitution of the United States to protect the freedmen's status.

Historically, the U.S. Constitution had been the source of civil liberties for citizens of the United States. The first eight amendments to the Constitution provided for a variety of freedoms. The First Amendment granted the freedoms of speech, religion, and assembly, as well as the right to petition the government for the redress of grievances. The Second, Third, and Fourth Amendments provided for a federal militia, the right to own private property, and the right to be protected from unreasonable seizures and searches of private property. The Fifth Amendment provided for the right of due process, ensured that one need not present evidence against oneself, and prevented double jeopardy in court (that is, one can-

Citizens outside the galleries of the U.S. House of Representatives celebrating the House's passage of the Civil Rights Bill in 1866. (Library of Congress)

CIVIL RIGHTS ACT OF 1866

The first section of the Civil Rights Act of 1866, reproduced below, established the civil rights due every United States citizen. The other nine sections of the law defined crimes against civil rights, designated punishments for those crimes, and established the jurisdiction of federal officers and federal courts to enforce the law.

An Act to protect all Persons in the United States in their Civil Rights, and furnish the Means of their Vindication.

Be it enacted by the Senate and House of Representatives of the United States of America in Congress assembled, That all persons born in the United States and not subject to any foreign power, excluding Indians not taxed, are hereby declared to be citizens of the United States; and such citizens, of every race and color, without regard to any previous condition of slavery or involuntary servitude, except as a punishment for crime whereof the party shall have been duly convicted, shall have the same right, in every State and Territory in the United States, to make and enforce contracts, to sue, be parties, and give evidence, to inherit, purchase, lease, sell, hold, and convey real and personal property, and to full and equal benefit of all laws and proceedings for the security of person and property, as is enjoyed by white citizens, and shall be subject to like punishment, pains, and penalties, and to none other, any law, statute, ordinance, regulation, or custom, to the contrary notwithstanding.

not be tried for the same offense twice). The Sixth through Eighth Amendments provide for further fair and equitable treatment by the judicial system. The purpose of various civil rights acts has been to extend these rights to all people, particularly those groups for whom these rights were originally withheld, and provide for their enforcement.

SIGNIFICANCE

In addition to its role in Reconstruction, the Civil Rights Act of 1866 set an important precedent for the enactment and protection of civil rights by statute rather than through the Constitution. Several civil rights acts have been passed in the United States since 1866. The Civil Rights Act of 1871 made it a crime to deny equal protection under the law through duress or force. Civil rights legislation passed in 1875, which guaranteed black people the right to use public accommodations, was ruled unconstitutional eight years after it was passed. This continued a downhill turn in the rights of African Americans, eventually leading to the Supreme Court's "separate but equal" decision in *Plessy v. Ferguson* (1896). This was the rule until 1954, when the Supreme Court determined that separate but equal was inherently unequal, in *Brown v. Board of Education of Topeka, Kansas*. It was not until 1964, and again in 1968, that any additional civil rights legislation was enacted at the national level. The 1964 and 1968 acts prohibited discrimination in employment, in use of public accommodations such as hotels, and in housing and real estate.

When President Andrew Johnson vetoed civil rights legislation aimed at granting rights to freed blacks, he began a two-year campaign that would end with an impeachment trial. Congressmen became increasingly concerned with Johnson's apparent plan to subvert and sabotage Reconstruction. His appointment of former Confederate leaders who had not vowed allegiance to the union, his lack of tact in dealing with those with whom he disagreed, his efforts to circumvent Congress and extend presidential powers, and his veto of important civil rights legislation resulted in a special meeting of the House of Representatives on March 2, 1867. Two measures were passed at this special session. One deprived Johnson of his responsibilities as commander in chief of the military; the second deprived him of the right to remove those with whom he disagreed from their cabinet positions. Finally, a resolution was passed to impeach Johnson for alleged violations of these measures. The senate failed to convict Johnson by one vote. However, Johnson was more compliant in the Reconstruction process after this trial.

—*Sharon L. Larson*

FURTHER READING

Abernathy, M. Glenn. *Civil Liberties Under the Constitution*. 5th ed. Columbia: University of South Carolina Press, 1989. Discusses the Bill of Rights and the historical relevance of civil rights legislation.

Asch, Sidney H. *Civil Rights and Responsibilities Under the Constitution*. New York: Arco, 1968. Analysis of amendments, such as the right-to-vote amendment, in light of ethical questions of the day.

Bardolph, Richard, ed. *The Civil Rights Record: Black Americans and the Law, 1849-1870*. New York: Thomas Y. Crowell, 1970. Presents legal documentation of the African American move toward legal equality.

Blaustein, Albert P., and Robert L. Zangrando, eds. *Civil Rights and the American Negro: A Documentary History*. New York: Trident Press, 1968. Discusses the civil rights legislation that has been passed specifically in relation to the end of slavery.

Chalmers, David M. *Hooded Americanism: The First Century of the Ku Klux Klan*. 3d ed. Durham, N.C.: Duke University Press, 1987. A historical and political examination of the Ku Klux Klan. Lends validity to the discussion of the civil rights and emancipation legislation of the post-Civil War era.

Franklin, John Hope, and Alfred A. Moss, Jr. *From Slavery to Freedom: A History of African Americans*. 8th ed. Boston: McGraw-Hill, 2000. Explores the progress of African Americans through slavery, emancipation, Reconstruction, and the early 1960's Civil Rights movement.

McKissack, Patricia, and Frederick McKissack. *The Civil Rights Movement in America, from 1865-Present*. 2d ed. Chicago: Children's Press, 1991. A discussion of the progress in civil rights since the end of the Civil War and slavery in the United States.

Trefousse, Hans Louis. *Impeachment of a President: Andrew Johnson, the Blacks, and Reconstruction*. New York: Fordham University Press, 1999. Focuses on the reasons why the Congress was unable to convict Johnson, the consequences of this acquittal, and the relationship of impeachment to the failure of Reconstruction. Trefousse argues that Johnson knowingly risked impeachment so he could thwart Reconstruction and maintain white supremacy in the South.

Weinstein, Allen, and Frank Otto Gatell. *Freedom and Crisis: An American History*. 2 vols. New York: Random House, 1978. Volume 2, chapter 24 discusses the dramatic events surrounding Lincoln's assassination, Johnson's impeachment trial, and congressional Reconstruction.

SEE ALSO: Jan., 1804: Ohio Enacts the First Black Codes; Mar. 6, 1857: *Dred Scott v. Sandford*; Apr. 12, 1861-Apr. 9, 1865: U.S. Civil War; Jan. 1, 1863: Lincoln Issues the Emancipation Proclamation; Dec. 8, 1863-Apr. 24, 1877: Reconstruction of the South; Mar. 3, 1865: Congress Creates the Freedmen's Bureau; Dec. 6, 1865: Thirteenth Amendment Is Ratified; 1866: Birth of the Ku Klux Klan; July 9, 1868: Fourteenth Amendment Is Ratified; Oct. 15, 1883: Civil Rights Cases; 1890: Mississippi Constitution Disfranchises Black Voters; May 18, 1896: *Plessy v. Ferguson*.

RELATED ARTICLES in *Great Lives from History: The Nineteenth Century, 1801-1900:* Andrew Johnson; Abraham Lincoln; Thaddeus Stevens; Charles Sumner.

May and July, 1866
MEMPHIS AND NEW ORLEANS RACE RIOTS

Economic and social disparities between black and white citizens combined with white resentment against the presence of federal troops and largely corrupt municipal police forces to create tensions and anger that led to lethal violence in Memphis and New Orleans that proved to be a harbinger of the violence that was to come during the Reconstruction era.

LOCALE: Memphis, Tennessee; New Orleans, Louisiana

CATEGORIES: Wars, uprisings, and civil unrest; civil rights and liberties

KEY FIGURES

Absalom Baird (1824-1905), military commander of federal troops in New Orleans

Andrew Johnson (1808-1875), president of the United States, 1865-1869

Philip H. Sheridan (1831-1888), military governor of Louisiana

George Stoneman (1822-1894), officer in charge of the East Tennessee military district

James Madison Wells (1808-1899), governor of Louisiana, a Union sympathizer

SUMMARY OF EVENT

Soon after Confederate general Robert E. Lee surrendered his army at Appomattox Courthouse in April, 1865, legislatures in the South passed a series of black codes. These laws were intended to maintain control over the lives of the newly freed African Americans and, in effect, keep them enslaved. For example, harsh vagrancy laws allowed police to arrest black people without cause and force them to work for white employers. President Abraham Lincoln's Emancipation Proclama-

White rioters shooting African Americans fleeing their burning homes in Memphis. (Library of Congress)

tion, on January 1, 1863, had, on paper, freed the slaves in the Confederate states, and the U.S. Congress formally abolished slavery throughout the nation with the Thirteenth Amendment to the Constitution in 1865. Congress then created the Freedmen's Bureau to assist the former slaves and was in the process of enacting, over the strong opposition of Lincoln's successor, President Andrew Johnson, a series of Reconstruction Acts intended to repeal the South's black codes. President Johnson resisted congressional attempts to admit African Americans to full citizenship, but Congress ultimately overrode his veto and took control of the Reconstruction program in the South.

Many former slaves, rejecting the life they had known on the plantation, moved to the cities of the South. Most were refugees without any economic resources, competing with Irish and German immigrants for scarce jobs in the war-torn South. Southern white Protestants feared both the new immigrants and the former slaves as threats to their social order.

Conditions in Memphis were especially volatile in May, 1866. The city had a reputation as a rowdy river town known for heavy drinking, gambling, prostitution, and fighting. In 1865, the black population of Memphis had rapidly increased to between twenty and twenty-five thousand people, many of whom lived in a run-down district near Fort Pickering. Memphis's white citizens were alarmed by incendiary newspaper accounts of crime and disorder caused by the black residents.

The Memphis police, mostly Irish immigrants, were corrupt and ill-trained and had a record of brutality toward black people. Added to this already explosive mixture was a body of federal troops, four thousand of whom were black soldiers stationed at Fort Pickering waiting to be mustered out of the army. The violence began on April 29, with a street confrontation between black soldiers and white policemen. On May 1, the violence escalated, with more serious fights breaking out between groups of soldiers and city police. By May 2, the mob included a number of people from the surrounding countryside as well as white citizens of Memphis. The mob rampaged through the black district of the city, attacking families, raping women, and burning homes. Civil authorities took no steps to curb the disturbance.

After a long delay, Major General George Stoneman, who was in command of local federal troops, brought the city under control. The three days of mob violence resulted in the deaths of forty-six African Americans and two white people. An estimated seventy to eighty other people were injured, and some ninety homes of black people, along with several African American churches and schools, were destroyed. Southern newspapers and civic officials blamed the black soldiers for the violence. A committee appointed by Congress, however, attributed the disturbances to the hatred of white people for the "colored race."

While the Memphis riots were the result of local conditions, the New Orleans disturbance of July 30 was caused by state politics and had national significance. Louisiana governor James Madison Wells, a Union sympathizer who needed to consolidate his power over the Confederates in the city and state, supported a plan to reassemble the state constitutional convention that had been disbanded in 1864. This convention, supported by Unionists, planned to gain votes by enfranchising African Americans. Sympathetic to Confederate politics, the city was armed, and the corrupt police force had a record of false arrests and mistreatment of free African Americans. The local newspapers, using highly emotional language, incited the fear of white citizens that African Americans would gain political control.

The commander of the federal troops, General Absalom Baird, should have foreseen the impending violence but apparently ignored the problem. When the delegates to the state convention began to assemble on July 30, fighting broke out between the city police and black marchers demonstrating in support of the right to vote. Delegates were dragged from the convention hall and assaulted by people in the street and by the police, who joined in the mob violence. The police attacks on African Americans were savage; the wounded were dragged to the city jail and beaten, and the bodies of the dead were mistreated. As the violence escalated, fueled by the drunkenness of the mob, African Americans were dragged from their homes and beaten.

The death toll in the one-day riot included thirty-four African Americans and three white people; approximately 136 people were injured. Although General Baird declared martial law, his action was too late. Several observers, including General Philip H. Sheridan, who was called in to restore order, described the mob violence as a "slaughter." As in the case of the Memphis riots, the overwhelming majority of the dead and injured were African Americans.

SIGNIFICANCE

The racial disturbances that erupted in Memphis and New Orleans were the result of economic, social, and political issues that troubled the nation during Reconstruction. Given the upheaval in the lives of defeated southerners after the Civil War (1861-1865), the racial disturbances are hardly surprising. In the simplest terms, one of the major tasks of Reconstruction was to assimilate the more than four million former slaves into U.S. society. A more complex view must consider the problems faced by the newly freed African Americans who had to achieve a new identity in a society that had allowed them almost no control over their own lives. White southerners had to live with the economic, social, and political consequences of defeat. The military occupation of the South by federal troops during Reconstruction after the Civil War angered southerners, who believed in their right to rebuild and rule their own society without interference from the North. The presence of federal troops—many of whom were African Americans—an armed citizenry, and the psychological difficulty of accepting the end of the world they had known created explosive conditions that erupted into violence.

While the Memphis riots were caused by local conditions, the disturbances in New Orleans had state and national political consequences. The Republican Party lost power in Louisiana, paving the way for Democratic control of the state. Precedents for the racial violence that would mark the years of Reconstruction and beyond had been established.

—*Marjorie J. Podolsky*

FURTHER READING

Foner, Eric. *Reconstruction: America's Unfinished Revolution, 1863-1877*. New York: Harper & Row, 1988. Analytical interpretation of the scholarly history of Reconstruction that combines older views with newer scholarship.

Franklin, John Hope. *Reconstruction: After the Civil War*. Chicago: University of Chicago Press, 1961. Presents a revised view that rejects the carpetbagger stereotype and argues for a more positive representation of African Americans during Reconstruction.

Franklin, John Hope, and Alfred A. Moss, Jr. *From Slavery to Freedom: A History of African Americans*. 8th ed. Boston: McGraw-Hill, 2000. Widely accepted record of the role of African Americans in U.S. history.

Litwack, Leon F. *Been in the Storm So Long: The Aftermath of Slavery*. New York: Vintage Books, 1980.

Provides a unique perspective, as it is based on the accounts of former slaves interviewed by the Federal Writers' Project in the 1930's.

Rable, George C. *But There Was No Peace: The Role of Violence in the Politics of Reconstruction.* Athens: University of Georgia Press, 1984. This survey of Reconstruction history includes detailed accounts of the events in Memphis and New Orleans that draw on contemporary newspaper articles to bring the story to life and connect the disturbances with similar events in the twentieth century.

Simpson, Brooks D. *The Reconstruction Presidents.* Lawrence: University Press of Kansas, 1998. Compares the role that Presidents Abraham Lincoln, Andrew Johnson, Ulysses S. Grant, and Rutherford B. Hayes played in post-Civil War Reconstruction policies.

Trelease, Allen W. *White Terror: The Ku Klux Klan Conspiracy and the Southern Reconstruction.* Baton Rouge: Louisiana State University Press, 1995. Scholarly study of the disruptive and violent role of the Ku Klux Klan during post-Civil War Reconstruction.

See also: Dec. 8, 1863-Apr. 24, 1877: Reconstruction of the South; Mar. 3, 1865: Congress Creates the Freedmen's Bureau; Nov. 24, 1865: Mississippi Enacts First Post-Civil War Black Code; Dec. 6, 1865: Thirteenth Amendment Is Ratified; 1866: Birth of the Ku Klux Klan; Apr. 9, 1866: Civil Rights Act of 1866; July 9, 1868: Fourteenth Amendment Is Ratified.

Related article in *Great Lives from History: The Nineteenth Century, 1801-1900:* Andrew Johnson.

May 10, 1866
Suffragists Protest the Fourteenth Amendment

Feeling betrayed by the explicit limitation of suffrage to male citizens in the text of what would become the Fourteenth Amendment to the U.S. Constitution, participants in the Eleventh National Woman's Rights Convention drafted a protest to Congress. Although that protest did not change the wording of the amendment, it contributed to eventual winning of universal suffrage in the United States.

Also known as: Eleventh National Woman's Rights Convention

Locale: Church of the Puritans, New York, New York

Categories: Civil rights and liberties; women's issues; laws, acts, and legal history

Key Figures

Elizabeth Cady Stanton (1815-1902), vice president of the National Woman's Rights Convention

Lucretia Mott (1793-1880), president of the convention

Susan B. Anthony (1820-1906), teacher and woman suffrage advocate

Horace Greeley (1811-1872), editor of the *New York Tribune*

Julia Ward Howe (1819-1910), writer, lecturer, and social reformer

Wendell Phillips (1811-1884), abolitionist and orator

Lucy Stone (1818-1893), speaker and agitator for women's rights

Summary of Event

On May 10, 1866, the Eleventh National Woman's Rights Convention was held at the Church of the Puritans in New York City's Union Square. The convention was called by such prominent activists for women's rights as Elizabeth Cady Stanton. Active for many years in abolitionist and reformist circles, Stanton had worked to abolish slavery, bring about labor reform, and secure equal property, labor, and voting rights for women. Many participants in the women's convention also had participated in the 1848 Women's Rights Convention at Seneca Falls, New York, and most of them were prominent in the movement to secure the rights of African Americans in the aftermath of the Civil War (1861-1865). Almost from the beginning, the battles to abolish slavery and to enfranchise women both legally and socially had gone hand in hand. In 1865, however, those goals began to diverge, and this divergence directly prompted the convention of 1866.

In the spring of 1865, the U.S. Congress began considering legislation for what would become the Fourteenth Amendment to the U.S. Constitution in 1868. Section 2 of that amendment specifically stated that if "the right to vote at any election . . . is denied to any male inhabitants . . . or in any way abridged," the representation of such states would be reduced proportionately. The inclusion of the word "male" allowed individual states to deny women the right to vote without penalty, leaving women no constitutional foundation for their claims to suffrage. As longtime workers for the emancipation of slaves, many women felt betrayed by the new legislation. Stanton was incensed that such a clause would be considered in a constitutional amendment and rallied the support of many followers to combat the implicitly sexist ideals represented by the new amendment.

Other prominent abolitionist leaders disagreed with Stanton's position. For example, Horace Greeley, the editor of the *New York Tribune* and one of the country's foremost antislavery leaders, believed that including the idea of the vote for women in the debate over the Fourteenth Amendment would only serve to make passage of voting rights for African Americans less likely. Likewise, Wendell Phillips, the leader of the American Anti-Slavery Society, believed that woman suffrage would never be approved in the political climate of the day, so it was unwise to endanger the passage of voting rights for black men by linking the two issues together. Neither of these men seemed moved by Stanton's arguments that half of the recently freed slaves were women, and that female slaves had been more abused by the slave system—particularly through sexual assault and the selling of their children—than had male slaves.

When the women's convention met in May of 1866, the participants were concerned with woman suffrage and women's rights in general, and specifically with the explicit limitation of suffrage to male citizens in the Fourteenth Amendment to the Constitution, which was then under consideration in Congress. The convention listed as its main aim the securing of "equal rights to all American citizens . . . irrespective of race, color, or sex."

Julia Ward Howe. (Library of Congress)

As the meeting convened, Stanton was elected president, but she declined, stating that she would prefer the first president to be Lucretia Mott, so that, in Stanton's words, "The office of President . . . might ever be held sacred in the memory that it had first been filled by one so loved and honored by all." Mott was a longtime worker for universal rights, a famous speaker on the abolitionist circuit, and a well-respected woman by all sides in the suffrage debate; she was elected president by unanimous vote. Although Mott was more than seventy years old and somewhat feeble, Mott agreed to accept the presidency, especially since Stanton, as vice president, would carry out most of the actual leadership duties. Mott praised the movement under way for being broad enough to encompass class, race, and sex, and reminded the participants that progress would likely be slow and ultimately would be advanced only by "the few in isolation and ridicule."

Mott's presidency of the convention was a brilliant compromise move on Stanton's part to head off a division between two rival groups in the convention's membership, one of which was led by Stanton herself and her longtime friend and colleague Susan B. Anthony. Stanton and Anthony were the most radical members of the group, who refused any compromise on the issues of universal suffrage and equality under the law. The other faction, led by Lucy Stone and Julia Ward Howe, was more conservative and willing to compromise on major issues. In later years, these two groups divided even further and worked separately for the passage of the Nineteenth Amendment and other legislation affecting women's rights.

The most significant outcome of the 1866 convention was the adoption of an address to Congress regarding the issues of African American male suffrage and woman suffrage. This document stated the majority opinion of the convention participants, including their belief that

> The only tenable ground of representation is universal suffrage, as it is only through universal suffrage that the principle of "Equal Rights to All" can be realized. All prohibitions based on race, color, sex, property, or education, are violations of the republican idea; and the various qualifications now proposed are but so many plausible pretexts to debar new classes from the ballot-box.

Although the 1866 convention's address was received by Congress, it did not alter the tenor of the congressional debate on the Fourteenth and Fifteenth Amendments, which were passed and eventually ratified by the states. The convention's seeds had been sown, however, and continued to bear fruit. In 1868, Stanton and Anthony founded the Woman Suffrage Association of America, which continued to work on both a state-by-state and a national basis for woman suffrage. Later called the National Woman Suffrage Association, this group also published a journal called *Revolution*, edited by Stanton and Anthony, that supported women's legislative causes. Another group, the American Woman Suffrage Association, worked for suffrage and other rights for women through its own magazine, *The Woman's Journal*, edited by Lucy Stone, Mary Livermore, and Julia Ward Howe.

SIGNIFICANCE

In August, 1920, the efforts of these and other women's rights organizations resulted in the ratification of the Nineteenth Amendment, granting all U.S. women the right to vote in all elections. The 1866 convention was instrumental in effecting the ratification of universal suffrage laws in the United States, by calling attention to the unfairness of the Fourteenth Amendment and similar laws that explicitly excluded women. The convention also helped organize and inspire former abolitionists to begin a new fight for women's freedom and rights, just as they previously had worked for the rights of former slaves. The ideals expressed in the address to Congress would later be rediscovered by twentieth century feminists and formed the foundation of the modern movement for full legal, social, and economic equity for women throughout the world.

—*Vicki A. Sanders*

FURTHER READING

Baker, Jean H, ed. *Votes for Women: The Struggle for Suffrage Revisited*. Oxford, England: Oxford University Press, 2002. Well-researched study of the history of the woman suffrage movement.

Banner, Lois W. *Elizabeth Cady Stanton: A Radical for Woman's Rights*. Boston: Little, Brown, 1980. Describes the atmosphere in which the 1866 women's rights convention took place and important events growing from it.

Blackwell, Alice Stone. *Lucy Stone: Pioneer of Woman's Rights*. 2d ed. 1930. Reprint. Charlottesville: University Press of Virginia, 2001. Alice Stone Blackwell, Lucy Stone's daughter, presents an insightful and personal view of her mother's personal and public life.

Buhle, Mari Jo, and Paul Buhle, eds. *The Concise History of Woman Suffrage: Selections from the Classic Work of Stanton, Anthony, Gage, and Harper*. Urbana: University of Illinois Press, 1978. Abridged edition of a six-volume work that includes the texts of the call for the convention and the address to Congress adopted by the 1866 women's rights convention.

Cromwell, Otelia. *Lucretia Mott*. Cambridge, Mass.: Harvard University Press, 1958. Describes Mott's lifelong work for abolition and women's rights, and explains why she was chosen as the convention's spokesperson.

Du Bois, Ellen Carol, ed. *Women Suffrage and Women's Rights*. New York: New York University Press, 1998. Diverse collection of essays that provide an excellent overview of the woman suffrage movement in the United States.

McFadden, Margaret, ed. *Women's Issues*. 3 vols. Pasadena, Calif.: Salem Press, 1997. Comprehensive reference work with numerous articles on woman suffrage, women's rights organizations, and related issues.

Schneir, Miriam, ed. *Feminism in Our Time: The Essential Writings, World War II to the Present*. New York: Vintage Books, 1994. Contains major writings by most of the participants in the convention; helps establish the historical context in which the convention took place.

Sherr, Lynn. *Failure Is Impossible: Susan B. Anthony in Her Own Words*. New York: Times Books, 1995. Excerpts from the speeches and letters of the leading figure of the nineteenth century women's rights movement, with a commentary on Anthony's life and career.

SEE ALSO: July 19-20, 1848: Seneca Falls Convention; May 28-29, 1851: Akron Woman's Rights Convention; Dec. 6, 1865: Thirteenth Amendment Is Ratified; July 9, 1868: Fourteenth Amendment Is Ratified; May, 1869: Woman Suffrage Associations Begin Forming; Dec., 1869: Wyoming Gives Women the Vote; June 17-18, 1873: Anthony Is Tried for Voting; Mar. 9, 1875: *Minor v. Happersett*; July 4, 1876: Declaration of the Rights of Women; Feb. 17-18, 1890: Women's Rights Associations Unite.

RELATED ARTICLES in *Great Lives from History: The Nineteenth Century, 1801-1900:* Susan B. Anthony; Matilda Joslyn Gage; Lucretia Mott; Elizabeth Cady Stanton; Lucy Stone.

June, 1866-1871
FENIAN RISINGS FOR IRISH INDEPENDENCE

The Irish revolutionary society known as the Fenian Brotherhood formed to liberate Ireland from its subjection to Great Britain. Organized simultaneously in Ireland and the United States, the Fenians sought a major rebellion in Ireland to topple the British government. Fenians in the United States planned to occupy British Canada to use as a bargaining chip to force Great Britain out of Ireland. Although initially unsuccessful, the movement kept alive the passion for freedom and independence in Ireland and sparked Canada's call for independence from Britain as well.

ALSO KNOWN AS: Irish Republican Brotherhood
LOCALE: Ireland; United States; Canada
CATEGORIES: Wars, uprisings, and civil unrest; government and politics

KEY FIGURES

James K. Stephens (1825-1901), founder of the Fenian movement in Ireland
John O'Mahony (1816-1877), founder of the Fenian movement in the United States
William R. Roberts (1830-1897), planner of Fenian invasion of Canada
Thomas W. Sweeny (1820-1892), military planner for invasion of Canada
John O'Neill (1834-1878), Fenian general

SUMMARY OF EVENT

The Fenian movement that arose in Ireland and the United States after 1850 sought the total elimination of British dominion in Ireland. Irish nationalists had long found much inspiration in the successful American and French Revolutions, and many were also radicalized by the harshness and injustices of British rule. Militant groups such as the Young Irelanders had periodically raised armed revolts, including the rising of 1848, although these were, without exception, crushed by the British army.

The Fenian rebellion promised more from the outset, however, because its strong anti-British message struck a chord not only in Ireland but also, and more so, among the large Irish Catholic immigrant communities in the United States. Memories of persecution were still vivid, as was the bumbling response of the British government to the horrors of the Great Irish Famine. Between 1845 and 1854 more than one million Irish died of disease and starvation while another million were forced overseas, mostly to the United States.

Two Irish nationalists, James Stephens and John O'Mahony, were most instrumental in the creation of the Fenian movement. Both had fought in the ill-fated Young Irelanders' insurrection of 1848. By the mid-1850's, Stephens in Dublin and O'Mahony in New York City were again plotting the overthrow of the British regime. In 1858 they joined in a transatlantic alliance to form a new society, called the Irish Republican Brotherhood (IRB). Later, O'Mahony discovered in Irish folklore the term "fenian," which he deemed more inspirational and fitting in describing the mission of the new organization. "Fenian" is derived from an old Gaelic word that referred to legendary pre-Christian Irish warriors pledged to die in defense of their land and its people. "Fenian" quickly became the most popular term for both the Irish and the U.S. wings of the organization.

Under Stephens's skillful leadership, Fenian "circles" were organized and, soon, membership rolls steadily expanded across Ireland. In the United States, meanwhile, substantial sums were raised to recruit, arm, and transport volunteers to Ireland to support the native Fenian militias in the struggle for liberation. Also, an estimated 150,000 Irish-born Union troops ready for demobilization and possible recruitment to the Fenian cause were available after April, 1865, the end of the U.S. Civil War.

In September, 1865, Stephens was in Dublin, ready to strike. He claimed that several thousand supporters in Ireland were waiting for word to rise up. At the last moment, a double agent serving as Stephens's aide tipped off the British, and on the night of September 14, 1865, troops raided Stephens's newspaper office and arrested most of his top deputies. Stephens himself escaped, but the Irish wing of the movement collapsed in disarray. If Ireland were to be liberated, it would have to come through the Fenian Brotherhood in the United States.

Meanwhile, O'Mahony, stunned at the collapse of the Fenian rising in Ireland, found his leadership of the U.S. wing under increasing criticism because of alleged timidity and indecision. When, in late 1865, O'Mahony continued to insist that the time was still not ripe, he was deposed from office and replaced by a fellow Irish-born militant named William R. Roberts. Roberts promptly named as his secretary of war a former Union general named Thomas W. Sweeny, whose motto was "deeds not words."

Roberts himself had already decided that the best way to free Ireland was to proceed not directly there but through British Canada. He regarded that land as thinly defended and very vulnerable. A successful Fenian conquest would be followed by the establishment of an Irish republican government-in-exile. Full British withdrawal from Ireland would be required as the price for the return of Canada. O'Mahony called the plan pure folly, but he could not change it.

Roberts charged Sweeny with devising the military strategy that would best achieve the conquest of Canada. Sweeny envisioned a multipronged assault that involved many thousands of Fenian troops attacking various points along a thousand-mile frontier that ran from the U.S. state of Vermont in the east to Michigan in the west. The ultimate goal was to capture the major Canadian cities of Toronto and Montreal, which would, in theory, end the war and prepare the way for the necessary deal with the British government. Sweeny was convinced, wrongly as it turned out, that Irish and French Catholics living in Quebec province would actively assist the Fenians.

At any rate, Sweeny's master plan could not be implemented. First, the Fenian leadership believed that a U.S. government bitterly resentful of England's tilt toward the Confederacy during the Civil War would not enforce a neutrality law that barred private military forces from invading another country from U.S. soil. President Andrew Johnson had privately assured the Fenians that he would recognize the "accomplished facts" of any such incursions. In fact, he intended to use the Fenian threat to Canada to pressure the British to pay large indemnities for damage done to Union forces during the Civil War by Confederate ships purchased in Britain.

Certainly, the U.S. government had no intention of starting a war with England over the Fenian incursions. Hence, when the first Fenian raids actually began in early June, 1866, U.S. troops intervened, blocking Fenian supply lines and arresting the leaders. The Fenians felt betrayed. Several Fenian leaders were jailed by U.S. authorities but quickly released in deference to the large Irish American vote that politicians had to respect.

The actual raids, three of which took place during the

Battle between John O'Neill's Fenian followers and a Canadian militia unit near Ridgeway, Ontario, on June 2, 1866. (Library of Congress)

first week of June, 1866, ended in disaster. Only the invasion led by Colonel John O'Neill had even temporary success. On June 2, O'Neill's force of six hundred Fenians decisively defeated a Canadian militia unit near Ridgeway, Ontario. However, when U.S. forces cut his supply lines and prevented reinforcements from reaching him, O'Neill returned to New York state, where he was promptly arrested and briefly jailed by U.S. authorities. In 1867, the Fenians in Ireland staged a series of unsuccessful rebellions that led to the capture, imprisonment, and execution of various local Fenian leaders.

Four years later in North America, the irrepressible O'Neill led four hundred men in an attack from Vermont into Quebec province, only to suffer a similar fate. This raid, and a smaller and also ineffective raid in 1871, marked the ignominious end of the Fenian venture into Canada. As a result, the movement lost much of its prestige among the Irish American populace and faded rapidly in influence.

A number of factors figured most prominently in the final outcome. First, the whole grandiose enterprise of the invasion of Canada was ill-conceived and mismanaged from the start. Another critical obstacle was the unwavering hostility of the Catholic Church because of the Fenian reliance on violence and its sometimes anticlerical outlook. Even more basic were the shifting policies of the U.S. government toward Fenian operations at the borders. Finally, there was the serious damage done to the Fenian cause by spies who often informed the British and Canadian authorities of prospective Fenian moves.

Significance

Although the Fenian rising in Ireland and the Fenian raids into Canada both failed miserably in their original purpose of liberating Ireland, they each left their marks on history. In Ireland the memory of Fenianism kept alive the passion for freedom and resistance to oppression. Further, the militant Fenian spirit, along with many former Fenians, lived on in fraternities like the Clan na Gael and, ultimately, in the Irish Republican Army (IRA), which early in the twentieth century blazed the path to Irish independence.

In Canada the Fenian raids had a major unintended consequence. The various Canadian provinces that comprised British North America displayed sharply contrasting characteristics that reflected a great diversity in geography, economy, and ethnic composition. As a result, most Canadians had traditionally preferred the loose political arrangement of the status quo, with its close dependence on the British crown.

The Fenian raids of 1866 shattered this equanimity. The threat of recurrent incursions from the United States helped to resurrect the long dormant idea of a confederation of Canada that would forge much closer ties among the provinces and provide more effectively for the common defense. In effect, the move to unite was born of the desire to survive. The British North America Act of 1867 created a Dominion of Canada, a confederation of provinces in a new nation whose government enjoyed much greater powers of self-determination within the British Commonwealth.

—*Donald Sullivan*

Further Reading

Moody, T. W. *The Fenian Movement*. Cork, Ireland: Mercier Press, 1968. Particularly valuable on the origins and early phases of the Fenian movement in Ireland.

Neidhardt, Wilfried. *Fenianism in North America*. University Park: Pennsylvania State University Press, 1975. Evenhanded account of the genesis, course, and impact of the movement as a whole. Frequent use of contemporary newspaper articles provides a vivid sense of immediacy and of the shifting forces of the Fenian cause.

Rafferty, Olivier. "Fenianism in North America in the 1860's: The Problems of Church and State." *History* 84 (1999): 257-277. Focuses on the significant role played by the U.S. and Canadian Catholic bishops in diminishing the appeal of Fenianism to their Irish immigrant populations.

Steward, Patrick J. "Erin's Hope: Fenianism in the North Atlantic, 1858-1876." Unpublished Ph.D. dissertation, University of Michigan, 2003. This work vividly relates events in North America to the broader political context in Ireland.

See also: 1829-1836: Irish Immigration to Canada; May 6-July 5, 1844: Anti-Irish Riots Erupt in Philadelphia; 1845-1854: Great Irish Famine; July 1, 1867: British North America Act; Sept.-Nov., 1880: Irish Tenant Farmers Stage First "Boycott"; May 2, 1882: Kilmainham Treaty Makes Concessions to Irish Nationalists; Dec. 6, 1884: British Parliament Passes the Franchise Act of 1884; June, 1886-Sept. 9, 1893: Irish Home Rule Debate Dominates British Politics.

Related articles in *Great Lives from History: The Nineteenth Century, 1801-1900:* William Ewart Gladstone; John Philip Holland; Daniel Mannix; Daniel O'Connell; Charles Stewart Parnell.

June 13, 1866-November 6, 1868
RED CLOUD'S WAR

In one of the most successful episodes of Native American resistance to white encroachments, the Sioux chief Red Cloud organized a pantribal coalition that forced the federal government to abandon its forts along the newly opened Bozeman Trail. However, Red Cloud's success merely hastened the process of forcing his people onto reservations.

ALSO KNOWN AS: Bozeman Trail War
LOCALE: Powder River country, Dakota Territory
CATEGORIES: Indigenous people's rights; wars, uprisings, and civil unrest

KEY FIGURES

John M. Bozeman (1835-1867), settler who laid out the route that started the war
Red Cloud (1822-1909), Sioux chief who led the opposition to the Bozeman Trail
Patrick E. Connor (fl. mid-nineteenth century), U.S. Army general
Henry Beebee Carrington (1824-1912), builder and commander of forts on the Bozeman Trail
William Judd Fetterman (c. 1833-1866), army captain killed with his entire command at Fort Kearny
Crazy Horse (1842?-1877), key Sioux strategist in the Fetterman battle

SUMMARY OF EVENT

In 1862, John M. Bozeman sought a more direct route to connect the newly discovered goldfields around Virginia City, Montana, with the east. After leaving Virginia City, he located a pass that led him to the headwaters of the Yellowstone River, then went southeast, along the eastern flank of the Bighorn Mountains, where he traversed the headwaters of the Bighorn, Tongue, and Powder Rivers. Continuing to the southeast, he intersected the Oregon Trail along the North Platte River seventy miles west of Fort Laramie. This new trail, which became known by Bozeman's name, cut directly through the best hunting grounds of the Teton Dakota Sioux—Red Cloud's people.

The Powder River country that the new Bozeman Trail traversed was a hunter's paradise, home to the great northern bison herd. Guaranteed to the Sioux by the Fort Laramie Treaty of 1851, it was the site of Sioux people's free-ranging lifestyle, and the Sioux meant to keep it. However, in responding to growing pressure from miners and settlers, the federal government was keenly interested in securing the Bozeman Trail but was uncertain of the best method to achieve that goal. Using force to subjugate or exterminate native peoples was a popular idea in the West. Alternatively, an approach based on peace through justice gained support, especially in the East after the Civil War (1861-1865), when humanitarians who previously had been devoted to the abolition of slavery turned their attention to the so-called Indian problem. This East-West rift led to a schizophrenic policy toward American Indians, in which both approaches were tried, often at the same time.

Pursuing an aggressive policy, the federal government built a string of three forts along the Bozeman Trail. Fort Reno was the first, built seventy miles up the Bozeman Trail in late summer of 1865 by General Patrick E. Connor. Best known for his slaughter of 273 Paiutes at Bear Creek in 1863, Connor issued the directive to "accept no peace offers and kill any male over twelve." However, with the help of his Cheyenne and Arapaho allies, Red Cloud mauled Connor's columns. The columns then withdrew, but the fort remained. On July 10 of the following year, Colonel Henry Beebee Carrington established Fort Phil Kearny forty miles north of Fort Reno at the fork of the Piney Creeks. In early August, he built Fort C. F. Smith ninety miles beyond that.

The peace process was tried also. On October 28, 1865, a commission under Governor Newton Edmunds of Dakota Territory announced peace with the Sioux, producing a treaty signed by chiefs already friendly to the settlers. None of the Powder River chiefs signed, however, as they were all fighting Connor. Red Cloud did go to Fort Laramie the next spring to discuss peace, trade, and Fort Reno. In the middle of peace negotiations, Colonel Carrington arrived at Fort Laramie on June 13, 1866, in a masterpiece of bad timing. He had seven hundred troops, more than two hundred wagons, and orders to build his Bozeman forts. Red Cloud then accused the commissioner, E. B. Edwards, of having already stolen what they were negotiating. Red Cloud and his entire camp were gone the next morning.

Meanwhile, Edwards collected the signatures of some other chiefs and blithely informed Washington that a satisfactory treaty had been concluded with the Sioux. While Colonel Carrington went on to build his forts, Red Cloud was galvanizing opposition with stunning oratory:

Red Cloud and other Sioux and Arapaho leaders in an undated picture of an Indian delegation. From left to right, seated: Yellow Bear, Red Cloud, Big Road, Little Wound, Black Crow; standing: Red Bear, Young Man Afraid of His Horse, Good Voice, Ring Thunder, Iron Crow, White Tail, and Young Spotted Tail. (Library of Congress)

> Hear Ye, Dakotas! . . . before the ashes of the council fire are cold, the Great Father is building his forts among us. You have heard the sound of the white soldier's axe upon the Little Piney. His presence here is an insult and a threat. It is an insult to the spirits of our ancestors. Are we then to give up their sacred graves to be plowed for corn? Dakotas, I am for war!

After Red Cloud assembled a coalition of three thousand warriors, his war against the Thieves' Road began in earnest.

Within days of their completion, Carrington's forts were beset with unrelenting guerrilla warfare. During the first five weeks, the colonel reported thirty-three whites killed. By December, ninety-six soldiers and fifty-eight civilians had been killed, many were wounded, and nearly one thousand oxen, cows, mules, and horses had been lost. Carrington reported fifty-one separate attacks on Fort Kearny alone.

The worst loss came on December 21, 1866, when the command of Captain William Judd Fetterman was completely annihilated. Having once boasted that he could ride through the whole Sioux nation with eighty good men, Fetterman led exactly eighty soldiers out of Fort Kearny to relieve an embattled party of woodcutters. In direct violation of Carrington's orders not to ride out of view of the fort, Fetterman could not resist chasing Chief Crazy Horse, who, acting as a decoy, lured Fetterman's contingent into an ambush by two thousand Sioux, Cheyennes, and Arapahos. In the ensuing Battle of One Hundred Slain, Fetterman's arrogance handed the U.S. Army its worst defeat in the Plains Wars to that date.

On August 1, 1867, the Cheyennes attacked hay cutters at Fort Smith. On the next day, Red Cloud's Sioux attacked a woodcutters' camp at Fort Kearny. Although these Hayfield and Wagon Box fights were standoffs, the federal government began to understand that the treaties negotiated by Edmunds and Taylor were meaningless. John Bozeman himself had been caught in 1867 by Blackfoot warriors and killed on his own road.

In 1867, Red Cloud rebuffed major peace initiatives from the federal government. He persistently refused to sign anything until the forts were gone. Concerned about the cost of a full military campaign and the safety of the new railroads then moving westward, Congress decided to concede the Bozeman overland route. On July 29, 1868, soldiers left Fort Smith. Fort Kearny was abandoned a month later, and Fort Reno a few days after that. Jubilant Indian warriors then burned the three forts to the ground, and the Bozeman Trail was closed. On November 6, 1868, Red Cloud signed the Sioux Treaty of 1868 at Fort Laramie. Red Cloud had won his war.

In 1870, Red Cloud and other Sioux were invited to Washington, D.C., to discuss the treaty. There Red Cloud heard for the first time of provisions calling for permanent Sioux settlements on a reservation. Although deeply upset, he was persuaded to make an address at the Cooper Institute in New York City before an audience of social reformers. At noon on June 16, he began with a prayer to the Almighty Spirit, then recited wrongs done to his people, and asked for justice. Praised for its piety, charisma, and sincerity, the speech was an immense success.

Significance

Red Cloud's growing influence with the eastern peace and reform circles allowed him to extract future concessions for his people from the government. The treaty articles that had not been explained to him, however, hastened the movement of the Sioux toward becoming "reservation Indians." Nevertheless, the success of Red Cloud's implacable opposition to the Bozeman Trail has made his name an appropriate eponym for Red Cloud's War.

—*Gary A. Olson*

Further Reading

Allen, Charles Wesley. *Autobiography of Red Cloud: War Leader of the Oglalas*. Edited by R. Eli Paul. Helena, Mont.: Montana Historical Society Press, 1997. First publication of an autobiography narrated by Red Cloud in 1893, a quarter of a century after he waged war over the Bozeman Trail.

Armstrong, Virginia Irving, comp. *I Have Spoken: American History Through the Voices of the Indians*. Chicago: Swallow Press, 1971. Collection of Native American orations that includes Red Cloud's 1866 Powder River exhortation and his 1870 Cooper Institute speech in New York City.

Brown, Dee. *Bury My Heart at Wounded Knee*. New York: Holt, Rinehart and Winston, 1970. Impassioned overview of the nineteenth century wars from the Native American point of view that includes a chapter on Red Cloud's War.

Goodyear, Frank H., III. *Red Cloud: Photographs of a Lakota Chief*. Lincoln: University of Nebraska Press, 2003. Collection of more than eighty photographs of Red Cloud by Mathew Brady, Edward Curtis, and others. Red Cloud allowed himself to be photographed many times because he believed that photographs helped him serve as a mediator between his people and the federal government.

Hyde, George E. *Red Cloud's Folk: A History of the Oglala Sioux Indians*. Rev. ed. Norman: University of Oklahoma Press, 1976. Originally published in 1937 and revised in 1957, this book is considered to be a definitive history of the Oglala Sioux. It includes extensive background for the events on the Bozeman Trail.

Lazarus, Edward. *Black Hills, White Justice: The Sioux Nation Versus the United States, 1775 to the Present*. New York: HarperCollins, 1991. History of Sioux struggles against the federal government that includes the full text of the Fort Laramie Treaty of 1868.

McDermott, John D. "Price of Arrogance: The Short and Controversial Life of William Judd Fetterman." *Annals of Wyoming* 63, no. 2 (Spring, 1991): 42-53. A look at Fetterman's character and its fatal consequences.

________, ed. "Wyoming Scrapbook: Documents Relating to the Fetterman Fight." *Annals of Wyoming* 63, no. 2 (Spring, 1991): 68-72. Gives details of the most significant Army loss in the war.

Olson, James C. *Red Cloud and the Sioux Problem*. Lincoln: University of Nebraska Press, 1965. The best and most complete account of Red Cloud. Except for some background information on the Lakota and Red Cloud's early life, it begins with the period immediately after the Civil War and ends with the death of Red Cloud in 1909.

See also: Aug. 17, 1862-Dec. 28, 1863: Great Sioux War; Nov. 29, 1864: Sand Creek Massacre; Dec. 21, 1866: Fetterman Massacre; 1876-1877: Sioux War; June 15-Oct. 5, 1877: Nez Perce War; Dec. 29, 1890: Wounded Knee Massacre.

Related articles in *Great Lives from History: The Nineteenth Century, 1801-1900:* Crazy Horse; Red Cloud.

June 15-August 23, 1866
AUSTRIA AND PRUSSIA'S SEVEN WEEKS' WAR

In the course of the Seven Weeks' War, Prussia defeated Austria's forces and those of her German allies. As a result, Prussia acquired considerable territory through annexations and henceforth played a dominant role in the new North German Confederation. In return for supporting the Prussian cause, Italy received the province of Venetia from Austria.

ALSO KNOWN AS: Autro-Prussian War
LOCALE: Langensalza, Germany; Custozza, Italy; Eastern Bohemia (now in the Czech Republic)
CATEGORIES: Wars, uprisings, and civil unrest; diplomacy and international relations

KEY FIGURES

Otto von Bismarck (1815-1898), prime minister of Prussia, 1862-1871, and later chancellor of the German Empire, 1871-1890
Helmuth von Moltke (1800-1891), chief of the Prussian general staff
Ludwig August von Benedek (1804-1881), commander in chief of the Austrian North Army
Francis Joseph I (1830-1916), emperor of Austria, r. 1848-1916
Napoleon III (1808-1873), emperor of France, r. 1852-1870
Frederick William (1831-1888), Prussian crown prince, 1861-1888, and later Emperor Frederick III of Germany, r. 1888
Eduard Vogel von Falkenstein (1797-1885), Prussian general

SUMMARY OF EVENT

Following the end of the Danish-Prussian War over control of the two provinces of Schleswig and Holstein, Austria and Prussia agreed in the Convention of Gastein (1865) to hold joint sovereignty over those provinces, with the understanding that Austria would administer Holstein while Prussia would control Schleswig. However, Otto von Bismarck, the minister-president (prime minister) of Prussia, immediately began to prepare the ground for a conflict with Austria. Already on friendly terms with Russia, Bismarck obtained the neutrality of France in the coming conflict during a meeting with Emperor Napoleon III by hinting at some territorial compensation along the Rhine. In April of 1866, Bismarck got Italy to promise to attack Austria should an Austro-Prussian war break out within three months. He promised Italy Venetia in return. Thus, by mid-1866, Austria was left with allies only in the German Confederation.

When an Austrian violation of the Gastein Convention provided a pretext, Prussian troops occupied Holstein. On June 15, 1866, the German Confederation under Austrian prompting voted for immediate military action against Prussia. In response, Bismarck dissolved the German Confederation, and armies began to move in three theaters of war: Germany, Italy, and Eastern Bohemia.

While most contemporaries expected the war to last for some time, in part because the opposing forces were numerically about even, the rapid movement of the Prussian forces came as a surprise to Austria. The war plans worked out by General Helmuth von Moltke depended heavily on Prussia's extensive rail network in combination with the telegraph. The Prussian armies were moved separately by rail to the theater of war to be united only shortly before battle. Moltke, assisted by an efficient general staff, could coordinate all troop movements by telegraph from Berlin.

On June 16, the Prussian West Army under General Eduard Vogel von Falkenstein invaded Hanover and Electoral Hesse and, after some initial setbacks, gained the upper hand during the Battle of Langensalza (June 27-29). After forcing the Hanoverians to surrender, the Prussian forces turned south toward Austria's German allies. At the same time, three Prussian armies began to move south toward Saxony and Bohemia: the Army of the Elbe under General Karl Herwarth von Bittenfeld occupied Dresden and, like the First Army under Friedrich Karl, the Iron Prince, also moved south, pursuing the retreating Saxons. The Second Prussian Army, commanded by Crown Prince Frederick William, moved south through Silesia and entered Bohemia through passes in the Riesengebirge.

Field Marshal August Ludwig von Benedek, the Austrian commander of the North Army, was, unlike the relatively inexperienced Moltke, a seasoned veteran of many campaigns. However, he lacked Moltke's organizational and war-planning skills. Having spent most of his time in northern Italy, he was unfamiliar with the Bohemian terrain and was hampered by an inferior railroad system, serious command problems, poorly trained and often incompetent staff officers, and a general staff that was one in name only. His forces were further handicapped by old-fashioned muzzle-loading rifles, while the Prussians enjoyed breech-loading guns that enabled them to deliver a much greater rate of fire. A further challenge facing Austrian commanders stemmed from the fact that many of the troops, often poorly educated and drawn from all parts of the multilingual Habsburg empire, frequently could not follow the orders of their officers.

The Austrians possessed excellent artillery, however, and their superior cavalry fought with great distinction. In the Battle of Custozza (June 24), an Austrian army under Archduke Albert defeated a numerically larger Italian force. Later, in the naval Battle of Lissa (July 20), an Austrian naval squadron under Admiral Wilhelm von Tegetthoff sank three Italian ironclads, whereupon the Italians left the scene. The Bohemian theater of war, however, presented some serious challenges for Benedek. Prior to the decisive Battle of Könniggrätz on July 3, a number of smaller engagements revealed the strengths and weaknesses of the opposing armies.

In the Battle of Nachod on June 27, twenty-one thousand Austrians suffered a disastrous defeat at the hands of ten thousand Prussians, in large part because many of the Austrian troops had not rested or eaten for twenty-four hours, while their Prussian opponents were rested and ready to do battle. However, in the Battle of Trautenau (Trutnov) on the same day, the Prussians suffered a defeat that Moltke attributed to a lack of reconnaissance and poor leadership. In the Battle of Skalitz (June 28), the Austrian side was hampered by confusion, insubordination, and the incompetent leadership of Archduke Leopold. The Austrians suffered more than five thousand casualties, while Prussian losses came to about one-fourth of that number. Another Austrian defeat on the following day at Gitschin (Jicin) was due in large part to communication and command problems that prompted Benedek at one point to ask Francis Joseph I, the Habsburg emperor, to make peace with Prussia at once. Francis Joseph refused.

Realizing the hopelessness of the situation after the Battle of Könniggrätz, an anxious Napoleon III sought to mediate and bring about an armistice as early as July 5.

King William leading Prussian troops in the decisive Battle of Könniggrätz. (Francis R. Niglutsch)

Prussian armies, however, continued their drive south in preparation for crossing the Danube River and marching on Vienna. Eventually, the parties agreed in the Armistice of Nikolsburg on July 26 that Austria would relinquish its role in German affairs and consent to the creation of a North German Confederation under the leadership of Prussia. The South German states would be allowed to retain their independence. The parties to the armistice also agreed to Prussia's direct annexation of Schleswig, Holstein, Hanover, Frankfurt, Electoral Hesse, and Nassau.

Bismarck, opposed to the wishes of his king, the belligerent William I, insisted that no Austrian lands be annexed, although he demanded that Austria and her southern German allies pay cash indemnities. However, when Napoleon III presented his claims for compensation, Bismarck rejected his requests out of hand. The provisions of the Armistice of Nikolsburg were confirmed by the Treaty of Prague on August 23, which formally ended the Seven Weeks' War. A formal peace treaty between Austria and Italy was signed in Vienna on October 12. Austria agreed to the transfer of Venetia to Italy and officially recognized the Kingdom of Italy.

SIGNIFICANCE

The Seven Weeks' War resulted in a major realignment of political, economic, and military power in central Europe, establishing Prussia as the dominant nation in the German-speaking lands. Austria, having been effectively removed from German affairs, was compelled to look eastward and engage in long-overdue internal structural reforms. Designed to meet the demands of its restless subject nationalities, those reforms led to the Austrian Ausgleich in 1867. This political reorganization created the Austro-Hungarian Empire, a dual monarchy consisting of two independent states with one ruler who would be both emperor of Austria and king of Hungary.

Prussia's substantial territorial annexations after the war established a physical link between the eastern and the western halves of the kingdom. The addition of these rich lands with a population of some seven million people enabled Prussia to triple the size of its armed forces. The formation of the Prussian-dominated North German Confederation extended Prussia's control to the River Main. The southern German states, already tied to Prussia in a customs union, entered into military alliances with Prussia, thereby providing Bimarck with the tools to pursue his next objective, the unification of Germany under Prussian leadership. Supported by the rising tide of German nationalism and confident of Napoleon III's diplomatic isolation, Bismarck pursued a course of action that culminated in the Franco-Prussian War, the defeat of France, and the proclamation of a German Empire in January of 1871 in the Palace of Versailles.

—*Helmut J. Schmeller*

FURTHER READING

Bucholz, Arden. *Moltke and the German Wars, 1864-1871*. New York: Palgrave, 2001. Focuses on Moltke's planning and execution of the Austro-Prussian conflict. Detailed information.

Carr, William. *The Origins of the Wars of German Unification*. New York: Longman, 1991. Offers balanced treatment of the war of 1866, including its economic and ideological aspects. Maps.

Craig, Gordon A. *The Battle of Koeniggraetz. Prussia's Victory over Austria, 1866*. Philadelphia: J. B. Lippincott, 1964. Judicious and well-written analysis of the conflict in Bohemia. Maps.

Showalter, Dennis E. *Railroads and Rifles. Soldiers, Technology and the Unification of Germany*. New York: Archon Books, 1975. Discusses impact of railroads and of improvements in weapons technology on Prussia's military efficiency.

Wawro, Geoffrey. *The Austro Prussian War. Austria's War with Prussia and Italy in 1866*. Cambridge, England: Cambridge University Press, 1996. Comprehensive study, based on archival research. Maps and illustrations.

SEE ALSO: July 11, 1859: Napoleon III and Francis Joseph I Meet at Villafranca; Sept. 24, 1862: Bismarck Becomes Prussia's Minister-President; Feb. 1-Oct. 30, 1864: Danish-Prussian War; 1866-1867: North German Confederation Is Formed; July 3, 1866: Battle of Könniggrätz; May 29, 1867: Austrian Ausgleich; July 19, 1870-Jan. 28, 1871: Franco-Prussian War; Jan. 18, 1871: German States Unite Within German Empire; May 20, 1882: Triple Alliance Is Formed.

RELATED ARTICLES in *Great Lives from History: The Nineteenth Century, 1801-1900:* Otto von Bismarck; Francis Joseph I; Napoleon III.

July 3, 1866
BATTLE OF KÖNNIGGRÄTZ

The Battle of Könniggrätz was a decisive Prussian victory in the Seven Weeks' War between Austria and Prussia. Austria's loss forced it to sue for peace and acquiesce to Prussia's demands for suzerainty over the German states, while excluding Austria from the North German Confederation. The battle also demonstrated the superiority of rapid-fire, breech-loading rifles, rifled artillery, and open, flexible tactics.

ALSO KNOWN AS: Battle of Sadowa
LOCALE: Between Sadowa and Könniggrätz, Bohemia (now Sadova and Hradec Králové, Czech Republic)
CATEGORY: Wars, uprisings, and civil unrest

KEY FIGURES

Helmuth von Moltke (1800-1891), Prussian chief of staff
Ludwig August von Benedek (1804-1881), Austrian commander of the Army of the North
Frederick William (1831-1888), Prussian crown prince, 1861-1888, and later Emperor Frederick III of Germany, r. 1888
Karl Eberhard Herwarth von Bittenfeld (1796-1884), Prussian commander of the Army of the Elbe
Eduard von Fransecky (1807-1890), Prussian commander of the Seventh Division

SUMMARY OF EVENT

In June of 1866, Prussia maneuvered Austria into a war for dominance of the German states. Austria was able to achieve some successes in the brief war, now known as the Seven Weeks' War, especially in battles against the Prussians' Italian allies. The Austrians struggled, however, in the Bohemian theater. From June 27 to June 29, they lost three battles in three days at Nachod, Trautenau (Trutnov), and Gischin (Jicin), respectively. By early July, Austria was at a clear disadvantage in the war, both militarily and diplomatically.

Prussian Chief of Staff Helmuth von Moltke seized the initiative, wishing to finish off his opponents. He sent three widely placed armies into Bohemia to converge quickly on Austrian forces before they could respond. This stratagem risked each army being defeated separately, but Austrian North Army commander General Ludwig August von Benedek failed to respond decisively. Instead, he played right into Moltke's hand by massing his forces north of Vienna and moving slowly northwest toward Josephstadt while he gathered reserves and supplies.

The Prussian forces converged quickly, and Benedek found his army enclosed by the enemy in a great arc from the northeast to the west. He retreated southward on July 1 to a position between Sadowa on the Bistritz River and Könniggrätz on the River Elbe.

Benedek's Army of the North consisted of some 195,000 Austrians and 25,000 Saxons in eight corps, with five cavalry divisions and more than 700 guns. They deployed on a four-mile front facing the Bistritz River on a series of low hills running northeast to southwest. Benedek anchored his right flank by placing troops in the villages of Lipa and Chlum, which sat on hills astride the main road from Sadowa to Könniggrätz. Behind them, he placed two more corps of troops. He further spread troops in the center and left positions, while behind his left center he placed three corps, most of which had been mauled in previous battles. One cavalry division watched each flank, with the rest of the cavalry held in reserve.

Moltke accompanied the Prussian forces that approached Benedek from the northwest, consisting of the First Army of six infantry and two cavalry divisions and the Army of the Elbe of three infantry divisions, a total force of 140,000 troops, including some 400 artillery pieces. Approaching Benedek's right flank from the north was the Second Army of some 115,000 troops and 300 guns, commanded by Crown Prince Frederick William.

Moltke initially feared that Benedek had fallen back behind the Elbe River and its forts, which would have been a strong defensive position. He planned to instruct the Second Army to cross the Elbe in order to outflank the Austrians. To Moltke's delight, however, he received intelligence on July 2 that Benedek had placed his back to the Elbe, exposing his right flank. Moltke quickly sent notice to the crown prince to turn his army southward and strike the exposed Austrian right flank. In the meantime, Moltke intended that the First Army should advance in a frontal assault to hold the Austrian Army in place, drawing in their reserves. To the south, he would have the Army of the Elbe under General Karl Eberhard Herwarth von Bittenfeld cross the Bistritz River and push back the Saxons holding Benedek's left flank.

In short, with the Second Army attacking the exposed Austrian right flank and the Army of the Elbe turning the Austrian left flank, Moltke planned to surround and annihilate Benedek's army. His plan relied on delicate

The Battle of Könniggrätz. From a painting by Anton von Werner (1843-1915). (P. F. Collier and Son)

timing, however, and depended as well on the Prussian commanders understanding Moltke's strategy. When the battle began on the morning of July 3, 1866, the Second Army was still some twenty miles away. It would have to move quickly to fulfill its role in the conflict.

Benedek's deployment invited disaster. He had placed his back against an unfordable river with few bridges, allowing little room for retreat. His troops were in an inverted "V" formation that practically invited the enemy to push in his flanks. He also failed to occupy several key positions. On his right front was a wood, the Swiepwald, that could threaten his right flank, while on his left, he had only a small force holding the forward crossing over the Bistritz River, three miles in front of the Saxon positions.

On the morning of July 3, Bittenfeld's army overcame the small force on the Bistritz River and began moving on Benedek's left flank. Around 8:00 A.M., the Prussian First Army's artillery began exchanging fire with the Austrians' artillery in a terrific cannonade. Around 9:00 A.M., the Prussian First Army began its advance along the Bistritz River line. The Austrian artillery was rifled, with superior range and accuracy over the smoothbores that composed much of the Prussian artillery. As a result, the Prussians were punished terribly. Conversely, Austrian troops were devastated by Prussian infantry armed with breech-loading rifles that had a greater rate of fire (five to six rounds a minute) than the Austrian muzzle-loading rifles (two to three rounds a minute). Austrian tactics emphasized bayonet attacks in densely massed columns, presenting ideal targets for Prussian fire. Prussian infantry tactics, on the other hand, emphasized gaining fire superiority utilizing skirmishers and open order formations.

Around 8:30 A.M., one of Benedek's corps commanders decided on his own initiative to occupy the Swiepwald Wood and turn the Prussian left flank on the Bistritz River before the Prussian Second Army could arrive. The Prussian Seventh Division under Lieutenant General Eduard von Fransecky counterattacked, and there began a bloody seesaw battle in the Swiepwald Wood. It lasted all day, with Fransecky barely holding on against superior Austrian numbers. Moltke refused him reinforcements, as he wished to retain his reserves while the Austrians expended theirs. Fransecky understood Moltke's plan, and his dogged defense of the wood was crucial. If Benedek had launched a general attack on the Prussian First Army at that time, he could have crushed it before the Second Army arrived, but he refrained.

About midday, the Prussian Second Army began to arrive and put pressure on the Austrian right flank. Austrian troops in the rear were stunned by the unexpected arrival of the Second Army and withdrew across the Elbe. In the south, the Saxons attempted to drive back

Bittenfeld's army, but they were outflanked and driven back by the Prussians, who now began to turn the Austrian left flank. Simultaneously, Moltke ordered the First Army reserves forward.

The Austrians were being squeezed in a tight box. In desperation, they launched a series of ferocious attacks against Lipa and Chlum, now held by the Prussians and forming a crucial link between their Second and First Armies. The Austrian attacks nearly succeeded in breaking the Prussian lines, but they were driven back. Prussian infantry, with their rapidly firing breechloaders, checked a final attack in the center by Austrian cavalry. By 3:00 P.M., the Austrian army began to disintegrate, and hordes of panicked troops began fleeing down the road to the bridge at Könniggrätz on the Elbe.

The Austrian army was utterly routed and demoralized, having lost some twenty-five thousand killed and wounded and another twenty thousand as prisoners, as well as hundreds of guns. The Prussians had lost around nine thousand troops total.

SIGNIFICANCE

The shattering defeat of the Austrian army at Könniggrätz convinced Austrian emperor Francis Joseph I that his situation was hopeless. As a result, the Seven Weeks' War was quickly brought to an end by the Treaty of Prague, signed August 23. The battle was the largest land battle to that date, involving 475,000 troops.

The sheer size of the armies involved called for a shift in strategies. The traditional strategy of massing armies together would constrict the movement and strategic options of such large forces and would make supplying them nearly impossible. Moltke's strategy revealed the possibilities of widely placed but quickly converging armies, reacting flexibly to contingencies as they arose. This strategy, however, placed absolute importance on coordination and timing; despite Benedek's failures, the Prussian victory at Könniggrätz had been far from assured. Moltke's strategy was tested with apprehension by the Prussian high command against the Austrians in 1866. It would be fully embraced by the Prussians and used with devastating effect against the French in 1870 in the Franco-Prussian War.

The rapidly firing breech-loading rifles used by the Prussians also signaled a change in warfare. These weapons allowed the Prussians to combine open, flexible formations with superior firepower to defeat massed columns of infantry using shock tactics. Such columns could now be shot to pieces before they had a chance to reach the enemy. Rifled artillery had proven itself as well, and by 1870, all of Prussia's guns would be rifled. Cavalry, meanwhile, had shown itself hopelessly vulnerable to firepower and nearly useless as a shock weapon in battle. It was increasingly restricted to the role of reconnaissance, screening, and communications.

From a geopolitical perspective, this decisive battle in the Seven Weeks' War resulted in Prussian domination of the German-speaking lands of central Europe. This set the stage for the unification of Germany under Prussian dominance in 1871.

—*Nathan J. Latta*

FURTHER READING

Craig, Gordon Alexander. *The Battle of Koniggratz: Prussia's Victory over Austria, 1866*. Philadelphia: University of Pennsylvania Press, 2003. A clear narrative of the battle, with a survey of the opposing armies, the campaign in Bohemia, its operational movements, and prior battles leading to Könniggrätz.

Showalter, Dennis E. *Railroads and Rifles: Soldiers, Technology, and the Unification of Germany*. Hamden, Conn.: Archon Books, 1975. Illustrates the importance of changing technology in the period and how it affected military thinking on strategy and tactics.

_______. *The Wars of German Unification*. London: Arnold, 2004. A study of the wars in the context of the transitions enacted by Otto von Bismarck and others in Prussian political and military policies from 1848 to 1871.

Wawro, Geoffrey. *The Austro-Prussian War: Austria's War with Prussia and Italy in 1866*. Rev. ed. New York: Cambridge University Press, 1997. A study of the entire war, its political origins, and its consequences, with an analysis of period strategy and tactics in the light of changing technology.

SEE ALSO: 1866-1867: North German Confederation Is Formed; June 15-Aug. 23, 1866: Austria and Prussia's Seven Weeks' War; July 19, 1870-Jan. 28, 1871: Franco-Prussian War; Jan. 18, 1871: German States Unite Within German Empire.

RELATED ARTICLES in *Great Lives from History: The Nineteenth Century, 1801-1900:* Otto von Bismarck; Francis Joseph I.

July 27, 1866
FIRST TRANSATLANTIC CABLE IS COMPLETED

This new communications link between North America and Great Britain opened a new era of political and economic cooperation by making possible nearly instantaneous communications.

LOCALE: Atlantic Ocean
CATEGORIES: Communications; engineering; science and technology

KEY FIGURES

Frederick N. Gisborne (1824-1892), English-born Canadian engineer who proposed the transatlantic cable
Cyrus West Field (1819-1892), principal American organizer of the cable venture
Isambard Kingdom Brunel (1806-1859), English engineer who built the SS *Great Eastern*
Matthew D. Field (fl. mid-nineteenth century), engineer who linked Newfoundland and Nova Scotia by telegraphic cable
Matthew Fontaine Maury (1806-1873), American oceanographer who surveyed the Atlantic cable route
Samuel F. B. Morse (1791-1872), inventor of the telegraph

SUMMARY OF EVENT

Among the most important developments of the nineteenth century were the invention of the magnetic telegraph, a simple electrical device that revolutionized the field of communications, and the launching of the steamship *Great Eastern*, which made possible the laying of the first transatlantic cable. Samuel F. B. Morse invented the electric telegraph in 1837. In less than a decade, his telegraph made possible almost instantaneous communication over long distances. In 1845, Morse secured a congressional appropriation of thirty thousand dollars to set up the first telegraph line in the United States, between Washington, D.C., and Baltimore.

The first successful underwater cable of any substantial length was completed in 1850; it connected Dover, England, and Calais, France, across the English Channel. That accomplishment inspired similar projects in Scandinavian waters and in the Mediterranean Sea. The English engineer Frederick N. Gisborne was the first person publicly to propose a transatlantic communication cable. In 1854, he encouraged the English engineer Sir Isambard Kingdom Brunel to visit New York to persuade the young businessman Cyrus West Field to form a cable company, after being assured by Morse that great distances would not hinder the telegraph's operation. Lieutenant Matthew Fontaine Maury, now regarded as the founder of oceanography, had previously surveyed the Atlantic depths between Newfoundland and Ireland and was able to offer precise recommendations for the best route.

The task of promoting capital and organizing a company to carry forward the venture was taken up primarily by Field, who had risen to a junior partnership in a New York wholesale paper business. In 1841, after the firm declared bankruptcy, he established his own company. Within ten years he had amassed one-quarter of a million dollars—enough to enable him to retire at the age of thirty-three. His interest in the possibility of a transatlantic cable was stimulated by his meeting, in 1854, with Gisborne.

After that meeting, Field organized a company to connect St. John's, Newfoundland, telegraphically with New York and the eastern seaboard. That telegraphic link alone would shorten by forty-eight hours the time required to bring European news to the United States. Field then pondered the next step: direct communication with Europe through a twenty-three-hundred-mile-long cable between Newfoundland and Ireland. This project received the support of a group of wealthy businessmen, and in May, 1854, the New York, Newfoundland, and London Electric Telegraph Company was organized and financed with $1.5 million in subscriptions. In the summer of 1856, the company established a telegraph link between Newfoundland and Nova Scotia, under the direction of engineer Matthew D. Field.

In 1856, Cyrus Field went to England to seek the assistance of the British government for his latest project. He was favorably received, and the British promised to supply both ships and funds. Field then was able to obtain similar commitments from the U.S. government. He immediately set up the Atlantic Telegraph Company, a joint stock company in England, which took over the New York, Newfoundland, and London Telegraph Company's monopoly for the laying of cables. Possessing capital of more than £350,000, and the support of both governments, the Atlantic Cable Company was ready to begin its herculean task. Field commissioned three British companies to make three thousand miles of heavily insulated steel thread cable, which weighed 1,860 pounds—nearly one ton—per mile.

Field's first attempt at laying the cable began on August 5, 1857, when a flotilla of nine ships sailed from Valentia Bay on the west coast of Ireland. One American ship, the *Niagara*, and one British vessel, the battleship *Agamemnon*, were assigned the difficult task of paying out the cable as the British-American ships moved westward. All went well for six days, but when the flotilla was 355 miles out to sea, the inferior cable snapped in a heavy swell, and the operation had to be abandoned. Experts from the two nations blamed the failure on each other, but Field and his associates remained confident of ultimate triumph.

For the next attempt, in the summer of 1858, it was decided that the two cable ships should start by meeting together in mid-ocean. There, they would splice together the separate ends of two lines, and each would go in an opposite direction, thereby cutting in half the distance over which any one ship would have to lay cable. On June 26, 1858, the *Agamemnon* proceeded toward Ireland and the *Niagara* toward Newfoundland. When the ships were some forty miles apart, the cable again broke after six recovery attempts, with the loss of 290 miles of cable. By that time, Cyrus Field's company had lost $2.5 million.

Improved equipment was installed, another attempt at splicing was initiated, and the *Agamemnon* and the *Niagara* again gingerly steamed away from each other and in opposite directions. This time the cable held together. After the *Niagara* safely reached North America, the *Agamemnon* completed the line when it reached Ireland on August 4, 1858. The English directors of the Atlantic Cable Company sent the first message: "Europe and America are united by telegraphic communication."

Later on that same day, U.S. president James Buchanan and British queen Victoria exchanged congratulatory remarks, and messages of all sorts were communicated between England and the United States. Most messages expressed the hope that the Atlantic cable would unite the two countries in eternal friendship. After a brief period, however, signals over the cable grew faint and finally gave out completely, after only three hundred messages had been transmitted. It was later determined that the cable failed because of inadequate insulation, but Field was accused of fraud, and his company faced financial collapse for a time. Without conceding defeat, Field continued to promote his idea, but the intervention of the Civil War (1861-1865) caused a delay in restarting.

In 1864, Field joined with Brunel and secured the now infamous twelve-thousand-ton steamship *Great Eastern*, "the unappeasable whale that ate men and gold." Often called "an elephant spinning a cobweb," the *Great Eastern* was the daily subject for caricatures and mali-

Arrival of the Great Eastern *at Heart's Content, Newfoundland.* (C. A. Nichols & Company)

cious press cartoons. By July 14, 1865, however, everything was ready as the ship lay at Sheerness, England, after taking on great spools of wire cable wrapped in a tar-manila insulation that was carried by navy hulks down from London. Even the Prince of Wales came aboard and said, "I wish success to the Atlantic Cable," a taped message that took two seconds to travel the 1,395 nautical miles of still-coiled, blemish-free cable. With fifteen hundred tons of coal and a dead load of twenty-one thousand tons, the *Great Eastern* left its berth, accompanied by a flotilla of English steamer ships to the accompaniment of fiddles, bagpipes, and cheering crowds.

Initially, the ship laid the new cable at a speed of six knots, but the entire operation was fraught with gales, broken cable, and even "flagrant evidence of mischief." On many occasions, long sections of the cable were lost and had to be laboriously retrieved from the ocean bottom with five-pronged anchors. Each section had to be carefully inspected for flaws, which then required tedious splicing.

On August 2, the *Great Eastern* crossed the Atlantic's halfway point. Then the operation, which was beset by rumors of sabotage, had to stop until an improved cable could be manufactured and the weaknesses and problems of laying the cable had been eliminated. The ship had laid 1,186 miles of trailing cable that was only partially alive. The area was marked with a red sea buoy with a black ball before the *Great Eastern* left.

On July 13, 1866, after Field reorganized the cable company, the *Great Eastern* resumed laying new cable and joined its new cable to the shore end off Valencia, and completed laying the cable in fourteen days. On Friday, July 27, the final splice was made successfully, after the cable was carried ashore at Heart's Content relay station in Newfoundland. On its return voyage, the *Great Eastern* located the red buoy with the black ball, and after grappling thirty times, the lost cable was retrieved. One crew member said, "Only God can know the sensation of this moment."

SIGNIFICANCE

The social, economic, and political effects of the transatlantic cable were almost immediate in both the United States and Great Britain, as government communications and growing numbers of commercial messages increased. Meanwhile, technical improvements in telegraphy permitted growing numbers of messages to be sent simultaneously on the same lines, including messages traveling in opposite directions. By the end of the century, numerous undersea cable lines were connecting virtually the entire globe.

—*Theodore A. Wilson, updated by John Alan Ross*

FURTHER READING

Babcock, F. Lawrence. *Spanning the Atlantic*. New York: Alfred A. Knopf, 1931. Sold narrative of the efforts to lay the first Atlantic cable.

Coe, Lewis. *The Telegraph: A History of Morse's Invention and Its Predecessors in the United States*. Jefferson, N.C.: McFarland, 1993. Well-researched history of the development of the telegraph by a former telegrapher. Gives special attention to the telegraph's role during the Civil War—the period during which the laying of the transatlantic cable was delayed.

Emmerson, George S. *The Greatest Iron Ship: S.S. Great Eastern*. Newton Abbot, England: David & Charles, 1980. Thorough account of the world's then largest iron ship, which was converted to lay the first Atlantic cable.

Fox, Stephen. *Transatlantic: Samuel Cunard, Isambard Brunel, and the Great Atlantic Steamships*. New York: HarperCollins, 2003. Narrative history of transatlantic steamships that looks closely at the builder of the *Great Eastern*, which completed the first transatlantic cable.

Hearn, Chester G. *Circuits in the Sea: The Men, the Ships, and the Atlantic Cable*. Westport, Conn.: Praeger, 2004. History of the eleven-year effort to lay a transatlantic telegraph cable, including Brunel's participation in the process. Describes the ships used, the technology involved, and the initial failures of the venture.

_______. *Tracks in the Sea: Matthew Fontaine Maury and the Mapping of the Oceans*. Camden, Maine: International Maritime/McGraw-Hill, 2002. Comprehensive biography of the pioneering American oceanographer who plotted the route for the first transatlantic cable.

McDonald, Philip B. *A Saga of the Seas: The Story of Cyrus W. Field and the Laying of the First Atlantic Cable*. New York: Wilson-Erickson, 1937. History of the first transatlantic cable that emphasizes the obstacles that had to be overcome.

Tyler, David B. *Steam Conquers the Atlantic*. New York: Appleton-Century-Crofts, 1939. Places the laying of the Atlantic cable in the wider context of the early years of the transatlantic steamships.

SEE ALSO: Jan. 10, 1840: Great Britain Establishes Penny Postage; May 24, 1844: Morse Sends First

Telegraph Message; Jan. 31, 1858: Brunel Launches the SS *Great Eastern*; Apr. 3, 1860-Oct. 26, 1861: Pony Express Expedites Transcontinental Mail; Oct. 24, 1861: Transcontinental Telegraph Is Completed; June, 1896: Marconi Patents the Wireless Telegraph.

RELATED ARTICLES in *Great Lives from History: The Nineteenth Century, 1801-1900:* Isambard Kingdom Brunel; William Fothergill Cooke and Charles Wheatstone; Matthew Fontaine Maury; Samuel F. B. Morse.

December 21, 1866
FETTERMAN MASSACRE

After ignoring warnings against pursuing American Indian decoys, a U.S. Army captain and eighty of his men were ambushed and killed near Fort Phil Kearny in the worst Indian massacre of whites before the Battle of the Little Bighorn a decade later.

LOCALE: South of Sheridan, Wyoming
CATEGORIES: Atrocities and war crimes; wars, uprisings, and civil unrest

KEY FIGURES

William Judd Fetterman (c. 1833-1866), U.S. Army captain
Henry Beebee Carrington (1824-1912), commander of Fort Phil Kearny
Red Cloud (1822-1909), Sioux chief
Philip St. George Cooke (1809-1895), commander of the Department of the Platte in Omaha, Nebraska
William Tecumseh Sherman (1820-1891), former Union general and commander of the Division of the Missouri

SUMMARY OF EVENT

At the end of the U.S. Civil War, the West was divided into two geographical areas for the purpose of military operations. Major General Henry W. Halleck headed the Division of the Pacific, and Lieutenant General William Tecumseh Sherman commanded the Division of the Missouri. The peacetime army increasingly faced the prospect of Indian wars on the Western frontier.

An 1865 peace treaty with the Sioux guaranteed them use of areas that included southeastern Montana, northeastern Wyoming, and the western Dakotas. However, when emigrants began the move west, particularly after finding gold in 1862, settlers began using the Bozeman Trail through Wyoming to Montana. The Indians in the area, however, considered the constant stream of migrants along the trail a violation of the treaty because the travelers repeatedly trespassed on their traditional hunting grounds. Sioux chief Red Cloud organized other tribes and began to make small raids on wagon, supply, and wood trains. In the spring of 1866, the U.S. Army ordered Brevet Brigadier General Philip St. George Cooke, commander of the Department of the Platte (which included the Bozeman Trail) and the Eighteenth Infantry Regiment, to secure the trail against such attacks by establishing two other forts along the Powder River.

Henry B. Carrington, a former lawyer and recruiting administrator in Ohio during the Civil War, was assigned the task of building the additional posts to protect westward settlers. His first objective was to construct the central stockade of Fort Phil Kearny on the plateau between the forks of Piney Creek. Carrington also faced inadequate supplies and manpower issues. Recruits were difficult to get, and they received little training, low pay, and few promotions. Complicating logistics was the postwar political climate and the question of Indian relations. A public dispute erupted between the Department of War and the Department of Interior about developing a cohesive Indian policy; the dispute often fluctuated between negotiating and using force.

Carrington lacked battlefield experience, and he took a decisively defensive strategy in dealing with these attacks. Oftentimes men were engaged in construction, guard, or escort duty, which left little time for training drills. The commander also gave strict orders to not pursue Indians because he feared he did not have enough manpower or weapons to repel them.

Carrington was an efficient organizer, but morale and discipline began to suffer at the fort, a matter that upset Captain William J. Fetterman. Fetterman was an aggressive and decorated soldier who marched with Sherman in the Georgia campaign during the Civil War. He detested Carrington's passivity in military matters and openly criticized his leadership abilities before fellow officers. Fetterman allegedly boasted to his commander that he could take down the entire Sioux nation with eighty men.

In late November, Cooke ordered that the army begin strikes against the Indians while they were in winter

General William T. Sherman. (Corbis)

camp. By early December, the fort was nearly complete, and Carrington did make plans for offensive movements against them. This led to a series of engagements. On December 6, one hundred Indians attacked another wood train. Carrington and Fetterman encountered them near Peno Creek. The troops panicked; two officers were killed and five soldiers were wounded in the melee, reinforcing for the Sioux that their decoy tactics were successful. Erring on the side of caution, the commander then gave explicit orders for the men not to pursue under any circumstances.

Thirteen days later, the Indians attacked again, and the troops, following Carrington's orders, failed to follow them. On December 21, Fetterman was sent with seventy-nine soldiers and two civilians to help reinforce a wood train attacked earlier that morning. This time Fetterman fell for the trap, and he decided to pursue Crazy Horse and the other decoy over a range of hills known as Lodge Trail Ridge. Fetterman led his men right into an ambush by a force of up to 2,500 Cheyenne, Arapaho, and Sioux warriors. The infantry and cavalry soon became separated into two groups, attempting to set up defensive positions, but were overtaken three miles from the fort. The shooting could be heard at the fort, but by the time Carrington dispatched cavalry to the ridge's summit, Fetterman and his entire detachment were dead—they had been killed within an hour. The Fetterman Massacre, known by Indians as the battle "100 in the Hand," represented the climax of Red Cloud's War.

Significance

The Fetterman Massacre was the worst defeat on the Western frontier until the time of George Armstrong Custer's Battle of the Little Bighorn in 1876. A court of inquiry exonerated Carrington of any fault for the massacre, but he was relieved of command nonetheless. Carrington retired from the military three years later, but he spent the remainder of his life trying to restore his reputation by altering the historical account of the massacre.

The forts along the Bozeman Trail were eventually abandoned during the next few years; Fort Phil Kearny closed in 1868. Railroads would eventually serve as the main form of transportation in the West. The U.S. government also agreed to restore unceded territory to the American Indians.

—*Gayla Koerting*

Further Reading

Brown, Dee. *The Fetterman Massacre, Formerly Fort Phil Kearny: An American Saga*. Lincoln: University of Nebraska Press, 1971. Recounts the events that preceded the massacre. A well-documented book based on Army records and reports. Scholars consider this work the definitive account of the massacre.

Calitri, Shannon Smith. "'Give Me Eighty Men': Shattering the Myth of the Fetterman Massacre." *Montana: The Magazine of Western History* 54, no. 4 (Autumn, 2004): 44-59. Refutes the claim that Carrington was completely reviled by Fetterman, his fellow officers, and subordinates as commander at Fort Phil Kearny. Calitri contends that Fetterman lived by a gentleman's code of conduct and would have behaved as a professional officer despite having misgivings about Carrington.

Johnston, Terry C. *Sioux Dawn: A Novel of the Fetterman Massacre*. New York: St. Martin's Press, 1990. A fictional work about the history and circumstances surrounding the Fetterman Massacre.

Longstreet, Stephen. *War Cries on Horseback: The Story of the Indian Wars of the Great Plains*. New York: Doubleday, 1970. This work examines the battles and clashing cultures from 1865 to 1900 between whites and American Indians. Both groups were fighting to control the Western frontier.

Olson, James C. *Red Cloud and the Sioux Problem.* 1965. New ed. Lincoln: University of Nebraska Press, 1975. Provides an account of Red Cloud's life. The author contends that Red Cloud was a transitional figure whose traditional warrior way of life was diminishing, and who was eventually forced to acquiesce to government demands to save his people.

Partridge, Robert B. "Fetterman Debacle—Who Was to Blame?" *Journal of the Council on America's Military Past* 16, no. 2 (1989) 36-43. Partridge contends that Fetterman and Carrington are case studies for conflicting military leadership abilities, the importance of loyalty, and the dangers of disobedience.

Utley, Robert M. *Frontier Regulars: The United States Army and the Indians, 1866-1891.* 1973. Reprint. Lincoln: University of Nebraska Press, 1984. In a meticulously documented book, Utley examines the Regular Army's role to subdue American Indians during the latter half of the nineteenth century. Utley addresses policy decisions, recruitment, military operations, maneuvers, and equipment.

Vaughn, J. W. *Indian Fights: New Facts on Seven Encounters.* Norman: University of Oklahoma Press, 1966. A reexamination of seven engagements during the Indian wars. Chapter 2 addresses the Fetterman Massacre.

Wenzel, Nikolai. "The Fetterman Massacre of December 21, 1866." *Journal of the Council on America's Military Past* 28, no. 1 (2001): 46-59. Wenzel concentrates on the personality clash between Fetterman and Carrington. He believes Fetterman was a rash officer whose thirst for glory was placed above the safety of his men.

See also: Aug. 17, 1862-Dec. 28, 1863: Great Sioux War; Aug., 1863-Sept., 1866: Long Walk of the Navajos; Nov. 15, 1864-Apr. 18, 1865: Sherman Marches Through Georgia and the Carolinas; Nov. 29, 1864: Sand Creek Massacre; June 13, 1866-Nov. 6, 1868: Red Cloud's War; 1867: Chisholm Trail Opens; Oct. 21, 1867: Medicine Lodge Creek Treaty; Nov. 27, 1868: Washita River Massacre; Mar. 3, 1871: Grant Signs Indian Appropriation Act; 1876-1877: Sioux War; June 25, 1876: Battle of the Little Bighorn; Dec. 29, 1890: Wounded Knee Massacre.

Related articles in *Great Lives from History: The Nineteenth Century, 1801-1900:* Black Hawk; Crazy Horse; George A. Custer; Red Cloud; William Tecumseh Sherman; Sitting Bull; Tecumseh.

1867
Chisholm Trail Opens

An eight-hundred-mile route from southern Texas to Abilene, Kansas, the Chisholm Trail expanded cattle markets, opened the Midwest to transport, and closed open ranges. The trail's importance began to wane with the arrival of the railroad through the region twenty years later.

Locale: Great Plains, United States
Categories: Transportation; trade and commerce

Key Figures

Jesse Chisholm (c. 1806-1868), Scottish-Cherokee trader and guide who pioneered the trail

John Clay (1851-1934), manager and inspector of British-owned ranch properties

Richard King (1824-1885), founder of the King Ranch in southern Texas

Joseph Geating McCoy (1837-1915), Illinois stockman who developed Abilene

Charles Russell (1864-1926), artist and chronicler of the West and ranch life

Summary of Event

At the end of the Civil War (1861-1865), astute and ambitious Texans conceived a plan whereby the numerous herds of longhorn cattle overrunning the southern part of the state could be rounded up and driven north to markets where they would command a higher price. Foremost among these Texans was a former steamboat captain, Richard King, whose original tract of 75,000 acres increased to 500,000 acres by the time of his death in 1885.

First introduced into California, New Mexico, and Texas by the Spaniards, the scrawny range cattle had been valuable mainly for their hides. For years, small herds had been driven every other year from Texas to New Orleans, St. Louis, or Kansas City by many south-Texas Mexican American ranchers. New England shippers frequented Pacific coast ports to gather hides for eastern tanneries. The Civil War, however, brought many changes to this area. Railroads began pushing westward across the Great Plains; the meat-packing industry was being consolidated by a few leading packers in urban centers such as Kansas City, Omaha, and Chicago, which dominated the national market.

Joseph G. McCoy, an Illinois stockman, assumed the leadership in working out a mutually satisfactory arrangement among the cattle owners, the railroads, and the meat packers. Cattle worth five dollars a head in Texas were to be driven northward, fattened on the nutritious short grass of the public domain en route, and then delivered to the railhead for shipment to eastern markets, where they would bring forty to fifty dollars each. McCoy chose Abilene, Kansas, the terminal town on the Kansas Pacific Railroad in 1867, as the initial shipping point. McCoy ordered lumber from Missouri and built stock pens stout enough to hold three thousand restless longhorns. He placed ten-ton scales that could weigh twenty cows at a time. Besides enlarging Abilene with a livery stable, barns, and an office, he also built the Drovers' Cottage, an eight-room hotel.

The Chisholm Trail was the name given to the route by which the cattle were driven northward from southern Texas, entering the Indian Territory at Red River Crossing, and continuing into Abilene. Jesse Chisholm, a Scottish-Cherokee wagon driver, first marked this trail, which he used to trade buffalo robes with midwestern tribes. Chisholm, who never raised cattle, knew the need for grass and water on a cattle trail. In 1868, Chisholm died from eating bad bear grease, without ever completing a trip on the trail named for him. As the railroad moved farther west, alternative routes were made. The Shawnee Trail followed the route of the Chisholm Trail until it veered to Baxter Springs, Kansas. The West Chisholm Trail led into western Kansas and Ellsworth, Kansas. The Panhandle Trail fought its way across the arid mesas of western Texas. The original routes ran from the central part of Indian Territory to the railhead at Ellsworth.

The pressure of farmers taking up homesteads near the railroads forced the cattlemen to relocate their long drives ever farther to the west. Construction of the Atchison, Topeka, and Santa Fe Railroad provided a shorter drive along the Great Western Trail to southwestern Kansas, first to Newton and later to Dodge City, the recognized "cowboy capital" between 1875 and 1885. If the cattle market was overcrowded in Dodge City, some cattle owners drove their herds northward to meet the Union Pacific. After Kansas was closed to the cattle owners, ranchers developed the Goodnight-Loving Trail, which ran westward across Texas to the Pecos River country and then northward through eastern New Mexico and Colorado into Wyoming, where there was less competition.

The drives started early in the spring, immediately following the roundup. Usually a herd of twenty-five hundred to three thousand head of cattle was placed in the charge of the trail boss, who hired a dozen cowboys accompanied by a chuck wagon. The cattle were moved along the trail between ten and fifteen miles per day at a pace that would permit them to gain flesh off the rich, nutritious short grass of the Great Plains. Cowboys preferred driving the longhorns. The span of the long horns kept the cattle spaced farther apart, preventing excess body heat and flesh loss. Before leaving on a drive, owners would brand their animals, so separating them at the terminal was simplified.

Numerous dangers were encountered along the trail, including American Indian attacks, stampedes, Quantrell's Raiders, jayhawkers, swollen rivers that had to be crossed, and attacks from farmers who did not want the herds crossing their lands and spreading the dreaded Texas fever to their own stock. This fever was caused by ticks, but it was attributed mistakenly to causes ranging from thorny shrubs scratching infected animals to deliberate sabotage.

Despite these hazards, between 1868 and 1871 almost 1.5 million head of cattle were loaded on the trains in the Abilene yards. From 1872 to 1875, Newton, on the Santa Fe line, received 1.5 million animals, and Dodge shipped 1 million of them to the eastern markets during the succeeding four years. No business was more widely advertised and romanticized. Tales of cattle kings building large estates and herds, cowboys engaging in the roundups and long drives, lawbreakers congregating in the cow towns to challenge authority and each other, and sheriffs' and marshals' attempts to maintain law and order were legion.

By 1880, the cattle industry was firmly established throughout the Great Plains. Rumors had circulated about the enormous profits that were available, with estimates running as high as a 40 percent return on capital in a single year. Investors in the East and abroad, primarily in England and Scotland, organized mammoth companies that bought acreage in New Mexico, Texas, and Colorado totaling eight thousand square miles with herds numbering more than 150,000 head.

Between 1881 and 1885, the British invested approximately $45 million in the cattle business and employed

John Clay to oversee their interests. In the process, a mad scramble ensued to obtain land strategically located to control the essential and limited water supply. Some companies resorted to leasing American Indian reservation lands and to enclosing sections of public domain that alternated with those areas that they had purchased from the western railroads. The aggressive and sometimes illegal activities of the cattle barons made them unpopular with farmers and small ranchers, as well as with the federal government.

In an attempt to bring order to the industry, southern and Great Plains cattle owners organized regional and territorial associations to supervise roundups, organize detective bureaus to prevent cattle rustling, institute inspection systems to oversee joint shipments of cattle from range to market, and lobby for political concessions. The collective efforts of these associations led to the creation of the Bureau of Animal Industry by the federal government. The boom could not last. Northern ranges were overcrowded, and steps were taken to shut off the long drives from Texas. Even so, overproduction caused prices on the domestic market to tumble steadily between 1884 and 1887.

To make a bad situation worse, climatic conditions in 1885 and 1886 were disastrous. The summers were hot and dry, reaching 110 degrees. One Fourth of July, there was a hailstorm that killed jackrabbits, yearlings, and antelope, and left cowboys with frozen and scarred faces and hands. In Montana, fifty thousand acres of good grassland burned. In the winter of 1886, three-fourths of some herds were destroyed. In November, a blizzard left snow up to the eaves of cabins. In January, a chinook caused the snow to melt, then on January 28, 1887, the temperatures dropped to fifteen degrees below zero, with winds of sixty miles per hour. More snow fell, isolating men and animals for six weeks. Small animals smothered in the drifts; Texas cattle froze, unaccustomed to severe winters; heartier cattle could not break the ice to get grass. Some animals resorted to eating tar paper off shacks and the wool off the bodies of dead sheep. Charles Russell, the famous western artist, did his first watercolor, *Waiting for a Chinook*, depicting a humped-up cow circled by wolves, during this winter storm.

Significance

The basic economic law of supply and demand on the open range and the whims of the weather dramatized the Chisholm Trail's end. Cattlemen reduced the size of their herds, fenced their ranches, made plans for feeding their animals during the winter months, and concentrated on improved breeding. Even with the number of cattle reduced, the market price did not rise during the 1890's. The industry struggled for survival in the decade of transition. The true story of cowboys and ranches has, over time, evolved into Hollywood fiction for the general populace.

—*W. Turrentine Jackson, updated by Norma Crews*

Further Reading

Adams, Ramon F. *The Old-Time Cowhand.* 1961. Reprint. Lincoln: University of Nebraska Press, 1989. A western historian gives insight into the everyday life of cowboys, stressing the differences in geographical locations.

Drago, Harry Sinclair. *Great American Cattle Trails: The Story of the Old Cow Paths of the East and the Longhorn Highways of the Plains.* New York: Dodd, Mead, 1965. Discusses the development of famous national trails, specifically addressing the business of driving stock.

Fuller, John H. "Ben Kinchlow: A Trail Driver on the Chisholm Trail." In *Black Cowboys of Texas*, edited by Sara R. Massey. College Station: Texas A&M Press, 2000. A chapter on African American cowboys of the West.

McCoy, Joseph G. *Historic Sketches of the Cattle Trade of the West and Southwest.* Kansas City, Mo.: Ramsey, Millett, & Hudson, 1874. A contemporary narrative of the cattle trade by the developer of Abilene, Kansas, the Chisholm Trail's endpoint. Available on the Web site of the Kansas Collection. http://www.kancoll.org/books/mccoy/. Accessed January 18, 2006.

O'Neal, Bill. *Cattlemen vs. Sheepherders: Five Decades of Violence in the West, 1880-1920.* Austin, Tex.: Eakin Press, 1989. Discusses the sheep wars that covered a large part of the West in the period after the drives to shipping points further developed the livestock industry.

Pirtle, Caleb, and Texas Cowboy Artist Association. *XIT, Being a New and Original Exploration, in Art and Words, Into the Life and Times of the American Cowboy.* Birmingham, Ala.: Oxmoor House, 1975. Discusses cowboys, trails, ranchers, and their legacy. Informally written, covering the period when the cattle industry was at its peak. Heavily illustrated, with an extensive bibliography.

Sanford, William R. *The Chisholm Trail in American History.* Berkeley Heights, N.J.: Enslow, 2000. A historical overview of the Chisholm Trail, written especially for younger readers. Includes maps, a bibliography, and an index.

Sherow, James E. "Water, Sun, and Cattle: The Chisholm Trail as an Ephemeral Ecosystem." In *Fluid Arguments: Five Centuries of Western Water Conflict*, edited by Char Miller. Tucson: University of Arizona Press, 2001. Examines the environmental impact of the trail, in the context of the struggle for water in the West.

Stiles, T. J. *Warriors and Pioneers*. New York: Berkley, 1996. A collection of primary sources, including "Up the Chisholm Trail" by John Wesley Hardin. Part of the In Their Own Words series. Includes maps and a bibliography.

SEE ALSO: July 15, 1806-July 1, 1807: Pike Explores the American Southwest; Sept., 1821: Santa Fe Trail Opens; 1822-1831: Jedediah Smith Explores the Far West; May, 1842-1854: Frémont Explores the American West; June 30, 1846-Jan. 13, 1847: United States Occupies California and the Southwest; Apr. 3, 1860-Oct. 26, 1861: Pony Express Expedites Transcontinental Mail; Dec. 21, 1866: Fetterman Massacre; May 10, 1869: First Transcontinental Railroad Is Completed; Sept. 10-Dec. 17, 1877: Texas's Salinero Revolt.

RELATED ARTICLE in *Great Lives from History: The Nineteenth Century, 1801-1900:* Wild Bill Hickok.

1867
LISTER PUBLISHES HIS THEORY ON ANTISEPTIC SURGERY

Joseph Lister's promotion of antiseptic surgery challenged other physicians to adopt procedures that would eventually effect a revolution in medicine by saving the lives of thousands of patients.

LOCALE: Glasgow, Scotland
CATEGORIES: Health and medicine; inventions; science and technology

KEY FIGURES

Joseph Lister (1827-1912), English surgeon
Louis Pasteur (1822-1895), French discoverer of the germ theory of disease
Ignaz Philipp Semmelweis (1818-1865), Hungarian physician who was an early discoverer of the principle of antisepsis
Sir James Young Simpson (1811-1870), Scottish physician who opposed Lister's principles

SUMMARY OF EVENT

Joseph Lister was the son of Joseph Jackson Lister, a Scottish optician, but he himself was interested in the study of medicine and obtained his medical degree in 1852. He then became assistant to James Syme, professor of clinical surgery at the University of Edinburgh. Lister held a responsible position as a lecturer and assistant surgeon in the university hospital, but he found time to occupy himself with his own researches in medicine and the causes of death that occurred after seemingly simple surgical procedures. One of the directions in which his research led him was to the problems of inflammation and death-causing infection after surgery.

Nineteenth century surgery was a precarious undertaking. The problem of pain during operations had been solved by the introduction of anesthetics such as chloroform and ether. However, there remained the so-called hospital diseases—often fatal infections that commonly appeared shortly after successful surgery. Surgeons did not know what caused these diseases, but many assumed that death was inevitable. Modern medical histories divide the nineteenth century into two periods: pre-Listerian, when surgery patients often died from infections, and Listerian, after the acceptance of antiseptic procedures promoted by Lister, Louis Pasteur, and Ignaz Philipp Semmelweis.

Apart from tetanus, the hospital diseases included gangrene, erysipelas, pyemia, and septicemia, all of which could cause death or leave patients permanently debilitated or disabled. All four were also epidemic. During the so-called erysipelas season in America, which lasted from January until March, surgery was avoided. In Great Britain, all surgery came to a complete halt when gangrene became epidemic within a hospital. In addition to these diseases that followed surgery, there was puerperal fever, which often affected women who gave birth to their children in hospitals; it was usually fatal.

Semmelweis, a Hungarian doctor who joined the staff of a Vienna hospital in 1846, concluded that puerperal fever came from within hospital wards, not from outside.

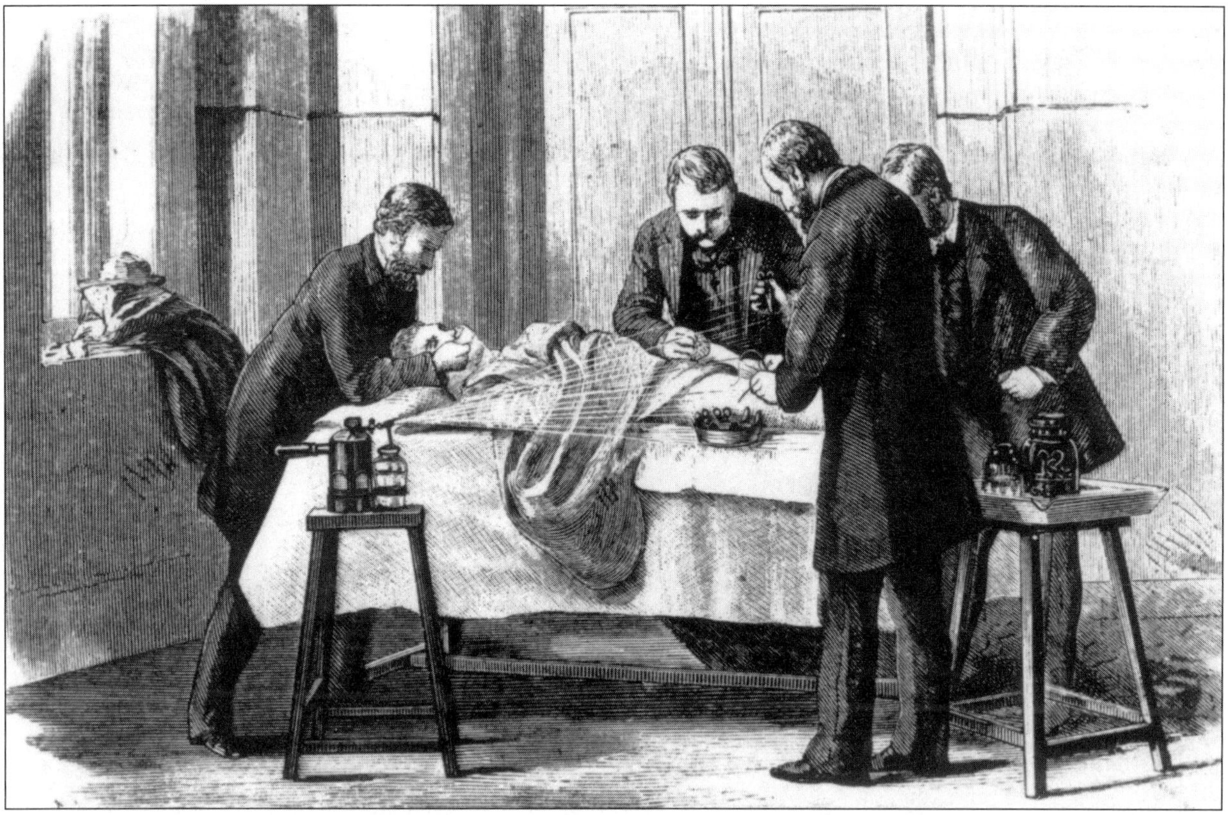

Early operation performed in antiseptic conditions. As the patient's face is covered with a cloth soaked in chloroform, a steam apparatus sprays a carbolic solution over the surgical area. (Hulton Archive/Getty Images)

He further concluded that the fever was carried by doctors and medical students who transmitted it to mothers during prenatal examinations. The answer was higher standards of cleanliness in hospitals and the disinfecting of examiners' hands before touching patients. Semmelweis made enemies, however, and although hospital mortality statistics showed that his antiseptic methods saved lives, his methods failed to gain acceptance. Semmelweis was astute in his judgment. In 1847, he insisted that all who attended surgery wash their hands in chloride of lime. This procedure reduced surgical deaths from 15 percent to 3 and then to 1 percent. Lister apparently did not find out about the work of Semmelweis until years after his own discovery.

In 1864, while Lister was lecturing and practicing surgery in Glasgow, he became acquainted with Pasteur's work on putrefaction. He believed that some of his questions might be answered by a study of Pasteur's works. This turned out to be so, for Lister conducted, for his own satisfaction, Pasteur's experiments and realized that Pasteur's germ theory also applied to hospital diseases. What he now needed to find was an agent that would kill germs (microbes) before they could penetrate deeply into body tissues.

The actual word "microbe" was not formally introduced to the medical community until February 26, 1878, when a military surgeon named Sedillot published a treatise on the treatment of purulent infection, a very common problem in military surgery. In that same paper Sedillot wrote,

> We shall have seen the conception and birth of a new surgery, a daughter of Science and of Art, which will be one of the greatest wonders of our century and with which the names of Pasteur and Lister will remain gloriously connected.

Lister obtained some carbolic acid, which he knew had been used successfully to treat garbage in the city of Carlisle. One of its remarkable effects had been to stop the sickening of cattle who grazed in fields near the city's garbage dumps. In 1865, he used carbolic acid on his first patient, but the man died. The next four cases were all very serious surgical problems, but they all survived, thanks in part because they did not develop any of the hospital diseases. Afterward, Lister continued to treat surgical cases with carbolic acid solutions and bandages. Lister soaked his bandages and cotton wool in carbolic acid, and carbolic vapor was blown over his hands and patients' wounds during surgery. Wounds were then wrapped in carbolic-soaked towels, and surgical instruments were kept in carbolic solutions. In 1867, Lister presented his evidence in an article published in *The Lancet*, the journal of British medicine: "On a New Method of Treating Compound Fracture, Abcess, etc."

SIGNIFICANCE

A considerable opposition was mobilized against Lister, particularly by Dr. James Young Simpson. However, as increasing numbers of physicians adopted Lister's methods, opposition collapsed, and antiseptic surgery gained general acceptance. The work of Louis Pasteur from 1844 to 1895 was to affect the medical field in England, Germany, and France. In the United States, the Mayo Clinic used the surgical and antiseptic techniques developed by Pasteur and refined by Lister.

The impact of antisepsis on war wounds saved thousands of lives. After centuries of losing casualties to infection, the use of Listerian methods made it possible to save lives and limbs. Much was to be learned from the results of wounds received in different battle conditions. Pre-Listerian surgeons had to learn different methods of wound treatment to suit the different places in which they worked. For example, researchers noticed that bacteria that flourished in damp conditions diminished in arid lands. Methods were argued, and as bacteria were identified, the doctors who were convinced that bacteria was the cause worked with diligence to use antisepsis to save lives.

—*Robert F. Erickson, updated by Norma Crews*

FURTHER READING

Cameron, Hector Charles. *Joseph Lister: The Friend of Man*. London: William Heinemann, 1949. English view of human attitudes toward antisepsis.

Cartwright, Frederick F. *Development of Modern Surgery*. London: Arthur Barker, 1967. History of surgery from the early nineteenth century through the 1960's by an English physician. Cites many examples of failures and successes as surgical techniques were developed.

Debré, Patrice, *Louis Pasteur*. Translated by Elborg Forster. Baltimore: Johns Hopkins University Press, 1998. Exploration of the life and work of the discoverer of germ theory by a French immunologist. Describes Pasteur's experiments in simple, understandable language.

Dormandy, Thomas. *Moments of Truth: Four Creators of Modern Medicine*. Hoboken, N.J.: John Wiley & Sons, 2003. Biographies of four physicians and scientists who made major contributions to the advancement of medical science, including Joseph Lister and Ignaz Philipp Semmelweis.

Gaw, Jerry L. *"A Time to Heal": The Diffusion of Listerism in Victorian Britain*. Philadelphia: American Philosophical Society, 1999. History of the adoption of Lister's antiseptic surgery techniques in mid-nineteenth century Britain.

Guthrie, Douglas. *Lord Lister: His Life and Doctrine*. Baltimore: Williams and Wilkins, 1949. Detailed look at Lister's accomplishments and their profound impact on the medical professions.

Mactavish, Douglas. *Joseph Lister*. New York: Franklin Watts, 1992. Comprehensive biography of Joseph Lister's life and work.

SEE ALSO: 1816: Laënnec Invents the Stethoscope; Oct. 5, 1823: Wakley Introduces *The Lancet*; Oct. 16, 1846: Safe Surgical Anesthesia Is Demonstrated; May, 1847: Semmelweis Develops Antiseptic Procedures; Nov. 4, 1854: Nightingale Takes Charge of Nursing in the Crimea; 1857: Pasteur Begins Developing Germ Theory and Microbiology; 1882-1901: Metchnikoff Advances the Cellular Theory of Immunity; Mar. 24, 1882: Koch Announces His Discovery of the Tuberculosis Bacillus; Aug. 20, 1897: Ross Establishes Malaria's Transmission Vector.

RELATED ARTICLES in *Great Lives from History: The Nineteenth Century, 1801-1900:* Joseph Lister; Louis Pasteur; Ignaz Philipp Semmelweis; Marie Elizabeth Zakrzewska.

1867
MARX PUBLISHES *DAS KAPITAL*

The first volume of Karl Marx's Das Kapital *provided the theoretical basis for a scientific socialist philosophy. Although some elements of Marx's theory—particularly the labor theory of value and the inevitability of communist revolution—have since been called into question,* Das Kapital *remains arguably the single best description of capitalism and the single most effective diagnosis of its flaws ever produced.*

ALSO KNOWN AS: *Capital: A Critique of Political Economy*
LOCALE: Hamburg (now in Germany)
CATEGORIES: Economics; philosophy

KEY FIGURES

Karl Marx (1818-1883), German philosopher
Friedrich Engels (1820-1895), German philosopher
Karl Kautsky (1854-1938), German-Austrian socialist political leader

SUMMARY OF EVENT

In 1867, Karl Marx published the first volume of his most ambitious work, *Das Kapital* (1867, 1885, 1894; *Capital: A Critique of Political Economy*, 1886, 1907, 1909; better known as *Das Kapital*). The mammoth volume represented the summation of his thinking about capitalism, its effects on society, and its future. This first volume was the only one that Marx himself saw through the press. Volumes 2 and 3 were edited from Marx's manuscripts by his intellectual partner Friedrich Engels and were published after Marx's death. A further volume of the philosopher's manuscripts, edited by the German socialist leader Karl Kautsky, was published early in the next century under a different title.

A German philosopher and social theorist, Marx was born in 1818 in Trier, Prussia. By the time he was thirty, he had become the prophet of European socialism. In 1848, Marx and Engels published *Manifest der Kommunistischen Partei* (*The Communist Manifesto*, 1850), one of the most brilliantly successful political tracts ever written. The ghost of communism, Marx and Engels wrote, was "haunting Europe." For almost a century and a half afterward, Marx's prophetic curse on the European bourgeoisie haunted not only Europe but also most of the world. In the meantime, Marx's doctrines, in one form or another, were embraced by untold numbers of the world's intelligentsia.

Das Kapital takes the form of a long and often rambling study of capitalist society. Marx based his study on economic history and detailed accounts of the behavior of European entrepreneurs ("capitalists"), their business enterprises, and the laboring classes ("the working class" or "proletariat"), who provided the sweat and muscle allowing European factories to produce an avalanche of goods. In addition, Marx studied profits, rents, the production and sale of commodities, the operation and circulation of money, markets, economic competition, the function of factory labor and its effects on laborers, capitalists' reaction to labor organizations, and many other topics related to modern industrial capitalist society. In *Das Kapital*, he dissected each of these topics in minute detail. Marx claimed to have discovered a number of laws that characterized the capitalist system as a whole. *Das Kapital* was written to lay bare these laws and the consequences of their operation.

While the whole of Marx's magnum opus defies brief summary, two key themes vital to Marx's enterprise can be identified. The first is the idea of *surplus value*. A tone of moral condemnation runs throughout *Das Kapital*. Much of it derives from Marx's view that capitalists unjustly appropriate—rob—from workers a significant portion of the value they produce. He based his view on a doctrine essential to Marxism—the labor theory of value. According to this theory, all economic value is derived from labor. Marx did not invent this theory, which was created by John Locke in his *Two Treatises of Government* (1690) and adopted by economists such as Adam Smith.

Economists since Marx have pointed to more sources of economic value than labor alone, but for Marx, capitalism cannot exist without the wanton theft of a portion of the laborer's work. Since laborers must work to live, capitalists have coercive power over them and use it to exploit them. Capitalists do this by paying labor only as much as is required for basic subsistence—the minimum required to raise a family, reproducing their labor for a new generation. The difference between what labor needs to subsist and the amount it actually produces is what Marx calls surplus value. In capitalism, Marx says, surplus value is taken away ("expropriated") from workers by capitalists, for whom it represents their profit. The expropriation of surplus value from its producer is, in Marx's theory, the technical definition of "exploitation." Moreover, Marx argued that employers are coerced by the inexorable competition of capitalism to squeeze progressively more surplus value from workers, so that exploitation increases as capitalism continues.

To accomplish this increase in surplus value, Marx argued, capitalists take advantage of "the reserve army of the unemployed." In demanding longer hours or lower wages, capitalists point out to workers the legions of unemployed people who are anxious to replace them and willing to take less for the privilege of doing so. The result is the increasing misery of the working class. The theory of surplus value forms the foundation for Marx's description of capitalism as morally bankrupt and thus accounts for the moralizing tone of *Das Kapital*.

The second key element of the work is Marx's theory of the economic crises of capitalist societies. He argues that these crises (cycles of boom, followed by bust or depression) are endemic to capitalism. Marx describes the spectacle, during economic depressions, of unemployed workers deprived of the necessities of life, while factory machines that could remedy this deprivation are left idle. This is but one of a series of contradictions found within capitalist society that define for Marx that society's fundamental irrationality, even as entrepreneurs seek to apply reason to every aspect of economic activity.

"Contradiction" is a key term for Marx, who believes that, far from mounting an external critique of capitalism, he is merely furnishing an objective description of the ways in which capitalism resists itself. Borrowing from Georg Wilhelm Friedrich Hegel, Marx sees the internal self-contradictions of a society as the driving force of history. While he believes that capitalism is unjust, it is not that injustice that will bring about the downfall of capitalist society in Marx's view. Rather, it is the fact that capitalism, containing as it does contradictions between the means of production and the relations of production, is inefficient. As it grows, the society's inefficiency increases—eventually, it is this inefficiency arising from contradictions inherent in its structure that will bring about its downfall.

THE FETISHISM OF THE COMMODITY AND ITS SECRET

One of the central concepts in Karl Marx's analysis of capitalism is what he calls "commodity fetishism." In this excerpt from Das Kapital, *Marx explains the phenomenon, which amounts to people forgetting that commodities are mere objects that have been endowed with conventional value by humans and instead treating them as if they had value in and of themselves.*

The mysterious character of the commodity-form consists therefore simply in the fact that the commodity reflects the social characteristics of men's own labour as objective characteristics of the products of labour themselves, as the socio-natural properties of these things. Hence it also reflects the social relation of the producers to the sum total of labour as a social relation between objects, a relation which exists apart from and outside the producers. Through this substitution, the products of labour become commodities, sensuous things which are at the same time suprasensible or social. In the same way, the impression made by a thing on the optic nerve is perceived not as a subjective excitation of that nerve but as the objective form of a thing outside the eye. In the act of seeing, of course, light is really transmitted from one thing, the external object, to another thing, the eye. It is a physical relation between physical things. As against this, the commodity-form, and the value-relation of the products of labour within which it appears, have absolutely no connection with the physical nature of the commodity and the material relations arising out of this. It is nothing but the definite social relation between men themselves which assumes here, for them, the fantastic form of a relation between things. In order, therefore, to find an analogy we must take flight into the misty realm of religion. There the products of the human brain appear as autonomous figures endowed with a life of their own, which enter into relations both with each other and with the human race. So it is in the world of commodities with the products of men's hands.

Source: Karl Marx. *Capital* (New York: Vintage Books, 1976), vol. 1, pp. 164-165.

Thus, in *Das Kapital*, Marx argues that the economic laws to which the owners of the means of production are coerced into submitting decree that the crises of capitalism must grow increasingly worse. In Marx's vision of the future, economic downturns become more cataclysmic, the sufferings of the working class likewise increase, and the irrationality of capitalism grows clearer to the world at large. The theory of the inevitable crises of capitalism points to the resolution of its contradictions through the advent of socialism, provoked by catastrophic suffering into which even fallen members of the bourgeoisie are swept up.

In *The Communist Manifesto*, Marx and Engels had written, famously, "All history is the history of class struggle." In *Das Kapital*, Marx analyzed the socioeconomic processes that he believed explained how and why class struggle was unfolding in contemporary society. Foreseeing the end of class struggle in a new post-capitalist society, Marx established his own version of "the end of history," related to but divergent from that of Hegel, from whom he inherited the model. Marx believed that socialism would overcome the increasingly apparent irrationalism of capitalism. History would end when socialism itself evolved into full-fledged communism, which would fulfill humanity's age-old quest for abundance and social peace.

Significance

The significance of *Das Kapital* to the subsequent history of Marxism—and therefore of the twentieth century—can scarcely be exaggerated. In the eyes of Marx's followers, the book provided the empirical evidence that Marxism required to be a scientific system of knowledge and not merely one more political ideology. *Das Kapital* set out to take its place in the pantheon of great writings on economics, among works by Adam Smith, David Ricardo, and others.

The fact that few persons could completely traverse the vast forests of words that flowed from Marx's prolific pen into *Das Kapital* was hardly to the point. With the work's publication, believers in Marxism had found their bible, which proved to their satisfaction that Marx was a scientist and not just a visionary and prophet. What he showed for these audiences was that socialism was an inevitable feature of the fast-approaching future. With the triumph of the Bolsheviks in Russia in 1917 and the rise of communist parties in western Europe both before and after World War II, the significance of *Das Kapital*, whose pages buttressed the faith of Marxists both in Europe and beyond, was enormous.

In *Das Kapital*, readers found that capitalist societies would find themselves in increasingly serious cyclical crises and that these societies were powerless to prevent a complete social and economic breakdown, which would set the stage for socialism and the eventual development of communist society. Communism would be characterized by material abundance (achieved through what Marx argued was the necessary intermediate stage of capitalism) and, since it abolished the division of labor, the absence of class struggle.

Well before the end of the twentieth century, however, the major governments that had embraced the label of "communism" were found to be abject failures. The only two major countries to claim to embrace communist doctrines, Russia and China, ultimately rejected those doctrines. The arguments of *Das Kapital* relating to communism thus seemed to be refuted. It has often been said since, however, that historians will never agree as to whether true communism failed or was simply never attempted. The greatest excesses of capitalism described by Marx, meanwhile, have been meliorated by welfare state benefits. Nevertheless, *Das Kapital* remains as a mighty indictment of the dehumanizing aspects of industrialization and the suffering they have caused. Equally, however, it stands as monument to the human tendency to intellectual hubris and the propensity to grasp at the hallow salvation offered by false prophets.

—Charles F. Bahmueller

Further Reading

Brewer, Anthony. *A Guide to Marx's "Capital."* Cambridge, England: Cambridge University Press, 1884. A clear and careful examination of *Das Kapital* that is useful for students.

Eastman, Max. Introduction to *"Capital," "The Communist Manifesto," and Other Writings by Karl Marx.* Reprint. New York: Modern Library, 1959. Written in 1932, Eastman's introduction provides a succinct, nontechnical introduction to Marx's argument.

Foley, Duncan. *Understanding Capital: Marx's Economic Theory.* Cambridge, Mass.: Harvard University Press, 1986. A step-by-step exploration of the subject matter of *Das Kapital*, written to guide students through subject matter somewhat opaque in Marx's presentation.

Marsden, Richard. *The Nature of Capital: Marx After Foucault.* London: Routledge, 1999. An examination of Marx and his *Das Kapital* in the light of the new historicist thought of Michel Foucault, whose notion of "discourse" was meant directly to contest Marx's notion of "ideology."

Rockmore, Tom. *Marx After Marxism: The Philosophy of Karl Marx.* Malden, Mass.: Blackwell, 2002. Seeks to interpret Marx's philosophy from an apolitical perspective, without the ideology that dominated many previous analyses. Focuses on Marx's relationship with Hegel.

See also: Apr., 1807: Hegel Publishes *The Phenomenology of Spirit*; 1817: Ricardo Identifies Seven Key Economic Principles; 1819: Schopenhauer Publishes *The World as Will and Idea*; 1839: Blanc Publishes *The Organization of Labour*; Feb., 1848: Marx and Engels Publish *The Communist Manifesto*; Feb. 22-June, 1848: Paris Revolution of 1848; Mar. 3-Nov. 3, 1848: Prussian Revolution of 1848; Sept. 28, 1864: First International Is Founded; 1868: Bakunin Founds the Social Democratic Alliance; Jan., 1884: Fabian Society Is Founded; Mar., 1898: Russian Social-Democratic Labor Party Is Formed; 1900: Freud Publishes *The Interpretation of Dreams*.

RELATED ARTICLES in *Great Lives from History: The Nineteenth Century, 1801-1900:* Friedrich Engels; Karl Marx; David Ricardo.

March 2, 1867
U.S. DEPARTMENT OF EDUCATION IS CREATED

The creation of the U.S. Department of Education was the first federal involvement in public education but it did little more than collect and disseminate information.

ALSO KNOWN AS: U.S. Office of Education
LOCALE: Washington, D.C.
CATEGORIES: Education; organizations and institutions

KEY FIGURES

Henry Barnard (1811-1900), educator, journalist, and first U.S. commissioner of education
James A. Garfield (1831-1881), Ohio congressman and later president, 1881
Andrew Johnson (1808-1875), president of the United States, 1865-1869
E. E. White (1829-1902), Ohio commissioner of common schools

SUMMARY OF EVENT

On March 2, 1867, President Andrew Johnson signed an act that created a federal department of education to collect and diffuse statistics and facts on the progress and condition of education in the several states and territories that would help establish and maintain efficient school systems and "promote the cause of education throughout the country." The act provided for the appointment of a federal commissioner of education charged with reporting annually to Congress the results of investigations and recommendations to carry out the statute's purposes.

The story behind the creation of the U.S. Department of Education is, in many ways, the story of Henry Barnard, a native of Connecticut, who, when only twenty-six years old, dedicated himself to the cause of promoting and improving public school education in America. Reasonably well off, Barnard attended both public and private schools in his home state. He graduated from Yale University in 1830, was admitted to the Connecticut bar, and made a grand tour of Europe in 1835. Barnard's extensive travels and his own educational experience convinced him that New England's public schools, although among America's best, were seriously deficient. He concluded that in no respect could the highly decentralized, ungraded, and miserably taught public institutions in the United States compare favorably with the state-controlled, generously supported, and professionally staffed educational systems he had observed in Europe.

After Barnard was elected to the Connecticut state legislature in 1837, he sponsored two educational reform bills. Both failed, but in 1838 his proposal to create a state Board of Commissioners of Common Schools passed unanimously. The board elected Barnard himself secretary and defined his duties: to collect by inspection

Henry Barnard. (Library of Congress)

and correspondence all possible information on conditions of the common schools; to propose plans relative to the organization and administration of the schools for consideration by the board and the state legislature; to meet with parents, teachers, and administrators in each county; to edit a common school journal; and to promote among the public, in any way possible, interest and information regarding the subject of education.

While seeking comparative data for his report, Barnard solicited information from several agencies of the federal government regarding education in other states. To his amazement, he discovered that no federal office gathered educational statistics of any kind. This discovery prompted him to visit Washington, D.C., where he prevailed upon the Van Buren administration to include a few educational items, particularly regarding literacy, in future census questionnaires. Barnard, his friend Horace Mann of Massachusetts, and others interested in common school education used the information so obtained to dramatize the dismal state of American education. They hoped ultimately to persuade influential persons, in and out of government, that gathering data on a national scale could contribute substantially to the improvement of public education at the local level.

The task was not an easy one. Those who favored formal recognition by the national government of common school education and some degree of national responsibility for its promotion disagreed as to the form that recognition should take. Should the federal government establish, support, and administer a comprehensive educational system, as many European nations did, or should it confine itself strictly to collecting and diffusing statistics concerning state and local systems? Even more difficult to overcome than such differences among friends were the objections raised by opponents, who interpreted any plan for federal participation in the educational sphere as an attempt to invade states' rights. Somewhere between these extremes lay the vast majority of Americans. They were either skeptical, apathetic, or unaware that the country had an educational problem.

Barnard appears to have first proposed the establishment of a special federal agency to collect and disseminate educational information during a speaking tour he made in 1842. In 1845 and again in 1847 he tried without success to interest the trustees of the Smithsonian Institution, which was then being organized, in his project. Later, at the National Convention of the Friends of Common Schools meeting in Philadelphia in 1849, Barnard helped draft a resolution urging congressional action. Over the next fifteen years he continued to promote his bureau in lectures, at conventions, and in the pages of his famous *American Journal of Education*.

Illness kept Barnard away from the convention that finally secured the attention of Congress. In February, 1866, at a Washington meeting of the National Association of State and City School Superintendents, Ohio's school commissioner, E. E. White, read a paper advocating the establishment of a national bureau for educational affairs. Joined by the National Teachers' Association, the superintendents voted to present White's proposal to Congress. There it found a sponsor in General James A. Garfield, a Republican representative from White's home state of Ohio.

On February 14, 1866, Garfield introduced a bill to establish a federal department of education. The House approved an amended measure on June 19 after a brief speech in which Garfield cited current illiteracy figures among the American population and reminded his colleagues that the country's political system depended upon an intelligent and informed electorate. Senate approval came early the next year, and on March 2, 1867, President Andrew Johnson signed the bill into law, naming Henry Barnard the first commissioner of the U.S. Department of Education.

SIGNIFICANCE

To the embittered Andrew Johnson, who was already hard pressed by a hostile Congress and soon to be the subject of impeachment proceedings, creation of the Department of Education—which later became the U.S. Office of Education in the Health, Education and Welfare Department—probably seemed relatively insignificant. For Commissioner Barnard, however, it represented the end of a thirty-year-long battle to achieve national recognition for what he considered the country's most important task: the establishment of "schools good enough for the best and cheap enough for the poorest."

—*Germaine M. Reed*

FURTHER READING

Annual Report of the United States Commissioner of Education for 1902. Vol. 1. Washington, D.C.: Government Printing Office, 1903. This volume contains two articles dealing with Barnard and his service as commissioner of education. The first, by W. T. Harris, who served as commissioner between 1889 and 1906, is "The Establishment of the Office of the Commissioner of Education of the United States and Henry Barnard's Relation to It." The second article, by A. D. Mayo, is "Henry Barnard as First U.S. Commissioner of Education." Both are basic to a detailed study of the circumstances contributing to creation of the agency and the personalities involved.

Blair, Anna Lou. *Henry Barnard: School Administrator*. Minneapolis: Educational Publishers, 1938. Balanced biography of Barnard's career. Blair attempts to place Barnard's life in context with the American public school movement of the nineteenth century.

Gutek, Gerald L. *Historical and Philosophical Foundations of Education: A Biographical Introduction*. 4th ed. Englewood Cliffs, N.J.: Prentice Hall, 2004. This historical overview of education throughout the world includes a biography of Horace Mann that explores his philosophy and impact upon education.

Kursh, Harry. *The United States Office of Education: A Century of Service*. 1965. Reprint. Westport, Conn.: Greenwood Press, 1977. History of the Department of Education and its successors that contains a chapter devoted to Barnard and the creation of the agency.

Lee, Gordon Canfield. *The Struggle for Federal Aid, First Phase: A History of the Attempts to Obtain Federal Aid for the Common Schools, 1870-1890*. New York: Teachers College, Columbia University, 1949. Gordon Canfield Lee's slim volume is worth consulting because it places the creation of the Office of Commissioner of Education in perspective.

Lykes, Richard Wayne. *Higher Education and the United States Office of Education, 1867-1953*. Washington, D.C.: Bureau of Postsecondary Education, United States Office of Education, U.S. Government Printing Office, 1975. Official history of the agency through the mid-twentieth century.

Pulliam, John D., and James J. Van Patten. *History of Education in America*. 8th ed. Upper Saddle River, N.J.: Merrill, 2003. Textbook covering the entire history of American education that has enjoyed enduring success because of the clarity with which it is written.

Smith, Darrell H. *The Bureau of Education: Its History, Activities, and Organization*. Baltimore: Johns Hopkins University Press, 1923. Only a few pages deal with the establishment of the Department of Education, but considerable attention is paid to its evolution.

Smith, Theodore C. *The Life and Letters of James Abram Garfield*. 2 vols. New Haven, Conn.: Yale University Press, 1925. The second volume contains a brief but good discussion of Garfield's efforts to push the department of education bill through Congress and afterward to protect it from its opponents, who opposed it as unconstitutional and unnecessary.

Steiner, Bernard C. *Life of Henry Barnard: The First United States Commissioner of Education, 1867-1870*. Washington, D.C.: Government Printing Office, 1919. Scholarly biography of Barnard that is very readable, but somewhat uncritical of its subject. Gives brief treatment to Barnard's career as commissioner.

Warren, Donald R. *To Enforce Education: A History of the Founding Years of the United States Office of Education*. Detroit: Wayne State University Press, 1974. Study of the issues surrounding the founding of the Department of Education.

SEE ALSO: 1820's-1830's: Free Public School Movement; May, 1823: Hartford Female Seminary Is Founded; Nov., 1828: Webster Publishes the First American Dictionary of English; Aug. 10, 1846: Smithsonian Institution Is Founded; Oct. 4-6, 1876: American Library Association Is Founded; Nov. 1, 1897: New Library of Congress Building Opens.

RELATED ARTICLES in *Great Lives from History: The Nineteenth Century, 1801-1900:* Henry Barnard; James A. Garfield; Horace Mann.

March 30, 1867
RUSSIA SELLS ALASKA TO THE UNITED STATES

The United States acquired a vast territory of abundant natural resources and immense strategic importance when it bought Alaska from the Russians for $7.2 million. Although the purchase was condemned by many Americans, that opposition gradually subsided after the discovery of gold in the region at the end of the nineteenth century.

ALSO KNOWN AS: Treaty with Russia; Russian America; Seward's Folly; Seward's Icebox
LOCALE: Washington, D.C.
CATEGORIES: Expansion and land acquisition; diplomacy and international relations

KEY FIGURES

William H. Seward (1801-1872), secretary of state, who negotiated the treaty for the U.S. government
Alexander II (1818-1881), czar of Russia, r. 1855-1881, who authorized the sale of Russian America
Nathaniel Prentiss Banks (1816-1894), chairman of the House Committee on Foreign Affairs
Aleksandr Mikhailovich Gorchakov (1798-1883), Russian foreign minister and chancellor
Edouard de Stoeckl (fl. mid-nineteenth century), Russian minister to the United States
Charles Sumner (1811-1874), chairman of the Senate Committee on Foreign Relations
Robert John Walker (1801-1869), former U.S. senator and lawyer, who helped secure passage of the appropriation bill

SUMMARY OF EVENT

Unofficial negotiations regarding the sale of Russian America—as Alaska was then called—to the United States were conducted in at least two instances before the Civil War (1861-1865), in 1854 and in 1860. Following the war, the discussion was renewed through the efforts of Baron Edouard de Stoeckl, Russian minister to the United States. Stoeckl believed that the transfer of Russian America was in the best interest of Russia and the future of Russian-United States friendship. Stoeckl received permission to negotiate the sale of Alaska after discussions with Czar Alexander II, Foreign Minister Aleksandr Gorchakov, and other Russian officials during his home leave late in 1866.

The minimum price for the land was set at five million dollars. The Russian willingness to sell was apparently motivated by the failure of the Russian American Company, a chartered company organized to exploit Russian America; a fear that the British might take the defenseless territory in the event of war; and a desire to minimize the possibility of clashes between U.S. and Russian interests in the Pacific.

U.S. secretary of state William H. Seward was an ardent expansionist who was interested in obtaining overseas possessions for the United States in the Caribbean and in the Pacific. When Stoeckl returned to Washington in March, 1867, Seward requested U.S. fishing rights in Russian-American territorial waters. When Stoeckl refused, Seward inquired whether Russia would be willing to sell Alaska. Stoeckl responded positively. Seward consulted President Andrew Johnson and the cabinet, which unanimously agreed to open negotiations. Seward's initial bid was five million dollars, but Stoeckl asked twice that amount for the 586,000 square miles of territory. The two men finally agreed on seven million

Secretary of State William H. Seward. (Library of Congress)

ALASKA PURCHASE TREATY

The United States entered into agreement with Russia in 1867 to purchase from the Russian Empire the Alaska Territory for $7.2 million. The treaty, excerpted here, includes a provision for Russian inhabitants to either return to their homeland or become U.S. citizens. An exception was made for "uncivilized native tribes," however, who were to be administered by the U.S. government as necessary.

Article I.

His Majesty the Emperor of all the Russias agrees to cede to the United States, by this convention, immediately upon the exchange of the ratifications thereof, all the territory and dominion now possessed by his said Majesty on the continent of America and in the adjacent islands, the same being contained within the geographical limits herein set forth. . . .

Article III.

The inhabitants of the ceded territory, according to their choice, reserving their natural allegiance, may return to Russia within three years; but if they should prefer to remain in the ceded territory, they, with the exception of uncivilized native tribes, shall be admitted to the enjoyment of all the rights, advantages, and immunities of citizens of the United States, and shall be maintained and protected in the free enjoyment of their liberty, property, and religion. The uncivilized tribes will be subject to such laws and regulations as the United States may, from time to time, adopt in regard to aboriginal tribes of that country.

Article V.

Immediately after the exchange of the ratifications of this convention, any fortifications or military posts which may be in the ceded territory shall be delivered to the agent of the United States, and any Russian troops which may be in the territory shall be withdrawn as soon as may be reasonably and conveniently practicable.

dollars, but when Stoeckl insisted that the United States also take over the Russian American Company, Seward added $200,000 to escape the obligation. Hence, the final purchase price was $7.2 million.

Stoeckl cabled the details of the sale to Foreign Minister Gorchakov, who authorized the signing of the treaty. Stoeckl brought the news to Seward on the evening of March 29 and suggested that the treaty be concluded the next day. Seward was anxious to proceed and wanted to draw up the treaty immediately. The Russian and United States plenipotentiaries summoned their clerks, and the treaty was signed at 4:00 A.M. on March 30, 1867.

A few hours after the signing, President Johnson forwarded the treaty to the Senate for ratification. It initially appeared that the necessary two-thirds vote would not be forthcoming, because Congress and President Johnson had reached an impasse concerning Reconstruction politics. Charles Sumner, chairman of the Senate Foreign Relations Committee, championed the bill, and on April 9, he made an effective three-hour speech that summarized the arguments for the purchase. Later the same day, the Senate gave its approval by a vote of thirty-seven to two. Ratifications were exchanged on June 20.

Most Americans were caught by surprise when the proposed treaty was revealed. There was some hostility and a good deal of criticism. Many newspapers denounced the proposed purchase, calling it "Johnson's Polar Bear Garden," "Seward's Icebox," "Seward's Folly," and "Walrussia," but some New England sea captains and West Coast defenders testified in its favor. Friendship with Russia was also a persuasive reason for accepting the treaty. Many people in the United States had regarded the calling of the Russian fleet at U.S. ports during the Civil War as an act of friendship at a time when England and France appeared hostile toward the cause of the Union. Although later research in Russian archives indicates that Russian ships had been dispatched to U.S. ports for strategic reasons, the idea of Russian-American friendship was not entirely illusory.

The formal transfer of Alaska to the United States took place on October 18, 1867, at Sitka, the capital of Russian America on the west coast of Baranof Island, before the agreed price had been paid to Russia. The delay in payment was caused by the failure of the House of Representatives to vote the necessary appropriation. Some members argued that, although the Constitution gave the Senate the exclusive right to approve treaties, it also gave the House the right to originate money bills. These congressmen believed that the House should have been consulted before the treaty was confirmed. Disputes between the executive and legislative branches, which eventually culminated in the impeachment trial of President Johnson, further delayed House action. Both Seward and Stoeckl, however, worked effectively to secure the appropriation.

Seward conducted a campaign to educate the newspapers and the public, while Stoeckl retained former senator Robert J. Walker as a lobbyist. Some newspapers and public officials may have received payments for their support of the treaty. Under the management of Seward's friend Nathaniel P. Banks, chairman of the House Committee on Foreign Affairs, the House passed the appropriation bill on July 14, 1868, by a vote of 113 to 43, with 44 abstaining. The Senate concurred on July 17, and the bill became law on July 27. Payment to Russia was finally made on August 1, 1868.

Estimates of the population of Alaska at the time of purchase put the Russian population at about five hundred, the number of Creoles (those of mixed Russian and indigenous descent) at about fifteen hundred, and the number of indigenous Alaskans at between twenty-four and thirty thousand. The treaty of purchase permitted inhabitants of Alaska who remained after the Russians departed the option of becoming U.S. citizens within three years, with the exception of members of the so-called "uncivilized tribes," who would be treated according to the laws that governed "aboriginal tribes" in the United States.

In general, native Alaskans had fared better under Russian rule than they did under initial U.S. rule. The Russians had extended citizenship to the Creoles and allowed some form of tribal government to remain intact among the settled native tribes. Although at first mistreated by the Russian fur traders, who conscripted Aleuts to hunt sea otters, native peoples had begun to gain increasingly benign treatment under the succession of charters that the Russian government granted to the Russian American Company beginning in 1799. The Russians strove to avoid serious conflict with the native Alaskans during much of the time that Alaska was under Russian rule.

SIGNIFICANCE

For the first seventeen years of rule by the United States, U.S. policy toward Alaska was one of neglect. Alaska officially became a customs district and was placed under military control. The War Department dispatched five hundred troops to Sitka and Fort Wrangell under the command of General Jefferson Davis. The army was unrestrained in its conduct and introduced a period of general lawlessness into a territory that had enjoyed orderly rule under the Russians. U.S. soldiers introduced disease, alcohol, and firearms to native Alaskans. It was not until the passage of the Organic Act of 1884, which provided limited government for Alaska, that some semblance of civil order was reestablished.

The founding of schools and churches by U.S. missionaries during the late nineteenth century, encouraged by Sheldon Jackson, a Presbyterian minister, significantly benefited native Alaskans at a time of neglect by the federal government. The Russian Orthodox Church, which continued to hold the allegiance of native Alaskans after the departure of the Russians, remains the most notable heritage of Russian rule in Alaska.

—Mark A. Plummer,
updated by Anne-Marie E. Ferngren

FURTHER READING

Bolkhovitinov, Nikolai N. *Russian-American Relations and the Sale of Alaska, 1834-1867*, edited and translated by Richard A. Pierce. Fairbanks, Alaska: Limestone Press, 1996. Originally published in 1991.

_______. "The Sale of Alaska in Context of Russo-American Relations in the Nineteenth Century." In *Imperial Russian Foreign Policy*, edited by Hugh Ragsdale. New York: Cambridge University Press, 1993. Two works that explore the Alaska purchase in the context of Russian-American relations before the 1867 sale and acquisition.

Chevigny, Hector. *Russian America: The Great Alaskan Venture, 1741-1867*. 1965. Reprint. Portland, Oreg.: Binford & Mort, 1979. A comprehensive survey of the Russian period of Alaskan history.

Dickerson, Donna Lee. *The Reconstruction Era: Primary Documents on Events from 1865 to 1877*. Westport, Conn.: Greenwood Press, 2003. A collection of primary source documents relating to late nineteenth century America, with documents on the Alaska purchase. Includes an introduction.

Elliott, Henry W. "Alaska: Ten Years' Acquaintance With, 1867-1877." *Harper's New Monthly Magazine* 55, no. 333 (1887). Available through the Library of Congress's Primary Documents in American History Web site.

Farrar, Victor J. *The Annexation of Russian America to the United States*. Washington, D.C.: W. F. Roberts, 1937. A brief, standard treatment of the purchase.

Jensen, Ronald J. *The Alaska Purchase and Russian-American Relations*. Seattle: University of Washington Press, 1975. Places the treaty in the larger context of Russian-American relations.

Miller, David Hunter. *The Alaska Treaty*. Kingston, Ontario: Limestone Press, 1981. An important and comprehensive study of the treaty.

Sherwood, Morgan B., ed. *Alaska and Its History*. Seattle: University of Washington Press, 1967. Contains several important articles dealing with the purchase.

Shiels, Archie W. [Archibald Williamson]. *The Purchase of Alaska.* Seattle: College, University of Alaska Press, distributed by University of Washington Press, 1967. Contains many documents pertaining to the purchase of Alaska.

Sumner, Charles. "The Cession of Russian America to the United States." Washington, D.C.: Congressional Globe Office, 1867. Sumner's speech to Congress on occasion of the Alaska purchase. Available through the University of Michigan Digital Library's Making of America Web site at http://name.umdl.umich.edu/AAZ9604.0001.001. Accessed January 17, 2006.

Van Deusen, Glyndon G. *William Henry Seward.* New York: Oxford University Press, 1967. An outstanding biography of the secretary of state who was the chief proponent of the purchase of Alaska.

SEE ALSO: Dec. 31, 1853: Gadsden Purchase Completes the U.S.-Mexican Border; Feb. 24-May 26, 1868: Impeachment of Andrew Johnson; Feb. 8, 1887: General Allotment Act Erodes Indian Tribal Unity; Aug. 17, 1896: Klondike Gold Rush Begins.

RELATED ARTICLES in *Great Lives from History: The Nineteenth Century, 1801-1900:* Alexander II; Jefferson Davis; Andrew Johnson; William H. Seward; Charles Sumner.

May 29, 1867
AUSTRIAN AUSGLEICH

A negotiated compromise between the Austrian Empire's German-Austrian and Hungarian segments, the Ausgleich created a dual monarchy under which almost all internal government functions were separated and coordinated national policies became almost impossible.

ALSO KNOWN AS: Austrian Compromise of 1867
LOCALE: Austria; Hungary
CATEGORY: Government and politics

KEY FIGURES

Francis Joseph I (1830-1916), emperor of Austria, r. 1848-1916, and king of Hungary, 1867-1916

Ferencz Deák (1803-1876), Hungarian politician and nationalist leader

Lajos Kossuth (1802-1894), leader of the Hungarian Revolution of 1848

Count Gyula Andrássy (1823-1890), first prime minister of Hungary

Count Friedrich von Beust (1809-1886), prime minister and chancellor of the Austrian Empire

František Palacký (1798-1876), leader of the Czechs within the Austrian Empire

SUMMARY OF EVENT

The Austrian Empire, as the Habsburg realms were officially known after 1804, consisted of several sets of crownlands, many ethnically heterogenous and all with a rich, distinct historical tradition. Brought together under the Habsburg Dynasty chiefly by judicious royal marriages arranged between the fifteenth and eighteenth centuries, these kingdoms and principalities and their eleven nationalities, including Germans, Magyars in Hungary, and various Slavic peoples, among others, made up a genuinely multiethnic realm. Internal peace was largely assured as long as its ethnic groups remained nationalistically quiescent.

However, with the national awakenings during the nineteenth century, the domestic tranquillity of the Habsburg monarchy became gravely jeopardized. Revolution swept across the Austrian Empire in 1848, as its various nationalities made vociferous demands for autonomy within, if not complete independence of, the empire. The most serious challenge to the Habsburgs was the revolt of the Magyars, who sought the virtual independence of Hungary. The Magyar revolt culminated in the declaration of a Hungarian Republic under the charismatic leadership of Lajos Kossuth. This revolution was the last to be put down, and required the aid of Russian troops. Hungary had traditionally been the most autonomous unit of the Austrian Empire. After the suppression of its revolt, it became completely subordinate to the highly centralized, neo-absolutistic regime established in Vienna under new emperor Francis Joseph I, whose feeble-minded predecessor Ferdinand I had been forced to abdicate.

The Hungarian Revolution of 1848 represented the initial effort of the Magyars to establish a new constitutional relationship with the rest of the Austrian Empire based on the historic rights of Hungary as a separate kingdom, whose Habsburg ruler enjoyed the title of king of Hungary only after formal election by the Hungarian "legislature," a body comprising representatives of the Hungarian nobility and landed gentry. The neo-absolutistic rule imposed on Hungary after 1848 relegated Hungary to the position of a mere province of Austria—a sharp contrast to Magyar hopes for all but complete independence of the Habsburgs. After 1848, Hungarians generally relapsed into a sullen passive resistance, and the government in Vienna made no attempt to ensure the legality of its monarchy in Hungary by securing its acceptance of the new monarch by the Hungarian legislature, and his coronation in Budapest.

Meanwhile, the Vienna regime, which had established this absolutistic regime in a moment of military strength, could only maintain it by remaining strong. Defeats suffered by the Austrian army in Italy in 1859 forced the government in Vienna to consider liberalizing its governmental structure. Austria's defeat in Italy cost it half of its possessions in northern Italy, the province of Lombardy, and necessitated a rapprochement with an increasingly restive Hungary that would acknowledge the real importance and the historical constitutional rights of the largest political unit of the Austrian Empire. During the early 1860's, however, the leading Magyars rejected the two constitutional experiments tried by the Vienna government because both failed to grant Hungary autonomy as a unitary kingdom within the empire.

Austria experienced a second setback when it was defeated by Prussia in the Seven Weeks' War of 1866. In the peace settlement that enabled the unification of Germany under Prussian leadership but without Austrian participation, Austria was forced to rethink its entire role as a state. Instead of looking west toward Germany, it now would have to look east, taking on a role of guaranteeing stability in eastern, and especially southeastern, Europe. Nevertheless, if Austria was to do that, it was imperative that its differences with the Hungarian leaders be resolved. Finally, on May 29, 1867, the Austrians, who were represented by Count Friedrich von Beust, and the Hungarians, represented by Count Gyula Andrássy and Ferencz Deák, concluded the Ausgleich, the political compromise that established the dual monarchy of Austria-Hungary.

The compromise finally worked out in 1867 was as complicated and cumbersome as the realms to which it applied, and the issue it addressed, namely, Hungary's place within the Habsburg Empire. According to the terms of the compromise, the Magyar kingdom, under its revived constitution, became a separate unit that was to be autonomous in its purely domestic affairs. The "Austrian" parts of the empire, Alpine Austria, Bohemia, Galicia, and Bukovina, were to be similarly autonomous. In addition to sharing Francis Joseph as their sovereign, Austria and Hungary were united through such common state functions as the military, foreign affairs, and finance. Expenditures for common functions were to be based on quotas that were to be negotiated every ten years. This decennial negotiation system made long-term national planning difficult, if not impossible, and it enabled each side to frustrate pet proposals of the other side. It would be largely responsible for the immobility that afflicted Austrian government through the half century that the empire lasted.

Ferencz Deák. (Library of Congress)

SIGNIFICANCE

At first glance, the compromise worked out in 1867 between Austrians and Hungarians appears to have been a politico-constitutional agreement between two kingdoms contained within a large empire. It also represented an agreement between the two most powerful national groups in Austria and Hungary, the Germans and the Magyars. This circumstance, however, made it an obstacle to any further constitutional development, since each of these two groups blocked further concessions to other ethnic groups, most notably the Slavs, as such concessions would have diminished the paramount position the 1867 compromise granted to the Germans and the Hungarians.

Because the empire's Slavic populations were divided, for governmental purposes, between Austria and Hungary—Croatians were delivered to the mercy of the Hungarians, although supposedly on terms providing for a limited degree of autonomy, and the Czechs, Poles, and Slovenians to the Austrians—any creation of a third entity, comprising all the Slavic peoples within the empire, was effectively foreclosed. Although the German-Austrians gradually yielded some power to their Slavic compatriots, who were not numerous enough to pose a threat, the Hungarians rigidly declined to make similar concessions to the Slavs in their part of the empire.

The compromise of 1867 was driven by the emperor's determination to preserve, at all costs, Austria-Hungary's status as a "great power." It achieved that goal, but only at the price of undermining the long-term preservation of the empire. In the light of subsequent history, revealing the deep-seated ethnic animosities in southeastern Europe, it is doubtful if any arrangement could have been crafted that would have held together such disparate political entities. However, the centrifugal forces at work throughout the region demonstrate the truth of the sage observation of the Czech leader František Palacký: "If the Austrian Empire had not already existed, it would have had to be invented." Even if it proved a short-term solution, the compromise of 1867 may have been its own justification.

—*Edward P. Keleher, updated by Nancy M. Gordon*

FURTHER READING

Gordon, Harold J., Jr., and Nancy M. Gordon. *The Austrian Empire: Abortive Federation?* Lexington, Mass.: D. C. Heath, 1974. Section 2 contains three different views of the compromise.

Kann, Robert A. *Dynasty, Politics and Culture: Selected Essays*. Edited by Stanley B. Winters. Boulder, Colo.: Social Science Monographs, 1991. Contains a chapter on the compromise, its causes and effects.

Kann, Robert A., and Zdenek V. David. *The Peoples of the Eastern Habsburg Lands, 1526-1918*. Seattle: University of Washington Press, 1984. Kann, the foremost historian writing in English on the Habsburg monarchy, died in 1981; the work was continued by David. This work is an extensive historical survey, and is volume 6 of *A History of East Central Europe*.

Lendvai, Paul. *The Hungarians: A Thousand Years of Victory in Defeat*. Translated by Jefferson Decker. Princeton, N.J.: Princeton University Press, 2004. Lively survey of the last one thousand years of Hungarian history, with several chapters on the Ausgleich era.

Pamlenyi, Ervin, ed. *A History of Hungary*. London: Collet's, 1975. Although issued under the auspices of the History Institute of the Hungarian Academy of Sciences, this book gives a balanced description of the evolution of Hungary under the compromise.

Sked, Alan. *The Decline and Fall of the Habsburg Empire, 1815-1918*. London: Longman, 1989. The last half of this book is devoted to the compromise and its effects; considers various historical interpretations.

SEE ALSO: June 15-Aug. 23, 1866: Austria and Prussia's Seven Weeks' War; Jan. 18, 1871: German States Unite Within German Empire; May 6-Oct. 22, 1873: Three Emperors' League Is Formed; May 20, 1882: Triple Alliance Is Formed.

RELATED ARTICLES in *Great Lives from History: The Nineteenth Century, 1801-1900:* Friedrich von Beust; Ferencz Deák; Francis Joseph I.

July 1, 1867
BRITISH NORTH AMERICA ACT

The British North America Act created of the Dominion of Canada, formally marking the birth of Canada as a nation within what would come to be known as the British Commonwealth.

ALSO KNOWN AS: Constitution Act of 1867
LOCALE: London, England; Ottawa, Canada
CATEGORIES: Laws, acts, and legal history; government and politics; colonization

KEY FIGURES

Sir George Étienne Cartier (1814-1873), leader of the Quebec delegation immediately before and after the creation of the Canadian confederation
Sir John Alexander Macdonald (1815-1891), first prime minister of Canada, 1867-1873, 1878-1891
Alexander Mackenzie (1822-1892), second prime minister of Canada, 1873-1878
Queen Victoria (1819-1901), queen of Great Britain, r. 1837-1901

SUMMARY OF EVENT

After the British defeat of French forces in the Seven Years' War (1756-1763), the terms of the 1763 Treaty of Paris forced France to yield its former colony, Canada, to Great Britain. For the first century after the Treaty of Paris, Canada was ruled as a British colony, and almost all important political decisions affecting Canadians were made by the British parliament in London or by the governor-general, who was the Crown's official representative in Canada.

Various British governments saw no reason to change this situation of overt colonial rule from London, until the outbreak of the U.S. Civil War (1861-1865) in the United States in 1861. Henry Palmerston, the British prime minister from 1859 to 1865, and his chancellor of the Exchequer, William Ewart Gladstone, expressed overt support for the Confederates and even considered granting diplomatic recognition to the Confederate government of Jefferson Davis. Moreover, British shipyards built ships for the Confederate navy. These were considered hostile acts in Washington, D.C. The overt distrust between Washington and London became much worse when, in 1861, a U.S. warship stopped the British steamer *Trent* during a trip from Canada to England and removed two Confederate agents, whose goal was to seek active support from England for the Confederates. This almost provoked a third war between the United States and Great Britain, after the Revolutionary War (1775-1783) and the War of 1812.

After the Union victory in the Civil War, the British government realized that the victorious North was angry with it but still felt positively toward Canadians, who had helped greatly in protecting escaped slaves. Prominent British politicians feared that U.S. forces might invade Canada in retaliation for British support of the Confederates during the Civil War, but believed that no such invasion would take place if Canada became an independent country. U.S. citizens in the North generally wished to maintain good relations with Canada. Thus, it was in Great Britain's self-interest to create, as quickly as possible, an independent form of government in Canada.

The British encouraged two leading Canadian politicians—Sir John Alexander Macdonald from Ontario (Upper Canada) and Sir George Étienne Cartier from Quebec (Lower Canada)—to propose a political system to unify the various Canadian provinces under a single federal system. The challenge for Macdonald and Cartier was to balance federal and provincial interests while preserving the best elements of the British parliamentary system. The recent experience of the Civil War convinced Macdonald and Cartier that it would be extremely unwise for Canada to grant excessive powers to individual provinces, but they both realized that certain matters needed to be resolved at the provincial level. Unless individual provinces saw economic, social, or political advantages for themselves in a new Canadian union, they would not join the new confederation, as it came to be called. Prince Edward Island, for example, chose not to join the Canadian confederation in 1867, but joined the Dominion of Canada six years later, only when the federal government offered to pay off the large debts the province had incurred as a result of railroad construction on the island.

The negotiations in Canada before the approval of the British North America Act of 1867 took place at conferences held in Charlottetown, on Prince Edward Island, and in Quebec City. It eventually was decided to recommend a legislature with two chambers: a House of Commons with elected members, and a Senate composed of appointed members. The linguistic and religious rights of Canadians were to be protected, and it was specified that either French or English could be used in the Houses of Parliament and in all Canadian courts. The founders of the Canadian confederation granted to the national government the power to regulate trade and commerce, to impose taxes, to control the criminal justice system, to appoint judges, and to overrule decisions rendered by provincial governments. The various provinces were to be responsible for education in their provinces. This section was important because it permitted the French Roman Catholic majority in Quebec to continue subsidizing Catholic schools in Quebec.

Unlike the U.S. Constitution, the British North America Act of 1867 specifically assigned to the federal government, not to the provinces, all powers not especially enumerated in the North America Act. The clear intention was to avoid in Canada disagreements about provincial and federal powers similar to the conflicts between federal and state powers that had created so many problems, and even a civil war, in the United States.

The North America Act did not contain a specific bill of rights, but reaffirmed the reality of the unwritten British tradition of protecting basic civil rights. (A specific Charter of Rights and Freedoms was, however, approved by the Canadian parliament in 1982. Similar to the U.S. Bill of Rights, it also established the equality in law between the French and English languages in Canada.) The British North America Act had restricted the ability of the Canadian parliament to change its basic provisions without the approval of the British parliament. In reality, the British government stopped interfering directly in Canadian domestic affairs early in the twentieth century, but the very possibility of British involvement in internal Canadian matters bothered many Canadians, and this requirement was eliminated by the Canada Act of 1982, by which the British government formally recognized Canada's complete independence from Great Britain.

On July 1, 1867, the British North America Act took effect, and the confederation of Ontario, Quebec, Nova Scotia, and New Brunswick created the Dominion of Canada. Because of its historical importance, July 1—Canada Day, as it is now known—became the Canadian national holiday. At the suggestion of Queen Victoria herself, John A. Macdonald, who had played the leading role in the creation of the Canadian confederation, was appointed Canada's first prime minister.

THE DOMINION OF CANADA, 1873

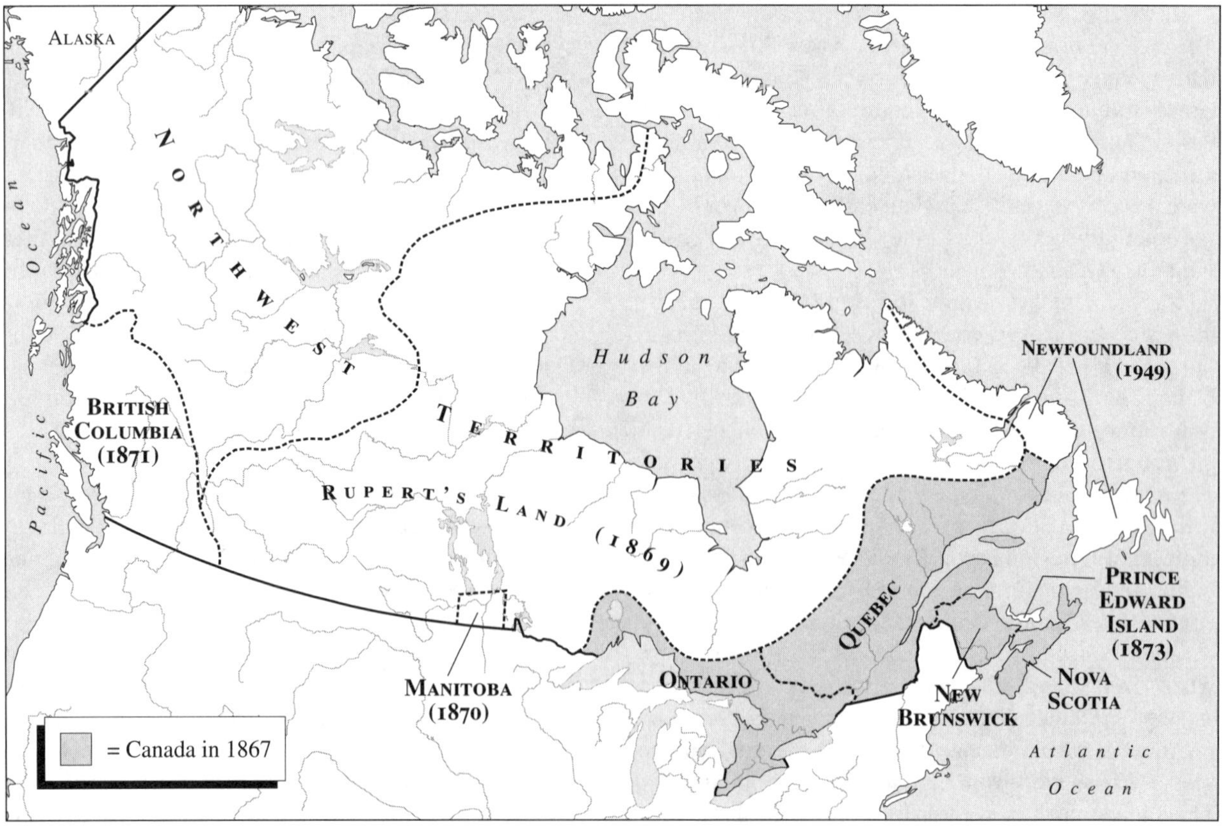

SIGNIFICANCE

As prime minister, Macdonald strove to unify Canada both politically and culturally. He was an English-speaking Protestant from Ontario and understood that the unity of Canada required that both major language groups (French and English) and religious groups (Catholic and Protestant) be included at all levels of the federal government. Until his death in 1873, George Étienne Cartier was Macdonald's most important adviser, and most historians feel that the French-speaking Catholic Cartier and the English-speaking Macdonald governed Canada together for the first six years of its independence.

Macdonald's government spent large sums of money to complete the construction of the Canadian Pacific Railway in order to permit travel and trade between eastern and western Canada. During his first six years as prime minister, the Northwest Territories, Manitoba, British Columbia, and Prince Edward Island all joined the Canadian confederation. Although Macdonald served as the leader of the opposition party in the House of Commons from 1873 to 1878, when Alexander Mackenzie served as Canada's prime minister, the years between 1867 and 1891 have generally been called the Macdonald era because of his great influence in creating the modern country of Canada.

—*Edmund J. Campion*

THE DOMINION OF CANADA

The British North America Act—now know as the Constitution Act, 1867—unified the provinces of Canada, Nova Scotia, and New Brunswick into a dominion of the British crown.

3. It shall be lawful for the Queen, by and with the Advice of Her Majesty's Most Honourable Privy Council, to declare by Proclamation that, on and after a Day therein appointed, not being more than Six Months after the passing of this Act, the Provinces of Canada, Nova Scotia, and New Brunswick shall form and be One Dominion under the Name of Canada; and on and after that Day those Three Provinces shall form and be One Dominion under that Name accordingly.
4. The subsequent Provisions of this Act shall, unless it is otherwise expressed or implied, commence and have effect on and after the Union, that is to say, on and after the Day appointed for the Union taking effect in the Queen's Proclamation; and in the same Provisions, unless it is otherwise expressed or implied, the Name Canada shall be taken to mean Canada as constituted under this Act.
5. Canada shall be divided into Four Provinces, named Ontario, Quebec, Nova Scotia, and New Brunswick.
6. The Parts of the Province of Canada (as it exists at the passing of this Act) which formerly constituted respectively the Provinces of Upper Canada and Lower Canada shall be deemed to be severed, and shall form Two separate Provinces. The Part which formerly constituted the Province of Upper Canada shall constitute the Province of Ontario; and the Part which formerly constituted the Province of Lower Canada shall constitute the Province of Quebec.
7. The Provinces of Nova Scotia and New Brunswick shall have the same Limits as at the passing of this Act.
8. In the general Census of the Population of Canada which is hereby required to be taken in the Year One thousand eight hundred and seventy-one, and in every Tenth Year thereafter, the respective Populations of the Four Provinces shall be distinguished.

FURTHER READING

Hutchison, Bruce. *Macdonald to Pearson: The Prime Ministers of Canada.* Don Mills, Ont.: Longmans Canada, 1967. Useful chapters on Macdonald's years of service as prime minister.

"John A. Macdonald." *Maclean's* 114, no. 27 (July 1, 2001): 37. A profile of Macdonald, describing his career, role in the confederation of Canada, and involvement in Canadian politics.

Martin, Ged. *Britain and the Origins of Canadian Confederation, 1837-1867.* London: Macmillan, 1995. Excellent analysis of the reasons that Great Britain was so eager to create the Dominion of Canada after the Civil War in the United States.

Smith, Cynthia M., and Jack McLeod, eds. *Sir John A.: An Anecdotal Life of John A. Macdonald.* Toronto: Oxford University Press, 1989. Contains numerous comments on John Macdonald from many different contemporary sources.

Swainson, Donald. *John A. Macdonald: The Man and the Politician.* Toronto: Oxford University Press, 1971. An excellent and well-documented biography of Macdonald.

Taylor, M. Brook, and Doug Owram, eds. *Canadian History: A Reader's Guide.* 2 vols. Toronto: University of

Toronto Press, 1994. Presents an excellent analysis of important studies of Canadian politics and society, both before and after the confederation of 1867.

Waite, P. B. *The Life and Times of Confederation, 1864-1867: Politics, Newspapers, and the Union of British North America*. 3d ed. Toronto: Robin Brass Studio, 2001. Recounts the events leading to the 1867 confederation of the Canadian provinces, examining the role that politics and newspapers played in the process.

SEE ALSO: Oct. 23-Dec. 16, 1837: Rebellions Rock British Canada; Feb. 10, 1841: Upper and Lower Canada Unite; Apr. 25, 1849: First Test of Canada's Responsible Government; June, 1866-1871: Fenian Risings for Irish Independence; 1872: Dominion Lands Act Fosters Canadian Settlement; 1873: Ukrainian Mennonites Begin Settling in Canada; Nov. 5, 1873-Oct. 9, 1878: Canada's Mackenzie Era; 1875: Supreme Court of Canada Is Established; 1876: Canada's Indian Act; Sept., 1878: Macdonald Returns as Canada's Prime Minister; Mar. 19, 1885: Second Riel Rebellion Begins; July 11, 1896: Laurier Becomes the First French Canadian Prime Minister.

RELATED ARTICLES in *Great Lives from History: The Nineteenth Century, 1801-1900:* Sir John Alexander Macdonald; Alexander Mackenzie; Lord Palmerston; Queen Victoria.

August, 1867
BRITISH PARLIAMENT PASSES THE REFORM ACT OF 1867

The Reform Act of 1867 extended a basically democratic franchise to the boroughs, giving the British urban and middle classes a major role in politics. It nearly doubled the number of eligible voters in Great Britain.

ALSO KNOWN AS: Representation of the People Act of 1867

LOCALE: London, England

CATEGORIES: Laws, acts, and legal history; social issues and reform; civil rights and liberties; government and politics

KEY FIGURES

Benjamin Disraeli (1804-1881), earl of Beaconsfield, Conservative leader of the House of Commons, 1866-1868, and later prime minister, 1868, 1874-1880

Fourteenth Earl of Derby (Edward George Geoffrey Smith Stanley; 1799-1869), Conservative prime minister, 1866-1868

William Ewart Gladstone (1809-1898), Liberal Party leader, 1859-1866, and later prime minister, 1868-1874, 1880-1885, 1886, 1892-1894

John Bright (1811-1889), middle-class Radical leader of the Reform League

John Russell (1792-1878), Liberal prime minister, 1865-1866

SUMMARY OF EVENT

Since the passing of the Great Reform Act of 1832, various opinions had existed about the furtherance of franchise reform in Great Britain. Chartists and working-class Radicals, such as Ernest Jones, proposed universal manhood suffrage, annual parliaments, the abolition of the property qualifications for election to Parliament, the secret ballot, and salaries for elected members. Liberals, such as William Ewart Gladstone and John Russell, sought reduction in the existing property qualifications from an annual rent payment of ten pounds sterling to six pounds. Middle-class Radicals, such as John Bright and Joseph Hume, sought a modified household suffrage franchise. Progressive Tories, such as Benjamin Disraeli, wanted to create a more balanced Parliament of "the more meritorious classes" by extending the vote to some workers by the so-called fancy franchises based on savings, tax payments, and education.

A number of reform bills introduced by Liberals or Radicals or Conservatives during the 1850's failed for a variety of reasons, including public apathy. A Conservative bill proposed by the fourteenth earl of Derby and by Disraeli failed in 1859 by only thirty-nine votes. Henry John Temple, Lord Palmerston, was prime minister from 1855 to 1865, and he dominated the political scene. Because he was strongly opposed to any reform, the matter was temporarily dropped.

The year 1864 witnessed a revival of Radicalism and agitation over reform because of Northern victories in the U.S. Civil War (1861-1865) and a visit to London by Giuseppe Garibaldi, the Italian patriot and revolutionary. Until then, prosperous times had lessened appeals for reform. Also in 1864, Gladstone, a leading Liberal, announced his conversion to franchise reform. In March, 1864, John Bright formed the Reform Union at Manchester and soon started formidable agitation. This middle-class Reform Union was joined in February, 1865, by the working Reform League led by Edmond Beales. Despite occasional class differences and some disagreements about methods of enfranchisement, the two reform groups cooperated well, since they both sought the enfranchisement of working men.

A bad harvest and economic problems gave rise to more agitation. Palmerston's death in October of 1865 made some reform almost certain. The succeeding Liberal government, with Lord Russell as prime minister and Gladstone as Chancellor of the Exchequer and leader of the House of Commons, set to work to prepare a reform bill. On March 12, 1866, Gladstone introduced a mild reform bill, which lowered the borough franchise from those who paid an annual rent of ten pounds sterling down to seven pounds. Gladstone's bill, however, ran into stiff opposition from a group of Whig-Liberals led by Robert Lowe, who objected strongly to any change toward democracy or working-class votes. A Conservative motion to change the voting system from ownership or rental of property to mere payment of tax passed with Lowe's aid, by 315 votes to 304 in June of 1866, and Russell's cabinet resigned over the defeat.

REFORM ACT OF 1867

Part 1 of the Representation of the People Act, 1867, commonly known as the Reform Act of 1867, expanded the voting franchise in England. The first two sections of part 1, excerpted below, enfranchised tenants of urban dwellings.

3. Every man shall, on and after the year one thousand eight hundred and sixty-eight, be entitled to be registered as a voter, and, when registered, to vote for a member or members to serve in parliament for a borough, who is qualified as follows; (that is to say,)
   1. Is of full age, and not subject to any legal incapacity; and
   2. Is on the last day of July in any year, and has during the whole of the preceding twelve calendar months been, an inhabitant occupier, as owner or tenant, of any dwelling house within the borough; and
   3. Has during the time of such occupation been rated as an ordinary occupier in respect of the premises so occupied by him within the borough to all rates (if any) made for the relief of the poor in respect of such premises; and
   4. Has on or before the twentieth day of July in the same year bona fide paid an equal amount in the pound to that payable by other ordinary occupiers in respect of all poor rates that have become payable by him in respect of the said premises up to the preceding fifth day of January:

   Provided that no man shall under this section be entitled to be registered as a voter by reason of his being a joint occupier of any dwelling house. . . . [or]
   1. Is of full age and not subject to any legal incapacity, and
   2. As a lodger has occupied in the same borough separately and as sole tenant for the twelve months preceding the last day of July in any year the same lodgings, such lodgings being part of one and the same dwelling house, and of a clear yearly value, if let unfurnished, of ten pounds or upwards; and
   3. Has resided in such lodgings for the twelve months immediately preceding the last day of July, and has claimed to be registered as a voter at the next ensuing registration of voters.

The Liberal ministry was succeeded by a minority Conservative government led by Lord Derby as prime minister and Disraeli as Chancellor of the Exchequer and leader of the House of Commons. The Reform Union and Reform League continued their agitation, which was aided by worsening economic conditions. A minor riot at a Reform League meeting at Hyde Park in London on July 23, 1866, caused considerable alarm. By the end of 1866, Disraeli and Derby agreed on the need for a reform bill, and general resolutions were introduced on February 23, 1867. Disraeli and Derby sought extensive reform, but part of the cabinet, led by Lord Cranbourne, threatened to resign. In an attempt to maintain unity in the cabinet, a milder bill was introduced but was quickly withdrawn. Disraeli then introduced the more extensive original Reform Bill on March 18, 1867, and Cranbourne and two other ministers resigned.

The Reform Bill established household suffrage in the boroughs or towns for those paying any Poor Law taxes directly and for those qualifying for the "fancy franchises" (fifty pounds in savings, a university degree, professional status, or payment of one pound in annual taxes). It also lowered property qualifications in the counties. In its original form, the Reform Bill would have enfranchised about five hundred thousand new voters and given double votes to two hundred thousand. The purpose was to create social balance in the electorate, since the workers and the aristocrats would each have one-fourth of the votes and the middle classes would have nearly one-half.

Gladstone, the leader of the Liberal opposition, tried at first to weaken the bill, but many Liberals refused to support him; he then tried to liberalize it further, intending to extend the vote to the entire middle class. John Bright and the Radicals also sought additional extensions. Lowe and Cranbourne bitterly opposed the bill. Disraeli took advantage of the confusion of the opposition and steered the bill through the Second Reading, the stage before voting amendments, by twenty-one votes. A number of Radical amendments were then offered. Disraeli declined some but decided to accept one that abolished compounding, a practice by which landlords paid the Poor Tax for their tenants. This amendment made all tenants taxpayers, thus adding almost five hundred thousand urban voters, most of whom were workers.

The change was consistent with the tax-rating basis of the bill, but it transformed the bill from a class-balanced measure to a democratic measure. Disraeli then dropped the now unnecessary "fancy franchises" and the dual votes. A mild redistribution of seats was added, and the county franchise was lowered to twelve pounds in property qualifications. In this form, the Reform Bill of 1867 passed the Commons by a comfortable margin. Lord Derby then steered it through the Conservative-controlled House of Lords by August, 1867, with only one minor change—a system of minority representation in three-member districts. Derby conceded some uncertainty about the results of the bill, using a phrase earlier coined by Disraeli, that it was "a leap in the dark." A separate Reform Bill in 1868 brought Scottish and Irish voting qualifications more in line with English ones and gave some extra seats to Scotland and Ireland.

SIGNIFICANCE

The Representation of the People Act of 1867 was one of the most important political reforms in modern British history. This Reform Act was significant for bringing a basically democratic franchise to the English boroughs. It also gave the urban working classes a major role in politics and completed the franchisement of the middle classes. The electorate was almost doubled by the addition of approximately 938,000 voters to the one million already voting. The Reform Act of 1867 also made Parliament more responsible to the electorate and led to strengthened party organization. The changed electorate did not radically change relative party strength, although it probably aided the Conservatives to some extent. The role of the Conservative Party in the reform helped to make it a more forward-looking party capable of enough popular appeal to remain a powerful party. As Conservative leader, Disraeli seemed unperturbed by a measure viewed as radical by many proponents of reform, and he was confident that he had secured his party's dominance.

The reform also struck a further blow at the still-common election-by-arrangement in small boroughs. The electorate was doubled in the boroughs, with a part of every class now entitled to vote. Long-term effects of the Reform Act of 1867 included the growth of party organization. The influence of constituents on their members of Parliament grew, and outside

Editorial cartoon by John Leech (1817-1864) commenting on William Ewart Gladstone and John Russell's failed attempt to lower the property requirements for the franchise from ten to six pounds in 1860. The cartoon is captioned, "The new Russell six-pounder." "Six-pounder" was also a term for a cannon that fired six-pound balls.

opinion came to have more influence on Parliament's actions. Since both parties now had many working-class members, the workers were in a position to demand democracy from both parties. These effects, however, came about only gradually. The Reform Act of 1867 did not bring democracy to the counties of England. It added some voters in rural regions, but among those still lacking a vote were agricultural workers, miners in rural areas, and poorer suburbanites. Worker influence did not immediately become significant, and aristocratic and middle-class dominance continued. Although historians disagree about who was responsible for it among Disraeli, Bright, Derby, and Gladstone, it is nevertheless clear that the Reform Act of 1867 was an important step toward democracy.

—James H. Steinel, updated by Carl Rollyson

FURTHER READING

Blake, Robert. *Disraeli*. New York: St. Martin's Press, 1967. Less of a psychological study than Weintraub's work listed below, this biography includes a good summary of the course of the Reform Bill of 1867 through Parliament, emphasizing the role played by Lord Derby.

Briggs, Asa. *Victorian People: A Reassessment of Persons and Themes, 1851-1867*. Chicago: University of Chicago Press, 1955. Excellent studies of Disraeli, Bright, and Lowe are included in an analysis of the Reform Bill of 1867 and a narrative of its passage.

Langley, Helen, ed. *Benjamin Disraeli, Earl of Beaconsfield: Scenes from an Extraordinary Life*. Oxford, England: Bodleian Library, 2003. Anthology of essays written to accompany an exhibit of Disraeli's papers at Oxford University's Bodleian Library.

Park, Joseph. *The English Reform Bills of 1867*. New York: Columbia University Press, 1920. A detailed account of the political and parliamentary development of the Reform Bill, and the relationship of English reform efforts to movements in the United States, France, Germany, and Italy.

Richmond, Charles, and Paul Smith, eds. *The Self-Fashioning of Disraeli: 1818-1851*. New York: Cambridge University Press, 1998. Collection of essays by historians, psychiatrists, and experts in literature that combine to profile the "self-made" Disraeli. Topics include his educational background and politics.

Seymour, Charles. *Electoral Reform in England and Wales*. London: Oxford University Press, 1925. Five chapters about the Reform Bill of 1867 give the best account of the actual provisions of the measure as well as able summaries of the earlier reform bills of the 1850's and 1860's.

Shannon, Richard. *The Age of Disraeli, 1868-1881: The Rise of Tory Democracy*. New York: Longman, 1992. See especially part 1, "From Derby to Disraeli," in which Shannon succinctly shows how Disraeli successfully challenged the supremacy of the Liberals in the boroughs and used the Reform Bill to establish himself as a new kind of Tory leader.

Weintraub, Stanley. *Disraeli: A Biography*. New York: E. P. Dutton, 1993. Chapter 21 emphasizes Disraeli's commitment to the Reform Bill and his insistence that only a "bold line" would succeed. An excellent narrative of the legislative process and political maneuvering that resulted in Disraeli's triumph.

SEE ALSO: Dec. 11-30, 1819: British Parliament Passes the Six Acts; 1824: British Parliament Repeals the Combination Acts; May 9, 1828-Apr. 13, 1829: Roman Catholic Emancipation; June 4, 1832: British Parliament Passes the Reform Act of 1832; 1833: British Parliament Passes the Factory Act; Aug. 14, 1834: British Parliament Passes New Poor Law; Sept. 9, 1835: British Parliament Passes Municipal Corporations Act; May 8, 1838-Apr. 10, 1848: Chartist Movement; June 15, 1846: British Parliament Repeals the Corn Laws; Aug. 28, 1857: British Parliament Passes the Matrimonial Causes Act; June 2, 1868: Great Britain's First Trades Union Congress Forms; Dec. 3, 1868-Feb. 20, 1874: Gladstone Becomes Prime Minister of Britain; Dec. 6, 1884: British Parliament Passes the Franchise Act of 1884.

RELATED ARTICLES in *Great Lives from History: The Nineteenth Century, 1801-1900:* John Bright; Fourteenth Earl of Derby; Benjamin Disraeli; William Ewart Gladstone; John Russell.

October, 1867
NOBEL PATENTS DYNAMITE

The commercial use of high explosives in the excavating and mining industries was established by the inventions of dynamite and the blasting cap. Alfred Nobel mixed nitroglycerin, a very unstable high explosive, with silica powder, forming a stable paste that he called "dynamite." Dynamite, which could be shaped into cylindrical charges that were safely detonated by a blasting cap, replaced black gunpowder, which had less than half of dynamite's blasting power.

LOCALE: Stockholm, Sweden
CATEGORIES: Inventions; chemistry; science and technology

KEY FIGURES
Alfred Nobel (1833-1896), Swedish industrialist, engineer, and inventor
Ascanio Sobero (1812-1888), Italian inventor of nitroglycerin
Immanuel Nobel (1801-1872), engineer, armaments producer, and Alfred Nobel's father
Emil Nobel (1843-1864), cofounder of the first nitroglycerin company and younger brother of Alfred Nobel
Théophile-Jules Pelouze (1807-1867), French chemist
William Bickford (1774-1834), inventor of the safety fuse

SUMMARY OF EVENT

Dynamite is an absorbent material that has been soaked in nitroglycerin, a substance so unstable that it can easily explode with a slight impact or a small change in temperature or pressure, making it unsafe for practical use. Alfred Nobel found that the absorbent material—dynamite—stabilized the nitroglycerin to the point that it needed a detonator to trigger its explosive power. In 1863, he invented the blasting cap, a detonator that was triggered by a burning fuse. The smaller explosion of the blasting cap generated a shock wave that was sufficient to detonate the larger explosion of the nitroglycerin within the dynamite.

Nobel's father, Immanuel Nobel, was an engineer and inventor. He built bridges and buildings in Stockholm, where the blasting of rocks was common practice. He also experimented with explosives, inventing and manufacturing naval mines made of black powder for the Russians during the Crimean War. Immanuel, who wanted his sons to join the family business, gave Alfred a first-class education. As part of his training in chemical engineering, Alfred researched explosives in the private laboratory of Théophile-Jules Pelouze, a professor of chemistry at the University of Torino in Paris, France. Here, in 1850, Alfred met Ascanio Sobero, an Italian chemist, who several years earlier had invented nitroglycerin, the first high explosive.

Explosives are materials that react extremely fast, producing a large amount of hot gas that expands so rapidly it creates a high-pressure wave. Some explosives, such as gasoline, utilize the oxygen in air to burn. The air-burning explosives react at such a slow rate that they are considered low-level explosives. The composition of high explosives already contains the oxygen needed for rapid "burning" within their chemical makeup, and their explosive reaction is considered a decomposition reaction. Nitroglycerin has a chemical formula of $C_3H_5(ONO_2)_3$; the oxygen in the compound combines with carbon and hydrogen and releases hot nitrogen gas during decomposition. The gases generated occupy more than twelve hundred times the original volume, and the heat generated by the reaction can raise the temperature to about 9,000 degrees Fahrenheit. The combined effect produces a local pressure of nearly 20,000 atmospheres that travels in a pressure wave at a speed of more than 17,000 miles per hour.

Early nitroglycerin was made by mixing glycerol with a mixture of sulfuric and nitric acids. The reaction that produced the nitroglycerin generated so much heat that it would cause the forming nitroglycerin to explode instantly. Attempts to run the reaction at cold temperatures were often unsuccessful because nitroglycerin is a liquid that would freeze at temperatures below 55 degrees Fahrenheit, and solid nitroglycerin is even more unstable than its liquid counterpart. Thus, Sobero viewed his invention as commercially worthless.

Alfred Nobel, along with his brother Emil and his father Immanuel, decided to experiment with a safer method of producing nitroglycerin, hoping that nitroglycerin could be made in commercial quantities, allowing for the utilization of its highly explosive character in the blasting industry. In 1862 the Nobels formed a research laboratory and plant in Stockholm, Sweden, to produce nitroglycerin. They found that cooling the reaction to lower temperatures could stabilize the forming nitroglycerin. Although Alfred worked to overcome safety issues, during the next few years his laboratory experienced several explosions (one in 1864 killed five people, including his younger brother Emil). Because of repeated explosions the city of Stockholm forced Alfred to move his laboratory outside city limits, where he continued his research in a floating laboratory on a barge anchored on Lake Mälaren. By 1864, Alfred was producing nitroglycerin in commercial quantities in his newly formed company, Nitroglycerin AB.

The use of nitroglycerin for blasting was now possible because of Alfred Nobel's blasting cap, an igniter for the main explosion. The Nobel patent detonator used a strong shock rather than heat combustion to detonate the main explosive. His early blasting cap was a cylinder of black powder that was surrounded by a larger vessel containing the nitroglycerin. A burning safety fuse, of the type invented by William Bickford, ignited the black powder and generated a low-level explosion, which produced sufficient impact to cause the high-level explosion of the nitroglycerin in a more manageable environment. Alfred continued his research to improve the blasting cap and eventually settled on a copper capsule containing a charge of mercury fulminate. The basic structure of this blasting cap remained in general use until the mid-1920's.

The instability of nitroglycerin continued to be a safety problem. Nitroglycerin was an oily, highly volatile liquid that was soluble in alcohol but not water. Alfred mixed the nitroglycerin with diatomite. Diatomite is a natural sedimentary material made of microscopic shells from diatoms (algae) composed of silica (SiO_2). The high porosity of the shells wicked the nitroglycerin into the microcavities, reducing the surface area for volatilization of the liquid. The silica shells protected the microscopic droplets from impact denotation, and the material now could be safely transported.

The mixture was a paste that could be molded by hand into cylindrical tubes that could easily be inserted into drill holes. The blasting caps could then be pushed and embedded into the paste. The impact of the explosion of the blasting cap would then detonate the pasty mixture of nitroglycerin and silica. Nobel called this new mixture dynamite and applied for a patent in 1867. In October of that year, Nobel received U.S. patent no. 78,317 for his dynamite.

Dynamite was soon recognized as the explosive of choice in the excavation and mining industries. Because it was impractical to transport explosives long distances and because of government restrictions on international shipments of explosives, dynamite had to be manufactured locally.

Luckily for Nobel, he was an excellent business entrepreneur. During the next two decades he founded or acquired more than ninety factories to produce dynamite in twenty different countries. So successful was Nobel that he became a multimillionaire. Many of his companies have become industrial enterprises that remain prominent in the world economy, including the Bofors-Gullspang Company in Sweden, a world-renowned manufacturer of munitions and firearms; Imperial Chemical Industries (ICI) of Great Britain; and Dyno Nobel in Norway.

Significance

Dynamite, detonated by a blasting cap, was the first high-explosive material that could be safely used for controlled blasting in the fields of civil engineering and mining. While dynamite saved thousands of lives in the long run, it was not free from causing accidents. The overall effects of blasting with dynamite increased, however, as fewer blasts were needed to accomplish the same amount of work.

Nobel's work established the modern initiation sequence, or firing train, for the safe use of high explosives. The ignition sequence is a chain reaction that cascades from relatively low levels of energy (Nobel's blasting cap) to the final detonation of the main charge of a high-energy explosive (Nobel's dynamite). Although the explosives involved in the firing train have changed since their inception, the initiation sequence established by Nobel remains in use.

—Dion C. Stewart and Toby Stewart

Further Reading

Cooper, Paul W., and Stanley R. Kurowski. *Introduction to the Technology of Explosives*. New York: Wiley-VCH, 1997. Gives details on the explosive reaction for the decomposition of nitroglycerin, written for the nonscientist.

Fant, Kenne. *Alfred Nobel: A Biography*. New York: Arcade, 1993. Tells the story of how Nobel invented dynamite and discusses his business ventures.

Gleasner, Diana C. *Dynamite: Inventions That Changed Our Lives*. New York: Walker, 1982. Gives an account of the significance of the development of dynamite. Good for younger readers.

Kelly, Jack. *Gunpowder: Alchemy, Bombards, and Pyrotechnics: The History of the Explosive That Changed the World*. New York: Basic Books, 2004. Relates the significance of dynamite's replacement of gunpowder as the blasting material of choice in the 1870's.

Meyer, Rudolf, et al. *Explosives*. New York: Wiley-VCH, 2002. This reference book provides scientific details about 120 different explosive materials, including dynamite and nitroglycerin, although it lacks details on the chemistry and physics of explosives. Written for those with some knowledge of chemistry.

SEE ALSO: Oct., 1893-October, 1897: British Subdue African Resistance in Rhodesia; Nov. 27, 1895: Nobel Bequeaths Funds for the Nobel Prizes.

RELATED ARTICLES in *Great Lives from History: The Nineteenth Century, 1801-1900:* Alfred Nobel; Bertha von Suttner.

October 21, 1867
MEDICINE LODGE CREEK TREATY

An attempt to bring a final settlement to the conflicts on the southern Great Plains, the Medicine Lodge Creek Treaty required the members of five major tribes to go to reservations but did not end violent conflicts.

LOCALE: Southwestern Kansas

CATEGORIES: Laws, acts, and legal history; indigenous people's rights

KEY FIGURES

Black Kettle (1803?-1868), leading Cheyenne chief at Medicine Lodge Creek

Satank (Sitting Bear; c. 1800-1871), Kiowa chief and orator at Medicine Lodge Creek

Satanta (White Bear; c. 1830-1878), Kiowa chief and orator at Medicine Lodge Creek

Nathaniel G. Taylor (1819-1887), U.S. commissioner of Indian affairs

Ten Bears (1792-1872), Comanche chief and orator

SUMMARY OF EVENT

For many years, the Comanche, Kiowa, Kiowa-Apache, Southern Cheyenne, and Arapaho peoples roamed the vast area of the southern Great Plains, following huge buffalo herds. This region later made up parts of Texas, Oklahoma, New Mexico, Colorado, and Kansas. The Northern Cheyenne, Sioux, and other peoples also lived similar lives on the northern Great Plains. Warfare was a part of the daily life of these peoples, generally as a result of intertribal rivalries and disputes concerning control of certain sections of the plains.

The traditional life styles of the Indians began to change when Europeans began arriving on the Great Plains during the sixteenth century. Until the early nineteenth century, however, the changes were limited to such things as the acquisition of horses, steel knives, guns, and other products from European traders. The tribes soon became dependent on these items, but their day-to-day lives changed little.

The most dominant Indians in the region were the Comanches, who were known as the Lords of the Southern Plains. Joined by the Kiowas, with whom they established friendly relations around the year 1790, the Comanches controlled the smaller Kiowa-Apache tribe and the region south of the Arkansas River. Their chief rivals north of the Arkansas River were the Southern Cheyenne. In 1840, however, the Comanches and Cheyennes established a fragile peace that also included the Arapahos, the less numerous allies of the Cheyennes. This peace came at the beginning of a decade that would change forever the face of the southern Great Plains.

In 1846, the United States annexed Texas. The end of the Mexican War in 1848 added New Mexico, Arizona, and other areas of the Southwest to the United States. Over the next half century, the fragile Native American peace of 1840 became a strong bond of brotherhood for the southern plains tribes as they fought to defend themselves and their land against the encroachments of Euro-American settlers, railroads, buffalo hunters, soldiers, and other intruders.

With the acquisition of Texas, the United States inherited a long and bloody conflict between Texans and Comanches, who were described by some observers as the best light cavalry in the world. The Comanches had long hunted between the Arkansas River and the Rio Grande. In 1821, the government of Mexico began giving land grants in west Texas to settlers from the United States who soon challenged the Comanches for control of the area.

The first attempt to confine the Comanches to reservations was a May, 1846, treaty that created two small reservations on the Brazos River. The few Comanches who settled on the reservations soon yearned for the free-spirited life on the vast plains. By 1850, discoveries of gold and silver between the southern Rocky Mountains and California were drawing numerous wagon and pack trains through the southern plains. These were soon followed by stagecoach lines and later by railroads. The increase in traffic was paralleled by increased confrontations with the Indian tribes, who were accustomed to unhindered pursuit of the buffalo.

Between 1846 and 1865, several treaties were signed between the Native Americans of the southern plains and the government of the United States. However, lack of mutual confidence, sarcasm, and open contempt on both

CHEYENNES SHAKING HANDS WITH THE COMMISSIONERS.

INTERIOR VIEW OF THE COUNCIL TENT.

SATANTA DELIVERING A SPEECH BEFORE THE COMMISSIONERS IN THE COUNCIL TE T.

very lovely place, and many have felt as though the prospect of a long life in this place would not be insupportable.

THE CEREMONY OF SHAKING HANDS

interesting sight, and it is an important cere-

THE GREAT CHIEF SATANTA,

in delivering his address, which has already appeared in the daily newspapers, spoke with a dignity and force that could not but be appreciated. He is a great orator and of unbounded influence in the council.

ISSUE OF CLOTHING TO THE COMANCHE INDIANS AT TIMBER MOUNTAIN FORK, KANSAS.

COLONEL LEAVENWORTH ISSUING GOODS TO THE CHEYENNES,

was a scene of rare interest. Pots, kettles and pans, nails, brushes, and every conceivable article of use to the Indians, were here given to them; as well as coffee,

quietly for their turns to come. The Cheyennes have been delayed a week, making medicine, at a point thirty miles below, on Medicine Lodge Creek.

THE INTERIOR VIEW OF THE COUNCIL TENT

shows the relative position of the whites and Indians

COL. LEAVENWORTH ISSUING GOO TO THE COMANCHE AND KIOWA INDIANS.

THE GREAT MEDICINE LODGE ON ME CINE LODGE CREEK, NEAR THE COUNCIL GROUNDS, KANSAS.

Scenes from the Medicine Lodge Creek treaty council published in Frank Leslie's Illustrated Newspaper. (Library of Congress) sides doomed these treaties to failure. The frustration felt by the Native Americans increased when cholera and other diseases introduced by Europeans began devastating the native populations.

In March of 1863, a party of Native American chiefs from the southern plains went to Washington, D.C., and met with President Abraham Lincoln. Returning home loaded with gifts, these leaders believed that coexistence with Euro-Americans was possible. However, their confidence was hard to maintain after the bloody and unprovoked massacre of Cheyennes at Sand Creek, in Colorado, the following year. Nevertheless, Ten Bears of the Comanches, who had met President Lincoln, Black Kettle of the Cheyennes, who had escaped from Sand Creek, and other chiefs still believed that peace was their best protection and was possible to achieve.

The next effort toward a peace settlement was the Little Arkansas Treaty in October, 1865. Representatives of the five southern plains tribes met with U.S. commissioners at the mouth of the Little Arkansas River near Wichita, Kansas. The government wanted to end Native American disruptions of movements in and through the plains. Little more than a stopgap measure, this treaty consigned the tribes to reservations—the Cheyennes and Arapahos in northern Indian Territory (Oklahoma) and the Comanches, Kiowas, and Kiowa-Apaches in western Texas and southwestern Indian Territory. These boundaries were impossible to enforce and did not end the violence, but the treaty set the stage for a more important meeting two years later.

In July, 1867, Congress created a peace commission to establish permanent settlements of grievances between Native Americans and Euro-Americans on the Great Plains. The commission was led by Commissioner of Indian Affairs Nathaniel G. Taylor and included a U.S. senator and three Army generals. The group chose to meet Indian representatives on the banks of Medicine Lodge Creek in southwestern Kansas. Joining them there were more than four thousand Native Americans. These people represented all five tribes but not all the bands of the tribes. Noticeably absent were the Quahadi, members of a Comanche band that wanted no peace with the U.S. government.

The council opened on October 19, 1867, with Senator John B. Henderson delivering the opening remarks. Under a large brush arbor, he referred to reservation homes, rich farmland, livestock, churches, and schools for all Native Americans. Although most tribal leaders accepted the promises as positive, the idea of being restricted to reservations covering only a fraction of their beloved Great Plains was sickening to them. The Kiowa chief Satanta (White Bear) lamented, "I love to roam over the prairies. There I feel free and happy, but when we settle down we grow pale and die." The Yamparika Comanche chief Ten Bears gave one of the most eloquent statements, declaring,

> I was born where there were no inclosures and where everything drew a free breath. I want to die there and not within walls. . . . when I see [soldiers cutting trees and killing buffalo] my heart feels like bursting with sorrow.

In spite of such emotional appeals, Ten Bears and other Comanche chiefs signed the Treaty of Medicine Lodge Creek on October 21, 1867, thereby committing their people to life on the reservation. With the horrors of the 1864 Sand Creek Massacre fresh on his mind, Black Kettle represented the Cheyennes at the council. He would not sign the treaty until other Cheyenne chiefs arrived on October 26. Although less happy with the treaty than the Comanche and Kiowa leaders, the Cheyenne chiefs also signed, primarily so they could get ammunition for firearms for their fall buffalo hunt. The Arapaho chiefs soon did likewise. At the end of the council meeting, Satank rode alone to bid farewell to the federal Peace Commission. He expressed his desire for peace and declared that the Comanches and the Kiowas no longer wanted to shed the blood of the white man.

SIGNIFICANCE

The Treaty of Medicine Lodge Creek restricted the five southern plains tribes to reservations in the western half of Indian Territory. However, vague terminology and unwritten promises made the treaty impossible fully to understand or enforce. New violence soon erupted on the southern plains. One year after Medicine Lodge Creek, Black Kettle was killed in a confrontation similar to the Sand Creek Massacre, this time on the Washita River in Indian Territory. The violence escalated for several years, then dwindled to isolated incidents before ending at Wounded Knee in 1890.

A poignant illustration of the ultimate effect of the treaty occurred on June 8, 1871, when the seventy-year-old Satank—who along with Satanta and a young war chief named Big Tree had been arrested for attacking a mule train carrying food that the ration-deprived Indians sorely needed—was being transported to Texas to stand trial for murder. Chewing his own wrists in order to slip out of his manacles, Satank then attacked a guard and was shot dead, fulfilling a prophecy that he had uttered only minutes before to fellow prisoners: "Tell them I am dead. . . . I shall never go beyond that tree."

—*Glenn L. Swygart*

Further Reading

Brown, Dee. *Bury My Heart at Wounded Knee*. New York: Holt, Rinehart and Winston, 1970. Impassioned history of Indian resistance to white encroachments that places the Treaty of Medicine Lodge Creek in the full context of Native American history in the western United States.

Grinnell, George Bird. *The Fighting Cheyennes*. 1915. Reprint. Norman: University of Oklahoma Press, 1956. An author who observed the Cheyennes at first hand presents their history up to 1890.

Hagan, William T. *United States-Comanche Relations*. New Haven, Conn.: Yale University Press, 1976. The most complete coverage of the council and treaty at Medicine Lodge Creek.

Hatch, Thom. *Black Kettle: The Cheyenne Chief Who Sought Peace but Found War*. New York: John Wiley & Sons, 2004. Biography of the chief who represented the Cheyennes at Medicine Lodge Creek.

Hoig, Stan. *The Peace Chiefs of the Cheyennes*. Norman: University of Oklahoma Press, 1980. Brief but well-illustrated study of the efforts of the Cheyennes to find peace, with particular attention to Black Kettle.

Josephy, Alvin M., Jr. *Five Hundred Nations: An Illustrated History of North American Indians*. New York: Alfred A. Knopf, 1994. Well-illustrated history of North America from its original inhabitants' viewpoint. Includes a brief section on the Medicine Lodge Creek Treaty that contains direct quotations from Indian leaders.

Mooney, James. *Calendar History of the Kiowa Indians*. 1898. Reprint. Washington, D.C.: Smithsonian Institution Press, 1979. Provides a chronology of the Kiowa tribe.

Rollings, Willard H. *The Comanche*. New York: Chelsea House, 1989. Describes the change in Comanche life after the Medicine Lodge Creek Treaty.

Williams, Jeanne. *Trails of Tears: American Indians Driven from Their Lands*. Dallas, Tex.: Hendrick-Long, 1992. Study of the forced removal to reservations of a variety of Native American tribes, including the Comanches and Cheyennes.

See also: Apr. 30, 1860-1865: Apache and Navajo War; Aug., 1863-Sept., 1866: Long Walk of the Navajos; Nov. 29, 1864: Sand Creek Massacre; Dec. 21, 1866: Fetterman Massacre; Nov. 27, 1868: Washita River Massacre; c. 1871-1883: Great American Buffalo Slaughter; Mar. 3, 1871: Grant Signs Indian Appropriation Act; June 27, 1874-June 2, 1875: Red River War; Feb. 8, 1887: General Allotment Act Erodes Indian Tribal Unity; Dec. 29, 1890: Wounded Knee Massacre.

Related article in *Great Lives from History: The Nineteenth Century, 1801-1900:* Abraham Lincoln.

December 4, 1867
National Grange Is Formed

The National Grange was the first major organization in the United States to address the social, economic, and educational needs of rural farming populations. Local chapters often became involved in business ventures and political affairs as well, helping to drive down farming costs. The organization also was instrumental in the passage of the Interstate Commerce Act of 1887.

Also known as: Order of Patrons of Husbandry; the Grange; National Grange of the Patrons of Husbandry

Locale: Washington, D.C.

Categories: Agriculture; organizations and institutions; social issues and reform; trade and commerce

Key Figures

Oliver Hudson Kelley (1826-1913), main organizer of the National Grange movement

William M. Ireland (fl. late nineteenth century), founder and the first treasurer of the National Grange

Caroline A. Hall (1838-1918), Kelley's niece and secretary

William Saunders (1822-1900), first master of the National Grange

Summary of Event

A federal bureaucrat and former farmer, Oliver Hudson Kelley founded the National Grange of the Patrons of Husbandry during the late 1860's out of a deep concern for the plight of persons living in rural areas of the United States. He believed that a fraternal organization for farmers and other country folk would contribute to their social and economic well-being. A tour of the southern states in 1866 confirmed what Kelley had already grasped through his ownership of a farm in Minnesota: Rural life was hardly a paradise.

The Jeffersonian vision of the small farm and contented citizen-farmers had crumbled along the more sparsely settled frontier and backwoods areas. Many rural men and women experienced intense isolation, and although they might travel long distances to overcome it, social life and community were difficult to sustain. As a member of the Benton County Agricultural Society, Kelley also had come to understand the harsh economic realities of agriculture and had begun plans to improve the farmers' lot. Whether Kelley expected it or not, the Grange would provide the basis for a widespread Agrarian movement for political and economic reform that would rock the major political parties for decades.

In 1867, Kelley left Minnesota to accept a position as a clerk in the U.S. Post Office in Washington, D.C. There, he and William M. Ireland, another clerk who, like Kelley, was a Freemason, began to plan the organization and ritual for a secret society of farmers that would both bind farmers together and advance agriculture. At the suggestion of his niece, Caroline A. Hall, and others, Kelley decided to admit both men and women into the organization. With several other interested government employees, Kelley quickly worked out a constitution. On December 4, 1867, five of the seven men later designated as founders constituted themselves as the National Grange of the Patrons of Husbandry and proceeded to elect officers. William Saunders, a horticulturist in the agriculture bureau, became the first master, but Kelley continued to play the leading role in the organization.

In 1868, Kelley resigned his government position and began promoting the formation of local Granges. He and his team first organized a local chapter, the Potomac Grange, and used it to experiment with the rituals and other organizational aspects. Letters and circulars to farmers around the country, however, elicited only a meager response. Kelley then toured the Midwest, attempting to sell charters at fifteen dollars each for the establishment of local Granges. He met with almost complete failure and was able to continue only by borrowing money and drawing on his wife's small inheritance. Before 1870, only a handful of local Granges had sprung up, mostly in Minnesota and Iowa, and in the next year, only scattered chapters existed in nine states.

Kelley's persistence paid off starting in 1872. The growth rate of the Grange increased sharply. Although only 132 new Granges appeared in 1871, about thirteen thousand formed within the next three years. Most of the Granges were located in the Midwest, but the network extended into almost every state. Deteriorating economic conditions undoubtedly drove many farmers to seek out organizational remedies. A few months before the Panic of 1873, a farm depression had foreshadowed the national business slowdown. Farmers who may have been looking at the Granges as a social opportunity now spotted the potential for economic mobilization.

Although the early motivations for the Granges may have been social and educational, local chapters often became involved in business ventures and political affairs. The local and state Granges experienced some success in eliminating or reducing the fees of the middleman in purchasing farm equipment and supplies. In some cases, state organizations appointed agents to deal directly with manufacturers. Montgomery Ward and Company, a Chicago-based retailer, incorporated with the express purpose of trading with the Grangers. Spurred by their success in cooperative buying, many state and local Granges expanded into retailing, manufacturing, and insurance.

When the national-level Grange had amassed a surplus from charter fees, it lent $50,000 to state Granges to assist in their expansions. Most of these enterprises eventually failed, however, because farmers lacked experience in selling and manufacturing; some Granges suffered mismanagement, lost membership confidence, and went into bankruptcy. Moreover, manufacturers, wholesalers, and retailers resisted the Granger initiatives. On the whole, however, the movement was successful in forcing down prices, despite limited success in business ventures.

During the 1870's, several farm-state legislatures passed so-called Granger Laws, which placed maximum limits on railroad and warehouse rates. In *Munn v. Illinois* (1877) and similar cases, the U.S. Supreme Court ruled that state rate-fixing was constitutional. The Supreme Court later reversed itself in *Wabash, St. Louis and Pacific Railway Company v. Illinois* (1886), but the pressure from the Granges helped push Congress to create the Interstate Commerce Commission in 1887, which helped pass the Interstate Commerce Act (1887).

Pressing state legislatures to enact maximum rate legislation enhanced the prestige of the Grange movement nationally. Although the constitution of the Grange forbade political activity, state and local Granges often were active politically. Other farm-oriented organizations were

Contemporary print celebrating the values of the National Grange movement. (Library of Congress)

operating at the same time, sometimes more effectively than the Grange in the political arena, but they lacked the national organization and ready identification of the Grangers. To the American public, the farmer-sponsored legislation concerning railroad rates were Granger Laws.

SIGNIFICANCE

Despite these perceived political successes, membership in the Grange decreased between 1875 and 1880 almost as rapidly as it had grown from 1872 to 1875. By 1877, membership was down to 411,000 (half the 1875 total), and by 1880, rosters reflected only 124,000 dues-paying members. Ironically, many of the once-attractive features of the Grange became liabilities in the second half of the decade. Rural Americans had found the cooperative features attractive, but when these business endeavors failed, the overall organization lost credibility. Similarly, when political action associated with the Grange movement was successful, the membership grew, but when Granger legislation proved ineffective, many farmers withdrew their support.

After 1880, the Grange continued to function as a social and educational outlet for rural populations, a civic center in small towns, and a bastion of the rural lifestyle in the face of urbanization and modernization. Granger-associated insurance companies remained strong into the next century. Granges also worked closely with the expanded state and federal agricultural extension services.

In politics, other farmers' organizations superseded the Granger movement. The Northern, Southern, and Colored Farmers' Alliances of the 1880's became powerful political forces, as did the Populist Party, which hit its peak during the early 1890's. In many ways, these later farmers' organizations were descendants of the National Grange of the Patrons of Husbandry, the first large-scale attempt at agricultural organization in the United States.

—*Mark A. Plummer, updated by Thomas L. Altherr*

FURTHER READING

Barns, William D. "Oliver Hudson Kelley and the Genesis of the Grange: A Reappraisal." *Agricultural History* 41 (July, 1967): 229-242. Overturns the interpretation that Kelley suddenly conceptualized the Grange in 1867 and established it for mainly social and educational ends.

Blanke, David. *Sowing the American Dream: How Consumer Culture Took Root in the Rural Midwest*. Athens: Ohio University Press, 2000. A history of the economics of consumerism and consumption in the rural Midwest, with a chapter called "A Battle of Standards: The Renunciation of the Rural Consumer Ethos by the Patrons of Husbandry, 1875-1882." Includes an extensive bibliography and an index.

Buck, Solon J. *The Granger Movement: A Study of Agricultural Organization and Its Political, Economic, and Social Manifestations, 1870-1880*. Lincoln: University of Nebraska Press, 1963. The first serious scholarly history of the Grangers.

Gilman, Rhoda R., and Patricia Smith. "Oliver Hudson Kelley: Minnesota Pioneer, 1849-1868." *Minnesota History* 40 (Fall, 1967): 330-338. Explores Kelley's agricultural experiences prior to leaving Minnesota to start the Grange.

Goodwyn, Lawrence. *Democratic Promise: The Populist Moment in America*. New York: Oxford University Press, 1976. Contrasts the perceived radical strategies of the Farmers' Alliances with the conservative strategies of the Grange.

Nordin, Dennis Sven. *Rich Harvest: A History of the Grange, 1867-1900*. Jackson: University Press of Mississippi, 1974. Argues that Kelley was a reluctant advocate of cooperatives and radical strategies.

Woods, Thomas A. *Knights of the Plow: Oliver H. Kelley and the Origins of the Grange in Republican Ideology*. Ames: Iowa State University Press, 1991. Maintains that Kelley, consistent with his Republican ideology, envisioned the Grange from the outset as a more political and radical organization.

SEE ALSO: 1820's-1830's: Free Public School Movement; Nov. 24, 1832-Jan. 21, 1833: Nullification Controversy; July 2, 1862: Lincoln Signs the Morrill Land Grant Act; Aug., 1872: Ward Launches a Mail-Order Business; Dec. 8, 1886: American Federation of Labor Is Founded; Feb. 4, 1887: Interstate Commerce Act; 1890: U.S. Census Bureau Announces Closing of the Frontier.

RELATED ARTICLES in *Great Lives from History: The Nineteenth Century, 1801-1900:* Robert Owen; Montgomery Ward.

1868
BAKUNIN FOUNDS THE SOCIAL DEMOCRATIC ALLIANCE

When Mikhail Bakunin could not find a home for his anarchist socialism within the First International that was under Karl Marx's communist leadership, he founded an underground organization to achieve his political ends. His Social Democratic Alliance proved short-lived, however, as he was expelled from the First International in 1872 and then retired from political life. The ensuing conflict within socialism between anarchism and communism has never been resolved.

LOCALE: Geneva, Switzerland
CATEGORIES: Social issues and reform; government and politics

KEY FIGURES

Mikhail Bakunin (1814-1876), Russian anarchist revolutionary
Karl Marx (1818-1883), German political philospher
Pierre-Joseph Proudhon (1809-1865), French journalist and social reformer

SUMMARY OF EVENT

Mikhail Bakunin's writings influenced many of the young Russian revolutionaries of the late nineteenth and early twentieth centuries. Bakunin rejected what he perceived as the dangerous and dehumanizing structure of nineteenth century European society. As a result of this rejection, he engaged in revolutionary theory and practice designed to bring about a better society. He was as critical of other revolutionaries as he was of their mutual enemies, and he produced critical analyses of both the Paris Commune and the First International. In 1868, he founded the Social Democratic Alliance as an underground organization within the First International. It operated in that capacity until 1872, when Bakunin and his fellows were expelled from the First International after losing a power struggle with Karl Marx.

Bakunin dedicated his life to the destruction of Europe's economic, political, and social structure, as well as to the creation of a new socialist system. In 1867, he joined the League of Peace and Freedom. This antiwar organization was created in an attempt to stop what its members believed was the nationalistic carnage of Otto von Bismarck's wars of German unification. Everyone in Europe knew that Bismarck's next target would be France and that, if he was successful, a new, highly militaristic German empire would occupy an advantageous geopolitical position in the center of Europe.

Bakunin's reputation as an activist had preceded him; therefore, the league awarded him the important position of chairman of the committee that was to create a general European peace initiative. He spent the next few months writing one of his most important revolutionary tracts, entitled *Federalism, Socialism, and Anti-Theologism* (1867). The basic argument of this work was that Europe would continue to experience the brutality of war and the exploitation of the masses for labor as long as the current economic, political, and social system existed. Bakunin stated that the only hope for a peaceful future was the elimination of the nation-state and the nationalistic and patriotic impulses it engendered. Both in his writing and in his speeches, he advocated the use of violence as an acceptable means of destroying the old order.

Most of the members of the League of Peace and Freedom were middle-class intellectuals who believed in social reform and rejected the use of violence. The philosophical incompatibility between these members and Bakunin forced the anarchist and his revolutionary committee to withdraw from the league. In the spring of 1868, Bakunin and his followers traveled to Geneva, Switzerland, and began to take an active role in a series of worker strikes. In the summer of that same year, they joined the First International and proposed a new operational model for the socialist organization. His plan called for the First International, under the leadership of Karl Marx, to concentrate on the development of revolutionary economic policy using Marx's *Das Kapital* (1867, 1885, 1894; *Capital: A Critique of Political Economy*, 1886, 1907, 1909; better known as *Das Kapital*) as the model. Bakunin and his committee, meanwhile, would direct the First International's policy concerning philosophical, political, and religious issues. Together the two groups would direct the course of the international socialist revolution.

With his Machiavellian personality, Marx realized the potential danger that Bakunin and his comrades posed to Marx's leadership of the First International. Therefore, he quickly rejected Bakunin's proposal. Shortly thereafter, the General Council of the First International denounced the revolutionary thesis expressed in Bakunin's *Federalism, Socialism and Anti-Theologism*.

Bakunin and his followers decided to create an alternative socialist front. A secret central committee that would exercise complete and unquestioned control over all policy decisions would lead this new alliance. The

BAKUNIN'S MATERIALIST ANARCHISM

Mikhail Bakunin was a rigorous materialist and socialist, but against Karl Marx's communism he espoused anarchism as the only responsible form of political practice. While both men believed in what they called "science" (meaning objectively grounded knowledge of any subject), Bakunin emphasized that such science should never license political authority; rather, it should only be used to persuade radically free subjects to accede to a given course of action.

While rejecting the absolute, universal, and infallible authority of men of science, we willingly bow before the respectable, although relative, quite temporary, and very restricted authority of the representatives of special sciences, asking nothing better than to consult them by turns, and very grateful for such precious information as they may extend to us, on condition of their willingness to receive from us on occasions when, and concerning matters about which, we are more learned than they. In general, we ask nothing better than to see men endowed with great knowledge, great experience, great minds, and, above all, great hearts, exercise over us a natural and legitimate influence, freely accepted, and never imposed in the name of any official authority whatsoever, celestial or terrestrial. We accept all natural authorities and all influences of fact, but none of right; for every authority or every influence of right, officially imposed as such, becoming directly an oppression and a falsehood, would inevitably impose upon us, as I believe I have sufficiently shown, slavery and absurdity.

In a word, we reject all legislation, all authority, and all privileged, licensed, official, and legal influence, even though arising from universal suffrage, convinced that it can turn only to the advantage of a dominant minority of exploiters against the interests of the immense majority in subjection to them.

This is the sense in which we are really Anarchists.

Source: Michael Bakunin, *God and the State* (New York: Mother Earth, 1916), section 2.

public face of the new organization was to be known as the Social Democratic Alliance. The main goal of the organization was the destruction of all existing nation-states and of the European social order based upon property. The targets of these revolutionaries would be the social, economic, and political infrastructure that supported the nationalistic, exploitive system. Political parties, the court system, government bureaucracies, and banks and other financial institutions had to be completely destroyed. The Social Democratic Alliance was formed in 1868, and as its membership was composed largely of Bakunin's faction in the First International, the alliance functioned essentially as an underground movement within the First International.

The members of the alliance sought to bring about a new world order based on the decentralized model of Pierre-Joseph Proudhon known as "mutualism." In this system, a federation of small political units, which would enter into economic and political agreements with one another for their mutual benefit, would replace the nation-state. The Social Democratic Alliance declared itself an atheist organization and called for the abolition of organized religion, which was to be replaced with belief in the laws of science. Similarly, the Western emphasis on the supremacy of divine justice was to be displaced by the concern for human justice.

The major goal of the Social Democratic Alliance was to achieve political, social, and economic equality for all people. This was to be accomplished by ending the right to inheritance and eventually placing all property under the control of the community—not the state, which was to be abolished. Material resources, whether agricultural or industrial, would then be used by all workers for the benefit of the entire society. The new structure would also provide equal education for both genders, so that over time intellectual and technological equality would develop. The alliance also called for the abolition of the existing political order and for the creation of associations of free citizens. Most important, the alliance emphasized that violent action should be directed against the existing structure and not against the people.

The failure of Emperor Napoleon III's government in the Franco-Prussian War (1870-1871) set off a series of events that culminated in the establishment of the Paris Commune. It also precipitated a revolutionary period that Bakunin and the Social Democratic Alliance hoped would begin the destruction of the old European order. The capture of Napoleon III after the Battle of Sedan (1870) led to the creation of an interim government that failed to bring the conflict with Prussia to a quick and successful conclusion. The citizens of Paris received little economic or military support; therefore, thousands of them died when the Prussian army, under the leadership of Otto von Bismarck, laid siege to the city.

In response to this perceived betrayal, the Parisians took revolutionary action and elected their own municipal government, which was to rule the city as a separate political entity. A public proclamation was issued that listed the reasons for this radical act. Its authors stated that the current conditions in France were the result of seven decades of conquest and expansion, as well as of the failure of the liberal, bourgeois government of Napoleon III. The new municipal leaders adopted a worldview in accord with that of the Social Democratic Alliance: They proclaimed that the time had come to dissolve the nation-state and to replace it with a new social order based upon a general association of independent communes, which would cooperate with one another for the general good. Socialism was to be the guiding philosophy of this new order, and for the first time in modern history, there would be true economic, political, and social equality. The French government sent troops to Paris to put down the insurrection. Thousands of people were killed, and the capital was eventually brought back under the control of the National Assembly.

Bakunin viewed the creation of the Paris Commune as an opportunity to place before Europe's radical community the differences between the communists, led by Karl Marx, and the anarchists of the Social Democratic Alliance. He described two major areas in which these two socialist camps differed: their attitudes toward the nation-state and the working classes. Bakunin rejected the communist principle of using the state to achieve the revolutionary goals of a free and equal society. He feared that a communist state would over time become just as repressive as the state-based system the radicals intended to overthrow, and thought it crucial to eliminate the state altogether. Bakunin also believed that he had more confidence in both the revolutionary zeal and the common sense of the working class than did Marx. He feared the Marxist concept of a revolutionary elite, believing that once such an elite attained power, it would become just another repressive oligarchy. Marx responded by referring to Bakunin as a "sentimental idealist."

The situation came to a head at the 1872 congress of the First International in The Hague. Marx engaged in internal politicking and, through maneuvers that had little to do with the substantive difference between the two men, he was able to have Bakunin and his associates expelled from the First International. At the same time, however, Marx transferred the seat of the organization's general council to New York, removing it so far from the political realities of Europe that some French delegates suggested it might as well be on the moon. The First International was dissolved four years later; Bakunin died the same year.

SIGNIFICANCE

The Social Democratic Alliance had little direct success, but its founder, Mikhail Bakunin, and his followers stand as the most important voices of anarchism within the history of the international socialist movement. They believed, that is, that the state was an irredeemable blight upon humanity and that for true social justice to be achieved, human sovereign communities would have to be much smaller than nations. Indeed, Bakunin believed such communities should be small enough that each member could be directly answerable to each other member and that larger communities could only be formed as cooperative alliances of small communities. Marx, by contrast, wrote far less about political structures than he did about economic structures. He did not require a communist state to exist after the end of history, but he thought such a state would be useful in achieving history's end. He certainly had no objection to states as such.

On a theoretical level, this divide between Bakuninian anarchism and Marxist communism has represented a significant debate within socialism since the 1860's. On a practical level, however, Bakunin's beliefs have proven nearly impossible to test. With the exception of a few, short-lived utopian socialist communities, socialism has only ever been attempted within the framework of the nation-state. The fate of these attempts may indicate that Bakunin was right to distrust the state, but they also establish just how difficult the state is to eliminate completely.

—*Richard D. Fitzgerald*

FURTHER READING

McLaughlin, Paul. *Mikhail Bakunin: The Philosophical Basis of His Theory of Anarchism.* New York: Algora, 2002. Examination of Bakunin's theory and its underpinnings that challenges Marxist and liberal interpretations of his philosophy.

Marks, Steven. *How Russia Shaped the Modern World: From Art to Anti-Semitism, Ballet to Bolshevism.* Princeton, N.J.: Princeton University Press, 2003. Contains an excellent account of Bukunin's revolutionary activities. Index.

Morland, David. *Demanding the Impossible? Human Nature and Politics in Nineteenth-Century Anarchism.* London: Cassell, 1997. Examines the philosophies of Bakunin, Pierre-Joseph Proudhon, and other nineteenth century anarchists, as well as the practical political consequences of those philosophies.

Ulam, Adam. *Russia's Failed Revolutionaries: From the*

Decembrists to the Dissidents. New York: Basic Books, 1981. Excellent account of the history of Russian revolutionary movements. Index.

Walicki, Andrzej. *A History of Russian Thought: From the Enlightenment to Marxism*. Stanford, Calif.: Stanford University Press, 1993. The best one-volume history of modern Russian thought. Index.

SEE ALSO: 1840's-1880's: Russian Realist Movement; Feb., 1848: Marx and Engels Publish *The Communist Manifesto*; Sept. 28, 1864: First International Is Founded; 1867: Marx Publishes *Das Kapital*; July 19, 1870-Jan. 28, 1871: Franco-Prussian War; Jan. 18, 1871: German States Unite Within German Empire; Mar. 18-May 28, 1871: Paris Commune; Mar., 1898: Russian Social-Democratic Labor Party Is Formed.

RELATED ARTICLES in *Great Lives from History: The Nineteenth Century, 1801-1900:* Mikhail Bakunin; Otto von Bismarck; Karl Marx; Napoleon III; Pierre-Joseph Proudhon.

1868
LAST CONVICTS LAND IN WESTERN AUSTRALIA

Although the colonies in the eastern part of Australia had banned the importation of convicts, Western Australian officials requested that transportation be revived to provide labor for their struggling colony's development. Nearly ten thousand felons arrived on the western shore from 1852 until the penal system officially ended in 1868.

LOCALE: Western Australia
CATEGORIES: Colonization; laws, acts, and legal history

KEY FIGURES

James Stirling (1791-1865), sea captain
Thomas Peel (1793-1865), English aristocrat
Solomon Levey (1794-1833), English financier
Charles Howe Fremantle (1800-1869), sea captain
John West (1809-1873), Congregational minister

SUMMARY OF EVENT

The British Transportation Act of 1718 provided for the seven-year expulsion of criminals from Great Britain to its colonies in North America. The act had not been fully realized in Great Britain's Australian colonies until the first fleet, carrying one thousand passengers, sailed in 1787. One year later, on January 20, 1788, 780 convicts, both men and women, along with their jailers, stepped off two warships to establish a prison on the site of what is now Sydney.

The original colony, New South Wales, which then encompassed the eastern part of the continent, took in eighty thousand convicts. The remaining seventy thousand were taken to Van Dieman's Land, an island colony that was renamed Tasmania in 1855. New South Wales stopped receiving convicts in 1840, and in 1852, Van Dieman's Land no longer admitted England's unwanted felons.

Just as transportation ceased in the flourishing eastern colonies, the settlers three thousand miles to the west saw the practice as a means of salvation for their floundering colony. For the next sixteen years, Western Australia, which covers approximately one-third of the continent, took in 9,668 able-bodied male convicts. They went to work building their own jails, even though thc superintendent of convicts described Western Australia as "a vast natural prison." The port town of Fremantle, facing the Indian Ocean and situated on the Swan River, served as the headquarters for the penal system. The workers spread through the colony, mainly along the coast, to work on the ranches and to build infrastructure such as bridges, roads, and public buildings.

In spite of the enthusiasm of Western Australian settlers for free labor, those in the eastern colonies objected to the continued importation of felons for that labor. The protests, along with economic factors, eventually stopped transportation to Western Australia and put an end to the brutal system in 1868.

That Western Australia in desperation continued to foster a system that was no longer acceptable remains consistent with the colony's early history. Its founding in 1829 had been fueled more by colonial fantasy and personal ambition than by practicality, which made it a financial burden both to Great Britain and to the other Australian colonies. When an adventurous British sea captain, James Stirling, stopped off briefly at the mouth of the Swan River in 1827, he considered the region promising and set out to promote a privately financed settlement there, which he would head as lieutenant-governor. His first patron, English landowner Thomas Peel, nurtured aspirations as an empire builder but lacked the necessary capital to fund his ambitions. Stirling's second backer, Solomon Levey, had the money but the wrong connections. Not only was he Jewish—a concern for many at the time—but also a former convict who had made a fortune in Sydney after his release. Living in London, he joined the enterprise as a silent partner.

The *Parmelia* sailed into the mouth of the Swan River in 1829 carrying an assemblage of free men and women who had been promised a paradise. Instead, they soon discovered they had been led into a wilderness that had not been surveyed or mapped. Even nature seemed incongruous to the newcomers, for the swans from which the river took its name were black with red bills. Either unproductive or covered with growth that defied clearing, the land resisted cultivation. In spite of Stirling's assurances that all would be well, desolation and misery mounted. Through importing basic supplies from South Africa and Van Dieman's Land, the colonists survived, and by 1850, Western Australia had a population of 5,886, all of whom would have gladly left the colony immediately according to a report the governor sent to London.

Finally, some of the frantic colonists requested that Western Australia be turned into a penal settlement in order to provide free labor to rescue the region from its hopeless state. This petition pleased London authorities who had been rebuffed by the eastern colonies, especially by the efforts of the Anti-Transportation League. Believing that the voluntary reception of convicts in the west would weaken the league and restore the transportation system to its former scale, the British began dispatching shiploads of men to Western Australia. The region's remoteness and instability offered nothing but misery, isolation, hard work, and deprivation to the hapless felons.

The Anti-Transportation League, founded by John West, a Congregational minister, had played an important role in ending transportation to New South Wales and Van Dieman's Land. The league's arguments did not focus on the system's inhumanity but stressed the moral pollution—or "the stain," as it was called—that the criminal class spread among the colonies full of decent folk. Never mind that many of the folk who protested the system were direct descendants of convicts. Yet the league found its arguments ignored by the same Western Australians who embraced the labor but ignored "the stain."

Significance

Historians acknowledge that importing convicts into the free settlement of Western Australia, which had started out with such grandiose plans, saved the colony from falling into oblivion. Through the infusion of nearly ten thousand laborers, the coastal region at last became productive. Most of the interior remains uninhabited and undeveloped into the twenty-first century.

While leaders of the Anti-Transportation League continued to preach against the penal system, their efforts actually played a minor part in ending convict importation. The decision makers in London concluded that the system was no longer practical from a financial standpoint. Because Western Australians did not have the funds to pay for much-needed laborers, the burden fell on the British government. Expenditures for transporting felons were ten times greater than the cost for imprisoning them in Great Britain.

After 1868, Reverend West and his associates turned their attention toward building a nation that would be loyal to the Crown. The defunct Anti-Transportation League would serve as a forerunner to the federation movement, which in 1901 united the scattered Australian colonies into a single entity.

Even though the penal system had been abolished, the convicts remained. The "old lags," as they were called in the Australian vernacular, met various fates. Many integrated into the communities, marrying, having children, and contributing to society. Others ended up in prison again or in mental institutions, often suffering illnesses such as acute alcoholism. Some vanished into the bush and joined the roving gangs of bushrangers who robbed and plagued settlers. A fortunate few made their way back to England.

For generations, the convicts, whom Australian novelist Kylie Tennant (1912-1988) aptly called "the reluctant pioneers," were denigrated, along with their offspring; no one would admit to having a convict ancestor. In later years this shame changed radically to a sort of pride. Contemporary Australians proudly claim their convict heritage, going to great lengths to prove that they are descendants of the once-invisible victims of a cruel system that played so significant a role in founding the nation.

—Robert Ross

Further Reading

Bosworth, Michal. *Convict Fremantle: A Place of Promise and Punishment*. Perth: University of Western Australia Press, 2004. Re-creates the old city and de-

Australia at the End of the Nineteenth Century

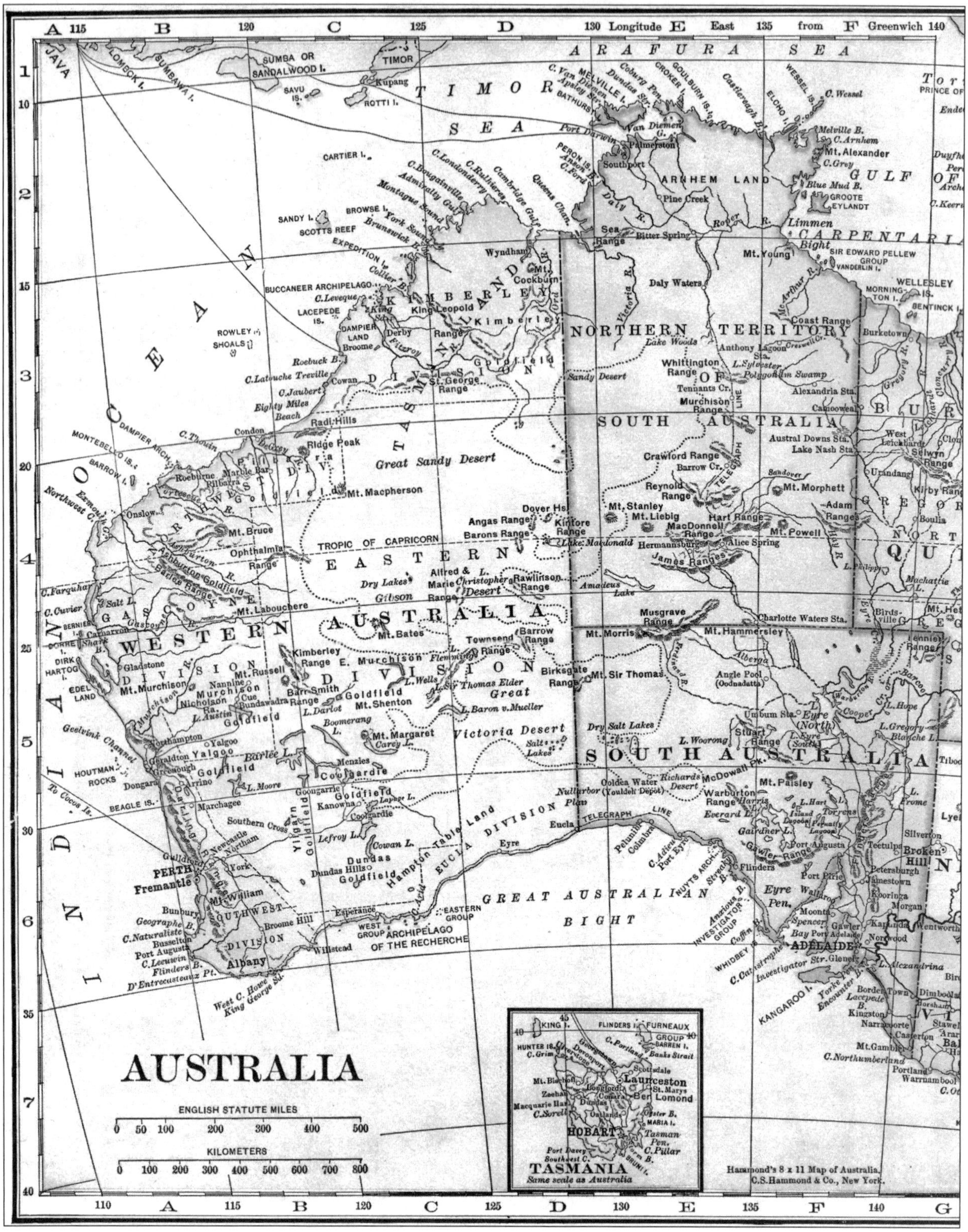

East 135 from Greenwich 140
CORAL SEA
PACIFIC OCEAN
GULF OF CARPENTARIA
Torres Strait
Gulf of Papua
NEW GUINEA
SOLOMON IS.
LOUISIADE ARCHIPELAGO
D'ENTRECASTEAUX IS.
TROBRIAND IS.
WOODLARK I.
TAGULA I.
WELLS REEF
Port Moresby (Granville)
MURRAY IS.
PRINCE OF WALES I.
C. York
Cape York Peninsula
COOK
BURKE
NORTH KENNEDY
SOUTH KENNEDY
GREGORY NORTH
MITCHELL
QUEENSLAND
LEICHHARDT
WARREGO
MARANOA
DARLING DOWNS
BURNETT
GREAT BARRIER REEF
Cooktown
Peter Botte
Port Douglas
Townsville
Charters Towers
Bowen
Mackay
Rockhampton
Keppel Bay
Port Curtis
Gladstone
Bundaberg
Maryborough
Gympie
Brisbane
Toowoomba
Warwick
Roma
Charleville
Longreach
Normanton
Burketown
Croydon
Cloncurry
Hughenden
Winton
Clermont
Emerald
Blackall
Tambo
Cunnamulla
St. George
Hungerford
HOLMES REEFS
WILLIS ISLETS
CORINGA IS.
DIAMOND IS.
LIHOU REEF & CAYS
FLINDERS REEF
TREGROSSE ISLETS & REEFS
CUMBERLAND ISLES
NORTHUMBERLAND ISLES
SWAIN REEFS
FREDERICK REEF
KENN REEF
SAUMAREZ REEF
WRECK REEF
BIRD ISLET
BELLONA REEFS
S. BELLONA REEFS
CATO I.
BAMPTON REEFS
AVON IS.
CHESTERFIELD IS.
SANDY IS.
CAPRICORN GROUP
To New Caledonia
MORETON I.
STRADBROKE I.
GR. SANDY I.
NORTHERN TERRITORY OF SOUTH AUSTRALIA
ARNHEM LAND
C. Wessel
WESSEL IS.
GROOTE EYLANDT
SIR EDWARD PELLEW GROUP
WELLESLEY IS.
MORNINGTON I.
BENTINCK I.
Alice Spring
Charlotte Waters Sta.
Mt. Hammersley
Angle Pool (Oodnadatta)
L. Eyre (North)
L. Eyre (South)
L. Frome
L. Torrens
L. Gairdner
Port Augusta
Port Pirie
Broken Hill
Silverton
ADELAIDE
KANGAROO I.
L. Alexandrina
NEW SOUTH WALES
WESTERN DIVISION
CENTRAL DIVISION
Bourke
Cobar
Wilcannia
Dubbo
Bathurst
Orange
Lithgow
Tamworth
Armidale
Grafton
Newcastle
SYDNEY
Goulburn
Wagga Wagga
Albury
Mt. Kosciusko
Port Macquarie
Sugar Loaf Pt.
VICTORIA
MELBOURNE
Ballarat
Geelong
Bendigo
Port Phillip
Wilsons Prom.
Port Albert
Bass Strait
KING I.
FLINDERS I.
FURNEAUX GROUP
TASMANIA
C. Howe
Hammond's 8 x 11 Map of Australia.
C.S.Hammond & Co., New York.
NEW ZEALAND
Same scale as Australia
NORTH ISLAND
SOUTH ISLAND
Auckland
WELLINGTON
Christchurch
Dunedin
Mt. Egmont
Napier
New Plymouth
Nelson
Cook Strait
Foveaux Strait
STEWART I.
C. Maria van Diemen
GREAT BARRIER I.
Bay of Plenty
To Sydney
E 135 F 140 G 145 H 150 J 155 K 160 L 165 M

scribes significant structures from the convict era to recapture life in the penal colony. An engaging and informative book. Illustrations.

Erickson, Rica, and Gillian O'Mara, comps. *Dictionary of Western Australians: Convicts in Western Australia 1850-1887*. Perth: University of Western Australia Press, 1999. Lists the convicts who came to Western Australia and provides information on their lives in the colony.

Fremantle Prison. http://www.fremantleprison.com. Accessed February 3, 2006. An excellent permanent Web site that offers a comprehensive history of the penal colony in Western Australia, personal information on the convicts and jailers, genealogical charts, and details about daily life. Includes illustrations and sketches.

Hughes, Robert. *The Fatal Shore*. 1987. Reprint. New York: Vintage Books, 1996. A classic work that provides the most thorough account of the penal system in Australia. A standard and important work that is notable for its readability.

Laugeson, Amanda. *Convict Words*. New York: Oxford University Press, 2003. Illuminates the British penal settlements in Australia through analyzing the language the convicts used, especially the slang and argot that developed.

Macintyre, Stuart. *A Concise History of Australia*. New York: Cambridge University Press, 2000. Includes a succinct account of the penal system and its role in colonization, which Stuart sees as a form of invasion.

O'Reilly, John Boyle. *Moondyne*. 1879. Reprint. Sydney: University of Sydney Press, 2000. O'Reilly's novel, based on his experiences as a convict in Western Australia, provides a rare, personal account of life in the penal colony. An Irish activist and political prisoner, O'Reilly escaped imprisonment and settled in Boston in the United States.

SEE ALSO: Dec. 6, 1801-Aug., 1803: Flinders Explores Australia; Sept. 7, 1803: Great Britain Begins Colonizing Tasmania; Aug. 16, 1835: Melbourne, Australia, Is Founded; 1851: Gold Is Discovered in New South Wales.

RELATED ARTICLES in *Great Lives from History: The Nineteenth Century, 1801-1900:* Sir Edmund Barton; Sir Henry Parkes; A. B. Paterson; W. C. Wentworth.

January 3, 1868
JAPAN'S MEIJI RESTORATION

After two-and-a-half centuries of increasingly ineffective shogunal rule, the emperor of Japan was restored to power by committed politicians and lower-ranking samurai who feared encroachment by the Western powers if Japan's government were to become too weak. The Meiji emperor instituted a policy of Westernization that allowed Japan to rise to become a world power in the next century.

LOCALE: Kyōto, Japan
CATEGORY: Government and politics

KEY FIGURES

Mutsuhito (1852-1912), emperor of Japan as Meiji, r. 1867-1912
Tokugawa Yoshinobu (1837-1913), last shogun of Japan, r. 1867
Ii Naosuke (1815-1860), Japanese politician and diplomat
Sakamoto Ryōma (1835-1867), Japanese rural samurai
Saigō Takamori (1827-1877),
Kido Takayoshi (Kōin Kido; 1833-1877), and
Ōkubo Toshimichi (1830-1878), Japanese statesmen known collectively as the Three Heroes of the Meiji Restoration

SUMMARY OF EVENT

While the Japanese imperial line could be traced back to quasi-historical times as early as the fifth or sixth century, military dictators, or shoguns, held most political power in Japan from 1192 until 1867. These regents supposedly ruled in the name of the emperor, but in reality an emperor usually had little control over a shogun. The power of the shogunate reached its apogee once the various feudal domains of the country were unified in 1600, ending almost one hundred years of civil war. This unification was completed by the Tokugawa family, which dominated the Japanese government for the next 250 years, supplying the nation with fifteen hereditary shoguns beginning in 1603. Until the nineteenth century, these shoguns kept control over the several hundred vassal warlords (daimyos) and their domains, ruling from the eastern city of Edo (modern day Tokyo), while the

The emperor Mutsuhito around 1904. (Library of Congress)

imperial court continued its rituals and ceremonies from the southern city of Kyōto, the ancient capital.

Ironically, in some ways the Tokugawa shoguns were undermined by their own success. The centuries of peace they brought about sapped the military vigor of the ruthless samurai warriors who had unified Japan. The Tokugawa gradually became more proficient as administrators than as fighters, and by the early nineteenth century signs of weakness were beginning to show. Droughts, famines, and other natural disasters wreaked havoc with the nation's economy, and the Tokugawa shoguns could do little to help. Peasants starved, and many samurai were dismissed by their warlords, as the central government tried to squeeze more tribute from the local domains. Many of these young disgruntled samurai became the vanguard of the Meiji revolution that was to come.

The immediate cause of the Tokugawa government's collapse, however, was the increasing presence of Westerners in the islands. In 1853, Commodore Matthew C. Perry and his squadron of U.S. Navy steamships forced their way into Edo Bay, demanding trade and other privileges. Other Western powers followed, and the country flew into a panic. Having seen what happened to China and other Asian countries after concessions had been extracted from them, samurai from three distant domains—Satsuma, Chōshū, and Tosa—began to consider the overthrow of the Tokugawa shogun and the restoration of the emperor to true power. The phrase *sonnō jōi*—"revere the Emperor, expel the barbarians"—became a nationalist rallying cry.

The shogun asked Ii Naosuke, a loyal vassal, to quell dissent in the ranks and negotiate more favorable treaties with the Westerners. Although he was initially successful, Ii's assassination in 1860 encouraged other patriots and idealistic young samurai to further action. While most warlords stood on the sidelines to see how the situation would be resolved, Chōshū forces rebelled and tried to take the emperor's palace by force. Saigō Takamori negotiated a settlement between the Chōshū domain and the shogun, but it was clear that a revolution was coming. With Saigō and Ōkubo Toshimichi acting for Satsuma, Kido Takayoshi acting for Chōshū, and Sakamoto Ryōma acting for Tosa, a strong if cautious and ambivalent alliance between these domains was struck. (History remembers Saigō, Kido, and Ōkubo as the Three Heroes of the Meiji Restoration.)

At the same time, the death of the childless shogun placed the Tokugawa order of succession into question. The appointment of Tokugawa Yoshinobu as shogun precipitated action, as it was thought that his support by Westerners would make him too powerful to overthrow later. When Yoshinobu proved unwilling or unable to expel the Westerners—as was demanded of him by the emperor and other warlords—the rebellious domains issued an ultimatum, ordering his resignation. The shogun complied, resigning in November, 1867. On January 3, 1868, Satsuma forces stormed the imperial palace in Kyōto and declared that the fifteen-year-old emperor, Mutsuhito, was restored to power. The young emperor issued an edict supporting their action after the fact and chose as his imperial name Meiji, or "enlightened rule." While the civil war did not actually end until June 27, 1869, when forces loyal to the shogun in the northern island of Hokkaido finally surrendered, it was clear by early 1868 that power had shifted and the shogunate had collapsed.

The decade after the reinstatement of imperial rule was one of drastic change and social experiment. Almost overnight, centuries-old institutions were torn down in an attempt instantly to modernize Japan. It was believed, ironically, that a modernized Japan would be less vulnerable to Western encroachment. Many momentous changes took place as a result. Feudalism was abolished, altering both Japan's system of government and its basic social structure. There had been four social classes officially established in Tokugawa Japan: samurai warriors, farmers, artisans, and merchants, as well as nobles and a small group of social outcastes. These distinctions were abolished, and the 6 percent of the population that had been samurai lost both their swords and their privileges.

The feudal domains were eliminated—as were their daimyos. The domains became prefectures, administratively similar to states or provinces in the West. With the disappearance of the feudal domains, however, the central government needed a new source of income, so a new system of taxation was devised. Land values were assessed, and a national land tax of 3 percent was implemented.

Once the samurai were eliminated, it became necessary to find a new way to defend the country. Universal military conscription was therefore established, as was compulsory education designed to provide both warriors and workers with necessary skills and talents. Finally, the new government pledged to learn from the world, especially the West. Several missions were sent abroad, and foreign experts from many technical fields and the humanities began to be imported. The distinctions between what was "modern" and what was "Western"—though sometimes contentiously debated—were often ignored in the race to make Japan as strong a power as possible in the shortest period of time.

Significance

In a sense, the name Meiji Restoration is misleading, as the emperor reigned more than he ruled. True power lay in the strong executive branch and in the fledging houses of the new imperial diet. Still, with the power to make important political appointments and to oversee the military, the emperor was more than just the symbolic figurehead he had been in Tokugawa Japan.

While the Meiji Restoration eliminated some of the gross inequities of the old feudal system, the rapid modernization it instituted was not without cost. Many farmers suffered because of the new tax code and the loss of manpower due to the draft. Instant industrialization caused the same urban and social problems that plagued Europe and America, only more quickly. Some important early revolutionary leaders—such as Saigō—became disenchanted with the new Meiji government and withdrew their support or openly rebelled. Still, with the restoration of imperial rule, the system of governing by shoguns and warlords was eliminated. This made possible the reforms necessary for Japan to become a major international economic and military power. By the time the Meiji period ended just before World War I, Japan was indeed a world power.

—*James Stanlaw*

Further Reading

Akamatsu, Paul. *Meiji, 1868: Revolution and Counter-revolution in Japan*. New York: Harper & Row, 1972. An older but detailed account, covering the whole set of changes in government, from the Tokugawa reforms in the 1840's to the last civil uprising in 1877.

Jansen, Marius. *The Making of Modern Japan*. Cambridge, Mass.: Harvard University Press, 2000. Perhaps the best single-volume history of modern Japan by one of the period's most knowledgeable American historians. Jansen gives a very detailed but understandable explanation of how the imperial restoration occurred.

_______. *Sakamoto Ryōma and the Meiji Restoration*. Stanford, Calif.: Stanford University Press, 1961. A classic study of the mind-set of the pro-imperial reformers and their world.

Keene, Donald. *Emperor of Japan: Meiji and His World*. New York: Columbia University Press, 2002. An exhaustive biography, using official Japanese records, of the young emperor who was restored to power, written by America's premier specialist on Japanese literature.

Ravina, Mark. *The Last Samurai: The Life and Battles of Saigō Takamori*. Hoboken, N.J.: John Wiley & Sons, 2004. A biography of one of the most colorful characters of the restoration, on whom the Tom Cruise movie of the same name is (very) loosely based.

Walthall, Anne. *The Weak Body of a Useless Woman: Matsuo Taseko and the Meiji Restoration*. Chicago: University of Chicago Press, 1998. A rare glimpse of the revolution through the eyes of a peasant woman, who was enshrined as the exemplar "good wife and wise woman" by later nationalists.

Wilson, George. *Patriots and Redeemers in Japan: Motives in the Meiji Restoration*. Chicago: University of Chicago Press, 1992. Wilson takes the view that the restoration was a redemptive millenarian social movement as much as a political power struggle.

See also: Mar. 31, 1854: Perry Opens Japan to Western Trade; Apr. 6, 1868: Promulgation of Japan's Charter Oath; 1870's: Japan Expands into Korea; Jan.-Sept. 24, 1877: Former Samurai Rise in Satsuma Rebellion; Feb. 11, 1889: Japan Adopts a New Constitution; July 8, 1894-Jan. 1, 1896: Kabo Reforms Begin Modernization of Korean Government; Aug. 1, 1894-Apr. 17, 1895: Sino-Japanese War.

Related articles in *Great Lives from History: The Nineteenth Century, 1801-1900:* Mutsuhito; Matthew C. Perry; Saigō Takamori.

February 24-May 26, 1868
IMPEACHMENT OF ANDREW JOHNSON

Motivated primarily by partisan political differences, this first attempt to impeach a U.S. president created a constitutional crisis that crippled Andrew Johnson's presidency and weakened federal Reconstruction policy in the defeated southern states.

LOCALE: Washington, D.C.
CATEGORIES: Government and politics; crime and scandals

KEY FIGURES

Andrew Johnson (1808-1875), president of the United States, 1865-1869
Salmon P. Chase (1808-1873), chief justice of the United States
Ulysses S. Grant (1822-1885), commanding general of the U.S. Army and Johnson's successor as president
Edwin M. Stanton (1814-1869), U.S. secretary of war
Thaddeus Stevens (1792-1868), Republican congressman from Pennsylvania
Charles Sumner (1811-1874), Whig senator from Massachusetts

SUMMARY OF EVENT

On February 24, 1868, when the U.S. House of Representatives passed a resolution declaring that President Andrew Johnson should be impeached, few observers were surprised. Angry Republicans, especially members of the radical faction who saw Johnson as the great enemy of their program, had put through the House a resolution directing the Judiciary Committee to inquire into Johnson's conduct in January, 1867. Among the many charges made against Johnson was the accusation that he had been involved in the Lincoln assassination plot. However, although the committee recommended impeachment at that time, the full House had voted it down.

The impeachment campaign arose over Johnson's alleged violation of the Tenure of Office Act passed by Congress on March 2, 1867, and subsequently passed again over the president's veto. This act made the removal of cabinet officers subject to approval by the Senate. Even supporters of the bill declared that its provisions referred only to cabinet members appointed by a president in office and not to those who had been appointed by his predecessor. Thus, the law should not have applied to cabinet appointees of Lincoln still serving under Johnson in 1867.

The conflict grew out of Johnson's determination to replace Edwin M. Stanton as secretary of war and to test the constitutionality of the Tenure of Office Act in court. A holdover from Lincoln's cabinet whom Johnson considered disloyal, Stanton supported the Reconstruction program of Congress, not that of the president. In the summer of 1867, Johnson asked Stanton to resign, but Stanton refused to do so. Johnson thereupon suspended Stanton from office pending concurrence by the Senate, the procedure required by the Tenure of Office Act. He then appointed General Ulysses S. Grant as the interim secretary of war. If the Senate did not concur in his action, Johnson planned to challenge the Tenure of Office Act in court in order to test its constitutionality.

Grant accepted the cabinet post but soon became unhappy because he supported the congressional party and knew that he was its choice for the Republican presidential nomination in 1868. As his discomfort increased, his relations with the president worsened. As a consequence, modern historians have debated Grant's integrity, or lack of it, in the episode. When the Senate, as expected, refused to concur in Stanton's ouster, Grant turned the office back to him. Johnson, however, remained determined to rid himself of Stanton. He then invited General William Tecumseh Sherman to take over from Stanton, but Sherman refused. At last, the adjutant general of the Army, garrulous old Lorenzo Thomas, agreed to take Stanton's place. On February 21, 1868, Johnson fired Stanton and appointed Thomas. However, since Stanton refused to give up his office, Thomas would not take it.

At that point, the Radical Republicans in the House saw their chance to strike at Johnson. On February 24, 1868, the House passed, by a large majority, the Covode Resolution, which declared that the president should be impeached. For many, it was a psychological catharsis to bring down the great opponent of Reconstruction and the great sustainer of rebellion. Some powerful legislators, such as Senator Charles Sumner of Massachusetts and Representative Thaddeus Stevens of Pennsylvania, considered Johnson, a Union Democrat originally from North Carolina, to be too closely allied with former Confederates who had only recently laid down their arms.

Another motive of the Republicans in Congress was to deal with the real problem of military Reconstruction. In his capacity as chief executive, Johnson had removed Union generals in the South who had been enthusiastic about military Reconstruction and replaced them with men of his own temper. Congressional Republicans

Congressional sergeant-at-arms George T. Brown serving President Andrew Johnson with a summons to appear for impeachment proceedings. (Library of Congress)

wanted the secretary of war to be someone who supported their own program of Reconstruction. When Johnson moved against Stanton, they concluded that they had to stop the president. To many, impeachment seemed to be the only solution. The resolution that the House finally passed had eleven articles. The first nine articles dealt with the president's alleged violation of the Tenure of Office Act, and the last two charged Johnson with making speeches designed to denigrate Congress and with failing to enforce the Reconstruction laws.

After the House had done its work by initiating Johnson's impeachment, it was left to the Senate to convict or acquit him. The U.S. Constitution stipulated that a two-thirds majority vote was necessary for conviction. In 1868, that meant that the votes of thirty-six senators were needed. In early March, with Chief Justice Salmon P. Chase presiding, the senators took the oath to try the president. As this was the first impeachment trial ever conducted against a president, there was a long debate about whether the Senate sat as a court or as a political body. To Chase, the Constitution clearly indicated that the Senate sat as a court, so he conducted the proceedings as a formal trial.

On March 30, the trial opened. The prosecution, composed of important Radical Republicans, claimed that Johnson had subverted the will of Congress, the will of the Republican Party, and the will of the people. As the defense duly noted, the prosecution made no effort to pin any specific crime on the president. Emphasizing that fact, Johnson's defense counsel argued that Johnson had done nothing to warrant impeachment under the Constitution.

Voting took place on May 16; the result was one vote short of the number needed to convict. Two more votes were taken on May 26, with the same result. Thirty-six votes were needed, but each time the outcome was only thirty-five to nineteen. Johnson was saved by seven Republicans who supported Reconstruction in Congress but who did not believe there were legal grounds for conviction in this case. Typical of the Republican senators who reluctantly opposed conviction was Kansas's Edmund G. Ross. Although Ross was no supporter of Johnson, he opposed the president's removal from office because he believed the office of the presidency itself would be seriously damaged if Thaddeus Stevens and Sumner succeeded in their struggle with Johnson.

SIGNIFICANCE

President Johnson was acquitted by the narrowest of margins. He served the remainder of his term with little further direct influence on Reconstruction policies. The office of the presidency survived this constitutional crisis, but the direction of Reconstruction remained firmly in the hands of the leaders of Congress. There would not be another impeachment trial of a U.S. president until 1998, when the House voted to impeach President Bill Clinton on charges of perjury and obstruction. As with Johnson's trial, Clinton was acquitted by the Senate on all charges.

—William J. Cooper, Jr.,
updated by Joseph Edward Lee

FURTHER READING

Beale, Howard K. *The Critical Year: A Study of Andrew Johnson and Reconstruction*. New York: Frederick Ungar, 1958. Clearly explains the positions taken by the executive and legislative branches as the crisis erupted.

Benedict, Michael Les. *The Impeachment and Trial of Andrew Johnson*. New York: W. W. Norton, 1973. Exceptionally good study of Johnson's impeachment. Concludes, with much supporting evidence, that the impeachment was justified and conviction would have been proper.

Brodie, Fawn M. *Thaddeus Stevens: Scourge of the South*. New York: W. W. Norton, 1959. Well-written and balanced biography of Johnson's chief nemesis.

Hearn, Chester G. *The Impeachment of Andrew Johnson*. Jefferson, N.C.: McFarland, 2000. One of several books about Johnson's impeachment written after Congress initiated impeachment proceedings against President Bill Clinton. Hearn focuses on the political turmoil after the Civil War that led to Johnson's impeachment.

McPherson, James M. *Ordeal by Fire: The Civil War and Reconstruction*. 2d ed. New York: McGraw-Hill, 1992. Analysis of the war and the political intrigue that flourished after Lincoln's assassination.

Simpson, Brooks D. *The Reconstruction Presidents*. Lawrence: University Press of Kansas, 1998. Comparative study of the presidencies of Andrew Johnson, Abraham Lincoln, Ulysses S. Grant, and Rutherford B. Hayes—the four presidents who presided over the Union's Reconstruction policies in the defeated South.

Trefousse, Hans Louis. *Impeachment of a President: Andrew Johnson, the Blacks, and Reconstruction*. New York: Fordham University Press, 1999. Study of Johnson's impeachment that examines why Congress failed to convict Johnson, the consequences of his acquittal, and connections between the impeachment and failure of Reconstruction.

SEE ALSO: Dec. 8, 1863-Apr. 24, 1877: Reconstruction of the South; Apr. 9 and 14, 1865: Surrender at Appomattox and Assassination of Lincoln; Dec. 6, 1865: Thirteenth Amendment Is Ratified; Apr. 9, 1866: Civil Rights Act of 1866; Mar. 30, 1867: Russia Sells Alaska to the United States; July 9, 1868: Fourteenth Amendment Is Ratified; Sept. 24, 1869-1877: Scandals Rock the Grant Administration.

RELATED ARTICLES in *Great Lives from History: The Nineteenth Century, 1801-1900:* Salmon P. Chase; Ulysses S. Grant; Andrew Johnson; William Tecumseh Sherman; Edwin M. Stanton; Thaddeus Stevens; Charles Sumner.

March, 1868
LARTET DISCOVERS THE FIRST CRO-MAGNON REMAINS

Excavations in France's Cro-Magnon rock shelter led to the discovery and establishment of Cro-Magnon humans as the earliest known example of the subspecies Homo sapiens sapiens *in Europe and added a new stage to the cultural sequencing of early human hisory.*

LOCALE: Les Eyzies-de-Tayac, Dordogne, France
CATEGORIES: Biology; genetics; archaeology

KEY FIGURES

Édouard Lartet (1801-1871), French archeologist, lawyer, and a founder of modern paleontology
Louis Lartet (1840-1899), French geologist and paleontologist, son of Édouard Lartet
Henry Christy (1810-1865), English ethnologist

SUMMARY OF EVENT

Édouard Lartet made three significant contributions to what had been the new field of paleontology. Believing that the Stone Age was not a single phase in human evolution, he proposed dividing it into a series of phases and established a system of classifications to that end. His research led to the establishment of the Upper Paleolithic as a distinctive period of the Stone Age. He discovered the first evidence of Paleolithic art. Although Lartet completed a degree in law after studying at Auch and Toulouse and began the practice of law in Gers, his real interest lay in science. Inspired by the work of Georges Cuvier, he began doing excavations around Auch, France, in 1834. There he found fossil remains that led him to devote his time to excavation and research. He began a systematic investigation of the caves in the area.

In 1858, Lartet was joined by his friend Henry Christy, an Englishman who had been working in ethnology. The son of a London hatter, Christy had joined his father's firm but became interested in ethnology because of his travels. He attended the Great Exhibition of 1851 and was so impressed that, like Édouard, he changed careers and devoted the rest of his life to travel and research into human evolution. Lartet and Christy focused their work in the caves located in the valley of the Vezere, a tributary of the Dordogne River. By 1861, Lartet began publishing his research. His "Sur l'ancienneté géologique de l'espèce humaine dans l'Europe occidentale" (1860; the antiquity of humans in western Europe) appeared, and the following year he published the results of his investigations and excavations in the cave of Aurignac. In *New Researches on the Coexistence of Man and of the Great Fossil Mammifers Characteristic of the Last Geological Period* (1861) he presented evidence that human beings existed during the same time period that saw other mammals, which are now extinct.

In 1863, Lartet and Christy were involved in a series of excavations in the Dordogne Valley, with sites at Gorge d'Enfer, Laugerie Haute, La Madeleine, Le Moustier, and Les Eyzies. They published several articles on their findings, the most important of which was an article in the journal *Revue archéologique* and the short work *Cavernes du Périgord: Objets gravés et sculptés des temps pré-historiques dans l'Europe Occidentale* (1864). They had planned to publish a book on their research but Christy died of lung inflammation on May 4, 1865. The book was partially written but Édouard continued working on it. It was finally completed by Rupert Jones only after Lartet's death and published as *Reliquiae Aquitanicae: Being Contributions to the Archaeology and Paleontology of Périgord and the Adjoining Provinces of Southern France* in 1875.

Lartet continued his work in archaeology and paleontology until his health began to fail in 1870. He died the following year. Before then, his son Louis Lartet, who was also a paleontologist and a geologist, had begun working with him. In 1868, a railway was being built through the hilly countryside of Les Eyzies-de-Tayac. In March of that year, a crew of workers who were excavating the hillsides found chipped flints, animal bones, and human remains in a rock shelter called Cro-Magnon. The contractors in charge of building the railway contacted Louis Lartet, who took charge of a scientific excavation of the shelter.

NEANDERTHAL AND CRO-MAGNON EXCAVATION SITES IN GERMANY AND FRANCE

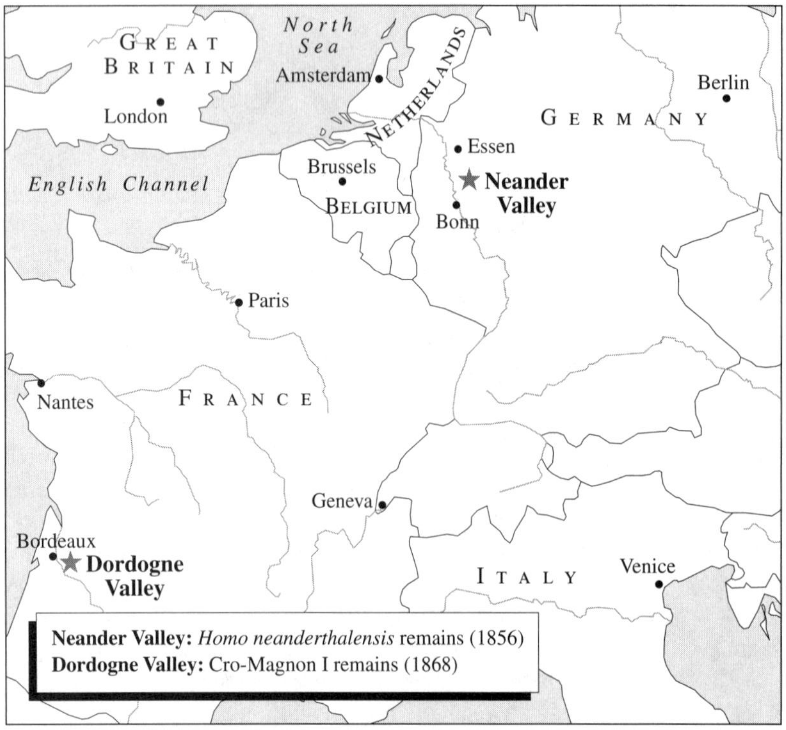

The younger Lartet's excavations revealed that the shelter contained five archaeological layers. The human remains, bones of animals belonging to extinct species, and flint, which showed evidence of having been worked with tools, were found in the topmost layer. Lartet determined that these remains and flints were from the Upper Paleolithic (a period dating from approximately 35,000 to 10,000 years ago). In the back of the shelter he found five skeletons, or parts of skeletons, decorated with ornaments, many of which were made from pierced seashells.

It is possible that there were remains of ten skeletons found in the shelter but the fragments of only five were preserved and studied. The excavators found the partial skeletons of four adults and one newborn child. Among the skeletal remains were the cranium and mandible of a male believed to have been about fifty years old at the time of his death. This specimen became known as the Old Man of Cro-Magnon (or Cro-Magnon I) and is considered a typical example of the peoples now known as Cro-Magnon.

CRO-MAGNON REMAINS

In 1868, Édouard and Louis Lartet recalled their discovery of Cro-Magnon remains in a cave near the Vezère River.

At the back of the cave was found an old man's skull, which alone was on a level with the surface, in the cavity not filled up in the back of the cave, and was therefore exposed to the calcareous drip from the roof, as is shown by its having a stalagmitic coating on some parts. The other human bones, referable to four other skeletons, were found around the first, within a radius of about 1.50 meters. Among these bones were found, on the left of the old man, the skeleton of a woman, whose skull presents in front a deep wound, made by a cutting instrument, but which did not kill her at once, as the bone has been partly repaired within; indeed our physicians think that she survived several weeks. By the side of the woman's skeleton was that of an infant which had not arrived at its full time of foetal development. The other skeletons seem to have been those of men. . . .

Whence came these ancient men of the Vezère? Here the geologist must be silent. His duty is to confirm the facts forming the subject of this introductory notice, as far as they belong to his domain. To the anthropologist we look to enlighten us on the characters of the race. It may, however, be remarked that the seashells associated with the sepulture at Cro-Magnon are in no wise of Mediterranean origin, but belong only to the Atlantic Ocean. . . . This fact may be taken in consideration from the Cro-Magnons together with the circumstance of there being in this sepulture several pebbles of basalt, which could not have been taken from the valley of the Vezère, but might well have been brought from that of the Dordogne. Hence we are led to suppose that before coming to the Cave District, where they found conditions so favorable for their mode of life, the reindeer-hunters had sojourned on our Atlantic coasts, and that they arrived at the banks of the Vezère after having ascended the Valley of the Dordogne.

Source: From *Reliquiae Acquitanicae*, 1868. Quoted in *Eyewitness to Discovery*, edited by Brian M. Fagan (New York: Oxford University Press, 1996), pp. 62-68.

SIGNIFICANCE

The remains that Louis Lartet found in the rock shelter at Cro-Magnon were the first human remains recognized as from the Upper Paleolithic period. Lartet's discovery made important contributions to the work that his father had done on the cultural sequencing of human beings. Édouard Lartet and Henry Christy had found evidence of art that was created during the Paleolithic period. Louis Lartet's discovery of the skeletons decorated with ornamentation and the pierced seashells gave further evidence of the intellectual and creative abilities of the human beings of the period. In addition, the findings at Cro-Magnon revealed that the people living during this period were deliberately burying their dead. Not only had they situated the dead in special places, but they also prepared the bodies with ornamentation.

Thus, the discoveries made in the rock shelter at Cro-Magnon helped to complete the definition of Upper Paleolithic humans as toolmakers, artists, and thinking individuals who had some conscious understanding of life and death. In Lartet's opinion the flint tools he found with the skeletons linked the Cro-Magnons to the Aurignacian culture he had identified a few years earlier. The tools had many features characteristic of the tool industry of the Aurignacian period.

Louis Lartet's findings at Cro-Magnon also added a new phase to the cultural sequencing of human evolution, which his father had created. The Cro-Magnon skeletal remains are the earliest known examples in Europe of the subspecies to which humankind belongs. Although Cro-Magnon originally indicated the site at which the rock shelter was located, the term has come to be used in a general sense to refer to the oldest modern peoples of Europe.

—*Shawncey Webb*

FURTHER READING

Clos, Lynne. *Field Adventures in Paleontology*. Boulder, Colo.: Fossil News, 2003. Although this book does not specifically cover Cro-Magnon, it addresses the work of paleontologists in an easily understandable form. Useful for the general reader.

Dawkins, Richard. *The Ancestor's Tale: A Pilgrimage to the Dawn of Evolution*. New York: Houghton Mifflin, 2004. Includes a chapter on Cro-Magnon. Using the format of Chaucer's *The Canterbury Tales*, Dawkins looks at discoveries and developments in human evolution.

Diamond, Jared. *The Third Chimpanzee: The Evolution and Future of the Human Animal*. New York: Harper-

Collins, 1992. Treats evolution of human social development.
Lynch, John, and Louise Barrett. *Walking with Cavemen: Eye-to-Eye with Your Ancestors*. New York: DK Adult, 2003. Based on James Burke's Discovery Science series. Examines human evolution from its beginnings in Africa, and includes accounts of archaeological discoveries. Illustrated with live-action photography and computer-generated graphics.
Olson, Steve. *Mapping Human History: Genes, Races, and Our Common Origins*. New York: Houghton Mifflin, 2002. Discusses physical anthropology and human migration, with an emphasis on the common ancestry of all human beings. Explores the early species in Europe.
Wells, Spencer. *The Journey of Man: A Genetic Odyssey*. Princeton, N.J.: Princeton University Press, 2002. Discusses the discovery of Cro-Magnon. Scientifically accurate yet easily read by general readers. Includes excellent maps and diagrams. Companion volume to a PBS National Geographic special.

SEE ALSO: 1809: Lamarck Publishes *Zoological Philosophy*; 1830's-1840's: Scientists Study Remains of Giant Moas; 1854-1862: Wallace's Expeditions Give Rise to Biogeography; Aug., 1856: Neanderthal Skull Is Found in Germany; Nov. 24, 1859: Darwin Publishes *On the Origin of Species*; 1861: *Archaeopteryx Lithographica* Is Discovered; 1871: Darwin Publishes *The Descent of Man*.
RELATED ARTICLES in *Great Lives from History: The Nineteenth Century, 1801-1900:* Karl Ernst von Baer; Charles Darwin; Sir Edwin Ray Lankester.

April, 1868
BRITISH EXPEDITION TO ETHIOPIA

After three years of inconclusive negotiations to secure the release of British citizens and other Europeans held captive in Ethiopia, the British government sent a military expedition to rescue the prisoners and to restore British honor and image. The best-organized and most modern expeditionary force that Great Britain had ever assembled, the expedition braved the rugged Ethiopian terrain and secured the release of the captives.

LOCALE: Magdela, Ethiopia
CATEGORIES: Diplomacy and international relations; wars, uprisings, and civil unrest

KEY FIGURES

Tewodros II (Theodore II; 1818-1868), emperor of Ethiopia, r. 1855-1868
Robert Napier (1810-1890), British general who commanded the Ethiopia expedition
Benjamin Disraeli (1804-1881), British Chancellor of the Exchequer and later prime minister
Kassa Mercha (1831-1889), rival to Tewodros who later became emperor Yohannes IV, r. 1872-1889
Charles Cameron (d. 1870), British consul to Ethiopia
Hormuzd Rassam (1826-1910), British envoy to Ethiopia

SUMMARY OF EVENT

When Tewodros II ascended the Ethiopian throne in 1855, he had grand plans for reforms to modernize his backward northeast African country and restore the central authority that had been shattered by the resurgence of feudal anarchy that characterized the Ethiopian political scene since the late eighteenth century. Tewodros sought to achieve his objective with European support. Accordingly, he tried to contact several European governments soliciting alliances against Ethiopia's hostile Muslim neighbors and seeking technical support. His approach, however, was rebuffed. The French, whom Tewodros assiduously courted, instead supported rebel chiefs in the north who were sympathetic to Roman Catholic missionaries.

Tewodros was particularly incensed by the failure of the British government to answer a letter that he sent to Queen Victoria in 1862 through the British consul, Captain Charles Cameron. In an apparent attempt to retaliate against European indifference and to extract concessions from the British, he arrested the British consul and his staff as well as several other Europeans. On receiving news of the detention of its consul in 1864, the British Foreign Office made an effort to mollify the emperor by sending a letter from Queen Victoria with a request to release the prisoners and a promise that preparations were being made to send craftsmen to Ethiopia. Hormuzd

Rassam, a member of the British consular staff in nearby Aden, was selected to lead the mission to Tewodros. Rassam reached Ethiopia in January, 1866.

Although the initial meeting between Rassam and Tewodros went well, the emperor changed his mind about releasing the prisoners and instead added Rassam and his party to his collection of detainees. This threw the British government into a quandary. The detention of British officials in the hands of an African leader was considered a major affront to British prestige and detrimental to British image, especially in the eyes of the Middle East and Asia. Many colonial officials, especially in India, argued that European prestige would remain under grave threat everywhere as long as the Ethiopian emperor continued to defy Britain. On the other hand, the forbidding mountainous terrain of Ethiopia and the exorbitant cost of mounting a rescue expedition made many in Parliament and the British government less sanguine to try to liberate the prisoners by force.

Romantic contemporary depiction of Tewodros's suicide. (Francis R. Niglutsch)

The military option came to the forefront with the coming to power of the Tory government under Prime Minister Derby and his Chancellor of the Exchequer, Benjamin Disraeli. The latter in particular was determined to use the issue of the captives in Ethiopia to achieve several other objectives, including sending a message to France, which was busy building the Suez Canal in Egypt, that Great Britain was capable of sending major military expeditions into the African hinterland. In addition, Disraeli calculated that a popular foreign war could be used to divert his fellow countrymen's attention from the domestic crisis surrounding the Reform Act of 1867. In August, 1867, the British cabinet decided on war.

Since the construction of the Suez Canal was not yet complete, sending a large force directly from England was ruled out. Instead, the British governor of Bombay was instructed to mount an expeditionary force consisting of British and Indian units. The task of organizing the force was given to Lieutenant General Robert Napier, a noted engineer and commander-in-chief of the Bombay army. Napier worked out elaborate plans for moving his army, which included 13,000 British and Indian soldiers and several thousand camp followers and working parties. In all, 62,220 men and 36,094 animals, including 44 elephants, were transported to the African coast at Zula in 205 sailing vessels and 75 steamers. The British soldiers were equipped with the recently issued Snider rifles—which would be used for the first time in battle—modern artillery, and rockets.

The British expedition had to traverse some four hundred miles of an extremely precipitous terrain to reach Magdela, where the European prisoners were kept. While the eventual success of the expedition owed a great deal to Napier's brilliant organizational skills and the vast British superiority in logistics, firepower, and discipline, the advance of the British force was unhindered because the emperor's power had nearly evaporated long before the arrival of the British troops. By 1868, much of Ethiopia had fallen into the hands of rebel chiefs. By the time that the British expedition landed on the coast, Emperor Tewodros was left with only a few thousand soldiers on his side, and he controlled little more than the fortress at Magdela, where he kept his European prisoners. The collapse of Tewodros's authority allowed General Napier to gather intelligence easily and to secure the cooperation of dissident chiefs, including Kassa Mercha, a powerful rebel lord who controlled the area through which the expedition traveled.

After the expedition reached the foothills of the Magdela plateau, it engaged Tewodros's army on April 10, 1868. British rockets and breech-loading Snider-Enfield rifles were more than a match for the poorly equipped Ethiopian force. Tewodros's small army was nearly annihilated, with minimal British losses. Tewodros released his European prisoners and committed suicide shortly before the British stormed his fortress. Napier returned in triumph with the freed hostages and the spoils of war, including the emperor's gold crown and more than a thousand ancient Ethiopian Coptic Christian manuscripts. A grateful British government bestowed numerous honors on Napier, including a peerage that made him Baron Napier of Magdela. Although Parliament had authorized the expediture of only £2 million for the expedition, the operation actually cost £8.6 million.

SIGNIFICANCE

The Battle of Magdela was a contest between a technologically backward traditional polity and one of the most modern imperial powers of the nineteenth century. The British expedition's performance in Ethiopia was a convincing display of the power of modern technology and of Britain's capability to penetrate foreboding hinterlands in any part of the world. The success of this expedition removed the inhibitions against venturing into the interior of Africa. The confidence and experience gained through this expedition encouraged Britain and other European powers to embark on extensive military intervention in all corners of Africa. Ironically, however, the worst military defeat that European imperial powers would suffer in Africa later occurred in Ethiopia in 1896, when Emperor Menelik II's army nearly annihilated a large Italian invasion force.

The British expedition to Ethiopia was also a strong proof that Britain had at last succeeded in subjugating India to its interest. Only a decade before the expedition, British rule over India had been engulfed in a crisis during the 1857-1858 Sepoy Mutiny. The fact that Indian troops and resources played such a vital role in the Ethiopian expedition is testimony to how well the British had succeeded in pacifying India and making it into an effective instrument of British power.

—*Shumet Sishagne*

FURTHER READING

Arnold, Percy. *Prelude to Magdala: Emperor Theodore of Ethiopia and British Diplomacy*. Edited by Richard Pankhurst. London: Bellew, 1992. An extensive account of the background to the detention of Europeans by Emperor Tewodros, the reaction of the British press and public, and the British military intervention to secure the release of the European captives.

Bates, Darrell. *The Abyssinian Difficulty: The Emperor Theodorus and the Magdala Campaign, 1867-68*. Oxford, England: Oxford University Press, 1979. An informative book with a useful survey of the rise to power of Emperor Tewodros and the challenges he faced, followed by a detailed description of the British campaign against the Ethiopian emperor.

Blanc, Henry. *A Narrative of Captivity in Abyssinia: With Some Account of the Late Emperor Tewodros, His Country, and People*. 1868. Reprint: London: Frank Cass, 1970. Firsthand account of the captivity of Europeans in Ethiopia by an English surgeon who accompanied the official British envoy to Tewodros and found himself detained with the rest of the group.

Harcourt, Freda. "Disraeli's Imperialism, 1866-1868: A Question of Timing." *Historical Journal* 23, no. 1 (1980). Engaging article that links the 1868 British expedition to Ethiopia with the policy of the Tory Party to divert attention from domestic social and political troubles.

Holland, Trevenen J., and Henry Hozier, comps. *Records of the Expedition to Abyssinia*. London: Her Majesty's Stationery Office, 1870. 2 vols. Official government record of the British expedition against Tewodros. Contains official reports, detailed campaign plans, and excellent maps.

Markham, Clements R. *A History of the Abyssinian Expedition*. 1869. Reprint. Farnborough, Hants., England: Gregg International Publishers, 1970. Contemporary account of the expedition written by a British geographer who accompanied it in an official capacity. The book contains an excellent description of the Ethiopian countryside through which the expedition traveled.

SEE ALSO: 1848-1889: Exploration of East Africa; May 10, 1857-July 8, 1858: Sepoy Mutiny Against British Rule; Aug., 1867: British Parliament Passes the Reform Act of 1867; Sept. 13, 1882: Battle of Tel el Kebir; Mar. 1, 1896: Ethiopia Repels Italian Invasion.
RELATED ARTICLES in *Great Lives from History: The Nineteenth Century, 1801-1900:* Fourteenth Earl of Derby; Benjamin Disraeli; Menelik II.

April 6, 1868
PROMULGATION OF JAPAN'S CHARTER OATH

Japan's Charter Oath abolished the country's rigid system of social classes and the privileged military classes of shogun and samurai. In place of the traditional feudal system, the oath instituted a new centralized government heavily influenced by Western models. It promised individual freedoms for Japanese citizens to pursue any vocation they desired, as well as broad public discussions to achieve political consensus.

ALSO KNOWN AS: Imperial Oath of Five Articles; Meiji Charter Oath
LOCALE: Tokyo, Japan
CATEGORIES: Government and politics; laws, acts, and legal history; social issues and reform

KEY FIGURES

Sakamoto Ryōma (1835-1867), Japanese rural samurai and one of the Three Heroes of the Meiji Restoration
Fukuoka Takachika (1835-1919), Japanese politician and samurai and one of the authors of the Charter Oath
Mutsuhito (1852-1912), emperor of Japan as Meiji, r. 1867-1912
Kido Takayoshi (1833-1877), Japanese politician and samurai and one of the Three Heroes of the Meiji Restoration

SUMMARY OF EVENT

The American commodore Matthew C. Perry arrived in Edo Bay (later Tokyo) with four Navy ships on July 8, 1853, ending nearly two centuries of Japanese isolation. The superiority of Western military technology immediately impressed the Japanese, including the shogun (military dictator) and the figurehead emperor. The Americans had steamships, powerful cannons, guns, and advanced navigational equipment. The emperor of Japan lived in Kyōto, and his power was mostly symbolic and ceremonial. The powerful shoguns of the Tokugawa dynasty had ruled in Edo since 1603, but they had failed to prevent the foreign intrusion. Perry's arrival sparked the downfall of the shogun's government, known as the shogunate, or *bakufu*.

Less than fifteen years after Perry's incursion, on January 3, 1868, forces from the province of Satsuma, supported by the provinces of Chōshū and Tosa, stormed the imperial palace in the Meiji Restoration. They declared that Emperor Mutsuhito—who took the reign name Meiji—was once again the supreme power in Japan, superceding the shogun. The imperial capital moved from Kyōto to Edo, which was renamed Tokyo. The demise of the shogunate and the rise of the imperial government would not be officially achieved, however, until April 6, 1868, when the emperor promulgated the Charter Oath. In the intervening fifteen years between 1853 and 1868, Japanese citizens perceived the emperor as weak and the shogun as corrupt and ineffectual. People blamed the government for allowing foreign incursions from the West and perceived that Japan had fallen far behind Western nations in military technology, education, and political philosophy.

Sakamoto Ryōma, from the Tosa domain, was one of many political activists who organized secret plots, assassinations, and military coups against the Tokugawa shogun in the years following Perry's surprise visit. The rebels argued that Japan should "revere the emperor and expel the barbarians" (*sonnō jōi*). The words of the slogan indicated that the shogun and samurais had failed to protect Japan.

For a while, Sakamoto worked on diplomatic missions to strengthen ties among feudal lords (daimyos) and samurais who wanted to eradicate the shogunate, concentrating on the provinces of Chōshū, Satsuma, and Tosa. Sakamoto softened from his earlier radicalism and believed that peaceful discussions could lead to the creation of a new government. He thought the shogun might still be involved in a new government, in a reduced role, but impatient samurais in Chōshū and Satsuma argued that the decadent Tokugawa dynasty needed to be abolished completely. Sakamoto's study of European governments led him to formulate a detailed plan for the new government in 1867 based on the general opinion of Japanese citizens: Two legislative bodies and a new constitution would be created. Power would be balanced among elected committees, officials, and a restored emperor. Sakamoto's blueprint for a new government would appear in the language of the Charter Oath.

Government leaders of the Meiji Restoration believed that Japan should restore itself from the "humiliation" of Perry's uninvited mission. The Charter Oath was drawn up to inspire the Japanese to embrace common goals of unity, improvement, and the long-term ideal of "rich country, strong army" (*fukoku kyōhei*). The oath signed by Emperor Meiji (whose name literally meant "enlightened ruler") assured citizens that the few warriors in Satsuma, Chōshū, and Tosa who had been behind the restoration would not dominate the new government. The Charter Oath was also known as the Imperial Covenant of Five Articles, indicating both its length and the fact that it was a compact between the emperor and his people.

Although the Charter Oath was written by men from the southwestern provinces, such as Tosa's Fukuoka Takachika and Chōshū's Kido Takayoshi, it was designed to include all of Japan in the political process. In the future, the government would be based on common opinion and consensus, not the whims of a ruling shogun and samurais. The new constitution that followed on the heels of the Charter Oath established the emperor as the supreme head of state, who nevertheless ruled under the advisement of a Western-style government with judicial, executive, and legislative branches. Compulsory education, universal military service, and a merit system for achievement were also established in the new constitution.

The text of the Charter Oath is remarkable for its brevity and openness to new ideas. The five articles were given added importance by Emperor Meiji's signature, and it is sometimes called the Meiji Charter Oath. While its language is abstract, the document is concise, and the oath emphasizes four major themes: Government would thenceforth be based solely upon consultation and public opinion; people were placed at liberty to pursue their own vocations; national interests were to be placed above those of the individual; and "evil customs" of history (meaning feudalism and the samurai class) would be supplanted by modern democratic institutions.

Given Japan's long history of feudalism and aristocratic rule by shoguns, emperors, daimyos, and samurais, the Charter Oath sparked an amazing transformation. The Meiji Restoration came to stand for rapid modernization in government, military technology, industry, and scientific education. The Charter Oath underlined the shift from feudalism to freedom, democracy, and opportunity for everyone. However, beneath the progressive and egalitarian language, the Charter Oath obscured a complex political reality: The ideal of uplifting national interests and sacrificing individual will for the good of Japan was more important than freedom of occupation and improving technology. The "rich country, strong army" doctrine made clear that social equality was not the ultimate concern of the government.

The social revolution, then, would not be accomplished so easily. Sometimes, however, social liberalization happened as an indirect result of attempts to centralize authority. For example, abolishing the samurai class could be seen as a move toward egalitarianism, but it really represented a new way to professionalize the military and establish an army of drafted men from all classes instead of an army of privileged elites. A new concentration of power in the emperor and centralization of government in Tokyo went against the tradition of regional and local fiefdoms. Also, the rule of the shogun did not end without bloodshed. Civil wars between loyalists to the shogun in the northeast and the new imperial armies from the southwest raged on for two years until the *bakufu* forces were finally defeated.

Although the Charter Oath reads as a document promoting modernization and consensus, it employs enough vagueness to serve as a model that can be adapted with changing times. The Charter Oath attempts to unite "all classes, high and low" and involve all citizens in "public discussions" about the nature of government. Many of the Meiji bureaucrats and military leaders had suffered under a corrupt shogunal regime based on family lineage rather than merit. In the era promised by the oath, opportunity would be provided for everyone; at the same time, the new government would "strengthen the foundations of imperial rule."

SIGNIFICANCE

The Charter Oath was the first step in Japan's leap into the modern world. The oath balanced two contradictory goals of inventing a modern plan for government (including formerly disenfranchised groups) and maintaining continuity with the past and the traditional power of the elite classes. The overriding need was to gain legitimacy for the new government and to put aside loyalty to the old Tokugawa shogunate. The brief five-article text was followed by a lengthy new constitution, both of which announced to the world that Japan valued Western knowledge, a centralized government with a democratic political process, and a strong military as its highest priorities. The Charter Oath paved the way for Japan to renew its imperial honor and, with the greatest ambitions, to join European nations in the race toward the twentieth century.

—*Jonathan L. Thorndike*

FURTHER READING

Allinson, Gary D. *The Columbia Guide to Modern Japanese History*. New York: Columbia University Press, 1999. Extremely useful book divided into four major sections: a) historical narrative from 1850 to the present; b) topical compendium on a wide range of issues from politics, military, business, education, and noteworthy writers; c) resource guide with a list of printed and electronic sources on Japan; and d) an appendix with historical documents like the Charter Oath and lists of major political figures.

Burma, Ian. *Inventing Japan*. New York: Modern Library, 2003. Focusing on the period 1853-1964, this book documents how Japan in barely more than one hundred years modernized through a process of cultural reinvention, borrowing, and imagining a shared mythology.

Duus, Peter. *Modern Japan*. 2d ed. Boston: Houghton Mifflin, 1998. Effective survey of the rise of Japan to world power status and postwar emergence as an economic superpower.

Jansen, Marius B., ed. *The Nineteenth Century*. Vol. 5 in *The Cambridge History of Japan*. Cambridge, England: Cambridge University Press, 1989. This authoritative work is the standard in the field of Japanese history. This volume expertly brings together the best scholars in nineteenth century history; other volumes cover Japan from its origins to the present.

SEE ALSO: Mar. 31, 1854: Perry Opens Japan to Western Trade; Jan. 3, 1868: Japan's Meiji Restoration; 1870's: Japan Expands into Korea; Jan.-Sept. 24, 1877: Former Samurai Rise in Satsuma Rebellion; Feb. 11, 1889: Japan Adopts a New Constitution; Aug. 1, 1894-Apr. 17, 1895: Sino-Japanese War; Nov. 14, 1897: Scramble for Chinese Concessions Begins.

RELATED ARTICLES in *Great Lives from History: The Nineteenth Century, 1801-1900:* Mutsuhito; Matthew C. Perry; Saigō Takamori.

June 2, 1868
GREAT BRITAIN'S FIRST TRADES UNION CONGRESS FORMS

The organization of British trade unions had received a number of setbacks in the first part of the nineteenth century. It was not until 1868 that a small group of trade union leaders were able to call together a small number of delegates from other unions around the country to form the Trades Union Congress, to discuss common problems and concerns.

ALSO KNOWN AS: TUC
LOCALE: London, England
CATEGORIES: Business and labor; organizations and institutions

KEY FIGURES

George Howell (1833-1910), first secretary of the Trades Union Congress and later a member of Parliament

William Allan (1813-1874), first treasurer of the Trades Union Congress and leader of the Amalgamated Society of Engineers

George Potter (1832-1893), first chairman of the Trades Union Congress and editor of the *Beehive*

SUMMARY OF EVENT

British trade unionism enjoyed mixed fortunes during the nineteenth century. At first prohibited, then enjoying a sudden mushrooming growth in the 1830's, it collapsed in the 1840's. A much slower growth in the 1850's by the unions representing skilled craftsmen established a more solid foundation on which to build a labor movement that by the end of the century numbered many millions of workers, skilled and unskilled, from all over Great Britain. The calling of the first Trades Union Congress was a significant event contributing to this later development.

The Combination Acts introduced by the government of William Pitt the Younger in 1799-1800 effectively prohibited all unions of working men. When they were repealed in 1824, there was a sudden surge of union activity. Workers formed large local unions, such as the National Union of Cotton Spinners formed in 1829, based in Lancashire. There were demands for higher wages, often backed by strikes that sometimes became quite violent. Robert Owen, a visionary industrialist, tried to unite the unions into his Grand National Consolidated Trades Union, which gained one-half million members in a few weeks after its founding in 1833. It had a radical political program, however, and immediately incurred government hostility.

In 1834, five members of an agricultural union were arrested and deported for their union membership. The case of these so-called Tolpuddle Martyrs was followed in 1837 by the arrest and imprisonment of the leaders of the Glasgow Cotton Spinners. In response to the realization of their lack of legal immunity, a downturn in the economy, and their own poor organization, the membership of Owen's union quickly dissolved. Reforming zeal transferred itself to the overtly political Chartist movement and later to the Cooperative movement and the Reform League. The latter succeeded in achieving passage of the 1867 Reform Act.

Cartoon by John Tenniel (1820-1914)—who illustrated the first edition of Lewis Carroll's Alice's Adventures in Wonderland *(1865)—published in* Punch *in 1867. The cartoon is captioned "The Road to Sheffield" and has the policeman (with the face of Punch) saying, "Now, then, stop that, I say! We'll have no intimidation here."*

The British economy did not pick up until the 1850's, a decade that saw the emergence of "model" unions, formed by the national amalgamation of local unions of skilled workmen. These unions acted more like medieval guilds, protecting the craft element of their trade and eschewing strike action in favor of negotiation and arbitration. Although they avoided political activity, they made contacts with sympathetic members of Parliament and soon gained a reputation for respectability. The leading model union was the Amalgamated Society of Engineers, founded in 1851 and led by William Allan. The visionary Robert Applegarth led the Carpenters and Joiners Union, which had ten thousand members by 1870.

Much union activity remained at a local level, where interunion cooperation was organized through local trade councils. The leading such council, formed in 1860, was in London, where many skilled union organizers worked and where many unions had their headquarters. Five leaders emerged, including Allan, Applegarth, and George Odger, leader of the Shoemakers' Union, a brilliant orator and part-time secretary for the London Trades Council. These were later named the Junta: They met secretly, forming a larger grouping called the Confederation of Amalgamated Trades (CAT). By and large, CAT policy was for unions to register as friendly societies, legal bodies set up for the common welfare of their members. However, not all London unionists agreed. George Potter, the militant leader of the Progressive Carpenters, had been involved in strike action in 1859-1860, and in his newspaper, the *Beehive*, opposed unions registering as friendly societies in order to gain legal legitimacy.

In an effort to heal this division, especially in the light of a hostile 1867 report by the Royal Commission on Trades Unions and Employers' Associations, the Manchester and Salford Trades Council, led by Sam Nicholson, sent out a letter on February 21, 1868, proposing a "Congress of Trades Councils" and inviting delegates from such councils and also from individual trade unions or federations to a meeting in London on May 4. The meeting was later postponed until June 2, 1868, to provide its participants with more time to prepare. The term "congress" was taken from the Social Sciences Associations'

Congress, which met annually to discuss papers of common concern. Twelve items for discussion were proposed for the first meeting, including regulation of the hours of labor, technical education, arbitration and courts of reconciliation, and the necessity of an annual congress.

Thirty-four delegates accepted the invitation, mainly from the provincial trade councils. The London Junta initially opposed the meeting, as did George Potter, and only two delegates from London attended. No formal organization was set up at the first congress, but it was recommended that the congress be held annually. The Birmingham Trades Council was asked to arrange the next congress in Birmingham, which turned out to be a more successful representation of British trade unionism.

Government and public hostility to unions was being fueled at that time by the "Sheffield outrages," a set of pro-union acts of violence committed in Sheffield that culminated in an anti-union home being blown up with gunpowder. A labor backlash against the public's hostility, however, brought disparate union factions together, and both the London Trades Council and George Potter's group were represented at the Birmingham meeting as a result. All told, the forty delegates present in 1869 represented one-quarter million workers.

The London Trades Council was invited to arrange the third Trades Union Congress, where a basic organization for the congress was established. George Potter became chairman, George Howell was made secretary, and William Allan assumed the post of treasurer. A political advisory group called the Parliamentary Action Committee was also formed, which was to have great influence at future Royal Commission hearings. The Parliamentary Action Committee of the Trades Union Congress effectively took over from the Junta, which dissolved itself.

Significance

A number of significant developments followed the organization of the Trades Union Congress (TUC). At a political level, a number of acts of Parliament followed, most based on Royal Commission reports in which TUC opinion was well represented. The most significant pieces of legislation were the 1871 Trades Union Act, giving the unions a legal basis, although the Criminal Law Amendment Act of the same year still curbed trade union activity; the 1875 Employer and Worker Act, which gave employees equal legal status with employers and decriminalized breaches of contract; and the 1875 Conspiracy and Protection of Property Act, which allowed for peaceful picketing.

In the 1874 national elections, the Parliamentary Action Committee canvassed every candidate on his views on trade unions, and several candidates in that election stood explicitly representing trade unionism. Gradually, individual members of Parliament were elected with the backing of the trade unions. The first of these were Radicals, but in the 1890's, the unions backed several candidates of the nascent Labour Party.

In terms of union membership, the success of the model unions encouraged semiskilled and unskilled workers to demand unions for themselves. For example, in 1872, Joseph Arch established the National Agricultural Labourers Union. By the 1880's, such unions had become part of the TUC and led to its rapid expansion. The annual congress became a very significant meeting over the next century. Indeed, in the decades after World War II, TUC meetings could significantly influence government policy, especially that of Labour governments. The TUC secretary general became as important as any government cabinet minister.

Although its influence declined beginning in the 1980's, the TUC is still a significant influence in British labor relations and legislation. The non-Marxist socialism its founders embraced, its focus on nonpolitical activity, and its mature early leadership contributed to the reputations of British trade unionism in general and of the TUC in particular. The TUC assumed a central and respected place among British institutions and avoided the divisiveness of extreme left-wing politics or the corruption of power that bedeviled the trade union movements of some other countries.

—David Barratt

Further Reading

Fraser, W. Hamish. *A History of British Trade Unionism, 1700-1998*. New York: St. Martin's Press, 1999. A very useful survey of the full extent of the trade union movement in Great Britain and the role of the TUC in that movement.

Jackson, Michael P. *Trade Unions*. New York: Longman, 1982. A good introductory survey of the history and importance of trade unions with full bibliography.

Laybourn, Keith. *A History of British Trades Unionism*. Stroud, England: Sutton, 1992. A history of trade unionism, setting the first Trades Union Congress in its historical context and explaining its significance to the movement.

Musson, A. E. *British Trades Unions, 1800-1875*. Basingstoke, Hampshire, England: Macmillans, 1972. A more traditional account of the rise of the trade unions and events leading up to the first Trades Union Congress.

Pelling, H. *A History of British Trades Unionism*. London: Penguin Books, 1963. Still one of the best introductory accounts of the subject; discusses the history of the labor movement and the role of trade unionism within the larger movement.

Reid, Alistair J. *United We Stand: A History of Britain's Trade Unions*. London: Allen Lane, 2004. An extremely full account of the history of trade unionism and the significance of the first Trades Union Congress.

Rule, John, ed. *British Trade Unionism, 1750-1850*. New York: Longman, 1988. A collection of detailed essays describing the events that led up to the first Trades Union Congress.

SEE ALSO: Mar. 11, 1811-1816: Luddites Destroy Industrial Machines; 1824: British Parliament Repeals the Combination Acts; 1833: British Parliament Passes the Factory Act; May 8, 1838-Apr. 10, 1848: Chartist Movement; Sept. 28, 1864: First International Is Founded; Aug., 1867: British Parliament Passes the Reform Act of 1867; Dec. 8, 1886: American Federation of Labor Is Founded; May 15, 1891: Papal Encyclical on Labor; Aug. 3, 1892: Hardie Becomes Parliament's First Labour Member; Feb. 27, 1900: British Labour Party Is Formed.

RELATED ARTICLE in *Great Lives from History: The Nineteenth Century, 1801-1900:* Robert Owen.

June 23, 1868
SHOLES PATENTS A PRACTICAL TYPEWRITER

Development of the first prototype of a letter-printing machine led to the invention of the first successful commercial typewriter. The early device, which was sold first by E. Remington & Sons, revolutionized office work by helping to increase workflow and efficiency. The typewriter also led unprecedented numbers of women into the white-collar workforce.

LOCALE: Milwaukee, Wisconsin
CATEGORIES: Inventions; communications

KEY FIGURES

Christopher Latham Sholes (1819-1890), inventor of the first practical typewriter
Carlos Glidden (1834-1877), co-inventor of the typewriter
Samuel W. Soulé (fl. mid-nineteenth century), co-inventor of the typewriter
James Densmore (1820-1889), lawyer who promoted the typewriter to investors

SUMMARY OF EVENT

Christopher Latham Sholes was born on a farm near Mooresburg, Pennsylvania, in Montour County. His parents, Orrin, a cabinet maker, and Catherine (Cook), moved to Danville when Sholes was seven. After finishing school, he became a printer's apprentice. By the time he was eighteen years old, he was helping his brothers print their newspaper, the *Wisconsin Democrat*, in Green Bay. Six years later Sholes became the editor of Madison's *Wisconsin Enquirer*.

Sholes moved to Southport (later Kenosha) to run another newspaper, and, eventually, President James K. Polk appointed him postmaster in 1843. Sholes then decided to enter politics, serving two terms in the state legislature. By 1857 he was the editor of the *Milwaukee Sentinel*, and, in 1863, Sholes accepted an appointment by President Abraham Lincoln to become the port collector of the city. This position was fortuitous for Sholes because it allowed him ample time to tinker with inventions in a machine shop on West State Street. He and his partner, Samuel W. Soulé, a civil engineer and draftsman, were granted a patent for a page numbering machine. Another partner, Carlos Glidden, after seeing a demonstration of the machine, suggested that Sholes create a machine that prints letters.

Sholes's next inspiration came from a *Scientific American* article of July 6, 1876, describing an early version of the typewriter by American inventor John Pratt. A few months later, Sholes, having worked on a primitive typing machine, asked his friend, Charles E. Weller of Western Union Telegraph, to stop by his office in the federal office building. Weller visited Sholes during his lunch break, and Sholes showed him his new invention. The device, which originally looked like a telegraph machine, typed four successive "w's" on a piece of carbon paper upon Sholes hitting a lever. Each letter of the alphabet, Sholes told Weller, could be placed on a separate hammer key. Sholes, Soulé, and Glidden soon began work on the prototype.

The prototype was built on a large, cumbersome, bulky, and heavy frame. The type bars struck upward against the platen (or typewriter/printer roller) and prevented the person typing from seeing the typed page until it was nearly complete; this early model was often referred to as a "blind typewriter." Sholes soon encountered another problem. He had arranged the letters alphabetically on the keyboard, but the type bars kept jamming as the typist increased speed and proficiency. He accidentally discovered that spreading the letters out in as many common diagraphs (for example, "ed," "er," "th," and "tr") as possible on the keyboard greatly reduced the jamming, especially when the first six keys—QWERTY—were placed in the third row. ("QWERTY" keyboards remain the standard on computers into the twenty-first century.) Also, Sholes's early typewriter did not have a key for the number 1; instead, the typist used the letter "l." In addition, the early model typed only in upper case letters because there was no shift key. There were other problems: The hand-inked ribbon did not always produce clean, clear type, and the strings used on the machine often broke. The collaborators had to refine the typewriter over the next few years, producing two other models.

Typist operating one of the earliest typewriters in 1872. (Hulton Archive/Getty Images)

Sholes eventually typed a letter and sent it to James Densmore, a promoter from Meadville, Pennsylvania, who made his money investing in oil tankers for railroad cars. At the time, Densmore was working as an attorney for the Corry Machine Company. He was so impressed by the invention that he agreed to pay Sholes and his partners their $600.00 in expenses. He also agreed to help them with future financing. Densmore secured two patents for Sholes, Glidden, and Soulé on June 23, 1868.

Despite setbacks in selling the early models, Densmore believed in the typewriter and its future prospects. Sholes sold off his patent rights to Densmore for $12,000 because he had ten children, five boys and five girls, to support. Finally, Densmore found success with E. Remington & Sons of Ilion, New York. Remington made its fortune during the Civil War producing munitions, but it later manufactured sewing machines. Remington began producing the typewriter for a commercial market on March 1, 1873. One year later, it produced a perfected model with a shift key for lower case letters and with a carriage that enabled the printed page to be viewed in its entirety while typing; the carriage could also be returned by depressing a foot pedal. The market was slow in the beginning—the company, by that time called Remington Arms, sold only 5,000 typewriters in 1886, but by 1900, sales skyrocketed to 100,000.

SIGNIFICANCE

The typewriter found its way into offices throughout the country, revolutionizing office workflow and efficiency in record keeping and leading women into white-collar jobs in business and other institutions. The Young Men's Christian Association (YMCA) in New York City soon offered typing courses for women, and, by 1888, the number of women employed as typists grew to sixty thousand. Mark Twain became the first writer to submit a typewritten manuscript, for *Life on the Mississippi* (1883), to the work's publishers.

Sholes eventually received additional payments from Remington for his typewriter, but his grave at Forest Home Cemetery in Milwaukee remained unmarked until 1919. The National Shorthand Reporter's Association arranged for a marker to commemorate his invention on the centennial of his birth.

—*Gayla Koerting*

FURTHER READING

Bliven, Bruce. *The Wonderful Writing Machine*. New York: Random House, 1954. Traces the history of the typewriter from early models in 1820 to models of 1950, and addresses how the invention revolutionized the American business world, especially for working women during the late nineteenth century.

Current, Richard N. *The Typewriter and the Men Who Made It*. Urbana: University of Illinois Press, 1954. Current examined papers from the Densmore family to trace the development of the typewriter. The book includes an annotated bibliography of primary and secondary sources.

Foulke, Arthur Toye. *Mr. Typewriter: A Biography of Christopher Latham Sholes*. Boston: Christopher, 1961. An account of Sholes's personal life, his career, and inventions. This work contains a chronology of developments for the writing machine, Sholes's family tree, and photographs of various typewriter models.

McMann, Dennis. "Milwaukee Man's Invention was the First Draft of the Modern Typewriter." *Milwaukee Journal Sentinel* 5 (April, 1998). The author focuses on how the typewriter created career paths for women during the late nineteenth century.

Rehr, Daryl. *Antique Typewriters and Office Collectibles*. Paducah, Ky.: Collector Books, 1997. A guide to the history of typewriters, written as an introduction to those interested not only in collecting the early devices but also in their history. Includes discussion of Sholes, his co-inventors, and the Remington company. Well-illustrated, with an index that is selectively annotated.

Roby, Henry W. *Henry W. Roby's Story of the Invention of the Typewriter*. Edited by Milo M. Quaiffe. Menasha, Wis.: George Banta, 1925. Roby, a contemporary court reporter and stenographer who became an acquaintance of Sholes, provides a narrative about Sholes and his invention.

Romeno, Frank J. *Machine Writing and Typesetting: The Story of Sholes and Mergenthaler and the Invention of the Typewriter and the Linotype*. Salem, N.H.: GAMA, 1986. Addresses the development of mechanical approaches to writing and typesetting. The author explains the roles that both inventions played in communication. Written to celebrate the centennial of the Linotype.

Snow, Richard F. "American Characters: Christopher Latham Sholes." *American Heritage* 33, no. 5 (August-September, 1982): 78-79. A brief article that provides a good overview of Sholes's attempts to develop a workable model of the typewriter.

Weller, Charles E. *The Early History of the Typewriter*. LaForte, Ind.: Chase and Shepherd, 1919. A memoir about Sholes and his development of the first practical typewriter.

SEE ALSO: 1819-1833: Babbage Designs a Mechanical Calculator; Sept. 10, 1846: Howe Patents His Sewing Machine; May 10-Nov. 10, 1876: Philadelphia Hosts the Centennial Exposition; Dec. 24, 1877: Edison Patents the Cylinder Phonograph; June, 1896: Marconi Patents the Wireless Telegraph.

RELATED ARTICLES in *Great Lives from History: The Nineteenth Century, 1801-1900:* Charles Babbage; Louis Braille; Ottmar Mergenthaler; Mark Twain.

July 9, 1868
FOURTEENTH AMENDMENT IS RATIFIED

The most important addition to the U.S. Constitution since adoption of the Bill of Rights, the Fourteenth Amendment was prompted by the need to protect the rights of former slaves; it defined citizenship and established a principle that would later be used to apply the protections of the Bill of Rights to actions by state governments.

LOCALE: Washington, D.C.
CATEGORIES: Civil rights and liberties; laws, acts, and legal history

KEY FIGURES

Andrew Johnson (1808-1875), president of the United States, 1865-1869

Thaddeus Stevens (1792-1868), Republican congressman and radical leader who helped draft the Fourteenth Amendment

Charles Sumner (1811-1874), Republican senator and prominent radical

SUMMARY OF EVENT

Ratified on July 9, 1868, the Fourteenth Amendment to the U.S. Constitution was part of the Reconstruction plan formulated by the Republican majority in the Thirty-ninth Congress. Before Congress met in December, 1865, President Andrew Johnson had authorized the restoration of white self-government in the former Confederate states, and congressmen and senators from those states waited in Washington to be seated in Congress.

Meanwhile, southern state legislatures elected under Johnson's program had met to develop a series of laws called black codes, which restricted the rights of the former slaves. Although the Republican majority in Congress had no intention of permitting the Johnson approach to Reconstruction to prevail or allowing the seating of the unrepentant white southern representatives, they had no comprehensive counterproposal. To gain time and to work out a positive approach, Republicans in the House and the Senate created the Joint Committee of Fifteen on Reconstruction. This committee was composed of six senators and nine representatives.

The Republican majority rejected Johnson's plan because, as the black codes demonstrated, the old Confederate politicians could not be trusted to respect the rights of the freedmen. Moreover, the Republicans had no intention of permitting white southerners, whom they regarded as rebels and traitors, to increase the representation in the House of Representatives of the southern Democrats. The abolition of slavery had destroyed the old compromise under which five slaves counted as three free persons in apportioning representation in the House and the electoral college, and the Republicans wanted to make sure that the South did not add to its numbers in the House and thereby profit from rebellion.

Between December, 1865, and May, 1866, Republicans attempted to hammer out a program that would accomplish their purposes in the South, unite members of their party in Congress, and appeal to northern voters. Given the diversity of opinion within the Republican Party, this undertaking proved to be difficult. The radical wing of the party wanted African American suffrage, permanent political proscription of former Confederate leaders, and confiscation of the property of former Confederates. Some Republicans maintained they were authorized in these actions by the Thirteenth Amendment, which, they believed, gave Congress the power to abolish the "vestiges of slavery." Moderate Republicans, on the other hand, feared political repercussions from African American suffrage, as such a requirement would result in beginning the Reconstruction process over again. Many moderates also believed that an additional amendment to the Constitution was needed to provide precise authority for Congress to enact civil rights legislation.

From deliberations of the joint committee and debate on the floor of the House came the Fourteenth Amendment. Many Republicans believed that the proposal was in the nature of a peace treaty, although this view was not explicitly stated. According to this view, if the South accepted the amendment, the southern states were to be readmitted and their senators and representatives would seated in Congress. In other words, Reconstruction would end. Republicans presented a united front during the final vote as a matter of party policy. Because the amendment was an obvious compromise between radicals and moderates, it was too strong for some and too weak for others.

The Fourteenth Amendment became the most important addition to the constitution since the Bill of Rights had been adopted in 1791. It contains five sections.

Section 1, the first constitutional definition of citizenship, states that all persons born or naturalized in the United States are citizens of the United States and of the states in which they reside. It includes limits on the power of states, by providing that no state may abridge

FOURTEENTH AMENDMENT TO THE U.S. CONSTITUTION

SECTION 1. All persons born or naturalized in the United States and subject to the jurisdiction thereof, are citizens of the United States and of the State wherein they reside. No State shall make or enforce any law which shall abridge the privileges or immunities of citizens of the United States; nor shall any State deprive any person of life, liberty, or property, without due process of law; nor deny to any person within its jurisdiction the equal protection of the laws.

SECTION 2. Representatives shall be apportioned among the several States according to their respective numbers, counting the whole number of persons in each State, excluding Indians not taxed. But when the right to vote at any election for the choice of electors for President and Vice President of the United States, Representatives in Congress, the Executive and Judicial officers of a State, or the members of the Legislature thereof, is denied to any of the male inhabitants of such State, being twenty-one years of age, and citizens of the United States, or in any way abridged, except for participation in rebellion, or other crime, the basis of representation therein shall be reduced in the proportion which the number of such male citizens shall bear to the whole number of male citizens twenty-one years of age in such State.

SECTION 3. No person shall be a Senator or Representative in Congress, or elector of President and Vice President, or hold any office, civil or military, under the United States, or under any State, who, having previously taken an oath, as a member of Congress, or as an officer of the United States, or as a member of any State legislature, or as an executive or judicial officer of any State, to support the Constitution of the United States, shall have engaged in insurrection or rebellion against the same, or given aid or comfort to the enemies thereof. But Congress may by a vote of two-thirds of each House, remove such disability.

SECTION 4. The validity of the public debt of the United States, authorized by law, including debts incurred for payment of pensions and bounties for services in suppressing insurrection or rebellion, shall not be questioned. But neither the United States nor any State shall assume or pay any debt or obligation incurred in aid of insurrection or rebellion against the United States, or any claim for the loss or emancipation of any slave; but all such debts, obligations and claims shall be held illegal and void.

SECTION 5. The Congress shall have power to enforce, by appropriate legislation, the provisions of this article.

the privileges and immunities of citizens, deprive any person of life, liberty, or property without due process of law, or deny to any person within its jurisdiction the equal protection of law. This section was intended to guarantee African Americans the rights of citizenship, although the amendment's framers did not define exactly which rights were included. Nor did they define "state action" to specify whether the term meant only official acts of state government or the actions of individuals functioning privately with state approval.

The courts later interpreted the amendment's due process clause to extend the rights of the accused listed in the Bill of Rights, which had applied only to the federal government, to the states. They would eventually expand the notion of equal protection to include other categories, such as sex and disability, as well as race. They also interpreted the word "person" to include corporations as legal persons; under this interpretation, corporations found protection from much state regulation.

Section 2 gave a new formula of representation in place of the old three-fifths compromise of the Constitution, under which five slaves were counted as equal to three free persons in determining a state's representation in the House of Representatives and the electoral college. All persons in a state were to be counted for representation, but if a state should disfranchise any of its adult male citizens, except for participation in rebellion or any other crime, the basis of its representation would be reduced proportionately. Although not guaranteeing suffrage to African Americans, this provision threatened the South with a loss of representation should black men be denied the vote.

Section 3 declared that no person who had ever taken an oath to support the Constitution (which included all who had been in the military service or held state or national office before 1860) and had then participated in the rebellion against the Union could be a senator or representative or hold any civil or military office, national or state. This disability could be removed only by a two-thirds vote of both houses of Congress. This section took away the pardoning power of the president, which congressional Republicans believed Andrew Johnson had used too generously.

Section 4 validated the debt of the United States, voided all debts incurred to support rebellion, and invalidated all claims for compensation for emancipated slaves made by their former owners.

Section 5 gave Congress authority to pass legislation to enforce the provisions of the Fourteenth Amendment.

Significance

After the Civil War (1861-1865), the framers of the Fourteenth Amendment desired to protect the former slaves and boost Republican Party strength in the South by barring old Confederates from returning to Congress and bolstering the electoral college with increased voting strength. They hoped to do this without threatening the federal system or unduly upsetting the relationship between the central government and the states. At the same time, Republicans wanted to unify their party and project a popular issue for the approaching electoral contest against Andrew Johnson.

Since its passage in 1868, the U.S. Supreme Court has used the due process and equal protection clauses of the Fourteenth Amendment to expand both the number and breadth of rights protecting individuals. More than any other amendment, the Fourteenth has provided the basis for the range of rights that Americans came to take for granted during the twentieth century.

—William J. Cooper, Jr., updated by Mary Welek Atwell

Further Reading

Benedict, Michael Les. *A Compromise of Principle: Congressional Republicans and Reconstruction, 1863-1869*. New York: W. W. Norton, 1974. Emphasizes the Republicans' concern that the Fourteenth Amendment maintain the role of the states in the federal system.

Cox, LaWanda, and John H. Cox. *Politics, Principle, and Prejudice: Dilemma of Reconstruction America, 1865-1866*. New York: Free Press, 1963. Argues that civil rights, rather than merely partisan politics, was the central issue during Reconstruction.

Hensley, Thomas R., Christopher E. Smith, and Joyce A. Baugh. *The Changing Supreme Court: Constitutional Rights and Liberties*. St. Paul, Minn.: West Publishing, 1997. Study of the U.S. Supreme Court's evolving protections of citizen rights that closely examines issues relating to the Fourteenth Amendment.

Hyman, Harold M., and William Wiecek. *Equal Justice Under Law: Constitutional Development, 1835-1875*. New York: Harper & Row, 1982. Includes a thorough discussion of the Fourteenth Amendment as a logical and necessary extension of the Thirteenth Amendment.

Lively, Donald E. *The Constitution and Race*. New York: Praeger, 1992. Focuses on the association of attitudes toward race and constitutional interpretation. A positive interpretation of the motives of framers of the Fourteenth Amendment.

Nieman, Donald G. *Promises to Keep: African-Americans and the Constitutional Order, 1776 to the Present*. New York: Oxford University Press, 1991. A survey of issues of race and constitutional law that highlights the contributions of African Americans to its development.

Perry, Michael J. *We the People: The Fourteenth Amendment and the Supreme Court*. New ed. New York: Oxford University Press, 2002. Examines the controversies surrounding interpretation of the Fourteenth Amendment by the Supreme Court.

See also: Dec. 8, 1863-Apr. 24, 1877: Reconstruction of the South; Mar. 3, 1865: Congress Creates the Freedmen's Bureau; Nov. 24, 1865: Mississippi Enacts First Post-Civil War Black Code; Dec. 6, 1865: Thirteenth Amendment Is Ratified; 1866: Birth of the Ku Klux Klan; Apr. 9, 1866: Civil Rights Act of 1866; May 10, 1866: Suffragists Protest the Fourteenth Amendment; Feb. 24-May 26, 1868: Impeachment of Andrew Johnson; May, 1869: Woman Suffrage Associations Begin Forming; Oct. 15, 1883: Civil Rights Cases; 1890: Mississippi Constitution Disfranchises Black Voters; May 18, 1896: *Plessy v. Ferguson*.

Related articles in *Great Lives from History: The Nineteenth Century, 1801-1900:* Andrew Johnson; Abraham Lincoln; Thaddeus Stevens; Charles Sumner.

July 28, 1868
Burlingame Treaty

The Burlingame Treaty established reciprocal rights between China and the United States, including respect for territorial sovereignty and bilateral immigration.

Locale: Washington, D.C.

Categories: Diplomacy and international relations; trade and commerce

Key Figures

Anson Burlingame (1820-1870), U.S. minister to China, 1861-1867, appointed in 1868 to head the Chinese delegation to the United States and Europe

William H. Seward (1801-1872), United States secretary of state

Prince Gong (Prince Kung; 1833-1898), coregent with the dowager empress of China

Cixi (Tz'u-hsi; 1835-1908), dowager empress of China

Summary of Event

Formal United States interest in China dates from the thirteen-thousand-mile voyage of the U.S. ship *Empress of China*, under the command of Captain John Green, which departed from New York City on February 22, 1784. The vessel returned from Canton in May, 1785, with tea, silks, and other trade goods of the Orient. Merchants in Philadelphia, Boston, Providence, and New York quickly sought profits in the China trade. By the late 1830's, "Yankee clippers" had shortened the transit time from America's Atlantic ports to Canton from a matter of many months to a mere ninety days.

Political problems, however, hindered commercial relations. The Manchu, or Qing, Dynasty (1644-1912), fearful of Western intentions, restricted trade to one city, Canton, and sharply curtailed the rights of foreigners in China. Chafing at these limits, especially China's refusal to deal with Europeans on terms of equality, caused Great Britain to begin hostilities with the Qing Dynasty, occasioned by the "unsavory issue" of England's trade in opium with China. The Opium War (1839-1842) resulted in the Treaty of Nanjing (August 24, 1842), a triumph for the political and commercial interests of Great Britain in eastern Asia. Britain obtained the cession of the island of Hong Kong and the opening of four additional cities—Amoy, Ningpo, Foochow, and Shanghai—to British trade. The U.S. government desired similar rights and obtained them in the Treaty of Wanghia (named for a village near Macao) on July 3, 1844. Commissioner Caleb Cushing, although not formally received by China as a minister, was permitted to negotiate this landmark agreement. The United States secured access to the newly opened ports and was extended the right of extraterritoriality; that is, U.S. citizens were to be tried for offenses committed in China under U.S. law by the U.S. consul.

Within the next twenty years, trade with China grew. The United States acquired Washington, Oregon, and California, and, with Pacific ports, had greater access to Chinese markets. The California gold rush (1849) and the construction of the Central Pacific Railroad (completed in 1869), with its need for labor, encouraged Chinese emigration to the United States. Meanwhile, U.S. missionaries, merchants, travelers, and adventurers were arriving in China. Conditions in the "Middle Kingdom," however, were not good. The authority of the central government had been challenged by the anti-Western Taiping Rebellion (1851-1864) and was suppressed only with outside help. Further European incursions into China, epitomized by the Anglo-French War with the Manchus (1854-1858), threatened to curtail U.S. cultural and commercial opportunities in China. If the United States did not act, it would face the prospect of being excluded from China by European imperialism.

Secretary of State William H. Seward believed that it was time for the United States to have formal representation at the Manchu court. His fortunate choice was Anson Burlingame. Born on November 14, 1820, in rural New York, the son of a "Methodist exhorter," Burlingame had grown up in the Midwest, graduating from the University of Michigan. After attending Harvard Law School, Burlingame went into practice in Boston. With a gift of oratory and exceptional personal charm, Burlingame served in the U.S. House of Representatives (1855-1861) and was a pioneer of the new Republican Party. As a reward for his labor and in recognition of his talents, Burlingame was offered the post of U.S. minister to Austria, but the Habsburgs refused him because of his known sympathies with Lajos Kossuth, the Hungarian revolutionary. As a second choice and a compensatory honor, Burlingame was given the assignment to China.

Because the United States was distracted with the Civil War (1861-1865), Burlingame was left on his own and could count on little U.S. military might to support his actions. Acquiring a great admiration for and confidence in the Chinese, Burlingame won the trust and respect of Yixin, known as Prince Gong. the coregent of China with the dowager empress Cixi. When Burlingame resigned as the U.S. minister to China, in November, 1867, the Imperial Manchu court asked him to head China's first official delegation to the West. The Burlingame mission toured the United States, being warmly received, and arrived in Great Britain as William Ewart Gladstone was assuming the prime ministership of that nation. Burlingame's brilliant career was cut short during a subsequent visit to Russia, where he contracted pneumonia, dying in St. Petersburg on February 23, 1870. Few had served their own country so well, and it was said that none had given China a more sincere friendship.

The most outstanding accomplishment of the Burlingame mission was the Burlingame Treaty, signed on July 28, 1868, in Washington, D.C. This document dealt with a variety of issues between China and the United States. The United States pledged itself to respect Chinese sovereignty and territorial integrity, a position in sharp contrast to that of the European powers and one that anticipated the subsequent "open door policy" of the United States (1899). The Burlingame Treaty accepted bilateral immigration between China and the United States, and by 1880 there were 105,000 Chinese living in the United States.

SIGNIFICANCE

By the standards of the 1860's, the Burlingame Treaty was a landmark of fairness and justice. However, the United States did not honor its spirit or letter. Anti-immigrant feeling focused on a fear of Chinese "coolie" labor. The infamous Sandlot Riots in San Francisco, in June, 1877, were symptomatic of both the mistreatment of Asian immigrants and the rising sentiment for Asian exclusion. On March 1, 1879, President Rutherford B. Hayes vetoed a congressional bill limiting the number of Chinese passengers on board ships bound for the United States as a violation of the Burlingame Treaty. Hayes did, however, send a mission to China to work for the revision of the Burlingame Treaty. In 1880, China recognized the right of the United States to regulate, limit, and suspend, but not absolutely forbid, Chinese immigration.

Two years later, President Chester A. Arthur vetoed a twenty-year suspension of Chinese immigration as being a de facto prohibition, but on May 6, 1882, the Chinese Exclusion Act passed, suspending the importation of Chinese labor for a ten-year period. In 1894, another ten-year exclusion period was enacted; in 1904, exclusion was extended indefinitely. When, on December 17, 1943, Chinese immigration was permitted by an act of Congress, it was within the strict limits of the 1920's

Canton, the only Chinese port open to American trade during the mid-nineteenth century. (R. S. Peale/J. A. Hill)

quota system, allowing the entrance of only 105 Chinese annually. Not until the mid-twentieth century did the United States depart from an immigration policy centered on ethnic origin, thus allowing the original intent of the Burlingame Treaty to be realized.

—*C. George Fry*

FURTHER READING

Dulles, Foster Rhea. *China and America: The Story of Their Relations Since 1784*. Princeton, N.J.: Princeton University Press, 1946. This brief, classic history places the Burlingame Treaty in the broad context of United States-Chinese trade and diplomacy over a period of one hundred fifty years.

Fairbank, John K. *China Perceived: Images and Policies in Chinese-American Relations*. New York: Alfred A. Knopf, 1974. A noted Harvard scholar compares the contrasting sensitivities, traditions, aims, and means of the United States and China as they have affected foreign policy.

Fairbank, John K., Edwin O. Reischauer, and Albert M. Craig. *East Asia: Tradition and Transformation*. Rev. ed. Boston: Houghton Mifflin, 1989. This profusely illustrated and thoroughly documented survey, a standard introduction to the history of Asia's Pacific Rim, illuminates the Chinese situation in 1868.

Miller, Stuart Creighton. *The Unwelcome Immigrant: The American Image of the Chinese, 1785-1882*. Berkeley: University of California Press, 1969. A succinct analysis that explains why the Chinese were the only immigrants other than Africans to be forbidden by law from entering the United States during the nineteenth century.

Mosher, Steven W. *China Misperceived: American Illusions and Chinese Reality*. New York: Basic Books, 1990. This combination of psychohistory and political analysis examines the varied U.S. perceptions of China, ranging from infatuation to hostility. Carefully annotated.

Tsai, Shih-shan Henry. *China and the Overseas Chinese in the United States, 1868-1911*. Fayetteville: University of Arkansas Press, 1983. Well-documented, concise study of the key issue between the United States and China during the late nineteenth century: immigration.

SEE ALSO: 1849: Chinese Begin Immigrating to California; Mar. 31, 1854: Perry Opens Japan to Western Trade; Nov. 1-2, 1861: Cixi's Coup Preserves Qing Dynasty Power; May 8, 1871: Treaty of Washington Settles U.S. Claims vs. Britain; Mar. 3, 1875: Congress Enacts the Page Law; May 9, 1882: Arthur Signs the Chinese Exclusion Act; Nov. 12, 1882: San Francisco's Chinese Six Companies Association Forms; May 4, 1892: Anti-Japanese Yellow Peril Campaign Begins; May 10, 1895: Chinese Californians Form Native Sons of the Golden State; May, 1900-Sept. 7, 1901: Boxer Rebellion.

RELATED ARTICLE in *Great Lives from History: The Nineteenth Century, 1801-1900:* William H. Seward.

September 30, 1868
SPANISH REVOLUTION OF 1868

Spain's 1868 revolution overthrew the monarchy to install a short-lived republican government in a transformation that brought to the surface the divisive influences of regionalism and demonstrated the continuing importance of the army.

LOCALE: Spain

CATEGORIES: Government and politics; wars, uprisings, and civil unrest

KEY FIGURES

Isabella II (1830-1904), queen of Spain, r. 1833-1868

Don Carlos (1788-1855), uncle of Isabella, whom he challenged for the throne

Amadeo (1845-1890), first duke of Aosta, who became king of Spain, r. 1870-1873

Leopoldo O'Donnell (1809-1867), leader of the conservative Moderates who helped form the Liberal Union

Francisco Pi y Margall (1824-1901), Federalist leader of the Republicans and president of the First Spanish Republic in 1874

Juan Prim y Prats (Marqués de los Castillejos; 1814-1870), leader of the Progressives

Manuel Ruíz Zorrilla (1834-1895), leader of the radical wing of the Progressive Party

Francisco Serrano y Domínguez (1810-1885), leader of the Liberal Union

The duke of Aosta entering Madrid, where he was welcomed as King Amadeo. (Francis R. Niglutsch)

SUMMARY OF EVENT

Isabella's reign as queen of Spain began with a war of succession and ended in a coup. From 1833, when she ascended the throne at the age of three, with her mother as regent, she was challenged by her uncle, Prince Carlos, who waged a five-year war to unseat her. Aided by the people of the northern province of Navarre and Roman Catholics who hated the liberal constitution of 1812, which had been restored, Don Carlos and twelve thousand soldiers attacked Madrid in 1837. During that same year, a new constitution was promulgated recognizing Roman Catholicism as the faith of all Spaniards. The combination of political compromise and military defeats led Don Carlos to withdraw. In 1843, the Cortes declared thirteen-year-old Isabella of age to rule.

Isabella reigned during one of the most chaotic periods of Spanish history. The mid-nineteenth century saw violent swings between forces of change and reactionary traditionalism. Liberal land reforms, the beginnings of the industrial revolution and an industrial working class, the growth of regionalist sentiments, and passionate conflicts over the role of the Church all occurred during her reign. Moreover, Isabella herself was responsible for many of Spain's problems.

Isabella was an avaricious woman, subject to her passions, who made and unmade ministers at will. Her reign saw many and varied palace intrigues, and many of her closest advisers were Carlists—supporters of Don Carlos. Isabella often relied on the military and its leaders, especially General Leopoldo O'Donnell, to maintain her power. By the late 1860's, most Spanish politicians had come to believe that Isabella was a hindrance to progress in Spain and that overthrow of the Bourbon Dynasty, which she represented, would solve many problems.

A revolutionary coalition formed with the aim of deposing Isabella and calling a representative Cortes, or parliament, to create an alternative form of government. The instigators of this coalition were General Francisco Serrano y Domínguez, who took over as the leader of the conservative Liberal Union after General O'Donnell's death in 1867, and General Juan Prim y Prats, marqués de los Castillejos, leader of the liberal Progressive Party. With the help of army and navy leaders, they forced Isabella to abdicate in September, 1868.

In 1869, a representative Cortes framed a new constitution making Spain a constitutional monarchy with universal suffrage and a bill of rights. The Spanish Bourbons were to be excluded from the throne, and a regency was to be formed until a suitable monarch could be found. Serrano became the regent and Prim the prime minister of this new government. Meanwhile, the search for a monarch revealed a new political group, the Republicans. Dominated by Francisco Pi y Margall, the Spanish Republicans were extreme federalists, anticlericals, and antimilitarists. They appealed to the substantial number of Spaniards who favored provincial rights over control by the central government. Furthermore, their reform program was attractive to many.

Prim and Serrano found a monarch in the Italian nobleman Amadeo, the first duke of Aosta, who proved to be a conscientious ruler with no unconstitutional ambitions. However, he was deprived of his most important adviser when Prim was assassinated on the day on which Amadeo arrived in Spain. Political rivalry between Serrano's Liberal Unionists and the Progressives under Prim's political heir, Manuel Ruíz Zorrilla, made any hope of moderate constitutional government impossible. In addition, the new Carlist pretender, Carlos VII, initiated the Second Carlist War in 1872. Unable to maintain an effective government, Amadeo abdicated the throne in February, 1873.

Although only a minority of its members were Republicans, the Cortes decided in desperation to proclaim a republic. Francisco Pi y Margall was made president of the First Spanish Republic. He was only the first of four presidents during the republic's solitary year of existence. To remain in power, the Republicans were forced to ally with the centrist Radical Progressives of Ruíz Zorrilla. This alliance lost them the support of the Provincialists, and their anticlericalism lost them the neutrality of the clergy. The Carlists continued their rebellion against this regime. Even radical proletarian support was lost when the Anarchists became active. Spain was in a state of civil war.

Finally, in January of 1874, when the republic had endured for only one year, President Emilio Castelar was defeated in a parliamentary vote and resigned. At that point, the army dismissed the deputies and dissolved the Cortes. The First Republic had ceased to exist.

SIGNIFICANCE

The failure of the republic created by the revolution of 1868 and the Second Carlist War over royal succession left the Spanish nation eager for order and political stability. The coup that overthrew the republic was widely supported, and there was little opposition to the appointment of General Francisco Serrano y Domínguez as temporary chief of state. In 1876, Spain adopted a new constitution that gave the nation some long-term political stability.

—José M. Sánchez, updated by James A. Baer

FURTHER READING

Brenan, Gerald. *The Spanish Labyrinth: An Account of the Social and Political Background of the Civil War*. Canto ed. New York: Cambridge University Press, 1990. Begins with the end of the reign of Isabella and the revolution of 1874. Explains the link between the failed republic and the restoration.

Carr, Raymond. *Spain, 1808-1939*. Oxford, England: Clarendon Press, 1966. Although a general history of modern Spain, one chapter focuses on the Revolution of 1868, recognizing the revolution's link to a depression in 1867 and the impracticality of the Federalists' program.

Crow, John A. *Spain, the Root and the Flower: An Interpretation of Spain and the Spanish People*. 3d ed. Berkeley: University of California Press, 1985. Chapter 10 focuses on the Bourbon Dynasty in Spain during the nineteenth century. Extremely useful for its combination of political and cultural history.

Flynn, M. K. *Ideology, Mobilization, and the Nation: The Rise of Irish, Basque, and Carlist Nationalist Movements in the Nineteenth and Early Twentieth Centuries*. New York: St. Martin's Press, 2000. Broad study of the development of nationalism in Ireland and Spain during the nineteenth century that illuminates the rise of nationalism among Spain's Carlists.

Hughes, Robert. *Barcelona*. New York: Vintage Books, 1993. Chapter 6 gives a regionalist picture of Spain's history during the period by focusing on the impact of national events in Barcelona.

Madariaga, Salvador de. *Spain: A Modern History*. New York: Frederick A. Praeger, 1958. Despite its age, this work is a very personal, interpretive history of Spain by a Spaniard, and is valuable for its perspective.

Smith, Rhea Marsh. *Spain: A Modern History*. Ann Arbor: University of Michigan Press, 1965. This general history of Spain has specific chapters on the reign of Isabella II, Amadeo and the First Republic, and the reign of Alfonso XII.

SEE ALSO: May 2, 1808: Dos de Mayo Insurrection in Spain; Sept. 29, 1833-1849: Carlist Wars Unsettle Spain; 1876: Spanish Constitution of 1876.

RELATED ARTICLES in *Great Lives from History: The Nineteenth Century, 1801-1900:* Don Carlos; Isabella II.

October 10, 1868-February 10, 1878
CUBA'S TEN YEARS' WAR

The Ten Years' War was the first of the three revolutionary conflicts that led to Cuba's independence from Spain in 1902. Although the insurgents acquiesced to a treaty with Spain in 1878, the Ten Years' War galvanized nationalist and abolitionist sentiment, politically mobilized patriots both slave and free, and produced several of Cuba's most important revolutionary heroes.

LOCALE: Eastern Cuba
CATEGORIES: Wars, uprisings, and civil unrest; social issues and reform

KEY FIGURES

Carlos Manuel de Céspedes (1819-1874), Cuban planter who initiated the Ten Years' War when he freed his slaves
Antonio Maceo (1845-1895), Cuban nationalist and military leader in the Ten Years' War
Máximo Gómez y Báez (1836-1905), Dominican-born commander in chief of insurgent forces in the Ten Years' War

SUMMARY OF EVENT

Cuban nationalist uprising against Spanish rule began with the Ten Years' War in 1868 and ended with the Spanish-American War and U.S. intervention in 1898. By the middle of the nineteenth century, Cuba was among Spain's few remaining colonial possessions, and, economically, Cuba was most important for Spain.

Some Cubans had grown increasingly resentful of the demands and restrictions of the declining Spanish Empire, and, in 1866, Spanish authorities established the Junta de Información to respond to the growing concerns of creole Cuban reformists: reducing taxation, expanding free trade, and increasing Cuban political liberties and representation. Cuban nationalists also called for a gradual transition toward self-government and the abolition of slavery. Spanish authorities met the junta commission's calls for colonial concessions with increased taxes, increased repression, and a ban on all reformist meetings in Cuba. For many Cubans, Spain's response indicated that armed protest would be more effective than calls for political and economic reform. The atmosphere of revolution may have been bolstered with the deposition of Spain's Queen Isabella II in July, 1868, as well as earlier nineteenth century attempts at Cuban rebellion led by Narciso López.

On October 10, 1868, Carlos Manuel de Céspedes, a poet, lawyer, and sugar planter, made a speech declaring freedom for his slaves, inviting them to join in a war for Cuban independence. His speech, which mobilized approximately thirty-seven like-minded planters and their slaves, became known as the Grito de Yara (Cry of Yara) and the opening salvo of the Ten Years' War. The Cuban Liberation Army (CLA) and the provisional revolutionary government that followed were composed of eastern planters, many of whom were unable to compete economically with the mechanized, large-scale sugar plantations of western Cuba; slaves, some of whom liberated themselves while others were freed by their owners or insurgent forces; and free Cubans of color, who composed a substantial part of the eastern population.

By November the rebel army had some twelve thousand men. These rebel fighters in the CLA became known as *mambíses*. Separatist insurgents sought release from Spanish imperial policies, especially those surrounding taxation and representation, and many fought for the abolition of slavery as a crucial element of an independent and free Cuba (*Cuba libre*). The ten-year struggle was a guerrilla war fought in the eastern part of Cuba. A primary tactic of the rebel forces was burning sugar plantations and mills. The insurgents were able to occupy some eastern towns like Bayamo and Guáimaro in spite of much larger and better-provisioned Spanish forces (the Spanish military and civilian volunteers exceeded 100,000). Loyalists maintained control of the major cities in the east as well as western Cuba.

While Cuban emigré separatists in New York City were unable to secure U.S. diplomatic or material support, the United States became involved in the Ten Years' War through the *Virginius* affair in 1873. Sympathetic Americans leased the vessel *Virginius*, a Confederate blockade-runner built during the U.S. Civil War, to New York-based Cuban patriots. On October 27, 1873, the *Virginius* illegally flew the American flag as it set off from Jamaica to Haiti with Cuban patriots, arms, supplies, and a predominantly British and American crew. Alerted by spies in Kingston, the Spanish warship *Tornado* captured the *Virginius* off the coast of Jamaica and took all 155 on board as prisoners to Santiago de Cuba, where they were charged with piracy; fifty-three were executed. As tensions between the United States and Spain mounted, U.S. secretary of state Hamilton Fish crafted a settlement that ultimately forced Spain to release the remaining prisoners and the ship and to pay an $80,000 indemnity to the families of the eight Americans who were executed.

Antonio Maceo, a Cuban of African descent, quickly ascended the ranks of the CLA during the Ten Years' War and served as an exceptional leader in Cuba's struggles for independence. Maceo's powerful leadership, the extensive ranks of supporters—including the Cuban nationalist leader José Martí—and the multiracial character of the insurgent army at all levels prompted Spanish authorities to propagandize, playing on the racial anxieties of some Cubans and their fears of a race war, "another Haiti," and black supremacy. Spanish counterinsurgency campaigns further disabled rebel forces and the creole populace through policies of execution, persecution, expropriation, deportation, imprisonment, and the forced removal of rural populations from regions with armed conflict. By 1877 growing tensions among rebel leaders inflamed by Spanish propaganda, a lack of material resources, insurgent capitulation, and failure to engage insurgents in western Cuba had severely weakened the rebel forces.

On February 10, 1878 the provincial leaders of the CLA in Camagüey signed a peace pact with Spain, the Treaty of Zanjón. Because the treaty, which promised reforms (many of which were never realized), stopped short of independence and full abolition, Maceo publicly denounced the armistice at a meeting with Spanish authorities in Baraguá and in a circular titled "Protest of Baraguá" (March 23, 1878). Maceo and his corps of approximately one thousand men, the majority of whom were Cubans of color, continued to resist Spanish forces in the eastern province of Oriente, but by the end of May, most of the holdouts had surrendered or retreated. Approximately 160,000 died in the course of the decade-long conflict. Despite the surrender of the CLA in 1878, the Ten Years' War commenced a thirty-year struggle for Cuban independence.

SIGNIFICANCE

Cuba's Ten Years' War was an anticolonial revolution that failed militarily and politically but nevertheless had a profound and long-lasting ideological impact. Antiracist rhetoric and the multiracial character of the insurgency undermined the early support of some white revolutionaries.

The intertwining of independence and abolition as the primary aims of revolution, however, first signaled by Carlos Manuel de Céspedes's Grito de Yara speech and reinforced by Antonio Maceo's "Protest of Baraguá," transformed the meaning of Cuban nationalism as it linked the end of colonialism with the end of slavery and established a rhetoric of social equality, justice, and national identity that transcended race. The significant participation of slaves in the Ten Years' War and the ensuing Spanish policies that formally recognized their legal freedom hastened the advent of full abolition in 1886. The political mobilization and extensive participation of Cubans of color in the Ten Years' War engendered a racially inclusive conception of Cuban citizenship.

The Ten Years' War laid the ideological groundwork for future revolution (the Guerra Chiquita or Little War of 1879-1880 and the War of Independence of 1895 that became the Spanish-American War in 1898) and generated several of Cuba's most important national heroes and military leaders, most notably Maceo, Máximo Gómez y Báez, and Calixto García Íñiguez. To this day, the word *mambí*, first used to refer to Cuba's nineteenth century freedom fighters, remains a fundamental symbol of Cuban patriotism.

—Christina Proenza-Coles

FURTHER READING

Bradford, Richard. *The Virginius Affair*. Boulder: Colorado Associated University Press, 1980. A detailed account of the *Virginius* affair and late nineteenth century diplomatic relations between the United States and Spain.

Ferrer, Ada. *Insurgent Cuba: Race, Nation, and Revolution, 1868-1898*. Chapel Hill: University of North Carolina Press, 1999. A book-length study of the Ten Years' War that examines the political mobilization of Cubans of color as well as discourses of nationalism and issues of race.

Gott, Richard. *Cuba: A New History*. New Haven, Conn.: Yale University Press, 2004. Offers a chapter summarizing the events of the Ten Years' War and provides a concise overview of its major issues and participants.

Quiroz, Alfonso. "Loyalist Overkill: The Socioeconomic Costs of 'Repressing' the Separatist Insurrection in Cuba, 1868-1878." *Hispanic American Historical Review* 78, no. 2 (May, 1998). Provides a summary of the grievances preceding the Ten Years' War and the counterinsurgency tactics employed by Spanish loyalists.

Schmidt-Nowara, Christopher. *Empire and Antislavery: Spain, Cuba, and Puerto Rico, 1833-1874*. Pittsburgh: University of Pittsburgh Press, 1999. Traces the development of revolutionary ideology in nineteenth century Cuba within the broader context of Spanish and Puerto Rican abolitionism and politics.

See also: Feb. 24, 1895-1898: Cuban War of Independence; Apr. 24-Dec. 10, 1898: Spanish-American War; Feb. 4, 1899-July 4, 1902: Philippine Insurrection.

Related articles in *Great Lives from History: The Nineteenth Century, 1801-1900:* Miguel Hidalgo y Costilla; Isabella II; José Martí.

November 27, 1868
Washita River Massacre

The Washita Massacre marked what was believed to be at the time a decisive step toward the reduction of Indian attacks on white settlers moving into the western frontier.

Also known as: Battle of Washita River
Locale: Washita River, Indian Territory (near Cheyenne, Oklahoma)
Categories: Atrocities and war crimes; terrorism and political assassination; indigenous people's rights; wars, uprisings, and civil unrest

Key Figures

Black Kettle (1803?-1868), Cheyenne chieftain
George A. Custer (1839-1876), commander of the Seventh Cavalry Regiment
Joel H. Elliott (1840-1868), second in command of the Seventh Cavalry Regiment
Philip Sheridan (1831-1888), commander of the Department of the Missouri
William Tecumseh Sherman (1820-1891), commander of the Division of the Missouri
Edward W. Wynkoop (1836-1891), agent for the Cheyenne and Arapaho tribes

Summary of Event

At dawn on November 27, 1868, troops of the Seventh U.S. Cavalry, led by Lieutenant Colonel George A. Custer, attacked and massacred a Cheyenne village on the banks of the Washita River in the Indian Territory. In this village of fifty-one lodges were some of the survivors of the 1864 Sand Creek Massacre, including the great Cheyenne chieftain Black Kettle.

Custer had set out on an expedition to "hunt" Indians and follow what he thought was the trail of a large war party. He found the village, which was located on the south side of the river and surrounded by thick woods. Custer divided his force of seven hundred men into four groups; under cover of darkness, on the night of November 26, he positioned them to the north, south, east, and west of the village. All through the bitterly cold and snowy night, the soldiers waited in absolute silence, without fires, for Custer's signal to attack. Troops G, H, and M, under Major Joel Elliott, were deployed to the north, while troops B and F were south of the village. Troops E and I were down the Washita River, to the right of Elliott's command. Custer, with the regimental band, the color guard, a special sharpshooter company, all the scouts, and troops A, C, D, and K, waited in the center.

Just before dawn, the soldiers crept closer to the village and, at first light, swept down upon the sleeping Cheyennes to the accompaniment of the strains of "Garry Owen," the theme song of the Seventh Cavalry. Custer, on his black stallion, charged through the village and onto a knoll, from where he watched the fighting. As the Cheyennes ran from their lodges, they were cut down by gunfire or saber, with no quarter given and no distinction made between men, women, or children. Chief Black Kettle and his wife were both shot as they attempted to escape on his pony. Caught entirely by surprise and with few weapons other than bows and arrows, the Cheyennes' only hope was flight—but most were killed by the sharpshooters positioned among the trees. Some did escape by plunging into the icy waters and making their way down the river channel to the Arapaho village of Chief Little Raven. Within a short time, the village fell to the soldiers, who set about killing or capturing those Cheyennes who had taken up defensive positions in the woods.

At about 10:00 A.M., Custer noticed that warriors were beginning to gather atop the neighboring hills and, looking for an explanation, questioned one of the female captives. He learned that Black Kettle's village was not the only one on the banks of the Washita River, as he had thought, but was one of many Cheyenne, Arapaho, and Kiowa villages in the area. Shortly after, an officer who had been supervising the roundup of Cheyenne ponies reported that he had seen a very large Arapaho village down river. Nevertheless, Custer directed his troops to

Arapaho chief Little Raven. (National Archives)

gather up the spoils of war, which included saddles, buffalo robes, bows and arrows, hatchets, spears, a few revolvers and rifles, all the winter supply of food, most of the Cheyennes' clothing, and all of their lodges. After making an inventory and choosing some personal souvenirs, including one of the lodges, Custer had all the rest burned.

Almost nine hundred of the Cheyennes' horses and mules had now been rounded up. Custer gave the best horses to his officers and scouts, provided mounts for the female captives, then ordered four companies of his men to slaughter the rest of the animals. He had no intention of leaving the horses behind for the warriors and reasoned that taking them along when he left the area would surely provoke attempts by the Cheyennes to recapture them.

During the late afternoon, Custer was informed that Major Elliott, with seventeen men, had chased a small band of fleeing Cheyennes down the river and had not returned. Custer sent out a search party, but no trace of the missing men was found. Custer then called off the search—a decision that added to the growing resentment and anti-Custer sentiments among some of his officers.

As night approached, Custer realized his command was in a precarious position. Besides being burdened with prisoners and their own wounded, his troops were cold and hungry, their mounts were exhausted, and warriors from the other villages had gathered in the surrounding hills. Thus, unprepared for further battle, Custer knew that he could not simply retreat toward his supply train, left behind at a safe distance from the fighting, without alerting the warriors to its location and risking that they would reach it first. The stratagem he devised was to convince them that he was advancing down river to attack again; at the head of his regiment, with band playing, he traveled east until darkness fell. Seeing this, the warriors hurried back to protect their villages, leaving only a few scouts behind. Custer then reversed back to the battlefield and up the Washita Valley, finally stopping at 2:00 A.M. to camp for the night. The next day, the troops rejoined the supply train and two days later reached Camp Supply, the fort from which Custer had started and at which General Philip H. Sheridan waited for news of the expedition.

In his official report of the Washita action, Custer stated that 103 Cheyennes had been killed and 53 women and children, some of them wounded, had been taken prisoner. Among the dead were two Cheyenne chieftains, Black Kettle and Little Rock. During the fighting in the village, one officer and three enlisted men of the Seventh Cavalry had been killed. Custer also reported the deaths of Major Elliott and his seventeen men, although at the time he had no actual knowledge of their fate. Their bodies were discovered in the woods by a later expedition.

Opinions differ as to whether Custer's attack upon the Cheyennes was simply another unprovoked massacre such as that at Sand Creek four years earlier. William Tecumseh Sherman, Philip Sheridan, and Custer, among others, believed that the Washita action was justified because of Cheyenne raids on white settlements along the Saline and Solomon Rivers in Kansas in August, 1868. During a three-day rampage, two hundred Cheyenne warriors had committed murder and rape and abducted women and children. When Black Kettle and two chiefs of the Arapaho had arrived at Fort Cobb in mid-November, seeking sanctuary and subsistence for their people under the terms of the Medicine Lodge Creek Treaty, they had been refused because General Sheridan now considered both tribes to be hostile after the recent raids. They were told to leave the Indian Territory and warned that troops were in the field.

On the other hand, Indian agent Edward W. Wynkoop

and others insisted that an entire tribe should not be punished for the acts of a few. They further argued that the promises made at Medicine Lodge had led the Cheyenne and Arapaho to expect fair treatment at Fort Cobb, which had not been forthcoming. Furthermore, it has since been established that the trail Custer followed, which he later claimed was that of a Cheyenne war party, actually had been made by Kiowas returning from a raid against the Utes in Colorado.

SIGNIFICANCE

To place the Washita Massacre in historical perspective, scholars point out that the U.S. Army had failed to subdue the plains tribes in battle on the prairie, and efforts to achieve peace through treaty had been largely unsuccessful. Thus, the invasion of the Indian Territory, of which the Washita Massacre was a decisive first step, represented a change of tactics in the U.S. government's efforts to achieve its ultimate goal: the removal of the plains tribes as an obstacle to white settlement of the Great Plains.

—*LouAnn Faris Culley*

FURTHER READING

Barnitz, Albert Trovillo Siders, and Jennie Barnitz. *Life in Custer's Cavalry, Diaries and Letters of Albert and Jennie Barnitz, 1867-1868.* Edited by Robert M. Utley. New Haven, Conn.: Yale University Press, 1977. An account of the massacre completed from the writings of one of Custer's troop commanders and his wife.

Brady, Cyrus. *Indian Fights and Fighters.* Lincoln: University of Nebraska Press, 1971. A narrative of the plains wars, including the Washita Massacre. Includes many eyewitness accounts not available elsewhere.

Brill, Charles. *Conquest of the Southern Plains.* Millwood, N.Y.: Kraus Reprint, 1975. A fully illustrated account of all events related to the massacre, with the texts of both Sheridan's and Custer's reports.

Custer, George Armstrong. *My Life on the Plains.* London: Folio Society, 1963. Contains Custer's account of the events before, during, and after the Washita Massacre.

Greene, Jerome A. *Washita: The U.S. Army and the Southern Cheyennes, 1867-1869.* Norman: University of Oklahoma Press, 2004. Part of the Campaigns and Commanders series, this work examines the Washita Massacre and the Sand Creek Massacre of 1864.

Hoig, Stan. *The Battle of the Washita.* Garden City, N.Y.: Doubleday, 1976. A thoroughly documented account of the Sheridan-Custer campaign. Maps and photographs.

SEE ALSO: May 6, 1850: California's Bloody Island Massacre; Feb. 6, 1861-Sept. 4, 1886: Apache Wars; Aug. 17, 1862-Dec. 28, 1863: Great Sioux War; Nov. 29, 1864: Sand Creek Massacre; Dec. 21, 1866: Fetterman Massacre; Oct. 21, 1867: Medicine Lodge Creek Treaty; Mar. 3, 1871: Grant Signs Indian Appropriation Act; 1876-1877: Sioux War; June 25, 1876: Battle of the Little Bighorn; 1890: U.S. Census Bureau Announces Closing of the Frontier.

RELATED ARTICLES in *Great Lives from History: The Nineteenth Century, 1801-1900:* Kit Carson; Crazy Horse; George A. Custer; Geronimo; William Tecumseh Sherman; Sitting Bull.

December 3, 1868-February 20, 1874
GLADSTONE BECOMES PRIME MINISTER OF BRITAIN

Prime Minister William Ewart Gladstone's activist approach to governing transformed British politics, especially during his first of four ministries. He supported the evolutionary growth of democracy in Great Britain and introduced an agenda for social and economic improvement, and he introduced and passed legislation that remedied unjust and inhumane conditions in Ireland.

LOCALE: London, England
CATEGORIES: Government and politics; laws, acts, and legal history; social issues and reform; economics

KEY FIGURES

William Ewart Gladstone (1809-1898), British prime minister, 1868-1874, 1880-1885, 1886, 1892-1894
Benjamin Disraeli (First Earl of Beaconsfield; 1804-1881), British prime minister, 1868, 1874-1880
Edward Cardwell (1813-1886), British secretary of state for war, 1868-1874

SUMMARY OF EVENT

William Ewart Gladstone came to power in 1868 after Benjamin Disraeli's first ministry collapsed after a few months. Gladstone's first ministry (1868-1874) not only brought much needed stability to the British government but also emerged as an activist government bent on eliminating abuses and corruption, improving the quality of life for citizens, and expanding the role of government in society. In part, this agenda was motivated by Gladstone's personal values through which he hoped to improve the political, economic, and social life of the nation.

Gladstone also was keenly aware that the new political parties—his Liberals and Disraeli's Conservatives—had to conduct business within a different framework than did the earlier Whig and Tory Parties. The new reality of the late nineteenth century was the continuing growth of democracy in a Britain that saw an increasing number of voters who were better educated and more demanding than in the past. Gladstone recognized that party identity was critical for long-term success, and he directed his policies and developed alliances with that consideration in mind. In foreign affairs, Gladstone looked on as the French were defeated by the Prussians in the Franco-Prussian War in 1870, the German Empire and the Kingdom of Italy were proclaimed, and Parisians experimented with communism in the Commune.

Early in his first ministry, Gladstone focused on Ireland. In 1869 the Irish Church Disestablishment Act dismantled the Anglican Church of Ireland and the much despised tax that supported it. Until this act was passed, Catholic Irish were compelled to support the Protestant church through a required tax; after the Irish Church Disestablishment Act was enacted, another tax was levied that supported Catholic, Presbyterian, and Anglican churches, none of which was considered to be the "official" Irish church. In 1870, Isaac Butt established the Irish Home Rule movement that was directed at establishing an Irish parliament so that the Irish could control their own affairs. Butt argued that Ireland would remain within the British Empire. From its inception, Gladstone considered Irish home rule a concept that might provide stability, but he had not, for more than one decade, formally embraced it. In August, 1870, Gladstone's government enacted the Landlord and Tenant Act for Ireland, which specified that a given tenant had the right to re-

William Ewart Gladstone in 1866, at the age of fifty-six. (The S. S. McClure Company)

ceive compensation for any improvements that were made during a given tenancy.

In 1870, Gladstone's government introduced a wide range of reforms. Initial steps were taken to improve the quality of the civil service, steps that included the introduction of testing for employment and suggestions for testing as the basis for promotions. Similarly, in 1870, Gladstone's secretary of state for war, Edward Cardwell, succeeded in gaining support for reducing the size of the standing army and establishing an army reserve. Later, in 1871, Cardwell managed to eliminate the long-standing tradition of purchasing army commissions.

Also in 1870, Gladstone's government passed the First Married Women's Property Act, which provided wives with some property rights. It would take two additional laws and twenty-three more years before married women would gain the same property rights as single women. Perhaps the most significant enactment in 1870 was the Education Act. Under this measure, local elected school boards were enabled to establish schools that were supported by taxes and fees; religious instruction in these public schools would not be compulsory nor could it be sectarian. Parliament increased its support for voluntary schools. The Education Act was the initial step in a national strategy that would improve literacy rates; in 1881, under another Gladstone government, attendance in elementary school was made compulsory.

In 1871, Gladstone continued the reform momentum with the Trades Union Act, which gave labor unions legal status before the law, and the Criminal Law Amendment Act, which established strike regulations for labor unions. In 1872, Gladstone focused on political reform and the protection of children. Through the Ballot Act, Gladstone enhanced the integrity of British democracy by establishing the secret ballot in all British elections; no longer could employers impinge upon an individual's right to vote through intimidation, whether explicit or implied.

The Infant Life Protection Act of 1872 required that women register as a foster parent if they had more than one foster child. Other measures required the maintenance of data on infant deaths, supported single mothers in obtaining child support from fathers, and allowed for legal action against a father in the event he did not provide support. In the next year the Agricultural Children's Act was passed; it prohibited the employment of children in agriculture who were under the age of eight.

Throughout the nineteenth century, Parliament had passed several laws that addressed some of the problems associated with the administration of justice in the British courts. To a large extent these changes were required because of the rapid transformation of Great Britain during the first six decades of the century. In 1873, Gladstone's government aligned these reforms in a series of measures that provided clarity and a reasonable degree of judicial stability; the Common Law and Equity courts were combined and the Court of Appeal and the High Court of Justice were formalized.

The energy that these reform efforts required took a toll on Gladstone. He lost the February, 1874, general election to Benjamin Disraeli and gave up the leadership of the Liberal Party. Gladstone would return, however, during the late 1870's and spend another fifteen years as Britain's most influential political force.

SIGNIFICANCE

William Gladstone's first ministry transformed British politics by its response to needed reform measures in Ireland and in education, the military, and the structure and administration of the British government. Gladstone understood the impact of the Reform Acts of 1867-1868 extending the vote, and he recognized democracy as a historical force that would be further evident in 1885, which saw additional legislation, giving all men the right to vote.

Gladstone's domestic agenda during his first ministry set the tone for British politics to 1914, when World War I began; Gladstone's Liberals and the Conservatives vied with one another in their attempts to gain and sustain the loyalty of the voters. Gladstone also recognized the importance of building and reinforcing the Liberal Party at all levels—boroughs, counties, municipalities, regional (Scotland, Wales, and Ireland), and national. While his Liberal Party did not survive as a major political party beyond the Great Depression, it attained significant domestic achievements and improved the quality of life for most Britons; the seeds of those later gains were visible during Gladstone's first ministry.

Gladstone's hope that Britain would restrain its imperial ambitions and avoid entangling alliances and alignments with European powers did not succeed. Indeed, Liberal governments prior to 1914 were actively, though secretly, involved in expanding Britain's diplomatic commitments.

—*William T. Walker*

FURTHER READING

Beeler, John F. *British Naval Policy in the Gladstone-Disraeli Era, 1866-1880*. Stanford, Calif.: Stanford University Press, 1997. An important scholarly work on how Gladstone and Disraeli developed naval pol-

icy within the context of national security and imperial considerations.
Biagini, Eugenio F. *Gladstone*. New York: St. Martin's Press, 2000. Part of the British History in Perspective series, this book is useful as an introduction to many of the issues that were reflected in Gladstone's policies and decisions.
Feuchtwanger, E. J. *Gladstone*. London: Allen Lane, 1975. A very readable and still-useful introduction to the life of William Gladstone.
Jagger, Peter John, ed. *Gladstone*. London: Hambledon Press, 1998. A series of essays on Gladstone's life, his politics, and his tenure as prime minister.
Jenkins, Roy. *Gladstone: A Biography*. New York: Random House, 1997. A worthwhile and readable biography of Gladstone by the late Labour Party leader and Chancellor of the Exchequer.
Matthew, Henry Colin Gray. *Gladstone, 1809-1898*. New York: Oxford University Press, 1997. Originally published in two volumes (*Gladstone, 1809-1874*, and *Gladstone, 1875-1898*), Matthew's biography remains the most authoritative and comprehensive work on Gladstone.
Partridge, Michael Stephen. *Gladstone*. New York: Routledge, 2003. A solid biography of Gladstone that provides a balanced and critical analysis of the Liberal leader.
Willis, Michael. *Gladstone and Disraeli: Principles and Policies*. New York: Cambridge University Press, 1989. A scholarly comparative analysis of the concepts that motivated William Gladstone and Benjamin Disraeli and how those values were reflected in their domestic and foreign policies.
Winstanley, Michael. *Gladstone and the Liberal Party*. New York: Routledge, 1990. A useful guide for undergraduate students that focuses on issues related to Gladstone as a politician.

SEE ALSO: June 4, 1832: British Parliament Passes the Reform Act of 1832; Sept. 2, 1843: Wilson Launches *The Economist*; Aug., 1867: British Parliament Passes the Reform Act of 1867; Sept.-Nov., 1880: Irish Tenant Farmers Stage First "Boycott"; Dec. 6, 1884: British Parliament Passes the Franchise Act of 1884; June, 1886-Sept. 9, 1893: Irish Home Rule Debate Dominates British Politics.

RELATED ARTICLES in *Great Lives from History: The Nineteenth Century, 1801-1900:* Lord Acton; F. H. Bradley; John Bright; Joseph Chamberlain; Benjamin Disraeli; William Edward Forster; William Ewart Gladstone; Lord Palmerston; Charles Stewart Parnell; Sir Robert Peel; John Russell; Third Marquis of Salisbury; Queen Victoria.

1869
BASEBALL'S FIRST PROFESSIONAL CLUB FORMS

The Cincinnati Red Stockings startled the baseball world by fielding an all-paid team and winning eighty-three consecutive games, becoming organized baseball's first fully professional club. The Red Stockings helped revolutionize the game and set the standard for excellence in the sport.

LOCALE: Cincinnati, Ohio
CATEGORIES: Sports; organizations and institutions

KEY FIGURES

Aaron Champion (d. 1943), nominal owner of the Red Stockings
Harry Wright (1835-1895), English-born team manager and player
Asa Brainard (1841-1888), team pitcher
Charlie Gould (1847-1917), team member
George Wright (1847-1937), team member

SUMMARY OF EVENT

By 1867, Ohioans were feverish for baseball, as the sport exploded in popularity after the U.S. Civil War. Cincinnati started to field respectable clubs by that year. The club that would become the professional Red Stockings in 1869 faced stiff competition from the equally able Buckeyes.

The 1860's was a time of city boosterism, and urban areas looked to gain civic prestige. At the time, Cincinnati was locked in a struggle with Chicago for regional economic dominance. Often called Porkopolis because it was a bustling Ohio River meatpacking center, Cincinnati feared that it was losing the battle to the Great Lakes city. However, baseball success was quickly becoming a reflection of the city's image and prospects.

In 1867, during what was otherwise a successful season for the Red Stockings, a Washington, D.C., club bombarded the home team with a score of 53-10. The following season, in 1868, the Cincinnati club hired four professionals and toured in the east. It won forty-one out of forty-eight games, providing a glimpse of things to come. Determined to avenge those seven losses and the 1867 drubbing by the Washington team, the club declared itself a fully professional team in 1869. Aaron B. Champion, a young lawyer who was also a commissioner for Ohio baseball, became the team's nominal owner. He empowered the team's manager, Harry Wright, to recruit the players and pay them accordingly.

This was not the first time that ballplayers received payment for their skills. Jim Creighton, a young player for the New York Excelsiors, may have been receiving a salary as early as 1858. During the 1860's, clubs such as the Philadelphia Athletics reportedly had three or four paid players, attempting to mask the salaries with indirect charity collections. For example, at the game there might be a collection for shortstop Dickey Pearce's sick aunt, a ruse to put money in Pearce's pocket. By 1866, players were jumping from team to team, seeking better deals so frequently that it precipitated a scandal of "revolving." Club owners clamped down on player mobility with the 1879 Reserve Rule. No team, however, challenged the doctrine of the National Association of Base Ball Players concerning the game's amateur status as boldly as did the Red Stockings.

The decision to become professional was timely. Especially after the Civil War, Americans were eager for professional entertainment. Before the war, customers would pay to see the best Shakespeare troupes, hear singers such as Jenny Lind, and experience P. T. Barnum's circuses, but the desire grew as the decade progressed. Postwar crowds demanded even better performances and were willing to pay for them. The Red Stockings fulfilled part of the public demand.

Harry Wright, born in England, was the son of a cricket player. Once in the United States, he developed his skills as a cricketer, but by 1858, he switched to the rising sport of baseball. He played with the famous Knickerbocker Club of New York City, but by 1866, he moved west to Cincinnati. A jeweler by trade, baseball commanded most of his attention. He fielded the finest team money could buy. Searching for a shortstop, Harry selected his younger brother George, who had established himself as a star with the Washington Nationals. George, with his flashing speed, quickly became professional baseball's first true superstar. He was also its most highly paid with a listed annual salary of $1,400, although he confessed later that the actual amount was more than $2,000.

Harry Wright also recruited Charlie Gould, the only Cincinnati native on the squad. Having only one local player was somewhat of a departure from baseball norms because clubs usually drew all or most of their players from the local community. Gould was a defensive wizard at first base at a time when the absence of gloves made fielding an adventure. The unpredictable Asa Brainard handled the pitching duties expertly. Although underhanded pitching was still the style of the day, Brainard threw very hard and included a curveball in his repertoire of pitches. He reportedly drew a salary of $1,100. Rounding out the squad were talented star players lured from other Eastern teams: Doug Allison at catcher, Fred Waterman at third base, Charlie Sweasy at second base, and Andy Leonard, Cal McVey (from Indianapolis, Indiana), and Harry Wright in the outfield. A substitute player, Dick Hurley, had a $600 contract.

The Red Stockings revolutionized the game, both on and off the field. At practice, they drilled incessantly, simulating hit-and-run plays and hitting a relay man on throws from the outfield. Harry Wright maintained a tight rein on his team off the field as well. The Red Stockings had to conform to a morality code, which included a curfew. Even their uniforms reflected the new approach to the game. Prior to 1869, ballplayers usually wore long pants. Outfitted in flannel knickers, the team was not only speedy on the base paths and on the field but also flashy in their red stockings.

For the 1869 season the Red Stockings remained undefeated, and it was not until June 14, 1870, that the team lost a contest on an error and an overthrow, which permitted the Brooklyn Atlantics an 8-7 extra-innings win. The winning streak of 1869-1870 totaled eighty-three games (ninety-five games since losing in October, 1868). One game, in Troy, New York, ended in a controversial 17-17 tie, as gamblers pulled their home team off the field after six innings to avoid losing bets. Thus, the Red Stockings did not win that match technically. In any case, their eighty-three-game streak stands as the all-time record for a professional sporting franchise. The Red Stockings showed the rest of the nation how to win at baseball.

The only disappointment for the Red Stockings was financial. The club entered the 1869 season heavily in debt, not only because of the new payroll but also because of the construction of a stadium the year before. Transportation costs were substantial. The Red Stockings were among the first passengers on the newly constructed transcontinental railroad, as their tour took them to California. Shady dealings at a couple of games and missing gate receipts undercut potential profits. Owner Aaron Champion, after subtracting all operating expenses, found that the 1869 net profit was a measly $1.25, but the club's winning ways pointed the way to profitability for other clubs in the future.

For all their glory, the Cincinnati Red Stockings did not stay together for long. After finally losing a game in June, 1870, they started to face tougher competition. Losses came more frequently, as other clubs caught up to their standard. After the 1870 season, many of the star players left Cincinnati, several of them heading for Boston, taking the name Red Stockings with them and establishing the preeminent team of the newly created National Association, baseball's first professional league. The Cincinnati Red Stockings had helped complete the inevitable transformation to professionalism.

SIGNIFICANCE

By the 1860's baseball had become the national pastime, a term linked to it by the 1850's. The older ideal of amateur play, however, was under severe pressure from competition and from commercial forces. When the Cincinnati Red Stockings recruited an all-professional team for the 1869 season and vanquished virtually all challengers for a year and a half, professionalization of organized baseball was set. Some older, more traditional clubs, such as the New York Knickerbockers, tried to keep amateur baseball alive, but they were fighting a rearguard action.

—*Thomas L. Altherr*

FURTHER READING

Alvarez, Mark. *The Old Ball Game*. Alexandria, Va.: Redefinition Books, 1992. A useful survey of the early trends in the game.

Block, David. *Baseball Before We Knew It: A Search for the Roots of the Game*. Lincoln: University of Nebraska Press, 2005. The definitive study of baseball's origins.

Brock, Darryl. *I Don't Care If I Never Get Back*. New York: Crown, 1990. delightful fictionalization of the 1869 Red Stockings season told in the context of a time-travel episode by a modern sportswriter.

Brown, Randall. "How Baseball Began." *National Pastime* 24 (2004): 51-54. A discussion of William Wheaton's connection to baseball and the Knickerbockers.

Goldstein, Warren Jay. *Playing for Keeps: A History of Early Baseball*. Ithaca, N.Y.: Cornell University Press, 1989. A sociological and historical study of the amateur period in early baseball and the trend toward professionalization.

Guschov, Stephen D. *The Red Stockings of Cincinnati: Base Ball's First All-Professional Team*. Jefferson, N.C.: McFarland, 1998. The best book focusing on the history of the Red Stockings.

Kirsch, George B. *The Creation of American Team Sports: Baseball and Cricket, 1838-1872*. Urbana: University of Illinois Press, 1989. A scholarly study of the decline of cricket and the rise of baseball in the United States.

Wright, Marshall D. *The National Association of Base Ball Players, 1857-1870*. Jefferson, N.C.: McFarland, 2000. Examines the early history of the first organization to manage baseball.

SEE ALSO: c. 1845: Modern Baseball Begins; Aug. 22, 1851: *America* Wins the First America's Cup Race; 1891: Naismith Invents Basketball; Apr. 6, 1896: Modern Olympic Games Are Inaugurated.

1869
FIRST MODERN DEPARTMENT STORE OPENS IN PARIS

The first department stores radically changed retail marketing and linked commerce, culture, and social activity. Department stores epitomized the nineteenth century's culture of consumption, changed attitudes toward buying and selling, and created the idea of shopping as a pleasant activity, especially for women.

LOCALE: France; United States
CATEGORIES: Marketing and advertising; business and labor; social issues and reform; fashion and design

KEY FIGURES

Aristide Boucicaut (1810-1877), French merchant who found the first department store
Jules Jaluzot (1834-1916), merchant and founder of Le Printemps in Paris
Ernest Cognacq (1839-1928), merchant and founder of La Samaritaine in Paris
Alexander Turney Stewart (1803-1876), merchant who founded A. T. Stewart Stores in New York City
John Wanamaker (1838-1922), merchant and founder of Wanamaker Stores in Philadelphia
Marshall Field (1834-1906), merchant and founder of Marshall Field's in Chicago

SUMMARY OF EVENT

Retail marketing and, consequently, consumerism underwent a drastic change with the creation of department stores. Before these new stores, keepers of small shops specialized in a single item or type of item. Milliners sold hats, tailors and dressmakers sold clothing, and drapers sold cloth. Customers entered stores only when they needed and intended to make a purchase. Prices were not marked on goods, and shopkeepers often set prices according to what they believed the individual customer could pay, resulting in a considerable amount of haggling over prices between buyer and seller. There were no refunds, reduced-price "sales," or home deliveries.

During the 1830's and 1840's, Paris saw the development of a new kind of store that paved the way for the department store and served as a transition from the small specialty shops to the multi-item stores. These new stores were called *magasins de nouveautés* (dry-goods stores) and carried wider varieties of goods than did the traditional shops. However, their stocks were limited, primarily, to cloth, clothing, and similar items. The proprietors of these new stores did some experimenting with the innovations that would become associated with modern department stores.

The history of the department store, however, begins with Aristide Boucicaut, who would build the first true department store in 1869. He arrived in Paris in 1835 and found employment at Le Petit Thomas, *magasin de nouveautés*, where he rose to the position of department head. In 1852 he left Le Petit Thomas and became co-owner of the Bon Marché with Paul Videau. Here he began to put into practice the innovative retailing techniques that would become characteristic of department stores: extensive varieties of merchandise attractively displayed in specialized departments, prices marked on items, entry without obligation to buy, return and refund, special sales at regular intervals, and home deliveries. He bought out his partner in 1863 and by 1869 had acquired enough space adjacent to the Bon Marché to build a much larger new store with the same name, which is considered the first department store.

Boucicaut was not the only merchant implementing new retailing techniques. On July 9, 1855, Les Magasins du Louvre opened with a salon and buffet and soon added household items to its stock. In 1856, Xavier Ruel expanded the shops of the corner of the Rue de Rivoli and Rue des Archives into Le Bazar de l'Hôtel de Ville and introduced the *prix fixe* (fixed prices). In 1865, Jules Jaluzot, a former employee of Bon Marché, opened Le Printemps. The store was an immediate success. By 1872, Le Printemps had extensive mail-order sales from seven different catalogs, which included a general catalog and six specialized catalogs. In 1869, Ernest Cognacq and his wife, Louise Jay, who were trained at Bon Marché, opened a small shop near the Pont Neuf. Madame Cognacq's experience with Boucicaut served her well, as she and her husband successfully built their shop into the department store La Samaritaine.

This retailing phenomenon was occurring at the same time in the United States. In 1846, Irish-born merchant Alexander Turney Stewart built a store in New York that was referred to as the Marble Palace. Faced in Tuckahoe marble, with imported French plate-glass windows on the ground floor and a construction of cast iron, the innovative building became the model for American department stores. Stewart employed many of the French retailing techniques in his own store, including fixed prices, free entry, and returns. In 1862, Stewart built a new store, which occupied a full city block; it had eight

Interior of Marshall Field's flagship department store in Chicago, around 1910.

floors and nineteen departments. His store was soon followed by other stores. In 1858, Rowland Hassey Macy moved Macy's from Haverhill, Massachusetts, to New York. By the 1880's, there were so many retail stores along a stretch of Broadway in New York City that the stretch became known as the Ladies Mile.

Department stores flourished in other areas of the United States as well. John Wanamaker, usually considered the founder of the American department store, converted an abandoned railroad depot into his first such store in Philadelphia, Pennsylvania, in 1875. He established a second store in New York in 1896. Chicago became the home of what was to be the world's largest department store, Marshall Field and Company. In 1881, Marshall Field, a former employee and later partner of Palmer Potter, the store's founder, became sole owner of the store and named it Marshall Field's.

The nineteenth century provided the perfect climate for the thriving of department stores. It was a time of economic prosperity, growth, and urbanization. Improved transportation systems, mass production of goods, and the rise to prominence of the bourgeois, or middle class, all contributed to the success of the stores. The department store in turn affected every aspect of life: economic, social, cultural, and intellectual. These large stores stimulated the economy, providing a significant number of jobs and an outlet for an enormous quantity of goods. Store owners such as Boucicaut, who provided an emergency fund for employees and free medical care, contributed to social reforms that benefited workers.

Department stores were more than just places to purchase goods. With their elaborate storefronts and ornate interiors such as Stewart's marble and cast iron facade, Boucicaut's skylights, and Field's Tiffany Dome, they set the standard for the architecture of commercial buildings in general. The stores had restaurants, separate lounges for men and women, and reading rooms, which encouraged socialization. They catered particularly to women, providing them with more "public" space. Courtesy and pleasing the customer were the first concerns of employees. Fashion shows and full-length mirrors in the ladies' lounge at Stewarts and a bridal registry and the option to take merchandise home on approval at Field's were meant to entice female clients. The stores also encouraged and supported the arts. Evenings saw concerts in front of Bon Marché; both Bon Marché and Le Printemps had art exhibits, and Macy's held its first Thanksgiving Day Parade in 1854, a parade that continues into the twenty-first century.

SIGNIFICANCE

The department store was a great innovation of the nineteenth century. The new commercial institution represented the essence of the culture and lifestyle of the time. It reflected the period's materialism, consumerism, and practices of consumption.

Focusing on pleasing female customers, the stores established women as experts in selecting quality goods: The idea of women-as-shoppers has become commonplace. French novelist Émile Zola's contemporary naturalistic novel about commerce during the nineteenth century, *Au Bonheur des dames* (1883; *The Ladies' Delight*, 1957), depicted women's pleasure in shopping. The practice of free entry and the emphasis on courtesy to customers opened the activity of shopping to all social classes.

With their insistence on storefronts of enormous size and a selection of the widest variety of goods possible under one roof, department stores paved the way for twentieth century mass marketing, shopping centers, and superstores.

—*Shawncey Webb*

FURTHER READING

Crossick, Geoffrey, and Serge Jaumain, eds. *Cathedrals of Consumption: The European Department Store, 1850-1939*. Burlington, Vt.: Ashgate, 1999. A comprehensive collection. Discusses store architecture, training of personnel, the cult of shopping, the culture of consumption, and how stores permitted women more public space. Explores the expansion of department stores from France and Britain to Germany, Belgium, and Hungary.

Lancaster, William. *The Department Store: A Social History*. London: Leicester University Press, 1995. Chronicles the development of department stores in Great Britain, the influence of Parisian grand *magasins*, the importance of Harry Gordon Selfridge (who left Marshall Field's in 1906) to British department stores, the role of women, and the paternalistic attitudes of store owners toward workers.

Leach, William R. *Land of Desire: Merchants, Power, and the Rise of a New American Culture*. New York: Vintage Books, 1994. Leach examines entrepreneurs such as Field and Wanamaker, who turned shopping into a religion, and the merchants' interactions with religious leaders to make buying a celebration of happiness.

Madsen, Axel. *The Marshall Fields: The Evolution of an American Business Dynasty*. Hoboken, N.J.: John Wiley & Sons, 2002. The story of the Marshall Field's department store, from its founding to the twenty-first century. Also chronicles the personal life of Marshall Field, his success as a businessman, and his failure as a family man. Traces five generations of Fields family.

Miller, Michael Barry. *The Bon Marché: Bourgeois Culture and the Department Store, 1869-1920*. Princeton, N.J.: Princeton University Press, 1981. A history of Bon Marché, its role in French commerce, and its social and cultural influences.

Schwartz, Vanessa R. *Spectacular Realities: Early Mass Culture in Fin-de-Siècle Paris*. Berkeley: University of California Press, 1999. An excellent recounting of the social and cultural atmosphere in which department stores and the cult of shopping developed and thrived.

Tamilia, Robert D. "The Wonderful World of the Department Store in Historical Perspective: A Comprehensive International Bibliography Partially Annotated." An eighty-nine page bibliography on the history of the department store, compiled by a marketing professor at the University of Quebec, Montreal. Available as a PDF document. http://faculty.quinnipiac.edu/charm/dept.store.pdf. Accessed January, 2006.

SEE ALSO: Mar. 23, 1857: Otis Installs the First Passenger Elevator; Aug., 1872: Ward Launches a Mail-Order Business; 1883-1885: World's First Skyscraper Is Built; May 8, 1886: Pemberton Introduces Coca-Cola; 1896: Brooks Brothers Introduces Button-Down Shirts.

RELATED ARTICLES in *Great Lives from History: The Nineteenth Century, 1801-1900:* Marshall Field; Montgomery Ward.

c. 1869
GOLDEN AGE OF FLAMENCO BEGINS

The three-part musical form—voice, accompanied by guitar and dance—transcended the small-group, folk-song styles and places of the Spanish underclass, particularly the Gitanos, or Gypsies, to become an art form and widespread phenomenon. Flamenco melded with the Spanish lyric theater, was represented in literature, and won many aficionados among all social groups.

LOCALE: Spain, especially Andalucía
CATEGORIES: Music; dance; art; theater

KEY FIGURES

Mariano Soriano Fuertes (1817-1880), Spanish composer
Silverio Franconetti (1831?-1889), Italian-born singer
Antonio Machado y Álvarez (1846-1893), Franconetti biographer
Juan Breva (Antonio Ortega Escalona; 1844-1918), folk-style singer and first flamenco celebrity
Antonio Chacón (1869-1929), child singer

SUMMARY OF EVENT

From the time of its ancient history, Spain has been characterized by not only multicultural diversity but also a rigid socioeconomic hierarchy. The resulting estrangement and anomie of most of its inhabitants led to voices of dissatisfaction, complaint, and suffering in rustic social settings expressed in the works of the musical form flamenco.

Flamenco was originally *cante*, a type of vocal expression. Later, flamenco was accompanied by *toque de palmas*, or hand clapping with guitar playing, and *baile*, or dance. Traditionally associated with intense emotion (*duende*) and the individual style of the performer, flamenco has always been inextricably tied to ethnicity, marginality, eroticism, substance abuse, and rebellion against all manner of social norms.

José Cadalso was the first writer to mention flamenco in literature in his *Cartas marruecas* (1774). Flamenco schools became more prevalent between the mid-eighteenth and nineteenth centuries in cities such as Cádiz, Jérez de la Frontera, and Seville. Until that time, flamenco had been a lower-class phenomenon of southern Spain, especially of the province of Andalucía, and was originally performed in tawdry *juergas*, or bordellos, of the slums.

During the self-proclaimed Siglo de Oro, the Golden Age of Spanish culture, the seventeenth century apex of all things Spanish, the public had begun to suffer because of the country's downward spiral in terms of loss of world prestige, economic privations, and socioreligious repression, which led to a national identity crisis. Then, in 1849, Mariano Soriano Fuertes wrote the pivotal comic opera *El tío Caniyitas*, which was performed in Seville. Appealing to every level of society with its music, dance, and humor, the work featured a poor Gypsy, the Uncle Caniyitas of the title, who initiated a young rich woman into the social milieu of the Gitanos, including the ribald language and the morally edgy flamenco. This work, and the later *¡Cante Hondo!* (1882), tied flamenco to the lyric theater, thus initiating social acceptability and a new cultural form.

However, not everyone approved of flamenco, some because of the sexual tension inherent in the dance and some because of the shady beginnings and overlay of the genre. Several members of the Generation of 1898 writers, including Pío Baroja, opposed writing about the fashionable genre because they believed that to do so would feed negative international stereotypes.

Concurrent nineteenth century *costumbrismo* (1820-1860) literature, by such writers as Armando Palacio Valdés, Salvador Rueda, Alarcón, Fernán Caballero, and Serafín Estébañez Calderón, had been dedicated to writing about Spanish life and practice, had made extensive references to Andalucía, and had portrayed scenes of flamenco. For example, Estébañez Calderón's *Escenas andaluzas* (1847) contains two stories so dedicated, mentioning mythical singers of the time, El Planeta and El Fillo, and describing aspects of flamenco.

Much of Spain had begun to identify with flamenco. Around 1869, it began to move into *cafés cantantes*, or musical cafés, and spread throughout the south and central provinces. It had even been performed in elegant bars like Los Fornos and Los Gabrieles in Madrid, the capital. The patronage of the *señoritos*, the young and disaffected male dandies of the period, and the *majos*, descendants of Andalusian immigrants to Madrid, played a role in this transformation.

During the last third of the nineteenth century, a series of nonethnic, nonpeasant singers, among them Silverio Franconetti, Juan Breva, and Antonio Chacón, both revolutionized the style and content of flamenco and broadened and popularized it as a uniquely Spanish cultural form. Franconetti's singing initiated the change by stylistically blurring the line between the peasant folk variations and the so-called outcast (ethnic or criminal) protest-element style, as well as by incorporating operatic conventions. Breva called attention to the flamenco by his flamboyant behaviors on and off the stage, gaining something of a "rock star" notoriety complete with groupies. Chacón, a star as a teenager, brought real acceptability to the form with great musical talent and an ability to incorporate prior elements into his own style.

In 1881, Antonio Machado y Álvarez wrote the first flamenco biography, that of Franconetti, and published a collection of songs. The same year, Manuel Balmaseda, who was barely literate and mainly dictated his lyrics, published *Primer Cancionero Flamenco*. Writers outside Spain picked up on the fashion as well; a work in German, *Die Cantes Flamencos*, by Hugo Schuchardt, was published a few months later.

SIGNIFICANCE

The golden age of flamenco eased Spain's national identity crisis by providing an acceptable, yet appealingly risky, artistic form around which the Spanish could rally. The fusion of styles incorporated those of diverse groups. The geographic spread and change of venue from the bordello to the lyric theater and the musical café led to social acceptance. The period also saw the fine-tuning of technique and the addition of variations like the intense *cante jondo*.

The golden age of flamenco led also to a complete reevaluation of the genre as a valid scholarly pursuit. In 1922, Granada, Spain, held a *cante jondo* competition, with the presentation of scholarly papers, a performance of classical-music adaptations by Manuel de Falla and Federico García Lorca that were inspired by flamenco, and performances of flamenco *guitarra* works by Andrés Segovia and others. Many books followed, among them a study of flamenco subgenres, *De cante grande y cante chico* by José Carlos de Luna (1926); a study of the sociopolitical milieu, *Andalucía, su comunismo y su cante jondo* by Carlos y Pedro Caba Landa (1933); and a collection of biographies, *Arte y artistas flamencos* by Fernando of Triana (1935).

"Flamencology" became something of a fashion in 1955 with the publication of *Flamencología* by Anselmo González Climent. The majority of works thereafter have dealt with the dance and guitar aspects. Non-Spanish scholars, too, have addressed the genre, with the majority of these works addressing the origins and history of flamenco. Other scholars have looked at flamenco's many other angles: linguistic (Manuel Ropero Nuñez), sociological (Francisco Carrillo Alonso, Gerhard Steingress), anthropological (Cristina Cruces, Génesis García Gómez), literary (Francisco Gutiérrez Carbajo), musical (José Romero, Norberto Torres, Faustino Nuñez, Miguel Espín), and cinematographic (Angel Custodio Gómez).

In 1997, the Centro Andaluz de Flamenco organized a congress, where experts analyzed several representative works from the various periods. Flamenco has become respectable in the twenty-first century, but it has also been commercialized as a so-called ethnic art form and consequentially distanced from its emotional roots through an international emphasis instead on its technical aspects.

—Debra D. Andrist

FURTHER READING

Haas, Ken, and Gwynne Edwards. *¡Flamenco!* New York: Thames and Hudson, 2000. A work on the genre that presents a combination of photographs and technical explanations.

Leblon, Bernard. *Gypsies and Flamenco: The Emergence of the Art of Flamenco in Andalusia*. Hertfordshire, England: University of Hertfordshire Press, 2003. Biographies of two hundred famous Gitano flamenco artists, plus terms and a bibliography of recorded flamenco music.

Martínez, Emma. *Flamenco . . . All You Wanted to Know*. Pacific, Mo.: Mel Bay, 2003. Focuses on the song and music aspects of the genre.

Mitchell, Timothy. *Flamenco Deep Song*. New Haven, Conn.: Yale University Press, 1994. Mitchell's application of critical theories to flamenco illuminates the genre as not only a historical phenomenon but also a psychological one.

Pohren, Donn. *The Art of Flamenco*. 1962. Reprint. Hertfordshire, England: University of Hertfordshire Press, 1999. Pohren's work is considered the bible of flamenco. A classic.

_______. *Lives and Legends of Flamenco: A Biographical History*. 1964. Rev. ed. Madrid: Society of Spanish Studies, 1988. Highlights the lives of the best-known singers, guitarists, and dancers in the flamenco tradition.

Totten, Robin. *Song of the Outcasts*. Portland, Oreg.: Amadeus Press, 2003. A technical guide plus a historical approach to the genre's emotional aspect from the point of view of the best-known component of the flamenco experience, the Spanish Gitanos.

SEE ALSO: 19th cent.: Spread of the Waltz; c. 1820-1860: *Costumbrismo* Movement; Mar. 12, 1832: *La Sylphide* Inaugurates Romantic Ballet's Golden Age; Jan. 27, 1895: Tchaikovsky's *Swan Lake* Is Staged in St. Petersburg.

RELATED ARTICLES in *Great Lives from History: The Nineteenth Century, 1801-1900:* Carolina Coronado; Rubén Darío.

1869-1871
MENDELEYEV DEVELOPS THE PERIODIC TABLE OF ELEMENTS

Dmitry Ivanovich Mendeleyev formulated a law describing a recurrent pattern in the properties of chemical elements that became apparent when they were organized according to their atomic weights. He devised a periodic table depicting this pattern that enabled him both to understand the relationships of elements and to predict the characteristics of unknown elements.

LOCALE: St. Petersburg, Russia
CATEGORIES: Chemistry; science and technology

KEY FIGURES

Dmitry Ivanovich Mendeleyev (1834-1907), Russian chemist
Julius Lothar Meyer (1830-1895), German chemist
Johann Wolfgang Döbereiner (1780-1849), German chemist
John Alexander Reina Newlands (1837-1898), English chemist
William Ramsay (1852-1916), Scottish chemist

SUMMARY OF EVENT

For more than two thousand years, most natural philosophers believed that only four elements—earth, air, fire, and water—existed, and they attempted to fit all newly discovered substances into this quadripartite scheme. During the eighteenth century, Antoine-Laurent Lavoisier, who helped create modern chemistry, listed thirty-three substances as provisionally elemental, and by 1830, chemists recognized fifty-five substances as elements. This recognition proved an embarrassment of riches, since the known elements varied widely in properties, and no system existed for making sense of them. As more substances were added to the list of elements, questions arose about how many elements actually existed and what principles regulated their properties and interrelationships.

The first person to discover some order among the elements was Johann Wolfgang Döbereiner, who, from 1816 to 1829, noticed that strontium had an atomic weight halfway between calcium and barium, and that the newly discovered element bromine had properties intermediate between those of chlorine and iodine. He discovered other triads that exhibited similar gradations of properties, and over the next twenty-five years other chemists expanded Döbereiner's scheme to include further triads and some four- and five-membered families of elements. In the 1860's, the English chemist John Alexander Reina Newlands found that, when he arranged the elements in order of their increasing atomic weights, similar physical and chemical properties appeared after seven elements, but members of the British Chemical Society ridiculed his "law of octaves" for its implied analogy to music. It took twenty-three years for English scientists to honor Newlands for his prescient attempt to formulate a periodic law.

The actual periodic system of the elements was discovered independently in Russia by Dmitry Ivanovich Mendeleyev and in Germany by Julius Lothar Meyer. During the late 1860's, both Mendeleyev and Meyer were preparing textbooks on chemistry. Meyer based his on the atomic theory and the systematization of elemental properties. Mendeleyev, skeptical of atomism, initially organized his *Osnovy khimii* (1868-1871; *The Principles of Chemistry*, 1891) around chemical practice rather than any theories of the classification of elements. It was not until early in 1869, when he was writing the second volume of the textbook, that he realized that he needed a better way of organizing the fifty-five elements, which he had not yet discussed.

During the first few weeks of February, 1869, while he was writing his second volume's first two chapters on the alkali metals, Mendeleyev listed sodium and potassium along with the recently discovered rubidium and cesium in order of their increasing "elemental" (his preferred term), or atomic, weights. He compared this arrangement with a similar one for the halogens (fluorine, chlorine, bromine, and iodine) and for the alkaline earths (magnesium, calcium, strontium, and barium). This comparison revealed to Mendeleyev an important pattern governed by elements' atomic weights.

Precisely how Mendeleyev arrived at his recognition of the importance of atomic weight as a classificatory tool is controversial, since the paucity of contemporary documents leaves room for various interpretations. In some accounts, a dream played a role. Some scholars claim that Mendeleyev put the elements and their properties on cards, arranged them in rows according to increasing atomic weights, and then noticed regular repetitions of physical and chemical properties. Other scholars believe that he grouped elements into natural families, such as the halogens, and then noticed their dependence on atomic weight. Still other scholars hold that he was acting as a pedagogue and he was looking for a method of discovery rather than a system of classification. However Mendeleyev arrived at his breakthrough, his account of it was made public when a friend presented a paper describing it on his behalf at a meeting of the Russian Chemical Society on March 6, 1869. It was soon published both in Russian and, in abbreviated form, in German.

Over the next three years, Mendeleyev gradually realized the deficiencies of his early formulations of the periodic law and table, and he grasped how to remove many of these defects while increasing the power of his systematization of the elements to make useful predictions. When arranged strictly in order of increasing atomic weights, some elements appeared to be out of place, and Mendeleyev assumed that erroneous atomic weights were responsible for these anomalies. Some of his ad-

ПЕРИОДИЧЕСКАЯ СИСТЕМА ЭЛЕМЕНТОВ

Периоды	Ряды	ГРУППЫ ЭЛЕМЕНТОВ I	II	III	IV	V	VI	VII	VIII			0
1	I	H 1 1,008										He 2 4,003
2	II	Li 3 6,940	Be 4 9,02	5 B 10,82	6 C 12,010	7 N 14,008	8 O 16,000	9 F 19,00				Ne 10 20,183
3	III	Na 11 22,997	Mg 12 24,32	13 Al 26,97	14 Si 28,06	15 P 30,98	16 S 32,06	17 Cl 35,457				Ar 18 39,944
4	IV	K 19 39,096	Ca 20 40,08	Sc 21 45,10	Ti 22 47,90	V 23 50,95	Cr 24 52,01	Mn 25 54,93	Fe 26 55,85	Co 27 58,94	Ni 28 58,69	
	V	29 Cu 63,57	30 Zn 65,38	31 Ga 69,72	32 Ge 72,60	33 As 74,91	34 Se 78,96	35 Br 79,916				Kr 36 83,7
5	VI	Rb 37 85,48	Sr 38 87,63	Y 39 88,92	Zr 40 91,22	Nb 41 92,91	Mo 42 95,95	Ma 43 —	Ru 44 101,7	Rh 45 102,91	Pd 46 106,7	
	VII	47 Ag 107,88	48 Cd 112,41	49 In 114,76	50 Sn 118,70	51 Sb 121,76	52 Te 127,61	53 J 126,92				Xe 54 131,3
6	VIII	Cs 55 132,91	Ba 56 137,36	La 57 * 138,92	Hf 72 178,6	Ta 73 180,88	W 74 183,92	Re 75 186,31	Os 76 190,2	Ir 77 193,1	Pt 78 195,23	
	IX	79 Au 197,2	80 Hg 200,61	81 Tl 204,39	82 Pb 207,21	83 Bi 209,00	84 Po 210	85 —				Rn 86 222
7	X	— 87	Ra 88 226,05	Ac 89 227	Th 90 232,12	Pa 91 231	U 92 238,07					

* ЛАНТАНИДЫ 58–71

Ce 58 140,13	Pr 59 140,92	Nd 60 144,27	61 —	Sm 62 150,43	Eu 63 152,0	Gd 64 156,9
Tb 65 159,2	Dy 66 162,46	Ho 67 164,94	Er 68 167,2	Tu 69 169,4	Yb 70 173,04	Cp 71 174,99

Mendeleyev's original periodic table. (The Granger Collection, New York) justed atomic weights proved helpful, but others were simply wrong (three atomic weight inversions exist in the modern periodic table, which is based on atomic number rather than atomic weight).

By November of 1870, Mendeleyev had heard of Meyer's work, published eight months earlier, in which Meyer had arranged fifty-six elements in vertical columns according to their increasing atomic weights. Meyer's horizontal families clearly showed the periodic recurrence of elemental properties. In the same paper, he presented a graphical illustration of periodicity by plotting atomic volumes (the space occupied by atoms) as a function of atomic weights. In this illustration, the analogous relationships of elemental properties occurred as waves, with the alkali metals at the peaks of each curve.

Mendeleyev became so convinced of the lawlike nature of his system that he published a periodic table with empty spaces for unknown elements, and because his law of periodicity brought out the dependence of properties on atomic weight, he was able to characterize these unknown elements with precision. For example, he reasoned that the unknown element in the empty space following calcium should be related to boron, and he gave this unknown element the provisional name "eka-boron" (after the Sanskrit *eka*, meaning "first"). He predicted the properties of two other unknown elements, eka-aluminum and eka-silicon.

When, late in 1871, Mendeleyev published an improved and expanded periodic table, he was convinced that he had discovered a new law of chemistry. This table, which had twelve horizontal rows and eight vertical columns, showed that most of the elements' properties had a periodic dependence on their atomic weights. Nevertheless, perplexing problems remained. For example, Mendeleyev failed to understand the few rare-earth elements that were then known, since these abundant metals have closely similar properties (once all fourteen were discovered, they needed a separate section in the periodic table). However, when Lecoq de Boisbaudran found eka-aluminum in 1875 and named it gallium, the power of Mendeleyev's formulation of his periodic table and law began to generate admirers, including Meyer. With the discovery of scandium (eka-boron) in 1879 and germanium (eka-silicon) in 1886, both of which had properties that Mendeleyev had predicted, chemists became satisfied that Mendeleyev's periodic table was much more than the simple teaching tool that he had initially envisioned. It was a new way of making sense of chemistry's rich past and of creating a fertile future.

SIGNIFICANCE

Although it took time for the periodic table of elements to assume its modern form, the table provided throughout its history a way for physicists and chemists to understand accumulated information about the elements. It also helped teachers to communicate to students the nature and properties of the basic building blocks of matter, and it enabled researchers to make discoveries of new elements. A good early example of its value as a research tool was the discovery by William Ramsay and Lord Rayleigh of the inert gases: helium, neon, argon, krypton, and xenon. A good later example was the discovery by Glenn Seaborg and others of such transuranic elements as plutonium, curium, and americium.

New advances in chemistry, such as the discovery of atomic numbers by Henry Moseley, helped scientists more rationally to organize the periodic table. When scientists discovered the spin of electrons and the shared-electron-pair bond, these new ideas helped deepen their understanding of the periodic law. Mendeleyev himself gave his estimate of the significance of his discovery by emphasizing the table's ability to elucidate unexplained phenomena and to make verifiable predictions. The periodic law's value to modern scientists has increased with the increased understanding of the nature of the atom brought about by the theories of quantum mechanics. What was a ridiculed idea during the nineteenth century has become a much-valued part of the foundations of modern science.

—*Robert J. Paradowski*

FURTHER READING

Gordin, Michael D. *A Well-Ordered Thing: Dmitrii Mendeleev and the Shadow of the Periodic Table*. New York: Basic Books, 2004. The author, a historian, elucidates Mendeleyev and his achievements by situating him in the complex political, cultural, and intellectual contexts of nineteenth century Europe. Extensive set of notes, a thirty-nine-page bibliography, and an index.

Morris, Richard. *The Last Sorcerers: The Path from Alchemy to the Periodic Table*. Washington, D.C.: Joseph Henry Press, 2003. Morris, a physicist and science writer, emphasizes the human beings behind the discoveries that led to chemists' modern understanding of elements in the periodic table. An appendix on the elements, a "further reading" section, and an index.

Strathern, Paul. *Mendeleyev's Dream: The Quest for the Elements*. New York: Berkeley Books, 2000. The sometimes quixotic quest to understand the world's elements by Mendeleyev and others is the theme that unifies this popular history of chemistry. A "further reading" section and an index.

Van Spronsen, J. W. *The Periodic System of Chemical Elements: A History of the First Hundred Years*. Amsterdam: Elsevier, 1969. Published to commemorate the centennial anniversary of the discovery of the periodic system, this narrative account, based largely on original sources, reveals how periodicity was discovered, how it absorbed old knowledge, and how it helped create new knowledge. References at the ends of chapters, name and subject indexes.

Weeks, Mary Elvira. *Discovery of the Elements*. 7th ed. Easton, Pa.: Journal of Chemical Education, 1968. This classic text on how each of the elements was discovered has been updated and reorganized by the historian of chemistry Henry M. Leicester, who consolidated chapters around each element or groups of elements. Chapter 14 is specifically on the periodic system of the elements. A "chronology of element discovery," and name and subject indexes.

SEE ALSO: 1803-1808: Dalton Formulates the Atomic Theory of Matter; 1850-1865: Clausius Formulates the Second Law of Thermodynamics; Dec. 14, 1900: Articulation of Quantum Theory.

RELATED ARTICLE in *Great Lives from History: The Nineteenth Century, 1801-1900:* Dmitry Ivanovich Mendeleyev.

April, 1869
WESTINGHOUSE PATENTS HIS AIR BRAKE

The development of the air brake permitted the rapid and reliable stopping of trains, which not only increased the safety and speed of railroad travel and transportation but also increased the ride's overall comfort for passengers and train workers.

LOCALE: Pittsburgh, Pennsylvania

CATEGORIES: Inventions; transportation; engineering; science and technology; trade and commerce

KEY FIGURES

George Westinghouse (1846-1914), American inventor

Cornelius Vanderbilt (1794-1877), American railroad tycoon

SUMMARY OF EVENT

One of the most problematic factors limiting the growth of the railroad in its early years was the problem of stopping a moving train quickly and safely. For decades, the only way to bring a train to a halt was a system of handbrakes at the front and the back of each car, and a brakeman who would turn a wheel to activate them, jumping between the two cars on which he was stationed.

Although brakemen tried to apply their brakes in unison upon the engineer's "down brakes" signal, inevitably there was unevenness, which led to lurching and to cars bumping into each other. Passengers could be knocked from their seats, while fragile freight could be smashed. Worse, the process was dangerous for the brakemen, who could fall from their perches or be crushed between cars that bumped. Furthermore, the latencies inherent in the system meant that brakes could not be applied rapidly. Many disastrous collisions were caused simply because the brakemen could not apply the brakes fast enough after the engineer saw a danger and signalled them to act.

Shortly after the end of the U.S. Civil War (1861-1865), the braking problem was brought to the attention of an ambitious young inventor by the name of George Westinghouse. He was trying to sell a device by which derailed cars could be quickly and easily re-placed on the tracks, and the superintendent of one company pointed out to him that the real problem facing the railroad industry was difficult braking. The truth of that statement was brought home not long after, when Westinghouse witnessed a horrific accident caused solely because the engineers could not get the brakes applied on their trains in time to prevent a collision, in spite of having seen each other well in advance.

Westinghouse applied his capable mind to the problem, trying several possibilities, including a bumper sensor and steam-driven brakes. All of them had fatal flaws, which soon became obvious upon further study. He was beginning to despair when he came across a magazine containing an account of a pneumatic drill used to dig a tunnel through a mountain in the Alps. Almost immediately he recognized the potential of compressed air to operate the brakes on an entire train, smoothly and simultaneously, at the command of the train's engineer.

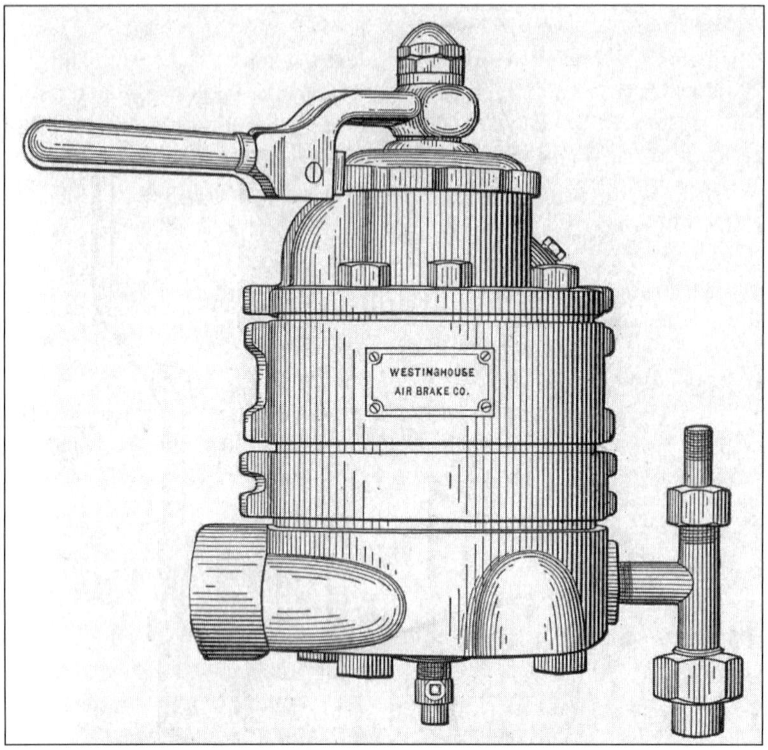

Handle and control valve of a Westinghouse air brake.

With that conceptual breakthrough, he would design a system by which a single air valve in the cab of the locomotive could apply the brakes on every car simultaneously. However, he had no means to build a working prototype. Worse, his concept was so revolutionary that he had great difficulty convincing people of the feasability of his idea. Furthermore, to top all his other problems, he was removed from the company he had created to manufacture and market the train car re-placer, leaving him without an income to fund his research.

Westinghouse visited Cornelius Vanderbilt, the head of the New York Central Railroad and one of the leading industrialists of the Gilded Age. Although it was not Vanderbilt's habit to grant interviews to people off the street, Westinghouse's persistence won him an appointment. However, his carefully prepared speech fell flat, for Vanderbilt saw only absurdity in the idea of using air to operate a brake. To him the wind was too weak to do such work, never mind that wind had moved whole ships in the age of sail.

Refusing to be defeated, in April, 1869, Westinghouse took out his own patent on the air brake. An old associate, Ralph Baggaley, advanced him enough money to build a working prototype of his design. As he was considering how to approach railroads with his invention, an executive of the Panhandle Railroad came to him with a proposal. The Panhandle Railroad would make a train available for a test of Westinghouse's new brake. In return, Westinghouse had to install the system at his own expense and promise to pay for any damages incurred if the brakes failed to work as advertised. The installation proved a financial strain, but by careful economies, Westinghouse was able to accomplish the work.

On the appointed test day, a number of Panhandle executives boarded the test train, headed toward Philadelphia for the test. Westinghouse's plan was to demonstrate the brakes at pre-set points, which would provide varying conditions of grade. However, chance provided a far more dramatic opportunity: A drayman's horses had stopped on the tracks and stubbornly refused to proceed. As the test train approached, the horses panicked and finally moved, but with a lurch that threw the driver onto the track. There was simply no way the driver, with the wind knocked out of him, could recollect his wits and jump clear before the locomotive would crush him under its wheels. Westinghouse and the train's engineer saw him in time, though, and a quick application of the new air brakes brought the train safely to a halt. Although the executives in the last car were tossed about by the force of such a sudden application of the brakes, all was quickly forgiven when they discovered that it was to save human life.

Although the effectiveness of the air-brake system had been amply proved, Westinghouse still insisted on going through the full demonstration he had planned. He wanted the executives swayed by the logic of reliable performance as well as the emotional impact of having saved the drayman's life.

With the success of his invention, Westinghouse was able to capitalize a new company, the Westinghouse Air Brake Company, to manufacture and install the brakes. His ferocious work ethic, however, kept him from being completely satisfied with the success of his invention. Rather, he would look for ways to improve it, and he did just that.

Westinghouse developed a special valve system that

would apply the brakes if the air pressure in the system were to fail. Strictly speaking, the new triple-valve system used air pressure to keep the brake shoe from applying rather than using air pressure to apply the brake shoe as had been the case in earlier systems. Because of this change, a train would stop automatically whenever the air-brake system was deprived of compressed air. Rather than leaving the engineer with a false sense of safety, only to discover that there was no braking capacity when it was needed, the new braking system would automatically revert to a safe state in case of failure. That is, if the brakes lost compressed air, they would engage and, therefore, brake, making the system virtually fail-safe.

SIGNIFICANCE

Not only did the development of the air brake completely transform the railroad, it also completely transformed the life of George Westinghouse. Although it made him rich, he did not choose to dissipate that wealth in high living. Instead, he reinvested the money in further research and invention. As he perfected the air brake, he moved to other railroad-related work, such as developing modern signaling systems.

Westinghouse also developed an interest in electricity, which led him to join forces with Croatian-born American inventor Nikola Tesla to create the modern alternating-current (AC) electrical distribution system, in opposition to Thomas Alva Edison's direct-current (DC) system, which was in fact a technological dead end. Westinghouse also modified some of his earlier air experiments to create the modern compressed-air shock absorber for automobiles, thus making the early roads much easier to drive.

—*Leigh Husband Kimmel*

FURTHER READING

Grant, H. Roger. *The Railroad: The Life Story of a Technology*. Westport, Conn.: Greenwood Press, 2005. An overview of the development of the railroad from its earliest beginnings to the twenty-first century, including the role of air brakes in making rail transportation and rail travel safer.

Jonnes, Jill. *Empires of Light: Edison, Tesla, Westinghouse, and the Race to Electrify the World*. New York: Random House, 2003. Although it focuses mostly on the later years of Westinghouse's company, when he was moving into electrical generation and distribution, this work discusses to some degree his invention of the air brake.

Leupp, Francis E. *George Westinghouse: His Life and Achievements*. Boston: Little, Brown, 1918. A detailed biography that includes details often passed over in later works. Includes several plates of photographs.

Levine, I. E. *Inventive Wizard: George Westinghouse*. New York: Julian Messner, 1962. An overview of Westinghouse's career as an inventor, including a discussion of his invention of the air brake.

Usselman, Steven W. "Air Brakes for Freight Trains: Technological Innovation in the American Railroad Industry, 1869-1900." *Business History Review* 58 (Spring, 1984): 30-50. The best single source available on how Westinghouse developed and promoted the air brake.

Wilmerding and the Westinghouse Air Brake Company. Charleston, S.C.: Arcadia, 2002. A history of the company and its impact upon Wilmerding, the southwest Pennsylvania town where Westinghouse's air-brake business was based.

Wormser, Richard. *The Iron Horse: How Railroads Changed America*. New York: Walker, 1993. A historical overview of railroading, including the role of the air brake in making railroads safer.

SEE ALSO: Mar. 24, 1802: Trevithick Patents the High-Pressure Steam Engine; September 27, 1825: Stockton and Darlington Railway Opens; July 21, 1836: Champlain and St. Lawrence Railroad Opens; Nov. 10, 1852: Canada's Grand Trunk Railway Is Incorporated; Mar. 23, 1857: Otis Installs the First Passenger Elevator; Jan. 10, 1863: First Underground Railroad Opens in London; May 1-Oct. 30, 1893: Chicago World's Fair.

RELATED ARTICLES in *Great Lives from History: The Nineteenth Century, 1801-1900:* Thomas Alva Edison; Nikola Tesla; Richard Trevithick; George Westinghouse.

May, 1869
WOMAN SUFFRAGE ASSOCIATIONS BEGIN FORMING

After the emancipation of African American slaves was achieved, American women's rights activists focused their attention on the goal of woman suffrage. Their first organizations, the National Woman Suffrage Association and the American Woman Suffrage Association, adopted different strategies but shared the same goal and eventually combined.

LOCALE: New York, New York; Cleveland, Ohio
CATEGORIES: Women's issues; organizations and institutions

KEY FIGURES

Susan B. Anthony (1820-1906) and
Elizabeth Cady Stanton (1815-1902), founders of the National Woman Suffrage Association
Carrie Chapman Catt (1859-1947), twice president of the National American Woman Suffrage Association
Alice Paul (1885-1977), founder of the National Woman's Party
Anna Howard Shaw (1847-1919), suffragist, minister, and medical doctor
Lucy Stone (1818-1893), cofounder of the American Woman Suffrage Association

SUMMARY OF EVENT

The struggle for woman suffrage, marked from start to finish by internal controversy, was first publicly articulated in the United States in a resolution drafted by Elizabeth Cady Stanton, one of the organizers of the first Woman's Rights Convention at Seneca Falls in 1848, and passed at that convention. The early struggle for women's rights paralleled the struggle for the rights of African Americans, and many of the same people were initially involved in both movements, forming the Equal Rights Association. At the outbreak of the Civil War (1861-1865), some rights advocates believed that it was more important to work for abolition of slavery than for women's rights. Women were told, "This is the Negroes' hour."

This split in emphasis resulted in the Thirteenth Amendment (1865) to the U.S. Constitution, which ended slavery once and for all. It also led to ratification of the Fourteenth Amendment (1868), which guaranteed equal protection to all American citizens and guaranteed the vote to all men, regardless of race, and the Fifteenth Amendment (1870), which guaranteed that the franchise could "not be denied or abridged by the United States or by any State on account of race, color, or previous condition of servitude," while saying nothing about sex. Efforts by Stanton and Susan B. Anthony to show that the Fourteenth Amendment included "women" in its word "persons" resulted in a Supreme Court decision in 1874 ruling that such was not the case.

At the close of a meeting of the Equal Rights Association in New York City, in May, 1869, women from nineteen states, led by Stanton and Anthony, formed the National Woman Suffrage Association (NWSA) to work for the emancipation of women through a new amendment to the U.S. Constitution. Stanton was the group's president, and Anthony was on the executive committee. Because of a division of opinion on tactics, Lucy Stone, another of the original Seneca Falls organizers, Julia Ward Howe, and others called for another convention in Cleveland, Ohio, in November, 1869. There they formed the American Woman Suffrage Association (AWSA), with the prominent Protestant cleric Henry Ward Beecher as president and Stone as chairman of the executive committee.

Lucy Stone. (Library of Congress)

The NWSA argued that the federal government was responsible for protecting women from states that denied them suffrage, just as the federal government protected the voting rights of black men with the Fourteenth Amendment. Thus, a federal amendment was needed. In addition, the NWSA continued to discuss issues that the movement had begun considering before the Civil War: equal pay, prostitution, sexual and physical victimization of women and children, and the role of the church in maintaining the oppression of women. Cut off from most former abolitionists, the NWSA consciously reached out to new groups of women. Although attempts to build alliances with working-class women foundered on the deep differences of class, a great deal of interest developed among middle-class professionals. The vote was seen as a tool women could use to gain other rights. The strategies were confrontation and civil disobedience.

By contrast, the more conservative reformers in the AWSA, who later included the Women's Christian Temperance Union, centered their work on obtaining suffrage for women through amendments to individual state constitutions and limited their work to the single issue of woman suffrage. The vote was an end in itself. The AWSA appealed mostly to wealthy, educated whites. It believed the vote could be won only by avoiding issues that were irrelevant and calculated to alienate the support of influential sections of the community. It did not organize working women, criticize the churches, or concern itself with the question of divorce.

In 1890, the two organizations united to form the National American Woman Suffrage Association (NAWSA). Stanton was its president, Anthony the vice president, and Stone the executive committee chair. When Stanton resigned due to her advancing age, Anthony was elected her successor, and when she resigned at eighty years of age in 1900, Carrie Chapman Catt became president. Catt was succeeded after four years by the Reverend Dr. Anna Howard Shaw and went on to head the International Woman Suffrage Alliance but later returned to the helm of NAWSA. The merger put an end to the confrontational tactics of the NWSA. State emphasis won out. The movement's arguments broadened: No longer was suffrage promoted as an equal right, but as a means to clean up corruption and give women the vote to protect their own special interests as mothers concerned for the education of their children, as working women subjected to exploitation without protection, or as the abused wives of drunkards.

The movement gradually waned. Between 1870 and 1910, 480 state campaigns resulted in only seventeen referenda in eleven states, only two of which succeeded. In 1913, Alice Paul formed a congressional committee within the organization. However, a new schism formed when NAWSA offered Congress a compromise amendment. In 1914, Paul formed the independent Congressional Union for Woman Suffrage, which launched the radical National Woman's Party (NWP) in 1916. The NWP mobilized women through the state organizations to come to Washington, D.C., for suffrage marches, to picket the White House, and to organize against the Democratic Party and its sitting president, Woodrow Wilson, simply because it was the party in power and had not passed the amendment. The 1918 elections gave the Republicans a majority in Congress, and President Wilson gave his first address supporting woman suffrage. The NWP kept the pressure on him until he translated his words into action. Finally, the Nineteenth Amendment, giving women the vote, as written and submitted by Anthony in 1875, was approved by Congress in 1919 and was ratified in 1920.

Significance

Even during the period when suffrage activity was centered in the NAWSA, women in the movement were divided as to methods and philosophy. There was disagreement as to whether emphasis on national or state ratification was best; whether traditional or confrontational methods should be employed; and whether woman suffrage should be the sole issue for which women worked, or if the movement should be put aside for issues such as emancipation and the World War I effort, or combined with all of women's needs. Some historians believe that the presence of dual organizations working for woman suffrage split and weakened the movement; others argue that the duality was positive because it provided a broader base and offered women a choice of conservative or radical feminism.

Because it took woman suffrage supporters fifty years to achieve the goal of a federal amendment, either interpretation may be correct. However, the state-by-state campaign emphasized by the more conservative leaders resulted in political power available to and used by the radical National Woman's Party in the final successful push for ratification. After the Nineteenth Amendment was ratified, the NWP was reorganized to work for equal rights. Alice Paul had the first Equal Rights Amendment introduced into Congress in 1923. The League of Women Voters was organized at the jubilee convention of the NAWSA in 1919. Catt joined this organization, and the schism continued: She thought there was no more need for an organization specifically concerned with women's rights. Both organizations continued to exist in the 1990's, but the League of Women Voters is much better known.

—*Erika E. Pilver*

FURTHER READING

Baker, Jean H, ed. *Votes for Women: The Struggle for Suffrage Revisited.* Oxford, England: Oxford University Press, 2002. Well-researched general history of the woman suffrage movement.

Clinton, Catherine. *The Other Civil War: American Women in the Nineteenth Century.* New York: Hill & Wang, 1984. Although comparatively brief, a comprehensive and excellent treatment of the women's rights movement during the nineteenth century.

DuBois, Ellen Carol. *Feminism and Suffrage: The Emergence of an Independent Women's Movement in America, 1848-1869.* Ithaca, N.Y.: Cornell University Press, 1978. Discusses the early years of the women's movement, showing the events that led to the formation of the woman suffrage movement.

Flexner, Eleanor. *Century of Struggle: The Woman's Rights Movement in the United States.* New York: Atheneum, 1970. Detailed history of the women's rights struggle, with some attention to the woman suffrage organizations.

Gurko, Miriam. *The Ladies of Seneca Falls: The Birth of the Woman's Rights Movement.* New York: Schocken Books, 1974. Emphasizes the early years and the personalities of the individual leading women in the women's rights movement.

McFadden, Margaret, ed. *Women's Issues.* 3 vols. Pasadena, Calif.: Salem Press, 1997. Comprehensive reference work with numerous articles on woman suffrage, women's rights organizations, individual leaders, and many related issues.

Wagner, Sally. *A Time of Protest: Suffragists Challenge the Republic, 1870-1887.* 2d ed. Carmichael, Calif.: Sky Carrier Press, 1988. Study of the woman suffrage movement between the time that the NWSA and AWSA formed and their amalgamation. Includes direct quotations from resolutions, facsimiles of broadsides, proclamations, and other interesting material.

Zink-Sawyer, Beverly Ann. *From Preachers to Suffragists: Woman's Rights and Religious Conviction in the Lives of Three Nineteenth-Century American Clergywomen.* Louisville, Ky.: Westminster John Knox Press, 2003. Examines the lives of Shaw and two other clergywomen—Olympia Brown and Antoinette Louise Brown Blackwell—whose involvement in the women's rights movement was an extension of their call to the ministry.

SEE ALSO: July 19-20, 1848: Seneca Falls Convention; May 28-29, 1851: Akron Woman's Rights Convention; May 10, 1866: Suffragists Protest the Fourteenth Amendment; July 9, 1868: Fourteenth Amendment Is Ratified; Dec., 1869: Wyoming Gives Women the Vote; June 17-18, 1873: Anthony Is Tried for Voting; Mar. 9, 1875: *Minor v. Happersett*; July 4, 1876: Declaration of the Rights of Women; Feb. 17-18, 1890: Women's Rights Associations Unite; Sept. 19, 1893: New Zealand Women Win Voting Rights; Oct. 27, 1893: National Council of Women of Canada Is Founded.

RELATED ARTICLES in *Great Lives from History: The Nineteenth Century, 1801-1900:* Susan B. Anthony; Anna Howard Shaw; Elizabeth Cady Stanton; Lucy Stone.

May 10, 1869
First Transcontinental Railroad Is Completed

The completion of the first railroad to connect the East and West Coasts greatly accelerated the development of the West and signaled a major step in the closing of the western frontier.

Locale: Promontory Point, Utah Territory
Categories: Transportation; economics; engineering

Key Figures

Oliver Ames II (1807-1877) and
Oakes Ames (1804-1873), Boston financiers who controlled the Union Pacific Railroad
Grenville M. Dodge (1831-1916), U.S. Army officer responsible for constructing the Union Pacific Railroad
Thomas C. Durant (1820-1885), organizer of the Crédit Mobilier for the Union Pacific Railroad
Theodore Dehone Judah (1826-1863), civil engineer who surveyed across the Sierra Nevada

Summary of Event

During the 1850's, the desirability of constructing railroads that would connect the East and West Coasts of the United States was widely recognized. However, many Americans thought that such schemes were merely visionary because of the great distances that would have to be covered, the engineering obstacles to be overcome, and the tremendous outlays of money that would be required. Realistic businessmen knew that government aid would be necessary to complete any such railroad. Both politicians and others concluded that the nation would be fortunate if financial support could be obtained to build even a single line, and therefore determination of which route would be followed became a major sectional consideration. It was believed that this problem could be resolved by the natural topography, and that one route would prove to be superior to all others on the basis of its more desirable terrain and climate. To find such a route,

Central Pacific Railroad construction workers standing on flatcars near Promontory Point, where the transcontinental railroad would be joined the following year. (Library of Congress)

THE TRANSCONTINENTAL RAILROAD IN 1869

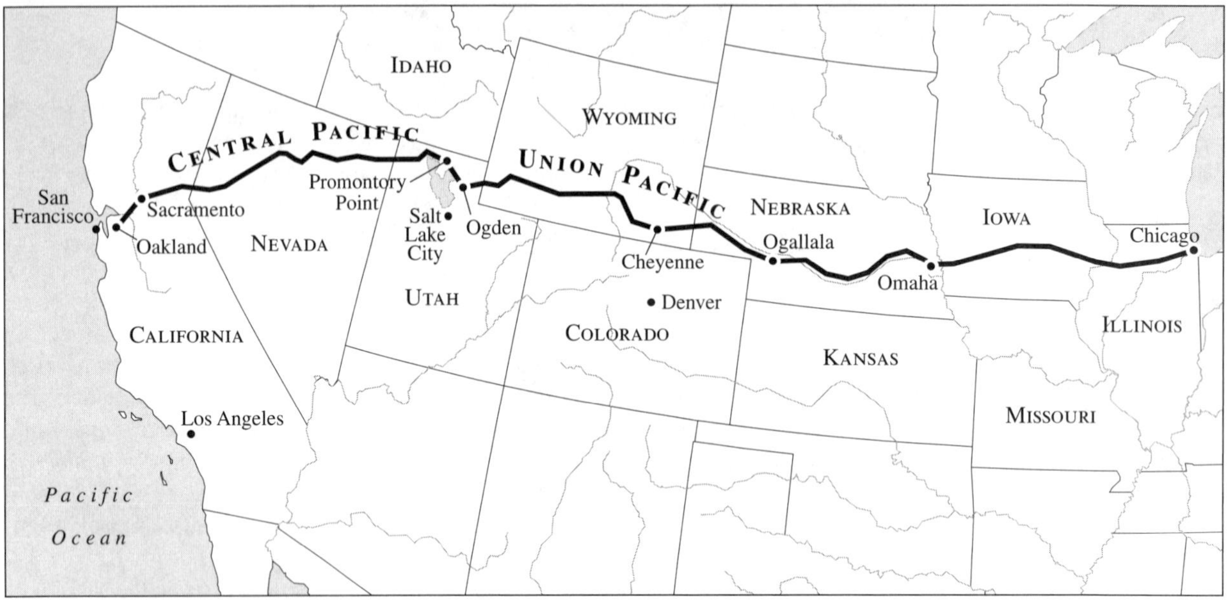

Congress authorized a survey by the U.S. Army Topographical Corps of all the feasible routes to the Pacific Ocean in 1853.

The multivolume report of these expeditions revealed that at least four routes seemed to be practical for a transcontinental railroad, and two were particularly noteworthy. One of these would connect either St. Louis or Chicago with San Francisco; the other would link New Orleans with Los Angeles. Southerners insisted on the desirability of the latter idea and pointed out that it, unlike the northern route, would not traverse any unorganized territories. The Kansas-Nebraska Act of 1854, which organized these territories, was meant to answer the southern challenge.

Meanwhile, the question of slavery in the territories, which the Kansas-Nebraska Act aggravated, delayed any decision on a transcontinental railroad route. California residents became impatient with the delay. In order to placate agitation on the Pacific coast, Congress approved the creation of the Pacific Wagon Road Office to improve the transcontinental wagon roads under the Department of the Interior. However, with the outbreak of the Civil War in 1861, a railroad connection with California became a more urgent necessity. With southern interests out of the federal government, the location of the line was quickly decided.

On July 1, 1862, Congress stipulated that two companies should build the first transcontinental railroad. One was the Central Pacific Company, organized a year earlier in California to carry out the construction plans of Theodore Dehone Judah to cross the Sierra Nevada eastward to tap the rich trade of the Comstock silver mines of Nevada. The other was the Union Pacific Railroad, which was to extend westward from the hundredth meridian to meet the Central Pacific at the California-Nevada line. Each company was granted a one-hundred-foot right-of-way along its routes and five alternate sections of land on each side within ten miles of the railroad. All necessary building supplies could be taken from the public domain. The federal government agreed to lend the railroad companies, on a first-mortgage basis, sixteen thousand dollars per mile for construction on level terrain, thirty-two thousand dollars per mile in foothills, and forty-eight thousand dollars per mile in mountains. The completion date was set for 1876.

Construction of the Union Pacific began in Omaha in December, 1863, but only forty miles of line were built in 1864 and 1865. The chief problem was one of finance, because private capitalists thought the project too risky an investment, despite generous government loans and land grants. In 1864, Congress came to the aid of the railroad by doubling the size of the land grants and by agreeing to a second mortgage to secure its loans, thus permitting borrowing elsewhere on a first-mortgage basis. The law required that the Union Pacific sell its bonds at par. To resolve this difficulty, Crédit Mobilier of America was organized to handle construction contracts, accepting payment in Union Pacific bonds which it, in turn, placed on the market for whatever they would bring.

Almost all the labor in building the Union Pacific and the Central Pacific was provided by human workers and draft animals. Steam shovels became available only toward the end of construction. Hence, the railroad was built by armies of men creating whole communities as they moved. Added to this was conflict resulting from the presence on the plains of the Sioux, who had no intention of giving up their lands to the settlers and their iron horse.

The Central Pacific also began construction in 1863, with the aid of the Pacific Railroad Fund raised by a special property tax in California. The state agreed to pay the interest for the following twenty years on the first $1.5 million worth of bonds issued by the company, a total of $2.1 million. Subsidies also were provided by the counties through which the line ran. President Abraham Lincoln decreed that because the Sierra Nevada extended westward into the Sacramento Valley, the railroad promoters could borrow the maximum of forty-eight thousand dollars per mile from the federal government.

Construction moved slowly between 1863 and 1867, and the difficult terrain was overcome only by employing seven thousand Chinese immigrants, who labored patiently on salaries of only thirty to thirty-five dollars per month, with a minimum of equipment. About nine-tenths of the workforce was Chinese. Many of these laborers had come to California in the wake of the gold rush of 1849, but after they proved to be exceptional workers, the railroad sent agents to China to recruit more of them.

By the summer of 1867, the crest of the Sierra Nevada was reached and easier downgrades lay ahead. Anticipating this situation, the Central Pacific had obtained from Congress the right to continue building through Nevada to meet and connect with the Union Pacific. A race then ensued between the two companies, each trying to obtain as much land and government loans as it could as it raced to lay more track than its rival.

By 1866, the Union Pacific reached Fort Kearney, Nebraska. The pace of construction increased the following summer, after a struggle for control of the railroad was resolved between Thomas C. Durant, the organizer of the Crédit Mobilier of America, and the Boston financiers Oliver Ames II and Oakes Ames. The Chicago and Northwestern Railroad by then had reached Council Bluffs, ending the expensive transportation of rails and supplies up the Missouri River by steamboat.

Meanwhile, Civil War veterans and Irish immigrants were moving west and seeking work as construction crews. They were described as first-rate but were a constant source of trouble in their free time. There was a great contrast between these uproarious army veterans and the sober, industrious Chinese workers on the Central Pacific. Grenville M. Dodge, an army officer with an aptitude for handling men, assumed responsibility for construction and, when necessary, armed his war veterans to fight off those interfering with construction.

In the spring of 1869, Union Pacific and Central Pacific construction crews finally came in sight of each other. When the two roads' surveys began to parallel each other, they started building two roadbeds side by side in the hope of obtaining more government aid. However, Congress intervened and selected Promontory Point in Utah, northwest of Ogden, as the junction of the two lines. There a ceremony celebrating the connection of the rails took place on May 10, 1869, in the presence of railroad officials and distinguished guests. At least one dozen spikes of gold and silver were driven into a polished laurel tie by various speakers, and then the engines came together nose to nose as their whistles blew, bells rang, and the crowd cheered. A war-weary nation had cause to celebrate. Split by secession less than a decade before, the nation now celebrated a new joining.

SIGNIFICANCE

Completion of the first transcontinental railroad introduced a new era in the settlement of the West. Rapid, comfortable, and comparatively safe transportation across the continent freed prospective settlers and traders from having to reach the frontier in slow, arduous, and often dangerous crossings by wagon train and stagecoach. The railroad also made possible shipment of goods from coast to coast that was faster and cheaper than shipping around Cape Horn. By the end of the nineteenth century, a vast network of railroads crisscrossed the continent and the era of the frontier was over.

—W. Turrentine Jackson,
updated by Stephen B. Dobrow

FURTHER READING

Ambrose, Stephen E. *Nothing Like It in the World: The Men Who Built the Transcontinental Railroad, 1863-1869.* New York: Simon & Schuster, 2000. History of the transcontinental railroad that offers considerable information about the financiers and engineers responsible for its construction.

Douglas, George H. *All Aboard! The Railroad in Ameri-*

can Life. New York: Paragon House, 1992. Lively social history of railroads in the United States.
Griswold, Wesley S. *A Work of Giants: Building the First Transcontinental Railroad*. New York: McGraw-Hill, 1962. Appreciative history of the transcontinental railroad that concentrates on the actual building of the railroad. Rich in colorful detail and anecdote.
McCague, James. *Moguls and Iron Men: The Story of the First Transcontinental Railroad*. New York: Harper & Row, 1964. Discusses the plans and work that were involved in building the first transcontinental railroad.
Mayer, Lynn Rhodes, and Ken Vose. *Makin' Tracks: The Saga of the Transcontinental Railroad*. New York: Barnes & Noble Books, 1995. Tells the story of the transcontinental railroad through illustrations and words of contemporary diaries, newspaper accounts, speeches, handbills, reports, and gossip.
Ogburn, Charlton. *Railroaders: The Great American Adventure*. Washington, D.C.: National Geographic Society, 1977. Discusses U.S. railroads and the people who built them, ran them, and made their fortunes by owning them.
Robertson, Donald B. *Encyclopedia of Western Railroad History*. Caldwell, Idaho: Caxton Books, 1986. Includes facts on the rise and decline of the railroad in the West, from the earliest times.
Strom, Claire. *Profiting from the Plains: The Great Northern Railway and Corporate Development of the American West*. Seattle: University of Washington Press, 2003. Detailed scholarly study of the forces behind the construction of the northern transcontinental railroad route.
Williams, John H. *A Great and Shining Road: The Epic Story of the Transcontinental Railroad*. New York: Times Books, 1988. Provides a dramatic history of the building of railroads across the United States and discusses what it meant to the states they crossed.

SEE ALSO: Mar. 24, 1802: Trevithick Patents the High-Pressure Steam Engine; September 27, 1825: Stockton and Darlington Railway Opens; Jan. 7, 1830: Baltimore and Ohio Railroad Opens; July 21, 1836: Champlain and St. Lawrence Railroad Opens; c. 1845: Clipper Ship Era Begins; 1849: Chinese Begin Immigrating to California; Nov. 10, 1852: Canada's Grand Trunk Railway Is Incorporated; Mar. 2, 1853-1857: Pacific Railroad Surveys; Apr. 3, 1860-Oct. 26, 1861: Pony Express Expedites Transcontinental Mail; Oct. 24, 1861: Transcontinental Telegraph Is Completed; 1890: U.S. Census Bureau Announces Closing of the Frontier.
RELATED ARTICLES in *Great Lives from History: The Nineteenth Century, 1801-1900:* J. P. Morgan; Leland Stanford; Cornelius Vanderbilt.

September 24, 1869-1877
SCANDALS ROCK THE GRANT ADMINISTRATION

Although President Ulysses S. Grant was himself an honest politician, the scandals in which members of his administration and other government officials were involved diminished the stature of the presidency, undermined the Republican Party's credibility, and prompted a movement to reduce political corruption.

ALSO KNOWN AS: Whiskey Ring scandal
LOCALE: United States
CATEGORIES: Government and politics; crime and scandals

KEY FIGURES

Ulysses S. Grant (1822-1885), president of the United States, 1869-1877
Orville E. Babcock (1835-1884), Grant's private secretary
William Worth Belknap (1829-1890), secretary of war, 1869-1876
George S. Boutwell (1818-1905), secretary of the Treasury, 1869-1873
Abel Rathbone Corbin (fl. mid-nineteenth century), Grant's brother-in-law, who was involved in the Black Friday gold speculation
Jay Gould (1836-1892) and
James Fisk (1834-1872), stock speculators
Oakes Ames (1804-1873), congressman censured for his role in the Crédit Mobilier scandal

SUMMARY OF EVENT

During President Ulysses S. Grant's two terms in office, much corruption was exposed at all levels of government—national, state, and local. Even allowing for exaggeration or misrepresentation by the various political opponents, such as southern conservatives and liberal reformers, or by sensation-mongering journalists, the record of Grant's administration is arguably the worst in U.S. presidential history.

Grant himself was personally above reproach, but he lacked essential qualities of political leadership. A poor judge of character, he gathered around him clever politicians with little regard for their moral reputation. His sense of loyalty to his subordinates limited his effectiveness in dealing with their corruption. The way in which he understood the Constitution depreciated the power of the presidency, and in his exercise of the office, he diminished its respect.

Grant's close associates were often involved in acts of doubtful legality. For example, his brother-in-law Abel Rathbone Corbin participated in a scheme with speculators Jay Gould and James Fisk to corner the gold market in 1869. To be successful, the manipulators needed assurance that the government would not interfere by selling gold from the Treasury. When Corbin implied that he had the necessary promise from the president, Gould and Fisk began buying gold with the intention of forcing the price up and selling at high profits to those who had made commitments payable only in gold. This manipulation led to a stock exchange panic on what became known as Black Friday, September 24, 1869. Grant authorized George S. Boutwell, then secretary of the Treasury, to sell government gold to protect business, and the scheme to corner the gold market was broken. Nevertheless, many brokers went bankrupt because of the actions of Gould and Fisk.

Although the most serious scandals of the Grant administration were not exposed until after Grant's reelection in 1872, there was significant opposition within the Republican Party to Grant's renomination. Civil service reformers, opponents of Radical Reconstruction, and party leaders disappointed with their shares of federal patronage joined forces in an attempt to deny Grant a second term. When they failed to prevent his renomination by the Republican Party, they formed the Liberal Republican Party and nominated newspaper editor Horace Greeley for president. The Democratic Party also nominated Greeley. However, Greeley's eccentric behavior and Grant's stature as a Civil War hero combined to secure Grant's reelection with an impressive 286 electoral votes out of a possible 352.

Although neither Grant nor his close associates were involved directly, the Republican Party was discredited by the investigation in 1872-1873 of the Crédit Mobilier affair, a scandal that seemed to epitomize the Grant era.

President Ulysses S. Grant. (Library of Congress)

Crédit Mobilier was a construction company designated to build the transcontinental railroad for the Union Pacific Company. To ensure the continuation of generous government grants, stock in the Crédit Mobilier was given, or sold at a favorable price, to important politicians, including Grant's two vice presidents, Schuyler Colfax and Henry Wilson, and to many senators and congressmen. The stock paid an annual dividend several times greater than its original cost, as the Crédit Mobilier bilked the Union Pacific and the government of millions of dollars. Congressman Oakes Ames of Massachusetts was censured after a congressional investigation for having been a leader in the scheme, and the episode undermined the reputations of both Congress and the administration.

Suspicions about the greed of congressmen were not allayed by the "Salary Grab" Act of March 3, 1873, by which Congress voted itself not only a needed raise but also, through a retroactive clause, a large cash bonus. This act later seemed even more inappropriate after the Panic of September 18, 1873. The financial crisis brought on a depression and the repeal of the Salary Grab Act. The Panic of 1873, which was largely precipitated by international financial conditions beyond the control of the Grant administration, was linked with the corruption of the time in the mind of the public.

Grant's Treasury Department, under William Richardson, carried common corruption to remarkable levels of audacity. John D. Sanborn, a protégé of Benjamin Franklin Butler, a Massachusetts congressman, was rewarded for campaign contributions with contracts for the collection of delinquent taxes. His commission was an exorbitant 50 percent. Sanborn even "earned" $213,500 for collecting taxes that would have been paid if he had done nothing.

Among the many scandals of the Grant administration, none came closer to implicating the president himself than the exposure of the activities of the Whiskey Ring. General John McDonald, an old friend whom Grant had appointed supervisor in the Internal Revenue Service at St. Louis and from whom Grant received political contributions, was indicted in 1875 for having defrauded the government of millions of dollars by conspiring with the distillers to avoid federal taxes. Colonel Orville E. Babcock, Grant's trusted private secretary, was also involved. Grant defended Babcock and allowed him to continue in an official position, although he no longer served as presidential secretary.

Another serious scandal of the Grant administration implicated Secretary of War William Belknap, who had accepted bribes to keep an Indian post trader in office. Belknap resigned and the House of Representatives impeached him, but the Senate failed to find him guilty because a number of senators believed that they lacked jurisdiction over a resigned officeholder.

SIGNIFICANCE

Much of the corruption of the Grant era was beyond the control of the president. He depended for political support upon the Stalwarts within the Republican Party, a group that included party bosses such as Roscoe Conkling of New York and Oliver Morton of Indiana, whose state organizations dispensed vital federal patronage. State governments, both North and South, were characterized by astounding corruption: Senate seats were sometimes purchased from the members of state legislatures who elected the U.S. senators. Local government was no better. The Tweed Ring of New York City plundered the city of millions of dollars.

An industrial and urban United States was emerging. The transitional character of the era, with its uncertain rules of conduct, encouraged corruption. Hampered by a misguided sense of loyalty, obstinacy, and lack of competence, Grant was unable to cope with the tendencies of his time.

—*Mark A. Plummer, updated by Charles H. O'Brien*

FURTHER READING

Bunting, Josiah, III. *Ulysses S. Grant*. New York: Times Books, 2004. Part of a series on presidential administrations, this study acknowledges Grant's flaws but grants him high marks for "nobility of character" and for his achievements in attaining civil rights for African Americans.

Cashman, Sean Dennis. *America in the Gilded Age: From the Death of Lincoln to the Rise of Theodore Roosevelt*. 3d ed. New York: New York University Press, 1993. A well-rounded and lively account of the economic, social, and political history of the late nineteenth century.

Korda, Michael. *Ulysses S. Grant: The Unlikely Hero*. New York: Atlas Books/HarperCollins, 2004. Brief but well-written and balanced biography that covers Grant's early life, military career, and presidency.

McFeely, William S. *Grant: A Biography*. New York: W. W. Norton, 1981. An authoritative study of Grant as a common man with uncommon ambition that places Grant in his times and offers a detailed account of the scandals of his administration.

Summers, Mark Wahlgren. *The Era of Good Stealings*. New York: Oxford University Press, 1993. A well-documented study of the Grant era that challenges its reputation for common or systemic corruption.

Trefousse, Hans L. *Carl Schurz: A Biography*. Knoxville: University of Tennessee Press, 1982. As senator from Missouri and advocate of civil service reform, Schurz spoke out against the corruption of the Grant administration. He also was active in the Liberal Republican Party of 1872.

Van Deusen, Glyndon G. *Horace Greeley: Nineteenth Century Crusader*. New York: Hill & Wang, 1964. The last part of this biography deals with the period after the Civil War and the 1872 presidential campaign, in which corruption in the Grant administration was a major issue.

SEE ALSO: Feb. 24-May 26, 1868: Impeachment of Andrew Johnson; May, 1869: Woman Suffrage Associations Begin Forming; May 10, 1869: First Transcontinental Railroad Is Completed.

RELATED ARTICLES in *Great Lives from History: The Nineteenth Century, 1801-1900:* Ulysses S. Grant; Horace Greeley; J. P. Morgan; Thomas Nast; Carl Schurz; William Marcy Tweed.

October 11, 1869-July 15, 1870
FIRST RIEL REBELLION

The resistance of the multiethnic Metis people to the incorporation of their ancestral homes into the new Dominion of Canada and the threat of being swamped by new immigrants led to some concessions to their demands when the province of Manitoba was created, but their unresolved grievances would later lead to a second rebellion.

ALSO KNOWN AS: Red River Rebellion; First Metis Rebellion
LOCALE: Red River, Manitoba
CATEGORIES: Wars, uprisings, and civil unrest; indigenous people's rights

KEY FIGURES

Louis Riel (1844-1885), Metis leader who was the second president of the government of Assiniboia
John Alexander Macdonald (1815-1891), first prime minister of Canada, 1867-1873, 1878-1891
William McDougall (1822-1905), first lieutenant governor of the Northwest Territories
Andre Nault (1829-1924), member of the provisional government of Assiniboia
Thomas Scott (1846-1870), militant Orangeman hanged for treason by the Metis provisional government

SUMMARY OF EVENT

During the fall of 1869, the Metis living in and around the Red River Valley in what is now Manitoba prevented a party of government land surveyors from continuing their work. They declared a provisional government and barred the new Canadian government's appointee from taking up his post as territorial governor. This act marked the start of the uprising known as the First Riel, or Red River, Rebellion. The background to the rebellion and the Canadian government's response are complex, and its outcome had important implications for both the Metis and the Dominion of Canada.

Descendants of French fur traders and American Indian women, the Metis blended elements of both cultures. Metis society flourished on the northern prairies in the late eighteenth and early nineteenth centuries. They were particularly noted for the highly militaristic organization of their twice-annual buffalo hunts.

The late 1860's was a period of great transition for people living in Great Britain's North America territories. The Dominion of Canada was created by the British North America Act on July 1, 1867. British Columbia prepared to join the Canadian Confederation as a province, on the condition that a transcontinental railroad would be built. With the fur trade era at an end, the Hudson's Bay Company prepared to give up its claim to Rupert's Land—the part of northern Canada whose rivers drain into Hudson Bay—and the northwest. The new dominion government had two goals: to build the railroad and to prevent the company lands from becoming part of the United States Under its first prime minister, John Alexander Macdonald, Canada entered into negotiations to acquire the territories. The government agreed to pay the Hudson's Bay Company £300,000, and the land transfer was set to occur on December 1, 1869. However, this was done without consulting the ten thousand Metis and English so-called half-breeds living in the Red River region.

Tensions between French Roman Catholics from Quebec and English-speaking Protestants in Ontario—which have continued into the twenty-first century—affected relations within Red River. Ontario had many new Protestant immigrants in need of land, and Red River, located immediately to the west of Ontario, seemed an ideal place to settle them. Although residents of mixed Indian-white ancestry formed more than 80 percent of the population of Red River, a great deal of racism was directed against them. The French-speaking and Roman Catholic Metis were held in particular disdain by the immigrants from Ontario. The rate at which these new immigrants were arriving made the Metis fear that they would soon be a minority in their own ancestral homeland. Moreover, several crop failures and the destruction of the buffalo herds had created economic stress among the Metis.

Although the official date of land transfer was several months away, the Canadian government sent land surveyors to the Red River in the summer of 1869. Despite government promises to respect Metis land tenure, the activities of the surveyors indicated that this would not be the case. The Metis had for many years occupied long, narrow farmsteads extending back from the Red River. Disregarding this practice, the surveyors delineated square township lots. On October 11, 1869, the surveyors reached the farmstead of Andre Nault. After securing the assistance of eighteen other Metis, Nault forced the surveyors off his land—the first action in the brief Red River Rebellion.

Under the leadership of Montreal-educated Louis Riel,

the Metis formed the Council of Assiniboia, which one month later declared itself the government of the region. On November 2, the Metis stopped William McDougall, who had been appointed lieutenant governor of the territory by Prime Minister Macdonald, at the U.S. border with Assiniboia, which had the only passable road into the territory from Ontario. They then seized Upper Fort Garry, which was located near the site of near present-day Winnipeg. No shots were fired, and the fort's occupants retreated to Lower Fort Garry.

The next move occurred on December 7, 1869, when the Metis seized Lower Fort Garry and arrested approximately fifty white Protestant settlers. Three militant Orangemen among the arrested—John Schultz, Charles Boulton, and Thomas Scott—were tried, convicted of treason, and sentenced to death. Boulton's sentence was commuted, and Schultz escaped to Ontario. Only Scott was hanged, on March 4, 1870. Scott's death made him a martyr and reinforced white Protestant opposition to the French Catholic Metis.

Leaders within the government of Assiniboia apparently did not plan to remain independent of Canada, but merely wished to guarantee that the rights of the Metis would be respected in an orderly transition of power. Militant Protestants in Ontario urged the dominion government to crush what they viewed as a French Catholic uprising, but Macdonald had no desire to upset the delicate balance of power that existed between Protestant Ontario and Catholic Quebec. In January of 1870, Macdonald's government entered into negotiations with Riel's provisional government. Among Metis proposals were demands for Assiniboia to enter the confederation as a province rather than as a territory, for both French and English to be official languages, and for high officials to be required to be bilingual. They also demanded a recognition of Metis property rights. In addition, they wanted amnesty for the members of the Metis government.

In May of 1870, the Canadian parliament passed the Manitoba Act, and the transfer of Rupert's Land from the Hudson's Bay Company to the Dominion of Canada, originally set for the previous December, occurred on July 15, 1870. On that same day, Manitoba became a Canadian province. Although the establishment of the province should have met many of the Metis' demands, in practice it did not. The province was limited to one hundred thousand square miles; Canada's parliament, not the new Manitoba legislature, retained control of the public lands; and the conveyance of the Metis' land titles was delayed so long that many Metis sold their rights to land speculators and moved farther west. Racism continued to be rampant, and many of the leaders of the Metis government were attacked and murdered. Riel himself fled to Montana and became a U.S. citizen. Andre Nault was assaulted and left for dead. He fled over the border and was arrested upon his return in 1883.

SIGNIFICANCE

So many white Protestant immigrants flooded into Manitoba that only 7 percent of the population was of mixed ancestry by 1885. Although Riel and his followers thought they had ensured a multiethnic society in which the Metis could participate as equals, Metis society was in disarray only fifteen years after passage of the Manitoba Act. Poverty and fear of further displacement led the Metis to the Second Riel Rebellion. This time, Cree and Assiniboine Indians—starving because of withheld treaty rations—joined the Metis in their revolt. Riel was summoned from his exile to lead the Metis. The Canadian government, fearing a general Indian uprising on the prairies, responded with swift military action rather than with negotiation. Riel was arrested, convicted of treason, and hanged on November 16, 1885.

The great Metis society of the prairies was dispersed. Some Metis joined American Indian tribes; others remained in Canada, disenfranchised and impoverished. During the last decades of the twentieth century, Metis renewed their claims for the lands and rights lost at the time of Canadian confederation.

—*Pamela R. Stern*

FURTHER READING

Brown, Jennifer S. H., Jacqueline Peterson, Robert K. Thomas, and Marcel Giraud, eds. *New Peoples: Being and Becoming Métis in North America*. St. Paul: Minnesota Historical Society, 2001. Ethnographic study of Manitoba's Metis people.

Charlebois, Peter. *The Life of Louis Riel*. Toronto: NC Press, 1975. Illustrated, very sympathetic, and readable biography of the most prominent Metis leader.

Friesen, John W. *The Riel/Real Story*. Ottawa: Borealis Press, 1996. Biography of Louis Riel that focuses on his contributions to the shaping of Metis culture.

Giraud, Marcel. *The Metis in the Canadian West*. Translated by George Woodcock. 2 vols. Lincoln: University of Nebraska Press, 1986. Primary source on the Metis, originally published in French in 1945. Volume 2 deals with the period of the rebellion.

McDougall, John. *In the Days of the Red River Rebellion*. Edmonton: University of Alberta Press, 1983. Mem-

oir of a Methodist missionary during the time of the First Riel Rebellion.
Miller, J. R. *Skyscrapers Hide the Heavens: A History of Indian-White Relations in Canada.* Rev. ed. Toronto: University of Toronto Press, 1991. General history of interethnic relations in Canada that contains a full chapter on the First Riel Rebellion.
Owram, Doug. *Promise of Eden: The Canadian Expansionist Movement and the Idea of the West, 1856-1900.* Toronto: University of Toronto Press, 1980. Chapter 4 discusses the politics of the Canadian response to the rebellion.
Purich, Donald. *The Metis.* Toronto: James Lorimer, 1988. Highly readable treatment of the Metis that contains three chapters on the two Riel Rebellions.

SEE ALSO: June 1, 1815-Aug., 1817: Red River Raids; 1873: Ukrainian Mennonites Begin Settling in Canada; May 23, 1873: Canada Forms the North-West Mounted Police; Sept., 1878: Macdonald Returns as Canada's Prime Minister; Mar. 19, 1885: Second Riel Rebellion Begins; July 11, 1896: Laurier Becomes the First French Canadian Prime Minister.
RELATED ARTICLES in *Great Lives from History: The Nineteenth Century, 1801-1900:* Sir John Alexander Macdonald; Louis Riel.

November 17, 1869
SUEZ CANAL OPENS

The opening of the Suez Canal reduced seafaring travel distances between Europe and the Indian Ocean and Far East by several thousand miles, enhancing world trade while easing global military operations and enhancing the strategic importance of Northeast Africa and the Red Sea.

LOCALE: Isthmus of Suez, Egypt
CATEGORIES: Engineering; science and technology; transportation

KEY FIGURES

Louis-Maurice-Adolphe Linant de Bellefonds (1800-1883), French explorer and Egyptian government official
Ismāʿīl Pasha (1830-1895), viceroy of Egypt, 1863-1879
Jean-Baptiste Lepère (1761-1844), French architect
Ferdinand de Lesseps (1805-1894), French engineer and diplomat in Egypt who organized and supervised canal construction
Saʿīd Paşa (1822-1863), viceroy of Egypt, r. 1854-1863
Napoleon III (Louis Napoleon Bonaparte; 1808-1873), emperor of France, r. 1852-1871
Eugénie (Eugénia Maria de Montijo de Guzmán; 1826-1920), empress of France, r. 1853-1871
Alois Negrelli (1799-1858), Austrian engineer
Lord Palmerston (1784-1865), British foreign minister, 1831-1851, and prime minister, 1855-1865

SUMMARY OF EVENT

By means of an indirect route, a water link existed during ancient times between the Mediterranean Sea and the Red Sea, about one hundred miles south in Egypt. Over the millennia, however, this connection deteriorated and became inoperable. Interest in restoring this link was revived beginning in 1798, during French general Napoleon Bonaparte's expedition to Egypt. The idea was relinquished at that time because of the mistaken belief that the differential between the two sea levels made the plan impractical. Nevertheless, speculation about the possibility of a waterway continued.

Surveys by the French architect Jean-Baptiste Lepère, French explorer Louis-Maurice-Adolphe Linant de Bellefonds (1840), and Austrian engineer Alois Negrelli showed that it would be possible to dig a waterway across the Isthmus of Suez. Scientific computations indicated that the water-level differential between the two seas would not present an obstacle to the project. Ferdinand de Lesseps, a French engineer and diplomat familiar with these precedents, arrived in Egypt in 1854 and dedicated himself to linking the two seas. Using his friendship with Saʿīd Paşa, the new Egyptian khedive (viceroy), de Lesseps obtained a concession to form a company to construct the canal.

A number of problems plagued the project, particularly the strong British opposition to the canal's construction, expressed most forcefully by Lord Palmerston, the British prime minister. Great Britain objected to the canal, fearing that it would facilitate and shorten the route to the Indian Ocean and jeopardize British colonial control of India—a threat posed earlier by Napoleon and not yet excluded in the age of imperial expansion. At the same time, any weakening of the Ottoman Empire, under whose sovereignty Egypt fell, would encourage Russia's expansionist aims in the areas controlled by the Ottomans. Britain also feared that construction of the canal would encourage the separatist tendencies of local Egyptian centers of political power.

Accordingly, although the British themselves would have benefited enormously from a shorter sea route to their eastern possessions, they believed that their national interest would be better served by preventing any developments that might upset the delicate balance of power existing among the competing European states. Palmerston and his subordinates in the British foreign office and abroad exerted maximum pressure on the Ottoman sultans in Constantinople, on Emperor Napoleon III of France, and on the Egyptian khedive to veto de Lesseps's canal project.

Not willing to be dissuaded, de Lesseps used his friendship with Saʿīd Paşa to obtain broad licenses in 1854 and 1856 to build the waterway. Despite the lack of approval by Saʿīd's overlord in Constantinople and the fear of offending any of the great powers (including France), de Lesseps created a corporate entity called the Compagnie Universelle du Canal Maritime de Suez (Universal Suez Ship Canal Company; now known as SUEZ), which, beginning on December 15, 1858, operated the waterway until its nationalization on July 26, 1956. The company raised capital through its stock issues and began actual construction in April, 1859. Progress was slow, largely because of mounting British diplomatic pressure.

Eventually, the terms of the concessions granted by Khedive Saʿīd Paşa were confirmed by the Turkish sultan, and the digging of the "world ditch" resumed at full throttle after its interruption from 1863 to 1866.

In the meantime, Ismāʿīl Pasha, Saʿīd Paşa's successor, had reneged on his obligation to provide Egyptian forced labor on the corvée system for the project in 1863. Napoleon III's arbitration award made Ismāʿīl Pasha in-

Port Said entrance to the Suez Canal during the late 1850's, before the canal's completion. Two ancient obelisks can be seen in the background. (Library of Congress)

demnify the Suez Canal Company with eighty million francs in exchange for his release from such obligation. Despite numerous technical and other difficulties and the necessity of building a freshwater canal from the Nile River to supply the Suez Canal Zone, the world-famous waterway was inaugurated with great fanfare. A galaxy of international guests, led by Napoleon III and Empress Eugénie of France, witnessed the opening of the canal on November 17, 1869. The distance of sea voyages was reduced by an average of two-thirds between Europe and the East, representing several thousand miles.

By a twist of irony, British prime minister Benjamin Disraeli took advantage of the extravagance of Khedive Ismāʿīl Pasha and his consequent need to raise funds by purchasing a controlling 44 percent share of stock in the Suez Canal Company for the British government in 1875. In 1882, the British took physical control of the canal zone when they defeated a native Egyptian force. The British did not evacuate the canal zone until 1956. By that time, the waterway's original depth of twenty-six feet and bottom width of seventy-two feet had been sharply increased, a process that continued under Egyptian control of the canal in order to meet the demands of contemporary ship traffic.

To do justice to one of the engineering feats of modern times, several other aspects of the canal project must be mentioned, particularly its political and social dimensions. With regard to its impact on diplomacy, it is important to consider the varying attitudes of the other great powers, especially Prussia and Austria, toward the canal project. As to the canal's impact on personal relations, the friendship of Saʿīd Paşa and de Lesseps stands in marked contrast to the antipathy of Saʿīd Paşa's successor Ismāʿīl Pasha toward de Lesseps and his Suez Canal Company. Also critical was Napoleon III's own shift from a position of neutrality to one of active support of de Lesseps and the pressure employed by British envoys to persuade the Ottoman sultan and members of his cabinet to oppose the project.

The social dimensions of the project, however, are most often overlooked. The human cost of the project was borne primarily by unskilled Egyptian workers, many of them peasants, who were seized from their villages and transported to the construction site. There, they worked under extreme conditions and lived in miserably unsanitary camps. Many of these workers never returned home. It was to them that President Gamal Abdel Nasser of Egypt referred in his speech announcing the nationalization of the Suez Canal on July 26, 1956, when he declared that the waterway had been built on the skulls of 100,000 of his countrymen and that Egypt had benefited very little from the project since that time. De Lesseps died a few years after the liquidation of the company that was backing his failed Panama Canal project. His statue, which had stood at the northern entrance of the canal in Port Saʿīd, was toppled by the Egyptian populace on the occasion of Nasser's speech.

SIGNIFICANCE

The Suez Canal engineering project, along with other projects such as the transcontinental railroad in the United States, opened the door for increased world trade, allowing for the transportation of goods across and through vast landscapes. The canal also allowed colonial powers to reach farther into Africa to establish colonies throughout the continent.

—Peter B. Heller

FURTHER READING

Beatty, Charles. *Ferdinand de Lesseps*. London: Eyre & Spottiswoode, 1956. This biography of the French engineer includes a political and financial history of the Suez Canal, focusing on the individual who, despite all odds, was most responsible for completing the project.

Farnie, D. A. *East and West of Suez: The Suez Canal in History, 1854-1956*. Oxford, England: Clarendon Press, 1969. In this thorough and well-documented study, there are three chapters relevant to the construction of the waterway. Includes a useful bibliography.

Karabell, Zachary. *Parting the Desert: The Creation of the Suez Canal*. New York: Alfred A. Knopf, 2003. A history of the canal. Karabell depicts de Lesseps as a shrewd salesperson who viewed construction of the canal as a means of achieving his place in history.

Kinross, Lord. *Between Two Seas: The Creation of the Suez Canal*. New York: William Morrow, 1969. A former British diplomat in Egypt, Kinross focuses his account on the role of Ferdinand de Lesseps in overcoming political intrigues as well as the financial and technical obstacles to completing the waterway. Contains attractive illustrations, including a map published on the canal's opening in 1869.

Marlowe, John. *World Ditch: The Making of the Suez Canal*. New York: Macmillan, 1964. Written by a British historian of imperialism, this study is still one of the most authoritative books on the waterway and touches on the various dimensions of the project. Illustrated, with a modest bibliography.

Schonfield, Hugh J. *The Suez Canal in Peace and War, 1869-1969*. Coral Gables, Fla.: University of Miami Press, 1969. First published in 1939, this updated edition focuses on the role of the waterway in world affairs and chronicles the construction of the canal in five chapters. This study is enhanced by an appendix containing the text of all the pertinent documents, beginning with Saʿīd Paşa's concessions of 1854 and 1856.

Stewart, Gail. *The Suez Canal*. San Diego, Calif.: Lucent Books, 2001. Part of the Building History series, this brief work is written especially for younger readers. Presents the project as one of intense diplomacy as well as of engineering and construction. Includes a historical overview of the times leading up to the project and examines conditions encountered by the workers. Also includes sidebar discussions and extensive quotations from primary and secondary sources.

SEE ALSO: 1814-1879: Exploration of Arabia; Oct. 26, 1825: Erie Canal Opens; c. 1845: Clipper Ship Era Begins; Jan. 31, 1858: Brunel Launches the SS *Great Eastern*; Apr., 1868: British Expedition to Ethiopia; Sept. 13, 1882: Battle of Tel el Kebir; June 20, 1895: Germany's Kiel Canal Opens; Mar., 1896-Nov., 1899: Sudanese War; July 10-Nov. 3, 1898: Fashoda Incident Pits France vs. Britain.

RELATED ARTICLES in *Great Lives from History: The Nineteenth Century, 1801-1900:* Benjamin Disraeli; Ferdinand de Lesseps; Napoleon III; Lord Palmerston.

December, 1869
WYOMING GIVES WOMEN THE VOTE

Long before ratification of the Nineteenth Amendment in 1920 guaranteed all American women the right to vote, western territories and state, beginning with Wyoming, granted woman suffrage.

LOCALE: Wyoming
CATEGORIES: Women's issues; laws, acts, and legal history

KEY FIGURES

Susan B. Anthony (1820-1906), leader of the National Woman Suffrage Association
Carrie Chapman Catt (1859-1947), founder of the League of Women Voters
Esther Morris (1814-1902), woman suffrage leader in Wyoming who became the first female justice of the peace
Lucretia Mott (1793-1880) and
Elizabeth Cady Stanton (1815-1902), organizers of the Seneca Falls convention

SUMMARY OF EVENT

When John Adams was helping to draft the Declaration of Independence in 1776, his wife, Abigail Adams, wrote to him, "In the new code of laws which I suppose it will be necessary for you to make, I desire you would remember the ladies." Despite her gentle prodding, however, the ladies were not remembered. When the U.S. Constitution was drafted eleven years later, there was considerable debate concerning who would be eligible to vote. In the end, the decision about who could vote was left to the individual states to decide. The vote was extended to those in each state qualified to vote for state legislature members. This effectively limited the vote to men.

In 1848, Elizabeth Cady Stanton and Lucretia Mott organized the Seneca Falls Convention, the first women's convention organized with the express purpose of improving the position of women through education, suffrage, and more liberal marriage laws. At that gathering, the Declaration of Sentiments was formulated, paralleling the writing of the Declaration of Independence. Woman suffrage was a specific point included in this resolution. Finally, two decades later, a territory known for its rugged frontier philosophy granted suffrage to women.

When the Union Pacific Railroad entered Wyoming in 1867, thousands of people poured into the area. Lawlessness abounded, with murders, robberies, holdups, and other criminal activity running rampant. Local settlers petitioned Congress for the right to establish a territorial government, and the request was approved by Congress and President Andrew Johnson. A territorial government officially was established in Wyoming in May, 1869.

Wyoming's first election was held in September, 1869, to select the delegates to the first legislature for Wyoming. Esther Morris, a transplant from the East, had an understanding of woman suffrage issues and had only recently heard a lecture by Susan B. Anthony. With information at hand, she invited twenty of the most influential men in the state to dinner. With a clarity of purpose and persuasive skill, she exacted from each guest a promise to support woman suffrage if he was elected. Morris herself later became the first female justice of the peace in the nation.

William H. Bright, one of Morris's dinner guests, was elected president of the council when the legislature later convened. Bright told his wife, "I have made up my mind that I will do everything in my power to give you the ballot." He soon set about the task of convincing the all-Democrat legislature of the gain associated with presenting a vote for woman suffrage for all the world to see. On November 27, 1869, Bright introduced the suffrage bill. Before the year was out, Wyoming became the first territory to adopt woman suffrage and. In 1890, Wyoming became the first state to be admitted to the union with general woman suffrage.

In 1876, as Colorado prepared for statehood at its constitutional convention, the question of woman suffrage was submitted. The amendment, which came up for vote in early 1877, was defeated. Much discussion at that time centered on the fact that African Americans had recently been enfranchised and some indemnity was therefore due to women. Although the 1877 measure failed, the idea of suffrage for women never really died out in Colorado.

In 1893, a nonelection year, a new discussion of the women's vote developed in Colorado. Populists were in control of the Senate and Republicans of the House. Wyoming, directly to the north, had not experienced the problems many had predicted would ensue from women voters. It was in this climate that a referendum granting the vote to women was proposed. According to Colorado's 1876 constitution, women could be granted suffrage if confirmed by referendum. Voters were simply asked to confirm or deny women's right to vote. The measure was confirmed by a margin of more than six thousand votes. Women gathered in front of suffrage headquarters upon hearing of their victory and sang "Praise God from Whom All Blessings Flow." Suffragists left that gathering believing that the battle that had been won in Colorado could be won in every western state.

Earlier, the women of Utah had held the right to vote.

Women voting in Cheyenne, Wyoming. (Library of Congress)

In February of 1870, the acting governor of Utah had signed the Act Conferring Upon Women of Utah the Elective Franchise in the Territory of Utah. This act admitted nearly forty times as many women voters as Wyoming had admitted. However, the road to permanent suffrage for the women of Utah was rocky. In 1887, seventeen years after passage of this act, suffrage for women was withdrawn by congressional action. The federal Edmunds-Tucker Bill disfranchised people who were involved in plural marriages, which were condoned by the Mormon Church.

At that time, Utah was attempting to gain statehood and was deeply embroiled in political issues revolving around the Mormon religious practice of polygamy. Mormon women who had voted were accused of voting the Mormon ticket and therefore not generally supporting the national suffrage movement. It was not until 1896 that the women of Utah could legally vote again. When Utah was finally admitted to statehood, the state constitution, submitted to Congress for review, contained an equal-suffrage clause, which was approved by 67 percent of the male voters.

In November, 1896, the voters of Idaho were asked, "Shall Section 2, of Article VI, of the constitution of the state of Idaho be so amended as to extend to women an equal right of suffrage?" When voters went to the polls, the amendment was carried by almost two to one. Elizabeth Ingram, a schoolteacher from a small Idaho town, formed the first woman suffrage organization of Idaho in 1893. However, it was the strong involvement of national woman suffrage workers, such as Susan B. Anthony and Carrie Chapman Catt, that was ultimately responsible for passage of women's vote legislation in Idaho.

SIGNIFICANCE

In 1910, more than eight million American women participated in the paid labor force, yet most could not vote in general elections. By the time the Nineteenth Amendment was passed in 1920, guaranteeing women the right to vote throughout the United States, many states had already passed woman suffrage legislation. Among these states were Washington, which granted women the vote in 1910; California, 1911; Oregon, Arizona, and Kansas, 1912; Montana and Nevada, 1914; New York, 1917; and South Dakota, Oklahoma, and Michigan, 1918. Clearly, the West and Midwest dominated the country in advancing the right of women to vote. Numerous other states had approved some woman suffrage. Most southern states had no statewide enfranchisement of women. The year 1920 was a presidential election year, and for the first time, women across the country were able to participate in the election.

—*Sharon L. Larson*

FURTHER READING

Baker, Jean H, ed. *Votes for Women: The Struggle for Suffrage Revisited*. Oxford, England: Oxford University Press, 2002. Solidly researched work that examines the entire history of the woman suffrage movement.

Beeton, Beverly. *Women Vote in the West: The Woman Suffrage Movement, 1869-1896*. New York: Garland, 1986. Provides a thorough discussion of the states that first granted suffrage to women. Gives particular attention to Utah's woman suffrage fight.

Catt, Carrie Chapman, and Nettie Rogers Shuler. *Woman Suffrage and Politics*. New York: Charles Scribner's Sons, 1926. Firsthand information on the fight for woman suffrage, written by a founder of the woman suffrage movement.

Coolidge, Olivia. *Women's Rights: The Suffrage Movement in America, 1848-1920*. New York: E. P. Dutton, 1966. Shows the tone of the early years of the movement and provides a time line of suffrage events.

Gurko, Miriam. *The Ladies of Seneca Falls: The Birth of the Woman's Rights Movement*. New York: Macmillan, 1974. An early history, with particular emphasis on Elizabeth Stanton and Lucretia Mott. Contains the wording of the Declaration of Sentiments.

McFadden, Margaret, ed. *Women's Issues*. 3 vols. Pasadena, Calif.: Salem Press, 1997. Comprehensive reference work with numerous articles on woman suffrage and related issues.

Schneir, Miriam. *Feminism: The Essential Historical Writings*. New York: Random House, 1972. Contains excerpts of writings by well-known suffragists and brief discussions of the history of these women.

SEE ALSO: Feb. 4, 1846: Mormons Begin Migration to Utah; July 19-20, 1848: Seneca Falls Convention; May 28-29, 1851: Akron Woman's Rights Convention; May 10, 1866: Suffragists Protest the Fourteenth Amendment; May, 1869: Woman Suffrage Associations Begin Forming; June 17-18, 1873: Anthony Is Tried for Voting; Mar. 9, 1875: *Minor v. Happersett*; July 4, 1876: Declaration of the Rights of Women; Feb. 17-18, 1890: Women's Rights Associations Unite; Sept. 19, 1893: New Zealand Women Win Voting Rights; Oct. 27, 1893: National Council of Women of Canada Is Founded.

RELATED ARTICLES in *Great Lives from History: The Nineteenth Century, 1801-1900:* Susan B. Anthony; Olympia Brown; Matilda Joslyn Gage; Lucretia Mott; Elizabeth Cady Stanton; Lucy Stone.

December 8, 1869-October 20, 1870
VATICAN I DECREES PAPAL INFALLIBILITY DOGMA

During an era when liberal ideas, political and religious, were gaining acceptance, the Vatican decreed that the pope was infallible in matters of doctrine and morality. The dogma reaffirmed that the pope was the absolute spiritual ruler of the Roman Catholic Church at a time when his role as temporal ruler of the Papal States was being effectively eliminated.

ALSO KNOWN AS: First Vatican Council
LOCALE: Rome (now in Italy)
CATEGORY: Religion and theology

KEY FIGURES

Pius IX (Giovanni Maria Mastai-Ferretti; 1792-1878), Roman Catholic pope, 1846-1878
Henry Edward Manning (1808-1892), English prelate
Johann Joseph Ignaz von Doellinger (1799-1890), German church historian

SUMMARY OF EVENT

In the wake of the French Revolution (1789), a rationalist worldview that had been generated in the preceding Enlightenment spread across Europe, challenging traditional Roman Catholic beliefs and the position of the Church in relation to civil governments. The Papal States were placed at risk, as nationalism swept the the Italian peninsula, and by 1861, Victor Emmanuel II, ruler of Piedmont-Sardinia, had become king of a united Italy. This nationalist triumph cost the papacy dearly, as its properties were absorbed into the new kingdom. Only Rome and its environs remained under the temporal rule of the pope, and the security of the Holy City depended upon the protection of French troops maintained there by Emperor Napoleon III.

In 1870-1871, France became embroiled in the Franco-Prussian War, requiring it to withdraw its forces from Rome. With no one to oppose it, the kingdom of Italy promptly invade Rome, annexing the last of the Papal States. Efforts to placate Pope Pius IX—now essentially barricaded within the Vatican—failed, leaving a hostile relationship between church and state that would prevail until 1929, when Benito Mussolini negotiated the Lateran Treaty with Pius XI.

Concurrent with the political and territorial problems confronting the Vatican, the pope had to deal with ideological currents that threatened the sanctity of the Church's doctrine as well as his own position at its head. Modern philosophies had strongly influenced the study and teaching of theology. At the same time, liberalism in politics was leading to democratic changes in many states.

When Pius IX became pope in 1846, Italy was bristling with revolutionary fervor, and the Papal States did not escape the effects of that fervor. The new pontiff at first granted concessions to dissidents, but they used their enhanced freedom to agitate for revolution. At one point, uprisings forced Pius to flee, leaving Rome in the grip of rebels. It was then that France responded to his plea for help and sent troops to restore his rule. This experience ended the pope's sympathy for political liberalism, and for the rest of his reign he opposed rationalism, secularism, and materialism, which he regarded as the roots of democracy. The pope's paternalism toward his subjects did not satisfy his critics, as he continued to claim sovereignty over lands lost to the emerging kingdom of Italy. The pope condemned the new national government and forbade Catholics to participate in its affairs.

Currier & Ives print of Pope Pius IX. (Library of Congress)

In the midst of Italy's turmoil but while Rome was still in his hands, Pius IX summoned the first Vatican Council. The purpose of the council was announced only vaguely as being to address modern errors and to advance the purity of morals. Only the pope's closest advisers knew that he intended the council to define papal infallibility, a doctrine to which most bishops subscribed that held that a pope was always correct in his interpretation of and pronouncements about Christian beliefs and practices. Many of the bishops, however, did not favor the definition and promulgation of that principle as Roman Catholic dogma at a time when Europe was unstable and liberals regarded the Church an obstacle to progress.

Catholics of an ultramontane persuasion—that is, champions of papal supremacy—for some time prior to the call for a council had urged making papal infallibility a dogma. Some, moreover, hoped the council would confirm the Syllabus of Errors, in which Pius IX had denounced eighty propositions of modern belief that he considered to be expressions of rationalism. The Jesuits, publishers of *Civiltà Cattolica*, were vigorous ultramontanes, and their influence with the pope was paramount. English archbishop Henry Edward Manning wrote to rebut the argument that the time was not opportune to make infallibility a dogma, for which the editors of *Civiltà Cattolica* commended him. Manning's influence was to be decisive at the council.

When participants gathered for the opening session on December 8, 1869, it was clear that a substantial minority opposed the dogmatic promulgation of the doctrine of papal infallibility at that time, even though the pope had claimed it in an 1846 encyclical and had declared the Immaculate Conception of the Virgin Mary a dogma without concilliar action in 1854. A preparatory commission set the agenda and rules of procedure so as to ensure success for Pius's intention, and 710 bishops, abbots, and generals of religious orders, a large majority of them Italians, assembled for the occasion.

The proceedings of the Vatican Council were secret, while its decisions were announced in public sessions. Latin was the language of discourse. Four areas of consideration occupied the councillors: doctrine, discipline, religious orders, and rites. In each matter, the purpose was to rebut contemporary deviations from Catholic tradition. Ultramontanes promoted a formal definition of papal infallibility as the best means to accomplish that end.

The pope's expectation of a brief, compliant council was not fulfilled. Several noteworthy ecclesiastics who opposed defining the dogma obstructed progress toward the pope's goal. Among them was the dean of the theological faculty in Paris, whose resistance prompted the rebuke of Archbishop Manning. American bishops from St. Louis, Cincinnati, and St. Augustine also joined the minority, and opposition among prelates in Germany and the Austro-Hungarian Empire was pronounced.

Although he did not attend the council, Johann Joseph Ignaz von Doellinger, a distinguished church historian at the University of Munich, was a determined critic of the Vatican Council whose erudition scholars would not ignore. The professor published a series of articles against infallibility per se, rather than merely contending that the time for promulgation of the dogma was inopportune. Doellinger's essays eventually appeared as a book assailing the ultramontane position in general and infallibility in particular. The vigor of his contentions aroused such consternation that some ultramontanes accused him of heresy, and the bishop of Regensburg prohibited theological students to attend his classes. When Doellinger refused to accept the dogma as affirmed by the council, the Church excommunicated him, but his university elevated him to the position of rector.

During the discussions about infallibility, many bishops of the minority were denied an opportunity to speak, and about eighty of them, to no avail, issued a complaint against the closure of debate. On July 13, 1870, the council voted on the *Schema de Ecclesia*, which contained the definition of infallibility. Of the 601 participants present, 451 affirmed the document, 88 denied it, and 62 accepted it with reservations. Next, 56 members of the minority indicated they would not change their position but would absent themselves from the public proceedings. Some 535 council members attended the final session on October 20, 1870, where all but 2 endorsed the dogma. Bishop Edward Fitzgerald of Little Rock, Arkansas, and Bishop Luigi Riccio of Sicily cast the only dissenting votes, but both submitted to the decision of the council.

Although it was a general council that authorized the promulgation of the dogma of papal infallibility, that action did not signify conciliar supremacy, nor even that the pope required such a council's validation to promulgate the dogma. Indeed, the official pronouncement asserted the primacy of the pope and proclaimed anathema on all who would deny it. In repetition of the Council of Florence (1439), the first Vatican Council (now known as Vatican I) affirmed papal primacy over the whole world. It proclaimed that the pope's judgment in matters of doctrine and morality was final, for he was subject to God alone.

Chapter 4 of the official proclamation cited the pope

as guardian of orthodoxy whenever he speaks *ex cathedra* (that is, from the throne, or in his official capacity as pope) on faith and morals as the shepherd and teacher of all Christians. His decrees of this nature are irreformable, because they are licensed by divine authority. The pope, however, is not considered to be infallible in ecclesiastical administration and discipline, and he alone decides when his pronouncements are or are not pronoucements *ex cathedra*. He is bound to act in accord with divine revelation and must rule in harmony with earlier definitions and creedal statements.

Significance

An immediate effect of Vatican I was the secession of a group of dissidents who formed the Old Catholic Church rather than accept the dogma of papal infallibility. Against the advice of Doellinger, the Old Catholics established congregations across Germany, Switzerland, and Austria, but these congregations won only a few thousand adherents.

Vatican I left the Roman Catholic Church securely in the control of a papal monarch, who at that time was committed to ideological combat with the modern world. Other Christian churches recoiled in contempt when the council issued its decrees. At the very time that other Christian bodies were drawing together in ecumenical relations, the Roman Catholic Church stood aloof, maintaining that it alone possessed the true Christian faith. Within the Church, the ultramontane faction had triumphed, to the delight of the Jesuits. In the era since the promulgation of the infallibility dogma, the pope has invoked *ex cathedra* only once—in 1954, when Pius XII declared the bodily assumption of the Virgin Mary into heaven a dogma of the faith.

—*James Edward McGoldrick*

Further Reading

Bokenkotter, Thomas. *A Concise History of the Catholic Church*. Rev. ed. New York: Doubleday Image Books, 1990. A lucid survey by a liberal Catholic author, this work includes substantial coverage of Vatican I.

Bressolette, Claude. "Vatican I." In *Encyclopedia of Christian Theology*. 3d ed. Edited by Jean-Yves Lacoste. New York: Routledge, 2005. This excellent summary offers a methodical coverage of the first Vatican Council and the dogma of papal infallibility.

Bury, J. B. *History of the Papacy in the Nineteenth Century*. Edited by R. H. Murray. London: Macmillan, 1930. This secularist history and interpretation emphasizes papal hostility to modern ideas.

Kueng, Hans. *Infallible? An Unresolved Enquiry*. Rev. ed. Translated by Eric Mossbach. London: SCM Press, 1994. The work of a controversial Catholic theologian in disfavor with the Vatican, this book expresses the concerns of many modern Church members.

MacGregor, Geddes. *The Vatican Revolution*. London: Macmillan, 1958. After a critical Protestant analysis of the issues, this book offers the full text of the Vatican decrees.

Pottmeyer, Hermann J. *Towards a Papacy in Communion: Perspectives from Vatican Councils I and II*. Translated by Matthew J. O'Connell. New York: Crossroad, 1998. An analysis of the doctrines issued by the first two Vatican Councils and their effects upon the history of the Roman Catholic papacy.

Tierney, Brian. *Origins of Papal Infallibility*. Leiden, Netherlands: E. J. Brill, 1972. This thorough study reflects the liberal view of an unorthodox Catholic historian often at odds with his church.

See also: 1820: Jesuits Are Expelled from Russia, Naples, and Spain; Jan. 12, 1848-Aug. 28, 1849: Italian Revolution of 1848; Dec. 8, 1854: Pius IX Decrees the Immaculate Conception Dogma; Feb. 11-July 16, 1858: Virgin Mary Appears to Bernadette Soubirous; Mar. 17, 1861: Italy Is Proclaimed a Kingdom; Dec. 8, 1864: Pius IX Issues the Syllabus of Errors; July 19, 1870-Jan. 28, 1871: Franco-Prussian War; 1871-1877: Kulturkampf Against the Catholic Church in Germany; 1881-1889: Bismarck Introduces Social Security Programs in Germany; May 15, 1891: Papal Encyclical on Labor.

Related articles in *Great Lives from History: The Nineteenth Century, 1801-1900:* Count Cavour; Napoleon III; Pius IX.

1870's
AESTHETIC MOVEMENT ARISES

English intellectuals and artists established the principles of art for art's sake and experience for experience's sake as a form of rebellion against Victorian moral judgment and Victorian restrictions on art, literature, and life.

LOCALE: England
CATEGORIES: Literature; art; cultural and intellectual history; crime and scandals

KEY FIGURES

Walter Pater (1839-1894), English essayist
Théophile Gautier (1811-1872), French poet, novelist, and critic
Oscar Wilde (1854-1900), Irish poet, playwright, and essayist
Arthur Symons (1865-1945), English essayist and poet
James McNeill Whistler (1834-1903), American painter
Gustave Flaubert (1821-1880), French novelist
Joris-Karl Huysmans (1848-1907), French novelist
Charles Baudelaire (1821-1867), French poet
Paul Verlaine (1844-1896), French poet
Stéphane Mallarmé (1842-1898), French poet

SUMMARY OF EVENT

The aesthetic movement's intellectual roots can be found in the writings of German Enlightenment philosopher Immanuel Kant and German poet, playwright, and novelist Johann Wolfgang von Goethe. Breaking with a centuries-old tradition regarding the function of art as a tool of instruction, both suggested that great art need not be didactic, or instructional. The concept that art, and literature, need not be didactic, coupled with the Romantic notion that art not only was mimetic but also expressive and reflective of a writer's experience of life, was influential in shaping the ideas of the first exponent of aestheticism, French writer Théophile Gautier.

Although Gautier earned his living as a critic, he thought of himself as a poet and also wrote fiction. Dismayed by the low status in which art was held in a growing materialistic society, he argued in the preface to his novel *Mademoiselle de Maupin* (1835-1836; English translation, 1887) that art is valuable only if it is useless. Artists must be free to deal with any subjects they choose; insofar as a poem, novel, play, musical composition, or painting serves as a vehicle for improving morals or social conditions, it is not really art. This revolutionary theory—art for art's sake—appealed to a select group who shared Gautier's Romantic sensibilities but was met with strong negative reaction in France and later in England; hence, the belief in art for art's sake became the rallying cry for a small coterie of practitioners and critics known as proponents of aestheticism.

While the French reading public continued to prefer the social realism of novelist Honoré de Balzac and the Romanticism of novelist Victor Hugo, Gautier's philosophy attracted a group of writers whose works reflect his advocacy of the care for form and the freedom from social constraints. Novelists Gustave Flaubert and Joris-Karl Huysmans, and poets Charles Baudelaire, Paul Verlaine, and Stéphane Mallarmé, were among the more noted practitioners of aesthetics. Several of these writers came to believe that artistic language should be different from everyday speech and writing, so they began to develop their own special meanings for common terms and to invest their work with meanings often not apparent to the general reader. Eventually, those who adopted these principles became known as Symbolists. Many broke with established conventions regarding subject matter, too, addressing taboo topics such as sexual relationships, heterosexual as well as homosexual, with a degree of frankness that scandalized their contemporaries.

Before the movement had attracted wide-scale attention from the English-speaking public, a handful of American and English writers had already begun to promote doctrines similar to those of Gautier. American writer and poet Edgar Allan Poe, an early devotee of Symbolist poetry, wrote in the posthumously published essay "The Poetic Principle" (1850) that art should be judged by standards other than moral or social; his ideas made him a kind of intellectual godfather to the generation of writers who would openly embrace aesthetic principles in the last three decades of the nineteenth century. Similarly, poets such as Dante Gabriel Rossetti and Algernon Charles Swinburne rebelled against strictures concerning subject matter and celebrated the kind of lifestyle that would become associated with the aesthetic movement by the century's end.

In England, the aesthetic movement can be understood best as a reaction to the dominant ideas held by the Victorians regarding the function of art, ideas promoted in the work of literary giants John Ruskin and Matthew Arnold. Although Ruskin concentrated on the visual arts and Arnold was mainly concerned with literature, both agreed that for art to be great, it must be useful in educating and uplifting its viewers and readers. Ruskin wrote in the third volume of his multivolume *Modern Painters* (1843-1860) that great art always included great ideas and could be produced only by those who possessed a noble nature.

Similarly, Arnold believed great literature possessed a quality he called high seriousness, the ability to help readers improve themselves (intellectually, if not materially) through the experience of engaging with a novel, poem, or play. In *Essays in Criticism* (1865 and 1888) he defined the critic's task as seeing "the object as in itself it really is," implying that it was possible for an artist's message to be understood and used as a guide for living. Hence, from Ruskin and Arnold the Victorians had learned that great art must be clear in its meaning and moral in its import. These notions were turned upside down by Walter Pater, an Oxford scholar whose 1873 work *Studies in the History of the Renaissance* became the bible for the English aesthetic movement.

In examining the work of a number of Renaissance artists, Pater abandons the practice of comparing works with one another, or looking to established external principles for determining value in a work of art. Instead, he tells the reader how he was affected by particular paintings, sculptures, and writings.

The ideas Pater advances in *Studies in the History of the Renaissance* were revolutionary in at least two ways. First, his call for art to exist for its own sake, as an object of beauty for contemplation by those of refined sensibilities, flew in the face of current theory about the function of art. Playfully reversing Arnold's premise, Pater insists that for the aesthetic critic, "the first step towards seeing one's object as it really is, is to know one's own impression as it really is." Reality, he goes on to argue, is simply a series of impressions, and the best one can do is to appreciate the impact of those impressions. This insight led to his second radical premise.

Pater argues that the way to make life worth living in the dreary, mechanistic world of Victorian Britain is to cultivate intense impressions, and to not follow conventional moral principles. Endorsing the notion that the goal of life is to pursue "not the fruit of experience, but experience itself," Pater announced in the conclusion to *Studies in the History of the Renaissance* that "to burn always with this hard, gemlike flame"—to seek experience for its own sake—would lead to happiness. For Pater there was no right or wrong experience; all were equally possible of promoting keen sensations, which in turn would give meaning and joy to life. Pater's pronouncement spawned a celebration of a lifestyle that would shock and offend "proper" Victorians: the life of the aesthete.

The reaction from mainstream Victorians to Pater's new doctrine was swift and negative. He was denounced in the *Quarterly Review* for substituting personal impressions for traditional critical principles. He was attacked for trying to set up the critic as a mediator between the artist and the world at large, thus investing critics with special knowledge. He was accused of promoting a philosophy of hedonism that encouraged people to pursue pleasure as the only end in life. These harsh commentaries, and others like them, caused Pater to withdraw the conclusion from several subsequent editions of *Studies in the History of the Renaissance*, but by that time his

James McNeill Whistler. (Library of Congress)

ideas had reached a generation of young artists already rebelling against the constraints of Victorian society.

What Pater stated explicitly as a theory had been the practice of several of his predecessors and contemporaries. The world of the visual arts had always had its iconoclasts, and several painters, most notably the Pre-Raphaelites, had been, since midcentury, creating art and living according to the principles promoted by Pater. Rossetti and other Pre-Raphaelites broke with convention in choosing their subjects and establishing their lifestyles before Pater identified the principal tenets of the aesthetic movement. The "aesthetic" works and lives of painters and designers such as Albert Joseph Moore, Sir Edward Coley Burne-Jones, and E. W. Godwin led to their being associated with the movement.

The visual artist who achieved perhaps the greatest notoriety as a practitioner of aestheticism was American painter James McNeill Whistler, who had emigrated to Europe in 1855. Whistler publicly promoted the idea that painting was concerned principally with composition, color, and form, a principle conveyed in his most famous painting, *Arrangement in Grey and Black, No. 1: The Artist's Mother* (1871), which is often erroneously called "Whistler's Mother." Whistler also cultivated an eccentric lifestyle that flouted convention and brought criticism from established art critics who were as scandalized by his behavior as they were chagrined by his artistic practices. Whistler sued Ruskin for libel when the critic wrote an unflattering review of one of his paintings.

Pater's impact on the rising generation of writers and artists in the last three decades of the nineteenth century was notable. Numbered among those who openly professed an affinity for aestheticism were the artist Aubrey Beardsley and poets Ernest Dowson and Lionel Johnson. During these decades, however, the aesthetic movement came to be associated with a lifestyle that promoted eroticism and even homosexuality. In that context, the most important figures were Arthur Symons and Oscar Wilde. Symons's essay "The Decadent Movement in Literature" (1893) and his book *The Symbolist Movement in Literature* (1899) not only provided a rationale for aestheticism but also developed a vocabulary for judging works produced according to the principles set forth by Pater and his disciples.

Wilde emerged as the most celebrated symbol of what became known as the Decadent movement of the last decades of the nineteenth century and into the early twentieth century in England. His outrageous dress and habits, as well as his rapier wit, earned him a worldwide reputation. He went out of his way to poke fun at Victorian conventions, writing a number of plays and essays that challenged Victorian values. His novel *The Picture of Dorian Gray* (1891), modeled on Huysmans's novel *Á Rebours* (1884; *Against the Grain*, 1922), offers a seductive portrait of a man named Des Esseintes who lives for sensual experiences. Wilde's homosexuality eventually led to public disgrace; in 1895 he was arrested for an affair with the son of a nobleman, was tried, convicted, and then sentenced to two years in jail for his crime. Those who had remained unconvinced in the value of aestheticism either as a critical principle or as a lifestyle frequently pointed to Wilde's eccentric rebellion as an object lesson in the bankruptcy of the concept.

SIGNIFICANCE

The effects of the aesthetic movement, although waning after Oscar Wilde's arrest, were nevertheless lasting and significant. Writers and critics adopted the concept put forth by Henry James in *The Art of Fiction* (1884) that the reader must grant artists the right to choose any subject, judging a work only by how well artists achieve the ends they set for themselves.

Aesthetic principles inspired the members of the Rhymers' Club, a group of poets organized in the 1890's by William Butler Yeats. The twentieth century modernists, especially members of the Bloomsbury Group, promoted ideas about art that derived from Pater's writings. The idea that perfection of form, not suitability of content, was the principal criterion for achieving greatness of art became one of the foundational tenets of New Criticism, a literary movement stressing form and technique over subject matter. The New Critics influenced academic study for nearly two-thirds of the twentieth century, making Pater's legacy as a literary critic exceptionally lasting.

—*Laurence W. Mazzeno*

FURTHER READING

Bell-Villada, Gene. *Art for Art's Sake and Literary Life*. Lincoln: University of Nebraska Press, 1996. Analyzes the development of aestheticism as a philosophical and literary movement from its origins in the eighteenth century to its persistence in the postmodern theory of the late twentieth century. Includes chapters on the diffusion of the doctrine in England, the United States, and continental Europe.

Chai, Leon. *Aestheticism: The Religion of Art in Post-Romantic Literature*. New York: Columbia University Press, 1990. Traces the development of the aesthetic movement from its roots in France through

English proponents such as Pater and Wilde. Demonstrates aestheticism's persistence in twentieth century literature and literary studies.
Court, Franklin E. *Pater and His Early Critics*. Victoria, B.C.: University of Victoria Press, 1980. Examines the reaction of important mainstream Victorian critics to Pater's work and provides a sense of the British public's understanding of the aesthetic movement.
Donoghue, Denis. *Walter Pater: Lover of Strange Souls*. New York: Alfred A. Knopf, 1995. A critical biography of Pater outlining the development of his ideas about art. Places his work in the context of nineteenth century literary and cultural criticism and traces his relationship with artists of his own and succeeding generations.
Robbins, Ruth. *Pater to Forster, 1873-1924*. Houndsmill, England: Palgrave Macmillan, 2003. Examines the importance of Pater's work in undermining Victorian ideas about morality and certitude. Also explores the work of disciples such as Symons and Wilde in reshaping attitudes about art and literature.
Shaffer, Talia. *The Forgotten Female Aesthetes: Literary Culture in Later Victorian England*. Charlottesville: University Press of Virginia, 2000. Traces the contributions of women to the development of the aesthetic movement and discusses a number of their works. Highlights differences in the reception given by the public to women and men practicing aestheticism.

See also: c. 1830's-1860's: American Renaissance in Literature; Fall, 1848: Pre-Raphaelite Brotherhood Begins; 1855: Courbet Establishes Realist Art Movement; 1861: Morris Founds Design Firm; c. 1865: Naturalist Movement Begins; 1884: New Guilds Promote the Arts and Crafts Movement; c. 1884-1924: Decadent Movement Flourishes; 1886: Rise of the Symbolist Movement; Nov. 8, 1900: Dreiser Publishes *Sister Carrie*.
Related articles in *Great Lives from History: The Nineteenth Century, 1801-1900:* Matthew Arnold; Honoré de Balzac; Charles Baudelaire; Aubrey Beardsley; Samuel Butler; Charles Dickens; Gustave Flaubert; John Keats; William Morris; Walter Pater; Edgar Allan Poe; John Ruskin; Percy Bysshe Shelley; James McNeill Whistler; Oscar Wilde; Émile Zola.

1870's
Japan Expands into Korea

Japan sought to expand its imperialistic ambitions and rival the great powers of Europe. Because Korea was considered a logical place for increased economic and political involvement around the world, Japan believed its expansion there could "liberate" Korea from Chinese influences, introduce modern technology to the peninsula, and send a statement to the world that Japan had newfound confidence and global aspirations.

Locale: Korean Peninsula
Categories: Expansion and land acquisition; colonization; diplomacy and international relations

Key Figures

Kuroda Kiyotaka (1840-1900), statesman and second prime minister of Japan, 1888-1889
Saigō Takamori (1827-1877), samurai leader
Enomoto Takeaki (1836-1908), Japanese admiral and statesman

Summary of Event

To satisfy its aspirations for modern statehood, much like that enjoyed by Great Britain, France, and Germany, the new Meiji government in Japan needed to take steps to define its territory. Doing so was considered a way to strengthen political will and to unite Japanese citizens under an umbrella of common national identity. Japan needed to reinvent itself into a modern, democratic nation instead of continuing the old ways of feudalism, shogun rule, samurai warriorship, and clan rivalry.

One way for Japan to reinvent itself was by colonization, just as the European powers had done in Asia and Africa. Although Japan was a latecomer in the race toward imperialism, the colonies could still be of benefit as markets for Japanese goods and as resources for raw materials to be manufactured in Japan. Colonies could be populated with new Japanese citizens loyal to both Japan and Emperor Meiji. The new military leaders in the Japanese army and navy looked at military expeditions to gain new colonies as a way to strengthen their reputations at home and to gain higher government positions once they returned from service abroad.

Japan's prestige rose with its rapid modernization and its scramble for new territory during the late nineteenth century. During the earlier Tokugawa era and rule by shoguns (1600-1868), Japan defined itself as the territory of the four major islands: Honshū (the mainland), Hokkaidō, Shikoku, and Kyūshū. The country had sought to unify politically the four islands and to add more territory from surrounding islands. The Sakhalin and Kuril Islands to the north were claimed by Russia but were only sparsely populated. The Okinawa Islands to the south were linguistically distinct from Japan though culturally related to both Japan and China. Okinawa had its own king and political structure, but it was weak and easy prey for the larger neighbor to the north. Japan made a move to annex Okinawa and subjugate the islanders under Emperor Meiji, after negotiations and limited conflict with Taiwan and China.

Japanese admiral Enomoto Takeaki had successfully bargained with Russia in 1875 to gain control over the Kurils by "giving back" Sakhalin in exchange for sole ownership of the Kuril Islands. Inhabitants on the Kuril Islands and Okinawa Islands would be considered subjects of Japan. The bargain with Russia marked the first major pact Japan had struck with a Western power that also had treated Japan as an equal. With new islands to control in 1875, Japan was eager for more colonies.

The next three obvious targets for Japanese territorial ambition were Taiwan, Korea, and China. A Japanese military force battled the Taiwanese in 1874 in response to a massacre of Japanese fisherman who had blown off course and drifted to Taiwan. Japan decided to punish the Taiwanese for their rash act. The success of this expedition and easy victory inspired confidence at home in the new Meiji government and the new military. Although more Japanese soldiers died from tropical disease than gunfire in the battle with Taiwan, the Meiji government used the victory as a stepping-stone to greater goals. China lost prestige in the conflict over Taiwan because Taiwan was considered Chinese culturally and politically. China acknowledged that Japan, because of its victory in Taiwan, had dominion over Okinawa. As a result, Japan had begun to feel more powerful and free to continue its imperial conquests.

The rivalry with China set the stage for Japanese expansion into Korea. Japan wanted the rest of the world to know that it had a modern government and a well-equipped army and navy. Japan saw itself as the one to bring modern industry and technology to Korea, which was being held back by a complacent Chinese government and stagnant Confucian cultural ways. Japan believed it had to take the lead in Asian development and expand its territory and not wait on the conservative regimes of Korea and China. Japanese government leaders wanted their country to be seen as a progressive, industrial, and imperial power. Some Japanese believed Japan was obligated to expand its influence and prevent European nations from further colonization.

Early Japanese diplomatic missions to Korea in 1873 had returned empty-handed. The Koreans had not respected Japan as much as it respected China. China was a much older civilization than was Japan, and most of the culture of Korea and Japan was Chinese in origin. Japan discussed engaging in a military intervention into Korea like the one it had engaged in Taiwan. Japan also wanted to "liberate" Korea from stifling Chinese influence. The plan was canceled, however, over fear of inciting a British counterreaction.

Many Japanese leaders, such as Saigō Takamori, argued for an invasion of Korea to strengthen Japan's image at home and abroad. Saigō, however, was suspicious of the Western values championed by other Meiji bureaucrats. In frustration over the canceled invasion, Saigō returned to his native province of Satsuma in 1877 and led a rebellion against his own Meiji government. The Satsuma Rebellion pitted the national army of Japan (which had superior training and modern weapons) against Saigō's army of traditional samurai. The national army easily defeated Saigō, and he committed ritual suicide on the battlefield.

Meiji government leaders viewed the Korean issue in different ways. Some, like Saigō, supported the political movement, known as the Seikanron debate (1873), which favored an armed invasion to liberate and improve Korea. In 1875, Japan had arranged for a high-level diplomatic venture to Korea to make clear Japan's aggressive foreign policy. To add seriousness to the mission, the diplomats traveled with three navy gunboats, but the Koreans were unimpressed with the Japanese show of force and fired upon one of their ships in Kanghwa Bay. Japan responded with a coastal bombardment, which led to the need for another diplomatic mission.

Kuroda Kiyotaka, the main diplomat to Korea after the conflict, regarded his mission to Korea as similar to the mission of Commodore Matthew C. Perry, who had helped "open" Japan to the West in 1854. Three gunboats escorted Kuroda, and he negotiated the Treaty of Kanghwa (1876), which authorized Japanese expansion onto the Korean peninsula. The treaty not only stated that Korea was independent and free from Chinese meddling; it also authorized the opening of three Korean ports for Japanese trade and established Japanese jurisdiction over Korea.

SIGNIFICANCE

Japan's drive to expand into Korea was a major move that would culminate in the global disaster of World War II (1939-1945). Japan's gaining a foothold in Korea had freed Korea from dependence on China and made a statement about Japan's strength and modernization. When Japan began to administer Korea, it made secret plans to invade China and bring its own version of "improvement" to the innocent citizens of Manchu province. In this relationship, Japan emerged as dominant and Korea as a weak and dependent state. Japan had endured such humiliation on the other side of the table in previous treaties with European powers during the 1850's. Now the tide had turned.

Historians argue that Korean expansion was not one piece of a larger plan to colonize all of Asia, but, instead, more of an effort to legitimize and shore up the authority of the new Meiji government at home. However, it seems clear that Japan also had imperialistic plans and wanted to acquire territory for more than political reasons.

—*Jonathan L. Thorndike*

FURTHER READING

Dudden, Alexis. *Japan's Colonization of Korea: Discourse and Power*. Honolulu: University of Hawaii Press, 2005. Includes a bibliography and an index.

Jansen, Marius B. *The Making of Modern Japan*. Cambridge, Mass.: Harvard University Press, 2000. Emphasis on Japan as a political entity emerging from Sekigahara and Tokugawa institutions that focused on domestic issues and moving through foreign relations and reform in education, industry, and culture toward modern statehood.

_______, ed. *The Emergence of Meiji Japan*. New York: Cambridge University Press, 1995. Major chapters on Tokugawa culture, the Meiji Restoration, opposing forces in Japanese society, and Japan's move toward imperialism and militarism.

Kim, Ki-Jung. "The Road to Colonization: Korea Under Imperialism." In *Korean History: Discovery of Its Characteristics and Developments*, edited by Korean National Commission for UNESCO. Elizabeth, N.J.: Hollym Press, 2004. Part of the Anthology of Korean Studies series. Explores the history of Korea under Japanese colonialism.

Lew, Young Ick. "Japanese Challenge and Korean Response, 1876-1910: A Brief Historical Survey." In *Korean History: Discovery of Its Characteristics and Developments*, edited by Korean National Commission for UNESCO. Elizabeth, N.J.: Hollym Press, 2004. Part of the Anthology of Korean Studies series. Explores the history of Korea under Japanese colonialism from the time of the Treaty of Kanghwa to 1910.

Pyle, Kenneth B. *The Making of Modern Japan*. Lexington, Mass.: D. C. Heath, 1996. Analysis of the political reform during the Meiji period that allowed for Japan's transformation into a modern nation rivaling nations of the West.

Strand, Wilson. "Opening the Hermit Kingdom: The Many Attempts to Open Korea to Western Trade in the Nineteenth Century." *History Today* 54, no. 1 (January, 2004): 20-29. A readable examination of how Korea was faced with modernizing forces that wanted to open its ports to Western trade.

Totman, Conrad. *A History of Japan*. London: Basil Blackwell, 2000. Explores Japan from ancient times, including its geographical and natural features. Extensive consideration of Japan's political, cultural, and social issues, from the industrial age to the end of the twentieth century.

SEE ALSO: Mar. 31, 1854: Perry Opens Japan to Western Trade; Jan. 3, 1868: Japan's Meiji Restoration; Apr. 6, 1868: Promulgation of Japan's Charter Oath; Jan.-Sept. 24, 1877: Former Samurai Rise in Satsuma Rebellion; July 23, 1882-Jan. 9, 1885: Korean Military Mutinies Against Japanese Rule; July 8, 1894-Jan. 1, 1896: Kabo Reforms Begin Modernization of Korean Government; Aug. 1, 1894-Apr. 17, 1895: Sino-Japanese War.

RELATED ARTICLES in *Great Lives from History: The Nineteenth Century, 1801-1900:* Itō Hirobumi; Mutsuhito; Matthew C. Perry; Saigō Takamori.

1870-1871
WATCH TOWER BIBLE AND TRACT SOCIETY IS FOUNDED

The founding of Jehovah's Witnesses by American Charles Taze Russell saw the emergence of a unique Christian group formed from early Bible study groups. By the beginning of the twenty-first century, the number of the sect's adherents had grown to more than six million people.

ALSO KNOWN AS: Zion's Watch Tower Tract Society; Watch Tower Bible and Tract Society
LOCALE: Allegheny, Pennsylvania
CATEGORIES: Religion and theology; organizations and institutions

KEY FIGURES

Charles Taze Russell (1852-1916), founder of the Watch Tower Bible and Tract Society
William Miller (1782-1849), founder of the Seventh-day Adventist Church
Joseph Franklin Rutherford (1869-1942), Russell's successor as leader of the movement

SUMMARY OF EVENT

The Watch Tower Bible and Tract Society that Charles Taze Russell founded in 1871 became officially known as the Jehovah's Witnesses in 1931. The society was originally inspired by the Seventh-day Adventist Church, whose adherents were part of a larger Christian millennial movement of the nineteenth century. Born into a Presbyterian family in Pennsylvania in 1852, Russell struggled with his faith as a young man. He joined a Congregational church at the age of fifteen but continued to question the Christian doctrines of predestination and eternal punishment. By the age of seventeen, he was very skeptical of Christianity in general and of the Bible in particular.

In 1870, Russell's faith was reestablished when he attended a Bible study meeting of Second Adventists. The Second Adventists (predecessors of the modern Seventh-day Adventist Church) can be traced to the Millerite movement of the 1830's. William Miller of upstate New York preached that the Bible contained encoded information that proved that the second coming of Jesus Christ would occur in 1843; many Americans believed him, and these Millerites (who called themselves Adventists) awaited the world's end and Christ's second coming. Miller withdrew from public life after his predictions were not manifested. Some of his followers maintained that Miller had been correct in that the end of the world and the second coming would be complete only after an indefinite period of "investigative judgment" in which Christ would judge the righteousness of the living and the dead.

Inspired by the Adventists, Russell organized and conducted his own Bible study meetings in 1870 and 1871. Disenchanted with the failed predictions of the Adventists, however, he emphasized that the second coming would be a spiritual and invisible event rather than an actual one. Russell wrote the pamphlet "The Object and Manner of the Lord's Return," in which he outlined his views on Christian theology. Reading similar views in Nelson H. Barbour's journal *The Herald of the Morning*, the two men agreed to jointly edit the journal. Russell and Barbour wrote *Three Worlds, and the Harvest of This World* (1877), in which they argued that Jesus Christ had returned to Earth invisibly in 1874 and that a forty-year period would elapse before the arrival of the end-time.

Charles Taze Russell around 1910. (Library of Congress)

By the end of the 1870's, Russell began to disassociate himself from Barbour and *The Herald*, and in 1879 he began publishing *Zion's Watch Tower and Herald of Christ's Presence* (later the *Watch Tower*). The new journal was very influential in the formation of thirty more congregations of Russell's followers in seven states. In 1881, Zion's Watch Tower Tract Society was informally established, and in 1884 the society was incorporated as an official religious organization. "Zion" was dropped from the name in 1896 and, in 1931, the name Jehovah's Witnesses was adopted. The 1884 charter stated that the group's purpose was for the "dissemination of Bible truths in various languages by means of the publication of tracts, pamphlets, papers and other religious documents."

In 1886, Russell began writing his *Studies in the Scriptures*. He would later write that true Christians needed to read both the Bible and his Scripture studies and that neither was sufficient without the other. *Studies in the Scriptures* was originally published in the *Watch Tower* and was republished in six separate volumes. The Bible was considered infallible by Jehovah's Witnesses. (In 1961, the group published its own English-language version of the Bible called the *New World Translation of the Holy Scriptures*.)

Russell's interpretation of Christianity held that God (called "Jehovah") was the all-powerful and all-knowing entity of the Hebrew Scriptures and did not recognize the Trinity. Russell preached that Satan is the enemy of Jehovah and that the way to resist the devil is by learning about Jehovah. He argued that the soul is mortal and that the resurrection will be of both body and soul. He argued that salvation came from accepting Jesus as Lord but that failing to meet Jehovah's requirements could result in the loss of salvation; only members of Jehovah's Witnesses would, however, achieve salvation in Heaven.

Hell, on the other hand, did not exist in Russell's teachings; he argued that a loving god would not subject souls to such torture. Those who did not qualify for salvation would simply disappear at the second coming. Finally, Jehovah's Witnesses cannot celebrate holidays such as Thanksgiving, Christmas, Easter, or birthdays because, as Russell and his followers believed, they are remnants of ancient false religions. The one day Witnesses were encouraged to celebrate is the anniversary of the death of Jesus Christ during Passover.

Russell lived to see the forty-year period of the invisible second coming reach an end in 1914. According to Jehovah's Witnesses doctrine, Christ did return to establish a heavenly paradise; Satan and his evil angels were banished from heaven and now live on Earth. This is how Jehovah's Witnesses explain crime and violence in the world today.

Russell died in 1916 and was succeeded as the president of the Jehovah's Witnesses by the group's lawyer, Joseph Franklin Rutherford. It was under Rutherford's presidency that the group became more centrally organized and also suffered schisms. Under his leadership the name "Jehovah's Witnesses" was adopted, and members were discouraged from joining the armed forces. Rutherford died in 1942 and was succeeded as president by Nathan Homer Knorr, who served during the publication of the *New World Translation*. Knorr was succeeded in 1977 by his vice president, Frederick W. Franz; he was succeeded in 1992 by Milton G. Henschel.

SIGNIFICANCE

The nineteenth century was a time in which many Americans reexamined the doctrines of their Christian faith. During the 1820's, after increasing industrialization greatly disrupted traditional social and economic structures in the United States, evangelists across the nation began encouraging people to rededicate themselves to their beliefs in God and Jesus Christ.

The series of religious revivals that followed during the next decades (commonly known as the Second Great Awakening) saw many schisms in established churches, as well as the formation of new religious groups and utopian communities (including those at Brook Farm in Massachusetts, Oneida in New York, and New Harmony in Indiana). Some of the new groups explained the disruptions within society (including the carnage of the U.S. Civil War) as proof that the world was to come to an end soon and that the second coming of Jesus Christ was imminent. These millennialist groups, including the Millerites, the Seventh-day Adventists, and Jehovah's Witnesses, attracted large numbers of adherents, but most of them lost large numbers of members when appointed days for the end-time came and went without incident.

Jehovah's Witnesses successfully weathered the religious storm that confronted many of the millennialist religious groups of the nineteenth century. The doctrines of Charles Taze Russell allowed for the second coming of Jesus Christ into a modern world that seems to have proved the particulars of his theology.

—*Kay J. Carr*

FURTHER READING

Horowitz, David. *Pastor Charles Taze Russell: An Early American Christian Zionist*. New York: Philosophical Library, 1986. A biography of the founder of the Jehovah's Witnesses.

New World Translation of the Holy Scriptures, Rendered from the Original Languages by the World Bible Translation Committee. Brooklyn, N.Y.: Watchtower Bible and Tract Society of New York, 1961. The translation of the Bible by a committee of Jehovah's Witnesses.

Penton, M. James. *Apocalypse Delayed: The Story of Jehovah's Witnesses*. 2d ed. Buffalo, N.Y.: University of Toronto Press, 1997. A survey of the history and theology of Jehovah's Witnesses.

Russell, Charles Taze. *Studies in the Scriptures*. 6 vols. Philadelphia: P. S. L. Johnson, 1937. The doctrinal writings of Russell, the founder of Jehovah's Witnesses.

SEE ALSO: May 8, 1816: American Bible Society Is Founded; 1820's-1850's: Social Reform Movement; c. 1826-1827: First Meetings of the Plymouth Brethren; Apr. 6, 1830: Smith Founds the Mormon Church; 1835: Finney Lectures on "Revivals of Religion"; July, 1865: Booth Establishes the Salvation Army; Sept., 1875: Theosophical Society Is Founded; Oct. 30, 1875: Eddy Establishes the Christian Science Movement; Feb., 1896-Aug., 1897: Herzl Founds the Zionist Movement.

RELATED ARTICLES in *Great Lives from History: The Nineteenth Century, 1801-1900:* William Booth; Alexander Campbell; Mary Baker Eddy; Joseph Smith; Brigham Young.

January 10, 1870
STANDARD OIL COMPANY IS INCORPORATED

John D. Rockefeller and his associates turned their partnership into the joint-stock corporation Standard Oil, which planned to use stock to facilitate purchase of competitive refineries. Within two years, Standard controlled more than 30 percent of American refining capacity.

LOCALE: Cleveland, Ohio
CATEGORIES: Business and labor; economics

KEY FIGURES

John D. Rockefeller (1839-1937), president of Standard Oil
William Rockefeller (1841-1922), vice president of Standard Oil
Henry M. Flagler (1830-1913), secretary-treasurer of Standard Oil
Thomas A. Scott (1823-1881), vice president of the Pennsylvania Railroad

SUMMARY OF EVENT

On January 10, 1870, the oil refining partnership of Rockefeller, Andrews & Flagler dissolved and reconstituted itself as the Standard Oil Company, a joint-stock corporation organized under the laws of the state of Ohio. The founders did not intend to sell stock to the public but planned to use stock to pay for acquiring other refineries while maintaining control in the hands of John D. Rockefeller, William Rockefeller, and Henry M. Flagler.

The new corporation, capitalized at $1,000,000, may already have been the largest oil company in the world. Its two great Cleveland refineries contained one-tenth of the petroleum refining capacity of the United States; it occupied sixty acres of land, operated its own large barrel-making factory and shipping facilities on the Great Lakes, owned tank cars and warehouses in the oil regions of Pennsylvania, and owned tanks and lighters in the Port of New York.

John D. Rockefeller, the dominant manager, early recognized the value of economies of scale and built the largest possible plants, stressing maximum efficiency. Standard became noted for the detailed records it kept of its operations and costs. (Rockefeller would boast in his memoirs of how much profit the company had accumulated over the years because he found a way to save one cent on the construction of each barrel.) Large-scale operation provided savings in the production of kerosene for lamps, then the predominant refinery product, and the residual matter that smaller refineries treated as waste could be profitably manufactured into lubricants, waxes, candles, and other salable by-products.

The company charter had one serious disadvantage: Ohio corporations were forbidden to own property outside the state, and Standard Oil had to use subterfuge and secrecy to cover its Pennsylvania and New York branches. Secrecy, however, could be a useful business tactic, and it became characteristic of Standard's operations, permitting the corporation to engage in activities it preferred not to admit. Standard would be accused of having secret subsidiaries undersell competitors and drive them out of business, and of using unacknowledged firms to surreptitiously buy opponents who contemptuously rejected direct offers from Standard.

Because oil production was then limited to northwestern Pennsylvania, the oil-producing regions and Pittsburgh appeared to be the best locations for refineries. However, the cost of shipping to port cities was a major factor affecting refinery profitability at a time when the United States, the world's largest producer of petroleum, exported two-thirds of the kerosene it produced. The oil regions and Pittsburgh mostly depended on the Pennsylvania Railroad for access to ports. Cleveland refiners, served by three railroads—the New York Central-Lake Shore combination, the Erie, and the Pennsylvania—and with access to the Great Lakes and Erie Canal water route to New York City, successfully bargained for lower rates, despite their greater distance from markets.

Railroads competed for business by offering secret discounts from official rates to favored shippers. Although not explicitly illegal until the Interstate Commerce Act of 1887, such rebates were never published or put in writing. Their existence, however, was common knowledge; all shippers strove for the biggest discounts they could get, but no one received as many or on as large a scale as Rockefeller and his associates. In 1868, Flagler won a rate of $1.65 per barrel to New York City, instead of the official $2.40, in exchange for agreeing to regularly ship sixty carloads per day. Critics of Standard claimed that insistence on secrecy proved rebates were unethical and immoral, even if not technically criminal, while defenders argued everybody did it and Standard deserved its special privileges because of the volume of traffic it generated.

In November, 1871, Rockefeller learned of a plan proposed by Thomas A. Scott of the Pennsylvania Railroad to end railroad price wars, raise rates to a profitable level, and guarantee each participating road a fair share of the oil traffic. Standard Oil, and the Pittsburgh and Philadelphia refiners also invited to join the South Improvement Company, would act as "eveners," distributing their shipments among the three oil-carrying railroads according to fixed percentages. In return, the preferred refiners would receive not only a substantial rebate from the increased official rate but also a comparable drawback on shipments by nonmembers of the South

John D. Rockefeller and his son, John D. Rockefeller, Jr., in 1915. (Library of Congress)

Improvement Company. Allan Nevins, in his favorable biography of John D. Rockefeller, wrote, "Of all devices for the extinction of competition, this [the drawbacks] was the cruelest and most deadly yet conceived by any group of American industrialists."

Although hesitant at first to join the scheme, Rockefeller and other Standard Oil officers took nine hundred of the two thousand shares issued by the South Improvement Company. On January 1, 1872, anticipating opportunities for expansion, the Standard Oil board increased its capitalization to $2.5 million, authorizing issuance of another $1.5 million in stock.

Word of the plot began to circulate in mid-February, 1872. When the railroads confirmed the rumors by announcing joint rate increases, producers and refiners in the oil regions reacted with fury, holding mass meetings, petitioning the state to revoke the South Improvement Company charter, and organizing a boycott of the offending refiners that cut off crude oil supplies to Standard, forcing it to drastically reduce production. Not until early April, after Rockefeller confirmed he was abandoning the scheme, did oil again flow to Cleveland.

Rockefeller always rejected assertions that the South Improvement device explained the growth of Standard Oil. He stressed that railroads, not Standard Oil, originated the idea, and because no oil ever shipped under the scheme, no one paid increased rates or suffered from drawbacks. Both assertions were correct, but Rockefeller carefully ignored the role played by fear of the South Improvement Company in his 1872 consolidation of Cleveland refineries, a move later called the Cleveland Massacre.

Between February 17, when rumors of the plan began to circulate, and March 28, when the railroads canceled their rate increases, Standard bought twenty-two of Cleveland's twenty-six independent refineries. To reduce the glut of kerosene on the market, Rockefeller planned to close most of the newly purchased refineries—only four of the acquired refineries were still operating at year's end. Standard then appraised most plants at scrap value, usually a quarter or less of what they had cost to build. It is difficult to explain the willingness of owners to accept such harsh terms, absent the climate of fear created by knowledge of Standard Oil's overwhelming competitive advantage under the South Improvement scheme.

SIGNIFICANCE

John D. Rockefeller and his associates were planning growth when they incorporated on January 10, 1870, but no one, not even the ambitious Rockefeller, could have foreseen such spectacular success. Taking advantage of economic distress during the depression of 1873-1878, Standard expanded its ownership share to 90 percent. To evade restrictions in the Ohio charter, managers of newly acquired plants were told to pretend they were still independent.

As they reorganized the refining industry, the managers of Standard Oil continued a policy of operating only the largest, most efficient, and technologically advanced plants. They preferred stable prices and steady income to spectacular profits that would encourage newcomers to enter the field. Despite the negative effect on the fortunes of competitors, there is no evidence that Standard adversely affected the economy of the United States during the nineteenth century.

The massive size of the company, however, and its monopoly over a major sector of the economy aroused uneasiness among opinion makers; the secrecy with which Standard carried out its coups magnified into fear. Rockefeller's stoic refusal to answer personal attacks enhanced the problem, as his very silence seemed both arrogant and proof he was hiding something. Standard Oil became the most hated corporation and Rockefeller the most reviled person in the country. Governmental investigations in the 1880's revealed enough questionable activity to stimulate the nineteenth century antimonopoly, trust-busting movement that eventually led to a judicial order breaking up the corporation in 1911.

—*Milton Berman*

FURTHER READING

Bradley, Robert L., Jr. *Oil, Gas & Government: The U.S. Experience*. 2 vols. Lanham, Md.: Rowman & Littlefield, 1996. Bradley, an economist, uses private enterprise ideology to defend Standard Oil Company against all criticisms, except that of poor public relations management.

Chernow, Ron. *Titan: The Life of John D. Rockefeller, Sr.* New York: Random House, 1998. In this thoroughly researched biography, Chernow skeptically examines Rockefeller's defensive explanations of the growth of Standard Oil.

Nevins, Allan. *Study in Power: John D. Rockefeller, Industrialist and Philanthropist*. 2 vols. New York: Charles Scribner's Sons, 1953. The first biographer to have access to company and family source material on Rockefeller, Nevins defends most of Standard Oil's actions.

Tarbell, Ida M. *The History of the Standard Oil Company*. 1904. Reprint. Edited by David M. Chalmers. New York: Dover, 2003. The classic Progressive period attack—abridged for this reprint—on Standard Oil condemns the company as unethical when not criminal, claiming it made ruthless use of South Improvement Company methods throughout its existence.

Weinberg, Arthur, and Lila Weinberg, eds. *The Muckrakers*. Urbana: University of Illinois Press, 2001. Words from muckrakers, or critics, of corporate and other scandals and political corruption, including two articles by Ida Tarbell on the Standard Oil Company.

Whitten, David O., and Bessie E. Whitten. *The Birth of Big Business in the United States, 1860-1914: Commercial, Extractive, and Industrial Enterprise*. Westport, Conn.: Praeger, 2006. An economic and standard history of major business in the United States before World War II. Includes a chapter on Standard Oil.

See also: 1850: First U.S. Petroleum Refinery Is Built; Aug. 27, 1859: Commercial Oil Drilling Begins; Jan. 2, 1882: Standard Oil Trust Is Organized; Jan. 29, 1886: Benz Patents the First Practical Automobile; Feb. 4, 1887: Interstate Commerce Act; July 20, 1890: Harrison Signs the Sherman Antitrust Act; Feb., 1892: Diesel Patents the Diesel Engine.

Related articles in *Great Lives from History: The Nineteenth Century, 1801-1900:* Andrew Carnegie; Rudolf Diesel; Dmitry Ivanovich Mendeleyev; John D. Rockefeller; Cornelius Vanderbilt.

April, 1870-1873
Schliemann Excavates Ancient Troy

The excavation of the legendary city of Troy, the Hissarlik archaeological site in what is now Turkey, began with media hype and questionable archaeological practices, both perpetrated by Heinrich Schliemann.

Locale: Hissarlik, Turkey; Greece
Categories: Archaeology; science and technology

Key Figures

Heinrich Schliemann (1822-1890), amateur archaeologist and businessman
Frank Calvert (1828-1908), archaeologist and antiquarian

Summary of Event

The son of a schoolmaster and clergyman in the north German area of Mecklenburg-Schwerin, Heinrich Schliemann mythologized much of his own life. Apparently his childhood was harsh and his schooling minimal, which destined him for a career in the trades. He was, however, bright and industrious, was a voracious reader, and had an early flair for languages—he reportedly learned a dozen or so through his years.

Schliemann studied business clerking in Amsterdam and at twenty-two years of age joined a major mercantile firm. Sent to St. Petersburg, Russia, by the firm, he became a very successful commodities dealer there. Following family footsteps to California during the gold rush, Schliemann opened a bank there to trade in prospectors' gold. Back in St. Petersburg, he married a Russian woman, with whom he had three children. During the Crimean War (1853-1856) he profited enormously from dealings in wartime commodities. He made another fortune in cotton and other products during the U.S. Civil War (1861-1865).

Several rounds of international travel and the frequenting of museums stimulated Schliemann's interest in past cultures. On one tour, he carried off a stone from the Great Wall of China in his fascination with the structure. Sufficiently wealthy to retire from business by the age of forty-one, Schliemann hungered to enter some area of scholarly endeavor. In Paris he pursued some formal studies, making intellectual contacts, reading widely, and developing a taste for antiquities. The science of archaeology was still in its infancy, and Schliemann was drawn to it as much as a collector as for scholarly discovery. Beginning a new tour of Mediterranean lands in early 1868, Schliemann studied archaeological undertakings in Rome and Pompeii. It was the world of early Greece, though, to which he was attracted.

Like many well-read Europeans of his time, Schliemann was familiar with the ancient Greek epics of Homer. Like a good romantic of his time he was prepared to accept them as factual accounts, even though serious scholars had long rejected them as legends. Identifying himself with Homer's wandering Odysseus (Ulysses), Schliemann proceeded to the Ionian island of Ithaca, where he made his first primitive venture into some archaeological digging, on what he imagined was the site of Odysseus's palace.

Hungering for new sites and objects, Schliemann stopped in Athens, where a local scholar suggested the Troad at the Dardanelles, the northwestern corner of Asia Minor, in the heart of the Ottoman Empire (now in Turkey). Schliemann was directed to the hill of Pinarbashi (Bunarbashi), which some antiquarians thought was the site of ancient Troy. He was also advised to consult a local expert, the Englishman Frank Calvert, who was then serving as the U.S. vice-consul for the region. Making his way to Pinarbashi in August, 1868, Schliemann initially avoided Calvert, reconnoitering and then undertaking some ill-defined and fruitless excavations. Only when about to leave did he meet Calvert. Calvert had spent years exploring the area's topography and sites. First interested in Pinarbashi, he rejected it as the site of Troy, which he now firmly believed was the hill called Hissarlik. He had even purchased a portion of the hill and wanted to excavate it himself but lacked financial means.

Schliemann was given a crash course by the Englishman on what Hissarlik represented. Calvert recognized that this wealthy enthusiast had the means to do what he himself could not afford to do, while Schliemann recognized a golden opportunity at hand. In proposing a partnership with Schliemann, however, Calvert not only shared his dream but sacrificed it to an opportunist whose character he did not understand.

While Schliemann spent months in correspondence and securing permissions from local Turkish authorities, he began consolidating his standing. He published a book exaggerating his work on Ithaca but staking his claims as a serious archaeologist. With that he secured an honorary doctorate from the University of Rostock, thus acquiring instant scholarly stature that Calvert, the gentleman-antiquarian, lacked. Moreover, in a quick trip to the United States, Schliemann gained U.S. citizenship, which he used deviously to obtain a divorce from the Russian wife who had refused to follow him in his adventures. Thus freed to extend his philhellenism, the forty-seven-year-old Schliemann found himself a new Greek bride, seventeen-year-old Sophia Engastromenos from Athens.

In April, 1870, Schliemann began serious excavations at Hissarlik. From the start, he engaged in constant duplicity, breaking agreements with Calvert, and practicing forms of digging that would be considered vandalism by twenty-first century archaeological standards. Ignoring Calvert's advice, he had large trenches dug that created a huge north-south gash across the hill. The successive campaign years turned up numerous finds that reinforced the hill's identification with Troy. However, Schliemann was quite unprepared for the complex layering of strata in his quest to identify the Troy of Homer's King Priam. Further conflicts developed over Schliemann's cheating Calvert out of his share of treasures, and there was even a rupture between them when Calvert argued in print against reckless interpretations of the site that Schliemann was circulating with his self-serving publicity.

TROY IN THE MODERN MEDITERRANEAN REGION

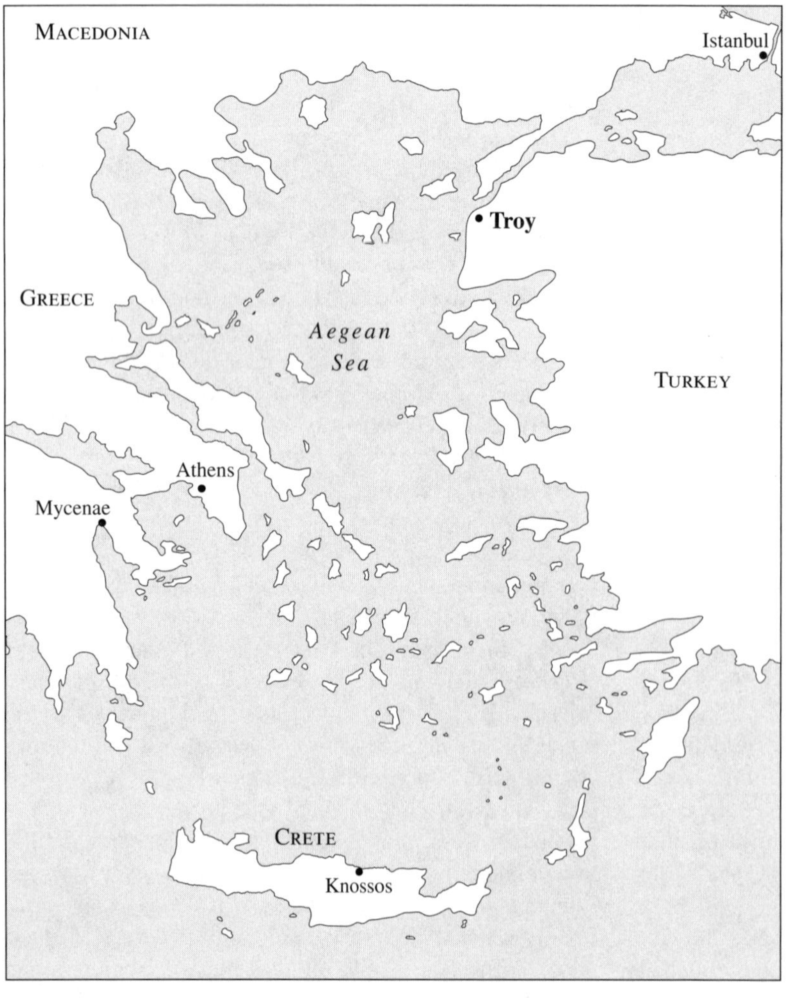

The climax of Schliemann's excavations came on May 31, 1873, when he came upon a body of copper and gold objects, including jewelry. He called this trove "Priam's treasure," reporting that he had recovered it with the help of his wife. In fact, Sophia was in Athens at the time of the discovery. Some critics have speculated that the so-called treasure was never actually found and that it was actually made up of objects Schliemann had purchased on the black market and placed on the site for discovery. Defying his

Contemporary woodcut showing Heinrich Schliemann's excavations around the southeastern gate of ancient Troy. (North Wind Picture Archives)

contract with the Turkish government, Schliemann smuggled these objects to Athens, to install them in his home there for exhibition and photography. A picture of his wife bedecked in the so-called "Helen's jewels" was circulated worldwide at the peak of Schliemann's self-promotion. The objects eventually found their way to Berlin, from which they were later carried off into obscurity by the Russians after World War II. In 1993, they were found to be preserved at Moscow's Pushkin Museum.

Schliemann faced fury and long legal actions from Constantinople, and only after a financial settlement was he allowed further access to Troy. In 1874, he published his excavation reports. The book, *Troja und seine Ruinen* (*Troy and Its Remains: A Narrative of Researches and Discoveries Made on the Site of Ilium and in the Trojan Plain*, 1875), consolidated his fame as the discoverer of Homer's Troy and, in the process, buried any credit due Calvert. Indeed, in his autobiographical writings, Schliemann even appropriated from Calvert the story that he had nourished since childhood the determination to find and reveal Homer's Troy.

On the basis of his sensational work at Troy, Schliemann was allowed to conduct excavations in Greece at Mycenae in 1876, where he cleared the grave circle and discovered its famous burial masks. In 1878-1879, amid uneasy reconciliation with Calvert, Schliemann pursued new excavations at Troy. He also ventured some further "Homeric" explorations at Ithaca (1878), Orchomenos (1881), and Tiryns (1884-1885), while continuing his prolific outpouring of writings and publications. A celebrity of worldwide standing, and now one of the great men of Greece, he built himself and Sophia a grand mansion (still standing) in downtown Athens.

Meanwhile, the perplexities of Troy continued to draw Schliemann. With Calvert's collaboration, he undertook new explorations of the area in 1882. He continued his involvement with the site, attending an international conference held there in 1889 to clarify the identity of Hissarlik. His plans for further investigations in 1890 were cut short by his death during a visit to Naples. Schliemann's remains were brought to Athens and buried in a grandiose neoclassical mausoleum on a hilltop in the city's main cemetery.

SIGNIFICANCE

The tangled explications of the various layers of Hissarlik's settlements were resumed by Schliemann's assistant, architect Wilhelm Dörpfeld, and they continue into the twenty-first century, albeit on a more scientific scale. Schliemann had demonstrated that the stories of a Trojan War corresponded to tangible evidence, and that Hissarlik was the site of the ancient Troy, but his brutal excavation techniques ironically destroyed much of what remained of the Trojan city.

Acclaimed as the founder of archaeology, Schliemann awakened a broad public to this new science. His methods, however, now evoke horror, and his shameful suppression of Calvert's role is now evident.

—*John W. Barker*

FURTHER READING

Allen, Susan Heuck. *Finding the Walls of Troy: Frank Calvert and Heinrich Schliemann at Hisarlik*. Berkeley: University of California Press, 1999. The fullest account of the pivotal relationship between Schliemann and Calvert.

Blegen, Carl W. *Troy and the Trojans*. Ancient Peoples and Places 33. New York: Praeger, 1963. Analysis of the site and its history by one of the leading twentieth century excavators.

Calder, William M., III, and David A. Traill, eds. *Myth, Scandal, and History: The Heinrich Schliemann Controversy*. Detroit: Wayne State University Press, 1986. Collection of scholarly essays that evaluate Schliemann's career, achievements, and image.

Deuel, Leo. *Memoirs of Heinrich Schliemann*. New York: Harper & Row, 1977. Thorough analysis of Schliemann's life, with generous selections from his own works, letters, and diaries. Balanced, with careful criticism and analytical sections, full notes, and a bibliography.

Ludwig, Emil. *Schliemann: The Story of a Gold-Seeker*. Translated by D. F. Tait. Boston: Little, Brown, 1931. One of the few biographies of Schliemann in English, and the first to raise some critical questions about his methods and intentions.

Moorehead, Caroline. *The Lost Treasures of Troy*. London: Weidenfeld & Nicolson, 1994. A history of the materials that Schliemann uncovered at Troy, describing how his finds were handled from their excavation through the early 1990's.

Runnels, Curtis. *The Archaeology of Heinrich Schliemann: An Annotated Bibliographic Handlist*. Boston: Archaeological Institute of America, 2002. An eighty-one-page reference source for works related to Schliemann and his work, archaeology, and the city of Troy. Includes a map.

Schliemann, Heinrich. *Troy and Its Remains: A Narrative of Researches and Discoveries Made on the Site of Ilium, and in the Trojan Plain*. Edited by Philip Smith. New York: Arno Press, 1976. A translated edition of the archaeologist's excavation reports of Troy, originally published in 1874. Includes bibliographic footnotes and an index.

Stone, Irving. *The Greek Treasure: A Biographical Novel of Heinrich and Sophia Schliemann*. Garden City, N.Y.: Doubleday, 1975. Best-selling novel about Schliemann's archaeological work that is most useful for providing vivid images of his digs and contemporary Greek culture.

Traill, David A. *Schliemann of Troy: Treasure and Deceit*. New York: St. Martin's Press, 1995. The most thorough myth-busting biography of Schliemann.

Wood, Michael. *In Search of the Trojan War*. Berkeley: University of California Press, 1988. Based upon a BBC television series. A very readable survey of Troy's lure and its attraction to archaeologists.

SEE ALSO: 1803-1812: Elgin Ships Parthenon Marbles to England; Mar. 22, 1812: Burckhardt Discovers Egypt's Abu Simbel; 1814-1879: Exploration of Arabia; 1839-1847: Layard Explores and Excavates Assyrian Ruins; Nov., 1839: Stephens Begins Uncovering Mayan Antiquities; Sept. 12, 1853: Burton Enters Mecca in Disguise; Mar. 23, 1900: Evans Discovers Crete's Minoan Civilization.

RELATED ARTICLES in *Great Lives from History: The Nineteenth Century, 1801-1900:* Sir Richard Francis Burton; Sir Arthur Evans; Heinrich Schliemann.

July 19, 1870-January 28, 1871
FRANCO-PRUSSIAN WAR

The result of failed diplomacy, the Franco-Prussian War made possible German unification, upset the balance of power in Europe, and laid the basis for the twentieth century's world wars.

LOCALE: France; Prussia; southern Germany
CATEGORY: Wars, uprisings, and civil unrest

KEY FIGURES

Otto von Bismarck (1815-1898), chancellor of the North German Confederation, minister-president of Prussia, and chancellor of the German Empire, 1871-1890

Napoleon III (Louis Napoleon Bonaparte; 1808-1873), emperor of France, r. 1852-1870

Antoine-Agénor-Alfred Gramont (1819-1880), French minister of foreign affairs

Léon Gambetta (1838-1888), French republican politician

Leopold (1835-1905), candidate for the Spanish throne and distant relative of Prussia's King William I

Marie-Edme-Patrice-Maurice de MacMahon (1808-1893), French general

William I (Wilhelm I; 1797-1888), Hohenzollern king of Prussia, 1861-1888, and emperor of Germany, r. 1871-1888

SUMMARY OF EVENT

The July, 1870, outbreak of war between France and Prussia and the latter's German allies resulted from factors that had been building for more than a decade. Prussia and France had gradually moved toward a decisive struggle for hegemony on the Continent as other European countries stood aloof for various reasons. Great Britain concentrated on its overseas empire and paid little attention to the balance of power on the Continent. Austria was recovering from the defeat administered in 1866 by Prussia, which unified all of northern Germany (North German Confederation). Russia was suffering still from its defeat in the Crimean War. The newly formed kingdom of Italy was guided by its nationalist aspirations, especially the goal of making Rome the capital of its secular state despite the objections of the pope. For these and other reasons, no other European powers entered the struggle that erupted between Prussia and France.

From the time of Prussia's defeat of Austria in 1866, many French and German citizens believed that war between France and Prussia was inevitable. The prospect of German unification under the leadership of a powerful Prussia not only was contrary to traditional French foreign policy but also was a threat to French dominance of Europe. France traditionally maintained excellent relations with the Roman Catholic states of southern Germany, such as Bavaria, whose governments often distrusted the militaristic government of Protestant Prussia. Southern Germans shared the dream of a united Germany, however, and Prussia had clearly assumed the lead in the German nationalist movement.

Napoleon III, the French emperor, apparently believed that political unification of the major national groups would lead to international cooperation. Although he was not totally opposed to the goal of German unification, he realized that Prussia's recent victories had increased Prussian power at the expense of French prestige. He attempted to redress the balance through negotiations whereby France would gain territory by annexing French-speaking areas such as Luxembourg. Prussia first approved and then rejected these arrangements in 1867. Afterward, the French government grew increasingly hostile to Prussian initiatives.

With this background of tension, the crisis that finally led to war was the Spanish provisional government's search for a monarch to replace the ousted Queen Isabella II. As one candidate after another proved either unworthy or unwilling to occupy the Spanish throne, the Spaniards turned to Prince Leopold of Hohenzollern-Sigmaringen, a Prussian infantry officer and distant relative of King William I of Prussia. Both King William and his family were hesitant to permit Leopold to ascend the shaky Spanish throne. Only the combined efforts of the Spanish emissaries and of Prussian chancellor Otto von Bismarck persuaded the king to allow Leopold's candidacy.

There is no doubt that from at least May of 1870, Bismarck encouraged Leopold's candidacy, hoping it might provoke a crisis useful to the process of German unification. Bismarck apparently feared that France was growing stronger. In a May referendum, French voters had overwhelmingly endorsed both the leadership of Emperor Napoleon III and the creation of a constitutional monarchy. As Bismarck had expected, the French were enraged over their diplomatic defeat and the potential threat that placing a German prince on the Spanish throne posed to their security. Both the French government and

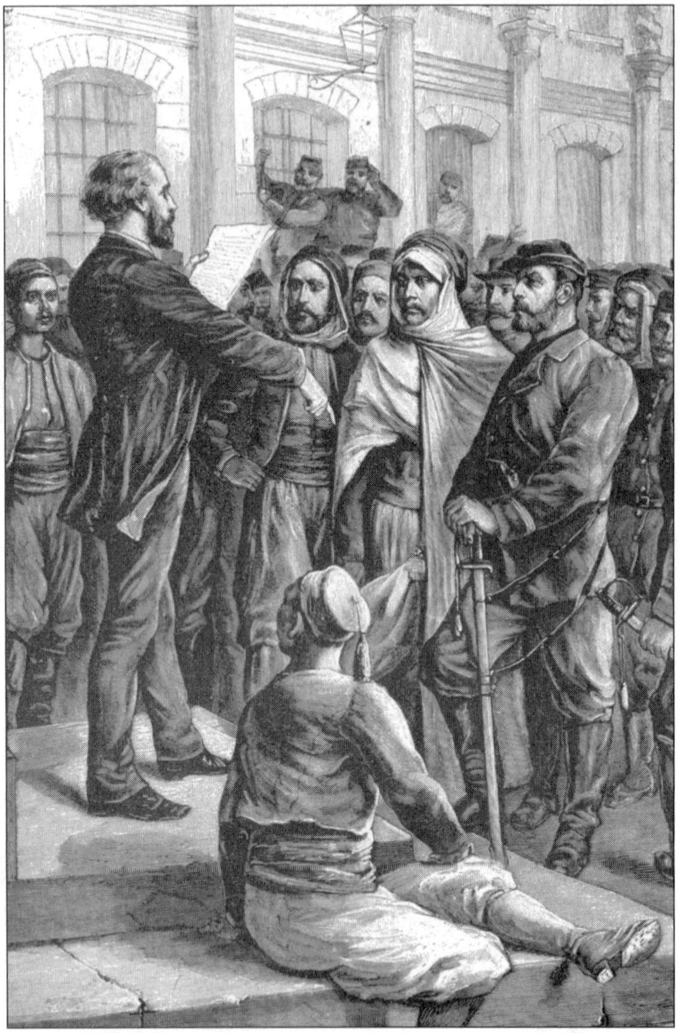

Léon Gambetta rallying fresh troops at Tours. (Francis R. Niglutsch)

French public opinion vigorously protested the prospect of Hohenzollern kings encircling France. The fervor of their protest caused Leopold to withdraw his candidacy, with the approval of King William.

Antoine-Agénor-Alfred Gramont, the French foreign affairs minister, then ordered the French ambassador to Berlin to obtain a promise from King William that he would never permit Leopold's candidacy to be renewed. The ambassador met William I at Ems, where the king was vacationing. By editing the telegraphed account of this encounter, Bismarck made the episode appear more forceful and dramatic than it really was. When it appeared in newspapers, the condensed version aroused national passions in both countries, and France declared war on Prussia on July 19, 1870. Clearly Gramont and Bismarck each wished to humiliate the other, when peace might otherwise have been preserved.

The Prussians already had plans in place for invading their neighbors, while the French had not. The southern German states joined the northern states. The army of the North German Confederation was technologically advanced, highly efficient, well organized, and staffed with able officers. On the other side, a major reform proposed for the French military in 1867 had been left underfunded and incomplete. French generals had become complacent and unimaginative since their last major campaigns during the 1850's.

The French placed two major armies in the field, and they were beaten in major battles at Sedan and Metz. Napoleon III, who was extremely ill from kidney disease and in constant pain, joined the army of Marshal Marie-Edme-Patrice-Maurice de MacMahon. Political pressure from the ministers in Paris dictated the decision to attempt to assist the forces besieged at Metz rather than retreat toward Paris and raise fresh troops. The Prussians encountered and defeated MacMahon's force near Sedan with superior artillery. Facing a disastrous defeat, Napoleon sought death in combat but was captured. He surrendered the French forces on September 1.

Opposition politicians in Paris immediately abolished the empire and declared a republic on September 4. Even as the French capital was besieged, these politicians formed a protest government, known as the Government of National Defense, to continue the fight against the Prussians. A fiery leader of resistance, Léon Gambetta, escaped in a balloon. At Tours, he rallied fresh troops, who fought bravely until January 28, 1871, when Paris surrendered. An armistice was signed on the same day, but France's Fort Belfort held out until February 16.

Meanwhile, Italy had seized the opportunity to take over Rome, where French troops had previously ensured the pope's control of the entire city. The German princes and kings met at Versailles's Hall of Mirrors and declared William I the emperor of a united Germany. German unification was thus achieved in the heat of military conquest and under an authoritarian government. The Germans refused to negotiate until the French formed a new government, so a hurried election for a National Assembly was held in February; it resulted in a conservative majority. The assembly appointed a conservative monarchist to head its executive and negotiate peace terms. This government's authority was later rejected by Democratic-Socialists in Paris, who formed the Commune and fought the assembly's troops.

SIGNIFICANCE

The peace terms imposed on France in the Treaty of Frankfurt, which was signed in May of 1871, were considered severe by prevailing standards. The Germans seized the French province of Alsace and one-third of the province of Lorraine. These border areas contained rich iron ore deposits, well-developed industries, and a population who wished to remain French. France was also required to pay a large sum of reparations in gold and accept a German occupation army.

In many ways, the peace terms of the Franco-Prussian War haunted Europe for decades. The Germans never governed Alsace-Lorraine in the same way as the rest of their empire and ceaselessly worried about French revenge. Feeling isolated and threatened by German power, France built a system of powerful allies which, in turn, alarmed the German government and helped precipitate World War I in 1914. When the Germans lost that war in 1918, they had to return Alsace-Lorraine to France, pay reparations to the victors, and accept an occupation force. These conditions, in turn, helped lead to World War II. The Franco-Prussian War left Europe more inclined to seek military solutions to problems, less democratic, more competitive, and more narrowly nationalistic than it otherwise might have been.

—*Harold A. Schofield, updated by Sharon B. Watkins*

FURTHER READING

Bury, J. P. T. *Gambetta and the National Defence: A Republican Dictatorship in France*. Reprint. Westport, Conn.: Greenwood Press, 1971. First published in 1936, this work provides a look behind the lines at besieged Paris and the French resistance after the battle of Sedan.

_______. *Napoleon III and the Second Empire*. New York: Harper & Row, 1968. An overview of the reign of Napoleon III with a clear treatment of the war.

Craig, Gordon A. *Europe, 1815-1914*. 3d ed. Fort Worth, Tex.: Harcourt Brace Jovanovich College Publishers, 1989. This textbook gives a clear analysis of origins and results of the war.

Gall, Lothar. *Bismarck: The White Revolutionary*. Translated by J. A. Underwood. 2 vols. Boston: Unwin Hyman, 1990. This German writer stresses the essentially conservative nature of Bismarck's policies.

Howard, Michael E. *The Franco-Prussian War: The German Invasion of France*. New York: Dorset Press, 1990. This is the single most instructive and balanced book on the war in English.

Lerman, Katharine Anne. *Bismarck*. New York: Pearson Longman, 2004. Careful examination of Bismarck's exercise of power as a crucial means of understanding his personality and statecraft.

Medlicott, W. N. *Bismarck and Modern Germany*. London: English Universities Press, 1965. A concise account of the great chancellor's role in founding unified Germany.

Price, Roger. *The French Second Empire: An Anatomy of Political Power*. New York: Cambridge University Press, 2001. Chronicles Napoleon's political career, examining how he was elected president, devised a coup to establish the Second Empire, and used the empire's power to initiate liberal reforms and wage a disastrous war against Prussia.

Taithe, Bertrand. *Citizenship and Wars: France in Turmoil, 1870-1871*. London: Routledge, 2001. Study of the political culture of France during its Third Republic, at the time of the Franco-Prussian War.

SEE ALSO: Dec. 2, 1852: Louis Napoleon Bonaparte Becomes Emperor of France; Feb. 1-Oct. 30, 1864: Danish-Prussian War; 1866-1867: North German Confederation Is Formed; June 15-Aug. 23, 1866: Austria and Prussia's Seven Weeks' War; Sept. 1, 1870: Battle of Sedan; Sept. 20, 1870-Jan. 28, 1871: Prussian Army Besieges Paris; 1871-1877: Kulturkampf Against the Catholic Church in Germany; Jan. 18, 1871: German States Unite Within German Empire; Feb. 13, 1871-1875: Third French Republic Is Established; Mar. 18-May 28, 1871: Paris Commune; May 20, 1882: Triple Alliance Is Formed; Jan., 1886-1889: French Right Wing Revives During Boulanger Crisis.

RELATED ARTICLES in *Great Lives from History: The Nineteenth Century, 1801-1900:* Otto von Bismarck; Louis Faidherbe; Léon Gambetta; Friedrich von Holstein; Wilhelm Liebknecht; Napoleon III.

September 1, 1870
BATTLE OF SEDAN

In one of the initial battles of the Franco-Prussian War, Prussian forces surrounded the city of Sedan and encircled a French army, which included French emperor Napoleon III. After a day of failed breakout attempts, Napoleon surrendered; the French army capitulated and effectively was wiped out. French citizens would soon depose the government and create the Third Republic. A subsequent Prussian siege of Paris ended in France's defeat and the creation of a new German state dominated by Prussia.

LOCALE: Sedan, France
CATEGORIES: Wars, uprisings, and civil unrest; government and politics

KEY FIGURES

Napoleon III (Louis Napoleon Bonaparte; 1808-1873), emperor of France, r. 1852-1870
Marie-Edme-Patrice-Maurice de MacMahon (1808-1893), French marshal
Helmuth von Moltke (1800-1891), general and chief of the Prussian general staff
Achille-François Bazaine (1811-1888), French marshal
Auguste Ducrot (1817-1882), French general

SUMMARY OF EVENT

The French declaration of war against Prussia and its allies was orchestrated by Prussian chancellor Otto von Bismarck as a way to persuade the independent states within the German geographic area to work together to defend one another under Prussian leadership. The French emperor, Napoleon III—Emperor Napoleon I's nephew—saw war as a way to stifle internal discontent through heightened patriotism. At the time, military and political observers saw France as a great power with a long and glorious military heritage. Prussia was seen as a second-tier power that, although growing, was incapable of defeating France on its own.

In reality, the French and Prussian militaries were not evenly matched. Although France had a large, well-trained, and well-equipped army, it was a force riddled with weaknesses. Command at the higher levels was based primarily on seniority, so average French field commanders were often ten to thirty years older than their Prussian counterparts. The social divide between enlisted men and their officers meant that the men were often treated as the dregs of society and not encouraged to rise in the ranks. The French army lacked an established staff system for prewar planning and training officers. Technologically the French had an exceptionally fine service rifle, the chassepot, but their muzzle-loading brass artillery pieces were outranged and outperformed by Prussian breech-loading cannon.

In contrast, Prussian society lionized military service and invested respect in soldiers of all ranks. Universal conscription ensured that able-bodied men received training and could be rapidly mobilized in a time of war. When war was declared, Prussia's 300,000-man army was reinforced with more than 900,000 reservists and militiamen known as the Landwehr. The Prussian general staff system trained officers and promoted on the basis of merit rather than seniority or social origin. During years of peace, staff officers planned for future operations against potential enemies, so that any given war would begin with war plans in hand. The staff officers also effectively integrated into their operations new technologies such as the railroads and the telegraph. The result was that the staff could operate the Prussian army at a faster tempo than the French anticipated. Finally, although the Prussian needle rifle was outranged by the French chassepot, Prussian artillerists had adopted modern Krupp made breech-loading guns that had more range, a greater rate of fire, and more lethality than the French artillery pieces.

For France the only hope for victory was speed, for in the opening days of the war the French outnumbered the Prussians by 400,000 to 300,000. Unfortunately, this advantage was wasted by the lack of prewar plans and divisions among the French high command. Napoleon III proved more skillful as a dogged politician than as a decisive commander. In the 1830's and 1840's he had been involved in failed coups, and not until after the revolutions of 1848 was he successful in claiming the mantle of emperor. His successes were sustained by opportunism and good fortune rather than by decisive leadership.

During the Franco-Prussian War, Napoleon proved to be indecisive in the field, and his dithering contributed significantly to what appeared to be a paralysis of the high command. His personal failings were highlighted by his inability to select or promote skilled military leaders. France's premier marshal was Achille-François Bazaine, but because of Napoleon's mistrust and political need to be associated with military glory like his uncle, Bazaine was initially given only a secondary role in operations.

France's primary force was called the Army of the Rhine. The sluggish pace of French mobilization contrasted unfavorably with Prussia's rapid mobilization. The chief of the Prussian general staff, General Helmuth von Moltke, seized and maintained the initiative. Throughout July and August, the French and Prussian forces fought a series of battles that resulted in Prussian advances. Bazaine, apparently unhappy with his limited role and never before having commanded such large forces, proved hesitant in the field. After the major battles of Mars-la-Tour and Gravelotte-St. Privat, Bazaine retreated into the fortress city of Metz.

The pace of the Prussian advance intimidated Napoleon III, who suddenly gave Bazaine command of the Army of the Rhine and then departed for the interior of France. While there, Napoleon III joined with Marshal Marie-Edme-Patrice-Maurice de MacMahon, who was vested with the command of the Army of Chalons. This force was to march on Metz and end the Prussian siege. MacMahon took a northerly route with the intent of encircling the Prussians, but these plans were reported in French newspapers. Faster-moving Prussian columns intercepted the Army of Chalons, and MacMahon beat a hasty retreat toward the Belgian border. Von Moltke maintained the Siege of Metz while moving with other Prussian forces against MacMahon.

MacMahon's forces retreated into the area around Sedan. Napoleon, vacillating as usual, left planning the battle to MacMahon. Even though pursued by the speedy Prussian columns, MacMahon decided to give his troops a day of rest. This gave the Prussians enough time to encircle the city. On August 30 and 31 the two forces began skirmishing, and on September 1, MacMahon was wounded. Thus, the French began the battle without clear leadership because Napoleon had ceded control of the battle to MacMahon. Because of his wounds, however, MacMahon was replaced by General Auguste Ducrot. Command was further muddled with the arrival from Paris of General Emmanuel de Wimpffen, who had been appointed by the French minister of war as MacMahon's replacement should MacMahon fall.

Throughout the day numerous French units launched

French troops in retreat at Sedan. (Francis R. Niglutsch)

Formal French capitulation at Sedan. (P. F. Collier and Son)

attacks to break through the Prussian encirclement. Without a coherent command structure, however, these attacks were uncoordinated. The Prussians seized the high ground surrounding Sedan and concentrated large numbers of artillery pieces in batteries overlooking the critical spots on the battlefield. Superior Prussian logistics provided ample stocks of ammunition, and throughout the day French units were deluged by accurate artillery fire from guns sited outside the range of their own ordnance. Well-coordinated Prussian infantry counterattacks, made under covering fire from the Prussian batteries, were launched along decisive points in the French perimeter.

Napoleon, acting as an individual rather than as a commander, courted a battlefield death as he rode around dispiritedly from French attack to French attack, but he remained unwounded. By late afternoon, heavy casualties and despair over lackluster leadership drove some French units to disintegration, and a despairing Napoleon contacted the Prussians to ask for terms of surrender.

While Napoleon would later claim that he offered to surrender himself only, in effect his surrender allowed the entire army to capitulate. The battle was a major humiliation for France. While the Prussians saw some nine thousand soldiers either killed, wounded, or missing, the French casualties included more than seventeen thousand soldiers dead or wounded and twenty-one thousand captured during the battle. Napoleon's surrender led eighty-three thousand more French soldiers into captivity.

With Napoleon captured, the Prussians marched onto Paris. When the people of Paris heard about the debacle, they immediately deposed Napoleon and declared the Third Republic. France continued to fight the Prussians, and popular fury over the incompetence of Napoleon and his generals fueled a burst of patriotism that prolonged the war and caused considerable destruction and bitterness. The defeat of the Army of Chalons compelled Bazaine to surrender. The capitulation of these two armies—which had constituted the bulk of France's organized and equipped forces—virtually ensured that French resistance would be unable to defeat the Prussians.

SIGNIFICANCE

The day-long struggle around Sedan was dominated by superior Prussian military organization, logistics, morale, artillery, and leadership. Napoleon III's surrender at

Sedan ended both his career and the Second Empire. From the ashes of defeat, the Third Republic arose, and popular patriotism reinvigorated the nation.

Despite its defeat in 1870-1871, the Third Republic would last until 1945. For Prussia, victory confirmed its skill and leadership and provided the impetus for the creation of a unified German state under the aegis of the king of Prussia and his selected subordinates. The new Germany would be a major power in world affairs until 1945 and the end of World War II.

—*Kevin B. Reid*

FURTHER READING

Badsey, Stephen. *Essential Histories: The Franco-Prussian War, 1870-1871*. London: Osprey, 2003. This volume in the Osprey Essential Histories series provides a short, yet detailed, look at the origins and events of the war as well as the weapons and tactics used in the major battles.

Howard, Michael. *The Franco-Prussian War: The German Invasion of France, 1870-1871*. New York: Routledge, 1988. The classic work on the war upon which all other related works have depended.

Price, Roger. *The French Second Empire: An Anatomy of Political Power*. New York: Cambridge University Press, 2001. Chronicles Napoleon's political career, examining how he devised a coup to establish the Second Empire and used the empire's power to wage the disastrous war against Prussia.

Wawro, Geoffrey. *The Franco-Prussian War*. New York: Cambridge University Press, 2003. Provides clear insights into how the different armies were raised, organized, equipped, and led. Wawro offers a first-rate analysis of commanders and the war's individual battles.

SEE ALSO: 1866-1867: North German Confederation Is Formed; July 19, 1870-Jan. 28, 1871: Franco-Prussian War; Sept. 20, 1870-Jan. 28, 1871: Prussian Army Besieges Paris; Jan. 18, 1871: German States Unite Within German Empire; Feb. 13, 1871-1875: Third French Republic Is Established; Mar. 18-May 28, 1871: Paris Commune.

RELATED ARTICLES in *Great Lives from History: The Nineteenth Century, 1801-1900:* Otto von Bismarck; Léon Gambetta; Napoleon III; Adolphe Thiers.

September 20, 1870-January 28, 1871
PRUSSIAN ARMY BESIEGES PARIS

When the leaders of the French Third Republic rejected Prussia's cease-fire terms during the Franco-Prussian War, the city of Paris became the focus for a new round of fighting. The French capital endured a siege of more than four months before the defending garrison finally capitulated. The city's fall ended the conflict and confirmed Prussia's status as the dominant military power on the Continent.

LOCALE: Paris, France
CATEGORY: Wars, uprisings, and civil unrest

KEY FIGURES

Otto von Bismarck (1815-1898), prime minister of Prussia, 1862-1890, and later chancellor of the German Empire, 1871-1890
Auguste Ducrot (1817-1882), French general
Jules Favre (1809-1880), French vice president and foreign minister
Frederick William (1831-1888), crown prince of Prussia and later emperor of Germany as Frederick III, r. March-June, 1888
Léon Gambetta (1838-1882), French interior and war minister
Helmuth von Moltke (1800-1891), Prussian chief of staff and later field marshal
Adolphe Thiers (1797-1877), French statesman and negotiator
Louis Jules Trochu (1815-1896), French president and commander of the Paris garrison to January 22, 1871
Joseph Vinoy (1803-1880), commander of the French Third Army and, after January 22, 1871, commander of the Paris garrison
William I (1797-1888), king of Prussia, r. 1861-1888, and later emperor of Germany, r. 1871-1888

SUMMARY OF EVENT

The surrender of Emperor Napoleon III's army—and of Napoleon himself—at Sedan on September 1, 1870, was initially believed to be the final act of the Franco-Prussian War. However, events in the war abruptly spun out of the control of politicians and diplomats alike. On September 4, in reaction to the news of the imperial capitulation at Sedan, a swift, bloodless uprising overthrew Napoleon's regime and proclaimed, for the third time, a French republic.

The republic's initial government was makeshift in many respects; General Louis Jules Trochu, who had been named military governor of Paris on August 17, was elevated to the post of president in the newly created Government of National Defense. Jules Favre, a veteran politician, took up the posts of vice president and foreign minister; a radical firebrand named Léon Gambetta assumed control of the Ministries of War and the Interior. Seventy-three-year-old Adolphe Thiers, a former prime minister under King Louis Philippe, served, without portfolio, as a special, roving ambassador. Uncertain of which direction the new French regime might take, Prussian chief of staff General Helmuth von Moltke ordered German units westward with the intent of gradually encircling Paris. The united German army was nominally under the command of Prussian king William I, but for all practical purposes it was von Moltke and Prussian prime minister Otto von Bismarck who set the military and political agendas.

Bismarck demanded that France cede the entire province of Alsace and the northern portion of the province of Lorraine, including the city of Metz. His terms were indignantly rejected by Favre. All the while, German troops took position around Paris between September 17 and 18, the army of Prussian crown prince Frederick William swung south and west to complete the entrapment, and his father, King William I, established a military headquarters at Versailles. Trochu had been prudently deploying forces at his disposal in case it became necessary to defend the capital. This eventuality came to pass on September 20, after negotiations had totally collapsed and the Siege of Paris officially began. Trochu's tenure was controversial, in that his focus was purely defensive; to some, he appeared to have ruled out the possibility of victory and seemed to be playing for time, in the hope that German resolve might flag. Others believed he acted out of a sense of honor that obligated him to offer at least a measure of resistance to the invaders.

Trochu's halfhearted defense contrasted sharply, however, with the energy shown by his military and ministerial colleagues. General Auguste Ducrot, Trochu's second in command, was outspoken, defiant, and aggressive, consistently pushing for attacks upon German positions. On October 7, Gambetta dramatically lifted off in a hot air balloon, which was the only way personnel and dispatches could travel to and from the world outside the besieged Paris. His mission was to rouse the countryside, recruit new armies, and send them to the relief of the capital. The elderly Thiers had slipped out in time and traveled from country to country, trying to kindle sympathy from foreign governments and perhaps secure aid or intervention. Unfortunately for Thiers, Napoleon III had alienated many potential allies over various issues prior to the Franco-Prussian War; in the end, only the United States expressed a desire to render assistance, and this offer proved to be too little, too late.

However, Gambetta's charisma and oratorical talents bore some fruit, and a large though ill-trained army was formed at Tours and won a victory at Coulmiers on November 9. Inside Paris, a "grand sortie" was planned to coordinate with this army's advance, and on November 28, Ducrot was to launch his offensive. All went awry: Trochu and Gambetta were only vaguely aware of each other's movements, so they were never able to coordinate their efforts. The crown prince was able to discern the intentions of the French, and he anticipated the attack. Meanwhile, flooding on the River Marne delayed operations for one crucial day. On November 29, Ducrot's sortie achieved initial success but faltered in the face of withering fire from a well-entrenched enemy; it had failed by nightfall. Meanwhile, Gambetta's army had been halted and thrown back beyond the city of Orléans.

The sortie of late November marked the last serious attempt by France to lift the siege of its capital. Thereafter, it became a matter of waiting for events that never materialized. Shortages within the beleaguered capital became acute. Nearly all the animals in the Paris Zoo were devoured, and meat from dogs, horses, cats, and even rats became regular fare displayed in butcher shops. Deaths from malnutrition, disease, and (as winter commenced) the elements rose dramatically—particularly among children. Nonetheless, by January, 1871, the dynamics of the situation were beginning to work against Germany. News of the privations of the citizens of Paris was starting to capture the sympathy of the outside world, and the Germans were increasingly perceived as heavy-handed and brutal.

To forestall imminent intervention by Great Britain, Russia, and the United States by speedily breaking down Parisian resistance, Bismarck ordered massive deliberate artillery bombing of civilians. Although internationally condemned, the bombardment had the desired effect. On January 22, 1871, the largely moribund Trochu, who seemed intent on enduring the siege regardless of the circumstances, was replaced by General Joseph Vinoy of the French Third Army. Negotiations between

Otto von Bismarck (left), Adolphe Thiers (center), and Jules Favre negotiating peace terms. (Francis R. Niglutsch)

Favre and Bismarck led to the city's formal capitulation on January 28, 1871, and the signing of the Treaty of Frankfurt. Germany acquired Alsace and northern Lorraine, and France paid two million francs in reparations, having to endure the presence of German occupation forces until the balance was delivered. William I was declared emperor of a freshly united Germany, of which Bismarck became chancellor.

Significance

The bloody, exhausting Siege of Paris and the resulting humiliation of France left in its wake a climate of anger and recrimination and set the stage for the horrific Communard Revolution in Paris that spring. In the long term, though, the heroic defense of the French capital redeemed much of the shame arising out of the debacle of Sedan and ultimately buttressed the fledgling Third Republic through its early years against attacks from legitimist, Orléanist, Bonapartist, and radical elements. Gambetta, in particular, was to attain legendary status. The memories of the civilian bombardment also added another bone of contention to the political culture of *revanche* (revenge) in France, which factored into the coming of World War I.

—*Raymond Pierre Hylton*

Further Reading

Badsey, Stephen. *The Franco-Prussian War, 1870-1871.* London: Osprey, 2003. This study of the Franco-Prussian War is succinct and accessible to lay readers.

Becker, George J., ed. *Paris Under Siege, 1870-1871: From the Goncourt Journal.* Ithaca, N.Y.: Cornell University Press, 1969. Edited version of one of the best-known and most lucidly written firsthand accounts of the siege.

Bury, J. P. T. *Gambetta and the National Defense: A Republican Dictatorship in France.* New York: Howard Fertig, 1970. Analytical study of the political figure who most energetically contributed to the anti-German resistance.

Christiansen, Rupert. *Paris Babylon: The Story of the Paris Commune.* New York: Penguin Books, 1996.

Although this volume concerns itself more with the Paris Commune, it nonetheless contains as background one hundred pages of useful information on the Siege of Paris.

Horne, Alistair. *The Fall of Paris: The Siege and the Commune*. New York: Penguin Books, 1981. The most thorough rendition of the diplomatic and political maneuverings relating to the siege, which are effectively tied into the military action. Bismarck is depicted in a less-than-creditable light.

Kranzberg, Melvin. *The Siege of Paris, 1870-1871: A Political and Social History*. Westport, Conn.: Greenwood Press, 1971. A more succinct account than that of Horne, but one that is equally insightful and judicious in its use of sources.

Stone, David J. A. *"First Reich": Inside the German Army During the War with France, 1870-1871*. London: Brassey's, 2002. Studies the Franco-Prussian War and the Siege of Paris from the point of view of the German soldiers investing the capital.

SEE ALSO: Dec. 2, 1852: Louis Napoleon Bonaparte Becomes Emperor of France; 1866-1867: North German Confederation Is Formed; July 19, 1870-Jan. 28, 1871: Franco-Prussian War; Sept. 1, 1870: Battle of Sedan; Jan. 18, 1871: German States Unite Within German Empire; Feb. 13, 1871-1875: Third French Republic Is Established; Mar. 18-May 28, 1871: Paris Commune.

RELATED ARTICLES in *Great Lives from History: The Nineteenth Century, 1801-1900:* Otto von Bismarck; Léon Gambetta; Napoleon III; Adolphe Thiers.

1871
DARWIN PUBLISHES *THE DESCENT OF MAN*

A continuation of Charles Darwin's earlier On the Origin of Species, The Descent of Man *argued that humans evolved from lower animals and that all of the features typically used to distinguish humans from animals originated through natural evolutionary processes. The work provided an impetus to the growth of materialist analyses of humanity and of scientific investigations into the origins of human nature.*

ALSO KNOWN AS: *The Descent of Man and Selection in Relation to Sex*

LOCALE: Downe, Kent, England

CATEGORIES: Biology; science and technology

KEY FIGURES

Charles Darwin (1809-1882), English naturalist who originated the theory of evolution

Thomas Henry Huxley (1825-1895), English comparative anatomist

John Lubbock (1834-1913), English banker, statesman, and naturalist

Edward B. Tylor (1832-1917), English anthropologist

Sir Charles Lyell (1797-1875), English barrister and geologist

Ernst Haeckel (1834-1919), German biologist

SUMMARY OF EVENT

Charles Darwin's *On the Origin of Species by Means of Natural Selection: Or, The Preservation of Favoured Races in the Struggle for Life* (1859; commonly known as *On the Origin of Species*) postulated that all life on Earth evolved from a common ancestor by means of natural selection. This theory provoked a flood of controversy because it implied that humanity also arose from lower animals by purely naturalistic mechanisms, rather than through supernatural means. Even though Darwin scrupulously avoided the question of human origins in that book, the issue of human evolution generated most of the controversy over his theory. Darwin was nevertheless eager to apply his theory to humans. From 1859 to 1871, he gathered valuable information by corresponding with scientists around the world and conducting his own experiments. What he learned during this time provided material for *The Descent of Man and Selection in Relation to Sex* (1871; commonly known as *The Descent of Man*).

The Descent of Man begins by asserting that there are no fundamental qualitative differences between the anatomies and development of humans and higher mammals. Comparative anatomical work on humans and nonhuman primates by Thomas Henry Huxley, Darwin's friend and most loyal defender, tended to support a common ancestry for these two groups. Darwin depended on Huxley's *Evidence as to Man's Place in Nature* (1863) for the first section of his own book. He also used Huxley's extensive anatomical data to show that there are no distinctly human structures and to argue that hu-

Charles Darwin. (Courtesy, University of Texas at Austin)

mans are even more closely related to apes than apes are to monkeys. This assertion shrank the physical gulf between humans and nonhuman primates. Darwin also argued that human populations possessed great variability and that natural selection could operate upon these differences.

In his book's next few chapters, Darwin argues that human mental capacities differ only in degree, not in essence, from those of animals. He provides several admittedly anthropomorphic anecdotal examples from animal behavior to support this claim. He believed that the origin and development of characteristics thought to distinguish humans from the animals, such as religion, language, and morality, can be reasonably explained by evolutionary mechanisms. Some found Darwin's line of argumentation convincing because by the late 1850's, many people were beginning to believe that humanity was more ancient than previously presumed. To establish the ancient age of humanity firmly, Darwin relied upon the research of three English scientists: archaeologist John Lubbock, anthropologist Edward B. Tylor, and geologist Sir Charles Lyell.

Another friend and defender of Darwin, Lubbock subdivided the Stone Age into the Neolithic and Paleolithic periods, based on progressive improvements in toolmaking, with the oldest remains of human activity displaying the most primitive levels of technology. Darwin also corresponded regularly with Edward Tylor, whose anthropological studies suggested that cultural differences between Europeans and non-European societies were well explained by an evolutionary model of inheritance, diffusion, and independent innovation. Drawing on Tylor's work, Darwin hypothesized that religious belief in humans originated from a primitive need to find a cause for things that evade simple explanation.

Yet another friend and sometime defender of Darwin, Charles Lyell, the author of *The Geological Evidences of the Antiquity of Man with Remarks on the Theories of the Origin of Species by Variation* (1863), cataloged, in great detail and with tremendous clarity for any educated Victorian, the accumulated evidence for the antiquity of humankind. His book was the first work after *On the Origin of Species* to cause a reevaluation of what it meant to be human. All these discoveries made degenerationism—the popular belief of the time that human culture had originated at a relatively high level of social organization and sophistication, after which some cultures degenerated to simpler states while others advanced to more complex states—untenable. They also made evolutionary accounts of the rise of modern humans from more primitive ones seem much more plausible.

In the matter of language, Darwin referenced the evolutionary genealogy of Indo-European languages constructed by August Schleicher. Schleicher's analyses intimated that all modern languages had evolved from earlier ones. Darwin postulated that human language originated from social sounds—similar to those produced by apes—that gradually developed when primitive humans began to imitate natural sounds. To explain the origin of morality, Darwin argued that right and wrong are relative and are learned by children when they are young, and that there is no innate sense of morality in humans. He used many examples from so-called uncivilized peoples and their practices to corroborate his claims.

Darwin was unsure of the identity of the actual biological ancestor of humanity, as he knew almost nothing about fossil primates. He suspected that the Old World monkeys gave rise to humans, but he had little evidence other than anatomical similarities to support that contention. He referred to the embryological work of Ernst Haeckel, the most enthusiastic promoter of Darwinism in Germany, to unite the evolutionary ancestors of primates

THE DESCENT OF MAN

In the first chapter of The Descent of Man, *Charles Darwin considers the evidence regarding whether human beings did or did not evolve from so-called lower species.*

He who wishes to decide whether man is the modified descendant of some pre-existing form, would probably first enquire whether man varies, however slightly, in bodily structure and in mental faculties; and if so, whether the variations are transmitted to his offspring in accordance with the laws which prevail with the lower animals. Again, are the variations the result, as far as our ignorance permits us to judge, of the same general causes, and are they governed by the same general laws, as in the case of other organisms; for instance, by correlation, the inherited effects of use and disuse, etc.? Is man subject to similar malconformations, the result of arrested development, of reduplication of parts, etc., and does he display in any of his anomalies reversion to some former and ancient type of structure? It might also naturally be enquired whether man, like so many other animals, has given rise to varieties and sub-races, differing but slightly from each other, or to races differing so much that they must be classed as doubtful species? How are such races distributed over the world; and how, when crossed, do they react on each other in the first and succeeding generations? And so with many other points.

The enquirer would next come to the important point, whether man tends to increase at so rapid a rate, as to lead to occasional severe struggles for existence; and consequently to beneficial variations, whether in body or mind, being preserved, and injurious ones eliminated. Do the races or species of men, whichever term may be applied, encroach on and replace one another, so that some finally become extinct? We shall see that all these questions, as indeed is obvious in respect to most of them, must be answered in the affirmative, in the same manner as with the lower animals.

Source: Charles Darwin, *The Descent of Man and Selection in Relation to Sex* (London: J. Murray, 1874).

with those of marsupials, monotremes (egg-laying mammals such as the duckbill platypus), reptiles, amphibians, and fishes. Darwin suggested that the ancestor of the vertebrates was the lowly tunicate (ascidian), whose larval stage possesses a notochord, the dorsally located cartilage rod, found in the embryos of all vertebrates, that serves as the embryological precursor to the backbone that is lost upon metamorphosis to the adult form in tunicates.

Darwin also devoted the latter part of *The Descent of Man* to the concept of sexual selection. Original to Darwin, sexual selection postulates that the evolution of particular traits is driven by competition for mates between individuals of the same sex. Darwin theorized that human beings, like the animals, possess a variety of superfluous traits that exist because they aid reproductive success. With sexual selection, Darwin attempted to explain most of the geographical and behavioral distinctions among human societies. He saw differences in physical appearance, such as skin color, hair texture, and body size, and divergent behavioral traits, such as bravery, social cohesion, maternal feelings, work ethic, obedience, and altruism, as explainable by means of applying sexual selection to humans. Like most Europeans of his day, Darwin believed that men were intellectually superior to women and that European society, whose set the evolutionary direction for humanity, was the most advanced kind of society.

By the time of Darwin's death in 1882, his theory of common descent, which included humans, enjoyed almost universal acceptance among scientists. However, natural selection, his proposed mechanism of evolutionary change, was heavily disputed and widely disbelieved. In 1891, Dutch anthropologist Eugene Dubois discovered a skull cap near Trinil, in central Java. This fossil seemed to belong to a species possessing anatomical features that were intermediate between those of apes and modern humans and was named *Pithecanthropus erectus* by Dubois. Its modern designation is *Homo erectus*, and it is commonly known as Java Man. Although disputed at first, Dubois's find was eventually viewed as vindicating Darwin's theories and initiated other efforts to find fossil human ancestors.

SIGNIFICANCE

The Descent of Man deals with questions regarding humanity's origins that had never been asked before Darwin's time. In this regard, the book was truly pioneering, even if some of its arguments were less than convincing. Darwin's book also spurred scientific investigation into the origin of humanity, particularly in areas that were formerly thought to be outside the purview of science. Biological investigations of human reasoning, consciousness, and moral motivations had their inauguration with *The Descent of Man*. Darwin's ideas also generated great controversy, since many people were appalled by the thought that they had descended from apelike creatures. In the United States, this controversy culminated in the 1925 Scopes "Monkey" Trial. The application of Darwin's theories to other fields, such as the social sciences and humanities, stimulated new avenues of research but also dehumanized them to some extent, which caused much of the controversy that surrounds Darwin's theories—a controversy that rages in the twenty-first century and shows no signs of abating.

—*Michael A. Buratovich*

Further Reading

Adler, Jerry. "Charles Darwin: Evolution of a Scientist." *Newsweek*, November 29, 2005, 50-58. Well-illustrated examination of Darwin's personal struggle to reconcile his developing theories on evolution with his Christian beliefs, with attention to modern challenges to Darwinism.

Bowler, Peter J. *Charles Darwin: The Man and His Influence*. Cambridge, England: Cambridge University Press, 1996. Brief but important biography of Charles Darwin that focuses on the lasting influence of his ideas.

Browne, Janet. *Charles Darwin: The Power of Place*. New York: Alfred A. Knopf, 2002. Authoritative and exhaustive biography of the later years of the life of Charles Darwin by a distinguished Darwin scholar.

Darwin, Charles. *From So Simple a Beginning: The Four Great Books of Charles Darwin*. Edited by Edward O. Wilson. New York: W. W. Norton, 2006. First one-volume edition of Darwin's most important books. Includes an introductory essay by Pulitzer Prize-winning author Edward O. Wilson, who also contributes a new introduction for each book and an afterword discussing evolutionary theory in the context of modern religious conservatism. Other features include a comprehensive index, reproductions of the original illustrations in Darwin's books, and a map.

Desmond, Adrian. *Huxley: From Devil's Disciple to Evolution's High Priest*. Reading, Mass.: Perseus Books, 1997. Nearly definitive biography of Thomas Henry Huxley and his role in the human origins debates.

Hodge, Jonathan, and Gregory Radick, eds. *The Cambridge Companion to Darwin*. New York: Cambridge University Press, 2003. Collection of original essays that examine Darwin's major theories, the development of his thinking, and how his thought has influenced philosophical, religious, and social debate.

Ruse, Michael. *The Darwinian Revolution: Science Red in Tooth and Claw*. 2d ed. Chicago: University of Chicago Press, 1999. Lively description and analysis of the scientific history of the inception of biological evolution.

See also: 1809: Lamarck Publishes *Zoological Philosophy*; July, 1830: Lyell Publishes *Principles of Geology*; 1850-1865: Clausius Formulates the Second Law of Thermodynamics; 1854-1862: Wallace's Expeditions Give Rise to Biogeography; Aug., 1856: Neanderthal Skull Is Found in Germany; Nov. 24, 1859: Darwin Publishes *On the Origin of Species*; 1861: *Archaeopteryx Lithographica* Is Discovered; 1862: Spencer Introduces Principles of Social Darwinism; 1865: Mendel Proposes Laws of Heredity; Mar., 1868: Lartet Discovers the First Cro-Magnon Remains; 1899-1900: Rediscovery of Mendel's Hereditary Theory.

Related articles in *Great Lives from History: The Nineteenth Century, 1801-1900:* Charles Darwin; Ernst Haeckel; Thomas Henry Huxley.

1871-1876
DÍAZ DRIVES MEXICO INTO CIVIL WAR

Porfirio Díaz led two rebellions against the Mexican government. The first, against Benito Juárez, was unsuccessful, but the second, against Sebastián Lerdo de Tejada, led to Díaz's heavy-handed presidency, Mexico's economic riches and its modernization, and, ultimately, the Mexican Revolution of 1910-1920.

LOCALE: Republic of Mexico
CATEGORIES: Wars, uprisings, and civil unrest; government and politics; diplomacy and international relations

KEY FIGURES

Benito Juárez (1806-1872), president of Mexico, 1861-1872
Sebastián Lerdo de Tejada (1827-1889), president of Mexico, 1872-1876
Porfirio Díaz (1830-1915), president of Mexico, 1876-1880, 1884-1911

SUMMARY OF EVENT

The Republic of Mexico experienced several decades of fratricidal warfare after achieving its independence from Spain in 1821. The two opposing parties, the liberals and the conservatives, fought each other for the control of the country's political and economic future. The liberals sought to introduce democratic government to Mexico while the conservatives hoped to preserve power in the hands of an elitist group that would guide the country to economic development without interference from the general public.

By December, 1860, the liberals, under the Zapotec Indian Benito Juárez, finally seized control of the central government. As president, Juárez sought to break the power of the Roman Catholic Church by confiscating its tremendous wealth. The conservatives responded by seeking to establish a Mexican monarchy. European powers Spain, France, and Great Britain, owed money by the Mexican government, joined conservatives in late 1861, persuading an Austrian archduke, Ferdinand Maximilian Joseph van Habsburg, to become emperor of Mexico. French emperor Napoleon III furnished Maximilian with an army to help him secure the throne. At first the imperialists succeeded, winning several pitched battles against the poorly armed and poorly led Mexican regulars. Juárez, however, did not give up.

Using guerrilla tactics, Juárez began a war of attrition against the French. Napoleon became disenchanted with the struggle and ultimately withdrew the French army. Lacking support among the Mexican population, Maximilian was forced to abdicate in 1867 and was executed by Juárez in June. Finally, Juárez once again resumed his leadership of the country and continued with his democratic reforms.

Mexico did not remain at peace long, however. Porfirio Díaz, one of Juárez's most successful generals, chose to run against him in the presidential elections of 1867. A mestizo (of mixed race), Díaz enjoyed tremendous popularity with the Mexican people. He had beaten French invasion forces in three open-field battles in May, 1862, and had confused them with his hit-and-run guerrilla tactics. Nevertheless, Juárez won the presidential election with 72 percent of the popular vote. He won

Porfirio Díaz. (R. S. Peale/J. A. Hill)

again in 1871, when he was again opposed by Díaz, who split the remaining votes with Sebastián Lerdo de Tejada, another of Juárez's followers.

Arguing that the 1871 election was not an honest one, Díaz attempted to organize a revolt, called the Plan de La Noria, named for his hacienda in Oaxaca. Díaz began organizing the insurrection months before. Despite his appeal to his old comrades-in-arms, Díaz garnered little support among the military. Federal forces defeated the Díaz forces at Puebla in 1871 and at Zacatecas in 1872.

Fortunately for Díaz and his political future, Juárez, regarded by many Mexicans as their greatest hero because of his defeat of Maximilian and the French, died after a heart attack in mid-1872. The followers of Juárez and Lerdo quickly secured Lerdo's appointment as interim president. Lerdo, who had held the office of president of the Mexican supreme court to this point, quickly granted amnesty to Díaz's followers, and they accepted the offer. Lerdo added to his laurels by winning the 1872 presidential election as well. Although the new president had the reputation for being an intellectual, he lacked, as it turned out, both the perception of what needed to be done as well as the necessary charisma to manage the presidency itself.

In December, 1875, while Díaz was headquartered in what is now Brownsville, Texas, he began a carefully planned rebellion (now called the revolution of Tuxtepec) to overthrow the Lerdo government. He and his followers asserted that Lerdo had violated the tenets of the sacrosanct constitution of 1857 and, therefore, should be removed from office. On November 16, 1876, Díaz commanded the insurrectionist army that defeated the federal troops at Tecoac, Puebla.

Díaz was to hold the office of president until 1911, with the exception of the 1880 to 1884 period, when he permitted a subordinate, General Manuel Gonzalez, to hold the office. Gonzalez, however, proved unequal to the task of running the country, so Díaz assumed the presidency once more. From 1884 until forced out of office by the Mexican Revolution of 1910, Díaz maintained tight political control over the country, allowing no civil disruption of any consequence to interrupt Mexico's strong economic growth. The days of frequent rebellions had come to an end.

Sensing an investment opportunity, foreign interests began to pour money into what had become a peaceful and well-governed country. Soon Mexico had a thriving import-export trade, with hundreds of factories, a countrywide railway system, and modern port facilities to move the exports. The president made it a point to reward those of his followers who helped him build and maintain the country's industrial growth. He also selected the candidates for appointment as electors to ensure his continuation in office. He sought and supported the candidacy of governors, who were prepared to work within his program as well. The Díaz government also maintained a balanced budget, ensured sustenance by an effective system of taxation. Under the pragmatic political management system of the Díaz regime, Mexico became a modern nation.

Significance

Although Porfirio Díaz's administration played a major role in ushering Mexico into the modern world of the twentieth century, its activities also led to the country's greatest upheaval, the Mexican Revolution of 1910. The major cause of the revolution, an economic and political disaster, lay in the uneven distribution of wealth generated by the administration's recently established economic program. Only a chosen few derived the program's benefits. Factory owners repressed their workers, plantation owners exploited the rural peasants under their control, and political power was concentrated solely in the hands of Díaz and his supporters.

During the presidential elections of 1910, Francisco Madero, a wealthy landowner from the northern state of Coahuila, launched a movement to open Mexico to democracy. He formed the Antireelectionist Party, seeking to defeat Díaz at the polls. The government arrested and jailed Madero for his stand, and the incumbent Díaz again won the presidency in an election that he closely controlled.

Escaping to the United States the same year, Madero began to organize an armed revolution to break Díaz's hold on the country. Soon the armies of the revolution, led by now-legendary figures such as Francisco (Pancho) Villa and Emiliano Zapata, defeated the federal armies in the field. Soon thereafter, in 1911, Díaz was forced to resign and leave the country. Madero had started Mexico on the road to democracy.

—*Carl Henry Marcoux*

Further Reading

Beals, Carleton. *Porfirio Díaz, Dictator of Mexico*. Philadelphia: J. B. Lippincott, 1932. The author conducted extensive interviews with Porfirio Díaz, providing an intimate look at the personality of the president

Creelman, James. *Díaz, Master of Mexico*. New York: D. Appleton, 1911. A pro-Díaz study written prior to the 1910 Mexican Revolution.

Garner, Paul. *Porfirio Díaz: Profiles In Power.* Harlow, England: Pearson Education, 2001. A modern biography based on previously unreleased archival documents.

Godoy, Jose F. *Porfirio Díaz, President of Mexico.* New York: G. P. Putnam's Sons, 1910. Published during the 1910 Mexican Revolution and at the end of the Díaz presidency.

Krauze, Enrique. *Mexico: Biography of Power.* New York: HarperCollins, 1997. A history of modern Mexico that includes an overview of the nineteenth and early twentieth century.

Perry, Laurens Ballard. *Juárez and Díaz: Machine Politics in Mexico.* De Kalb: Northern Illinois University Press, 1978. One of the better biographies on Díaz.

Turner, John Kenneth. *Barbarous Mexico.* Austin: University of Texas Press, 1969. A biased and extremely negative view of Díaz, his presidency, and the state of Mexico during his administration.

Wasserman, Mark. *Everyday Life and Politics in Nineteenth Century Mexico: Men, Women, and War.* Albuquerque: University of New Mexico Press, 2000. Part 2, "The Age of Civil Wars," describes Mexican history, politics, economics, and everyday life from 1848 through 1876.

SEE ALSO: Sept. 16, 1810: Hidalgo Issues El Grito de Dolores; Sept. 16, 1810-Sept. 28, 1821: Mexican War of Independence; Oct. 2, 1835-Apr. 21, 1836: Texas Revolution; May 13, 1846-Feb. 2, 1848: Mexican War; Sept. 12-13, 1847: Battle of Chapultepec; June 16, 1855-May 1, 1857: Walker Invades Nicaragua; Oct. 31, 1861-June 19, 1867: France Occupies Mexico.

RELATED ARTICLES in *Great Lives from History: The Nineteenth Century, 1801-1900:* Fanny Calderón de la Barca; Porfirio Díaz; Miguel Hidalgo y Costilla; Benito Juárez; Maximilian; Napoleon III; Antonio López de Santa Anna.

1871-1877
KULTURKAMPF AGAINST THE CATHOLIC CHURCH IN GERMANY

A conflict between the German imperial government and the Roman Catholic Church in Germany was launched by the imperial chancellor, Otto von Bismarck. His policy of national unification required the Church to be subordinate in authority to the state. He failed to achieve this subordination of the Church, primarily because of an inept bureaucracy and effective passive resistance sustained by the Church despite extensive persecution.

LOCALE: German Empire (now in Germany)

CATEGORIES: Government and politics; religion and theology

KEY FIGURES

Otto von Bismarck (1815-1898), chancellor of the German Empire, 1871-1890

William I (1797-1888), emperor of Germany, r. 1871-1888

Ludwig Windthorst (1812-1891), German Catholic politician

Adalbert Falk (1827-1900), Bismarck's minister of religion and education

Pius IX (Giovanni Maria Mastai-Ferretti; 1792-1878), Roman Catholic pope, r. 1846-1878

SUMMARY OF EVENT

The Kulturkampf, or "cultural conflict," against the Roman Catholic Church in Germany took place against the background of two brilliant military and foreign policy triumphs by Otto von Bismarck as prime minister of Prussia. Over a five-year span from 1866 to 1871, Bismarck's armies had delivered crushing defeats to Austria and France, Prussia's chief rivals for supremacy in continental Europe. Prussia's defeat of Austria in the Seven Weeks' War of 1866 had given Prussia control of the North German Confederation, a loose conglomeration of industrial cities and duchies in the Rhineland. Based on these acquisitions, William I, king of Prussia, had assumed the title of king of Germany. The delicate balance-of-power system under Austria that had kept the peace in Europe for more than one-half century after the defeat of Napoleon I was permanently shattered by the Seven Weeks' War.

Four years later, Bismarck provoked France into the Franco-Prussian War of 1870-1871. At the 1871 Treaty of Versailles, which confirmed Prussia's triumph, King William I of Germany was, at Bismarck's urging, crowned emperor of Germany. Two French duchies and several southern German states, including Bavaria, were absorbed into the new German Empire. Bismarck himself became imperial chancellor, the emperor's chief executive in the realm. He would preside over a federal system of states and cities effectively dominated by Prussia. The official reunification of the German lands after more than seven centuries of fragmentation was the supreme achievement of Otto von Bismarck, who was soon to be called the Iron Chancellor.

Despite his astonishing foreign policy successes up to 1871, Bismarck had no desire for further conquests. He was a conservative nationalist whose prime goal as chancellor was to consolidate the new German nation he had created. At the outset, however, the staunchly Protestant Bismarck saw an imminent threat from a resurgent Roman Catholic Church under the dynamic Pope Pius IX. Particularly troubling to Bismarck was the recently promulgated doctrine of papal infallibility, according to which the pope could not err when pronouncing on matters of Catholic faith and morals. Bismarck was convinced that this doctrine empowered any pope, as defender of the faith, to intervene even in the internal politics of a sovereign nation. This possibility the German chancellor found intolerable. He also believed that a potentially deadly coalition might be forming against him, foremost among them the vengeful Austrians and French, possibly directed by the pope.

In any case, Bismarck regarded the Roman Catholic Church in Germany as the major obstacle to his dream of a powerful Protestant German nation under the firm guiding hand of his native Prussia. He strongly suspected the loyalty of a church whose members constituted nearly one-third of the population of the empire, gave their religious allegiance to the pope, and enjoyed virtual independence from German state authorities in religious matters.

In his campaign against the Catholic peril in the German Empire, the pragmatic Bismarck found a ready ally in the National Liberal Party in the Prussian parliament. Founded in 1867, the party was committed to an agenda that included the national unification of Germany, state control of the schools, and the strict separation of church and state. Its members sought to advance the secular values of the urban, middle-class Germans who formed the party's base constituency. They were even more hostile to the Catholic Church than Bismarck. While Bismarck did not share the overall secular orientation of the National Liberals, he found their majority position in the Prussian parliament indispensable to obtaining the legislation he needed to carry out his Kulturkampf.

Between 1871 and 1877, Chancellor Bismarck, through his agents and his parliamentary allies, waged a wide-ranging program of intimidation and open persecution upon the Catholic Church, especially in Prussia. Bismarck's goal was to reduce the Church and its ally, the Catholic Center Party, to complete subservience to the government. Following a few preliminary moves in 1871, Bismarck launched a barrage of anti-Church legislation, which was introduced for him by a compliant National Liberal majority in parliament. His chief agent in implementing these measures was a Prussian civil official named Adalbert Falk. In January, 1872, Falk was appointed *Kulturminister*, or minister for religion and education, in charge of the department of the Prussian bureaucracy directly responsible for dealing with the churches and the religious schools of the state. Falk, well known for his liberal, anticlerical views, eagerly assumed this position.

From 1872 through 1874, Falk's Ministry for Religion and Education relentlessly targeted the Catholic clergy and the Catholic schools. Seminaries were taken over by the government in order to imbue seminarians with the nationalist and broadly secular values of the state. All church appointments had to be approved by the government, especially appointments of teachers conducting religious instruction in Catholic schools. Between 1872 and 1875, nearly 250 Catholic priests were arrested in Prussia, most for disobeying the Kulturkampf decrees. By 1875, all 11 Prussian bishops were either in jail or exiled. Pope Pius IX declared the Kulturkampf laws invalid and threatened to excommunicate any Catholics who accepted their legality.

Other laws struck at old enemies of the liberals, such as the Jesuits. Their schools and residences were shut down throughout the German Empire, and Jesuit priests were forced to flee the country. Other priestly orders later endured the same fate, along with all Prussian monasteries. The Catholic laity suffered as well. Nearly 150 Catholic newspaper editors were arrested, 20 newspapers were seized, and 210 members of the Catholic Center party were jailed at various points after 1871, mostly for their public opposition to the Kulturkampf. Probably the most controversial of the new laws affected both the Catholic laity and their church. The Civil Marriage Act of 1875 specified that only a purely secular service, conducted under state auspices, was legally valid in Prussia. Thenceforth, the state would control the official records, removing the church from another of its traditional functions.

By 1875, the government campaign against the Catholic Church was in serious trouble. Exasperated by mounting opposition to his policies, Bismarck took personal charge. Adalbert Falk was marginalized and pressured to resign. One clear sign of the chancellor's predicament was the large volume of church properties forfeited to the state in lieu of unpaid fines. Church officials regularly refused any cooperation with the Kulturkampf. Passive resistance proved to be the most effective tactic for Catholics in Germany. The nonviolent reaction to persecution was for many Catholics personified by Ludwig Windthorst, the leader of the Catholic Center Party. Many Protestant Germans, increasingly resentful of the harshness and ruthlessness of so many of the prescribed measures, came to sympathize with the plight of their Catholic countrymen.

Probably the most important single factor in the failure of the Kulturkampf was the inability of the sluggish, tradition-bound Prussian bureaucracy to compel compliance. Bismarck could not correct this problem. He had also badly underestimated the resiliency of the Catholic Church to weather systematic persecution. In the process, German Catholics had built a more cohesive and committed religious community and had even experienced a notable spiritual renewal. By 1878 Bismarck, ever the pragmatist, had determined to cut his losses and move on to other pressing problems, such as the economy and the challenge of socialism. Falk became the scapegoat for Bismarck's failure, while most of the Kulturkampf measures were repealed outright or allowed to languish. Only the laws on civil marriage and the state control of education remained permanently on the books.

SIGNIFICANCE

The Kulturkampf in Germany was part of a broader European conflict between Catholicism and liberalism during the late nineteenth century. In Germany, this conflict was complicated by the presence of a solid conservative Protestant element led by Bismarck. Bismarck's greatest achievement was to make the German Empire a world power. Among his worst setbacks was his failure to reduce the German Catholic Church to the position of state servant. He had found that there were severe limits to the means he could muster to this end. In short, Bismarck's genius in foreign policy was not matched by his understanding of the power of religious faith. He lost prestige from this episode, although it was not a complete debacle. Kulturkampf laws on state control of schools and mandatory civil marriages survived in modified form.

—*Donald Sullivan*

FURTHER READING

Anderson, Margaret Livinia. *Windthorst: A Political Biography*. Oxford, England: Clarendon Press, 1986. Sympathetic, scholarly assessment of the career of the German Catholic politician who most effectively opposed Bismarck's Kulturkampf.

Lerman, Katherine Anne. *Bismarck*. New York: Pierson and Longman, 2004. Places the Kulturkampf within the context of Bismark's overall political motives and goals.

Ross, Ronald J. *The Failure of Bismarck's Kulturkampf: Catholicism and State Power in Wilhelmine, Germany*. Washington, D.C.: Catholic University of America Press, 1998. Contends that Bismarck's Kulturkampf failed largely because of the government's inability to enforce its laws and decrees

Smith, Helmut W. *German Nationalism and Political Conflict, 1870-1912*. Princeton, N.J.: Princeton University Press, 1995. First section describes the impact of the Kulturkampf on the national unification of Germany.

SEE ALSO: 1820: Jesuits Are Expelled from Russia, Naples, and Spain; 1835-1836: Strauss Publishes *The Life of Jesus Critically Examined*; Sept. 24, 1862: Bismarck Becomes Prussia's Minister-President; 1866-1867: North German Confederation Is Formed; Dec. 8, 1869-Oct. 20, 1870: Vatican I Decrees Papal Infallibility Dogma; July 19, 1870-Jan. 28, 1871: Franco-Prussian War; Jan. 18, 1871: German States Unite Within German Empire; Oct. 19, 1878: Germany Passes Anti-Socialist Law; 1881-1889: Bismarck Introduces Social Security Programs in Germany.

RELATED ARTICLES in *Great Lives from History: The Nineteenth Century, 1801-1900:* Otto von Bismarck; Napoleon I; Pius IX.

c. 1871-1883
GREAT AMERICAN BUFFALO SLAUGHTER

Within a space of a little more than a decade, the numbers of buffalo roaming the plains of North America were reduced from what may have been as many as thirty million animals to only a few thousand. In addition to driving the buffalo to near extinction, mass killings of the animals destroyed the traditional way of life of the Plains Indians.

ALSO KNOWN AS: Bison slaughter
LOCALE: American Great Plains
CATEGORIES: Environment and ecology; expansion and land acquisition

KEY FIGURES

William Cody (Buffalo Bill; 1846-1917), frontier scout and buffalo hunter
Philip H. Sheridan (1831-1888), U.S. Army general
William Tecumseh Sherman (1820-1891), U.S. Army leader in the West

SUMMARY OF EVENT

In 1853, an estimated sixty to seventy million buffalo still roamed the plains of North America. Within thirty years, that number was reduced to a few thousand animals. The precipitous decline of the buffalo was the result of human greed, uncontrolled exploitation, and a U.S. government policy.

Known to scientists as the American bison, buffalo are the largest land animals native to North America. Before Europeans settled in North America, buffalo ranged from the Rocky Mountains to the Atlantic shoreline and from northern Mexico to southern Canada. The greatest concentration of the animals was on the grasslands of the Great Plains. Buffalo provided the basis for a complete way of life for Native Americans living on the plains. They provided food, clothing, tools, and shelter. An important part of the culture of the nomadic Plains Indians was the buffalo-hide tepee, which could be collapsed quickly and easily transported when communities were ready to relocate. Indians also used hides for blankets, clothing, and shoes. They used the animals' horns to make utensils, cups, powder horns, toys, and decorative items. They used buffalo hair to make rope, halters, pads, and other items. They also used other parts of the buffalo to make soaps, oils, cosmetics, glues, bow strings, pouches, and much more. On the largely treeless plains, the dried droppings of buffalo provided fuel for cooking and heating. Throughout history, few human societies have developed cultures that depended on a single species of animal as strongly as the cultures of the Plains Indians depended on buffalo.

On the northern Great Plains, where the terrain was rugged, buffalo herds feeding near cliffs were often driven over precipices by Indian men and boys waving buffalo robes and shouting, an event known as a buffalo jump. Other people then rushed in to butcher as many of the animals as they could. Indians rarely intentionally killed more animals than they needed, but buffalo jumps frequently left more animals dead or dying than their pursuers could handle. Contemporary observers described slaughters of from two hundred to two thousand buffalo in such hunts. However, because of the relatively small numbers of Native Americans in North America and the primitiveness of their weapons, the impact of Indians on buffalo populations was slight.

After the U.S. Civil War ended in 1865, U.S. Army troops were freed to go west to battle the Cheyennes, Lakota Sioux, Crows, and other tribes on the frontier. Army units contracted with local settlers to supply their troops with buffalo beef for provisions. Workers constructing the new transcontinental railroad also had to be fed. Contractors included William Cody, who would become better known as Buffalo Bill, who was probably the best known of all the buffalo killers. Hunters frequently skinned the buffalo, cut out their tongues, and took only small portions of the animals' meat, leaving the remainder to rot on the prairie.

Dressed hides from animals shot by professional hunters were shipped east to be sold as lap robes for winter sleigh and buggy rides or were turned into overcoats. Highly romanticized stories by eastern writers about the exploits of Buffalo Bill and other buffalo hunters quickly made buffalo robes a status symbol. Demand increased, and ever more buffalo were slaughtered. Often only the animals' skins were taken, while their carcasses were left to scavengers. Every year, hundreds of thousands of buffalo were killed for food and hides.

Many buffalo were also killed for sport, as it became popular for people to travel to the Great Plains simply to shoot buffalo. The railroads that linked the East and West cut across the ancient north-south routes of the buffalo. The seemingly endless herds were an annoyance to train crews and a temptation to the passengers. When trains were delayed, passengers often fired into the massed animals, killing some and wounding many more. The rail-

Passengers on a Kansas-Pacific Railroad train shooting buffalo in 1871. (Library of Congress)

roads encouraged this, with advertising to induce people to ride their trains.

It is difficult to obtain accurate data on the number of buffalo slaughtered. Accurate records were rarely kept, and killings took place over a wide area. However, partial statistics can suggest what the overall picture may have been. For example, in western Kansas in 1872, approximately two thousand hide hunters each killed about fifteen buffalo a day. At that rate, hunters were killing thirty thousand buffalo per day in that one small region. As soon as herds in one area were reduced so much that hunting became unprofitable, hunters moved elsewhere, seeking larger herds. An 1869 report noted that during a good year, about 250,000 hides were shipped to the New York market alone. That figure is equivalent to the total number of buffalo estimated to be alive in North America at the turn of the twenty-first century. Total railroad shipments to the East between 1872 and 1874 were estimated at 1,378,359 hides.

A peculiarity in buffalo behavior made them particularly easy targets for hunters. Although buffalo could be easily stampeded, hunters firing from ambush could pick off the animals one by one without upsetting herds because the animals simply stood where they were as fellow buffalo were shot and dropped around them. Hide hunters called such a shooting "a stand." Some members of herds simply poked their noses at their fallen comrades and then calmly returned to grazing. Good hunters could kill seventy-five to one hundred buffalo per day. One especially skillful hunter won a bet with other hunters by shooting at a stand from ambush, killing 120 buffalo in only forty minutes.

The slaughter of the buffalo was far from a managed or controlled affair. Hunters indiscriminately shot the adults and subadults. Calves were ignored except, possibly, for camp meat. Unweaned, orphaned calves, not yet able to graze the abundant grasses, were left to starve to death. After one particularly large herd was killed, five hundred to one thousand calves wandered off to starve.

While the introduction of professional hunters alone threatened buffalo with extinction, an even more nefarious threat appeared. The U.S. government took the position that the still-warring Native Americans could be subdued if buffalo were denied to them. The U.S. Army began a program of interdiction of the herds. General Philip H. Sheridan spoke out strongly in favor of continuing the slaughter of the buffalo "to settle the Indian question." Sheridan's Civil War comrade, General William Tecumseh Sherman, echoed these sentiments. He stated that the only way to force Native Americans to reservations and turn them into peaceful farmers was to clear the prairies of buffalo. The government further encouraged the slaughter of buffalo by providing free ammunition to hunters.

As early as 1873, significantly fewer buffalo were observed in western Kansas. Hide hunters moved to the northern Great Plains territories and continued the slaughter. The decline spread throughout the range of the buffalo, and it soon became obvious to most observers that the great herds were gone.

The intensive slaughter for hides was brief, occurring mostly from 1872 to 1874, but the activity extended from 1871 through 1883. Most herds were wiped out within about four years, and the hunters then moved on to other areas. Although a few buffalo survived, their numbers clearly slipped below the level that ecologists regard as a minimum viable population size. For many animals, more than one male and one female are required to begin a breeding population. The great slaughter left the prairies littered with buffalo skeletons. For years, farmers gathered cartloads of bones to sell to fertilizer processors. One bone buyer estimated that from 1884 to 1891, he bought the bones of as many as six million buffalo skeletons.

SIGNIFICANCE

While the killings were winding down, neither settlers nor Native Americans could believe that the buffalo were really gone. Many settlers thought that the herds had migrated to Canada and would soon return. Native Americans, drawing on their mythologies, believed that the animals had returned to a great cavern in the ground to reappear when the right prayers were said and the right supplications were made. However, the great herds were, in fact, gone. The impact of the hide hunters' indiscriminate slaughter and the U.S. government's interdiction policy destroyed not only the buffalo but also the Native American nomadic way of life. Reluctantly, but with resignation, Indians were compelled to become farmers on reservations as the U.S. government had sought. Perhaps the worst blow to the Plains Indians, however, was their loss of the religious and cultural relationship they had had with the buffalo. Their entire civilization and lifeways had been destroyed along with the animals on which they depended.

Only a few scattered buffalo and some in private herds escaped the slaughter. Later, brought together in national parks, preserves, and other protected areas, they survived and multiplied. During the late twentieth and early twenty-first centuries, commercial breeding of buffalo for hides and food was greatly increasing their number. By the year 2005, it was estimated that more than one million buffalo were alive in North America.

—*Albert C. Jensen*

FURTHER READING

Carter, Robert A. *Buffalo Bill Cody: The Man Behind the Legend.* New York: John Wiley & Sons, 2000. Popular biography of the most famous buffalo hunter of them all.

Dary, David A. *The Buffalo Book: The Full Saga of the American Animal.* Chicago: Swallow Press, 1974. Detailed account of buffalo in North America. Black-and-white photos, index, bibliography.

Foster, John, ed. *Buffalo.* Edmonton, Canada: University of Alberta Press, 1992. Small collection of papers by specialists in ecology and sociology detailing the relationship between the Plains Indians and the American buffalo. Illustrations.

Isenberg, Andrew C. *The Destruction of the Bison: An Environmental History, 1750-1920.* New York: Cambridge University Press, 2000. Illuminating multidisciplinary study of the natural and human causes of the near-extinction of North American buffalo, which the author believes may have numbered as many as thirty million animals. Illustrations and maps.

McHugh, Tom. *The Time of the Buffalo.* New York: Alfred A. Knopf, 1972. Factual and readable revision of a professional wildlife biologist's dissertation. Illustrations, index, and detailed bibliography.

Matthews, Anne. *Where the Buffalo Roam.* New York: Grove Weidenfeld, 1992. Describes a plan to restore the Great Plains to their natural condition and the buffalo to their former numbers. Illustrations and index.

Wetmore, Helen Cody, and Zane Grey. *Buffalo Bill: Last of the Great Scouts.* Commemorative ed. Lincoln: University of Nebraska Press, 2003. New edition of a biography written by Cody's sister that was originally published in 1899. Includes the original illustrations by Frederic Remington and other notable artists of the Old West.

SEE ALSO: June 1, 1815-Aug., 1817: Red River Raids; Oct. 21, 1867: Medicine Lodge Creek Treaty; June 27, 1874-June 2, 1875: Red River War; 1876-1877: Sioux War; 1890: U.S. Census Bureau Announces Closing of the Frontier.

RELATED ARTICLES in *Great Lives from History: The Nineteenth Century, 1801-1900:* William Cody; Sitting Bull.

1871-1885
PRZHEVALSKY EXPLORES CENTRAL ASIA

Russian explorer Nikolay Mikhaylovich Przhevalsky completed four arduous journeys to Chinese Turkestan, Mongolia, and Tibet, surveying previously unexplored regions and discovering flora and fauna new to Western science. The secondary aim of his expeditions, facilitating Russian political expansion into disputed territories, was not realized.

LOCALE: Eastern Siberia; western China; Tibet; Mongolia
CATEGORY: Exploration and discovery

KEY FIGURES

Nikolay Mikhaylovich Przhevalsky (1839-1888), Russian military officer and explorer
Pyotr Kozlov (1863-1935), Russian explorer and protégé of Przhevalsky
Dmitrii Alekseevich Miliutin (1816-1912), Russian minister of war, 1861-1881
Pyotr Semenov-Tianshansky (1827-1914), Russian explorer, editor, and social reformer

SUMMARY OF EVENT

In 1870, three European powers—Great Britain, France, and Russia—stood poised on the margins of the crumbling Chinese empire, eager to acquire new territory and establish commercial hegemony. The British sent forays northward from their base in India. Meanwhile, over the course of the preceding two decades, the Russians had occupied formerly Persian territory in Central Asia, from the Caspian Sea westward and southward to the crest of the Tian Shan Mountains. Between the Russian border and the British outposts in the southern reaches of the Himalayas lay a vast expanse of unexplored territory, impenetrable from the south because of Tibetan isolationism and inaccessible to the Russians because of the sheer distances and physical barriers involved.

The old caravan routes, running east-west from Kashgar across the Tarim Depression and from Lake Baikal south across the Gobi Desert to Beijing, had fallen into disuse when oceanic transport from China to Europe burgeoned. For Russia, reopening and controlling one of these routes for rail or river transport represented a plausible strategy in the economic development of eastern Siberia. In order to do so, the Russians needed an accurate geographical survey of the territory, and they needed someone who could conduct such a survey in the face not only of incredible physical hardships but also against the backdrop of a bloody civil war. In 1864, the Tungans, a group of Chinese-speaking Muslims settled in western China, rebelled against a corrupt Chinese administration. Allying themselves with the Turkic-speaking Muslim Uighurs, they established a short-lived independent state under the ruthless Zaman Beg. The Tungans destroyed the Chinese infrastructure, and the Chinese massacred the Tungans.

The Russian War Department, headed by the expansionist Dmitrii Alekseevich Miliutin, saw the troubles in Chinese Turkestan as an opportunity for territorial acquisition. Pyotr Semenov-Tianshansky, who headed the quasi-governmental Russian Geographical Society, was eager to build upon his own earlier researches in the Tian Shan Mountains. A progressive who was instrumental in the liberation of Russia's serfs in 1863, Semenov-Tianshansky believed that accurate knowledge of physical geography and a comprehensive census were keys to the development of a modern state.

In 1871, a modest surveying expedition funded by these two organizations left Kyakhta, south of Lake Baikal, and proceeded across Mongolia toward Beijing, intent on securing permission from the Chinese government to explore Western China and Tibet. At its head was Nikolay Mikhaylovich Przhevalsky, an adventurous young military officer who had already made a name exploring along the Amur and Ussuri Rivers in extreme eastern Siberia. His Siberian expedition had established Przhevalsky as someone able to amass prodigious amounts of accurate physical data and plant and animal specimens with minimal assistance in the face of great physical hardship. However, working in a region populated mainly by Chinese outlaws and adventurers had also instilled in him an attitude of contempt and hostility toward the Chinese in general.

After procuring the necessary documents, Przhevalsky, accompanied by the first of a series of young protégés and two Cossacks, proceeded north and westward to the Qilian Shan mountains at the northeastern extremity of Tibet. They were able to survey these mountains and to sample rich flora and fauna from a base in the Lamasery at Choibseng. Storing their specimens, the party turned southward along a treacherous pilgrim route toward Lhasa. Their camels proved unequal to the elevation, fires could not be lit, and the party, pursued by ravenous wolves, was forced to turn back. The return route traversed areas devastated by the Tungan rebellion, a nightmare of poisoned wells and abandoned settlements.

Przhevalsky's bravado and reputation as a crack shot at times served him in good stead. Caravans welcomed him as an escort, supposing him to be effective protection against bandits. Use of Western medical knowledge and the ability to predict weather from a barometer led some to call him a magician. This was sometimes a hindrance; surveying became a furtive venture, because local nomads suspected there was some sinister magical purpose to it. Despite his failure to reach Lhasa, Przhevalsky mapped three thousand miles of route and collected several tons of specimens that still furnish botanists and zoologists with material for analysis. Back in Irkutsk, Przhevalsky published an account of his travels. Combining a flair for drama with a lively writing style, he captured the Russian public's imagination; this helped secure better funding for subsequent expeditions.

A second expedition originated in Kashgar and proceeded up the Ili Valley, then temporarily under Russian jurisdiction, across the Tian Shan Mountains, and into the Tarim Basin, aiming to enter Tibet from the northwest. Przhavelsky determined that the rivers running southward and eastward from Tian Shan terminated in a large brackish lake, Lop Nur, reported by Marco Polo to be at a different location. Subsequent surveying vindicated both explorers' observations: The rivers of the Taklimakan Desert periodically shift their courses, accounting for the change in the lake's position. Polo's Lop Nur is today a barren salt pan. Ill health forced Przhevalsky to cut his second expedition short.

A third expedition, in 1876-1877, produced the discovery of the primitive horse that now bears Przhevalsky's name. A relict population of the wild forebear of domestic horses roamed the Junggar Desert near Urumqi. When native hunters brought him a skin and skull from one of these horses, Przhevalsky immediately recognized their significance. He subsequently saw, but failed to capture, living specimens. He also assiduously

CENTRAL ASIA DURING THE LATE NINETEENTH CENTURY

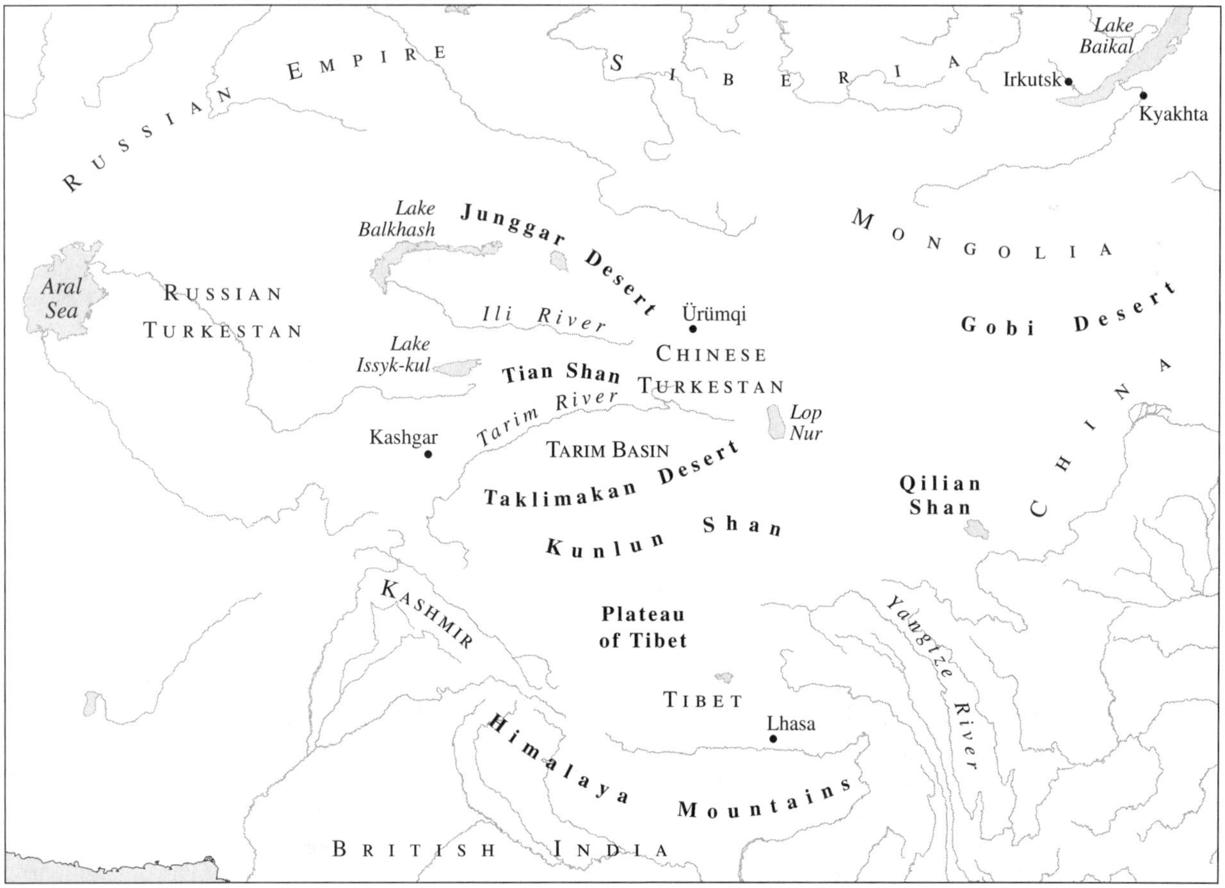

sought the fabled yeti or ape-man, no authentic specimens of which were forthcoming.

Proceeding across the Taklimakan Desert, Przhevalsky entered Tibet from the north, crossed the Plateau of Tibet, and reached a point twenty-six miles from Lhasa before being turned back by the Chinese authorities, who feared that the supposedly purely scientific expedition was a prelude to Christian evangelism, military conquest, or both. The British had probably encouraged this suspicion in order to prevent the Russians from gaining an advantage over them in the region. Przhevalsky was able to repay the British for this stratagem: He showed the Chinese maps of Tibet that had been prepared by Indian surveyors disguised as pilgrims.

In 1884, Przhevalsky again returned to the Tarim Basin and northern Tibet, surveying additional territory and collecting more biological specimens. His survey was the first general account of northern Tibet to reach the West. Upon his return in 1885, he published an outline of conditions in Central Asia that was so ardent in its Eurocentric chauvinism and imperialistic designs that Russian policy makers were quick to repudiate it.

In 1888, Przhevalsky was in the process of organizing a fifth expedition. Then forty-nine years old and losing some of his legendary physical stamina, he expressed a wish not to live to see old age and retirement in Russia. A bout of typhoid obliged: He died on the shores of Lake Issyk-Kul, in Kyrgyzstan, surrounded by his companions of the field. These included Pyotr Kozlov, a former clerk who accompanied Przhevalsky on his last two expeditions and later became a distinguished explorer in his own right.

SIGNIFICANCE

To Russians of his generation, Przhevalsky was a hero. A young Anton Chekhov wrote a glowing obituary; later, he modified his opinions, as firsthand accounts of the Chinese and indigenous Siberian peoples exposed hero's arrogance and narrow chauvinism. Soviet-era Russian sources emphasized the contributions of the progressive liberal Semenov-Tianshansky and downplayed the role of Przhevalsky in the exploration of Central Asia.

Two aspects of the Przhevalsky's narrative, one probably false, have attracted the attention of popular historians. Based on his dogged determination, aggressive character, residence in the Caucasus at the relevant time, and a certain facial resemblance, a rumor arose that Przhevalsky was Joseph Stalin's natural father. Serious biographers of both men doubt this. Rather, his never having married and his close relationship with a series of handsome young protégés are seen as evidence that he was homosexual, although no direct evidence exists to confirm this theory.

Przhevalsky's scientific discoveries, including but by no means limited to the famous wild horse, are probably his most lasting contribution to posterity. The laboriously completed surveys of physical geography would have facilitated military incursions and Russian development of the region, but these never materialized. The assassination of Alexander II and resignation of Miliutin introduced a more conservative spirit into the Russian administration, putting a stop to further expansion into Chinese Turkestan.

—*Martha A. Sherwood*

FURTHER READING

Meyer, Karl E., and Shareen Blair Brysac. *Tournament of Shadows: The Great Game and the Race for Empire in Central Asia*. Washington, D.C.: Counterpoint, 1999. Broad in scope, covering the entire nineteenth and early twentieth centuries; puts Przhevalsky's explorations in the context of Anglo-Russian rivalries.

Przhevalsky, Nikolai. *From Kulja Across the Tian Shan to Lob-Nor*. Translated by E. Delmar Morgan. 1879. Reprint. New York: Greenwood Press, 1969. This firsthand account conveys a sense of the explorer's style; includes a large foldout map.

Rayfield, Donald. *The Dream of Lhasa: The Life of Nikolay Przhevalsky, 1839-1888, Explorer of Central Asia*. Athens: Ohio University Press, 1976. Well-researched, thorough, and vividly written; provides necessary background and technical detail.

Stockwell, Foster. *Westerners in China: A History of Exploration and Trade, Ancient Times Through the Present*. Jefferson, N.C.: McFarland, 2003. Includes a chapter on Przhevalsky, drawn largely from work done by Rayfield.

Wieczynski, Joseph, ed. *Modern Encyclopedia of Russian and Soviet History*. Gulf Breeze, Fla.: Academic Press, 1975-1983. Good source for biographies of Kozlov, Miliutin, and Semenov-Tianshansky.

SEE ALSO: 1854-1862: Wallace's Expeditions Give Rise to Biogeography; Winter, 1855-Jan. 2, 1878: Muslim Rebellions in China; Nov. 14, 1897: Scramble for Chinese Concessions Begins.

RELATED ARTICLES in *Great Lives from History: The Nineteenth Century, 1801-1900:* Alexander II; Anton Chekhov.

January 18, 1871
GERMAN STATES UNITE WITHIN GERMAN EMPIRE

In the wake of three successful wars that solidified Prussia's status as a great European power, the German states were unified under the dominance of Prussia into the German Empire. The empire, a strong military and economic entity in central Europe, altered the traditional European balance of power and revolutionized European trade and diplomacy.

LOCALE: Berlin, Prussia (now in Germany); Versailles, France
CATEGORIES: Government and politics; expansion and land acquisition

KEY FIGURES

Otto von Bismarck (1815-1898), minister-president of Prussia, 1862-1890, and chancellor of the German Empire, 1871-1890
William I (1797-1888), king of Prussia, r. 1861-1888, and German emperor, 1871-1888
Napoleon III (Louis Napoleon Bonaparte; 1808-1873), emperor of France, r. 1852-1870
Francis Joseph I (1830-1916), emperor of Austria, r. 1848-1916, and king of Hungary, r. 1867-1916
Friedrich von Beust (1809-1886), Austrian foreign minister, 1866-1871

SUMMARY OF EVENT

On January 18, 1871, the rulers of the various German states assembled in the Hall of Mirrors of the ancient palace of French kings at Versailles for a momentous event. Otto von Bismarck, minister-president of Prussia, was about to proclaim the formation of the Second German Empire with his king, William I of Prussia, as its emperor. Bismarck's proclamation fulfilled the dreams cherished in the hearts of many Germans for more than a half century, a dream of uniting the German states into a powerful nation.

When Napoleon I's armies had occupied many of the German states in 1804-1806, he had organized most of those outside Austria and Prussia into the Confederation of the Rhine with himself as its "Protector." The French troops who occupied the German states introduced to the Germans the political ideals of constitutionalism, parliamentarianism, the natural rights of man, and nationalism. Bonaparte's oppressive policies toward the Germans and the arrogant behavior of the French troops awoke the spirit of German nationalism, especially among young Germans.

Initially German nationalism took a Romantic form. Its proponents—the most vocal of whom were the students and faculties of German universities—argued that every human ethnic group possessed unique characteristics. These characteristics, they said, had to develop free of any outside interference. Only then could the ethnic group make its contribution to the progress of the human race. This Romantic nationalism in Germany was inextricably intertwined with liberal political views. The young Germans who championed these ideas wanted to establish a national state that would include all ethnic Germans ruled by a constitution and a parliament based on universal manhood suffrage.

With the defeat of Napoleon at the Battle of Waterloo in 1815, nationalists and liberals in the German states expected their dreams of a united Germany to be realized. Instead, the leaders of the great powers of Europe created the Germanic Confederation, a loose union of thirty-nine German states, dominated by Austria and Prussia. Neither the confederation nor any of its members had elected legislative bodies or constitutions. The states that composed the confederation maintained their own armies, erected tariff barriers against one another, coined their own money, and passed their own laws. The hereditary aristocracies in all of the states continued to enjoy special privileges before the law. The failure of the great powers to create a unified, liberal German state frustrated the dreams of German nationalists and liberals and turned them on a course of revolutionary activity that culminated in the Prussian Revolution of 1848.

Despite press censorship and restrictions on German professors, liberal and nationalist ideas continued to spread between 1815 and 1848. The nationalists found allies among the German bourgeoisie during the 1830's because of the tariff barriers erected by the governments of the small states. Such tariffs greatly hindered economic and industrial development. In 1834, economic concerns forced seventeen of the German states to join the Prussians in creating the Zollverein (German customs union), a customs union which expedited economic development among its members. The bourgeoisie joined the faculties and students at the German universities to furnish the leadership for the Prussian revolution.

In 1848, several factors, chief among them frustrated nationalism and liberalism, contributed to the outbreak of revolutions in most of the European states. The revolutionaries overthrew autocratic governments from Hungary to France and from Italy to Germany, and they proceeded to create new national states based on liberal political ideas. After the overthrow of aristocratic governments in the German states, most of the new governments sent delegates to a meeting charged with writing a constitution for a united German nation. The delegates convened the Frankfurt parliament on May 18, 1848, and debated the exact form and extent of the new nation for more than a year. By March, 1849, the parliament had drafted the constitution for a united Germany. A delegation from the parliament offered the throne of this German empire to Frederick William IV of Prussia on April 3, 1849. Frederick William declined, however, saying he would accept such a crown only from the aristocratic rulers of the German states. Dejected, the representatives went back to Frankfurt, and the parliament dissolved some months later. Liberal and nationalist Germans found their dreams once again unrealized.

During the 1850's, the chances for a united Germany seemed more remote than ever. Reactionary governments were firmly established in the German states, which were too jealous of their privileges to contemplate national unification. The situation began to change toward the end of the decade when the new Prussian regent, William I, came into conflict with the Prussian parliament.

Hoping to break the stalemate, William appointed Otto von Bismarck as minister-president of Prussia in 1862. Bismarck had little regard for liberalism or parliamentarianism and was a Prussian patriot rather than a German nationalist. Nevertheless, he embarked on aggressive new foreign and domestic policies that resulted in the unification of the German states in an empire similar to that envisioned by the members of the Frankfurt parliament.

Bismarck embarked on the course that led to German

THE UNIFICATION OF GERMANY

Proclamation of William I (on platform) as emperor of Germany at Versailles. (Francis R. Niglutsch)

unification by defying the Prussian parliament and disregarding the constitution. He collected taxes for the expansion and reequipment of the Prussian army without the approval of parliament. He used the expanded army to win a victory over Denmark in the Danish-Prussian War (1864), when the Danish king tried to annex a member state of the German Confederation. The victory made Bismarck a hero in Prussia and throughout the German states. Two years later, he led Prussia in the Seven Weeks' War, this time against the Austrian emperor Francis Joseph I.

According to many historians, Bismarck had maneuvered the Austrian government into a position in which it was forced to declare war against Prussia. Immediately before the war, Bismarck had made sure that no other nation would intervene on Austria's behalf in the struggle. He signed an alliance with the Italians, received assurances from the Russians that they would remain neutral, and convinced Emperor Napoleon III that France would gain territory along the Rhine River in the international conference that would follow the war.

The Seven Weeks' War resulted in a defeat for the Austrians. At the conclusion of hostilities, Bismarck secured a quick and mild peace with the Austrian government, now led by Friedrich von Beust, to prevent Napoleon III from playing a role in the peace proceedings. Bismarck then organized twenty-two of the German states into a new political entity called the North German Confederation. The constitution of the new state established a national parliament elected by universal manhood suffrage, with executive power exercised by a president in the person of the Prussian king, William. Bismarck became the chancellor of the new state.

The south German states joined with the Austrians in forming the South German Confederation, essentially a continuation of the old German Confederation in a diminished form. Beust, the Austrian foreign minister, spent the next five years trying to prevent Bismarck from incorporating the south German states into the North German Confederation. Napoleon III, embittered by what he considered to be a betrayal by Bismarck, joined Beust in opposing further Prussian expansion. If Bismarck did set out to unify the German states under Prussian leadership in 1862, he must have realized after 1866 that his goals could not be achieved without a war with France.

The immediate cause of the Franco-Prussian War of 1870-1871 was a dispute over the Spanish throne in 1866-1870. Members of the Spanish government invited Leopold von Hohenzollern to become their new monarch. Leopold, a relative of William of Prussia, was not acceptable to Napoleon III, who forced Leopold's withdrawal as a candidate for the Spanish throne. In 1870, the Spanish again invited Leopold to become their king. Napoleon III demanded that William withdraw his relative's candidacy and promise that never again would a Hohenzollern become a candidate for the Spanish throne. William's reply was not satisfactory to Napoleon III, who declared war against Prussia. Some historians maintain that Bismarck engineered the affair in such a way that Napoleon III had no choice but to declare war. However true this thesis may be, the Franco-Prussian War was the final step in the unification of Germany.

The Prussian army defeated the French forces and besieged Paris. Through diplomatic and military pressure, Bismarck forced the princes of the south German states to become members of the North German Confederation. Bismarck made his famous proclamation of the formation of the Second German Empire during an outburst of patriotic enthusiasm in the German states that accompanied the defeat of the French. The new empire adopted the constitution and form of the North German Confederation, the only difference being that the executive powers were vested in the hands of a hereditary emperor, William I of Prussia.

Significance

With the formation of the German Empire, all the German states were finally unified under a central authority. Territories that had traditionally been rivals or at best temporary allies became incorporated into a single entity that incorporated significant military and economic resources. In a relatively brief period of time, Europe's balance of power had shifted dramatically. The German Empire would continue to exist as the dominant force in central Europe until it entered World War I in 1914.

—Paul Madden

Further Reading

Carr, William. *The Origins of the Wars of German Unification.* London: Longman, 1991. Examines the multitudinous causes of the series of wars that led to the formation of the German Empire.

Feuchtwanger, Edgar. *Bismarck.* London: Routledge, 2002. Concise biography, reassessing Bismarck's historical significance.

Hargreaves, David. *Bismarck and German Unification.* Houndmills, England: Macmillan, 1991. Shows the importance of Bismarck's own personality in determining the nature of the new nation he created.

Lerman, Katharine Anne. *Bismarck.* New York: Pearson Longman, 2004. One of the titles in the Profiles in Power series, this book focuses on Bismarck's exercise of power as a crucial means of understanding his personality and statecraft.

Pflanze, Otto. *Bismarck and the Development of Germany: The Period of Unification, 1815-1871.* Princeton, N.J.: Princeton University Press, 1971. Surveys the events leading to the formation of the German Empire and Bismarck's role in shaping those events.

Sellman, Roger Raymond. *Bismarck and the Unification of Germany.* London: Methuen, 1973. A concise account of the formation of the Second Reich based on secondary sources and designed for college courses.

Simpson, William. *The Second Reich: Germany, 1871-1918.* New York: Cambridge University Press, 1995. The most recent history of the Second German Empire, based on the latest scholarship.

See also: June 8-9, 1815: Organization of the German Confederation; Jan. 1, 1834: German States Join to Form Customs Union; Mar. 3-Nov. 3, 1848: Prussian Revolution of 1848; Sept. 24, 1862: Bismarck Becomes Prussia's Minister-President; Feb. 1-Oct. 30, 1864: Danish-Prussian War; 1866-1867: North German Confederation Is Formed; June 15-Aug. 23, 1866: Austria and Prussia's Seven Weeks' War; July 19, 1870-Jan. 28, 1871: Franco-Prussian War; 1871-1877: Kulturkampf Against the Catholic Church in Germany; May 6-Oct. 22, 1873: Three Emperors' League Is Formed; May 20, 1882: Triple Alliance Is Formed.

Related articles in *Great Lives from History: The Nineteenth Century, 1801-1900:* Friedrich von Beust; Otto von Bismarck; Francis Joseph I; Napoleon III.

February 13, 1871-1875
THIRD FRENCH REPUBLIC IS ESTABLISHED

With the downfall of the Second Empire of Napoleon III, France again established a constitutional republican system of government. The creation of this Third French Republic was fraught with political confrontation and maneuverings between royalists and republicans that set the tone for the long period of political control that followed.

LOCALE: France
CATEGORY: Government and politics

KEY FIGURES

Adolphe Thiers (1797-1877), first president of the Third French Republic, 1871-1873
Marie-Edme-Patrice-Maurice de MacMahon (1808-1893), second president of the Third French Republic, 1873-1879
Henri Dieudonné d'Artois (Duc de Bordeaux and Comte de Chambord; 1820-1883), Bourbon claimant to the throne of France
Léon Gambetta (1838-1888), radical republican leader
Jacques-Victor-Albert Broglie (1821-1901), French premier and minister of foreign affairs, 1873-1874
Louis-Philippe-Albert d'Orléans (Comte de Paris; 1838-1894), Orléanist pretender to the throne of France

SUMMARY OF EVENT

While France continued to battle in the Franco-Prussian War (1870-1871) after Napoleon III's surrender on September 1, 1870, its chances for any military success became increasingly remote in the last months of that year. In the face of mounting despair and against the wishes of the fiery radical Léon Gambetta, the provisional government began negotiations with Prussia and arranged a truce on January 28, 1871. France was to hold national elections while the truce was in force in order to create a legal government that could negotiate a formal peace. The elections were held on February 13; those elected began to assemble in Bordeaux shortly thereafter.

Two factors combined to make this National Assembly predominantly royalist in tone. First, France was war-weary, and its citizens, remembering Gambetta's stubborn refusal to surrender, associated republicanism with war. Second, the extreme shortness of the electoral campaign period encouraged the peasants to vote for those men who enjoyed the greatest prestige in the community, often members of the local aristocracy. Once convened, the National Assembly elected Adolphe Thiers, the old Orléanist minister, as its provisional executive, then moved from Bordeaux to Versailles and began work on a final peace treaty with Germany.

A well-known historian, Thiers had been in the assembly since 1863 as a deputy and had constantly sat with the liberal opposition to the empire. As a conservative republican, Thiers tried to strike a balance between the fiery republicans who were under the sway of Gambetta and the royalists. In August of 1871, with the grudging support of the royalists, Thiers became the president, but by 1873 he was alienated by the extreme positions of the royalists and ultraconservatives. It was in Thiers's nature to try to moderate and reach political consensus, but this proved to be increasingly difficult.

After it had determined itself empowered to act as a constituent assembly, the National Assembly had to agree on what form the new government should take. The overwhelming royalist majority was hampered in its desire to create a monarchy by three factors. First, they were unable to agree whether the crown belonged to Louis-Philippe-Albert d'Orléans, comte de Paris and grandson of the former King Louis-Philippe, or to Henri Dieudonné d'Artois, the grandson of King Charles X. Second, Thiers, a political conservative, appeared to be agreeable to continuing a republic, especially if he himself were president of it. Third, the republicans seemed to convince the electorate that royalist support of the papal cause in Italy might lead to war. This last factor identified the royalists with war and the republicans with peace, so that in successive elections the republicans cut deeply into the royalist majority.

The royalists, worried by increasing republican strength, overthrew Thiers in 1873 and had him replaced with Marshal Marie-Edme-Patrice-Maurice de MacMahon, an old imperial general. MacMahon then selected Jacques-Victor-Albert Broglie as premier and minister of foreign affairs. Royalist hopes for establishing a monarchy were dashed when the obstinate Dieudonné d'Artois announced that he would accept the throne only on terms that everyone in France knew would be unacceptable. Marshal MacMahon was approached by Dieudonné d'Artois about a possible coup d'état, but MacMahon remained loyal to his oath as president. Dieudonné d'Artois left France in a state of irritation with MacMahon and other royalists who were not inclined to act illegally for him. The threat of a Bourbon restoration faded, mainly because of Dieudonné d'Artois's rigidity and his own imperious personality.

Antimonarchist revolutionaries tearing down a statue of Napoleon III in Paris. (Francis R. Niglutsch)

When this attempt at establishing a monarchy failed, the moderates took over the leadership of the National Assembly, and in 1875 they established the Third French Republic on a permanent basis. The constitution of 1875 was designed to prevent the radical republicans from gaining power, but aided by certain precedent-establishing events of the next few years it prevented anyone from gaining personal power.

SIGNIFICANCE

The precarious new republic was bolstered in the wake of the events of May 16, 1876, when President MacMahon forced Premier Jules Simon, a moderate, to surrender his office to a conservative who was acceptable to MacMahon and the right. Republicans of all persuasions resisted the royalists in the Chamber of Deputies, refusing to recognize the change. MacMahon responded by dissolving the chamber and calling for new elections. At this point, the royalists were confident of an electoral victory, as the republicans were able to unite.

In a surprise move, Adolphe Thiers and Léon Gambetta campaigned together vigorously, but during the campaign Thiers died. Thiers, who had never been liked by the staunch Gambettist republicans, became a martyr, a rallying point. Although the republicans never gained the overwhelming victory for which they had hoped, they at least stanched the royalist tide. MacMahon's powers were reduced, and the high tide of royalist sentiment had been reached. The elections of October 14, 1877, were indeed conclusive for the republicans, who received more than 54 percent of the vote. This victory ended the confrontation that dominated the early days of the Third Republic and also settled the political confusion that had marked the establishment of the republic. France had finally achieved a reasonably stable government.

—*Harold A. Schofield, updated by James J. Cooke*

FURTHER READING

Bury, J. P. T. *Gambetta and the Making of the Third Republic*. London: Longman, 1973. Bury's work contains a great number of facts surrounding Léon Gambetta's role in the creating of the republic.

Elwitt, Sanford. *The Making of the Third Republic*. Baton Rouge: Louisiana State University Press, 1975. In this work, Elwitt focuses on the so-called bourgeois founders of the republic.

Fortescue, William. *The Third Republic in France, 1870-1940: Conflicts and Continuities*. London: Routledge, 2000. Chapters 1 and 2 cover the emergence of the Third Republic and the political climate in the republic's earliest years.

Lehning, James R. *To Be a Citizen: The Political Culture of the Early French Third Republic*. Ithaca, N.Y.: Cornell University Press, 2001. A history of the early years of the republic, in which the French government worked to implement political reforms, including universal male suffrage.

Taithe, Bertrand. *Citizenship and Wars: France in Turmoil, 1870-1871*. London: Routledge, 2001. Examination of the concept of citizenship during the period of social and political upheaval surrounding the establishment of the French Third Republic.

Thomson, A. M. *Democracy in France Since 1870*. London: Oxford University Press, 1964. Thomson's presentation of the foundation of the republic examines all factions and their positions.

Wright, Gordon. *France in Modern Times: From the Englightenment to the Present*. 5th ed. New York: W. W. Norton, 1995. This classic work examines France of 1870 from every aspect of French culture, politics, and society.

Zeldin, Theodore. *Ambition, Love and Politics*. Vol. 1 in *France, 1848-1945*. Oxford, England: Clarendon Press, 1973. Zeldin recounts the chaos and confusion of the 1870's in France.

SEE ALSO: Apr. 11, 1814-July 29, 1830: France's Bourbon Dynasty Is Restored; Feb. 22-June, 1848: Paris Revolution of 1848; Dec. 2, 1852: Louis Napoleon Bonaparte Becomes Emperor of France; Sept. 1, 1870: Battle of Sedan; Sept. 20, 1870-Jan. 28, 1871: Prussian Army Besieges Paris; Mar. 18-May 28, 1871: Paris Commune; Jan., 1886-1889: French Right Wing Revives During Boulanger Crisis.

RELATED ARTICLES in *Great Lives from History: The Nineteenth Century, 1801-1900:* Léon Gambetta; Napoleon III; Adolphe Thiers.

March 3, 1871
GRANT SIGNS INDIAN APPROPRIATION ACT

In one of the most wrenching shifts in federal policy toward Native Americans, the Indian Appropriation Act unilaterally ruled that Native Americans no longer belonged to their own sovereign nations, ending treaty making between U.S. and tribal governments.

LOCALE: Washington, D.C.

CATEGORIES: Indigenous people's rights; laws, acts, and legal history

KEY FIGURES

Felix R. Brunot (1820-1898), head of the Board of Indian Commissioners

Henry Laurens Dawes (1816-1903), Massachusetts congressman who opposed the treaties

Ulysses S. Grant (1822-1885), president of the United States, 1869-1877

Ely Samuel Parker (c. 1828-1895), Seneca leader who served as Grant's commissioner of Indian affairs

William Windom (1827-1891), Minnesota congressman who supported the treaty system

Richard Yates (1815-1873), Illinois senator who opposed the treaty system

SUMMARY OF EVENT

In 1871, the U.S. Congress voted to stop entering into treaties with Native American peoples. Since the origins of the republic, the U.S. government had dealt with tribes by recognizing each one as a sovereign nation living within the United States. Hence, ambassadors were sent out from Washington, D.C., to negotiate treaties, and each agreement had to be ratified by a two-thirds majority of the Senate, as provided in the U.S. Constitution. In *Worcester v. Georgia* (1832), Chief Justice John Marshall had determined that this process had to be followed because each tribe was self-governing and sovereign within its own territory.

The change took place because many Americans had come to believe that Native American nations no longer acted like sovereign states. They were too weak to assert their sovereignty, post-Civil War whites believed, and many had become dependent on the federal government for their very survival. Members of Congress expressed that view in a series of debates on Indian policy in 1870-1871. In the House of Representatives, the feeling also grew that the House was being ignored in the development of Indian policy. The only way the House could influence Native American relations would be by renouncing the treaty concept. The attack on treaty making gained strength during the debate over the money to be appropriated for the United States Board of Indian Commissioners, the agency created in 1869 to oversee expenditures on Indian programs.

Seneca leader Ely Samuel Parker. (Library of Congress)

The commissioners' first report suggested major changes in Indian policy. It called for ending the treaty system and dealing with the so-called "uncivilized" native peoples as "wards of the government." Board chairperson Felix R. Brunot echoed the views of many U.S. citizens when he declared that it was absurd to treat "a few thousand savages" as if they were equal with the people and government of the United States. President Ulysses S. Grant supported that view, as did his commissioner of Indian affairs, Ely Samuel Parker, who was himself a member of New York's Seneca nation. Parker believed that it was a cruel farce to deal with the tribes as equals. In his view, most tribes were "helpless and ignorant wards" of the federal government.

Resentment of members of the House of Representatives at their exclusion from Indian policy making became apparent during debates over new treaties negotiated in 1868 and 1869. For example, a May, 1868, agreement with the Osage Nation in Kansas had ceded eight million acres of land to the government. The land then was then to be sold to a railroad company for twenty cents per acre. The House voted unanimously to recommend that the Senate not ratify the treaty because the land transfer had taken place outside the traditional methods of selling public property. The Senate responded to the House plea by rejecting the treaty. Later, however, the land was sold to the railroad company with the approval of the House.

The House again took up the issue of treaty making in 1869 during a violent debate over the Indian appropriation for 1870. The appropriation provided money for food, clothes, and education for tribal members living on reservations. The House refused to accept an increase in funds voted by the Senate. Representatives also began to question whether native peoples were capable of signing official treaties with the United States. Most representatives attacked the traditional system, although three congressmen spoke in favor of the treaty process. Representative William Windom of Minnesota argued that changing the process would be a breach of faith with the tribes and that revoking the process would confuse Native Americans and add to their distrust of the U.S. government.

Representative John J. Logan, Republican of Illinois, responded for the majority, however, by declaring that "the idea of this Government making treaties with bands of wild and roving Indians is simply preposterous and ridiculous." Amid loud cheers and laughter, Logan attacked the character of native peoples and suggested that they were an inferior race that should not be treated as equal in status to the people of the United States. The House refused to approve the appropriation bill, and the Senate refused to compromise; therefore, no Indian appropriation bill passed Congress in 1869.

In the debate over the 1871 appropriation, both sides raised the same arguments. In the Senate, supporters of the treaty system argued that any change would severely injure any goodwill that native peoples still held toward the U.S. government system. Senator Richard Yates reiterated the antitreaty sentiment, declaring that the tribes were not civilized and that making treaties with them had been a mistake. The Senate, however, passed an appropriation bill and sent it to the House. While the debate took place, many tribes were waiting for the money due to them under treaties negotiated in 1868 and 1869. However, unless Congress agreed to an appropriation bill, they would receive nothing. Finally, in a compromise arranged between the two legislative branches, a sum of two million dollars was appropriated to pay off prior obligations. However, debate over the appropriation for the next year bogged down in the House.

The Board of Indian Commissioners then helped the House position by calling for an end to treaty making and for abrogating all existing agreements. Only Representative Eugene M. Wilson of Minnesota spoke in favor of continuing the historic policy. If Native Americans were not protected by treaties, he argued, they would be cheated out of their lands by white speculators and end up with nothing. Debate in the Senate and the House seemed far more concerned with constitutional technicalities than with the welfare of native peoples. Once more, no bill seemed possible. On the last day of the session, President Grant urged a compromise, or, he warned, a war with the tribes was sure to break out. Under this threat, Congress agreed to put aside its differences temporarily and passed a bill.

When the new Congress opened on January 4, 1871, Representative Henry Laurens Dawes of Massachusetts led the call for change. Dawes, who in 1887 would author a major bill in the Senate drastically changing policy toward native peoples, called for a quick program of assimilation in this earlier debate. If Native Americans were to become Americanized—a policy that he supported—they should be treated as individuals rather than as members of foreign nations. So far as he was concerned, Native American nations were not and never had been equal to the United States. The House then passed a bill denouncing what were worded as "so-called treaties."

In the Senate, an amendment to delete the words "so-called" before "treaties" led to a vigorous debate. Senator William Stewart of Nevada objected to the amendment. "The whole Indian policy of feeding drunken, worthless, vagabond Indians, giving them money to squander . . . has been a growing disgrace to our country for years." Treaties with "irresponsible tribes" were no treaties at all. However, only a few senators agreed with the amendment, and "so-called" was eliminated. This angered the House, which refused to accept the Senate version.

Meanwhile, many congressmen and senators were growing tired of the endless debate and seemed willing to compromise. A conference committee of senators and representatives agreed that past treaties would be accepted or the integrity of the United States would be compromised. The members of the committee agreed that no more treaties should be negotiated with Native Americans, however. Most conferees agreed that the tribes with which treaties had not yet been signed scarcely seemed like legitimate nations, as they were too small, weak, and miserable.

The final compromise asserted the validity of prior agreements but provided that in the future, "no Indian nation or tribe within the territory of the United States shall be acknowledged or recognized as an independent nation, tribe, or power with whom the United States may contract by treaty." Both the Senate and the House accepted the compromise, and President Grant signed it into law on March 3, 1871.

SIGNIFICANCE

After passage of the Indian Appropriation Act, treaties were no longer to be negotiated with Native American peoples. From that date, Native Americans were instead considered by the federal government to be "wards of the state." The next major shift in federal policy toward Native Americans would come in 1887, with passage of the General Allotment Act, which allowed, for the first time, the allotting of land to individual members of tribes.

—*Leslie V. Tischauser*

FURTHER READING

Cohen, Fay G. *Treaties on Trial: The Continuing Controversy Over Northwest Indian Fishing Rights*. Seattle: University of Washington Press, 1986. Shows the continuing importance of treaties and the bitterness still evoked by pre-1871 agreements.

Heizer, Robert F. "Treaties." In *California*. Vol. 8 in *Handbook of North American Indians*. Washington, D.C.: Smithsonian Institution Press, 1978. A brief description of treaty making before 1871.

Jones, Dorothy V. *License for Empire: Colonialism by Treaty in Early America*. Chicago: University of Chicago Press, 1982. Discusses abuses of the system and how native peoples failed to understand the process.

Kvasnicka, Robert M. "United States Indian Treaties and Agreements." In *History of Indian-White Relations*, edited by Wilcomb E. Washburn. Vol. 4 in *Handbook of North American Indians*. Washington, D.C.: Smithsonian Institution Press, 1988. A short discussion of the debate over treaties and how the process was ended.

Prucha, Francis Paul. *American Indian Treaties: The History of a Political Anomaly*. Berkeley: University of California Press, 1994. The full story of treaty making and how it was ended in 1871. Index and list of treaties.

SEE ALSO: May 28, 1830: Congress Passes Indian Removal Act; Apr. 30, 1860-1865: Apache and Navajo War; Feb. 6, 1861-Sept. 4, 1886: Apache Wars; Dec. 21, 1866: Fetterman Massacre; Oct. 21, 1867: Medicine Lodge Creek Treaty; Nov. 27, 1868: Washita River Massacre; June 27, 1874-June 2, 1875: Red River War; 1876: Canada's Indian Act; Feb. 8, 1887: General Allotment Act Erodes Indian Tribal Unity.

RELATED ARTICLES in *Great Lives from History: The Nineteenth Century, 1801-1900:* Ulysses S. Grant; Lewis Henry Morgan.

March 18-May 28, 1871
PARIS COMMUNE

The short-lived Paris Commune failed as an attempt by French revolutionaries to seize control of France, but it provided future generations of socialists with an inspirational symbol.

LOCALE: Paris, France
CATEGORY: Wars, uprisings, and civil unrest

KEY FIGURES

Auguste Blanqui (1805-1881), leading revolutionary theorist
Gustave Courbet (1819-1877), French painter who tried to organize artists to support the revolt
Louise Michel (1830-1905), foremost woman participant in the insurrection
Adolphe Thiers (1797-1877), president of the French National Assembly
Pierre-Joseph Proudhon (1809-1865), leading French socialist

SUMMARY OF EVENT

During the spring of 1871, a bitter civil war between the people of Paris and the national government erupted. The background to the revolt included several interrelated factors. Paris had just emerged from the Franco-Prussian War, angry because the so-called Government of National Defense had failed to break the four-month-long siege of the city and defeat the Germans. Traditionally republican Paris was also fearful that the royalist majority in the National Assembly at Bordeaux would attempt to restore the monarchy. Paris was also outraged over the concessions that Adolphe Thiers, the president of the National Assembly, had made to the Prussian chancellor, Otto von Bismarck, while negotiating the treaty that ended the war. Moreover, many Parisians were threatened with ruin after the assembly passed several laws that forced immediate payment on overdue promissory notes and ended the moratorium on the payment of back rent.

Disturbed by this growing Parisian hostility, the National Assembly, which had just relocated to Versailles, tried to recapture some cannons held by local National Guard units in Paris. The failure of this attempt to disarm Paris on March 18, 1871, marked the beginning of the insurrection. On March 26, elections to the Paris Commune were held. Elected members of the Commune held a variety of beliefs. Moderate republicans jostled for position of power with radical republicans, and various socialist groups argued about the ideas of Auguste Blanqui and Pierre-Joseph Proudhon, and the nascent Marxist concepts expressed by some leaders of the First International.

From its inception, the Paris Commune was weakened by serious internal divisions. Disagreements over the source of ultimate authority between official and semiofficial governmental institutions were part of the problem. A clash of interests and political philosophies between the Jacobin majority and the socialist minority within the Commune was another. As a result of these conflicts, members of the Commune could not come to any understandings on such basic questions as the role and aims of government.

Many socialists, especially the Proudhonists, looked upon the Commune as the first step toward the creation of a decentralized state. The Jacobins, however, saw the Commune as a revival of the First French Republic when radical Paris, working through a dictatorship, forced its views on the rest of the nation. In terms of its aims, the Jacobin majority not only adopted the same terminology but also wished to concentrate on the same type of political and social issues that had confronted the leaders of 1793.

In opposition, the socialist minority, led by members of the First International, were more concerned with using the Commune as a means to combat the new problems introduced by industrialization, such as the increasing disparity of wealth between the possessors and the nonpossessors. Inspired by their ideas, the Paris Commune did represent a brilliant, although short-lived, period of social experimentation. Female workers, led by Louise Michel, formed political groups to push for an improvement in conditions for women, and even artists, led by the realist painter Gustave Courbet, attempted to marshal their collective talents for the betterment of the human condition.

In the end, however, the Commune failed to do the one thing that every revolutionary government must do in order to succeed: It did not carry the fight to its enemy. Unwilling to assume the offensive, the Commune waited until the strength of Thiers's army was overwhelming, while members debated petty issues and ignored the all-important question of survival. Given this failure, the destruction of the Commune was almost inevitable, and it came during the week of May 21-28, known as Bloody Week, when the Versailles army mercilessly crushed all Parisian opposition to the national government. Scholars have estimated that the number of Communards killed during Bloody Week may have been as high as thirty thousand, many of whom were summarily executed after they surrendered.

Pierre-Joseph Proudhon. (Library of Congress)

Significance

The original outbreak of revolution in Paris in March of 1871 also inspired a number of similar revolts in several other French cities, notably Toulouse, Lyon, Marseille, Saint-Étienne, and Narbonne. Plagued by the same internal difficulties that weakened the Paris Commune, these local insurrections also succumbed quickly to armed repression organized by the government in Versailles. As a result, none of these provincial communes lasted more than a month.

—Harold A. Schofield,
updated by Christopher E. Guthrie

Further Reading

Aminzade, Ronald. *Ballots and Barricades: Class Formation and Republican Politics in France, 1830-1871.* Princeton, N.J.: Princeton University Press, 1993. Best English-language account of the "provincial" communes that appeared in March, 1871, in response to the outbreak of insurrection in Paris.

Christiansen, Rupert. *Paris Babylon: A Social History of the Paris Commune.* New York: Viking, 1995. Detailed account, based on diaries, letters, and photos, of everyday life in Paris during the Prussian siege and Commune.

Edwards, Stewart. *The Paris Commune, 1871.* Chicago: Quadrangle Books, 1971. Edwards presents a sympathetic leftist interpretation of the Commune that incorporates the findings of many French studies.

Ehrenberg, John. *Proudhon and His Age.* Atlantic Highlands, N.J.: Humanities Press, 1996. Social biography that places the life of the leading French socialist thinker of his time within the context of a changing French society.

Horne, Alistair. *The Fall of Paris: The Siege and the Commune 1870-71.* New York: Pan Macmillan, 2002. Compelling narrative history of the Paris Commune that brings its dramatic events to life.

Jellinek, Frank. *The Paris Commune of 1871.* London: Victor Gollancz, 1937. In this classic English-language analysis of the Commune, Jellinek essentially accepts the Marxist interpretation of the event.

Lissagaray, Prosper. *History of the Commune.* New York: Monthly Review Press, 1975. Account of the Commune written by an important participant who later participated in radical exile politics in London.

Marx, Karl, and Frederick Engels. *On the Paris Commune*. Moscow: Progress Publishers, 1971. Collection that brings together the classic Marxist writings on the Paris Commune of 1871, most notably Marx's *Civil War in France*, whose publication was a turning point in the history of the International Working Men's Association.

Mason, Edward S. *The Paris Commune: An Episode in the History of the Socialist Movement*. New York: Macmillan, 1930. A basically unsympathetic account of the Commune by a historian who is clearly in opposition to those who argue that the event represented a major turning point in the history of socialism.

Schulkind, Eugene. "Socialist Women During the 1871 Paris Commune." *Past and Present* 106 (February, 1985): 124-165. Detailed and nuanced analysis of the role of women during the Commune.

SEE ALSO: Feb. 22-June, 1848: Paris Revolution of 1848; Dec. 2, 1852: Louis Napoleon Bonaparte Becomes Emperor of France; Sept. 28, 1864: First International Is Founded; 1868: Bakunin Founds the Social Democratic Alliance; July 19, 1870-Jan. 28, 1871: Franco-Prussian War; Sept. 1, 1870: Battle of Sedan; Sept. 20, 1870-Jan. 28, 1871: Prussian Army Besieges Paris; Feb. 13, 1871-1875: Third French Republic Is Established.

RELATED ARTICLES in *Great Lives from History: The Nineteenth Century, 1801-1900:* Mikhail Bakunin; Gustave Courbet; Pierre-Joseph Proudhon; Adolphe Thiers.

April 10, 1871
BARNUM CREATES THE FIRST MODERN AMERICAN CIRCUS

Although circuses originated in ancient Rome, the modern traveling circus is a largely American institution that owes its roots to the legendary nineteenth century showman P. T. Barnum.

LOCALE: Brooklyn, New York
CATEGORIES: Theater; organizations and institutions

KEY FIGURES

P. T. Barnum (1810-1891), American showman
Philip Astley (1742-1814), innovator of the modern circus in England
James A. Bailey (1847-1906), American part owner of the Great London Circus and later Barnum's partner
W. C. Coup (1837-1895), circus manager who persuaded Barnum to form a traveling circus
Joice Heth (c. 1760-1836), female slave who was Barnum's first exhibit
Jenny Lind (1820-1887), Swedish soprano whose American tour Barnum sponsored
John Bill Ricketts (d. 1799), promoter who staged the first American circus
Charles Sherwood Stratton (General Tom Thumb; 1838-1883), dwarf who performed in Barnum's museum and circus

SUMMARY OF EVENT

Ancient Romans first used the Latin word *circus* ("round") for entertainments held in round arenas. The three elements of the modern circus—ring-shaped arenas, acts, and clowns—were combined first in 1768 by Philip Astley in London. Thomas Pool staged a simple horse and clown show in Philadelphia in August, 1785, but John Bill Ricketts staged the first show in the United States that was called a circus in Philadelphia in April, 1793. Ricketts's most famous attraction was Jack, the white horse George Washington had ridden in the American Revolution (1775-1783).

Although the circus in the United States drew from Astley's innovations and the traditions of Europe, certain features were indigenous. Informative as well as entertaining, early American circuses featured menageries as their central attractions but also usually had troupes of acrobats, jugglers, and minstrels. Early American circuses were wholly rural, traveling by horse and wagon as far as fifteen to twenty miles per day between small towns. Traveling tent shows provided entertainment for the rural towns, just as formal theaters and variety halls did for the cities.

Circus parades were adopted as the primary means of advertising the arrival of circuses in town during the early nineteenth century. By the mid-1830's, no fewer than thirty-two circus shows were touring the United States. As cities grew, traveling shows merged with urban horse shows, and during the 1850's, the entertainments often were staged in city amphitheaters. However, the city shows lacked the excitement of travel and the allure of the tent shows.

The greatest moment in American circus tradition

may have occurred on April 10, 1871, in Brooklyn, New York, when P. T. Barnum invested this ancient tradition with his own spectacular showmanship. A sixty-one-year-old New Englander, Barnum had tried a variety of occupations before becoming a showman and had even edited an abolitionist newspaper. In 1834, he went to New York City and launched his career as a showman by purchasing and exhibiting an African American slave named Joice Heth, whom he advertised as the 161-year-old former nurse of George Washington. The woman—who was actually only about seventy-six years old at the time of her death in 1836—was a perfect example of Barnum's genius at creating public curiosity and excitement. His exploitation of an elderly black woman as a curiosity was also an example of the deeply entrenched racism of the times.

Circus poster from the mid-1890's. (Library of Congress)

In 1841, Barnum purchased the American Museum, an amalgamation of the old Scudder's Museum and Peale's Museum that was located in central Manhattan at the corner of Broadway Avenue and Ann Street. This museum, to which Barnum would devote most of his career, was an urban forerunner of the grand circus. Before the days of the Metropolitan Museum or the Museum of Natural History, curious travelers found little refuge in New York. In Barnum's establishment they could, for a small admission fee, gaze at stuffed animals from all corners of the world, relics purchased from sea captains returning from Asia and the South Pacific, and a gallery of paintings that Barnum advertised as a national portrait gallery.

Most famous for his freaks-of-nature exhibits, Barnum transformed the American Museum into a great cultural sideshow. He exhibited a family of "trained fleas" and a "Feejee" mermaid, which was the upper half of a monkey sewn to the lower half of a fish. He also staged the first American Punch-and-Judy show and offered concerts and temperance lectures. Just before beginning his European tour in 1843, Barnum met the twenty-five-inch-tall, four-year-old dwarf Charles Sherwood Stratton, whom he nicknamed General Tom Thumb and hired at a starting weekly salary of three dollars. The American Museum soon became the most popular tourist attraction in New York City.

Barnum's promotion of the American circus was foreshadowed by his sponsorship of Swedish soprano Jenny Lind's enormously successful 1850 singing tour. Soon afterward, Barnum received a shipment of exotic animals, which he marched up Broadway, led by five harnessed pairs of Ceylonese elephants pulling a gaudy gilded chariot. Barnum's Great Asiatic Caravan, Museum, and Menagerie lasted in New York until 1854. Two separate fires destroyed the museum, but after each fire Barnum rebuilt.

Barnum had decided to retire in 1870, when W. C. Coup, a dedicated young circus manager, talked him into forming the "P. T. Barnum Travelling Exhibition and World's Fair on Wheels," which began its first tour in Brooklyn on April 10, 1871. Coup also suggested transporting the circus by railroad, enabling it to visit larger towns. Huge crowds flocked to Barnum's circus, which showed a profit of more than one million dollars in six months. The circus's popularity soon outgrew its ability to accommodate spectators. Expanding the forty-two-foot-diameter ring would have required retraining all of the animals, so as early as 1872, Barnum added a second ring, and then a third, thereby creating the famous "three-ring circus." The three rings were surrounded by a hippodrome track, used for displays of horsemanship and drama.

Barnum's expanded show traveled by rail in more than sixty cars and could accommodate twenty thousand spectators. Its gross receipts averaged between one and two million dollars each season. Railroads ran excursions to its performances from all nearby points. In many rural areas of the United States, its appearance was the great event of the year, with its parade and almost inevitable advance guard of elephants.

Barnum's circus combined virtually all forms of nineteenth century popular entertainment into one show. Each performance began with the Congress of Nations, a theatrical spectacle in which actors impersonated world leaders and acted out great historical events. These "specs," which typically represented events from ancient history, could last up to thirty minutes and use as many as one thousand actors. One of Barnum's greatest competitors, Adam Forepaugh, Sr., was famous for elaborate spectacles; his reenactment of the American Revolution was greater than any Barnum produced.

Further competition came from the rise of Buffalo Bill's Wild West Show, in which actors dressed as cowboys and Indians acted out recent frontier battles. Competition among circuses became so fierce that advertising brigades containing several railroad cars of posters and handbills preceded the circus trains themselves by as much as a full week. Advertisements were typically exaggerated and misleading, and circuses not only promoted their own acts but also posted "ratsheets" denouncing their competitors' acts as frauds.

In 1872, Barnum moved his circus to the Hippotheatron on Fourteenth Street in New York, which he hoped would become the show's permanent home. Five weeks later, a fire destroyed almost all the animals and the performers' costumes and equipment. Barnum reopened the show early the following spring but suffered great losses. After another fire struck the circus in 1880, Barnum sought a spectacular attraction. At that time, Barnum's closest competitor—James A. Bailey's Great London Circus—featured Columbia, the first baby circus elephant born in captivity. Barnum allegedly offered Bailey $100,000 for it, but Bailey turned down the offer. During the 1881 season, however, the two circuses merged to form Barnum and Bailey's Circus—"The Greatest Show on Earth." Having lived with circus performers most of his life, Bailey organized the show as a traveling village that provided for all of its members' needs.

The attraction that may have been the one most closely associated with Barnum's circus was an enormous African elephant that Barnum purchased from the London Zoo for ten thousand dollars in 1882. Billed as the world's largest elephant, Jumbo was Barnum's most popular attraction. It was so popular, in fact, that its name added a new word to the English language, as "jumbo" became synonymous with great size. People traveled great distances merely to see Jumbo and spread his name and image throughout North America. Jumbo's success did not last long, however. After an Ontario performance on September 15, 1885, Jumbo was accidentally killed by a freight train. The circus's financial loss was devastating. Trainers tried to compensate by teaching surviving elephants to carry black hankies in their trunks and wipe their eyes, as if crying. Jumbo's stuffed skin and separately reassembled skeleton traveled with the circus for several years but never drew the same crowds.

SIGNIFICANCE

Bailey took over the circus after Barnum's death in 1891. After Bailey died in 1906, the five Ringling brothers of Baraboo, Wisconsin, bought the show and ran it independently until 1919, when they merged it with their own show to form the Ringling Brothers and Barnum & Bailey Circus. By then, with the development of motion pictures and the growing mobility offered by cars, trains, and airplanes, the circus's popularity diminished because people no longer needed to have the wonders of the world brought to them. By the turn of the twenty-first century, the diminishing number of circuses played only in the largest cities and usually performed in sports arenas, rather than in the circus tents that had been known as "big tops." By that time, circuses were also losing public favor because of the growing animal rights movement, which vilified animal acts in circuses as exploitative. However, although circuses have declined in popularity in modern culture, circus lore remains a strong part of the American popular culture heritage.

—Geralyn Strecker

FURTHER READING

Adams, Bluford. *E Pluribus Barnum: The Great Showman and the Making of Popular Culture*. Minneapolis: University of Minnesota Press, 1997. Exploration of P. T. Barnum's contributions to American popular culture that examines the cultural context of his mass entertainment.

Barnum, Phineas T. *The Life of P. T. Barnum*. Introduction by Terence Whalen. Urbana: University of Illinois Press, 2000. One of many editions of Barnum's autobiography, which he published under different titles and frequently revised.

Cook, James W. *The Arts of Deception: Playing with Fraud in the Age of Barnum*. Cambridge, Mass.: Har-

vard University Press, 2001. Analysis of nineteenth century mass entertainment in the United States that pays special attention to Barnum, who earned notoriety for the often wildly exaggerated and distorted claims he made about his shows and museum displays.
Culhane, John. *The American Circus: An Illustrated History*. New York: Henry Holt, 1990. A profusely illustrated history of the American circus that contains much information on Barnum.
Dennett, Andrea Stulman. *Weird and Wonderful: The Dime Museum in America*. New York: New York University Press, 1997. Colorful history of Barnum's American Museum in New York City that he twice had to rebuild after fires.
Fitzsimons, Raymund. *Barnum in London*. New York: St. Martin's Press, 1970. Biography focusing specifically on Barnum's time in England and how his "Yankee Doodle" character Americanized Great Britain.
Harding, Less. *Elephant Story: Jumbo and P. T. Barnum Under the Big Top*. Jefferson, N.C.: McFarland, 2000. History of the famed African elephant that was briefly the star attraction in Barnum's traveling circus.
Harris, Neil. *Humbug: The Art of P. T. Barnum*. Boston: Little, Brown, 1973. Biography focusing on Barnum's showmanship and business practices.
Saxon, A. H. *P. T. Barnum: The Legend and the Man*. New York: Columbia University Press, 1989. This heavily illustrated scholarly biography offers a critical consideration of Barnum in context with other nineteenth century events.

See also: c. 1801-1850: Professional Theaters Spread Throughout America; Feb. 6, 1843: First Minstrel Shows; 1850's-1880's: Rise of Burlesque and Vaudeville; May 10-Nov. 10, 1876: Philadelphia Hosts the Centennial Exposition.
Related articles in *Great Lives from History: The Nineteenth Century, 1801-1900:* P. T. Barnum; William Cody; Jenny Lind; Adah Isaacs Menken; Annie Oakley.

May 8, 1871
Treaty of Washington Settles U.S. Claims vs. Britain

This treaty, which settled U.S. claims against Great Britain for having violated its neutrality during the Civil War, as well as several other disputes, was a milestone in international conciliation that helped to define the responsibilities of neutral nations in future international conflicts.

Also known as: *Alabama* Dispute
Locale: Washington, D.C.; Geneva, Switzerland
Category: Diplomacy and international relations

Key Figures

Hamilton Fish (1808-1893), U.S. secretary of state, 1869-1877
Ulysses S. Grant (1822-1885), president of the United States, 1869-1877
Charles Sumner (1811-1874), Massachusetts senator who and chaired the Senate Foreign Relations Committee
Charles Francis Adams (1807-1886), U.S. commissioner to the Geneva arbitration tribunal
Alexander Cockburn (1802-1880), lord chief justice of England who was British commissioner at Geneva
John Rose (1820-1888), British-Canadian statesman

Summary of Event

During the years immediately following the U.S. Civil War (1861-1865), British-American relations were dangerously tense. The principal cause was the lasting bitterness of Americans who had supported the Union toward what they regarded as Great Britain's shamefully unneutral support of the Confederacy. On several occasions, Britain had come perilously close to recognizing the independence of the Confederate States of America—an act that would have been tantamount to intervening on the South's behalf.

Although that step was never taken, British sympathy for the Confederacy was manifested by the government's toleration of repeated evasions of Britain's Foreign Enlistment Act of 1819, especially the section that prohibited British construction of warships for belligerent foreign powers. The Confederacy hoped to break the Union's naval blockade of its ports and drive Union commerce from the seas by building its own navy in Great Britain. The gamble almost succeeded. During the war, Confederate warships that had been built in Britain sank or seized about 250 Union merchant ships. Three fast commerce destroyers, the *Florida*, the *Shenandoah*, and

On June 19, 1864, the notorious CSS Alabama *was sunk off the coast of Cherbourg, France, by the USS* Kearsage. (Francis R. Niglutsch)

especially the notorious *Alabama*, accounted for almost one-fourth of the sinkings.

The case of the *Alabama* was so blatant a violation of Great Britain's neutrality that just before its scheduled launching in July, 1862, the British government began proceedings to detain the ship. However, the *Alabama* escaped to begin an amazing career that would prove extremely embarrassing to the British government. Although the British government soon closed the loopholes in its neutrality laws, the U.S. government considered that the damage had already been done and that Britain should pay for its callous disregard of its neutrality obligations.

During the remainder of the war, Union claims for indemnity arising from Confederate depredations committed by the *Alabama* and other British-built warships mounted steadily, but the government of Lord Palmerston refused to accept responsibility for the Confederate cruisers' activities. The determination of the U.S. government to gain satisfaction culminated in the suggestion in 1869 by Senator Charles Sumner, chairman of the Senate Foreign Relations Committee, that Great Britain be made to pay for the estimated $15 million in damage caused by the Confederate cruisers, plus the cost of catching them and an addition $110 million for the destruction caused to U.S. merchant vessels. Moreover, because the cruisers' actions had prolonged the war by two full years, Britain should pay an additional $2 billion to cover the cost to the Union of the war for those extra years.

Sumner's real aim was not to bankrupt the British treasury but to force Britain to satisfy American demands by ceding Canada to the United States. The British government dismissed Sumner's demands as utter insanity but was forced to note that both President Ulysses S. Grant and his new secretary of state, Hamilton Fish, supported Sumner's claims.

When Britain decided to negotiate, Secretary Fish adopted a more moderate position, asking only for payment of existing American claims and an expression of regret. Informal conversations were begun between Fish and Sir John Rose, a British-Canadian statesman and businessman residing in England, whom the British Foreign Office had chosen to convey its interest in pacific settlements of the various disputes. It was soon agreed that a joint commission should be convened to deal with all unresolved issues: the *Alabama* claims, a long-standing conflict over American fishing rights off the Canadian coast, the matter of ownership of the San Juan Islands in Puget Sound, and other minor problems.

On February 27, 1871, official Washington shrugged off late winter dreariness to celebrate the beginning of a momentous gathering of American and British dignitaries. The social festivities that took place did much to dissipate the feelings of bitterness and suspicion that had dominated British-American relations since the war. The Washington conference had been called to deal with the U.S. claims against Britain. Proceedings began on a surprisingly cordial note, and within three months the two delegations had reached solutions or provided for later agreement on almost all matters at issue. Neither side would have believed when the negotiations were first arranged that such an explosive issue as the *Alabama* claims could be resolved with so little difficulty.

Comprising five American and five British representatives, the commission met in Washington from February 27 to May 8, 1871. Buoyed by foxhunting weekends, liberal ministrations of fine liquor, and superb food, the commissioners agreed without serious difficulty on a fair settlement. Most important was the treaty provision regarding the *Alabama* claims. Great Britain offered to express its formal regrets for the escape of the *Alabama* and other warships and agreed to submit the claims to binding arbitration. Furthermore, it accepted a definition of rules to govern neutral obligations toward belligerents.

Arbitration of the *Alabama* claims took place in Geneva, Switzerland, in December, 1871. The discussions nearly collapsed at the outset, for Charles Francis Adams, the United States commissioner, carrying out express instructions from Secretary of State Fish, revived an issue that the British had thought dead and buried, that of indirect damages. Fish's motivation was neither gaining more money nor acquiring Canada, but satisfying the needs of American domestic politics. He wanted the tribunal to deal with and reject the matter of indirect damages. Otherwise, he feared that the U.S. Congress might throw out the treaty. Although the British representative, Sir Alexander Cockburn, lord chief justice of England, was enraged by this tactic, the tribunal exceeded its jurisdiction and ruled out the indirect claims. This act allowed for adjudication of the direct claims. The court found in favor of the United States and awarded damages of $15.5 million.

Significance

Although these regulations were not retroactive, the British were conceding victory to the American position in the forthcoming arbitration proceedings. This British-American agreement was a historic one for the future of neutrality. The treaty also provided for a temporary resolution of the quarrel over fishing privileges, an agreement to submit the question of the San Juan Islands to arbitration, and numerous other economic and territorial agreements. The Washington Treaty was a remarkable accomplishment and had been termed by some as the greatest example of international conciliation ever known. It also represented a significant diplomatic victory for the United States.

—*Theodore A. Wilson*

Further Reading

Allen, Harry C. *Great Britain and the United States: A History of Anglo-American Relations, 1783-1952.* New York: St. Martin's Press, 1955. Useful survey of British-American relations from the time of the American Revolution through the Korean War of the twentieth century.

Boykin, Edward C. *Ghost Ship of the Confederacy: The Story of the "Alabama."* New York: Funk & Wagnalls, 1957. Popular account of the notorious British-built Confederate warship *Alabama*.

Cushing, Caleb. *The Treaty of Washington: Its Negotiation, Execution, and the Discussions Relating Thereto*. Freeport, N.Y.: Books for Libraries Press, 1970. First published in 1873, this contemporary analysis of the Washington negotiations by the American diplomat who served as U.S. counsel at the Geneva tribunal is still valuable, especially for understanding the personalities and political issues involved.

Duberman, Martin B. *Charles Francis Adams, 1807-1886*. Boston: Houghton Mifflin, 1961. Comprehensive biography based on exhaustive research in the Adams papers. Describes the crucial role Adams played in the resolution of the Geneva tribunal.

Jones, Howard. *Great Britain and the Confederate Navy, 1861-1865.* Bloomington: Indiana University Press, 2004. Scholarly examination of the British role in the development of the Confederate navy.

Luraghi, Raimondo. *A History of the Confederate Navy.* Translated by Paolo E. Coletta. Annapolis, Md.: Naval Institute Press, 1996. Fullest account yet published on the Confederate navy, by a leading European historian of the U.S. Civil War. Pays particular attention to Confederate innovations in technology

and tactics during its unequal struggle against the Union navy.
Smith, Goldwin A. *The Treaty of Washington, 1871: A Study in Imperial History*. 1941. New York: Russell & Russell, 1971. Study of the treaty that focuses on Canada's role in the negotiations over the *Alabama* claims. Also clarifies numerous aspects of the diplomatic engagement.
Still, William N., Jr., ed. *The Confederate Navy: The Ships, Men, and Organization, 1861-65*. Annapolis, Md.: Naval Institute Press, 1996. Well-illustrated guide to the ships of the Confederate navy, edited by a distinguished naval historian. A good companion to Raimondo Luraghi's narrative history.
Winks, Robin W. *Canada and the United States: The Civil War Years*. Baltimore: Johns Hopkins University Press, 1960. This excellent monograph places in context difficulties between the United States and Canada.

SEE ALSO: Feb. 17, 1815: Treaty of Ghent Takes Effect; Aug. 9, 1842: Webster-Ashburton Treaty Settles Maine's Canadian Border; June 15, 1846: United States Acquires Oregon Territory; Apr. 12, 1861-Apr. 9, 1865: U.S. Civil War.

RELATED ARTICLES in *Great Lives from History: The Nineteenth Century, 1801-1900:* Caleb Cushing; Ulysses S. Grant; Lord Palmerston; Charles Sumner.

October 8-10, 1871
GREAT CHICAGO FIRE

A devastating fire began a deadly three-day sweep through the heart of downtown Chicago, taking three hundred lives and the homes of ninety thousand residents, causing more than $200 million in damage, and destroying more than eighteen thousand buildings and other structures. Remembered especially in the legend of Mrs. O'Leary's cow, the disaster led to building reforms and Chicago's growth as a major urban center.

LOCALE: Chicago, Illinois
CATEGORIES: Disasters; architecture

KEY FIGURES

Roswell B. Mason (1805-1892), mayor of Chicago
Robert A. Williams (fl. mid- to late nineteenth century), city of Chicago's chief fire marshal
Philip H. Sheridan (1831-1888), U.S. Civil War veteran
Catherine O'Leary (c. 1827-1895), Irish immigrant

SUMMARY OF EVENT

In 1871, Chicago was a fast-growing boomtown, thanks to its advantageous geographic position between the eastern and western United States. Nicknamed the Queen of the West, the city was home to ten railroad lines, and its ports provided access to the Great Lakes. By the last decades of the nineteenth century, more than half of its residents were immigrants, and Chicago's factories, stockyards, lumberyards, and grain silos provided work for thousands of people seeking a better life.

Because most of Chicago was built on swampland, the roads and sidewalks were frequently choked with mud. To combat the quagmire, the city began paving the roads with wooden planks and constructing raised wooden sidewalks. By the late nineteenth century, Chicago had 561 miles of wooden sidewalks and fifty-seven miles of wood-paved streets. In addition, nearly two-thirds of Chicago's buildings were made of wood, and many of the stone structures had wooden roofs coated with tar to make them rainproof. There were few building codes, and unscrupulous builders took advantage of the population boom to construct and sell substandard homes and businesses. Despite urging by the chief fire marshal, Robert A. Williams, city officials refused to pass and enforce stricter building codes because doing so would have meant raising taxes.

Chicago's summer of 1871 was dry; only one and one-half inches of rain had fallen by early July. By fall, the city's firefighters were battling an average of twenty fires per week, including a fire on October 7 that destroyed four city blocks. This massive blaze also damaged two fire engines, a hook truck, and a ladder wagon, and left the 185 men of the Chicago fire department exhausted and understaffed.

The blaze that would become known as the Great Chicago Fire began in the west division of the city at about 9:00 P.M., on October 8, 1871, a Sunday. Even though Chicago had a new telegraph-based fire alarm system, miscommunication delayed the arrival of firefighters and equipment. Seven fire companies arrived within the first hour, but they could not contain the blaze. Fanned by southwesterly winds, the fire grew and spread through the neighborhood, consuming cottages and barns filled with hay and grain saved up for the coming winter. With the help of police and civilians, the firefighters were able to prevent the fire from moving west but could not stop the branch that spread to the northeast, which included lumber and coal yards. Within hours, the wood mills and furniture factories were on fire.

Hopes of containing the fire in the western division of Chicago fell when strong winds carried embers and flaming chunks of wood across the south branch of the Chicago River. One of the first casualties in the south division was the gasworks, where a massive fuel tank exploded, causing the city's gas lights to go out.

Mayor Roswell B. Mason had been summoned to his office at the Cook County Courthouse and was monitoring the fire's progress; he was also trying to get help from the surrounding cities. His telegrams read: "Chicago Is In Flames. Send Your Whole Department to Help Us." Fire departments from Wisconsin, Illinois, Ohio, and even as far as Pennsylvania responded with men and equipment.

Attempts to fight the fire with explosives failed, and desperate residents took to the rooftops, extinguishing flying embers and pieces of debris as they landed and dampening down the tar and wood roofs as best they could. The fire reached the courthouse shortly before 2:00 A.M., and Mayor Mason ordered an evacuation. Within twenty minutes the courthouse tower collapsed, sending the 7,200-pound bell that sounded the fire alarms crashing into the basement.

CHICAGO TRIBUNE REPORT ON THE FIRE

Three days after being burned out of its own offices, the Chicago Tribune *published its first news story, excerpted here, of the great fire. The October 11, 1871, edition of the paper came with the headline "FIRE! Destruction of Chicago! 2,600 Acres of Buildings Destroyed. Eighty Thousand People Burned Out." The headline continued: "Over a Hundred Dead Bodies Recovered from the Debris. Tens of Thousands of Citizens Without Home, Food, Fuel or Clothing."*

[T]his city has been swept by a conflagration which has no parallel in the annals of history, for the quantity of property destroyed, and the utter and almost irremediable ruin which it wrought. A fire in a barn on the West Side was the insignificant cause of a conflagration which has swept out of existence hundreds of millions of property, has reduced to poverty thousands who, the day before, were in a state of opulence, has covered the prairies, now swept by the cold southwest wind, with thousands of homeless unfortunates, which has stripped 2,600 acres of buildings, which has destroyed public improvements that it has taken years of patient labor to build up, and which has set back for years the progress of the city, diminished her population, and crushed her resources. But to a blow, no matter how terrible, Chicago will not succumb. . . .

From the west side of Jefferson street, as far as the eye could reach, in an easterly direction—and that space was bounded by the river—a perfect sea of leaping flames covered the ground. The wind increased in fierceness as the flames rose, and the flames wailed more hungrily for their prey as the angry gusts impelled them onward. . . . Meanwhile, the people in the more southern localities bent all their energies to the recovery of such property as they could. With ample time to move all that was movable, and with a foreboding of what was coming, in their neighborhood at least, they were out and in safety long before the flames reached their dwellings. They were nearly all poor people, the savings of whose lifetime were represented in the little mass of furniture which blocked the streets, and impeded the firemen. They were principally laborers, most of them Germans or Scandinavians. Though the gaunt phantom of starvation and homelessness, for the night, at least, passed over them, it was singular to observe the cheerfulness, not to say merriment, that prevailed. Though mothers hugged their little ones to their breasts and shivered with alarm, yet, strange to say, they talked freely and laughed as if realizing the utter uselessness of expressing more dolefully their consciousness of ruin.

Source: Chicago Tribune, October 11, 1871.

The fire continued to move eastward through the business district and was by now so hot that even the fireproof buildings of stone and marble were destroyed. Spectators quickly became refugees, and survivors fled to the north division or eastward toward the shores of Lake Michigan. Some were able to hire wagons, but most fled with what they could carry, and the streets were littered with expensive possessions that had been abandoned during the escape.

The same blaze that destroyed the courthouse sent a spark across the northern branch of the Chicago River. A railroad car filled with kerosene burst into flames, and in no time the fire raged in the northern division, advancing toward the waterworks, a stone structure with a wooden roof. At 3:00 A.M., the roof collapsed in flames and the massive pumps that provided the water to the hydrants

People fleeing across the Chicago River as central Chicago burns.

ground to a halt. Once the station was destroyed, it was nearly impossible for firefighters to continue to battle the blaze anywhere other than areas close to the Chicago River.

With nothing left to stop it, the fire continued to blaze after dawn and into the day. People who had lost their homes gathered in the open prairie west and northwest of the city, as well as on the banks of Lake Michigan, just north of the Chicago River. The fire continued to burn until it reached the northern city limits. Fortunately, a light rain began to fall at about 11:00 P.M., and a few hours later, the sky opened with a downpour. Small fires continued to burn for the next several days, but for the most part, the Great Fire was out.

The so-called Burnt District covered more than two thousand acres, including twenty-eight miles of streets. Eighteen thousand buildings were destroyed. Losses were estimated at more than $200 million dollars, one-third of the city's property value. Only half of the property owners carried insurance, but most of the locally owned insurance companies perished in the aftermath of the fire, making insurance policies worthless.

SIGNIFICANCE

As the Great Chicago Fire still blazed, city officials began organizing relief efforts for those who had lost their homes. Mayor Mason declared martial law and placed a U.S. Civil War veteran, Lieutenant General Philip H. Sheridan, in charge of restoring and maintaining order. Temporary city offices were set up in the western division at the First Congregational Church, and the Chicago Relief and Aid Society was established to distribute money and goods flowing in from across the United States and around the world. Despite his efforts during the fire and in the days following, Mason lost the mayoral election the following month to Joseph Medill, who ran on the Fireproof Party platform.

The cause of the blaze was never established, but, like the fire, rumors spread quickly. Even before the flames were completely extinguished, newspaper accounts had fixed the blame on an Irish immigrant family named O'Leary. Patrick O'Leary was a laborer, and his wife Catherine sold the milk of a handful of cows kept in their barn behind their cottage. Although it was true that the blaze began in the vicinity of the O'Leary barn, no proof exists to show that, as the legend says, one of the cows kicked over a lantern, igniting the blaze.

Reporters, politicians, and other officials seized the opportunity to make scapegoats of the O'Learys rather than place the blame on the city's substandard housing codes or the consequences of trying to work an overworked and understaffed fire department. Catherine O'Leary's name was not cleared until 1997, when the Chicago City Council passed a resolution absolving her from responsibility in the Great Chicago Fire.

—*P. S. Ramsey*

FURTHER READING

Bales, Richard F. *The Great Chicago Fire and the Myth of Mrs. O'Leary's Cow*. Jefferson, N.C.: McFarland, 2002. A modern-day forensic-style analysis of the fire's origin and spread, as well as the finger-pointing that followed.

Cromie, Robert. *The Great Chicago Fire*. Nashville, Tenn.: Rutledge Hill Press, 1994. A detailed account of the events during the fire, including photographs and illustrations from the actual time period.

Lowe, David, ed. *The Great Chicago Fire: In Eyewitness Accounts and Seventy Contemporary Photographs and Illustrations*. Mineola, N.Y.: Dover, 1979. A collection of firsthand accounts of the Great Fire.

Miller, Ross. *The Great Chicago Fire*. Chicago: University of Illinois Press, 2000. A historical perspective on how the Great Fire affected the city of Chicago throughout the next century.

Sawislak, Karen. *Smoldering City: Chicagoans and the Great Fire, 1871-1874*. Chicago: University of Chicago Press, 1995. A look at the aftermath of the fire, the years immediately following it, and the rebuilding of Chicago.

SEE ALSO: Aug., 1872: Ward Launches a Mail-Order Business; 1883-1885: World's First Skyscraper Is Built; May 31, 1889: Johnstown Flood; Sept. 8, 1900: Galveston Hurricane.

RELATED ARTICLES in *Great Lives from History: The Nineteenth Century, 1801-1900:* Daniel Hudson Burnham; Marshall Field; Louis Sullivan; Montgomery Ward.

1872
DOMINION LANDS ACT FOSTERS CANADIAN SETTLEMENT

Canada's Dominion Lands Act encouraged immigrant farmers to settle in the recently acquired western part of the country. It was modeled after the U.S. Homestead Act of 1862, but it was less successful than the latter act in attracting immigrant settlers and increasing agricultural production until close to the turn of the twentieth century.

LOCALE: Canada

CATEGORIES: Laws, acts, and legal history; immigration; agriculture; expansion and land acquisition

KEY FIGURES

Sir John Alexander Macdonald (1815-1891), Canadian prime minister, 1867-1873, 1878-1891
Henry Youle Hind (1823-1908), Canadian explorer
John Macoun (1831-1920), Canadian surveyor
John Palliser (1817-1887), British explorer

SUMMARY OF EVENT

The Dominion Lands Act of 1872 was intended to attract settlers to a large area in western Canada formerly known as Rupert's Land. In 1670, Charles II (r. 1660-1685) of England had granted a charter that gave the Hudson's Bay Company control of the land, rivers, and lakes—and a monopoly on the fur trade—in this area of 1.5 million square miles that included parts of what are today western Ontario, Saskatchewan, Manitoba, Nunavut, and Alberta, constituting more than one-third of modern Canada. This arrangement was in force until the mid-nineteenth century, when Canada became interested in creating farming settlements and new provinces in the area.

Accordingly, Sir John Alexander Macdonald, minister of militia affairs for the Province of Canada, drafted the British North American Act, which was passed by the British parliament in 1867. This act created the Dominion of Canada, which included Ontario, Quebec, New Brunswick, and Nova Scotia. An election that same year made Macdonald the first prime minister and gave his Conservative Party control of the government. Macdonald created an ambitious agenda for nation-building and economic growth called the National Policy. It included adding Rupert's Land and British Columbia to Canada and building a transcontinental railroad. In 1857, expeditions headed by British captain John Palliser and Canadian Henry Youle Hind surveyed Rupert's Land. Palliser's report was extremely negative regarding the agricultural potential of the area, but Hind's more positive report eventually led to the revocation of the Hudson's Bay Company's charter in 1869, when the territory became part of Canada.

The province of Manitoba was created from a portion of the newly acquired territory in 1870, and the rest was designated the North-West Territories of Canada. In 1871, British Columbia became Canada's sixth province. Land and settlement policy debates focused on the concerns of skeptics, who believed that the semiarid western plains were not suitable for farming. John Macoun, a civil servant, was commissioned to survey western Canada and assess its agricultural potential. His report in 1872 (which some said was based on a period of unusually high precipitation) indicated that all regions of the territory were well suited for farming. This report led to the passage of the Dominion Lands Act of 1872.

The law was designed to help populate Canada's western prairies and dramatically to increase agricultural productivity. It provided that any head of household or male at least eighteen years old who paid a ten dollar fee could have 160 acres of free land, provided the homesteader resided there for three years, kept at least thirty acres under cultivation, and built a permanent dwelling. The act also established the Dominion Lands Survey, which divided the territory into square townships made up of thirty-six sections of 640 acres each, which were then subdivided into the 160 acre quarter-section farms. Dominion Lands policy also stipulated that the Hudson's Bay Company would retain title to about 10 percent of the land, that a large amount of land would be given to the Canadian Pacific Railway to finance its construction, and that several sections in each township would be reserved for schools and other public buildings.

The provisions of the Dominion Lands Act of 1872 closely paralleled those of the U.S. Homestead Act of 1862, which was also part of a comprehensive strategy for settlement of the western plains and economic development. Both laws gave 160 acres to any head of household who would live on, cultivate, and improve the land (five years, rather than three, was the residency requirement under the U.S. act). However, for many years, the Homestead Act was far more successful in attracting settlers than was the Dominion Lands Act, in spite of the fact that the Canadian act allowed homesteaders to purchase at a low price 160 acres adjoining their free parcel in order to double the size of their farms. In Canada, the settlement rate was disappointing, with homestead applications numbering only about three thousand per year from 1872 to 1896. Approximately the same number of homesteaders gave up and left their land annually during the same period. By contrast, the plains of the United States were filling up with homesteaders at that time, and an estimated 120,000 of them were emigrants from Canada.

There were several reasons for the fact that immigration to western Canada was slower than that to the plains of the United States. Canada experienced an economic

CANADA'S VAST LANDSCAPE

In this extract from the final chapter of Roughing It in the Bush *(1852), English writer and Canadian pioneer Susanna Moodie expresses some of her feelings about her life in Canada and predicts a prosperous future for the new land. Western immigration would be opened by the Dominion Lands Act of 1872 and would thrive in the last decades of the nineteenth century.*

When I say that Canada is destined to be one of the most prosperous countries in the world, let it not be supposed that I am influenced by any unreasonable partiality for the land of my adoption. Canada may not possess mines of gold or silver, but she possesses all those advantages of climate, geological structure, and position, which are essential to greatness and prosperity. Her long and severe winter, so disheartening to her first settlers, lays up, amidst the forests of the West, inexhaustible supplies of fertilising moisture for the summer, while it affords the farmer the very best of natural roads to enable him to carry his wheat and other produce to market. It is a remarkable fact, that hardly a lot of land containing two hundred acres, in British America, can be found without an abundant supply of water at all seasons of the year; and a very small proportion of the land itself is naturally unfit for cultivation. To crown the whole, where can a country be pointed out which possesses such an extent of internal navigation? A chain of river navigation and navigable inland seas, which, with the canals recently constructed, gives to the countries bordering on them all the advantages of an extended sea-coast, with a greatly diminished risk of loss from shipwreck!

Source: Susan Moodie, *Roughing It in the Bush* (3d ed., London, 1854), chapter 28.

recession that began shortly after the confederation of the country, and there was much more frost-free land available in the United States. The U.S. transcontinental railroad was completed before the Canadian Pacific Railway, whose lack initially restricted the transportation of Canadian farm produce.

In addition, when the Canadian Pacific Railway was completed, Dominion Lands Act policy mandated that the free land had to be more than twenty miles from a railway because of the railroad land grants, which increased farmers' transportation costs. In fact, less than half of the farmland in Canada's plains was available for homesteading or for sale at low prices because of the extensive landholdings of the railroad, the Hudson's Bay Company, and "colonization companies," which were granted land in hopes of speeding up the process of development. The need to create 320-acre farms to make wheat farming profitable and the restricted availability of adjacent land parcels frustrated potential settlers and contributed to the high failure rate of homesteads.

Ironically, one of the main reasons for the Canadian government's very limited success in populating its western plains was the promotional campaign that was designed to encourage settlement. The advertisements in this campaign depicted the area as being so rich in resources, including water, wood, gold, silver, and fertile soil, that an utterly inexperienced farmer could realize a profit starting in the first year that would continue to increase thereafter. The unrealistic, romanticized vision of homesteading life presented in these ads even portrayed the cold climate as beneficial, because the water freezing in the ground would expand and break up the soil without the need for tilling.

Thus, many settlers wooed by these advertisements started their farms completely unprepared to deal with the real challenges and hardships of farming in the Canadian West. Typically, water had to be hauled long distances daily. There was no wood for construction or fuel, so cow or buffalo dung was used for cooking and heating, and homes built from sod were damp, insect- and worm-infested, and poorly insulated from the cold. Protectionist tariffs that eliminated American competition allowed profiteers of every type to overcharge for farming implements, supplies, and transportation. Loan payments were demanded on a schedule designed to flood the market with grain, so speculators could buy it at low prices and reap most of the profits from its production. It is no wonder, then, that each year a large proportion of Canada's homesteaders gave up and left their land until almost the turn of the twentieth century.

As a result of all of these factors, the increase in wheat prices during the early 1880's created an enormous upsurge in the homesteading population of the United States, but there was very little corresponding growth in Canada. After 1896, new dry-farming techniques and more rapidly maturing varieties of wheat resulted in a dramatic increase in Canadian homesteaders and wheat production.

SIGNIFICANCE

By 1930, when the repeal of the Dominion Lands Act ended Canadian homesteading, the goals of Prime Minister Macdonald's National Policy had been achieved. After 1896, when much of the prime land on the prairies of the United States was exhausted, the Canadian West saw a tremendous increase in immigration that populated all of what had once been Rupert's Land and made Canada a unified nation whose borders stretched from coast to coast. Thriving towns and cities were created, and unprecedented economic growth was experienced, as Canada became one of the leading wheat producers in the world.

In addition, this influx of settlers into Canada during the late nineteenth and early twentieth centuries included many immigrants from the United States, western Europe, and other parts of the world. The result was the cultural transformation of Canada into the nation of significant ethnic, linguistic, and religious diversity that it is today.

—*Jack Carter*

FURTHER READING

Richardson, Heather Cox. *The Greatest Nation on Earth: Republican Economic Policies During the Civil War*. Cambridge, Mass.: Harvard University Press, 1997. An examination of the domestic policy agenda in the United States during and following the U.S. Civil War, including the Homestead Act of 1862, the Union Pacific Railroad Act, antislavery legislation, and the Land Grant College Act.

Rollings-Magnusson, Sandra. "Canada's Most Wanted: Pioneer Women on the Western Prairies." *Canadian Review of Sociology and Anthropology* 37, no. 2 (2000): 223-238. Discuses Canada's National Policy, which was designed to encourage immigration to western Canada during the late nineteenth century with an emphasis on the important contributions of women in the settlements.

Swainger, Jonathan. *The Canadian Department of Justice and the Completion of Confederation, 1867-*

1878. Vancouver: University of British Columbia Press, 2000. Shows how the Department of Justice, created by Prime Minister Sir John Alexander Macdonald to reform the criminal justice system, came to be very influential in creating the National Policy.

SEE ALSO: 1818-1854: Search for the Northwest Passage; 1829-1836: Irish Immigration to Canada; Feb. 10, 1841: Upper and Lower Canada Unite; Mar. 23, 1858: Fraser River Gold Rush Begins; May 20, 1862: Lincoln Signs the Homestead Act; July 2, 1862: Lincoln Signs the Morrill Land Grant Act; July 1, 1867: British North America Act; 1873: Ukrainian Mennonites Begin Settling in Canada; May 23, 1873: Canada Forms the North-West Mounted Police; 1875: Supreme Court of Canada Is Established; Sept., 1878: Macdonald Returns as Canada's Prime Minister; 1896: Immigrant Farmers Begin Settling Western Canada.

RELATED ARTICLE in *Great Lives from History: The Nineteenth Century, 1801-1900:* Sir John Alexander Macdonald.

February 20, 1872
METROPOLITAN MUSEUM OF ART OPENS

The Metropolitan Museum of Art was the first public art museum in the United States. Founded as a collaboration between the city of New York and several of the city's most prominent citizens, the museum was touted both as a sign of the city's newfound wealth and prestige and as a means of educating and uplifting the city's working classes.

LOCALE: New York, New York
CATEGORIES: Organizations and institutions; art

KEY FIGURES

John Jay (1817-1894), American foreign minister and president of the Union League Club
Andrew Haswell Green (1820-1903), American comptroller of Central Park
William Cullen Bryant (1794-1878), American journalist and poet
John Frederick Kensett (1816-1872), American landscape painter

SUMMARY OF EVENT

By the mid-nineteenth century, New York City was the largest and most prosperous city in the Western Hemisphere. The recently completed Erie Canal linked the Great Lakes with the Hudson River and positioned New York City as the gateway between the Midwest and the Atlantic Ocean. Rapidly developing industrialization, coupled with increasing trade with Europe, created a generation of newly wealthy New Yorkers who were eager to compete with "old money" New Yorkers for social status at home and with their European counterparts for cultural recognition abroad.

Unlike Europe at the time, the United States had no important public cultural institutions such as the Louvre Museum in Paris. Wealthy American art collectors displayed their treasures in their homes, so those treasures remained inaccessible to the public. The closest things the United States had to public museums were "curiosity cabinets"—small displays of oddities and natural-science specimens gathered by travelers and explorers—and art galleries. Both were open only to persons of high social rank. For the average New Yorker, art was both inaccessible and inexplicable.

The period during and following the U.S. Civil War brought a new sense of social consciousness to the United States. The wealthy classes saw the sacrifices and suffering of the common soldiers who had fought to keep the country together. Civic leaders began to organize benefits and to establish organizations to help these soldiers. In some instances, this new social consciousness extended beyond veterans to ordinary workers and their families. It was in this era of social awakening that the idea of public museums for the edification and education of the people emerged, giving rise to the Museum of Fine Arts in Boston, the Corcoran Museum in Washington, D.C., and the Metropolitan Museum of Art in New York City.

The Metropolitan Museum of Art had its origins in the 1864 Metropolitan Fair, which was organized to raise funds for the medical care of Union soldiers. Of particular success at the fair was the Picture Gallery, which was attended by thousands of New Yorkers, rich and poor alike. This public display of interest in the arts inspired members of New York's prestigious Union League Club to begin discussions regarding the establishment of an art museum in New York. Not only would a museum in New York serve the important social function of enlightening and educating the populace, but it would also elevate New York's international social standing to compete with those of London and Paris.

The proposal for the new museum was presented on July 4, 1866, at a dinner party in Paris, which was attended by many wealthy American businessmen and politicians. The speaker for the evening was John Jay, a grandson of the first chief justice of the United States, who was also named John Jay. Jay took advantage of the festive occasion to promote and solidify his fellow New Yorkers' ambitions to construct a cultural monument at home that would rival the famed Louvre Museum in Paris.

Once the wealthy Americans were back in the United States, the Union League Club assumed leadership in planning the new museum. The members of the club and their associates included famous artists, such as Thomas Worthington Whittredge, Sanford Robinson Gifford, Frederick Edwin Church, and John Frederick Kensett; well-known art collectors, such as William A. Aspinwall and William T. Blodgett; the famous poet William Cullen Bryant; and numerous wealthy businessmen and civic leaders. In spite of their differing backgrounds, all the participants agreed that in addition to the important purpose of fostering an aesthetic appreciation for the arts, the new art museum would take on the social role of educating and refining the public through exposure to the arts. On January 31, 1870, the first officers of the proposed new museum were elected, and on April 13 of the same year, the state legislature of New York approved the incorporation of the Metropolitan Museum of Art.

The plan to create a new museum from the ground up was financially ambitious to say the least, even for men of considerable wealth, so they looked to the government to provide assistance. As the first negotiations with the city commenced, donations of three private European collections, including 174 paintings, formed the nucleus of the new museum's holdings and necessitated finding temporary quarters capable of housing the paintings. The museum first opened on February 20, 1872, at 681 Fifth Avenue. During the following year, it moved to the Douglas Mansion at 128 West 14th Street. Neither loca-

Metropolitan Museum of Art during the early twentieth century. (Library of Congress)

tion had been built as a museum, and each was less than ideal for the display of art.

The museum needed a building of its own—a building that was designed specifically as a museum and that was centrally located for convenient public access. Andrew Haswell Green, the comptroller of Central Park, was the first to propose that the new museum be constructed on the grounds of the city-owned park. After many complex negotiations, the city finally consented to provide the museum with land and a building, provided that the museum would permit the public free access to the collections on mutually agreed upon days and times. The land and the building would be owned by the city, while the collections and the museum would remain under the trusteeship and control of the museum's board of trustees. The collaboration between the city of New York and the Metropolitan Museum of Art was the first such public-private arrangement for a museum in the United States.

In 1880, the Metropolitan Museum of Art moved to its new building in Central Park, situated along Fifth Avenue between 80th and 84th Streets, where it still resides today. The original Gothic-revival style building, designed by the American architects Calvert Vaux and Jacob Wrey Mould, was expanded upon as early as 1888, as generous donors, eager to participate in the new cultural institution, bequeathed their collections to the nascent museum.

Over time, the city's contribution to the museum increased to include providing funds for the running of the museum and its security and utilities. The city's generosity was not without strings—the city demanded that the museum open its doors on Sundays, the one day that most New Yorkers had free to enjoy Central Park and its new museum. In return for the city's added financial support, the museum trustees agreed, albeit reluctantly, to open its doors on Sunday, something that many of the museum's Protestant founders had steadfastly refused to do. During the early twenty-first century, in an ongoing spirit of mutual cooperation, the city of New York continued to provide the land and the building, as well as paying for the museum's heat, light, and electricity and for a portion of the costs for the security and maintenance of both the facility and the collections. In return, the museum was open to the public every day except Mondays and major holidays.

Significance

The decision to construct an art museum for the benefit of the public marked a point of maturation in American society, when more advantaged citizens turned their attention away from their own well-being toward the well-being of the public at large. The importance of civic engagement and an emphasis on the cultural and social value of the arts became inherent qualities of the American spirit. The museum that began during the mid-nineteenth century as a volunteer effort on the part of the prominent citizens of New York City grew into one of the largest and most prestigious cultural institutions in the United States. The continued relationship between New York City and the Metropolitan Museum of Art serves as a testimony to the dedication and determination of the civic and cultural leaders of New York City.

Since its founding in 1870, the Metropolitan Museum of Art's collections have increased in quality and number to include more than two million works of art representing all periods of history and many cultures from around the world. The museum that started in a small structure built in a city park expanded dramatically through the years to encompass approximately two million square feet of museum space. During the early twenty-first century, more than five million persons per year visited "the Met," as it was affectionately called. The Metropolitan Museum of Art ranked among the world's greatest museums.

—*Sonia Sorrell*

Further Reading

Howe, Winifred E., and Henry Watson Kent. *A History of the Metropolitan Museum of Art*. 2 vols. New York: Gillis Press, 1946. The best and most comprehensive study of the history of the museum, from its founding to 1912; illustrated.

Lerman, Leo. *The Museum: One Hundred Years and the Metropolitan Museum of Art*. New York: Viking Press, 1969. A comprehensive history of the museum, divided into time periods, accompanied by photographs of works in the collections.

Metropolitan Museum of Art. *The Metropolitan Museum of Art, New York*. Introduction by A. Hyatt Mayor. New York: Newsweek & Arnoldo Mondadori Editore, 1979. Overview of the museum's collections with a brief introduction explaining the history of the museum.

The Metropolitan Museum of Art, New York. http://www.metmuseum.org/. Official Web site of the Metropolitan Museum of Art; includes extensive artistic resources, in addition to details of the institution and its current exhibitions.

Tomkins, Calvin. *Merchants and Masterpieces: The Story of the Metropolitan Museum of Art*. New York:

Henry Holt, 1980. A history of the museum's founders, contributors, and collections.

See also: 1824: Paris Salon of 1824; Aug. 10, 1846: Smithsonian Institution Is Founded; 1855: Courbet Establishes Realist Art Movement; May 15, 1863: Paris's Salon des Refusés Opens; Apr. 15, 1874: First Impressionist Exhibition; Nov. 1, 1897: New Library of Congress Building Opens.

Related article in *Great Lives from History: The Nineteenth Century, 1801-1900:* William Cullen Bryant.

March 1, 1872
Yellowstone Becomes the First U.S. National Park

After the Washburn-Langford-Doane expedition explored the watershed of the Yellowstone River and documented and mapped the area's natural wonders in 1870, its recommendations led to a congressional act of dedication, creating the first national park in the United States and initiating policies for the preservation and conservation of such parks.

Also known as: Act of Dedication, Yellowstone National Park

Locale: Montana and Wyoming Territories

Categories: Environment and ecology; exploration and discovery; government and politics; laws, acts, and legal history

Key Figures

Henry D. Washburn (1832-1871), surveyor-general of Montana Territory

Nathaniel P. Langford (1832-1911), first superintendent of Yellowstone National Park

Gustavus C. Doane (1840-1892), American soldier

Ferdinand Vandeveer Hayden (1829-1887), American geologist

Thomas Moran (1837-1924), American artist

John Colter (c. 1775-1813), American mountain man and explorer

Summary of Event

Accounts by mountain men of strange phenomena in the Yellowstone area of the Rocky Mountains led to scientific exploration and documentation of the natural wonders of the area. Expedition team reports from the area led conservationists to join the scientists in petitioning the U.S. Congress to place the lands in the public domain in order to preserve the wilderness and prevent hunters, sightseers, and developers from destroying the scenic environment and habitat of fish and wildlife. This led to an act of Congress in 1872, creating Yellowstone National Park—two million acres in the Yellowstone watershed area of the Wyoming and Montana Territories—as the first U.S. national park.

The creation of Yellowstone National Park in turn established a pattern for setting aside areas of natural wonders and ancient archaeological sites, protecting them from private ownership and commercial development. Congress vested authority in the secretary of the interior to develop policies and procedures to carry out its mandate to preserve and conserve national forests, prehistoric civilization sites, and natural wonders. These conservation efforts led to the founding of the National Park Service in 1916 as the agency for identifying, establishing, maintaining, and protecting from destruction dedicated lands and wildlife.

During the early nineteenth century, mountain men trapping and trading furs in the Yellowstone area reported fire pits, shooting geysers, boiling springs, and other strange phenomena in the northwest corner of the Louisiana Purchase territory (located in the present-day states of Montana and Wyoming). John Colter, who left the expedition of Meriwether Lewis and William Clark in 1810 to venture on his own, described the unusual landscape of what historians now believe was the Firehole area east of Yellowstone Lake. Journalists, reacting with disbelief and ridicule to his reports, labeled the area "Colter's Hell." In September, 1869, Charles W. Cook, David E. Folsom, and William Peterson, who were involved in mining operations in the area, launched the first organized expedition into the Gallatin River Valley. Their published reports spurred public and scientific interest.

In the summer of 1870, the Washburn-Langford-Doane expedition set forth to survey and document the Yellowstone area. The party was led by Henry D. Washburn, surveyor-general of Montana Territory, and Nathaniel P. Langford, Montana bank examiner and avid Yellowstone enthusiast. U.S. Army lieutenant Gustavus C. Doane led the six-man military escort for the expedi-

YELLOWSTONE NATIONAL PARK

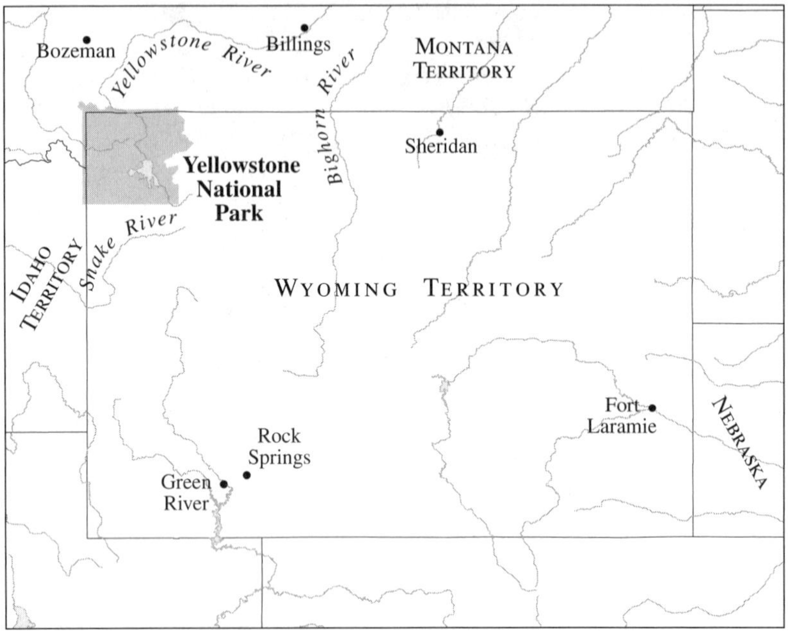

tion. In September, 1870, as they prepared to leave Yellowstone, the team discussed the area's potential as a huge tourist attraction and foresaw the environmental damage that would be caused if large-scale development occurred. They agreed that the federal government should be asked to remove the entire area from private ownership and commercial development and to preserve it in its original condition for the people of the United States.

Upon the expedition's return to Helena, Montana, Langford went east to visit influential officials in Minneapolis, New York, and Washington, D.C. He made public speeches and gave interviews to members of the news media, advocating that Yellowstone be set apart as a national park for the enjoyment of the people. Langford's efforts resulted in a government-sponsored exploration of Yellowstone in 1871 conducted by the Geological Survey of the Territories. One of the officials approached by Langford was Dr. Ferdinand Vandeveer Hayden, a geologist, who agreed to conduct the official survey of Yellowstone if Congress voted to finance the expedition.

In 1871, Congress appropriated the funds for the U.S. Geological Survey and the U.S. Army Corps of Engineers to survey the region and document it with maps, drawings, and photographs. In addition to Hayden, the team included two botanists, a zoologist, an entomologist, a mineralogist, a meteorologist, and a topographer, as well as two photographers and artist Thomas Moran. Moran's sketches and paintings of the area became important in publicizing the scenic wonders of the American West.

On July 15, 1871, the Hayden-Moran expedition got under way. The scientists identified and classified plants and animals, noted the geologic features of the area, mapped and sketched its topography, and named the geysers and other natural wonders they encountered. Upon their return, team members' individual accounts, photographs, and maps were widely published and inspired additional explorations, as well as public interest.

The Hayden-Moran expedition team joined forces with the earlier Washburn-Langford-Doane team in a formal proposal that Congress create a system of national parks, beginning with the Yellowstone area, to protect the nation's natural wonders and ancient archaeological sites from commercial development and private profit-making schemes. Legislation to create Yellowstone National Park was introduced in Congress in December, 1871, and endorsed by the secretary of the interior on January 29, 1872. On March 1, 1872, the U.S. Congress passed the Act of Dedication, Yellowstone National Park, setting aside 2.2 million acres (3,400 square miles) of the Montana and Wyoming Territories as the first U.S. national park.

The law gave authority to the secretary of the interior to draw up policies and procedures to effect the preservation of forests, mineral deposits, natural curiosities, and scenic wonders in a natural, undisturbed condition and to protect the lands and wildlife from destruction for commercial purposes. However, Congress created a severe problem, in that it provided no money to operate the park, nor did it provide a means for enforcing the conservation regulations. Langford became the first superintendent of Yellowstone, and he served for several years without pay. The revenues collected on-site, comprising public utility fees and taxes on concessions operated for public benefit, did not begin to cover the park's operating budget. No revenue could be gained from hunting and fishing licenses, leases, or permits, because local cattlemen, timber men, and hunters were barred from grazing, removing timber, hunting, or fishing on park lands.

Without enforcement authority, the superintendent could not stop the poaching of fish and game. Nor could he prevent the wild animals either from attacking human intruders into their habitat or from fleeing beyond the park's boundaries to escape them. Thousands of human visitors crossing the lands each year made it impossible to preserve the park in its natural state. The superintendent's annual report of February 4, 1873, stated that without funds to hire personnel or authority to prosecute offenders, he could not comply with the congressional mandates of conservation and facilitation of public enjoyment of the park.

After its creation in 1872, the park was visited by rapidly increasing numbers of expeditions and sightseers. Sightseers took five-day guided tours, traveling over dirt roads by horseback, wagon, or stagecoach. In 1881, 200 miles of roads and 150 miles of bridle paths were completed, but visitors complained of the dust and stumps in the roads. In March, 1883, Congress responded to complaints by authorizing a paid superintendent and ten part-time assistants. Road and bridge construction was assigned to the U.S. Army Corps of Engineers, and the secretary of the interior was instructed to request troops from the secretary of war to protect the park and its visitors. This action left the secretary of the interior in charge of managing a park partially funded and staffed through the War Department. Conservation was neglected.

In 1886, because of budget concerns, Congress eliminated all civilian jobs and turned Yellowstone over to the War Department. In 1890, Congress appropriated fifty thousand dollars to build Fort Yellowstone and empowered the military park authorities to enforce its conservation regulations and prosecute violators of poaching and vandalism laws. Although a civilian superintendent was authorized again in 1901, members of the U.S. Cavalry served as both park rangers and law enforcement officers until the National Park Service was founded in 1916.

SIGNIFICANCE

The establishment of Yellowstone National Park led to conservation efforts to save and preserve the nation's wilderness areas, archaeological sites, and forests. Expeditions to such sites have increased knowledge and contributed to the conservation of historic sites, natural habitats, and wildlife. The Antiquities Act of 1906 set aside additional national parks and historic areas for preservation. In 1916, the National Park Service was created to preserve, conserve, and manage the national parks and other significant historic sites and landmarks. The Department of Interior was charged with developing selection criteria, management policies, and conservation practices. Artist Thomas Moran's paintings of Yellowstone not only helped persuade Congress to preserve Yellowstone but also helped establish a global image of the American West.

—*Marguerite R. Plummer*

FURTHER READING

Fishbein, Seymour L. *Yellowstone Country: The Enduring Wonder*. Washington, D.C.: National Geographic Society, 1989. A photographic overview of Yellowstone National Park and its environs.

Frantz, Joe B. *Aspects of the American West*. College Station: Texas A&M Press, 1976. Explores the philosophical idea of preserving wilderness areas and the practical effects of this idea.

Haines, Aubrey L. *Yellowstone National Park: Its Exploration and Establishment*. Washington, D.C.: Government Printing Office, 1974. Provides a detailed history of the early explorations and creation of Yellowstone National Park.

Kirk, Ruth. *Exploring Yellowstone*. Seattle: University of Washington Press, 1972. Discusses issues of public access to and conservation of the first national park in the United States.

Murphy, Thomas D. *Three Wonderlands of the American West*. Boston: Page, 1919. Features maps and photographs of Hayden's expedition and Thomas Moran's influential paintings of Yellowstone National Park.

Nabokov, Peter, and Lawrence Loendorf. *Restoring a Presence: American Indians and Yellowstone National Park*. Norman: University of Oklahoma Press, 2004. Explores the claims to ownership of Yellowstone lands by Native Americans and the consequences of those claims to conservation and preservation of the park, as well as to tribal culture.

Saunders, Richard L., ed. *A Yellowstone Reader: The National Park in Popular Fiction, Folklore, and Verse*. Salt Lake City: University of Utah Press, 2003. A collection of stories and poems about Yellowstone National Park.

SEE ALSO: May 14, 1804-Sept. 23, 1806: Lewis and Clark Expedition; June 15-Oct. 5, 1877: Nez Perce War.

RELATED ARTICLES in *Great Lives from History: The Nineteenth Century, 1801-1900:* Ferdinand Vandeveer Hayden; Meriwether Lewis and William Clark.

August, 1872
WARD LAUNCHES A MAIL-ORDER BUSINESS

Montgomery Ward established the first successful mail order business and built the largest distribution house during the late nineteenth century. His company provided a model to other entrepreneurs, transforming both commerce and advertising in the United States.

LOCALE: Chicago, Illinois
CATEGORIES: Trade and commerce; business and labor; marketing and advertising

KEY FIGURES

Montgomery Ward (1844-1913), American entrepreneur
George R. Thorne (1837-1918), Ward's brother-in-law and cofounder of Montgomery Ward and Company
Alvah C. Roebuck (1864-1948), cofounder of Sears, Roebuck, and Company
R. W. Sears (1863-1914), cofounder of Sears, Roebuck, and Company

SUMMARY OF EVENT

Montgomery Ward was born in Chatham, New Jersey. His father, Sylvester Ward, later moved the family to Niles, Michigan. Ward finished his schooling at the age of fourteen and became an apprentice in a barrel factory and later stacked bricks in a kiln. Eventually, he relocated to St. Joseph and went to work at a shoe store.

Ward discovered that he was a good salesman and began working for a general store; after three years of employment, he rose to the position of manager. The retail experience was important for Ward. By 1865, Ward relocated to Chicago, Illinois, the hub for wholesale dry goods, and began working for a lamp house called Case and Sobin. A few years later, he joined Field, Palmer, and Lieter, which later became Marshall Fields. He worked for them for two years, then went to work as a traveling salesman for the mercantile dry-goods business of Wills, Greg, and Company.

In the post-Civil War era, the United States was still primarily agrarian. Ward visited rural communities throughout the Midwest; he noticed the unfair practices of local storeowners. Merchants kept prices for their products high as a result of the costs to suppliers of bringing items to rural areas. The variety of stock available for purchase was also limited. This forced farmers to buy goods on credit until their crops were harvested, creating a continuous cycle of debt. In order to reduce the costs associated with the middleman and to meet consumer demand, Ward decided to try direct mail sales, offering more products, and delivering the orders to the nearest railroad station.

Ward's idea got off to a rocky start after his first inventory was destroyed by the Great Chicago Fire in 1871, but by the next year, he had received sixteen hundred dollars in capital. Accordingly, in August, 1872, Ward and two others, George S. Drake and Robert P. Caufield, rented a small room on North Clark Street. Their first catalog was a single-sheet flyer that listed 163 products and gave instructions for ordering them by mail. However, both of Ward's partners left the business within a short time, because they believed it was not lucrative enough. George R. Thorne, a good friend of Ward who had lost his own grocery and lumber business, decided to join Ward as a full partner.

Three events soon worked to the advantage of Ward. First, the *Chicago Tribune* ran a story on November 8, 1873, about his company and accused Ward of fraudulent practices. Ward responded that the newspaper should investigate his operations. The reporter who came to Ward's supply house was so impressed with his business

Montgomery Ward. (Library of Congress)

acumen that the paper wrote an endorsement, and Ward reprinted the article in his 1874 catalog.

The National Grange, or Patrons of Husbandry, formed in 1867 by Oliver H. Kelley in Minnesota, was a growing political force in agricultural areas. It rallied farmers against monopolistic practices of the railroads, emphasizing the need for fair pricing, regulation, and the creation of cooperatives for creameries, warehouses, and elevators in order to sell crops. Ward was able to win the trust of the unified rural community when he introduced a money back guarantee on all his products.

Finally, printing and typesetting innovations, such as the Linotype, aided Ward in making the merchandise in his catalogs look attractive to consumers. Thanks to these technologies, high-quality images and illustrations could be reproduced in great quantity. Ward's copy was as high in quality as his images: As company head, he proofread every catalog for accuracy and approved the final copy sent to the printers.

At first, Ward offered only dry goods, but as the business grew, the catalog began to offer home and farm accessories. Eight years later, the company's catalog had grown to 240 pages and listed ten thousand items; consumers referred to it as the "wish book." By the late 1880's, the business had grown so fast that Ward had to buy a six-story warehouse on Michigan Avenue that employed more than one hundred clerks and one thousand workers. By 1904, the company distributed three million catalogs that weighed four pounds each.

In 1896, Montgomery Ward and Company confronted major competition in the mail-order business from R. W. Sears and Alvah C. Roebuck. Four years later, Ward had total sales of $8.7 million versus Sears, Roebuck, and Company's $10 million. This rivalry endured into the twentieth century, and both companies struggled for dominance in the marketplace. Providing such convenience met with complaints by local merchants, who believed large mail-order companies were hurting the local economy. Storeowners printed flyers and advertisements urging townspeople to start campaigns against Montgomery Ward and Company and Sears, Roebuck, and Company. In some instances, there were public burnings of catalogs, but the majority of these protests were of little or no use. Montgomery Ward and Company remained a mail-order company until 1926, when it opened its first retail store in Plymouth, Indiana.

SIGNIFICANCE

Ward's mail-order company increased the standard of living for the American middle classes and brought wholesale prices from urban centers to the rural sector. The success of Montgomery Ward and Company, and later Sears, Roebuck, and Company, reflected the Industrial Revolution's innovations in mass production and printing. In addition, by offering low prices and guaranteeing the quality of the merchandise he offered, Ward became an industry icon. Such commitment to consumers is still the underlying notion in direct mail-order firms today. The company was not able to maintain its success into the late twentieth century, however. In 1985, Montgomery Ward and Company closed its cataloging department, and by the late 1990's, the company had lost ground to low-cost competition from Wal Mart, K-Mart, and Target. Montgomery Ward and Company announced it was closing its stores on December 28, 2000, in one of the largest retail bankruptcy liquidations in U.S. history.

—*Gayla Koerting*

FURTHER READING

Baker, Nina Brown. *Big Catalogue: The Life of Aaron Montgomery Ward*. New York: Harcourt, Brace, 1956. Juvenile biography about Ward's life.

Boorstin, Daniel J. "A Montgomery Ward's Mail-Order Business." *Chicago History* 2 (Spring-Summer, 1973): 142-152. Boorstin, a history professor, analyzes the economic, social, and political forces that allowed Ward to become successful in the mail order business during the late nineteenth century.

Herndon, Booton. *Satisfaction Guaranteed: An Unconventional Report of Today's Consumer*. New York: McGraw-Hill, 1972. Explains how Montgomery Ward and Company modified and improved its catalog over time to meet the demands of its customers. States that Ward's was the first business in the United States to use the concepts of merchandising and mass marketing in an effective manner.

Hoge, Cecil C. *The First Hundred Years Are the Toughest: What Can We Learn from the Century of Competition Between Sears and Wards*. Berkeley, Calif.: Ten Speed Press, 1988. Examines the management successes and hardships of Montgomery Ward and Company and Sears, Roebuck, and Company, emphasizing how both companies created modern marketing. Contains extensive bibliography.

Kaufman, Leslie. "Montgomery Ward to Close Its Doors After 128 Years in Retailing." *The New York Times*, December 29, 2000. Addresses the demise of the company and provides a brief history of the retailer.

Latham, Frank B. *1872-1972, a Century of Serving Cus-*

tomers: The Story of Montgomery Ward. Chicago: Montgomery Ward Public Relations Department, 1972. Centennial history of Montgomery Ward and Company. Latham, former editor of *Look*, observes how the company adapted its cataloging and marketing campaigns in order to meet American consumer demands over the course of one hundred years.

Talaski, Karen. "Montgomery Ward Closes After 128 Years." *Detroit News*, December 29, 2000. Provides a brief history of the rise and downfall of Montgomery Ward and Company. Article includes key dates in the company's history.

SEE ALSO: Dec. 4, 1867: National Grange Is Formed; 1869: First Modern Department Store Opens in Paris; Oct. 8-10, 1871: Great Chicago Fire; May 8, 1886: Pemberton Introduces Coca-Cola; 1896: Brooks Brothers Introduces Button-Down Shirts.

RELATED ARTICLE in *Great Lives from History: The Nineteenth Century, 1801-1900:* Montgomery Ward.

1873
UKRAINIAN MENNONITES BEGIN SETTLING IN CANADA

To populate Manitoba and produce needed agricultural products, the Canadian government recruited Mennonites to immigrate from the Ukraine. The migration to Canada proved just one in a succession of Mennonite migrations, as the members of this religious denomination attempted to find a home free of persecution.

LOCALE: Manitoba, Canada

CATEGORIES: Immigration; agriculture; expansion and land acquisition; government and politics

KEY FIGURES

Alexander II (1818-1881), czar of Russia, r. 1855-1881

William Hespeler (1830-1921), Canadian emissary who recruited Ukrainian Mennonites

Jacob Y. Shantz (1822-1909), Mennonite from Ontario who oversaw the settlement of Mennonites in Manitoba

David Klassen (1813-1900), Mennonite leader

John Lowe (fl. late nineteenth century), secretary in the Canadian Department of Agriculture

John Henry Pope (1824-1889), Canadian secretary of agriculture

SUMMARY OF EVENT

In 1873, when many Mennonites left the Ukraine for Manitoba, Canada, it was the latest in a series of migrations for a people whose religion forbade the swearing of oaths, involvement in secular civic affairs, and the bearing of arms. The pattern of Mennonite history, one of withdrawal, flight, and emigration, began in Switzerland and continued in the Netherlands, Prussia, and the Ukraine, when those countries posed serious threats to the Mennonite faith. The Mennonites were drawn to the Ukraine when, in 1762-1763, Catherine the Great of Russia invited foreigners, except for Jews, to the so-called New Russia, the Ukraine, which Russia had won in a war with Turkey.

Thousands of Mennonites accepted this invitation, and for more than one hundred years they enjoyed prosperity and the freedoms promised them by Catherine. They regulated their own affairs, were free to have their own schools—where lessons were taught in German—and were not subject to military conscription. However, in 1870, Czar Alexander II decided to "Russianize" the German-speaking Mennonites and rescinded those freedoms, which had been reaffirmed by Czar Paul I: Russian replaced German as the language of commerce, secular government replaced church government, and universal conscription was instituted, although Mennonites were allowed to serve in the medical corps rather than fight in the military service. Although the Mennonites were given ten years to comply with the altered situation, many of them decided to emigrate.

Mennonite John Funk began a correspondence with Cornelius Janzen, an American Mennonite who was interested in having the Ukrainian Mennonites immigrate to the United States, but the Canadians were more aggressive in their recruitment of the Mennonites. At the time, the province of Manitoba had much to gain from an influx of settlers. The Canadians were concerned about the possibility of American settlers moving across the border, possibly leading to an annexation like the one in Texas. They also needed farmers in the West to supply the more populous eastern Canada with foodstuffs, and they wanted a population base for the intercontinental railroad they had planned.

The Canadian government sent William Hespeler,

one of their immigration agents then in Germany, to Berdiansk in the Ukraine. Hespeler conducted a secret meeting with the Mennonites, providing them with information and advice about a move to Canada. Despite Russian opposition after his first meeting, he returned to meet with the Mennonites again. Hespeler's efforts were supplemented by those of Jacob Y. Shantz, a Mennonite from Ontario who toured Manitoba and issued an 1873 report touting the advantages Manitoba offered to his Mennonite brethren. These included cheaper land (free or one dollar per acre, as opposed to three dollars per acre in the United States) and better protection against lawlessness and against Native Americans.

In the spring of 1873, twelve Mennonite delegates from closely knit colonies in the Ukraine arrived to visit the United States and Canada. When they arrived in Fargo, North Dakota, they were met by Hespeler and Shantz, who accompanied them on their tour of Manitoba. There were problems with the land they were offered: Mosquitoes and grasshoppers were rampant in the marshy land, which lacked timber for construction. Livestock and farm implements were more expensive in Canada than they were in the United States, and the native Metis also claimed the land. In fact, there was an encounter between the twelve Mennonites and the Metis, who surrounded them at House's Tavern after a brawl; the Mennonites, though, were protected by Hespeler, who summoned provincial troops to disperse the attackers.

Eight Mennonite delegates promptly left for the United States, but two from the Bergthal colony, Jacob Peters and Heinrich Wiebe, and two from the Kleine Gemeinde colony, Cornelius Toews and David Klassen, went to Ottawa to ratify an agreement with the Canadian authorities, probably because they shared Heinrich Wiebe's belief that the United States would not grant the Mennonites the military exemption they sought or the freedom of religion they needed. The letter that John Lowe, a Canadian agent, sent the Mennonites on July 25, 1873, granted them exemption from military service, gave them the opportunity to affirm rather than sign legal affidavits, offered them exclusive rights to eight free townships with the option of exchanging them if they proved unsuitable, and allowed them to run their own schools. John Henry Pope, minister of agriculture, amended the letter three days later, reducing the concessions, but his emendations remained secret for forty-five years.

Between 1873 and 1878, about fifteen thousand Mennonites, representing about 30 percent of the total Ukrainian Mennonite population, emigrated to the United States and Canada; seven thousand (about twelve hundred peasant households) emigrated to Manitoba, some directly and some after a winter stopover in Ontario. By 1881, Mennonites composed 13 percent of Manitoba's population. The emigration succeeded despite the financial losses the Mennonites experienced when they sold their property in Russia for less than it was worth and despite the cost of travel to the United States, including passage, passports, exit permits, bribes, and advance Russian tax payments.

The Bergthal colony, which was a poor colony in the Ukraine, had financial problems, but these were overcome through the assistance of the richer Mennonite emigrants, the Ontario Mennonites, and the *Waisenamt* (a kind of welfare bank), and by a $100,000 loan from the Canadian government, most of which was repaid with interest. The Mennonites settled in an Eastern Reserve, which lacked timber, and a Western Reserve, where some of the Eastern Reserve Mennonites eventually moved. From their arrival in Canada, when they spent money on livestock and farm implements, through the early twenty-first century, they have had a significant impact on the Canadian economy. They quickly made the change from a subsistence to a capitalistic economy; flax was the first crop they grew commercially.

SIGNIFICANCE

The Mennonite immigration to Manitoba, which peaked between 1873 and 1883, increased substantially the population of Canada, supplied necessary foodstuffs to eastern markets, and made the Canadian Pacific Railway feasible and financially successful. Canadian Mennonites eventually encountered the same problems they had faced earlier in their history, however. From the start, their unfamiliar customs (for example, women working in the fields) bothered their neighbors; their exemption from military service in both world wars also brought criticism, and their educational system came under attack by the government.

Increases in Mennonite immigration after both world wars were offset by the loss of traditional Mennonites, who emigrated to Mexico and Paraguay. The impact of the Mennonites on Manitoba may be measured by their status as a large immigrant group, by the place-names of towns and cities, and by their effects upon Canadian agricultural practices, some of which derive from the Ukrainian Mennonites' experiences. The assimilation experience, so common to immigrants, was especially difficult for them but was eventually largely resolved.

—*Thomas L. Erskine*

FURTHER READING

Ens, Adolf. *Subjects or Citizens? The Mennonite Experience in Canada, 1870-1925*. Ottawa: University of Ottawa Press, 1994. Focuses on the military and educational issues that brought the Mennonites into conflict with their neighbors and the Canadian government. Ens also supplies information about the cause and extent of the Mennonite emigration from Canada to Mexico and Paraguay. Extensive bibliography.

Francis, E. K. *In Search of Utopia: The Mennonites in Manitoba*. Glencoe, Ill.: Free Press, 1955. Early history of Mennonite emigration, covering Mennonite history into the first half of the twentieth century.

Gerbrandt, Henry J. *Adventure in Faith*. Altona, Man.: D. W. Friesen and Sons, 1970. The first one hundred pages cover the historical background through the emigration in the 1870's; the rest of the book concerns Mennonite churches in the twentieth century. Gerbrandt offers a detailed account of the Dominion Day brawl involving the twelve Mennonite delegates and the Metis.

Klippenstein, Lawrence. *David Klassen and the Mennonites*. Agincourt, Canada: Book Society of Canada, 1982. Part of the "We Built Canada" series designed for secondary school students, the book contains the story of the emigration plus details about farming implements, church services, and the schools. Many early photographs and maps.

Neufeld, William. *From Faith to Faith*. Hillsboro, Kans.: Kindred Press, 1989. Part 1 provides historical background and a brief account of the Mennonite emigration to Manitoba. The rest of the book concerns the Mennonite Church in the United States and the development of the Mennonite Church in North America after 1888.

Schroeder, William. *The Bergthal Colony*. Rev. ed. Winnipeg, Man.: CMBC, 1986. Focuses primarily on the Bergthal colony, its government, schools, church, and community life, but the book has one chapter entitled "Migration to Manitoba," which contains edited diaries about the initial visit of the twelve Mennonite delegates and their trip from the Ukraine to Manitoba. Shroeder also includes Czar Paul's "Charter of Privileges" granted to the Russian Mennonites and John Lowe's letter of July 3, 1873, specifying Canadian concessions made to the Mennonites.

SEE ALSO: 1829-1836: Irish Immigration to Canada; July 1, 1867: British North America Act; Oct. 11, 1869-July 15, 1870: First Riel Rebellion; 1872: Dominion Lands Act Fosters Canadian Settlement; 1896: Immigrant Farmers Begin Settling Western Canada.

RELATED ARTICLE in *Great Lives from History: The Nineteenth Century, 1801-1900:* Alexander II.

1873-1880
EXPLORATION OF AFRICA'S CONGO BASIN

Through the 1870's, the exploration, mapping, and establishment of trading posts and treaties in the Congo Basin began to spark political interest in the region, especially from Belgium, France, and Portugal, that led to the partition of the region among European powers during the following decade.

LOCALE: Central Africa

CATEGORIES: Exploration and discovery; diplomacy and international relations; expansion and land acquisition

KEY FIGURES

Henry Morton Stanley (1841-1904), British American newspaper correspondent and explorer

Pierre-Paul-François-Camille Savorgnan de Brazza (1852-1905), Italian-born French explorer

Leopold II (1835-1909), king of Belgium, r. 1865-1909

Verney Lovett Cameron (1844-1894), Scottish explorer

Alexandre Alberto da Rocha de Serpa Pinto (1846-1900),

Hermenegildo Carlos de Brito Capello (1841-1917) and

Roberto Ivens (1850-1898), Portuguese naval explorers and scientists

SUMMARY OF EVENT

From the late fifteenth century through the mid-nineteenth century, central Africa's Congo Basin was an important focus for trade with Europeans, especially in slaves. As the Atlantic slave trade was gradually abolished during the nineteenth century, European interest in controlling the Congo began to grow, at the same

EXPLORERS' ROUTES IN THE CONGO BASIN

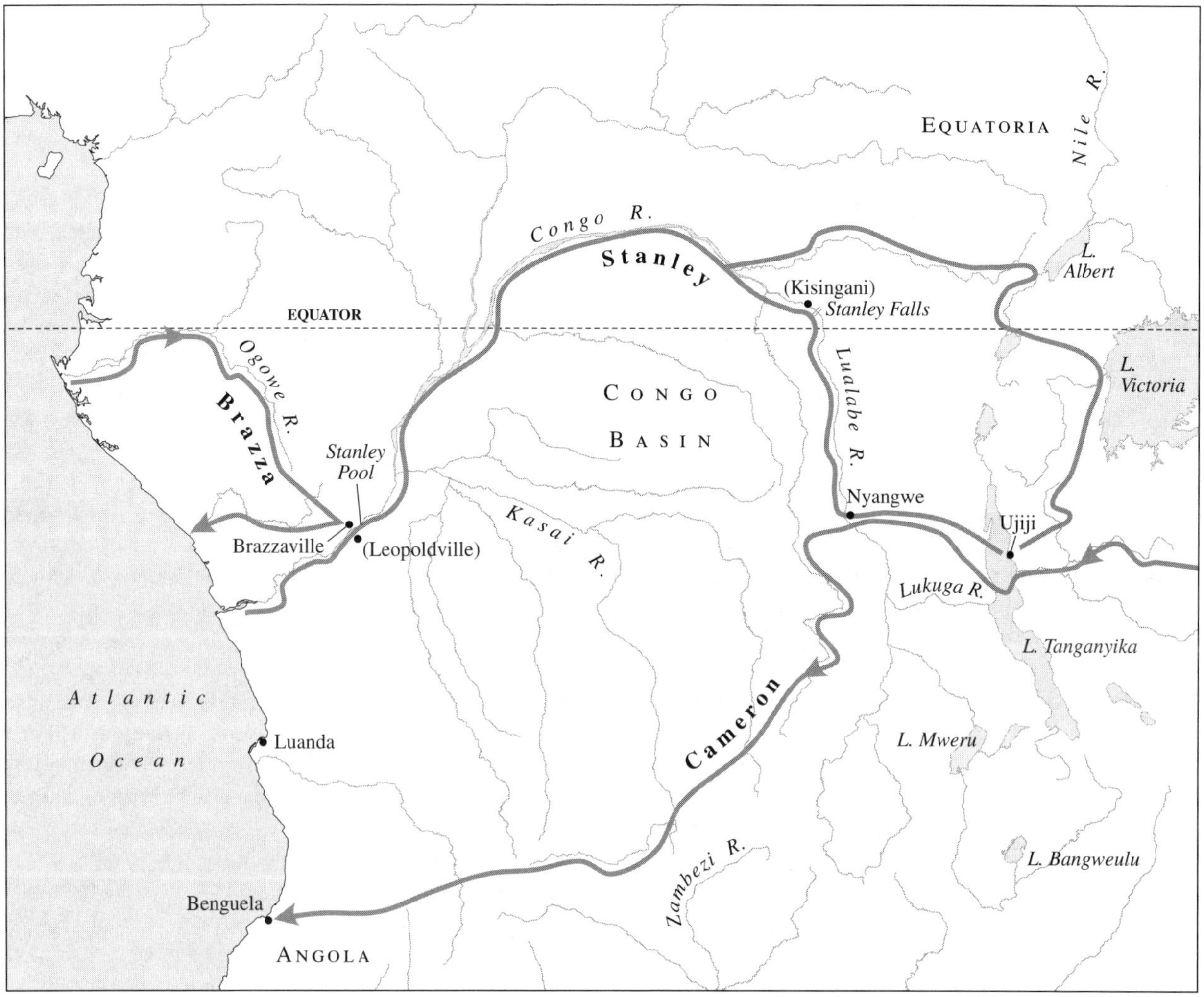

time that many of the region's African societies were becoming eager to unify under a European power for protection against their neighbors. Exploration of the region prepared the way for political jostling during the late 1870's.

The story of nineteenth century central African exploration begins with David Livingstone, who made Africa a subject of wonder to the Western world during the late 1850's and 1860's. In 1868 he lost contact with Europe while searching for the source of the Nile in the interior of East Africa. The Welsh-born American journalist Henry Morton Stanley was sent by the *New York Herald* to find him. In 1871, Stanley found Livingstone at Ujiji, on the eastern shore of Lake Tanganyika, one of the great central African lakes east of the Congo Basin.

In 1872, before Stanley's news reached Great Britain, the Scottish explorer Verney Lovett Cameron was also sent to find Livingstone. By then Livingstone had died. After Cameron found Livingstone's grave in 1873, he located Lake Tanganyika's western outlet, the Lukuga River. Before heading southwest, he went farther west, to the Lualaba River, which some geographers thought might feed into the Nile. Although he went only a short distance on the Lualaba, he rightly surmised that it flowed into the Congo River, not the Nile.

In 1875, Cameron made a several-hundred-mile journey along the Congo-Zambezi watershed, noting the wealth of copper in Katanga on his way to the west coast, which he reached on November 7, 1875, near Benguela. He also discovered that tribal leaders appeared to be eager to unify for peace, and he obtained agreements from several chiefs to cede their rights to their land in return for protection. However, as Cameron was later to learn, Great Britain apparently was not greatly interested in establishing a protectorate over that part of Africa. However, Belgium's King Leopold II was.

Seeing an opportunity to make money and secure a colony for his tiny European country, Leopold met with Cameron in 1876 and garnered support from several European countries in Brussels to establish the International African Association (IAA), which presented itself as an international humanitarian effort to bring Western civilization to the people of Africa. The participating countries formed national committees to raise money for their own delegations, but they all eventually pursued their own political interests in the region. Soon, it became clear that the IAA was merely the first of several organizations that Leopold was forming to enrich himself.

By 1877, Leopold concluded that the best way to suppress slave trafficking and tribal warfare in central Africa was to establish European-controlled trade in goods along the Congo River. No longer interested in Cameron, he tried to recruit the Italian-born French explorer, Pierre-Paul-François-Camille Savorgnan de Brazza for an African venture. As a French naval officer, de Brazza had explored the Ogowe (Ogoué) River basin inland from the coast of Gabon, to the north of the Congo River mouth. In 1877, he had gone up the Ogowe to its source and reached the Alima River, a tributary of the Congo. De Brazza, however, apparently wished to remain loyal to France, for nothing came of Leopold's overtures to him. The king then approached Stanley, who by 1877 had become a well-known explorer.

Stanley had already circumnavigated Lake Victoria and explored Lake Tanganyika to its southwest during the mid-1870's. He confirmed what Cameron had surmised: that the Lualaba River was in fact part of the Congo River system. He followed the Lualaba down to the Congo and reached the Atlantic coast in August, 1877. After failing to find financial support in Britain for further exploration work, Stanley accepted Leopold's commission in 1879. He work was to be conducted under the auspices of Leopold's Comité d' Études du Haut-Congo, Survey Committee for the Upper Congo, which later became known as the International Congo Association. The organization was founded and ultimately financed by Leopold himself, not the Belgian government.

De Brazza felt that French interests were being threatened by Leopold and Stanley's plans to create a west-to-east trading route along the Congo River, so he planned a new expedition of his own while he was in Paris. He decided to search for the Upper Congo from the source of the Ogowe and then travel by land to Stanley Pool (now Pool de Malebo) on the Lower Congo. He succeeded in reaching the Upper Congo ahead of Stanley in 1879. By the following year, he had obtained numerous treaties ceding control of the area to France, including one from Makoko, a tribal chief with wide hereditary claims to the surrounding territory. He built a fort on a village on the north side of Stanley Pool. The French protectorate he labored to establish officially became the French Congo in 1891, and the location where he built the fort became the colony's capital, which was named Brazzaville in his honor.

Meanwhile, Stanley made his way upriver from the Congo's mouth in 1879 and unexpectedly met de Brazza at Vivi, one of several trading and administrative stations Stanley had founded on his way upriver. Among de Brazza's motives in moving downriver was to explore the possibility of building a railroad that would connect the trading posts in the region, an idea that Stanley had also championed. Not surprisingly, Stanley was annoyed to discover that de Brazza had reached the Upper Congo ahead of him. Meanwhile, King Leopold's agents were intercepting de Brazza's letters. When Leopold learned of de Brazza's plans, he urged Stanley to hurry. Stanley finally reached the Upper Congo in 1881. He also secured treaties near Stanley Pool that would ultimately secure the south bank of the region for Leopold.

As Portugal observed the speed with which France and Leopold's agents were establishing posts in the Congo Basin, its government began to assert its claims to territories with which it had deep historical connections through centuries of missionary work and trading near the coast and along the mouth of the Congo River. Portugal launched its own scientific explorations to map the southwestern region of the Congo Basin, notably with the journeys of naval officers and scientists Alexandre Alberto da Rocha de Serpa Pinto, Hermenegildo Carlos de Brito Capello, and Roberto Ivens. These three men departed from Benguela and headed toward central Angola, but Capello and Ivens soon separated from Pinto, who set off to the southeast and eventually reached the coast. Capello and Ivens meanwhile explored the southwestern part of the Congo Basin, mapping out the territory between the Upper Zambezi and the Upper Congo before returning to Lisbon in 1880. During the 1880's, Portugal petitioned Great Britain to recognize its claims in the Congo, an issue that would not be settled for another decade.

SIGNIFICANCE

The European explorations of the Congo Basin paved the way for the partition of central Africa during the 1880's among France, Portugal, and Leopold's International Congo Association. De Brazza's work led to the establishment of the French Congo, which became part of French Equatorial Africa after 1910, in the area making up much of the present-day Republic of the Congo. Portugal's claim to the land between Mozambique and Angola was officially recognized by France and Germany in 1886, but Britain, by threatening violence, forced Portugal out of the interior in 1890.

During the early 1880's, Stanley completed a road from Vivi to the west coast and collected more than 450 treaties from tribal chieftains that ceded most of the Congo Basin to the International Congo Association. The association's central African domain became the Congo Free State after the Berlin West Africa Conference met in 1884-1885. The United States and thirteen other countries recognized the area as an independent state headed by Leopold II. The association agreed to abide by certain humanitarian principles, including the suppression of the slave trade. However, in order to build a railroad and continue a profitable trade in rubber and ivory, the Congo Free State's extensive monopoly exacted what was essentially forced labor from Africans. Responding to pressure from Christian missionaries and the Congo Reform Association, the Belgian parliament annexed the region in 1908, establishing the Belgian Congo, which limited the power of the king over the region. The Belgian Congo remained a colony until 1960, when it became the independent Democratic Republic of the Congo. That country later changed its name to Zaire, but by the twenty-first century, it had reverted to the name it had at independence.

—*William Gahan*

FURTHER READING

Cameron, Verney Lovett. *Across Africa*. 1877. Reprint. New York: Negro Universities Press, 1969. Firsthand account of the Scottish explorer's travels, with maps and illustrations.

Capello, Hermenegildo Carlos de Brito, and Roberto Ivens. *From Benguella to the Territory of Yacca*. Translated by Alfred Elwes. 1882. Reprint. New York: Negro Universities Press, 1969. This early translation of the Portuguese explorers' account of their travels from 1877-1880 is still the best source in English for details about Capello and Ivens. Includes maps and illustrations.

Hochschild, Adam. *King Leopold's Ghost: A Story of Greed, Terror, and Heroism in Colonial Africa*. London: Pan, 2002. Scholarly but accessible work that focuses on the atrocities committed by the Congo Free State under the direction of Leopold II. Includes a section discussing the events that led up to creation of Leopold's private African domain.

Newman, James L. *Imperial Footprints: Henry Morton Stanley's African Journeys*. Washington, D.C.: Brassey's, 2004. Illustrated study of Stanley that concentrates on his journeys themselves, rather than on the psychology and personality of the explorer.

West, Richard. *Congo*. New York: Holt, Rinehart and Winston, 1972. Illustrated study of the French, British, Belgian, and German explorations in the region includes an entertaining chronicle of de Brazza and Stanley's personal rivalry.

SEE ALSO: May 4, 1805-1830: Exploration of West Africa; 1822-1874: Exploration of North Africa; 1848-1889: Exploration of East Africa; Nov. 17, 1853: Livingstone Sees the Victoria Falls; Nov. 15, 1884-Feb. 26, 1885: Berlin Conference Lays Groundwork for the Partition of Africa.

RELATED ARTICLES in *Great Lives from History: The Nineteenth Century, 1801-1900:* Mary Kingsley; Leopold II; David Livingstone; Henry Morton Stanley.

1873-1897
ZANZIBAR OUTLAWS SLAVERY

Ruled by a regime that had its origins in southern Arabia, Zanzibar built its prosperity on control of the East African ivory and slave trades during the nineteenth century, only to come under increasing Western pressure to abolish the slave trade and then the institution of slavery itself. It responded to that pressure first by outlawing the slave trade and, nearly one-quarter of a century later, abolishing domestic slavery.

LOCALE: Zanzibar (now in Tanzania)
CATEGORIES: Social issues and reform; civil rights and liberties

KEY FIGURES

Sa'īd ibn Sulṭān (1791-1856), Omani sultan, r. 1804-1856, who moved the capital to Zanzibar in the 1830's
Arthur Henry Hardinge (1859-1933), British consul general at Zanzibar, 1894-1898
Joseph Pease (1799-1872), leader of abolitionist movement
Khalid ibn Barghash (1874-1927), claimant to Zanzibari sultanate
Barghash (c. 1834-1888), sultan of Zanzibar, r. 1870-1888

SUMMARY OF EVENT

The East African offshore island of Zanzibar had a long history of involvement in the slave trade. Between the twelfth and fifteenth centuries Zanzibar was a powerful city-state with trade links to the Middle East, India, and other parts of Asia. During the mid-seventeenth century, the rules of southern Arabia's Omani sultanate began involving themselves in the east coast of Africa, especially by providing coastal towns with naval support against the Portuguese. In 1840, Sultan Sa'īd ibn Sulṭān moved his capital from Oman to Zanzibar in order to exercise closer control over Oman's growing East African trade.

The main commodities brought by caravans from the interior of East Africa to the coast were ivory and slaves. Around the mid-nineteenth century, more than 10,000 slaves—many from as far inland as Lake Tanganyika—were taken through the coastal town of Bagamoyo and sold in the Zanzibar markets every year. Overall, some 600,000 slaves were sold in Zanzibar between 1830 and 1873, the year in which Zanzibar prohibited the trade.

Meanwhile, Oman's increasing trade attracted Western interest. In 1798, Great Britain and Oman established trade agreements. In 1833, the United States signed an amity and commerce treaty with Oman that gave the latter most-favored-nation privileges and established an American consulate in Zanzibar town. Britain followed with a similar treaty in 1839 and France in 1844. Along with Western trade came opposition to the institution of slavery.

During the first half of the nineteenth century, Britain concentrated its efforts to intercept slave ships along Africa's western coast. The British then moved to help eradicate the slave trade on the other side of the continent. One of the first British consuls in Zanzibar, Colonel Atkins Hamerton, used his diplomatic influence to pressure the sultan. In 1845, Sultan Sa'īd signed a treaty with Britain agreeing to limit the slave trade within his possessions. However, this agreement left him free to channel slaves through ports in the Persian Gulf.

After Sultan Sa'īd died in 1856, he was succeeded by his first son, Majid, who had no interest in limiting the slave trade. In fact, he founded the city of Dar es Salaam on the coast of the mainland and expanded its harbor with the purpose of increasing trade. However, he died in 1870 before achieving his goals. One of his brothers, Barghash, succeeded him as sultan and found his power decreasing. In 1872, a hurricane destroyed his naval fleet. Afterward, the sultanate was formally partitioned, making Zanzibar completely separate from Oman. British opposition to slavery was also increasing as David Livingstone's reports of his 1856 expedition to East Africa raised awareness of the cruelties of the slave trade and as European missionaries such as Johann Ludwig Krapf and Johann Rebmann began working on the mainland. In 1873, Barghash finally issued a decree ending the export of slaves from Zanzibar.

Anglican agents of the Universities' Mission to Central Africa took over the large slave market in Zanzibar town throughout which hundreds of thousands of slaves had passed. In 1876, they built an Anglican cathedral on that site that has ever since stood as a memorial to the victims of the slave trade. Meanwhile, the institution of slavery would continue on Zanzibar for another quarter of a century.

Zanzibar's economy had already undergone a major transformation. During the 1830's, cloves had been introduced to Zanzibar. No longer was the focus on Zanzibar town alone, as plantations sprang up throughout Zanzibar and the neighboring island of Pemba. Zanzibar soon became the world's leading exporter of cloves, with markets not only in Asia but also in Europe and the Americas. Slaves brought from the mainland were now purchased to serve the growing plantations on Zanzibar. In addition to clove production, coconut plantations expanded the economic base. At the same time, more Arabs relocated from Oman during the late 1870's to run the plantations.

The end of slave exports in the 1873 decree was in some ways a natural development, but slavery on Zanzibar continued to flourish. Barghash's decree had outlawed the import of slaves from the mainland, leaving only the slaves who had lived in Zanzibar and their offspring as legal under the law. However, it was difficult to enforce the ban on importing slaves, and the numbers of slaves on Zanzibar continued to increase. In 1895, a British official estimated that of the 200,000 inhabitants of the island, three-quarters were slaves.

In 1890, Great Britain established a protectorate over Zanzibar, reducing the sultan to a figurehead. The British then began a major debate on the status of slavery on the island. In London, abolitionists led by Joseph Pease lobbied Parliament to take action. However, in Zanzibar Consul General Arthur Henry Hardinge opposed forcing any major changes, taking the side of the plantation owners. Reports sent back to Britain generally painted a glowing picture of conditions in Zanzibar. Even a number of missionaries from the Church Mission Society expressed reluctance to go against the status quo. However, when the Society of Friends established a mission in Zanzibar in 1895, eyewitness reports about the facts on the ground were shared with the British public.

The impetus for a complete ban on slavery came in September, 1896, when France announced the abolition of slavery in Madagascar. During the previous month, Zanzibar's Sultan Hamid ibn Thuwain had died. Khalid ibn Barghash, a strong proponent of slavery, proclaimed his own succession and took over the palace. However, British naval vessels bombarded the palace, killing about five hundred defenders and removing the new sultan. The British then installed their own candidate for sultan,

Muslim slave traders marching their captives to the East African coast during the early 1870's. (Arkent Archive)

Hamoud ibn Muhammad. Hardinge was recalled to London for instructions. When he returned to Zanzibar in early 1897 the transformation was enacted. On April 6, 1897 the new sultan issued a decree abolishing slavery in Zanzibar. Slave owners were to be paid compensation for the loss of legally held slaves.

SIGNIFICANCE

The abolition of slavery in Zanzibar in 1897 was the final step in the century-long British effort to end Africa's slave trade. However, even then, the issue of slavery was not fully resolved. Zanzibar's emancipation decree required slaves to apply for their freedom and prove that they had both places to live and means of support. Moreover, a series of vagrancy laws were written into the decree to restrict the lives of newly freed slaves. Within the first year, only 10 percent of Zanzibar's slaves had bothered to complete the paperwork. Other slaves negotiated for better working conditions and remained on their plantations.

The decree did, however, have a lasting effect on life in Zanzibar. Following years of prosperity, the early part of the twentieth century showed signs of struggle. The plantations at first suffered from labor shortages. Many switched from clove to coconut production because the latter was less labor-intensive. Many large plantations broke up and were replaced by small farmers who were more concerned with subsistence or small business operations. Meanwhile, the city of Zanzibar expanded as former slaves left the countryside to find work in the city.

The end of slavery on Zanzibar was a victory for several generations of abolitionists who had lobbied tirelessly against the institution. However, the 1897 decree did not apply to the coastal areas of the mainland under British control, where the effort to abolish slavery continued for another decade. In many areas the concern for slavery shifted to working conditions for free laborers.

—*Fred Strickert*

FURTHER READING

Bennett, Norman Robert. *The Arab State of Zanzibar: A Bibliography.* Boston: G. K. Hall, 1984. Comprehensive bibliography of Zanzibar, with many references to works on nineteenth century events.

Cooper, Frederick. *From Slaves to Squatters: Plantation Labor and Agriculture in Zanzibar and Coastal Kenya, 1890-1925.* New Haven, Conn.: Yale University Press, 1981. Examination of Zanzibar's transformation from a slave economy to a wage-based economy.

Depelchin, James. "The Transition from Slavery, 1873-1914." In *Zanzibar Under Colonial Rule*, edited by Abdul Sheriff and Ed Ferguson. Athens: Ohio University Press, 1991. Essay on Zanzibar's transition to a free economy that argues that the motivation for abolishing slavery in Zanzibar was economic, not humanitarian.

Fair, Laura. *Pastimes and Politics: Culture, Community, and Identity in Post-Abolition Urban Zanzibar, 1890-1945.* Athens: Ohio University Press, 2001. Study of changes in Zanzibar after the legal abolition of slavery.

Grant, Kevin. *A Civilized Savagery: Britain and the New Slaveries in Africa, 1884-1926.* Philadelphia: Taylor & Francis, 2004. Scholarly study, based on archival sources, of attempts by the British government and evangelical churches to end slavery and forced-labor practices in Africa during the first decades of its colonial involvement in the continent.

Sheriff, Abdul. *Slaves, Spices, and Ivory in Zanzibar.* Athens: Ohio University Press, 1987. Broad economic history of trade in Zanzibar.

SEE ALSO: Mar. 2, 1807: Congress Bans Importation of African Slaves; Aug. 28, 1833: Slavery Is Abolished Throughout the British Empire; Nov., 1862: Slave Traders Begin Ravaging Easter Island; Dec. 6, 1865: Thirteenth Amendment Is Ratified; Nov. 15, 1884-Feb. 26, 1885: Berlin Conference Lays Groundwork for the Partition of Africa.

RELATED ARTICLES in *Great Lives from History: The Nineteenth Century, 1801-1900:* David Livingstone; Saʿīd ibn Sulṭān; Tippu Tip.

January 22, 1873-February 13, 1874
SECOND BRITISH-ASHANTI WAR

The second in a series of nineteenth century wars between the British and the Ashanti Kingdom, the 1873-1874 conflict temporarily weakened the Ashanti kingdom and strengthened the British position on the Gold Coast but did not provide a lasting solution to strained relations between the British and the Ashanti.

ALSO KNOWN AS: Second Ashanti War
LOCALE: Gold Coast and Ashanti territory in West Africa (now Ghana)
CATEGORY: Wars, uprisings, and civil unrest

KEY FIGURES

Kofi Karikari (Kofi Kakari; 1837-1883), king (*asantehene*) of the Ashanti, r. 1867-1874
Amankwatia (d. 1874), general who led the Ashanti invasion of 1873
Garnet Joseph Wolseley (1833-1913), commander of the British forces in the war
Sir John Hawley Glover (1829-1885), commander of eastern column of British forces

SUMMARY OF EVENT

The Ashanti War of 1873-1874, sometimes called the Second Ashanti War, was one of a series of conflicts during the nineteenth century between the British and the West African people known as the Ashanti, or Asante. The British and the Dutch had established posts along what was then called the Gold Coast in territory controlled by the Fante people. The Ashanti controlled territory inland from the coast and frequently came into conflict with the Fante. Throughout the century, the British tended to align themselves with the Fante and clashed with the Ashanti, who were friendlier with the Dutch.

During the late 1860's and early 1870's, the British and the Dutch arranged to exchange several of their forts, including the Dutch fort at Elmina. The transfer of Elmina to the British took place on April 6, 1872, over the protests of the Ashanti king Kofi Karikari, who said that Elmina belonged to his kingdom. At the same time, Karikari asserted Ashanti sovereignty over the border states between Ashanti and Fante territory, even though the Ashanti had recognized the independence of those states by a treaty in 1831.

On December 9, 1872, the Ashanti assembled an army estimated to have had as many as forty thousand men and marched it out of their capital, Kumasi, Led by General Amankwatia, the Ashanti army reached the recognized boundary of Ashanti territory at the River Pra on December 22. Exactly one month later, it crossed over into the border state of Assin. On February 9, 1873, the Ashanti defeated an Assin army at Assin Nyankumasi. One month later, the Ashanti defeated a combined Assin and Fante force at Fante Nyankumasi. Two inconclusive battles ensued on April 8 and 14 at Dunkwa. Finally, on June 5, 1873, the Ashanti routed the Fante at Jukwa. Thousands of panicked Fante then fled to the British fort at Cape Coast Castle.

The British at first reacted to the crisis slowly. Governor John Pope Hennessy even said he did not think an Ashanti invasion was under way. Eventually, however, the British began to take the situation more seriously and a sent out a small marine detachment under Lieutenant Colonel Francis Festing. It arrived in time to thwart an Ashanti attack on Elmina on June 13, 1873. In August, the British government took additional steps, sending Captain John Glover to raise African forces to attack the Ashanti from the east. Garnet Joseph Wolseley was placed in control of all British and allied forces on the Gold Coast, with orders to raise African levies to fight the Ashanti.

Wolseley arrived on the Gold Coast on October 2, 1873. Eleven days later, he led a successful raid on Ashanti forces at Elmina. Shortly afterward, the Ashanti decided to withdraw to their own territory, in part because of their reverses in battle but also because of losses they suffered from smallpox and dysentery. As they withdrew from Fante territory and the border states, the Ashanti stopped to fight a battle at Abrakrampa on November 5, and were soundly defeated. However, Wolseley was able to recruit few African troops and could do little more than harry the Ashanti from the rear as they retreated. In order to carry the war to Ashanti territory, he wrote home asking for more British troops and was sent three regiments, which arrived in December.

The original British plan of attack was based on the idea of transporting the troops by railroad into the bush, and tracks were even sent out to build a railroad line for this purpose. However, the terrain was found to be too hilly to make the plan practical, so the plan was abandoned. Any idea of invading by water was also abandoned after a disastrous reconnaissance mission up the River Pra led by Commodore John Commerell in August. Instead, the Royal Engineers constructed roads, bridges, and staging areas. In January, 1874, Wolseley

Leaders of the Abrakrampa people toast the queen of Great Britain with several British missionaries after the British defeat of the Ashanti. (Hulton Archive/Getty Images)

began marching his troops north from Cape Coast, crossing the Pra River into Ashanti territory on January 20. During the march, King Karikari sent messages asking Wolseley to slow down and negotiate. However, Wolseley continued marching until his forces met the Ashanti army at Amoafo on January 31 for the major battle of the war.

Despite having lost half their army in their 1873 invasion, the Ashanti still outnumbered the British at Amoafo. However, the British had superior weapons, including breech-loading rifles and artillery. The Ashanti had antique muzzle-loading muskets and poor gunpowder. Lacking lead bullets, they used shells and stones instead. The Ashanti held out for hours, but when the British brought their artillery into play and launched a bayonet charge, the Ashanti fell back.

The Ashanti did not give up immediately, however. After falling back, they pursued their usual tactic of encircling their enemy from the rear, in the process disrupting British supply lines. Deprived of supplies, Wolseley decided that his best course of action would be to make a quick dash to capture the Ashanti capital and not stay there long. There then followed battles at Bekwai on February 1 and Odasu on February 4, after which the British were able to enter Kumasi without opposition.

Once in the capital, Wolseley sent messages to King Karikari asking him to present himself to agree to terms, but the king remained in the bush with the bulk of his forces. Lacking the supplies his force needed for a long stay and fearing the onset of the rainy season, Wolseley withdrew his troops from Kumasi and began returning south. The British feared that the Ashanti might attack them as they retreated, but King Karikari sent a message on February 9 begging Wolseley to call off the attacks by Captain Glover and agreeing to make peace. With a small force of Hausa troops, Glover had reached Kumasi, causing the Ashanti to think that a second major British army was in the field. The Ashanti agreed to surrender and agreed to a treaty on February 13 that they signed at Fomena on March 14. Under the terms of this treaty, the Ashanti agreed to renounce their claims to Elmina and the border states and to pay the British an indemnity of fifty thousand ounces of gold.

SIGNIFICANCE

In the short term, the war weakened the Ashanti and strengthened the position of the British. Afterward, civil war broke out in the Ashanti kingdom, and Karikari was deposed. Meanwhile, Wolseley was celebrated as a hero in Great Britain, where the Ashanti War was seen as a great victory. The result of the war also led to the British to declare the Gold Coast to be a colony, thus solidifying their control over the area. The war also showed that superior technology could triumph over superior numbers, and it ended Ashanti claims to the border states.

The British did not, however, pursue their advantage after the war. They were uncertain if it was in their interest to encourage divisions among the Ashanti or to seek a more peaceful and stable situation. In the end, they pursued a noninterventionist course, and the Ashanti eventually rebuilt and reunited. Twenty years later more fighting between the Ashanti and the British broke out, and the British wars with the Ashanti did not end until the British annexed the Ashanti territory in 1901.

On a more technical level, the war was significant for introducing innovations in warfare. Wolseley got the British troops to switch from tight-fitting scarlet uniforms to loose-fitting gray clothes and sun helmets that were more practical in tropical climates. Wolseley also broke with custom by breaking his military companies into small sections and by introducing a healthier and more substantial diet for his troops. He paid a great deal of attention to the health of his troops in an attempt to ward off attacks of malaria. In this, however, he was not very successful, as 71 percent of his troops fell ill—in part because it was not then known that malaria was transmitted by mosquito bites.

—*Sheldon Goldfarb*

FURTHER READING

Claridge, W. Walton. *A History of the Gold Coast and Ashanti from the Earliest Times to the Commencement of the Twentieth Century*. 2d ed. 2 vols. London: Frank Cass, 1964. Reprint of the massively detailed 1915 edition, focusing on British activity. Includes maps.

Edgerton, Robert B. *The Fall of the Asante Empire: The Hundred-Year War for Africa's Gold Coast*. New York: Free Press, 1995. Offers considerable detail about the Ashanti and the war from their point of view but has a poor index. Includes maps.

Keegan, John. "The Ashanti Campaign, 1873-4." In *Victorian Military Campaigns*, edited by Brian Bond. London: Hutchinson, 1967. Provides details on British strategy and tactics, background material, and numbers.

Kochanski, Halik. *Sir Garnet Wolseley: Victorian Hero*. London: Hambledon Press, 1999. Biography of Wolseley that also includes short biographical sketches of his fellow officers. Also includes illustrations and statistics.

Lloyd, Alan. *The Drums of Kumasi: The Story of the Ashanti Wars*. London: Longmans, Green, 1964. Lots of detail on the fighting, especially from the British side. Much material on Captain Glover.

Maxwell, Leigh. *The Ashanti Ring: Sir Garnet Wolseley's Campaigns, 1870-1882*. London: Secker & Warburg, 1985. Detailed description of the military campaigns, focusing on the British side. Includes maps.

Ward, W. E. F. *A History of Ghana*. 3d ed. London: Allen & Unwin, 1966. Standard history of Ghana that offers precise dates and considerable information on the Ashanti wars and other events.

SEE ALSO: May 4, 1805-1830: Exploration of West Africa; Nov. 15, 1884-Feb. 26, 1885: Berlin Conference Lays Groundwork for the Partition of Africa; Nov., 1889-Jan., 1894: Dahomey-French Wars.

RELATED ARTICLE in *Great Lives from History: The Nineteenth Century, 1801-1900:* Sir Robert Stephenson Smyth Baden-Powell.

February 12, 1873
"CRIME OF 1873"

The so-called Crime of 1873 was an emotion-laden slogan used by proponents of the free coinage of silver to express their hostility toward the federal Coinage Act that made gold the sole monetary standard, with no provision for the coining of silver dollars. The debate over silver coinage would continue into the twentieth century.

ALSO KNOWN AS: Coinage Act
LOCALE: Washington, D.C.
CATEGORIES: Banking and finance; crime and scandals; laws, acts, and legal history

KEY FIGURES

John Jay Knox (1828-1892), comptroller of the currency
Henry Richard Linderman (1825-1879), special assistant to the comptroller of the currency
William Morris Stewart (1827-1909), U.S. senator from Nevada
George M. Weston (fl. late nineteenth century), secretary of the National Monetary Commission

SUMMARY OF EVENT

The U.S. money controversy that the shibboleth "Crime of 1873" dramatized raged between 1865 and 1896 and can best be understood in the context of the nation's antebellum and Civil War monetary policies. Until the Civil War, the United States functioned under bimetallism—a monetary system based on silver and gold, supplemented by the notes of its banks. The use of the two kinds of specie as money was deemed desirable because there were insufficient quantities of precious metals for the requirements of trade, commerce, and exchange. Under bimetallism, both silver and gold were acceptable for the payment of debts at rates fixed by the government. The Currency Act of 1834 established a legal ratio between the two metals of sixteen ounces of silver to one ounce of gold. Under this so-called mint ratio, the Treasury was obligated to purchase both metals at the established prices.

Bimetallism presented a problem, in that the values of silver and gold fluctuated on the world market in response to changes in supply. New supplies of gold from Russia, Australia, and California during the 1840's, for example, caused gold gradually to decline in value. Therefore, silver was undervalued if priced at the mint ratio of sixteen to one. As predicted by Gresham's law—that cheaper currency drives higher-valued currency out of circulation—silver coins disappeared from circulation, because silver producers preferred to sell their bullion on the world market, where the price was higher than at the mint. By 1853, the market ratio of silver to gold was 15.4-1. In other words, silver producers needed sixteen ounces of silver to exchange for an ounce of gold at the mint, but only 15.4 ounces on the bullion market. After having been out of circulation for years, silver was reduced by Congress in 1853 to a subsidiary metal. Silver remained scarce and undervalued as coin until the 1870's.

Under great pressure to raise money during the Civil War, the government abandoned the specie standard and passed the Legal Tender Acts of 1862, which authorized the printing of fiat money (greenbacks), unsupported by specie but acceptable legal tender for all debts except interest on government bonds and excise taxes. During the war, the Treasury circulated more than $450 million in greenbacks, which inflated precipitously by 1864. The

John Jay Knox, the comptroller of the currency. (Library of Congress)

use of gold became limited primarily to international trade.

When the war ended, the Treasury began urging a program of deflation leading to the eventual retirement of the greenbacks and a return to a specie standard. Resistance in Congress to this hard-money scheme came from a group of soft-money advocates, who opposed a return to specie but differed among themselves over the issue of inflation. Consequently, the Treasury received authority to retire only small quantities of greenbacks. Some soft-money advocates who favored inflation demanded the printing of more greenbacks to be used for payment of the national debt, a proposal that was written into the Democratic Party platform of 1868.

By that time, the money controversy had caused factions to grow in the business community (among farmers, bankers, and manufacturers), in geographical regions, and to some extent in political parties, with soft-money supporters generally showing greater strength in the states west of the Appalachians. However, the Greenbackers suffered serious reverses with the passage of the Public Credit Act of 1869, which pledged payment of the national debt in gold, and the Resumption Act of 1875, which ordered the redemption of greenbacks with gold by 1879.

In the midst of the greenback controversy, John Jay Knox, the comptroller of the currency, aided by special assistant Henry Richard Linderman, the former director of the U.S. mint at Philadelphia, began preparing a revision of the laws dealing with the mints and coinage. One aspect of their work appeared in the federal Coinage Act that Congress passed on February 12, 1873, which discontinued the coinage of silver dollars. The following year, the *Revised Statutes of the United States* demonetized silver by limiting its legal tender function to debts of not more than five dollars. Both laws gave belated recognition to the fact that silver had not circulated since the 1840's. At the time, the legislation disturbed no one, not even the silver miners who preferred to sell on the open market. Indeed, Senator William Morris Stewart of the silver-producing state of Nevada, who later used the slogan "Crime of '73," failed to oppose either law.

Even as the legislation was passed, however, new mines were opening in the western states, augmenting the world supply of silver. The market ratio, 15.9-1 in 1873, climbed to 16.1-1 in 1874, and to 16.6-1 by 1875, or about ninety-six cents in gold. As silver prices dropped, mining interests discovered to their dismay that the Currency Act of 1873 blocked the profitable sale of silver to the mint at 16-1.

On March 2, 1876, George M. Weston, the secretary of the U.S. Monetary Commission, charged in a letter to the *Boston Globe* that the demonetization of silver was a conspiracy by the creditor class against the people. Weston's letter, which attached the word "crime" to the federal law for the first time, began the controversy over silver. Other advocates of silver took up the charge, demanding the free coinage of silver. Later, Greenbackers and other inflationists, fighting losing battles against resumption, also began supporting silver.

Agitation for the free coinage of silver continued until 1896, when new gold supplies began inducing the price increases that post-Civil War inflationists had desired. Congress, however, previously had passed legislation permitting limited silver coinage. The Bland-Allison Act of 1878 required the Treasury to buy between two and four million ounces of silver per month at the prevailing market price. According to the Sherman Silver Purchase Act of 1890, four million ounces had to be purchased each month. This legislation demonstrated that those who favored silver had far greater strength than the Greenbackers had had a decade earlier.

SIGNIFICANCE

The conspiracy charge against the Currency Act of 1873, which alleged that British financiers plotted to influence Congress, was rejected by most nineteenth century economists and writers. The issue was raised again in 1960 with the discovery of new evidence that seemed to indicate that Linderman foresaw an increase in silver output and, as a monometallist, allegedly plotted to omit silver coinage from the 1873 legislation. Nevertheless, most modern scholarship continues to reject the conspiracy thesis.

—Merl E. Reed, updated by Charles H. O'Brien

FURTHER READING

Barrett, Don Carlos. *The Greenbacks and Resumption of Specie Payments, 1862-1879.* Cambridge, Mass.: Harvard University Press, 1931. Although dated in some ways, this work, which treats the gold standard almost as a moral issue, is still a useful reference.

Friedman, Milton, and Anna J. Schwartz. *A Monetary History of the United States, 1867-1960.* Princeton, N.J.: Princeton University Press, 1963. This massive study by two economists combines economic analysis with economic history. Its first three chapters discuss the greenback and silver controversy.

Hixson, William F. *Triumph of the Bankers: Money and Banking in the Eighteenth and Nineteenth Centuries.*

Westport, Conn.: Praeger, 1993. Contends that the dominating theme of U.S. monetary history is a perennial conflict between creditors and debtors. Two chapters deal with monetary policy from 1865 to 1896.

Laughlin, J. Laurence. *The History of Bimetallism in the United States*. 4th ed. New York: Greenwood Press, 1968. The author, who was one of the most scholarly writers on the silver issue during the nineteenth century, was a gold supporter. His work still serves as a useful and necessary reference.

Rothbard, Murray N. *A History of Money and Banking in the United States: The Colonial Era to World War II*. Auburn, Ala.: Ludwig Von Mises Institute, 2002. One of the best general histories of U.S. banking and the money supply, by a distinguished economist.

Studenski, Paul. *Financial History of the United States*. New York: McGraw-Hill, 1952. This general work contains four chapters on the Civil War and Reconstruction periods that general readers should find helpful before undertaking more complex studies, such as those by Unger or Friedman and Schwartz.

Timberlake, Richard H. *Monetary Policy in the United States: An Intellectual and Institutional History*. Chicago: University of Chicago Press, 1993. Discusses the evolution of governmental control of the U.S. monetary and banking system. Chapters 10 through 12 discuss the greenback and silver issues.

Unger, Irwin. *The Greenback Era: A Social and Political History of American Finance, 1865-1879*. Princeton, N.J.: Princeton University Press, 1964. Authoritative treatment of the post-Civil War period. Challenges the view of the era as a struggle between embattled farmers and rising capitalists, arguing that it was far more complex and confused.

Van Ryzin, Robert R. *Crime of 1873: The Comstock Connection*. Iola, Wis.: Krause, 2001. Popular history of the minting of Morgan and Silver Trade dollars. Apart from the author's views on corruption in the U.S. Mint, this book will be of interest mainly to numismatists.

Weinstein, Allen. *Prelude to Populism: Origins of the Silver Issue, 1867-1878*. New Haven, Conn.: Yale University Press, 1970. Focuses on the politics and social conflicts involved in the first drive to restore silver as a monetary standard.

SEE ALSO: Aug. 1, 1846: Establishment of Independent U.S. Treasury; Feb. 25, 1863-June 3, 1864: Congress Passes the National Bank Acts; Apr. 22, 1864: "In God We Trust" Appears on U.S. Coins; July 4-5, 1892: Birth of the People's Party; Nov. 3, 1896: McKinley Is Elected President.

RELATED ARTICLE in *Great Lives from History: The Nineteenth Century, 1801-1900:* John Peter Altgeld.

March 3, 1873
CONGRESS PASSES THE COMSTOCK ANTIOBSCENITY LAW

The Comstock Law amended U.S. postal regulations and banned the use of the mail to advertise, publish, or sell sexually suggestive material, including information about contraception and abortion. The law had the effect of severely retarding the dissemination of birth-control information.

LOCALE: United States

ALSO KNOWN AS: Federal Anti-Obscenity Act; Comstock Act

CATEGORIES: Laws, acts, and legal history; women's issues; health and medicine; communications

KEY FIGURES

Anthony Comstock (1844-1915), social reformer and author of the Comstock Law

Jacob Collamer (1791-1865), Vermont senator and author of the 1865 Postal Act

Margaret Sanger (1879-1966), nurse, author, and founder of the American Birth Control League

SUMMARY OF EVENT

On March 3, 1873, the U.S. Congress passed a bill that led to the Comstock Law, which amended the 1865 Postal Act. The 1865 act had made it a crime to send "publication[s] of a vulgar or indecent character" through the mail. The Comstock Law strengthened these restrictions, establishing special antiobscenity agents with the power to seize material deemed obscene by law.

The Comstock Law stipulated that for the first obscenity offense, offenders found guilty could be sentenced for a term of up to five years in prison or fined up to two thousand dollar, well over a year's salary for most individuals at the time. The definition of "obscenity," always a matter of subjective judgment, came to be regarded as any sexually suggestive material that made reference to what nineteenth century Victorian American society regarded as lewd or lascivious.

In effect, the Comstock Law criminalized not only the distribution of contraceptives through the U.S. postal system but also information on contraceptives and abortion through the mail. The stated purpose of the law was to prevent the circulation of pornography, and its supporters argued about the "immorality" of birth control. The argument on birth control was also tied to women's rights, eugenics, Malthusianism, neo-Malthusianism, Christian morality, and the growing power of the Catholic Church.

The nineteenth century, powered by industrialization and immigration, was a time of profound social change. Social theories that had gestated in England were transplanted to the United States, where they affected attitudes and laws on social and personal morality. The neo-Malthusian writings of Robert Dale Owen in the United States emphasized that the fundamental problem of poverty was not overpopulation but maldistribution of wealth and the oppression of the poor.

Malthusian theories evolved later in the century into the pseudoscientific but popular concept of eugenics, which advocated methods for curtailing population growth among the poor and working classes while encouraging more births to middle- and upper-class families. Eugenics influenced John Humphrey Noyes, a follower of "perfectionism" and founder of the socialist utopian colony at Oneida, New York, in 1848. Noyes advocated that contraception should not be mechanical but should instead consist of self-control on the part of the male partner. He also attempted to practice eugenics through the process of choosing partners who were to create children.

Free-love advocates, along with a growing women's movement in the United States, which had begun during the 1840's, supported "voluntary motherhood." Voluntary motherhood recognized the import of female sexuality and a woman's right to control her own reproduction. Advocates adopted either Noyes's concept of male self-control or the right of a woman to insist on abstinence. Both movements opposed "mechanical" methods of contraception, fearing that these methods would encourage promiscuity and provide a means whereby men could exploit and even rape women with impunity.

During the same period, white, middle-class women were getting abortions at increasing rates. As tolerance for abortion increased, physicians moved to establish a monopoly over women's reproduction and to diminish the use of midwives and herbalists. Consequently, between 1860 and 1880, every state had enacted laws stipulating that abortion could be performed by physicians only, and only when the pregnant woman's life was in danger. Some historians see these developments as constituting a backlash against women's search for greater reproductive power and, therefore, freedom.

Congress acted on this matter in 1842, when it passed a tariff act authorizing customs officials to seize "obscene" or "immoral" imported prints and pictures. This act thereby implied that pornography was a foreign, primarily European, phenomenon. By the 1860's there had been a brisk domestic trade in domestically produced photographs, pamphlets, and novels. Soldiers during the U.S. Civil War (1861-1865) made use of the mail system to order this material, much of it originating in New York City.

In 1865, at the behest of Senator Jacob Collamer of Vermont, a former postmaster general, Congress had passed a law making the mailing of any "obscene book, pamphlet, picture, print or other publication" of "vulgar

TEXT OF THE COMSTOCK LAW

Be it enacted . . . That whoever, within the District of Columbia or any of the Territories of the United States . . . shall sell . . . or shall offer to sell, or to lend, or to give away, or in any manner to exhibit, or shall otherwise publish or offer to publish in any manner, or shall have in his possession, for any such purpose or purposes, any obscene book, pamphlet, paper, writing, advertisement, circular, print, picture, drawing or other representation, figure, or image on or of paper of other material, or any cast instrument, or other article of an immoral nature, or any drug or medicine, or any article whatever, for the prevention of conception, or for causing unlawful abortion, or shall advertise the same for sale, or shall write or print, or cause to be written or printed, any card, circular, book, pamphlet, advertisement, or notice of any kind, stating when, where, how, or of whom, or by what means, any of the articles in this section . . . can be purchased or obtained, or shall manufacture, draw, or print, or in any wise make any of such articles, shall be deemed guilty of a misdemeanor, and on conviction thereof in any court of the United States . . . he shall be imprisoned at hard labor in the penitentiary for not less than six months nor more than five years for each offense, or fined not less than one hundred dollars nor more than two thousand dollars, with costs of court.

and indecent character" a misdemeanor punishable by a fine or imprisonment or both. In 1872, Congress had strengthened the law by adding envelopes and postcards to the prohibited list.

It was in this social atmosphere that Anthony Comstock came of age. Comstock had been born in New Canaan, Connecticut, in 1844, the son of a prosperous farmer and a devout Congregationalist mother. He had joined the Christian Commission during the Civil War and campaigned against tobacco, alcohol, gambling, and atheism. After the war, he had moved to New York City, joined the Young Men's Christian Association (YMCA). Through the YMCA, he met like-minded but wealthier men, who employed him full time as an agent for the newly formed New York Society for the Suppression of Vice, headed by Samuel Colgate.

In 1872, while still in his twenties, Comstock wrote the first of two books, with a telling, lengthy title: *Frauds Exposed: Or, How the People Are Deceived and Robbed, and Youth Corrupted, Being a Full Exposure of Various Schemes Operated Through the Mails, and Unearthed by the Author in a Seven Years' Service as a Special Agent of the Post Office Department and Secretary and Chief Agent of the New York Society for the Suppression of Vice* (pb. 1880). In this book he characterized his view of the problem: a systemized business, newspapers teeming with their advertisements, inadequate laws, and public sentiment "worse than dead." Incensed by his failure to prosecute Victoria Woodhull and her sister Tennessee Claflin for their publication *Woodhull and Claflin's Weekly* because newspapers were exempt from pornography laws, Comstock traveled to Washington, D.C., to start lobbying for a stronger law at the federal level.

The following year, 1873, Congress passed the Comstock Act, which classified as obscene all physical instruments, visual images, and written material pertaining to contraception or abortion. Additionally, President Ulysses S. Grant appointed Comstock a "special agent" of the U.S. Post Office empowered to enforce the new law through mail inspection. After his first year on the job, he boasted of having destroyed hundreds of thousands of obscene

COMSTOCKERY MUST DIE!

Nurse, social reformer, and birth control advocate Margaret Sanger wrote a polemic in 1915, excerpted here, against the Comstock Law of 1873, which criminalized the use of the U.S. mail to send material deemed by the federal government to be obscene or vulgar. Obscene literature included birth control information.

America stands in the eyes of the younger generations of the various countries of Europe as a great hope and inspiration for the development of a free race. What, then, is their surprise and disappointment to learn that an American woman, born on American soil, must leave the "land of the free and home of the brave" to escape imprisonment for discussing the subject of Family Limitation. . . .

[A] large family of children is one of the greatest obstacles in the way to obtain economic freedom for her class. It is the greatest burden to them in all ways, for no matter how spirited and revolutionary one may feel, the piteous cry of hunger of several little ones will compel a man to forego the future good of his class to the present need of his family. . . .

The Woman Rebel [Sanger's early twentieth century magazine] told the Working Woman that there is no freedom for her until she has this knowledge which will enable her to say if she will become a mother or not. The fewer children she had to cook, wash and toil for, the more leisure she would have to read, think and develop. That freedom demands leisure, and her first freedom must be in her right of herself over her own body; the right to say what she will do with it in marriage and out of it; the right to become a mother, or not, as she desires and sees fit to do; that all these rights swing around the pivot of the means to prevent conception, and every woman had the right to have this knowledge if she wished it. . . .

I resolved, after a visit to France, where children are loved and wanted and cared for and educated, to devote my time and effort in giving this information to women who applied for it. I resolved to defy the law, not behind a barricade of law books and technicalities, but by giving the information to the workers directly in factory and workshop.

This was done by the publication of a small pamphlet, "Family Limitations," of which one hundred thousand copies were distributed in factories and mines throughout the U. S. . . .

Comstockery must die! Education on the means to prevent conception and publicity on [Anthony] Comstock's actions is the surest weapon to strike the blow. When people have the knowledge to prevent conceptions then the law becomes useless and falls away like the dead skin of a snake.

Source: "Comstockery in America," 1915 (New York University, Margaret Sanger Papers Project, 1999).

pictures, tons of sexually suggestive books, and thousands of condoms and supposed aphrodisiacs. Between 1873 and 1880, Comstock arrested more than fifty-five abortion providers, many business owners advertising birth control, and many persons supplying contraceptives.

However, judges, juries, and prosecutors were lenient in their rulings and findings. Various types of contraceptives—from herbs and vaginal douches to crude condoms and "pessaries" (diaphragms)—had been marketed through newspapers and magazines since the 1830's. Ironically, Samuel Colgate's company (now known for toothpaste and other toiletries) began a newspaper campaign that spoke about the contraceptive benefits of its new product, Vaseline.

SIGNIFICANCE

In response to the passage of the Comstock Law, twenty-four states enacted "mini-Comstock" laws. Publishers grew fearful of running afoul of Comstock, leading to media self-censorship. Perhaps most important, however, was the impact of the law on women's rights advocates who attempted to mail information about birth control.

One famous advocate was Margaret Sanger, who is often credited as the mother of birth control in the United States. She was, however, preceded by a number of women who distributed birth control remedies. Sanger, who opened the first birth control clinic in the United States in 1916, saw her mother die at the age of fifty, after she had given birth to eleven children. Sanger later became a nurse and a socialist, working with poor, working-class women in the Lower East Side of New York City. She saw the despair of poorer women who had to give birth to children they did not want and could not support. She was unable to save those who would die from self-inflicted abortions.

By 1912, Sanger would give up nursing to devote herself full-time to providing birth control information, which violated the Comstock Law. She was initially indicted on nine counts. The day before her trial, she managed to leave the country under an assumed name (Bertha Watson) and traveled to Great Britain, where she met Marie Scopes, who was doing similar work. The following year, Sanger was arrested once again and sent to a workhouse after being found guilt of creating a "public nuisance." In 1917, she formed the American Birth Control League (ABCL), which supported doctors in disseminating contraceptives "to prevent disease." In 1948, the ABCL became the Planned Parenthood Federation of America (PPFA).

In 1938, sixty-five years after the passage of the Comstock Law, the Supreme Court ruled that contraceptives were presumed not to be obscene unless proved otherwise—the understanding being that doctors would prescribe them only for moral purposes, that is, within the bounds of marriage. Family planning now had meaning on two levels: as the personal choice of families and as social planning to limit rates of population growth.

In 1961, the PPFA took the fight to the state that had the most reactionary law: Connecticut, where contraceptives and information about them was still illegal, for married as well as unmarried couples. Connecticut authorities arrested the clinic director, and in the resulting case of *Griswold v. Connecticut*, the U.S. Supreme Court ruled the law unconstitutional because it interfered with the right of privacy of married couples. In 1977 the last vestige of state Comstock laws was invalidated in *Carey v. Population Services International*, which limited distribution and sale of contraceptives to minors.

—*Erika E. Pilver*

FURTHER READING

Beisel, Nicola Kay. *Imperiled Innocents: Anthony Comstock and Family Reproduction in Victorian America.* Princeton, N.J.: Princeton University Press, 1997. Looks at Comstock's crusade against the movement toward reproductive knowledge in nineteenth century America.

Boyer, Paul S. *Purity in Print: The Vice-Society Movement and Book Censorship in America.* New York: Scribner, 1968. Examines government book censorship and the suppression of vice in the United States.

Brodie, Janet Farrell. *Contraception and Abortion in Nineteenth-Century America.* Ithaca: Cornell University Press, 1994. An extensive look at the full range of options for contraception and abortion during the nineteenth century.

Gordon, Linda. *The Moral Property of Women: A History of Birth Control Politics in America.* Urbana: University of Illinois Press, 2002. A general history of birth control in the United States, stressing the unity of political thinking during the past two centuries.

McBride-Stetson, Dorothy. *Women's Rights in the USA: Policy Debates and Gender Roles.* New York: Routledge, 2004. Puts birth control into the context of U.S. history and the women's movement.

Mackey, Thomas C. *Pornography on Trial: A Handbook with Cases, Laws, and Documents.* Santa Barbara, Calif.: ABC-Clio, 2002. A detailed collection of documents from relevant cases and laws regarding pornography.

Shapiro, Thomas M. *Population Control Politics: Women, Sterilization, and Reproductive Choice*. Philadelphia: Temple University Press, 1985. Addresses the dynamics of class, race, and gender in birth control issues.

Tone, Andrea. *Controlling Reproduction: An American History*. Wilmington, Del.: SR Books, 1997. Short selections, including coverage of court cases, spanning the arguments on reproductive rights.

_______. *Devices and Desires: A History of Contraceptives in America*. New York: Hill & Wang, 2001. Details the history of "bootleg" birth control.

SEE ALSO: 1807: Bowdler Publishes *The Family Shakespeare*; 1882: First Birth Control Clinic Opens in Amsterdam; 1883: Galton Defines "Eugenics."

RELATED ARTICLES in *Great Lives from History: The Nineteenth Century, 1801-1900:* Annie Besant; Francis Galton; Charles Goodyear; Thomas Robert Malthus; Victoria Woodhull.

May 6-October 22, 1873
THREE EMPERORS' LEAGUE IS FORMED

An informal alliance among the rulers of Germany, Austria-Hungary, and Russia, the Three Emperors' League was an attempt to preserve the status quo in eastern and central Europe and maintain French isolation before it was superseded by the Dual Alliance of Germany and Austria and by another Three Emperors' alliance in 1881.

ALSO KNOWN AS: League of the Three Emperors; Schönbrunn Convention

LOCALE: Berlin, Germany; St. Petersburg, Russia; Vienna, Austria

CATEGORY: Diplomacy and international relations

KEY FIGURES

Alexander II (1818-1881), czar of Russia, r. 1855-1881

Count Gyula Andrássy (1823-1890), foreign minister of Austria-Hungary, 1871-1879

Otto von Bismarck (1815-1898), chancellor of the German Empire, 1871-1890

Francis Joseph I (1830-1916), emperor of Austria, r. 1848-1916, and king of Hungary, r. 1867-1916

Aleksandr Mikhailovich Gorchakov (1798-1883), minister of foreign affairs and chancellor of the Russian Empire

William I (Wilhelm I; 1797-1888), emperor of Germany, r. 1871-1888

SUMMARY OF EVENT

The formation of the Three Emperors' League was a joint effort by Germany's William I, Russia's Alexander II, and Austria's Francis Joseph I to adjust their foreign policies to the status quo of the year 1871. As a result of the victory of Prussia over France during that year, Otto von Bismarck, who was then the chancellor of the North German Confederation, achieved the unification of Germany and the coronation of William I, king of Prussia, as the first emperor of Germany.

Bismarck was satisfied with his achievement at home. He had no further territorial ambitions. For him, the German Empire was a "saturated" power. Consequently, his domestic policy was aimed at consolidating the new Germany, but on the international front, he had to restore good relations with Austria-Hungary and continue Prussia's friendship with Russia to ensure the perpetual isolation of France. Given Germany's central location in Europe, the realization of such policies were, in Bismarck's mind, essential for the survival of the state that he had created.

It was fortunate for Bismarck that the rulers of Russia and Austria-Hungary were also eager to cement relations among the three empires. Despite the defeat of Austria by Prussia in the Seven Weeks' War of 1866, the Austrian emperor Francis Joseph I did not find it difficult to accept Bismarck's offer of a rapprochement. He was conscious that Bismarck had treated the Habsburg Empire with consideration in the Peace of Prague in 1866, and he accepted Bismarck's assurances that he had no designs for annexing the German provinces of Austria-Hungary.

In 1871, Francis Joseph appointed Count Gyula Andrássy, who was known to be pro-Prussian, as the new foreign minister of his Dual Monarchy. This appointment conciliated Bismarck, and it was also regarded with approval by Prince Aleksandr Mikhailovich Gorchakov, minister of foreign affairs and chancellor of the Russian Empire, who liked Andrássy personally and who also appreciated the legitimate interests of Austria in the Balkans. The willingness of Gorchakov to reconcile the rival Austrian and Russian claims in the Balkans enabled Bismarck in 1873 to create the Three Emperors' League.

This alliance resulted from several imperial conferences and meetings of the emperors in 1872 and 1873. The most important was attended by all three emperors in Berlin from September 6-12, 1872, at which time Gorchakov and Andrássy agreed to promote the maintenance of the status quo in the Balkans. The fact that the meeting was held in Berlin and that Francis Joseph of Austria and Alexander of Russia were eager to come not only added luster to William's new imperial title but also served to exalt the major role of Germany in the international affairs of Europe.

Together with other conferences, this meeting of the emperors led first to a Russo-German military convention, signed by William and Alexander in St. Petersburg on May 6, 1873. The contracting parties to this pact promised mutual aid in the event that either was attacked by another power. One month later, on June 6, Austria and Russia signed the Schönbrunn Convention. Accepted by Germany on October 22, 1873, this convention provided for joint consultation and cooperation in the event of an attack on one of the empires by another country. The imperial states also agreed to preserve the status quo and repress any revolutionary movements. The Holy Alliance of 1815 was thus revived in a new and altered form.

Significance

More than an entente but less than a full military alliance of the type to come later, the Three Emperors' League lasted only five years. The Balkan Crisis of 1877 and the subsequent Congress of Berlin of 1878 revived the Austro-Russian struggle for supremacy in southeastern Europe. Bismarck then realized that he would have to choose which power he wanted as his primary ally: Austria-Hungary or Russia. He chose Austria-Hungary, which was eager for German support of its new involvement in the Balkans. The result, therefore, was the con-

Central and Eastern Europe

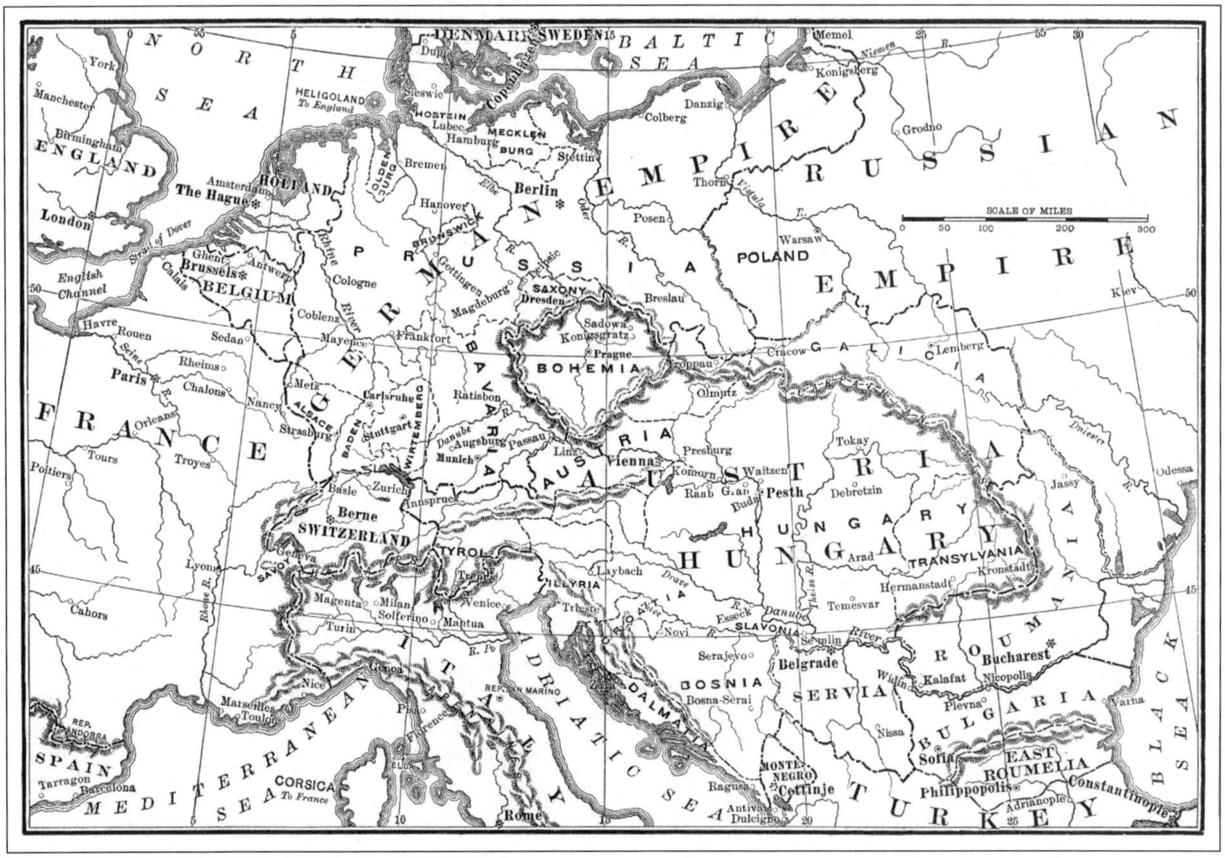

clusion of a much tighter and much more durable pact in 1879 between Austria and Germany, the Dual Alliance, which lasted until the end of World War I.

—*Edward P. Keleher, updated by John Quinn Imholte*

FURTHER READING

Beller, Steven. *Francis Joseph.* London: Longman, 1996. Part of a series of biographies of rulers, this volume examines Francis Joseph's long reign and attempts to put it in a broad historical perspective.

Calleo, David. *The German Problem Reconsidered: Germany and the World Order, 1870 to the Present.* Cambridge, England: Cambridge University Press, 1978. Argues that the "German Problem," or Germany's diplomatic culpability, has been distorted by favoring Germany's victors. German aggressiveness can be best explained by the international order of nations. Places the league in its international context. Erudite and challenging.

Feuchtwanger, Edgar. *Bismarck.* London: Routledge, 2002. Brief biography that offers an accessible evaluation of Bismarck's role in nineteenth century European history.

Langer, William L. *European Alliances and Alignments, 1871-1890.* 2d ed. New York: Alfred A. Knopf, 1950. Provides background of the league. Describes the goal of monarchical solidarity on one hand, with the inability of the league to address problems, especially those in the Balkans, on the other. Both descriptive and interpretative.

Lerman, Katharine Anne. *Bismarck.* New York: Pearson Longman, 2004. A contribution to the publisher's Profiles in Power series, this volume examines Bismarck's exercise of power as way to understand his complex personality and statecraft.

Moss, Walter G. *A History of Russia.* 2d ed. 2 vols. London: Anthem Press, 2002. General history of Russia that offers a useful overview of Alexander II's government reforms and foreign policies.

Palmer, Alan. *Twilight of the Habsburgs: The Life and Times of Emperor Francis Joseph.* New York: Grove Press, 1995. Comprehensive biography of the ruler of Austria-Hungary that seeks to provide a balanced portrayal of Francis Joseph.

Waller, Bruce. *Bismarck.* London: Basil Blackwell, 1985. Brief but substantive account of Bismarck's leadership in establishing the league, but at the same time, his difficulty in balancing the contrary interests of Russia and Austria, Germany's partners in the league. A concise biography.

SEE ALSO: Nov. 20, 1815: Second Peace of Paris; Sept. 24, 1862: Bismarck Becomes Prussia's Minister-President; 1866-1867: North German Confederation Is Formed; May 29, 1867: Austrian Ausgleich; Jan. 18, 1871: German States Unite Within German Empire; May, 1876: Bulgarian Revolt Against the Ottoman Empire; June 13-July 13, 1878: Congress of Berlin; May 20, 1882: Triple Alliance Is Formed; Jan. 4, 1894: Franco-Russian Alliance.

RELATED ARTICLES in *Great Lives from History: The Nineteenth Century, 1801-1900:* Alexander II; Otto von Bismarck; Francis Joseph I.

May 23, 1873
CANADA FORMS THE NORTH-WEST MOUNTED POLICE

The North-West Mounted Police, later known as the Royal Canadian Mounted Police, was formed as the national law enforcement agency of Canada, charged with keeping the peace, serving as a border patrol and customs agency, and supervising treaties with indigenous peoples. The agency was instrumental in the development and westward expansion of Canada.

ALSO KNOWN AS: Royal Canadian Mounted Police; Royal Northwest Mounted Police; Mounties
LOCALE: Canada
CATEGORIES: Organizations and institutions; expansion and land acquisition; government and politics; military history

KEY FIGURES

Sir John Alexander Macdonald (1815-1891), first prime minister of Canada, 1867-1873, 1878-1891
Sir George Arthur French (1841-1921), police commissioner
Louis Riel (1844-1885), Meti leader
Samuel Benfield Steele (1849-1919), police superintendent
James Morrow Walsh (1840-1905), police superintendent

SUMMARY OF EVENT

The North-West Mounted Police (NWMP) were created in 1873 to establish Canadian authority, law, and order in the Northwest Territories (present-day Saskatchewan and Alberta). The agency's initial duties were to control the illegal whiskey trade, serve as border patrol, and supervise and enforce agreements with First Nations (indigenous) peoples. During Canada's nineteenth century westward expansion, the NWMP evolved into a national and federal law enforcement agency. Among its additional responsibilities were customs services, federal law enforcement, and contracting to serve as municipal and provincial police in Canada's western territories and provinces.

Sir John Alexander Macdonald, the first prime minister of Canada, initiated the formation of the North-West Mounted Police by an act of Parliament on May 23, 1873. The primary purpose of the NWMP was to assert Canadian sovereignty and ensure law and order. Magisterial authority was conferred on the NWMP by having the commanding officer sworn in as justice of the peace in the territory under his jurisdiction. Sir George Arthur French was appointed to organize the NWMP in September, 1873, and began selecting officers and recruiting members. On July 8, 1874, Commissioner French, with 275 mounted officers and men, left Dufferin, Manitoba, for the historic March West to present-day southern Alberta, where they arrived in October, 1874.

The NWMP struck first at the illegal whiskey traders who had settled at Fort Whoop-Up (officially Fort Hamilton) near Lethbridge, Alberta. Acting on a native's complaint about the high-priced, outlawed Whoop-Up Bug Juice (alcohol spiked with ginger, molasses, and red pepper, then boiled with black chewing tobacco to make "firewater"), the NWMP rounded up and punished the perpetrators, thus establishing Canadian authority in the Alberta-U.S. borderlands.

The Mounties, as the NWMP troops came to be known, were successful in establishing good relations with the First Nations peoples in the Northwest Territories. In 1876, the Sioux chief Sitting Bull and thousands of his followers escaped the U.S. military by fleeing across the U.S.-Canada border into southern Saskatchewan, settling in the area of Wood Mountain. Officer James M. Walsh and his unit were assigned to watch over the encamped Sioux and keep the peace. Walsh earned Sitting Bull's trust and friendship and was able to maintain peaceful relations, though he could never persuade Sitting Bull to return to the United States.

The NWMP established a patrol system and assigned law enforcement detachments throughout the region. In 1870, the force helped to put down the First Riel Rebellion of 1869-1870, led by Louis Riel, leader of the Metis people, a multiracial First Nations tribe made up of descendants of French and British trappers and traders who married Indian women. In 1870, when the British parliament merged the Hudson's Bay Company (HBC) land holdings of Rupert's Land with the Canadian colony in Ontario, Riel led the Metis into battle against the NWMP, declared a provisional government, and ultimately set the terms under which the province of Manitoba joined the Canadian Confederation. Because he executed Thomas Scott during the First Riel Rebellion, Riel was forced into exile in the United States. While in exile, he was elected three times to the Canadian House of Commons, but he never assumed his seat.

In 1884, Riel returned to Canada's Saskatchewan province and led the Metis in another resistance movement. This resistance escalated into the Second Riel Re-

Member of the Royal Canadian Mounted Police during the early twentieth century. (Library of Congress)

bellion (also called the Northwest Rebellion) of 1885, in which the NWMP, under the command of Superintendent Samuel Benfield Steele and aided by Canadian army troops sent in by railroad, defeated the Metis. The last battle was fought when Steele's group of Mounties engaged Big Bear's rebels on the shores of Loon Lake. The Metis's leader, Riel, was convicted of treason and hanged on November 16, 1885, ending the rebellion and the Metis provisional government.

In 1895, the Yukon Territory was added to the NWMP's jurisdiction. In 1896, the discovery of gold along the Klondike River brought thousands of miners into the area that extended from present-day Dawson City into Alaska. Steele became commanding officer in the Yukon and served from July, 1898, to September, 1899. Under his leadership, the Mounties maintained law and order during the Klondike gold rush, ran the mails, organized firefighters, installed drainage and sanitary systems, and ensured a pure water supply for Dawson City. The NWMP's success made possible Canada's dominion over the Yukon Territory, which was established officially by the Yukon Act of June 13, 1898.

In 1896, the Canadian government began encouraging settlement of the Western prairies by offering free land and cost of passage to Europeans. By the end of the nineteenth century, a flood of new settlers had arrived. Among them were Poles, Russians, Ukrainians, Hungarians, Germans, Mennonites, and Icelanders. Additional settlers from Ontario and the western United States added to the growing population of the Western prairies. The NWMP assisted this development by ensuring the safety and welfare of the settlers, fighting disease, poverty, and prairie fires that threatened the early settlements.

The Mounties on horseback in their colorful uniforms became the dominant image associated with Canada all over the world. The NWMP uniforms featured red serge tunics in the standard British military style. At first, the NWMP wore buff trousers, but later they adopted dark blue trousers with yellow-gold stripes in the British cavalry tradition. The British foreign service helmet (pith helmet) proved to be impractical in the Canadian west, and frontier Mounties preferred the wide flat brim Stetson hat for camp and patrol wear. The NWMP contingent that paraded at Queen Victoria's Diamond Jubilee also wore the Stetson, although it was not adopted officially until 1904. Black riding boots were later changed to brown, and black cross belts were changed to the still-worn Sam Brown belts. Weapons, though not used often in the early years, soon became standard gear. The Mounties would come to call their organization "the Force" and to refer to one another as "members of the Force."

The Musical Ride, a ceremonial tradition developed by the NWMP members to display their riding skills, began in 1886. The maneuvers to music were drawn from the cavalry's precision drills. The first officially recorded Musical Ride was performed in Regina in 1887, under Inspector William George Matthews. Musical Ride performances have attracted large audiences throughout Canada. After the NWMP's name was changed to the Royal Northwest Mounted Police (RNWMP) in June, 1904, the Musical Ride was performed in many international arenas.

SIGNIFICANCE

The North-West Mounted Police was instrumental in Canada's westward expansion during the nineteenth century. By providing law and order, border security, assistance to immigrants, and supervision of First Nations' treaties with the Canadian government, the NWMP provided the peace that was essential to Canada's successful development and expansion to the west. By operating as both a law enforcement agency and a military force, the NWMP was able to assert Canadian authority over the Canadian territories and maintain the peace necessary for growth and stability in the Northwest Territories.

As the Northwest Territories grew in population, Canada was able to establish in 1905 two new provinces, Alberta and Saskatchewan. The NWMP, having been renamed the Royal Northwest Mounted Police in 1904 by British king Edward VII (r. 1901-1910), was given responsibility for law enforcement in the new provinces. In the reorganization of federal police in 1920, the RNWMP absorbed the Dominion Police and became the Royal Canadian Mounted Police (RCMP).

The RCMP was assigned responsibility for federal law enforcement in all provinces and territories of Canada. The Canadian regions policed by the RCMP were the Atlantic (Newfoundland, Labrador, Prince Edward Island, Nova Scotia, and New Brunswick), central (Quebec and Ontario), Northwestern region (Manitoba, Saskatchewan, Alberta, Nunavit, and Northwest Territories), and Pacific (British Columbia and Yukon Territory). The RCMP, successor to the NWMP, eventually became the largest police force in Canada, with more than twenty-two thousand members.

—*Marguerite R. Plummer*

FURTHER READING

Beahan, William, and Stanley Horrall. *Red Coats on the Prairies: The North-West Mounted Police, 1886-1900*. Regina, Sask.: Centax Books, 1998. Relates activities of the NWMP in the new settlements and among the First Nations.

Cruise, David, and Alison Griffiths. *The Great Adventure: How the Mounties Conquered the West*. Toronto: Viking Press, 1996. Comprehensive account of the creation of the NWMP in 1873 and of the March West in 1874.

Dobrowolsky, Helene. *Law of the Yukon: A Pictorial History of the Mounted Police in the Yukon*. Whitehorse, Y.T.: Lost Moose, 1995. Describes the NWMP role in policing the Klondike gold rush.

Macleod, Rod. *The North-West Mounted Police and Law Enforcement, 1873-1905*. Toronto: University of Toronto Press, 1976. Recounts the story of the NWMP in the context of the early development and settlement of western Canada.

Wallace, Jim. *A Trying Time*. Winnipeg, Man.: Bunker to Bunker Books, 1998. Describes the NWMP's role in the Northwest Rebellion of 1884-1885.

SEE ALSO: Mar. 23, 1858: Fraser River Gold Rush Begins; Oct. 11, 1869-July 15, 1870: First Riel Rebellion; 1872: Dominion Lands Act Fosters Canadian Settlement; Nov. 5, 1873-Oct. 9, 1878: Canada's Mackenzie Era; 1876: Canada's Indian Act; Sept., 1878: Macdonald Returns as Canada's Prime Minister; Mar. 19, 1885: Second Riel Rebellion Begins; Aug. 17, 1896: Klondike Gold Rush Begins.

RELATED ARTICLES in *Great Lives from History: The Nineteenth Century, 1801-1900:* Sir John Alexander Macdonald; Alexander Mackenzie; Louis Riel; Sitting Bull.

June 17-18, 1873
ANTHONY IS TRIED FOR VOTING

After being arrested for voting, Susan B. Anthony hoped to carry her case to the U.S. Supreme Court, where she could make a national appeal for woman suffrage, but because of purely procedural matters, her case quietly died after her conviction and the women's movement had to adopt a different strategy.

LOCALE: Rochester, New York
CATEGORIES: Civil rights and liberties; women's issues

KEY FIGURES

Susan B. Anthony (1820-1906), suffragist and activist for women's rights
Victoria Woodhull (1838-1927), radical suffragist
Ward Hunt (1810-1886), U.S. associate justice
Henry R. Selden (1805-1885), appeals court judge
Virginia Louisa Minor (1824-1894), suffragist who sued to establish woman's constitutional right to vote

SUMMARY OF EVENT

During the mid-nineteenth century women activists hoped that with the enfranchisement of African American men by the Civil War amendments, the enfranchisement of women would follow. However, the Fourteenth and Fifteenth Amendments proved to be severe blows to women's hopes because nothing in their language implied that women should be guaranteed the franchise. Outraged, many women turned their energies with a new urgency toward winning the right to vote. However, disagreements over the best means to achieve this goal split the women's rights movement. Elizabeth Cady Stanton and Susan B. Anthony founded the National Woman Suffrage Association to work for passage of a Sixteenth Amendment granting women throughout the United States the vote. Meanwhile, Lucy Stone organized the American Woman Suffrage Association to work for enfranchisement on a state-by-state basis.

A third line of attack, which crossed organizational lines, was working to demonstrate that the U.S. Constitution already granted women suffrage. To this end, Victoria Woodhull spoke before the House of Representatives' Judiciary Committee in January, 1871. She pointed out that the Fourteenth and Fifteenth Amendments, despite the former's linkage of the word "male" to enfranchisement, also guaranteed the vote regardless of "race, color, or previous condition of servitude." She argued that all women belong to a race and are a color, and were therefore guaranteed the right to vote. The Judiciary Committee was not persuaded by Woodhull's argument.

Despite Woodhull's failure, Anthony hoped that the presidential election of 1872 could set the stage for another showdown testing the interpretation—and perhaps the constitutionality—of the Fourteenth and Fifteenth Amendments. She and other women determined to attempt to vote in that election, knowing that they would likely not even be allowed to register. Anthony planned, if refused, to file suit against the election registrars and have the matter become one that the courts must decide.

In all, some fifty women from Rochester, New York, tried to register to vote in the November, 1872, presidential election. Early on voter registration day, Anthony and her three sisters went to their local voter registration site, where Anthony demanded that they be allowed to register. Their right, she explained, was guaranteed both by the Fourteenth Amendment to the U.S. Constitution and by the New York State constitution. She told the registrars that she had sought legal counsel from former appeals court judge Henry R. Selden, a respected citizen of Rochester who supported her claims. She threatened to sue anyone who turned her away. The women were allowed to register.

On election day, November 5, 1872, Anthony and fifteen other women from her ward cast ballots (Anthony voted for Republican candidate Ulysses S. Grant). By that time, local feelings were running so high that none of the other fifty women from Rochester who had registered to vote was allowed to vote. Three weeks later Anthony, the fifteen other women who voted, and two voting inspectors were arrested. When an embarrassed deputy marshal assured Anthony that she could proceed to the district attorney's office without an escort, the fifty-two-year-old suffragist responded, "I prefer to be arrested like anybody else. You may handcuff me as soon as I get my coat and hat."

Anthony had planned to sue any inspector who refused her the right to vote; she had not expected to be arrested herself. Nevertheless, she quickly saw the use to which she could put her arrest. With luck, she could use her ensuing trial to bring the case before the U.S. Supreme Court and get a national hearing for the cause of woman suffrage. However, her hopes were dashed in this ambition. After two hearings, Anthony had Selden apply for a writ of habeas corpus, arguing that the government had no legal right to hold her because no crime had been committed. The court adjourned to consider its response to the writ.

In late January, 1873, a district judge denied the writ and sentenced Anthony to jail until her trial could be held. He placed her bail at one thousand dollars. Anthony promptly refused to pay bail, but Selden insisted on paying. At the time, Anthony did not understand the importance of this act, but she found out minutes after she left court that by paying bail Selden had forfeited all chance of using the writ of habeas corpus as a route to the Supreme Court. Selden later said that he understood the legal ramifications but could not bear to have a lady detained in jail. The following day a grand jury indicted Anthony, and her trial was set for May 13.

Convinced that she would not get a fair hearing, Anthony spent the time before the trial taking her case to the people. Making speeches at each of the twenty-nine districts in her county, she proclaimed:

> The Declaration of Independence, the U.S. Constitution, the constitutions of the several States and the organic laws of the Territories, all alike propose to *protect* the people in the exercise of their God-given rights. Not one of them pretends to bestow rights.

When the judge realized what Anthony had done, he ordered the trial moved to Ontario County, saying that it would be impossible to find local jurors unprejudiced by Anthony's speeches. He also delayed the trial until June. Anthony spent the extra time in Ontario County giving the same speeches she had delivered earlier in Monroe County.

Anthony's trial opened on June 17, 1873, and was presided over in an unorthodox and questionable manner by U.S. associate justice Ward Hunt. When Selden called Anthony to the witness stand, the prosecution objected, calling Anthony an incompetent witness. Hunt sustained the objection, so Selden spoke as a witness in Anthony's behalf, pointing out, among other things, that as her legal adviser he had counseled Anthony to vote.

At the end of Selden's defense and the district attorney's response, Hunt read his opinion, which he had written *before* the trial even began. He stated, "under the 14th amendment, which Miss Anthony claims protects her, she was not protected in a right to vote." The statement concluded with Hunt issuing an illegal order to the jury, "to find a verdict of guilty." Selden again objected, but to no avail. His request that the individual jury members be polled was also rejected, as was his request for a new trial.

Hunt then asked the prisoner if she had anything to say. Anthony accused Hunt of having "trampled under foot every vital principle of our government." She continued, "My natural rights, my civil rights, my political rights, my judicial rights, are all alike ignored. Robbed of the fundamental privilege of citizenship, I am degraded from the status of a citizen to that of a subject." Although ordered to be silent several times, she continued, pointing out that she had been denied a jury of her peers, for as long as women were denied equal rights of citizenship, no man could be her peer. Instead, she said, "each and every man [connected with the trial—lawyers, judge, and jury members] was my political superior; hence, in no sense, my peer." Law itself, she insisted, was "all made by men, interpreted by men, administered by men, in favor of men and against women."

When Anthony finished her statement and sat down, Justice Hunt fined her one hundred dollars plus the cost of the prosecution. Anthony retorted, "I will never pay a dollar of your unjust penalty." Had Hunt ordered An-

Susan B. Anthony. (Library of Congress)

thony held until her fine was paid, she would again have had recourse to appeal to the Supreme Court. Considering the blatant disregard of legalities during her hearing Anthony would almost certainly have gained the right to a new trial. However, Hunt knew that, so he let her go and never tried to collect her fine, thus ending her hopes of a Supreme Court hearing.

SIGNIFICANCE

During 1871 and 1872, at least 150 women in ten different states and Washington, D.C., attempted to vote. Only a handful were successful in having their ballots counted. Anthony's case, however, was the most publicized and the only one targeted for prosecution, no doubt because of her status as a suffragist leader. Meanwhile, a far less publicized case was making its way to the Supreme Court—that of Virginia Louisa Minor, the president of the Missouri Woman Suffrage Association.

Minor filed suit against a St. Louis, Missouri, registrar who refused to let her register to vote. She argued that states had no right to bar U.S. citizens who were women from voting, as that was to give states power to rescind "the immunities and privileges of American citizenship [which] are National in character. . . ." Her stance that citizenship and the right to vote are synonymous was not upheld by the Supreme Court, which in October, 1874, ruled that citizenship did not necessarily guarantee suffrage. That ruling closed off interpretation as an avenue toward gaining woman suffrage.

By the end of 1874, the only routes remaining for gaining the vote for women were state-by-state legislation or an amendment to the U.S. Constitution. In either case suffragists would have to sway the votes of already enfranchised male adults—hardly, as Anthony had pointed out, a jury of peers. Following Wyoming's lead in 1869, a number of western territories and states began granting woman suffrage, but it would be almost a half century before the Nineteenth Amendment finally guaranteed all American women the franchise in 1920.

—*Grace McEntee*

FURTHER READING

An Account of the Proceedings of the Trial of Susan B. Anthony of the Charge of Illegal Voting, at the Presidential Election in Nov., 1872, and on the Trial of Beverly W. Jones, Edwin T. Marsh and William B. Hall, the Inspectors of Election by Whom Her Vote Was Received. Rochester, N.Y.: Daily Democrat and Chronicle Book Print, 1874. This transcript of the trial is an invaluable primary source.

Baker, Jean H., ed. *Votes for Women: The Struggle for Suffrage Revisited.* Oxford, England: Oxford University Press, 2002. Solidly researched work that examines the entire history of the woman suffrage movement.

Barry, Kathleen. *Susan B. Anthony: A Biography of a Singular Feminist.* New York: Ballantine Books, 1988. This scholarly and sympathetic biography dispels earlier portraits of Anthony as self-serving, while outlining Anthony's involvement in the abolition and suffrage movements.

Flexner, Eleanor. *Century of Struggle: The Woman's Rights Movement in the United States.* Cambridge, Mass.: Harvard University Press, 1959. Comprehensive and still standard history of the women's rights movement that places specific incidents into the larger historic picture.

Lehman, Godfrey D. "Susan B. Anthony Cast Her Ballot for Ulysses S. Grant." *American Heritage* 37 (1985): 25-31. Engaging and dramatic description that includes often omitted information about public response and the fate of the voting inspectors.

McFadden, Margaret, ed. *Women's Issues.* 3 vols. Pasadena, Calif.: Salem Press, 1997. Comprehensive reference work with numerous articles on Susan B. Anthony, woman suffrage, and related issues.

Sherr, Lynn. *Failure Is Impossible: Susan B. Anthony in Her Own Words.* New York: Times Books, 1995. Excerpts from Anthony's speeches and letters with commentaries about her life and career.

Stanton, Elizabeth Cady, Susan B. Anthony, and Matilda Joslyn Gage, eds. *History of Woman Suffrage.* Vol. 2. New York: Fowler & Wells, 1882. Reprint. New York: Arno Press, 1969. Part of an eleven-volume set, this invaluable primary source is edited by women who worked for woman suffrage for the better part of their long lives, including Anthony and her closest friend and associate, Stanton.

SEE ALSO: July 19-20, 1848: Seneca Falls Convention; May 10, 1866: Suffragists Protest the Fourteenth Amendment; May, 1869: Woman Suffrage Associations Begin Forming; Dec., 1869: Wyoming Gives Women the Vote; Mar. 9, 1875: *Minor v. Happersett*; July 4, 1876: Declaration of the Rights of Women; Feb. 17-18, 1890: Women's Rights Associations Unite; Oct. 27, 1893: National Council of Women of Canada Is Founded.

RELATED ARTICLES in *Great Lives from History: The Nineteenth Century, 1801-1900:* Susan B. Anthony; Elizabeth Cady Stanton; Lucy Stone; Victoria Woodhull.

November 5, 1873-October 9, 1878
CANADA'S MACKENZIE ERA

In Canada's early years of nationhood, conservative dominance was temporarily interrupted with the election of the liberal Mackenzie as prime minister. The liberals enacted the secret ballot, provided for same-day elections, passed consumer protection laws, created a supreme court, created the nation's first military academy and founded the North-West Mounted Police, and completed surveys for the Canadian Pacific Railway.

LOCALE: Ottawa, Canada
CATEGORY: Government and politics

KEY FIGURES

Alexander Mackenzie (1822-1892), liberal prime minister, 1873-1878
John Alexander Macdonald (1815-1891), conservative prime minister, 1867-1873 and 1878-1891
George Brown (1818-1880), Liberal Party founder
Sir George Étienne Cartier (1814-1873), Quebec politician and political ally of Macdonald
Hugh Allen (1810-1882), Montreal businessman and financier
Lord Dufferin (Frederick Temple Hamilton-Temple Blackwood; 1826-1902), governor-general of Canada, 1872-1878
Edward Blake (1833-1912), former premier of Ontario, minister of finance, 1875-1877, and later Liberal opposition leader

SUMMARY OF EVENT

The year 1873 witnessed a dramatic shift of power in Canadian national politics with the fall of Prime Minister John Alexander Macdonald's conservative government. Canada had become a self-governing dominion of the British crown in 1867, largely as a result of a cooperative effort by bitter political rivals such as Macdonald (a conservative) and George Brown (a reformer), who forged a temporary alliance to gain this end.

After Quebec, Ontario, and the Maritime Provinces joined in a federal structure and national parliament, this political unity ultimately gave way to partisan party politics. On one side stood the reformers and "Clear Grits" who established the Liberal Party. Their opponents, the conservatives, or Tories, were headed by Macdonald, a pragmatic Ontario attorney. As party leader, Macdonald attempted to bridge Canadian ethnic, language, and religious divisions through compromise, concessions, and liberal use of patronage to cement political loyalty. The politically astute and charismatic Macdonald put together a diverse combination of Anglo-Protestants, big business, and conservative Roman Catholic French Canadian nationalists in a truly national party.

In contrast, the liberals were still largely a regional party, with their strongest base, in rural Ontario, consisting of a loose association of provincial rights advocates linked by distrust of powerful central government.

These advantages allowed Macdonald's party to dominate the early years of Canadian political history. The conservatives advocated strong central government that could defend national interests in competition with the more powerful United States and secure control of the vast but sparsely populated western region. Macdonald governed by promoting ambitious, expensive megaprojects and pork-barrel legislation to keep his coalition of interests unified, appeal to business supporters, and build an economically sound nation. The prime minister's most grandiose and visionary scheme was the construction of a transcontinental railroad to create the dominion stretching from sea to sea. This project would unite the sparsely settled and remote West to the rest of Canada, lay the foundation for future immigration and settlement, and promote exploitation of western natural resources.

Macdonald's strenuous efforts on behalf of this dream brought his downfall. To induce the lightly populated Pacific coast colony of British Columbia into confederation in 1871, the prime minister made extravagant, expensive, and impossible commitments to begin building the transcontinental railroad in two years and to complete the project by 1881. Growing public dissatisfaction was reflected in the 1872 elections, which saw the liberals nearly destroy the government's majority. After the election, the liberals came into possession of damning evidence against their foes. Hugh Allen, the head of one of two business syndicates competing for the lucrative government contract to build the Canadian Pacific Railway line, had given the governing party a bribe of $300,000 to aid in the tough election battle and ensure his being granted the contract. Sir George Étienne Cartier, leader of the party organization in Quebec, and Macdonald himself were directly involved in this affair, known as the Pacific Scandal.

As new evidence and public furor mounted, and Macdonald suffered defection from party ranks, Canada's governor-general, Lord Dufferin, finally called upon op-

Alexander Mackenzie.

position leader Alexander Mackenzie to form a new government on November 5, 1873. When national parliamentary elections were held, the conservatives were soundly routed as the liberals received a commanding parliamentary majority of 138 to 67.

Canada's new prime minister was a stubborn, self-made, highly principled, and moralistic Scottish immigrant. Arriving in Upper Canada in 1842, the former stonemason had established himself as a building contractor. Mackenzie became a supporter of George Brown's Reform Party, a liberal journalist, and eventually a member of the legislative assembly of Canada. In 1867, he won a seat in the first Dominion House of Commons and also assumed leadership of the liberals when Brown gave up this role.

Mackenzie presented a sharp contrast to the convivial and talented, but hard-drinking and morally flawed, Macdonald. Macdonald's successor was a devout Baptist who exuded Victorian piety, an austere, utilitarian outlook, and great earnestness. His nineteenth century liberalism included egalitarian sentiments and a distrust of entrenched class privilege, monopoly, and unchecked institutional power. He also was an advocate of free trade, individual enterprise, thrifty government, and democratic political reforms.

Although Mackenzie applied himself to the task of governing the nation with great diligence and earnestness, he suffered from a combination of bad luck and some personal shortcomings as a leader. One major difficulty was the task of putting together a strong, cooperative cabinet and turning the Liberal Party into a truly national and cohesive organization. It was hard to find experienced and highly qualified liberals to fill ministerial positions. Quebec was not strongly represented, and the party remained weak in that province.

Because only a few cabinet members, such as Edward Blake and Finance Minister Richard Cartwright, were of outstanding quality, much of the burden of debate in Parliament fell upon the prime minister's shoulders. Mackenzie also experienced problems with prominent colleagues such as Blake, the most capable liberal politician, who thought he was more qualified to head the party and occasionally undermined Mackenzie's authority.

Power had fallen into Mackenzie's lap at an inopportune moment. After the Panic of 1873, Canada, like the United States, had entered a period of economic slump and depression that would persist intermittently for two decades. This situation, although not of his making, made it difficult for Mackenzie to fulfill Macdonald's overly generous contract with British Columbia regarding the railroad connection. The country now had to settle for piecemeal construction of the line as financial considerations permitted.

Another setback for Mackenzie was his failure to obtain a reciprocity agreement with the United States on the lowering of tariffs and customs duties. When this attempt to benefit some groups with lower prices and expanded markets for Canadian products went for naught, as a result of lack of interest in Washington, D.C., the government was left with no economic policy to offer voters in these hard times other than retrenchment.

SIGNIFICANCE

In spite of these difficulties, the Mackenzie era produced several sound legislative accomplishments. In an effort to reduce electoral fraud and manipulation, which were common occurrences, the government enacted the secret ballot and provided for elections to be held on the same day. Consumer protection laws were passed. The creation of a supreme court and the nation's first military academy enhanced Canadian self-rule and lessened dependence on Great Britain. The North-West Mounted Police, created by Macdonald in 1873, became firmly established in the West under the new government. In spite of financial constraints, necessary surveying for the transcontinental railroad was completed. Mackenzie also pursued government construction of important and difficult sections of the line when private interests were not forthcoming.

The government's electoral mandate came to an end in 1878, and Mackenzie called a national election for September 17. The prime minister hoped the country would reward his hard efforts and record of relatively honest government. However, the unfavorable economic situation and Macdonald's affable and easy manner with audiences enabled him to rebound from the disgrace of the Pacific Scandal. In contrast to the government's tightfisted economic policy, he championed a vision of prosperity, security, and economic strength through his national policy of protective tariffs, railroad building, and settlement and development of the West.

Mackenzie was stunned as the results of 1873 were reversed, resulting in a conservative parliamentary landslide. The voting public apparently preferred the personable and eloquent, if scandal-tainted, Macdonald to the scrupulously honest but lackluster and plodding Mackenzie. A bitter and disappointed prime minister resigned office on October 9, bringing the short-lived Mackenzie era to a close. Macdonald's conservatives resumed their dominance until shortly after the old leader's death during the 1890's.

—*David A. Crain*

FURTHER READING

Brown, R. Craig, ed. *The Illustrated History of Canada*. Toronto: Key Porter, 2002. A good survey of Canadian history that places Mackenzie in the context of his times. Contains black-and-white and color illustrations and bibliographical essays.

Dictionary of Canadian Biography Online. "Mackenzie, Alexander." http://www.biographi.ca/EN/ShowBio.asp?BioId=40374. Accessed January 24, 2006. A good Web source for more information on Mackenzie and his accomplishments.

See, Scott W. *The History of Canada*. Westport, Conn.: Greenwood Press, 2001. A short survey of Canadian history, supplemented with appendices and a bibliographic essay, which criticizes Mackenzie's leadership as ineffective.

Stanley, G. F. G. "The 1870's." In *The Canadians, 1867-1967*, edited by J. M. S. Careless and R. C. Brown. Toronto: Macmillan of Canada, 1967. Overview of the political issues, events, and personalities of this era by a noted Canadian academic.

Thompson, Dale C. *Alexander Mackenzie, Clear Grit*. Toronto: Macmillian of Canada, 1960. A detailed narrative account that does a good job of depicting Mackenzie's problems with matters such as his cabinet, the ethnic issue, and political reform.

Waite, Peter B. *Canada, 1874-1896: Arduous Destiny*. Toronto: McClelland & Stewart, 1971. Chapters 2 through 5 provide a readable and colorful account of Canadian national politics during the 1870's, by a prominent Canadian historian.

SEE ALSO: Apr. 25, 1849: First Test of Canada's Responsible Government; July 1, 1867: British North America Act; May 23, 1873: Canada Forms the North-West Mounted Police; 1875: Supreme Court of Canada Is Established; 1876: Canada's Indian Act; Sept., 1878: Macdonald Returns as Canada's Prime Minister; July 11, 1896: Laurier Becomes the First French Canadian Prime Minister.

RELATED ARTICLES in *Great Lives from History: The Nineteenth Century, 1801-1900:* George Brown; Sir John Alexander Macdonald; Alexander Mackenzie; William Lyon Mackenzie; Sir Charles Tupper.

April 15, 1874
FIRST IMPRESSIONIST EXHIBITION

At the first Impressionist exhibition, a group of painters committed to naturalistic representation, color theory, and experimentation with photography mounted a show meant to challenge the Parisian art establishment's aesthetics. Although not initially a success, the exhibition announced the emergence of modernist art, paving the way for post-Impressionism, abstract expressionism, Fauvism, cubism, and a host of other movements that owe their existence in part to French Impressionism.

LOCALE: Paris, France
CATEGORIES: Art; photography

KEY FIGURES
Claude Monet (1840-1926), French painter
Édouard Manet (1832-1883), French painter
Camille Pissarro (1830-1903), French painter
Pierre-Auguste Renoir (1841-1919), French painter
Berthe Morisot (1841-1895), French painter
Edgar Degas (1834-1917), French painter and sculptor
Alfred Sisley (1839-1899), English expatriate painter
Paul Cézanne (1839-1906), French painter
Jean-Frédéric Bazille (1841-1870), French painter
Louis Leroy (1812-1885), French artist and critic

SUMMARY OF EVENT

On April 15, 1874, thirty artists who had joined forces the previous December as the Société Anonyme des Artistes (anonymous association of artists) opened an independent exhibition at 35 Boulevard des Capucines in Paris. Their show challenged the authority of the French Academy of the Fine Arts, the prestigious, state-sponsored institution whose annual exhibition, or Salon, had long been indispensable for launching and maintaining a successful career in painting, sculpture, or engraving. The acceptance or rejection of one's submissions to the academy depended on the decisions of a jury of previous exhibitors. Unsurprisingly, the system led to extreme conformity in both subject matter and technique. As a result, most paintings accepted to the Paris Salon were moralizing, idealized versions of historical, religious, and mythological subjects, rendered in balanced compositions and distinct lines on smoothly finished canvases.

The prime movers behind both the Société Anonyme des Artistes and the exhibition were members of a small group of painters who were discouraged by persistent official rejection of their work. They had become determined to loosen the academy's strangehold on the Parisian art world's aesthetics and sales. Claude Monet, perhaps the most ambitious of the group, had met Camille Pissarro and Paul Cézanne in 1862 at the Académie Suisse, a studio for impoverished students. Soon afterward, he had befriended Pierre-Auguste Renoir, Jean-Frédéric Bazille, and Alfred Sisley at the Atelier Gleyre—where their teacher, Charles Gleyre (1808-1874), though capable and generous, nevertheless upheld academic dogma. The following year, provoked by Gleyre's conventional insistence that "[i]n drawing a figure, one should always think of the antique," Monet persuaded the others to abandon the master's studio.

The six friends, soon joined by the like-minded Berthe Morisot and Edgar Degas, became a close-knit circle of innovators. As of 1866, most of them regularly gathered at the Café Guerbois, on Rue de Batignolles, where they spent countless evenings in debates about art with such colleagues as Édouard Manet, who had already established himself as a leading avant-garde artist and enjoyed periodic academic success. Thanks to the neighborhood in which they gathered, these artists were initially known as the Batignolles group.

As early as 1867, the Batignolles artists dreamed of having their own group show. Given their poverty, however, they had to content themselves with occasionally getting their more conservative works accepted by the Salon and having small, one-artist shows in private galleries. In 1873, however, they felt more than usually disgusted with the Salon jury, which seemed to be repeating the extreme intolerance it had shown a decade earlier, when it had dismissed 70 percent of the five thousand submissions it received. In the earlier decade the government of Napoleon III had responded to the protests of hundreds of artists by arranging for the rejected works to be displayed separately in the Salon des Refusés (exhibition of rejects). Pissarro, Cezanne, and Manet had all participated in the Salon des Refusés, the last causing a sensation with his subversively classical yet anticlassical *Déjeuner sur l'herbe* (1863). Ten years later, wary of associating their reputations with another "reject" Salon, the Batignolles decided to form their own society and to exhibit independently.

A sixty-franc annual membership fee brought in enough money to fund the 1874 exhibition—a month-long display of 165 oil paintings, watercolors, pastels, prints, and sculptures in a studio on loan from a photographer. Whereas Degas had been particularly active in recruiting members for the association, it was Renoir who hung most of the paintings in the studio's five red-wallpapered rooms, because the rest of the organizing committee did not show up. More than one-fourth of the displayed pieces were pictures by the core group, including twelve by Monet, ten by Degas, nine by Morisot, seven by Renoir, five by Pissarro, three by Cézanne, and two by Sisley. Manet neither joined the association nor exhibited with them, but he did lend his friends his copy of Morisot's *Cache-cache* (1873; hide and seek).

The exhibition's oil paintings in particular established the movement's iconoclastic trademarks. These included representing contemporary people and ordinary scenes; capturing fleeting moments in middle- or working-class life or in nature's rhythms; using bold colors on canvases free of the dark under-painting beloved by the academy; conveying the light, motion, or energy of the subject through short, rapid brushstrokes; intensifying the immediacy of scenes through cropped figures and props or through flattened perspective; painting entire pictures outdoors (*en plein air*), rather than finishing them in the studio; and rendering shadows through complementary pigments rather than black—for instance, blue-green shade for trees in an orange sunset.

To encourage working-class visitors, the society kept the exhibition open from eight to ten o'clock in the evenings. Although they managed to attract thirty-five hundred people (paying 1 franc apiece) and to sell 3,600 hundred francs' worth of pieces, after costs their 949-franc profit did not even cover all the members' dues. Worse, their venture provoked extreme hostility from most critics, who especially attacked what, by academic standards, they considered the unfinished quality of the paintings.

Monet's seascape *Impression: Soleil levant* (1872; impression: sunrise) was the painting that most outraged fellow artist and critic Louis Leroy. On April 25, reviewing the exhibition for the satirical paper *Le Charivari*, Leroy scathingly commented that the painting was less finished than "wallpaper in its embryonic state" and contemptuously dismissed all the exhibitors as "Impressionists." It was in this review that the term Impressionist was first coined to describe the works of the society. Although it began as a pejorative label, the name stuck, and it was eventually embraced by some (though not all) members of the movement.

Leroy denigrated Monet's representation of people in *Boulevard des Capucines* (1873) as "black tongue-lickings." Other subsequently famous oil paintings on display in 1874 included Degas's *Aux Courses en province* (1869; at the races in the country), Pissarro's *Le Verger* (1872; the orchard), Morisot's *Le Berceau* (1872; the cradle), and Renoir's *La Loge* (1874; the theater box). Although these last two paintings were among the few that received praise, it was arguably Monet's *Impression: Soleil levant* that proved most influential. Within the year, the label it had inspired Leroy to coin so contemptuously had lost its stigma and had become a reputable term for the movement.

While the 1874 exhibition was hardly a financial or critical success, it led to seven more group showings in the next twelve years, as well as to the 1879 creation of a journal dedicated to Impressionism, *La Vie moderne* (modern life), with an art gallery adjoining the journal's offices. The public debut also encouraged the group's select supporters, among them the art dealer Paul Durand-Ruel (1831-1922) and the writers Stéphane Mallarmé (1842-1889) and Émile Zola (1840-1902), to continue

Pierre-Auguste Renoir. (Library of Congress)

championing the movement. By the time of the last exhibition, in 1886, there was no question that Impressionism had become a force to be reckoned with in the art world.

SIGNIFICANCE

The first Impressionist exhibition was a crucial step in liberating its participants and their successors from the academy's long dictatorship over French art. The painters of the next artistic generation (some of whom were the same age as the Impressionists) started out as Impressionists and only eventually found their individual paths into the various styles titled Post-Impressionism. They included Cézanne, Paul Gauguin, Vincent van Gogh, Georges Seurat, and Henri de Toulouse-Lautrec. Even after abandoning Impressionism's essentially realist concern with recording the world as it appeared to pursue their more subjective visions, these artists remained indebted to the movement's innovations.

By insisting on portraying the world they lived and worked in—both urban and rural—the participants in the first Impressionist exhibition introduced and privileged the modern moment as a an inspiration equal to traditional subjects. By displaying their experimentation with different techniques for best capturing the flux of this moment, they also opened up new directions in representing space and time. While their interest in both photography and Japanese prints led to a flatter, more immediate rendering of spatial dynamics, their reliance on short, broken brushstrokes to indicate changes in light, movement, and energy endowed painting with a new temporal dimension. The prominence of these rough brushstrokes, the way they attracted attention to the canvas surface, looked ahead to the emphasis on medium, rather than on content, in abstract art. Finally, the Impressionists' bold use of color likewise laid the foundations for the vibrant canvases of the next generation, especially those of van Gogh, Gauguin, and Seurat.

—*Margaret Bozenna Goscilo*

FURTHER READING

Bomford, David, Jo Kirby, John Leighton, and Ashok Roy. *Art in the Making: Impressionism.* New Haven, Conn.: Yale University Press, 1990. A technical but accessible analysis of fifteen paintings from London's National Gallery, with an introductory essay on the materials, studios, and traditions of the nineteenth century art world.

Brettell, Richard R. *Impression: Painting Quickly in France, 1860-1890.* New Haven, Conn.: Yale University Press, 2000. This lavishly illustrated book by a professor of aesthetic studies focuses on the theory, meaning, and technique behind particularly "unfinished," or quickly executed, Impressionist paintings.

Denvir, Bernard. *The Chronicle of Impressionism: An Intimate Diary of the Lives and World of the Great Artists.* London: Thames and Hudson, 2000. A journal-format survey of the movement's origins, exhibitions, career divergences, and legacy. Excerpts from critical reviews, letters, and diaries provide a fascinating cultural context for more than four hundred paintings.

_______. *The Thames and Hudson Encyclopedia of Impressionism.* London: Thames and Hudson, 1990. Covers the movement's people, places, events, and techniques in admirably precise entries.

Tinterow, Gary, and Henri Loyrette. *Origins of Impressionism.* New York: Metropolitan Museum of Art, 1994. Nine essays focus on the movement's achievements in different genres of nineteenth century painting.

SEE ALSO: 1824: Paris Salon of 1824; c. 1830-1870: Barbizon School of Landscape Painting Flourishes; Oct.-Dec., 1830: Delacroix Paints *Liberty Leading the People*; 1839: Daguerre and Niépce Invent Daguerreotype Photography; May 15, 1863: Paris's Salon des Refusés Opens; Feb. 20, 1872: Metropolitan Museum of Art Opens; Late 1870's: Post-Impressionist Movement Begins; 1892-1895: Toulouse-Lautrec Paints *At the Moulin Rouge*; 1893: Munch Paints *The Scream.*

RELATED ARTICLES in *Great Lives from History: The Nineteenth Century, 1801-1900:* Paul Cézanne; Edgar Degas; Paul Gauguin; Vincent van Gogh; Édouard Manet; Napoleon III; Camille Pissarro; Pierre-Auguste Renoir; Georges Seurat; Henri de Toulouse-Lautrec; Émile Zola.

June 27, 1874-June 2, 1875
RED RIVER WAR

During the Red River War, the U.S. Army defeated three of the American West's most formidable Indian tribes, opening large areas of the Southwest to settlement by the United States. The war confirmed the success of the doctrine of "total war," launching the army on a mission of destruction of any Native American culture that resisted U.S. expansion.

ALSO KNOWN AS: Red River Indian War
LOCALE: Texas; Oklahoma; Kansas
CATEGORIES: Wars, uprisings, and civil unrest; expansion and land acquisition

KEY FIGURES

Quanah Parker (c. 1845-1911), Comanche war chief
Philip H. Sheridan (1831-1888), American commander of the Military Division of the Missouri
William Tecumseh Sherman (1820-1891), commanding general of the U.S. Army
Ranald Slidell Mackenzie (1840-1889), American military commander
Nelson A. Miles (1839-1925), American military commander
Gray Beard (d. 1875), Cheyenne war chief
Lone Wolf (c. 1820-1879), leader of the Kiowa war faction
William R. Price (fl. 1874),
John Wynn Davidson (1823-1881), and
George P. Buell (fl. 1870's), U.S. military commanders

SUMMARY OF EVENT

Despite good intentions expressed in the 1867 Medicine Lodge Creek Treaty, the southern Great Plains remained a hotbed of hostile Native American activity, lawlessness, and punitive military action. Kiowa and Comanche bands continued to raid into Texas and Mexico, while southern Cheyenne and Arapaho braves still threatened parts of Kansas, often returning to the protection of reservations after their raids. Meanwhile, the U.S. Army, frustrated by restrictions imposed under President Ulysses S. Grant's Quaker Peace Policy, labored to control the volatile situation.

By 1874, the inadequacies of the reservation system and other outside influences combined to trigger a major tribal uprising. For most members of the plains tribes, reservation life and the imposition of Anglo-American values threatened the most basic tenets of their existence, depriving them of freedom, mobility, and dignity. This proved especially problematic for young men, whose status largely depended on demonstrations of bravery in war or prowess on the hunt. Reservation Indians suffered from poor food; frequently, promised rations were never delivered. Whiskey traders and horse thieves preyed on reservations with relative impunity. Most grievous to the American Indians was the wholesale slaughter of the buffalo by hide-hunters and sportsmen who were killing the beasts by the hundreds of thousands, leaving stripped carcasses to litter the prairie. With the arrival of spring, the South Plains erupted in violence, as American Indians left their reservations in large numbers.

On June 27, 1874, several hundred Cheyenne and Comanche warriors attacked a group of twenty-eight buffalo hunters in the Texas Panhandle at an old trading post known as Adobe Walls. Prominent among the attackers was Quanah Parker, the son of an influential Comanche chief and his captured wife, Cynthia Ann Parker. Despite

Kiowa war leader Lone Wolf. (National Archives)

overwhelming odds, the well-protected buffalo hunters devastated the attackers with high-powered rifles. Although never confirmed, American Indian casualties probably exceeded seventy.

The attack at Adobe Walls signaled the beginning of the Red River War. In July, Lone Wolf's Kiowas assailed a Texas Ranger detachment, Cheyenne warriors struck travel routes in Kansas, and Comanches menaced Texas ranches. As hostile action intensified, the army received permission to pursue raiders onto previously protected reservations and take offensive action to end the uprising. On July 20, 1874, Commanding General William Tecumseh Sherman issued orders initiating a state of war, the prosecution of which fell to Lieutenant General Philip Sheridan, whose massive jurisdiction included the South Plains. Sheridan, like Sherman an advocate of total war, quickly devised the most ambitious campaign yet mounted by the army against American Indians in the West.

Sheridan's plan called for five independent columns to converge on American Indian camps in the Texas Panhandle, surround them, and punish the Indians to such an extent as to discourage future uprisings. Accordingly, Colonel Nelson A. Miles marched from Fort Dodge, Kansas, with a large force of cavalry and infantry; Colonel Ranald Slidell Mackenzie, with eight companies of cavalry and five infantry companies, moved northward from Fort Concho, Texas; Major William R. Price led a squadron of cavalry eastward from New Mexico; and Lieutenant Colonels John Wynn Davidson and George P. Buell prepared their commands, comprising several companies of Buffalo Soldiers (African American troops from the Ninth and Tenth Cavalries), to strike westward from Indian Territory. The total force numbered more than two thousand soldiers and Indian scouts.

In August, Army units moved onto reservations to separate peaceful Indians from the hostile. Although almost all Arapahos enrolled as friendly, most Cheyennes refused to submit. Troubles at the Fort Sill agency triggered a confrontation between Davidson's cavalry and a band of Comanches supported by Lone Wolf's Kiowas. Most of these Indians escaped to join hostile factions on the Staked Plains. The Army listed almost five thousand Indians as hostile; of these, roughly twelve hundred were warriors.

A severe drought made water scarce, and late August temperatures reached 110 degrees as Colonel Miles eagerly pushed his men southward. On August 30, near Palo Duro Canyon, the column clashed with Cheyenne warriors, who were soon joined by Kiowas and Comanches. The soldiers prevailed, driving the warriors onto the plains. Miles could not exploit the opportunity, however; supply shortages forced him to retire in search of provisions. The drought gave way to torrential rains and dropping temperatures as Miles linked with Price's column on September 7. Two days later, a band of Kiowas and Comanches assailed a supply train en route to Miles. Following a three-day siege, the American Indians abandoned the effort unrewarded, but the incident complicated the supply crisis.

The Red River War

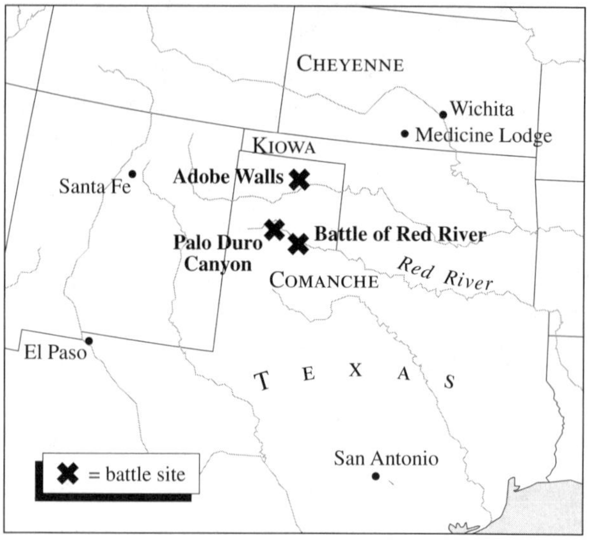

With Miles temporarily out of action, Mackenzie and his crack Fourth Cavalry Regiment took up the fight. After stockpiling supplies, Mackenzie moved, in miserable conditions, to the rugged canyons of the Caprock escarpment. On September 26, Mackenzie thwarted a Comanche attempt to stampede his horses. Two days later, the crowning achievement of the campaign came as Mackenzie struck a large encampment in Palo Duro Canyon. Following a harrowing descent, wave after wave of cavalry swept across the canyon floor. The soldiers inflicted few casualties but laid waste to the village, burning lodges, badly needed food stocks, and equipment. Mackenzie's troopers completed the devastation by capturing fifteen hundred of the tribe's ponies, one thousand of which the colonel ordered destroyed to prevent their recapture.

Over the next three months, Army units scoured the Texas Panhandle, despite freezing temperatures and intense storms. In November, a detachment from Miles's command destroyed Gray Beard's Cheyenne camp, recovering Adelaide and Julia German, two of four sisters seized in a Kansas raid. Catherine and Sophia German were released the following spring. Hungry and demoralized, Indians began to trickle into the reservation by October, but most remained defiant until harsh weather and constant military pressure finally broke their resistance. In late February, 1875, five hundred Kiowas, including Lone Wolf, surrendered. On March 6, eight hundred Cheyennes, among them the elusive Gray Beard, capitulated. In April, sixty Cheyennes bolted from their reservation in an effort to join the Northern Cheyennes; twenty-seven of these, including women and children, were killed by a cavalry detachment at Sappa Creek in northwestern Kansas. Finally, on June 2, 1875, Quanah Parker and four hundred Comanches—the last organized band fighting in the Red River War—surrendered to Mackenzie at Fort Sill.

After a dubious selection process, seventy-four Indians, ostensibly the leading troublemakers, including Gray Beard and Lone Wolf, were shipped to prison in Florida. Gray Beard was later killed trying to escape; others perished in captivity, but some accepted the benevolent supervision and educational efforts of Lieutenant Richard Pratt. Several Red River War veterans remained with Pratt after their release to assist him in establishing the Carlisle Indian School in 1879.

Significance

The Red River War was among the most successful campaigns ever conducted against American Indians. It brought almost complete subjugation to three of the most powerful and revered tribes in North America. It also provided a model for future army campaigns and boldly confirmed the doctrine of total war. Now less concerned with inflicting casualties, the Army would focus on destroying the American Indians' means and will to resist. Combined with the annihilation of the buffalo, this campaign of eradication made it impossible for American Indians to exist in large numbers outside reservations. Finally, the campaign's successful completion opened vast areas to white settlement and ranching.

—*David Coffey*

Further Reading

Haley, James L. *The Buffalo War: The History of the Red River Indian Uprising of 1874*. Garden City, N.Y.: Doubleday, 1976. Provides substantial background information and military analysis. Maps, illustrations, notes, bibliography, and index.

Hutton, Paul Andrew. *Phil Sheridan and His Army*. Lincoln: University of Nebraska Press, 1985. An expansive study of Sheridan's post-Civil War career, including his role as the Red River War's chief architect. Maps, illustrations, notes, bibliography, and index.

Jauken, Arlene Feldmann. *The Moccasin Speaks: Living as Captives of the Dog Soldier Warriors, Red River War, 1874-1875*. Lincoln, Nebr.: Dageforde, 1998. Account of the experiences of the German family, who were captured by the Cheyenne during the Red River War.

Leckie, William H. *The Buffalo Soldiers: A Narrative of the Negro Cavalry in the West*. Norman: University of Oklahoma Press, 1967. Discusses the considerable role played by African Americans in the frontier Army, devoting an entire chapter to the Red River War. Maps, illustrations, notes, bibliography, and index.

Robinson, Charles M., III. *Bad Hand: A Biography of General Ranald S. Mackenzie*. Austin, Tex.: State House Press, 1993. A comprehensive study that treats Mackenzie's pivotal role in the Red River War in suitable detail. Maps, illustrations, notes, bibliography, and index.

_______. *The Plains Wars, 1757-1900*. New York: Routledge, 2003. The Red River War features prominently in this book from the Essential Histories series. Bibliographic reference and index.

Utley, Robert M. *Frontier Regulars: The United States Army and the Indian, 1866-1891*. Lincoln: University of Nebraska Press, 1984. An essential study of the frontier Army and the Indian wars. Includes a chapter on the Red River War and a wealth of other pertinent information. Maps, illustrations, notes, bibliography, and index.

_______. *The Indian Frontier of the American West, 1846-1890*. Albuquerque: University of New Mexico Press, 1984. This authoritative treatment of cultures in conflict includes a discussion of the causes and effects of the Red River War. Maps, illustrations, notes, bibliography, and index.

Wooster, Robert. *Nelson A. Miles and the Twilight of the Frontier Army*. Lincoln: University of Nebraska Press, 1993. Includes a chapter on the controversial soldier's extensive Red River War operations.

See also: Apr. 30, 1860-1865: Apache and Navajo War; Feb. 6, 1861-Sept. 4, 1886: Apache Wars; Aug. 17, 1862-Dec. 28, 1863: Great Sioux War; Aug., 1863-Sept., 1866: Long Walk of the Navajos; Nov.

29, 1864: Sand Creek Massacre; Oct. 21, 1867: Medicine Lodge Creek Treaty; c. 1871-1883: Great American Buffalo Slaughter; Mar. 3, 1871: Grant Signs Indian Appropriation Act; 1876-1877: Sioux War; June 25, 1876: Battle of the Little Bighorn; June 15-Oct. 5, 1877: Nez Perce War; Dec. 29, 1890: Wounded Knee Massacre.

RELATED ARTICLES in *Great Lives from History: The Nineteenth Century, 1801-1900:* Ulysses S. Grant; William Tecumseh Sherman.

November 24, 1874
GLIDDEN PATENTS BARBED WIRE

Joseph Glidden's invention of a new type of barbed wire for fencing had an immediate impact on the American West. The wire's production and proliferation forever transformed the grazing era, revolutionized the physical demarcation of borders, and developed a new symbolism of containment and even oppression.

LOCALE: De Kalb, Illinois
CATEGORIES: Inventions; science and technology; agriculture

KEY FIGURES
Joseph Glidden (1813-1906), American inventor
Charles F. Washburn (1798-1893), American steel producer
Isaac L. Ellwood (1833-1910), American inventor and businessman
John W. Gates (1855-1911), American financier
Jacob Haish (1826-1926), American inventor

SUMMARY OF EVENT
Upon arriving in the Americas, colonists defined boundaries by heaping stones, brushes, and trees excavated from their fields on an agreed border. Settlers who moved into eastern prairies and the Great Plains found few familiar resources and resorted to earthen barriers, imported Osage orange brush, and other poor substitutes. With the advent of barbed wire, and its subsequent mass production, fencing quickly littered the West, acting still as a critical physical barrier in domestic, industrial, correctional, and military facilities.

Late nineteenth century industrialization and the mass production of steel provided the potential for a new durable divider. Between 1860 and 1873 at least nine fence patents were recorded. By 1881 some 1,229 fence designs received recognition from the U.S. Patent Office. The first in the barbed-wire family was actually a picket fence with sharp tacks embedded to block livestock. Later, the Hunt Patent (1867) employed two smooth steel wires with rotating spurs of sheet metal affixed throughout. The Kelly Patent (1868) included the first twisting wires complemented by small spikes and was perhaps the true first modern barbed wire.

Joseph Glidden was born in 1813 in New Hampshire. A year after birth his family relocated to New York State, where he was raised and received an education. Glidden went on to teach school before moving to Illinois in 1842, claiming six hundred acres of land in De Kalb County. After thirty years of farming and community involvement, Glidden stumbled upon his famous invention—barbed wire. Three varying stories recount the origin of his idea. In one narrative the invention was more an accidental discovery as he worked to untangle two crossed smooth wires; in a second story, Glidden invented barbed wire as a practical means to protect his wife's garden; in yet a third explanation the invention came as inspiration after visiting a county fair in which inventor Henry M. Rose demonstrated a smooth wire fence on which hung thin sixteen-foot wooden panels embedded with sharp brands. Other soon-to-be rivals likewise attended the same fair and envisioned products similar to Glidden's barbed wire.

Glidden's barbed wire was functional, durable, and eventually became quite cheap to produce. The patent describes the invention as "a twisted fence-wire having the transverse spur wire *D* bent at its middle portion about one of the wire strands of *a* of said fence-wire, and clamped in position and place by the other wire strand *z*, twisted upon its fellow, substantially as specified." More simply put, the invention consisted of barbs evenly placed upon a single smooth steel wire with a second wire wrapped around the first to hold the barbs in place, the wires then attached to posts every fifteen to fifty feet (depending on the topography). Intertwining two wires allowed the fence to expand and contract with the fluctuation of temperature while remaining durable and successfully deterring livestock. Furthermore, Glidden's wire did not aid in the making of snow drifts, nor did it block vision or oppose otherwise damaging winds—a perfect fit for the plains.

The Glidden patent was challenged several times, most critically by fellow De Kalb resident Jacob Haish. Glidden's first application to the Patent Office dates to October, 1873. On technical grounds of organization, however, the application was rejected, corrected, and resubmitted twice before being granted approval on November 24, 1874 (Patent No. 157, 124). Haish, on the other hand, submitted his application of a similar design after Glidden's original but immediately received the patent in June, 1874, as no other conflicting claim had yet been completed. A legal battle ensued between the two rivals. As late as 1880, Glidden testified against Haish, claiming Haish sent a mechanic to copy his specifications in May of 1874. The legal suit was eventually resolved by no less than the U.S. Supreme Court in an 1892 decision upholding Glidden's patent.

The barbed-wire industry pushed forward, even with the litigation. In 1874, Glidden partnered with inventor and businessman Isaac Ellwood, who purchased half the rights to the patent. The two then founded the Barbed Fence Company. They quickly acquired previous necessary patents and, in December, 1874, bought the rights to P. W. Vaughan's barbed-wire machine (a step up from Glidden's original converted coffee grindstone). Employing seventy workers in a small two-story building, the company's increasing demand for processed smooth steel wire caught the notice of their supplier, Washburn & Moen Manufacturing Company of Worchester, Massachusetts. After several visits, Washburn & Moen's vice president, Charles F. Washburn, was sufficiently impressed by the design. Finding it easy to mass-produce with advanced machinery, Washburn & Moen partnered with Ellwood in 1872 and bought out Glidden's interests.

Public acceptance of barbed wire was slow initially, but eventually the fence was everywhere in the prairies and plains. Many opposed "the devil's rope" for fear that it would harm the cattle and horses that wandered into the barbs. On the eve of the Texas legislature's motion to outlaw the product, Ellwood dispatched salesmen Henry B. Sanborn and John "Bet-a-Million" Gates to persuade ranchers of its value. In 1875, Gates organized a demonstration of barbed wire in San Antonio's main plaza, wherein he corralled several Longhorns. Impressed by the product's durability and the evident safety of the cattle, as well as the temporary offer to sell the wire at wholesale, Texans quickly converted to the wire. To persuade southern ranchers to adopt it, Glidden and Sanborn organized a ranch fenced with barbed wire in Texas; the ranch led to the development of Amarillo. Soon the product was in widespread use across the plains, by ranchers and farmers seeking to protect their lands.

After Glidden's work ended, Washburn & Moen continued to play a primary role in barbed-wire production, buying out and intimidating its competitors. Haish, who lacked comparable production and financial backing, faded into obscurity. In December of 1880, Washburn won a test case before a federal district court that recognized the primacy of its patent and required all competitors to lease rights and recompense back-payment penalties.

In 1887, recently successful competitor (and former employee) Gates pressed Washburn & Moen for a corporate merger. After being rejected, Gates went on to incorporate steel producers, refiners, and barbed-wire companies in an enormous monopoly-holding firm named the American Steel and Wire Company of New Jersey. In April of 1899, Washburn & Moen reconsidered and, with the support of other companies, it joined American Steel and Wire. The merger led the newly organized company to control 96 percent of barbed-wire production in the United States.

Significance

The effects of barbed wire have been expansive and far-reaching. Barbed-wire fencing rapidly covered the prairie and plains states. In Texas, immense cattle ranches formed to dominate the cattle industry and state politics, in large part facilitated by the new wire. On the northern plains, barbed fences posted by ranchers and farmers created a patchwork that increasingly denied cattle access to grazing fields, water holes, and general passage to railheads, eventually transforming the plains into the agricultural entity of the twentieth century. Quite literally, barbed wire closed the open range, and though barbed wire did not see widespread use outside the United States, ranchers in Argentina and Australia often employed the fence as well.

Military uses for the wire may have begun after its mention in an 1888 British war manual. Teddy Roosevelt's Rough Riders also used the fencing to protect their camps during the Spanish-American War (1898).

Because barbed wire is a common tool for enclosure, it has come to symbolize containment and oppression, evoking uneasy emotions. Perhaps most apparent, barbed wire remains a standard deployment for high-wire entanglements on the battlefield, and it frequently serves to protect and partition military, industrial, correctional, and domestic boundaries. Whether surrounding pastures, prisons, or factories, barbed wire is a surrounding feature of life, even into the twenty-first century.

—*Matthew R. Garrett*

FURTHER READING

Clifton, Robert T. *Barbs, Prongs, Points, Prickers, and Stickers: A Complete and Illustrated Catalog of Antique Barbed Wire*. Norman: University of Oklahoma Press, 1970. Almost one thousand classified drawings, complete with indexes to patents, inventors, and manufacturers.

Dreicer, Gregory K., ed. *Between Fences*. Washington, D.C.: National Building Museum and Princeton Architectural Press, 1996. An exhibition catalog with essays that include "Barbed Wire Fences and the American West" by historian J. B. Jackson, a pioneer in the field of cultural landscape studies.

Krell, Alan. *The Devil's Rope: A Cultural History of Barbed Wire*. London: Reaktion Books, 2002. A history of barbed wire that emphasizes modern applications, collectors, symbolism, and the wire's social and cultural impact.

McCallum, Henry D., and Frances T. McCallum. *The Wire That Fenced the West*. Norman: University of Oklahoma Press, 1965. Discusses the development, legal issues, and early production of barbed wire.

McFadden, Joseph M. "Monopoly in Barbed Wire: The Formation of the American Steel and Wire Company." *Business Historical Review* 52, no. 4 (Winter, 1978): 465-489. Traces the rise of the American Steel and Wire Company as it incorporated smaller businesses and grew to dominate wire manufacturing in the United States.

Mather, Eugene, et al. "Fences and Farms." *Geographical Review* 44, no. 2 (April, 1954): 201-223. A brief history that also discusses the various types of fences prevalent in the United States during the mid-twentieth century.

Netz, Reviel. *Barbed Wire: An Ecology of Modernity*. Middletown, Conn.: Wesleyan University Press, 2004. Examines the functional and symbolic use of barbed wire, with sections on "expansion," "confrontation," and "containment."

U.S. Patent and Trademark Office. "Joseph F. Glidden's Barbed Wire Patent." Patent Description, National Archives and Records Administration, Records of the Patent and Trademark Office, Record Group 241. A facsimile of Glidden's first patent application, dated October, 1873.

SEE ALSO: Sept. 20, 1811: Krupp Works Open at Essen; 1855: Bessemer Patents Improved Steel-Processing Method; Dec. 4, 1867: National Grange Is Formed; Apr. 24-Dec. 10, 1898: Spanish-American War.

RELATED ARTICLES in *Great Lives from History: The Nineteenth Century, 1801-1900:* Sir Henry Bessemer; Sir Robert Abbott Hadfield.

1875
SUPREME COURT OF CANADA IS ESTABLISHED

The Parliament of the Dominion of Canada passed a statute creating a Supreme Court. A controversial law, the Supreme Court Act began the process of defining Canada's judicial independence from Great Britain.

ALSO KNOWN AS: Supreme Court Act
LOCALE: Ottawa, Canada
CATEGORIES: Laws, acts, and legal history; organizations and institutions; government and politics

KEY FIGURES

Edward Blake (1833-1912), Canadian minister of justice

Alexander Mackenzie (1822-1892), prime minister of Canada, 1873-1878, and leader of the Liberal Party

Sir John Alexander Macdonald (1815-1891), prime minister of Canada, 1867-1873, 1878-1891

SUMMARY OF EVENT

In 1867, Canada became a dominion of Great Britain with the passage of the British North America Act. The act provided Canada with a constitution and a federal government, but the constitution could be changed only by the British parliament, which thereby retained ultimate control of the structure and law of the country. The British North America Act gave the Canadian Parliament the ability to create a general court of appeal "for the better administration of the Laws of Canada." However, the precise limits of such a court's jurisdiction would be vague, since the Judicial Committee of the

Privy Council of Great Britain would remain the highest appellate court for the dominion.

In 1875, Parliament passed the Supreme Court Act, a statute establishing a general court of appeal in accordance with the right granted to it by the British North America Act. This court was referred to as the Supreme Court of Canada. The proposal of this law, as well as its passage, caused sharp debate among the founders of the dominion. Sir John Alexander Macdonald argued that the Canadian constitution did not anticipate the creation of such a Supreme Court when it described a court of appeal. Since Canada was still a dominion of Great Britain, it was unclear precisely which laws were "the Laws of Canada" and which were British laws. Many Liberals and Conservatives alike opposed a Supreme Court, fearing the possible consequences for provincial rights. By establishing a Supreme Court, Parliament could conceivably be providing itself with a constitutional interpreter. The impartiality of such an interpreter was questionable, because the federal government would appoint its members and would determine the court's field of competency.

The Liberal government of Alexander Mackenzie finally persuaded Parliament to vote in favor of a Supreme Court. It argued both the need for standardized Canadian law and the need to provide constitutional interpretation on issues that would affect the evolution of the new federation. An unsuccessful attempt was made by Canadian minister of justice Edward Blake to abolish appeals to the Judicial Committee when the Supreme Court was established. However, the Supreme Court was an institution of the Dominion of Canada rather than Great Britain, and as such it was to remain bound by the decisions of the Judicial Committee of the Privy Council until 1949.

The Supreme Court of Canada included a chief justice and eight junior justices appointed by the governor-in-council. Members could be selected from among provincial superior court judges or from among those barristers and advocates who had been members of a provincial bar for at least ten years. The Supreme Court Act required that at least three of the judges be appointed from Quebec. It is now traditional for three other judges to come from Ontario, one from the Maritime Provinces, and two from the western provinces.

Under the Supreme Court Act, the Supreme Court of Canada not only pronounced judgment and advised federal and provincial governments on questions of law and of fact concerning constitutional interpretation but also functioned as the general court of appeal for criminal cases. However, appeals in criminal cases were abolished in the Dominion of Canada in 1888, and they remained illegal until 1926, when their abolition was determined to be invalid. The Statute of Westminster (1931) gave Canada the authority to reenact this regulation.

The Supreme Court could choose the cases it would hear, with one major exception, called the "reference case." The Court was required to consider and advise on questions referred to it by the federal cabinet or by any provincial cabinet, on any matter that directly concerned the interpretation of the Canadian constitution. This device permitted a speedy answer to doubtful constitutional questions without the need to wait until an actual dispute arose. The creation of a class of cases that the Supreme Court is required to hear remains unique to Canada.

For much of its existence, the precise position of the Canadian Supreme Court relative to the Judicial Committee of the British Privy Council was a matter of dispute. Arguments against Canadian appeals being heard by the Judicial Committee rather than the Supreme Court rested on claims that it was demeaning for Canada to be forced to rely on a body beyond its borders and its national sovereignty for final judicial decisions, that the Privy Council was ill equipped to consider problems of Canadian federalism, and that the Judicial Committee had misinterpreted the British North America Act in many of its more than 170 judgments. Nevertheless, given its status as a dominion state of the British Empire, with a constitution created by an act of the British parliament, Canada lacked the sovereign authority to deny the Judicial Committee jurisdiction over any legal proceeding over which the committee chose to assert its authority.

SIGNIFICANCE

Sovereignty was the central issue behind Canadians' desire to render the Supreme Court the ultimate authority and court of final appeal for their nation. This issue had come to a head by the 1930's, but World War II caused a delay in the move toward completely ending appeals to the Judicial Committee of the Privy Council. In 1949, an amendment to the Supreme Court Act transferred ultimate appellate jurisdiction to Canada. The Supreme Court of Canada has been the highest court for all legal issues of federal and provincial jurisdiction since 1949. The Supreme Court frequently refers to the judgment of the Judicial Committee, but it is no longer legally bound to follow those decisions. This allows the Supreme Court greater creativity and flexibility in decision making. On the other hand, it can prove problematic in constitutional matters, given the difficulties that may arise from a disregard for the federalist principles that were firmly established by the Judicial Committee.

By a decision in November of 1969, the Supreme Court of Canada put itself in a position to play a new and enlarged role in Canada's political life. In *Regina v. Drybones*, the Supreme Court rendered inoperative a provision of the Indian Act, basing its judgment on the "equality before the law" clause of the Canadian Bill of Rights. The Court ruled that, if a federal statute cannot be reasonably interpreted and applied without abolishing, limiting, or infringing upon one of the rights or liberties recognized in the Bill of Rights, it is inoperative unless Parliament expressly declares that is is to apply notwithstanding the Bill of Rights. The Court concluded that Joseph Drybones, who had been found drunk off reserve land in a lobby of a hotel, had been punished because of race under a law whose scope and penalty differ from that for other Canadians.

—*Susan M. Taylor*

FURTHER READING

Canada Supreme Court. *The Supreme Court of Canada and Its Justices, 1875-2000: A Commemorative Book/ La Cour suprême du Canada et ses juges, 1875-2000: Un Livre commémoratif.* Toronto: Author, 2000. Bilingual commemorative text detailing the history of the Canadian Supreme Court and listing each of the justices who has occupied the Bench.

Creighton, Donald. *Canada's First Century, 1867-1967.* New York: St. Martin's Press, 1970. A comprehensive account of political events and contrasts between the economic growth and erosion of the fundamental national institutions.

________. *Dominion of the North: A History of Canada.* Toronto: Macmillan of Canada, 1957. Discusses events from the founding of New France through World War II.

McCormick, Peter. *Supreme at Last: The Evolution of the Supreme Court of Canada.* Toronto: James Lorimer, 2000. Discussion of the history of courts of last resort in Canada and the development of the authority of the Supreme Court.

Saywell, John T. *The Lawmakers: Judicial Power and the Shaping of Canadian Federalism.* Toronto: University of Toronto Press, 2002. Extensive discussion of the relationship between the Canadian Supreme Court, the Canadian constitution, and federalism in Canada.

SEE ALSO: Feb. 10, 1841: Upper and Lower Canada Unite; Apr. 25, 1849: First Test of Canada's Responsible Government; July 1, 1867: British North America Act; 1872: Dominion Lands Act Fosters Canadian Settlement; Nov. 5, 1873-Oct. 9, 1878: Canada's Mackenzie Era; 1876: Canada's Indian Act; Sept., 1878: Macdonald Returns as Canada's Prime Minister.

RELATED ARTICLES in *Great Lives from History: The Nineteenth Century, 1801-1900:* Sir John Alexander Macdonald; Alexander Mackenzie.

March 3, 1875
BIZET'S *CARMEN* PREMIERES IN PARIS

The first performance of Georges Bizet's opera Carmen *was not well received, but the work soon became one of the mainstays of the operatic repertoire. It continues to be performed in many languages on stages around the world, and it has been adapted for film, ballet, and musical theater.*

LOCALE: Paris, France
CATEGORIES: Theater; music

KEY FIGURES

Georges Bizet (1838-1875), French operatic composer
Henri Meilhac (1831-1897), French librettist
Ludovic Halévy (1834-1908), French librettist
Prosper Mérimée (1803-1870), French historian and author
Ernest Guiraud (1837-1892), French composer
Oscar Hammerstein II (1895-1960), American lyricist

SUMMARY OF EVENT

The premiere of the opera *Carmen* by the French composer Georges Bizet on March 3, 1875, was poorly received. The audience was shocked by the portrayal of lower-class characters in Seville, Spain—particularly by the onstage depiction of the murder of the title character by her lover. However, audiences at a production staged later that year in Vienna, Austria, were drawn to the strong characters, exotic locales, colorful gypsy scenes, and engaging music, and *Carmen* soon became one of the favorite and most often performed works in the operatic repertoire.

The story of Carmen traces its roots to 1830, when French author Prosper Mérimée—traveling through the Andalusia region of Spain—first heard a tale about a gypsy girl who was killed by a jealous lover. This story developed into the novella *Carmen* (1845). In the novella, the soldier José Navarro falls in love with the headstrong gypsy Carmen and follows her into a life of crime and murder after he deserts his regiment. When she does not remain faithful to him, he kills her. Before his execution, he tells his story to the narrator, a historian touring Spain.

Belgian opera singer Marguerita Sylva (1876-1957) as Carmen. (Library of Congress)

In 1873, when Bizet had the opportunity to work with two of the leading librettists in France, Henri Meilhac and Ludovic Halévy, he suggested they adapt Mérimée's novella. Meilhac and Halévy changed many aspects of Mérimée's work, adding characters and eliminating scenes to enhance its dramatic impact. Bizet was much more involved in the crafting of the text than were many opera composers, taking advantage of his previous experience composing *Les Pêcheurs de perles* (1863; the pearl fishers), *La Jolie Fille de Perth* (1867; the fair maid of Perth), and *Djamileh* (1872).

The directors of the Opéra-Comique, the theater where *Carmen* was to be staged, were not pleased with the choice of subject matter, rightly sensing that the unconventional story populated with thieves, gypsies, and the climactic murder of Carmen by her lover, Don José, would be scandalous to the French public. Additional revisions to the opera were made during rehearsals against Bizet's wishes, some at the insistence of the theater directors.

The opera is in four acts and adds two characters that barely appear in Mérimée's novella. Don José's former girlfriend, Micaela, becomes a moral foil that accentuates the immorality of Carmen, while Carmen's next conquest, the bullfighter Escamillo, embodies the virtues that José turns away from in his obsession with Carmen. Perhaps the most dramatic change from the novella is that José's last confrontation with Carmen before he kills her takes place outside a bullring instead of on a remote mountainside. The cheers of the crowd inside for Escamillo's victory render Carmen's death even more tragic. Bizet's music brings the characters to life for the audience, as in Carmen's first aria, which is accompanied by the seductive rhythms of the Habañera, a slow Cuban dance.

While the audience applauded act 1 of *Carmen* at its premiere on March 3, 1875, they became more cool and almost hostile by the end of the production. Newspaper reviews of the performance were overwhelmingly critical. The Mérimée story was considered too obscene for the stage, and Bizet's music was said to lack drama and original melodies, although a few reviews praised the music in specific scenes. Bizet himself considered the opera to be a failure, although it was performed forty-seven more times at the Opéra-Comique, albeit with fewer people in the audience over the course of its run.

Bizet did not live to see the eventual success of *Carmen*. He succumbed to heart failure exactly three months after the opera's premiere, on June 3, 1875. The score of the opera was still incomplete when Bizet died, with the various revisions made during the first production not yet consolidated. As a result, different versions of *Carmen* exist, and many subsequent productions have been quite different from Bizet's original conception of the work.

The Paris version of *Carmen* employed spoken dialogue between Bizet's aria and ensemble numbers, but for the production in Vienna in October of 1875, sung dialogue, or recitative, was added in order to conform to the tradition of grand opera. The new recitatives were composed by Bizet's friend Ernest Guiraud. It was primarily this version of the opera that was published and that most productions since have followed. The Vienna production also added ballet music from a previous Bizet opera, a parade of bullfighters, and even men on horseback. The success of Carmen in Vienna was followed by a production in Brussels, Belgium, and the opera was soon performed across Europe and the United States. An 1883 revival in Paris finally brought *Carmen* critical praise in the French press. Later performances during the nineteenth century were often sung in the vernacular, with productions in Spanish, English, Italian, and Czech.

SIGNIFICANCE

The success of *Carmen* can be attributed to at least three factors. The first is the compelling, psychologically realistic characterization of Carmen herself. She is a strong woman, comfortable using her sexual appeal to get what she wants and determined to preserve her freedom, leading her to reject the possessive Don José. She stays true to her beliefs, even when faced with death at the hands of her jealous lover. The exotic setting of southern Spain also appeals to audiences, with colorful costumes and characters and the mystery that the opera associates with gypsy culture. The third factor in *Carmen*'s success is in the compelling music of Bizet, who adapted folk melodies and Spanish dance rhythms to compose his original music, which is both lively and sensuous.

Even though *Carmen* was not immediately successful during its first performances, it soon entered into the repertoires of opera companies around the world, and it became one of the most popular operas of the twentieth century. Many productions translated the original French libretto into other languages, including Croatian, Chinese, Hebrew, and Japanese.

The popularity of the story has also inspired many non-operatic versions of *Carmen*. Oscar Hammerstein II retained Bizet's music but adapted the story into a Broadway musical called *Carmen Jones* (1943) set in a World War II parachute factory with an African American cast; a film version directed by Otto Preminger was released in 1954. Other film versions of *Carmen*, some with little or none of Bizet's music, have appeared in France, Italy, Spain, England, Russia, and the United States. One film employs Bizet's music but is sung and spoken in the South African language of Xhosa. These adaptations are examples of the global appeal of Bizet's engaging musical score and of the timeless characters that were first introduced on the Paris opera stage in 1875.

—*R. Todd Rober*

FURTHER READING

Baker, Even. "The Scene Designs for the First Performances of Bizet's Carmen." *Nineteenth-Century Music* 13, no. 3 (Spring, 1990): 230-242. Provides illustrations of the likely stage sets employed in the first production of *Carmen*.

Curtiss, Mina Kirstein. *Bizet and His World*. New York: Vienna House, 1974. A comprehensive and well-documented biography that provides context for the music of Bizet through firsthand accounts from letters and other original documents.

Dean, Winton. *Georges Bizet: His Life and Work*. 3d ed. London: J. M. Dent & Sons, 1975. A thorough recounting of Bizet's biography and discussion of his music with many musical examples for illustration.

Gould, Evlyn. *The Fate of Carmen*. Baltimore: Johns Hopkins University Press, 1996. A complex reading of three versions of Carmen: Mérimée's novella, Bizet's opera, and the film of Carlos Saura; aimed at an academic audience.

Lowe, David A. "Pushkin and Carmen." *Nineteenth-Century Music* 20, no. 1 (Summer, 1996): 72-76. A compelling argument that the libretto for the opera Carmen was influenced by the Aleksander Pushkin poem *The Gypsies* in addition to Mérimée's novella.

McClary, Susan. *Georges Bizet: Carmen*. Cambridge, England: Cambridge University Press, 1992. A detailed analysis of the work that offers insights into issues of gender, race, and class in the opera and also later film versions.

SEE ALSO: Feb. 20, 1816: Rossini's *The Barber of Seville* Debuts; Jan. 2, 1843: Wagner's *Flying Dutchman* Debuts; Aug. 13-17, 1876: First Performance of Wagner's Ring Cycle; Oct. 22, 1883: Metropolitan Opera House Opens in New York; Jan. 14, 1900: Puccini's *Tosca* Premieres in Rome.

RELATED ARTICLE in *Great Lives from History: The Nineteenth Century, 1801-1900:* Georges Bizet.

March 3, 1875
Congress Enacts the Page Law

Originally designed to prohibit Chinese contract workers and prostitutes from entering the United States, this federal law eventually excluded Asian women in general.

Also known as: Act Supplementary to the Acts in Relation to Immigration
Locale: Washington, D.C.
Categories: Immigration; civil rights and liberties; diplomacy and international relations; women's issues

Key Figures

Horace F. Page (1833-1890), California congressman
David Bailey (b. c. 1813), U.S. consul general in Hong Kong
H. Sheldon Loring (b. 1824), Bailey's successor as consul general in Hong Kong
John S. Mosby (1833-1916), Loring's successor

Summary of Event

On February 10, 1875, California congressman Horace F. Page introduced federal legislation designed to prohibit the immigration of female Asian prostitutes into the United States. Passed by Congress on March 3 as "An Act Supplementary to the Acts in Relation to Immigration," the Page law evolved into a more general restriction against vast numbers of Chinese immigrants into the country, whether they were prostitutes or not. It subjected any person convicted of importing Chinese prostitutes to a maximum prison term of five years and a fine of not more than five thousand dollars.

An amendment to the Page law prohibited individuals from engaging in the "coollie trade," the importation of all illegal Chinese contract laborers. Punishment for that type of violation, however, was both less severe and much more difficult to effect, given the large numbers of immigrant Asian men in the United States at that time. As a consequence of this division of penalties, the law was applied in a most gender-specific manner, effectively deterring the immigration of Asian women into the United States. During the seven years following the implementation of the law, the average number of Chinese women who entered the United States dropped to one-third of its previous level.

An elaborate bureaucratic network established to carry out the Page law's gender-specific exclusions was a catalyst for the decline in Chinese immigration rates. American consulate officials supported by American, Chinese, and British commercial, political, and medical services made up the law's implementation structure. Through intelligence gathering, interrogation, and physical examinations of applicants, the consulate hierarchy ferreted out undesirable applicants for immigration and those suspected of engaging in illegal human trafficking.

This investigative activity evolved well beyond the original intent of the law's authors. Any characteristic or activity that could be linked, even in the most remote sense, to prostitution became grounds for denial to immigrate to the United States. Most immigration applications came from women from the lower economic strata of Chinese society. Low economic status therefore became a reason for immigration exclusion. The procedure was a complicated one.

Many roadblocks were placed in the way of prospective immigrants. Acquiring permission to immigrate took much time and effort. Passing stringent physical examinations performed by biased health care officials was often impossible. Navigating language barriers through official interviews aimed at evaluating personal character often produced an atmosphere of rigid interrogation, bringing subsequent denial of the right to immigrate. Such a complex system aimed at uncovering fraudulent immigrants placed a hardship upon those wishing to leave China.

Because Hong Kong was the main point of departure for Chinese emigrating to the United States, all required examinations were performed there with a hierarchy of American consulate officials determining immigrant eligibility. In a sense, the Page law actually expanded consulate authority beyond any previous level. Such increased power of the consular general in implementing the law provided an opportunity for possible abuses of power.

In 1878, the U.S. consul general in Hong Kong, John S. Mosby, accused his predecessors of corruption and bribery. According to Mosby, David Bailey and H. Sheldon Loring had been guilty of embezzlement. Both men were accused of setting up such an intricate system to process immigration applications that bribery soon became the natural way to obtain the necessary permission to do so. Mosby went on to charge that Bailey had amassed thousands of dollars in extra income by regularly charging additional examination fees, regardless of whether examinations were performed. Mosby also accused Bailey of falsifying test results and encouraging medical personnel to interrogate applicants in order to deny immigration permission to otherwise legal immigrants.

Most of the allegations of corruption concerned the fact that moneys allotted by the federal government for implementation of the Page law were far below the amounts that Bailey required to administer the law. Given that situation, the U.S. government scrutinized Bailey's conduct. No indictments came from the official investigation, however, and Bailey, who had previously been promoted to vice-consul general in Shanghai, remained in that position. Later examinations of Bailey's tenure in Hong Kong have suggested that he was, if anything, an overly aggressive official who made controlling the immigration of Chinese women to the United States a top priority of his tenure there rather than an opportunity for profit.

Bailey was replaced in Hong Kong by H. Sheldon Loring. Loring did not enforce the Page law with as much vigor as his predecessor and allowed a slight, but still insignificant, increase in the annual numbers of Chinese immigrants. Nevertheless, Loring did enforce the law in an efficient manner, publicly suggesting that any ship owner who engaged in the illegal transport of women would be dealt with to the fullest extent of the law. Even so, Loring was accused of sharing Bailey's enthusiasm for the unofficial expensive design of the immigration procedure.

EXTRACTS FROM THE PAGE LAW

Be it enacted by the Senate and House of Representatives of the United States of America in Congress-assembled, That in determining whether the immigration of any subject of China, Japan, or any Oriental country, to the United States, is free and voluntary, as provided by section two thousand one hundred and sixty two of the Revised Code, title "Immigration," it shall be the duty of the consul-general or consul of the United States residing at the port from which it is proposed to convey such subjects, in any vessels enrolled or licensed in the United States, or any port within the same, before delivering to the masters of any such vessels the permit or certificate provided for in such section, in ascertain for a term of service within the United States, for lewd and immoral purposes; and if there be such contract or agreement, the said consul-general or consul shall not deliver the required permit or certificate. . . .

SEC. 3. That the importation into the United States of women for the purposes of prostitution is hereby forbidden; and all contracts and agreements in relation thereto, made in advance or in pursuance of illegal importation and purposes, are hereby declared void; and whoever shall knowingly and willfully hold, or attempt to hold, any woman to such purposes, in pursuance of such illegal importation and contract or agreement, shall be deemed guilty of a felony, and, on conviction thereof, shall be imprisoned not exceeding five years and pay a fine not exceeding five thousand dollars.

SEC. 5. That it shall be unlawful for aliens of the following classes to immigrate into the United States, namely, persons who are undergoing sentence for conviction in their own country of felonious crimes other than political or growing out of or the result of such political offenses, and women "imported for the purposes of prostitution." Every vessel arriving in the United States may be inspected under the direction of the collector of the port at which it arrives . . .

During Loring's tenure, questions about his character surfaced, mostly on account of his past relationships with individuals who engaged in questionable business practices in Asia. By the time that Mosby replaced him, such questions had become more than a nuisance. The new U.S. consul to Hong Kong began to describe his predecessor as a dishonest taker of bribes. Once again, the official dynamics of such charges brought forth an official inquiry from Washington. Like the earlier investigation of Bailey, however, this investigation produced no official indictment against Loring. The only blemish concerned an additional fee that Loring had instituted for procuring official landing certificates. However, as precedents for such fees existed, Loring, like his predecessor, was exonerated of all charges.

After deciding that his predecessors were indeed corrupt, but unable to prove it, Mosby enforced the Page law with relentless energy. Keeping a posture that was above accusations of corruption, Mosby personally interviewed each applicant for immigration, oversaw relations between the consulate and the health examiners, and eliminated the additional charges for the landing permits. In the end, the numbers of Chinese immigrants that he allowed remained similar to those of Loring and below those of Bailey, with the numbers of Chinese female immigrants continuing to decline. Aside from being free from charges of corruption, Mosby's tenure in office was as authoritative and unilaterally considerate as those of his predecessors.

SIGNIFICANCE

Regardless of the personalities of the consulate officials in charge of implementing the Page law, the results were the same: The numbers of Chinese who immigrated to the United States decreased dramatically between the 1875 enactment of the law and the enactment of the Chinese Exclusion Act of 1882, which superseded it. Furthermore, the law's specific application to Chinese women ensured a large imbalance between numbers of male and female immigrants during the period under consideration. In the long run that imbalance negatively affected Asian American families who had settled in the United States. The barriers that the Page law helped to erect against immigrant Chinese women made strong nuclear family structures within the Asian American community an immigrant dream rather than a reality.

—*Thomas J. Edward Walker and Cynthia Gwynne Yaudes*

FURTHER READING

Cheng, Lucie, and Edna Bonacich. *Labor Immigration Under Capitalism*. Berkeley: University of California Press, 1984. Examines the development and intent of political movements among immigrants in the United States before World War II.

Foner, Philip, and Daniel Rosenberg. *Racism, Dissent, and Asian Americans from 1850 to the Present*. Westport, Conn.: Greenwood Press, 1993. A documentary history that traces the political and social segregation of immigrants. Indicates the existence of more than one view among people not of Asian descent on the position of Asians in the United States. Extensive historiographical essay, index.

Gordon, Charles, and Harry Rosenfield. *Immigration Law and Procedure*. Albany, N.Y.: Banks Publishers, 1959. An excellent history of immigration and immigration law. Covers the period from the 1830's to the 1950's, with special discussions of Asian immigrant experiences.

LeMay, Michael C., and Elliott Robert Barkan, eds. *U.S. Immigration and Naturalization Laws and Issues: A Documentary History*. Westport, Conn.: Greenwood Press, 1999. History of U.S. immigration laws supported by extensive extracts from documents.

Peffer, George Anthony. "Forbidden Families: Emigration Experience of Chinese Women Under the Page Law, 1875-1882." *Journal of American Ethnic History* 6 (Fall, 1986): 28-46. Solidly documented research article showing the relationship between the Page law and engendered immigration of Chinese during the first seven years of its existence.

_______. *If They Don't Bring Women Here: Chinese Female Immigration Before Exclusion*. Urbana: University of Illinois Press, 1999. Study of the special problems faced by female Chinese immigrants in the years leading up to the Chinese Exclusion Act of 1882.

Tung, William L. *The Chinese in America, 1820-1973*. Dobbs Ferry, N.Y.: Oceana, 1974. Provides chronological and bibliographical references on the changing status of Chinese in American society. Contains good primary source materials.

SEE ALSO: 1849: Chinese Begin Immigrating to California; July 28, 1868: Burlingame Treaty; May 9, 1882: Arthur Signs the Chinese Exclusion Act; Nov. 12, 1882: San Francisco's Chinese Six Companies Association Forms; 1892: America's "New" Immigration Era Begins; May 4, 1892: Anti-Japanese Yellow Peril Campaign Begins; May 10, 1895: Chinese Californians Form Native Sons of the Golden State.

March 9, 1875
MINOR V. HAPPERSETT

In this setback to the woman suffrage movement, the U.S. Supreme Court held that states could constitutionally forbid women to vote, despite their holding U.S. citizenship.

LOCALE: Washington, D.C.
CATEGORIES: Women's issues; laws, acts, and legal history

KEY FIGURES

Virginia Louisa Minor (1824-1894), suffragist who brought suit to establish woman's constitutional right to vote
Reese Happersett (fl. mid- to late nineteenth century), registrar who refused Virginia Minor permission to register to vote
Susan B. Anthony (1820-1906), American suffragist leader
Horace Bushnell (1802-1876), author of a book arguing against women's right to vote
Tennessee Celeste Claflin (1845-1923), author of a polemic in favor of women's right to vote and sister of Victoria Woodhull
Ralph Waldo Emerson (1803-1882), noted essayist who supported woman suffrage
Elizabeth Cady Stanton (1815-1902), suffragist leader
Victoria Woodhull (1838-1927), radical suffragist and member of the National Party

SUMMARY OF EVENT

Long before the concerted effort for woman suffrage developed during the nineteenth century, American women had exercised the right to vote. In January, 1648, Margaret Brent had petitioned the Maryland assembly for permission to vote in their proceedings, and the assembly agreed. The governor of Maryland vetoed the decision, and Brent lodged an official protest. In the same decade, in Rhode Island and New York, women participated in community affairs by voting. In 1776, in New Jersey, all references to gender were omitted from suffrage statutes. During the first fourteen years after the laws were passed, women did not vote, thinking that the laws referred only to men. By 1800, women were voting throughout New Jersey. However, a legislature made up entirely of white men voted in 1807 to change the New Jersey law to include only white male voters, with the strange argument that allowing women to vote produced a substantial amount of fraud.

During the first half of the nineteenth century, some U.S. women joined with the abolitionist movement in an attempt to blend their search for legal rights for themselves with rights for the slaves. At the time, these women were more concerned with obtaining rights to own property and to enter into contracts than with the right to vote. At the women's first convention in Seneca Falls, New York, in 1848, Elizabeth Cady Stanton did mention as part of the platform that women should have the right to vote, but this right did not become a paramount issue until after the Civil War (1861-1865). At that time, when the slaves were freed and all male citizens were given the right to vote, women were shocked to discover that in spite of all the work that they had done on behalf of the slaves, they themselves had been denied that right. The right to vote thus became the central issue to concerned women over the next seventy years.

Woman suffrage was an issue that divided the country along race, gender, religious, and political lines. Among the many men opposed to granting women the right to vote was Horace Bushnell, who wrote *Women's Suffrage; The Reform Against Nature* (1869). In that tract, he argued a traditional nineteenth century position that men and women lived in separate spheres, public and private. Men inhabited the public sphere, women, the private. If women entered into the public sphere, the moral nature of current life would be jeopardized. He asserted that it was a historic fact, extending back to biblical times, that women were unsuited to any role in the government of countries. Last, he argued that granting suffrage to women would have a negative effect upon married life. Because men were the accepted heads of households at that time, to grant women the right to vote might threaten this arrangement. Such thinking exemplified that of many men who opposed woman suffrage.

The noted nineteenth century essayist Ralph Waldo Emerson rejected such thinking. He believed that because all humans are fallible and biased about one issue or another, granting women the right to vote would only be correcting the biases. He believed that if one brought together all of the various opinions existing in the country, such a franchise would produce something better.

Two parties existed that women could join in their fight for suffrage. One, the American Party, remained a single-issue party. The other, the Nationals, opened itself to other issues, so as to attract wider membership. Among the people it attracted were the sisters Victoria

Woodhull and Tennessee Celeste Claflin. Woodhull advocated women's rights, in addition to free love, spiritualism, and faith healing, and argued before Congress that women already had the right to vote under the privileges and immunities clause of the Fourteenth Amendment to the Constitution. Claflin wrote a treatise in support of woman suffrage, *Constitutional Equality*. She argued that women and men should not exist in separate spheres, and that if it were feared that the entrance into politics would corrupt women, it was time that women entered into, discovered, and exposed what was so corrupting about politics. She also argued that the refusal of men to relinquish their claims to dominance over women was selfishness on their part.

In early 1872, Thomas Nast pilloried Victoria Woodhull in this cartoon by depicting her as a devil offering salvation through free love. (Library of Congress)

For a time, both parties published newspapers. In 1869, *The Revolution*, the newspaper of the Nationals, published a set of resolutions that stated, as Woodhull had declared before Congress, that the Constitution already conferred the right to vote upon women because of its privileges and immunities clause. Francis Minor, an attorney from St. Louis, Missouri, wrote the resolution. His wife, Virginia Louisa Minor, was president of the Missouri Woman Suffrage Association. When Virginia was turned away from the polls by registrar Reese Happersett in November, 1872, she and Francis, who was required to participate in any legal action his wife might bring, petitioned the courts of St. Louis for damages in the amount of ten thousand dollars.

While Minor's suit was making its way through the courts, other suffragists were challenging the law. In 1871 and 1872, at least 150 other women tried to vote in various states throughout the country. Among these was Susan B. Anthony, who headed a group of sixteen women in Rochester, New York, in first registering and then voting in the presidential election of 1872. The women did this knowing that they risked being fined up to three hundred dollars and imprisoned for up to three years. Anthony was not allowed to testify at her trial and was denied the right to a genuine decision by the jury when the judge directed the jury to return a guilty verdict. After the jury returned the verdict, the judge refused to commit Anthony to jail. She therefore lost the right she would have had to appeal her case to the U.S. Supreme Court.

The Supreme Court, however, did eventually hear the *Minor* case and passed down its ruling on March 9, 1875. However, it summarily rejected the couple's claims under the Fourteenth Amendment's privileges and immunities clause. The Court held that Virginia Minor, like all American women, was a citizen of the United States, but it dismissed her additional claim that citizenship conveyed upon her the right to vote. This right was not intended as part of the privileges and immunities clause in the Constitution, according to the Court's decision.

SIGNIFICANCE

The Supreme Court's ruling ignored the social factors that were at the root of arguments over whether women should have the vote. These factors, as expressed by Bushnell, Emerson, and Claflin, for example, continued to disturb the country after the *Minor* case was decided and until women achieved suffrage in 1920. The *Minor* case merely indicated to those who were determined to obtain woman suffrage how far they had to go before achieving that right.

—*Jennifer Eastman*

FURTHER READING

Agonito, Rosemary. "Ralph Waldo Emerson." In *History of Ideas on Woman: A Source Book*. New York: G. P. Putnam's Sons, 1977. Emerson, a firm suffragist, believed that the right to vote for women was an inevitable and positive change in society.

Baker, Jean H, ed. *Votes for Women: The Struggle for Suffrage Revisited*. Oxford, England: Oxford University Press, 2002. Scholarly history of the woman suffrage movement.

Bushnell, Horace. *Women's Suffrage; The Reform Against Nature*. New York: Charles Scribner, 1869. Opposes woman suffrage on the grounds that it would undermine women's natural and moral position in society, that is, the private sphere of domesticity.

Claflin, Tennessee C. *Constitutional Equality: A Right of Woman*. New York: Woodhull, Claflin, 1871. This early feminist tract expounded on woman's right to equality and to vote in a world where men and women would share the same life, if men would allow it.

Flexner, Eleanor. *Century of Struggle: The Woman's Rights Movement in the United States*. Cambridge, Mass.: Belknap Press of Harvard University Press, 1959. Comprehensive study of the women's movements of the nineteenth and early twentieth century, which places the struggle for woman suffrage in a historical context.

Frost-Knappman, Elizabeth, and Kathryn Cullen-DuPont. *Women's Suffrage in America: An Eyewitness History*. New York: Facts On File, 1992. Contains many primary sources concerning woman suffrage, including the *Minor* petition to the lower courts and the later opinion in the *Minor* case by the Supreme Court.

Goldstein, Leslie Friedman. *The Constitutional Rights of Women: Cases in Law and Social Change*. Rev. ed. Madison: University of Wisconsin Press, 1988. Includes little-known commentary on woman suffrage, as well as the Supreme Court opinion in the *Minor* case.

Lewis, Thomas T., and Richard L. Wilson, eds. *Encyclopedia of the U.S. Supreme Court*. 3 vols. Pasadena, Calif.: Salem Press, 2001. Comprehensive reference work on the Supreme Court that contains substantial discussions of *Minor v. Happersett* and many related subjects.

McFadden, Margaret, ed. *Women's Issues*. 3 vols. Pasadena, Calif.: Salem Press, 1997. Comprehensive reference work with numerous articles on Susan B. Anthony, woman suffrage, and related issues.

SEE ALSO: July 19-20, 1848: Seneca Falls Convention; May 10, 1866: Suffragists Protest the Fourteenth Amendment; May, 1869: Woman Suffrage Associations Begin Forming; Dec., 1869: Wyoming Gives Women the Vote; June 17-18, 1873: Anthony Is Tried for Voting; July 4, 1876: Declaration of the Rights of Women; Feb. 17-18, 1890: Women's Rights Associations Unite.

RELATED ARTICLES in *Great Lives from History: The Nineteenth Century, 1801-1900:* Susan B. Anthony; Elizabeth Cady Stanton; Lucy Stone; Victoria Woodhull.

September, 1875
THEOSOPHICAL SOCIETY IS FOUNDED

Reacting against the secularism that arose in the wake of Charles Darwin's theories about evolution, the Theosophical Society sought to unite numerous religious traditions and put its members into contact with higher, mystical truths.

LOCALE: New York, New York
CATEGORIES: Religion and theology; philosophy

KEY FIGURES

Helena Petrovna Blavatsky (1831-1891), Russian noble and occultist
Henry Steel Olcott (1832-1907), cofounder and first president of the Theosophical Society
William Quan Judge (1851-1896), cofounder of the Theosophical Society and later general secretary of its American section
Annie Besant (Annie Wood; 1847-1933), feminist author and secularist who converted to Theosophy
Jiddu Krishnamurti (1895-1986), influential teacher of Theosophy who later broke from the society to found his own philosophical school

SUMMARY OF EVENT

The rise of the Theosophical Society to a position of importance during the nineteenth century may be traced to several converging factors. First, the impact of the evolutionary theories of Charles Darwin left many people in Europe and the United States feeling that religious support for their ethical and metaphysical views had been undermined. Second, a hoax propagated by Margaretta, Kate, and Leah Fox in Hydesville, New York, in 1848 led to a vogue in spiritualism, messages from "the other world," and belief in hidden powers. Finally, there was the undeniable impact and inventiveness of a charismatic member of the minor Russian nobility, Helena Petrovna Blavatsky.

Madame Blavatsky, as she later came to be known, developed a belief in her own occult powers from a very early age. While she was on a trip to Cairo with the opera singer Agardi Metrovich, Metrovich was killed, and Blavatsky remained behind. She supported herself in Egypt by creating an occult society, the Société Spirite (spirit society), in 1871. In 1873, scandals involving accusations of fraud caused Blavatsky to emigrate from Egypt to New York City, where she once again gained recognition as a clairvoyant and medium.

In 1874, Blavatsky met a lawyer and author who believed deeply in occult phenomena, Henry Steel Olcott. Together, the two "chums," as they referred to themselves, established a joint residence known as the Lamasery. They began to attract other individuals with similar interests in spiritualism. Both in Cairo and in New York, Blavatsky had advanced her theory that communicating with the dead was not the highest purpose to which psychic ability could be dedicated. She began to claim that she was in spiritual contact with "Hidden or Ascended Masters." She originally asserted these beings were located in Egypt but later said they resided in the Himalayas and Tibet.

Among the most frequently mentioned of these so-called Hidden Masters were Koot Hoomi and El Morya, figures who, it was later claimed, had visited the earth in earlier incarnations as the Egyptian pharaoh Thutmose III, Abraham, Pythagoras, King Arthur, Sir Percivale, Saint Bernard of Clairvaux, Saint Francis of Assisi, Saint Thomas More, and other distinguished philosophical and religious leaders. The Hidden Masters were said to exist on a higher spiritual plane and to speak through psychic mediums, not merely to convey messages from departed relatives or to provide proof of an afterlife but to guide those still living "on this side" in their struggles to find a deeper truth about themselves and the universe.

The precise nature of the truth revealed by Blavatsky's Hidden Masters seemed to vary considerably according to the individual medium, the audience being addressed, and the period when the Masters' teaching was being manifested. Nevertheless, there was sufficient belief in Blavatsky's claims that, in September of 1875, the Theosophical Society was formed in her apartment in order to promote the study of psychic phenomena and the revelations of the Hidden Masters.

Almost from the beginning, the Theosophical Society attempted to serve two largely incompatible missions simultaneously. To some of its members, it was a scientific society, created to investigate claims of psychic experiences to determine if they were genuine. To other members, the legitimacy of occult phenomena was beyond question, and the society's purpose was not to challenge claims of extraordinary experiences but to promulgate them. As a result of these differences, during the late nineteenth century, various splinter groups began to split off from the Theosophical Society, creating a vast web of competing but related occult societies.

In 1879, the Theosophical Society launched a journal,

Annie Besant. (Library of Congress)

The Theosophist, which soon began generating considerable profit. In 1882, a new center for the society was established at Adyar, near Madras, India, which later became the society's international office. Additional branches (or "lodges," as they were called, in imitation of the Masonic model) were established throughout the world during the 1880's, and membership in the society quickly rose into the thousands. The rapid growth of the society, the isolation of its international office from the large urban centers of Europe and the United States, and the society's repeated pattern of attracting idiosyncratic but highly charismatic individuals to positions of leadership diluted any unity that the Theosophical Society's teachings could possibly have attained.

Struggles for leadership within the society among Olcott, William Quan Judge, and Annie Besant resulted in increasing acrimony and produced conflicting "revelations" from the Hidden Masters. These competing leaders adopted ever more complex rituals, which appealed to some members while exasperating others. A confusing amalgamation of overlapping societies developed. Accusations of pederasty and other deviant sexual practices on the part of several leaders of the society surfaced, and those leaders also undertook a series of seemingly bizarre new initiatives—such as the formation of the Liberal Catholic Church in 1915. All these developments alienated many of Theosophy's early supporters.

As these scandals continued, they were intensified by accusations that the very "spirit manifestations" on which the society was founded were little more than fraudulent displays of stage trickery. The society's membership soon began to wane. Nevertheless, the impact of the Theosophical Society continued to be felt in the many occult movements that it spawned and even in the phenomenon of New Age mysticism that arose in the late twentieth century.

SIGNIFICANCE

The Theosophical Society demonstrated the hunger for deeper meaning that numerous Americans and Europeans felt after attempting to relate their former beliefs to Darwinism, the Industrial Revolution, and the decline of "divine right" government—to name just a few of the many cultural upheavals of the nineteenth century. Theosophy suggested that hidden spiritual truths were still important and that these truths could be within reach of nearly every person. As a result, the Theosophical Society helped provide hope to generations of people who felt cut off from the moorings of earlier religious society.

Furthermore, nearly every occult and mystical movement that began in the twentieth century could ultimately trace its roots to Madame Blavatsky and the Theosophical Society. The reestablishment of the Rosicrucian Order, the teachings of George Ivanovitch Gurdjieff (1866-1949) and Peter D. Ouspensky (1878-1947), the Anthroposophy of Rudolph Steiner (1861-1925), the antiwar philosophy of Jiddu Krishnamurti, and the entire range of New Age mysticism are almost impossible to imagine without the foundations laid by Blavatsky, Olcott, and Judge in the Theosophical Society of the late nineteenth century.

—*Jeffrey L. Buller*

FURTHER READING

Buescher, John B. *The Other Side of Salvation: Spiritualism and the Nineteenth-Century Religious Experience*. Boston: Skinner House, 2004. Places the Theosophical movement and other spiritualist beliefs in the context of late Romantic movements involved with the abolition of slavery, women's rights, temperance, prison reform, and labor reform.

Caldwell, Daniel, ed. *The Esoteric World of Madame Blavatsky*. Wheaton, Ill.: Quest Books, 2001. Collection of reminiscences about Blavatsky and her circle; provides insight into contemporary views about the origins of the Theosophical Society.

Goodrick-Clarke, Nicholas, ed. *Helena Blavatsky*. Berkeley, Calif.: North Atlantic Books, 2003. General biography of Blavatsky with an extended section on Theosophy and the origins of the Theosophical Society.

Jinarajadasa, C., ed. *Golden Book of the Theosophical Society*. Whitefish, Mont.: Kessinger, 2003. The Theosophical Society's own account of its history from 1875 until 1925.

Washington, Peter. *Madame Blavatsky's Baboon*. New York: Schocken Books, 1993. The best place to begin a study of the Theosophical Society. Elaborately researched and clearly presented, this work connects Blavasky's movements with numerous other occult and philosophical movements of the nineteenth and twentieth centuries.

SEE ALSO: 1804: British and Foreign Bible Society Is Founded; Nov. 24, 1859: Darwin Publishes *On the Origin of Species*; 1870-1871: Watch Tower Bible and Tract Society Is Founded; 1871: Darwin Publishes *The Descent of Man*; Oct. 30, 1875: Eddy Establishes the Christian Science Movement.

RELATED ARTICLES in *Great Lives from History: The Nineteenth Century, 1801-1900:* Annie Besant; Charles Darwin.

October 30, 1875
EDDY ESTABLISHES THE CHRISTIAN SCIENCE MOVEMENT

In 1875, Mary Baker Eddy published the first edition of Science and Health, *a book stating her unique theology.* Science and Health *put forward a religious system that became the basis of the movement known as Christian Science.*

ALSO KNOWN AS: Church of Christ, Scientist
LOCALE: Lynn, Massachusetts
CATEGORY: Religion and theology

KEY FIGURES

Mary Baker Eddy (Mary Baker Glover or Mary Baker Patterson; 1821-1910), founder of the Christian Science movement

Phineas Parkhurst Quimby (1802-1866), American health practitioner

Julius Dresser (1838-1893), a leader of the New Thought school of mental healing

Edward Arens (fl. late nineteenth century), a follower of Eddy

SUMMARY OF EVENT

The Church of Christ, Scientist (commonly known as Christian Science) developed duirng the late 1870's, beginning as a religious movement before it became an official organization. The movement was established by the publication of *Science and Health* on October 30, 1875. The book, published by Mary Baker Glover (who would become Mary Baker Eddy when she married Asa Gilbert Eddy fourteen months later) laid out the principles of its author's religious system. In 1876, the Christian Scientist Association was founded; it was later chartered as the Church of Christ, Scientist, in 1879.

Eddy traced the movement's origins to 1866, when she experienced what was, by all accounts, a miraculous cure from a fall that had left her near death. While reading the Bible, she had discovered the true meaning of the Gospel and was suddenly restored to health. In the days following her recovery, she began an intense study of healing in the Bible and devoted herself to studying, writing, healing, and, finally, to organizing and leading a church.

Since childhood, Mary Baker Eddy had suffered from chronic invalidism and various physical complaints, and as an adult, she suffered many personal losses. She struggled to understand how a good and omnipotent God could allow suffering and pain in the world and reasoned that if God created matter, then God would be responsible for suffering, which she found to be an unacceptable conclusion. After her accident, she had a new understanding that the only reality is spiritual. God could not have created evil, because God is spirit, or divine mind, and God's Creation was therefore completely spiritual, not physical.

Eddy deduced that disease resulted from a false belief

in a material universe. Jesus had become like God and had been able to heal through the power, or mind, of God, because he had understood the nature of God. The true Gospel had been lost to the church over the years through error and misunderstanding, but all people could become like God, just as Jesus was like God, through a correct understanding. Eddy called this "rediscovery" of primitive Christianity, with its power to heal, Christian Science. *Science and Health* contained all the doctrine her followers would need to understand it.

In 1878, Eddy began leading services in Lynn, Massachusetts, and she gave sermons at the Baptist Tabernacle in Boston. She attracted a large following, and by 1879, the members of the Christian Scientist Association voted to form the Church of Christ, Scientist. Eddy was ordained pastor of the church in 1881 and moved to Boston.

Boston's Mother Church of Christian Science at the end of the nineteenth century. (Library of Congress)

That same year, she opened the Massachusetts Metaphysical College, where she taught faith healing. The success of Christian Science practitioners created numerous converts to the movement. In 1886, the National Christian Science Association (NCSA) was formed.

Hostile critics sought to discredit Eddy and her movement through public meetings and sensational newspaper attacks. Protestant clergy accused her of using apparently Christian language to create an entirely different religion. She was denounced by the medical community and rival mental healers, and many of her followers defected. The so-called Quimby controversy plagued the movement for years. A former student, Edward Arens, who had instigated a number of disastrous lawsuits on Eddy's behalf and later turned on her, together with the founder of New Thought, Julius Dresser, began a campaign in 1883 to establish Phineas Parkhurst Quimby as the founder of Christian Science. Quimby was a mental healer from Portland, Maine, who had successfully treated both Dresser and Eddy in 1862 and had become their mentor.

Dresser accused Eddy of stealing Quimby's ideas and plagiarizing his writings. Because Quimby had died in 1866 without publishing anything and his son refused to release the few writings in his possession, it was impossible for Eddy to prove her ideas were original. Although Eddy was influenced by Quimby, her Christian Science was primarily a religion, relying on spiritual power alone to heal. Quimbyism, by contrast, was a more general belief in mind over matter that might use religion, mesmerism, or any other form of mental influence to effect a physical cure.

In 1889, Eddy resigned as pastor of the Boston church in order to gain a firmer control over the movement. She formally disorganized the Church of Christ, Scientist, dissolved the National Christian Science Association, and closed the Massachusetts Metaphysical College. She focused on defining her doctrine more precisely and, in 1891, published a landmark fiftieth edition of *Science and Health*. Next, the church was formally reorganized, and the Mother Church, First Church of Christ, Scientist, in Boston was dedicated in 1895, the same year the *Manual of the Mother Church*, regulating all matters of worship and practice, was published.

In 1908, Eddy instructed the board of trustees of the Mother Church to launch a newspaper, the *Christian Science Monitor*. It became a leading newspaper in the United States. The Church of Christ, Scientist, had almost 100,000 members when Mary Baker Eddy died in 1910.

SIGNIFICANCE

Christian Science is one of several lasting religious movements, indigenous to the Americas, that continues to be both a respected religion and a politically powerful force with a significant international following. At a time when scientific materialism was seriously weakening Protestant Christianity, Christian Science answered the needs of many Christians who looked to the Scriptures for comfort and guidance but no longer accepted the literal interpretation of the Bible or believed in an angry God, predestination, or damnation. The movement revitalized the early Christian message of the power of faith to heal and contributed to the later rise of Protestant denominations, such as the Pentecostals, that stressed faith healing.

The use of faith healing, especially in normal obstetrics, provided an alternative to the inadequate and often harmful medical interventions of the late nineteenth century. On the other hand, the movement has caused intermittent public outcries and ongoing legal and ethical debates over health-related religious practices. It has become an accepted principle that Christian Scientists have the right to refuse medical treatment for themselves. The most prominent of the debates about religion and medicine, however, have involved the right of a parent to refuse medical treatment for a child based upon the parent's religious beliefs. Ensuring a child's right to medical care while respecting the parents' right to practice their religion continues to be a serious concern.

Christian Science owes its origins to the intellectual and organizational skills of a relatively self-educated woman in a male-dominated society. Although Eddy was not a feminist, she was certainly liberated, and she gave equal roles to men and women in the Church of Christ, Scientist. Her example has empowered women who sought a voice in religious matters. The *Christian Science Monitor*, founded in 1908 under the auspices of the Church of Christ, Scientist, as a protest against the sensationalism of the popular press, is perhaps the most significant accomplishment of the movement. It has become one of the most respected newspapers in the United States.

—*Edna B. Quinn*

FURTHER READING

Eddy, Mary Baker. *Science and Health: With Key to the Scriptures*. Boston: Writings of Mary Baker Eddy, 2000. Complete explanation of Christian Science by its founder and leader. Textbook for the study and practice of Christian Science.

Fraser, Caroline. *God's Perfect Child: Living and Dying in the Christian Science Church*. New York: Henry Holt, 1999. Critical view of the Christian Science movement by a former member.

Gill, Gillian. *Mary Baker Eddy*. Reading, Mass.: Perseus Books, 1998. Extensive, well-researched biography by a non-Christian Scientist who had access to archives of The Mother Church. Includes helpful chronology and detailed notes.

Gottschalk, Stephen. *The Emergence of Christian Science in American Religious Life*. Berkeley: University of California Press, 1973. First significant comparison of Christian Science to other American religious movements.

Henneman, Richard A. *Persistent Pilgrim: The Life of Mary Baker Eddy*. Etna, N.H.: Nebbadoon Press, 1997. The development of Christian Science, as well as Mary Baker Eddy's personal story, is described by a former editor of the *Christian Science Monitor*.

Peel, Robert. *Christian Science: Its Encounter with American Culture*. Garden City, N.Y.: Anchor Books, 1965.

_______. *Mary Baker Eddy*. 3 vols. New York: Holt, Rinehart and Winston, 1966, 1971, 1977. These two works represent the definitive history of the development of Christian Science and the most complete biography of its founder; written by a loyal Christian Science historian.

Twain, Mark. *Christian Science*. 1907. Reprint. New York: Oxford University Press, 1996. Facsimile reprint of Mark Twain's scathing attack on Mary Baker Eddy contains some humorous passages, but it is most interesting as a statement against Christian Science written at a moment when both Eddy and her church were in the ascendant.

SEE ALSO: Apr., 1808: Tenskwatawa Founds Prophetstown; Apr. 9, 1816: African Methodist Episcopal Church Is Founded; May 8, 1816: American Bible Society Is Founded; May, 1819: Unitarian Church Is Founded; c. 1826-1827: First Meetings of the Plymouth Brethren; Apr. 6, 1830: Smith Founds the Mormon Church; 1870-1871: Watch Tower Bible and Tract Society Is Founded; Sept., 1875: Theosophical Society Is Founded.

RELATED ARTICLE in *Great Lives from History: The Nineteenth Century, 1801-1900:* Mary Baker Eddy.

Late 1870's
POST-IMPRESSIONIST MOVEMENT BEGINS

Painting both during and after the Impressionist period in France, the post-Impressionists sought to create representations less focused on the ephemeral nature of perception than were the Impressionists. The movement formed a bridge between the early modernism of the Impressionists and the mature modernism of the twentieth century.

LOCALE: France; Tahiti
CATEGORY: Art

KEY FIGURES
Paul Cézanne (1839-1906), French painter
Paul Gauguin (1848-1903), French expatriate painter
Vincent van Gogh (1853-1890), Dutch painter
Henri de Toulouse-Lautrec (1864-1901), French artist
Georges Seurat (1859-1891), French painter

SUMMARY OF EVENT

Post-Impressionism was a movement in France that represented both an extension and a rejection of Impressionism. The term "post-Impressionism" was coined by English art critic Roger Fry to describe the work of such painters as Paul Cézanne, Paul Gauguin, Vincent van Gogh, Henri de Toulouse-Lautrec, and Georges Seurat. These painters began as Impressionists, but each abandoned that style to form his own personalized style.

Impressionism was itself a revolt against tradition and did not conform to conventional academic requirements, emphasizing instead the fleeting effect of light and color through the use of thick applications of paint, distinctive broad brushstrokes, and subject matter drawn directly from life. A basic principle of Impressionism was painting outdoors (*en plein air*), directly from nature, in order to portray subtle atmospheric changes. The Impressionists contended that a painting that sought to capture an outdoor scene should not be constructed in the studio. In order to capture fleeting atmospheric conditions, an artist had to work quickly, before the light changed. Thus, there was no time to mix colors carefully or to portray objects in great detail. This is what gives Impressionism its sense of spontaneity.

Post-Impressionism is a much more diverse movement than is Impressionism. Its style is therefore difficult to characterize. The post-Impressionists were disinterested in recording light and color phenomena faithfully. Thus, although post-Impressionism is characterized by bright color and sharply outlined edges, color is used to infuse a painting with emotion and expression, rather than to capture an effect observed in nature. The artists felt that art should have a deeper and more permanent significance than that of an "impression." Unlike the Impressionists, however, they were not a cohesive group working together and exhibiting together with a common philosophy or aesthetic. Rather, in an effort to reorganize nature, each post-Impressionist artist set out independently to create order from the haphazard form that existed, using whatever technique seemed right to him.

Cézanne is the earliest painter to be labeled post-Impressionist, and in fact he produced his first such works during the late 1870's, while Impressionism itself was still in full swing. He even exhibited several works now thought of as post-Impressionist at Impressionist exhibitions. Cézanne's revolutionary style of painting equated color and form. Each dab of paint assumed a definite and predetermined position in space. He was not interested in imitating the real world. Rather, he was interested in re-creating three-dimensional shapes and the spaces between them without interrupting the flatness of the canvas. To do so, he placed objects in front of one another, overlapped them, and used warm reds and yellows, which seemed to jump forward in a painting, in contrast to cold blues and greens, which receded.

Cézanne showed all sides of an object at once, making them seem to come out of the painting. Whether the subject of his painting was human or the assemblage of objects forming a still life, he ignored surface detail and reduced his subject matter to basic geometric shapes—cube, sphere, cylinder. This facet of his art was to form the basis of the movement called cubism during the early twentieth century. Cézanne painted landscapes as well as numerous still lifes. Although the objects in these still lifes seemed to be placed haphazardly, he would spend hours arranging and rearranging them so that the final effect would be exactly what he desired. His entire life was spent struggling to develop the technical competence to express on canvas what he experienced in nature. His struggle resulted in techniques so innovative that he has been called the founder of modern art.

Gauguin reacted differently against Impressionism and nineteenth century French realism. Like Cézanne, he felt that the two-dimensional quality of the canvas should be maintained and that painting should not be treated as if it were sculpture. Gauguin's own style, called *cloisonnisme*, first emerged in paintings from Brittany characterized by bright, flat color patterns and strong outlines. He wanted to express the world around him in a realistic and straightforward way, so he used bold shapes and vivid colors. His style was primitive, partly because he had no formal training.

Eventually, Gauguin traveled to Tahiti, and he painted representations of Tahitian women. The beauty of the South Sea Islanders made a huge impact on Gauguin, and he painted them repeatedly. His style remained the same, but his colors became more resonant and his design simpler. He freed art from some of its conventional limitations, rejecting the relatively new idea that art must portray something seen in the real world, often using color unnaturally to set an emotional tone and create an atmosphere or expressive effect.

Van Gogh began painting in the Impressionist manner of applying paint in small dashes but later painted in swirls and waves, applying the paint thickly to express his strong feelings and exaggerate his vibrant palette. His technique of often applying paint directly from tube onto canvas and then molding it with his brush (called *impasto*) became a hallmark of his work. Yellow was his favorite and most used color. It represented the sun, creation, and fields of wheat. The other colors most common to his palette (blue and purple) only served to intensify the effect of his yellow. His well-known sunflowers were painted almost entirely in yellow.

The term "expressionism" was coined to describe van Gogh's work. When he was painting in Arles in the south of France, he painted with violent passion and energy. His broad and strong brushstrokes vibrated energy and, at the same time, distorted reality by exaggerating what he considered essential while leaving surface detail vague. His canvases showed the torment of his repeated seizures, conveyed by writhing, twisting forms against turbulent skies. Many consider his mental instability to have been key to his emotional expressiveness.

Toulouse-Lautrec's art depicted the "night people" of Paris, particularly Montmartre: actors, circus performers, dancers, nightclub entertainers, pimps, and prostitutes. He chronicled the gaiety of Parisian night life and lived the life he pictured. Toulouse-Lautrec often por-

A famous example of Georges Seurat's use of pointillism is his 1886 painting Sunday Afternoon on the Island of La Grande Jatte.

trayed figures as silhouettes placed off-center and simplified almost to caricature. As a result of two accidents in his teens, the growth of Toulous-Lautrec's legs was stunted, so as he matured, his torso and head developed normally, but his legs did not. His dwarfish, grotesque appearance caused him to be excluded from conventional society and thrust into the world of his paintings.

Toulouse-Lautrec's work was devoid of emotion and was so detached that he appeared to be an outside observer of the life he portrayed. Obeying no taboos, he was unconcerned about the subject matter portrayed in his paintings and considered the more unattractive aspects of life fit subjects for art. His sharp eye captured the bohemian life with humor, energy, and color. His greatest art was in his lithographs. Using a few colors and simple outlines, his posters usually advertised entertainers in such innovative ways that they resembled candid snapshots. They were, in fact, the result of many carefully prepared sketches.

Seurat developed the method of painting called "pointillism," in which thousands of tiny dots of brilliant unmixed color were applied to the canvas side by side. Theoretically, the eye of the viewer would mix the colors, so that a person looking at an image of a flower composed of tiny blue and red dots would see a purple flower. His method was slow and meticulous, and he hoped to achieve greater accuracy of detail, as well as to indicate the vibrancy of colors in bright sunlight. Seurat is sometimes criticized for his impartiality and dryness, but he was a sharp observer of contemporary Parisian life. He sought to restore solidity and architectural order to Impressionist painting through a new and innovative technique.

Significance

Several twentieth century artistic movements were influenced by post-Impressionism, including Fauvism, led by Henri Matisse (1869-1954), a short-lived movement characterized by bold distortions of forms and exuberant color. The beginning of the Fauvist movement in the first decade of the twentieth century is often taken to mark the end of the post-Impressionist movement. Cubism followed Fauvism: Paint texture and color were abandoned by the cubists, as were emotionally charged subject matter and concern about the play of light on form, movement, and atmosphere.

The cubist palette was limited to black, brown, gray, and off-white, in rigid geometric composition. The aim was to appeal to the intellect by showing everyday objects as the mind rather than the eye perceived them—from all sides at once. Late cubism (1913-1920's) used brighter colors and more decorative effects with fewer and simpler forms. Cubism was a form of abstract art, or art which is not an accurate representation of form or object. The artist simplifies or exaggerates the object using various shapes, colors, or forms. Notable cubists were Pablo Picasso and Georges Braque.

As art developed through Fauvism and cubism to abstract expressionism and utterly nonrepresentational forms, artists came to be concerned more explicitly with the canvas and less explicitly with the world beyond it. The end result of this trend was to be found in the paintings of Jackson Pollock and Jasper Johns, which represented nothing other than paint on canvas. This concern with representing the medium itself had roots in the work of the post-Impressionists.

—Marcia J. Weiss

Further Reading

Athanassoglou-Kallmyer, Nina Maria. *Cézanne and Provence: The Painter in His Culture*. Chicago: University of Chicago Press, 2003. Examines how Cézanne's alliance with the region of Provence affected his innovative painting style and critical reputation. Illustrated with 120 color plates and halftones.

Cézanne and the Post-Impressionists. New York: McCall, 1970. Informative text and illustrations of the post-Impressionists.

Druick, Douglas W., et al. *Van Gogh and Gauguin: The Studio of the South*. Chicago: Thames and Hudson and Art Institute of Chicago, 2001. Catalog accompanying an exhibit of the two artists' work that was displayed at the Art Institute of Chicago and the Van Gogh Museum in 2001-2002.

Halliwell, Sarah, ed. *Who and When? Impressionism and Postimpressionism: Artists, Writers, and Composers*. London: Marshall Cavendish, 1998. Overview with illustrations written in simple narrative fashion.

Herbert, Robert L. *Seurat: Drawings and Paintings*. New Haven, Conn.: Yale University Press, 2001. Examines the full range of Seurat's work, concentrating on the personal and social meaning of his individual paintings and drawings.

Rewald, John. *Post-Impressionism: From Van Gogh to Gauguin*. Garden City, N.Y.: Doubleday, 1962. Classic text with illustrations on the history and influence of post-Impressionism.

Thomson, Belinda. *The Post-Impressionists*. Secaucus, N.J.: Chartwell Books, 1983. A detailed survey of the period, analyzing the artists, their rivalry, their subject matter, and major themes.

See also: 1824: Paris Salon of 1824; c. 1830-1870: Barbizon School of Landscape Painting Flourishes; Oct.-Dec., 1830: Delacroix Paints *Liberty Leading the People*; 1855: Courbet Establishes Realist Art Movement; May 15, 1863: Paris's Salon des Refusés Opens; Apr. 15, 1874: First Impressionist Exhibition; 1892-1895: Toulouse-Lautrec Paints *At the Moulin Rouge*; 1893: Munch Paints *The Scream*.

Related articles in *Great Lives from History: The Nineteenth Century, 1801-1900:* Paul Cézanne; Paul Gauguin; Vincent van Gogh; Henri de Toulouse-Lautrec; Georges Seurat.

1876
Canada's Indian Act

The Indian Act was the first comprehensive post-confederation law to establish Canadian policy toward Native Americans. That policy stipulated a goal of integrating Native Americans into Euro-Canadian society—a goal that met both with mixed success and with mixed reactions on the part of Native Canadians.

Also known as: Act to Amend and Consolidate the Laws Respecting Indians
Locale: Canada
Categories: Laws, acts, and legal history; indigenous people's rights; government and politics

Key Figures

Alexander Mackenzie (1822-1892), prime minister of Canada, 1873-1878
Sir John Alexander Macdonald (1815-1891), prime minister of Canada, 1867-1873, 1878-1891
Jeannette Lavelle (b. 1942), Ojibwa woman who fought the enfranchisement provision of the Indian Act
Jean Chrétien (b. 1934), minister of Indian Affairs and Northern Development during the administration of Prime Minister Pierre Trudeau

Summary of Event

The British North America Act of 1867, which created the Dominion of Canada, gave the federal government sole jurisdiction in all issues related to Native Canadians. This long-held British colonial policy had been established initially in recognition of the fact that indigenous peoples, when treated in an inconsistent and often unscrupulous manner, posed a military threat to British colonies. Even after Indians ceased to be an obstacle to British settlement, the policy was continued with the twin goals of the protection and eventual assimilation of the Native Canadians.

With the passage of the Act to Amend and Consolidate the Laws Respecting Indians, better known as the Indian Act of 1876, the government of Prime Minister Alexander Mackenzie continued the policies established during British colonial rule. As prime minister, Mackenzie's primary aim was nation building—to which Native Canadians, particularly those in the newly acquired prairies, presented an obstacle. With regard to the Indian Act, Mackenzie's predecessor and successor, Prime Minister Sir John Alexander Macdonald, was later quoted as saying, "the great aim of our legislation has been to do away with the tribal system and assimilate the Indian people in all respects with the other inhabitants of the Dominion." Consequently, Native Canadian policy under both Mackenzie and Macdonald placed less emphasis on protection and more on assimilation. Ironically, the goals worked at cross-purposes. Paternalistic efforts to protect indigenous peoples emphasized the distinctions between them and the Euro-Canadians, thereby discouraging assimilation. The Indian Act was amended nine times between 1914 and 1930. Nearly every change in the act placed greater restrictions on the activities of Native Canadians.

The Indian Act set out a series of reserved lands that were to be laboratories to test various techniques for training Native Canadians in the ways of the European settlers. The first reserves were established away from areas of white settlement in an effort to protect Indians from the unsavory elements of Euro-Canadian society. When it became clear that this policy hindered assimilation, new reserves were created near towns populated by whites, in the hopes that Native Canadians would learn from their Euro-Canadian neighbors.

Another element of the Indian Act provided for the establishment of elected band councils. Although these councils had little power, they were meant to supplant traditional native leadership. The act permitted the superintendent general for Indian Affairs or his agent to remove any elected councillor deemed unfit to serve for reasons of "dishonesty, intemperance, or immorality."

The native peoples of British Columbia were forbidden from engaging in potlatches or any other give-away feasts, in part because such ceremonies helped to perpetuate traditional leadership roles. This ban on ceremonies was quickly extended beyond the tribes of British Columbia and the northwestern coast to nearly all traditional religions and cultures. Native Canadians also were prohibited from consuming alcohol.

In order to protect tribal lands from being sold to non-native people, title to those lands was held by the Crown rather than by the tribes. Reserve lands were exempt from property and estate taxes, and income earned on reserves was exempted from taxation. Although these provisions protected Native Canadian property from seizure, they also hindered economic development on the reserves. Because Native Canadians were unable to mortgage their lands, it was often difficult for them to raise capital for development projects. Indian agents, who retained power to make nearly all economic decisions with regard to tribal lands, often resorted to harsh measures (such as withholding relief rations) in efforts to force adoption of Euro-Canadian beliefs and practices.

Although many of the provisions of the Indian Act were intended to ease Native Canadians into a Euro-Canadian lifestyle, others were purely racist. In British Columbia, for example, native peoples had been denied the treaty rights and land tenure provisions afforded native peoples in much of the rest of Canada. In order to prevent court action to secure those rights, the Indian Act was amended to prohibit fund-raising for the purposes of pursuing land claims.

DEFINING "INDIAN"

The Indian Act of 1876 enacted a specific and somewhat indiosyncratic definition of "Indian" for the purposes of Canadian law.

The term "Indian" means

First. Any male person of Indian blood reputed to belong to a particular band;

Secondly. Any child of such person;

Thirdly. Any woman who is or was lawfully married to such person:

(a) Provided that any illegitimate child, unless having shared with the consent of the band in the distribution moneys of such band for a period exceeding two years, may, at any time, be excluded from the membership thereof by the band, if such proceeding be sanctioned by the Superintendent-General:

(b) Provided that any Indian having for five years continuously resided in a foreign country shall with the sanction of the Superintendent-General, cease to be a member thereof and shall not be permitted to become again a member thereof, or of any other and, unless the consent of the band with the approval of the Superintendent-General or his agent, be first had and obtained; but this provision shall not apply to any professional man, mechanic, missionary, teacher or interpreter, while discharging his or her duty as such:

(c) Provided that any Indian woman marrying any other than an Indian or a non-treaty Indian shall cease to be an Indian in any respect within the meaning of this Act, except that she shall be entitled to share equally with the members of the band to which she formerly belonged, in the annual or semi-annual distribution of their annuities, interest moneys and rents; but this income may be commuted to her at any time at ten years' purchase with the consent of the band:

(d) Provided that any Indian woman marrying an Indian of any other band, or a non-treaty Indian shall cease to be a member of the band to which she formerly belonged and become a member of the band or irregular band of which her husband is a member:

(e) Provided also that no half-breed in Manitoba who has shared in the distribution of half-breed lands shall be accounted an Indian; and that no half-breed of a family (except the widow of an Indian, or a half-breed who has already been admitted into a treaty), shall, unless under very special circumstances, to be determined by the Superintendent-General or his agent, be accounted an Indian, or entitled to be admitted into any Indian treaty.

SIGNIFICANCE

The Indian Act was significantly revised in 1951 to eliminate much of the blatant discrimination resulting from previous amendments to the 1876 act. Some discrimination remained, however. One onerous aspect of the Indian Act that was retained codified the category "Indian" as a legal rather than a racial or cultural designation and gave the government the legal power to determine who qualified as an Indian. It also provided that a man could surrender Indian status for himself, his wife, and his children in exchange for Canadian citizenship and a plot of land. Very few Native Canadians chose to relinquish their Indian status voluntarily, however.

An Indian woman who married a non-Indian (either a man not of indigenous descent or a Native Canadian who had legally become a non-Indian) involuntarily surrendered her own Indian status and benefits, and her children were precluded from claiming Indian status. Non-Indian women who married Indians, however, became legal Indians themselves. This provision of the Indian Act was challenged in 1973 by Jeannette Lavelle, an Ojibwa from Manitoulin Island who had lost her Indian status through marriage. Lavelle based her case on Canada's Charter of Rights and Freedoms. Although Lavelle did not prevail in court, her case and others exposed Canada to condemnation by several international human rights organizations and led to the 1985 passage of Bill C-31, which restored to thousands of Native Canadian women and their children the legal Indian status they had lost through marriage to non-Indians.

The issue of Indian legal status divides Native Canadians as well. Although many acknowledge that maintaining a legal status distinct from that of other Canadians creates opportunities for discrimination, others believe that they have inherent aboriginal rights that must be recognized. Despite the flaws and failures of the Indian Act, there has been only one serious attempt to discard it. In 1969, Jean Chrétien, minister of the Department of Indian Affairs and Northern Development, proposed a repeal of the Indian Act. This initiative, which became known as the White Paper, proposed eliminating many of the legal distinctions between native and non-native Canadians and requiring the provinces to provide the same services to Native Canadians that they provide to other citizens. Fearing that the provinces would be even more likely to discriminate against Native Canadians and that the federal government would abandon its responsibilities for native welfare, many Indian groups fought the White Paper proposals until they were withdrawn in 1971.

—Pamela R. Stern

Further Reading

Dickason, Olive Patricia. *Canada's First Nations: A History of Founding Peoples from Earliest Times*. Norman: University of Oklahoma Press, 1992. Contains several lengthy discussions of the policies generated by the Indian Act.

Lawrence, Bonita. *"Real" Indians and Others: Mixed-Blood Urban Native Peoples and Indigenous Nationhood*. Lincoln: University of Nebraska Press, 2004. Detailed discussion of the Indian Act, its amendments and legacy, and the legal status of Native Canadians.

McMillan, Alan D. *Native Peoples and Cultures of Canada: An Anthropological Overview*. Vancouver, B.C.: Douglas & McIntyre, 1988. Chapter 12 discusses both the Indian Act and issues related to the status of Native Canadians.

Satzewich, Vic, and Terry Wotherspoon. *First Nations: Race, Class, and Gender Relations*. Scarborough, Ont.: Nelson Canada, 1993. Contains a thoughtful discussion of the impact of the Indian Act on native women in Canada.

Tennant, Paul. *Aboriginal Peoples and Politics: The Indian Land Question in British Columbia, 1849-1989*. Vancouver: University of British Columbia Press, 1990. A thorough discussion of the history of Native Canadian policy and relations between Native Canadians and whites in the province of British Columbia. Several sections deal specifically with the Indian Act.

Tobias, John L. "Protection, Civilization, Assimilation: An Outline History of Canada's Indian Policy." In *Sweet Promises: A Reader on Indian-White Relations in Canada*, edited by J. R. Miller. Toronto: University of Toronto Press, 1991. This article, reprinted from the *Western Canadian Journal of Anthropology*, provides a critical overview of legislation and policy making with regard to Native Canadians.

See also: Feb. 10, 1841: Upper and Lower Canada Unite; Mar. 23, 1858: Fraser River Gold Rush Begins; July 1, 1867: British North America Act; May 23, 1873: Canada Forms the North-West Mounted Police; Nov. 5, 1873-Oct. 9, 1878: Canada's Mackenzie Era; 1875: Supreme Court of Canada Is Established; Sept., 1878: Macdonald Returns as Canada's Prime Minister.

Related articles in *Great Lives from History: The Nineteenth Century, 1801-1900:* Sir John Alexander Macdonald; Alexander Mackenzie.

1876
SPANISH CONSTITUTION OF 1876

Spain's 1876 constitution created a stable political system that lasted for half a century, but it was based on a prearranged sharing of power by rival political parties through electoral fraud.

LOCALE: Spain
CATEGORY: Government and politics

KEY FIGURES

Alfonso XII (1857-1885), king of Spain, r. 1874-1885
Francisco Serrano y Domínguez (1810-1885), head of the provisional government in 1874
Antonio Cánovas del Castillo (1828-1897), leader of Spain's Liberal-Conservative Party
Arsenio Martínez de Campos (1834-1900), leader of military forces that proclaimed Alfonso XII king
Fernando Primo de Rivera (fl. mid-nineteenth century), Spanish military leader
Práxedes Mateo Sagasta (1825-1903), leader of the Fusionist Liberal Party
Manuel Ruíz Zorrilla (1834-1895), leader of the republican movement against Alfonso XII

SUMMARY OF EVENT

After the Spanish Revolution of 1868, the failed Spanish Republic, and the Second Carlist War over succession to the throne, Spaniards longed for order and stability. There was therefore widespread public support for the military coup that overthrew the republican government in January, 1874, and made General Francisco Serrano y Domínguez temporary chief of state, pending a decision on what form the government was to take.

Meanwhile, Serrano had to go north to fight the Carlists, who had risen against the Spanish Republic and continued to fight after the coup. The chief civilian leader in Madrid was Antonio Cánovas del Castillo, a leader of the old Conservative Party. A historian who understood many of Spain's problems, Cánovas wanted to keep the military out of politics and to force the Roman Catholic Church to be obedient to civil power. He believed that the military and the Church had been responsible for much of Spain's political turmoil since the insurrection of 1808. Both he and the army favored a restoration of a Bourbon monarchy, but Cánovas did not want the army to effect a restoration through a coup.

In December of 1874, a young officer, Arsenio Martínez de Campos, proclaimed for Alfonso XII, the son of the exiled Queen Isabella. Still fighting in the north, General Serrano asked the other army leaders to reject Martínez de Campos's coup, but they refused. The commander of the Madrid garrison, General Fernando Primo de Rivera, supported the coup and contributed to its success. Alfonso, who was then a seventeen-year-old cadet at the Royal College of Infantry and Cavalry at Sandhurst in England, arrived in Spain in January, 1875, and made a joyful entry into Madrid.

Because the army had no plans other than a restoration, and was still in the midst of war with the Carlists, Cánovas was able to keep power in the hands of civilians. Two years later, in February of 1876, Charles VII withdrew from Spain with ten thousand soldiers and supporters. With the support of the new Spanish king, Cánovas summoned a committee to draft a new constitution. The resulting Spanish constitution of 1876 would be so well designed that it would serve Spain until 1923—the longest period that any Spanish constitution had lasted.

Spain's 1876 constitution was a compromise between radical liberal documents, such as the constitution of 1812, and more conservative ones, such as the constitution of 1837. It provided for a parliamentary system of ministerial responsibility and limited monarchy, much like the British system. Suffrage was based on property ownership, and the legislature was to be bicameral. Some individual rights were guaranteed. Ardent republicans, however, were unwilling to accept this new government and continued to plot its overthrow from their headquarters in Paris. Manuel Ruíz Zorrilla, the leader of the exiled republicans, planned a revolution for 1878, but it failed, and its leaders were jailed.

Political stability was not maintained by the constitution but by Cánovas's "system," a pragmatic reliance on an outward show of constitutionality that manipulated the electoral process. Fearing a return of military coups by opposition parties and desiring no more radical political transitions, he provided for a peaceful turnover of ministries between his party, the conservative Liberal-Conservatives, and the liberal Fusionist Liberals of Práxedes Mateo Sagasta. It was agreed that Cánovas would govern for a few years, and then Sagasta would take his turn as prime minister.

All elections were rigged to provide this peaceful transition. At the base of Cánovas's plan was the cacique system. Caciques were rural political bosses who could deliver votes according to the dictates of the ministry in Madrid. Although the caciques held little sway in the towns, they had sufficient strength to control the elections. After the votes had been counted by local committees appointed by the government, results were left blank and district governors could fill in the totals as required. Even after Sagasta's ministry provided universal suffrage during the 1880's, Cánovas's system still worked to thwart the desires of a growing electorate, which included workers and peasants. Whatever their internal bickering, the Liberal-Conservatives and the Fusionist Liberals shared a common belief that Spain could be governed only by fraud. Thus, the very strength of Cánovas's system eventually weakened the status of the monarchy in Spain.

Cánovas was shrewd enough to keep the army from interfering with political life. His premise was that the army had no praetorian ambitions, but served simply as a force to restore order in times of anarchy and disorder. So long as civilian governments could provide order, there was no need for the army to intervene. Nevertheless, in order to maintain power, the government became increasingly dependent on the army to preserve order in the face of republican opposition and a growing response to the corruption.

The Roman Catholic Church, long interested in a political settlement favorable to itself, had supported the clerical Carlist movement. Cánovas pacified the clergy with a constitutional provision that provided for clerical salaries to be paid by the state. Since the clergy had lost their landed wealth during the period of liberal confiscations, this method of payment pleased them. Furthermore, members of the clergy were unlikely to oppose a government that supported them, and they were content to accept a provision of the constitution that provided limited toleration for other sects but retained Catholicism as the official religion of the state.

Significance

The forces of change, both reactionary and progressive, were neutralized for almost half a century by the Spanish constitution of 1876. Although it accomplished Cánovas's goal of providing stability, his system perverted the political system and created a monarchy that was insensitive and unresponsive to the majority of the Spanish people.

—*José M. Sánchez, updated by James A. Baer*

The youthful king Alfonso XII entering Madrid. (Francis R. Niglutsch)

FURTHER READING

Brenan, Gerald. *The Spanish Labyrinth: An Account of the Social and Political Background of the Civil War.* New York: Cambridge University Press, 1990. The first chapter of this study of forces leading to the Spanish Civil War of the 1930's deals with the Bourbon restoration and the impact of Cánovas del Castillo's system on Spanish politics.

Carr, Raymond. *Spain, 1808-1939.* Oxford, England: Clarendon Press, 1966. History of Spain from the insurrection of 1808 through the accession to power of Francisco Franco in 1939. A leading historian of Spain, Carr defends Cánovas's use of caciques, or political bosses, as a way to provide political stability.

Carr, Raymond, ed. *Spain: A History.* New York: Oxford University Press, 2000. Collection of essays that provide an excellent overview of the political climate in Spain before, during, and after Isabella's thirty-five year reign.

Flynn, M. K. *Ideology, Mobilization, and the Nation: The Rise of Irish, Basque, and Carlist Nationalist Movements in the Nineteenth and Early Twentieth Centuries.* New York: St. Martin's Press, 2000. Comparative study of Spanish and Irish nineteenth century nationalism that examines the rise of nationalism among Spain's Carlists.

Madariaga, Salvador de. *Spain: A Modern History.* New York: Frederick A. Praeger, 1958. Opinionated history of Spain that criticizes Cánovas's regime for returning the Roman Catholic Church and the army to political power.

Payne, Stanley G. *Politics and the Military in Modern Spain.* Stanford, Calif.: Stanford University Press, 1967. General survey of the military's role in Spanish politics that offers a good discussion of military participation in the events of the restoration and the constitution of 1876.

Smith, Rhea Marsh. *Spain: A Modern History.* Ann Arbor: University of Michigan Press, 1965. Comprehensive work on Spanish history with two chapters on the failure of the republic and the reign of Alfonso XII.

SEE ALSO: May 2, 1808: Dos de Mayo Insurrection in Spain; Sept. 29, 1833-1849: Carlist Wars Unsettle Spain; Sept. 30, 1868: Spanish Revolution of 1868.

1876-1877
SIOUX WAR

The Dakota, or Sioux, peoples, along with the Cheyenne, Arapaho, and other indigenous peoples of the northern Great Plains, rose up in a mass armed rebellion against the U.S. government, the last great mass armed stand by the Sioux peoples to remain free. In the end, the U.S. government would prevail and the American Indian tribes of the plains were faced with a new life forced upon them.

LOCALE: South Dakota; Wyoming; Montana

CATEGORIES: Wars, uprisings, and civil unrest; expansion and land acquisition; indigenous people's rights

KEY FIGURES

Crazy Horse (1842?-1877), Oglala Lakota warrior and leader

Sitting Bull (1831-1890), Lakota medicine man and chief

Alfred Terry (1827-1890), lawyer and U.S. Army officer

George A. Custer (1839-1876), U.S. cavalry officer

Ulysses S. Grant (1822-1885), eighteenth president of the United States

George Crook (1829-1890), U.S. Army officer

Nelson A. Miles (1839-1925), U.S. Army officer

SUMMARY OF EVENT

By the 1870's, the American Indian tribes of the northern Great Plains were keenly aware of the fate of the eastern tribes that had been forced by the U.S. government to leave their traditional lands for reservations during white settlement in the West. The Bureau of Indian Affairs, which had been the government agency established to protect the Indians, frequently violated agreements by failing both to deliver on promises of goods and to defend the interests of the tribes they were mandated to protect.

The peace between the plains tribes and the federal government had been precarious. Under the Fort Laramie Treaty (1851), white settlers were allowed safe travel across tribal lands in exchange for tolls and other considerations. Just three years into the agreement, the first of many conflagrations occurred when Lakotas killed a

U.S. troops deploying at the Battle of Wolf Mountain in January, 1877. (Library of Congress)

lame cow, thought to have been discarded by settlers. Troops who had been sent out to investigate the claims of the disgruntled settler were attacked. The U.S. Army responded with a punitive attack on the Lakotas, thus beginning a cycle of distrust, violence, hostility, and cultural misunderstandings that would last for generations.

During the early 1860's, Minnesota's four Dakota tribes, who had their lands confiscated, had been relocated to reservations in the West for waging war against settlers who violated treaties. As whites moved farther into the interior of the continent, they continued to encroach on Indian lands in violation of treaties.

Outraged by the construction of the Bozeman Trail, which traversed Lakota lands located between modern-day Omaha, Nebraska, and Montana—a blatant violation of the Treaty of Fort Laramie—Oglala Lakotas, led by Crazy Horse, attacked federal forces near Fort Phil Kearney in Wyoming in December of 1866. The ensuing conflicts led to many deaths, and the U.S. military had limited success in subduing the Lakota. Federal officials, whose will to fight had been depleted by years of fighting a civil war with the southern states, eventually capitulated, signing the Sioux Treaty of 1868 at Fort Laramie. Under the agreement, spearheaded by Lakota warrior Red Cloud and his fierce fights against U.S. troops during Red Cloud's War, 1866-1868, the Oglala Lakota agreed to give up their weapons and move to a reservation in western South Dakota. In exchange, the federal government would abandon the Bozeman Trail and provide food and supplies to the Lakota. The sporadic violence continued as more settlers moved West.

The discovery of gold in the Black Hills of the Dakota Territory in 1874, however, accelerated to a frenzy the trickle of whites crossing into Indian lands. Gold prospectors, who were determined to cross these lands, did not care if doing so would be illegal, especially if doing so also meant getting a good mining claim before others beat them to it.

Almost overnight, the Black Hills area was teeming with miners. The vast bison herds, which had provided the Sioux with food, clothing, and shelter, were suddenly being emaciated in the course of buffalo hunting. The bison not only served as a food source for the new arrivals but also were fast becoming major resources, as demand for leather and hides fueled a hunting spree that all but eliminated the herds. The bison, a long-time primary source of food for the native plains people, suddenly had become scarce. By 1876 more than twenty-five thousand whites resided in the Black Hills, competing with the Indians for the area's already limited resources.

In response to the continued territorial violations as well as the destruction of their primary source of food and clothing, tribes of the northern Great Plains rose up in rebellion. Led by Sitting Bull, a chief and spiritual leader who had long spurned the promises and gifts of whites, and Crazy Horse, a force estimated at thirty thousand gathered in 1875 to make a stand. Efforts by representatives of the U.S. government to regain control of the situation proved futile. In December of 1875, the secretary of the interior ordered all Indians to return to their reservations, or face repercussions. When the warning was not heeded, the U.S. Army was called in to force the Indians to comply. General George Crook sent several expeditions in early 1876, but with few results. A battle at Rosebud River against forces led by Crazy Horse seemed only to aggravate the situation.

A second expedition led by General Alfred Terry, assisted by Colonel George A. Custer, a West Point graduate and veteran of the U.S. Civil War, led U.S. troops into what is now eastern Montana to try forcing the tribes into submission. On June 25, 1876, a detachment of troops led by Custer attacked the Sioux at the Little Bighorn River. Sitting Bull's force easily overtook Custer and his soldiers, killing the entire detachment before reinforcements could arrive.

Emboldened by their victory over Custer, the Sioux and their allies attacked settlements throughout the northern Great Plains during the late summer and fall of 1876. As conditions deteriorated, white settlers became desperate. Local governments responded by offering bounties for Indians—captured dead or alive—who were found within local, non-Indian, jurisdictions. Miners and settlers in the Black Hills called upon the territorial governor and President Ulysses S. Grant for protection from the new threat. In response, General Crook established a camp at Bear Butte Creek, near Sturgis, which became known as Fort Meade. Colonel Nelson A. Miles led the Fifth Infantry in a relentless pursuit of Crazy Horse and his followers, wearing them down and making it difficult for them to rest or to obtain a regular supply of food.

In January of 1877, at Wolf Mountain in southern Montana, Crazy Horse led eight hundred men in a surprise attack against Miles and his troops. Facing howitzers disguised as wagons, Crazy Horse withdrew and, when counterattacked, retreated under the cover of a snowstorm. Unable to achieve victory, more and more of Crazy Horse's allies surrendered. After receiving a promise from General Crook that if he surrendered, his people would have a reservation of their own, Crazy Horse led some followers to Fort Robinson, Nebraska, in the spring of 1877, where he was killed under questionable circumstances two months later.

SIGNIFICANCE

Although a great victory for Sitting Bull and Crazy Horse, Custer's defeat increased the resolve of the United States. Many more treaties were signed at gunpoint, and the tribes were forced back on the reservations. The Black Hills were forcibly ceded by the tribes to the United States in February of 1877. Detachments of U.S. troops had flooded the Great Plains to find Sitting Bull and any followers who refused to live on the reservations. Sitting Bull eventually made his way to Canada, where U.S. forces would not follow. He surrendered in 1881.

Confrontations with the U.S. government would continue, most notably with the controversial Battle of Wounded Knee in 1890, but the Sioux War marks the last great mass armed stand by the Sioux people to remain a free people. In the end, the U.S. government would prevail and the American Indian tribes of the northern Great Plains would try to cope with their new lives. The resentment toward, and distrust of, the U.S. government continues.

—Donald C. Simmons, Jr.

FURTHER READING

Ambrose, Stephen E. *Crazy Horse and Custer: The Parallel Lives of Two American Warriors*. New York: Anchor Books, 1996. Ambrose, a historian who has written several popular biographies and military histories, examines the similarities between Crazy Horse and Custer.

Hyde, George E. *Red Cloud's Folk: A History of the Oglala Indians*. Norman: University of Oklahoma Press, 1957. The author does not address events after 1878. Detailed appendices, brief bibliography, illustrations, index.

Marshall, Joseph M., III. *The Journey of Crazy Horse: A Lakota History*. New York: Viking Books, 2004. A refreshing new perspective on Crazy Horse and the Lakota people, written from a Lakota perspective by a Lakota. Detailed bibliographical references, index.

Nylander, August. *Survival of a Noble Race*. Chamberlain, S.D.: St. Joseph's Indian School, 1991. The authors, twenty-six-year veteran civil servants of the Bureau of Indian Affairs, offer a perspective that adds much to the literature. The chapters "History of Indian Policy" and "A Chronology and Summary of Indian Affairs" are wonderful synopses. Index.

Sandoz, Mari. *These Were the Sioux*. New York: Hastings House, 1961. An interesting, albeit elementary, overview of Sioux social culture, with references to the effects of wars on soldiers. Illustrations by Amos Bad Heart Bull and Kills Two.

Utley, Robert M. *The Last Days of the Sioux Nation*. New Haven, Conn.: Yale University Press, 1963. The primary focus of this work is after 1877, and some statements are questionable, but the introductory chapters are worthy of review. Illustrations, bibliography, index.

Vestal, Stanley. *Sitting Bull: Champion of the Sioux*. Norman: University of Oklahoma Press, 1969. As explained in the introduction, the book claims to be the first biography of the "American Indian soldier." Detailed appendix, bibliographical essay, illustrations, index.

_______. *Warpath: The True Story of the Fighting Sioux Told in a Biography of Chief White Bull*. Lincoln: University of Nebraska Press, 1984. The autobiography of Joseph White Bull, chief of the Lakota, as told to the author. Detailed appendix, bibliography, illustrations, index.

SEE ALSO: Aug. 17, 1862-Dec. 28, 1863: Great Sioux War; Aug., 1863-Sept., 1866: Long Walk of the Navajos; Nov. 29, 1864: Sand Creek Massacre; June 13, 1866-Nov. 6, 1868: Red Cloud's War; Dec. 21, 1866: Fetterman Massacre; Nov. 27, 1868: Washita River Massacre; c. 1871-1883: Great American Buffalo Slaughter; June 27, 1874-June 2, 1875: Red River War; June 25, 1876: Battle of the Little Bighorn; June 15-Oct. 5, 1877: Nez Perce War; 1890: U.S. Census Bureau Announces Closing of the Frontier; Dec. 29, 1890: Wounded Knee Massacre.

RELATED ARTICLES in *Great Lives from History: The Nineteenth Century, 1801-1900:* Black Hawk; Crazy Horse; George A. Custer; Red Cloud; Sitting Bull.

May, 1876
BULGARIAN REVOLT AGAINST THE OTTOMAN EMPIRE

At a time when the Ottoman Empire was weakening, Bulgarian nationalists attempted a revolt that was ruthlessly suppressed but which nevertheless led to the establishment of an independent Bulgarian state in 1878, while contributing to national animosities that would help provoke the Balkan Wars in the early twentieth century.

LOCALE: Balkan Mountains, Bulgaria
CATEGORIES: Wars, uprisings, and civil unrest; government and politics

KEY FIGURES

Khristo Botev (1847-1876), Bulgarian poet and revolutionary
Vasil Levski (1837-1873),
Lyuben Stoychev Karavelov (1834-1879),
Georgi Sava Rakovski (1821-1867), and
Stefan Nikolov Stambolov (1854-1895), Bulgarian revolutionaries
Mahmud II (1785-1839), Ottoman sultan, 1808-1839

SUMMARY OF EVENT

The Turkish conquest of Bulgaria in 1396 resulted in nearly five hundred years of virtually complete Ottoman domination of Bulgaria. However, some elements of the Bulgarian population, through the activity of the Eastern Orthodox Church and traditions of village culture, managed to keep alive the cultural life of the country. By the late eighteenth century, Turkish power was seriously weakening, and a movement of national revival and autonomy was growing among the Bulgarians.

The Ottoman sultan's constant warfare had reduced the Turkish male population, as had disease and a low birthrate, at a time when improving economic and social opportunities were providing the Bulgarians with increasing trade and manufacturing possibilities. On the other hand, the proximity of Turkey to Bulgaria, and the presence in the Bulgarian countryside of former Janissaries, bandits, and other lawless mercenaries, had turned much of Bulgarian territory into a wasteland. It was also a scene of frequent warfare. The Russians and the Ottomans clashed on Bulgarian territory between 1806 and 1812 and again from 1828 to 1829.

The destruction of the Turkish Janissary corps, which had become a serious threat to Ottoman stability and military capability, was followed in 1826 by the creation of a modern army by Sultan Mahmud II. Supplies to equip and feed this new military force came largely from Bulgaria, and economic prosperity from the export of textiles, agricultural products, leather, and manufactured articles provided the material basis from which social change became possible.

Uprisings in Greece and Serbia during the first decades of the nineteenth century led to an atmosphere of change throughout the Ottoman Empire. Although the Bulgarians did not figure largely in these struggles, an unforeseen benefit from the Greek uprising was the removal of Greeks from positions of trust in the empire. This benefited Bulgarian merchants economically. It also removed Greek as the language of education and religion in Bulgaria, opening the door to the use of the vernacular in these spheres. The Bulgarians thus began to experience a national revival in economic matters, education, and the arts.

Schools offering instruction in the Bulgarian language and making it freely available to all were opened in various Bulgarian communities. There was a resurgence of activity in book and journal publication, the writing of poetry, religious and secular painting, music, wood-carving, and architecture. Reading rooms were opened, which not only made available literary offerings but also provided dramas, musical events, lectures, and other intellectual stimuli to a population newly awakened to a sense of their own national identity. Freed from the dominance of Greek in their cultural life, the Bulgarians began to formulate their own literary language, based on the dialect of eastern Bulgaria.

The Bulgarians also began to resist the domination of their church by Greek clergy. Public protests complained about the excesses of the Greek priests and a desire for a return to a Bulgarian national church. In 1870, the sultan extended recognition of a separate Bulgarian church headed by an exarch. Since the patriarchate refused to recognize this new church and even excommunicated many of its leaders, the creation of the exarchate precipitated a national crisis. The new Bulgarian Orthodox Church, however, soon became a focus in Bulgarian national life and was firmly allied with advances in education and enlightenment.

Although some Bulgarians had participated in political opposition to the Turks earlier in the century, for the most part Bulgaria was not heavily involved in the anti-Ottoman movements in the Balkans during the early years of the nineteenth century. There was some peasant unrest sporadically, but it was largely based on dissatisfaction with the system of taxation and land tenure. Such unorganized rebellions were easily put down by the Ottoman authorities. Within the Ottoman Empire itself, the 1840's and subsequent decades were a period of reform, during which the rights of non-Muslim religious groups became an important issue. In 1839, the Tanzimat reforms began working to change abuses in taxation and the treatment of national groups throughout the empire.

A more immediate cause of revolutionary activity was the aftermath of the Crimean War (1853-1856). Russia's defeat in that war meant that Bulgaria could not depend on Russian assistance for its internal problems. There were also conflicting interests between merchants and craftsmen who benefited from increased trade with the Ottomans and others who saw in the example of the Greeks and Serbs a possibility for greater autonomy. The young intelligentsia in particular were affected by liberal and national ideologies they had encountered in their studies abroad, particularly in some of the revolutionary circles within czarist Russia.

In 1862, a Bulgarian legion was formed in Belgrade with the aid of the Serbian government under the leadership of Georgi Sava Rakovski. The conspirators moved their operations to Romania a few years later after some disagreements with the Serbs over clashing territorial ambitions. After Rakovski's death from tuberculosis in 1867, the Bulgarian secret central committee, under the leadership of Lyuben Stoychev Karavelov and Vasil Levski, espoused the goal of fomenting a national uprising among the peasants.

A new organization, the Bulgarian Revolutionary Central Committee, was formed with the program of establishing a federation of autonomous Balkan nations to achieve liberation from Ottoman control by revolutionary means. Levski returned to Bulgaria to try to achieve this goal but was apprehended by the Ottomans and hanged in Sofia. His martyrdom made him a national hero to the Bulgarians. His work was continued outside of Bulgaria by Karavelov, the poet Khristo Botev, Stefan Nikolov Stambolov, and Georgi Benkovski.

When Serbia and Turkey went to war in 1876, many Bulgarians joined the Serbs against the Turks. The Bulgarian revolutionary leaders determined that this was the time to provoke an uprising in Bulgaria as well, with simultaneous outbreaks planned in the four revolutionary districts that they had set up. Although the uprising was planned for May, the Ottoman authorities learned of the conspiracy, which caused the revolt to break out sooner than anticipated. Fighting broke out in April in Koprivshtica but remained confined to the Balkan Mountain region.

This premature uprising was a failure in that it led to the deaths of a large number of Bulgarians and failed to instigate a general peasant uprising. Atrocities were committed on both sides, with mass killings of resident

The Balkans at the End of the Nineteenth Century

Turks followed by massacres of Bulgarians by Turkish forces. The atrocities perpetrated against the Bulgarians enlisted European sympathies to the cause of Bulgaria and strengthened the feeling of national consciousness among the Bulgarians themselves.

SIGNIFICANCE

The Ottoman atrocities also contributed indirectly to the expansion of Bulgaria's borders in the aftermath of Russia's victory in the Russo-Turkish War of 1877-1878. According to the provisions of the Treaty of San Stefano of March 3, 1878, negotiated between Russia and Turkey, Bulgaria was to get territory north and south of the Balkan Mountains, Thrace, and most of Macedonia. The great powers, as well as the other Balkan states, saw this greatly enlarged Bulgaria as a threat to the security of Europe, however, since it offered an opportunity for Russia to enlarge its sphere of influence in the Balkans. Thus, a new treaty, the Treaty of Berlin, was proposed and signed, under which a much smaller Bulgaria was created, Eastern Rumelia (south of the Balkan Mountains) was to be a semiautonomous province, and Thrace and Macedonia remained under Ottoman control. The provisions of this treaty caused much bitterness among Bulgarians, contributing to the national antagonisms that eventually led to the Balkan Wars of 1912-1913. After the Congress of Berlin, there were major alliance shifts among the great powers to effect a new equilibrium.

—*Gloria Fulton*

FURTHER READING

Clark, James Franklin. *The Pen and the Sword: Studies in Bulgarian History*. New York: Columbia University Press, 1988. Collection of essays on Bulgarian history that includes discussions of the Bulgarian national revival and its consequences.

Crampton, R. J. *A Short History of Modern Bulgaria*. New York: Cambridge University Press, 1987. Although focusing on events after the Treaty of Berlin, the first chapter of this book treats the important developments in Bulgaria that led up to the massacres of 1876.

Jelavich, Charles. *The Establishment of the Balkan National States, 1804-1920*. Seattle: University of Washington Press, 1977. Treats the historical development of the Balkan nations from ancient cultures, through nearly five hundred years of Turkish domination, and the national movements of the nineteenth and early twentieth centuries.

Karpat, Kemal H. *The Politicization of Islam: Reconstructing Identity, State, Faith, and Community in the Late Ottoman State*. New York: Oxford University Press, 2001. Study of the transformation of the Muslim world under the late nineteenth and early twentieth century Ottoman Empire, the period during which Bulgaria was forging its independence from the empire.

MacDermott, Mercia. *A History of Bulgaria, 1393-1885*. London: Allen & Unwin, 1962. Focuses on the years of Ottoman domination, the cultural revival, and the movements to liberate Bulgaria from the Turks.

Tzvetkov, Plamen. *A History of the Balkans: A Regional Overview from a Bulgarian Perspective*. San Francisco, Calif.: Edwin Mellen Press, 1993. Volume 1 covers Bulgaria through the Ottoman period, with detailed information on the revolutionary movement and the conspirators.

Yasamee, F. A. K. *Ottoman Diplomacy: Abdülhamid II and the Great Powers*. Istanbul: Isis Press, 1996. Study of the complicated foreign policy of Sultan Abdülhamid II, who came to power shortly after the Bulgarian Revolt was suppressed.

SEE ALSO: 1808-1826: Ottomans Suppress the Janissary Revolt; Sept. 24, 1829: Treaty of Adrianople; Oct. 4, 1853-Mar. 30, 1856: Crimean War; Oct. 17, 1854-Sept. 11, 1855: Siege of Sevastopol; Oct. 25, 1854: Battle of Balaklava; 1863-1913: Greece Unifies Under the Glücksburg Dynasty; May 6-Oct. 22, 1873: Three Emperors' League Is Formed; Apr. 24, 1877-Jan. 31, 1878: Third Russo-Turkish War; June 13-July 13, 1878: Congress of Berlin; 1894-1896: Ottomans Attempt to Exterminate Armenians.

RELATED ARTICLES in *Great Lives from History: The Nineteenth Century, 1801-1900:* Abdülhamid II; Benjamin Disraeli; William Edward Forster.

May, 1876
OTTO INVENTS A PRACTICAL INTERNAL COMBUSTION ENGINE

In his efforts to improve the efficiency of the Lenoir engine, Nikolaus August Otto built the first four-stroke piston cycle, internal combustion engine. As the prototype for all modern internal combustion engines, Otto's engine helped to revolutionize transportation.

LOCALE: Deutz, German Empire (now in Germany)
CATEGORIES: Inventions; science and technology

KEY FIGURES

Nikolaus August Otto (1832-1891), German engineer and inventor
Étienne Lenoir (1822-1900), Belgian-French inventor
Eugen Langen (1833-1895), German technician and businessman
Alphonse Beau de Rochas (1815-1893), French engineer and inventor
Gottlieb Daimler (1834-1900), German engineer and inventor
Wilhelm Maybach (1846-1929), German engineer, automobile builder, and industrialist
Carl Benz (1844-1929), German mechanical engineer and inventor
William Crossley (1844-1911), British car manufacturer
Francis Crossley (1839-1897), British car manufacturer

SUMMARY OF EVENT

While a young man, Nikolaus August Otto developed a keen interest in technology and mechanical objects. After dropping out of high school at the age of sixteen, he became a traveling salesman. During one of his trips, he heard about an internal combustion engine that had been developed by Étienne Lenoir in 1860. It was a two-stroke engine that drew in a mixture of fuel and air during the first stroke. The mixture was ignited by a low-tension electric ignition, and it expanded during the second stroke, impelling the pistons. The Lenoir engine was not very efficient and was limited to relatively small sizes, because it had to be cooled by a water jacket placed around the cylinder.

Otto attempted to improve the Lenoir engine using a carburetor that he had invented. He then conducted several experiments with a four-stroke engine, but his initial attempts failed. In 1861, he filed for a patent for his own two-cycle gasoline engine. In 1864, Otto was joined in his engine-building efforts by German industrialist Eugen Langen. They became partners and formed the first engine manufacturing company in the world, N. A. Otto and Company, in Cologne, Germany. Between 1866 and 1876, the company manufactured a free-piston, atmospheric, two-cycle engine that was much more efficient than the Lenoir engine. The engine's piston movement was independent of the main shaft. Its fuel mixture was ignited with an open flame in the combustion chamber. This flame-ignition system would be used by a number of engine manufacturers until around 1900.

Rather than generating power from the gaseous fuel explosion itself, the operational cycle of the Otto-Langen engine developed its power from atmospheric pressure. Production engines never exceeded three horsepower. A two-horsepower engine weighed almost four thousand pounds and stood about 10.5 feet tall. Competing against fourteen other gas engines, N. A. Otto and Company was awarded a gold medal for its engine at the World's Fair in Paris in 1867. Less than five thousand Otto-Langen engines were manufactured. Almost half of those were built by a British company owned by William and Francis Crossley. The Otto-Langen engine was not yet a reasonable alternative to the steam engine, because it was much noisier and could generate only a few horsepower. It was an important stepping-stone, however, toward the development of a four-stroke engine.

In 1869, N. A. Otto and Company built a new factory, the Gasmotorenfabrik (fuel-powered engine factory), in Deutz, Germany. Two prominent German engineers, Gottlieb Daimler and Wilhelm Maybach, joined N. A. Otto and Company in 1872. With their assistance and returning to some of the ideas that he had experimented with in 1861, Otto built the first practical alternative to the steam engine in May, 1876. It was a four-stroke piston cycle, internal combustion engine.

Otto's engine carried out four piston strokes in one cycle. During the first stroke, an intake valve opened, the piston moved outward in the cylinder, and the pressure inside the cylinder dropped. The lowered pressure caused a fuel mixture of air and vaporized gasoline to be sucked into the cylinder. When the cylinder reached its maximum volume, the intake valve closed and the pressure increased. In the second stroke, the piston moved inward. This inward motion of the piston in the cylinder compressed the gasoline-air mixture, which in turn raised the temperature of the mixture. Since the compression stroke occurred very quickly, only a small amount of the energy was transferred to the environment.

Near the end of the compression stroke, the fuel mixture was ignited and the power stroke initiated. During this third stroke, the ignited gas expanded rapidly, increasing the pressure against the piston and driving it outward to produce mechanical work. This process again occurred rapidly, so little energy was lost to the environment. At the end of the power stroke, the exhaust valve was opened. The hot exhaust gases were expelled through the exhaust valve during the final stroke, the exhaust stroke. The piston moved inward in the cylinder and the temperature and pressure decreased. The cycle then started over again.

The Otto engine was much more efficient than the Lenoir engine and could be made in much larger sizes. The four-stroke piston cycle became known as the Otto cycle. It became the prototype used by modern internal combustion engines. The efficiency of an engine may be measured as the net work produced during a cycle divided by the heat that is absorbed during ignition. For a typical compression ratio of eight to one, the theoretical maximum efficiency achievable is 56 percent. In practice, as a result of friction, conductive heat loss, and the incomplete combustion of the fuel, efficiencies are about 20-30 percent. In order to control the speed of the engine, Otto and his colleagues tried various ways to regulate the action of the intake and exhaust valves, as well as a variety of methods for regulating the gas-air ratio.

Otto was granted a patent for his four-stroke engine in 1877. The English licensees for manufacturing N. A. Otto and Company engines were the Crossleys. They built many thousands of Otto engines, and they sold more than thirty thousand of them between 1876 and 1886.

Otto's patent for the Otto engine was revoked in 1886, when it was discovered that French inventor Alphonse Beau de Rochas had described the four-cycle principle in 1861 in a rather obscure, privately published pamphlet. From all available evidence, Otto developed his engine independently of the work done by Beau de Rochas. Nevertheless, he was left without a defendable patent. Many manufacturers began building engines based on the Otto cycle.

Carl Benz established the first practical automobile manufacturing company in 1885 and used the Otto engine design in his automobiles. Daimler and Maybach, who left N. A. Otto and Company in 1882, formed their own company. Daimler used the Otto engine to build the first gas-engine motorcycle in 1885. In 1890, Maybach used the Otto engine design to manufacture the first four-cylinder internal combustion engine. With the Otto cycle as a model, Rudolf Diesel developed the diesel engine in 1893. It was an internal combustion engine that used high compression ignition instead of flame or electric ignition.

SIGNIFICANCE

Otto's four-stroke engine provided the first practical alternative to the steam engine. Since steam engines were too expensive and not well suited for portable or small applications, the Otto engine marked the beginning of a new era of industrial development and laid the foundation for the manufacture of modern engines. By 1886, more than thirty thousand Otto engines had been sold. By 1890, the Otto internal combustion engine had been developed to the point where it was suitable for small fabrications and powerful enough for most portable, remote operations. As a result, it was universally adopted for the production of petroleum-fueled automobiles. The diesel engine developed in 1893 is an internal combustion engine that resulted from Otto's design. By 1900, internal combustion engines were beginning to replace steam engines for electric generation and were being used in all but the largest installations by 1915.

Modern internal combustion engines are the most commonly used engines for mobile propulsion systems. A wide variety of internal combustion engines has been developed for a variety of applications. These include reciprocating engines, such as the two-stroke, four-stroke, and diesel engines, as well as rotary engines, such as the Wankel engine. The gas turbine, jet engine, ramjet engine, and rocket engine, meanwhile, are internal combustion engines in which combustion occurs continuously. They are all patterned after Otto's invention. Internal combustion engines are used in almost all automobiles and motorcycles, many boats, and a wide variety of aircraft and locomotives. In jet aircraft and large ships, they occur mostly in the form of gas turbines. They are also used for electric generators and in a variety of industrial applications.

—*Alvin K. Benson*

FURTHER READING

Baierlein, Ralph. *Thermal Physics*. Cambridge, England: Cambridge University Press, 1999. Explains the basic thermodynamic principles associated with the operation of Otto's internal combustion engine.

Lumley, John L. *Engines: An Introduction*. Cambridge, England: Cambridge University Press, 1999. Describes the operation of a variety of engines, including the four-stroke engine.

Pulkrabek, Willard W. *Engineering Fundamentals of the Internal Combustion Engine*. Upper Saddle River,

N.J.: Pearson/Prentice Hall, 2004. Discusses the history, operating principles, and applications of the internal combustion engine.

Schroeder, Daniel V. *An Introduction to Thermal Physics*. New York: Addison Wesley Longman, 2000. Reviews Otto's development of the practical internal combustion engine, the components of the Otto cycle, and the efficiency of the Otto engine.

Sturge, M. D. *Statistical and Thermal Physics: Fundamentals and Applications*. Natick, Mass.: A K Peters, 2003. Sturge reviews some of the important history of the internal combustion engine, including the detailed operation and practical limitations of the Otto cycle.

See also: Mar. 24, 1802: Trevithick Patents the High-Pressure Steam Engine; Sept. 20, 1811: Krupp Works Open at Essen; 1850: First U.S. Petroleum Refinery Is Built; Aug. 27, 1859: Commercial Oil Drilling Begins; 1860: Lenoir Patents the Internal Combustion Engine; Jan. 29, 1886: Benz Patents the First Practical Automobile; Dec. 7, 1888: Dunlop Patents the Pneumatic Tire; Feb., 1892: Diesel Patents the Diesel Engine.

Related articles in *Great Lives from History: The Nineteenth Century, 1801-1900:* Carl Benz; Gottlieb Daimler; Rudolf Diesel; Étienne Lenoir; Nikolaus August Otto.

May 10-November 10, 1876
Philadelphia Hosts the Centennial Exposition

The United States held its first world's fair to celebrate the one-hundredth anniversary of the nation's independence from Great Britain. The exposition focused on industry, which had been a new strength for the United States. It also signaled America's entry into the world of international trade and diplomacy by showing that it could compete with and often surpass other nations in a post-Industrial Revolution world.

Also known as: Centennial Exhibition; International Exhibition of Arts, Manufactures, and Products of the Soil and Mines

Locale: Philadelphia, Pennsylvania

Categories: Science and technology; trade and commerce; organizations and institutions

Key Figures

Hermann J. Schwarzmann (1846-1891), German architect, chief architect of the Centennial Exposition

Joseph R. Hawley (1826-1905), politician, president of the Centennial Commission

Sir Alfred T. Goshorn (1833-1902), businessman, director-general of the Centennial Commission

John Welsh (1805-1886), merchant and president of the exposition's board of finance

Summary of Event

The United States held its first international exposition in 1876 to celebrate the one-hundredth anniversary of the nation's independence. The Centennial Exposition, which ran from May 10 to November 10 in Fairmount Park, Philadelphia, had more than nine million visitors and introduced many new inventions, setting the stage for the rise of the United States to international industrial predominance.

Plans for the event began in 1871, when the U.S. Congress authorized an international exposition, or world's fair, to celebrate the centennial; Congress, however, did not appropriate funds for the event. A centennial commission, also created by Congress, chose Philadelphia as the fair site. The city of Philadelphia provided $50,000, while Congressman D. J. Morrell of Pennsylvania, who had pushed through the original legislation, helped create the centennial board of finance to sell up to $10 million in stocks.

The fair took enormous planning. Joseph R. Hawley served as the president of the centennial commission, Sir Alfred T. Goshorn served as director-general, John Welsh led the board of finance, and German-born architect Hermann J. Schwarzmann became the chief architect. Welsh and his team managed to sell only $2.5 million in stocks, but they did persuade the city of Philadelphia to contribute $1.5 million and Congress to loan the commission $1.5 million.

Schwarzmann, who had been instrumental in designing Philadelphia's Fairmount Park, designed the fair's layout. Unlike previous expositions, which had one main building, the Centennial Exposition used a new arrangement of several large buildings surrounded by smaller pavilions. Schwarzmann also designed the two permanent buildings that would remain after 1876—Memorial Hall and Horticulture Hall.

Machinery Hall formed the exposition's focal point and covered thirteen acres. It showcased the wonders of the American Industrial Revolution: electric lights and elevators powered by the 1,400 horsepower Corliss steam engine, a prototype slice of cable for the Brooklyn Bridge, the first telephone and typewriter, locomotives, printing presses, mining equipment, and much more. U.S. exhibits filled 80 percent of Machinery Hall and overwhelmed visitors. The other major buildings included the main building, which showcased manufactures, Memorial Hall for the fine arts, Agricultural Hall, and Horticultural Hall. All exhibitors were classified into one of seven departments: Mining & Metallurgy, Manufactures, Education and Science, Art, Machinery, Agriculture, or Horticulture. Each classification was further subdivided and classified, and even may have been a model for the Dewey decimal system.

The fair area was laid out roughly in a triangle with the West End Railway running around the edge, allowing visitors to view the grounds. There were seventeen state buildings, nine foreign government buildings, and many restaurants, food stands, and other small kiosks. Visitors could also ride the first monorail, the Saddleback Railroad, which connected Horticultural Hall with Agricultural Hall. The grounds also had an internal telegraph system.

When the exposition opened on May 10, 1876, building exteriors were finished, but some of the interiors lagged behind schedule. The exposition's defining moment came on opening day in Machinery Hall. The Brazilian emperor, the only foreign head of state in attendance, turned handles that set into motion a giant Corliss engine standing seventy feet high. American inventor George Corliss had built the engine specifically for this exposition. The engine, twenty-three miles of shafting, and forty miles of belting turned on all the machinery in the hall at once. Machinery Hall held engines, boilers, printing presses, forges, hoists, machine tools, steam fire engines, internal combustion engines, mechanical refrigeration, and dynamo-electric machinery. American industry had awoken with its own revolution and was ready to challenge the world.

The other buildings housed many wonders as well. The Moorish-style Horticultural Hall was a grand Victorian edifice that housed the largest hothouse conservatory in the world. The main building held exhibits of furniture, ceramics, glassware, silver, textiles, clocks, musical instruments, tools, vehicles, and scientific appa-

Opening of Philadelphia's Centennial Exposition. (C. A. Nichols & Company)

ratus. The U.S. Government Building held exhibits from the Smithsonian Institution, the War Department, the Navy Department, the Coast Survey, and the Light House Board. Many of the exhibits in this building would find their way to permanent exhibition in Washington, D.C., and provide a firm foundation for a national museum.

A unique building at the exposition was the Women's Pavilion. A women's centennial executive committee was established to campaign and raise funds for a building devoted to items designed and made by women and to items of special interest to women. The Centennial Exposition was the first fair that included the products of enterprising women. The pavilion was filled with "the product of her own thought and labor." Also, women's rights activists and organizations distributed literature that demanded, among other things, women's participation on juries, no taxation of women without representation, and the removal of the word "male" in state constitutions.

Outside the exposition grounds an unofficial midway, dubbed "Centennial City," developed with beer halls, cheap hotels, and sideshows. One show presented the Wild Men of Borneo, and another re-created the 1870 German siege of Paris. Midways, and particularly displays of "primitives," became a mainstay of expositions after 1893.

The Centennial Exposition broke almost all previous world's fair attendance records. It had the largest number of visitors, the most paid admissions, and the largest single-day attendance. The board of finance had a $2 million surplus before repaying the government loan. The stage had been set for several international expositions that would follow in the United States.

SIGNIFICANCE

The 1876 Centennial Exposition had a great impact at home and abroad. The United States had been a country still recovering from its devastating Civil War (1861-1865) and had been disturbed anew by the scandals of the Grant administration. The exposition gave Americans a sense of pride in their progress and confidence in a strong future based on their substantial industrial power.

In part because of the successful world's fair, the United States sought increased global standing as an internationally important industrial power. The exposition succeeded in astonishing foreign visitors with a show of American industrial ingenuity and productivity. The United States could now compete industrially and economically with the major European powers. Reports in London newspapers noted that, in many cases, the economic success of American industry began to surpass that of British industry. In large part, the American foreign trade balance, which changed dramatically in favor of the United States from 1875 to 1877, can be attributed to the fair.

After 1876, the United States was on its way to earning an international reputation as a land of innovation. The telephone, electrical systems, vast engines, and other items remained powerful images of American innovativeness long after the end of the exposition, as the United States showed that it had moved from its image as an agrarian nation to a nation of inventors and industrialists on a par with the rest of the industrialized world.

—*Linda Eikmeier Endersby*

FURTHER READING

Findling, John E., ed. *Historical Dictionary of World's Fairs and Expositions, 1851-1988*. Westport, Conn.: Greenwood Press, 1990. A good synopsis of the 1876 fair as well as synopses on numerous other fairs in the United States and around the world.

Giberti, Bruno. *Designing the Centennial: A History of the 1876 International Exhibition in Philadelphia*. Lexington: University Press of Kentucky, 2002. Detailed analysis of the planning and design of the 1876 exposition.

Maass, John. *The Glorious Enterprise: The Centennial Exhibition of 1876 and H. J. Schwarzmann, Architect-in-Chief*. Watkins Glen, N.Y.: American Life Foundation, 1973. Describes the exposition and Schwarzmann's career. Contains numerous plates and engravings. Good examples of European views of the United States and the exposition.

Post, Robert C., ed. *1876: A Centennial Exhibition: A Treatise Upon Selected Aspects of the Great International Exhibition Held in Philadelphia on the Occasion of Our Nation's One-Hundredth Birthday, with Some Reference to Another Exhibition Held in Washington Commemorating the Epic Event, and Called 1876*. Washington, D.C.: Smithsonian Institution, 1976. A detailed description of some of the buildings and exhibits at the 1876 fair.

Rydell, Robert W. *All the World's a Fair: Visions of Empire at American International Expositions, 1876-1916*. Chicago: University of Chicago Press, 1984. An in-depth analysis of the 1876 and other American-based world's fairs, with a focus on the connections between the fairs and American imperialism.

Rydell, Robert W., John E. Findling, and Kimberly D.

Pelle. *Fair America: World's Fairs in the United States*. Washington, D.C.: Smithsonian Institution Press, 2000. A brief, readable analysis of all the international fairs in the United States. Provides a rich context for the 1876 fair.

SEE ALSO: May 1, 1851-Oct. 15, 1851: London Hosts the First World's Fair; June 23, 1868: Sholes Patents a Practical Typewriter; Apr. 10, 1871: Barnum Creates the First Modern American Circus; June 25, 1876: Bell Demonstrates the Telephone; Oct. 28, 1886: Statue of Liberty Is Dedicated; May 1-Oct. 30, 1893: Chicago World's Fair.

RELATED ARTICLES in *Great Lives from History: The Nineteenth Century, 1801-1900:* P. T. Barnum; Alexander Graham Bell; Melvil Dewey.

June 25, 1876
BATTLE OF THE LITTLE BIGHORN

The end of the Sioux wars marked the destruction of traditional Sioux lifeways.

ALSO KNOWN AS: Custer's Last Stand
LOCALE: Southeastern Montana
CATEGORY: Wars, uprisings, and civil unrest

KEY FIGURES

George A. Custer (1839-1876), commander of the Seventh Cavalry at the Little Bighorn
Sitting Bull (c. 1831-1890),
Crazy Horse (c. 1842-1877), and
Gall (c. 1840-1894), Sioux leaders at Little Bighorn
Frederick W. Benteen (1834-1898), commander of a cavalry force at Little Bighorn
George Crook (1829-1890), commander of troops marching from Fort Fetterman
John Gibbon (1827-1896), commander of troops marching from Fort Ellis
Marcus A. Reno (1835-1889), commander of a force at Little Bighorn
Joseph J. Reynolds (1822-1899), commander of attack at Powder River
Alfred H. Terry (1827-1890), commander of troops marching from Fort Abraham Lincoln

SUMMARY OF EVENT

In 1875, the Sioux, or Lakota, people—a confederation of seven Native American tribes—had many grievances against the United States. Conditions on their reservations were deplorable, chiefly because of maladministration by the Bureau of Indian Affairs. Supplies promised to the Sioux by treaty were inadequate, consisting chiefly of shoddy blankets and food unfit for human consumption. This situation caused many Native Americans to leave their reservations, which resulted in confrontations with miners, cattlemen, and settlers.

The gold rush that followed the discovery of gold in the Black Hills in 1874 goaded the Sioux into rebellion. The first prospectors who entered the hills, which the Sioux regarded as a holy land, had been evicted but were determined to return. When U.S. general William T. Sherman ordered Lieutenant Colonel George A. Custer to lead an expedition into the Black Hills in 1874 and report on conditions there, a considerable number of gold seekers accompanied Custer's men. The Indian Office tried to purchase Sioux lands and open hunting rights along the Platte River. When negotiations broke down, the federal government opened the area to all miners willing to enter at their own risk.

By 1875, the Black Hills were being overrun by prospectors. Knowing that many young warriors who were eager to fight were leaving their reservations, officials from the Department of the Interior ordered all Sioux to return to their reservations by January 31, 1876, despite prior treaties that permitted the Sioux to hunt on the northern plains. The major Sioux leaders Sitting Bull (who was a Hunkpapa), Crazy Horse (an Oglala), and Gall (a Hunkpapa) ignored the order and established an encampment on the Little Bighorn River to the west that included large numbers of Sioux and Cheyenne followers. The Department of the Interior, viewing these actions as hostile, turned the entire situation over to the U.S. Army.

Army leaders made plans for a punitive expedition against the Sioux. Troops were to converge upon the enemy in the Bighorn country from three directions: General George Crook was to move north from Fort Fetterman, located on the North Platte River in Wyoming; Colonel John Gibbon was to march east from Fort Ellis, Montana; and a third column was to head west from Fort Abraham Lincoln at Bismarck, North Dakota, under General Alfred H. Terry, who was to have overall command of the campaign. Terry was not eager to undertake the assignment. Custer, in command of the Seventh Cavalry under Terry, had hoped for the command, but he was out of favor with President Ulysses S. Grant. Grant had publicly rebuked Custer for testifying at congressional investigations against the secretary of war and the president's brother, who had been engaged in fraudulent Indian trading activities. Aggrieved by this personal attack, Custer sought to regain his prestige by distinguishing himself on the battlefield.

In March, 1876, Crook left Fort Fetterman, moving north toward the rendezvous until he came upon an Indian camp on Powder River that contained about a hundred lodges of Sioux and Cheyenne. Colonel Joseph J. Reynolds, in immediate command of the attack, burned half the village, destroyed much of its food supply, and captured its herd of ponies. Reynolds then unaccountably withdrew his troops from the battle, allowing many Indians to escape. When a blizzard developed, the Indians reorganized and even regained many of their lost ponies. They then headed east to unite with Crazy Horse. The demoralized soldiers returned to Fort Fetterman.

Late in May, Crook moved his force north a second time. He engaged the Sioux on the South Fork of the Rosebud River on June 17, 1876. By that time, the Indians could no longer tolerate the encroachment of whites. Their anger was reinforced by reports of Sitting Bull's dreams, which depicted a great Indian victory over the white soldiers. One of Sitting Bull's visions during the Sun Dance not only predicted a total victory for the Sioux but also forewarned them not to desecrate the bodies of their enemies.

The Indian warriors attacked Crook's forces during the soldiers' midmorning coffee break. The Indians' tactics and tenacious advances astounded and confused Crook's men. Crazy Horse actively participated in the Battle of the Rosebud, while Sitting Bull, whose arms were weakened by his sacrifices of flesh during the Sun Dance, rallied his men and inspired them to action. As a result of the hard-fought battle, Crook's army left the battlefield and he was delayed from joining Terry and Gibbon. The victorious Indians buried their dead and celebrated their triumph for several days. Later they relocated their camp at Greasy Grass, which was known to the white Americans as Little Bighorn.

Indians advancing on the cavalry position at the Little Bighorn. From a 1903 painting by Charles M. Russell (1864-1926). (Library of Congress)

Terry left Fort Abraham Lincoln in May and late in the month joined forces with Gibbon along the Yellowstone River at the mouth of the Powder River. Gibbon reported that his scouts had seen signs of a Native American trail along the Rosebud River. Terry immediately dispatched Custer to follow the Indians' path up the Rosebud River. Despite later interpretations to the contrary, Custer did not disobey Terry. His standing orders were to engage the enemy in battle when he came in contact with them. Terry had hoped that Custer would not attack until he arrived with the main force, because he wanted time to ascend the river to the Indians' camp and prevent their escape into the Bighorn Mountains. This plan, however, was not realized.

On June 25, 1876, Custer came upon a large encampment of Sioux and Cheyenne along the valley of the Little Bighorn. Approximately one thousand Indian lodges housed seven thousand people, of whom two thousand were warriors. Although vastly outnumbered, Custer ordered a charge. Major Marcus A. Reno, leading three troops of cavalry, was sent across the valley floor to attack the Indians, while Custer took five units along the nearby hills in an encircling movement to shut off the Indian retreat. Captain Frederick W. Benteen led three companies to scout the south.

As Reno's troops approached the Indian village, he was met by superior forces, which caused him to dismount and fight on foot. When promised support from Custer did not materialize, Reno retreated to a safer position, where Benteen's forces later joined him. Meanwhile, Custer moved along the bluffs overlooking the village. Although there is uncertainty about his exact actions, he attempted to join the attack. However, he was forced to withdraw to higher ground because of overwhelming forces sent against him. Soon, the warriors of Sitting Bull, Crazy Horse, and Gall surrounded and killed Custer and his 225 men.

Gall later recalled that the battlefield was a dark and gruesome sight and related the effectiveness of the warriors' charges against Custer's dismounted men. A similar fate would undoubtedly have befallen Reno's command had not General Terry's column arrived.

SIGNIFICANCE

The Battle of the Little Bighorn, popularly known as Custer's Last Stand, was a short-lived victory for the Sioux. Despite the destruction of Custer's force, General Terry's campaign, as well as others led by General Nelson A. Miles and Crook, relentlessly pursued the Sioux and Cheyenne. For example, Terry entrapped them in the Tongue River Valley and forced them to surrender and return to the reservation. Crazy Horse himself was killed at Fort Robinson in 1877. Sitting Bull and his followers escaped to Canada, but the threat of starvation forced them to return to the reservation in 1881.

The Indian victory at the Little Bighorn can be attributed to their inspirational leaders, their superior numbers, and their determination to fight. Although Custer must bear major responsibility for the debacle, he was not solely responsible. He certainly underestimated the enemy's numbers and ability to fight. His earlier attacks on Indian villages had usually resulted in the Indians panicking and fleeing, so his orders to attack the village were tactically sound. However, the Indians did not scatter but launched a counterattack of their own. In addition, Custer's relationships with Reno and Benteen were strained as a result of his inclination to practice favoritism among officers.

The Battle of the Little Bighorn aroused the ire of the United States, as whites sought reasons for the annihilation of Custer's forces. However, the battle proved ultimately to be a defeat: It ended the freedom and independence that the western Sioux cherished and ushered in the devastating dependence and restraints of the reservation era.

—*W. Turrentine Jackson,*
updated by Sharon K. Wilson and Raymond Wilson

FURTHER READING

Ambrose, Stephen E. *Crazy Horse and Custer: The Parallel Lives of Two American Warriors*. New York: Anchor Books, 1996. Comparative biography of two of the major leaders in the Battle of the Little Bighorn; written for general readers.

Carroll, John M., ed. *General Custer and the Battle of the Little Bighorn: The Federal View*. Mattituck, N.J.: J. M. Carroll, 1986. Collection of official government documents relating to the battle.

Gray, John S. *Centennial Campaign: The Sioux War of 1876*. Ft. Collins, Colo.: Old Army Press, 1976. Provides the best synthesis of the campaign and battle at Little Bighorn.

Hatch, Thom. *The Custer Companion: A Comprehensive Guide to the Life of George Armstrong Custer and the Plains Indian Wars*. Mechanicsburg, Pa.: Stackpole Books, 2002. Comprehensive reference work on Custer's life and military career that devotes considerable space to controversies surrounding Custer's disastrous defeat at the Little Bighorn.

Marshall, Joseph, III. *The Journey of Crazy Horse: A*

Lakota History. New York: Viking Press, 2004. Biography of the Sioux chief Crazy Horse by Lakota raised on the Rosebud Sioux Reservation who drew on the recollections of his grandfather and other oral histories.

Sajna, Mike. *Crazy Horse: The Life Behind the Legend.* New York: John Wiley & Sons, 2000. Detailed biography, offering new perspectives on Crazy Horse's role in the battle at the Little Bighorn and his eventual surrender and murder.

Utley, Robert M. *Cavalier in Buckskin: George Armstrong Custer and the Western Military Frontier*. Rev. ed. Norman: University of Oklahoma Press, 2001. Revealing examination of Custer's complex personality that analyzes his actions at the Little Bighorn. Utley argues that Custer lost the battle because of poor intelligence and his underestimation of the ability and determination of his opponents.

________. *The Lance and the Shield: The Life and Times of Sitting Bull.* New York: Henry Holt, 1993. Describes the character of Sitting Bull and his prominent role in the Battle of the Little Bighorn.

SEE ALSO: Feb. 6, 1861-Sept. 4, 1886: Apache Wars; Aug. 17, 1862-Dec. 28, 1863: Great Sioux War; Dec. 21, 1866: Fetterman Massacre; Nov. 27, 1868: Washita River Massacre; June 27, 1874-June 2, 1875: Red River War; 1876-1877: Sioux War; Dec. 29, 1890: Wounded Knee Massacre.

RELATED ARTICLES in *Great Lives from History: The Nineteenth Century, 1801-1900:* Crazy Horse; George A. Custer; Sitting Bull.

June 25, 1876
BELL DEMONSTRATES THE TELEPHONE

Alexander Graham Bell's first public demonstrations of the telephone caused a sensation at Philadelphia's Centennial Exposition and captured the interest of scientists and inventors throughout the world, launching a new era in communications.

LOCALE: Philadelphia, Pennsylvania
CATEGORIES: Inventions; communications; science and technology

KEY FIGURES

Alexander Graham Bell (1847-1922), Scottish-born American inventor
Thomas Alva Edison (1847-1931), American inventor
Hermann von Helmholtz (1821-1894), German physiologist, physicist, and anatomist
Johann Philipp Reis (1834-1874), German inventor
Thomas Augustus Watson (1854-1934), Bell's laboratory assistant

SUMMARY OF EVENT

Alexander Graham Bell's path to his invention of the telephone began in his early interest in teaching speech to the deaf. He developed that interest as a result of his father's own work in the area and the influence of his mother, who was hearing-impaired. The elder Bell, like his father before him, devoted himself to the mechanics of sound and is regarded as a pioneer teacher of speech to the deaf. Alexander worked with his father in Edinburgh, Scotland.

After immigrating to the United States, Bell became a teacher at the Boston School for the Deaf and later became a professor of vocal physiology at Boston University. While in Boston, he improved his knowledge of electricity and continued the study he had begun before coming to the United States of the theories of Hermann von Helmholtz, a German physicist concerned with the mechanical production of sound. During the 1850's, Helmholtz had described the method by which the inner ear responds to differences in pitch and had shown that sound quality as recognized by the human ear is a product of a number of overtones that are developed from rapid vibrations over the original sound source.

Bell's invention of the telephone stemmed from his conviction that sound-wave vibrations could be converted into electric current, and that at the other end of an electric circuit, the current could be reconverted into identical sound waves. Thus, he believed, it would be possible to establish voice communications that would operate at the speed of light.

Prior to Bell's effort, Johann Philipp Reis, working in Frankfurt, Germany, had developed an apparatus he called a telephone, that could alter an electric current through sound power. His device, which was functioning successfully as a laboratory tool after 1860, reproduced audible sounds but did not transmit speech. His failing, apparently, was in not understanding that vibratory mechanisms were necessary at both the transmitting and receiving ends of a circuit in order to reproduce voices.

In 1874, Bell was able to describe to his father an "electric speaking telephone," but he was not then convinced that the human voice was strong enough to produce the necessary undulating electric current. However, as a result of experiments done the next year, he was able to give his laboratory assistant, Thomas Augustus Watson, the necessary instructions for building an electromagnetic transmitter and receiver.

On March 10, 1876, the first voice communication was made by means of impulses transmitted through wires when Bell, as a result of a laboratory accident, called out to his assistant, "Mr. Watson, please come here. I want you." Watson was on another floor of the building with the receiving apparatus, and distinctly heard this utterance. Bell's success after many experiments in what he called "telephony" came shortly after he began using a liquid transmitter. This discovery secured for Bell full credit for the development of the telephone. He had received a U.S. patent for his invention only a few days before.

Public demonstrations of the telephone soon followed. The most significant of these took place on June 25, at the Centennial Exposition in Philadelphia. The telephone was hardly a perfect instrument. For one thing, its liquid transmitter delivered only a feeble electric current and

Exhibit of Bell Telephone equipment at the Exposition Universelle in Paris in 1889. (Library of Congress)

made the instrument cumbersome and sensitive to motion. Even so, it was considered the most remarkable of all the exhibits at the 1876 exposition. Bell himself demonstrated the device, to the delight of those present, including the Brazilian emperor, Dom Pedro II, who exclaimed when he heard Bell's voice in the receiver: "It talks!" This statement found its way into numerous newspaper headlines, and news of Bell's invention soon spread throughout the scientific community as well. Back in Boston, Bell and Watson succeeded in holding the first telephone conversation in October of the same year.

Improvements in Bell's early instrument were soon forthcoming. Perhaps the most important of those made almost immediately was the carbon granule transmitter credited to Thomas Alva Edison. This device transmitted electricity by compressing or expanding the fluctuating air vibrations set up by sound. After Bell began demonstrating the telephone's ability to carry conversations over telegraph wires, interest in the telephone as a practical means of communication soon increased.

Technical improvements in the telephone led to its commercial development. The first telephone line was installed in 1877. It soon was possible to realize Bell's 1878 prediction that the day would come when a grand system of connecting lines would be established so that people not only could communicate with one another in the same city but could also communicate over long distances through central receiving and transmitting stations. The direct result of Bell's foresight was the establishment, within about ten years, of the framework of the twentieth century Bell Telephone system.

SIGNIFICANCE

Although Bell's imagination and scientific understanding led him to further innovations in the years following the invention of the telephone, none were to achieve commercial success. Not long after he invented the telephone, he rededicated his energies to his lifelong project of educating the deaf. He began a school for the deaf in Washington, D.C., formed a national society to promote the learning of speech by the hearing-impaired, and was influential in increasing public funding for deaf education in several states. However, the world chiefly remembers Bell for the remarkable device he made when he was only twenty-nine years of age. On the day of his burial in Scotland, in 1922, telephone service was brought to a halt for one minute in the United States in honor of Bell and his contribution to technology.

—Robert F. Erickson,
updated by Diane P. Michelfelder

FURTHER READING

Bruce, Robert B. *Bell: Alexander Graham Bell and the Conquest of Solitude*. Boston: Little, Brown, 1973. Nearly definitive biography of Bell. Thorough and engaging, it provides a clear, detailed look into the scientific and practical struggles associated with the development of the telephone.

Du Moncel, Theodore. *The Telephone, the Microphone, and the Phonograph*. 1879. Reprint. New York: Arno Press, 1974. Traces the history of the invention of the telephone, with special emphasis on the scientific knowledge involved in its development.

Fischer, Claude S. *America Calling: A Social History of the Telephone to 1940*. Berkeley: University of California Press, 1992. Comprehensive account of the history of the commercial development of the telephone in the United States. Discusses the role of the telephone in changing U.S. social life.

Giberti, Bruno. *Designing the Centennial: A History of the 1876 International Exhibition in Philadelphia*. Lexington: University Press of Kentucky, 2002. Detailed analysis of the Philadelphia exposition at which Bell gave his first public demonstrations of the telephone.

Grosvenor, Edwin S., and Morgan Wesson. *Alexander Graham Bell: The Life and Times of the Man Who Invented the Telephone*. New York: Harry N. Abrams, 1997. Lavishly illustrated biography of Bell that focuses on the early history of the telephone.

Mackay, James. *Alexander Graham Bell: A Life*. New York: John Wiley & Sons, 1997. Mackay depicts Bell as a man of great intelligence and curiosity, and describes his varied interests and inventions. Provides new information about Bell's early years and how they influenced his later life and work.

MacKenzie, Catherine. *Alexander Graham Bell: The Man Who Contracted Space*. Boston: Houghton Mifflin, 1928. Early biography of Bell, based in part on his own recollections of his struggle to invent the telephone, as told to the author.

Ronell, Avital. *The Telephone Book: Technology, Schizophrenia, Electric Speech*. Lincoln: University of Nebraska Press, 1989. The history and significance of the telephone considered from a variety of perspectives, including philosophy, history, literature, and psychoanalysis. Challenging, but valuable for its efforts to connect Bell's interest in deaf communications with his interest in the telephone.

Watson, Thomas A. *Exploring Life*. New York: D. Appleton, 1926. This autobiography of Bell's laboratory assistant provides a vivid account of the invention of the telephone and of the personality of its inventor.

SEE ALSO: Jan. 10, 1840: Great Britain Establishes Penny Postage; May 24, 1844: Morse Sends First Telegraph Message; Apr. 3, 1860-Oct. 26, 1861: Pony Express Expedites Transcontinental Mail; Oct. 24, 1861: Transcontinental Telegraph Is Completed; May 10-Nov. 10, 1876: Philadelphia Hosts the Centennial Exposition; Dec. 24, 1877: Edison Patents the Cylinder Phonograph; Mar. 11, 1891: Strowger Patents Automatic Dial Telephone System; June, 1896: Marconi Patents the Wireless Telegraph.

RELATED ARTICLES in *Great Lives from History: The Nineteenth Century, 1801-1900:* Alexander Graham Bell; Thomas Alva Edison; Samuel F. B. Morse.

July 4, 1876
DECLARATION OF THE RIGHTS OF WOMEN

The National Woman Suffrage Association's presentation of its Declaration of the Rights of Women at Philadelphia's Centennial Exposition had little immediate impact, but the declaration served to remind Americans of the nation's constitutional obligation to provide equal rights to all its citizens.

LOCALE: Philadelphia, Pennsylvania

CATEGORIES: Women's issues; civil rights and liberties; social issues and reform

KEY FIGURES

Elizabeth Duane Gillespie (fl. late nineteenth century), organizer of the Women's Centennial Committee

Susan B. Anthony (1820-1906), secretary of NWSA and editor of the *Revolution*

Matilda Joslyn Gage (1826-1898), vice president of NWSA and contributor to the *Revolution*

Elizabeth Cady Stanton (1815-1902), woman's rights activist, lecturer, and president of NWSA

Lucretia Mott (1793-1880), woman's rights activist

Joseph R. Hawley (1826-1905), politician who served as president of the United States Centennial Commission

Thomas W. Ferry (1827-1896), Michigan senator and acting vice president of the United States

SUMMARY OF EVENT

In 1872, a centennial commission was formed to prepare for the 1876 Philadelphia Centennial Exposition. Designed to celebrate one hundred years of U.S. independence, this exposition would prove to be a monumental and much-publicized affair. More than two hundred buildings were erected, and nearly six million dollars of private, local, state, and federal moneys were raised to fund the project.

Although the exposition's organizers reportedly advocated erecting a building for women's exhibits, no funds were allocated for that purpose. Nevertheless, Elizabeth Duane Gillespie organized the Women's Centennial Committee, whose members sold stock at local bazaars and concerts to raise nearly $100,000 to pay for their exhibition. In return, they were promised a display area in the main building of the exposition. Prior to the opening of the centennial, however, Gillespie's committee was told there was no room available for them. Undaunted, the women raised more money to erect a separate women's building. Although the pavilion they had built contained inventions and artwork by women, Elizabeth Cady Stanton, president of the National Woman Suffrage Association (NWSA), opposed the site because it ignored women's challenges to the legal system, particularly those of the suffrage movement.

As officers of the NWSA, Stanton, Susan B. Anthony, and Matilda Joslyn Gage were determined to represent women's efforts in the suffrage movement. Throughout the centennial's preparations, they prepared to issue a declaration of rights for women to counter the scheduled reading of the 1776 Declaration of Independence during the centennial's Fourth of July ceremonies. At the association's headquarters, the officers tirelessly worked sixteen-hour days. In consultation with Anthony, Stanton and Gage produced the new declaration. It included articles of impeachment against the government for its usurpation of women's rights.

Anthony, Stanton, and charter member Lucretia Mott organized a women's convention to be held on the same day as the exposition's Fourth of July celebration. Anthony resolved to interrupt the ceremonies at Independence Hall to present a copy of the declaration to Acting Vice President Thomas W. Ferry, who was delegated to officiate at the ceremony in President Ulysses S. Grant's absence. Anthony's measure of protest is significant, as a presentation of the Declaration of the Rights of Women ensured that the declaration would be officially recorded as part of the day's events.

Anthony wrote to General Joseph R. Hawley, president of the centennial commission, requesting seats on the platform for NWSA officers in order to display the representation of women at the event, but Hawley declined. Anthony then secured five press passes from her brother's Kansas newspaper, the *Leavenworth Times*. Stanton noted that the program was to host a visiting party of foreign dignitaries. She was unwilling to disrupt the scheduled event but was adamant about women's representation, so wrote to Hawley requesting permission to present the bill of rights after the reading of the Declaration of Independence. Fearing that the women's declaration would detract from the day's scheduled activities, Hawley declined the association's second request. Stanton, who was reportedly angry at the rebuff, refused to participate in Anthony's gesture of protest, choosing instead to wait with Mott at the First Unitarian Church, the site of the scheduled convention.

Anthony, Gage, and three other NWSA officers, Sara Andrews Spencer, Lillie Devereux Blake, and Phoebe W. Couzins, entered Independence Hall armed with press passes and an elaborate roll of parchment that housed the declaration, signed by thirty-one of the most prominent advocates of the suffrage movement. Richard Henry Lee of Virginia was scheduled to read the declaration of 1776, and the women determined that the close of his reading would be the best moment for presenting their declaration.

After Lee's delivery, a hymn was played that muffled the sound of the women's approach. As they marched to the speaker's stand, the women advanced upon the startled chairman; the foreign dignitaries and military officers before the podium moved to permit the women's arrival. Anthony then presented the declaration to Vice President Ferry, thereby officially registering the document as part of the day's proceedings.

Ferry evidently accepted the declaration without a word and turned pale. The women then quickly moved to the musicians' platform on the opposite side of Independence Hall, handing copies of the declaration to the outstretched hands of the male audience, while Hawley shouted "Order, order!" to the cries of the crowd. In front of the statue of George Washington and the Liberty Bell,

Reading of the Declaration of Independence at Philadelphia's Centennial Exposition. (C. A. Nichols & Company)

DECLARATION OF WOMEN'S RIGHTS

On July 4, 1876, Susan B. Anthony spoke before a crowd that had gathered at the Philadelphia Centennial Exposition to hear the recitation of the Declaration of Independence for the U.S. centennial. Anthony's reading of a women's rights declaration was met with enthusiastic applause and acceptance by the audience but met with shock by government and exposition officials.

[We, the women of the United States] do rejoice in the success, thus far, of our [the U.S.'s] experiment of self-government. Our faith is firm and unwavering in the broad principles of human rights proclaimed in 1776, not only as abstract truths, but as the corner stones of a republic. Yet we cannot forget, even in this glad hour, that while all men of every race, and clime, and condition, have been invested with the full rights of citizenship under our hospitable flag, all women still suffer the degradation of disfranchisement. . . .

The history of our country the past one hundred years has been a series of assumptions and usurpations of power over woman, in direct opposition to the principles of just government, acknowledged by the United States as its foundations. . . .

In making our just demands [in this declaration of rights], a higher motive than the pride of sex inspires us; we feel that national safety and stability depend on the complete recognition of the broad principles of our government. Woman's degraded, helpless position is the weak point in our institutions today; a disturbing force everywhere. . . .

And now, at the close of a hundred years, as the hour hand of the great clock that marks the centuries points to 1876, we declare our faith in the principles of self-government; our full equality with man in natural rights; that woman was made first for her own happiness, with the absolute right to herself—to all the opportunities and advantages life affords for her complete development; and we deny that dogma of the centuries, incorporated in the codes of nations, that woman was made for man, her best interests, in all cases, to be sacrificed to his will. We ask of our rulers, at this hour, no special favors, no special privileges, no special legislation. We ask justice, we ask equality, we ask that all the civil and political rights that belong to citizens of the United States, be guaranteed to us and our daughters forever.

Source: "Declaration of Rights," in Joan Hoff, *Law, Gender, and Injustice* (New York: New York University Press, 1991).

Anthony stood under the shade of an umbrella held by Gage and read the NWSA's Declaration of the Rights of Women to an enthusiastic crowd. Stanton sensed the latent symbolism of this act, noting with irony that during the same hour, men and women stood on opposite sides of Independence Hall and expressed their different views of democracy and its effects.

After receiving an ovation from the assembled crowd, the association's officers again distributed copies of their document and headed for the convention that was slated to begin at noon. There, in Philadelphia's historic First Unitarian Church, they again delivered their document before a large crowd, this time led by Stanton. The reading was followed by speeches regarding various points of the declaration. After five hours, the convention adjourned.

While demystifying the Founders' documents, which neglected to include women in their rubric of life, liberty, and the pursuit of happiness, the NWSA's declaration revealed men's usurpation of legislative power over women to be in direct opposition to the principles of democracy. The declaration criticized the introduction of the word "male" into state constitutions, thereby definitively excluding women through terminology and biology. It also attacked the writ of habeas corpus, which prioritized the marital rights of the husband to the exclusion of the woman's rights. The declaration criticized the constitutional principle of the right to trial by a jury of one's peers because the Sixth Amendment did not protect women for the reason that women were subject to judges, jurors, and legal counsel who were exclusively men. It charged that women were subject to taxation without representation because they were expected to pay taxes but were prohibited from voting.

The declaration also attacked the principle of drafting special legislation for women, because, the association asserted, women's rights had been subject to legislative caprice as laws varied from state to state. By 1876, twenty-four states had been admitted to the union, but not one of them recognized women's right to self-government. The declaration assailed universal manhood suffrage, which the suffrage movement asserted had established a despotism based on biology, and the judiciary of the nation, which opposed the spirit and letter of the Constitution.

SIGNIFICANCE

The Declaration of the Rights of Women was written twenty-eight years after Stanton had written the Declaration of Sentiments, with which she ceremoniously opened the first suffrage convention at Seneca Falls in

1848. The 1876 declaration prompted no tangible changes but served as a reminder to a nation that was celebrating its achievements over the past century that it still had much to do in the future—grant political enfranchisement to women.

—*Michele Mock Murton*

FURTHER READING

Clinton, Catherine. *The Other Civil War: American Women in the Nineteenth Century*. New York: Hill & Wang, 1984. Details Philadelphia's Centennial Exposition, noting Elizabeth Cady Stanton's opposition to the woman's pavilion because it ignored women's contributions to the legal system.

Griffith, Elisabeth. *In Her Own Right: The Life of Elizabeth Cady Stanton*. New York: Oxford University Press, 1984. Chronicles Stanton's life as a reformer, using her personal correspondence and diary to present additional information regarding the inception of the Declaration of the Rights of Women.

Lutz, Alma. *Created Equal: A Biography of Elizabeth Cady Stanton, 1815-1902*. New York: John Day, 1940. Early and insightful biography of Stanton. Provides great detail regarding the Centennial Exposition and the events surrounding the presentation of the women's declaration.

Palmer, Beverly Wilson, Holly Byers Ochoa, and Carol Faulkner, eds. *Selected Letters of Lucretia Coffin Mott*. Urbana: University of Illinois Press, 2002. Selection of letters that Mott wrote between 1813 and 1879, providing an understanding of her public and private lives.

Sherr, Lynn. *Failure Is Impossible: Susan B. Anthony in Her Own Words*. New York: Times Books, 1995. Chronicles, through speeches and letters, Anthony's participation in the NWSA and her crusade for women's rights.

Stanton, Elizabeth Cady. *Eighty Years and More: Reminiscences, 1815-1897*. 1898. Introduction by Ellen Carol DuBois. Afterword by Ann D. Gordon. Boston: Northeastern University Press, 1993. Details the motivation behind the creation of the Declaration of the Rights of Women. Unique in crediting Anthony for her participation in coauthoring the 1876 document.

Stanton, Elizabeth Cady, Susan B. Anthony, and Matilda Joslyn Gage, eds. *History of Woman Suffrage*. Vol. 3. Rochester, N.Y.: Mann, 1886. Chronicles the woman suffrage movement from 1840 to 1885. Offers first-person accounts of the events surrounding the conception and delivery of the Declaration of the Rights of Women. Includes the document in its entirety and newspaper accounts of the event.

SEE ALSO: July 19-20, 1848: Seneca Falls Convention; May 28-29, 1851: Akron Woman's Rights Convention; Aug. 28, 1857: British Parliament Passes the Matrimonial Causes Act; May 10, 1866: Suffragists Protest the Fourteenth Amendment; May, 1869: Woman Suffrage Associations Begin Forming; Dec., 1869: Wyoming Gives Women the Vote; June 17-18, 1873: Anthony Is Tried for Voting; Mar. 9, 1875: *Minor v. Happersett*; Feb. 17-18, 1890: Women's Rights Associations Unite; Sept. 19, 1893: New Zealand Women Win Voting Rights; Oct. 27, 1893: National Council of Women of Canada Is Founded.

RELATED ARTICLES in *Great Lives from History: The Nineteenth Century, 1801-1900:* Susan B. Anthony; Matilda Joslyn Gage; Lucretia Mott; Elizabeth Cady Stanton.

August 13-17, 1876
FIRST PERFORMANCE OF WAGNER'S RING CYCLE

Nearly thirty years in the making, Richard Wagner's cycle of four operas, The Ring of the Nibelung, *was a watershed event not only in Wagner's career, but also in the cultural history of Germany and the history of opera, expanding the boundaries of musical and dramatic expression.*

ALSO KNOWN AS: *Der Ring des Nibelungen*; *The Ring of the Nibelung*
LOCALE: Bayreuth, Bavaria, German Empire (now in Germany)
CATEGORIES: Theater; music

KEY FIGURES

Richard Wagner (1813-1883), German operatic composer
Hans Richter (1843-1916), conductor of the first Ring cycle
Louis II (1845-1886), king of Bavaria, r. 1864-1886

SUMMARY OF EVENT

Richard Wagner's *Der Ring des Nibelungen* (pr. 1869-1876; *The Ring of the Nibelung*, commonly known as the Ring cycle), comprising four nights of opera, represented a project unprecedented in scope, length, complexity, coherence between music and dramatic narrative, and stage design. It was the culmination of Wagner's lifelong attempts at operatic reform and at engaging in political commentary through music. Still performed both in its entirety and as individual operas worldwide, it has become one of the most discussed works of music in history, not only because of its complexity but also because of Wagner's controversial biography and the National Socialist Party's associations with the Bayreuth Festspielhaus, the opera house where the cycle premiered.

Wagner's intermittent work on what was to become the massive Ring cycle began in 1848, when he wrote a prose sketch of the Nibelung saga. This saga represented a distillation of the mythology and fairy tales that had fascinated Wagner during his last years in Dresden. The entire project was completed in November, 1874, when he completed the music for the fourth opera, thus culminating nearly three decades of work.

For the story of the Ring cycle, Wagner combined Norse and Teutonic mythology with German fairy tales to create a story of a hero, Siegfried, who despite his heroic deeds has fallen under the curse of the Nibelung's ring. The power-hungry dwarf Alberich, who himself stole the ring from the Rhine, was forced to give it up to the gods to save his own life, and in his anger, he cursed the ring so that anyone who came into its possession would die. Wagner had the text for the entire cycle written out by the end of 1852—it consisted of a "preliminary evening," *Das Rheingold* (the Rhinegold), followed by three "music dramas": *Die Walküre* (the valkyrie) *Der junge Siegfried* (the young Siegfried) and *Siegfrieds Tod* (Siegfried's death). The latter two pieces would have their names changed before being staged. Wagner began to compose the music for the operas early in 1853.

During the same period, Wagner wrote several prose works outlining his visions for operatic reform and proposing how he intended to "correct" all the shortcomings that he felt marred operas (including his own). He envisioned his four-opera Ring cycle as a chance to present this vision to the world. After composing the music for the first two operas and beginning work on the third, however, Wagner's optimism waned. His financial difficulties, his exile from his home country, and his struggles to get individual operas—let alone a cycle of four operas—performed began to wear on his will. With no foreseeable prospects for publishing his music or putting it onstage, Wagner decided to break off composition of the Ring cycle in 1857. He instead focused his energies on two other operas, *Tristan und Isolde* (1859) and *Die Meistersinger von Nürnberg* (1867; the meistersinger of Nuremberg).

By 1863, Wagner's hopes for his Ring project were rekindled; Crown Prince Louis of Bavaria read Wagner's publication of the Ring poem, which also included an introduction expressing his hopes to someday see the entire cycle performed at a theater designed specifically for its performance. The prince, who became King Louis II the next year, was fascinated with Wagner's work and vision and became a good friend, as well as an important, well-connected patron. Louis helped Wagner with his financial debts, and he helped Wagner secure the site for his special opera theater, the Bayreuth Festspielhaus.

Wagner accordingly resumed composition of the Ring cycle. The first two operas in the cycle were performed individually, as the composer continued to work on the final two. When he was finished and the new opera house was ready, the entire work finally received its premiere. The complete Ring cycle debuted at the Bayreuth Festspielhaus on August 13, 14, 16, and 17, 1876. It comprised

Das Rheingold (pr. 1869), *Die Walküre* (pr. 1870), *Siegfried* (pr. 1876), and *Götterdämmerung* (pr. 1876; twilight of the gods). It was conducted by Hans Richter. The premiere was a significant cultural event: A new cultural center in Germany had been established, and a revolutionary work of art was introduced to the world. No single musical work of this scope had ever been performed before, and the performance raised opera—or "music-drama," as Wagner referred to it—to new heights.

Wagner was able to maintain musical and dramatic continuity over a span of four operas and fourteen hours through his innovative compositional techniques. The innovative features of the Ring cycle were a result of Wagner's strong desire to reform opera and to create the perfect work of art, synthesizing poetry, drama, and music. The music itself was innovative because of its gradual abandonment of traditional harmony—in other words, the consonant chord progressions common in Baroque and classical music—especially in the last two works, *Siegfried* and *Götterdämmerung*. In place of such chord progressions, Wagner used nontraditional, dissonant progressions with increasing frequency over the course of the cycle, especially in the depiction of evil characters.

The cohesiveness of the Ring cycle is due in large part to Wagner's so-called leitmotif technique, in which short musical ideas represent various facets of the drama. Two famous examples of such motifs are the Sword motif—a majestic, major-key theme played by the trumpet—and the Curse motif—a dark, sinister, minor-key theme heard in the trombones with a timpani roll underneath it. Throughout the cycle, a complex network of some one hundred motifs dominates the orchestral accompaniment; these motifs provide a supplement to the onstage action and texts. Wagner took the technique of simple motivic repetition (seen in earlier operas, including his own) and raised it to another level in the Ring cycle, in which motifs evolve from and combine with one another in order to communicate nuanced dramatic content to the audience. The scope of the motivic system created by the Ring cycle represented an unprecedented musical and dramatic device. The motifs in the Ring cycle did not remain static in their recurrences. Rather, they changed,

Richard Wagner (standing) entertaining friends in his Bayreuth home. From an 1880 painting by Wilhelm Beckmann. (P. F. Collier and Son)

both independently and in combination with other motifs, as the drama developed.

Wagner's subtle social commentary in the Ring cycle has long fascinated scholars and audiences alike. Through the text and the music, Wagner commented on many aspects of society, including revolution, corruption, the dangers of lust, and the redemptive power of self-sacrifice. Wagner's precise meanings remain controversial, as scholars continue to argue about, for example, the use of the gods to represent the "old regime" of power that falls at the end of the cycle or the anti-Semitic undertones of the corrupt, power-hungry dwarves Alberich and Mime. Even more significant in Germany's cultural history were the connections between Wagner and the later National Socialist regime. In the 1930's, Adolf Hitler, who often professed his affinity for Wagner's music, particularly the Ring cycle, appropriated the composer's music in different ways. Hitler used Bayreuth and Wagnerian opera performances as meeting places for his followers, and he piped Wagner's music into the concentration camps.

Significance

Wagner's Ring cycle has generated a massive amount of literature since its premiere. Studies range from plot summaries and catalogs of its leitmotifs to complex interpretations of its plot, including George Bernard Shaw's socialist interpretation in and Robert Donington's Jungian analysis of the motifs. Wagner's controversial lifestyle and political views (particularly his vehement anti-Semitism) have also provoked numerous studies about the Ring cycles's cultural undercurrents. In addition, the history of Bayreuth and performances of the Ring cycle after Wagner's death, including the frequent presence of Adolf Hitler and the National Socialists at Bayreuth in the 1930's, has cast a dark shadow over the cultural history of the cycle.

However, the legacy of the Ring cycle remains—a turning point in the history of opera and the cultural life of Germany. Its unprecedented scope, complexity, harmonic innovations, and musical-dramatic coherence led to a new phase in music history—the post-Romantic era of composers such as Richard Strauss, Giacomo Puccini, and Gustav Mahler. Inspired by Wagner's challenges to musical and operatic traditions, these composers broke new ground in their own compositions. Viennese composer Arnold Schoenberg took Wagner's harmonic innovations a step further when he "abolished" traditional musical harmony altogether and created the twelve-tone system. In short, the Ring cycle represents a landmark event in the life of a revolutionary composer.

—*Graham G. Hunt*

Further Reading

Cooke, Deryck. *I Saw the World End: A Study of Wagner's "Ring."* New York: Oxford University Press, 1979. Detailed study of the origins of the Ring cycle and its music.

DiGaetani, John, ed. *Penetrating Wagner's "Ring": An Anthology*. Cranbury, N.J.: Associated University Presses, 1978. Wide-ranging collection of essays on the Ring cycle.

Holman, J. K. *Wagner's "Ring": A Listener's Companion and Concordance*. Portland, Oreg.: Amadeus Press, 1996. Detailed guide to the Ring cycle, including a glossary and motif listing.

Newman, Ernest. *The Wagner Operas*. Princeton, N.J.: Princeton University Press, 1949. Comprehensive studies of each of Wagner's works, particularly the Ring cycle.

Sabor, Rudolph. *Richard Wagner: "Der Ring des Nibelungen."* London: Phaidon Press, 1997. A five-volume companion to the Ring cycle, including textual and motivic guides to each opera.

Spencer, Stewart, and Barry Millington. *Wagner's "Ring of the Nibelung."* London: Thames and Hudson, 2000. Complete translation of the Ring cycle's text, as well as several essays on the cycle.

See also: Apr. 7, 1805: Beethoven's *Eroica* Symphony Introduces the Romantic Age; Feb. 20, 1816: Rossini's *The Barber of Seville* Debuts; May 7, 1824: First Performance of Beethoven's Ninth Symphony; Jan. 2, 1843: Wagner's *Flying Dutchman* Debuts; Mar. 3, 1875: Bizet's *Carmen* Premieres in Paris; Oct. 22, 1883: Metropolitan Opera House Opens in New York; Dec. 22, 1894: Debussy's *Prelude to the Afternoon of a Faun* Premieres; Jan. 27, 1895: Tchaikovsky's *Swan Lake* Is Staged in St. Petersburg; Jan. 14, 1900: Puccini's *Tosca* Premieres in Rome.

Related articles in *Great Lives from History: The Nineteenth Century, 1801-1900:* Engelbert Humperdinck; Richard Wagner.

October 4-6, 1876
American Library Association Is Founded

Leading American librarians established the American Library Association to promote librarianship and to set ethical standards for the profession, to promote libraries as intellectual institutions, and to encourage reading as a means to social improvement.

Locale: Philadelphia, Pennsylvania
Categories: Organizations and institutions; cultural and intellectual history

Key Figures

Melvil Dewey (1851-1931), college librarian who cofounded the American Library Association
Justin Winsor (1831-1897), Boston librarian who cofounded the association and served as its first president
William Frederick Poole (1821-1894), Chicago librarian who cofounded the association

Summary of Event

American libraries date back to the beginnings of colonial settlement. Benjamin Franklin founded the first public lending library in colonial America, and subscription libraries soon appeared throughout the colonies. John Harvard's personal collection became the foundation of Harvard College's growing library, which grew to be the largest academic library in the United States. Thomas Jefferson, who believed that legislators should have at their disposal as much factual material as possible to shape their governing decisions, donated his own book collection to form the foundation of the Library of Congress, now the nation's largest publicly funded research library. In 1833 the town of Petersborough, New Hampshire, created the first tax-supported public library.

The skills of library work were taught to some degree, and many of the foremost academic and public librarians corresponded regularly with one another and exchanged ideas. On the whole, however, the country's new libraries, as institutions, existed in isolation. No organization tied them together, and there were no uniform or otherwise guiding practices or standards. Each librarian was his or her own guide, and a person visiting a new library would often have to spend significant amounts of time to become acquainted with the peculiarities of a given collection. There were some hints of change in September of 1853, which saw the first national conference of librarians, a gathering that included a number of well-known names in early librarianship. The conference, however, produced no lasting organizational structure, and the U.S. Civil War (1861-1865) was to sideline follow-up meetings for more than one decade.

Into this situation of flux came a young firebrand by the name of Melvil Dewey, a graduate of Amherst who had become the librarian at his alma mater, where he created the first library school to teach librarianship as a profession. In addition to advocating the creation of an entire system of library schools, he had founded the first magazine related to librarianship and libraries, *Library Journal*, and almost single-handedly created the Dewey decimal classification system, which organized books and other printed materials systematically by subject rather than by an author's name, as had been common practice.

Although he had no formal authority to do so, Dewey was to lay the groundwork for creating a professional association of librarians along the lines of the American Medical Association and the American Bar Association. With Justin Winsor of the Boston Public Library, William Frederick Poole of the Chicago Public Library, and others, Dewey arranged for a discussion about creating a

Melvil Dewey. (Library of Congress)

AMERICAN LIBRARY ASSOCIATION CHARTER OF 1879

Be it known, that whereas Justin Winsor, C. A. Cutter, Samuel S. Green, James L. Whitney, Melvil Dui, Fred B. Perkins and Thomas W. Bicknell, have associated themselves with the intention of forming a corporation under the name of the American Library Association for the purpose of promoting [the] library interests [of the country] *throughout the world* by exchanging views, reaching conclusions, and inducing cooperation in all departments of bibliothecal science and economy; by disposing the public mind to the founding and improving of libraries; and by cultivating good will among its own members, *and by such other means as may be authorized from time to time by the Executive Board or Council of the American Library Association,* and have complied with the provisions of the statutes of this Commonwealth in such case made and provided, as appears from the certificate of the President, Treasurer and Executive Board of said corporation, duly approved by the Commissioner of Corporations, and recorded in this office. . . .

Source: Charter of 1879 (modified 1942). American Library Association, Governing and Strategic Documents. The ALA's 1942 modifications to the 1879 charter are indicated in the above excerpt by the following: Additions are in italic and the single deletion is in square brackets.

"library association." On October 4, 1876, in Philadelphia, Pennsylvania, more than one hundred people attended the first brainstorming meeting, which included thirteen women, reflecting the growing importance of women in the profession. On October 6, attendees produced a resolution that formally created the American Library Association (ALA). Winsor, who was as well known for his work as a historian as he was for his librarianship, was unanimously elected ALA president, and Dewey was made its first secretary. Dewey promptly announced that a representative of the bureau of education was bringing copies of the government's *Special Report on Libraries*.

The conference had been the stage for strong personality clashes between Poole, a midwesterner, and Dewey, a New Englander who sought social reform. Many of their arguments concerned the value of reading fiction as part of social reform. Poole had believed that good contemporary fiction could lead people toward quality nonfiction and ultimately to the great classics of ancient Greece and Rome. Dewey had regarded fiction as inherently suspect, as something that could corrupt readers' minds and morals. Dewey also disapproved of several of Poole's personal habits, in particular his fondness for tobacco. During the course of the conference, Poole left the meeting room to smoke a cigar. Subsequently, when he protested that the organization was promulgating resolutions upon which he had not voted, Dewey criticized him for having left the meeting to smoke and suggested that these absences explained his ignorance of the proposals in question.

The conference helped transform the concept of the library profession. No longer would librarians be merely custodians of a static collection of books. Rather, the librarian was to become an agent of social change by selecting and promoting books that had the capacity to change the way in which readers thought and acted. However, this transformation did not come about through the discussion of abstract principles of librarianship. The ALA had a practical orientation, and the question of quality fiction and its possible use in the transformation of society was probably the most theoretical discussion. Dewey and his fellow librarians were far more interested in concrete issues such as the establishment of uniform standards of practice across the library profession, as well as securing sources of supplies. As a result, Dewey established an organization known as the Library Bureau to provide ALA members and their libraries with quality library supplies at the lowest possible cost by plugging into economies of scale. Rather than each library going directly to the maker of each type of equipment, be it furniture or pencils or card stock, the Library Bureau would buy in bulk at wholesale prices and pass the savings on to the individual library. Dewey's driving energy was one of the major factors in the success of the fledgling ALA in those early years.

SIGNIFICANCE

The founding of the American Library Association marked a critical turning point in the perception of librarianship as a profession. The ALA was able not only to set standards of practice but also ethical standards, and it became one of the foremost defenders of intellectual freedom. By the middle of the twentieth century, the organization routinely served as a clearinghouse for information about complaints against the contents of books and how librarians could best respond to those complaints. The ALA also became an important proponent of information technology, from the central production of accurate and uniform catalog cards by the Library of Congress during the late nineteenth century to the development of the computer and databases for both staff and patron use.

—*Leigh Husband Kimmel*

FURTHER READING

Davis, Donald G. *Winsor, Dewey, and Putnam: The Boston Experience*. Champaign: University of Illinois Graduate School of Library and Information Science, 2002. A look at the relationship between the New Englanders who were among the founders of the American Library Association.

Utley, George Burwell. *Fifty Years of the American Library Association*. Chicago: American Library Association, 1926. A slender volume with a great deal of early material. The author was involved with many of the events of the ALA's early history.

Wiegand, Wayne A. *Irrepressible Reformer: A Biography of Melvil Dewey*. Chicago: American Library Association, 1996. Examines Dewey's activities in the ALA in the context of his general interest in social reform.

SEE ALSO: 19th cent.: Development of Working-Class Libraries; 1820's-1830's: Free Public School Movement; Mar. 2, 1867: U.S. Department of Education Is Created; Nov. 1, 1897: New Library of Congress Building Opens.

RELATED ARTICLES in *Great Lives from History: The Nineteenth Century, 1801-1900:* Melvil Dewey; William Holmes McGuffey; Daniel and Alexander Macmillan; Henry Hobson Richardson.

January-September 24, 1877
FORMER SAMURAI RISE IN SATSUMA REBELLION

The Satsuma Rebellion was the last of several uprisings against the new Meiji government by former samurai dissatisfied with state policies, the loss of former-samurai rights, and the modernization of Japan. The rebellion also marked the end of six centuries of feudalism in Japan.

LOCALE: Kyūshū, Japan

CATEGORIES: Wars, uprisings, and civil unrest; government and politics

KEY FIGURES

Mutsuhito (1852-1912), Meiji emperor of Japan, r. 1867-1912, whose restoration made Japan into a modern state

Saigō Takamori (1827-1877), Satsuma statesman, military leader, and major architect of the Meiji Restoration

Aritomo Yamagata (1838-1922), former prime minister and founder of Japan's modern army

SUMMARY OF EVENT

Japan's 1877 Satsuma Rebellion was the last in a series of battles fought between the new Meiji government and politicians and the former samurai who were disenchanted with the new policies and reforms that had been enacted one decade earlier. The rebels were some of the most important men in Japan in the last half of the nineteenth century, including the colorful Saigō Takamori, who became immortalized in the public consciousness as one of the last of the true samurai. He had committed ritual suicide on the field of battle when faced with certain defeat by the new Meiji army. The Meiji victory secured the new government militarily and gave it the confidence and tactical ability to proceed with its program of instant modernization.

There were two major reasons for the various rebellions in Japan in the 1870's. First, in an attempt to resist the growing Western economic and military threats, the old Tokugawa shogunate was overthrown by principled and idealistic midlevel samurai who sought to restore the emperor to power. With the restoration of Mutsuhito, the Meiji emperor, in 1867, Japan changed almost overnight; the new imperial government decided that to save the country it must immediately industrialize and discard all vestiges of the old social order. The samurai warrior class was abolished, and samurai lost their privileges, their stipends, and eventually even their swords. They were replaced by a new European-style army that the former samurai regarded as a group of mere "conscripted farmers." Ironically, some of the most important instigators of the Meiji revolution, such as Saigō Takamori, developed second thoughts about the new government and society they helped create.

The second factor behind the rebellions was the Seikanron debate (1873) over Japan's expansion into Korea by force. The new Meiji state tried to alter its formal rela-

Young samurai rebels in training. (Francis R. Niglutsch)

tions with Korea, believing that Korea was a country located naturally within its growing sphere of influence. The Koreans spurned these advances, seeing Japan as attempting to usurp traditional Chinese influence in the peninsula. The Koreans would not, for example, allow a Japanese consulate to be established in Pusan.

In 1873 members of the Japanese government had become divided over whether or not to punish Korea for these insults. Many permanent government officials were traveling to the United States and Europe on a goodwill mission at the request of the emperor, and more ambitious politicians, eager for military action, were in charge. These figures included Saigō Takamori, who offered to travel to Korea and provoke a violent incident there, perhaps even at the expense of his own life. Upon the return of those with cooler heads, Saigō's offer was dismissed, and he was sent away in disgrace to his home in Satsuma (modern-day Kagoshima prefecture) on the southern Japanese island of Kyūshū in October, 1873.

The 1870's saw several uprisings, mostly in Kyūshū. In the Saga Rebellion of 1874, three thousand former samurai in Saga prefecture had attacked a bank. Most wanted war with Korea, but probably one-third also were angry about the loss of samurai rights. Imperial troops quelled the disturbance within two weeks.

The Jimpūrun Rebellion of 1876 in Kumamoto prefecture concerned the samurai's right to wear swords. About 170 former samurai attacked the Kumamoto garrison on October 24, but they were subdued the next day. The Hagi Rebellion of October 26, 1876, occurred in Yamaguchi prefecture (across from Kyūshū). Several hundred former samurai had planned to attack the prefecture office over the loss of samurai privileges and over disagreements with the government's modernization policies. This rebellion was quickly repressed when the government uncovered the plot.

The Akizuki Rebellion had taken place in Fukuoka prefecture on October 27, 1876, concerning the ban on wearing swords and the cutting of samurai stipends. Several hundred people attacked the prefectural office and garrison, but the government learned of the plan and the rebels were soon captured.

The Satsuma Rebellion was the last, and largest, of the uprisings. Tensions between Satsuma and the central government had been rising throughout the fall of 1876. Satsuma still had not adopted many of the reforms ordered by the government in Tokyo, and it continued to retain its own armed forces under the guise of private military schools that Saigō Takamori had established to provide employment for the many jobless former samurai. The rebellion technically began on January 30, 1877, when one thousand students from these private military academies seized some Meiji government arsenals and a shipyard in Kagoshima City and Iso. The imperial government, suspecting trouble, had wanted to secretly move these munitions to safer quarters at the main arsenal in Osaka, but they were detected by Satsuma antigovernment forces, who immediately attacked them.

Saigō was sympathetic to the complaints of the former samurai and to the cause of the rebels in Satsuma and other prefectures. He also was concerned about the plight of the farmers who were suffering greatly under the Meiji government's new draconian land-tax system. Still, Saigō did not want another revolution. Although exiled from the national government several years earlier, his popularity remained strong both nationally and locally, and many believed that with his support the central government could still be brought down. Thus, when rebellions broke out, he deliberately kept himself in seclusion for fear that his appearance would be taken as a call to arms.

When his students and fellow Satsuma leaders, however, attacked the government powderhouse in Kagoshima, Saigō felt obligated to support them. The capture of several Meiji government spies thought to have come to Satsuma to assassinate Saigō likely also changed his mind. In February, he decided to raise an army, go to Tokyo to see the emperor, and confront the "enemies of the emperor," the new central government. He raised an army of some thirty thousand troops.

Although well trained and with high morale, the rebel army was limited by shortages of ammunition, artillery, food supplies, and money. In contrast, Aritomo Yamagata's new modern imperial army enjoyed better logistics, interior lines, control of the seas, and limitless supplies. Although initial advances were quick, the rebels became bogged down in a siege of the imperial garrison at Kumamoto, which lasted fifty days. This gave the government time to fully mobilize and force Saigō's retreat to the mountains. By September, all that was left of the Satsuma army was three hundred men. All perished in a final charge to their deaths on September 24.

SIGNIFICANCE

The suppression of the Satsuma Rebellion marked the true end of more than six centuries of feudalism in Japan. After suppressing the various rebellions of the 1870's, the new central government no longer had to face organized military resistance from the domains or clans. The new Meiji central government became legitimized internationally and gained strong national support. The loyalty of the people was no longer in doubt, and the samurai era had ended.

The new conscript army eventually proved itself a disciplined and well-trained force, pledging total allegiance to the emperor. The early criticisms made by the former samurai—that an army of commoners could not defend the nation—proved unfounded. This same army would lead Japan to victory against China in 1894 and Russia in 1905.

In its wisdom, the Meiji government held no special resentments toward the rebel provinces, which speeded healing and unification. Even many of the participants were pardoned, though most leaders and instigators were harshly punished. The government, did, however, posthumously pardon Saigō in 1891. He is still venerated as a hero—considered an upholder of traditional values rather than a rebel—and his statue stands in Ueno Park in Tokyo.

—*James Stanlaw*

FURTHER READING

Buck, James. "The Satsuma Rebellion of 1877: From Kagoshima through the Siege of Kumamoto Castle." *Monumenta Nipponica* 28, no. 4 (1973): 427-446. The classic, and most detailed, account in English of the actual battle of the Satsuma Rebellion.

Hacket, Roger. *Yamagata Aritomo in the Rise of Modern Japan, 1838-1922*. Cambridge, Mass.: Harvard University Press, 1971. The standard biography of one of the founders of the Meiji state and the architect of the modern army.

Ikegami, Eiko. *The Taming of the Samurai: Honorific Individualism and the Making of Modern Japan*. Cambridge, Mass.: Harvard University Press, 1995. Covers the one-thousand-year history of the samurai, their particular world view of loyalty and honor, and attempts to domesticate them (ending with the Satsuma Rebellion).

Ravina, Mark. *The Last Samurai: The Life and Battles of Saigō Takamori*. Hoboken, N.J.: John Wiley & Sons, 2004. The second biography of Saigō to appear in English (and the basis for Tom Cruise's movie of the same name) by a noted historian.

Yates, Charles. *Saigō Takamori: The Man Behind the Myth*. London: Kegan Paul, 1995. The first biography in English of Saigō, giving a good examination of his motivations in rebelling against the state he helped create.

SEE ALSO: Mar. 31, 1854: Perry Opens Japan to Western Trade; Jan. 3, 1868: Japan's Meiji Restoration; Apr. 6, 1868: Promulgation of Japan's Charter Oath; 1870's: Japan Expands into Korea; July 23, 1882-Jan. 9, 1885: Korean Military Mutinies Against Japanese Rule.

RELATED ARTICLES in *Great Lives from History: The Nineteenth Century, 1801-1900:* Itō Hirobumi; Mutsuhito; Matthew C. Perry; Saigō Takamori.

March 5, 1877
HAYES BECOMES PRESIDENT

In one of the most fiercely disputed elections in U.S. history, Democrat Samuel Tilden won the popular vote, but Republican Rutherford B. Hayes was awarded the presidency through a compromise in which he promised to end Reconstruction in the South.

ALSO KNOWN AS: Election of 1876; Compromise of 1877

LOCALE: United States

CATEGORY: Government and politics

KEY FIGURES

Rutherford B. Hayes (1822-1893), president of the United States, 1877-1881

Samuel Jones Tilden (1814-1886), Democratic presidential candidate in 1876

Ulysses S. Grant (1822-1885), president of the United States, 1869-1877

SUMMARY OF EVENT

Rutherford B. Hayes won the U.S. presidency through the Compromise of 1877, the last great compromise between the North and the South, and the compromise also ended Reconstruction in the South. This agreement, which had its antecedents in 1787, 1820, and 1850, came as a direct result of the disputed presidential election of 1876.

The 1876 presidential election found the Republicans attempting desperately to retain the power that they had held since their first victory in 1860, but it was no easy task in 1876. The party was rent by feuding between regulars, known as Stalwarts, who supported President Ulysses S. Grant, and reformers, who had supported the unsuccessful Liberal Republican candidacy of Horace Greeley in 1872. The Liberal Republicans had quit the party chiefly as a result of the issues of corruption, civil service reform, and southern policy.

In its search for a candidate in 1876, the Republican Party, conscious of the danger to its hegemony, steered between Stalwarts and reformers. It finally settled on Rutherford B. Hayes of Ohio, who had risen to the rank of brevet major general in the Union army during the Civil War and had served as both a congressman and a governor of Ohio. Hayes was a regular. He had not bolted in 1872, but he was not a spoilsman, and he had indicated that perhaps the southern policy needed revision. In his letter accepting the party's nomination, Hayes espoused reform of civil service and promised southerners the right to govern themselves without further federal interference.

The Democrats had gone into the presidential election believing that 1876 would be their year. They had been out of power since 1860, but their optimism in 1876 was based on political reality. During the 1870's, many northerners had grown tired of Reconstruction programs and Republican rule; they were eager for change. The existence of the Liberal Republicans in 1872 illustrated that feeling and reflected an underlying racism that had existed among northerners before the Civil War. Many northerners were willing to believe stories of the incompetence and corruption of "Negro-Carpetbag" governments in the South because they opposed any Republican government at all, honest or dishonest.

The promise of Reconstruction had failed, too, as a result of racism and economic and class considerations. The southern Republicans were divided within and from their larger base of support in the North on the basis of class differences. The Republican Party retreated from southern agrarian reform as it retreated from northern working-class reform during the 1870's. Immigrant factory workers and black field hands were both feared as threats to Republican order and individual property rights. Traditional Republican ideology warned against entrusting the propertyless masses with political power. Thus, it was easy for northerners to accept Democratic charges of corruption in the Republican South and to be unsympathetic to the demands of the southern poor for economic independence.

Furthermore, northern Republicans hoped that conciliation with the South would produce a coalition of northern and southern conservatives. Many former Whigs and Unionists in the Southern Democratic Party were business-oriented and had little in common with antebellum farmers. They shared the economic and political philosophies of the northern wing of the Republican Party. During the 1876 electoral crisis, they demanded railroads, manufacturing plants, banks, and internal improvements for the South. The promise of federal funds for their demands gave the South hope that industry and transportation would complement agriculture and produce unparalleled prosperity.

The Democrats therefore were able to capitalize on the northern eagerness for change. The return of Democratic control in all but three of the former Confederate states helped the party on a national level. In the congressional elections of 1874, the Democrats had won a majority of seventy seats in the House of Representatives and had almost gained control of the Senate. By 1876, the Democrats were poised to oust the Republicans through their presidential nominee Samuel Tilden, the governor of New York.

The election results were unprecedented. Tilden won a national majority of more than 250,000 popular votes, but the count of electoral votes failed to reveal a winner. With 185 electoral votes needed to win, Tilden had 184 undisputed votes, while Hayes had only 165. A serious dispute erupted over 19 electoral votes in the South: 8 in Louisiana, 7 in South Carolina, and 4 in Florida. Both parties claimed to have carried those three states, and conflicting sets of returns from each state had been sent to Washington, D.C. There was also a minor dispute over 1 electoral vote from Oregon, but the real battle occurred over the 19 from the three southern states.

A grave constitutional problem arose because the U.S. Constitution, while stipulating the procedure for counting electoral votes, gave no indication what should be done when more than one set of returns came in from a single state. The Constitution stated that the president of the U.S. Senate, in joint session of the House and Senate, should open the electors' certificates and then the votes should be counted, but it did not say who should count them. If the president of the Senate—at that time a Republican—were to count the votes, he would be expected to count the Republican electors' votes that were in dispute. If the Speaker of the House—a Democrat—were to do the counting, he presumably would count the disputed Democratic votes. With no specific guidelines and Congress divided between a Republican Senate and a Democratic House, there was real danger that inauguration day would arrive before some solution could be reached.

On January 29, 1877, after weeks of uncertainty, Congress established an electoral commission to determine which of the disputed returns should be counted. The commission was to comprise fifteen members: five from the Senate, five from the House, and five from the Su-

Currier & Ives campaign poster for Rutherford B. Hayes and his running mate, William A. Wheeler (1819-1887), a New York congressman who retired from public life after completing his term as vice president. (Library of Congress)

PRESIDENT HAYES ON THE POST-RECONSTRUCTION SOUTH

Excerpts from President Rutherford B. Hayes's first state of the union address (1877), alluding to conditions in the post-Reconstruction South.

To complete and make permanent the pacification of the country continues to be, and until it is fully accomplished must remain, the most important of all our national interests. The earnest purpose of good citizens generally to unite their efforts in this endeavor is evident. It found decided expression in the resolutions announced in 1876 by the national conventions of the leading political parties of the country. There was a widespread apprehension that the momentous results in our progress as a nation marked by the recent amendments to the Constitution were in imminent jeopardy; that the good understanding which prompted their adoption, in the interest of a loyal devotion to the general welfare, might prove a barren truce, and that the two sections of the country, once engaged in civil strife, might be again almost as widely severed and disunited as they were when arrayed in arms against each other.

The course to be pursued, which, in my judgment, seemed wisest in the presence of this emergency, was plainly indicated in my inaugural address. It pointed to the time, which all our people desire to see, when a genuine love of our whole country and of all that concerns its true welfare shall supplant the destructive forces of the mutual animosity of races and of sectional hostility. Opinions have differed widely as to the measures best calculated to secure this great end. This was to be expected. The measures adopted by the Administration have been subjected to severe and varied criticism. Any course whatever which might have been entered upon would certainly have encountered distrust and opposition. These measures were, in my judgment, such as were most in harmony with the Constitution and with the genius of our people, and best adapted, under all the circumstances, to attain the end in view. Beneficent results, already apparent, prove that these endeavors are not to be regarded as a mere experiment, and should sustain and encourage us in our efforts. Already, in the brief period which has elapsed, the immediate effectiveness, no less than the justice, of the course pursued is demonstrated, and I have an abiding faith that time will furnish its ample vindication in the minds of the great majority of my fellow-citizens. . . .

The results that have followed are indeed significant and encouraging. All apprehension of danger from remitting those States to local self-government is dispelled, and a most salutary change in the minds of the people has begun and is in progress in every part of that section of the country once the theater of unhappy civil strife, substituting for suspicion, distrust, and aversion, concord, friendship, and patriotic attachment to the Union. . . .

preme Court. There would have seven Democrats, seven Republicans, and one independent—David Davis, an associate justice of the United States. When the Illinois legislature elected Davis to the Senate, his place on the commission went to Associate Justice Joseph P. Bradley, a Republican.

Powerful forces operated to bring about the creation of the commission and agreement on a peaceful settlement. Northern businessmen, Republicans and Democrats alike, adamantly opposed any resort to violence. Equally important was the insistence by southern Democrats that threats of violence were absurd; one civil war had been enough for them. Tilden adopted an unyielding pacifist stance. Many southerners, eager for economic largesse for levees, river and harbor improvements, and a western railroad across Texas, hoped that Hayes would triumph, because his party was disposed to extend government economic aid.

When the commission met on February 9, it soon became apparent that the eight Republicans would stand united and award the presidency to Hayes. The Republican members insisted that the commission could not question the returns but had to accept those certified by the legal authorities of the states. Because Republicans controlled Florida, Louisiana, and South Carolina at the time of the election in 1876, all the legally certified returns were, in the commission's sense, for Hayes. Thus the commission allowed Hayes all the disputed votes and declared him the winner.

However, the commission's ruling was not final, as the electoral votes still had to be officially counted in a joint session of Congress. Many Democrats were unhappy about the commission's decision and threatened to filibuster or otherwise to disrupt the proceedings of Congress in order to prevent the legal election of Hayes. Cooler heads, influenced by the same forces that earlier had stood against violence, prevailed. Some southern Democrats worked out a compromise with the Republicans, whereby they would support Hayes's election in return for promises that federal troops would be withdrawn from Louisiana and South Carolina, that Hayes would appoint a southern Democrat to his cabinet, and that the Republicans would support a federal subsidy to build the Texas and Pacific Railroad. Hayes got the electoral votes that he needed.

SIGNIFICANCE

On March 5, 1877, Rutherford B. Hayes was inaugurated the nineteenth president of the United States. As promised, he appointed a southern Democrat to his cabinet. In April, he formally ended the Reconstruction era by ordering the withdrawal of federal troops from South Carolina and Louisiana. He had extracted promises from the southern Democrats who would control the state governments that they would observe the Fourteenth and Fifteenth Amendments' guarantees of African American civil rights, but southern politicians soon forgot those promises. Meanwhile, the United States would not see another presidential election whose results were as controversial as that of 1876 until 2000, when the U.S. Supreme Court intervened to declare another Republican, George W. Bush, the winner over the Democrat Al Gore, who had beaten him in the popular vote.

—*William J. Cooper, Jr., updated by Bill T. Manikas*

FURTHER READING

Bedford, Henry F., and Trevor Colbourn. *The Americans: A Brief History to 1877*. New York: Harcourt Brace Jovanovich, 1976. Chapter 11 discusses the radical, presidential, and congressional plans of reconstruction and the price paid for Hayes's election.

Davis, Allen F., and Harold D. Woodman. "Reconstruction." In *Conflict and Consensus in Early American History*. 7th ed. Lexington, Mass.: D. C. Heath, 1988. Examines the failure of Reconstruction and the flare-up of northern racism.

Hoogenboom, Ari. *Rutherford B. Hayes: Warrior and President*. Lawrence: University Press of Kansas, 1995. Revisionist history that refutes historians who depict Hayes as a southern sympathizer or an example of Gilded Age greed. Hoogenboom argues that Hayes was a devout and pragmatic supporter of civil rights.

Morris, Roy, Jr. *Fraud of the Century: Rutherford B. Hayes, Samuel Tilden, and the Stolen Election of 1876*. New York: Simon & Schuster, 2003. Written partly in response to the disputed presidential election of 2000, this study of the 1876 election provides information on the lives and characters of both candidates as well as the nature of the political process.

Patrick, Rembert Wallace. *The Reconstruction of the Nation*. New York: Oxford University Press, 1967. Provides a detailed, interpretive account of Reconstruction. Where necessary, emphasis shifts from the national to the local scene.

Polakoff, Keith Ian. *The Politics of Inertia: The Election of 1876 and the End of Reconstruction*. Baton Rouge: Louisiana State University Press, 1973. Superb study of the election that argues that negotiations between southern Democrats and Hayes's friends had no effect on the settlement, that both parties were faction-ridden, that Hayes held the Republicans together better than Tilden held the Democrats together, and that in actuality Congress drifted into a settlement.

Rehnquist, William H. *Centennial Crisis: The Disputed Election of 1876*. New York: Random House, 2004. Examination of the legal issues behind the 1876 election by the chief justice of the United States who presided over the Supreme Court's intervention in the 2000 election.

Richardson, Leon Burr. *William E. Chandler: Republican*. New York: Dodd, Mead, 1940. A detailed biography of the man who was the chairman of the Republican National Committee in 1876.

Trefousse, Hans L. *Rutherford B. Hayes*. New York: Times Books, 2002. Brief but informative account of Hayes's life and career, focusing on his Ohio governorship and his presidency. Part of a series of books about American presidents.

SEE ALSO: Sept. 25, 1804: Twelfth Amendment Is Ratified; Dec. 8, 1863-Apr. 24, 1877: Reconstruction of the South; Oct. 15, 1883: Civil Rights Cases; Nov. 4, 1884: U.S. Election of 1884; Nov. 3, 1896: McKinley Is Elected President.

RELATED ARTICLES in *Great Lives from History: The Nineteenth Century, 1801-1900:* Chester A. Arthur; Ulysses S. Grant; Rutherford B. Hayes.

April 24, 1877-January 31, 1878
THIRD RUSSO-TURKISH WAR

Russia and Turkey renewed their historical rivalry in the Balkan region, fighting their third war during the nineteenth century. Russian victories initially led to its influence in the area, but the leading powers of Europe opposed Russian expansion and forced it, through the Congress of Berlin, to relinquish some territorial and strategic advantages won on the battlefield and in diplomatic agreements.

ALSO KNOWN AS: Russo-Turkish War of 1877-1878
LOCALE: Southeastern Europe (Balkans)
CATEGORIES: Wars, uprisings, and civil unrest; diplomacy and international relations; expansion and land acquisition

KEY FIGURES

Mikhail Dmitriyevich Skobelev (1843-1882), Russian general
Joseph Vladimirovich Gourko (1828-1901), Russian cavalry commander
Abdülhamid II (1842-1918), Ottoman sultan, r. 1876-1909
Süleyman Paşa (1838-1892), Turkish army commander
Osman Nori Paşa (1837?-1900), Turkish military commander

SUMMARY OF EVENT

The Balkan region of southeastern Europe is made up of numerous groups of different ethnic, religious, and national backgrounds. The area, part of the Ottoman Empire (Turkey) for several centuries, had periodically erupted in violence, sometimes leading to harsh Turkish suppression. Two neighboring empires, Austria and Russia, had used these conditions to advance their own territorial and strategic interests in the area. The Crimean War (1854-1856) between Russia and Turkey had been a recent example.

A series of Balkan revolts and minor wars against Turkish rule had begun in 1875 and continued into 1876. Austria and Russia, along with Germany and Britain, demanded on several occasions that Turkey make reforms to cope with the grievances and aspirations of the repressed areas. Sultan Abdülhamid II often rejected these proposals. Seeing no diplomatic resolution to the crisis after months of broken promises, and eager to extend its influence in the region, Russia declared war on the Ottoman Empire in April 24, 1877.

The Russian strategy was to cross Romania, enter Bulgaria, and continue southward with the goal of forcing the Turkish government in Constantinople to surrender or make concessions. During the conflict that lasted less than one year, Russia also had limited military support from several small Balkan principalities: Serbia, Montenegro, and Romania. Three periods characterize the conflict: Russian invasion and initial success (April-June), increased Turkish resistance and Russia's campaign against Plevna (July-December), and final Russian victory (December, 1877-January, 1878).

Russian troops entered Romania in April and crossed the Danube River into Bulgarian territory in late June. The Turks failed to block the advancing Russians, who captured Svistov and Nikopol in July. Turkish forces under Osman Nori Paşa retreated to Plevna (Pleven), arriving before the Russians moved to capture this strategic location. Turkish defenses withstood initial Russian attacks on the town in late July. Two subsequent attacks against Plevna in August and September also failed, with large Russian casualties.

In the face of Turkish resistance, Russian commanders considered withdrawing from the region but in mid-September adopted a plan for a siege of Plevna. This lasted until the Turkish garrison of 43,000 surrendered in December, 1877. Russia suffered approximately 38,000 casualties during the Plevna operations, while Turkish figures are lower. During the siege, Russian czar Alexander II stayed with the attacking forces, determined to conquer this strategically important point in the Ottoman Empire.

The mountainous terrain in Bulgaria created difficulties for the Russian advance, especially because Turkish troops held several key mountain passes of the Balkan mountain chain through which the Russians had to move to reach the open plains to the south. Shipka Pass was an especially important objective, and General Josif Gurko's cavalry command successfully took the pass in mid-July against Turks commanded by Süleyman Paşa. Several major engagements occurred there between July, 1877, and January, 1878, as Turkish forces attempted but failed to recapture this vital position and slow the Russian advance southward. At the conclusion of the fourth battle of Shipka Pass, 32,000 Turkish troops surrendered. The battles at Plevna and Shipka Pass are among the most famous military engagements of the war.

Other notable military outcomes include the Battle of

Lovcha (September, 1877), when Russian troops successfully attacked and captured this strategic location. Another was at Gorni-Duybnik, when Gurko's forces captured the Turkish fortress in late October. During the Balkan campaigns, General Mikhail Dmitriyevich Skobelev commanded large numbers of Russian troops, and he became famous for his dashing and daring leadership at Plevna, Lovcha, and other places.

With Plevna's surrender in mid-December, sizeable Russian troops were available for the final push southward. They won a major battle against Süleyman Paşa at Plovdiv (Philippopolis) in January, 1878. About the same time, Gurko's forces captured the important Bulgarian city of Sofia. Skobelev's forces occupied Adrianople on January 22, not far from Constantinople. Facing imminent collapse and the possible capture of its capital city, the Turkish authorities requested an armistice. The combatants signed a cease-fire at Adrianople on January 31, 1878.

Another theater of military operations was fought along the east coast of the Black Sea to the south of the Caucasus Mountains. Russian forces crossed the border in June and attacked Turkish defensive positions in late summer and early fall. The conflict ebbed and flowed throughout the region before the fortress at Kars, a primary Russian objective, surrendered in November, 1877. Approximately seventeen thousand Turks surrendered there. Portions of the captured territories in the region were included as Russian annexations in the eventual peace settlement.

Russia's decisive victory over the Ottoman Empire in this relatively short conflict determined the conditions in the Treaty of San Stefano (March 3, 1878), which provided advantages to Russia and its allies. Notable features of the treaty included the creation of a large Bulgarian state and greater autonomy for Balkan states such as Serbia, Romania, and Montenegro. Russian influence increased significantly in the area, thereby upsetting the balance of power in the unstable region.

In response to these significant geographic changes and strategic shifts, several European powers (notably Great Britain, Austria, and Germany) attempted to counter and limit Russia's success. Facing diplomatic and possible military opposition, the Russian government

Russia's Cossack Imperial Guard advancing into Turkey. (Francis R. Niglutsch)

agreed to reconsider the San Stefano treaty. The Congress of Berlin (1878) extensively revised that agreement, permitting the creation of a small Bulgarian state as well as allowing Turkish authority to continue in much of southeastern Europe.

Comparing the two major combatants, the Turkish armament was equal to or better than that of the Russians, especially in the quality and accuracy of rifles and artillery. The top leadership on both sides, who were often members of the nobility or other privileged classes, usually is portrayed as marginal at best, permitting field commanders such as Skobelev, Joseph Vladimirovich Gourko, and Osman Nori Paşa to earn their reputations on the battlefield. The Russian strategy and tactics, while uneven, generally outclassed that of Turkey, which did not always utilize its forces effectively. The large geographic area involved in the Balkan and Caucasus campaigns was a serious challenge for the Turks, giving the Russians more opportunity to maneuver to outflank and defeat their rivals. Enlisted men on both sides fought bravely while coping with the great hardships of battle conditions, inadequate supplies, and the harsh winter of 1877-1878.

SIGNIFICANCE

The Russo-Turkish conflict of 1877-1878 showed that significant and historic changes were occurring in southeastern Europe and the eastern Mediterranean. The Ottoman Empire, a major state in the region during several centuries, steadily lost power and authority during the nineteenth century. Russia's success against the Turks showed that the balance of power in the region had shifted in its favor. Only French and British military assistance to Turkey in the Crimean War blocked Russia's advance, but the two European powers were not willing to aid the Turks in the 1870's as they had done two decades earlier.

In a broader context, the leading European powers were concerned that Balkan instability and growing Austro-Russian competition might trigger a future expanded conflict in the region. Consequently, the Berlin agreement sought to restore a balance of power in the area and provide some benefits to both Austria and to Russia to try to satisfy them. However, in relinquishing the benefits of a hard fought war and the Treaty of San Stefano, Russia reacted negatively to the Berlin settlement as a serious diplomatic and psychological blow to its strategic and political interests. While the Berlin treaty temporarily stabilized conditions in the Balkans, it continued to be a region of competition and instability. The situation deteriorated after 1900, and World War I began in the region in 1914.

—Taylor Stults

FURTHER READING

Crampton, R. J. *A Concise History of Bulgaria*. New York: Cambridge University Press, 1997. Discusses the emergence of Bulgarian nationalism and independence efforts during the ninenteenth century.

Furneaux, Rupert. *The Breakfast War: The 143 Day Siege of Plevna in 1877*. New York: Thomas Y. Crowell, 1958. Colorful account of the long siege, including an account of the presence of newspaper correspondents in the region.

Glenny, Misha. *The Balkans: Nationalism, War, and the Great Powers, 1804-1999*. New York: Penguin Books, 1999. Extensive description of the politics and competition of this complicated and unstable region.

Menning, Bruce W. *Bayonets Before Bullets: The Imperial Russian Army, 1861-1914*. Bloomington: Indiana University Press, 1992. Detailed assessment of the Russian military's capabilities and effectiveness in the 1877-1878 war, along with analysis of strategy and key battles.

Stavrianos, L. S. *The Balkans Since 1453*. New York: New York University Press, 2000. Includes four chapters on the diplomatic and military events of the 1870's.

Stojanovic, Mihailo D. *The Great Powers and the Balkans, 1875-1878*. New York: Cambridge University Press, 1968. Focuses on diplomatic maneuvering in the region.

Sumner, B. H. *Russia and the Balkans, 1870-1880*. Hamden, Conn.: Archon Books, 1962. Covers both diplomacy and military events of the period.

SEE ALSO: 1808-1826: Ottomans Suppress the Janissary Revolt; Mar. 7, 1821-Sept. 29, 1829: Greeks Fight for Independence from the Ottoman Empire; Apr. 26, 1828-Aug. 28, 1829: Second Russo-Turkish War; 1832-1841: Turko-Egyptian Wars; 1863-1913: Greece Unifies Under the Glücksburg Dynasty; May, 1876: Bulgarian Revolt Against the Ottoman Empire; June 13-July 13, 1878: Congress of Berlin; 1894-1896: Ottomans Attempt to Exterminate Armenians.

RELATED ARTICLES in *Great Lives from History: The Nineteenth Century, 1801-1900:* Abdülhamid II; Alexander II; Otto von Bismarck.

June 15-October 5, 1877
NEZ PERCE WAR

For more than three months, Chief Joseph conducted a war in retreat. He led his people for fifteen hundred miles as they fled a U.S. army that greatly outnumbered them—standing to fight occasionally before retreating once more—in one of the most remarkable Indian war campaigns of U.S. history. When they finally surrendered, the Nez Perce were exiled from their homeland.

LOCALE: Oregon; Idaho; Montana
CATEGORIES: Wars, uprisings, and civil unrest; expansion and land acquisition

KEY FIGURES

Joseph the Elder (1786-1871), chief of the Nez Perce
Chief Joseph (1840-1904), chief of the Nez Perce and son of Joseph the Elder
Looking Glass (c. 1823-1877), Nez Perce tribal chief and warrior
Alokut (1842-1877), Nez Perce tribal war leader and brother of Chief Joseph
Nelson A. Miles (1839-1925), U.S. military commander
Oliver O. Howard (1830-1909), U.S. military commander

SUMMARY OF EVENT

During the nineteenth century, the Nez Perce tribes occupied various areas of the American Northwest, including Washington, Idaho, and Oregon. There were five separate groups, each under the leadership of an autonomous chief. One group occupied Oregon territory in the Imnaha and Wallowa Valleys and was under the leadership of Joseph the Elder, or Old Chief Joseph. In 1855, the governor of the Oregon Territory signed a celebrated treaty with Joseph and numerous other Nez Perce leaders, allowing the tribe ownership of all the land in the Imnaha and Wallowa Valleys. The treaty was ratified by the U.S. Senate.

The treaty of 1855 proved short-lived, however: The Civil War (1861-1865) and the discovery of gold at Orofino, Idaho, in 1860, led to a surge in the migration of white settlers into the valleys and territories claimed by the Nez Perce. Because of increasing tensions between the whites and the Indians, in 1863 a new treaty was negotiated. The new terms excluded the Imnaha and Wallowa Valleys and other vast areas of land that had been dedicated to the Indians in 1855. The revised treaty was signed by James Reuben and Chief Lawyer, but Chiefs Old Joseph, White Bird, and Looking Glass refused to ratify it. Thus, the 1863 treaty resulted in a distinction between "treaty Indians" and "nontreaty Indians."

In 1871, Old Chief Joseph died, leaving the leadership of the Nez Perce to his son, Joseph the Younger, commonly known simply as Chief Joseph. The continuing influx of white immigrants into the Nez Perce lands caused increasing problems between Indians and whites. In 1876, a commission was appointed to investigate complaints, and it was decided that the nontreaty Nez Perce had no standing and that all groups should move onto designated reservations. In 1877, the U.S. Department of the Interior issued instructions to carry out the commission's recommendations. Preparing for the transition, a council of tribal leaders and U.S. government officials was set to meet on May 3, 1877. Chief Joseph and his brother, Alokut, represented the Nez Perce, while General Oliver O. Howard represented the U.S. government. The final understanding was that the nontreaty Indians would be on their designated reservations by June 14, 1877.

On June 15, 1877, word was received at Fort Lapwai, Idaho, that the Nez Perce had attacked and killed several settlers around Mount Idaho, Idaho. U.S. Army troops were sent from Fort Lapwai to counterattack. On June 17, troops headed into Whitebird Canyon and engaged in a bitter encounter with the Nez Perce. The U.S. Army lost thirty-four troops and numerous horses; the Nez Perce, numbering only seventy warriors, had only four wounded in the battle. On July 1, regular troops and Idaho volunteers under Captain Stephen C. Whipple attacked Looking Glass's village. The troops shot, destroyed property, and looted at random. As a result, Looking Glass joined the war effort with Chief Joseph.

By then, Chief Joseph and his people had already left their home. They had begun the extended retreat for which they would become famous on the day the army first attacked, June 17, 1877, and all their subsequent battles with the army took place in the course of retreating. By July 13, after numerous skirmishes with General Howard's troops and other soldiers, Chief Joseph, with approximately four hundred of his people in tow, moved eastward toward the Lolo Trail in the Bitterroot Mountains. On July 15, Looking Glass urged escape to Montana and proposed joining with the Crow of the plains. Chief Joseph agreed, Looking Glass became supreme war leader, and on July 16, the nontreaty Nez Perce summarily left the boundaries of their traditional homeland.

Chief Joseph and Looking Glass kept track of Howard's position and were able to stall and otherwise frustrate Howard's advance. As a result, the chiefs led the Nez Perce through Lolo Trail and into the Missoula area. General Howard subsequently contacted Colonel John Gibbon at Fort Shaw, Montana, and instructed him to take up the pursuit. Gibbon was able to muster 146 men of the Seventh Infantry and 34 civilians.

Chief Joseph and Looking Glass crossed the Continental Divide and encamped their weary followers in the Big Hole Valley, unaware of Colonel Gibbon's pursuit and position. On August 9, Colonel Gibbon's troops made a surprise attack on the Nez Perce's camp and engaged in a long and difficult battle. Many Nez Perce lives—mostly of women and children—were lost in the initial confrontation. Chief Joseph and White Bird outflanked Gibbon's troops and led the families to safety, while the warriors under Alokut and Looking Glass split Gibbon's forces. After holding the army in siege for several days, the warriors eventually broke off the engagement, and the Nez Perce continued their retreat through the Montana territory.

By August 27, Chief Joseph had led the Nez Perce into Yellowstone National Park, with General Howard and his troops in continuing pursuit. By September 6, Chief Joseph and Looking Glass had made their retreat through the northeast corner of Yellowstone Park. Continuing north, Chief Joseph led his people up through the Snowy Mountains and finally into the northern foothills of the Bear Paw Mountains, an easy day's ride from the Canadian border. Unknown to Chief Joseph, Colonel Nelson A. Miles had been notified by General Howard and was in pursuit from Fort Keogh, paralleling Chief Joseph's trail from the north. On September 30, Colonel Miles's troops made a surprise attack on the Nez Perce's camp. The fighting during the Bear Paws Battle was intense. The army lost fifty-three men and the Nez Perce lost eighteen warriors, including Alokut, Tulhulhutsut, and Poker Joe. On the night of October 4, General Howard rode into Miles's camp and provided the reinforcements that would ensure a final surrender from Chief Joseph.

On October 5, General Howard sent terms of surrender to the Nez Perce. A brief skirmish evolved, and Looking Glass was fired on and killed. Colonel Miles assured Chief Joseph that he and his tribe would be allowed to return home to the Northwest in peace. Feeling that he could do so with honor, Chief Joseph offered one of the most famous surrendering speeches ever documented. Turning to the interpreter, Chief Joseph said:

FLIGHT OF THE NEZ PERCE IN 1877

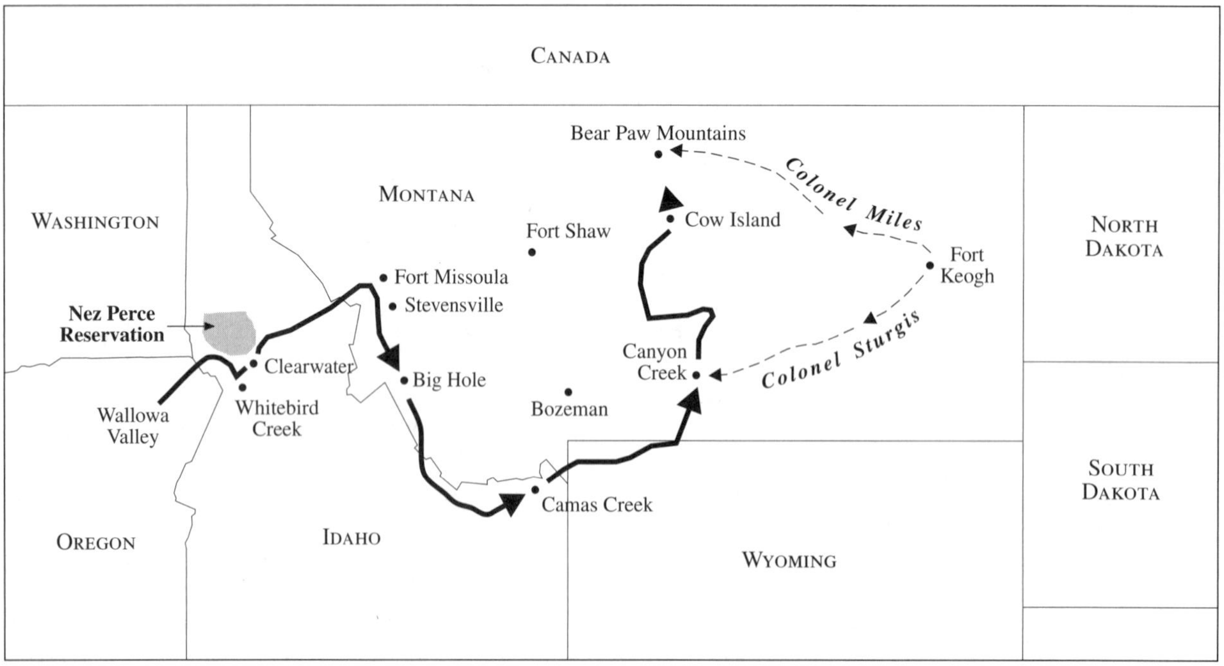

Contemporary magazine illustration of Chief Joseph and his principal chiefs surrendering to U.S. Army general Nelson A. Miles on October 5, 1877. (Library of Congress)

> Tell General Howard I know what is in his heart. What he told me before, I have in my heart. I am tired of fighting. Our chiefs are killed. Looking Glass is dead. Tulhulhutsut is dead. The old men are all dead. It is the young men who say yes or no. He [Alokut] who led on the young men is dead. My people, some of them, have run away to the hills and have no blankets, no food; no one knows where they are—perhaps freezing to death. I want to have time to look for my children and see how many of them I can find. Maybe I shall find them among the dead. Hear me, my chiefs. I am tired; my heart is sick and sad. From where the sun now stands I will fight no more, forever.

Thus ended the Nez Perce War, one of the most remarkable Indian war campaigns of U.S. history.

SIGNIFICANCE

Chief Joseph surrendered with 86 men, 148 women, and 147 children. The Nez Perce were transported to Fort Keogh for temporary holding. On November 1, despite Colonel Miles's assurances that the tribe would be allowed to return to the Northwest, he was ordered to take his prisoners farther south, to Fort Lincoln, near Bismarck, North Dakota. On November 27, Chief Joseph and his people were moved again (by train) to Fort Leavenworth, Kansas. Kept in unsanitary conditions, plagued by disease and twenty deaths, in July, 1878, Chief Joseph and his people were again moved to the Quapaw Reservation in Kansas territory. By the end of the year, nearly fifty more tribe members had died from disease.

After repeated requests to return to the Northwest, in 1885, eight years after their surrender, the 268 survivors of the nontreaty bands taken into captivity were allowed to return to the Northwest. About half of them were housed at Lapwai, Idaho, and Chief Joseph's Wallowa band was housed at Nespelem on the Colville Reservation in eastern Washington. From the time of his return to the Northwest until his death, September 21, 1904, Chief Joseph attempted in vain to gain permission to return his people to his homeland in the Wallowa Valley in eastern Oregon.

—*John L. Farbo*

FURTHER READING

Adkison, Norman B. *Indian Braves and Battles with More Nez Perce Lore*. Grangeville, Idaho: Idaho County Free Press, 1967. This brief history chronicles events of the Nez Perce from actual correspondence, journals, and interviews.

________. *Nez Perce Indian War and Original Stories*. Grangeville, Idaho: Idaho County Free Press, 1966. Another brief chronicle of events of the Nez Perce from actual correspondence, journals, and interviews.

Beal, Merrill D. *I Will Fight No More Forever: Chief Joseph and the Nez Perce War*. Seattle: University of

Washington Press, 1963. Detailed history of Chief Joseph and the Nez Perce War.

Chalmers, Harvey, II. *The Last Stand of the Nez Perce*. New York: Twayne, 1962. Detailed history of Chief Joseph and the Nez Perce War.

Gidley, Mick. *Kopet: A Documentary Narrative of Chief Joseph's Last Years*. Seattle: University of Washington Press, 1981. This brief history well documents various photographs, journals, and correspondence.

Moeller, Bill, and Jan Moeller. *Chief Joseph and the Nez Perces: A Photographic History*. Missoula, Mont.: Mountain Press, 1995. Color photos and text depict the places in Idaho and Montana where the Nez Perce Indians camped, followed trails, and sought refuge from government troops between June and October, 1877.

Moulton, Candy. *American Heroes: Chief Joseph: Guardian of the People*. New York: Forge Books, 2005. Well-documented biography, recounting Chief Joseph's attempt to lead his people to safety in Canada and his subsequent diplomatic initiatives to regain his people's homeland.

SEE ALSO: June 15, 1846: United States Acquires Oregon Territory; Apr. 30, 1860-1865: Apache and Navajo War; Feb. 6, 1861-Sept. 4, 1886: Apache Wars; Apr. 12, 1861-Apr. 9, 1865: U.S. Civil War; Aug. 17, 1862-Dec. 28, 1863: Great Sioux War; Aug., 1863-Sept., 1866: Long Walk of the Navajos; June 13, 1866-Nov. 6, 1868: Red Cloud's War; Mar. 1, 1872: Yellowstone Becomes the First U.S. National Park; June 27, 1874-June 2, 1875: Red River War; 1876-1877: Sioux War.

RELATED ARTICLE in *Great Lives from History: The Nineteenth Century, 1801-1900:* Chief Joseph.

September 10-December 17, 1877
TEXAS'S SALINERO REVOLT

Anglo-American entrepreneurs entered the trans-Pecos area of Texas to mine the region's salt lakes, disturbing traditional Mexican and Tejano salt-gathering practices. The salineros, *or salt miners, revolted in response to the encroachment, leading to battles between the* salineros *and local authorities, including the Texas Rangers.*

ALSO KNOWN AS: Salt Wars
LOCALE: San Elizario, Trans-Pecos region of Texas, United States
CATEGORY: Wars, uprisings, and civil unrest

KEY FIGURES

Thomas Blair (fl. late nineteenth century), U.S. Army captain
Louis Cardis (1825-1877), Italian-born Texas merchant and political leader
Charles H. Howard (1842-1877), lawyer and district judge
Richard B. Hubbard (1832-1901), governor of Texas
Ramón Ortiz (1813-1896), priest and pacifist
John B. Tays (fl. late nineteenth century), commander of the Texas Rangers

SUMMARY OF EVENT

For years, the people of the trans-Pecos region of Texas and Mexico, also known as the El Paso area, had traveled to the *salinas*, or salt lakes, to get salt. The *salinas* were situated about one hundred miles east of El Paso, in the foothills at the base of Guadalupe Peak. Records indicate that as early as 1800, the inhabitants of the area made regular treks from ranches and villages to gather rock salt. To harvest the salt, people—including *salineros*, or salt miners—would handpick chunks of rock salt from the edges of the *salinas*.

During the late 1860's, Anglo-Americans began moving into the area, acquiring large landholdings and taking political control. The ensconced Tejano population began to lose political and social dominance. Both the Anglos and the Tejanos (Texans of Mexican descent) depended on joint efforts from their Mexican neighbors and the military, who came and went to and from Fort Bliss, to maintain an active economy.

Louis Cardis, who was born in Italy, settled in El Paso in 1854 and became a merchant and contractor who supplied goods to the barracks at Fort Bliss. He spoke Spanish and knew the Mexican character well. His business put him in contact with many people on the border: Anglo-Americans, Mexicans, and Mexican Americans. He became an adviser and friend to many people in the region, although his contacts with the newcomer Anglo-Americans were not as successful. Anglos, seeing commercial opportunities in the area, showed resentment toward the Tejano population that had long provided the needs of the people of the trans-Pecos. This attitude caused friction between the newly arrived "gringos" and the established Tejanos, a division that formed based on race and political cronyism. The steady immigration of Europeans, Middle Eastern merchants, Confederate war veterans, and others expanded Cardis's business, giving him daily contacts with the diverse groups.

Charles H. Howard, a Missouri lawyer who had served in the Confederate army, came to El Paso in 1872. He was a man of imposing appearance, had a powerful physique, and was determined, rather reckless, and forceful. A Democrat, Howard became a district judge in 1874. Cardis, a Republican, was delegate to the lower house in 1864, attended the constitutional convention in 1875, and was elected to the legislature in 1876. As Cardis's political tenure had preceded Howard's arrival in El Paso, a political struggle between these two men ensued. Howard had political position, but not the large, multiethnic following of Cardis. Howard saw opportunity in the growth of the region. To take advantage of this opportunity, he enlisted the help of his father-in-law, Major George B. Zimpleman, to acquire title to the salt lakes. Howard then began charging the local residents for harvesting the salt.

This attempt to acquire title angered the people, who had always taken all the salt they needed, free of charge. As a result, these ordinarily law-abiding people began to take matters into their own hands. They met and made plans to storm the *salinas* and take salt by force. Using his political influence, Judge Howard had two prominent Tejanos in this protest group arrested. The storming of the *salinas* took place on September 10, 1877, at San Elizario, a stagecoach stop and resting spot for the military located midway between El Paso and the *salinas*. The mob was so incensed that they arrested and imprisoned Howard, the district and county judges with him, and then organized their own court to try them. Cardis and Father Ramón Ortiz, the well-known curate of Mission Nuestra Señora de Guadalupe in El Paso del Norte, interceded for the two men, who were released on the condition that they leave the area and never return. Howard signed his abdication with reluctance. He had no intention of yielding the salt lakes.

Howard fled to New Mexico. Four of his friends put up a $12,000 bond that guaranteed Howard would stand by his word and would allow free salt harvesting. From New Mexico, Howard appealed continuously to the Texas legislature and Texas governor Richard B. Hubbard to allow him to return to El Paso. His demands included unrestricted control of the salt lakes and military or Texas Ranger intervention in the "race war" and the "invasion from Mexico." Howard created news statewide by publicly accusing Cardis of plotting his assassination.

On October 10, 1877, Howard returned to the trans-Pecos, although he faced death threats if he returned to the region. On that day, in the store of a merchant friend, Cardis had just finished writing a letter to Chico Barela, one of the mob leaders, pleading with him to stop the violence and above all to be lenient with Howard. Cardis placed the letter in his breast pocket and sat talking with two men, when Howard came in carrying a double-barreled shotgun. The merchant asked Howard not to shoot inside his store, but Howard ignored the plea. Cardis was hit in the heart with the second shot. Howard again fled to New Mexico and on October 25, 1877, again asked Governor Hubbard for military intervention in controlling the "mob."

Howard returned to El Paso in early December. The governor had sent twenty Texas Rangers, under the leadership of Lieutenant John B. Tays, who resented having to guard only one man. Howard's overbearing attitude did not help. Meanwhile, Hubbard had called on President Rutherford B. Hayes for assistance, which was granted. Because of slow communications, however, an Army attachment headed by Captain Thomas Blair did not receive the orders in time to arrive with Howard and the Rangers.

On his arrival at San Elizario, on a Monday, Tays found the village full of people who regularly harvested salt, armed and angry. The Texas Rangers took cover and shooting began. By Thursday, there were two dead. Howard's bondsmen and friends, betrayed by Howard, asked him to join them and the Rangers in giving in to the harvesters. This was the only time that Texas Rangers ever surrendered. On December 17, 1877, to avenge Cardis's death and for the free use of the salt lakes, the harvesters and villagers shot Howard and his bondsmen. The bondsmen were shot not because of guilt but because of their association with Howard.

Significance

By the time the United States military arrived, four men had been killed, many had been wounded, and the mob had dispersed. Indictments were made, but no one was arrested or brought to trial. A congressional investigation attempted to get the facts, but in the end nothing significant happened other than the reopening of Fort Bliss.

Eventually, the Tejanos returned to the *salinas* to take salt as they wished. This situation continued until 1891, when the Lone Star Salt Company bought the salt lakes and began processing salt with modern methods.

—*Norma Crews*

FURTHER READING

Matovina, Timothy M. *Tejano Religion and Ethnicity: San Antonio, 1821-1860*. Austin: University of Texas Press, 1995. Examines the interrelationship of religion, ethnicity, and economics during the transition period prior to the U.S. Civil War.

Meier, Matt S., and Feliciano Ribera. *Mexican Americans/American Mexicans: From Conquistadors to Chicanos*. Rev. ed. New York: Hill & Wang, 1993. A standard history survey of people of Mexican descent in the United States. Examines the patterns of economic intimidation practiced against Mexican Americans in the southwestern borderlands.

Metz, Leon. *El Paso Chronicles*. El Paso, Tex.: Mangan Books, 1993. A complete history of the El Paso area to modern times. Covers archaeological, political, military, and other aspects of the region.

________. *Roadside History of Texas*. Missoula, Mont.: Mountain Press, 1994. Includes coverage of little-known Texas historical events.

Sonnichsen, C. L. *The El Paso Salt War, 1877*. El Paso: Texas Western Press, 1961. A detailed study of each of the events that contributed to the eruption of the Salt War, its climax, and its ending.

________. *I'll Die Before I'll Run: The Story of the Great Feuds of Texas*. New York: Devin-Adair, 1962. A history of conflicts between individuals and groups in Texas from the early nineteenth century to the 1930's. Illustrations.

Webb, Walter Prescott. *The Texas Rangers: A Century of Frontier Defense*. 2d ed. Austin: University of Texas Press, 1965. A history of the Texas Rangers, their beginnings, and their major activities to the mid-1930's.

SEE ALSO: Oct. 2, 1835-Apr. 21, 1836: Texas Revolution; Aug.-Dec., 1857: Texas's Cart War; 1867: Chisholm Trail Opens.

RELATED ARTICLE in *Great Lives from History: The Nineteenth Century, 1801-1900:* Stephen Fuller Austin.

December 24, 1877
EDISON PATENTS THE CYLINDER PHONOGRAPH

Thomas Alva Edison's cylinder phonograph became an instant sensation but was not an immediate commercial success. However, with further development, the phonograph became the basis for the recording industry, one of the central forms of mass entertainment of the twentieth century.

LOCALE: Menlo Park and West Orange, New Jersey
CATEGORIES: Inventions; science and technology; music; cultural and intellectual history

KEY FIGURES

Thomas Alva Edison (1847-1931), American inventor and entrepreneur

Charles Batchelor (1845-1910), American inventor who was an associate of Edison

John Kruesi (1843-1899), Swiss machinist who was an associate of Edison

SUMMARY OF EVENT

Thomas Alva Edison invented the cylinder phonograph in Menlo Park, New Jersey, as an offshoot of his work on the telegraph and telephone. His was the first device capable of recording and playing back sound, and it created a worldwide sensation. The device helped Edison achieve worldwide celebrity and garner support for his future inventive work. However, his phonograph was not a practical commercial product until it was improved in the 1890's. The sale of phonographs soared after these improvements, and the resulting financial windfall helped Edison develop some essential technologies of the twentieth century, such as electrical systems and the storage battery.

By the 1870's, the telegraph had become an essential technology for U.S. industry and westward expansion, and Edison's work as a telegraph operator in various midwestern states had prompted him to attempt improvements to the device. His development of the quadruplex telegraph brought him sufficient financial resources to pursue his own interests. In early 1876, he moved to Menlo Park and set up a laboratory with a select team of technicians and craftsmen. Edison and his assistants had worked on an automatic telegraph that used a small wheel with a strip of treated paper. A stylus rested on it and chemically recorded the dots and dashes.

Alexander Graham Bell's exhibition of a telephone at the 1876 Centennial Exposition shifted the focus of Edison's research. He noted the problems with Bell's device and set to work on an improved device that would not interfere with Bell's patents. The Menlo Park team worked on a system in which the sound vibrations produced by the human voice hit a diaphragm and exerted varying pressure on a button of pressed carbon. They mounted the diaphragm in a frame with a mouthpiece, spoke into it, and tested the resulting vibration levels. Edison, moreover, recalled his automatic telegraph. When he saw how well its stylus indented sound vibrations into treated paper, he concluded that he should be able to reproduce the sound thus recorded. A similar stylus on the diaphragm of the Edison telephone would make indentations, or "voice impressions," on treated paper. When the paper was pulled through the device a second time, Edison reasoned, it should reproduce the sounds it had registered.

Thomas Edison with his cylinder phonograph. (Library of Congress)

From June through November, 1877, Edison and his assistants returned periodically to the device and worked on improvements. Charles Batchelor was Edison's primary assistant. Batchelor recorded much of the information on the development of the phonograph in his laboratory notebooks. His notes indicate that Batchelor aided Edison greatly in the development of the phonograph, although the original idea of combining the diaphragm, the human voice, and the special paper was Edison's.

By December, 1877, Edison was satisfied with the device's design and had the talented Swiss machinist working in his machine shop, John Kruesi, construct a phonograph. Edison later claimed that Kruesi believed the machine could not work. Despite his disbelief, Kruesi constructed the first phonograph from Edison's designs. The original phonograph consisted of a spiral-grooved, solid brass cylinder mounted on a long shaft with a screw pitch of ten threads per inch. A thin sheet of tinfoil was pressed firmly into the cylinder's grooves. The machine was hand cranked. The cylinder turned on the shaft and moved from right to left. Speaking into a funnel-like mouthpiece in the phonograph activated a diaphragm. A stylus connected to the diaphragm then pressed into the tinfoil, on which the vibrations occurring in the diaphragm were recorded. Once the recording was complete, the stylus was pulled back, the cylinder was rewound, and a stylus on the other side of the machine was applied to the tinfoil in order to read the information recorded on it. The original sound was then re-created, albeit only if the machine was cranked at the same rate as it had been during the recording. Later, the two styluses would be combined into a single mechanism capable of recording and playing sound.

Edison first demonstrated the phonograph in his Menlo Park laboratory on December 6, 1877, when he read from the nursery rhyme "Mary Had a Little Lamb." The machine reproduced the sound of Edison's voice reciting the words of the rhyme. The sound astonished the laboratory staff, as well as the editors of *Scientific American* to whom Edison demonstrated the machine the next day. Edison applied for a patent on the phonograph on December 24, 1877.

The initial tinfoil cylinder phonograph, while working, had problems that made it commercially unviable.

The operator had to apply just the right pressure when placing the tinfoil against the grooves, and the hand crank required a very consistent rate of cranking during both recording and playback. In addition, although everyone thought it was a wonderful invention, no one was quite sure what to do with it. Edison's initial thoughts for applications of the device had been to use it as a dictating machine or as a way to record telephone calls. The playback of music for entertainment came later.

The immediate effect of Edison's invention was to enhance his own reputation. Edison became known as the Wizard of Menlo Park and was world famous within months. Reporters flocked to Menlo Park and followed his every move. From that point on, even Edison's unsuccessful inventions garnered far more attention than other inventors' successful ones. Edison, relying on his new reputation, built a laboratory complex in West Orange, New Jersey, for the invention of new products. The laboratory's first output was an improved phonograph.

When Alexander Graham Bell and Charles Sumner Tainter demonstrated a wax-cylinder phonograph during the mid-1880's, Edison returned his attention to his own phonograph. The wax cylinder worked more consistently and proved more commercially practical. Edison's team developed a wax cylinder technically superior to that of Bell and Tainter, but it was also more expensive. In addition, Edison's machine was more difficult to operate. It found limited success as a dictating machine.

Teams developed the new wax cylinder phonograph in a fashion that would set the standard for twentieth century industrial research laboratories. One team focused on determining the best material for the cylinders. Another focused on duplicating them. There were also teams for the mechanics of the phonograph, the motor and battery, and the recording and playback portions. Eventually, the West Orange complex included a large phonograph and record factory. By the turn of the century, Edison's team had developed an improved phonograph that played music well and cost less than other models. They had also developed an improved record-duplication process. Agents demonstrating dictating phonographs installed coin slots in the devices and set up phonograph parlors in which to showcase them. They discovered that customers enjoyed listening to a recording for a nickel. The age of recorded musical entertainment had begun. Sales provided a steady stream of funds for further Edison inventions, and his company became the recording industry's leader.

The Edison laboratory continued to improve the phonograph. However, Edison insisted that cylinders were the best form for recording media. It was therefore another company that first developed disc records. Other companies were also able to acquire contracts with more popular singers than those recorded by Edison. Edison, although partially deaf, insisted on choosing potential recordings himself, and he focused on the quality of singers' voices rather than their popularity. By 1929, Edison had left the recording industry.

SIGNIFICANCE

Edison's invention of the phonograph inaugurated the era of recorded sound that would forever change history. The income and celebrity that Edison derived from his phonograph contributed to other innovations, such as the alkaline storage battery, a practical light bulb, and motion pictures. The phonograph's financial windfall and notoriety also helped build the first large-scale industrial research laboratory, which would set the model for industrial research, development, and invention in the twentieth century. Edison, the most heroic and best known of the individual inventors who characterized the nineteenth century, ushered in the laboratory and the team-focused research and development that would characterize the twentieth century.

—Linda Eikmeier Endersby

FURTHER READING

Baldwin, Neil. *Edison: Inventing the Century*. Reprint. Chicago: University of Chicago Press, 2001. Biography focusing on Edison's personality and family relations.

Israel, Paul. *Edison: A Life of Invention*. New York: John Wiley & Sons, 1998. Detailed technical biography focusing on Edison's inventions.

Jenkins, Reese V., et al, eds. *The Papers of Thomas A. Edison*. 5 vols. Baltimore: Johns Hopkins University Press, 1989- . An edition of edited and annotated documents written by Edison and his close associates.

Josephson, Matthew. *Edison: A Biography*. Reprint. New York: John Wiley & Sons, 1992. A standard biography of Edison.

Melosi, Martin V. *Thomas A. Edison and the Modernization of America*. Glenview, Ill.: Scott, Foresman, 1990. Biography focusing on the business side of the Edison enterprise.

Read, Oliver, and Walter L. Welch. *From Tin Foil to Stereo: The Evolution of the Phonograph*. Indianapolis: Howard Sams, 1976. A detailed analysis that puts Edison's invention of the phonograph into perspective with other phonograph inventions and developments.

SEE ALSO: 1839: Daguerre and Niépce Invent Daguerreotype Photography; June 23, 1868: Sholes Patents a Practical Typewriter; June 25, 1876: Bell Demonstrates the Telephone; 1878: Muybridge Photographs a Galloping Horse; Oct. 21, 1879: Edison Demonstrates the Incandescent Lamp; May, 1887: Goodwin Develops Celluloid Film; Mar. 11, 1891: Strowger Patents Automatic Dial Telephone System; Dec. 28, 1895: First Commercial Projection of Motion Pictures; June, 1896: Marconi Patents the Wireless Telegraph.

RELATED ARTICLES in *Great Lives from History: The Nineteenth Century, 1801-1900:* Alexander Graham Bell; Thomas Alva Edison.

1878
MUYBRIDGE PHOTOGRAPHS A GALLOPING HORSE

Eadweard Muybridge developed camera equipment and techniques to take high-speed photographs of animals and humans in motion and demonstrated for the first time in history that galloping horses lift all their feet off the ground simultaneously. He also invented an early predecessor to the motion picture projector.

LOCALE: Palo Alto, California

CATEGORIES: Photography; science and technology; motion pictures

KEY FIGURES

Eadweard Muybridge (Edward James Muggeridge; 1830-1904), British-born photographer

Leland Stanford (1824-1893), American industrialist who hired Muybridge to photograph horses

Étienne-Jules Marey (1830-1904), French scientist who also studied motion with photography

SUMMARY OF EVENT

Born in Kingston-on-the-Thames, England, Eadweard Muybridge came to the United States in 1852 as a representative of the London Printing and Publishing Company when he was twenty-two. Three years later, he settled in San Francisco, where he learned photography from a daguerreotype photographer, Silas Selleck, during the early 1860's. Muybridge next worked for Carleton Watkins, an important landscape photographer.

Muybridge first gained recognition for his dramatic photographs of California's Yosemite Valley. In 1868, he was selected as the official photographer for the U.S. military in Alaska, which the United States had purchased from Russia the previous year. From then until 1873, Muybridge took more than two thousand photographs of the American West—mostly of Yosemite, the San Francisco Bay Area, and Alaska. During those years, he invented one of the first mechanical camera shutters.

In the spring of 1872, Leland Stanford, who had made his fortune in railroading and served as governor of California, invited Muybridge to discuss a photographic project. Stanford wanted to use scientific methods to develop the greatest stable of racehorses in the American West. He particularly wanted to know how horses move their legs when they gallop—a motion so rapid that individuals watching horses run disagree about what they see. Stanford was especially curious about whether four of a horse's feet leave the ground at one time as it gallops. Stanford proposed that Muybridge use photography to freeze the movements of a galloping horse. As Muybridge later stated, he was "perfectly amazed at the boldness and originality of the proposition," and he accepted Stanford's challenge.

Other photographers had attempted to take pictures of rapid movements, but none had succeeded in capturing an event that occurred too rapidly to be seen with the human eye. The photographic plates available during the 1870's were not very sensitive to light, and the mechanical shutters of cameras were not very fast. Hence, exposure times of tens of seconds were common, making rapidly moving objects appear as blurs. To accomplish Stanford's objective, Muybridge had to develop new photographic techniques and instruments.

Muybridge began his efforts at Stanford's Sacramento, California, ranch. However, his work there was interrupted when he was arrested for killing an army officer named Harry Larkyns in 1874. A jury ruled Muybridge's act justifiable homicide, but Muybridge nevertheless decided to leave California temporarily. In 1875, he went to Central America and resumed landscape photography.

In 1876, Muybridge returned to California and resumed his project to photograph Stanford's horses. He developed a new type of camera shutter that made possible exposures of only one-thousandth of a second. His

Eadweard Muybridge's photographic studies of horses provided the first conclusive proof that a galloping horse lifts all its feet off the ground simultaneously. (Hulton Archive/Getty Images)

shutter consisted of two sliding pieces, each having a narrow, rectangular slit. The slides were pulled in opposite directions by rubber bands. Photographic plates were thus exposed only during the short intervals when one slit passed in front of the other.

In 1878, Muybridge's project moved to Palo Alto, where Stanford had established a stock ranch. During that same year, Muybridge used twenty-four cameras, spaced along a fifty-foot length of the track where Stanford's horse ran. Each camera, which took a single frame, was triggered by a trip-wire stretched across the track, activating its shutter as the horse passed before it. Muybridge was successful, not only in producing a sequence of photographs of a galloping horse, but in showing, for the first time, that a horse lifted all four of its legs off the ground at the same time. Afterward, Stanford arranged to have the results of Muybridge's work published in *The Horse in Motion* (1882), written by Jacob Stillman, who was Stanford's personal physician. Although the book included his photographs, Muybridge complained that it was published without his name on the title page. Because Stanford's Palo Alto stock farm later became the site of Stanford University, Muybridge's photographic studies are now regarded as the first research project on that site.

Muybridge's ideas for photographing horses appear to have been inspired, in part, by the work of the French scientist Étienne-Jules Marey. Marey had suggested in his book *La Machine animale: Locomotion terrestre et aérienne* (1873; *Animal Mechanism: A Treatise on Terrestrial and Aërial Locomotion*, 1874) that a sequence of images of animals in motion could be displayed using a zoetrope, a cylindrical device in which the viewer looks through a series of slits in a rotating drum at a sequence of pictures placed at equal distances on the opposite sides of the drum. As the drum rotates, the viewer sees a progression of images that create the illusion of a single picture in motion. After reading Marey's book, Muybridge invented a device he called the zoöpraxiscope, which projected a slow-motion sequence of images of objects in motion.

During the fall of 1881, Muybridge lectured in Europe, intent on establishing his reputation as the creator of the techniques for studying motion using photography. While in Paris, Marey introduced him to many artistic and scientific leaders. The enthusiastic response to his lectures inspired Muybridge to look for ways to continue his photographic studies. In February of 1883, he lectured at the Academy of the Fine Arts in Philadelphia, where he used his zoöpraxiscope to show images of humans and animals in motion. Fairman Rogers, the director of the Academy, and Thomas Eakins, a prominent American painter, persuaded William Pepper, the provost of the University of Pennsylvania, to hire Muybridge and provide the facilities and financial support he needed to continue his studies.

In a private demonstration in Stanford's house during the fall of 1879, Muybridge projected a sequence of images of Stanford's horse in motion using his new zoöpraxiscope, which can be considered to be a primitive motion picture projector. He demonstrated a zoöpraxiscope in public during a lecture at the California School of Fine Arts in San Francisco in 1880. Muybridge lectured and showed sequences of humans in motion in the Zoopraxographical Hall, a forerunner of the movie theater, which was a popular exhibit at the World's Columbian Exposition in Chicago in 1893. His invention of the zoöpraxiscope, the first device that projected a sequence of images of an object in motion, has given rise to the suggestion that he was the true founder of modern motion pictures.

Between 1884 and 1886, Muybridge worked in the courtyard of the Veterinary Hall and Hospital of the University of Pennsylvania. He used new technology including dry plates that were more sensitive to light than his earlier wet plates and worked with W. D. Marks to develop an electromagnetic clockwork shutter. By 1885, he was using three rows of twelve cameras each. One row was parallel to the subject, while the others were set at positions sixty and ninety degrees to the subject, thereby recording the motion from a variety of angles. At the University of Pennsylvania, Muybridge and his co-workers exposed more than twenty thousand negatives, many of which he published in a portfolio called *Animal Locomotion* (1887).

During his career, Muybridge photographically documented the movements of a wide variety of animals, including horses, goats, cats, gnus, eagles, gazelles, sloths, camels, and birds. Using these photographs, he identified 132 characteristic animal motions. He also studied human motion. He exhibited and sold these photographs to the public, as he had with his landscape photographs earlier in his career. Muybridge never regarded his motion studies to be completely successful, because he sold only twenty-seven complete sets of the *Animal Locomotion* portfolio. However, he sold many of his smaller, one-hundred-print sets, mostly to artists and libraries. Muybridge later returned to his birthplace, where he died in 1904.

Significance

Before Muybridge began his experiments on the photography of moving objects, he considered himself an artist. However, as his focus narrowed to motion studies, he regarded his work as scientific. That judgment has since been disputed by scholars who have noted the extreme lack of scientific rigor in Muybridge's studies when compared with those of Marey. Nevertheless, Muybridge's photographs ushered in an era of scientific uses of photography. His work also had a significant influence on the visual arts. His *Animal Locomotion* became an important resource for artists who were interested in accurately depicting animals and humans in their paintings and drawings. Moreover, while Muybridge himself had no great interest in creating moving images—which he saw as the opposite of his project of separating motion into discrete still moments, his work had a profound influence on the development of motion pictures by Thomas Alva Edison and the Lumière brothers.

—*George J. Flynn*

Further Reading

Haas, Robert. *Muybridge: Man in Motion.* Berkeley: University of California Press, 1976. Full account of Muybridge's life, his collaboration with Stanford, and his photography.

Hendricks, Gordon. *Eadweard Muybridge.* Mineola, N.Y.: Dover, 2001. Exploration of Muybridge's photographic work, recounting his early life in England and his work as a photographer in San Francisco. Hendricks also discusses his stormy relationship with Leland Stanford.

Muybridge, Eadweard. *Animals in Motion*. Mineola, N.Y.: Dover, 1957. Reprint of Muybridge's collection of more than 3,900 photographs of thirty-four different animals. Includes Muybridge's written observations on animal movements.

Prodger, Philip and Gunning, Tom. *Time Stands Still: Muybridge and the Instantaneous Photography Movement*. Oxford, England: Oxford University Press, 2003. Written to accompany an exhibition of Muybridge's photography, this book describes the improvements in photographic chemistry, optics, shutter technology, and other components required to make the study of animal motion possible.

Solnit, Rebecca. *River of Shadows: Eadweard Muybridge and the Technological Wild West*. New York: Viking Books, 2003. Controversial account of the development of technology in America that suggests that the high-technology industries of California's Silicon Valley and the Hollywood movie industry can be traced back to innovations by Stanford and Muybridge.

SEE ALSO: 1839: Daguerre and Niépce Invent Daguerreotype Photography; Dec. 24, 1877: Edison Patents the Cylinder Phonograph; May, 1887: Goodwin Develops Celluloid Film; May 1-Oct. 30, 1893: Chicago World's Fair; Dec. 28, 1895: First Commercial Projection of Motion Pictures; Feb., 1900: Kodak Introduces Brownie Cameras.

RELATED ARTICLES in *Great Lives from History: The Nineteenth Century, 1801-1900:* Mathew B. Brady; Jacques Daguerre; Thomas Alva Edison; Leland Stanford.

1878-1899
IRVING MANAGES LONDON'S LYCEUM THEATRE

Under the management of Henry Irving and the syndicate that briefly followed his tenure, London's Lyceum Theatre functioned as an unofficial British national theater and helped transform the acting profession in England from itinerant to established and from marginal to socially respectable. An official seal was set on the Lyceum's success when Irving became the first actor to be knighted in 1895.

LOCALE: London, England
CATEGORY: Theater

KEY FIGURES

Henry Irving (John Henry Brodribb; 1838-1905), British actor
Ellen Terry (1847-1928), Irving's most frequent leading lady
Bram Stoker (1847-1912), Irish novelist who was the Lyceum's stage manager and general factotum

SUMMARY OF EVENT

From his base at the Lyceum, Henry Irving dominated the London theater scene for nearly a quarter of a century. He also took his company on regular and exceptionally well-received tours of North America and performed by invitation for Queen Victoria at Windsor Castle. His after-show dinners at the theater's Beefsteak Club also became legendary, as they were attended by such dignitaries as the Prince of Wales; Germany's future kaiser, William II; Irving's right-hand man, author Bram Stoker; Sir Arthur Conan Doyle, and many others.

Irving first appeared at the Lyceum Theatre in 1871, in *The Bells*, a melodrama staged under the aegis of the American impresario H. L. Bateman. In that play, he played Mathias, a man who has committed a murder and escaped justice but is tormented by his own conscience. Irving was an instant success, and *The Bells* later became a permanent staple of the Lyceum's repertoire. Irving continued to act for Bateman until the latter's death in 1875, when his widow took over the management of the theater and ran it for a further two years. Irving then proposed taking it over himself, which he did in 1878.

To join him, Irving invited two people who were to prove crucial to the Lyceum's success. The first was the gifted and beautiful comic actress Ellen Terry, who was to act as his regular leading lady through the next quarter of a century. The second was Bram Stoker, a young Irish clerk who had been so affected by seeing Irving on tour in Dublin that he had volunteered to become Dublin's first, unpaid theater critic and had subsequently formed a strong bond with Irving. These two, and other staples of the Lyceum's management such as Austin Brereton, formed Irving's professional and personal support network. He became permanently estranged from his wife, Florence O'Callaghan, after she asked him the night that *The Bells* opened if he proposed to go on making a fool of himself all his life. However, both of Irving's sons by Florence, Laurence Irving and H. B. Irving, subsequently followed him into the theater.

Irving's most famous roles were Mathias in *The Bells*, a hit to which he could always turn in troubled periods and which he performed more than any other part; Mephistopheles in Johann Wolfgang von Goethe's *Faust: Eine Tragödie* (pb. 1808; *The Tragedy of Faust*, 1823); Eugene Aram, another guilt-tortured murderer; and Thomas à Becket in Alfred, Lord Tennyson's *Becket* (wr. 1879, pb. 1884, pr. 1893), which Tennyson wrote with Irving in mind. Irving also enjoyed notable successes in several historical dramas, including one on Charles I, and a number of Shakespearean roles, including Shylock, Macbeth, Hamlet, Cardinal Wolsey, and Iago and Othello—roles that he alternated with the American actor Edwin Booth.

Irving's mannered and eccentric delivery was best suited to melodrama, which was in any case popular and in which he seems to have exerted a quasi-hypnotic effect on the audience. However, this effect tended to marginalize the talents of Ellen Terry, who was best suited to comedy. Irving's repertoire was popular with audiences, but not always with critics. George Bernard Shaw accused Irving of conspiring to keep serious drama off the London stage by refusing to stage the plays of the great Norwegian naturalist Henrik Ibsen. That this was indeed Irving's sole decision was confirmed after the breakup of the Lyceum company, when Terry produced and acted in Henrik Ibsen's *Hærmænde paa Helgeland* (pr., pb. 1858; *The Vikings at Helgeland*, 1890). The Lyceum was also drawn into scandal when it was suggested that the gruesome Jack the Ripper murders might have been triggered by the theater's staging of a theatrical adaptation of Robert Louis Stevenson's *The Strange Case of Dr. Jekyll and Mr. Hyde* (1886).

Despite these occasional more negative notes, the impact of the Lyceum on the London theatrical, literary and social scenes can hardly be overestimated. In his two-volume memoir, *Personal Reminiscences of Henry Irving* (1906), Irving's faithful stage manager Stoker provided a list of people in Irving's social circle. It covers several pages and includes virtually every name of note in the London of the time, foreign royalty, and several American presidents, with whom Irving regularly dined during the eight major American tours that he and the Lyceum company undertook between 1883 and 1901.

During his years at the Lyceum, Stoker wrote his famous novel *Dracula* (1897), which is sometimes seen as either a homage to, or a critique, of Irving. Irving himself refused to play the lead role in a dramatization of *Dracula*, although Stoker hoped he would. Stoker also wrote several other novels and was instrumental in accepting the first play by Sir Arthur Conan Doyle.

Henry Irving and Ellen Terry as Benedick and Beatrice in William Shakespeare's Much Ado About Nothing. (Library of Congress)

England's poet laureate Tennyson was a close friend of Irving whose plays became two of Irving's successes. W. S. Gilbert and Sir Arthur Sullivan were other Lyceum regulars, as was the now forgotten but then hugely popular novelist Hall Caine, to whom Stoker dedicated *Dracula*. Irving was also a longstanding and active Freemason, a fact that helped win him the friendship of the Prince of Wales (future King Edward VII), the grand master of the United Grand Lodge of England. The prince was instrumental in procuring for Irving an invitation to give a private performance at Windsor Castle in front of his mother, Queen Victoria, and also in having him knighted in 1895—the apogee of Irving's success.

The end of the Lyceum followed soon after Irving's knighthood. In 1897, Irving suffered a bad fall and strained his knee. Afterward, he struggled to appear on stage. During the same year, he sponsored a production of a play about Russia's Peter the Great mounted by his son Laurence. However, it was a financial disaster. The death-knell of the theater was sounded by a disastrous fire on February 18, 1898, that destroyed many of the sets and costumes needed for productions. For a visual, effects-dominated theater such as Irving's this loss was a disaster from which the Lyceum company never recovered. In 1899, a consortium took over management of the theater, to the immense consternation of Stoker and others of Irving's faithful followers. The end came in 1902, when the company went into liquidation. At the age of sixty-five, Irving was forced to go on tour again. Three years later he died in Bradford, in northern England, after performing in Tennyson's *Becket*.

SIGNIFICANCE

Irving's reign at the Lyceum permanently changed the perception of the theater in England. Instead of being a marginal, rootless figure barely managing to scrape a living, at least one actor was seen to have acquired social status and, temporarily at any rate, financial success. The Lyceum and its repertoire became important cultural artifacts central to the social and artistic life of late Victorian London.

—*Lisa Hopkins*

FURTHER READING

Belford, Barbara. *Bram Stoker and the Man Who Was Dracula*. London: Da Capo Press, 2002. Obligatory reading for those interested in the suggestion that Irving inspired Stoker's title character in *Dracula*.

Brereton, Austin. *Life of Henry Irving*. London: Ayer, 1974. Originally published in 1908, this biography was written by a man who knew Irving well and was intimately involved in running the Lyceum. It is interesting to compare Brereton with Stoker, whom Irving seems sometimes to have pitted against him.

Irving, Laurence. *Henry Irving and His World*. 1951. Reprint. London: Virgin Books, 1988. Biography written by Henry Irving's grandson.

Richards, Jeffrey. *Sir Henry Irving: An Actor and His World*. London: Hambledon & London, 2005. Written by a leading English authority on Victorian theater, this biography is likely to become the standard work on Irving.

Stoker, Bram. *Personal Reminiscences of Henry Irving*. 2 vols. 1906. Reprint. London: Greenwood Press, 1970. More hagiography than biography, but a unique record by the man who may have been closer to Irving than anyone else.

SEE ALSO: c. 1801-1850: Professional Theaters Spread Throughout America; 1850's-1880's: Rise of Burlesque and Vaudeville; 1879: *A Doll's House* Introduces Modern Realistic Drama; Oct. 10, 1881: London's Savoy Theatre Opens; Oct. 14, 1898: Moscow Art Theater Is Founded.

RELATED ARTICLES in *Great Lives from History: The Nineteenth Century, 1801-1900:* Edwin Booth; Anton Chekhov; W. S. Gilbert and Arthur Sullivan; Henrik Ibsen; Henry Irving; William Charles Macready; Alfred, Lord Tennyson; Ellen Terry; Oscar Wilde.

June 13-July 13, 1878
CONGRESS OF BERLIN

The parties to the Congress of Berlin negotiated a compromise settlement balancing the interests of the Austro-Hungarian Empire, Great Britain, and Russia. They thereby averted a major war over the Ottoman Empire's Balkan possessions.

LOCALE: Berlin, Prussia, German Empire (now in Germany)

CATEGORY: Diplomacy and international relations

KEY FIGURES

Benjamin Disraeli (1804-1881), earl of Beaconsfield and prime minister of Great Britain, 1868, 1874-1880

Aleksandr Mikhailovich Gorchakov (1798-1883), chancellor of the Russian Empire

Count Gyula Andrássy (1823-1890), foreign minister of the Austro-Hungarian Empire, 1871-1879

Otto von Bismarck (1815-1898), chancellor of the German Empire, 1871-1890

Alexander II (1818-1881), czar of Russia, r. 1855-1881

William Ewart Gladstone (1809-1898), prime minister of Great Britain, 1868-1874, 1880-1885, 1886, 1892-1894

Nikolay Pavlovich Ignatyev (1832-1908), Russian ambassador to Constantinople

SUMMARY OF EVENT

The Congress of Berlin, held in the summer of 1878, marked the end of a serious crisis in the Middle East that

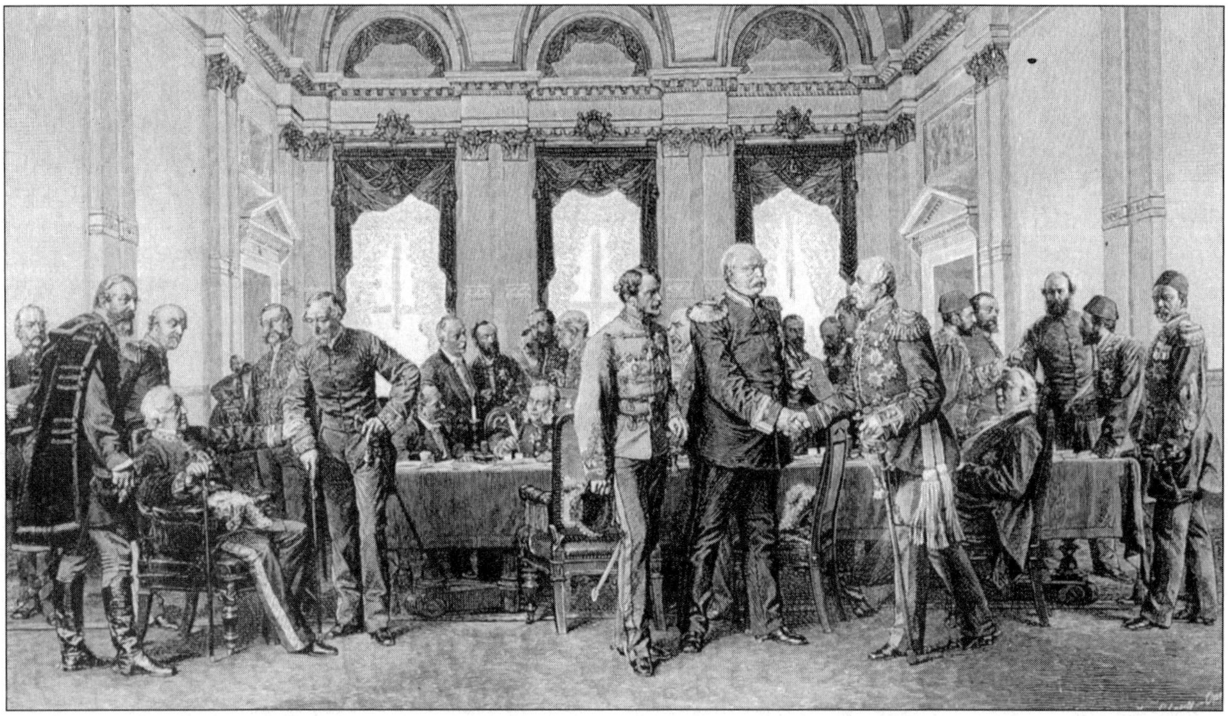

Conferees at the Congress of Berlin. (R. S. Peale/J. A. Hill)

had arisen in 1875 with the outbreak of rebellion in Bosnia and Herzegovina against Turkish rule. Increasingly throughout the nineteenth century, the various peoples of the Balkans had been asserting their national identities at the expense of a declining Ottoman Empire. The Greeks had achieved complete independence from the Turks in 1829, Serbia gained autonomous status in 1830, and the principalities of Wallachia and Moldavia by 1859 were united in the kingdom of Romania. Between 1866 and 1868, the people of Crete, in their effort to join Greece, waged an unsuccessful revolt against the Turks. By 1875, the fever of national independence had spread to the westernmost Turkish provinces of Bosnia and Herzegovina, whose mixed Croatian-Serbian population raised the standard of rebellion against the rule of the sultan in July of that year.

It was not long before the revolt spread, embroiling several of the Balkan states and the great European powers in a protracted Middle Eastern crisis, which was not settled until 1878. Russia and the Austro-Hungarian Empire, eager to preserve the Balkan status quo and with it the rapprochement they had worked out in entering the Three Emperors' League in 1873, acted in concert in attempts to mediate the conflict between the Slavs of Bosnia and Herzegovina and their Turkish masters. The combined efforts of the three allies came to naught, and by mid-1876 the rebellion had spread to Bulgaria, Serbia, and Montenegro. The formal declaration of war by Serbia and Montenegro on the Ottoman Empire inspired the Russian Pan-Slavs, led by Nikolai Pavlovich Ignatyev, the Russian ambassador to Constantinople, to press Czar Alexander II to render military assistance to the Balkan Slavs.

The brutality with which the Ottoman authorities dealt with the Bulgarian revolt further undermined diplomatic efforts to find a peaceful solution to the Balkan crisis. Turkish regular forces, which had been sent to restore order, destroyed about sixty villages and massacred between twelve and fifteen thousand people. Public outcries over these atrocities were particularly strong in Russia and Great Britain. The Bulgarian massacres strengthened the demands of the Pan-Slavs for the establishment of a Russian protectorate over the Balkan Christians. In Great Britain, popular outrage was fanned by former prime minister William Ewart Gladstone's pamphlet *The Bulgarian Horrors and the Question of the East* (1876). These sentiments made it difficult for the British government to mount effective opposition to a Russian war against the Ottoman Empire.

To prepare for such an eventuality and at the same

time prevent a conflict with Austria, the chancellor of the Russian Empire, Prince Aleksandr Mikhailovich Gorchakov, met with the foreign minister of the Austro-Hungarian Empire, Count Gyula Andrássy, on July 8, 1876, in Reichstadt, Bohemia. The two statesmen agreed that their governments should work together to regulate any territorial changes that might arise in case of a Turkish defeat at the hands of the southern Slavs.

Meanwhile, the war of 1876 in the Balkans had become, for the most part, a contest between Serbia and the Ottoman Empire, with the latter rapidly gaining the ascendancy. With the Turks about to seize the Serbian capital of Belgrade, Russia issued a forty-eight-hour ultimatum on October 31, 1876, demanding that the Turks stop their advance and grant the Serbs an armistice of at least six weeks. This they agreed to do. Despite the armistice, however, Alexander II remained torn between the demands of the Pan-Slavs to declare war on the Turks and his own desire for a peaceful settlement of the conflict. Consequently, he ordered preliminary preparation for war while making plans to participate in a conference of the great powers at Constantinople that would seek to find a diplomatic solution to the Serbian-Ottoman conflict. This conference was held from December 12, 1876, to January 20, 1877, but it was a failure.

Russia continued to seek a guarantee of Austrian neutrality in the event of a Russo Turkish war and, in the Budapest Convention of March, 1877, was successful. In return, Russia agreed to allow Austria to occupy Bosnia and Herzegovina and also agreed to refrain from establishing a large Slavic state in the Balkans should Austria defeat the Turks. Such terms placed Russia in the position of fighting for Austrian aggrandizement in the western Balkans. Meanwhile, despite the fact that the Serbs had concluded their war with the Turks in a formal treaty on February 28, 1877, Russia continued to press the Sublime Porte (diplomatic shorthand for the Turkish government) to introduce reforms throughout its Balkan provinces. However, the sultan, emboldened by outpourings of Turkish nationalism and Great Britain's policy of guaranteeing the integrity of the Ottoman Empire, emphatically refused. Therefore, on April 24, 1877, Russia declared war on Turkey.

Russia's resounding victory over the Turks, sealed in the Treaty of San Stefano on March 3, 1878, brought an immediate adverse reaction from Great Britain and Austria in the form of a demand that the government at St. Petersburg submit the peace settlement to an international congress of European states. The major reservation that Austria and Britain had regarding the Treaty of San Stefano was its provision for the creation of a greater Bulgaria with an outlet to the Aegean Sea. To Austria, this amounted to the establishment of Russian hegemony over the eastern Balkans, not to mention the violation of two Austro-Russian accords—those of Reichstadt and Budapest—forbidding the creation of an enlarged Slavic state. In the view of Prime Minister Benjamin Disraeli of Great Britain, the creation of an enlarged, Russian-dominated Bulgaria posed a potential threat to British interests in the eastern Mediterranean, especially the Suez Canal. Public outrage generated by Gladstone's pamphlet over the atrocities in Bulgaria, which had earlier hampered Disraeli's efforts to resist Russian expansionism in the Balkans, evaporated once Russia was seen as a serious threat to Britain's imperial communications.

After some preliminary arrangements between Britain, the Austro-Hungarian Empire, Russia, and the Ottoman Empire, a general European congress was convened in Berlin from June 13 to July 13, 1878, with German chancellor Otto von Bismarck serving as host and "honest broker." Andrássy represented the Austro-Hungarian Empire, Gorchakov represented Russia, and Disraeli represented Great Britain. The Congress of Berlin decided that the enlarged Bulgaria, whose boundaries had been drawn up in March as part of the Treaty of San Stefano, should be divided into three parts: Bulgaria proper, located north of the Balkan Mountains, which was to become an autonomous province of the Ottoman Empire; Eastern Rumelia, located south of the Balkan Mountains, which was somewhat more closely tied to the sultan; and Macedonia, which was to remain under direct Turkish rule. Bulgaria was thus reduced by two-thirds and completely cut off from the Aegean Sea. Other provisions gave Bessarabia to Russia and allowed Austria to occupy Bosnia and Herzegovina as well as to garrison the Sanjak of Novi Bazar, a strip of land lying between Serbia and Montenegro. Great Britain's occupation of Cyprus had previously been arranged on June 4, 1878, before the congress formally opened.

SIGNIFICANCE

The outcome of the Middle Eastern crisis of 1875-1878 in the Congress of Berlin had some far-reaching implications for the future of the Balkans, of Europe, and the world. Overall, the Austro-Hungarian Empire and Great Britain were able temporarily to stabilize the territorial integrity of the Ottoman Empire in the face of another historic Russian attempt to seize or outflank the Straits of the Dardanelles. Within this general framework, a serious consequence of the congress was that Russia had been deeply humiliated. True, Russia had knowingly and willingly overstepped the bounds of the Reichstadt and Budapest agreements in creating an enlarged Bulgaria under Russian influence. However, it is significant that Russia measured its forced retreat from the eastern Balkans (which did not actually begin until 1879) against the accession of Austrian hegemony in the west.

Although Austria's occupation of Bosnia and Herzegovina was likewise clearly in accord with the Budapest Convention, Austria nevertheless incurred the animosity of Russia, especially in Pan-Slav circles. At any rate, the Austro-Hungarian Empire became a leading power in southeastern Europe, where its interests would continue to clash with those of Russia. The Three Emperors' League did not survive the events of 1878. For Great Britain, the dissolution of this continental coalition was an added triumph.

Finally, the settlement of 1878 left all the Balkan states bitter toward each other and toward their shared adversaries, the Turks. The Bulgarians were embittered by the partition of their country, the Serbs by Austria's occupation of Bosnia and Herzegovina, and the Greeks by their failure to obtain any territorial compensation whatsoever. The stage was thus set for more national wars and strife in the Balkans, culminating in the assassination of Francis Ferdinand, the archduke of Austria, in Sarajevo, Bosnia, in June, 1914, which brought about World War I.

—Edward P. Keleher, updated by Richard D. King

FURTHER READING

Anderson, M. S. *The Eastern Question, 1774-1923: A Study in International Relations*. New York: St. Martin's Press, 1966. A comprehensive history of the problems and rivalries caused by the gradual decline of the Ottoman Empire during the nineteenth century.

Bridge, F. R. *The Habsburg Monarchy Among the Great Powers, 1815-1918*. New York: Berg, 1990. A history of Habsburg foreign policy during the century before World War I that emphasizes the Balkan ambitions of the monarchy and its leading statesmen.

Jelavich, Barbara. *Russia's Balkan Entanglements, 1806-1914*. New York: Cambridge University Press, 1991. Examines the reasons for Russian involvement in five wars in the Balkan Peninsula and their impact on internal developments in Russia.

Jelavich, Charles, and Barbara Jelavich. *The Establishment of the Balkan National States, 1804-1920*. Vol. 8 in *A History of East Central Europe*. Seattle: University of Washington Press, 1977. This work traces the history of the Balkan peoples' struggles for independence.

Langer, William L. *European Alliances and Alignments, 1871-1890*. 2d ed. New York: Alfred A. Knopf, 1950. A classic diplomatic history that focuses on Bismarck's efforts to prevent the emergence of an alliance system hostile to the newly created German Empire.

Medlicott, W. N. *The Congress of Berlin and After: A Diplomatic History of the Near East Settlement, 1878-1880*. 2d ed. Hamden, Conn.: Archon Books, 1962. A scholarly study that shows how Balkan rivalries continued after the Congress of Berlin as the great powers tried to implement the Berlin settlement.

Moss, Walter G. *A History of Russia*. 2d ed. Vol. 2. London: Anthem Press, 2002. Describes Alexander's reforms and his foreign policies in detail.

Seton-Watson, R. W. *Disraeli, Gladstone, and the Eastern Question: A Study in Diplomacy and Party Politics*. 1935. Reprint. New York: W. W. Norton, 1972. Studies the conflict between the principles of national self-interest and internationalism in British foreign policy toward the Balkans.

Yasamee, F. A. K. *Ottoman Diplomacy: Abdülhamid II and the Great Powers*. Istanbul: Isis Press, 1996. Traces the delicate balance in Turkish relations with Germany, Russia, France and Britain from the 1878 Congress of Berlin to 1909.

SEE ALSO: Dec. 3, 1868-Feb. 20, 1874: Gladstone Becomes Prime Minister of Britain; May 6-Oct. 22, 1873: Three Emperors' League Is Formed; May, 1876: Bulgarian Revolt Against the Ottoman Empire; Apr. 24, 1877-Jan. 31, 1878: Third Russo-Turkish War; Jan. 4, 1894: Franco-Russian Alliance.

RELATED ARTICLES in *Great Lives from History: The Nineteenth Century, 1801-1900:* Alexander II; Otto von Bismarck; Benjamin Disraeli; William Ewart Gladstone.

September, 1878
MACDONALD RETURNS AS CANADA'S PRIME MINISTER

The second administration by Canada's first prime minister, conservative John Macdonald, aimed to protect Canadian enterprises from foreign competition and encourage western settlement.

LOCALE: Ottawa, Canada
CATEGORY: Government and politics

KEY FIGURES

Sir John Alexander Macdonald (1815-1891), conservative prime minister of Canada, 1867-1873 and 1878-1891
Alexander Mackenzie (1822-1892), liberal prime minister of Canada, 1873-1878
Sir George Étienne Cartier (1814-1873), conservative minister of defense under Macdonald, 1867-1873
Charles Tupper (1821-1915), conservative prime minister of Canada, 1896
Wilfrid Laurier (1841-1919), liberal prime minister of Canada, 1896-1911

SUMMARY OF EVENT

It is difficult to overestimate the importance of John Macdonald in early Canadian history. Along with his two most influential associates, Sir George Étienne Cartier from Quebec and Charles Tupper from Nova Scotia, Ontarian John Macdonald played a central role in persuading the British government to approve the British North America Act, which ended Canada's colonial status and united the Canadian provinces under a single federal system. Alexander Mackenzie, Tupper, and Cartier created a political system that protected religious freedom, established English and French as the official languages of the new Dominion of Canada, and created a balance between the power of the federal and provincial governments.

On July 1, 1867, the British North America Act of 1867 took effect, and Macdonald became Canada's first prime minister. Macdonald was an English-speaking Protestant from Ontario, and Cartier was a French-speaking Roman Catholic from Quebec. They both understood that the unity of their new country required that representatives from Canada's major linguistic groups (English and French) and religions (Catholic and Protestant) be included at all levels of government. Although Macdonald was the prime minister, most historians believe that he and Cartier governed Canada together until Cartier's death in 1873. This cooperation contributed to the unity of Canada.

A scandal in 1873 that linked certain members of Macdonald's cabinet to bribes paid during the construction of the Canadian Pacific Railway weakened the influence of Macdonald's Conservative Party. Macdonald resigned as prime minister, and he was succeeded by Liberal Party leader Alexander Mackenzie in November, 1873.

Unfortunately for the honest and hardworking Mackenzie, Canada endured serious economic problems during the mid-1870's, and Canadian voters held him responsible for this depression. In the September, 1878, general election, Macdonald promised a new national

Sir John Alexander Macdonald. (Library of Congress)

policy that would protect Canadian business from unfair competition from U.S. and British companies. Macdonald and his major adviser, Charles Tupper, argued that unrestricted free trade with the United States and Great Britain had contributed significantly to the depression of the 1870's (which manifested itself in the United States as the Panic of 1873). This argument proved persuasive with the voters, who returned Macdonald to the office of prime minister. His Conservative Party kept its majority in Parliament until 1896, five years after Macdonald's death, when the liberals, under Wilfrid Laurier, defeated Prime Minister Tupper and the conservatives.

After Macdonald was again prime minister, the three major aspects of his national policy were revealed to the public. First, he imposed high tariffs on certain imported goods in order to protect Canadian companies from foreign competition. This did produce the desired effect of ensuring Canadian control over the Canadian economy, but it had the unavoidable side effect of creating inflation, because Canadian manufacturers felt no pressure to keep their prices low, since there was no real competition from other countries. Throughout the 1880's, Canadian voters were willing to accept high prices on products because they believed that low tariffs would have endangered Canadian economic independence by allowing U.S. and British companies to dominate the Canadian market.

A second important element of the national policy was the completion of the Canadian Pacific Railway, in order to link the eastern provinces to British Columbia. To obtain approval from the House of Commons for the large expenditures required for this massive project, Macdonald and Tupper, his minister of railroads and canals, gave overt preference to Canadian construction companies, even if their bids were higher than those received from U.S. or British companies. Macdonald and Tupper presented the nationalistic argument that Canadian economic independence justified the additional expense, and they questioned the patriotism of Edward Blake, the Liberal Party leader from 1880 to 1887, who had expressed serious doubts about what he considered to be the waste of tax dollars to protect uncompetitive Canadian companies.

After the creation of the Canadian Confederation in 1867, the new Dominion of Canada began expanding westward. Manitoba joined the confederation in 1870, and the following year, British Columbia became a province. Although Alberta and Saskatchewan were still territories and did not become provinces until September 1, 1905, they were an integral part of Canada during the second Macdonald government. Macdonald recognized that it was not sufficient to connect all of Canada physically by completing a transcontinental railroad system. He also had to encourage people to settle in large numbers in the provinces and territories west of Ontario, so that full economic development would be possible in the western part of Canada.

Macdonald actively encouraged immigration, but he gave overt preference to European immigrants over Asian immigrants and did little to discourage discrimination in British Columbia against Chinese and Japanese immigrants, who nevertheless were responsible for much of the construction of the British Columbia portion of the Canadian Pacific Railway.

Although Macdonald was successful in protecting emerging Canadian companies and in establishing a unified economic system in Canada, he began to pay less attention to the aspirations of the Maritime Provinces and Quebec. Residents in the provinces of Quebec, New Brunswick, Nova Scotia, and Prince Edward Island resented having to pay high prices for products in order to protect manufacturing companies located largely in Ontario and the western provinces, and they did not believe that eastern Canada had benefited significantly from the vast expenditure of tax dollars required for the construction of the Canadian Pacific Railway system.

In 1886, the provincial legislature of Nova Scotia seriously considered seceding from the Canadian Confederation. Large numbers of French speakers in Quebec were enraged when Macdonald approved the execution, in November, 1885, of Louis Riel, a Catholic French Canadian who had revolted against what he perceived to be the terrible mistreatment of French Canadian settlers in Saskatchewan. The hanging of Riel turned him into a martyr among Catholic and French Canadian voters. In hindsight, it appears that if Macdonald had still had an influential French Canadian adviser such as Cartier, who had helped him immensely during the early years of the Canadian Confederation, he would have pardoned Riel and would not have risked alienating French Canadian voters.

Growing dissatisfaction in Quebec and the Maritime Provinces with the national policy of the Conservative Party under Macdonald would contribute greatly to the victory of the liberal leader Wilfrid Laurier, a Catholic, French-speaking Quebecer, in the general election of 1896.

SIGNIFICANCE

Macdonald served as the prime minister of Canada for nineteen years. Although he was highly controversial, even his political opponents appreciated the importance of his central role in transforming Canada from a British colony into an independent country. In an eloquent and sincere eulogy given in the House of Commons on June 8, 1891, only two days after Macdonald's death, the opposition leader, Laurier, described Macdonald as "Canada's most illustrious son, and in every sense Canada's foremost citizen and statesman."

The high opinion in which Canadians have held Macdonald, their first prime minister, has not diminished. He remains an almost legendary figure in Canadian history.

—*Edmund J. Campion*

FURTHER READING

Creighton, Donald. *Canada's First Century, 1867-1967*. New York: St. Martin's Press, 1970. Contains a clear description of the profound changes that occurred in Canada between the creation of Canada in 1867 and Macdonald's death in 1891.

Donaldson, Gordon. *Fifteen Men: Canada's Prime Ministers from Macdonald to Trudeau*. Garden City, N.Y.: Doubleday, 1969. Describes succinctly the nature of John Macdonald's national policy, which transformed Canada from a collection of provinces into a unified transcontinental nation.

"John A. Macdonald." *Maclean's* 114, no. 27 (July, 1, 2001): 37. A profile of Macdonald, describing his career, role in the confederation of Canada, and involvement in Canadian politics.

Owram, Douglas, ed. *Canadian History: A Reader's Guide. Confederation to the Present*. Toronto: University of Toronto Press, 1994. Contains an excellent annotated bibliography of historical studies on Macdonald's importance, both to the creation of Canada as an independent country and for his accomplishments as prime minister.

Smith, Cynthia M., and Jack McLeod, eds. *Sir John A: An Anecdotal Life of John A. Macdonald*. Toronto: Oxford University Press, 1989. Despite its subtitle, this book does not merely contain anecdotes about the life of Canada's first prime minister. Includes numerous judicious assessments of Macdonald's career, by both contemporaries and later historians.

Swainson, Donald. *John A. Macdonald: The Man and the Politician*. New York: Oxford University Press, 1971. A sympathetic, well-documented biography of Macdonald. Discusses the many political and social problems caused by the implementation of his national policy.

Waite, P. B. *The Life and Times of Confederation, 1864-1867: Politics, Newspapers, and the Union of British North America*. 3d ed. Toronto: Robin Brass Studio, 2001. Recounts the events leading to the 1867 confederation of the Canadian provinces, examining the role played by politics and newspapers.

SEE ALSO: Oct. 23-Dec. 16, 1837: Rebellions Rock British Canada; Feb. 10, 1841: Upper and Lower Canada Unite; Apr. 25, 1849: First Test of Canada's Responsible Government; July 1, 1867: British North America Act; Oct. 11, 1869-July 15, 1870: First Riel Rebellion; 1872: Dominion Lands Act Fosters Canadian Settlement; May 23, 1873: Canada Forms the North-West Mounted Police; Nov. 5, 1873-Oct. 9, 1878: Canada's Mackenzie Era; 1875: Supreme Court of Canada Is Established; 1876: Canada's Indian Act; Mar. 19, 1885: Second Riel Rebellion Begins; July 11, 1896: Laurier Becomes the First French Canadian Prime Minister.

RELATED ARTICLES in *Great Lives from History: The Nineteenth Century, 1801-1900:* George Brown; Sir John Alexander Macdonald; Alexander Mackenzie; Louis Riel; Sir Charles Tupper; Queen Victoria.

October 19, 1878
GERMANY PASSES ANTI-SOCIALIST LAW

The Anti-Socialist Law of 1878 attempted to destroy the Social Democratic Party by prohibiting Social Democrats from forming associations, holding public meetings, collecting funds, or publicizing their views. The government allowed Social Democratic deputies to continue their work in the German parliament and to field candidates for election. The law remained in effect until 1890 but failed to stop the growth of the Social Democratic party.

LOCALE: Berlin, Prussia, German Empire (now in Germany)

CATEGORIES: Laws, acts, and legal history; civil rights and liberties; government and politics

KEY FIGURES

William I (1797-1888), king of Prussia, r. 1861-1888, and German emperor, r. 1871-1888

Otto von Bismarck (1815-1898), prime minister of Prussia, 1862-1890, and chancellor of the German Empire, 1871-1890

August Bebel (1840-1913), co-founder and leader of the Social Democratic Party

William II (1859-1941), king of Prussia and German emperor, r. 1888-1918

Rudolf von Bennigsen (1824-1902), leader of the National Liberal Party

SUMMARY OF EVENT

Germany's Law Against the Publicly Dangerous Endeavors of Social Democracy, commonly known as the Anti-Socialist Law or simply the Socialist Law, was essentially the brain child of Imperial Chancellor Otto von Bismarck. It prohibited all associations and societies that advocated social democratic, socialist, or communist endeavors, which were seen as threatening the existing political or social order. The prohibition applied not only to private societies but also to the Social Democratic Party. The law was first passed on October 19, 1878, and was subsequently renewed four times, in May, 1880, in May, 1884, in April, 1886, and—despite considerable opposition—in February, 1888. Its provisions remained in effect until September 30, 1890.

Enforcement of the law's sweeping provisions was entrusted to the State Police Authorities in the various states of the German Empire. They could attend all meetings of suspect societies, arrest and interrogate individuals, and prohibit or dissolve meetings. They also had the power to punish anyone who served as a member of a prohibited society or who carried out activities on its behalf. Offenders were subject to monetary fines or to imprisonment, depending on the gravity of the offense.

To curtail the spread of socialist propaganda, the police were given the power to confiscate all publications that could be viewed as threatening the public peace or as disturbing the peaceful relations among the various classes of society. Printers and distributors of such materials, as well as booksellers and even librarians in lending libraries or the owners of reading rooms, could be fined or imprisoned. Furthermore, innkeepers and persons engaged in the retail liquor business could be forbidden from continuing in their business if they participated in prohibited meetings.

To reduce the effectiveness of the Social Democratic Party, the authorities were also empowered to confiscate party assets. More serious was the provision that in larger cities like Berlin or Hamburg, which had an exceptionally high concentration of Social Democrats, the authorities could proclaim a so-called minor state of siege, during which persons deemed especially dangerous to the public order could be expelled from the city.

The law was implemented with brutality and ruthlessness and drove the Social Democratic Party underground. Many of its leaders, as well as rank and file members, were frequently given jail sentences or driven into exile. The party's newspaper, the *Sozialdemokrat* (social democrat), had to be published in Zurich, Switzerland, and smuggled into Germany, while the party leadership was compelled to hold its congresses abroad. At the same time, the law dealt a serious blow to the Independent Trade Unions, who were affiliated with the Social Democratic Party.

However, much to Bimarck's chagrin, the National Liberals in the Reichstag, or German parliament, had managed to limit the terms of the law to two and one-half years. Another obstacle in his efforts to silence the Social Democrats was that the law did not affect the Social Democratic deputies in the parliament, who were led by August Bebel. In addition to participating in the frequently heated debates, the deputies also functioned as the party's unofficial executive committee, since they could not be prevented from meeting together.

Bismarck's campaign against the Social Democrats derived from his conviction that as internationalists, republicans, and atheists, these "enemies of the empire" represented a danger to the stability of the state and to the security of the monarchy. The struggle against the Social Democrats was intertwined with Bismarck's plan to reduce the influence of Rudolf von Bennigsen's National Liberal Party, which was generally sympathetic to Social Democratic efforts to reform the German political system. Above all, Bismarck wanted to bring the National Liberals in line with his move toward protectionism.

The opportunity for Bismarck to advance his plans by instituting the Anti-Socialist Law had arisen on May 11, 1878, when one Max Hoedel, a deranged plumber's apprentice, had fired two shots at Emperor William I. He had missed, but Bismarck, undeterred by the fact that there was no evidence to connect Hoedel with the Social Democrats, had exploited the assassination attempt and blamed the party anyway. In short order, he had submitted a hastily drawn up bill that would outlaw the Social Democratic Party. The loosely worded bill had suffered an overwhelming defeat in the Reichstag.

However, on June 2, 1878, a second attempt on William's life was more successful, and the aging emperor was gravely wounded. The perpetrator, Karl Nobiling, an agronomist, shot himself before his motives could be established. Once again, Bismarck blamed the Social Democrats and started a vicious propaganda campaign against them. On June 11, he dissolved the Reichstag. The following elections resulted in a shift to the right, as both the National Liberals and their progressive allies lost mandates. The Social Democrats also lost some seats but managed to increase their votes in the larger cities.

On October 19, an anti-socialist bill passed the Reichstag by a vote of 221 to 149, although the law was not as sweeping as Bismarck and the Conservatives had hoped it would be. In the years to come, Bismarck repeatedly tried but failed to strengthen the bill and make it permanent. Realizing that the outlawed Social Democrats were in fact increasing in strength, Bismarck sought to wean the workers away from the party by portraying the Social Democrats as revolutionaries who had never proposed any legislation that would benefit the working classes. He attempted to demonstrate that his government would grant to the German workers what their own party with its few deputies was unable enact. In 1881, he started a program of social legislation that culminated in the passage of the Sickness Insurance Law (1883), the Amended Accident Insurance Law (1884), and the Old Age and Disability Insurance Law (1889), effectively bringing social security to the German Empire.

On January 25, 1890, Bismarck's effort to pass a new, permanent anti-socialist law failed in the Reichstag. The new emperor, William II, had already made it clear that, in spite of Bismarck's threat to resign, he was not interested in another anti-socialist law but rather in a reform of protective legislation for labor. In the elections of February-March, 1890, the Social Democrats managed to strengthen their position in the Reichstag: Indeed, during the period of suppression, they had managed to increase the number of seats they held from nine to thirty-five. Bismarck, now completely at odds with his sovereign and facing the fact that he had irretrievably lost control of the parliament, resigned in March of 1890. The existing Anti-Socialist Law expired on September 30.

SIGNIFICANCE

The major underlying reason for Bismarck's failure to crush the Social Democrats was his inability to appreciate the changing social dynamics inherent in Germany's growing industrialization. He believed that he could manage the growing conflict between parliamentary aspirations and monarchical power and assure the continued strength of the monarchy by threats, repression, and, if need be, by paternalistic and benevolent social legislation. By 1890, his Anti-Socialist Law had backfired and brought about the exact opposite of its original intent. At the same time, however, his attacks on the National Liberal Party had met with success and had dealt a serious blow to progressive forces.

Bismarck's ruthless parliamentary tactics and his contempt for democratic principles, which he displayed during the twelve years of the Anti-Socialist Law, did nothing to build confidence in the viability of democratic government in Germany. However, his successes in foreign policy as the unifier of Germany and his role at the Congress of Berlin (1878) as Europe's honest broker more often than not overshadowed, at least in the popular mind, the failures of his domestic policies and their negative impact on the growth of democracy.

—*Helmut J. Schmeller*

FURTHER READING

Craig, Gordon A. *Germany, 1866-1945*. New York: Oxford University Press, 1978. The chapter "The Campaign Against Social Democracy and Bismarck's Fall, 1879-1890," represents the standard treatment of the subject.

Kent, George O. *Bismarck and His Times*. Carbondale: Southern Illinois University Press, 1978. Brief account of Bismarck's policies, offering a summary of the literature on the topic since World War II.

Lee, Stephen J. *Imperial Germany, 1871-1918*. London:

Routledge, 1999. Each of the brief chapters offers a narrative section and a separate analytical section. Especially useful for undergraduates.

Lerman, Katharine Anne. *Bismarck.* New York: Pearson Longman, 2004. Contains a brief and balanced discussion of Bismarck's campaign against liberals and social democrats.

Litdke, Vernon L. "The Outlawed Party." In *Social Democracy in Germany, 1878-1890.* Princeton, N.J.: Princeton University Press, 1966. Well-documented and comprehensive account. An appendix of relevant documents includes the text of the Anti-Socialist Law. Indispensable.

Williamson, D.G. *Bismarck and Germany, 1862-1890.* 2d ed. London: Longman, 1998. Concise and readable account of Bismarck's domestic and foreign policies. Useful glossary, maps, and a collection of pertinent documents.

SEE ALSO: Sept. 24, 1862: Bismarck Becomes Prussia's Minister-President; 1866-1867: North German Confederation Is Formed; 1871-1877: Kulturkampf Against the Catholic Church in Germany; Jan. 18, 1871: German States Unite Within German Empire; 1881-1889: Bismarck Introduces Social Security Programs in Germany.

RELATED ARTICLE in *Great Lives from History: The Nineteenth Century, 1801-1900:* Otto von Bismarck.

1879
A DOLL'S HOUSE INTRODUCES MODERN REALISTIC DRAMA

With the controversial play A Doll's House, *which centered on the subjugation of a middle-class married woman, Henrik Ibsen introduced the language, characterization, and structure that came to be known as modern realistic drama. The popular theater would never again be devoted solely to verse dramas or overdone melodramas, and all serious dramatists would follow Ibsen's innovations in exploring realistic character psychology.*

ALSO KNOWN AS: *Et dukkehjem*
LOCALE: Christiana (now Oslo), Norway
CATEGORIES: Literature; theater; women's issues; social issues and reform

KEY FIGURE

Henrik Ibsen (1828-1906), Norwegian playwright and theater manager

SUMMARY OF EVENT

Before writing *Et dukkehjem* (1879; *A Doll's House*, 1880), Henrik Ibsen had become famous for highly romantic verse dramas about Norwegian myth and history. Indeed, his countryfolk were so proud of him for aggrandizing their culture that, although he was living abroad, the Norwegian parliament voted him a lifetime annual allowance. Ibsen's background was middle class, having been born into the family of a well-to-do Norwegian merchant. When he was a young boy, Ibsen's father lost his business and the family fell into poverty. Despite the problems of a poverty-stricken youth, Ibsen managed to obtain a reasonable education, and through his writings he became for a time a theater manager in Christiana, Norway. Always driven to writing, his work in the theater led him to create highly successful poetic plays.

In 1869, however, Ibsen, always a revolutionary at heart, abandoned verse for prose, and with *De unges forbund* (1869; *The League of Youth*, 1890), a satire on supposed liberals, he signaled a turn in the direction of social problems. There followed in 1877 a savage attack on the hypocrisy of the merchant class in *Samfundets støtter* (*The Pillars of Society*, 1880), which caused an uproar upon its production in Norway. Two years later the uproar would be even greater with the production in 1879 of his groundbreaking realistic drama, *A Doll's House*. What exactly prompted Ibsen to take up the cause of middle class women's rights is difficult to say, but it is known that he had read and been impressed with John Stuart Mill's *The Subjection of Women* (1869), in which women's subjugation and freedom are strongly argued.

To understand the extent of Ibsen's innovation in *The Doll's House* one should consider also the nature of popular theater during the late nineteenth century. Audiences had enjoyed Romantic verse drama, as well as William Shakespeare's works, but the stage in Norway had been virtually dominated by the popular melodrama. In melodrama during that time, the emphasis had been on highly contrived incidents and clearly defined and conventional emotions. Villains were always completely wicked, and women were divided into two categories: the simple and innocent girls and wives and the fallen and conniving courtesans. Men were either brave and strong or evil and scheming. The dialogue, even if it were in prose, tended to be overblown and rhetorical. *A Doll's House* soon appeared and caused a revolution in the theater world.

Set in a staid middle-class home headed by a dominant and domineering husband who is a successful banker, *A Doll's House* is centered on the life of Nora Helmer, a quiet and dutiful housewife and mother. Nora's husband, Torvald, regards her in a manner typical of the society of the day: as a grown child who is to be treated as such by her husband. Nora's home is a "doll's house," where she plays at being a mother and wife. In another innovation that comes out of the play, Ibsen presents this picture in the ordinary prose dialogue of everyday life.

Change appears in the Helmers' household, as Nora has a secret that her husband is about to discover. As the story goes, several years earlier, when Torvald had been very ill, Nora had to forge her father's name on a loan application to get enough funds to aid her husband medically. That secret ends up being revealed by the clerk who witnessed the forgery. Torvald discovers the secret and berates his wife unmercifully, as if she were a rebellious teenager, furious with her that she dared, as a "mere" woman, to make decisions about money without consulting him. The clerk then sends a letter saying he regrets having told the secret and promises not to discuss the matter further. Torvald, now relieved, apologizes to Nora for being so harsh. Nora, however, has had enough of being treated as a lesser human being. She leaves Torvald and the children, slams the door on her doll's house, and sets out to become the full human being she is.

In more modern times, Nora's decision to leave her children and husband would have been understood as, at minimum, psychologically sound. The full psychological complexity of Nora's situation is fully presented by Ibsen. Nora was acting in the best interests of her husband when she forged her father's name for the loan to help her husband. Torvald was too sick to be consulted, and Nora's father was also incapacitated. Nora loved her husband, and she was equally devoted to her children. Throughout the play, however, Nora

"I Have Been Your Doll-Wife"

In Henrik Ibsen's drama A Doll's House, *Nora finally confronts her belittling husband Torvald by sitting him down for a never-before-held conversation between the two. In the following excerpt, from Act III of the play, Torvald acts surprised by Nora's convictions, and Nora acts with an authority and assertiveness that shows she has broken out of the doll mold that has encased her life to this point.*

Nora (shaking her head). You have never loved me. You have only thought it pleasant to be in love with me.

Torvald. Nora, what do I hear you saying?

Nora. It is perfectly true, Torvald. When I was at home with papa, he told me his opinion about everything, and so I had the same opinions; and if I differed from him I concealed the fact, because he would not have liked it. He called me his doll-child, and he played with me just as I used to play with my dolls. And when I came to live with you—

Torvald. What sort of an expression is that to use about our marriage?

Nora (undisturbed). I mean that I was simply transferred from papa's hands into yours. You arranged everything according to your own taste, and so I got the same tastes as you—or else I pretended to, I am really not quite sure which—I think sometimes the one and sometimes the other. When I look back on it, it seems to me as if I had been living here like a poor woman—just from hand to mouth. I have existed merely to perform tricks for you, Torvald. But you would have it so. You and papa have committed a great sin against me. It is your fault that I have made nothing of my life.

Torvald. How unreasonable and how ungrateful you are, Nora! Have you not been happy here?

Nora. No, I have never been happy. I thought I was, but it has never really been so.

Torvald. Not—not happy!

Nora. No, only merry. And you have always been so kind to me. But our home has been nothing but a playroom. I have been your doll-wife, just as at home I was papa's doll-child; and here the children have been my dolls. I thought it great fun when you played with me, just as they thought it great fun when I played with them. That is what our marriage has been, Torvald.

Torvald. There is some truth in what you say—exaggerated and strained as your view of it is. But for the future it shall be different. Playtime shall be over, and lesson-time shall begin.

Nora. Whose lessons? Mine, or the children's?

Torvald. Both yours and the children's, my darling Nora.

Nora. Alas, Torvald, you are not the man to educate me into being a proper wife for you.

is considered an immature girl by her husband. One climactic scene shows her attempt to prevent her husband from reading the clerk's letter about the loan by dancing the tarantella, a dance considered a bit risqué for the period. She is stopped in her dance and berated by her husband for being immature and not showing restraint and dignity in his presence.

Nora leaves her "doll's house," but Ibsen does not allow for an easy solution to Nora's newfound problem. Nora declares her independence to herself and the world, but she has no way of making a living for herself. Furthermore, Victorian society would not have allowed that she ever again see her children. Her life would prove to be extremely difficult, and Ibsen ends the play on that note. The outcry that came with the play's performance when it opened in Norway is evidence of how difficult Nora's life would be in such a world. Indeed, under extreme pressure from critics, Ibsen had to agree to a different ending to the play, in which Nora repented her decision to leave. Nevertheless, *A Doll's House* started a literary revolution, and the play's fame, along with that of the playwright, spread across Europe and the United States, as audiences and dramatists embraced the new realistic prose drama.

Scene from the 1922 silent film adaptation of A Doll's House, *with Alan Hale (right) as Torvald Helmer and Alla Nazimova as Nora Helmer.* (Hulton Archive/Getty Images)

1870's

SIGNIFICANCE

During the late nineteenth century the Western world had become dominated by the middle class, and the middle class was built upon the institution of marriage. Moreover, marriage was seen as union between a significant male, who was head of the household, and a less significant female. The role of the husband was to earn a living for the couple and their children and to take part in the organization and government of his house and of society as a whole. The role of the female was to be a good mother and wife and to make a home that was pleasant for and supportive of her husband. For a woman, always, to violate this tradition was to call into question the whole social order. This ideal was without question psychologically unsound, and Ibsen revealed its indignities in a single play.

It has been said that when Nora closed the door on the doll's house she in turn opened the door for modern realistic drama. Ibsen quickly followed with other prose dramas exploring the psychology of the middle-class woman. Most notable are his works *Gengangere* (pb. 1881, pr. 1882; *Ghosts*, 1885) and *Hedda Gabler* (pb. 1890, pr. 1891; English translation, 1891). In doing so he led the way for major realistic playwrights such as George Bernard Shaw to create a continuing tradition of drama.

—*August W. Staub*

FURTHER READING

Clurman, Harold. *Ibsen*. New York: Macmillian, 1977. An excellent overall study by an important mid-twentieth century critic.

McFarland, James, ed. *The Cambridge Companion to Ibsen*. New York: Cambridge University Press, 1994. The most complete general work on Ibsen still available.

Shaw, George Bernard. *The Quintessence of Ibsenism*. London: Walter Scott, 1891. Despite its age, this book by the great English playwright is an excellent introduction to the realistic dramas of Ibsen. It clearly demonstrates the powerful immediate impact that Ibsen's new psychological realism had on modern drama.

Templeton, Joan. *Ibsen's Women*. New York: Cambridge University Press, 1997. The background and psychology of Nora and the other women in Ibsen's works are thoroughly explored and explicated.

SEE ALSO: Mar. 3, 1830: Hugo's *Hernani* Incites Rioting; 1850's-1880's: Rise of Burlesque and Vaudeville; Mar., 1852-Sept., 1853: Dickens Publishes *Bleak House*; 1855: Courbet Establishes Realist Art Movement; Oct. 1-Dec. 15, 1856: Flaubert Publishes *Madame Bovary*; c. 1865: Naturalist Movement Begins; 1878-1899: Irving Manages London's Lyceum Theatre; Oct. 14, 1898: Moscow Art Theater Is Founded; Nov. 8, 1900: Dreiser Publishes *Sister Carrie*.

RELATED ARTICLES in *Great Lives from History: The Nineteenth Century, 1801-1900:* Kate Chopin; Charles Dickens; Gustave Flaubert; Edvard Grieg; Victor Hugo; Henrik Ibsen.

1879
POWELL PUBLISHES HIS REPORT ON THE AMERICAN WEST

One of the most influential recommendations for government land management and disposition in the American West came out of an 1879 report made by scientist and explorer John Wesley Powell. He insisted in the report that most of the West was unsuited for settlement and farming as practiced in the humid East, and his work led to the idea of water management, including the use of dams and irrigation projects, as key to Western development.

LOCALE: Western United States
CATEGORIES: Expansion and land acquisition; exploration and discovery; geography

KEY FIGURE

John Wesley Powell (1834-1902), explorer, scientist, and director of the U.S. Geological Survey and the U.S. Bureau of Ethnography

SUMMARY OF EVENT

John Wesley Powell achieved national fame through his pioneering voyage down the Colorado River in 1869. Born in 1834 on a frontier farm in New York, he showed an early interest in education and was introduced to science by a farm neighbor in Ohio. He further developed his scientific interests as a student at colleges in Illinois and Ohio. His career as a schoolteacher and lyceum lecturer was interrupted by the U.S. Civil War (1861-1865). A wound that Powell received at Shiloh (Pittsburgh Landing) resulted in the amputation of his right arm, after which his wife and first cousin, Emma Dean Powell, accompanied him in the field. Mustered out of the Army, Powell joined Illinois Wesleyan College as a professor of natural history.

In 1867, after raising money from various state and federal institutions and private business, he set out on an exploratory trip to the Rocky Mountains. Powell and his wife climbed Pikes Peak and explored the Grand River (now the upper Colorado River) in Colorado. The next year, he returned to climb Longs Peak, explore the White River Valley, and visit Green River, Wyoming.

In early spring, 1869, faced by threats of desertion from his crew, Powell had to curb his wife's managerial

John Wesley Powell. (Library of Congress)

efforts. She never again accompanied him in the field. During 1869, Powell began collecting artifacts from the Utes, recording Ute legends, and compiling a Ute dictionary. In 1869, he descended the Colorado River from Green River, going through the Grand Canyon to the mouth of the Virgin River. Only two days before the trip's end, three discouraged men left the canyon, only to be killed by Paiutes.

On July 12, 1870, Congress had established the Geographical and Geological Survey of the Rocky Mountain Region, with Powell in charge. Powell's survey spent ten years mapping the Colorado Plateau in Utah and Arizona, publishing reports on natural history and indigenous tribes. Powell became alarmed by many of his observations and by events elsewhere in the West. Many farmers on the Great Plains, deceived by a series of unusually wet years during the 1860's and early 1870's, settled too far West, beyond the hundredth meridian, where normal rainfall, fewer than twenty inches per year, was insufficient to grow crops. When the weather cycle turned dry, many farmers were bankrupted and driven from the land. Much agricultural land also was eroded severely by wind and water. In the Rockies, irrigation companies were gaining control over water supplies, and timber cutters were denuding the mountainsides.

POWELL ON THE GREAT AND UNKNOWN GRAND CANYON

John Wesley Powell combined into one narrative the story of his two trips into the Grand Canyon and down the Colorado River with his survey crew. In this excerpt from his 1875 book, Exploration of the Colorado River of the West and Its Tributaries, *Powell introduces the reader to the start of the journey "down the Great Unknown."*

We are now ready to start on our way down the Great Unknown. Our boats, tied to a common stake, chafe each other as they are tossed by the fretful river. They ride high and buoyant, for their loads are lighter than we could desire. We have but a month's rations remaining. The flour has been resifted through the mosquito-net sieve; the spoiled bacon has been dried and the worst of it boiled; the few pounds of dried apples have been spread in the sun and reshrunken to their normal bulk. The sugar has all melted and gone its way down the river. But we have a large sack of coffee. The lightening of the boats has this advantage: they will ride the waves better and we shall have but little to carry when we make a portage.

We are three quarters of a mile in the depths of the earth, and the great river shrinks into insignificance as it dashes its angry waves against the walls and cliffs that rise to the world above; the waves are but puny ripples, and we but pigmies, running up and down the sands or lost among the boulders.

We have an unknown distance yet to run, and unknown river to explore. . . .

Source: Excerpted in *The Wilderness Reader*, edited by Frank Bergon (Reno: University of Nevada Press, 1980), p. 152.

1870's

As early as 1873, Powell expressed concern about future settlement in the arid West and recommended changing the land classification system of the United States. In 1879, he published his *Report on the Lands of the Arid Region of the United States, with a More Detailed Account of the Lands of Utah.* (An earlier version of the report was submitted to Congress in 1878 but was corrected and finalized by Powell; it was published as a second edition by the U.S. Government Printing Office in 1879. The second edition is considered definitive.) Because two-fifths of the United States was arid, Powell urged closing public lands to entry until they were topographically mapped and reclassified. Thereafter, the lands were to be distributed to the people according to regulations adapted to Powell's five proposed classes: mineral, coal, pasturage, irrigable, and timber lands.

Powell's report included two proposed laws for organizing irrigation districts and pasturage districts in the western lands. Groups of farmers were to be urged to locate together and form cooperatives, sharing the expense of building dams and ditches to conserve and use water resources. Land units in irrigation districts were to be eighty acres, rather than the accustomed 160. Water rights would inhere in the land, title to the water passing with the land.

Powell recommended abandonment of the rectangular system of survey so that irrigable land could be parceled out, giving each person access to water. He proposed organizing grazing units of twenty-five hundred acres, each unit to include water sufficient to irrigate twenty acres of winter hay or farm crops. Settlers would be allowed to file for holdings without charge, but if the water were not utilized within five years, the land and water rights would revert to the public domain. Powell also insisted that riparian rights under English common law, allowing land owners to take all the water they wished from streams crossing or bordering their property, would have to be modified or abrogated in the arid region. Thus, water rights would be limited to the amount required or used on land to be irrigated.

The report also described the lands of Utah and their development as directed by the Church of Jesus Christ of Latter-day Saints (the Mormons) as an example of how his recommendations might be implemented. This part of the report was written by members of Powell's survey: *Irrigable Lands of the Salt Lake Drainage System* by Grove Karl Gilbert, Powell's chief geologic assistant; *Irrigable Lands of the Valley of the Sevier River* by Clarence Edward Dutton, the geologist responsible for geologic reports on the Grand Canyon and the Colorado Plateau; and *Irrigable Lands of That Portion of Utah Drained by the Colorado River and Its Tributaries* by Powell's brother-in-law Almond H. Thompson. Thompson was a map maker and the chief topographer for the Powell surveys. Willis Drummond, Jr., contributed *Land Grants in Aid of Internal Improvements*.

Powell's proposals were unpopular with westerners. Many small farmers, too impatient to wait on government land reclassification, thought his program closed the door to opportunity. Others thought large land units for grazing favored big cattlemen. His reforms also were opposed by railroads, prospectors and mining companies, cattle associations, land companies, and irrigation companies. Thus, Congress failed to act on Powell's recommendations.

SIGNIFICANCE

Although Powell was ignored by Congress, he continued his efforts to reform land policy in the arid lands. He was instrumental in consolidating western geological exploration in the U.S. Geological Survey, which, starting in 1879, continued the topographic mapping he had recommended. He also organized and became director of the Bureau of Ethnology to study American Indian cultures. In 1881, he also became director of the Geological Survey.

In 1887, a decade of drought began, bringing disaster to arid-land farmers and demands for federal irrigation projects. Powell, with the aid of Senator William Stewart of Nevada, secured a congressional resolution in 1888, establishing an Irrigation Survey within the Geological Survey. This resolution also closed entry into most public lands until the irrigable lands had been identified and surveyed. In 1890, however, political opposition drastically reduced funds for the Irrigation Survey. Powell then retired from the Geological Survey and devoted the remainder of his life to the Bureau of Ethnology, which he served as director for twenty-three years.

More of Powell's 1879 proposals were enacted under conservation-minded administrations in the twentieth century. In 1902, the Newlands Act, creating the Bureau of Reclamation, provided for irrigation districts, dams, and canals more or less according to Powell's 1879 recommendations. The Soil Conservation Service, later the Bureau of Land Management, and the Tennessee Valley Authority (TVA), enacted in 1932, incorporate part of Powell's 1879 proposals. Opposition, however, persisted in the 1990's as Republicans called for selling the TVA and western public lands.

—W. Turrentine Jackson,
updated by Ralph L. Langenheim, Jr.

FURTHER READING

Darrah, William Culp. *Powell of the Colorado*. Princeton, N.J.: Princeton University Press, 1951. The first and best full-length biography of John Wesley Powell.

Dellenbaugh, Frederick S. *A Canyon Voyage*. New Haven, Conn.: Yale University Press, 1962. The most complete published narrative of Powell's second expedition along the Colorado River.

Goetzmann, William H. *Exploration and Empire: The Explorer and the Scientist in the Winning of the American West*. New York: Alfred A. Knopf, 1966. A chapter on Powell as an explorer and reformer is included in this Pulitzer Prize-winning book.

Powell, John Wesley. *Report on the Lands of the Arid Region of the United States, with a More Detailed Account of the Lands of Utah*. Edited by Wallace Stegner. Cambridge, Mass.: Belknap Press of Harvard University Press, 1962. A reprint of the second (1879), corrected edition, with an introduction by the editor.

________. *Seeing Things Whole: The Essential John Wesley Powell*. Edited by William de Buys. Washington, D.C.: Island Press/Shearwater Books, 2001. A collection of Powell's writings, including selections from *A Report on the Lands of the Arid Region of the United States*, and writings expressing his ideas about civilization, western settlement, and allocation of natural resources. Selections are annotated and have introductions placing them within the proper context.

Stegner, Wallace. *Beyond the Hundredth Meridian: John Wesley Powell and the Second Opening of the West*. Boston: Houghton Mifflin, 1954. This book abounds with special pleading for causes and people, lacks unity, and has a shaky conceptual framework, but is delightful reading and highly informative.

Udall, Stewart L. *The Quiet Crisis and the Next Generation*. Salt Lake City, Utah: Peregrine Smith Books, 1988. Discusses Powell's work as part of the conservationist and preservationist movements in the United States.

Watson, Elmo Scott. *The Professor Goes West*. Bloomington: Illinois Wesleyan University Press, 1954. Emphasizes Powell's first western expedition in 1867 and reprints the reports of expedition member J. C. Hartzell.

Worster, Donald. *A River Running West: The Life of John Wesley Powell*. New York: Oxford University Press, 2001. Thorough, detailed account of Powell's life from his childhood through his years directing the Bureau of American Ethnology.

SEE ALSO: May 14, 1804-Sept. 23, 1806: Lewis and Clark Expedition; July 15, 1806-July 1, 1807: Pike Explores the American Southwest; Sept. 8, 1810-May, 1812: Astorian Expeditions Explore the Pacific Northwest; Apr. 24, 1820: Congress Passes Land Act of 1820; 1822-1831: Jedediah Smith Explores the Far West; May, 1842-1854: Frémont Explores the American West; June 30, 1846-Jan. 13, 1847: United States Occupies California and the Southwest; Mar. 2, 1853-1857: Pacific Railroad Surveys; May 20, 1862: Lincoln Signs the Homestead Act; July 2, 1862: Lincoln Signs the Morrill Land Grant Act.

RELATED ARTICLES in *Great Lives from History: The Nineteenth Century, 1801-1900:* Kit Carson; John C. Frémont; Zebulon Pike; Jedediah Smith; Fanny Bullock Workman; Brigham Young.

January 22-23, 1879
BATTLES OF ISANDLWANA AND RORKE'S DRIFT

The first major engagement of the Zulu War, the Battle of Isandlwana was a Zulu victory that inflicted a devastating defeat on a British army. In the next day's battle at Rorke's Drift, a small British garrison repelled the assaults of an immensely larger Zulu force. Despite the great losses suffered by the British, the Zulu lost even more men, and the war would end in a decisive British victory.

LOCALE: Zululand and Natal, South Africa
CATEGORY: Wars, uprisings, and civil unrest

KEY FIGURES

Bartle Frere (1815-1884), governor of the Cape Colony and British high commissioner for South Africa, 1877-1880

Cetshwayo (1832-1884), king of the Zulu, r. 1872-1879

Second Baron Chelmsford (Frederic Augustus Thesiger; 1827-1905), British commander who led the invasion of Zululand

Anthony W. Durnford (1830-1879), British officer in the Royal Engineers

Henry Pulleine (1838-1879), British army officer

Dabulamanzi (1839-1886), Zulu commander at Rorke's Drift

John R. M. Chard (1847-1897), Lieutenant, Fifth Company, Royal Engineers, senior British officer defending Rorke's Drift

Gonville Bromhead (1845-1892) and

James Langley Dalton (1833-1887), British officers at Rorke's Drift

SUMMARY OF EVENT

Early in 1879, the British high commissioner in South Africa, Sir Bartle Frere, tried to establish a confederation of white-led states in Southern Africa. However, the Zulu Kingdom stood in the way of his plan. After giving an ultimatum to the Zulu king Cetshwayo that was ignored, Frere launched a military invasion of Zululand.

Under the command of Lieutenant General Lord Chelmsford, the invasion force consisted of three columns and two reserve units. The entire force was directed to converge on the royal Zulu military encampment at Ulundi. At the head of 4,700 men of the central column, Chelmsford crossed the Mzinyathi River on January 11, 1879, leaving behind a small contingent by the river to secure a depot at Rorke's Drift. The following day his column attacked a Zulu settlement near a large rock crag named Isandlwana and afterward made camp. The camp was considered temporary and unlikely to be attacked, so no defensive measures were undertaken. The column comprised more than 4,900 men and 300 wagons.

On January 17, 1879, 28,000 Zulu warriors crossed the White Mfolozi River near Ulundi. On January 18, 4,000 of the warriors left the main Zulu army, and the remaining 24,000 encamped at isiPhezi ikhanda. On January 19, the larger force split in two and began moving in parallel columns toward the Ngwebeni Valley. Upon reaching the valley on January 21, the army went into hiding.

On January 21, a scouting party of 150 men left the British camp at Isandlwana. At the same time, 1,600 mounted soldiers of the Natal Native Contingent left to scout to the southeast. During the same day, several skirmishes occurred with Zulu patrols, and both the British and Natal units chose to make camp in the field. The next morning, Chelmsford rode with 2,500 men to reinforce the British scouting party, leaving 1,800 men at Isandlwana under the command of Lieutenant Colonel Pulleine. A second British scouting force spotting a small group of Zulu began a pursuit, ending at an overlook of the Ngwebeni Valley. Spread below them was the 24,000-man Zulu army.

The Zulu intended to attack the British camp the next day, but when the scouting party began firing into them, and Zulu advanced quickly toward Isandlwana. The scouts reached Isandlwana in time to sound a warning. Pulleine established a thin defensive perimeter at the base of the crag. Colonel Anthony W. Durnford then led a mounted troop onto the plain in front of the crag.

The main Zulu attack began with about 20,000 men sweeping across the plain, while 4,000 were held in reserve. Durnford's position was indefensible, and Pulleine's force was spread out too far to form a defensive square. The Zulu attacked using their traditional encircling movement, which they likened to the horns of a bull, and quickly engulfed the British. Tactical errors by Pulleine's soldiers and Durnford's mounted force were magnified by slowness in distributing ammunition. The result was a complete British defeat after three hours of close-quarters fighting. Only six men of the regiment escaped, and nearly every British casualty was found to have run out of ammunition.

British soldiers attempting to escape from the carnage during the Battle of Isandlwana, in which more than one thousand of their comrades were killed. From a contemporary engraving. (Arkent Archive)

A partial solar eclipse during the battle added an unearthly quality to the struggle. The victorious Zulu looted the British camp of almost one thousand advanced Martini-Henry rifles and hundreds of thousands of rounds of ammunition, which the British had stored in heavy wooden boxes made to be opened with screwdrivers. More than 1,700 colonial troops were killed at Isandlwana. Zulu losses have been estimated at more than 2,000 men killed outright and another 2,000 who were mortally wounded.

Late in the afternoon of the next day, January 22, horsemen fleeing from Isandlwana arrived at the little post at Rorke's Drift with news of the disaster at Isandlwana and a warning that a large Zulu force was headed for Rorke's Drift. This Zulu force consisted of the 4,000 Zulu who had been held in reserve at Isandlwana. They were under the command of Dabulamanzi, Cetshwayo's half-brother, who was eager for a fight after having been denied action at Isandlwana.

Editorial cartoon by John Tenniel (1820-1914) commenting on the lesson that the British government learned from the Zulu War, in which it had badly underestimated the power of the Zulu.

At Rorke's Drift, Lieutenants John Chard and Gonville Bromhead and commissary officer James Dalton realized that escape was impossible and resolved that their garrison must defend itself until help could come. Their force consisted of only 140 men, 36 of whom were hospitalized. They had the garrison hastily fortified by erecting a breast-high, 100-yard-long barricade of 200-pound mealie bags, biscuit boxes, and wagons between the outpost store and hospital, both with loop-holed walls, connecting to a stone-walled enclosure kraal and a rocky terrace. Inside this fortification, they built a higher defensive redoubt. From behind these barricades, the British could direct fire in all directions with their Martini-Henry .450 caliber rifles. After the fighting began, the soldiers were allowed to fire at will and were continuously supplied with fresh ammunition.

The Zulu warriors had no artillery and few rifles in the hands of competent marksmen, so they repeatedly launched mass frontal attacks on the British position with the intent of breaking through so they could engage in hand-to-hand combat with their stabbing spears. During sixteen hours of intense fighting, the Zulu broke tradition by attacking at night, as well as by day, and managed to breach the barricades several times. Nevertheless, disciplined British rifle fire and bayonet charges repelled the attackers.

Firsthand accounts from both British and Zulu sources detail a battle of fierce combat and incredible acts of individual courage on both sides. More than 600 Zulu men were killed outright. The British casualties were 15 men killed and 10 wounded, including 2 who died later. Early on the morning of January 23, Chelmsford's relief column arrived at Rorke's Drift. Eleven Victoria Crosses were awarded for gallantry to the outnumbered British defenders at Rorke's Drift. It was the largest number of such awards made to one regiment for a single action in British military history.

SIGNIFICANCE

January 22, 1879, is remembered as one of the worst days in British colonial history. However, despite the magnitude of the British defeat at Isandlwana and the brutal struggle at Rorke's Drift, the British inflicted more than 5,000 casualties on the Zulu army. The loss represented about 15 percent of the available Zulu fighting force. Total military losses for the Zulu over six months of the Zulu War are estimated at between 10,000 and 20,000—approximately half of all Zulu warriors. Total British military losses during the war were fewer than 2,000 men.

The war resulted in a total British victory under which they imposed upon the Zulu an unworkable peace that divided the Zulu Kingdom into thirteen states. These separate states were denied the prosperity of a united kingdom and began warring against one another. By design, this kept the Zulu militarily impotent and thus unable to attack in force any nearby European colonies. The British victory in the Zulu War, and the imposed dividing of the once independent Zulu state, virtually destroyed the traditional ways of Zulu life.

The 1964 Metro-Goldwyn-Mayer motion picture *Zulu* reenacts the Battle of Rorke's Drift. Despite the film's dramatic excesses, its battle sequences are considered realistic depictions of the ferocity and courage shown in the fighting. The 1979 film *Zulu Dawn* reenacts the Battle of Isandlwana.

—*Randall L. Milstein*

FURTHER READING

Edgerton, Robert. *Like Lions They Fought.* New York: Free Press, 1988. Dramatic recounting of the battles of Isandlwana and Rorke's Drift. Contains many historical photographs.

Hanson, Victor. *Carnage and Culture: Landmark Battles in the Rise of Western Power.* New York: Anchor Books, 2001. Provides a riveting battle narrative of Rorke's Drift and a balanced perspective of the battle's aftermath.

Knight, Ian. *Great Zulu Battles: 1838-1906.* London: Orion, 1998. Analyses of a selection of diverse and significant battles throughout nineteenth century Zulu history, including the Battle of Isandlwana.

_______. *Rorke's Drift, 1879: Pinned Like Rats in a Hole.* Oxford, England: Osprey, 1996. Essential reference by the foremost researcher and author on the Battle of Rorke's Drift.

_______. *Rorke's Drift: The True Story.* London: Greenhill Books, 2005. Revelatory account that strips away imperial British political and press manipulations to show the tragedy of the battle that is in conflict with enduring images of British glory.

_______. *The Zulu War: 1879.* Oxford, England: Osprey, 2003. Informative volume in the Osprey Essential History Series. The book is richly illustrated and gives a concise account of the Zulu War.

Lock, Ron, and Peter Quantrill. *Zulu Victory: The Epic of Isandhlwana and the Cover-Up.* London: Greenhill Books, 2002. Detailed, almost minute-by-minute account of the Zulu victory at Isandlwana based on British sources and surviving Zulu testimonies.

Morris, Donald. *The Washing of Spears: The Rise and Fall of the Zulu Nation.* New York: Simon & Schuster, 1965. Popular account of the rise of the Zulu nation under Shaka and its fall under Cetshwayo in the Zulu War of 1879.

SEE ALSO: c. 1817-1828: Zulu Expansion; 1865-1868: Basuto War; Jan. 22-Aug., 1879: Zulu War; Dec. 16, 1880-Mar. 6, 1881: First Boer War; 1884: Maxim Patents His Machine Gun; Oct., 1893-October, 1897: British Subdue African Resistance in Rhodesia; Oct. 11, 1899-May 31, 1902: South African War.

RELATED ARTICLES in *Great Lives from History: The Nineteenth Century, 1801-1900:* Cetshwayo; Lobengula; Shaka.

January 22-August, 1879
Zulu War

The expansion of the British Empire into the interior of South Africa led the British into direct conflict with the strongest native African power, the Zulu Kingdom. After the British suffered a catastrophic defeat, they conquered the Zulu and thereby ended major resistance to white domination and ensured the ascendance of British imperial might in South Africa.

Also known as: Anglo-Zulu War; Zulu-British War
Locale: South Africa
Categories: Wars, uprisings, and civil unrest; expansion and land acquisition; colonization

Key Figures

Mpande (1798-1872), king of the Zulu, r. 1840-1872
Cetshwayo (1832-1884), Mpande's son and king of the Zulu, r. 1872-1879
Bartle Frere (1815-1884), governor of the Cape Colony and British high commissioner for South Africa, 1877-1880
Sir Theophilus Shepstone (1817-1893), British administrator of Natal, 1856-1876, and administrator of Transvaal, 1877-1879
Second Baron Chelmsford (Frederic Augustus Thesiger; 1827-1905), British commander who led the invasion of Zululand
Sir Garnet Joseph Wolseley (1833-1913), British lieutenant governor of Natal and high commissioner of Southeast Africa

Summary of Event

After Great Britain took control of the Cape of Good Hope from the Dutch in 1814, it was slow to develop a serious interest in expanding its authority far inland. All that began to change during the 1870's with the discovery of diamonds at Kimberley and with the later discovery of gold on the Transvaal's Witwatersrand. During the 1870's, British colonial officials began initiating steps toward their long-term objective to unite all the diverse polities of South Africa within a federation under British rule. By doing so, the British could ensure the safety of the precious minerals that had already begun to draw large amounts of British investment. Sir Theophilus Shepstone, the top British administrator in the Natal colony, was ordered by the British government to persuade the Afrikaners in the Transvaal's South African Republic to accept British rule. If that proved impossible, he was simply to annex the Transvaal. The Afrikaners were reluctant to accept British hegemony, so Shepstone announced the annexation of the Transvaal in 1877. All the Afrikaners could do at that time was protest. From that moment, only the Zulu stood in the way of British domination of South Africa.

Since an Afrikaner force had defeated the Zulu at the Battle of Blood River in 1838, the Zulu had slowly recovered from their defeat under the peaceful rule of Mpande. When Mpande died in 1872, he left no clear heir. His position was soon filled by his eldest son, Cetshwayo, who strove to continue maintaining peaceful relations with the British. In 1873, Shepstone "crowned" Cetshwayo—an unprecedented action that bestowed on Cetshwayo formal British recognition but which Shepstone also intended to symbolize British authority over the Zulu. With its annexation of the Transvaal four years later, Britain inherited unresolved land disputes between the Afrikaners and Zulu and sought to use these disputes to further its own imperial objectives. In the eyes of British schemers, subduing the Zulu nation would ease the way to a South African confederation by eliminating the primary African threat to Natal and the Transvaal. Furthermore, the British believed that such an action would increase Afrikaner acceptance of British rule and help provide African labor for the mines. In 1878, the British decided to act on these ideas.

Bartle Frere, the British governor of the Cape Colony, began looking for a pretext to wage war on the Zulu. The dispute between the Afrikaners and Zulu over land near Blood River appeared to offer an opportunity. The Afrikaners claimed that Mpande had ceded land to them, but Cetshwayo denied that claim. Frere and Shepstone supported the Afrikaner claim. However, when the conflict was arbitrated, a court ruled in favor of Cetshwayo and actually awarded more land to the Zulu than Cetshwayo had claimed.

Frustrated, Frere searched for another excuse for war. When a Zulu chief crossed into British Natal with an armed party to retrieve two women fleeing from punishment for marital infidelity, Frere used the incident as an opportunity to instigate a conflict. Citing border violations and inhumane acts, the colonial government pressed the issue. In an attempt to avoid conflict, Cetshwayo offered to make a payment for his perceived offense, but the British wanted war. With Frere's consent, Shepstone issued Cetshwayo an ultimatum that required him to turn over the men responsible for the border violation and

1870's

British troops advancing on the Zulu at the Tugela River. From a drawing by Max Klepper (1861-1907). (P. F. Collier and Son)

provide compensation. Additionally, and more important, he was to dismantle the Zulu army and accept British missionaries and officials into his land. Still eager for a peaceful solution, Cetshwayo agreed to meet the British demands that did not infringe upon the sovereignty of the Zulu nation. However, that response did not satisfy the British, who at last found a justification for war.

In January, 1879, the British general Chelmsford led seventeen thousand troops of mixed British regulars and colonial troops in an assault on Zululand. At Ulundi, the Zulu army mobilized to meet the aggressors. Confident that a quick victory would follow, the British then made several tactical errors in their advance. Chelmsford split his troops into two groups. One group chased a small Zulu party while the others remained at Isandlwana. On January 22, 1879, at least twenty thousand Zulu soldiers attacked an ill-prepared and thinly spread British line. Despite the superior firepower of the British, the Zulu army enveloped the British troops and overwhelmed them. Meanwhile, another Zulu force attacked a small British unit building a bridge near a Norwegian mission station at Rorke's Drift but was repelled in a heroic defense. Instead of pressing the Zulu advantage, Cetshwayo remained defensive in the hope that the British would withdraw and seek peace.

The British defeat at the hands of the Zulu at Isandlwana shocked the world, especially imperial policy makers in London. Some imperialists began to reevaluate the goal of a South African confederation. Frere received the most blame and was severely castigated. He remained governor of the Cape Colony, but a new position was created to deal with Natal and the newly annexed Transvaal. This office, High Commissioner of Southeast Africa, was extended to Sir Garnet Wolseley, effectively negating Frere's influence in Zululand.

Despite the setback, the British government believed that the only way to absolve its army's tarnished reputation was to continue the war and secure victory. As British reinforcements bolstered the ranks and marched onward, Cetshwayo repeatedly sued for peace—much as the Ndebele king Lobengula later would in what is now Zimbabwe. Zulu troops managed to win a small victory at Hlobane, but the British advance could not be stopped. The Gatling machine gun took its toll, and at Ulundi the Zulu finally fell to the British in August, 1879. In an effort to avoid further Zulu resistance, Wolseley then divided the kingdom among thirteen chieftaincies. Cetshwayo was captured and sent into exile. He was later reinstated briefly but died in 1884. The Zulu never recovered from their defeat in their war with the British and fell into disarray and civil war. In 1887, Great Britain annexed Zululand, destroying forever the independent Zulu nation.

Significance

Great Britain's crushing of the Zulu Kingdom signified a turning point in South African history. The Zulu had been the dominant African power in the region since the early nineteenth century. The Zulu were the most obvious rallying point for African resistance to white expansion, so their defeat was a major blow to African self-determination. White dominance in South Africa was assured from that point. The ensuing civil war among the Zulu people only exacerbated the situation, forcing many Zulu into the hands of white employers. Therefore, the Zulu followed the path of many Africans before them, becoming a labor pool for the diamond and gold mines.

The British war of expansion against the Zulu must be placed within the context of the mineral revolution and the British desire to control the wealth issuing from it. The destruction of the Zulu Kingdom was crucial for any plans to consolidate South Africa, but the British victory did not ensure consolidation. In 1881, the Transvaal's Afrikaners rebelled against British rule in what became known as the First Boer War, and the British abandoned the Transvaal until the outbreak of the South African War in 1899. The war against the Zulu serves as a fine example of the new imperial Britain—one motivated by mineral riches and expansion in the name of national pride.

—Branden C. McCullough

Further Reading

Cope, Richard. *Ploughshare of War: The Origins of the Anglo-Zulu War of 1879*. Pietermaritzburg: University of Natal Press, 1999. This study focuses on the British policies in South Africa that led to the war but offers little on the prosecution of the war itself.

Guy, Jeff. *The Destruction of the Zulu Kingdom: The Civil War in Zululand, 1879-1884*. London: Longman, 1979. Provides a detailed analysis of the consequences of the Zulu War.

Knight, Ian. *Great Zulu Battles: 1838-1906*. London: Orion, 1998. Analyses of a selection of diverse and significant battles throughout nineteenth century Zulu history, including battles during the Zulu War of 1879 and the internal Zulu conflicts that followed.

_______. *The Zulu War: 1879*. Oxford, England: Osprey, 2003. Informative volume in the Osprey Essential History series. Written by a specialist in Zulu military history, this book is richly illustrated and gives a concise account of the Zulu War.

Laband, John. *Kingdom in Crisis: The Zulu Response to the British Invasion of 1879*. New York: Manchester University Press, 1992. Focused study of the war primarily from the Zulu perspective.

_______. *The Rise and Fall of the Zulu Nation*. London: Arms and Armour Press, 1997. Comprehensive study of the Zulu nation that provides an account of the events leading up to and after the war.

Laband, John, and Paul Thompson, eds.. *Kingdom and Colony at War: Sixteen Studies on the Anglo-Zulu War of 1879*. Pietermaritzburg: University of Natal Press, 1990. Collection of individual essays covering specific aspects and circumstances of the war.

Mitford, Bertram. *Through the Zulu Country: Its Battlefields and People*. 1883. Reprint. Novato, Calif.: Presidio Press, 1992. Facsimile reprint of a firsthand account of a journey through Zulu War sites made three years after the war. A novelist who wrote extensively about the Zulu, Mitford interviewed many participants in the war and recorded vivid descriptions of both events and battle sites. This edition has a modern introduction by Ian Knight and many photographs not in the original edition.

Morris, Donald. *The Washing of Spears: The Rise and Fall of the Zulu Nation*. New York: Simon & Schuster, 1965. Frequently reprinted popular account of the rise of the Zulu nation under Shaka and its fall under Cetshwayo in the Zulu War of 1879.

See also: c. 1817-1828: Zulu Expansion; 1835: South Africa's Great Trek Begins; 1865-1868: Basuto War; Jan. 22-23, 1879: Battles of Isandlwana and Rorke's Drift; Dec. 16, 1880-Mar. 6, 1881: First Boer War; 1884: Maxim Patents His Machine Gun; June 21, 1884: Gold Is Discovered in the Transvaal; Mar. 13, 1888: Rhodes Amalgamates Kimberley Diamondfields; Oct., 1893-October, 1897: British Subdue African Resistance in Rhodesia; Dec. 29, 1895-Jan. 2, 1896: Jameson Raid; Oct. 11, 1899-May 31, 1902: South African War.

Related articles in *Great Lives from History: The Nineteenth Century, 1801-1900:* Sir Robert Stephenson Smyth Baden-Powell; Cetshwayo; Paul Kruger; Lobengula; Shaka.

April 5, 1879-October 20, 1883
WAR OF THE PACIFIC

In the War of the Pacific, Chile increased its territories and resources at the expense of neighboring Peru and Bolivia. Ironically, however, Chile's newly acquired lands and wealth were exploited by Great Britain at Chile's expense, so the nation's short-term gains ultimately weakened the Chilean government and economy.

LOCALE: Chile; Peru; Bolivia
CATEGORIES: Wars, uprisings, and civil unrest; expansion and land acquisition

KEY FIGURES

José Manuel Balmaceda (1840-1891), Chilean president, 1886-1891
Andrés Avelino Cáceres (1833-1923), Peruvian general
Hilarión Daza (1840-1894), Bolivian dictator who went to war with Chile
Aníbal Pinto (1825-1884), Chilean president, 1876-1881

SUMMARY OF EVENT

The War of the Pacific was fought for control of the lucrative nitrate deposits in the remote and desolate Atacama Desert, an area located along the central Pacific coast of South America. Peru and Bolivia were determined to keep their sovereignty over these regions, while Chile was eager to end its economic depression of the 1870's by taking possession of lands that were being developed largely by Chilean businesses flush with British capital. This corner of South America had largely escaped the constant border disputes that had plagued other formerly Spanish colonies in the previous generation, but Peru and Bolivia secretly allied in 1873 to thwart the aggressive penetration of Chilean capitalism within their boundaries.

Before that secret alliance, Chile and Bolivia had tried to resolve their differences diplomatically. Just seven years earlier, in 1866, a treaty between the two countries had fixed their border at the twenty-fourth parallel. This treaty had secured Bolivian possession of the province of Antofagasta, which not only contained the coveted nitrates but also gave the otherwise landlocked Bolivians their only unfettered access to the sea. Instead of limiting their mining in the wake of the treaty, however, Chilean businesses backed by British bankers went further into Bolivia and also expanded into the adjacent Tarapaca province of Peru.

The 1866 treaty had offered both Chilean and Bolivian firms equal opportunity to produce nitrates in the expansive zone between the twenty-third and twenty-fifth parallels while splitting any export tax monies derived from nitrates evenly between the two countries. However, overwhelming Chilean success and dominance of nitrate mining upset the balance established by the treaty. Thus, in a second treaty of 1874 meant to reestablish that balance, Chile agreed to give up its share of taxes from Bolivian lands in return for no new taxes being levied on Chilean companies working in Antofagasta.

In 1875, the bankrupt Peruvian government forcibly took over foreign-owned concerns in Tarapaca and merged them into a state monopoly over nitrates. The Chileans expropriated from Tarapaca moved into Antofagasta, increasing tensions there. This influx of Chilean companies was the last straw for Bolivia, which was emboldened not only by Peru's overt confiscation of Chilean resources but also by its covert deal with that seemingly formidable rival of Chile. In addition, Bolivia needed revenue quickly to rebuild its port of Antofagasta, which was heavily damaged by a tidal wave in 1877.

Accordingly, in 1878, Bolivia under the leadership of Hilarión Daza violated the treaty negotiated barely four years earlier by raising taxes on Chilean exports from Antofagasta. When the Chileans, led by President Aníbal Pinto, refused to pay these new if relatively small taxes, Bolivia threatened them with a repetition of the Peruvian confiscation and turned down any attempts at arbitration. In February, 1879, determined to avoid another Tarapaca, Chile preempted any Bolivian seizure of its nationals' businesses by occupying first the port of Antofagasta and then the entire province. Chile then rejected Peru's bid to mediate the crisis, as word of the secret Andean alliance reached Santiago. Energized by their easy triumph in Antofagasta and eager to recolonize Tarapaca, the Chileans declared war on both Peru and Bolivia on April 5, 1879.

The first and most decisive battles of the War of the Pacific were literally on the Pacific Ocean. At Iquique in May, 1879, and Cape Angamos five months later, Chilean ironclad warships trounced their outmaneuvered Peruvian opponents, capturing at Angamos the pride of the Peruvian navy, the *Huáscar*. By the start of 1880, Chilean naval supremacy meant that Santiago could transport large armies by sea without risk; in contrast, Peru and

Bolivia never overcame the logistical problems of moving and supplying regiments over the Andes Mountains and Atacama Desert.

Peru bore the brunt of the fighting with Chile, as Bolivians generally fought with each other without ever reaching the enemy. Accordingly, amphibious landings allowed Chilean warships to pick off disorganized and hungry Peruvian troops who had been left to fend for themselves in the desert. At the same time, emulating the Union in the U.S. Civil War nearly two decades earlier, Chile blockaded its enemy's coast, while it benefited

WAR OF THE PACIFIC

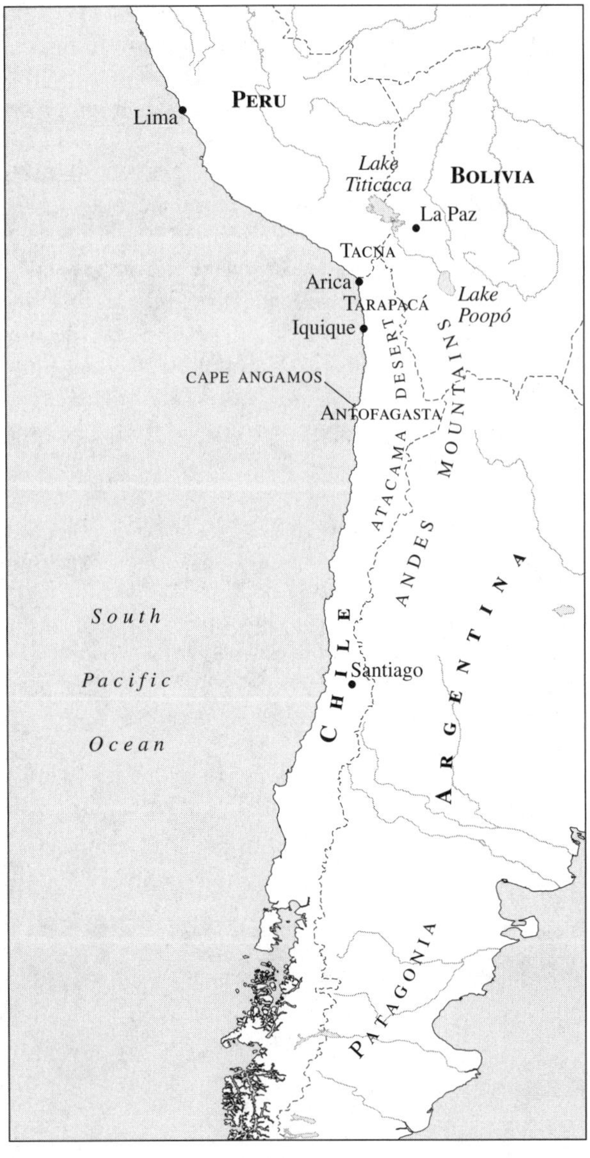

from increased trade with Europe and, in particular, more investment from Great Britain. Chile's easy victories by sea prompted the United States to consider intervening on behalf of Peru and Bolivia to prevent such an imbalance of power, but the assassination of President James A. Garfield in 1881 ushered in an administration that was more sympathetic toward Chile and that did not want to get involved.

The most stunning Chilean assault by sea led to the fall of the Peruvian port and capital of Lima in January, 1881. Any Chilean occupation beyond the nitrate coast was short-lived, however, as Peruvians resented and resisted Chilean attempts to take money and equipment south. A guerilla war led by the Peruvian general Andrés Avelino Cáceres ensued, and it made Chile's ultimate victory relatively costly in both blood and treasure. Although costly, the victory was assured by the crippling effects of Chile's blockade, which forced Peru to agree to the humiliating terms of the Treaty of Ancón on October 20, 1883.

The treaty, which ended the war between Chile and Peru, gave nitrate-rich Tarapaca to Chile in perpetuity and allowed Chile to hold on to the adjacent provinces of Tacna and Arica for at least another decade. Voters in Tacna and Arica were supposed to decide the latter two provinces' fate in 1893, but that plebiscite never came to pass. Chile kept governing the provinces until 1929, when the United States brokered a deal by which Tacna reverted to Peru and Arica remained Chilean.

Bolivia held out a little longer and, for many years, refused to sign a formal treaty ceding its territory to the Chileans. Nevertheless, a temporary cease-fire between the two countries was established in 1884. The cease-fire acknowledged by default Chile's control of Antofagasta province—a control that had been a reality since the beginning of the conflict. Twenty years later, in 1904, a formal treaty finally sealed the destiny of Antofagasta as part of Chile. In return for that settlement, Chile promised to build a railroad linking the Bolivian capital of La Paz to Arica. In 1913, Chile followed through on its promise and completed the railroad. This corridor was supposed to end Bolivia's isolation and to compensate for the loss of its sovereign access to the sea, but that did not stop the Andean country from unsuccessfully trying to wrest access to an ocean-bound river from Paraguay, another and even poorer neighbor, in the 1930's.

SIGNIFICANCE

From the War of the Pacific, Chile emerged as the "Prussia of the Pacific," emulating the quick and decisive victories of that German state over its neighbors Denmark, Austria, and France in the 1860's and early 1870's. That Chilean image belied several realities. First, unlike the Prussian war machine, Chilean seapower, not its small armies, won the war against countries with much larger populations. In that spirit, Chile was more like its main benefactor, Great Britain, than like Prussia, and its example would be cited by Admiral Alfred Thayer Mahan in his influential manual on the importance of naval supremacy (1890).

Moreover, unlike Prussia and the subsequent German Empire's pursuit of industrial might, Chile failed to benefit economically in the long term from its land grabs along the nitrate coast. Before the war, Chilean business owners had dominated the nitrate industry; in fact, that dominance was one of the preconditions for the conflict. By the 1890's, however, nearly 70 percent of the nitrate industry was in British hands. The capital from London that helped Chile win the war, then, had strings attached. The nitrate industry—and eventually the copper industry as well—siphoned labor and material from other Chilean industries, retarding the nation's entrepreneurial ventures in every sector except the export sector. Mining interests and their foreign investors combined with traditional landowning oligarchs in 1891 to depose the popularly elected President José Manuael Balmaceda, who had dared to tax the nitrate industry to build roads, schools, and other modern infrastructure.

Ultimately, then, the War of the Pacific turned out to be a Pyrrhic victory for Chile. The nation gained nitrate and copper resources by annexing territory from Peru and Bolivia. However, it became overly dependent on the fluctuating global demand for those commodities to its economic and political detriment. Chilean democracy would never really challenge the entrenched elites empowered by colonial industry until the election of Salvador Allende in 1970.

—*Charles H. Ford*

FURTHER READING

Burr, Robert N. *By Reason or Force: Chile and the Balancing of Power in South America, 1830-1905.* Berkeley: University of California Press, 1967. A little dry and old-fashioned, this book remains the most reliable in charting the diplomatic background leading up to the war.

Farcau, Bruce W. *The Ten Cents War: Chile, Peru, and Bolivia in the War of the Pacific, 1879-1884.* Westport, Conn.: Praeger, 2000. Although lacking maps, this book provides the best information on the actual battles and military strategies of the war.

Loveman, Brian. *Chile: The Legacy of Hispanic Capitalism.* 3d ed. New York: Oxford University Press, 2001. This overview's sixth chapter does the best job of explaining the centrality of nitrates to Chilean foreign policy.

O'Brien, Thomas F. "Chilean Elites and Foreign Investors: Chilean Nitrate Policy, 1880-1882." *Journal of Latin American Studies* 11, no. 1 (1979): 101-121. Clearly explains the crucial economic relationship between Chile and Great Britain and why the British displaced Chilean ownership by the end of the 1880's.

Sater, William F. *Chile and the War of the Pacific.* Lincoln: University of Nebraska Press, 1986. The first book to point out the long-term problems that Chile inherited because of the war; notes that the analogy of Chile as a South American Prussia obscures more than it explains.

SEE ALSO: Mar., 1813-Dec. 9, 1824: Bolívar's Military Campaigns; Jan. 18, 1817-July 28, 1821: San Martín's Military Campaigns; May 1, 1865-June 20, 1870: Paraguayan War.

RELATED ARTICLES in *Great Lives from History: The Nineteenth Century, 1801-1900:* Simón Bolívar; José de San Martín.

October 21, 1879
EDISON DEMONSTRATES THE INCANDESCENT LAMP

Thomas Alva Edison's incandescent lamp was not the first electric light to be invented, but it was the first that was practical, durable, and economical, and for that reason it made possible a world revolution in lighting and energy.

LOCALE: Menlo Park, New Jersey
CATEGORIES: Inventions; science and technology

KEY FIGURES

Thomas Alva Edison (1847-1931), American inventor
Moses Gerrish Farmer (1820-1893), early American experimenter with electrical lights
Grosvenor Lowrey (fl. early nineteenth century), Western Union general counsel who encouraged Edison's work
J. P. Morgan (1837-1913), American financier who helped fund Edison's experiments

SUMMARY OF EVENT

On October 21, 1879, Thomas Alva Edison and five associates at his laboratory in Menlo Park, New Jersey, passed one of the great milestones of modern science—a demonstration of an incandescent lamp that was at once economical, practical, and durable. The records of that day show that Edison had managed to manufacture an incandescent lamp that burned for thirteen and one-half hours. In the excitement of the discovery, notes were incomplete, and there was some talk of a bulb that burned for the then unimaginable time of more than forty hours. The light from Edison's first successful lamp gave only a feeble, reddish glow, but Edison had set out not merely to invent a new kind of light but to revolutionize the science of illumination and to bring electricity within the means of everyone.

The secret of Edison's incandescent lamp is best explained in his subsequent patent application:

> I have discovered that even a cotton thread, properly carbonized and placed in a sealed glass bulb, exhausted to one-millionth of an atmosphere, offers from one hundred to five hundred ohms resistance to the passage of current and that it is absolutely stable at a very high temperature.

Edison had made an incandescent lamp with a hairlike carbon filament for a burner, having the necessary high resistance and low current, and sealed in a permanent high-vacuum glass to allow the burner to glow without being destroyed by the heat. The importance of Edison's discovery is not that it was the first electric light or even the first incandescent lamp, but that it was the first electric bulb that had the potential to be universally and economically used for domestic lighting. This was especially true after Edison managed to distribute the great power generated by electrical dynamos to send it to individual users over wires. Nevertheless, when he later threw a switch at New York's Pearl Street power station in 1882, lighting four hundred lamps for eighty-five customers, few realized that he had replaced the steam age with the electric age.

It may have been only Edison who realized the full implications of his invention. A group of Wall Street financiers headed by J. P. Morgan had eagerly bankrolled his first work in electricity but had grown weary of waiting for results. When Edison revealed to them his astonishing success, they balked at adding to their previous investments, fearing that Edison had invented a mere laboratory toy, rather than the modern electric light and power industry, which at the time of Edison's death in 1931 would be valued in the United States alone at fifteen billion dollars.

Edison's friend and informal financial adviser, Grosvenor Lowrey, a Western Union attorney who specialized in patents, could get no more funds from Wall Street until Edison made his early success public. The news of Edison's invention finally reached the press on December 21, when the *New York Herald* announced that Edison "makes light without gas or flame, cheaper than oil." The aesthetic importance of Edison's lamp was captured by the *Herald* reporter, who described the effect as a "bright, beautiful light, like the mellow sunset of an Italian autumn."

The triumph of the incandescent lamp was also a personal triumph for Edison. His previous major success, his invention of the phonograph in 1877, had already brought him fame. In the course of a long career, Edison would eventually be responsible for more than one thousand patents, covering inventions or improvements of the storage battery, dictaphone, ore separator, electric dynamo, electric locomotive, composition brick, Sprauge separator, compressing dies, and a forerunner of the modern motion picture projector. In pure science, Edison was responsible for the discovery of the Edison effect, which contributed to the genesis of modern electronics.

Edison's method for inventing involved delegating

authority and supervising gifted associates in a well-equipped laboratory. Most of Edison's discoveries were collaborative ventures, but most of the imagination and creative impetus were supplied by Edison himself.

When Edison invented his incandescent lightbulb, harnessing electrical power was not itself new. Sir Humphry Davy had shown the possibility of electric illumination before the Royal Society of London in 1808. After the invention of the dynamo by Michael Faraday in 1831, electricity developed steadily but slowly. At the Philadelphia Centennial Exposition in 1876, Moses Gerrish Farmer demonstrated three large arc lights powered by a primitive transformer. Arc lighting resulted from the oxidation of carbon caused by the flow of current, which created a brilliant blue light. Incandescence relies instead upon heat applied in a vacuum to prevent the heated carbon from melting. The main problems in early incandescence concerned the supply of current and the search for a filament material that would not melt at a high temperature. Edison became fascinated by electricity after seeing Farmer's commercial application of arc lights at Wanamaker's Philadelphia department store in 1878.

Edison's genius was not that of pure science; he was always interested in commercial applications. His aim with electricity was not to compete with the arc-light manufacturers but rather to duplicate the success of the gas-distributing industry by using electricity. At the time, gas lighting was a major U.S. industry with annual revenues of more than $150 million. Arc lights were expected to threaten only 10 percent of this income. Edison wanted the other 90 percent.

In this endeavor, Edison was, in effect, working from first principles, because most research in electric lighting had been devoted to the arc-light principle. He needed financing, and with confidence and gall in equal proportions, he announced before the fact that he had invented a new and cheap electric light. With W. H. Vanderbilt, Morgan, and several other prominent financiers participating, the Edison Electric Light Company was formed on October 12, 1878. It was capitalized with 3,000 shares, 2,500 of which were Edison's. The financiers advanced $50,000 to Edison, who then proceeded to invent the light he had already announced as invented. Edison asserted that it would take only six weeks to make his lightbulb.

The fact that Edison accomplished his immediate goal in little more than one year was astonishing. However, so much publicity had preceded the actual invention that it was some time before it was taken seriously by the public or the financiers, in spite of occasional dramatic interludes, such as the lighting of all of Menlo Park, New Jersey, with the new incandescent lamp.

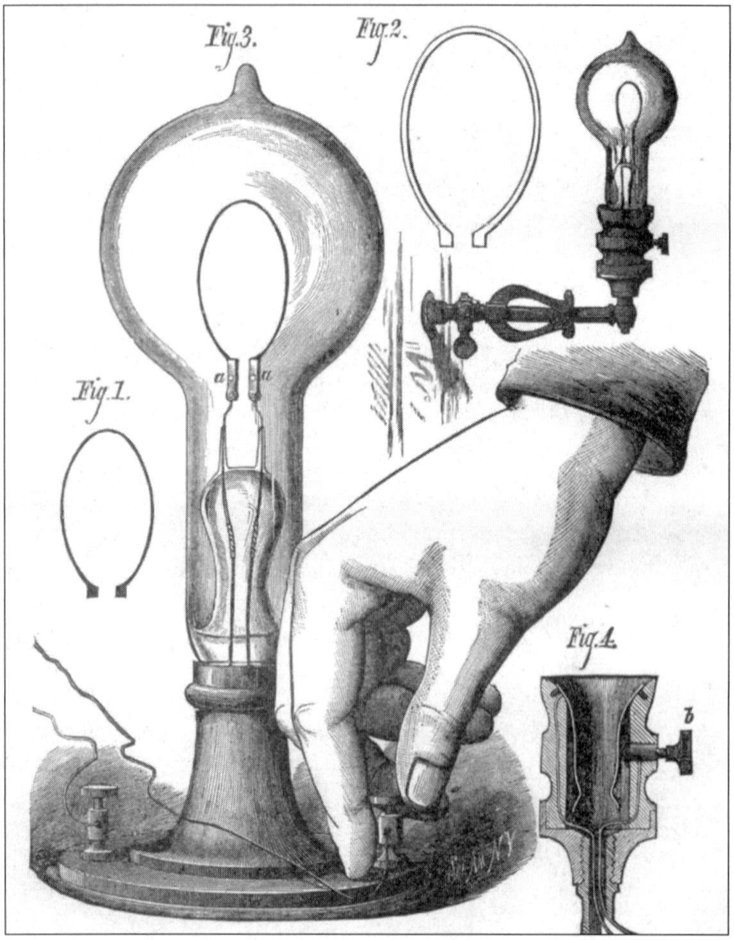

Edison's incandescent lamp. (Premier Publishing Company)

SIGNIFICANCE

After actually creating the electrical lightbulb, Edison's next challenge was demonstrating the ability of his incandescent lamp to light an entire urban area. On December 17, 1880, he founded the Edison Electric Illumination Company of New York, which evolved into Consolidated Edison. The laying of mains, the running of generators, and the convincing of a still dubious public absorbed all the inventor's energy. However, his discovery won first prize at the 1881 Paris Electrical Exposition, and soon, patches of electrical lighting throughout the world's cities announced the arrival of "Edison's lamps."

Before Edison was done, he had not only invented a successful incandescent light but had also developed an entire system to generate and distribute electric energy. Credit for bringing electricity to the world is also due to the likes of Alessandro Volta, Sir Humphry Davy, Michael Faraday, and others who had helped the realization of Edison's more dependable, durable, and reliable system.

—Richard H. Collin,
updated by Peter B. Heller

ELECTRIC LIGHT

A report, excerpted here, on the 1881 Paris Electricity Exposition, which featured Thomas Edison's newly invented incandescent lamp, lauds the electric light as nothing but ideal.

We normally imagine electric light to be blindingly bright light, whose harshness hurts the eyes. . . . Here, however, we have a light source that has somehow been civilised and adapted to our needs. Every individual light shines like gaslight, but this is a type of gas that has not yet been invented—a gas that gives a completely steady light but nevertheless shines vividly and brightly and places no strain on the retina. But then—how different from gas! Electric light leaves no combustion residues in the house—no carbon dioxide and carbon monoxide to pollute the air, no sulphuric acid and ammonia to damage paintings and fabrics. Electricity does not raise the air temperature, and does not give off the uncomfortable and fatiguing warmth associated with gas lighting. It puts an end to the danger of explosion or fire. It is not affected by fluctuations in the outside temperature or changes in mains pressure. . . . It shines evenly and steadily, irrespective of the season . . . and in water as well as in air. It is totally independent of all external influences.

Source: Henry de Parville, "L'Electricité et ses applications" (1883), quoted in Wolfgang Schivelbusch, *Disenchanted Night: The Industrialization of Light in the Nineteenth Century* (Berkeley: University of California Press, 1995), p. 60.

FURTHER READING

Baldwin, Neil. *Edison: Inventing the Century*. New York: Hyperion, 1995. This lightly illustrated account, with assistance from scores of individuals, such as Edison family descendants, is commendable for its vignettes and anecdotes. Includes a hundred pages of notes and bibliography.

Clark, Ronald W. *Edison: The Man Who Made the Future*. New York: G. P. Putnam's Sons, 1977. Attractively illustrated biography illuminated with fascinating vignettes and little-known facts make this an engaging book to read. Includes an entire chapter on Edison's invention of the lightbulb.

Dillon, Maureen. *Artificial Sunshine: A Social History of Domestic Lighting*. London: National Trust, 2002. Lively narrative of the impact that artificial lighting has made on human history.

Edison, Thomas A. *Menlo Park: The Early Years, April 1876-December 1877*. Vol. 3 in *The Papers of Thomas A. Edison*, edited by Robert A. Rosenberg et al. Baltimore: Johns Hopkins University Press, 1994. Includes Edison's own early notes on an electric lighting system.

Friedel, Robert D. *Edison's Electric Light: Biography of an Invention*. New Brunswick, N.J.: Rutgers University Press, 1986. History of Edison's invention that offers a clear explanation of the origins and nature of the electric lightbulb, whose genesis was helped by William Wallace's dynamo to generate power.

Israel, Paul. *Edison: A Life of Invention*. New York: John Wiley & Sons 1998. Israel draws on Edison's notebooks to describe Edison's working methods, portraying him as a tireless experimenter who produced his inventions with prodigious amounts of labor.

Jonnes, Jill. *Empires of Light: Edison, Tesla, Westinghouse, and the Race to Electrify the World*. New York: Random House, 2003. Explains how the three inventors who made the most important contributions to electrical lighting sought to create businesses that would provide safe, reliable electricity.

Josephson, Matthew. *Edison: A Biography*. 1959. Reprint. New York: John Wiley & Sons, 1992. Written in colorful but accessible language, this full biography is nearly encyclopedic in its coverage.

Millard, Andre. "Edison's Laboratory and the Electrical Industry." In *Edison and the Business of Innovation*. Baltimore: Johns Hopkins University Press, 1990. Well-researched and illustrated work that places the invention of Edison's high-vacuum incandescent bulb in the broader context of the entire electrical system.

Bazerman, Charles. *The Languages of Edison's Light*. Cambridge, Mass.: MIT Press, 1999. Describes how Edison and his colleagues created a system of symbols and communication to describe the new invention of electric lighting.

Wachhorst, Wyn. *Thomas Alva Edison: An American Myth*. Cambridge, Mass.: MIT Press, 1981. The few pages devoted to the incandescent lamp, and especially the encyclopedic Edison bibliography, are noteworthy.

SEE ALSO: c. 1801-1810: Davy Develops the Arc Lamp; 1802: Britain Adopts Gas Lighting; Oct., 1831: Faraday Converts Magnetic Force into Electricity; 1850: First U.S. Petroleum Refinery Is Built; Dec. 24, 1877: Edison Patents the Cylinder Phonograph; Oct. 10, 1881: London's Savoy Theatre Opens; May 1-Oct. 30, 1893: Chicago World's Fair; Dec. 28, 1895: First Commercial Projection of Motion Pictures; Nov. 16, 1896: First U.S. Hydroelectric Plant Opens at Niagara Falls; Dec. 15, 1900: General Electric Opens Research Laboratory.

RELATED ARTICLES in *Great Lives from History: The Nineteenth Century, 1801-1900:* Sir Humphry Davy; Thomas Alva Edison; Michael Faraday; Joseph Wilson Swan; Nikola Tesla; George Westinghouse.

1880's
BRAHMIN SCHOOL OF AMERICAN LITERATURE FLOURISHES

A small group of writers and academics, located principally in Boston, set out to define the qualities that would make a distinctly American literature. The group, which came to be called the Brahmins, called for writers to treat American subjects but to do so using the literary forms of Europe, particularly England, as models for constructing fiction and poetry. Brahminism's influence began diminishing with the rise of literary naturalism and realism in the United States.

LOCALE: New England
CATEGORY: Literature

KEY FIGURES

Oliver Wendell Holmes (1809-1894), American physician, poet, and essayist

Henry Wadsworth Longfellow (1807-1882), American poet and professor

James Russell Lowell (1819-1891), American poet, professor, and editor

SUMMARY OF EVENT

Through most of the nineteenth century, literary tastes in the United States were determined by a relatively small circle of men and women in and around Boston. Many were descendants of families who had settled in New England in the seventeenth or early eighteenth centuries. Most of the men had attended Harvard, where they were taught by professors such as Edward Everett, William Ellery Channing, and William's brother Edward Channing. These three men argued that the American man of letters should be cultivated, knowledgeable about art and literature, gentlemanly in deportment, and concerned with religion and morals.

Educated at Harvard during the 1820's, Oliver Wendell Holmes had readily adopted the prevailing ideas about the value and function of literature. Writing in 1859 for the newly established *Atlantic Monthly* magazine, Holmes had described the Brahmins as the untitled aristocracy of America, the class that produces the true scholars whose aptitude for learning is both congenital and hereditary. He used the term "brahmin," which refers to the highest caste of Hindu society (Brahman), to name the group. Bred for generations to appreciate the finer things in life, many believed that this class was well suited to determine what is best in American culture and society.

Holmes's friend and a fellow professor, poet James Russell Lowell, became the principal spokesperson for the Brahmins' philosophy of American literature. Lowell influenced the development of literary theory through numerous articles in publications such as the *North American Review* and, especially, the *Atlantic Monthly*, which he had helped found in 1857 and for which he had served as the first editor. If there exists any document that can be considered a manifesto of the Brahmins' ideology, it is Lowell's essay "Nationality in Literature," published in the *North American Review* (July, 1849). Intending to set the stage for future literary production in the United States, Lowell insisted that if American authors wish to distinguish themselves from English writers, they should choose American subjects. Lowell and other Brahmins believed, however, that the forms of English—and not American—poetry and fiction were most suitable for American writers, and they

Henry Wadsworth Longfellow. (Library of Congress)

encouraged aspiring authors to model their work on the English tradition.

Lowell made it clear that first-rate literature was not "national" at all, but instead appealed to people of all nations and of all times. He and others associated with the Brahmins also spoke firmly about the dual purpose of literature—it could serve as entertainment, but it also must provide readers moral, spiritual, social, and civic instruction.

Poet Henry Wadsworth Longfellow most exemplified the qualities the Brahmins expected in the new American literature. From the time he joined the Harvard faculty in 1836, Longfellow had been a leading figure on the Boston literary scene. His poems, such as "The Song of Hiawatha," "The Courtship of Miles Standish," and "Evangeline," used English meter and rhyme schemes to relate American tales. Longfellow was a staunch proponent of the idea that a poet needed to absorb the culture of other nations to be truly successful in his or her own land. While at Harvard, he instituted the study of comparative literature, and his efforts abroad to introduce European readers to American literature were matched by his work at home to champion the study of European writers.

Outside the immediate circle of the Brahmins, the writers whose works most closely approximated the criteria set by them were all from the northeast United States. The writers included poet William Cullen Bryant from Massachusetts and fiction writers Washington Irving and James Fenimore Cooper, both from New York. Bryant's poems, written in a stately, cadenced language, were hardly distinguishable from those of the Augustan poets of eighteenth century Great Britain. Irving's sketches had a certain regional flavor to them, but in almost every instance, he conveyed a genial underlying moral to his humorous tales that made his work acceptable to critics demanding that literature teach as well as delight.

Cooper chose American subjects as his themes. His series The Leatherstocking Tales introduced the reading public to the excitement of America's early days, when early settlers clashed with American Indians. His "savages," though, spoke with a diction and eloquence that would have made them at home in eighteenth century London drawing rooms. Nathaniel Hawthorne was admired by the Brahmins for his examination of the country's Puritan heritage, but there was also a certain sense of discomfort with the Gothic quality of much of his work.

By the 1880's the theories promoted by Lowell, Holmes, and Longfellow had taken hold of American literary production. Boston had become what Ralph Waldo Emerson had predicted several decades earlier: the city whose appointed destiny was to lead the process of civilization in America. Young writers such as William Dean Howells and Henry James accepted without question the idea that Boston was America's cultural capital. Howells, a native Ohioan, moved to Boston to be closer to the city's cultural life, eventually working as an editor at the *Atlantic Monthly*.

Howells and James, however, were part of a generation that would eventually replace the Brahmins' theories of literature and culture with ones that stressed concepts the Brahmins would have found uncomfortable. Realism, naturalism, and aestheticism gradually replaced the genteel tradition championed by the Brahmins, and new voices such as those of Mark Twain and other regional writers were given equal status with the accepted icons of American poetry and fiction.

SIGNIFICANCE

The influence of Lowell, Longfellow, Holmes and the other Brahmins on both the development and study of American literature extended well into the twentieth century, largely because the scholarly class, including college professors, had been familiar with the ideas promoted by the Boston-based intelligentsia whom these men represented. Lowell's influence as a critic remained strong for decades; George Saintsbury, England's most astute and influential critic of the late nineteenth century, called Lowell the best critic the United States had yet produced. Generations of schoolchildren have since read poetry by Longfellow and Bryant and fiction by Irving and Cooper as staples of the school curriculum.

The tide began to turn against the Brahmins after World War I. A new generation of scholars began to see in the writings of other nineteenth century figures a literature more distinctly American than that created by the Brahmins and their disciples. These new critics discovered that, parallel to the fiction and poetry of Brahminism, the United States had spawned another form of literature, which had been founded on Emersonian ideas about self-reliance and celebrations of the New Adam—a person whose character and values were shaped exclusively by the American experience.

The great revolution in literary studies elevated the work not only of Emerson and Nathaniel Hawthorne but also Herman Melville, Henry David Thoreau, Mark Twain, and Walt Whitman, as masterpieces of a truly American literature. People still read the Brahmins, but much of Brahminism is now considered a literature reflective of the cultural mores of the times in which they were composed.

—Laurence W. Mazzeno

AN AMERICAN LITERATURE?

In what is considered the definitive statement of what would become the Brahmin school of literature, James Russell Lowell argues that it is futile to claim a national literature. Excerpts from his article, an 1849 review of Henry Wadsworth Longfellow's Kavanagh, *follow.*

Literature survives, not because of its nationality, but in spite of it. . . .

Let us be thankful that there is no court by which we can be excluded from our share in the inheritance of the great poets of all ages and countries, to which our simply humanity entitles us. . . .

That Art in America will be modified by circumstances, we have no doubt, though it is impossible to predict the precise form of the moulds into which it will run. New conditions of life will stimulate thought and give new forms to its expression. It may not be our destiny to produce a great literature, as, indeed, our genius seems to find its kindliest development in practicalizing simpler and more perfect forms of social organization. We have yet many problems of this kind to work out, and a continent to subdue with the plough and the railroad, before we are at leisure for aesthetics. Our spirit of adventure will take first a material and practical direction, but will gradually be forced to seek outlet and scope in unoccupied territories of the intellect. In the meantime we may fairly demand of our literature that it should be national to the extent of being as free from outworn conventionalities, and as thoroughly impregnated with humane and manly sentiment, as is the idea on which our political fabric rests. Let it give a true reflection of our social, political, and household life. . . .

The error of our advocates of nationality lies in their assigning geographical limits to the poet's range of historical characters as well as to his natural scenery. There is not time or place in human nature, and Prometheus, Coriolanus, Tasso, and Tell are ours if we can use them, as truly as Washington or Daniel Boone. . . .

Source: "Kavanagh, A Tale: Nationality in Literature." *North American Review* 61, no. 1 (1849): 196-215.

FURTHER READING

Broaddus, Dorothy C. *Genteel Rhetoric: Writing High Culture in Nineteenth-Century Boston.* Columbia: University of South Carolina Press, 1999. Outlines the development of ideas about the role and characteristics of American literature and summarizes strategies used by Lowell, Holmes, and others to give legitimacy to their vision.

Buell, Lawrence. *New England Literature Culture: From Revolution Through Renaissance.* New York: Cambridge University Press, 1986. Discusses developments of the middle decades of the nineteenth century, a time when leaders of the Brahmins formulated their ideas about the nature and function of American literature. Demonstrates the influence of class and class consciousness in shaping the work of individual authors.

Calhoun, Charles C. *Longfellow: A Rediscovered Life.* Boston: Beacon Press, 2004. Thoughtful assessment of Longfellow's career. Outlines his influence on Americans' view of Europe and his efforts to serve as an unofficial ambassador of American culture to Europeans.

Duberman, Martin. *James Russell Lowell.* Boston: Houghton Mifflin, 1966. Contains a chapter on Brahmin society, detailing the relationships among the men whose ideas influenced the formation of culture in Boston during the nineteenth century.

Gibian, Peter. *Oliver Wendell Holmes and the Culture of Conversation*. New York: Cambridge University Press, 2001. Examines Holmes's principal methods for promoting his theories of literature and culture. Includes commentary on Holmes's development of the idea of the Brahmin caste in New England.

McGlinchee, Claire. *James Russell Lowell*. New York: Twayne, 1967. Reviews Lowell's career and assesses his ideas about the requirements for the development of a distinctively American literature.

Small, Miriam R. *Oliver Wendell Holmes*. New York: Twayne, 1963. Outlines Holmes's career as an author, highlighting his ideas about the importance of culture in shaping literature.

Story, Ronald. *The Forging of an Aristocracy: Harvard and the Boston Upper Class, 1800-1870*. Middletown, Conn.: Wesleyan University Press, 1980. Explains how Harvard served as a base for the writers whose work influenced the development of literary theory in Boston during the nineteenth century.

Williams, Cecil B. *Henry Wadsworth Longfellow*. New York: Twayne, 1964. Analyzes Longfellow's career as a poet and discusses his relationship with literary and academic figures of his day.

SEE ALSO: 1807-1850: Rise of the Knickerbocker School; 1819-1820: Irving's *Sketch Book* Transforms American Literature; c. 1830's-1860's: American Renaissance in Literature; 1851: Melville Publishes *Moby Dick*; c. 1865: Naturalist Movement Begins; Dec., 1884-Feb., 1885: Twain Publishes *Adventures of Huckleberry Finn*.

RELATED ARTICLES in *Great Lives from History: The Nineteenth Century, 1801-1900:* William Cullen Bryant; William Ellery Channing; James Fenimore Cooper; Ralph Waldo Emerson; Nathaniel Hawthorne; Oliver Wendell Holmes; Henry James; Henry Wadsworth Longfellow; Herman Melville; Henry David Thoreau; Mark Twain; Walt Whitman.

1880's
ROUX DEVELOPS THE THEORY OF MITOSIS

In the wake of discoveries by Charles Darwin and Gregor Mendel, investigations into the genetic basis for heredity increasingly centered on the role of chromosomes. Wilhelm Roux argued that differentiation of cell types was linked to the distribution of chromosomes following cell division in the process termed "mitosis." Although Roux would be proven wrong in suggesting chromosomes were distributed unequally, he was the first to demonstrate the sorting of chromosomes during division.

LOCALE: Breslau, Germany (now Wroclaw, Poland)
CATEGORIES: Biology; genetics; health and medicine

KEY FIGURES

Wilhelm Roux (1850-1924), German anatomist
Charles Darwin (1809-1882), English naturalist
Éduard Strasburger (1844-1912), German cytologist
August Weismann (1834-1914), German zoologist
Walther Flemming (1843-1905), German anatomist
Wilhelm Waldeyer (1836-1921), German anatomist
Theodor Boveri (1862-1915), German zoologist

SUMMARY OF EVENT

In 1859, the publication of Charles Darwin's *On the Origin of Species* led to what is arguably among the most important of modern scientific discoveries, an explanation of evolution as a result of natural selection. Darwin's theory of evolution suggested that physical traits that provide reproductive advantage to an organism will be maintained in a selective environment. Darwin's ideas initially applied primarily to complex organisms such as plants or animals, but the idea of natural selection was increasingly applied to other areas of biology, including that of individual cells.

Improvements in microscopes combined with the implementation of staining techniques during the nineteenth century allowed for more precise observational studies of cell structures and organelles. Using newly developed aniline dyes, Walther Flemming observed the presence of threadlike structures from the nucleus of animal cells. Since these structures became visible during cell division, Flemming named the process mitosis, from the Greek word meaning "thread." In 1888, Wilhelm Waldeyer named these structures chromosomes. Eduard Strasburger, carrying out similar observations using cells from plants, noted the presence of specific stages during cell division and, in 1884, named these phases prophase, metaphase, anaphase, and telophase, terms still used.

Wilhelm Roux was the only son of a university fencing master. Following service in the Franco-Prussian War (1870-1871), Roux entered a medical program at the University of Jena, completing his medical examinations in 1877. In 1879, he joined the institute at the University of Breslau, where he was to remain some ten years. Roux's work was primarily in the emerging field of embryology, and his designation as the founder of experimental embryology is a tribute to his contributions. He was well aware of the importance of Darwin's ideas on natural selection, and, incorporating his own work on the development and differentiation of the embryo, he began to apply these ideas at the microscopic level. In other words, he believed that events that occur at the cellular level represent the result of processes likely to increase the chances of survival of the cell.

Strasburger and Flemming had only recently described their work on mitosis. It was Roux's belief that the complex processes described by his colleagues could be accounted for in the context of natural selection—that there was a function behind mitosis that enhanced the survival of the cell and the more complex organism. One application of this idea, albeit incorrect, was that stronger cells would crowd out weaker ones in the developing embryo.

In an 1883 essay, Roux described the physiological processes associated with chromosomes during cell division. Each chromosome (a modern term) divides longitudinally, with the separated material distributed to each daughter cell. It had appeared to Roux that during this process, chromosomes were randomly distributed throughout the nuclear region, and they perhaps were passed in like manner to the daughter cells. That is, Roux was unsure whether distribution of the chromosomes during cell division was equal, and he speculated that differentiation may in part be the result of an unequal distribution.

The pattern of movement of chromosomes to daughter cells also led Roux to speculate that their primary role in the cell was heredity. This idea was further applied by August Weismann in his theories on the role of chromosomes in development; Weismann argued that the maintenance of hereditary characteristics over generations was the result of chromosomes being passed from parent to offspring, an idea largely proved correct. However, Weismann incorrectly believed each chromosome was the equivalent of the others.

Roux's incorrect assumption that differentiation is the result of alternative arrangements of chromosomes in cells is largely the reason why he remains a footnote in this area of biology. Much of his work during the later years at Breslau followed the same idea, that unequal chromosomal separation was necessary to explain the events during embryonic development. It remained for Theodor Boveri in the first years of the twentieth century to clarify the role played by chromosomes in development, as well as provide an explanation for their distribution.

After establishing that chromosomes were both necessary and sufficient to maintain genetic characteristics in fertilized sea urchin eggs, Boveri demonstrated that fertilization with two sperms resulted in the abnormal development of the organism. He concluded from these results that the inability of the sea urchin to develop normally was the result of unequal distribution of the chromosomes during cell division. If chromosomes were equivalent, as suggested earlier by Weismann, simply having extra chromosomes should not interfere with normal development. Boveri concluded that normal development required a precise number of chromosomes and that individual chromosomes probably carried specific characteristics. Boveri later refined this work in what would become his chromosomal theory of heredity.

SIGNIFICANCE

Roux's observation of processes associated with cell division—mitosis—led to one of the first reports explaining how chromosomal material is distributed to daughter cells. Only one year had passed, however, from the time Flemming had reported the presence of such structures in the nucleus of cells, and while some believed that chromosomes somehow played a role in heredity, the precise function of chromosomes needed confirmation.

Roux's work was significant in providing further evidence for the function of chromosomes, a function that allowed for a mechanism by which chromosomal material may be passed to daughter cells. The mechanism duplicated or divided chromosomes along a longitudinal axis, which ensured their distribution to daughter cells following the completion of mitosis. In the context of natural selection, Roux's ideas, largely theoretical, addressed the question of why such a complex mechanism might be beneficial for a cell.

One significant detail was absent from Roux's hypothesis: He did not explain the process of differentiation. In his studies of embryology, Roux showed that cells underwent two separate divisions, in which the final set of daughter cells did not contain the same quantity of chromosomes as the original parent cell. This led to the mistaken hypothesis by Weismann that differentiation is, in part, the result of unequal distribution of chromosomes. Roux's ideas required subsequent revision. Nevertheless, his work bridged the period between the discovery of chromosomes and the elucidation of their role in the heredity of both the cell and larger organisms.

—*Richard Adler*

Further Reading

Baltzer, Fritz. "Theodor Boveri." *Science* 144 (1964): 809-815. Biography of the scientist instrumental in developing a chromosomal theory of inheritance. Highlighted is his work in demonstrating the equal distribution of chromosomes during mitosis.

Becker, Wayne, Lewis Kleinsmith, and Jeff Hardin. *The World of the Cell.* 6th ed. New York: Pearson/Benjamin Cummings, 2006. Comprehensive examination of the history of the study of the cell, with photographs of the process of cell division.

Gillispie, Charles, ed. *Dictionary of Scientific Biography.* New York: Charles Scribner's Sons, 1975. Professional biographies of the major figures and the roles they played in cell history.

Harris, Henry. *The Birth of the Cell.* New Haven, Conn.: Yale University Press, 1999. History of cell theory and cell processes.

Nurse, Paul. "The Great Ideas of Biology." *Clinical Medicine* 3 (2001): 560-568. A brief but thorough and brilliant history of the development of cell biology and genetics by one of the top molecular cell biologists of modern times.

Portugal, Franklin, and Jack Cohen. *A Century of DNA.* Cambridge, Mass.: MIT Press, 1977. Authors describe the experiments that led to determining DNA's role in heredity. (DNA was discovered in 1869.) Roux's observations are included in the early history.

Sturtevant, A. H. *A History of Genetics.* Cold Spring Harbor, N.Y.: Cold Spring Harbor Press, 2001. An updated reprint of the subject of genetics, written by a key figure in the study of heredity. The author, a student of Thomas Hunt Morgan, the founder of modern genetics, played an important role in understandings of chromosomal theory.

Thompson, D'Arcy Wentworth. *On Growth and Form.* Mineola, N.Y.: Dover, 1992. Thompson's theory of transformation as an explanation of evolution was first described in 1917. Included is a history of cell theory, with reference to Roux's work.

See also: 1838-1839: Schwann and Virchow Develop Cell Theory; 1865: Mendel Proposes Laws of Heredity; 1882-1901: Metchnikoff Advances the Cellular Theory of Immunity; Dec. 11, 1890: Behring Discovers the Diphtheria Antitoxin; 1898: Beijerinck Discovers Viruses; 1899-1900: Rediscovery of Mendel's Hereditary Theory.

Related articles in *Great Lives from History: The Nineteenth Century, 1801-1900:* Karl Ernst von Baer; Charles Darwin; Francis Galton; Ernst Haeckel; Gregor Mendel; August Weismann.

1880's-1890's
RISE OF YELLOW JOURNALISM

In their competition to sell newspapers, William Randolph Hearst and Joseph Pulitzer engaged in yellow journalism—sensational or biased stories that often contained factual inaccuracies. The sensationalism of their newspapers influenced the outbreak of the Spanish-American War of 1898, as well as having a lasting influence on American journalism.

LOCALE: New York, New York
CATEGORIES: Journalism; communications; crime and scandals

KEY FIGURES

William Randolph Hearst (1863-1951), American newspaper publisher
Joseph Pulitzer (1847-1911), American newspaper publisher
Richard Felton Outcault (1863-1928), American comic strip creator
Frederic Remington (1861-1909), American foreign correspondent, painter, and sculptor
Richard Harding Davis (1864-1916), American foreign correspondent and writer

SUMMARY OF EVENT

Historians mark the era of yellow journalism as occuring roughly between 1895 and 1905, and its rise in 1895 is closely associated with journalistic practices in New York City in particular. The Industrial Revolution allowed publishers to utilize machines that could print thousands of newspapers overnight, creating an endless battle to win and keep readers. The term "yellow journalism" refers to a style of reporting based on this competition to sell newspapers: Renowned publishers of the day used sensationalized stories of murders, accidents, and even international conflicts in order to capture attention and entertain readers.

These sensationalized newspaper stories often made use of colorful language and exaggerated or even inaccurate information. Newspapers often hastily and sloppily gathered information in order to publish stories before their competitors did, and biased opinions usually took the place of balanced, objective accounts. Trivial stories with human interest or sensationalistic elements sometimes dominated the front pages, and the number of drawings and cartoons carried by newspapers increased. The yellow press also lowered prices and expanded the number of pages in each newspaper. It enjoyed higher sales than did the more unbiased newspapers of the day.

Joseph Pulitzer's *New York World* and William Randolph Hearst's *New York Journal American*, competing New York City newspapers during the late nineteenth century, are most closely associated with the rise of yellow journalism. When Hearst bought the *New York Journal American* in 1895, he began a competition with Pulitzer for the loyalty of New York readers. Both Pulitzer and Hearst sought to appeal to readers that other New York City newspapers had largely ignored, including women, laborers, Democrats, immigrants, and the poor. Hearst utilized tactics in his competition with Pulitzer that would later become associated with yellow journalism.

The term "yellow journalism" first appeared in 1895, the year Hearst purchased the *New York Journal American*. It originated with a comic strip called "The Yellow Kid," which first appeared in Pulitzer's *New York World*.

Joseph Pulitzer. (The Granger Collection, New York)

The comic strip's artist was well-known cartoonist Richard Felton Outcault, and his color comic was an innovation of its time, using special smear-proof yellow ink. Hearst lured Outcault, as well as the rest of Pulitzer's Sunday edition staff, to his rival newspaper. Pulitzer then hired George B. Luks to continue production of the comic without its original creator. Thus, "The Yellow Kid" appeared for a time in both newspapers. The competition for the comic strip, an early step in the battle to increase circulation, marked the beginning of yellow journalism's heyday.

The most famous incident of yellow journalism occurred during the Spanish-American War of 1898. In the years prior to the war, Cuban revolutionaries had been battling for the island's independence from Spain. American newspapers sent well-known foreign correspondents, called "traveling commissioners" at the time, to Cuba. These reporters and illustrators included Richard Harding Davis, Stephen Crane, Frederick Remington, George Rea, and Sylvester Scovel. Many of the reporters entered Cuba illegally, disguised as rebels or spies, and some were arrested, thrown out of the country, or killed in battle. Hearst sided with the Cuban revolutionaries and did not hide his bias.

Hearst sent the well-known writer Richard Harding Davis and the renowned artist and illustrator Frederic Remington to Cuba in 1897 in order to cover the Cuban rebellion for the *New York Journal American*. In a famous and often repeated anecdote, Remington wired Hearst that a war appeared unlikely and requested permission for the two men to return to the United States. Hearst then allegedly sent a telegrammed reply stating that if Remington furnished the pictures, Hearst would provide the war. This remark was widely repeated as evidence of yellow journalism's willingness to employ shady tactics and inaccurate reporting to get a story. Many historians, however, doubt the veracity of the anecdote regarding Hearst's famous telegram, which came from a book of reminiscences by one of Hearst's writers. Hearst himself denied its accuracy. Nevertheless, the anecdote led many historians to label the Spanish-American War "Mr. Hearst's War" or "The Newspapers' War."

Hearst's biased coverage of the growing rebellion remained one-sided in favor of the Cubans. Hearst would not print any news that came from Spanish sources, claiming they were untrustworthy. His articles included accounts of Spanish cruelty and brutality designed to outrage American readers and gain their support for the Cuban revolutionaries. When the American battleship *Maine* exploded in Havana Harbor on February 15, 1898, killing two hundred and sixty crewmembers, Hearst found another story to use in his attempt to gain the American public's support for U.S. entry into the conflict. While other city newspapers such as the *New York Times*, the *New York Tribune*, the *New York Herald*, and the *New York Evening Post* cautioned readers to wait for a Navy board of inquiry to determine the explosion's cause, Pulitzer's *New York World* and Hearst's *New York Journal American* carried stories of a "suppressed cable" that stated that the *Maine*'s explosion was not an accident. The cable later proved to have been manufactured. Such sensational and unfounded reports helped gain the public's support for U.S. action and put pressure on U.S. president William McKinley to declare war against Spain.

In another famous incident, Hearst was able to catch Pulitzer employing a common tactic of yellow journalism. Many newspapers routinely carried stories they had lifted directly from the pages of rival newspapers. In an attempt to catch Pulitzer in the act, Hearst ran an 1898 story about the death of a fictional Colonel Reflipe W. Thenuz, whose name was a corruption of the sentence "we pilfer the news." Pulitzer then unknowingly ran the article, even adding in a dateline for more authenticity. While most historians view Hearst as the one most responsible for the creation of yellow journalism, Pulitzer became an integral part of the pheonemon as a result of his role in reporting the Cuban revolution against Spain, the explosion of the *Maine*, and the subsequent Spanish-American War.

Significance

Many historians view the actions of Pulitzer and Hearst in reporting the Cuban revolution and the explosion of the *Maine* as key elements in the growing national pressure for American involvement that led to the Spanish-American War. The Remington telegram also became one of the best-known incidents in the history of the American news media. William Randolph Hearst and Joseph Pulitzer remained dominant names within the American media, and Pulitzer went on to create the famous literary and journalistic prizes that bear his name.

By the early twentieth century, circulation of the yellow press newspapers had dramatically declined, but individual tactics of yellow journalism have continued. The muckraking journalists of the early twentieth century Progressive movement wrote in the vein of yellow journalism in their scandalous exposés on such topics as worker safety, slum conditions, and food production. Legacies of yellow journalism also include the use of eye-catching headlines, comic strips, human-interest stories, stories that target special interest groups, investigative reports, and accusations of bias, factual inaccuracies, and fabrications. The era of yellow journalism also continues to serve as a cautionary tale in the media's efforts to remain unbiased and accurate in its reporting while still attracting a large audience.

—*Marcella Bush Trevino*

FURTHER READING

Campbell, W. Joseph. *Yellow Journalism: Puncturing the Myths, Defining the Legacies*. Westport, Conn.: Praeger, 2003. Provides an overview of the yellow journalism era and separates myths from realities.

Littlefield, Roy Everett. *William Randolph Hearst: His Role in American Progressivism*. Lanham, Md.: Rowman & Littlefield, 1980. Examines Hearst's influence on the Progressive movement of the late nineteenth and early twentieth centuries.

Milton, Joyce. *The Yellow Kids: Foreign Correspondents in the Heyday of Yellow Journalism*. New York: Harper & Row, 1989. Highlights the coverage of the Spanish-American War from the perspective of the reporters who served as foreign correspondents.

Nasaw, David. *The Chief: The Life of William Randolph Hearst*. Boston: Houghton Mifflin, 2000. Biography covering Hearst's life and career as a newspaper publisher, movie producer, and politician.

SEE ALSO: Sept. 3, 1833: Birth of the Penny Press; Sept. 18, 1851: Modern *New York Times* Is Founded; 1895-1898: Hearst-Pulitzer Circulation War; Feb. 24, 1895-1898: Cuban War of Independence; Apr. 24-Dec. 10, 1898: Spanish-American War.

RELATED ARTICLES in *Great Lives from History: The Nineteenth Century, 1801-1900:* Stephen Crane; William McKinley; Joseph Pulitzer; Frederic Remington.

September-November, 1880
IRISH TENANT FARMERS STAGE FIRST "BOYCOTT"

The social and economic ostracism of land manager Charles Cunningham Boycott by Irish tenant farmers in County Mayo was a new tactic that addressed the land reform debate in late nineteenth century Ireland. The practice of "boycotting" unpopular land or business owners carried over into the social and labor movements of the twentieth century.

LOCALE: Ballinrobe, County Mayo, Ireland

CATEGORIES: Business and labor; agriculture; social issues and reform

KEY FIGURES

Charles Cunningham Boycott (1832-1897), Irish estate manager

Michael Davitt (1846-1906), a leader of the Irish Republican Brotherhood and spokesman for the Irish National Land League, 1879-1881

James Daly (1835-1910), publisher and editor of the *Connaught Telegraph* and a leader of the Irish National Land League, 1879-1881

Charles Stewart Parnell (1846-1891), leader of the Irish Parliamentary Party, 1879-1890

John Henry Crichton (1802-1884), third earl of Erne and Irish landowner

William Ewart Gladstone (1809-1898), prime minister of Great Britain, 1868-1874, 1880-1885, 1886, 1892-1894

SUMMARY OF EVENT

During the Irish Land War (1879-1881), a group of tenant farmers engaged in actions designed socially and economically to isolate an estate manager and rent collector named Charles Cunningham Boycott. The action, which lasted from September to November, 1880, was well publicized, and as a result, "boycotting" entered both the lexicon and the arsenal of people attempting to protest actions or to effect change. In that first boycott, the agricultural workers, tenant farmers, and townspeople of Ballinrobe, County Mayo, were reacting to increases in rents and falling agricultural prices. Accordingly, they refused to work for or sell goods or services to Boycott and his family.

The Boycott episode of 1880 must be placed in the broader context of the organization and mobilization of Irish tenant farmers for land reform legislation, and the political struggle for Irish home rule, or self-governance, during the late nineteenth century. Most Irish landlords did not live on their estates and employed land managers to oversee rent collection and run the estates' day-to-day

Irish tenant farmers being evicted from their homes on the estate of a British absentee landlord. (Library of Congress)

affairs. Since the eighteenth century, nearly all Irish landlords were Protestant, and most tenant farmers were Catholic. In addition to this social and religious divide, there was economic tension as well. As a visible representative of the landlord, the estate manager was a magnet for threats to life and property from disgruntled tenant farmers. The mobilization of the rural populace against Boycott, as well as occasionally violent encounters between tenant farmers and their landlords or estate mangers during the Irish Land War, not only characterized the centuries-old struggle for the control of Irish land but also led to parliamentary reforms concerning land ownership, tenant rights, and the setting of fair land prices in Ireland between 1880 and 1903.

Boycott was born near Norfolk, England, in 1832. He purchased a commission in the British army and served out his commission in Ireland. After his discharge, Boycott and his Irish-born wife, Annie, managed a two-thousand-acre estate on Achill Island, County Mayo. In 1873, the Boycotts moved to Lough Mask Estate, near Ballinrobe, to manage some fifteen hundred acres and about forty tenant farmers for John Henry Crichton, the third earl of Erne.

The late 1870's was a period of falling crop prices, and many Irish tenant farmers who had difficulty in paying their yearly rents faced eviction. According to later testimony to a parliamentary commission in 1888, Boycott insisted that tenant farmers make full rent payment or face eviction, regardless of poor harvests. The difficulties over rent prices, payment, evictions, and land ownership came to a head in the summer of 1879. County Mayo farmers banded together in August, 1879, and formed the Mayo Tenants League. The league was led by Irish republican revolutionary Michael Davitt and newspaper owner James Daly, and it rapidly adopted a policy of socially and economically isolating land managers, their assistants, and persons who purchased an evicted farmer's land.

The protests in County Mayo and the general economic unrest in Ireland were noted by Charles Stewart Parnell, the leader of the Irish Parliamentary, or "Home Rule," Party. Parnell sought a way to gain broader political support, and in October, 1879, he married the issue of Irish independence with land reform legislation in a series of meetings with Davitt. Parnell was appointed president of the Irish National Land League and organized mass political rallies across Ireland through 1880 to promote the twin causes of independence from Great Britain and land reform. The practice of isolating land managers and farmers who purchased evicted rental lands was announced by Parnell September 19, 1880, at a speech in Ennis, County Clare. Five days later, on September 24, the ostracism of the Boycotts began at Lough Mask.

Boycott later testified to a parliamentary commission that all his household servants and agricultural workers had abandoned his service within a week's time after the boycott began. Moreover, local blacksmiths, mail carriers, and grocers refused business dealings with the Boycotts. Boycott reported being "hooted and booed" in the town of Ballinrobe and along the country lanes. Fences and enclosures on the estate were broken down, and livestock was led astray by persons unknown. By the end of September, the Boycotts, their son, and a family friend had to perform every task themselves, including milking the cows, herding the sheep, cooking, and cleaning.

With the harvest only weeks away, Boycott's case was publicized across Ireland and Britain by mainly Protestant, unionist, anti-home rule newspapers. Bernard Becker, a reporter for London's *Daily News*, traveled to Lough Mask in mid-October, 1880, and wrote the first article specifically dealing with the Boycott case. Becker's article was reprinted in major Irish newspapers, and Protestant unionists organized the "Boycott Relief Fund," as well as calling for Protestant volunteers to travel to Lough Mask to help with the harvest.

A group of some fifty Protestant laborers, guarded by more than one thousand British troops, arrived in Ballinrobe on November 11, 1880. The group of laborers and soldiers was greeted by a hail of insults from the locals as they marched to the Lough Mask estate. The harvest was completed by November 25. Several threatening letters had been sent to the Boycotts during that time, but the presence of British troops prevented any large-scale disturbance. On November 27, 1880, the Boycotts, the laborers, and the soldiers left Ballinrobe by train to the mixed cheering and jeering of locals.

The Boycotts headed to Dublin, but the threatening letters continued. The manager of the hotel where the Boycotts had lodged was threatened with death if he continued to provide them shelter. Charles Boycott and his family booked the first ferry for England and left Ireland on December 1, 1880. Boycott returned to Lough Mask in 1881 and was again treated to boos and hisses in public. The workers, however, returned to the estate. Boycott continued to manage Lough Mask until 1886 without further incident. He returned to England in 1886 to manage an estate near Suffolk. Boycott died June 19, 1897, on the Suffolk estate.

SIGNIFICANCE

The "boycott" of 1880 demonstrated the growing organizational power of Irish tenant farmers and the Irish Parliamentary Party against Protestant land owners and land managers, as well as increased support for Irish independence. This episode in Irish history also briefly united the militant Irish Republican Brotherhood with the moderate Irish Parliamentary Party. The event and others like it across Ireland also impelled the British government to enact a series of land reforms in Ireland (1880-1903), along with anti-coercion measures that targeted groups such as the National Land League as "revolutionary."

This carrot-and-stick approach adapted by British prime minister William Ewart Gladstone after the land war of 1879-1881 did little to alleviate the growing political tensions in Ireland. However, the Boycott affair and Irish tenant-farmer agitation did draw Parliament's attention to tenant rights, the conflict over rent prices, and the right of farmers to sell their lease. The Boycott affair emphasized the close ties between Irish nationalism and the Irish land question during the late nineteenth century.

The social practice of boycotting became a powerful, worldwide instrument for disenfranchised social and ethnic groups through the twentieth century. The practice of passive resistance posited an alternative, peaceful means to gain social, political, and economic objectives, or to at least bring attention to particular grievances.

—*Tyler T. Crogg*

FURTHER READING

Bew, Paul. *Land and the National Question in Ireland, 1858-1882*. Dublin: Gill & Macmillan, 1978. A critique of Irish tenant farmer organizations and the multiple internal divisions in Irish land reform movements.

Clark, Samuel. *Social Origins of the Irish Land War*. Princeton, N.J.: Princeton University Press, 1979. An analysis of the socioeconomic structures in late nineteenth century Ireland and the origins of "collective action" campaigns.

Jordan, Donald E., Jr. *Land and Popular Politics in Ireland: County Mayo from the Plantation to the Land War*. Cambridge, England: Cambridge University Press, 1994. A long-term analysis of tenant farmer organization and political activity in County Mayo. The most specific work dealing with the foundation of the Mayo Tenants League and socioeconomic conditions in County Mayo.

Marlow, Joyce. *Captain Boycott and the Irish*. London: Andre Deutsch, 1973. The most detailed narrative of Charles Boycott's career and the specific events of the "Boycott campaign" at Lough Mask Estate in 1880.

O'Day, Alan. *Irish Home Rule, 1867-1921*. Manchester, England: Manchester University Press, 1998. An examination of the evolution within the Irish home rule movement and its relationship with other nationalist groups in Ireland. Includes timeline and glossary of terms.

SEE ALSO: 1807: Bowdler Publishes *The Family Shakespeare*; 1845-1854: Great Irish Famine; June, 1866-1871: Fenian Risings for Irish Independence; Dec. 3, 1868-Feb. 20, 1874: Gladstone Becomes Prime Minister of Britain; June, 1886-Sept. 9, 1893: Irish Home Rule Debate Dominates British Politics.

RELATED ARTICLES in *Great Lives from History: The Nineteenth Century, 1801-1900:* William Ewart Gladstone; Charles Stewart Parnell.

December 16, 1880-March 6, 1881
FIRST BOER WAR

The first large-scale armed confrontation between British imperial forces and Afrikaners in a long series of British-Afrikaner conflicts, the First Boer War restored independence to the Transvaal's South African Republic but left unresolved questions about the future of British-Afrikaner relations, while intensifying Afrikaner nationalism and increasing tensions that led to the bloody South African War of 1899-1902.

ALSO KNOWN AS: First Boer War; First War of Freedom
LOCALE: Transvaal-Natal border region, South Africa
CATEGORIES: Wars, uprisings, and civil unrest; expansion and land acquisition

KEY FIGURES

Sir Theophilus Shepstone (1817-1893), British administrator of Natal, 1856-1876, and administrator of Transvaal, 1877-1879

Henry Howard Molyneux Herbert (Fourth Earl of Carnarvon; 1831-1890), British sectary of state for the colonies, 1874-1878

Paul Kruger (1825-1904), member of the Transvaal Triumvirate, 1877-1883, and later president of the South African Republic, 1883-1900

Petrus Jacobus Joubert (1831-1900), member of the Transvaal Triumvirate, 1877-1883, and commander in chief of Afrikaner forces, 1878-1881

Marthinus Wessel Pretorius (1819-1901), member of the Transvaal Triumvirate, 1877-1883, who was a former president of both the South African Republic and Orange Free State

Sir George Pomeroy Colley (1835-1881), commander of the British army in Natal and Transvaal, 1880-1881

SUMMARY OF EVENT

South Africa's so-called First Boer War—known to Afrikaners as the First War of Freedom—resulted from Great Britain's annexation of the Afrikaner-ruled South African Republic in the Transvaal in a British attempt to consolidate territorial holdings in South Africa. The war may be seen in the large contexts of the developing European imperial so-called scramble for Africa and the rising tensions among long-established native African communities, white Afrikaner settlers, and colonial authorities. Although this conflict was neither the first nor the last time that British forces and Afrikaners fought each other, the brief war set the stage for the South African, or Second Boer, War of 1899-1902 and helped to lift Afrikaner nationalism to a new political level.

The Afrikaner people, who were pejoratively called "Boers" (farmers) by the British, were descendants of Dutch, German, and French settlers who had begun immigrating to South Africa during the seventeenth century at the behest of the Dutch East India Company. The company built Cape Town as a victualling stop for ships sailing between Europe and Asia, and its administration was the only European government in what is now the Republic of South Africa until 1806, when Great Britain occupied its Cape Colony during the Napoleonic Wars in order to protect its own sea route to British India.

From 1835 to 1837, thousands of Afrikaner families left the British-ruled Cape Colony and headed north and east into the interior to escape unwelcome government interference in their lives. The emigrant Afrikaners eventually founded two independent republics, the Orange Free State, in the region between the Orange and Vaal Rivers, and the South African Republic, in the Transvaal region beyond the Vaal River. Both republics soon became targets of British attempts to impose colonial administration. British interest in the Afrikaner domains increased after the discovery of diamonds near the Orange River in 1867. Moreover, the British government eventually wished to unite South Africa under a single imperial authority. However, the Afrikaners persistently resisted all such attempts. British-Afrikaner treaties at Sand River in 1852 and at Bloemfontein in 1854 guaranteed limited Afrikaner independence, but the newfound mineral wealth and growing influx of British settlers brought matters to a head in 1877.

In April, 1877, under orders from British colonial secretary Lord Carnarvon, Theophilus Shepstone, the administrator of Britain's Natal colony, led a contingent of British troops into the Transvaal's capital, Pretoria. There he raised the British Union Jack and proclaimed that the republic was under British rule.

The irate Afrikaners rallied under Paul Kruger, a veteran political leader who called for nothing short of restoring independence. Kruger and two other leading Transvaal politicians, M. W. Pretorius and Petrus Jacobus Joubert, formed a triumvirate government to counter the British administration. Over the next several years, the members of the triumvirate presided over mass rallies of their increasingly disgruntled fellow Afrikaners. However, it was not until after the British seized an Afrikaner's wagon at Potchefstroom for sale in a public auction in November, 1880, that the first shots were fired in what became a war.

British troops trying to recapture Majuba Hill in the face of Afrikaner guns. (The Co-Operative Publishing Company)

News of the wagon seizure was immediately transmitted through the countryside. On November 11, 1880, a one-hundred-man Afrikaner commando—which was something like a mounted militia unit—confronted British officials. One month later, at a mass meeting at Paardekraal, Kruger, Joubert, and Pretorius were formally elected as the triumvirate and proclaimed that the restoration of the Transvaal's independence was vital.

Finally, on December 16, the first shots were fired between British troops and the local commando in Potchefstroom. The Afrikaners then rapidly organized and laid siege to several British garrisons in the Transvaal. A British relief column was ordered to Pretoria to assist the besieged garrison there. On December 20, the column of some 270 British troops and wagons was ordered to halt and go back by armed Afrikaners near the town of Bronkhorstspruit, about forty miles east of Pretoria. When the British commander refused to comply, about two hundred well-concealed Afrikaners opened fire. Within fifteen minutes, 156 British troops were killed or wounded. This battle demonstrated the tactics that the Afrikaners would use and foreshadowed the high casualties that the British would sustain throughout the ensuing war.

British forces under the command of Major-General Sir George Pomeroy Colley began marching to the Transvaal border January 19, 1881. Colley's objective was to clear and secure the main road to Pretoria. Knowing that this single road was vital to British relief forces coming from Natal, Afrikaners under the command of Joubert concentrated their forces near two high hills that overlooked the road crossing the Natal-Transvaal border, Laing's Nek and Majuba. On January 28, 1881, Colley's assault on Laing's Nek was repulsed by the Afrikaners. Again, the British suffered with high casualties, including four of Colley's five staff officers, and more than eighty killed and nearly 115 wounded.

Colley's troops retreated to a small encampment named Mount Prospect to await reinforcements, while the Afrikaners stepped up their raids on British dispatch riders. Recognizing the threat to his supply and communications lines, Colley marched about four hundred of his troops south to the Ingogo River on February 8 to counter Afrikaner raiding parties. He deployed his troops on a slight rise near the river, where they were surrounded by Afrikaner riflemen posted on small rises. There, the British soldiers suffered from both the accurate rifle fire of their enemies and a lack of water. This action cost the British another fifty-eight dead and more than sixty wounded. During a heavy evening thunderstorm, the Afrikaners pulled back, and Colley seized his chance to escape with his men back to Mount Prospect. There he awaited reinforcements from Great Britain and India.

With the arrival of fresh British troops at Mount Prospect on February 23, Colley planned the occupation of Majuba Hill, which overlooked both Laing's Nek and the Pretoria road. In a difficult night-time maneuver, Colley and about six hundred troops climbed the rough slopes of Majuba. At daybreak on February 27, Colley's troops could see the entire road and the Afrikaner camp below the hill. Joubert then called for an Afrikaner immediate attack to dislodge the British. At about 6:00 A.M., three separate commandoes, of about 150-200 men each, began threading their way along the gullies, ravines, and boulders toward the summit of Majuba. By noon, the British were under a barrage of accurate and heavy rifle fire from advancing Afrikaners. By 2:00 P.M., the Afrikaners had gained the summit and were firing down on the fleeing British troops. Majuba was a disaster for the British, who lost 240 killed and wounded. Among the dead was Major-General Colley himself. The Afrikaners counted fewer then 10 dead in the assault.

On March 6, 1881, the British accepted the Afrikaner offer of an armistice at Mount Prospect. During a meeting at a farmhouse near the base of Majuba Hill on March 21-23, British officers and Afrikaners leaders agreed to terms that would restore nominal independence to the Transvaal and withdraw British forces from the Transvaal. This agreement was officially guaranteed by the Treaties of Pretoria (1883) and London (1884).

SIGNIFICANCE

The First Boer War resulted from the developing strains between Britain's colonial rulers and the emigrant Afrikaners and added to those strains. Although the Treaties of Pretoria and London guaranteed Afrikaner independence, the discovery of gold in the Transvaal in 1884 attracted a large-scale influx of British prospectors and settlers, as well as British investment in both the economic and political sectors of the Transvaal. The British desire for revenge against the Transvaal Afrikaners, the continued British planning for federating South Africa, and Transvaal's informal alliance with Germany made for an uneasy peace between 1881 and 1899.

The war also demonstrated the prowess of highly mobile Afrikaner commando units against professional British soldiers in both guerrilla tactics and set-piece battles. Nevertheless, when the British fought the Afrikaners again in the South African War, they repeated many of the same military and political mistakes.

—Tyler T. Crogg

FURTHER READING

Castle, Ian. *Majuba 1881: Hill of Destiny*. London: Osprey Press, 1996. Well-illustrated and detailed text covering the 1880-1881 war, with useful information on the leaders, regiments, equipment, and weapons used in the war.

De Villiers, Marq. *White Tribe Dreaming*. London: Penguin Books, 1989. Part Afrikaner history and part genealogy, De Villier's work describes the evolution of the Afrikaner community and nationalism from the seventeenth to twentieth centuries.

Giliomee, Hermann. *The Afrikaners: Biography of a People*. Charlottesville: University Press of Virginia, 2003. Balanced study of the historical construction of Afrikaner identity.

Le May, G. H. L. *The Afrikaners: A Historical Interpretation*. Oxford, England: Basil Blackwell, 1995. Analysis of changing concepts of Afrikaner identity through three centuries.

Omer-Cooper, J. D. *History of Southern Africa*. 2d ed. London: James Currey, 1994. Solid general history of the numerous peoples of Southern Africa, their interactions and development.

Paulin, Christopher M. *White Men's Dreams, Black Men's Blood: African Labor and British Expansionism in Southern Africa, 1877-1895*. Trenton, N.J.:

Africa World Press, 2001. Examination of the exploitation of African workers that looks closely at competition between the British and the Afrikaners for control of the Transvaal.

SEE ALSO: 1835: South Africa's Great Trek Begins; 1865-1868: Basuto War; Jan. 22-23, 1879: Battles of Isandlwana and Rorke's Drift; Jan. 22-Aug., 1879: Zulu War; June 21, 1884: Gold Is Discovered in the Transvaal; Mar. 13, 1888: Rhodes Amalgamates Kimberley Diamondfields; Dec. 29, 1895-Jan. 2, 1896: Jameson Raid; Oct. 11, 1899-May 31, 1902: South African War; Oct. 13, 1899-May 17, 1900: Siege of Mafeking.

RELATED ARTICLES in *Great Lives from History: The Nineteenth Century, 1801-1900:* Paul Kruger; Cecil Rhodes.

1881-1889
BISMARCK INTRODUCES SOCIAL SECURITY PROGRAMS IN GERMANY

Otto von Bismarck, Imperial Germany's chancellor, attempted to preempt the rising Social Democratic movement in the empire by introducing various social welfare measures to benefit Germany's workers. Bismarck's social security programs marked the beginning of what would become known as the welfare state.

LOCALE: Berlin, Prussia, German Empire (now in Germany)

CATEGORIES: Government and politics; laws, acts, and legal history; social issues and reform

KEY FIGURES

Otto von Bismarck (1815-1898), Prussian prime minister, 1862-1890, and German chancellor, 1871-1890

William I (1797-1888), king of Prussian, r. 1861-1888, and emperor of Germany, r. 1871-1888

Theodor Lohmann (1831-1905), undersecretary of trade and the interior

SUMMARY OF EVENT

In 1881, Otto von Bismarck, chancellor of Imperial Germany since its formation in 1871, introduced into the German Reichstag, or parliament, the Accident Insurance Bill, which aimed to provide pensions for laborers who were injured while working in the nation's most dangerous industries. During the next several years, Bismarck's leadership led to the passage of several such insurance laws, together constituting the first comprehensive social welfare measures to be adopted in the industrial world.

Bismarck had been the primary force in bringing about the German Empire, or the Second Reich, in 1871. A conservative Prussian aristocrat, he had used his Machiavellian diplomatic skills in peace and war to weld the several German states into an empire dominated by Prussia. Together, the German states formed a nation in the heart of Europe that changed the political and military balance of power on the Continent. The industrial development of the empire's economy was such that by the 1880's, Germany was challenging Great Britain's economic supremacy. The Iron Chancellor, as Bismarck was known, continued to dominate the new Germany in the two decades after its unification. Under his guidance, the empire forged a series of alliances aimed at ensuring its international security by isolating France. Domestically, he was equally effective at overcoming potential opponents and challengers.

Always an advocate of a centralized, even authoritarian, state, Bismarck perceived two of his enemies during the 1870's to be the Roman Catholic Church and the socialists, including the government's Social Democratic Party. Bismarck was Prussian, and the kingdom of Prussia dominated Imperial Germany. Moreover, as a Protestant—like most Prussians—Bismarck was concerned about southern Germany's Catholic influence. Although Bismarck was conservative, most liberals in Germany and elsewhere were opposed to Pope Pius IX's condemnation of all forms of liberalism and modernism in his Syllabus of Errors (1864). They were also concerned by his dogma of papal infallibility, promulgated in 1870 by the First Vatican Council. A number of laws were passed during the Kulturkampf, or culture war, against the Catholic Church. These included the requirement of a civil rather than religious marriage, the banning of the Jesuits, and the monitoring of clerical education. However, by 1878, Bismarck had largely abandoned his campaign against the Catholic Church in favor of his new nemesis, the socialists.

Industrialization in Germany accelerated during the 1860's and 1870's, creating a sizeable industrial working class that made up a majority of the population in many German cities. The economic depression of the early 1870's led to the formation in 1875 of the Social Democratic Party, a socialist party with some Marxist influences. The party was adamantly opposed to the traditional liberal nostrums of lower tariffs and free trade as means to solve the empire's economic problems.

Bismarck attacked the Social Democratic Party's leaders, claiming they were committed to revolution, destruction, and anarchy. Bismarck, who knew little of Marxism, sincerely believed that socialism was a danger not only to those who owned property but also to the unity of Germany itself. Moreover, it was a good political strategy for Bismarck to isolate the socialists and gain the support of the middle classes. Two failed assassination attempts on the life of Emperor William I in 1878 gave Bismarck the opportunity to force through the Reichstag the Anti-Socialist Law, which outlawed all socialist, social democratic, and communist organizations. The Social Democratic Party was weakened, as were many labor unions, but the party survived, because its members could still run for office and could not be prevented from meeting at the Reichstag once they were elected.

Against the Catholics, Bismarck had relied upon the liberals, including the National Liberal Party. His move against the socialists had split the liberals, not because they had any sympathy for the socialist economic program, but rather because some liberals were advocates of laissez-faire practices and limited governmental power. These liberals were committed to civil rights and opposed Bismarck's heavy-handed repression of his political foes. After isolating the socialists and dividing the liberals, Bismarck turned to the conservative Center Party, a party that was mainly but not entirely made up of Catholics, his former opponents. He sought the Center Party's support, together with that of other political factions in the Reichstag, for his most radical measure in the domestic arena.

In 1881, Bismarck proposed a comprehensive state insurance plan for Germany's workers. The plan was radical, because it contradicted the prevailing laissez-faire liberalism of the day and because nothing of the kind had yet been attempted on the scale that Bismarck envisioned. The Accident Insurance Bill was presented to the Reichstag in March, 1881. It would provide workers in the most dangerous industries with pensions for injuries that either ended or reduced their incomes. These

Otto von Bismarck. (Library of Congress)

pensions would be awarded to the workers' dependents in the event of fatal injuries. Employers were to pay two-thirds of the insurance premiums, employees would pay one-third, and the government would provide an additional subsidy, as well as administering the program.

The few Social Democrats in the Reichstag opposed Bismarck's program because they thought it did not go far enough. The legislative body's liberals opposed it because it violated their commitment to laissez-faire government and liberal individualism. The bill was withdrawn, but a revised bill was submitted to a newly elected Reichstag in November. The revised bill was accompanied by an imperial message from William I, who did not author the document but who had influence upon it. The message included the emperor's policy statement that social reform would be an ongoing commitment of the government, which should continue to respond to whatever social needs existed rather than being satisfied with the passage of a single law. The revised accident insurance bill did not become law until June, 1884, taking effect on October 1, 1885. It covered more industries and trades than in the original bill, and the entire cost of the premiums was paid by the employers, who preferred not to have a government subsidy that could lead to additional bureaucratic interference with their businesses.

Bismarck introduced a comprehensive sickness insurance bill in May, 1882, that proposed two-thirds of the benefits were to be paid by employers and one-third by the workers. After considerable discussion and debate, it became law in May, 1883, and went into force in December, 1884. A compulsory old age and disability pension bill, with the cost divided equally between employers and employees along with a state subsidy, became law in May, 1889. Provisions for unemployment insurance were postponed and did not become law until the 1920's—during the Weimar Republic, after the demise of Imperial Germany.

There is no question that Bismarck was the driving force behind the social security legislation, although Theodor Lohmann, an undersecretary in the Ministry of Trade and the Imperial Office of the Interior, played a major role in drafting the accident and sickness insurance bills until he resigned in 1883. The old age pension bill was delayed until 1889 in part because Bismarck's interest in social matters waned during the mid-1880's. His motives had been debated since the social legislation was first introduced. Almost everyone has recognized the revolutionary nature of his proposals, but Bismarck's motives have often been seen to be merely the result of his authoritarianism and amoral political calculations. That is, some historians believe they were a tactic to reduce the lure of socialism and of the Social Democratic Party to Germany's industrial workers.

Such political considerations undoubtedly did play a role, but Bismarck had always doubted the moral efficacy of liberalism's individualist, self-help ethos. As an aristocrat and a Christian, there was an element of religious paternalism in Bismarck's actions, and he likely sincerely believed that the empire had an obligation to provide some security for its less fortunate citizens.

SIGNIFICANCE

Although it is likely that Bismarck did not fully understand the long-term implications of his own accomplishments, his social security programs, including accident, sickness, and old-age pension benefits, were revolutionary. They set the precedent followed by Great Britain in the early twentieth century and by the United States in the New Deal of the 1930's. Because he opposed any interference in the workplace between employers and employees—such as limiting hours, regulating working conditions, or eliminating child labor—Bismarck's reforms benefited what might be called the passive rather than active citizens and workers. By restricting his reforms to the unemployed rather than the employed, he failed to integrate Germany's working class into the politics of the empire, particularly in his attack on working-class leadership as exemplified by the Social Democratic Party and labor unions. Bismarck's legacy was a German Empire that was more oligarchic and elitist than democratic and that would collapse in the maelstrom of Germany's defeat in World War I.

—Eugene Larson

FURTHER READING

Ashley, Annie. *Social Policy of Bismarck: A Critical Study*. London: Longman, 1912. One of the earliest comparison studies of Bismarck's social reforms with those of Great Britain.

Crankshaw, Edward. *Bismarck*. New York: Viking, 1981. One of the most popular biographies of Bismarck.

Feuchtwanger, Edgar. *Bismarck*. New York: Routledge, 2002. Excellent discussion of Bismarck's motives and tactics in his attack on the Social Democrats and his social reforms, part of the Routledge Historical Biographies series.

Lerman, Katharine Anne. *Bismarck*. London: Pearson Longman, 2004. A volume in the Profiles in Power series, in this work the author argues that Bismarck's reforms were significant but only halfway measures.

Waller, Bruce. *Bismarck*. Oxford, England: Basil Blackwell, 1997. 2d ed. Part of the Historical Association Studies series, this well-written and insightful analysis claims that Bismarck's welfare legislation was his greatest achievement.

SEE ALSO: Sept. 24, 1862: Bismarck Becomes Prussia's Minister-President; Dec. 8, 1864: Pius IX Issues the Syllabus of Errors; Dec. 8, 1869-Oct. 20, 1870: Vatican I Decrees Papal Infallibility Dogma; 1871-1877: Kulturkampf Against the Catholic Church in Germany; Jan. 18, 1871: German States Unite Within German Empire; Oct. 19, 1878: Germany Passes Anti-Socialist Law.

RELATED ARTICLES in *Great Lives from History: The Nineteenth Century, 1801-1900:* Otto von Bismarck; Pius IX.

July, 1881-1883
STEVENSON PUBLISHES *TREASURE ISLAND*

Robert Louis Stevenson's coming-of-age novel about a young man searching for treasure while surrounded by pirates in the South Seas enjoyed enormous success amid a largely staid Victorian literary world and inspired a popular craze for adventure novels over the next two decades.

ALSO KNOWN AS: *The Sea Cook: Or, Treasure Island*
LOCALE: London, England
CATEGORY: Literature

KEY FIGURES

Robert Louis Stevenson (1850-1894), Scottish novelist
H. Rider Haggard (1856-1925), English novelist

SUMMARY OF EVENT

In 1881, Robert Louis Stevenson, recovering from a bout with tuberculosis in Braemar, Scotland, was entertaining himself by drawing a map with his twelve-year-old stepson, Lloyd Osbourne, when he had an idea for an adventure story set on the high seas. Stevenson had studied engineering and law but had never practiced either profession, instead building a modest career as a writer. By July of 1881, he had expanded his idea into a tale of pirates, mutiny, and hidden treasure and was publishing it as a serialized novel in the British children's magazine *Young Folks.*

The story, at that point entitled *The Sea Cook: Or, Treasure Island,* unfolded in weekly installments through June of 1882, but like many serialized novels of the day, it failed to attract any particularly loyal readership and was soon forgotten. Stevenson, who by that time had moved to Switzerland for additional treatment for his tuberculosis, rewrote the novel with an eye toward a more adult audience. The next year, 1883, Cassell & Company, Limited, a London publisher, released the novel in book form as *Treasure Island.*

The novel tells the story of a young boy named Jim Hawkins, son of an innkeeper on the west coast of England. The inn attracts a disreputable clientele, including a frightening group of pirates and an old buccaneer with a treasure map. The buccaneer, Billy Bones, dies at the inn after being presented with the "black spot," a mysterious message from pirates. Jim finds the treasure map inside the dead man's sea chest and shows it to two local authorities, Dr. Livesey and Squire Trelawney. The men identify it as belonging to an infamous pirate, Captain Flint.

Trelawney organizes an expedition to search for the treasure and hires a crew of sailors collected by a shady rogue named Long John Silver. Silver and his crew turn out to be pirates themselves and, well into the journey, begin plotting a mutiny. Jim overhears the plan and tells the captain of the ship, Captain Smollett. The captain tricks the pirates into leaving the ship, but Jim sneaks ashore with them. He sees Long John Silver murder one of the pirates and, frightened, flees into the island's interior, where he meets Ben Gunn, a former pirate marooned on the island years earlier.

Captain Smollett and the loyal sailors come ashore and take shelter in the pirates' empty stockade, where Jim and Ben soon join them. When the pirates attack the stockade, Jim takes Ben's boat back to the ship and cuts the ship's anchor. After some time, he struggles aboard and is confronted by Israel Hands, one of the watchmen. Israel tries to kill Jim, but Jim, despite being wounded,

Cover of an edition of Treasure Island *illustrated by N. C. Wyeth that was first published in 1911.*

kills Israel instead. Jim returns to the stockade and is captured by Long John Silver. Silver has acquired the treasure map from Trelawney but is being threatened with mutiny himself by the other pirates, so he enlists Jim in a plan to escape by pretending Jim is his hostage. Unconvinced, the pirates give Silver the black spot and relieve him of his command.

Desperate, Silver leads the pirates to the treasure, but the site has already been excavated and the treasure removed. Suddenly, Ben, Dr. Livesey, and the loyal sailors ambush the pirates, allowing Jim and Long John Silver to escape. After the group defeats the pirates, Ben leads them to the treasure, which he had discovered earlier and hidden in a cave. They set sail for home, leaving the pirates, with the exception of Long John Silver, marooned on the island. Silver sneaks off the ship, taking part of the treasure with him, and the group eventually arrives home, where Jim suffers from nightmares about the sea and swears off treasure hunting forever.

The novel enjoyed a stunning reception and soon became one of the most widely read books of the western world. It set off a wave of interest in adventure stories set in exotic locales and quickly inspired a host of imitators, including the immensely popular *King Solomon's Mines* (1885) by H. Rider Haggard. Much of the success of *Treasure Island* was rooted in two factors: the romanticized nature of the adventure and the strict conventions of Victorian children's literature.

For readers during the nineteenth century, the details of *Treasure Island* seemed to come from an idealized past. By the time of the novel's publication, piracy was largely a distant memory though a compelling one. Pirates had been a scourge on British shipping in the sixteenth and seventeenth centuries, so the British would not have soon forgotten them. In addition, colorful and notorious characters such as Captain Kidd and Blackbeard were prominent in pirate lore and helped establish the romanticized images of pirates that many Victorians possessed. For a nation racing into its future on newly invented locomotives and steamships, tales of the swashbuckling pirates of its past offered a romantic escape.

For a Victorian readership schooled in the conventions of the day, moreover, an adventure like *Treasure Island* was both innovative and provocative. Children's books in the Victorian Era were written for their moral lessons; any entertainment they might have provided was secondary or even deleterious. Many parents and educators of this period distrusted imaginative tales, so *Treasure Island* and its imitators—with their exotic and romantic geographical settings and their celebration of nationalistic, if not missionary, accomplishments—were deemed to possess an educational quality that lent the stories a degree of merit worthy of young readers. *Treasure Island* does embrace some moral values—responsibility, courage, and resourcefulness—but for its readers, it was primarily an exciting adventure, an engaging contrast to the dull world of Victorian children's literature. In spite of the book being identified as a "boy's novel," *Treasure Island* and Robert Louis Stevenson were well-respected by the most prominent literary voices of the day, including Henry James.

SIGNIFICANCE

The popularity of *Treasure Island* created an intense interest in adventure stories and inspired a flood of literary works with heroic explorers, dangerous quests, and exotic locales. The best known such work was Haggard's *King Solomon's Mines*, though even works of more obvious fantasy, such as James Barrie's *Peter Pan: Or, The Boy Who Wouldn't Grow Up* (pr. 1904, pb. 1928), grew out of the adventure craze inspired by *Treasure Island*. Even more popular were the "dime novel" adventures written primarily as inexpensive entertainment for young men. Largely forgotten now, these novels were published by the hundreds and found an enormous audience in their time. Their most successful authors were British war correspondent George Alfred Henty, who wrote more than 140 novels, and American Horatio Alger, whose 135 "rags-to-riches" novels made his name synonymous with the American Dream.

Novels such as *Treasure Island* and *King Solomon's Mines* also had an influence on popular perceptions of colonialism in Great Britain, particularly in their assumptions about and portrayals of Britain's overseas territorial possessions. Britain's colonial empire stretched around the world and included exotic and mysterious locations like India and Africa, so the successful adventures of fictional British explorers in such exotic locales encouraged the idea of British hegemony in those regions. As a result, adventure narratives provided an entire generation with an education, albeit distorted, regarding the cultural and economic exchange between Britain and its colonies. As a result, most Britons took great pride in being leaders in the global empire united by British cultural, moral, political, and commercial values.

—Devon Boan

FURTHER READING

Bloom, Harold, ed. *Robert Louis Stevenson*. Langhorne, Pa.: Chelsea House, 2005. A diverse compilation of essays reflecting the twentieth century's best literary criticism of Stevenson's major works, with an introduction by Bloom.

Colley, Ann C. *Robert Louis Stevenson and the Colonial Imagination*. London: Ashgate, 2004. Explores Stevenson's personal and cultural connections to the South Sea Islands and their influence on his writing, with an emphasis on the prevailing imperialistic values that were deeply embedded in the British mind-set of Stevenson's time.

Gray, William. *Robert Louis Stevenson: A Literary Life*. Basingstoke, Hampshire, England: Palgrave, 2004. Traces the evolution of Stevenson's writings in the context of the five dramatically different geographical locations in which he wrote the works.

Robinson, Roger, ed. *Robert Louis Stevenson: His Best Pacific Writings*. Honolulu: Bess Press, 2003. A compilation of Stevenson's many stories and essays about the South Seas, the setting of *Treasure Island* and Stevenson's home for the last years of his life.

See also: 1807: Bowdler Publishes *The Family Shakespeare*; 1807-1834: Moore Publishes *Irish Melodies*; 1814: Scott Publishes *Waverley*; Dec., 1816: Rise of the Cockney School; 1842: Tennyson Publishes "Morte d'Arthur"; 1851: Melville Publishes *Moby Dick*; Mar., 1852-Sept., 1853: Dickens Publishes *Bleak House*; Dec., 1884-Feb., 1885: Twain Publishes *Adventures of Huckleberry Finn*; Dec., 1887: Conan Doyle Introduces Sherlock Holmes.

Related articles in *Great Lives from History: The Nineteenth Century, 1801-1900:* Horatio Alger; H. Rider Haggard; Henry James; Robert Louis Stevenson.

October 10, 1881
London's Savoy Theatre Opens

Built as the home for the operettas of Gilbert and Sullivan by their business partner, the Savoy set new standards in theatrical technology, and it provided a home to the world-renowned partnership.

Locale: London, England
Categories: Theater; architecture

Key Figures

Richard D'Oyly Carte (1844-1901), English impresario and theatrical promotor
W. S. Gilbert (1836-1911), English playwright and librettist
Arthur Sullivan (1842-1900), English composer

Summary of Event

London's musical theater was a lively scene during the nineteenth century. Many of the latest operatic hits from the Continent were mounted upon the London stage, and popular theater was active and diverse. Its range extended from music-hall variety reviews and pantomimes to farces and burlesques, many parodying current operas or serious dramas. W. S. Gilbert's own first play was a nonmusical spoof of an opera by Gaetano Donizetti. English operetta, based on continental models, was slow to take root, but the importation of Jacques Offenbach's lively examples from 1857 onward stimulated local emulations.

On this scene the famous team of W. S. Gilbert and Arthur Sullivan quickly eclipsed all competition. Their collaboration was, however, forged and sustained by the third member of their partnership, the one too easily forgotten: Richard D'Oyly Carte. Carte came from a musical family and trained as a composer. He wrote three light operas in the years 1868-1876 but realized composition was not his forte. In 1870, he became an agent for performers, musical and otherwise, and over the years he handled such clients as singer Adelina Patti, lecturer Oscar Wilde, and composer Offenbach. He developed a sharp eye for talent and creative possibilities, joining it with a mastery of promotion.

In 1874, Carte became a theater manager, offering French operettas and English comedies. Running a leading singer's company in 1875, he was on the lookout for short program-fillers. A young writer proposed a text to him, and Carte immediately proposed the young composer best suited to write the music for it. The two had, in fact, already been collaborators in a failed production, *Thespis: Or, The Gods Grown Old* (pr., pb. 1871), but Carte was convinced they had a future as partners. Their names were W. S. Gilbert and Arthur Sullivan.

Gilbert and Sullivan had each been developing a promising career of his own. Gilbert had begun writing verses and plays in his student days. After grim years as a government clerk, he pursued legal studies and became a practicing trial attorney. At this calling, he had little success. To relieve boredom or fill dull stretches, he returned to scribbling verses and penning satirical drawings. He found publishers for such things and soon his literary and graphic endeavors took precedence over the law. He served as a newspaper correspondent, but during the mid-1860's, his plays were produced, while the first edition of his comic verses and drawings was published in 1869 as *The Bab Ballads* (later a source for plot and character ideas). He rapidly became a new force in London's theater world, at first writing parodies of literary or operatic works, but then graduating to original comedies and satires of his own. From the title of one political satire came the label "topsy-turvy," which characterized his style.

The son of a bandmaster, Sullivan was immersed early in music. His education as an Anglican choirboy led to training as a church musician. His capacities for composition were recognized, and scholarship support allowed him to study in Leipzig. Back in England and initially employed as a church organist, he made important contacts, soon winning attention for a number of concert and chamber compositions. As his reputation rose, Sullivan circulated in ever more prestigious circles and developed a taste for travel, the good life, and (later) heavy gambling. Responding to London's new excitement over Offenbach's operettas, Sullivan joined the humorist Francis Burnand in a little one-act farce, *Cox and Box: Or, The Long Lost Brothers* (pr. 1866). It led nowhere, confirming Sullivan's assumption that his destiny lay in "serious" composing, in which he won further success.

Gilbert and Sullivan first met in 1870, in a brief, cold encounter. The following year, mutual friends induced them to collaborate on *Thespis*, whose failure boded ill for any further endeavors. Richard D'Oyly Carte's positive recollection of the piece, however, prompted his decision to pair them to produce the courtroom spoof *Trial by Jury* (pr., pb. 1875). For the premiere, Gilbert directed and Sullivan conducted, setting a pattern that would continue into their future collaborations.

Although the audience loved *Trial by Jury*, the partnership did not crystalize immediately. Gilbert was caught up in various plays, including operettas with other

The inaugural production of Gilbert and Sullivan's Patience *in London's Savoy Theatre, in late 1881.* (Hulton Archive/Getty Images)

composers. Sullivan ventured another one-act piece, *The Zoo* (pr. 1875), with a different collaborator, but still regarded ventures into musical theater as a sideline that distracted him from his "serious" musical path. Carte, however, was now set on making the Gilbert and Sullivan partnership a continuing one. With great daring, Carte organized the financing of a new organization, the Comedy Opera Company, committed to fostering English light opera and specifically focused on Gilbert and Sullivan. From them, he drew a new operetta, their first full two-act production, *The Sorcerer* (pr., pb. 1877), which benefited from the new troupe of talents Carte was assembling. It was a substantial success, confirming that the partnership had a future.

HMS Pinafore: Or, The Lass That Loved a Sailor (pr., pb. 1878) had obstacles to overcome, but it soon caught on with the public and became an unprecedented sensation. The partners became rich, and Carte organized touring companies of the show. He still had to fight to keep the creative team together, however. To combat the rampant piracy of unauthorized productions and circulation, Carte arranged a double premiere of *The Pirates of Penzance: Or, The Slave of Duty* (pr. 1879, pb. 1880) for copyright purposes—a token one in Devon and the main one in New York. The partnership's pressures mounted, as Gilbert quibbled over profits and Sullivan yearned to pursue his "serious" career. Carte still fought to keep things together for *Patience: Or, Bunthorne's Bride* (pr., pb. 1881), their next smash hit.

With still grander dreams, Carte plunged into building a new London theater for his company and productions. Located off the Strand, above the Thames Embankment in the area of the old Savoy Palace, it was called the Savoy Theatre. The Savoy Theatre set new standards for theatrical equipment and safety, becoming the first public building in Great Britain to use electric lighting. It opened sensationally on October 10, 1881, with the *Patience* production transferred to it from its previously leased theater.

Thereafter, the Savoy Theatre became the continuing partnership of Gilbert and Sullivan's home base, from which touring companies now ranged the English-speaking world and beyond. At the Savoy Theatre were premiered the subsequent Gilbert and Sullivan collaborations: *Iolanthe: Or, The Peer and the Peri* (pr., pb. 1882), *Princess Ida: Or, The Castle Adament* (pr., pb. 1884), *The Mikado: Or, The Town of Titipu* (pr., pb. 1885), *Ruddigore: Or, The Witch's Curse* (pr., pb. 1887), *The Yeomen of the Guard: Or, The Merryman and His Maid* (pr., pb. 1888), and *The Gondoliers: Or, The King of Barataria* (pr., pb. 1889). Revivals were also mounted there.

With his profits from the partnership, Carte built the grand Savoy Hotel (opened 1889) adjacent to the theater. Modeled on new American designs he had observed, the hotel pioneered new levels of luxury and innovation. Cezar Ritz was its first manager, and Auguste Escoffier was its first chef.

Ever stress-ridden, the partnership between Gilbert, Sullivan, and Carte exploded over expenses for the Savoy Theatre in the notorious "carpet controversy" of 1890. Embittered, Gilbert went his own way, while Carte, to accommodate Sullivan's ambitions, built a new theater, the Royal English Opera House, where in 1891 his *Ivanhoe* was premiered. It never caught on, and the theater brought Carte such financial reverses that he had to sell it the following year. (It still exists as the Palace Theatre, and its current proprietor is Andrew Lloyd Webber.)

Sullivan still composed operettas for the Savoy Theatre (1892, 1894, 1898, 1899), but with other librettists, while Gilbert tried to work with other composers. Carte effected a reconciliation between Gilbert and Sullivan, but two late collaborations, *Utopia Limited: Or, The Flowers of Progress* (pr., pb. 1893) and *The Grand Duke: Or, The Statutory Duel* (pr., pb. 1896), could not repeat their earlier successes. After 1896, the three partners never worked together again. Sullivan and Carte died in successive years. Carte's family continued his company, and for a few years (1906-1909) Gilbert directed some revivals of his operettas, but they ended even before he died in 1910.

SIGNIFICANCE

From the Savoy Theatre has come the designation of "Savoyards" for performers and fans of the immortal Gilbert and Sullivan operettas. From Carte's success at persuading the public to make an orderly line at his box office has come that English institution, the queue. The D'Oyly Carte Opera Company, operated by Richard's descendants, controlled performance rights for the operettas, mounting regular revivals at the Savoy Theatre, until the copyrights expired in 1962. The company struggled on for a while, finally dissolving in 1982; an attempted renewal in 1988 failed. The theater itself, remodeled extensively in 1929, was gutted by fire in 1990, but was refurbished and returned to regular use.

—*John W. Barker*

FURTHER READING

Ainger, Michael. *Gilbert and Sullivan: A Dual Biography*. New York: Oxford University Press, 2001. A coherent treatment of the intertwining lives of Gilbert and Sullivan.

Allen, Reginald, ed. *The First Night Gilbert and Sullivan*. Rev. ed. Avon, Conn.: Cardavon Press, 1975. Includes all the librettos in original form, as well as background essays and period illustrations.

Brahms, Caryl. *Gilbert and Sullivan: Lost Chords and Discords*. Boston: Little, Brown, 1975. Good survey of the partnership, its vicissitudes, and its products.

Goodman, Andrew. *Gilbert and Sullivan's London*. New York: Hippocrene Books, 1988. Fascinating text with photos on London sites important to Gilbert and Sullivan, including the Savoy Theatre and Hotel.

Hibbert, Christopher. *Gilbert and Sullivan and their Victorian World*. New York: American Heritage, 1976. The operettas set vividly in period context.

Hyman, Alan. *Sullivan and His Satellites: A Survey of English Operettas, 1860-1914*. London: Chappell, 1978. Overview of the London context of light opera.

Jacobs, Arthur. *Arthur Sullivan: A Victorian Musician*. 2d ed. Portland, Oreg.: Amadeus Press, 1992. The authoritative biography of the composer.

Pearson, Hesketh. *Gilbert: His Life and Strife*. New York: Harper & Row, 1957. Classic study of the playwright.

Stedman, J. W. *W. S. Gilbert: A Classical Victorian and his Theatre*. New York: Oxford University Press, 1996. Important study of the writer, placing him in relation to British Victorian culture.

Wren, Gayden. *A Most Ingenious Paradox: The Art of Gilbert and Sullivan*. New York: Oxford University Press, 2001. Analysis of the operettas, discussing what is most distinctive about the work of Gilbert and Sullivan.

SEE ALSO: 1802: Britain Adopts Gas Lighting; 1878-1899: Irving Manages London's Lyceum Theatre; Oct. 21, 1879: Edison Demonstrates the Incandescent Lamp; Oct. 14, 1898: Moscow Art Theater Is Founded.

RELATED ARTICLES in *Great Lives from History: The Nineteenth Century, 1801-1900:* Gaetano Donizetti; W. S. Gilbert and Arthur Sullivan; Jacques Offenbach; Oscar Wilde.

1882
FIRST BIRTH CONTROL CLINIC OPENS IN AMSTERDAM

The establishment of the world's first birth control clinic in Amsterdam inspired the creation of similar clinics in other countries and helped to promote acceptance of contraception in many different cultures.

LOCALE: Amsterdam, the Netherlands

CATEGORIES: Health and medicine; social issues and reform; women's issues

KEY FIGURES

Aletta Jacobs (1854-1929), founder of the world's first birth control clinic

Annie Besant (1847-1933), member of the British Malthusian League

Charles Bradlaugh (1833-1891), member of the British Malthusian League

Charles Drysdale (1829-1907), president of the British Malthusian League

Charles Knowlton (1800-1850), author of *The Fruits of Philosophy*

Thomas Robert Malthus (1766-1834), author of *An Essay on the Principle of Population*

Margaret Sanger (1879-1966), American birth control activist

Samuel van Houten (1837-1930), Liberal member of Dutch Parliament

SUMMARY OF EVENT

Although various methods of contraception had been used for thousands of years to prevent pregnancy, the idea of using birth control as a means to limit human population growth to help end poverty did not arise until the nineteenth century. Up to that time, political economists saw human population growth as an indicator of prosperity. It was not until after Thomas Robert Malthus published *An Essay on the Principle of Population* (1798) that the first birth control movement began.

Malthus was an Anglican clergyman who postulated that population growth is geometric, while the supply of resources can only grow arithmetically. He foresaw a time when the rapid growth of the human population would outstrip natural resources, leading to widespread poverty and starvation. He saw the need for birth control,

Thomas Robert Malthus. (Library of Congress)

but due to his religious beliefs, he could support only delayed marriage and abstinence to achieve that goal.

In most industrialized countries of Malthus's time, the general public had no practical knowledge of birth control. The only published source of information was *The Fruits of Philosophy: Or, The Private Companion of Young Married People*, published by the American physician Charles Knowlton in 1832. Knowlton was promptly arrested on the book's publication. The book then traveled to Great Britain, where birth control activists Charles Bradlaugh and Annie Besant were arrested in 1876 for selling it. Their trial generated so much publicity that sales of the book in Britain leapt to the hundreds of thousands. Knowlton's book was concerned with family planning and was presumably aimed at members of the middle class who could purchase and read it.

The first organization to actively promote contraception among the poor as a means to control population took its name from Malthus when the Malthusian League formed in Great Britain in 1877. Unlike Malthus, however, the organization's founder, Charles Drysdale, and his supporters expressed the need for artificial methods of birth control. The Malthusian League lasted fifty years and had, at most, little more than one thousand members, yet these few members made their voice heard by writing incessantly to Parliament and various publications—which usually refused to publish the letters—lecturing and distributing tracts numbering in the millions. In many ways, however, their prodigious efforts were in vain. The members of the Malthusian League were largely middle class with no sympathy for the poor. They wanted to see the lower classes produce fewer children, yet their propaganda did not emphasize the benefits of small families to individual readers. In fact, their tracts did not even spread information about effective methods of birth control, from fear of censorship laws. During the early years, though, the league could boast of chapters in France, Germany, and the Netherlands.

The only European country in which it was not illegal to give out birth control information was the Netherlands. In 1879, upon receiving her medical degree, Aletta Jacobs, the first professionally trained woman physician of that country, visited England and became acquainted with the Malthusian League. During that same year Drysdale lectured in Amsterdam. Immediately the Dutch Neo-Malthusian League was formed; it became official in 1881.

Unlike the British Malthusian League, the Dutch Neo-Malthusian League from its beginning stressed family planning, admitted socialist members—who gave the league access to the poor)—and actively distributed two hundred thousand tracts that explained methods of birth control. Since Jacobs had always provided free medical care to the poor in her clinic, it was just one more step for her to offer free family planning advice to the poor as well as to the wealthier patrons of her private practice. Jacobs established her birth control clinic in Amsterdam in 1882; it was the world's first such clinic. Along with counseling, Jacobs also fitted women with diaphragms, a recent invention she perfected. However, it was the only form of artificial contraception she advocated.

Over the next several years, physician members of the Dutch Neo-Malthusian League established birth control clinics in The Hague, Rotterdam, and many other cities in the Netherlands by 1892. All were characterized by giving free birth control advice to poor patients and by hiring midwives to counsel and fit patients. By 1894, the midwives were treating more than five hundred women a year. In 1898 alone, more than fifteen hundred women used the clinic's services.

Near the turn of the twentieth century an organization of midwives opposed to Neo-Malthusianism formed in Amsterdam, and it excluded any woman associated with the league from practicing midwifery. The clinics responded by training poor women instead of midwives, and they encouraged these "lay-nurses" to go out and teach other poor women. Church and medical organizations went to the Dutch parliament to protest the clinics, and doctors faced difficulties if they showed any support of Neo-Malthusianism. However, the government subsequently passed no laws against birth control, most likely because of the efforts of Samuel van Houten, an influential Liberal member of the Dutch parliament who was also a vice president of the British Malthusian League. In 1911, the only law passed concerning contraception put some restrictions on vendors of birth control devices and created standards that birth control clinics had to meet. Workers at the clinics hailed the law, which would minimize false advertising from quacks and allow the public to see the clinics in a more positive light.

SIGNIFICANCE

The clinics were never shut down, and in 1925 Jacobs was able to report on their success. Around 1880, the birth rate in the Netherlands was 37.6 births for every 1,000 inhabitants. In 1920, the rate was 19.3 births. Birth control became accepted by the majority of the Dutch populace, and the league established the Aletta Jacobs Huis in 1931. This institute, the first large public birth control clinic in Amsterdam, was allowed to continue, and others followed.

Birth control took longer to find acceptance in other parts of the world, but it eventually did, thanks in large part to Margaret Sanger, an American birth control activist who visited the Netherlands and met Jacobs in 1914. Sanger was pleased by the improving birth rate statistics in the Netherlands and, being a registered nurse, she learned how to fit women with diaphragms. On her return to the United States, she established the first American birth control clinic in Brooklyn in 1916. Her efforts led to the first World Population Conference in Geneva in 1927. From Sanger's American Birth Control League, established in 1921, came the International Planned Parenthood Federation (IPPF), which was founded in 1953.

During the 1960's, governments throughout the world were committed to giving money to Planned Parenthood. In 1969, the United Nations Fund for Population Activities was established. The United Nations has hosted international conferences addressing the problem of overpopulation in Bucharest in 1974, in Mexico City in 1984, and in Cairo in 1994. Many governments, the most notable being China, adopted official policies regarding family planning. Birth rates began to fall in developed countries, and many international groups focused their attention on reducing birth rates in developing countries as well. By the twenty-first century, the use of birth control to control population growth as well as family size was generally accepted.

—*Rose Secrest*

FURTHER READING

Avery, John. *Progress, Poverty, and Population: Rereading Condorcet, Godwin and Malthus*. London: Frank Cass, 1997. Traces the history of the debate during the late eighteenth and early nineteenth centuries between utopian optimists, such as Condorcet and Godwin, and pessimists, such as Malthus, about the effects of population growth upon society.

Back, Kurt W. *Family Planning and Population Control: The Challenges of a Successful Movement*. Boston: Twayne, 1989. A thorough, easy-to-read account of the history of the birth control movement, stressing trends and mores shifting as the need for contraception became more obvious.

Besant, Annie, and Charles Knowlton. *"A Dirty, Filthy Book": The Writings of Charles Knowlton and Annie Besant on Reproductive Physiology and Birth Control and an Account of the Bradlaugh-Besant Trial*. Edited by Sripati Chandrasekhar. Berkeley: University of California Press, 1981. Includes Besant's *Law of Population* and her recantation *Theosophy and the Law of Population* (1891), as well as Knowlton's *Fruits of Philosophy*. The texts are prefaced by a useful introduction.

Bosch, Mineke, with Annemarie Kloosterman, eds. "Unity Above Nation, Race, or Creed: An Introduction to the International Woman Suffrage Alliance." In *Politics and Friendship: Letters from the International Woman Suffrage Alliance, 1902-1942*. Columbus: Ohio State University Press, 1990. A translated edition of a Dutch book of Jacobs's letters. Provides a well-researched account of her life and causes.

Elwell, Frank W. *A Commentary on Malthus's 1798 Essay on Population as Social Theory*. Lewiston, N.Y.: Edwin Mellen Press, 2001. An analysis of the essay that seeks to eliminate some of the dogma and misinterpretation surrounding Malthus's theories and present his ideas with more subtlety and complexity. Includes a reprint of the original essay

Jacobs, Aletta. "Birth Control in Holland." *The Nation* 120, no. 3118 (April 8, 1925): 392. Shows success of Dutch birth control clinics with statistics on birth rate, infant mortality, and illegitimate children.

_______. "The First Birth Control Clinic." In *European Women: A Documentary History, 1789-1945*, edited by Eleanor S. Riemer and John C. Fout. New York: Schocken Books, 1980. An account of how and why Jacobs went into birth control practice. Also explains its success and lack of acceptance as late as 1928.

Ledbetter, Rosanna. "Neo-Malthusians Abroad." In *A History of the Malthusian League, 1877-1927*. Columbus: Ohio State University Press, 1976. Incredibly detailed and well written, this chapter gives an outstanding brief account of the Dutch Neo-Malthusian League and the circumstances surrounding the birth control clinic.

See also: May, 1847: Semmelweis Develops Antiseptic Procedures; May 12, 1857: New York Infirmary for Indigent Women and Children Opens; Mar. 3, 1873: Congress Passes the Comstock Antiobscenity Law; 1883: Galton Defines "Eugenics"; 1897: Ellis Publishes *Sexual Inversion.*

Related articles in *Great Lives from History: The Nineteenth Century, 1801-1900:* Annie Besant; Thomas Robert Malthus; Francis Place; Marie Elizabeth Zakrzewska.

1882-1901
Metchnikoff Advances the Cellular Theory of Immunity

Elie Metchnikoff demonstrated that amoeboid white blood cells combat disease by engulfing and killing bacteria. He was the first modern pathologist to view inflammation as part of the healing process.

Locale: Italy; Russia; France
Categories: Biology; health and medicine

Key Figures

Élie Metchnikoff (1845-1916), Russian zoologist
Alexander Kovalevsky (1840-1901), Russian zoologist, founder of vertebrate embryology
Louis Pasteur (1822-1895), French bacteriologist, founder of modern microbiology
Paul Ehrlich (1854-1915), German chemist
Rudolf Virchow (1821-1902), German cellular pathologist

Summary of Event

The genius of science frequently manifests itself under unexpected circumstances. A line of research that to the layperson would probably be seen as obscure and peripheral to bettering the human condition can produce a result that, when viewed in a certain light, proves to hold the key to some fundamental physical or biological process. Such is the phenomenon of cellular immunity, whose significance the Russian zoologist Élie Metchnikoff stumbled upon in 1882 while studying the development of invertebrate embryos.

Thanks to the work of Louis Pasteur, Robert Koch, and others, the pathology of infectious disease and the microbial nature of many of the agents was already well known, but the crucial role of white blood cells in fighting infection was not. Immunity to diseases following infection was thought to arise primarily out of a host's production of specific antitoxins. Pasteur favored the depletion theory for recovery from primary infection, postulating that bacteria used up some vital growth factor and were no longer able to reproduce, thus limiting disease.

As professor of zoology at the university in Odessa, Russia, Metchnikoff labored far from the European centers of biomedical research. A passionate Darwinist, professed atheist, and political radical, he followed the lead of his fellow Russian Alexander Kovalevsky in choosing comparative embryology as the discipline most likely to elucidate evolutionary relationships in the animal kingdom.

Believing that "ontogeny recapitulates phylogeny," Metchnikoff reasoned that studying developmental stages of the simplest multicellular invertebrates would yield fundamental insights into the evolutionary process. At the same time, following the lead of Rudolf Virchow, who maintained that pathology ultimately derived from disturbances of cells and could be understood only at the cellular level, Metchnikoff directed his microscope at inflammation. At a congress of naturalists and physicians in Odessa in 1882, he first set forth his hypothesis that phagocytosis was the basis of the healing process. Following the assassination of Czar Alexander II, academic freedom at Russian universities took a sharp downturn. Metchnikoff chose to emigrate, settling first in Messina, Italy, where he had done his doctoral research. His wife's inheritance freed him from the necessity of paid employment, both in Italy and later at the Pasteur Institute in Paris.

While observing the development of starfish embryos, Metchnikoff noticed that amoeboid cells that migrated to form the digestive surface bore a strong resemblance to vertebrate leukocytes, and wondered if the amoeboid cells would behave in a similar manner. He verified that pricking the embryos with a fine thorn caused the cells to migrate to the site of the injury, and that the cells enveloped dye particles, thus providing further evidence that the ability of such cells to engulf foreign particles, including bacteria, played a role in protection against disease.

Metchnikoff next turned to Daphnia (water fleas), small, nearly transparent arthropods with a defined gut and body cavity. He noted that amoeboid cells in the cavity fluid engulfed and destroyed spores of a parasitic fungus to which the organism had some immunity. His first paper reporting these discoveries on the intracellular digestion of invertebrates (1883) attracted little attention from the medical community, but Metchnikoff persisted, extrapolating his findings to inflammation following trauma and maintaining that the migration of white blood cells to infection sites, pus formation, and changes in other cells associated with inflammation were part of an active process by which the body combated disease organisms. This ran contrary to prevailing medical opinion, and plunged Metchnikoff into the thick of a raging conflict between rival schools of pathology.

Metchnikoff's work attracted the attention of Louis Pasteur, who, in 1888, offered him a position with the newly opened Pasteur Institute. Metchnikoff became the institute's director following Pasteur's death in 1895, continuing an active research program until the outbreak of World War I all but closed the institute. While at the institute, he delivered a series of lectures and then published two major books summarizing his findings: *Leçons sur la pathologie comparée de l'inflammation* (1892; *Lectures on the Comparative Pathology of Inflammation*, 1893) and *L'immunité dans les maladies infectieuse* (1901; *Immunity in Infective Diseases*, 1905). In these books, he maintained that the phagocyte was the chief means of defense against disease and that circulating antibodies, the so-called humoral factors, were secondary in importance.

METCHNIKOFF'S NOBEL PRIZE

When Élie Metchnikoff was awarded the Nobel Prize in Physiology or Medicine in 1908, Alfred Peterson, a member of the Nobel committee, summarized Metchnikoff's contributions to medical science:

- Investigations into which cells in higher organisms function as phagocytes
- Determining which types of phagocytes functioned in various capacities
- Discovery that immune sera facilitate phagocytosis
- Discovery that leukocytes neutralize bacterial toxins
- Investigations into the complex nature of bacteriolysis and hemolysis
- Discovery of a new way of stimulating blood-forming organs

SIGNIFICANCE

By 1901, the two schools of immunology—cellular and humoral—had become sharply drawn along national lines, with the French, led by the Russian expatriate Metchnikoff, championing the role of the cell, and the Germans, headed by Koch's successor Paul Ehrlich, maintaining that circulating chemicals, rather than cells, constituted the key to defense against disease.

The German school was supported by the development of specific therapies. Ehrlich had demonstrated that guinea pigs fed increasing doses of lethal vegetable toxins developed immunity to them, and that the immunity derived from a chemical present in blood serum. Working with diphtheria and cholera, diseases whose causative agents produce potent toxins, Ehrlich's laboratory in Berlin was able to produce animal sera effective against these scourges. Cellular immunity, in contrast, appeared to be rather nonspecific.

By the time the Nobel Prize committee decided to award the Nobel Prize in Physiology or Medicine jointly to Metchnikoff and Ehrlich in 1908, the humoral theory of immunity appeared to have triumphed over cellular theory. Metchnikoff had become convinced that a well-balanced intestinal flora held the key to prolonging human life, and he devoted much of his energies in the last decade of his life to promoting the consumption of yogurt to achieve a condition he called orthobiosis.

In choosing to make a joint award to two rivals whose theories, in 1908, appeared to some extent to be in opposition, the Nobel committee anticipated the eventual integration of the two theories into a comprehensive model of immune system function. In his *History of Immunology* (1989), Arthur Silverstein noted that the controversy between humoral and cellular theories of immunity provided a striking example of the ways in which nonscientific events (notably the Franco-Prussian War) shape research. He considers it a case in which the triumph of one concept (the humoral theory) stifled developments dependent on the other, to the detriment of science. Metchnikoff's death in 1916 left no distinguished proponent of his theory to take up the mantle, and cellular immunology remained on the back burner for decades.

The discovery of antibiotics revived interest. Antibiotics function by depressing growth rates rather than killing bacteria outright, thereby giving white blood cells an advantage. Serum factors have little effect on antibiotic effectiveness, but a robust cellular immune system is essential.

—*Martha A. Sherwood*

FURTHER READING

Lagerkvist, Ulf. *Pioneers of Microbiology and the Nobel Prize*. River Edge, N.J.: World Scientific, 2003. Describes Metchnikoff's research and provides an insider's view of the workings of the Nobel committee that awarded him the prize in 1908.

Metchnikoff, Elie. *Lectures on the Comparative Pathology of Inflammation*. Translated by F. A. Starling and E. H. Starling. New York: Dover, 1968. Metchnikoff's book on the subject of inflammation, with a new introduction by scholar Arthur M. Silverstein.

Silverstein, Arthur M. *A History of Immunology*. New York: Academic Press, 1989. The long chapter on cellular versus humoral immunity integrates many threads, including philosophy and nationalism.

_______. *Paul Ehrlich's Receptor Immunology: The Magnificent Obsession*. San Diego, Calif.: Academic Press, 2002. Emphasis is on Ehrlich and the Berlin school, but contains considerable information on Metchnikoff, especially on his conflicts with Ehrlich.

Tauber, Alfred I. *Metchnikoff and the Origins of Immunology: From Metaphor to Theory*. New York: Oxford University Press, 1991. A thorough account of the scientific aspects of Metchnikoff's work.

SEE ALSO: 1838-1839: Schwann and Virchow Develop Cell Theory; May, 1847: Semmelweis Develops Antiseptic Procedures; 1867: Lister Publishes His Theory on Antiseptic Surgery; 1880's: Roux Develops the Theory of Mitosis; Mar. 24, 1882: Koch Announces His Discovery of the Tuberculosis Bacillus; Dec. 11, 1890: Behring Discovers the Diphtheria Antitoxin; Aug. 20, 1897: Ross Establishes Malaria's Transmission Vector; 1898: Beijerinck Discovers Viruses; June, 1900-1904: Suppression of Yellow Fever.

RELATED ARTICLES in *Great Lives from History: The Nineteenth Century, 1801-1900:* Emil von Behring; Ferdinand Julius Cohn; Robert Koch; Joseph Lister; Louis Pasteur; Ignaz Philipp Semmelweis; Rudolf Virchow.

January 2, 1882
STANDARD OIL TRUST IS ORGANIZED

The Standard Oil Trust centralized control of the fledgling oil industry in the hands of John D. Rockefeller and the rest of the trust's shareholders. It became the model for late nineteenth century American business, and its eventual dismantling was a landmark in U.S. antitrust law.

LOCALE: Cleveland, Ohio

CATEGORIES: Trade and commerce; business and labor

KEY FIGURES

John D. Rockefeller (1839-1937), dominant figure in the growth of the Standard Oil Company

Samuel C. T. Dodd (1836-1907), attorney who developed the Standard Oil Trust

Henry M. Flagler (1830-1913), Rockefeller partner credited with the early development of the trust

William Rockefeller (1841-1922), John's brother, who was also significant in the rise of the Standard Oil Company

Samuel J. Andrews (1817-1906), early Rockefeller partner and inventor of a more efficient refining process

George F. Chester (1813-1897),

Myron R. Keith (fl. late nineteenth century), and

George H. Vilas (1835-1907), Standard Oil trustees in 1879

SUMMARY OF EVENT

The importance of big business in the United States economy was confirmed during the last two decades of the nineteenth century as the United States became one of the world's major industrial powers. The petroleum industry played a leading role in this development and was, in many ways, a harbinger of the new age of U.S. economic supremacy. Although only about thirty years old by 1890, the industry was gigantic—characterized by concentrated ownership in refining and transportation facilities. This concentration had been brought about largely by one dominant organization, the Standard Oil Trust. Formed in 1882, it became the prototype for large-scale U.S. enterprise.

The rise of Standard Oil was brought about largely through the efforts of John D. Rockefeller. A Cleveland bookkeeper whose family fortune would surpass all, Rockefeller has been depicted both as the personification of the Horatio Alger myth of success through hard work and intelligence and as a ruthless, obsessive monster motivated by greed. On one hand, he was regarded as a man of great morality and piety. On the other hand, his businesses operated in a culture of secrecy, duplicity, rebates, drawbacks, and convenient memory loss. Undoubtedly, he had great genius at organization, foresight, considerable administrative talents, and the ability to choose able subordinates.

Starting his career at the age of sixteen in a small produce firm and later becoming a partner in a grain commission house during the U.S. Civil War (1861-1865), Rockefeller sensed the possibilities in the new oil regions of northwestern Pennsylvania but was appalled by the disorder and instability of the new industry. In 1860, one year after Edwin Drake built the first commercial oil well in Titusville, Pennsylvania, the price of a barrel of oil was twenty dollars. By the end of the next year, it had dropped to ten cents as a result of overproduction. By 1863, Cleveland was linked by rail to the oil fields, and Rockefeller invested in a refinery that soon became the city's largest. After buying out most of his partners, Rockefeller, his brother William Rockefeller, and Samuel J. Andrews built a second refinery. William moved to New York to develop the eastern and export trade. Henry M. Flagler became a partner in 1867 and negotiated extremely favorable railroad freight rate arrangements that facilitated the growth of the company.

In 1870, Rockefeller organized the Standard Oil Company (Ohio), which was incorporated as a joint stock company with a capitalization of one million dollars. Rockefeller had begun moving toward vertical integration of his operations. Almost fanatically dedicated to efficiency, he was convinced that destructive and wasteful competition must end if the company were to remain solvent. Therefore, he began acquiring other refineries, first in Cleveland, then in other cities. By the end of 1872, Rockefeller and his associates controlled all the major refineries in Ohio, New York, and Pennsylvania. Over the next decade, the company developed a pipeline system, purchased new oil-bearing lands, acquired extensive oil terminal facilities, and constructed an elaborate and efficient marketing system. By 1879, thirty-seven stockholders of the Standard Oil Company, through the parent, subsidiary, and associated companies, controlled more than 90 percent of U.S. refining capacity.

Operations of the Standard Oil Company and its affiliates developed so rapidly and with such complexity that they soon outgrew the structural framework of the parent company, a situation that distressed and perplexed Rockefeller. The Standard Oil Company (Ohio) was a manufacturing company with multitudinous operations outside the state, despite the fact that it had no legal right to own property or stock beyond the borders of Ohio. It was the nucleus of the richest and most powerful industrial organization in the country and was almost nationwide in scope.

The company's expansion, however, had developed in a somewhat haphazard fashion, and its structure lacked coherence and administrative centralization. Between 1873 and 1879, stock in other companies had been acquired in the names of Flagler, William Rockefeller, and others acting as trustees. In 1879, this structure was reorganized and systematized. The trustee device gave the Standard Oil Company a flexible means of expanding beyond the borders of Ohio and, equally important, permitted Rockefeller and his associates to camouflage their activities. Following a strict legal interpretation of the nature of trustees—that they were acting on behalf of stockholders and not of the company per se—Standard Oil Company officials, including Rockefeller himself, denied publicly and under oath that the company owned or controlled certain assets.

By 1879, this informal arrangement clearly had weaknesses that transcended its advantages. If a trustee died, there could be difficult legal problems, and disagreements within the management of the Standard Oil Company could create internal dissension. In 1879, a plan to overcome these dangers was developed, probably by Flagler. All Standard Oil Company properties held in the names of various individuals and all possessions outside Ohio were transferred to three trustees, George H. Vilas,

Myron R. Keith, and George F. Chester, who were minor employees at the Cleveland office. Theoretically, these men were to manage the various interests for the exclusive use and benefit of the stockholders of the Standard Oil Company, who would receive profits in the form of dividends proportionate to their holdings. This 1879 plan was legally satisfactory, because all the legal holdings of the Standard Oil Company then were concentrated in the Cleveland office, and the danger of conflict of interest among the trustees was minimized.

Cumbersome and risky, the arrangement did not provide adequate administrative centralization, solve many of the problems of planning and coordinating company activities outside Ohio, or deal with the possibility of double, triple, and even quadruple taxation of the same assets by several states. No provision was made for continuity among the trustees in case of resignations or deaths. There was no method or procedure for the transfer of trust certificates. Finally, Vilas, Chester, and Keith had no real power to control or direct the operations of subordinates, and unity or uniformity was maintained only through cumbersome devices such as occasional meetings of Standard Oil Company leaders in executive committees.

In early 1882, these problems were largely solved in a new trust agreement, apparently written by Samuel C. T. Dodd, the chief attorney for the Standard Oil Company, who refined Flagler's idea. Signed on January 2, 1882, the agreement welded separate Standard Oil corporations of various states together by pooling the stock of all. The signatories included the stockholders of the Standard Oil Company, together with Vilas, Chester, and Keith. All properties owned or controlled by the Standard Oil Company were placed in the hands of nine trustees, including John D. Rockefeller.

Each share of Standard Oil Company (Ohio) stock was exchanged for twenty trust certificates at a par value of one hundred dollars each, enabling investors to buy or sell portions of the pool. The trustees were to exercise general supervision over all Standard Oil companies and over other concerns whose stock was held in trust. In effect, a giant new centralized company, the Standard Oil Trust, had been created, although it did not have a legal existence. The new arrangement gave John D. Rockefeller and his associates the administrative flexibility to direct their worldwide activities effectively. By 1885, 70 percent of Standard Oil's business was overseas. The trust produced from wells in Pennsylvania, Texas, and California, and exported to Europe, the Far East, and, ironically, the Middle East.

Significance

The Standard Oil Trust served as the prototype for other monopolies, until the New Jersey legislature passed a law in 1889 permitting intercorporation stockholding and paving the way for the creation of giant holding companies. One of the first of these would be a successor to the Standard Oil Trust and the target of antimonopoly prosecution, Standard Oil (New Jersey). In a twenty-thousand-word decision rendered in May, 1911, in *Standard Oil Company of New Jersey et al. v. United States*, the Supreme Court gave Standard Oil six months to dismember its empire, leading to the formation of the major U.S. oil companies of the twentieth century.

As the U.S. economy expanded during the nineteenth century, there were numerous endeavors to consolidate businesses. The Standard Oil Trust of 1882 was the most dynamic product of these trends, exemplifying a milestone in the evolutionary chain stretching from primitive pooling agreements to the development of giant holding companies. Through the Standard Oil Trust, Rockefeller, Flagler, and Dodd pointed the way toward the complete centralization of giant industries, thus revolutionizing the structure of U.S. business.

—James E. Fickle, updated by Randall Fegley

Further Reading

Bradley, Robert L., Jr. *Oil, Gas, and Government: The U.S. Experience*. 2 vols. Lanham, Md.: Rowman & Littlefield, 1996. An Enron Corporation economist, Bradley defends the Standard Oil Company against all criticisms other than poorly managing public relations.

Chernow, Ron D. *Titan: The Life of John D. Rockefeller, Sr.* New York: Random House, 1998. Well-written, meticulously researched biography based on newly acquired archival materials. Chernow recounts the details of Rockefeller's life and career, describing his human side as well as his misdeeds.

Cochran, Thomas, and William Miller. *The Age of Enterprise: A Social History of Industrial America*. New York: Harper & Row, 1961. A well-written, general treatment of late nineteenth century industrial United States that contains a section on pools, trusts, and corporations.

Hidy, Ralph, and Muriel Hidy. *Pioneering in Big Business, 1882-1911*. Vol. 1 in *History of Standard Oil Company, New Jersey*. New York: Harper & Row, 1955. A detailed study of what would become the most prominent offspring of the Standard Oil Trust.

Kirkland, Edward. *Industry Comes of Age: Business, La-*

bor, and Public Policy, 1860-1897. New York: Holt, Rinehart and Winston, 1961. A useful survey of late nineteenth century U.S. economic structures and society. Includes an excellent chapter, "The Organization of Production," dealing with combination.

Nevins, Allan. *John D. Rockefeller*. Abridged by William Greenleaf. New York: Charles Scribner's Sons, 1959. A condensed version of Nevins's earlier works on Rockefeller.

________. *Study in Power: John D. Rockefeller, Industrialist and Philanthropist*. 2 vols. New York: Charles Scribner's Sons, 1953. A comprehensive, well-balanced biography of Rockefeller.

Sampson, Anthony. *The Seven Sisters*. New York: Viking, 1975. Standard Oil features prominently in this well-written history of the world's seven major oil companies, which has been revised several times.

Tarbell, Ida. *The History of the Standard Oil Company*. 2 vols. New York: McClure, Phillips, 1904. This classic polemic reflects the muckraking attitudes of its times.

Williamson, Harold, and Arnold Daum. *The American Petroleum Industry: The Age of Illumination, 1859-1899*. Evanston, Ill.: Northwestern University Press, 1959. This general study of the petroleum industry includes an excellent study on the Standard Oil Trust.

Yergin, Daniel. *The Prize*. New York: Simon & Schuster, 1992. Important history of the world petroleum industry.

SEE ALSO: 1850: First U.S. Petroleum Refinery Is Built; Aug. 27, 1859: Commercial Oil Drilling Begins; Jan. 10, 1870: Standard Oil Company Is Incorporated; May, 1876: Otto Invents a Practical Internal Combustion Engine; Jan. 29, 1886: Benz Patents the First Practical Automobile; Dec. 7, 1888: Dunlop Patents the Pneumatic Tire; July 20, 1890: Harrison Signs the Sherman Antitrust Act; Feb., 1892: Diesel Patents the Diesel Engine.

RELATED ARTICLE in *Great Lives from History: The Nineteenth Century, 1801-1900:* John D. Rockefeller.

March 24, 1882
KOCH ANNOUNCES HIS DISCOVERY OF THE TUBERCULOSIS BACILLUS

The first researcher to isolate the microorganisms that cause tuberculosis and cholera, Robert Koch firmly established the infectious nature of these diseases, making possible the study of their origins.

LOCALE: Berlin, Germany
CATEGORIES: Health and medicine; biology; science and technology

KEY FIGURES

Robert Koch (1843-1910), German physician and bacteriologist
Louis Pasteur (1822-1895), French chemist and founder of germ theory of disease
Pierre-Paul-Émile Roux (1853-1933), assistant to Pasteur and bacteriologist
Louis Thuillier (1856-1883), assistant to Pasteur
Jean Antoine Villemin (1827-1892), French physician who suggested contagious nature of tuberculosis
Rudolf Virchow (1821-1902), German pathologist who established science of cell pathology

SUMMARY OF EVENT

The period between 1870 and 1900 could arguably be called the golden age of bacteriology. It was during these years that the infectious nature of many forms of disease was firmly established. Further, with the development of techniques for growing microorganisms in pure culture, a process initiated by Robert Koch in his work with anthrax during the 1870's, it became possible to establish specific organisms as the etiological agents behind specific diseases. It was Koch's work on the isolation of the tuberculosis bacillus that indicated the necessity of growing microorganisms in pure culture in order to carry out such studies.

During the 1880's, tuberculosis became the scourge of Europe, as one of every seven deaths was linked to the disease. Many others were undoubtedly infected with the tuberculosis agent but were without symptoms; some of these people served as carriers for the disease. Tuberculosis had been known since antiquity; the Greeks in the time of Hippocrates (c. 400 B.C.E.) referred to it as phthisis (condition of wasting away). It was also referred to as the White Death, or as consumption (as it was known in England), reflecting its insidious nature.

Even into the mid-eighteenth century, the precise nature of the disease remained uncertain. The noted German pathologist Rudolf Virchow believed that what was called tuberculosis was actually any of several distinct diseases. In contrast, the French pathologist René Laennec argued that what appeared as distinct diseases actually represented the same process occurring in disparate parts of the body. In 1865, French physician Jean Antoine Villemin was able to transmit the disease to experimental animals, strong evidence for an infectious nature for tuberculosis. Nevertheless, both the cause and prevention remained unknown.

Koch began his career as a country physician, gaining experience in clinical studies during the Franco-Prussian War of 1870-1871. Upon his return, he began studies on anthrax, a scourge among farm animals. Koch confirmed the role of the anthrax bacillus as the cause of the illness; more important, he established the methodology for growing the organism in pure culture. Koch's 1881 paper on methods involved in studying organisms in such cultures, using his plate technique, became known as the bible of bacteriology; Koch himself became internationally known as a result.

Koch began his studies into tuberculosis in August, 1881. He was aware of Villemin's work on transmission of the agent to animals and had access to pathological material from patients at the Berlin Charite Hospital. There were two major technical problems with which Koch had to deal. First, the organism that caused tuberculosis, and Koch had no doubt that there was such an organism, was extraordinarily difficult to grow in the laboratory. Further, it resisted standard methods of staining, making it difficult to observe. Using samples obtained initially from phthisis patients at the hospital, Koch was able to infect guinea pigs. He then developed an unusual staining procedure involving strong alkali solutions, and was able to visualize rod-shaped bacteria in infectious material. The difficulty in staining suggested that these bacteria had unusual cell wall properties that made them unique among known bacteria. The bacillus subsequently became known as *Mycobacterium tuberculosis*.

After he developed a means to visualize the organism, Koch began a systematic study of diseased tissues. He quickly established that all specimens obtained from patients with tuberculosis contained the organism. As the disease progressed, either toward increased severity, or patient recovery, the number of organisms reflected the developments in the disease. If the disease became worse, the numbers increased; if the patient recovered, the number of organisms decreased.

Robert Koch. (Courtesy, University of Virginia Health System)

Koch then attempted to grow the organism in pure culture. He used a variety of nutrient media, but it was only when he added coagulated blood serum to the growth cultures that the organism began to grow. Even so, it required several weeks of incubation before colonies of bacteria could be observed to develop on the nutrient material. Koch then inoculated guinea pigs with samples obtained from his pure cultures. These animals developed tuberculosis, with symptoms and pathology identical to those observed in human patients; symptoms were also similar to those in guinea pigs inoculated with material from the human disease. The methodology of this work—isolation and growth of a suspected etiological agent in pure culture, followed by observation of the disease in animals inoculated with this material—became the basis for what is known as Koch's postulates.

Koch presented his work on isolation of the tubercle bacillus before the Berlin Physiological Society on March 24, 1882. It was fewer than eight months from the time when he had begun work on the problem.

In 1883, Koch turned his attention to the problem of cholera. Endemic in India for centuries, the disease did not reach Europe until 1831. By 1875, it had been associated with four major pandemics; Koch himself had observed the nature of the disease during the European epidemic between 1866 and 1875. The severity and rapid spread of the disease had already established it as one of the most dread diseases of humankind. In 1883, a fresh outbreak occurred in Egypt, threatening to spread again into the continent of Europe. By the request of the Egyptian government, the French established a commission to study the disease under the auspices of Louis Pasteur, but led by Pasteur's assistants, Pierre-Paul-Émile Roux and Louis Thuillier. The commission arrived in Alexandria during mid-1883.

Reflecting the ongoing rivalry with the French, the German government likewise established a commission, under the leadership of Koch, which arrived in Egypt in August, 1883. During the course of the epidemic in Egypt, between 60,000 and 100,000 people died. Among the deaths was that of Louis Thuillier. Thuillier had been so respected that Koch put aside his personal dislike for Pasteur and the French and attended Thuillier's funeral.

Ironically, the German commission arrived after the epidemic had peaked, and it became difficult to obtain sufficient clinical specimens for study. Koch received permission from his government to travel to India, the source of the cholera epidemics, and arrived there in December, 1883. The research program for isolation and identification of the cholera agent was similar to that utilized previously in his studies on tuberculosis. The availability of fresh material allowed Koch to quickly observe the cholera bacillus, and to grow it in pure culture. The agent he described, now called *Vibrio cholerae*, was identical in appearance to those he had previously observed in Egypt. Unlike the tuberculosis agent, the cholera bacillus could be grown in the laboratory with relative ease. Further, its unusual appearance, that of a curved or comma-shaped organism, made it easy to identify among the multitude of organisms in clinical specimens from the intestines.

In February, 1884, Koch reported the isolation of the cholera organism, but Pasteur and others were skeptical that he had indeed isolated the correct organism; Koch had been unable to reproduce the disease in animals. Nevertheless, the nature of the epidemiology of cholera, and the invariable presence of the organism in such epidemics, established the etiological nature of the comma bacillus.

SIGNIFICANCE

Robert Koch's discovery of the microorganisms—the bacteria—that cause both tuberculosis and cholera led to methods for containing tuberculosis and nearly eliminating cholera from the developed world. His laboratory methods, including unique staining techniques and his use of a pure culture to isolate organisms, make Koch the founder of modern bacteriology. In 1905, he was awarded the Nobel Prize in Physiology or Medicine, most notably for his work with tuberculosis.

—*Richard Adler*

FURTHER READING

Brock, Thomas. *Robert Koch: A Life in Medicine and Bacteriology*. 1988. Reprint. New York: AMS Press, 1999. Written by a noted microbiologist, this biography of Koch also presents a detailed study of his career, based on his correspondence, published work, and contemporary literature on bacteriology.

Bulloch, William. *A History of Bacteriology*. London: Oxford University Press, 1938. A classic work on the history of bacteriology. Provides a significant amount of detail on the works of Koch and Pasteur.

Daniel, Thomas M. *Pioneers of Medicine and Their Impact on Tuberculosis*. Rochester, N.Y.: University of Rochester Press, 2000. This history of tuberculosis and its treatment includes a chapter on Koch's pioneering work in bacteriology.

De Kruif, Paul. *Microbe Hunters*. New York: Harcourt, Brace & World, 1950. This readable yet detailed account includes the lengthy chapter "Koch: The Death Fighter." De Kruif makes the world of microbiology accessible to the general reader.

Dormandy, Thomas. *The White Death: A History of Tuberculosis*. New York: New York University Press, 2000. This history of tuberculosis examines Koch's role in isolating the cause of the disease.

Geison, Gerald. *The Private Science of Louis Pasteur*. Princeton, N.J.: Princeton University Press, 1995. A detailed biography of France's most famous chemist, and Koch's chief rival.

Golub, Edward. *The Limits of Medicine*. New York: Random House, 1994. Discusses the role of science and medicine in the treatment and prevention of disease.

Ryan, Frank. *The Forgotten Plague: How the Battle Against Tuberculosis Was Won—and Lost*. Boston: Little, Brown, 1992. A popular account of the story of tuberculosis. Emphasis is placed on the spread of the disease in the 1980's, but the work also includes an extensive history.

SEE ALSO: 1838-1839: Schwann and Virchow Develop Cell Theory; May, 1847: Semmelweis Develops Antiseptic Procedures; 1857: Pasteur Begins Developing Germ Theory and Microbiology; 1867: Lister Publishes His Theory on Antiseptic Surgery; 1882-1901: Metchnikoff Advances the Cellular Theory of Immunity; Dec. 11, 1890: Behring Discovers the Diphtheria Antitoxin; Aug. 20, 1897: Ross Establishes Malaria's Transmission Vector; 1898: Beijerinck Discovers Viruses; June, 1900-1904: Suppression of Yellow Fever.

Related articles in *Great Lives from History: The Nineteenth Century, 1801-1900:* Emil von Behring; Ferdinand Julius Cohn; Robert Koch; Joseph Lister; Louis Pasteur; Rudolf Virchow.

April, 1882-1885
French Indochina War

In an effort to rid Vietnam of French control, Emperor Tu Duc violated the 1862 Treaty of Saigon and renewed a vassal relationship with China, instigating the French to declare war.

Also known as: Sino-French-Vietnamese War; Sino-French War; Franco-Chinese War
Locale: Vietnam
Categories: Wars, uprisings, and civil unrest; expansion and land acquisition; diplomacy and international relations

Key Figures

Tu Duc (Nguyen Phuoc Hoang Nham; 1829-1883), emperor of Vietnam, r. 1847-1883
Henri Rivière (1827-1883), French captain
Amédée Courbet (1827-1885), French admiral
François-Jules Harmand (1845-1921), commissioner-general of Tongking

Summary of Event

Although the Vietnamese emperor Tu Duc ratified the Treaty of Saigon that his government made with France in 1862, it remained a source of resentment for him. He continued to do everything he could to rid Vietnam of the French. Unable to find a solution, Tu Duc focused on limiting the commercial imperialism of France and suppressing the Christian-led rebellion in Tongking (northern provinces, also called Tonkin). In 1873 a French trader was barred from proceeding up the Red River with his goods. Tu Duc saw the trader's action as a violation of the treaty, and tensions mounted. Vietnamese forces in Hanoi prepared for fighting, and Francis Garnier took strongholds on the Red River. This led to the signing of the "peace, friendship and perpetual alliance" treaty in 1874.

The treaty called for the withdrawal of French troops from Hanoi for a reprieve, which Tu Duc took as a weakness in French forces. As they withdrew, Tu Duc continued his policy of persecuting Christians. Vietnamese resentment of missionaries had substantially grown since France took power in Vietnam, and as the French left Hanoi, Christian villages were burned to the ground. Tu Duc signed the friendship treaty with no intention of honoring it, and, in 1874, he began to seek Chinese protection. In 1876, Tu Duc revived Chinese overlordship and in 1880 requested Chinese troops to quell Tongking rebels. The Vietnamese also continued to encourage insurgents to attack French commercial interests in an attempt to frustrate and drive them out.

The presence of Chinese troops and constant guerrilla attacks gave the French an excuse to intervene. The French decided to strengthen their forces in Hanoi. Captain Rivière took reinforcements there in April of 1882. Citing the need to protect his men from an oncoming attack, Rivière attacked Hanoi and seized the city. The French then took Nam Dinh outside Hanoi, followed by Hon Gay and its anthracite coal mines one year later. Tu Duc turned to guerrilla tactics and enlisted the help of Tongking bandits, the Black Flags, whose strength had already been diminished by French attacks. In March, 1883, the Black Flags attacked Hanoi, killing Rivière and shattering his troops.

Rivière's loss strengthened France's resolve to control Vietnam, and additional funds were given to establish a French protectorate by military force. Jules Ferry, the prime minister of France, was a staunch supporter of imperialism and sought to dominate Vietnam. General Bouet took over the French forces at Hanoi while they awaited Ferry's dispatch of three thousand troops from Europe. Under Ferry, Admiral Amédée Courbet took command of naval forces and François-Jules Harmand, a civilian, became commissioner-general.

Tu Duc died in July, and because he had no heirs, a succession crisis followed. Duc Duc received the title of

FRENCH INDOCHINA

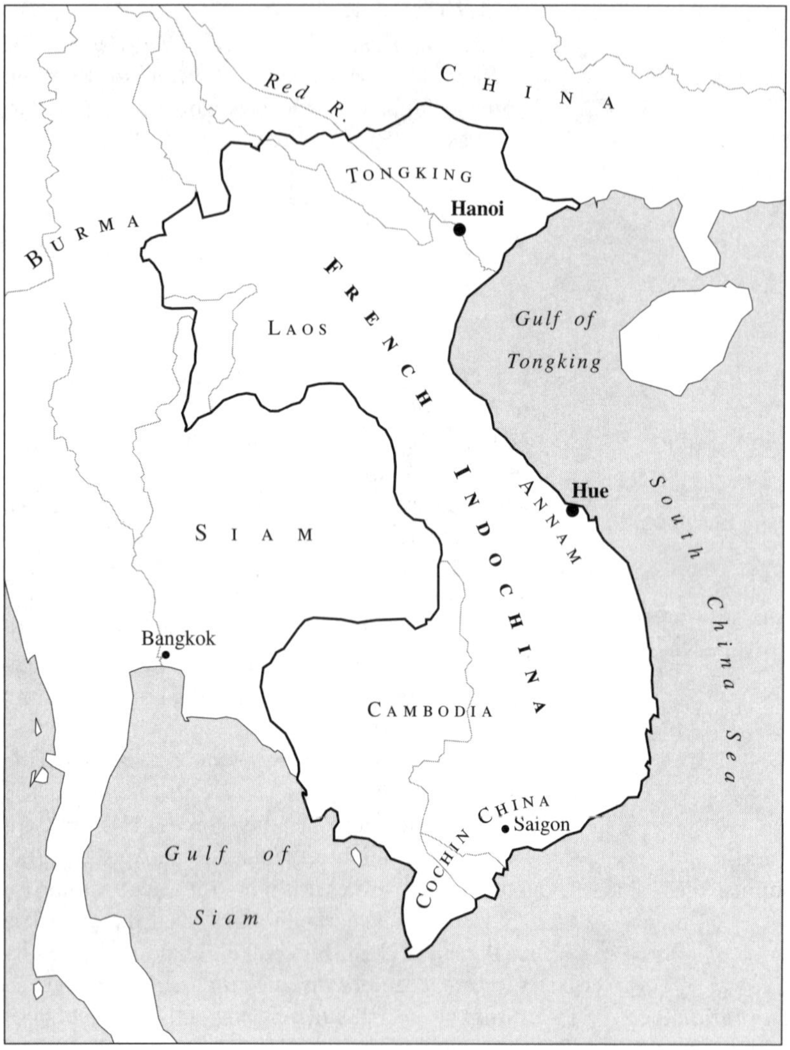

emperor from the council of regents, but he was deposed soon after. Hiep Hoa ascended the throne, but by then, French forces, led by Courbet, arrived at the Hue River in August. After a heavy bombardment, Vietnamese forces suffered heavy losses, and Hue fell in August. The substantial losses prompted the Court to send a mandarin (public official) to plea for a truce. The French demanded the surrender of all forts and vessels in the Hue area, and negotiations for a new treaty began.

Emperor Hiep Hoa signed a treaty of protectorate in August, 1883, which established a French protectorate over North (Tongking) and Central (Annam) Vietnam, and the independence of Vietnam ended. The French occupied as many forts along the Hue River and in Tongking as they saw necessary. The Red River went under French control and was promptly opened for trade. Vietnam also surrendered the province of Binh Thuan and all of its warships. In addition, all Vietnamese troops in Tongking were called back.

In June, 1884, the Hue treaty was signed. It modified and confirmed the treaty of protectorate. Binh Thuan was returned to Vietnam, Tongking was ruled by France, and Annam (central provinces) became a protectorate.

Because the Chinese had renewed their overlordship with Vietnam prior to these treaties, the Chinese minister in Paris protested the actions of France and opposed the treaty of protectorate. In an effort to seize back their vassal, the Chinese had prepared for war, ordering warships and sending reinforcements to Tongking. In December, 1883, French and Chinese forces collided when the French captured Son Tay, which the Chinese were defending. Bouct beheaded the captured Chinese. In early 1884, French troops captured Thai Nguyen, Bac Ninh, and the Black River region. In May the Chinese and French met for negotiations and drafted a treaty at Tientsin (Tianjin). The Chinese had to withdraw troops from Vietnam and never intervene in Vietnamese affairs, and France was to protect China's southern border if necessary.

Even with the convention of Tientsin treaty, clashes still existed between the Chinese and the Vietnamese. China did not necessarily want to give up its rights to Tongking and expose its border to the French. A misunderstanding of when the Chinese troops would withdraw led to hostilities between the two countries, and a major battle occurred in June at Bac Le in Lang Son. France lost this battle and demanded compensation from China. With China's refusal, tensions continued. In February, 1885, France took Lang Son and blockaded the Chinese territory of Formosa (Taiwan). The war waged on and eventually concluded without a clear winner. Eager to seek peace on both sides, negotiations reopened. Outside

Lang Son, French General François de Negrier was ambushed and wounded, and his second in command decided to evacuate the town. This latest incident increased France's desire to end the war, and the following month, a peace protocol was signed. The protocol was confirmed with the Treaty of Tientsin in June, which removed the French from Formosa, in addition to the agreements already ratified in 1884. The treaty between China and France solidified French control of Vietnam.

SIGNIFICANCE

The Treaty of Tientsin sealed Vietnam's fate as a French territory, beginning several decades of colonial rule. With colonial rule came subjugation and oppression and a complete denial of basic rights, such as the ability for the Vietnamese to freely move around their country and beyond the borders. The French, fearful of losing their lands to Great Britain, and in an effort to maintain control of Indochina, did whatever they felt was necessary to suppress dissidents and revolts.

By the twentieth century, as occurred with many countries under imperial rule, waves of nationalism grew. Groups that revolted early under imperial rule became symbols of nationalism. For Vietnam, any Vietnamese person who tried to overthrow an oppressor in history became a martyr to the nationalistic cause and a means to garner peasant support. As the French started to lose control over their territories, Vietnamese nationalism grew, until the First Indochina War of 1946-1954. This war marked the culmination of anti-French sentiment. Led by Ho Chi Minh, Vietnam regained control from the French.

Without the modes of imperialism, nationalism would not have culminated as it did, and the massacre of the French at Dien Bien Phu would not have occurred. In addition, the Vietnam War was an indirect result of French imperialism, because without the French, Ho Chi Minh would not have become a war hero and, therefore, also a political figure.

The Sino-French-Vietnamese War of the 1880's also had immediate effects. The tensions between China and France led to tensions between the Europeans. China was a major trade partner with Great Britain and other powers, and the fighting between France and China was affecting European trade. The fighting with China was also an embarrassment to the French prime minister, Jules Ferry, who wanted to expand France's empire into Laos and Siam. However, with British pressure to end the fighting and the embarrassment of the war, Ferry was forced from office. His removal led to the deterioration of imperial desires to acquire more land. Without Ferry, British and French tensions also eased slightly in Southeast Asia, possibly avoiding large-scale fighting in that area.

—*Tina Powell*

FURTHER READING

Duiker, William J. *Vietnam: A Nation in Revolution*. Boulder, Colo.: Westview Press, 1983. Brief discussion of the wars with France, but extended discussion of French colonialism in Vietnam. Emphasizes the twentieth century.

Sardesai, D. R. *Vietnam: Past and Present*. Boulder, Colo.: Westview Press, 2005. A detailed discussion of the history of Vietnam, with an emphasis on colonial expansion, the colonial period, and the rise of nationalism in Vietnam.

Tarling, Nicholas, ed. *From c. 1800 to the 1930's*. Vol. 2, part 1 in *The Cambridge History of Southeast Asia*. New York: Cambridge University Press, 2000. A detailed analysis of the war with a discussion of European motives, the political atmosphere in Europe, and how those two factors affected the colonization of Southeast Asia.

Tate, D. J. M. *The Making of Modern South-East Asia: The European Conquest*. Kuala Lumpur, Malaysia: Oxford University Press, 1977. A detailed discussion of the war from both angles, with an emphasis on events and dates.

SEE ALSO: Aug., 1858: France and Spain Invade Vietnam; July 23, 1882-Jan. 9, 1885: Korean Military Mutinies Against Japanese Rule; Aug. 1, 1894-Apr. 17, 1895: Sino-Japanese War; Nov. 14, 1897: Scramble for Chinese Concessions Begins.

RELATED ARTICLES in *Great Lives from History: The Nineteenth Century, 1801-1900:* Gia Long; Ho Xuan Huong; Napoleon III; Tu Duc.

May 2, 1882
KILMAINHAM TREATY MAKES CONCESSIONS TO IRISH NATIONALISTS

An agreement between the British government and Charles Stuart Parnell, the imprisoned leader of the Irish Parliamentary Party and the Irish National Land League, stipulated that upon release Parnell would openly support the 1881 Irish Land Act and would condemn violent tactics. In return, the 1881 act would be amended to include a large number of indebted Irish tenant farmers. The treaty, know popularly as the Kilmainham Jail Treaty, secured Parnell's leadership of the Irish Home Rule Party but divided Irish nationalist opinion.

ALSO KNOWN AS: Kilmainham Jail Treaty
LOCALE: Dublin, Ireland
CATEGORIES: Government and politics; agriculture; business and labor; social issues and reform

KEY FIGURES

Charles Stewart Parnell (1846-1891), leader of the Irish National Land League, 1879-1882, and leader of the Irish Home Rule Party, 1877-1890

William Ewart Gladstone (1809-1898), prime minister of Great Britain, 1868-1874, 1880-1885, 1886, and 1892-1894

Michael Davitt (1846-1906), a leader of the militant Irish Republican Brotherhood and spokesman for the Irish National Land League

John Dillon (1851-1927), Irish member of Parliament, 1880-1918, and supporter of the Irish National Land League

William O'Brien (1852-1928), Irish member of Parliament, 1883-1918, and chief secretary of Irish National Land League

SUMMARY OF EVENT

The Kilmainham Treaty of May 2, 1882, was a verbal compromise between Charles Stewart Parnell, the Irish Parliamentary Party and Irish National Land League leader, and the British government under Prime Minister William Ewart Gladstone concerning the 1881 Irish Land Act. The compromise ended what was called the Irish Land War of 1879-1881. The treaty foreshadowed not only the series of political negotiations and tough compromises that led to the ultimate political independence and division of Ireland in 1921 but also the tensions between Irish militant and constitutional groups. Moreover, with Parnell's acceptance of the 1881 act, the dismantling of the Irish Protestant land-owning class had begun.

Since the late seventeenth century, most Irish landlords were Protestants, and a majority of the tenant farmers were Roman Catholics. Within this religious and economic divide, Irish Catholics campaigned vigorously for complete political independence from Great Britain during the early nineteenth century. The combination of religious, political, and economic grievances among Irish Catholics spurred continued demands for broad-scale change either through constitutional or revolutionary methods.

To galvanize the numerous groups seeking Irish independence in a nationwide movement, Parnell and other home rule leaders attempted to find a singular issue on which to base their platform. Throughout Irish history, the key issue was land ownership and landlord-tenant relations. Rents, leasing terms, and rent increases by Irish landlords had been subject to previous legislation in the 1870 Irish Land Act, but fell short of Irish tenant expectations.

The 1870's were punctuated by several poor harvests and outright crop failures, particularly in western Ireland. Through 1879, County Mayo tenant farmers formed local organizations to pressure Irish landlords to redress grievances of increasing rents and evictions during periods of agricultural failures. The County Mayo tenant organization was expanded into a national organization by Parnell and Irish Republican Brotherhood member Michael Davitt in October, 1879. Through the Irish National Land League, Parnell and Davitt linked the issues of land ownership reform with the political campaign for Irish home rule.

Parnell campaigned vigorously in the British parliament, the United States, and across Ireland for legal and economic redress of the tenant-landlord relations and eventual Irish independence. However, sporadic violence and the murders of several Irish landlords and their land agents during 1879 and 1880 pressed Gladstone to enact stiff legal prosecution against Irish militants via the Protection of Persons and Property Act of March, 1881. Through this three-year "war," the British cabinet, the press, and popular opinion often viewed Parnell, home rule leaders, and the Land League as fronts for Irish militant groups, but Parnell distanced himself from any militant organization.

By early April, 1881, a new Irish land reform bill was completed and was passed by Parliament in August. The 1881 Irish Land Act incorporated the main points (the three "F's" as they were known) demanded by Parnell and the Land League—tenant right to fair rental price, tenant right to fixed tenure on rented land, and tenant right to freely sell their lease—but the act did not include provisions for indebted Irish farmers. In a series of public speeches across Ireland during the summer and autumn, Parnell denounced the new land act for this oversight.

Gladstone and his cabinet, feeling betrayed by Parnell for his public criticism and believing Parnell was stoking violence among the Irish crowds, ordered his arrest and imprisonment, along with other Land League leaders, including John Dillon and William O'Brien, and some one thousand other members on October 13-15, 1881, under the recently passed Protection of Persons and Property Act. On October 18, Parnell, O'Brien, and Dillon issued their No Rent Manifesto from Dublin's Kilmainham jail. The manifesto called on Irish tenant farmers to withhold rents due in protest of the Land League leaders' arrests.

Charles Stewart Parnell. (Library of Congress)

The following day, Gladstone declared the Irish National Land League an illegal organization. Through the autumn, violence continued in the Irish countryside not only between tenants and landlords but also between large-scale farmers included under the provisions of the land act and tenant farmers excluded from the act. By early 1882, Gladstone and his advisers believed the only way to limit these Irish "outrages" was to release Parnell and other Land Leaguers on the condition that they denounce any and all violent action in Ireland.

Intermediaries between Parnell and Gladstone communicated a willingness of both to reach a compromise by early April, 1882. Gladstone and some Irish officials believed Parnell could restore order to an increasingly militant Irish populace and convince them that legal and constitutional methods could attain much more progress in the land reform and home rule question. Parnell demanded from Gladstone that indebted farmers were included under the act. Although this would cost the British government and Irish landowners dearly, Gladstone finally accepted Parnell's terms in the face of increasing violence in Ireland and the stark disapproval of government officials and Irish landlords.

Parnell and other Land Leaguers were released from Kilmainham jail on May 2, 1882. Each party kept their word. Parnell officially dissolved the Irish National Land League and publicly supported the revised land act, while denouncing criminal activities. Gladstone implemented the necessary legal revisions to the act. However, on May 6, 1882, the newly installed Irish chief secretary, Lord Frederick Cavendish, and his under-secretary, Thomas Burke, were murdered by Irish militants known as the Invincibles while walking in Dublin's Phoenix Park. The gory publicity surrounding the Phoenix Park murders led to a series of recriminations against Parnell and Gladstone, though Parnell had no knowledge of this militant group, nor did he support violent action. The murders heightened the tension between Irish and British leaders and demonstrated the difficulties Parnell was to face in leading the home rule movement.

SIGNIFICANCE

The Kilmainham Treaty cemented Charles Stewart Parnell's position as leader of the home rule movement until his scandalous downfall in 1890. However, the Kilmainham Treaty split the British government and the Irish home rule movement. Some British and Irish officials resigned in protest on the release of Parnell, and some Irish militant and nationalist groups distanced themselves from what they viewed as Parnell's compromising tone toward the British government. In one sense, the Land War, the 1881 Land Act, and the treaty did more to divide than it did to unite the parties seeking resolution in Ireland.

Although Parnell's release from prison brought an overall decline to agrarian violence and set a constitutional path toward Irish self-governance, the long-term tension between constitutionalist and militant elements remained in Irish politics. The stresses and occasional overlaps between these forms of political activism remained a centerpiece in Irish and, later, Northern Irish, politics well into the twentieth century.

—*Tyler T. Crogg*

FURTHER READING

Bew, Paul. *Land and the National Question in Ireland, 1858-82*. Dublin: Gill & Macmillan, 1978. A critique of Irish tenant-farmer organizations and multiple divisions in the Irish land reform movement.

Clark, Samuel. *Social Origins of the Irish Land War.* Princeton, N.J.: Princeton University Press, 1979. An analysis of the socioeconomic structures in late nineteenth century Ireland and the origins of "collective action" campaigns.

Kee, Robert. *The Laurel and the Ivy: The Story of Charles Robert Parnell and Irish Nationalism.* New York: Penguin Books, 1993. Exhaustive biography, tracing Parnell's political career and analyzing his impact on Irish nationalism and British politics.

King, Carla, ed. *Famine, Land, and Culture in Ireland.* Dublin: University College Dublin Press, 2000. A history of land tenure and the general land question in Ireland, with chapters on Parnell and Davitt, evictions, the social conditions of rural life, agricultural laborers, and the "hidden history" of the land wars of the late nineteenth century.

O'Day, Alan. *Irish Home Rule, 1867-1921.* Manchester, England: Manchester University Press, 1998. An examination of the evolution of the Irish home rule movement and its relationship to other nationalist groups in Ireland. Includes a time line and a biographical dictionary.

SEE ALSO: 1845-1854: Great Irish Famine; June, 1866-1871: Fenian Risings for Irish Independence; Dec. 6, 1884: British Parliament Passes the Franchise Act of 1884; June, 1886-Sept. 9, 1893: Irish Home Rule Debate Dominates British Politics.

RELATED ARTICLES in *Great Lives from History: The Nineteenth Century, 1801-1900:* Joseph Chamberlain; Fourteenth Earl of Derby; William Edward Forster; William Ewart Gladstone; John Philip Holland; Daniel Mannix; Daniel O'Connell; Charles Stewart Parnell.

May 9, 1882
ARTHUR SIGNS THE CHINESE EXCLUSION ACT

A new wave of nativist xenophobia generated the first U.S. immigration law to discriminate on the basis of national origin. The act, which was renewed several times, severely restricted Chinese immigration—and barred immigration of Chinese women—and naturalization until 1943.

LOCALE: Washington, D.C.

CATEGORIES: Immigration; laws, acts, and legal history; social issues and reform

KEY FIGURES

James Burrill Angell (1829-1916), chairman of the U.S. Treaty Commission

Chester A. Arthur (1829-1886), twenty-first president of the United States, 1881-1885

John F. Miller (1831-1886), California senator who supported the exclusion movement

Denis Kearney (1847-1907), leader of the Workingmen's Party in California and a foe of Chinese immigration

Li Hongzao (Li Hung-tsao; 1820-1897) and *Baoyun* (Pao-yun; 1807-1891), Chinese plenipotentiaries for treaty negotiations in 1880

SUMMARY OF EVENT

In 1886, the United States dedicated the Statue of Liberty, a monument that stands in symbolic welcome to the "huddled masses" from foreign shores. However, even as the statue was dedicated, the citizenry had allowed its vision of the country as a refuge for all people to grow dimmer instead of brighter. Four years earlier, in 1882, the United States had taken the first steps to exclude immigrants from China and to restrict certain classes of immigrants from all foreign countries.

The closing of the door to Chinese immigrants had begun during the early 1850's. Responding to the thousands of Chinese workers who had crossed the Pacific Ocean after 1849 to seek their fortune in the California gold rush, the California state legislature enacted a series of discriminatory laws to discourage settlement and further immigration. The foreign miners' tax of 1852, immigration head tax of 1855, Chinese fishing tax of 1860, and police tax of 1862 imposed discriminatory fines on Chinese laborers, making it difficult for them to continue working in California. By the early 1860's, increased taxation, coupled with the discovery of gold in Australia, reduced the number of Chinese immigrants entering the United States from more than twenty thousand in 1852 to only twenty-seven hundred in 1864.

Editorial cartoon depicting President Rutherford B. Hayes standing on an ice drift representing the United States as he vetoes the 1879 Chinese exclusion bill of California senator Denis Kearney, who is shown standing on a piece of the ice drift, labeled "Kearneyfornee," that is breaking away from the United States. (Library of Congress)

Precisely at that time, however, a new source of employment was opening for Chinese in the United States. In 1865, the Central Pacific Railroad Company began employing Chinese laborers to lay track for the western portion of the transcontinental railroad. Within three years, the company hired ten thousand Chinese workers. The promise of good pay and steady work, far from city taxes and prejudice, again drew Chinese to the United States. Between 1868 and 1870, nearly thirty-five thousand Chinese immigrants passed through San Francisco customs, many directly recruited by U.S. railroad agents in China. With the completion of the transcontinental railroad in 1869, however, these thousands of Chinese laborers returned to the West Coast to seek work. Competition for jobs between Chinese and Euro-American workers in San Francisco and other Pacific coast cities led American workers to intensify their demands for restrictions on Chinese immigration.

Workers in California rallied for stricter control over Chinese immigration. They argued that the growing population and alien customs of the Chinese constituted a threat to basic American institutions. They claimed that Chinese houses and shops were opium dens in which innocent native Californians were debauched. They accused the Chinese of being a race of "coolies" (a derogatory term used to name unskilled laborers) who threatened the wages and dignity of native California labor. In San Francisco, "anti-coolie clubs" and "light hour leagues" organized anti-Chinese demonstrations.

Under the leadership of Denis Kearney, a firebrand orator from the sandlots of San Francisco, the Workingmen's Party of California became a potent exclusionist force in state politics and in anti-Chinese riots and demonstrations. Kearney's racist harangues incited workers all along the Pacific coast to rise up against the Chinese. Mob violence against the Chinese escalated throughout the 1870's, exemplified by a Los Angeles attack in which a mob of about five hundred assaulted and killed a score of the residents of the city's Chinatown.

During the early 1880's, California exclusionists turned the Chinese problem into a national issue, demanding that Congress enact a law that would prohibit Chinese immigration. Party politics gave added weight to the exclusionists' demands on the national level, as both Republicans and Democrats vied for western con-

CHINESE EXCLUSION ACT OF 1882

An Act to Execute Certain Treaty Stipulations Relating to Chinese

Preamble. Whereas, in the opinion of the Government of the United States the coming of Chinese laborers to this country endangers the good order of certain localities within the territory thereof: Therefore,

Be it enacted by the Senate and House of Representatives of the United States of America in Congress assembled, That from and after the expiration of ninety days next after the passage of this act, and until the expiration of ten years next after the passage of this act, the coming of Chinese laborers to the United States be, and the same is hereby, suspended; and during such suspension it shall not be lawful for any Chinese laborer to come, or, having so come after the expiration of said ninety days, to remain within the United States.

SECTION 2. That the master of any vessel who shall knowingly bring within the United States on such vessel, and land or permit to be landed, any Chinese laborer, from any foreign port or place, shall be deemed guilty of a misdemeanor. . . .

SECTION 14. That hereafter no State court or court of the United States shall admit Chinese to citizenship; and all laws in conflict with this act are hereby repealed.

SECTION 15. That the words "Chinese laborers," wherever used in this act, shall be construed to mean both skilled and unskilled laborers and Chinese employed in mining.

Source: The Avalon Project at Yale Law School. Documents in Law, History, and Diplomacy.

stituencies, which they believed to be crucial. In 1879, Congress responded to western pressure and passed a Chinese exclusion bill. President Rutherford B. Hayes vetoed the measure because it violated the terms of the Burlingame Treaty of 1868, which permitted unlimited Chinese immigration to the U.S.

Chinese plenipotentiaries Li Hongzao and Baoyun agreed to renegotiate the Burlingame Treaty to include the possibility of limiting Chinese immigration. In 1880, they concluded a treaty with the U.S. representative, James Burrill Angell, that granted the United States the right to regulate, limit, or suspend the immigration of Chinese laborers, but not absolutely prohibit such immigration.

The Angell Treaty opened the door for the creation of federal legislation restricting Chinese immigration. Without delay, California senator John F. Miller introduced a bill calling for the suspension of immigration for all Chinese laborers, skilled or unskilled, for a period of twenty years. The Senate heatedly debated the bill. New England senators argued that a founding tenet of the United States—free immigration from all nations for all peoples—was at stake. West Coast senators countered that the future of American laborers was in jeopardy. The bill finally passed the Senate but was vetoed by President Chester A. Arthur because it violated the spirit of the 1880 negotiations with China.

Congress immediately drafted another bill, which suspended immigration and naturalization of Chinese laborers, skilled and unskilled, for ten years. On May 9, 1882, President Arthur signed the Chinese Exclusion Act into law. The Exclusion Act was renewed for another ten-year period in 1892, again in 1902, and in 1904 was made permanent. The act was not rescinded until December 17, 1943, during World War II, when it became a source of embarrassment between the two allied nations.

SIGNIFICANCE

Chinese exclusion initiated a trend toward the passage of increasingly restrictive immigration legislation. President Arthur had signed into law the Immigration Act of 1882, the first general immigration law. This act imposed a tax on every immigrant and prohibited the entry of any convict, "lunatic," "idiot," or person unable to take care of himself or herself without becoming a public charge. Well into the twentieth century, Congress continued to pass legislation limiting the immigration of certain "undesirable" groups.

By 1882, the United States had excluded one nationality and had imposed limitations, however slight, on all potential immigrants. The Chinese question in California had been an explosive one, fueled by racism toward Chinese immigrants who could not and, exclusionists believed, would not assimilate. The interaction of social pressures, economic changes, and opportunistic politics in the United States closed the Pacific door to Chinese laborers. By prohibiting these Chinese from entering the United States, Congress had turned away "huddled masses" even before Emma Lazarus's poetry on the Statue of Liberty had bid them welcome.

—*Emory M. Thomas, updated by Daniel J. Meissner*

FURTHER READING

Barth, Gunther. *Bitter Strength: A History of the Chinese in the United States, 1850-1870*. Cambridge, Mass.:

Harvard University Press, 1964. Although it does not treat events after 1870, this book is important to an understanding of anti-Chinese sentiment in California.

Chan, Sucheng, ed. *Entry Denied: Exclusion and the Chinese Community in America, 1882-1943*. Philadelphia: Temple University Press, 1991. Explores the legal ramifications of the Exclusion Act and the act's effects on Chinese who were living in the United States.

Coolidge, Mary Roberts. *Chinese Immigration*. 1909. Reprint. New York: Arno Press, 1969. A dated but comprehensive book. Argues that the Exclusion Act was necessary to prevent unchecked Chinese immigration from undermining the U.S. economy.

Peffer, George Anthony. *If They Don't Bring Women Here: Chinese Female Immigration Before Exclusion*. Urbana: University of Illinois Press, 1999. A study of the special problems faced by female Chinese immigrants in the years leading up to the Chinese Exclusion Act.

LeMay, Michael C. *From Open Door to Dutch Door: An Analysis of U.S. Immigration Policy Since 1820*. New York: Praeger, 1987. Examines underlying causes of the anti-immigration movement in the United States in response to European and Chinese immigration since 1820.

Miller, Stuart Creighton. *The Unwelcome Immigrant: The American Image of the Chinese, 1785-1882*. Berkeley: University of California Press, 1969. Countering Coolidge's argument of an economic basis for the Exclusion Act, argues that racism was at the root of Californian and U.S. hostility toward Chinese immigrants.

Takaki, Ronald. *Strangers from a Different Shore: A History of Asian Americans*. 1989. Rev ed. Boston: Little, Brown, 1998. Chapter 3 succinctly examines the early years of Chinese immigration. Other chapters explore the Asian immigrant experience in detail. A comprehensive work.

SEE ALSO: 1840's-1850's: American Era of "Old" Immigration; Jan. 24, 1848: California Gold Rush Begins; 1849: Chinese Begin Immigrating to California; July 28, 1868: Burlingame Treaty; May 10, 1869: First Transcontinental Railroad Is Completed; Mar. 3, 1875: Congress Enacts the Page Law; May 9, 1882: Arthur Signs the Chinese Exclusion Act; Nov. 12, 1882: San Francisco's Chinese Six Companies Association Forms; 1892: America's "New" Immigration Era Begins; May 4, 1892: Anti-Japanese Yellow Peril Campaign Begins; May 10, 1895: Chinese Californians Form Native Sons of the Golden State; Mar. 28, 1898: *United States v. Wong Kim Ark*.

RELATED ARTICLES in *Great Lives from History: The Nineteenth Century, 1801-1900:* Chester A. Arthur; Stephen J. Field; Rutherford B. Hayes; Emma Lazarus.

May 20, 1882
TRIPLE ALLIANCE IS FORMED

The Triple Alliance among Austria-Hungary, Germany, and Italy was an agreement that each country would support and defend the other in case of military attack. The alliance remained in force into World War I.

LOCALE: Vienna, Austria
CATEGORY: Diplomacy and international relations

KEY FIGURES

Otto von Bismarck (1815-1898), chancellor of the German Empire, 1871-1890

Agostino Depretis (1813-1887), premier of Italy, 1881-1887

Count Gusztav Siegmund Kálnoky von Köröspatak (1832-1898), foreign affairs minister of Austria-Hungary

Pasquale Stanislao Mancini (1817-1888), Italian foreign affairs minister

Umberto I (1844-1900), king of Italy, r. 1878-1900

SUMMARY OF EVENT

A major contribution to the system of entangling alliances that prevailed in Europe from 1871 to 1914 was the expansion of the Dual Alliance of 1879 into the Triple Alliance of 1882. The Dual Alliance was negotiated by the German Empire and Austria-Hungary as a defensive pact directed explicitly against a possible Russian attack on either of the two signatories, and implicitly against France.

As soon as the Dual Alliance had been signed, Italy sought admission as a full-fledged member. There were two important reasons. Domestically, the Italians were concerned during the early 1880's over the possible restoration of the Papal States to the papacy, since Leo XIII, who had succeeded Pius IX in 1878, had reached a religious rapprochement with the anticlerical governments of Austria and Germany. Of even greater significance was the French occupation of Tunis in May, 1881, because Italy cast envious eyes on that territory as part of a future Italian Empire in North Africa. Waves of anti-French sentiment swept through Italy. The government, realizing that it must take prompt steps to quell popular unrest, discarded any misgivings it might have had about entering into an alliance with Austria, Italy's old enemy.

Indeed, Otto von Bismarck, the chancellor of the German Empire, made it clear to the Italians, whose partnership he was at first hesitant to accept, that they must negotiate their membership with Vienna before gaining admittance to the alliance. Accordingly in October, 1881, King Umberto I of Italy, his premier, Agostino Depretis, and his minister of foreign affairs, Pasquale Stanislao Mancini, journeyed to Vienna to begin negotiations with their traditional Habsburg adversary, represented by Count Gusztav Siegmund Kálnoky von Köröspatak, the minister of foreign affairs of Austria-Hungary. The negotiations lasted for months, but finally, on May 20, 1882, Germany, Austria, and Italy signed the treaty creating the Triple Alliance.

The terms of the Triple Alliance supplemented rather than supplanted those of the Dual Alliance of 1879. Explicitly a defensive pact, the Triple Alliance bound Germany and Austria to come to the aid of Italy if it were attacked by France; similarly, if France attacked Germany, Italy would come to its aid. In the event that one or two of the signatories were attacked by two or more powers, the other allies or ally would render armed assistance. If one of the allies were obliged to make war on a nonsignatory power, the other allies would observe a benevolent neutrality. Finally, if war became imminent for one of the contracting parties, all the parties were to consult together; if war broke out and all the allies became involved, none of them would conclude a separate peace. The treaty of alliance was to be kept secret and last for five years.

SIGNIFICANCE

The Triple Alliance brought advantages to each member. Italy gained the prestige of association with the two great powers of central Europe. However, the unlikelihood of a French invasion of Italy's Alpine northwestern frontier diluted the significance of Austria's and Germany's promise to come to the aid of their ally if France were to attack. Italy was more likely to fight for Germany than Germany for Italy. However, in the event of involvement in a defensive war against France, Italy, backed by Germany, could look forward to the possible annexation of French Nice and Savoy, and perhaps even Tunis in North Africa. Finally, the price of Italy's improved relations with Austria was the renunciation of Italy's irredentist claims.

More realistic advantages accrued to Austria and Germany as a result of the alliance. Austria, in the event of war with Russia, would not have to withhold part of its army to guard its southwestern frontier against an Italy fighting either for its irredentist claims or on behalf of a French ally. The ability of Austria to commit all its forces against Russia would prove invaluable to Germany in case Germany had to face Russia and France in a two-front war. A French attack on Germany would now prove difficult, as some French forces would have to be diverted to hold the Italian Alpine frontier. Neither Bismarck nor Kálnoky was impressed with Italian military strength, but both statesmen wanted Italy to threaten France's frontier rather than Austria's frontier. "Sparing the Austrian forces," as Bismarck put it, "rather than winning those of Italy is our aim."

There was, as Bismarck himself realized, a great deal of truth in the second part of this remark, for while Germany and Austria recognized the advantage in an alignment with Italy, neither power ever trusted Italy. The traditional Austro-Italian rivalry soon flared up over territorial questions in the northern Adriatic and the Balkans. Meanwhile, Franco-Italian relations improved to the point where, in 1900, Paris and Rome arrived at a rapprochement over their disputes in North Africa, followed in 1902 by an Italian promise to France to remain neutral in the event of an attack on France. These steps had the effect of nullifying Italy's participation in the Triple Alliance that, however, was renewed when required until 1914.

When World War I broke out and German troops threatened to break through to Paris, Italy remained neutral, an act that may well have spared France and Great Britain total defeat. In the Treaty of London in 1915, the two allies persuaded Italy to enter the war on the side of the Triple Entente. Hence, what Austria and Germany had feared and attempted to forestall—namely, an attack on Austria's frontier—actually took place, to the strategic disadvantage of the Central Powers throughout the remainder of World War I.

—Edward P. Keleher, updated by John Quinn Imholte

FURTHER READING

Albertini, Luigi. *The Origins of the War of 1914*. Vol. 1. London: Oxford University Press, 1952. Emphasis is on Italy's participation in the alliance. French occupation of Tunis was the main reason for Italy seeking a formal relationship with Germany and Austria.

Fay, Sydney B. *The Origins of the World War*. 2d rev. ed. New York: Macmillan, 1930. An analysis of the alliance. The author rejects the contention that Bismarck actively sought Italy as an ally.

Hayes, Carlton J. H. *A Generation of Materialism, 1871-1900*. New York: Harper & Row, 1941. Provides a useful synopsis of the reasons for Italy's entry into the alliance with Germany and Austria.

Langer, William L. *European Alliances and Alignments, 1871-1890*. 2d ed. New York: Alfred A. Knopf, 1950. Author devotes a chapter to the Triple Alliance and provides brief and substantial descriptions and interpretations.

Schmitt, Bernadotte E. *Triple Alliance and Triple Entente*. New York: Howard Fertig, 1971. Account of the background of the alliance and its effects. A valuable source both for description and interpretation.

Waller, Bruce. *Bismarck*. New York: Basil Blackwell, 1985. Biography of the statesman who was most directly responsible for the Triple Alliance. Places it within a more intimate context.

SEE ALSO: Sept. 24, 1862: Bismarck Becomes Prussia's Minister-President; 1866-1867: North German Confederation Is Formed; June 15-Aug. 23, 1866: Austria and Prussia's Seven Weeks' War; May 29, 1867: Austrian Ausgleich; July 19, 1870-Jan. 28, 1871: Franco-Prussian War; Jan. 18, 1871: German States Unite Within German Empire; May 6-Oct. 22, 1873: Three Emperors' League Is Formed; Jan. 4, 1894: Franco-Russian Alliance.

RELATED ARTICLES in *Great Lives from History: The Nineteenth Century, 1801-1900:* Otto von Bismarck; Friedrich von Holstein; Leo XIII.

July 23, 1882-January 9, 1885
KOREAN MILITARY MUTINIES AGAINST JAPANESE RULE

Korean resentment of widening Japanese influence and infighting at the royal court led to a military mutiny that turned against the Korean queen and the Japanese. Suppression of the rebellion brought in Japanese and Chinese troops and humiliated Korea. A later coup by Japanese and progressive Koreans, who were keen on modernization, failed because of Chinese intervention, and Japan and China agreed to withdraw their troops from Korea.

LOCALE: Seoul, Korea

CATEGORIES: Wars, uprisings, and civil unrest; diplomacy and international relations; government and politics

KEY FIGURES

Min (Myongsong Hwanghu; 1851-1895), queen of Korea, r. 1866-1895

Kojong (Myong-bok; 1852-1919), king of Korea, r. 1864-1897, emperor of Korea as Kwangmu, r. 1897-1907

Taewon-gun (Yi Ha-ung; 1821-1898), Korean grand prince and regent for his son Kojong, r. 1864-1873

Hanabusa Yoshimoto (1842-1917), Japanese minister to Korea in 1882

Li Hongzhang (Li Hung-chang; 1823-1901), Chinese statesman

Kim Ok-kyun (1851-1894),

Pak Yong-hyo (1861-1939), and

So Chae-p'il (Philip Jaisohn; 1866-1951), leaders of the 1884 progressive coup

Horimoto Reizō (d. 1882), Japanese commander of a Korean elite unit

SUMMARY OF EVENT

After 1876, when Japan forcibly opened the kingdom of Korea to foreign trade with the Treaty of Kanghwa, Japanese influence grew in Korea. The treaty ended Korea's status as a vassal state of China and made it independent. Yet Japan engineered the treaty to increase its own opportunities in Korea.

Kojong, the Korean king who signed the treaty, was a weak person. Initially, he was dominated by his father, who is known by the name for "grand prince," Taewon-gun. Taewon-gun selected a noble orphan girl, Myongsong Hwanghu, to be his son's wife. She was from the powerful Min clan, whom Taewon-gun sought to dominate. Myongsong Hwanghu became Queen Min at her wedding in 1866 at the age of fifteen. Queen Min suspected that Taewon-gun had poisoned their firstborn son, and in 1873, he pushed Kojong to assume power for himself.

Queen Min permitted Japanese lieutenant Horimoto Reizō to set up an elite Japanese-style Korean army unit in May, 1881. Quickly, the preferential treatment given to these one hundred Korean soldiers led by a Japanese commander caused resentment. On July 19, 1882, in Seoul, regular Korean soldiers were given their first salary in more than one year. Min Kyom-ho, a relative of Queen Min, sold the rice that was earmarked as the soldiers' pay and instead distributed to them an inedible mix of grains and sand. Early in the morning of July 23, angry soldiers marched toward Min Kyom-ho's house. He arrested their leaders and announced their pending execution.

Enraged by Min's orders, soldiers stormed his house and broke into an armory. Freshly armed, mutineers stormed Seoul prison and freed their comrades. Augmented by poor and dissatisfied citizens, the rebellion rose to three thousand men and developed an anti-Japanese character. Soldiers killed Lieutenant Horimoto, and then the rioters surrounded the Japanese legation. The Japanese minister to Korea, Hanabusa Yoshimoto, ordered the building to be burned as cover and escaped with his men to the harbor of Inchon. With six Japanese killed, Yoshimoto and his group fled to the sea, where they were rescued by a British ship.

On July 24, the mob stormed the royal palace, killing Min Kyom-ho and others. Queen Min escaped in disguise. After siding with the rebels, Taewon-gun assumed power, and soon ordered a state funeral for Queen Min, who was presumed dead. He then abolished the Japanese-led army unit.

Japan sent four warships and fifteen soldiers to accompany Minister Yoshimoto back to Seoul. Queen Min secretly contacted King Kojong to ask for Chinese help. Li Hongzhang, China's viceroy responsible also for Korea, sent three warships. A Japanese ship reached Inchon before the three Chinese warships arrived on August 10.

Li Hongzhang (right) with former U.S. president Ulysses S. Grant during the latter's visit to China in June, 1879. (The S. S. McClure Company)

When the main Japanese fleet arrived on August 12, the Chinese withdrew and then returned with reinforcements of four thousand infantry on August 22 and two hundred soldiers the next day. On August 22, Yoshimoto had met with King Kojong and conveyed Japan's demands. Among them, Korea was to pay 500,000 yen for the deadly anti-Japanese riot. King Kojong asked for more time, but Yoshimoto refused and returned to his fleet at Inchon. Japan then refused a Chinese offer at mediation.

On August 26, the Chinese asked Taewon-gun into their camp, but they kidnapped him upon his arrival and then deported him to China. He was interrogated by Li Hongzhang and kept for three years. After Chinese soldiers stormed the royal palace on August 29, killing nearly four hundred Korean soldiers and executing ten rebel leaders, Queen Min returned to power.

On September 30 Korea signed the Treaty of Chemulpo (now called Inchon) with Japan, agreeing to all Japanese demands, and Japan received the right to station soldiers to protect its rebuilt legation. Queen Min shifted her allegiance to the Chinese. In October, Korea and China signed an agreement on trade that restored Korea's vassal status to China.

The conservative policies of Queen Min antagonized a group of progressive Koreans around their intellectual leader Kim Ok-kyun, who began plotting a coup in 1883. A regional commander, fellow plotter Pak Yong-hyo, trained a five-hundred-man force that impressed the king. A suspicious Queen Min amalgamated the force into the regular army. Conspirator So Chae-p'il went abroad and returned a graduate from Japan's military academy in June, 1884.

The plotters saw their chance after China reduced its troop strength in Seoul in May, 1884, so that it could have more soldiers to block French claims over Vietnam. With the outbreak of the Sino-French-Vietnamese War over the status of Vietnam in September, 1884, the plotters moved ahead. The new Japanese minister to Korea, Takezoe Shinichiro, arrived in Seoul on October 30 and sided with the plotters. On December 4, the Kapsin coup—named for the year of the event in Korean—was staged. The plotters used the inauguration of Seoul's new post office to assassinate invited conservative politicians. The plotters failed to kill all their main targets but took King Kojong and Queen Min into custody in a small palace.

On December 5, the conspirators announced a new government. The Chinese contacted Queen Min, who agreed to receive their help. She advised King Kojong to ask to be moved to the large, less defensible main palace, and Takezoe agreed. On December 6, the king issued a fifteen-article reform proclamation drafted by the progressives. In the afternoon, Chinese troops and conservative Korean troops attacked the palace held by the insurgents. The troops of the progressives were overwhelmed. Under fire, the Japanese under Takezoe withdrew to Inchon after burning their legation, and they took Kim, Pak, and So with them to safety, and eventually to Japan.

Family members of the Korean plotters were executed in the plotters' stead. Japanese forces returned to Korea with seven warships and three thousand infantry. Restitution demands were small because the Koreans did not mention Japanese complicity in the Kapsin coup. The Protocol of Seoul between Japan and Korea was signed on January 9, 1885, and fifteen hundred Japanese soldiers landed in Korea. With both Chinese and Japanese troops in Korea, tension was resolved by negotiations. The Treaty of Tientsin (Tianjin) was signed in China on April 18, 1885, between Li Hongzhang and Japanese prime minister Itō Hirobumi. China and Japan agreed to remove their respective troops from Korea, agreed to train Korean soldiers, and agreed to notify the other if either country sent new troops to Korea.

SIGNIFICANCE

By 1882, the failure of Queen Min to do the near impossible and modernize Korea without giving in to Japanese aggression subjected her country to hardship. What began as a riot against a corrupt court official quickly turned into anti-Japanese violence. The killing of Japanese people gave Japan a pretext to humiliate Korea. Turning from one foreign power to the next for her survival, Queen Min brought in the Chinese, who saw a chance to help China reassert its own lost authority.

The Korean progressives who staged the Kapsin coup of 1884 sincerely believed in the benefits of modernizing Korea along Japanese lines. Queen Min's alignment with China was seen as a harmful tie to a stagnant nation. Kim Ok-kyun and his followers trusted the Japanese propaganda that promoted Japan as the Asian country whose modernization would enable it to prevent Western imperialism. What Kim failed to see was that Japan acted as an imperialist itself.

The Treaty of Tientsin brought temporary peace. In the end, the Sino-Japanese War (1894-1895) between China and Japan would break out over Korea's status. Japan's victory would threaten further Korean autonomy until Japan's subsequent victory over Russia in the early twentieth century ultimately led to Korea's annexation by Japan in 1910.

—R. C. Lutz

FURTHER READING

Hatada, Takahashi. *A History of Korea*. Translated by Warren Smith and Benjamin Hazard. Santa Barbara, Calif.: ABC-Clio, 1969. Chapter 6 places the event in the context of foreign imperialist ambitions in Korea. Appendix, index, maps, and tables.

Joe, Wanne. *A Cultural History of Modern Korea*. Elizabeth, N.J.: Hollym Press, 2000. Passionately pro-Korean, very detailed rendition of the event in chapter 2. Illustrations, maps, notes, bibliography, index.

Keene, Donald. *Emperor of Japan*. New York: Columbia University Press, 2002. Biography of the Meiji emperor of Japan. Chapter 36 and the beginning of chapter 44 give detailed accounts of the event from a Japanese point of view. Notes, index, bibliography, illustrations.

Oliver, Robert. *A History of the Korean People in Modern Times*. Newark: University of Delaware Press, 1993. Chapter 3 examines the event, outlining foreign interests in Korea and competition between imperialist nations. Notes, references, indexes.

Shin, Yong-ha. *Modern Korean History and Nationalism*. Translated by N. N. Pankaj. Seoul, Republic of Korea: Jimoondang, 2000. Chapter 2 provides a detailed analysis of the failed 1884 coup, which is seen as a progressive nationalist move independent of Japanese influence. Bibliography, glossary, index.

Tennant, Roger. *A History of Korea*. London: Kegan Paul, 1996. Chapters 27 through 29 examine and discuss the event. Very readable, with notes, a bibliography, and an index.

SEE ALSO: Oct. 23, 1856-Nov. 6, 1860: Second Opium War; May 10, 1857-July 8, 1858: Sepoy Mutiny Against British Rule; 1870's: Japan Expands into Korea; Jan.-Sept. 24, 1877: Former Samurai Rise in Satsuma Rebellion; Apr., 1882-1885: French Indochina War; July 8, 1894-Jan. 1, 1896: Kabo Reforms Begin Modernization of Korean Government; Aug. 1, 1894-Apr. 17, 1895: Sino-Japanese War.

RELATED ARTICLES in *Great Lives from History: The Nineteenth Century, 1801-1900:* Cixi; Itō Hirobumi; Mutsuhito.

September 13, 1882
BATTLE OF TEL EL KEBIR

Great Britain's victory in the Battle of Tel el Kebir ended the antiforeign, nationalist movement in Egypt known as the Arabi Revolution. Egypt was converted into a British protectorate in everything but name, and it remained under de facto British control until 1946.

ALSO KNOWN AS: Battle of El Tell el Kebîr; Battle of at-Tall al-Kabīr

LOCALE: Tel el Kebir, near Zagazig, Egypt

CATEGORIES: Wars, uprisings, and civil unrest; colonization; expansion and land acquisition

KEY FIGURES

Arabi Pasha (ʿUrābī Pasha; 1839-1911), Egyptian rebel, 1879-1881, and minister of war, 1882

Muḥammad Tawfīq Pasha (1852-1892), Egyptian khedive, r. 1879-1892

Ismāʿīl Pasha (1830-1895), Egyptian khedive, r. 1863-1879

Frederick Beauchamp Paget Seymour (Baron Alcester; 1821-1895), commander in chief of British naval forces in the Mediterranean, 1880-1883

Garnet Joseph Wolseley (1833-1913), British military commander

SUMMARY OF EVENT

Burdened by massive debts to Europeans and heavy taxes imposed by a Turko-Circassian alliance that had dominated their country since 1805, angry Egyptians rose against all these outsiders in 1882. The story of this revolution begins, however, in the 1870's, with the profligate Ismāʿīl, Egypt's governor, or khedive (a title granted to him by the Ottoman sultan in 1867). As the Ottoman Empire had declined, the Ottoman governor had become Egypt's de facto ruler, and Ismāʿīl had ruled in that capacity since 1863. When he ran out of cash in the 1870's, he sold government bonds and obtained loans, mainly from Western banks, until, saddled with a debt of £90 million, he could find no other sources of credit. Two immediate results were his sale of Egypt's shares in the Suez Canal Company to Great Britain and the creation of the Caisse de la Dette Publique (public debt fund). The former greatly enhanced Great Britain's interest in Egyptian affairs, while the latter created a board of European supervisors who took control of Egypt's national budget.

The main purpose of the Caisse de la Dette Publique was to pay Egyptian debts on time. By 1880, it used 66 percent of state revenues to meet this goal. Other government expenditures were cut drastically across the board: Even the police and armed forces were affected. Military officers and soldiers, already owed back pay, now found themselves out of a job. Heavy taxes, combined with a shortage of capital, helped stifle an already weak economy. By 1878, Egypt's peasant farmers, the *fellaheen*, were so heavily in debt that they were abandoning their farms and moving into large cities like Cairo or Alexandria. This in turn created food shortages and greatly increased tensions among the urban poor.

The next year saw Ismāʿīl forced out of office and replaced by his son, Muḥammad Tawfīq Pasha, who also assumed the title of khedive. Muḥammad Tawfīq seemed better equipped to get along with the Europeans and their debt fund, but he was in a small minority among local notables. Most resented the Europeans as outsiders who, although representing only 2 percent of the government bureaucracy, received 15 percent of the total outlay for salaries. With Egyptians either owed months of back pay or being released from their cherished government jobs altogether, they probably agreed with an American eyewitness who castigated the Caisse de la Dette Publique as "that oligarchy of carpetbaggers."

Egyptian gunners attempting a futile defense against the British naval bombardment of Alexandria. (The Co-Operative Publishing Company)

Several disturbances resulted directly from the streamlined budgets forced upon Egypt by the Caisse de la Dette Publique. The first such disturbance was in Cairo: On July 18, 1879, army officers, some owed more than a year's worth of back pay, staged a protest that almost turned into a riot. Blatant discrimination fueled the dissatisfaction of these Egyptian officers, as Turkish, Circassian, and Albanian officers were protected by the regime. These foreign officers, collectively referred to by Egypt's majority Arabic-speakers as "Circassians," represented a ruling elite whose collaboration was considered vital to the preservation of the khedival throne. In reality, they were an inefficient and corrupt combination that despised native Egyptians and made every effort to dominate important military commands.

With no more than twenty thousand Circassians in the nation, Egypt had to fill lower military positions with Arabs. The latter, along with Sudanese recruits, represented 100 percent of the Egyptian rank and file and also dominated low- to mid-ranking officer slots. A good example of the latter was Arabi Pasha, who had risen to the rank of colonel before running into an iron barrier of discrimination. Arabi was a pious Muslim whose charisma and plainspoken manner found considerable support among his fellow Arabs. Early in the 1880's, he openly criticized the Circassians as incompetent outsiders who had bungled the failed war against Abyssinia (Ethiopia) in 1876.

The Circassian leadership responded with charges against Arabi, and through one of their own, Minister of War ʿUthmān Rifki, they initiated orders for Arabi to be transfered away from Cairo. While this might have worked in the 1870's, the army by now held little respect for its senior leaders. A riot on February 1, 1881, demonstrated this change in attitude, as soldiers of the elite First Infantry Regiment refused to follow legal orders issued by ʿUthmān Rifki and instead beat him up and freed pro-Arabi officers from their regimental jail.

A showdown took place on September 9: Fearing he would be arrested and murdered by the Circassians, Arabi marched two infantry regiments to the center of khedival power in Cairo, the ʿAbdīn Palace. There he read his famous statement, "By the name of God, besides whom there is no other, we shall no longer be inheritable, and from this day on we shall not be enslaved." Faced with four thousand disgruntled soldiers, Muḥammad Tawfīq rightfully feared for his life. He instantly agreed to dismiss all current government ministers, increase the army to eighteen thousand troops, and call a legislative assembly.

Thus began the Arabi Revolution (also known as the ʿUrābī Revolution). A nationalist government was formed, and Arabi became the minister of war. The government focused on ending foreign influence over Egypt. This goal naturally worried European investors, who feared Arabi could use his influence to end the power of the Caisse de la Dette Publique. Their voices joined those of diplomats, businessmen, and European expatriates living in Egypt. All called for intervention. On January 6, 1882, France and Great Britain issued a joint note to Egypt declaring their support for the khedive, while a powerful naval force was prepared for dispatch to Alexandria.

The diplomatic note infuriated Egyptian nationalists and enhanced Arabi's political capital. Tensions only increased on May 20, 1882, when the British and French squadron entered Alexandria and Muḥammad Tawfīq fled to his summer palace there. The next day, the rest of Egypt's cabinet resigned, and Arabi effectively became the nation's dictator. On May 25, another joint note from Great Britain and France demanded that Arabi and his supporters leave the government and go into exile. Arabi's response was to order repairs to Alexandria's coastal defense system. Admiral Frederick Beauchamp Paget Seymour, commander in chief of Britain's Royal Navy in the Mediterranean, viewed these repairs as an act of aggression and requested the right to destroy the city's defenses before they were improved.

Alexandria was the flash point for conflict in the summer of 1882. Although mainly an Arab city, it also held a considerable minority of European residents. Religious, economic, political, and international rivalries boiled over in June, leading to a series of riots. Although these riots were described as "Christian massacres" by the European press, only fifty foreigners were killed or wounded in them. They caused nearly three thousand Egyptian casualties.

On July 10, Admiral Seymour issued an ultimatum: Arabi's men must stop their work, or the British fleet would open fire. Arabi refused, and on July 11, Seymour's ships launched an artillery assault against the city, now known as the Bombardment of Alexandria. As Seymour's ironclad warships were nearly impervious to the defenders' small guns, the bombardment was rather one-sided. Within four hours, Egyptian batteries were silenced and Arabi's forces were evacuating the city. Between the June riots and July shellings, about half of Alexandria was in ruins.

A British occupation of Alexandria followed, but it did not end the fighting. Arabi withdrew his soldiers into the Nile Delta, where myriad canals funneled transportation along just a few main lines. The Egyptians were well entrenched by the time a British expeditionary force arrived under the command of General Garnet Joseph Wolseley. Looking to avoid a bloody encounter against fixed defenses, Wolseley skillfully boarded 17,400 of his troops, moving via the Suez Canal so he could land at Ismailia and approach Cairo from the more open terrain of eastern Egypt. Although surprised by this maneuver, Arabi was able to prepare new defenses manned by twenty-two thousand men at Tel el Kebir. Covering almost four miles, these defenses were formidable, and they commanded the high ground overlooking the railroad tracks connecting Ismailia to Cairo.

Wolseley scouted the Egyptian position and instantly ruled out a conventional assault, as it would "have entailed very great loss." Instead, he opted for a night advance, hoping to surprise the Egyptians and overwhelm their defenses. His cavalry was held in reserve, with orders to race for Cairo as soon as the infantry won a clear victory. Setting off at 1:30 A.M. on the morning of September 13, 1882, two British columns advanced on the Egyptian trenches. Both veered off their planned axis, but this mistake turned out to be a stroke of luck, because it allowed the British to avoid the strongest enemy fortifications. When they were finally discovered by Egyptian picquets at 4:55 A.M., some British troops were already within two hundred yards of the main line. A sharp fire fight broke out, but Wolseley's novel tactics had paid off. The Egyptians were surprised, and Arabi himself was asleep in the rear. Fighting ended around 5:30 A.M., when—with 2,000 dead and numerous wounded—the remaining Egyptians fled. British losses amounted to 57 killed and 412 wounded.

SIGNIFICANCE

Great Britain's victory at Tel el Kebir was decisive, causing the surrender of Cairo and ending the Arabi Revolution. More important, it signaled the beginnings of the "veiled protectorate," in which Great Britain dominated Egyptian governments behind the scenes until 1914. Ironically, then, by forcing the issue and precipitating armed conflict, the Arabi Revolution brought about the consolidation of foreign control of Egypt. World War I caused the "veil" over this control to be lifted, making it clear that Egypt was nearly a British colony, a situation that did not end until 1946.

—*John P. Dunn*

Further Readings:

Asad, Talal. *Formations of the Secular: Christianity, Islam, Modernity*. Stanford, Calif.: Stanford University Press, 2003. Explores the history, practice, and politics of secularism in the Middle East and the West.

Dunn, John P. *Khedive Ismail's Army*. London: Frank Cass, 2005. Detailed analysis of why Egyptian armies of the 1870's and 1880's consistently failed.

Featherstone, Donald. *Tel el-Kebir 1882. Wolseley's Conquest of Egypt*. London: Osprey, 1993. Looks at the battle from a British perspective. Excellent illustrations and maps.

Royle, Charles. *The Egyptian Campaigns 1882-1885*. London: Hurst and Blackett, 1900. A standard British account, probably the best.

Scholch, Alexander. *Egypt for the Egyptians*. London: Ithaca Press, 1981. The best scholarly work in English.

See also: 19th cent.: Arabic Literary Renaissance; Mar. 1, 1811: Muḥammad ʿAlī Has the Mamlūks Massacred; 1822-1874: Exploration of North Africa; Apr., 1868: British Expedition to Ethiopia; Nov. 17, 1869: Suez Canal Opens; Mar. 13, 1884-Jan. 26, 1885: Siege of Khartoum; Mar., 1896-Nov., 1899: Sudanese War; Mar. 1, 1896: Ethiopia Repels Italian Invasion.

Related articles in *Great Lives from History: The Nineteenth Century, 1801-1900:* Muḥammad ʿAbduh; John Bright; Jamāl al-Dīn al-Afghānī.

November 12, 1882
San Francisco's Chinese Six Companies Association Forms

Anti-Asian nativism prompted Chinese immigrants, mainly wealthy merchants, to organize the Chinese Six Companies for political representation, social services, and physical protection of the Chinese in the San Francisco area. The association's reach would soon encompass the entire United States.

Also known as: Chinese Consolidated Benevolent Association
Locale: San Francisco, California
Categories: Social issues and reform; organizations and institutions; economics

Key Figure

Huang Zunxian (Huang Tsun-hsien; 1848-1905), poet and Chinese consul general in San Francisco

Summary of Event

During the early years of the United States, relations with China consisted of a small amount of trade in scarce goods. After the second Opium War (1856-1860) forced the Chinese emperor to open coastal areas to foreign trade and settlement in 1842, U.S. business interests began to view China as a potential market for exports.

News of the California gold rush of 1848-1849 was the first catalyst for large Chinese emigration across the Pacific to the United States. Many dreamed of streets of gold, but most Chinese emigrants arrived too late to capitalize on the limited riches of gold. Although some did mine for gold, often taking over claims that had been abandoned by miners who had moved on to richer deposits, many others worked as laborers building the transcontinental railroad under dangerous conditions. As more Chinese arrived in the West, some whites began to resent the diligent work habits of the Chinese immigrants and feared that their willingness to work would bring down wages for all workers. Like many other groups of newly arrived immigrants to the United States, many Chinese chose to cling to their native language and customs and live with fellow Chinese immigrants.

The Chinese population in the United States at that time was overwhelmingly male. By 1880, more than 100,000 Chinese lived in the western United States, of which only three thousand were women. Because of the preponderance of men, many whites saw the Chinese as transient workers who wanted temporary jobs in the United States to prepare for future marriages after they returned to China. The completion of the railroads and the Panic of 1873 had caused great economic difficulties in the West. Frustrated by political and economic difficulties, many Euro-Americans and elements of organized labor began to blame the Chinese for the lack of jobs and the economic recession.

Violence against Chinese in this period was widespread. In October, 1871, crowds of whites burned and looted the Los Angeles Chinatown after two white policemen were killed by Chinese assailants. Nineteen men, women, and children were killed and hundreds injured as angry whites randomly attacked crowds of Chinese.

Hostility toward Chinese immigrants was reflected in the immigration laws of the period. Under intense political pressure from white voters in the West, Congress moved to exclude Chinese and other foreign-born Asians from obtaining citizenship. The 1870 Nationality Act denied the Chinese the possibility of becoming naturalized U.S. citizens, specifying that only foreign-born "free whites" and "African aliens" were eligible for citizenship. In 1878, California convened a constitutional convention to settle what was called the "Chinese problem." The adopted constitution prohibited further Chinese immigration and granted local municipalities the right to exclude Chinese immigrants or confine them to specified areas. California also prohibited Chinese, American Indians, and African Americans from attending public schools.

Chinese immigrants were prohibited from owning property, obtaining business licenses, procuring government jobs, and testifying in any legal proceedings. At the urging of white voters in California, Congress in 1882 passed the first of a number of Chinese exclusion acts that prohibited the entrance of Chinese into the United States. The U.S. Supreme Court upheld the exclusion acts, ruling in 1889 that the Chinese were "a race that will not assimilate with us [and] could be excluded when deemed dangerous to peace and security." President Grover Cleveland supported that act and echoed the Court's description of Chinese immigrants' role in American society.

In San Francisco, anti-Chinese laws were supplemented to isolate the large Chinese community. Since the gold rush, San Francisco had been a center for recent immigrants to the United States. Attracted by tales of wealth in San Francisco—Jinshan, or "golden mountain"—newly arrived Chinese were forced to settle in the Chinatown area because of local laws and hostility from whites. Local regulations penalized attempts by Chinese merchants to expand by levying special taxes on businesses. There was even a local tax on the long braided hair worn by Chinese men. Segregated by these discriminatory laws, Chinatown began to establish structures to govern and protect its residents. San Francisco's Chinatown, made up primarily of men as a result of the immigration control acts, had developed a reputation as a center of vice. Although most leaders at the time did not encourage assimilation with white society, they did move to control the small criminal element that began to define Chinese society to the non-Chinese residents of San Francisco.

Unemployed men loitering in San Francisco's Chinatown around the year 1900, when the city had the largest concentration of Chinese immigrants in North America. (Library of Congress)

Most of the early Chinese immigrants to San Francisco's Chinatown came from the southern provinces of Guangdong and Fujian. Early on, wealthy merchants in Chinatown had organized around clan groups and district associations in their hometowns in China. By 1854, there were six main associations in Chinatown. The first, formed in 1849, was the Gangzhou Gongsi, named after the district in Guangdong province that was the source of most of its members. The second, the San Yi Gongsi, consisted of immigrants from the administrative districts of Nanhai, Panyu, and Shunde. Immigrants from the districts of Yanging, Xinning, Xinhui, and Kaiping made up the third association, the Si Yi Gongsi. Immigrants from the Xiangshan area formed the fourth association, the Yang He Gongsi. The fifth, the Ren He Gongsi, was made up of the so-called Hakka peoples from Guanxi province.

The formation in 1854 of the sixth association, the Ning Yang Gongsi, marked the informal beginnings of the Chinese Six Companies Association. Formed first as a *kung saw* (public hall), the Six Companies served as a public association for leaders of the major associations in Chinatown to mediate disputes between their members and serve as a representative of the Chinese community as a whole. Newly arrived immigrants from China who were in need of assistance sought out these family or district associations rather than turn to local social service agencies. When business or personal disputes developed between members of different associations, the Six Companies would provide a forum for peaceful mediation of disputes.

The anti-Chinese legislation of the 1880's forced the Six Companies to move toward a more overt role as representatives of Chinese interests in San Francisco. In 1882, the Chinese consul general in San Francisco, poet Huang Zunxian, recognized the group as the leading body in Chinatown. The Six Companies moved toward creating a formal representative body within Chinatown to represent Chinese interests. On November 19, 1882, the group formalized its existence by establishing an executive body drawn from members of the existing associations. The Six Companies, formally known as the Chinese Consolidated Benevolent Association (CCBA), adapted some of the representative principles of U.S. political culture. After its reorganization, the office of the president served a specified term and the presidency rotated between member associations that made up the Six Companies.

The CCBA was recognized by the state of California in 1901. At the time, the Six Companies sought to create a body above family clans or associations that would resist the growing anti-Chinese movements in California and the western United States. While it would carry on its role as a mediator in Chinatown, the group now took a more public role in its resistance to anti-Chinese legislation.

Significance

After the CCBA's formal establishment in 1882, Chinese diplomats encouraged Chinese communities across the United States, Canada, and South America to establish Chinese Consolidated Benevolent Associations. The Six Companies in San Francisco had limited success in challenging anti-Chinese legislation as violations of the Fourteenth Amendment to the Constitution. The Six Companies supported the 1896 case of *Yue Ting v. Hopkins*, which forced the Supreme Court to overturn San Francisco safety ordinances designed to harass Chinese laundrymen.

Anti-Chinese attitudes in San Francisco and across the United States did not diminish after 1900. In 1902, an amendment to extend the Chinese Exclusion Act indefinitely was passed by Congress without debate. China boycotted U.S. goods to protest the legislation.

During the first half of the twentieth century, the Six Companies in San Francisco supported measures to improve the quality of life in Chinatown. In 1905, the Six Companies established a school in Chinatown to teach children Chinese culture and language. In 1943, Congress passed an immigration act that repealed the exclusion laws, and barriers to Chinese Americans in the United States began to fall. In California, many Americans of Chinese ancestry moved to white neighborhoods after anti-Chinese laws were overturned.

—*Lawrence I. Clark*

Further Reading

Chinn, Thomas W. *Bridging the Pacific: San Francisco Chinatown and Its People*. San Francisco, Calif.: Chinese Historical Society of America, 1989. A detailed look at San Francisco from its founding to the late 1980's, by the cofounder of the Chinese Historical Association of America. Includes photographs, clan charts, notes on transliteration, business directories, maps, a bibliography, and an index.

Kinkead, Gwen. *Chinatown: A Portrait of a Closed Society*. New York: HarperCollins, 1992. A valuable resource for observers interested in the inner workings of New York's Chinatown. Provides a detailed portrait of the role of the New York CCBA in its Chinatown.

Lai, Him Mark. *Becoming Chinese American: A History of Communities and Institutions*. Walnut Creek, Calif.: AltaMira, 2004. Explores the historical and cultural development of Chinese immigrants to the United States, with special emphasis on community organizations. Chapter 4 covers the CCBA.

Nee, Victor, and Brett de Barry Nee. "The Establishment." In *Longtime Californ': A Documentary Study of an American Chinatown*. New York: Pantheon Books, 1973. Examines the founding of the Six Companies and its role in Chinatown in the twentieth century.

SEE ALSO: 1849: Chinese Begin Immigrating to California; Oct. 23, 1856-Nov. 6, 1860: Second Opium War; July 28, 1868: Burlingame Treaty; May 10, 1869: First Transcontinental Railroad Is Completed; Feb. 12, 1873: "Crime of 1873"; Mar. 3, 1875: Congress Enacts the Page Law; May 9, 1882: Arthur Signs the Chinese Exclusion Act; 1892: America's "New" Immigration Era Begins; May 4, 1892: Anti-Japanese Yellow Peril Campaign Begins; May 10, 1895: Chinese Californians Form Native Sons of the Golden State; Mar. 28, 1898: *United States v. Wong Kim Ark*.

RELATED ARTICLES in *Great Lives from History: The Nineteenth Century, 1801-1900:* Grover Cleveland; Stephen J. Field.

1883
GALTON DEFINES "EUGENICS"

Francis Galton's term "eugenics," with its associated movement, became a rallying cry for social improvement, including appeals across the political spectrum. The disadvantages of trying to put eugenic theory into practice led to its near demise, culminating in the revulsion against the Nazi sterilization practices during the twentieth century.

LOCALE: London, England
CATEGORIES: Biology; genetics; social issues and reform

KEY FIGURES
Francis Galton (1822-1911), English statistician
Charles Darwin (1809-1882), English naturalist
Karl Pearson (1857-1936), English statistician
Thomas Robert Malthus (1766-1834), English economist

SUMMARY OF EVENT

The late nineteenth century saw a great deal of discussion of the consequences of the theory of heredity for human development. Francis Galton wrote extensively on the subject and pointed out the advantages to humanity of interfering with human reproduction in the way that breeders of dogs and other animals had produced certain desired characteristics. His writings led to the field of "eugenics," named for the term Galton derived from a Greek word meaning "well born."

In the course of human history, hereditary aristocracies and monarchies had tended to defend the system that perpetuated power and wealth according to birth by claiming that there were characteristics that were passed along within families that guaranteed that the offspring of noble parents would behave nobly. Many examples, however, had showed that in practice there could be enormous differences between parents and children. As a result, by the nineteenth century political power had often been transferred to other individuals and institutions, even in countries where hereditary monarchies still existed.

Two nineteenth century thinkers had contributed to the shaping of the issues Galton addressed. The first was

Francis Galton. (Library of Congress)

Thomas Robert Malthus, who had argued, using mathematical calculation, that a calamity was facing human society. The food supply, he claimed, was increasing at a linear rate (an arithmetic progression), and the human population was increasing at an exponential rate (a geometric progression). He concluded that no matter how much extra food there might be at any given time, ultimately, the population would outgrow the food supply and lead to devastating consequences.

The second thinker was Charles Darwin, the naturalist who formulated the theory of evolution. In his discussion of human descent, Darwin argued that human beings transmitted characteristics from one generation to the next in the same way that animals do. As a result, if there was some mechanism for passing along eye color among human beings, there might be a similar mechanism for passing along something related to intelligence. Darwin's ongoing battle with theologians kept him from pursuing the detailed application of the theory of evolution of human beings.

That did not stop other individuals from claiming that Darwin's theory could be applied to institutions as well. Using phrases such as "survival of the fittest" and "social Darwinism," individual thinkers argued that institutions evolved just in the way humans did. Because of this, institutions had the right to indulge in the same kind of unrestricted competition that was visible in nature.

Francis Galton was primarily interested in questions about the statistical basis for heredity and the evidence for evolution. He was the leading statistician of his time, and he tried to find ways of representing populations that indicated both the average characteristics and the extremes within those populations. One subject he devoted particular attention to was that of the hereditary nature of intelligence, because he believed that the human species was in dire need of increasing the proportion of those at the upper end of the spectrum of intelligence.

Galton addressed the subject a number of times, but in his 1883 book *Inquiries into the Human Faculty and Its Development*, he introduced the word "eugenics" and argued for the importance of transmitting the genes of those who, from one generation to the next, had displayed special talents and abilities. He complained about the "dysgenic" policies of the Middle Ages, in which the most-able individuals had been condemned to a life of celibacy. By contrast, he was endorsing the notion that the talented should be encouraged to marry early and to have many children.

It is difficult to know how seriously one should take Galton's suggestions about eugenics. His 1883 book also included an essay on the statistical effects of prayer, claiming that the evidence did not favor the claim that human prayer had any effects on the health of those for whom the prayers were made. Still, while the article on prayer was omitted from subsequent editions of the volume, the essay using the term "eugenics" remained part of the book.

By the end of Galton's life, he had taken eugenic issues much more seriously, claiming that it could be a mixture of science, religion, and social reform. His view attracted a large following among those who were concerned about the future of the species and who believed Darwinian theory provided a partial solution to the problem. The end of the nineteenth century brought a great

THE QUESTION OF EUGENICS

In a 1904 scholarly article, Francis Galton defined "eugenics" as "the science which deals with all influences that improve the inborn qualities of a race; also with those that develop them to the utmost advantage." Twenty-one years earlier, however, Galton had introduced the term "eugenic," albeit in a footnote to his 1883 book on the human faculty. His definition is excerpted here.

I do not propose to enter further into the anthropometric differences of race, for the subject is a very large one, and this book does not profess to go into detail. Its intention is to touch on various topics more or less connected with that of the cultivation of race, or, as we might call it, with "eugenic" questions, and to present the results of several of my own separate investigations. . . .

[footnote:] That is, with questions bearing on what is termed in Greek, *eugenes* namely, good in stock, hereditarily endowed with noble qualities. This, and the allied words, *eugeneia,* etc., are equally applicable to men, brutes, and plants. We greatly want a brief word to express the science of improving stock, which is by no means confined to questions of judicious mating, but which, especially in the case of man, takes cognisance of all influences that tend in however remote a degree to give to the more suitable races or strains of blood a better chance of prevailing speedily over the less suitable than they otherwise would have had. The word *eugenics* would sufficiently express the idea; it is at least a neater word and a more generalised one than *viriculture* which I once ventured to use.

Source: "Eugenics: Its Definition, Scope, and Aims" (1904), and *Inquiries Into Human Faculty and Its Development* (1883).

deal of apprehension about the degeneration of human beings, and individuals in various countries saw those in other countries as examples of this sort of degeneracy. Clearly, however, a certain amount of this degeneracy was in the eye of the beholder.

SIGNIFICANCE

The beginning of the twentieth century saw the founding of the Eugenics Education Society (1907) and an international congress on eugenics. Galton's influence would soon spread to countries like the United States and Germany as well. It was unclear, however, what form eugenics should take in practice, and Galton was not eager to try to turn his theory into practice (as in instituting some sort of legislation). Galton's successor, Karl Pearson, tried to steer investigations toward the scientific foundations of the heredity of intelligence and away from politics. Those who were not statisticians, however, showed no such reluctance, and different countries took various roads to "improve" their populations by eugenic means.

In many countries measures were taken to sterilize those who were thought to be unfit to reproduce. The strict definition of that particular characteristic was usually not brought before the public at large. In the United States, Indiana was the first state to try to enact legislation on the subject, but it was ruled unconstitutional. In contrast, Virginia produced legislation that passed one round of the constitutionality test, enacting a eugenics law in 1924. By the end of the year, the law faced the constitutionality test before the U.S. Supreme Court. By an 8-1 vote the Court, in 1927, supported the legitimacy of Virginia's measure, upholding the statute; sterilizations began on a regular basis for the mentally "unfit" until the statute was repealed nearly fifty years later.

On an even larger scale the Nazis of Germany in the 1930's began to sterilize those thought to be unfit. The initial sterilizations apparently were unrelated to the anti-Semitic racism that drove Adolf Hitler's policies. As the anti-Semitism stepped into higher gear, however, sterilization was considered insufficient. Instead, individuals were put to death for the crime of not being fit to reproduce.

In its earliest days, eugenics had been supported by some of the leading socialists in England, but it took the Nazi atrocities to place eugenics in a bad light. After the Nazi regime's crimes were revealed, eugenics took some time to shake the stigma. The Eugenics Education Society resorted to changing its name to the Galton Institute to disassociate itself from the loaded term "eugenics."

—*Thomas Drucker*

FURTHER READING

Blacker, C. P. *Eugenics: Galton and After*. Cambridge, Mass.: Harvard University Press, 1952. Written in the aftermath of World War II, this book attempts to defend eugenics against the critics of its excesses.

Brookes, Martin. *Extreme Measures: The Dark Visions and Bright Ideas of Francis Galton*. New York: Bloomsbury, 2004. Comprehensive biography written by a former evolutionary biologist. The author is impressed by the breadth of Galton's achievements, but condemns Galton's racist ideas, Victorian prejudices, and failure to understand the statistical ideas he devised.

Bulmer, Michael. *Francis Galton: Pioneer of Heredity and Biometry*. Baltimore: Johns Hopkins University Press, 2003. Regards Galton's eugenics as simply an outcome of his hereditarian and evolutionary investigations rather than as part of a political program.

Forrest, D. W. *Francis Galton: The Life and Work of a Victorian Genius*. London: Paul Elek, 1974. Ties Galton's eugenical writings to the events of his life.

Gillham, Nicholas Wright. *A Life of Sir Francis Galton: From African Exploration to the Birth of Eugenics*. New York: Oxford University Press, 2001. Ends with the story of the first international congress on eugenics and seeks to explain the success of eugenics in its time.

Kevles, Daniel J. *In the Name of Eugenics: Genetics and the Uses of Human Heredity*. Cambridge, Mass.: Harvard University Press, 1995. The standard account of the interactions between biology and eugenics.

Keynes, Milo, ed. *Sir Francis Galton, FRS: The Legacy of His Ideas*. London: Macmillan, 1993. Collection of papers bearing witness to the continued interest in Galton and eugenics without taking his premises for granted.

SEE ALSO: 1809: Lamarck Publishes *Zoological Philosophy*; 1854-1862: Wallace's Expeditions Give Rise to Biogeography; 1862: Spencer Introduces Principles of Social Darwinism; 1865: Mendel Proposes Laws of Heredity; Mar. 3, 1873: Congress Passes the Comstock Antiobscenity Law; 1882: First Birth Control Clinic Opens in Amsterdam; 1899-1900: Rediscovery of Mendel's Hereditary Theory.

RELATED ARTICLES in *Great Lives from History: The Nineteenth Century, 1801-1900:* Charles Darwin; Francis Galton; Ernst Haeckel; Thomas Robert Malthus; Gregor Mendel; Herbert Spencer.

1883-1885
WORLD'S FIRST SKYSCRAPER IS BUILT

Chicago architect William Jenney built the world's first skyscraper, the Home Insurance Building in Chicago, utilizing new steel-frame technology and aesthetic innovations that would inspire a generation of architects and forever change the design of urban buildings.

LOCALE: Chicago, Illinois
CATEGORIES: Architecture; engineering; science and technology

KEY FIGURES
William Le Baron Jenney (1832-1907), architect
Louis Sullivan (1856-1924), architect
Sir Henry Bessemer (1813-1898), inventor of the process by which steel could be mass-produced
Dankmar Adler (1844-1900), architect
Daniel Hudson Burnham (1846-1912), architect
John Wellborn Root (1850-1891), architect

SUMMARY OF EVENT

After the Great Fire that nearly destroyed Chicago in 1871, the city began to rebuild with an eye toward the future. A growing population, the scarcity of space in the city's central area, and the dramatic increase in the cost of land suggested that city planners consider taller buildings, but buildings rising beyond five or six stories faced considerable obstacles. Water pressure could not provide running water beyond about four floors, and using stairs made offices on the higher floors unpopular with customers and difficult to rent.

The most formidable obstacle to building tall, however, was structural. At the time, a building's exterior walls bore the weight of the entire structure, so as buildings grew taller, their exterior walls needed to be thicker, and the resulting heavier walls brought design limitations of their own.

By 1881, one of the city's most revered architects, William Le Baron Jenney, discovered that a thin frame of steel could support a tall building as effectively as thick exterior walls. Twenty-five years earlier, Sir Henry Bessemer had invented a process for mass-producing steel by blowing air through molten pig iron to remove carbon, dramatically reducing the cost of steel. Jenney designed a metal skeleton of vertical columns and horizontal beams that allowed him to use the exterior wall merely as a decorative and protective cover for the building rather than as its load bearer. Because the steel skeleton supported the weight of the entire structure, Jenney was able to design a facade that contained more windows than any previous building. The innovative design frightened city officials, who grew so concerned that they halted construction, which began in 1883, to investigate the building's safety. When completed in 1885, the Home Insurance Building, as it came to be known, rose to a height of ten stories—138 feet—and would be considered the world's first skyscraper.

Across town, a young architect named Louis Sullivan was working on the problem of how a skyscraper should look. Most of the architecture of the time reflected a Gothic Revival style, but Sullivan, an unusually innovative designer, was developing a model by which buildings would not only rise far above ground level but also support his highly original terra-cotta and cast iron orna-

Chicago's Home Insurance Building.

1880's

mentation. His solution to the design problem was to envision the building not horizontally as a series of floors, but vertically, emphasizing the rise of each floor, similar to a classical Ionic or Corinthian column—with a distinct base, shaft, and ornate capital.

Typically, Sullivan's buildings consisted of a two-story base supporting a shaft of large windows topped by a decorative terra-cotta cornice as its capital. The extensive use of glass to replace exterior walls eventually led to the development of a window with a large fixed-glass panel flanked on each side by a double-hung operable sash, a design that came to be called a "Chicago window."

Many of the most ambitious and aesthetically innovative building projects of the period were designed by either Sullivan or his partner, Dankmar Adler. The Auditorium Building, constructed in 1889, was Chicago's tallest, largest, and heaviest building at the time, enclosing 63,500 square feet and weighing well over 100,000 tons. It was also the most technologically advanced building of its time, encompassing a hotel, office space, retail stores, and a state-of-the-art theater with a hydraulically operated stage, air conditioning, and acoustics that were considered nearly perfect.

The Transportation Building, constructed for the 1893 World's Columbian Exposition, was 960 feet long and had an enormous entryway called the Golden Door, consisting of a series of arches decorated with gold leaf ornamentation. The Guaranty Building in Buffalo, New York, designed in 1895 by Sullivan, is acknowledged as one of the era's most beautiful and ornate designs and a masterpiece of the Chicago School of Architecture, as is the Carson, Pirie, Scott Building, a Chicago department store designed by Sullivan in two phases between 1899 and 1903.

The most architecturally advanced of the early skyscrapers was the Reliance Building, designed by Daniel Hudson Burnham in 1895. Burnham and his business partner, John Wellborn Root, designed so many of the decade's most impressive buildings that Burnham and Root came to rival Adler and Sullivan as Chicago's premier architectural firm. In his design for the Reliance Building, Burnham eliminated all of the support functions of the exterior wall, creating a white terra-cotta facade that weaves in and out along all four sides and incorporates a creative and attractive variation on the Chicago window. Most critics consider it the masterpiece of the Chicago school's office buildings. Even more aesthetically creative was the Flatiron Building, New York City's first steel-frame skyscraper, built in 1902 in a triangular shape resembling the irons used at the time to press creases from clothing.

SIGNIFICANCE

With the wide availability of inexpensive steel, the "Chicago skeleton" became the urban architectural model for years to come, and by the turn of the twentieth century, all the developments necessary for skyscrapers to move to forty stories and beyond, including central heating, elevators, and pressurized plumbing, had been invented.

Just five years after the construction of the Home Insurance Building, Burnham and Root built Chicago's last high-rise to have load-bearing walls—the Monadnock Building. It rose to a height of sixteen stories but was entirely supported by conventional load-bearing walls, built six-feet thick at the base. Within a generation, skyscrapers were appearing around the world and had grown to heights unimaginable just a few decades earlier.

The New York World Building followed five years after the Home Insurance Building and doubled its height. At the beginning of the twentieth century, Manhattan had more than twenty buildings exceeding fifteen stories. By 1910, a mere twenty-five years after Jenney's first skyscraper, the Woolworth Building in New York, designed by Cass Gilbert in the Gothic Revival style, had reached more than 700 feet into the sky and was considered one of the world's great works of art. The Home Insurance Building was itself demolished in 1931 to make room for an even larger structure.

The aesthetic innovations that the new steel skeletons permitted came to represent the ideal in sophisticated architectural art. Replicas of Sullivan's terra-cotta designs were mass produced and used to decorate buildings throughout small-town America, as well as being widely copied by other architects, and the Chicago window was used in buildings across America until the 1960's, when the widespread use of air-conditioning eliminated the need to open windows.

—Devon Boan

FURTHER READING

Douglas, George H. *Skyscrapers: A Social History of the Very Tall Building in America*. Jefferson, N.C.: McFarland, 2004. A readable history of the skyscraper's influence on urban life, with an emphasis on the dynamics of their construction.

Hudson, Leslie A. *Chicago Skyscrapers*. Mount Pleasant, S.C.: Arcadia, 2004. A photographic history of Chicago's early (1880's-1930's) skyscrapers through the use of two hundred vintage picture postcards.

Lepik, Andres. *Skyscrapers*. New York: Prestel, 2004. A brief historical look at fifty of the world's most important skyscrapers. Beautifully photographed, this work includes photos of several early skyscrapers, beginning with the Reliance Building in Chicago.

Moudry, Roberta. *The American Skyscraper: Cultural Histories*. New York: Cambridge University Press, 2005. An examination of the skyscraper as a social, political, and architectural influence on cities, especially Chicago and New York, where the first skyscrapers were built.

Wells, Matthew. *Skyscrapers: Structure and Design*. New Haven, Conn.: Yale University Press, 2005. An engaging work by a structural engineer outlining the architectural principles behind the construction of skyscrapers, including environmental challenges such as high wind and earthquakes.

SEE ALSO: July 4, 1848: Ground Is Broken for the Washington Monument; 1855: Bessemer Patents Improved Steel-Processing Method; Mar. 23, 1857: Otis Installs the First Passenger Elevator; 1869: First Modern Department Store Opens in Paris; Oct. 8-10, 1871: Great Chicago Fire; Oct. 28, 1886: Statue of Liberty Is Dedicated; Mar. 31, 1889: Eiffel Tower Is Dedicated; May 1-Oct. 30, 1893: Chicago World's Fair; Nov. 1, 1897: New Library of Congress Building Opens.

RELATED ARTICLES in *Great Lives from History: The Nineteenth Century, 1801-1900:* Sir Henry Bessemer; Daniel Hudson Burnham; Louis Sullivan.

January 16, 1883
PENDLETON ACT REFORMS THE FEDERAL CIVIL SERVICE

The Pendleton Act created the U.S. Civil Service Commission in order to do away with the political spoils system and replace it with a merit-based system of employment by the federal government.

ALSO KNOWN AS: National Civil Service Act
LOCALE: Washington, D.C.
CATEGORIES: Government and politics; laws, acts, and legal history; terrorism and political assassination

KEY FIGURES

George Hunt Pendleton (1825-1889), Democrat from Ohio who sponsored the act bearing his name

Dorman Bridgman Eaton (1823-1899), secretary of the National Civil Service Reform League and first head of the Civil Service Commission

Chester A. Arthur (1829-1886), president of the United States, 1881-1885

James A. Garfield (1831-1881), president of the United States, 1881

Charles Julius Guiteau (1841-1882), disappointed office seeker who shot Garfield

SUMMARY OF EVENT

On July 2, 1881, President James A. Garfield prepared to leave Washington for a vacation in New York State. As the presidential party neared the waiting train, Garfield was shot in the back by Charles Julius Guiteau, an unsuccessful aspirant to the office of consul to Paris. He shouted, "I am a Stalwart, and Arthur is president now!"

Even in an age of widespread graft, Chester A. Arthur, the vice president, had been well known as the head of the New York Customs House, a classically corrupt government agency, and as a spoilsman in Roscoe Conkling's New York Republican political machine. Few expected him to change when he became president at Garfield's death on September 19, but he exhibited an unanticipated coolness toward the Stalwarts (professional machine Republicans) in selecting cabinet replacements and insisted on continuing the prosecution of the "Star Route" mail fraud case. These actions are credited with costing Arthur the presidential nomination in 1884, as well as with providing the Democrats with numerous victories in the elections of fall, 1882. As a result, the outgoing Republican Congress was impelled to adopt civil service reform legislation in 1883.

In the end, however, a confluence of factors was responsible for civil service reform. George Washington, when he was president, had initiated the idea that persons of high competence and integrity should be sought to fill public service jobs. This approach resulted in a stable and fairly skilled workforce but contributed to its elite quality. When Andrew Jackson became president in 1829, he operated under the belief that the "common man" had as much right to a government job as the wealthy and that most government jobs could be done by people without special training. He democratized the civil service but also helped justify the spoils system.

By the 1880's, the number of public jobs had greatly increased, and the quality of those serving in them had

THE PENDLETON ACT

The Pendleton Act brought an end to the so-called spoils system in the U.S. civil service, replacing it with a merit-based system in which candidates for government jobs had to pass examinations evaluating their competence. The section of the act excerpted below describes the rules that should be established to govern these examinations.

SECOND. And, among other things, said rules shall provide and declare, as nearly as the conditions of good administration will warrant, as follows:

First, for open, competitive examinations for testing the fitness of applicants for the public service now classified or to be classified here-under. Such examinations shall be practical in their character, and so far as may be shall relate to those matters which will fairly test the relative capacity and fitness of the persons examined to discharge the duties of the service into which they seek to be appointed.

Second, that all the offices, places, and employments so arranged or to be arranged in classes shall be filled by selections according to grade from among those graded highest as the results of such competitive examinations.

Third, appointments to the public service aforesaid in the departments at Washington shall be apportioned among the several States and Territories and the District of Columbia upon the basis of population as ascertained at the last preceding census. Every application for an examination shall contain, among other things, a statement, under oath, setting forth his or her actual bona fide residence at the time of making the application, as well as how long he or she has been a resident of such place.

Fourth, that there shall be a period of probation before any absolute appointment or employment aforesaid.

Fifth, that no person in the public service is for that reason under any obligations to contribute to any political fund, or to render any political service, and that he will not be removed or otherwise prejudiced for refusing to do so.

Sixth, that no person in said service has any right to use his official authority or influence to coerce the political action of any person or body.

Seventh, there shall be non-competitive examinations in all proper cases before the commission, when competent persons do not compete, after notice has been given of the existence of the vacancy, under such rules as may be prescribed by the commissioners as to the manner of giving notice.

Eighth, that notice shall be given in writing by the appointing power to said commission of the persons selected for appointment or employment from among those who have been examined, of the place of residence of such persons, of the rejection of any such persons after probation, of transfers, resignations, and removals and of the date thereof, and a record of the same shall be kept by said commission. And any necessary exceptions from said eight fundamental provisions of the rules shall be set forth in connection with such rules, and the reasons there-for shall be stated in the annual reports of the commission.

declined. Several reform attempts failed. The first serious attempt to reform the system was led by Thomas Allen Jenckes, a Republican congressman from Rhode Island. Jenckes was a patent lawyer by profession and also had financial interests in several companies. In both activities he had to rely on the federal mail service, which was inefficient and corrupt. In 1865 he introduced his first civil service reform bill covering all federal agencies, including the U.S. Post Office. His proposal was patterned after the British system and would have covered all federal officials except those appointed by the president with the consent of the Senate. A decade later a number of organized reform groups around the country, concerned first with local and then with national corruption, were formed. A national reform movement was spearheaded by the National Civil Service Reform League, presided over by George William Curtis.

The assassination of Garfield was the spark that lit the smoldering coals not only of the reformers' attempts but also of elected officials' weariness with long lines of people seeking jobs and patronage appointees' weariness with blatant assessments of percentages of their salaries for political party support. The Republican Congress's assessment that its power might be about to end in the wake of Arthur's presidency also contributed an impetus to reform, since its party would no longer be the one to benefit from the patronage system. Therefore, after the midterm elections, the outgoing Republican Congress passed an act drafted by Dorman Bridgman Eaton, secretary of the National Civil Service Reform League, and sponsored by Democratic senator George Hunt Pendleton of Ohio. Passed on January 16, 1883, the National Civil Service Act was commonly known as the Pendleton Act, after its sponsor.

The act had two purposes: to eliminate political influence from administrative agencies and to ensure more competent government employees. It established a three-member bipartisan Civil Service Commission appointed by the president with the consent of the Senate for indefinite terms. Eaton became the first chairman of the Civil Service Commission.

On July 2, 1881, President James A. Garfield was shot by Charles J. Guiteau, a frustrated office seeker. He lived until September 19. During the intervening eighty days, he lay gravely ill and the office of the presidency virtually ceased to function. (Library of Congress)

About 10 percent of the government positions were included initially, but other positions, to be designated by the president, could be "covered in"; that is, current patronage appointees could remain in their positions when those positions were included under the act. This provision gave outgoing presidents an incentive to "cover in" increasing numbers of positions over time, which is in fact what happened. The act provided that civil service positions were to be filled through open and competitive examinations; lateral entry was encouraged, and employees were assured tenure regardless of political changes at the tops of the organizations. Employees were also protected against political pressures such as assessments and required participation in campaign activities.

SIGNIFICANCE

The adoption of a merit system at the federal level was followed immediately by similar adoptions in some of the states. Widespread coverage at the state and local levels was subsequently brought about through requirements attached to most federal grant moneys. The spoils system gradually disappeared—at least as an acknowledged or accepted practice—at all levels of American governance.

Over the years, legislation was added to improve the civil service system. The Classification Act of 1923 established a system for classifying jobs according to qualifications needed to carry them out and tying them to various pay grades, thus providing uniformity throughout the federal system. The Hatch Political Activities Act of 1939 prohibited national civil service workers from taking an active part in politics, and later amendments extended the ban to state and local employees whose programs were financed fully or in part by federal funds. In 1978 the Civil Service Reform Act reassigned the Civil Service Commission's often contradictory functions to two agencies: a new Office of Personnel Management, responsible for policy leadership, and a Merit Systems

Protection Board, to handle investigations and appeals. A Senior Executive Service was also established, creating a separate personnel system for the highest-ranking civil service officials in an attempt to provide greater flexibility in assignments and incentives for top senior personnel.

—*Anne Trotter, updated by Erika E. Pilver*

FURTHER READING

Ackerman, Kenneth D. *Dark Horse: The Surprise Election and Political Murder of President James A. Garfield*. New York: Carroll & Graf, 2003. Focuses on the battling among Republicans for patronage and spoils, describing how this fighting resulted in Garfield's assassination by Charles Guiteau, a disappointed patronage seeker.

Cayer, N. Joseph. *Public Personnel Administration in the United States*. New York: St. Martin's Press, 1986. A good survey of the U.S. civil service to date.

Emmerich, Herbert. *Federal Organization and Administrative Management*. University: University of Alabama Press, 1971. A classic in the field, useful for coverage through the 1960's.

Hoogenboom, Ari. *Outlawing the Spoils: A History of the Civil Service Reform Movement, 1865-1883*. Urbana: University of Illinois Press, 1961. Attacks the stereotypes of the "evil" spoilsmen and the "noble" reformers.

Ingraham, Patricia, and Carolyn Ban, eds. *Legislating Bureaucratic Change: The Civil Service Reform Act of 1978*. Albany: State University of New York Press, 1984. An account of the act's provisions and an analysis of their implementation.

SEE ALSO: Dec. 3, 1828: U.S. Election of 1828; July 6, 1854: Birth of the Republican Party; Nov. 4, 1884: U.S. Election of 1884; Feb. 4, 1887: Interstate Commerce Act; July 20, 1890: Harrison Signs the Sherman Antitrust Act.

RELATED ARTICLES in *Great Lives from History: The Nineteenth Century, 1801-1900:* Chester A. Arthur; James A. Garfield; Andrew Jackson.

May 24, 1883
BROOKLYN BRIDGE OPENS

When the Brooklyn Bridge opened to traffic, it was considered an engineering marvel that set new standards for aesthetic design of utilitarian structures. More than a century later, its reputation remained undiminished.

LOCALE: New York, New York

CATEGORIES: Engineering; science and technology; transportation

KEY FIGURES

John Augustus Roebling (1806-1869), American engineer who designed suspension bridges

Washington Augustus Roebling (1837-1926), Roebling's son, who directed the Brooklyn Bridge's construction

Emily Roebling (1843-1903), Washington Roebling's wife

Charles Ellet (1810-1862), European-trained American engineer

SUMMARY OF EVENT

On May 24, 1883, U.S. president Chester A. Arthur and New York governor Grover Cleveland, together with the mayors of New York and Brooklyn, met with thousands of citizens in attendance to open the majestic Brooklyn Bridge, which was described as the eighth wonder of the world. A marvel of engineering, this suspension bridge seemed to many people to be a symbol of the American way of life—free, useful, and beautiful. The height of the bridge's Gothic towers, from which hung the great cables and suspenders that supported the roadway, was matched only by the tower of Trinity Church in lower Manhattan. Completion of the bridge made it possible to cross the entire North American continent without once having to use a ferry or get one's feet wet.

The person who envisioned this nineteenth century marvel was John Augustus Roebling, a man whose life in many ways exemplified the American Dream. Born in the Saxon town of Mülhausen in 1806, he acquired his training in engineering at Berlin's Royal Polytechnic Institute. There he was strongly influenced by the philosopher Georg Wilhelm Friedrich Hegel, who imbued him with liberal ideas and the belief that the United States was the land of hope and destiny. After becoming disillusioned with the repressive politics of Germany, Roebling emigrated to the United States with several friends in 1831.

The Brooklyn Bridge shortly after its completion. (R. S. Peale/J. A. Hill)

contracts. Roebling eventually won the title Master of the Suspension Bridge in 1854, after the bridge Ellet built over the Ohio River at Wheeling collapsed, and Roebling was hired to rebuild it. During the 1850's, Roebling's reputation soared. His bridge over the Niagara River, two miles below the falls, was an advanced structure that carried both railroad tracks and a highway. The hallmarks of his work were utility and grace.

By any standards, Roebling's greatest structure was the Brooklyn Bridge. Not only did he design it, but he also originated the project itself. He conceived the idea of linking New York City and Brooklyn by bridge in 1857 and did the preliminary planning but was unable to attract sufficient public support to begin construction. Interest in his project began to revive in 1865. When, during the following winter, the East River—which separated Manhattan and Brooklyn—iced over on several occasions and ferry service was disrupted, irate citizens demanded that something be done.

Roebling and his German friends settled in western Pennsylvania, where they established the town of Saxonburg, and most of them became farmers. In 1837, the year he became a naturalized citizen, he gave up farming to become a state canal surveyor. This work brought him into contact with a new invention that hauled railroad cars and heavy loads up steep inclines by means of a stationary engine and a heavy hemp rope. Noticing that the hemp constantly frayed and threatened to break, Roebling designed a superior rope made from metal wire and formed a company to manufacture it in 1841. Roebling's firm provided Saxonburg with a needed industry and gave Roebling an income that allowed him the financial independence to work only on projects that interested him.

In 1846, Roebling completed his first suspension bridge across the Monongahela River at Pittsburgh. By midcentury he had designed and constructed five others. For more than a decade, his chief rival in the field was Charles Ellet, the first native-born American to receive European training in engineering. The first competition between the two men had occurred in 1841, when both engineers submitted designs for a suspension bridge across the Schuylkill River at Fairmount. At the last minute, Ellet's proposal was adopted. Although an excellent engineer, Ellet never achieved financial independence because his abrasive temperament cost him numerous

Roebling's plans were then finally approved, and a company was commissioned in 1869 to build the bridge. However, the magnitude of the project was considered to be so great that pessimists said it could not be done. The total length of the structure was to be 1,596.6 feet (487 meters); its 86-foot-wide (26.2 meters) deck would accommodate two sets of railroad tracks, two electric tram lines, two roadways, and a footpath. Four cables and their accompanying suspenders would have to carry a weight of 18,700 tons.

Construction of the bridge began on January 3, 1870. The chief engineer was a Roebling, but not John. During the previous summer, John Roebling had been injured in an accident while selecting the site for the bridge's Brooklyn tower. Despite the amputation of several toes, he contracted tetanus and died. Directors of the construction company then selected his thirty-two-year-old son to succeed him. Washington Roebling, a graduate of Rensselaer Polytechnic Institute, had worked with his father on several projects, including the great Cincinnati Bridge. He had earned a reputation as a civil engineer in his own right while serving in the Union army during the Civil War (1861-1865).

Washington Roebling's first task in erecting the Brooklyn Bridge was to build the huge caissons on which the support towers were to rest. Working as much as eighty feet below the surface of the water was both difficult and extremely hazardous, the greatest danger being from the dreaded caisson disease known as the bends, which was caused by pressure changes. During the first five months of 1872, more than one hundred men were hospitalized with the ailment, and three died.

One of the most seriously affected by the bends was Washington Roebling himself. He was left disabled, almost mute, and in constant pain for the rest of his life. Unable to inspect work on the bridge personally, he relied upon his memory, a pair of binoculars, and his wife, Emily, who taught herself engineering in order to help him. Month after month he sat by a window watching the construction through binoculars, ordering adjustments as needed and sending messages to the workmen through Emily. The design of the bridge remained faithful to the drawings of his father but included numerous alterations devised by Washington Roebling.

With as many as six hundred workmen engaged on the bridge at one time, it slowly began to take shape, but its costs mounted considerably beyond expectations. In 1878, Washington Roebling announced that he had already spent $13.5 million—almost twice the amount of the original estimate. For six months, all work stopped until new funds could be raised. In 1881, Roebling almost was fired when he asked for an extra thousand tons of steel to reinforce the decking, and his demand was met only after a fight.

In 1882, Roebling faced the greatest crisis of his professional life. The newly elected mayor of Brooklyn called into question Roebling's competence and was determined to oust him as the bridge's chief engineer. The unexpressed fear was that, given Roebling's physical infirmity, some of the decisions relating to the bridge were being made by his wife. Many people questioned the ability of women to deal with technical matters. Emily maintained that she always consulted with her husband before instructions were given to his assistants. She now was determined to save both her husband's reputation and his position. She began a letter-writing campaign; she persuaded a key trustee to visit her husband to ascertain his mental capabilities. Largely as a result of her efforts, the effort to remove him failed by two votes. Roebling would still be the bridge's chief engineer when his masterpiece was completed.

Eight months later, on May 24, 1883, Roebling sat in his chair by a window to watch the ceremonies as the Brooklyn Bridge was opened to traffic. Celebrations followed.

Significance

Both the Roeblings and the principle of suspension-bridge design were amply vindicated. Clearly, this type of bridge could be used to span great distances. So soundly was the Brooklyn Bridge constructed that no substantial renovation was necessary until the late 1940's. Equally important was the establishment of the architectural principle that a utilitarian object should be attractively designed, a concept fully accepted by contemporary architects. In 1964, the Brooklyn Bridge was declared a national monument.

Important as it was, the building of the Brooklyn Bridge was but a single detail during an era of great industrial expansion in the United States after the Civil War, when the country emerged as a major industrial power. It was a period of corruption, greed, and the creation of great wealth. It was also the period of the political bosses. By the turn of the century, every major city had one. New York was among the first. However, the Brooklyn Bridge probably never would have been built had it not had the backing of the political bosses of both Brooklyn and New York. By the time William Marcy Tweed, New York's political boss, fell from power, the bridge had been declared a "public work" by the state legislature, and despite opposition, the project continued to completion.

—*Anne Trotter, updated by Nis Petersen*

Further Reading

Brooklyn Museum. *The Great East River Bridge, 1883-1983*. New York: Harry N. Abrams, 1983. Commemorative volume on the bridge's centennial. Contains primary source material, such as eyewitness accounts, cartoons, and articles, as well as reproductions of works of art with the bridge as subject.

Cadbury, Deborah. *Dreams of Iron and Steel: Seven Wonders of the Nineteenth Century, from the Building of the London Sewers to the Panama Canal*. New York: Fourth Estate, 2004. Popular history of notable construction projects of the nineteenth century, including the Brooklyn Bridge.

McCullogh, David G. *The Great Bridge: The Epic Story of the Brooklyn Bridge*. 1972. Reprint. New York: Simon & Schuster, 2001. One of the best all-around accounts of the building of the bridge. Deals with the technical details in an understandable manner, using a mystery writer's ability to build suspense.

Mandelbaum, Seymour J. *Boss Tweed's New York*. Chicago: Ivan R. Dee, 1990. Often misunderstood, the political bosses and their impact on U.S. political and economic life are being reexamined. This author discusses one of the best-known, most-criticized political bosses and finds much of what he did commendable.

Trachtenberg, Alan. *Brooklyn Bridge: Fact and Symbol*. New York: Oxford University Press, 1965. Extended essay on the Brooklyn Bridge that fits its construction into a socioeconomic context, not only as a cultural symbol but also as an indication of the transition of the United States from a rural to an urbanized economy.

Weigold, Marilyn E. *Silent Builder: Emily Warren Roebling and the Brooklyn Bridge*. Port Washington, N.Y.: Associated Faculty Press, 1984. Short but thorough study of Emily Roebling's role in building the bridge, which argues that she was in full charge at times.

See also: 1855: Bessemer Patents Improved Steel-Processing Method; Jan. 10, 1863: First Underground Railroad Opens in London; Oct. 28, 1886: Statue of Liberty Is Dedicated; Mar. 31, 1889: Eiffel Tower Is Dedicated.

Related articles in *Great Lives from History: The Nineteenth Century, 1801-1900:* Isambard Kingdom Brunel; Marc Isambard Brunel; James Buchanan Eads; Gustave Eiffel; John Augustus Roebling; Thomas Telford; William Marcy Tweed.

1880's

August 27, 1883
Krakatoa Volcano Erupts

The eruption of Krakatoa was one of the most powerful and deadly volcanic eruptions in recorded history, initially killing more than thirty-six thousand people in the region with its main blast. The eruption's aftereffects reached global proportions, as it triggered tsunamis, altered weather patterns and atmospheric conditions, and blurred and darkened skies.

Locale: Krakatoa Island, Dutch East Indies (now Indonesia)

Categories: Disasters; natural disasters; geology; earth science; environment and ecology

Key Figure

Rogier Verbeek (1845-1926), Dutch colonial official who published a major study of the eruption in 1886

Summary of Event

A 60,000-year-old volcanic island, Krakatoa exploded on Monday, August 27, 1883. Before its cataclysmic disappearance, Krakatoa was a 15-square-mile island with abundant wildlife and plants, about midway in the Sunda Strait. The strait separates the much larger islands of Java and Sumatra and is a major gateway to the Indian Ocean. Krakatoa island was 22 miles (35 kilometers) from Java and 30 miles (50 kilometers) from Sumatra.

The three islands, as well as many others directly east, were part of the former Dutch East Indies. The Dutch colonial government occupied Krakatoa at different times and for different reasons. It was used as a lookout station, a small shipyard, a base for a small fishing fleet, and a prison for indigenous peoples. The island, however, was uninhabited when it erupted.

The eruption's human tragedy occurred in the densely populated coastlines inside the Sunda Strait facing the volcano. Before the explosion, tens of thousands of people lived in small fishing villages and towns, Dutch-owned plantations, and small farms in the exposed areas. Virtually everyone in the blast zone thought that Krakatoa was a harmless silhouette of tropical green forest on the horizon, and it was relatively distant and had not erupted in more than two hundred years.

On May 20, Krakatoa's magma chamber hurled its first fiery cloud of pyroclasts (burning particles of rock, ash, and cinders). The explosion was the start of the island's great disappearing act, which would end dramatically on August 27. The May 20 eruption was large enough to destroy virtually all the island's vegetation. Showers of pyroclasts from the blast fell on passing ships, but there were no injuries on board. The Sunda Strait's Dutch, Chinese, and indigenous settlers were surprised, and some were even terrified, by the sound of the explosion, but they experienced only an annoying film of ash.

Just seven days after the eruption, a Dutch steamship company in Batavia (now Jakarta) loaded tourists on an excursion vessel that landed on the island. Aside from burning the soles of their shoes, the sightseers spent an uneventful afternoon on the still-fuming volcano. For the next three months, the volcano rumbled, spit out gas and steam, and provided delightful pyroclastic displays for people on Java and Sumatra and passers-by on ships. The last human being to stand on Krakatoa was a Dutch army captain sent there to begin mapping the altered island. Intent on returning, he left with a half-finished map on August 12.

The first of four larger convulsions began Sunday evening, August 26, 1883. The second and third explosions took place at around 5:30 A.M. and 7 A.M. on August 27. The same day, the sequence ended with the most violent explosion in recorded history at about 10 A.M. The final blast was especially powerful partly because earlier explosions tore fissures into the sides of the volcano. These ruptures allowed seawater to rapidly pour into the underground magma chamber. The mixture of superheated seawater and magma created a marked buildup of pressure inside. The mountain suddenly became like a giant pressure cooker. The flanks of the mountain gave way to the pent-up pressure by bursting outward and upward.

The energy released by the four explosions equaled the force of 100 million tons of dynamite. (The force of the Hiroshima nuclear bomb during World War II was about 20,000 tons of dynamite.) More than 6 cubic miles (25 cubic kilometers) of rock, ash, and pumice blew skyward. Furthermore, each of Krakatoa's explosions generated one large and several small tsunamis (seismic sea waves), which occur after the spastic motions of an exploding island volcano or the jolts of an earthquake on the sea floor pass energy into the water. These waves move through deep water practically undetected, but as they approach a shoreline through more shallow water, they gain height rapidly.

The tsunamis washed over small islands and completely wiped out their populations before reaching Java and Sumatra's coastline. Each wave's arrival must have been terrifying. If victims had not drowned right away, then thrashing water and swirling tree trunks and other debris pummeled them to death. Krakatoa's fourth and final eruption created by far the largest, most destructive wave, which reached heights up to 115 feet (35 meters) in some places. In comparison, Tambora, another Indonesian volcano, erupted in 1815 and killed ninety-two thousand people, during and after its main explosion. Krakatoa's toll of more than thirty-six thousand deaths came directly from the volcano's eruption. Tambora's main blast killed about 12,000 people; post-eruption starvation and disease took the remaining lives.

Evidence of the volcano's massive convulsion was obvious near and far. The volcano had disappeared, except for a small piece of its southern flank (now Rakata Island). The tsunamis destroyed 295 villages and killed more than 36,000 people in the Sunda Strait. A ship sailing west through the strait reported seeing bloated human corpses in groups of fifty to one hundred for two days. In the Indian Ocean, hundreds of miles from where the island once stood, ships navigated through acres of floating pumice (a porous lightweight volcanic rock). The skies as far east as Batavia—80 miles (130 kilometers) distant—were nearly pitch-black by midday on Monday, two hours after the largest explosion. Several hours later, a tsunami killed a woman while working in a rice paddy 2,000 miles (3,200 kilometers) away in Ceylon. She was probably the most distant casualty.

Twelve hours later, a tsunami of notable height—

KRAKATOA IN MODERN INDONESIA

Krakatoa before its eruption. (Library of Congress)

4 feet (1.2 meters)—struck the southeastern coast of Africa. Ocean currents washed pumice and the sun-bleached skeletons of victims onto the same coast more than one year after the eruption. Airborne shockwaves recorded on barographs traveled around Earth seven times and continued for fifteen days. Winds scattered volcanic aerosols—tiny particles of airborne dust and sulfuric acid—around the globe. The aerosols caused multihued and vermillion sunrises and sunsets for months. These atmospheric effects were reported from latitudes covering 70 percent of the globe, ranging from Reykjavik, Iceland, to Buenos Aires, Argentina.

In 1885-1886, Rogier Verbeek, a Dutch colonial official in Batavia, published a detailed study of the eruption called *Krakatau*. The Royal Society (Great Britain's national academy of science) collected reports of the eruption's effects from more than eight hundred locations around the world, presenting its own report in 1888.

SIGNIFICANCE

The Krakatoa eruption, infamous for its physical effects, remains the deadliest volcanic explosion in recorded history. The blast caused an immense sonic reverberation, as the sound of its main blast traveled 2,900 miles (4,660 kilometers). No other natural sound is known to have traveled so far. Additionally, modern tree-ring analyses suggest that Krakatoa's aerosols blocked enough solar energy from reaching Earth's surface to reduce average global temperatures to below normal. The average solar radiation in Europe decreased 10 percent and crop yields decreased as well.

Krakatoa's eruption stirred artistic passions as well as scientific interest. William Ascroft, an English watercolor artist, became famous for his prolific renderings of Krakatoa sunsets. Edvard Munch, a Norwegian artist, was reportedly inspired to paint his well-known work *The Scream* after hearing of the devastation. Other paintings, as well as poems, children's stories, and Hollywood films, also immortalized Krakatoa.

Historian Simon Winchester pointed out what is perhaps Krakatoa's major significance: It occurred during a science-conscious Victorian age, when Europeans were beginning to think about ecological links among people and place. Winchester noted that Krakatoa's eruption, "an event that intersected so much and affected so many, seemed all of a sudden to be an example of this newly recognized phenomenon," that is, the essential connections between Earth's inhabitants and Earth itself. Krakatoa's eruption, devastating as it was, led to increased understandings of Earth's ecosystem.

—Richard A. Crooker

FURTHER READING

Botkin, Daniel B., ed. *Forces of Change: A New View of Nature*, Washington, D.C.: National Geographic Society, 2000. Prominent scientists offer perspectives on global change and the processes that shape it, including the role of volcanic eruptions.

Francis, Peter. *Volcanoes: A Planetary Perspective*. New York: Oxford University Press, 1993. Presents a global history of volcanoes and volcanic eruptions.

Simkin, Tom, and Richard S. Fiske. *Krakatoa, 1883: The*

Volcanic Eruption and Its Effects. Washington, D.C.: Smithsonian Institution Press, 1983. A technical description of the eruption that incorporates the theory of plate tectonics to explain the blasts.

Simmons, G. J., ed. *The Eruption of Krakatoa, and Subsequent Phenomena*. Report of the Krakatoa Committee of the Royal Society. London: Trüber, 1888. Reprint. La Jolla, Calif.: University of California, Scripps Institution of Oceanography, 1952. Contains maps, tidal graphs, eyewitness accounts, and factual observations of the eruption and its aftermath.

Thornton, Ian W. B. *Krakatau: The Destruction and Reassembly of an Island Ecosystem*. Cambridge, Mass.: Harvard University Press, 1996. An award-winning work that explores the ecological effects of the eruption. Includes maps, illustrations, biographical references, and an index.

Verbeek, Rogier. *Krakatau*. 2 vols. Batavia: Government Printing Office, 1885. Includes original diagrams, tables, and maps documenting the eruption's timing and the distribution of its effects. In Dutch.

Winchester, Simon. *Krakatoa—The Day the World Exploded: August 27, 1883*. New York: HarperCollins, 2003. Examines Krakatoa's geological, geographical, and sociological settings. Includes the chapters "The Moments When the Mountain Moved" and "The Unchaining of the Gates of Hell." Illustrations, maps, bibliographical references, and index.

SEE ALSO: Apr. 5, 1815: Tambora Volcano Begins Violent Eruption; July, 1830: Lyell Publishes *Principles of Geology*; Apr., 1898-1903: Stratosphere and Troposphere Are Discovered; 1900: Wiechert Invents the Inverted Pendulum Seismograph.

RELATED ARTICLE in *Great Lives from History: The Nineteenth Century, 1801-1900:* Sir Charles Lyell.

October 15, 1883
CIVIL RIGHTS CASES

In a set of five cases consolidated in a single decision, the U.S. Supreme Court found the Civil Rights Act of 1875 unconstitutional. The decision affirmed the premise that the Fourteenth Amendment gave Congress the power to prohibit discrimination only by state governments and not by private individuals or businesses.

ALSO KNOWN AS: *United States v. Stanley*; *United States v. Ryan*; *United States v. Nichols*; *United States v. Singleton*; *Robinson and Wife v. Memphis & Charleston Railroad Company*

LOCALE: Washington, D.C.

CATEGORIES: Laws, acts, and legal history; government and politics; civil rights and liberties; social issues and reform

KEY FIGURES

Joseph P. Bradley (1813-1892), associate justice of the U.S. Supreme Court, 1870-1892

John Marshall Harlan (1833-1911), associate justice of the U.S. Supreme Court, 1877-1911

Robert Brown Elliott (1842-1884), African American U.S. representative from South Carolina

John Mercer Langston (1829-1897), head of the Equal Rights League and a civil rights advocate

Charles Sumner (1811-1874), Republican senator and civil rights advocate

SUMMARY OF EVENT

The Civil Rights Act of 1875 proved to be the last piece of Reconstruction law passed by Congress to ensure that former slaves and their descendants would not be denied their rights as citizens. Partly as a tribute to Senator Charles Sumner, who had fought tirelessly for civil rights during his lifetime and who had died the previous year, his fellow senators approved the legislation. Sumner had held that the Thirteenth Amendment, in addition to abolishing the institution of slavery, also raised former slaves to a status of legal equality. On that basis, Congress had the power to pass laws that would guarantee African Americans freedom from discriminatory treatment, whether by public authorities or by private individuals. As Congress debated the Civil Rights Bill during the early 1870's, the most visible signs of African Americans' legal inferiority were restrictions and segregation in public facilities. Hotels, inns, theaters, trains, and ships routinely denied accommodations to black patrons.

Anticipating questions about the constitutionality of his proposals, Sumner tied his advocacy of free access to public facilities directly to the abolition of slavery, arguing that because one of the disabilities of slavery was the prohibition against entering public places, the end of slavery should mean freedom to enter the establishments of one's choosing. Restrictions on that freedom based on race constituted a "badge of slavery."

Supporters of the public accommodations law also argued that it could be sustained on Fourteenth Amendment grounds. Representative Robert Brown Elliott insisted that the amendment's equal protection clause required that states secure equality before the law for all citizens as part of their responsibility to advance the common good. He cited the Supreme Court's position in the 1872 Slaughterhouse cases that the purpose of the Thirteenth and Fourteenth Amendments was to protect African Americans from those who had formerly enslaved them.

The Republicans lost their majority in Congress in the 1874 elections. They passed the Civil Rights Act in a lame duck session in early 1875, as a last effort to secure the rights of African Americans before Congress became dominated by Democrats and pro-white southerners. The original version of the bill was drafted by African American civil rights activist John Mercer Langston, who gave it to Sumner. As passed, the Civil Rights Act of 1875 included five sections. Section 1 provided for equal access for all Americans to public accommodations and places of amusement. Section 2 defined violations and penalties for violating the equal access provisions. Section 3 gave federal, rather than state, courts jurisdiction in civil rights cases and required that law-enforcement agencies cooperate to enforce the law. This section was an attempt to ensure that the act would be enforced and violations prosecuted even in states where local authorities were reluctant to do so. Section 4 forbade racial discrimination in federal or state juries, and section 5 provided for Supreme Court review of cases arising under the act. An additional provision extending the equal access guarantees to public education was dropped from the bill.

In the year after the passage of the Civil Rights Act, neither Republican presidential candidate Rutherford B. Hayes nor Democratic candidate Samuel Tilden received a majority of the electoral votes. As the outcome of the presidential election remained in doubt, a special commission was appointed to resolve the constitutional crisis. A settlement was reached that allowed Hayes to assume the presidency. This settlement included an agreement that the federal government would stop trying to enforce civil rights legislation, including the new law passed in 1875. Even so, the law remained on the books until a group of cases, known collectively as the Civil Rights Cases, came before the Supreme Court in 1883.

The challenges to the law arose from four criminal prosecutions of persons who had excluded African

The Civil Rights Cases

In the Civil Rights Cases, the Supreme Court limited the power of the federal government to outlaw racial discrimination by private individuals. The majority opinion, excerpted below, explained that there was a difference between a state government taking away someone's rights, which Congress could prevent, and a mere act by a private individual interfering with those rights, which Congress lacked the authority to outlaw.

In this connection it is proper to state that civil rights, such as are guarantied by the constitution against state aggression, cannot be impaired by the wrongful acts of individuals, unsupported by state authority in the shape of laws, customs, or judicial or executive proceedings. The wrongful act of an individual, unsupported by any such authority, is simply a private wrong, or a crime of that individual; an invasion of the rights of the injured party, it is true, whether they affect his person, his property, or his reputation; but if not sanctioned in some way by the state, or not done under state authority, his rights remain in full force, and may presumably be vindicated by resort to the laws of the state for redress. An individual cannot deprive a man of his right to vote, to hold property, to buy and to sell, to sue in the courts, or to be a witness or a juror; he may, by force or fraud, interfere with the enjoyment of the right in a particular case; he may commit an assault against the person, or commit murder, or use ruffian violence at the polls, or slander the good name of a fellow-citizen; but unless protected in these wrongful acts by some shield of state law or state authority, he cannot destroy or injure the right; he will only render himself amenable to satisfaction or punishment; and amenable therefor to the laws of the state where the wrongful acts are committed. Hence, in all those cases where the constitution seeks to protect the rights of the citizen against discriminative and unjust laws of the state by prohibiting such laws, it is not individual offenses, but abrogation and denial of rights, which it denounces, and for which it clothes the congress with power to provide a remedy. This abrogation and denial of rights, for which the states alone were or could be responsible, was the great seminal and fundamental wrong which was intended to be remedied. And the remedy to be provided must necessarily be predicated upon that wrong. It must assume that in the cases provided for, the evil or wrong actually committed rests upon some state law or state authority for its excuse and perpetration.

Americans from their hotels or theaters and a fifth case brought by a black woman who had been excluded from a white railroad car reserved for women. All five cases fell under sections 1 and 2 of the 1875 law, and the Supreme Court was asked to decide whether these provisions were constitutional under the Thirteenth and Fourteenth Amendments. Could private discrimination be prohibited as one of the "badges of slavery"? Could Congress prevent discrimination by individuals on the grounds that the state was involved when it tolerated or ignored such actions by its citizens?

On October 15, 1883, Justice Joseph P. Bradley delivered the opinion of the Court. Seven justices joined his opinion; only Justice John Marshall Harlan dissented. Bradley's ruling effectively established a narrow scope for the Fourteenth Amendment, which was determined to apply only to the official actions of state governments. Congress, he maintained, did not have the power to prohibit discrimination by private individuals. Bradley asserted that such legislation was a "municipal law for the protection of private rights," far beyond the scope of congressional authority. He considered that under the Fourteenth Amendment, Congress's power to ensure that no state deprived a citizen of equal protection of the law meant that Congress could provide relief only after a state agency had acted to deny equal protection.

Bradley's interpretation of the Fourteenth Amendment left African Americans largely at the mercy of state governments, since they could appeal to Congress for relief only after a state had acted to deprive them of their civil rights. As for the acts of individuals that interfered with other persons' enjoyment of their rights of other persons, the Court's opinion termed such situations "simply a private wrong." The remedy for such discrimination was to bring action in a state court. According to this ruling, private interference, even with the right to hold property, to vote, or to serve as a witness or a juror, could not be prohibited by federal law.

Bradley reasoned that federal laws could only prohibit or prevent the "denial" of rights—that is, the elimination of those rights in principle. Because a private individual did not have the power to deny rights but only to "interfere with the enjoyment of the right in a particular case," such an individual's actions fell outside the scope of federal power to enforce the Fourteenth Amendment. It remained up to each state to enforce its laws against instances of "force or fraud" that interfered with the enjoyment of civil rights, just as it was up to the state to enforce laws against any other instance of "force or fraud."

Bradley further denied that the Thirteenth Amendment had any relevance to the case. In the opinion of the Court, "mere discrimination on account of race or color" could not be considered among the badges of slavery. In abolishing slavery, the amendment was not intended to adjust the "social rights" in the community. According to Bradley's opinion, it was time for African Americans to stop being "the special favorite of the laws" and to assume "the rank of a mere citizen." In ruling the Civil Rights Act of 1875 unconstitutional, the Supreme Court advised African Americans that their rights would be protected in the same way as other citizens' rights, by the state governments.

Justice John Marshall Harlan, a former slave owner, wrote the only dissent in the Civil Rights Cases. As he would do later in *Plessy v. Ferguson*, Harlan criticized his colleagues for distorting the intent of the Fourteenth Amendment by their narrow definition of state action. He asserted that public establishments were agents of the state, as they operated under state licenses and regulations. Harlan also argued that, because race had served as a justification for slavery, racial discrimination qualified as a badge of slavery. Emancipation raised the former slaves to the status of freedom and entitled them to the same civil rights as their fellow citizens. The Thirteenth Amendment, in its enforcement clause, gave Congress the power to ensure the enjoyment of those rights, including equal access. Harlan concluded that the constitutional amendments passed after the Civil War had prohibited any race or class of people from deciding which rights and privileges their fellow citizens could enjoy.

SIGNIFICANCE

Through its narrow definition of state action and of the Fourteenth Amendment's equal protection clause, the Supreme Court effectively limited the federal government's power to outlaw racial discrimination. Rather than affirming that the federal government had the constitutional authority to ensure equal citizenship for African Americans, the justices supported the principle of states' rights, opting for a limited definition of congressional authority and deferring to the states to safeguard the welfare of their citizens.

Among those who protested the Court's decision in the Civil Rights Cases was a group of black lawyers called the Brotherhood of Liberty. They argued that leaving the enforcement of civil rights to the states would be a disaster for African Americans. They criticized Republican federal judges as well as Republican legislators for betraying the purposes of the Reconstruction amendments out of political self-interest. Some black journalists compared the Civil Rights Cases to the Court's decision in *Dred Scott v. Sandford* (1857), which had denied that any African American could ever be a U.S. citizen.

—*Mary Welek Atwell*

FURTHER READING

Hyman, Harold M., and William M. Wiecek. *Equal Justice Under Law: Constitutional Development, 1835-1875.* New York: Harper & Row, 1982. Emphasizes issues concerning the Thirteenth Amendment as a source of federal power to enforce civil rights.

Lewis, Thomas T., and Richard L. Wilson, eds. *Encyclopedia of the U.S. Supreme Court.* 3 vols. Pasadena, Calif.: Salem Press, 2001. Comprehensive reference work on the Supreme Court that contains substantial discussions of the Civil Rights Cases and of all of the Court's other major civil rights decisions.

Litwack, Leon, and August Meier, eds. *Black Leaders of the Nineteenth Century.* Urbana: University of Illinois Press, 1988. Profiles of prominent African American activists.

Lively, Donald E. *The Constitution and Race.* New York: Praeger, 1992. A careful analysis of constitutional interpretation based on primary sources.

Nelson, William E. *The Fourteenth Amendment: From Political Principle to Judicial Doctrine.* Cambridge, Mass.: Harvard University Press, 1988. A valuable study of the changing application and meaning of the amendment.

Perry, Michael J. *We the People: The Fourteenth Amendment and the Supreme Court.* New ed. New York: Oxford University Press, 2002. Examines the controversies historically surrounding interpretation of the Fourteenth Amendment by the Supreme Court.

SEE ALSO: Jan., 1804: Ohio Enacts the First Black Codes; Mar. 6, 1857: *Dred Scott v. Sandford*; Dec. 8, 1863-Apr. 24, 1877: Reconstruction of the South; Nov. 24, 1865: Mississippi Enacts First Post-Civil War Black Code; Dec. 6, 1865: Thirteenth Amendment Is Ratified; Apr. 9, 1866: Civil Rights Act of 1866; July 9, 1868: Fourteenth Amendment Is Ratified; Mar. 5, 1877: Hayes Becomes President; 1890: Mississippi Constitution Disfranchises Black Voters; May 18, 1896: *Plessy v. Ferguson*; Mar. 28, 1898: *United States v. Wong Kim Ark*.

RELATED ARTICLES in *Great Lives from History: The Nineteenth Century, 1801-1900:* Rutherford B. Hayes; Charles Sumner.

October 22, 1883
METROPOLITAN OPERA HOUSE OPENS IN NEW YORK

From its opening in 1883, the Metropolitan Opera House has featured the world's most famous performers. Despite a catastrophic fire in 1892 that shut it down for a year, the opera house became a significant musical and social landmark in New York City, one that remains central to the city's cultural life.

LOCALE: New York, New York
CATEGORIES: Architecture; music; theater

KEY FIGURES

Henry Abbey (1846-1896), American operatic theatrical director
Auguste Vianesi (1837-1908), Italian conductor
Christine Nilsson (1843-1921), Swedish soprano
Anton Seidl (1850-1898), conductor of the Metropolitan Opera House, 1884-1891
Lilli Lehmann (1848-1929), internationally known singer

SUMMARY OF EVENT

The impetus for the construction of the Metropolitan Opera House (commonly known as the Met) was the inability of wealthy Manhattan socialites to obtain box seats at the New York Academy of Music. These socialites resolved to found a new opera house—one that not only would provide them seats but also could measure up to the great opera houses of Europe. The house opened in 1883, and, despite being shut down in 1892 because of a fire, it became one of the world's most famous opera houses during the late nineteenth century, putting the world's finest singers onstage for sold-out performances that were both musical and social events.

Opera first came to New York City in 1825, when French and Italian operas were performed at the Park Theatre. The first concert venue dedicated specifically to opera performance was the Italian Opera House, which opened its doors in 1833; however, the Italian Opera House became merely one of three short-lived and only moderately successful opera houses in New York. It burned down just six years after its opening, and its two successors, Palmo's Opera House and the Astor Place Opera House, lasted for four and five seasons, respectively.

The Academy of Music opened on October 2, 1854, and became the mainstay for New York opera-goers for more than thirty years, as well as a venue for concert performances. It boasted the largest stage in the world. Audiences flocked to the Academy of Music, but only partly to see the operatic masterpieces being performed on the stage: One of the attractions of opera-going was seeing the wealthy socialites in their private boxes, which were in prominent view on either side of the stage. In essence, the occupants of the boxes, "old money" New York socialites of the so-called Knickerbocker aristocracy, were part of the show (and perhaps the entire show) for the rest of the audience.

Many wealthy New Yorkers, including members of the Vanderbilt and Roosevelt families, were unable to obtain boxes at the Academy of Music and thus were unable to show off themselves and their wives to the public. As the famous singer Lilli Lehmann once described it, the men wanted their wives to "dazzle" the audience from the boxes. Frustrated with this unavailability, as well as with the academy's reluctance to construct new boxes to their liking, a group of millionaires founded the board of directors for what was to become New York's central operatic institution, the Metropolitan Opera House. The house, located at Broadway and Thirty-Ninth Street, was to contain many boxes, to which board members would have free and constant access but which would also be available for purchase by other wealthy New Yorkers. The "family circle" would provide cheaper seats to the rest of the public.

After initially convening on April 10, 1880, the board of directors obtained their site the next year, and the doors to the Metropolitan Opera House opened on the night of October 22, 1883, with a performance of French composer Charles Gounod's *Faust* (pr. 1859). The performance featured the renowned Swedish soprano Christine Nilsson and was conducted by Auguste Vianesi. During the first season (1883-1884), mostly French and Italian operatic staples were performed, including Georges Bizet's *Carmen* (pr. 1875), Giuseppe Verdi's *Il trovatore* (pr. 1853), and Wolfgang Amadeus Mozart's *Don Giovanni* (pr. 1787). The acting director and producer for the Met was Henry Abbey, a noted theater producer who had little operatic experience. Abbey left after the first season, giving way to German producer Leopold Damrosch.

The Metropolitan Opera House, on the corner of Thirty-Ninth Street and Broadway in Manhattan. (Library of Congress)

For the next seven seasons, the Met produced almost exclusively German operas, including works by German composer Richard Wagner. A disciple and friend of Wagner, Anton Seidl, became music director of the Met in 1885, and directed the first American performance of Wagner's complete *Der Ring des Nibelungen* (pr. 1869-1876; *The Ring of the Nibelung*, commonly known as the Ring cycle) in January of 1889. The Ring cycle was taken on tour and performed in seven other cities during the 1888-1889 season. Notable singers who performed at the Met during this period included Christine Nilsson, Marianne Brandt, Lilli Lehmann, Amalie Materno, and Albert Niemann. At that time, New York had a very large German-speaking population, and the heavy emphasis on German operas brought large audiences to the house. By now, the Met had usurped the Academy of Music as the main opera house in New York, and the academy closed its doors in 1886.

However, the emphasis on German opera, including the long, heavy Wagnerian works that bored some audiences, ended in 1891, when the board decided to shift back to the Met's original emphasis on French and Italian opera; this decision coincided with the rehiring of Henry Abbey. Singers such as Emma Eames, Emma Albani, and Jean Lassalle were with the Met during the 1891-1892 season. Misfortune struck the Met on August 27, 1892, when a workman allegedly dropped a cigarette in a backstage paint room, starting a massive fire that caused major damage to the interior of the opera house and required it to be shut down for the 1892-1893 season.

Ironically, the fire brought about several much-needed improvements to the building. Board members and stockholders raised money to help with the reconstruction, which began in April, 1893. The one-season break in productions and the money raised for the Met's reconstruction allowed some of the budget issues that had arisen during the "German years" to be resolved. The Met reopened on November 27, 1893, again with a performance of Gounod's *Faust*, featuring the great Emma Eames in the lead female role and Jean and Edouard de Reszkes as Faust and Mephistopheles. The opera house quickly reassumed its role as the center of cultural life in New York City.

SIGNIFICANCE

Since its beginnings during the late nineteenth century, the Metropolitan Opera House has remained a musical, cultural, and social epicenter in New York City, attracting audiences from all levels of society to see the finest performers in the world. Its illustrious history in the twentieth century included the tenure of legendary conductor Arturo Toscanini (1908-1915); the tenure of perhaps the Met's greatest star, Enrico Caruso, who appeared in six hundred opera performances at the Met; and the relocation of the opera house to its current location at Lincoln Center in 1966. Lincoln Center now houses not only the Met but also the Avery Fisher Hall, the New York Public Library, and the prestigious Juilliard School of Music. In short, the Met is one of the world's preeminent opera houses and has been such since its opening in 1883.

—*Graham G. Hunt*

FURTHER READING

Allison, John. *Great Opera Houses of the World*. London: Rolls House, 2004. Contains a detailed architectural study of the Metropolitan Opera House.

Johanna Fiedler. *The Mayhem Behind the Music at the Metropolitan Opera*. New York: Nan A. Talese, 2001. A candid and entertaining look at the behind-the-scenes activities at the Met, told by a former press representative.

Kolodin, Irving. *The Metropolitan Opera, 1883-1966*. New York: A. A. Knopf, 1966. Examines the eighty-three years of opera at the original location at Thirty-Ninth Street and Broadway.

Mayer, Martin. *The Met: One Hundred Years of Grand Opera*. New York: Simon & Schuster, 1983. Well-illustrated study of the Met and its performances from 1883 to 1983.

The Metropolitan Opera. www.metopera.org. The official Web site of the Metropolitan opera, upgraded in March of 2005, whose history database contains detailed accounts of every performance since 1883, as well as facsimiles of programs, portraits, and stage set designs. Accessed February 20, 2006.

SEE ALSO: c. 1801-1850: Professional Theaters Spread Throughout America; Feb. 20, 1816: Rossini's *The Barber of Seville* Debuts; Jan. 2, 1843: Wagner's *Flying Dutchman* Debuts; Mar. 3, 1875: Bizet's *Carmen* Premieres in Paris; Aug. 13-17, 1876: First Performance of Wagner's Ring Cycle; Jan. 14, 1900: Puccini's *Tosca* Premieres in Rome.

RELATED ARTICLES in *Great Lives from History: The Nineteenth Century, 1801-1900:* Georges Bizet; Charles Gounod.

November 3, 1883
GAUDÍ BEGINS BARCELONA'S TEMPLO EXPIATORIO DE LA SAGRADA FAMÍLIA

Noted architect Antoni Gaudí began work on an immense church in Barcelona. His plans for the church evolved to incorporate Gaudí's distinctively Catalan modern aesthetic, making it a landmark work in the region. The project remains unfinished, but even in its unfinished state it has become a symbol of the vibrant culture of Barcelona.

LOCALE: Barcelona, Spain
CATEGORIES: Architecture; religion and theology

KEY FIGURES
Antonio Gaudí (1852-1926), Spanish architect
Joan Rubió i Bellver (1871-1952), Spanish architect and Gaudí's assistant
José María Bocabella Verdaguer (1815-1892), Spanish bookseller
Francisco de Paula del Villar y Lozano (fl. late nineteenth century), Spanish architect
José María Rodríguez (1817-1879), Spanish Roman Catholic priest

SUMMARY OF EVENT
The Templo Expiatorio de la Sagrada Família (Expiatory Church of the Holy Family) was conceived by a devout if eccentric bookseller, José María Bocabella Verdaguer, and a Roman Catholic priest of the Mercedarian order, José María Rodríguez. As envisioned by Bocabella, the church would be dedicated to the Holy Family of Joseph, Mary, and Jesus; to Joseph again, in his role as the patron saint of workers; and to the expiation of the sins of Bocabella's own generation. In order to raise money for the project, Bocabella founded a group known as the Asociación Espiritual de Devotos de San José (Spiritual Association of Devotees of Saint Joseph) in 1866. By 1881, the association was able to purchase a site in the Gracia suburb of Barcelona, the capital of Catalonia, Spain.

Bocabella apparently hoped that the temple would resemble the thirteenth century Italian shrine of Loreto, to which the bookseller had made a pilgrimage. Plans for a neo-Gothic structure were instead developed in 1882 by diocese architect Francisco de Paula del Villar y Lozano, and the temple's cornerstone was laid on March 19 of that year—Saint Joseph's Day. In November of 1883, however, a dispute between Villar and the church council, or junta, overseeing the project, led to Villar's replacement with a colleague and former student, thirty-one-year-old Antonio Gaudí.

Gaudí had been born in 1852 in the nearby Catalonian city of Reus and was already a noted member of the loosely knit movement known as *Renaixança* (renaissance). Although part of Spain, the region of Catalonia enjoys its own language and culture, and *Renaixança* was viewed by its adherents as a rebirth of the region's distinctive political, artistic, and linguistic character. A later Catalonian architectural movement known as *modernismo*, in vogue from 1885 to 1905, combined the aspirations of *Renaixança* with many aspects of the Art Nouveau style then popular throughout Europe.

In Gaudí, the church authorities had chosen a worthy architect, but they could not have imagined the convoluted course that the project was to follow. Gaudí began actual work on the Templo Expiatorio de la Sagrada Família on November 3, 1883, and was appointed official director of works for the project on March 28, 1884. Because workers and their families lived in the area in which the temple was to be built, and because they contributed faithfully to its construction, Gaudí called it the "Cathedral of the Poor." He and Bocabella shared a utopian vision of a spiritual community of craftsmen taking up residence in the neighborhood surrounding the structure.

Like other *modernista* architects, Gaudí drew on a variety of styles indigenous to the Iberian Peninsula, including Catalan and Moorish elements. His highly individual projects were strikingly sinuous and ornate, but although he had requested permission to abandon Villar's design on March 3, 1884, Gaudí seemed reluctant at first to make many changes. Work on the crypt of the church had begun in 1882, shortly before Gaudí's involvement, and the young architect chose to complete the structure in conventional terms. The first mass was celebrated in the crypt on St. Joseph's Day, 1885, and the chamber was finally vaulted in 1887. As time passed, however, Gaudí drew more and more upon an organic ideal far removed from Villar's original plan. At the same time, the projected structure grew larger and far more complex.

It is difficult to determine exactly when Gaudí's change of heart took place, since many of his papers and models were destroyed during the Spanish Civil War of 1936-1939. A drawing apparently made during the late nineteenth century by his assistant Joan Rubió i Bellver shows the church largely as it has been developed since. In place of Villar's plain and unimaginative design is a massive assemblage of gabled roofs and slender towers (four of them campaniles, or bell towers) whose appearance has been compared to the stalagmites of a cave and to gargantuan cone shells. As completed in the twentieth century, the towers are capped with fantastic sculptures and inlaid with materials such as tile and Venetian glass. Words sacred to Christianity such as "Excelsis" and "Hosanna" are spelled out in mosaics on the campaniles.

Gaudí gave the Templo Expiatorio de la Sagrada Família three enormous facades: the Nativity Facade, facing east; the Passion Facade, facing west; and the main, or Glory Facade, facing south. Of these, only the Nativity Facade (1893-1929) was even begun during the architect's lifetime. Its surface is heavily sculpted and roughly worked in a manner that recalls a cave or grotto, and it includes some one hundred varieties each of animals and plants in its details. Yet the facade also makes room for a variety of conventional statuary and symbols celebrating the birth and life of Christ. The overall effect of the immense structure is routinely described as surreal, even hallucinatory.

As the project progressed, the junta continued to raise funds, but the final decade of the nineteenth century was to prove especially difficult for the administration of the project. On April 22, 1892, José María Bocabella Verdaguer, the bookseller who had conceived the Templo Expiatorio de la Sagrada Família and who had become president of the junta, died. The junta presidency was then passed to his son-in-law, Manuel de Dalmases y de Riba, but when Dalmases himself died in 1893, his widow took control. She was destined to die the same year. The bishop of Barcelona assumed administrative control of the project in 1895.

At the end of the nineteenth century, the Templo Expiatorio de la Sagrada Família existed as only a shell—and a partial one at that. The crypt and a single chapel of a projected seven, the Rosario, had been completed, and only parts of the Nativity Facade and the exterior wall of the cloister had been erected.

SIGNIFICANCE

The Templo Expiatorio de al Sagrada Família embodies several seemingly contradictory trends in the history of Spain and particularly of Barcelona. Although the church's construction began in an era of accelerating commercialization and industrialization, Bocabella and Gaudí himself regarded it as a literal expiation of the moral failings that these socioeconomic changes entailed. Despite the extremely conservative religious beliefs of the pair, the style of their church and many of the techniques involved in its construction were distinctly modern.

Work on the Templo Expiatorio de la Sagrada Família occupied Gaudí off and on for most of his career. He completed numerous important projects after beginning work on the church—among them the Casa Milá and the Park Güell, both in Barcelona—but the church itself was unfinished at the time of his death in 1926. Although subsequent construction, including that of the Passion Facade (1954-1977), followed Gaudí's plans closely,

The Templo Expiatorio in 1955. (Hulton Archive/Getty Images)

1880's

the church remained unfinished at the beginning of the twenty-first century. Despite its incomplete state, however, the church has solidified Gaudí's international reputation, which was in decline at the time of his death. The structure has emerged as the signature landmark of Barcelona and continues to represent Catalonia's cultural, spiritual, and nationalistic aspirations.

—*Grove Koger*

FURTHER READING

Bury, Mark. *Expiatory Church of the Sagrada Família: Antoni Gaudí*. London: Phaidon, 1993. Oversize volume illustrated with numerous plans and photographs. Chronology, bibliography.

Crippa, Maria Antonietta. *Antoni Gaudí, 1852-1926: From Nature to Architecture*. Cologne, Germany: Taschen, 2004. A compact, profusely illustrated survey. Maps, bibliography.

Hughes, Robert. *Barcelona*. New York: Alfred A. Knopf, 1992. Treats Gaudí, his body of work, and the Sagrada Família as elements of Barcelona's history. Illustrations, extensive bibliography.

Lahuerta, Juan José. *Antoni Gaudí, 1852-1926: Architecture, Ideology, and Politics*. London: Phaidon, 2004. Extended consideration of Gaudí's *oeuvre* emphasizing its social, political, and philosophical context.

Mackay, David. *Modern Architecture in Barcelona, 1854-1939*. New York: Rizzoli, 1989. A survey placing Gaudí and other *modernista* figures within the wider context of Barcelona's modern architectural development. Plans, numerous photographs.

Solà-Morales, Ignasi de. *Gaudí*. New York: Rizzoli, 1984. Includes plans and photographs, some archival, including many of the Sagrada Família.

Van Hensbergen, Gijs. *Gaudí*. New York: HarperCollins, 2001. The standard life of the architect in English. Illustrations, notes, bibliography, chronology.

Zerbst, Rainer. *Gaudí, 1852-1926: Antoni Gaudí i Cornet—A Life Devoted to Architecture*. Cologne, Germany: Taschen, 1988. Sumptuous survey of the architect's work. Numerous photographs, maps, plans, chronology, short bibliography.

SEE ALSO: Apr. 27, 1840-Feb., 1852: British Houses of Parliament Are Rebuilt; July 4, 1848: Ground Is Broken for the Washington Monument; 1883-1885: World's First Skyscraper Is Built; Mar. 31, 1889: Eiffel Tower Is Dedicated.

1884
MAXIM PATENTS HIS MACHINE GUN

Hiram Stevens Maxim's invention of the machine gun, the first true automatic weapon, revolutionized warfare. He invented both of the two systems for automatic guns—gas operation and recoil operation—and extensively developed the latter. Nearly all contemporary machine guns are based on Maxim designs, and the recoil-operated guns are almost identical to his original model.

LOCALE: London, England
CATEGORIES: Inventions; manufacturing

KEY FIGURES

Hiram Stevens Maxim (1840-1916), American-born British engineer, inventor, and industrialist
Richard J. Gatling (1818-1903), American physician and inventor

SUMMARY OF EVENT

Hiram Stevens Maxim was born in a small town in Maine. Largely self-educated, he was an authentic mechanical genius. During his early years he successfully designed or participated in the design of carriages, water mills, mouse traps, gas lighting, automatic fire extinguishers, and electric lamps; indeed, the first electric lights used in New York City were designed and installed by one of Maxim's companies.

In 1882, Maxim traveled to Europe after a friend advised him to invent "something that will enable these Europeans to cut each other's throats with greater facility." According to his own account, he remembered the great recoil he felt while firing a .45-70 rifle. He hit upon the idea of harnessing that recoil energy to operate the gun's mechanism. He was able to experimentally convert a Winchester rifle into a semiautomatic rifle by using a recoil-propelled lever to work the rifle's action. This first invention received great attention in Europe; in 1884, Maxim was granted a patent in England on a recoil-operated breech system.

Although Maxim developed several autoloading rifles and pistols, he concentrated his design efforts on machine guns. A machine gun, or fully automatic gun, continues to fire if its trigger is held back and cartridges continue to be available at the feed mechanism. At the time Maxim began working on machine guns, the most similar working gun was one made by American physician Richard J. Gatling, who designed and patented his Gatling gun in 1862.

The Gatling gun had ten barrels mounted around a central axis. The barrels were revolved by a crank that had to be turned by hand. Cartridges were fed from a hopper mounted above the rotary mechanism. Later, a drum or rotary feed was devised. As the crank was turned a carrier behind each barrel picked up a fresh cartridge that was then chambered and locked by the breech block. When the loaded barrel reached the five or six o'clock position, the cartridge was fired. Gatling guns used one of the rifle cartridges of their day, a .58 caliber rim-fire black-powder round. With a full crew of skilled operators this gun could achieve a rate of fire of nearly one thousand rounds per minute.

Sir Hiram Maxim explaining how his machine gun works to his grandson in 1893. (Hulton Archive/Getty Images)

The Gatling gun was not used extensively in the U.S. Civil War because the War Department doubted Gatling's loyalty to the Union. Gatling contracted with the Colt Arms Factory to build one hundred of the guns in 1867 using a new .50 caliber center-fire cartridge. This weapon proved to be very effective. It was used in a number of colonial wars against a variety of tribesmen. Its most notable success was during the Zulu War of 1879 in which thousands of charging Zulus were killed by British troops.

The Gatling gun had several serious disadvantages. It was large and heavy and usually required a crew of four to operate it, although in a pinch, once the gun was emplaced, it could be worked by firer and loader alone. The gun stood high from the ground and afforded no shelter for the crew from long-range rifle fire. The vertical feed arrangements made it difficult to sight the weapon exactly. These deficiencies, together with a relative lack of reliability in action, ended with the invention of the Maxim machine gun.

Maxim developed what is called a short-recoil weapon. The bolt is locked to the barrel at the moment of firing. The bolt and barrel recoil together for a short distance and are then unlocked by a toggle mechanism. The bolt continues to the rear, extracts and ejects the fired case, picks up a new cartridge that is then is chambered as the bolt moves forward again and re-locks itself. When the barrel and bolt come into battery again the new cartridge is fired and the cycle begins anew. The operator need only hold the trigger back and the gun continues to fire automatically.

Maxim's achievement was extraordinary. In addition to using recoil operation for the first time, his gun was fed by cartridges loaded into belts, thus avoiding the clumsy vertical feed. Belt feed is universally used today. All the parts of the gun could be removed by hand by the operator for cleaning or replacement. Maxim devised a new and more reliable extractor, a means of adjusting the head space of the gun in the field, and a new ejector system. Finally, the gun could be carried and operated by a smaller crew able to lie closer to the ground. All the mechanical developments were patented by Maxim between 1883 and 1885.

Maxim machine guns were built by Vickers in England, Colt in the United States, and many other manufacturers around the world. These guns, or their successors, are in use in nearly every army of the world with only very minor changes in dimension or design. Maxim did little developmental work on gas-operated machine guns, which he patented, but the famous Browning machine guns, the standard of the U.S. armed forces, owe their inception to John M. Browning's development of Maxim's idea.

The Maxim gun quickly overtook and replaced the Gatling. In colonial or tribal wars it allowed small detachments of troops to prevent and control rebellions against colonial powers. A famous satiric rhyme by Hailar Bello ("The Modern Traveler," 1898) after Lord Horatio Kitchener's slaughter of the Dervishes at Omdurman in 1898 expresses the gun's significance: "Whatever happens, we have got The Maxim Gun, and they have not."

By the time of World War I the machine gun had become the most fearsome infantry arm. Emplaced machine guns with overlapping fields of fire were the cause of most of the huge battlefield slaughters of that war. Maxim's design was suitable for modern high-velocity smokeless cartridges as well as for the older black-powder ammunition. With these newer cartridges the effective range of machine gun fire could be as great as 1,800 meters if "plunging" (arched) fire were used or perhaps 1,000 meters for direct fire. The volume of fire compensated for inaccuracies at such great ranges. Until the development of armored vehicles the machine gun prevented offensive wars of movement, at least between roughly equal forces.

SIGNIFICANCE

As new weapons so often do, the Maxim machine gun changed the face of warfare. In its time it put the defensive into ascendancy. This brought about the dreadful experience of extended trench warfare during World War I and the enormous casualty lists of that conflict. It also—as new weapons so often do—brought about the development of countervailing weapons. Although the most notable example is the tank, which was explicitly designed to be immune from machine gun fire, the development of air bombing and strafing beginning during World War I and coming more fully to fruition in World War II was even more notable.

—*Robert Jacobs*

FURTHER READING

Armstrong, David A. *Bullets and Bureaucrats: The Machine Gun and the United States Army, 1861-1916.* Westport, Conn.: Greenwood Press, 1982. Discusses the Army's refusal to recognize the worth of either the Gatling gun or the Maxim gun, which resulted in the United States entering World War I without a single machine gun in commission.

Hogg, Ian V. *Machine Guns: Fourteenth Century to the Present.* ILA, Wis.: Krause, 2002. The author, a former master gunner and now military historian, explores the history of machine guns, including early models from the fourteenth century and Maxim's and Gatling's inventions.

Maxim, Hiram Percy. *A Genius in the Family: Sir Hiram Stevens Maxim Through a Small Son's Eyes.* New York: Harper & Bros., 1936. Reminiscences and anecdotes of Maxim's life by his son.

Mottelay, P. Fleury. *The Life and Work of Sir Hiram Maxim.* New York: John Lane, 1920. Biography with considerable detail of Maxim's work with the manufacturers Vickers and Vickers-Armstrong.

Smith, Anthony. *Machine Gun: The Story of the Men and the Weapon That Changed the Face of War.* New York: St. Martin's Press, 2003. Examines the work of the makers of the first rapid-fire and automatic weapons, including Colt, Gatling, and Maxim, and the military impact of the machine gun.

Smith, W. H. B., and Joseph E. Smith. *Small Arms of the World: A Basic Manual of Military Small Arms.* 7th ed. Harrisburg, Pa.: Stackpole, 1962. A good biographical summary of Maxim's life and work as part of a very extensive discussion of small arms development to the mid-twentieth century. Includes copious photographs and drawings.

Willbanks, James, and Spencer Tucker, eds. *Machine Guns: An Illustrated History of Their Impact.* Santa Barbara, Calif.: ABC-Clio, 2004. Written for the younger reader, this work provides an introduction to the development of machine guns and their role in warfare.

SEE ALSO: Feb. 25, 1836: Colt Patents the Revolver; Apr. 12, 1861-Apr. 9, 1865: U.S. Civil War; Jan. 22-23, 1879: Battles of Isandlwana and Rorke's Drift; Jan. 22-Aug., 1879: Zulu War; Oct., 1893-October, 1897: British Subdue African Resistance in Rhodesia.

RELATED ARTICLES in *Great Lives from History: The Nineteenth Century, 1801-1900:* Samuel Colt; Alfred Krupp.

1884
NEW GUILDS PROMOTE THE ARTS AND CRAFTS MOVEMENT

The Arts and Crafts movement arose among professional artists and architects in response to the dehumanizing effects of mass production and industrialization and industrialism's devaluation of handmade works. Members of the movement argued that good design, simplicity, and craftsmanship fostered individuality, worker integrity, and pride in one's work.

LOCALE: Great Britain
CATEGORIES: Art; architecture

KEY FIGURES

William Morris (1834-1896), architect and designer
Charles Robert Ashbee (1863-1942), architect
William Richard Lethaby (1857-1931), architect, design educator, and historian
John Ruskin (1819-1900), art critic and author
Arthur Mackmurdo (1851-1942), architect
Walter Crane (1845-1915), painter, illustrator, and designer

SUMMARY OF EVENT

The Arts and Crafts movement arose in Victorian Great Britain in reaction to what was perceived by many architects, designers, and theorists as the harsh transformation of a heretofore agrarian society to one that was industrialized. In 1804, painter William Blake spoke out against "the satanic character" of the mills that had been springing up throughout the country, and later, in Charles Dickens's novels, the main characters were often the destitute workers in those mills. Critics argued that individualism and pride in one's work had been destroyed by industrialization.

To restore what had been taken away, critics and artists such as John Ruskin and William Morris advocated replacing machine-made goods with those made by hand. Ruskin, in *The Stones of Venice* (1851-1853), was explicit in his hatred of machine-made products, labeling them as soulless and degrading and that which leaves workers without pride in their creations. Ruskin believed that the solution was a return to medieval art and to a time when craftsmen could take pride in their work.

A leader in the early stages of the Arts and Crafts movement, Morris wanted to apply Ruskin's love of the handmade to modern commerce. Morris challenged manufacturers to move away from the heavily ornate, factory-made products that had appeared at the Great Exhibition of 1851 in the Crystal Palace, London. He proposed that simplifying design would raise standards, bring the designer and craftsman into a closer working relationship, and lower the cost of items to a more affordable level. Ruskin's theories of a return to styles and customs of the medieval age, including restoration of the guild system, inspired Morris and his followers to develop not only an artistic style but also a lifestyle. This unashamedly utopian society would celebrate the individuality and integrity of craftsmanship and thereby improve the quality of life for all. Morris's goal of restoring dignity to workers who had been robbed of pride and satisfaction in their work by Victorian commercialism led to a form of socialism and political activism that his followers took up in varying degrees.

There were a number of Arts and Crafts guilds created in the 1880's. One of the first was the Century Guild, founded in 1882 by Arthur Mackmurdo. The Century Guild's workshop produced furniture, metalwork, enameling, and textiles. One of the most important contribu-

John Ruskin.

tions made by the guild was the publishing of the journal *The Hobby Horse*, which, by emphasizing printing as a craft in its own right, was an important influence on Morris's Kelmscott Press and others in the creation of the private-press movement.

Mackmurdo's goals differed from those of Morris in one important respect. Morris, in a democratic spirit, thought to match the status of painting and sculpture as "fine arts" to that of the crafts, while Mackmurdo wanted to "lift" the status of crafts, which were considered of "lower" status, to that of the exulted fine arts. Although the Century Guild lasted a few years only, it had an important influence on the formation of the Arts and Crafts movement and, with its emphasis on natural forms in design, predicted the development of the later Art Nouveau style.

The Art Workers' Guild was founded in London in 1884 by five architects—William Lethaby, Mervyn Macartney, Gerald Horsley, Ernest Newton, and E. S. Prior—and The Fifteen, a group of artists led by Lewis F. Day and Walter Crane. Although the stated goal of the Art Workers' Guild was to destroy barriers between the various practitioners of the arts (for example, artists, architects, designers, and craftsmen) in order to create artistic unity, the unstated goal was to oppose the Royal Academy, whose members refused to exhibit the crafts, and the Institute of British Architects, whose conservative members refused to recognize architects of the Arts and Crafts movement.

From its inception, membership (by election only) in the Art Workers' Guild was restricted to men, and a committee chaired by a "master" set the rules and goals. By 1886, however, members recognized that the guild's exclusive and private nature contradicted the organization's aims, so the guild set out to establish closer contact with the public by holding annual exhibitions of what were then called "combined arts." Book designer T. J. Cobden-Sanderson had suggested the phrase "arts and crafts" be used instead. Thus, a new organization, with the name Arts and Crafts Exhibition Society, was founded, with Walter Crane as chairman and a committee that included William Morris and painter Sir Edward Coley Burne-Jones.

The first exhibition of the new society was held in October, 1888, and invitations were sent to guild members and to the key personnel of manufacturing firms. The society's goal was to create a favorable status for Arts and Crafts artists and designers and to put them in touch with leaders of industry. The first exhibition also featured lectures and demonstrations by various members of the guild, an approach that proved successful because most artists recognized the need for commercial survival and were reluctant to adopt the more radical socialist position of Morris, preferring instead to practice a romantic kind of socialism.

Following the success of this first exhibition, the society organized annual exhibitions at the New Gallery on Regent Street in London, a gallery event that became a popular showcase for Arts and Crafts objects. Exhibition acceptance was not limited to the society's members, but all exhibitors were required to meet the strict criteria set down by the society, the most important being that all work must be entirely handmade.

Another organization founded to promote the Arts

SOCIALISM THROUGH THE EYES OF AN ARTIST

One of the most influential figures in the Arts and Crafts movement was the English designer William Morris. In 1883, he wrote a brief autobiographical sketch, "My Very Uneventful Life," excerpted here, in which he offered his views on the relationship between art and socialism.

Through all this time I have been working hard at my business, in which I have had a considerable success even from the commercial side; I believe that if I had yielded on a few points of principle I might have become a positively rich man; but even as it is I have nothing to complain of, although the last few years have been so slack in business.

Almost all the designs we use for surface decoration, wallpapers, textiles, and the like, I design myself. I have had to learn the theory and to some extent the practice of weaving, dyeing, & textile printing: all of which I must admit has given and still gives me a great deal of enjoyment.

But in spite of all the success I have had, I have not failed to be conscious that the art I have been helping to produce would fall with the death of a few of us who really care about it, that a reform in art which is founded on individualism must perish with the individuals who have set it going. Both my historical studies and my practical conflict with the philistinism of modern society have *forced* on me the conviction that art cannot have a real life and growth under the present system of commercialism and profit-mongering. I have tried to develop this view, which is in fact Socialism seen through the eyes of an artist, in various lectures, the first of which I delivered in 1878. . . .

Source: Gillian Naylor, ed., *William Morris by Himself* (Edison, N.J.: Chartwell Books, 2001), pp. 16-17.

and Crafts movement was the Home Arts and Industries Association (1884), an umbrella organization that supported both professional and amateur work produced by a number of new, small workshops in largely rural areas. The association provided, also, a London showcase for the products of these workshops. By 1886, there were similar regional associations throughout Wales, Ireland, and Scotland. There existed some similarities between the rural craft revival and Morris's urban commercial revolution, but, by and large, the home industries movement had little interest in Morris's socialism, which they believed was a threat to their newly acquired social stability.

The Guild and School of Handicraft was founded in 1888 by the architect Charles Robert Ashbee. The guild's headquarters were first in Essex House in the heart of London's working-class East End. In 1902, the guild, which by that time consisted of more than one hundred members, moved to the rural environment of Chipping Campden in the Cotswolds, where it remained for the next six years. Ashbee's goal was to achieve quality of design that, in his mind, depended upon good social conditions. In fact, more attention was given by the guild to developing good domestic conditions and leisure pursuits than to developing high standards of craftsmanship. Ashbee wrote, for example, that the real thing is the life and it does not matter so much if craftsmanship is second rate.

SIGNIFICANCE

By 1907, the aesthetic ideals of the Arts and Crafts movement had been internationally recognized, helped by the many artists of the movement who had attained positions in established art schools as well as in the new art colleges that opened throughout England, continental Europe, and the United States. William Richard Lethaby's philosophy of raising the standard of the craft arts while also providing an educational system for designers to enable them to meet the requirements of sympathetic commercial firms was being put to practical use.

In Edinburgh, Scotland, for example, the new School of Applied Art offered classes in both crafts and architecture. In Glasgow, Charles Rennie Mackintosh, architect and designer, created the Glasgow style with his designs for the Glasgow School of Art, a severe rectangular structure with long, simple curves and a plain, unadorned facade. He was also an important interior designer; his most famous work was the design scheme for the Cranston chain of tearooms in Glasgow.

In the United States, British Arts and Crafts influenced the work of the Roycrofters in upper New York state, a project under the leadership of Elbert Hubbard. Frank Lloyd Wright, considered by many the premier architect of the time, was deeply inspired by the British movement. In California, the brothers Charles and Henry Greene created the first important architectural style called the California bungalow style. Gustav Stickley, after a trip to England in 1898, where he was inspired by the theories of Ruskin and Morris, returned home to create the first truly American style in furniture, his handcrafted craftsman line, which was based on honesty and simplicity.

Wherever the Arts and Crafts style has appeared, it has generally remained true to the original goal expressed by Ruskin and Morris: to raise the level of the craft arts to that of the fine arts and to reverse the dehumanizing effects of the Industrial Revolution by returning to a society in which dignity and respect were again the lot of the craftsperson.

—LouAnn Faris Culley

FURTHER READING

Meyer, Barbara. *In the Arts & Crafts Style*. New York: Chronicle Books, 1992. Each chapter examines a different facet of the movement, with 150 color plates.

Naylor, Gillian, et al., eds. *The Encyclopedia of Arts and Crafts*. New York: Knickerbocker Press, 1998. Originally published in 1989, this brief but informative work surveys the movement in Europe and the United States. Includes illustrations and an index.

Parry, Linda. *William Morris*. New York: Harry N. Abrams, 1996. A scholarly analysis of William Morris's multifaceted achievements.

Rosenberg, John, ed. *The Genius of John Ruskin: Selections from His Writings*. Charlottesville: University Press of Virginia, 1998. The selections address John Ruskin in all important aspects of his work as art critic, social critic, and autobiographer.

Todd, Pamela. *The Arts & Crafts Companion*. New York: Bulfinch Press, 2004. Examines the movement with chapters on its "Philosophy and Background" and "The Makers of the Movement." Includes discussion of Arts and Crafts architecture, architectural interiors, furniture, textiles, wallpaper, stained glass and lighting, pottery, ceramics, metalwork, jewelry, literature, and gardens.

Waggoner, Diane, ed. *"The Beauty of Life": William Morris and the Art of Design*. New York: Thames and Hudson, 2003. Published to accompany an exhibition presented at the Huntington Library in San Marino, California, and the Yale Center for British Art. Contains essays about Morris's stained glass, interior decoration, and book making, his influence on British design and the Arts and Crafts movement in the United States.

SEE ALSO: Mar. 11, 1811-1816: Luddites Destroy Industrial Machines; c. 1815-1848: Biedermeier Furniture Style Becomes Popular; July 14, 1833: Oxford Movement Begins; Fall, 1848: Pre-Raphaelite Brotherhood Begins; May 1, 1851-Oct. 15, 1851: London Hosts the First World's Fair; 1861: Morris Founds Design Firm; 1870's: Aesthetic Movement Arises; c. 1884-1924: Decadent Movement Flourishes.

RELATED ARTICLES in *Great Lives from History: The Nineteenth Century, 1801-1900:* Aubrey Beardsley; Thomas Carlyle; William Morris; John Ruskin.

c. 1884-1924
DECADENT MOVEMENT FLOURISHES

The Decadents promoted a deliberately provocative, scandalous international movement in art and literature that emphasized a cult of the aesthetic and the artificial, disparaged social and familial commitments and traditions, encouraged wide-ranging sexual practices, promoted drug use, celebrated the cultivation of the Self, and affirmed the right of the genius toward destructive and self-destructive acts.

LOCALE: Western Europe

CATEGORIES: Literature; art; philosophy; crime and scandals

KEY FIGURES

Joris-Karl Huysmans (1848-1907), French novelist

Oscar Wilde (1854-1900), Irish playwright, poet, and novelist

Gustave Flaubert (1821-1880), French novelist

Gabriele D'Annunzio (1863-1938), Italian novelist, poet, and playwright

Arthur Schopenhauer (1788-1860), German philosopher

Charles Baudelaire (1821-1867), French poet

Rachilde (Marguerite Eymery; 1860-1953), French novelist

SUMMARY OF EVENT

The concept of "decadence" originated with the idea that all things, from nations to societies to family units to the arts, inevitably sicken, decay, and die from a natural aging process such as that of the human body. The decline and fall of the Roman and the Byzantine Empires provide striking examples of past decadence and they offered warnings for the future. Secondary influences for the Decadent movement include the gothic novel and the morbid stories of American writer Edgar Allan Poe (1809-1849). The hyperesthesia (extrasensitivity to physical sensations) of many Decadent protagonists reminds readers of two of Poe's characters, Roderick Usher and William Wilson.

In France, the birthplace of the Decadent movement, intellectuals felt a sense of futility and social decline coming after the loss of Napoleonic grandeur and undisputed supremacy in Europe, after the repeated failure of the revolutions of 1789, 1830, and 1848 to establish a lasting

Charles Baudelaire. (Library of Congress)

democracy, after the country's rapid and humiliating defeat in the Franco-Prussian War (1870-1871), and after the rise of stultifying middle-class commercial values. From sheer boredom, the Decadents contemplated destructive and self-destructive acts. Charles Baudelaire memorably evoked decadent thinking in "Au lecteur" ("To the Reader"), the opening poem of *Les Fleurs du Mal* (1857, 1861, 1868; *Flowers of Evil*, 1931).

After 1830, "frenetic" Romantics such as Pétrus Borel (1809-1859) and Théophile Gautier (1811-1872), followed by Gustave Flaubert and Baudelaire, foreshadowed the start of the Decadent movement in France and had enormous influence in England, Spain, Russia, and Italy. Gautier's novel *Mademoiselle de Maupin* (1835-1836; English translation, 1887) fictionalized the life of a bisexual transvestite from the seventeenth century. The novel's brilliant preface expounds the aesthetic doctrine of art for art's sake. Flaubert's immense, leprous, rotting, lustful general Hannon in *Salammbô* (1862; English translation, 1886) exemplifies the Decadent character, and the collapse of Carthage in this historical novel illustrates the Decadent historical vision.

Against the Grain

Joris-Karl Huysman's character Des Esseintes, in Against the Grain, *epitomizes the philosophy of Decadence: intense experience- and pleasure-seeking.*

Try what he would, an overpowering sense of ennui weighed him down. But still he persisted, and presently had recourse to the perilous caresses of the experts in amorousness. But his health was unable to bear the strain and his nerves gave way. . . .

The physicians he consulted terrified him. It was indeed high time to change his way of life, to abandon these practices that were draining away his vitality. For a while, he led a quiet existence; but before long his passions awoke again and once more piped to arms. Like young girls who, under stress of poverty, crave after highly spiced or even repulsive foods, he began to ponder and presently to practise abnormal indulgences, unnatural pleasures. This was the end; as if all possible delights of the flesh were exhausted, he felt sated, worn out with weariness; his senses fell into a lethargy, impotence was not far off. . . .

Decadence revels in the new and the artificial. In this excerpt, Des Esseintes expresses his abhorrence of nature, of sameness, of predictability.

To tell the truth, artifice was in Des Esseintes' philosophy the distinctive mark of human genius.

As he used to say, Nature has had her day; she has definitely and finally tired out by the sickening monotony of her landscapes and skyscapes the patience of refined temperaments. . . .

Yes, there is no denying it, she is in her dotage and has long ago exhausted the simple-minded admiration of the true artist; the time is undoubtedly come when her productions must be superseded by art.

Source: Joris-Karl Huysman, *Against the Grain* (New York: Dover, 1969), pp. 7 and 22.

The feast of sins in Flaubert's *Tentation de Saint Antoine* (1874; *The Temptation of Saint Anthony*, 1895), and the sadistic and macabre scenes in both Gautier's and Flaubert's works, inspired a literature of morbidity in several countries. In 1857, the national government indicted both Flaubert's *Madame Bovary* (1857) and Baudelaire's *Les Fleurs du Mal* for their alleged offenses against religion and public morals. Seven of Baudelaire's poems with lesbian or sadistic themes, along with sarcastically amoral passages in Flaubert, were suppressed.

Joris-Karl Huysmans's novel *À rebours* (1884; *Against the Grain*, 1922) became the bible of international Decadence, reinforced by the publication of the pessimistic poems of Jules Laforgue (1860-1887). Other influences include Rachilde, Rémy de Gourmont (1858-1915), Octave Mirbeau (1848-1917), Oscar Wilde, Gabriele D'Annunzio, and Robert, comte de Montesquiou-Fezensac (1855-1921), who was the probable model for Huysmans's Decadent protagonist Des Esseintes and for Marcel Proust's (1871-1922) Charlus in *À la recherche du temps perdu* (1913-1927; *Remembrance of Things Past*, 1922-1931, 1981). In his novel *Sixtine: Roman de la vie cérébrale* (1890; *Very Woman: A Cerebral Novel*, 1922), Gourmont's protagonist asserted that physical pleasure is all that matters, regardless how it is obtained, and that his guiding principle for life was to avoid having children.

Wilde issued some of the most compelling theoretical statements of the movement in 1891, including that of the separation of art from life, in "The Decay of Lying" and *The Picture of Dorian Gray*, 1891. In the intimate journal embedded within his novel *Il piacere* (1889; *The Child of Pleasure*, 1898), D'Annunzio spelled out what

Huysmans and Wilde had only suggested: He found an alternate source of inspiration within the Self—the unconscious.

In feminist circles, Marie Bashkirtseff (1858-1884), a brilliant musician and painter who died prematurely from tuberculosis, helped found a female *culte du moi* (cult of the Self), free from the imperatives of marriage, reproduction, and nurturance. The unexpurgated version of her journal, published in 1901, caused a scandal. Rachilde's *Mercure de France* (1890-1965), cofounded with her husband Alfred Vallette, became the dominant journal of the Decadent movement. As a novelist, Rachilde was an innovator who depicted a wide range of sexual behavior, more so than did her male counterparts. She turned fetishism (*Monsieur Vénus*, 1884), necrophilia (*La tour d'amour*, 1899), bestiality (*L'animale,* 1893), and cross-dressing into prominent literary subjects. The renowned Paris literary salon of Natalie Clifford Barney (1876-1972) celebrated lesbian sexuality, while the male writers of the Parisian cabaret and salon Le Chat Noir (The Black Cat) celebrated male homosexuality. Barney inspired at least three notorious romans à cléf, including a novel by dancer Liane de Pougy (1869-1950), *Idylle sapphique* (c. 1901).

During the belle époque, between 1880 and 1914, western Europe and the British Isles enjoyed a magnificent flowering of the arts and unprecedented peace, prosperity, and economic and technological progress. At the same time, the aesthetic movement of the midcentury, which had claimed that artistic creation should be an end in itself, independent of any moral mission and any moral restraint (art for art's sake), later developed into the international Symbolist movement, which subordinated life to art. Philosopher Arthur Schopenhauer, well known throughout Europe in the 1880's, encouraged a philosophy of pessimism, undermining sensitive souls' will to live and reproduce. The decadent title character of the Symbolist drama *Axël* (1890) by Auguste Villiers de l'Isle-Adam (1838-1889) persuades the woman he loves to join him in a suicide pact, arguing that living is worthy only of underlings.

The Decadents' protagonists withdrew from society, cultivated their own personalities, and dismissed conventional morality regarding sex and sexuality, respect for the body, and the sanctity of life. They explored bestiality, sadomasochism, and necrophilia (although group sexual experience became an overt topic only in the twentieth century). They treated suicide and gratuitous murder without compunction. Prominent in works by precursors such as Poe ("The Black Cat," 1843; "The Imp of the Perverse," 1845; "The Telltale Heart," 1843) and the comte de Lautréamont (Isidore Lucien Ducasse, 1846-1870), gratuitous murder returns in works of high Decadence including Jean Lorrain's (Paul Duval, 1855-1906) *Monsieur de Phocas* (1901), Octave Mirbeau's *Contes Cruels* (1885-1899), and Rachilde's *La Marquise de Sade* (1887).

SIGNIFICANCE

From its beginning, the Decadent movement contained the seeds of its demise. Its foundational work, Huysmans's *À rebours*, depicts a wealthy aristocratic protagonist who cultivates artificiality in every aspect of his life. Boredom and ill health eventually drive him from his shelter. Sequels with a new protagonist, Durtal, become increasingly autobiographical and trace the author's conversion to Roman Catholicism. Many other Decadent writers also converted, foreshadowing the Catholic Renaissance in France and the Anglican Renaissance in England during the first half of the twentieth century.

The salon of American expatriot Natalie Clifford Barney on the Left Bank of Paris remained intact far longer, exerting a strong international influence on women's rights movements until at least the 1930's.

After World War I, High Modernist authors such as T. S. Eliot, James Joyce, and Marcel Proust perpetuated the Decadent style, but they increasingly combined it with social critique. Eventually, Thomas Mann's (1875-1955) novella *Der Tod in Venedig* (1922; *Death in Venice*, 1925) and *Doktor Faustus* (1947; *Doctor Faustus*, 1948) rejected the exclusive cult of art and of the Self.

Decadence was seen once more in 1920's Chicago, Illinois, popularized by the *Chicago Tribune*'s book reviews and led by the crime reporter Ben Hecht (1894-1964), a circus acrobat as a child. Hecht later became close friends with Dada artist Georg Grosz in Berlin. Hecht's flamboyant novels *Fantazius Mallare: A Mysterious Oath* (1922), *Gargoyles* (1922), and *The Kingdom of Evil: A Continuation of the Journal of Fantazius Mallare* (1924) introduced a sensational, satanic form of Decadence to American popular culture. Hecht later became an influential Hollywood producer, with seventy novels and screenplays to his credit.

—*Laurence M. Porter*

FURTHER READING

Bernheimer, Charles. *Decadent Subjects: The Idea of Decadence in Art, Literature, Philosophy, and Culture of the Fin de Siècle in Europe*. Edited by T. Jefferson Kline and Naomi Schor. Baltimore: Johns

Hopkins University Press, 2002. A synthesis from the standpoint of poststructuralist criticism.

Calinescu, Matei. *Five Faces of Modernity: Modernism, Avant-Garde, Decadence, Kitsch, Postmodernism.* Rev. ed. Bloomington: Indiana University Press, 1987. A classic philosophical background to Decadence in Germany and Italy.

Constable, Liz, et al., eds. *Perennial Decay: On the Aesthetics and Politics of Decadence*. Philadelphia: University of Pennsylvania Press, 1999. Treats many major international figures, including writers from Nicaragua, Belgium, Spain, and Sweden.

Porter, Laurence M. "Decadence and the *Fin-de-Siècle* Novel." In *The French Novel from 1800 to the Present*, edited by Timothy Unwin. New York: Cambridge University Press, 1997. An overview of the Decadent movement in France.

_______. "Huysmans' 'À rebours': The Psychodynamics of Regression." *American Imago* 44, no. 1 (Spring, 1987): 51-65. Discusses how an unconscious drive toward health eventually reintegrates Des Esseintes with society.

_______. "Literary Structure and the Concept of Decadence: Huysmans, D'Annunzio, and Wilde." *Centennial Review* 22, no. 2 (Spring, 1978): 188-200. Discusses how the greatest Decadent writers symbolize and dramatize the role of the unconscious in their protagonists.

Weir, David. *Decadence and the Makings of Modernism.* Amherst: University of Massachusetts Press, 1995. Examines the aftermath of the Decadent movement in the United States.

SEE ALSO: 1807: Bowdler Publishes *The Family Shakespeare*; c. 1820-1860: *Costumbrismo* Movement; c. 1830's-1860's: American Renaissance in Literature; Fall, 1848: Pre-Raphaelite Brotherhood Begins; 1861: Morris Founds Design Firm; c. 1865: Naturalist Movement Begins; 1870's: Aesthetic Movement Arises; 1884: New Guilds Promote the Arts and Crafts Movement; 1886: Rise of the Symbolist Movement; Nov. 8, 1900: Dreiser Publishes *Sister Carrie*.

RELATED ARTICLES in *Great Lives from History: The Nineteenth Century, 1801-1900:* Charles Baudelaire; Gustave Flaubert; Walter Pater; Edgar Allan Poe; John Ruskin; Oscar Wilde.

January, 1884
FABIAN SOCIETY IS FOUNDED

Founded as a British socialist society, the Fabian Society became the most influential voice and meeting place of socialists in late nineteenth century Britain. During the early twentieth century, it evolved into the Labour Party, becoming a major force in British politics.

LOCALE: England

CATEGORIES: Organizations and institutions; government and politics; social issues and reform

KEY FIGURES

Sidney Webb (1859-1947), historian, social reformer, economist, and a founding member of the Fabian Society

George Bernard Shaw (1856-1950), Irish playwright and a founding member of the Fabian Society

Graham Wallas (1858-1932), political scientist, psychologist, and a founding member of the Fabian Society

Beatrice Webb (Beatrice Potter; 1858-1943), wife of Sidney Webb and a leader of the Fabian Society

H. G. Wells (1866-1946), British writer, member, and then a chief critic of the Fabian Society

SUMMARY OF EVENT

During the late nineteenth century, British socialism consisted of an aggregation of different theories and political positions with no guiding force or program. In January, 1884, a group of social thinkers and activists led by Sidney Webb, George Bernard Shaw, and Graham Wallas set out to rectify this lack of focus among British radicals by articulating a coherent vision of political practice and reform. The group called itself the Fabian Society, and the vision of its members would later be adopted by the Labour Party and successive Labour governments.

The members of the Fabian Society were influential both as writers and as organizers. The society attracted the greatest thinkers and authors of the day, such as H. G. Wells, and by 1889, when it published *Fabian Essays in Socialism*, it won its place as Great Britain's leading socialist organization. Fabian summer schools educated

"Why Are the Many Poor?"

In 1884, the Fabian Society published its first tract, "Why Are the Many Poor?" The tract, excerpted below, argued that competition was a fundamentally unjust basis for the distribution of wealth and called upon the rich and the poor to join together to fight this injustice and work for the creation of a better society in Great Britain.

What is Capital?

It is the sum of our instruments of production, and of the advantages of the work of former years. Its use is to be found in devoting it to the benefit of all; its abuse in leaving it in the hands of a few to waste its revenues in their own personal gratification. The present system gives to the few the power to take from the workers a huge portion of the product of their labor—the labor which alone makes fruitful the capital bequeathed by generations of social industry.

What does it give to the many?

Their portion is poverty. This is the inevitable outcome of their competition for wages, and none know so well as the workers the full burden of that terrible and long-continued demoralisation which is brought about not merely by the poverty of a generation, but by generations of poverty. With the smallest of chances the poor are expected to display the greatest of virtues. On scanty and undertain wages they must struggle to maintain the independence, self-respect, and honesty of men and women, and to put by something for the rainy day that is sure to come. . . .

This ceaseless labor of the workers continually enriches those already rich, until extreme wealth enables a privileged minority to live in careless luxury, undisturbed by the struggle for existence that goes on beneath them.

Have laborers no right under the sun but to work when capitalists think fit, and on such terms as competition may determine? If the competitive standard of wage be the true one, why is it not applied all round? What, for instance, would be the competitive value of a Duke, a Bishop, or a Lord-in-Waiting?

the younger members and nonmembers alike, so writers such as Rebecca West carried the Fabian message into such other radical journals as *The Freewoman* and *The Clarion*.

The Fabians opposed the status quo and the policies of the Conservative and Liberal governments that dominated the nineteenth and early twentieth centuries. Fabians also opposed revolution, however, and they repudiated the idea of class struggle that informed Karl Marx's model, arguing that the gradual permeation of their ideas into British institutions would bring about the natural evolution and dominance of socialism. At first, the Fabians took little notice of trade unionism, but their attitudes changed when Beatrice Potter married Sidney Webb and became one of the central forces in the Fabian movement. Through her efforts, the society established working-class connections that developed into the Labour Representation Committee (1900), the precursor of the Labour Party.

Under Sidney Webb's leadership, the Fabians argued against the expropriation of property and for progressive taxation, the means by which the state would be able to institute social, economic, and political reforms. Elected to the London County Council in 1892 and a founder of the London School of Economics in 1895, Webb put his ideas into practice, pointing out that socialism would triumph on both the local and national levels if its adherents sought both to articulate socialist policies and to attain political offices in which they could implement socialism.

Beatrice Webb acquired experience as a rent collector, investigated dock labor, and testified before Parliament about the poor conditions of the working class. She spoke for socialism with a religious fervor and used her private income to support several research projects, resulting in books such as *The History of Trade Unionism* (1894) and *Industrial Democracy* (1897). These books attacked the liberal, nineteenth century idea of individual contracts between employer and employee. Modern mass society could no longer function on the basis of such agreements, the Webbs argued, because the individual laborer lacked the power to negotiate a decent wage with huge industries. Consequently, they said, labor unions must develop comprehensive demands for a system that ensured the health, education, and economic well-being of workers and all other members of the public.

Through his plays and essays, George Bernard Shaw furthered the Fabian program. In *Major Barbara* (pr. 1905, pb. 1907), for example, he ridiculed the futility of organizations such as the Salvation Army, which depended on public charity to help the indigent and homeless. The piety of such organizations sentimentalized the poor but did nothing to change the structure of society that rendered them impoverished in the first place. The capitalists in Shaw's plays are often the most dynamic and fascinating characters, because, like the Webbs, he saw in them the power to change society, and he believed there was a way to harness that power to the socialist cause.

The Webbs practiced the equivalent of Shaw's romance with the capitalists by establishing a kind of salon to which they invited Liberals and Conservatives in power to come to discuss the Fabian program for social reform. H. G. Wells criticized the Webbs, Shaw, and other Fabians for indulging in what he regarded as a too cozy intrigue with the establishment. Wells then tried to take over the society, planning to broaden its membership, but he was ostracized as an interloper and adventurer.

Although there is no doubt that the Webbs exerted significant influence on the establishment, Wells's points were well taken. Despite their role in its formation, the Webbs and other Fabians were very slow to take the emerging Labour Party seriously. In this respect, the Webbs narrowed the scope of socialism. Even worse, they would become apologists in the 1930's for the Soviet brand of socialism. If they did not approve of revolution, they nevertheless lauded Joseph Stalin and apparently blinded themselves to his tyranny, so intent were they in finding a society that they believed had established the modern welfare state. Shaw joined them in this pro-Soviet line, willfully ignoring the evidence of Stalin's mass murders and coercive government.

Indeed, the Webbs and many of the other Fabians were a curious and not always salutary combination of pragmatic and idealistic qualities. They were formidable researchers and could submit social conditions to penetrating analysis, but they could easily blind themselves to the implications of their ideas and the consequences of a socialism unchecked by democratic values and a respect for human rights. The Fabians formed their own elite aimed at changing society for the better, and yet as an elite they removed themselves from many of the realities of the socialism they advocated.

SIGNIFICANCE

The vigor of Fabian socialism persisted throughout the early twentieth century, as evidenced by the founding in 1913 of *The New Statesman*, which became a central organ for socialist thinkers and activists. The founding of the magazine coincided with the Webbs' disillusionment with the Liberal Party and their move to support Labour instead. By 1916, Sidney Webb was a member of the Labour Party executive committee, and he assisted in the formulation of its policies throughout the post-World War I period.

By the mid-1930's, the Webbs and their fellow Fabians had been thoroughly absorbed by the Labour Party. The Webbs, close to the end of their work, were regarded more as sacred monuments than as vital influences. Their fawning comments about the Soviet Union seriously damaged their reputation, leading to speculation that their support of Soviet-style socialism revealed an excessive fondness for bureaucracy. However, their pro-Soviet line was adopted by many Fabians and Labour Party activists, who believed that capitalism was crumbling and that a workers' state was in the offing. This wishful thinking—a corruption of the turn-of-the-century Fabian position that rejected Marxism—resulted, as Rebecca West predicted in 1924, in the degradation both of socialism and of the Labour Party.

West, never a member of the Fabians, was a product of its summer schools and a believer in the original Fabian idea that socialism should be an indigenous British program, working for the gradual transformation of society at the grass-roots level, starting with local government and building toward a national movement. She believed that by the 1920's and the advent of the first Labour government, the Fabians had taken a wrong turn, relying increasingly on a centralized state and a top-heavy bureaucracy to enforce social, political, and economic change.

—*Carl Rollyson*

FURTHER READING

Cole, G. D. H. *Fabian Socialism*. London: Frank Cass, 1943. An account of one of the early Fabians, with chapters on persons and politics, socialism, the Fabian program for industry, the society's view of equality, foreign affairs, and democracy.

Cole, Margaret. *The Story of Fabian Socialism*. London: Heinemann, 1961. An extensive history by one of the society's important members, covering Fabian policies and personalities, the conflict with H. G. Wells, and the organization's impact on society and on political parties. Includes an index of persons.

Freemantle, Anne. *'This Little Band of Prophets': The Story of the Gentle Fabians*. London: Allen & Unwin, 1960. A concise narrative history with photographs of the principal Fabian leaders.

Jeffreys, Kevin, ed. *Leading Labour: From Keir Hardie to Tony Blair*. London: I. B. Tauris, 1999. Contains biographies of every leader of the Labour Party, beginning from its founding under the influence of the Fabian Society.

Mackenzie, Norman, and Jeanne Mackenzie. *The Fabians*. New York: Simon & Schuster, 1977. The most comprehensive and scholarly history of the society. Extensive notes.

Nord, Deborah Epstein. *The Apprenticeship of Beatrice Webb*. Amherst: University of Massachusetts Press, 1985. A careful study of Beatrice Webb's ideas and of her writing. Includes a detailed chronology and notes.

Pease, Edward R. *The History of the Fabian Society*. London: Frank Cass, 1963. A reprint of the 1918 edition. A firsthand account by one of the founders of the society. See especially the first chapter on the ideas of the 1880's that influenced the early Fabians.

Vernon, Betty D. *Margaret Cole, 1893-1980: A Political Biography*. Dover, N.H.: Croom Helm, 1986. Chapters 8 and 9 deal with the Fabian Society and the relationships between the Coles and the Webbs. Includes biographical notes and select bibliography.

SEE ALSO: 1824: British Parliament Repeals the Combination Acts; Feb., 1848: Marx and Engels Publish *The Communist Manifesto*; Sept. 28, 1864: First International Is Founded; 1867: Marx Publishes *Das Kapital*; July 4-5, 1892: Birth of the People's Party; Aug. 3, 1892: Hardie Becomes Parliament's First Labour Member; Mar., 1898: Russian Social-Democratic Labor Party Is Formed; Feb. 27, 1900: British Labour Party Is Formed.

RELATED ARTICLES in *Great Lives from History: The Nineteenth Century, 1801-1900:* Keir Hardie; Karl Marx.

January 25, 1884
INDIAN LEGISLATIVE COUNCIL ENACTS THE ILBERT BILL

British India's Ilbert Bill allowed Indians to try Europeans in courts of law. It caused an uproar among Europeans in India, who launched a successful protest movement. The bill was modified to favor Europeans, but the agitation over it helped develop India's national consciousness. The Indian National Congress was founded two years later, in 1885.

ALSO KNOWN AS: Criminal Procedure Amendment Code Bill

LOCALE: Calcutta, India

CATEGORIES: Laws, acts, and legal history; colonization; government and politics

KEY FIGURES

Sir Courtenay Peregrine Ilbert (1841-1924), law member of the Indian viceroy's executive council, 1882-1886

Lord Ripon (George Frederick Samuel Robinson; 1827-1909), first marquis and second earl of Ripon and viceroy and governor-general of India, 1880-1884

Sir James Fitzjames Stephen (1829-1894), legal member of the Indian viceroy's executive council, 1869-1872

Sir William Wilson Hunter (1840-1900), British historian and member of the Indian civil service

SUMMARY OF EVENT

Founded in 1600, the British East India Company became the dominant power in India after the Battle of Plassey in June, 1757. It established the three presidencies of Bengal, Bombay, and Madras, each of which had its own legal system and high court. In addition, on an ad hoc basis, the British established law courts in the districts that covered criminal and civil procedure for Indians based on Hindu, Islamic, or local common law. Such law was dispensed through British magistrates by members of the Indian civil service. It had been established that Europeans had the right to be tried in a high court before a jury of their (European) peers, and this practice was confirmed by the code of criminal procedure of 1861. Thus, in the event that an Indian had cause to engage in legal action against a British subject, both the British defendant and the Indian plaintiff would have to be transported as many as one thousand miles to one of the three presidencies' high courts.

The difficulty and expense of providing transportation to high courts persuaded the government in 1872 to allow district magistrates very limited powers to imprison and fine Europeans. Immediately, the question arose of whether Indian magistrates could try Europeans, but the issue was moot because all of the magistrates were British. In 1882, however, Behari Lal Gupta, an Indian member of the judicial section of the Indian civil service, was promoted to the post of sessions judge in upper Bengal, a post in which he would preside over European defendants. The promotion thus brought the issue to a head and led to the introduction of the Ilbert Bill, which was aimed at bringing fairness and uniformity to the legal system in Bengal by putting Indian judges on the same footing as British judges.

Lord Ripon had been sent to India as viceroy by the Liberal prime minister William Ewart Gladstone. He was instructed to reverse the conservative and belligerent policies of the previous viceroy, the first earl of Lytton (viceroy 1876-1880), and to reestablish good relations with leading Indian figures. The Ilbert Bill was one of several liberal measures he promoted. As soon as the legislation was proposed, however, a storm of protest arose from the European community in Calcutta. The idea of Europeans being tried by Indians was anathema to most of the British colonials. Ripon came in for enormous enmity, he was boycotted, and there were even threats to kidnap him and take him to England.

Editorial cartoon by John Tenniel (1820-1914). Titled "The Anglo-Indian Mutiny," the cartoon is captioned "A bad example to the elephant!" The cartoon comments on the anger felt by British residents of India who were outraged by the prospect that offering "equal rights" to native Indians might subject them to being tried by Indian magistrates.

On February 2, 1883, Sir Courtenay Peregrine Ilbert, the law member of the executive council, introduced the bill in the Imperial Legislative Council of India. Three days later, on February 5, the attack on the bill and the administration began. Opponents of the bill created the European and Anglo-Indian Defence Association to defend their privileges. Indians supported the bill, and the stage was set for a major confrontation.

The height of the protest movement was reached on the afternoon of February 28, when a large protest meeting against the bill was held in Calcutta's town hall. The meeting was attended by an estimated three to five thousand people. European shops and offices were closed so people could attend the meeting, which was presided over by the sheriff of Calcutta. A motion was made stating that, among other things, the bill was unnecessary, it was based on no sound principle, and it would stir up race antagonism and jealousy not seen since the Sepoy Mutiny (1857-1858). The speeches that followed were intemperate and generated a great deal of rancor, as speakers argued that Indians could never be trusted with power over Europeans.

Opponents of the bill in England, such as the jurist and former legal member of the viceroy's executive council Sir James Fitzjames Stephen, believed they were arguing not on racist grounds but on the principle that India was fundamentally different from Europe. The British had acknowledged this difference by earlier creating separate codes for Hindu and Muslim law. A country such as India with its diversity of people and traditions could not be governed by one uniform system of law. It was natural, then, to have a special code for Europeans.

Stephen's critics, especially Sir William Wilson Hunter, argued that British rule in India was committed to the eradication of special privileges for any one community and the creation of a common system of law applicable to all. The Ilbert Bill was one of a series of measures designed to whittle away class privilege. Stephen's reply to this was that if the British wanted to treat everyone equally then they had no right to rule India, because the British Raj (government in India) was an absolute government not based on consent but on conquest. The only way to establish equality in India, Stephen pointed out, would be for the British to leave the subcontinent.

The argument that if the British wanted equality in India they should leave was one that liberals could not answer and preferred to avoid. The debate on the issue was carried on in both the House of Commons in London and in the Imperial Legislative Council in Calcutta. Informally, it was the talk of the town in the clubs and homes of Europeans in India.

On December 22, a "concordat" was finally reached between Sir Griffith Evans (1840-1902), a member of the legislative council arguing on behalf of the European and Anglo-Indian Defence Association, and Sir Aukland Colvin (1838-1904), representing the government. The compromise established that session judges would be ex officio justices of the peace with the ability to try Europeans and to assess fines of up to two thousand rupees and imprisonment of up to six months. The most important component of the "concordat" was that European and British-born subjects had the right to be tried by a jury, half of which would consist of Europeans or Americans. As a result of this compromise, which had the reluctant blessing of Ripon, who had lost the support of his entire cabinet apart from Ilbert, the bill was finally passed on January 25, 1884, and became law.

SIGNIFICANCE

As a result of the Ilbert Bill controversy, Indians realized they could not expect justice or fairness from the British when it came to their own interests. They saw more explicitly than ever the connection between British colonialism and British racism. One of the major Indian political leaders of the time, Sir Surendranath Banerjea (1848-1925), said that when the Ilbert Bill was introduced no self-respecting Indian could sit idle, as it was a patriotic duty to oppose it. The controversy, therefore, helped crystallize Indian national consciousness. It taught Indians the power of organization. It showed them how the government could be forced to change its legislation through an organized campaign of opposition. The year following the passage of the bill, the first all-India political party, the Indian National Congress (INC), was founded at Bombay. The INC became the primary party of Indian nationalism and led India to independence in 1947. The Ilbert Bill was an important step in the nascence of the independence movement.

—Roger D. Long

FURTHER READING

Hirschmann, Edwin. *"White Mutiny": The Ilbert Bill Crisis in India and Genesis of the Indian National Movement*. New Delhi, India: Heritage, 1980. Standard study on the Ilbert Bill. Offers a detailed analysis of the crisis and its aftermath. Includes texts of the principal speeches given at the town hall meeting on February 28, 1883, and the final act of 1884.

Ilbert, Courtenay. *The Mechanics of Law Making*. Reprint. Union, N.J.: Lawbook Exchange, 2000. A handbook for law makers written by the man who introduced the Ilbert Bill in 1883.

Metcalfe, Thomas R. *Ideologies of the Raj*. Cambridge, England: Cambridge University Press, 1994. This volume in the New Cambridge History of India series deals with Great Britain's justification and legitimation of its rule in India.

Sinha, Mrinalini. "Reconfiguring Hierarchies: The Ilbert Bill Controversy, 1883-1884." In *Feminist Postcolonial Theory: A Reader*, edited by Reina Lewis and Sara Mills. New York: Routledge, 2003. A feminist reading of the Ilbert Bill controversy and its relationship to gender hierarchies in colonial India.

SEE ALSO: Apr. 10, 1802: Lambton Begins Trigonometrical Survey of India; Dec. 4, 1829: British Abolish Suttee in India; Apr., 1848-Mar., 1849: Second Anglo-Sikh War; May 10, 1857-July 8, 1858: Sepoy Mutiny Against British Rule; 1885: Indian National Congress Is Founded.

RELATED ARTICLES in *Great Lives from History: The Nineteenth Century, 1801-1900:* First Marquis of Dalhousie; William Ewart Gladstone; Sir James Outram.

March 13, 1884-January 26, 1885
SIEGE OF KHARTOUM

The siege of Khartoum by a Muslim fundamentalist army and the resulting death of General Charles Gordon was a defining moment in British imperial history that forced the collapse of William Ewart Gladstone's ministry and the establishment of an extended British interest and presence in Northeast Africa. The siege embodied a variety of values associated with religion, slavery, exploration, and control over the headwaters of the Nile River.

LOCALE: Khartoum, Sudan
CATEGORIES: Wars, uprisings, and civil unrest; diplomacy and international relations

KEY FIGURES

Charles George Gordon (1833-1885), British army officer who administered the Sudan, 1874-1880, and led the defense of Khartoum

The Mahdi (Muḥammad Aḥmad ibn as-Sayyid ʿAbd-Allāh; 1844-1885), Sudanese Islamic revolutionary

Romolo Gessi (1831-1881), Italian army officer and explorer

William Ewart Gladstone (1809-1898), Liberal prime minister of Great Britain, 1868-1874, 1880-1885, 1886, 1892-1894

Sir Garnet Joseph Wolseley (1833-1913), commander of the British expeditionary force to relieve Khartoum

Horatio Herbert Kitchener (1850-1916), member of the Khartoum relief force

SUMMARY OF EVENT

During the 1850's, British interest in Africa was reinvigorated by the explorations of Richard Francis Burton, David Livingstone, and others who sought to locate the source of the Nile River. During the 1870's, British imperial interest in Africa was renewed under the leadership of Prime Minister Benjamin Disraeli, who in 1876 acquired control of the Suez Canal for Great Britain.

Meanwhile, Egypt's Khedive Ismāʿīl Pasha hired Charles George Gordon to serve as governor of the Equatoria Province in the Sudan in 1873. A British army engineer, Gordon had earned a reputation as a warrior in the Crimean War (1853-1856) and in China, where his exploits earned him the name "Chinese" Gordon. In 1865, Gordon had returned to Britain. While continuing to serve in the army there, his interest in Christianity was transformed into a personal mystical Christianity through which he believed that he communicated directly with God. Gordon then took up the causes of the dispossessed and became a vehement opponent of slavery wherever it still existed throughout the world. This was the Charles Gordon whom the khedive hired to stabilize the Sudan.

During his tenure as governor, Gordon's accomplishments were extensive. Between 1874 and 1876, he explored the Nile, with the assistance of the Italian explorer Romolo Gessi, developed detailed maps, and reached as far south as present-day Uganda. In 1876, Gordon was elevated to the position of governor of the entire Sudan. For four years, he labored at establishing order, modernizing the government, and eliminating the slave trade. His adamant opposition to slavery and all of its vestiges resulted in his creating many enemies among Arab slave traders and slaveholders. At the same time, however, he earned a growing respect and admiration among the Sudanese peoples. Eventually, however, his strenuous efforts in the Sudan led to his physical collapse, so he returned to England in 1880.

In early 1881, a resurgence of radicalism Islam manifested itself in the Sudan. Under the leadership of Muḥammad Aḥmad ibn as-Sayyid ʿAbd-Allāh, who is better known as the Mahdi, fundamentalist and militant Islam targeted all infidels, both native and foreign. In 1883, the Mahdi's forces annihilated an Egyptian army led by British officers. The European and Egyptian survivors then took refuge in Khartoum and adopted a defensive posture as they awaited a relief force. However, the British response was slow. Prime Minister William Ewart Gladstone's government had little enthusiasm for further involvement in Northeast Africa.

Gladstone himself was an anti-imperialist and entertained suspicions about the accuracy of the reports coming out of the Sudan. However, the British press clamored for action to rescue those in Khartoum. Finally, Gladstone reluctantly agreed to send Gordon back to the Sudan to evacuate Khartoum. Once again appointed governor of the Sudan, Gordon accepted the assignment and arrived in Khartoum on February 18, 1884. During the following three weeks, he had more than two thousand foreigners—mostly women, children, and the older persons—evacuated down the Nile, toward the Egyptian frontier. On March 13, 1884, the Mahdi's forces surrounded the city, making additional evacuations extremely difficult. The Siege of Khartoum had begun.

Contemporary depiction of General Gordon's death at Khartoum. (Library of Congress)

Although Gordon did not comply with Gladstone's order to evacuate the garrison or report directly on what he found, he did transform the environment of Khartoum. He organized Khartoum's defenses and resources. Using his expertise as an engineer, he directed the construction of new fortifications and used the natural terrain and the Nile River itself to his advantage. He established a plan to conserve foodstuffs and even managed to increase the supply of food that was available. He inventoried his armaments and centralized control over stores of ammunition.

Gordon also introduced discipline among Khartoum's Egyptian-Sudanese defenders, trained them for the defense of Khartoum, and improved their morale. He permitted no dissension among his troops and had troublemakers shot or expelled from the city. On the larger question of whether Gordon ever intended to evacuate Khartoum himself there can be little question. By choosing to remain in Khartoum, Gordon meant to force Gladstone to send a relief force to the Sudan to rescue him. The relief force would then defeat the Mahdi, secure the region for British interests, and end slavery and the slave trade. To drum up public support for his cause, Gordon sent letters directly to British newspapers, which responded by calling for an army to be sent to the Sudan.

Gladstone was outraged by Gordon's tactic and, surprisingly—in Gordon's eyes—resisted the mounting political pressures, including pleas from Queen Victoria, until August, 1884, when his government finally approved forming a relief expedition. Under the leadership of General Garnet Wolseley, the British relief force took an inordinate amount of time to train for desert warfare after its arrival in Egypt. It finally advanced from its base at Wadi Halfa in October, 1884. Wolseley's force defeated the Mahdi's troops in two minor battles. Confronted with the choice of withdrawing from Khartoum to save his army from possible defeat by the British or attacking the city before the main British force could arrive, the Mahdi gambled and attacked Khartoum on January 26, 1885. After a fierce struggle, the city fell and Gordon and the defenders were slaughtered. Two days later, on January 28, 1885, advance units of the British force arrived; Colonel Horatio Herbert Kitchener and Lord Charles Beresford were among the first to arrive at Khartoum. After a brief struggle, both sides withdrew. The Mahdi and his army left Khartoum and made Omdurman, on the opposite side of the Nile, their base.

SIGNIFICANCE

The immediate consequences of the Siege of Khartoum were the deaths of Gordon and the defenders in the garrison, the collapse of Gladstone's government, enhanced reputations for Wolseley and Kitchener, and the suppression of the Mahdi and his militant Muslim forces. More significantly, however, the temporary establishment of a major British military force in the Sudan had a far-reaching impact upon the expansion of British imperial designs on Northeast and East Africa. Some pro-imperialists advocated a Cape-to-Cairo railroad, and that would necessitate British control of most of eastern Africa.

During the mid-1890's the French government decided to establish a foothold in the region and quietly sent an expeditionary force across the African continent. At the same time the followers of the Mahdi, who died in 1885, revolted against the Anglo-Egyptian regime in the Sudan. Finally, the British sent a large expeditionary force under General Kitchener that decisively defeated the so-called dervishes at the Battle of Omdurman on September 2, 1898. Kitchener's forces then moved on Khartoum, where they learned of a French garrison at Fashoda (now Kodok) on the White Nile. Kitchener moved on the French position, and a major Anglo-French crisis known as the Fashoda incident unfolded. This crisis almost led to war between the two great powers, but the French backed down and undertook to normalize relations with Britain. Eventually, the French persuaded the British to enter the Anglo-French Entente of 1904, which resolved their later colonial disputes in Africa.

—*William T. Walker*

FURTHER READING

Elton, Godfrey. *Gordon of Khartoum*. New York: Alfred A. Knopf, 1955. Well-written biography that makes no attempt to hide the author's admiration for his subject. Nevertheless, Elton does not overlook Gordon's shortcomings.

Gordon, Charles George. *The Journals of Major-General Charles George Gordon, C.B., at Khartoum*. Edited by Egmont A. Hake. Boston: Houghton Mifflin, 1885. These journals cover only September 10 through December 14, 1884, but they provide the best insight into Gordon's mind during his last days at Khartoum.

Johnson, Peter. *Gordon of Khartoum*. Wellingsborough, England: Patrick Stephens, 1985. Solid biographical study of Charles Gordon that is especially good for those with little knowledge of Gordon or the resurgence of militant Islam in the Sudan.

Moore-Harrell, Alice. *Gordon and the Sudan: Prologue to the Mahdiyya, 1877-1880*. Portland, Oreg.: Frank Cass, 2001. Examines the years preceding the Mahdist revolution in Sudan by focusing on Gordon's administration as governor-general. Provides details about the political, economic, and social developments under Gordon's leadership.

Neillands, Robin. *The Dervish Wars: Gordon and Kitchener in the Sudan, 1880-1898*. London: John Murray, 1996. Important contribution to the literature on Gordon and the British in Northeast Africa; a book that should be of interest to general readers as well as serious students of this period.

Nicoll, Fergus. *Sword of the Prophet: The Mahdi of Sudan and the Death of General Gordon*. Stroud, England: Sutton, 2004. Focuses on the Mahdi's role as the charismatic leader of the Sudanese independence movement, and examines Gordon's death from the Mahdi's perspective.

Thompson, Brian. *Imperial Vanities: The Adventures of the Baker Brothers and Gordon of Khartoum*. London: HarperCollins, 2001. Well-written account intended for general readers that approaches its subjects as explorers and adventurers.

Waller, John H. *Gordon of Khartoum: The Saga of a Victorian Hero*. New York: Atheneum, 1988. Sympathetic but not uncritical account of Gordon's activities in the Sudan that argues that the fall of Khartoum constituted a major turning point in British imperialism in Africa.

SEE ALSO: 1822-1874: Exploration of North Africa; Sept. 13, 1882: Battle of Tel el Kebir; Mar., 1896-Nov., 1899: Sudanese War; Mar. 1, 1896: Ethiopia Repels Italian Invasion; July 10-Nov. 3, 1898: Fashoda Incident Pits France vs. Britain; May 18-July, 1899: First Hague Peace Conference.

RELATED ARTICLES in *Great Lives from History: The Nineteenth Century, 1801-1900:* Benjamin Disraeli; William Ewart Gladstone; Charles George Gordon; the Mahdi.

June 21, 1884
GOLD IS DISCOVERED IN THE TRANSVAAL

The discovery of goldfields that would eventually make South Africa one of the world's largest gold producers rapidly transformed the obscure Transvaal's Afrikaner republic into a prosperous economic center that would attract a huge influx of outsiders and again make the Transvaal the object of British imperial designs.

LOCALE: Transvaal (now in South Africa)
CATEGORIES: Earth science; economics; expansion and land acquisition; trade and commerce

KEY FIGURES

Paul Kruger (1825-1904), Afrikaner president of the Transvaal's South African Republic, 1883-1902
Cecil Rhodes (1853-1902), English prime minister of Cape Colony, 1890-1896
David Mackay Wilson (b. c. 1852), early gold commissioner in Transvaal

SUMMARY OF EVENT

During the 1880's, South Africa's Transvaal region was governed under a republic that had been established by Afrikaner settlers of primarily Dutch descent several decades earlier. During the 1830's, thousands of Afrikaner families began leaving the British ruled Cape Colony, and most of them eventually settled in the Transvaal and in the region that became known as the Orange Free State. Under the terms of the 1852 Sand River Convention, Great Britain recognized that Afrikaners living north of the Vaal River were independent of the Cape Colony.

The Transvaal Afrikaners called their country the South African Republic, but it was better known to outsiders as the Transvaal. In 1877, Britain annexed the Transvaal, claiming that it was acting to protect its people from hostile Zulus and from government bankruptcy. The Afrikaners, however, perceived the annexation as an unwanted interference. Tensions rose until December, 1880, when the Afrikaners launched an armed revolt. Under the leadership of Paul Kruger, they inflicted a serious defeat on the British at Majuba Hill in February, 1881. In the Pretoria Convention that settled the conflict, which became known as the First Boer War, Great Britain permitted the Afrikaners to rule the Transvaal under its supervision. Kruger then won election as the Transvaal's president. In February, 1884, the London Convention declared that the South African Republic was fully independent.

Several months after the London Convention, the discovery of gold in the Transvaal abruptly changed the republic's future. Although many people had earlier found small quantities of gold in alluvial deposits, no substantial quartz lodes were known until 1884. Discoveries of substantial diamond deposits in nearby Kimberley during the late 1860's had inspired prospectors to seek sizable mineral riches rumored to exist underground in the Transvaal's mountain ranges. The Transvaal government encouraged prospecting by offering rewards as large as eight hundred pounds for discoveries of gold reefs.

On June 21, 1884, a prospector named Graham Barber notified the Transvaal government that he and his brothers had found a large gold deposit in the De Kaap valley. Other prospectors miners soon located the adjacent Umvoti Reef. By late July, officials verified the miners' finds. Gold Commissioner David Mackay Wilson

South African Republic president Paul Kruger. (Library of Congress)

christened the site Barberton. Mining engineers determined that subterranean goldfields stretched more than forty miles from the Limpopo River to the Vaal River, along the Witwatersrand. International publicity soon alerted people outside Africa of the potential riches to be found in the previously obscure Transvaal. Britain and other European countries again became interested in gaining control over the Transvaal in order to profit from its mineral wealth.

THE SOUTH AFRICAN REPUBLIC

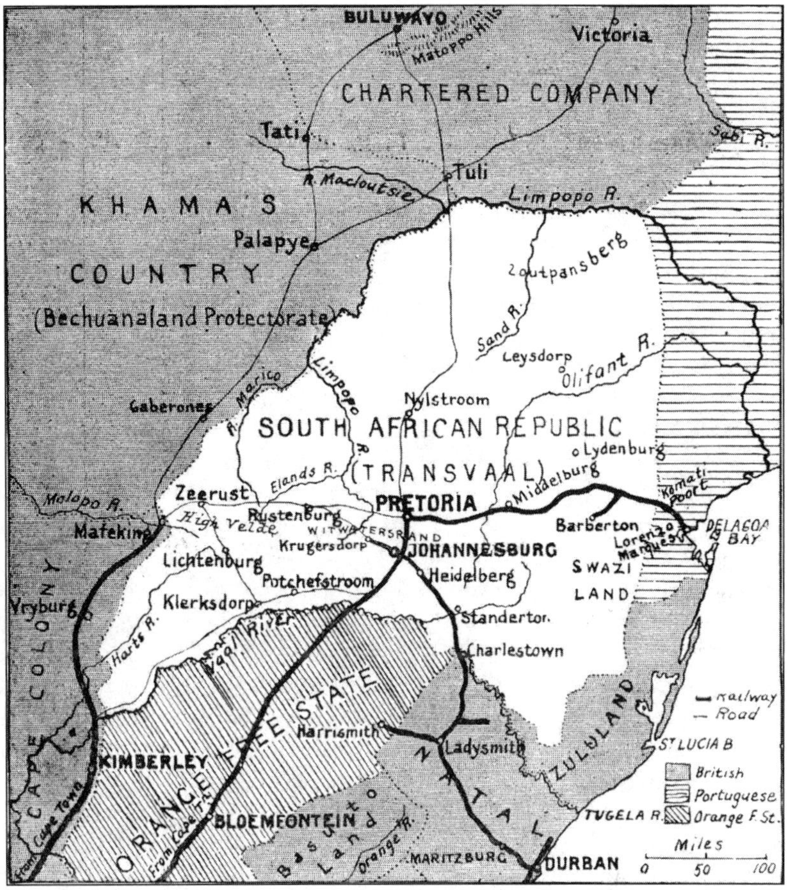

Prospectors armed with pickaxes flooded into the Transvaal, pegged claims, and jumped abandoned mining sites. Ordered to collect fees for the government, Wilson and mining officials sold licenses that soon began bringing into the government an average of ten thousand pounds per month from the goldfields. Wilson's staff included Afrikaners, Germans, and native Africans who helped with administrative duties and assisted with court sessions. Wilson rode his horse personally to view every claim. Miners were soon working about two thousand separate operations spread over about 4,500 square miles. Wilson drafted laws that specified rules for pegging and obtaining claims from farmers, defining the size and depth of claims, and outlawing claim jumping. President Paul Kruger visited the De Kaap Goldfields in 1885 and discussed opening a government mint.

Meanwhile, the Transvaal government delayed officially recognizing goldfields, thus permitting officials to seize miners' gold if they wanted. This outraged early prospectors who thought the government was taking advantage of them. Despite the risks of confiscation and other hazards, which included landslides and venomous snakes, miners continued seeking gold. By 1886, the government proclaimed public diggings on nine farms. Thousands of foreign prospectors, whom the Afrikaners called Uitlanders (outsiders), rushed into the Transvaal searching for gold. The mostly British Uitlanders soon outnumbered the Afrikaners, an imbalance that posed risks to the republic's stability.

Afrikaner leaders considered the miners to be temporary dwellers who might help rivals usurp power, and declared that Uitlanders could neither vote nor participate in the republic's government until they had resided in the Transvaal for fourteen years. Although the Transvaal had many native African districts, members of tribes were denied voting privileges. Angered by being excluded from policy making, high taxes, and unfair monopolies that favored Afrikaners, foreign miners reacted strongly. Some ripped down Transvaal flags, and others accused Afrikaner leaders of corruption.

The British resented the fact that Kruger contracted with German dynamite manufacturers for blasting supplies. A millionaire from his investments in gold, Kruger arranged monopolies with selected Transvaal and foreign vendors for goods ranging from bricks to liquor. High tariffs protected Transvaal industries from unwanted competition, and Kruger encouraged high fees for goods shipped to and from the British Cape Colony. Kruger practiced favoritism, offering contracts and positions to relatives and associates, even it they were not qualified to fulfill the contracts.

Language, cultural, and religious differences exacerbated tensions. As the Afrikaners became a minority in their own republic, Uitlanders, the new majority, complained to Cape Colony officials and later petitioned the queen. Uitlanders demanded representation rights because they contributed to the Transvaal's affluence. Afrikaners resented the Uitlanders for their frequently lawless and immoral behavior. Miners often damaged farmers' crops, and their crowded towns were dangerous. Everything in the Transvaal became more expensive. As Afrikaners sold their farms to miners and investors, they became landless but rich. These new upper-class elites often relocated elsewhere in South Africa.

Gold offered the Transvaal new economic opportunities. Land values soared. Produce sold for higher prices in markets. Businesses, stock exchanges, boardinghouses, and taverns mushroomed near goldfields to meet the needs of prospectors and take their money. Many entrepreneurs and financial speculators, hoping to profit, shifted from the Cape Colony to the Transvaal. Men who became known as "Randlords," after the Witwatersrand, became wealthy through buying land and establishing mining corporations. Many British investors had money, often from prior diamond investments, necessary to purchase and install mining technology, including hoists and shafts to extract ore deep underground. Nearby coal deposits fueled machinery.

The gold rush was also a catalyst for building better transportation and communication systems. The populations of mining villages at Pretoria and Johannesburg swelled. Locals benefited from jobs related to the mines and associated services for miners. Many native Africans, including Zulus, worked in mines, although they often were paid low wages or none at all. Black and Indian migrant workers traveled to the Transvaal from Mozambique and elsewhere for goldfield employment and encountered racism, often brutal and exploitative, from many Afrikaners and Uitlanders who considered themselves superior. However, Africans rarely complained about labor conditions, realizing that neither the British nor the Afrikaners would help them regain their ancestral lands or compensate them for their losses.

SIGNIFICANCE

Gold both enriched and altered the Transvaal, enabling its political leaders to assert claims of independence. Greed for wealth and power resulted in rivals contesting for control of other parts of Africa. European nations competed for African colonies to assert their prowess at imperialism and superiority. Gold enhanced the Transvaal's international stature and became South Africa's most important export, while lifting the Transvaal's economic and political assets to surpass all other parts of Southern Africa. Basically unknown before the gold rush, Transvaal had more then 100,000 mines by the 1890's and yielded gold valued at several million pounds annually. Like Kruger, other leaders realized that money represented political power. Gaining additional African land also appealed to greedy British imperialists. As European powers acquired African territories, they viewed the Transvaal and adjacent lands as prime property. Delegates met at the Berlin Conference in late 1884 through 1885 to address colonial disputes in Africa.

Gold and its associated political benefits also intrigued Cecil Rhodes, the Cape Colony prime minister, who had become rich at the Kimberley diamondfields. Concerned about German competitors in southwest Africa, he sought to reassert British control of the Transvaal and incorporate it in a confederated British-ruled Southern Africa. Kruger resisted. He wanted the Transvaal to retain its economic independence. Ultimately, his refusal to cooperate with British leaders resulted in the Transvaal's suffering its most devastating military defeat in the South African War (1899-1902). In May, 1902, the victories British made the Transvaal a colony. The 1910 South Africa Act joined the Transvaal with the Cape Colony and other areas to create the Union of South Africa. During the twenty-first century, the Transvaal's gold mining industry still continues to extract billions of dollars worth of gold every year.

—*Elizabeth D. Schafer*

FURTHER READING

Giliomee, Hermann B. *The Afrikaners: Biography of a People*. Charlottesville: University Press of Virginia, 2003. Study of Afrikaner history that explores the impact of gold on the people who settled the Transvaal and how they dealt with political rivals attempting to destroy their autonomy.

Hatch, Frederick H., and John A. Chalmers. *The Gold Mines of the Rand: Being a Description of the Mining Industry of Witwatersrand, South African Republic*. New York: Macmillan, 1895. Comprehensive contemporary account written by mining engineers familiar with the Transvaal. Contains historical, geological, metallurgical, and legal information supplemented with photographs, charts, mine plans, and maps.

Paulin, Christopher M. *White Men's Dreams, Black Men's Blood: African Labor and British Expansionism in Southern Africa, 1877-1895.* Trenton, N.J.: Africa World Press, 2001. Discusses how imperialism intensified demands for inexpensive, plentiful workers and how the British and Afrikaners both subjugated Africans as they sought control of the Transvaal.

Wilson, David Mackay. *Behind the Scenes in the Transvaal.* London: Cassell, 1901. Memoir of the Transvaal gold commissioner who was intimately familiar with the development of the goldfields. Wilson describes events, people, the violence associated with mining camps, and mistreatment of African workers.

Worger, William H., Nancy L. Clark, and Edward A. Alpers, eds. *Africa and the West: A Documentary History from the Slave Trade to Independence.* Phoenix, Ariz.: Oryx Press, 2001. Collection of primary sources including documents relating to European competition for African colonies, the Berlin Conference, and the Transvaal gold discoveries.

SEE ALSO: Jan. 24, 1848: California Gold Rush Begins; 1851: Gold Is Discovered in New South Wales; Mar. 23, 1858: Fraser River Gold Rush Begins; Jan. 22-Aug., 1879: Zulu War; Dec. 16, 1880-Mar. 6, 1881: First Boer War; Nov. 15, 1884-Feb. 26, 1885: Berlin Conference Lays Groundwork for the Partition of Africa; Mar. 13, 1888: Rhodes Amalgamates Kimberley Diamondfields; Dec. 29, 1895-Jan. 2, 1896: Jameson Raid; Aug. 17, 1896: Klondike Gold Rush Begins; Oct. 11, 1899-May 31, 1902: South African War.

RELATED ARTICLES in *Great Lives from History: The Nineteenth Century, 1801-1900:* Paul Kruger; Cecil Rhodes.

November 4, 1884

U.S. ELECTION OF 1884

After one of the dirtiest presidential election campaigns in U.S. history, Grover Cleveland's victory in 1884 broke the Republicans' twenty-four-year hold on the presidency, and Cleveland became known for his exceptional integrity.

ALSO KNOWN AS: Election of Grover Cleveland
LOCALE: United States
CATEGORY: Government and politics

KEY FIGURES

Grover Cleveland (1837-1908), governor of New York, 1883-1885, who was the Democratic presidential candidate

James G. Blaine (1830-1893), former Speaker of the House of Representatives who was the Republican candidate

Samuel D. Burchard (1812-1891), clergyman whose tactless comments about Democrats may have hurt Blaine

Benjamin Franklin Butler (1818-1893), nominee of the Greenback-Labor Party

John Pierce St. John (1833-1916), nominee of the Prohibition Party

Carl Schurz (1829-1906), Republican reformer who supported Cleveland

SUMMARY OF EVENT

The 1884 presidential election, which pitted Republican James G. Blaine against Democrat Grover Cleveland, was one of the dirtiest in U.S. history. The parties were evenly split as far as voter loyalties were concerned, so the race turned on the personal characters of the two major party nominees. The presidential election was won by Cleveland, a former mayor of Buffalo, New York, and the governor of New York. He was the first successful Democratic candidate for the presidency in twenty-four years. However, the voting was so close that a shift of six hundred votes in a single state would have reversed the outcome. During a time of electoral stalemate between the parties, narrow margins in the popular vote were typical. Public excitement in the campaign ran high, and spectacular episodes swayed the electorate throughout the campaign.

When the Republicans met in Chicago to nominate their candidate on June 3, 1884, the front-runner was the most popular figure of his time: James G. Blaine of Maine. The incumbent president, Chester A. Arthur, had little support. He had been an adequate president after succeeding the assassinated James A. Garfield in 1881, but the party regulars and the rank and file of the so-called Grand Old Party (GOP) preferred the more charismatic Blaine. Unfortunately for the party, however,

Blaine also had weaknesses. Charges circulated that he had used his offices for personal gain. His dealings with an Arkansas railroad while he had been Speaker of the House during the 1870's had been recorded in damaging letters that were owned by a man named Mulligan. These "Mulligan letters," on which Blaine had written, "Burn this letter when you have read it," dogged him throughout the election.

Blaine's nomination was relatively easy. He was selected on the fourth ballot, and John A. Logan of Illinois became his running mate. For Republican reformers—who were nicknamed mugwumps, after an Indian term for big chief—Blaine was an impossible choice. Their spokesman, Carl Schurz, said that electing Blaine would have evil results. These discontented Republicans prepared to support the Democratic nominee.

A month after the Republican convention, the Democratic Party met in Chicago. Sensing a victory after long years in the political wilderness, the Democrats had a fresh face in Grover Cleveland, who had gained a reputation in New York as a foe of corrupt politics and an enemy of an activist government. He had quarreled with the New York City political machine, Tammany Hall. Enemies called him the Veto Governor. Cleveland was a large man, whose family called him Uncle Jumbo. Cleveland seemed the clear choice during an era when the Democrats could win the presidency by carrying the solidly Democratic South, New York, and one or two midwestern states. Cleveland was nominated on the second ballot, and Thomas A. Hendricks of Indiana balanced the ticket as his midwestern running mate.

The campaign that followed quickly became dirty. In July, news broke that Cleveland had been involved with a woman named Maria Halpin and that he might be the

Democratic Party campaign poster for Grover Cleveland and Thomas A. Hendricks. (Library of Congress)

father of her illegitimate son. The story was true. Cleveland accepted responsibility for the child and paid for his upbringing. Republicans tried to capitalize on the episode in their political rallies. Marchers strode behind baby carriages and chanted, "Ma! Ma! Where's My Pa?" Cleveland responded to the allegations by urging his supporters to tell the truth. By admitting what had happened right away, Cleveland defused the scandal.

Meanwhile, the Democrats charged Blaine with corruption concerning the Mulligan letters, and further revelations during the campaign added to the force of the allegations. In the giant rallies that they staged, the Democrats shouted together as they walked through the streets of towns and cities:

> Blaine, Blaine, James G. Blaine
> The continental liar from the State of Maine
> *Burn this letter!*

The overall electoral picture in 1884 gave the edge to the Democrats. Their base in the South was so solid that they had to win fewer northern states than the Republicans did. The economy had slipped into a mild recession that favored the party out of power. Because the Republicans had been in power so long, accumulated grievances against the federal government worked against them. As a result of the defection of the mugwumps, many of the newspapers and magazines in the East that ordinarily would have favored the Republican candidate were in the Democratic camp.

In response, the Republicans looked to capitalize on perceived areas of Democratic weakness. Cleveland did not enjoy much support from labor. Accordingly, the Republicans provided money for the Greenback-Labor Party and its presidential candidate, Benjamin Franklin Butler of Massachusetts. The erratic Butler campaigned with great energy but was not an important factor in the outcome of the race.

A source of worry for the Republicans was the Prohibition Party and its standard-bearer, John Pierce St. John. Voters for the "dry" candidate usually came from among former Republicans, and St. John was particularly strong in upstate New York, which played a large role in the outcome of the contest.

Blaine became the central focus of the campaign. He wanted to make the protective tariff a major issue and stressed economic concerns in his letter accepting the nomination. His record of opposition to Great Britain in foreign affairs also won him support from among Irish American voters. Working against Blaine was Republican disunity. The leader of the GOP in New York, former senator Roscoe Conkling, had a hatred for Blaine dating back to arguments they had had in the House of Representatives during the 1860's. Conkling refused to campaign for Blaine, and his opposition to Blaine hurt Republican chances in the key state of New York.

To overcome these obstacles, Blaine decided to embark on a personal campaign swing. Although he was not the first presidential candidate to try this technique, it was an innovation for a major party candidate to woo the electorate directly. Democrats charged that Blaine was lowering the tone of the race for the White House. On the whole, the experiment was successful. Blaine drew large and enthusiastic crowds. The Republicans seemed to be ahead when they carried Maine and Vermont in September, and Ohio went Republican in October. (At that time, not all states voted for the president on the same days.)

The key state was New York, which Blaine had to carry to win. With reports coming in that the Democrats might win, Blaine decided to include New York on his speaking schedule. At the end of October, he spent a week in a determined effort to cover the vast expanses of the Empire State. He arrived in New York City on October 28 in a condition of near exhaustion.

On October 29, Blaine met with several hundred Protestant clergymen in his hotel lobby. When the designated speaker was delayed, the group called upon a Presbyterian minister named Samuel D. Burchard as a substitute. Burchard announced in his remarks that "We are Republicans and don't propose to leave our party and identify ourselves with the party whose antecedents have been rum, Romanism, and rebellion." In his answer, Blaine did not mention Burchard's comment.

Burchard's statement caused an uproar, because it attacked Roman Catholicism at a time when Blaine had been trying to woo the votes of predominantly Catholic Irish Americans. The Democrats spread the remark as widely as they could, and Republican disavowals were late and ineffective. Another public relations fiasco occurred when Blaine attended a dinner in his honor at Delmonico's restaurant in New York City, where his audience was made up of millionaires and business leaders. The Democrats promptly dubbed the occasion "The Boodle Banquet."

Election day on November 4 brought further problems for Blaine. In upstate New York, heavy rains kept Republican voters at home in an area where Blaine needed a big turnout. It was soon apparent that the election would be very close. Cleveland carried the Democratic South, and Blaine ran strongly in the Midwest. The key state was New York, whose returns trickled in slowly over several days. In the end, Cleveland won New York by a scant 1,149 votes. The Prohibition ticket had received 25,000 votes, the majority of which would have gone to Blaine under normal circumstances.

SIGNIFICANCE

Cleveland won the 36 electoral votes of New York, and his total of 219 put him into the White House. Blaine's total was 182 electoral votes. The popular vote was also close. Cleveland's majority was less than 25,000 ballots. After the election, and in historical accounts since 1884, the episode involving the Reverend Burchard was said to have cost Blaine the election. In fact, Blaine did better than any other Republican might have done. He ran 400,000 votes ahead of James A. Garfield's total in 1880. The real explanation for what happened in 1884 was that, in a Democratic year, Grover Cleveland kept his party united to achieve a narrow victory. Four years later, Cleveland would lose his bid for reelection, but in 1892, he became the first former president to come back and be elected again.

—Lewis L. Gould,
based on the original entry by Gustav L. Seligman

FURTHER READING

Crapol, Edward P. *James G. Blaine: Architect of Empire*. Wilmington, Del.: Scholarly Resources, 2000. Biography of Blaine that pays special attention to his tenure as secretary of state, including his relations with Latin America and his attempts to upgrade the merchant marine and U.S. Navy.

Gould, Lewis L. "1884." In *Running for President: The Candidates and Their Images*, edited by Arthur Schlesinger et al. Vol. 1. New York: Simon & Schuster, 1994. Brief account of the 1884 election that incorporates updated historical scholarship about the outcome of the Blaine-Cleveland race.

Graff, Henry F. *Grover Cleveland*. New York: Times Books, 2002. Solid contribution to a series of brief presidential biographies. Graff depicts Cleveland as a decisive president, a man of action and uncompromising integrity.

Jeffers, H. Paul. *An Honest President: The Life and Presidencies of Grover Cleveland*. New York: William Morrow, 2000. Jeffers portrays Cleveland as a staunch reformer, a man of high moral character and courage who restored dignity to the presidency.

Keller, Morton. *Affairs of State: Public Life in Late Nineteenth Century America*. Cambridge, Mass.: Belknap Press of Harvard University Press, 1977. Useful for understanding how the Blaine-Cleveland contest grew out of the political culture of the late nineteenth century.

McGerr, Michael. *The Decline of Popular Politics: The American North, 1865-1928*. New York: Oxford University Press, 1986. Discusses the 1884 election in the context of evolving campaign styles and methods of getting voters to the polls.

Morgan, H. Wayne. *From Hayes to McKinley: National Party Politics, 1877-1896*. Syracuse, N.Y.: Syracuse University Press, 1969. Readable, thorough account that places the 1884 election in the context of the battle between the Republicans and Democrats to secure a national majority.

Welch, Richard. *The Presidencies of Grover Cleveland*. Lawrence: University Press of Kansas, 1988. Discusses how the election of 1884 brought Cleveland to national power and considers the political appeal that twice took him to the White House.

SEE ALSO: Sept. 25, 1804: Twelfth Amendment Is Ratified; July 6, 1854: Birth of the Republican Party; Mar. 5, 1877: Hayes Becomes President; Jan. 16, 1883: Pendleton Act Reforms the Federal Civil Service; July 4-5, 1892: Birth of the People's Party; Nov. 3, 1896: McKinley Is Elected President.

RELATED ARTICLES in *Great Lives from History: The Nineteenth Century, 1801-1900:* Chester A. Arthur; James G. Blaine; Grover Cleveland; Carl Schurz.

November 15, 1884-February 26, 1885
BERLIN CONFERENCE LAYS GROUNDWORK FOR THE PARTITION OF AFRICA

A defining moment in the history of European involvement in Africa, the Berlin Conference brought together representatives of fourteen nations to work out mutually acceptable procedures and protocols for dividing Africa among themselves—without the benefit of consulting the views of Africa's peoples on their own future.

LOCALE: Berlin, Germany
CATEGORIES: Diplomacy and international relations; expansion and land acquisition; colonization

KEY FIGURES

Otto von Bismarck (1815-1898), chancellor of the German Empire, 1871-1890
Leopold II (1835-1909), king of Belgium, r. 1865-1909
Henry Morton Stanley (1841-1904), British American newspaper correspondent and explorer

SUMMARY OF EVENT

Between November 15, 1884, and February, 1885, representatives of all the European imperial powers met in Berlin in what was the first major colonial conference of the modern era. The conference seemingly resolved various contentious issues among several European nations that arose from their competing imperial ambitions and relationships in Africa. Fourteen nations were represented, including the United States. However, the major participants were France, Germany, Great Britain, and Portugal, as well as the International Association of the Congo, a private entry created by the Belgian king, Leopold II. Leopold himself did not attend the conference, but he would prove to be its primary beneficiary. However, the conference itself was something of an anticlimax because many crucial decisions had been made before it even opened. In any case, many of the decisions that the conference did make were soon superseded by subsequent events.

European involvement in sub-Saharan Africa went back hundreds, even thousands, of years. The ancient Greeks and Romans had sailed and traded along the continent's eastern shore, and Portuguese explorers and merchants had established a presence along the western coast of Africa in the late fifteenth century, and they began operating along the East African coast during the sixteenth century. During the mid-seventeenth century, the Dutch founded Cape Town in South Africa and began colonizing the region around it. Intense European colonization, however, did not begin until the nineteenth century. By the latter part of that century, European nations had claimed most of the African littoral, either directly or indirectly. However, much of the interior of Africa was still terra incognita to Europeans and other Westerners. That situation began to change with the explorations of Sir Richard Francis Burton, John Hanning Speke, and Henry Morton Stanley. The latter, a Welsh-born American journalist, became

Belgian king Leopold II. (Library of Congress)

1880's

Africa at the End of the Nineteenth Century

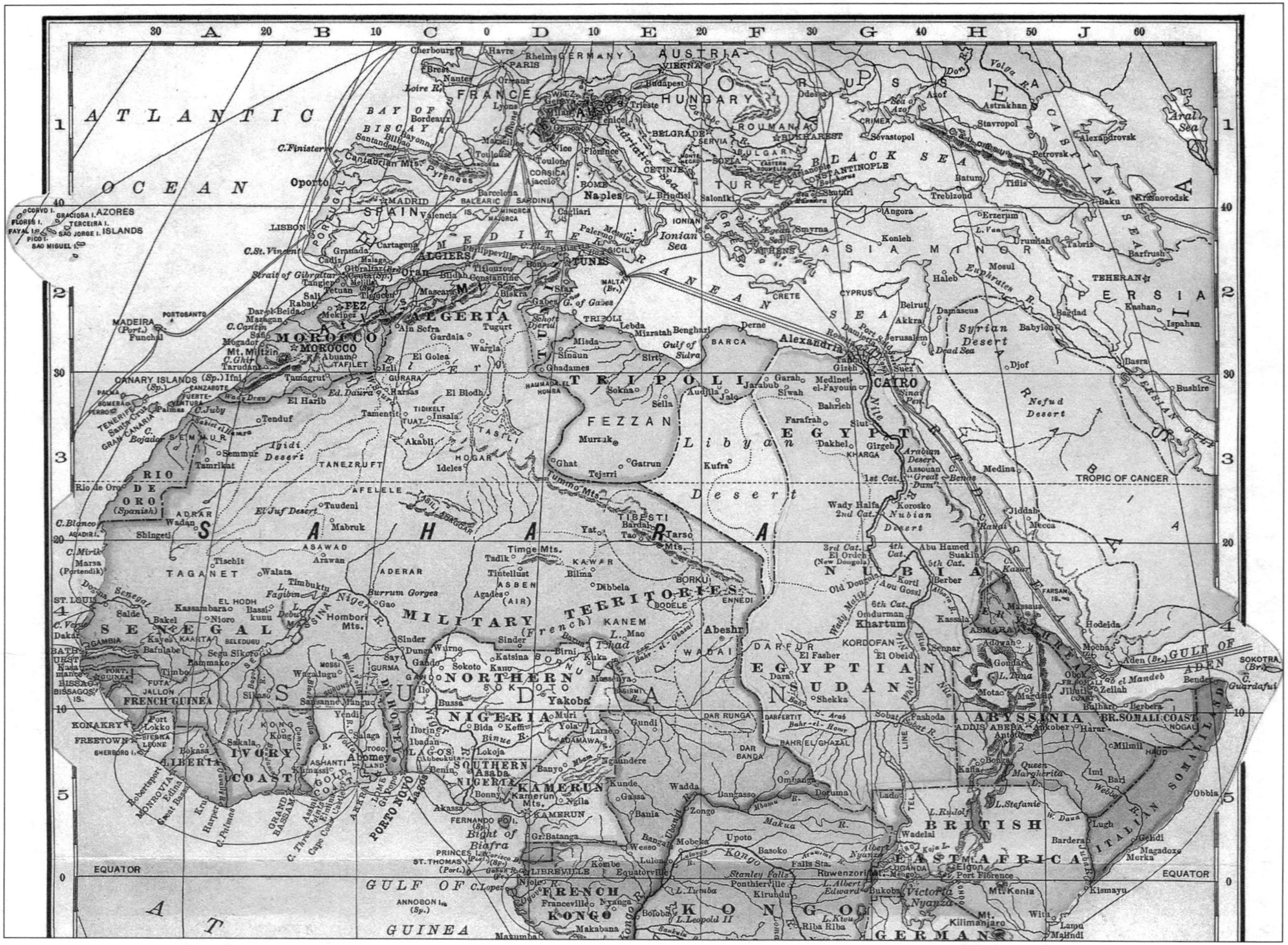

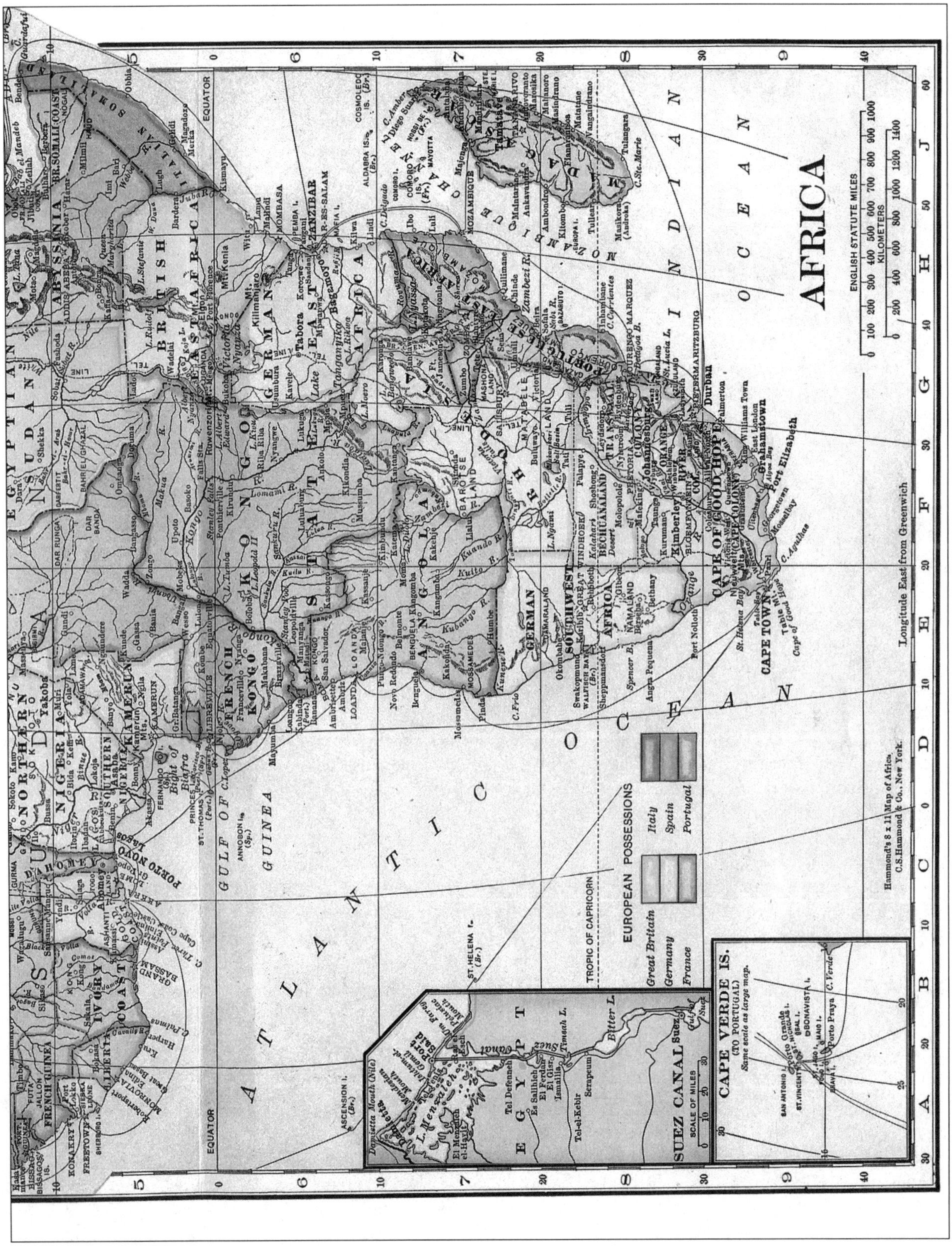
AFRICA
EUROPEAN POSSESSIONS
Great Britain
Germany
France
Italy
Spain
Portugal
ATLANTIC OCEAN
INDIAN OCEAN
SUEZ CANAL
CAPE VERDE IS.
(TO PORTUGAL)
Same scale as large map.
ENGLISH STATUTE MILES
KILOMETERS
Longitude East from Greenwich
Hammond's 8 x 11 Map of Africa.
C.S.Hammond & Co., New York.

1880's

world famous for his finding of the famed missionary-explorer David Livingstone in 1872. Meanwhile, Livingstone's "Three Cs"—Christianity, civilization, and commerce—became Europe's justification for its imperial endeavors in Africa.

The small nation of Belgium had few African connections, and most Belgians had little interest in that continent. The exception was Leopold II, who became their king in 1865. Leopold desired a larger world stage than his nation provided, and establishing an overseas empire appealed to him. Sub-Saharan Africa was a logical focus, but he disguised his imperial ambitions under the cloak of humanitarianism. In 1876, he sponsored a geographical conference in Brussels, attended by a number of notable explorers, with the exception of Henry Morton Stanley, who then crossing Africa from its east to its west coast. Under Leopold's leadership, the conference participants created the International African Association (Association International Africaine; AIA). With King Leopold as its first chairman, the association adopted a flag with a gold star on a blue background.

Meanwhile, in August, 1877, Stanley completed the crossing of the African continent, thereby becoming the first explorer to chart much of the Congo River to its mouth. Eager to capitalize on Stanley's fame, King Leopold signed him to a five-year contract to continue his explorations and to secure land concessions in the Congo Basin by making treaties with African rulers. To Stanley and others, Leopold's interest in Africa appeared to be mainly humanitarian. The ambitious king reconstituted his International African Association as the Association Internationale du Congo (AIC), or the International Congo Association, whose sphere of interest encompassed not only the region close to the Congo River but also the entire Congo basin. Thanks to Stanley's work, the association's flag was flying over a number of small settlements along the great river by the year 1884.

As Leopold developed his own private colony in the heart of Africa, other issues were threatening the African status quo. The desire for raw materials and new markets, a consequence of the Industrial Revolution, had quickened European interest in Africa. Portugal, which had had a long presence in sub-Saharan Africa, began fearing French ambitions in the region, so it opened negotiations with Great Britain in 1882 that would give Britain an unofficial protectorate over the Congo in exchange for British recognition of Portugal's own territorial claims along Africa's western coast. The British government was not eager to colonize the Congo, but it was adamant in defending the policy of free trade for its subjects, something that France was less likely to grant. In reaction to the proposed Anglo-Portuguese treaty, France and Germany—which had recently been opponents in the Franco-Prussian War (1870-1871)—increased their mutual diplomatic contacts because both opposed Britain's expanding its interests in Africa. Ultimately the Anglo-Portuguese treaty was not ratified, in large part because of the opposition of Germany's Chancellor Otto von Bismarck. In response to its failed treaty with Britain, Portugal proposed a general European conference concerning West African issues.

Unified only since 1871, Germany entered the colonial race late. Bismarck's personal enthusiasm for a German overseas empire was muted, but he was in the midst of a conflict with Britain over an inconsequential strip of territory in Southwest Africa, a dispute that had escalated when the British government failed to immediately respond to Bismarck's concerns. France had its own ambitions, notably the establishment of French colonial authority along the Niger River, north of the Congo. In October, 1884, with French support, Bismarck issued invitations to a conference to meet in Germany's capital, Berlin, in November. Unsure about the aims of the conference, the British were initially reluctant to participate and demanded guarantees of free trade and navigation along both the Niger and Congo Rivers.

While Portugal, Britain, France, and Germany engaged in their diplomatic maneuvers, Leopold II pursued his own Congo goals. He cleverly appealed to American sentiment on the issues of antislavery and free trade and suggested a parallel between the American-backed republic of Liberia and his own Congo project. In April, 1884, he gained formal American diplomatic recognition for his International Congo Association , thus giving what had been basically a private organization status as a sovereign power. A few days later France also granted Leopold's association diplomatic recognition, in exchange for the promise that in the event that it collapsed, France would have first rights to obtain its African territories. Leopold's resulting guarantee to France led to Bismarck's recognition of his quasi-state on November 8, 1884, immediately before the conference opened. On December 16, Britain also granted recognition to the association, motivated by fear of French ambitions in Africa.

Fourteen powers were represented at the Berlin Conference, including Leopold's International Congo Association, which actually had no legal status. The key participants were Britain, France, Germany, Portugal, and

Leopold's association. The initial stages of the conference dealt with the issue of freedom of commerce in the Congo Basin and at the mouth of the Congo River. The second stage dealt with freedom of navigation along the Congo and Niger Rivers, and the last stage, in February, 1885, considered the issue of what was mean by "effective occupation" of territory by colonial powers. Humanitarian concerns, including the abolishment of the slave trade, played little part in the conference discussions, despite earlier intimations to the contrary. Negotiations among the principal powers resulted in the creation of an extensive Congo state under the aegis of Leopold's International Congo Association, while France and Portugal were awarded limited adjacent territories, territories that did not seriously impinge upon Leopold's vision and ambitions.

A broader issue considered by the conference was that of effective colonial occupation. As established colonial powers, Britain and France favored a loose definition of "effective occupation," while Germany, which was initially not an imperial power, wanted to require would-be colonial powers to demonstrate effective political control over territories before claiming the territories as their colonies. After much discussion and compromise, the conferees agreed that any new colonial claims along the African coast required that the occupying state notify the other signatory states. In addition, when and if new colonies were claimed and established, existing rights must be respected and freedom of trade be guaranteed.

SIGNIFICANCE

In spite of what is often claimed about the Berlin Conference, Africa was not formally partitioned as a result of the Berlin Conference. The so-called scramble for Africa had begun earlier, and by the early twentieth century only Ethiopia, Liberia, and Morocco remained free from direct European control. Nevertheless, there were some clear winners at the conference. For example, Britain used the conference to prevent its rival France from occupying the Congo Basin. Although the German-French entente broke down over various issues, it succeeded in forcing Britain—which had recently occupied Egypt—to accept international regulation of both the Suez Canal and the Egyptian government debt.

During the period leading up the conference, Germany acquired several colonies in Africa and elsewhere. But it was the king of the Belgians, Leopold II, who emerged truly victorious. Diplomatic recognition of his International Congo Association resulted in international recognition of the sovereignty of his Congo Free State, a territory in the heart of Africa that was larger than Britain, France, Germany, Italy, Spain, and Belgium combined. The ultimate losers were Africa's native peoples, especially in the Congo. The Congo Free State regime soon became one of the most rapacious and inhumane regimes on the continent, and under its banner, slavery and other forms of human degradation became the norm in the quest for economic profits. In 1908, the Belgium government took the colony away from Leopold's control.

—Eugene Larson

FURTHER READING

Crowe, S. E. *The Berlin West African Conference, 1884-1885*. London: Longmans, Green, 1942. This study of the Berlin Conference remains the standard work on the subject.

Hochschild, Adam. *King Leopold's Ghost*. Boston: Houghton Mifflin, 1998. Brilliant exposition of the establishment of the Congo Free State and the tragic consequences that followed.

Newman, James L. *Imperial Footprints*. Washington, D.C.: Brassey's, 2004. Excellent discussion of Henry Morton Stanley's African exploratory expeditions, including those that he undertook for King Leopold II.

Pakenham, Thomas. *The Scramble for Africa*. New York: Random House, 1991. Well-written and comprehensive narrative of European imperialism in Africa from 1876 to 1912.

SEE ALSO: May 4, 1805-1830: Exploration of West Africa; 1822-1874: Exploration of North Africa; 1848-1889: Exploration of East Africa; Nov. 17, 1853: Livingstone Sees the Victoria Falls; 1873-1880: Exploration of Africa's Congo Basin; 1873-1897: Zanzibar Outlaws Slavery; Jan. 22, 1873-Feb. 13, 1874: Second British-Ashanti War; Sept. 13, 1882: Battle of Tel el Kebir; June 21, 1884: Gold Is Discovered in the Transvaal; Nov., 1889-Jan., 1894: Dahomey-French Wars; Mar., 1896-Nov., 1899: Sudanese War; July 10-Nov. 3, 1898: Fashoda Incident Pits France vs. Britain.

RELATED ARTICLES in *Great Lives from History: The Nineteenth Century, 1801-1900:* Otto von Bismarck; Sir George Goldie; Leopold II; David Livingstone; Henry Morton Stanley.

December, 1884-February, 1885
TWAIN PUBLISHES *ADVENTURES OF HUCKLEBERRY FINN*

Publication of Mark Twain's literary masterwork, Adventures of Huckleberry Finn, *marked a watershed in American literary history by introducing the rhythms of realistic American colloquial speech to fiction. During the twenty-first century, the book remains one of the most controversial and most widely read and studied works in American literature.*

LOCALE: London, England
CATEGORY: Literature

KEY FIGURES

Mark Twain (Samuel Langhorne Clemens; 1835-1910), American novelist and humorist
William Dean Howells (1837-1920), American writer and literary critic

SUMMARY OF EVENT

In 1876, Samuel Langhorne Clemens, better known by his pen name, Mark Twain, wrote to his friend and fellow writer William Dean Howells that he was working on a sequel to his recently completed novel, *The Adventures of Tom Sawyer* (1876). The protagonist of his new novel was to be Tom Sawyer's friend, Huckleberry Finn. Twain completed about a third of this new novel in 1876, stopped work on the manuscript for a few years, resumed writing in 1879 only to put the manuscript aside again, and finally completed the book, *Adventures of Huckleberry Finn*, in 1884. The novel was published in England in December, 1884, and the first American edition appeared in February, 1885.

Huckleberry Finn was very different from *Tom Sawyer*, which featured an omniscient narrator, as it was narrated by Huck himself in the coarse homespun dialect of an unschooled Missouri boy. Featuring a murder mystery and buried treasure, *Tom Sawyer* was a humorous boys' adventure story. By contrast, *Huckleberry Finn* grappled with one of America's most troubling moral issues, slavery. Set around the mid-1840's, *Huckleberry Finn* centers on the relationship between Huck, who has run away from his abusive father, Pap Finn, and Jim, a runaway slave. The two fugitives meet on an island in the Mississippi River, find a raft, and head downriver toward Cairo, Illinois, where they plan to sell the raft, buy passage on a steamboat, and head upstream on the Ohio River into the free states of Ohio and Pennsylvania. However, they drift past Cairo on a foggy night and head ever deeper into slave territory. Along the way, they experience a series of both humorous and harrowing adventures. Throughout the journey, Huck wrestles with his conscience, trying to decide whether to report Jim as a fugitive slave or to assist him in his quest for freedom. Eventually, Huck recognizes Jim's humanity and decides to help him gain his freedom, even if it means that he himself will go to hell.

Many early reviews of *Huckleberry Finn* were positive. Reviewers praised the authenticity of Huck Finn's voice, Twain's ability to capture the culture of Mississippi River communities, and the book's biting humor. Like Twain's earlier books—*The Innocents Abroad* (1869), *Roughing It* (1872), *Tom Sawyer*, and *Life on*

Frontispiece of the first edition of Adventures of Huckleberry Finn. *Mark Twain objected to an earlier version by illustrator Edward Kemble because he thought it made Huck look "too Irishy."* (Library of Congress)

the Mississippi (1883)—*Huckleberry Finn* sold well. The novel's first printing, which contained illustrations by E. W. Kemble, was set for 30,000 copies. However, shortly after the book's publication, it ran into trouble. In March, 1885, the trustees of the Concord, Massachusetts, public library decided to exclude *Huckleberry Finn* from the library's collection. The trustees cited as reasons the book's coarse humor, the unsuitable behavior of many of its characters, and Huck's ungrammatical diction. Some educators considered Huck a poor role model for American youngsters: Huck smokes, cuts school, can barely read, and speaks ungrammatically. Other libraries followed Concord's example, but Twain himself appeared to be unfazed by this form of criticism. He claimed that library bans would result in the sale of an additional 25,000 copies of his novel.

HUCK'S DISCOVERY OF JIM'S HUMANITY

One of the most moving passages in Mark Twain's Huckleberry Finn *occurs in chapter 23, when the young waif Huck awakens to the realization that a black person such as his companion Jim has the same feelings as a white person. The passage takes place during a quiet moment on Huck and Jim's raft.*

I went to sleep, and Jim didn't call me when it was my turn. He often done that. When I waked up, just at day-break, he was setting there with his head down betwixt his knees, moaning and mourning to himself. I didn't take notice, nor let on. I knowed what it was about. He was thinking about his wife and his children, away up yonder, and he was low and homesick; because he hadn't ever been away from home before in his life; and I do believe he cared just as much for his people as white folks does for their'n. It don't seem natural, but I reckon it's so. He was often moaning and mourning that way, nights, when he judged I was asleep, and saying, "Po' little 'Lizabeth! po' little Johnny! its mighty hard; I spec' I ain't ever gwyne to see you no mo', no mo'!" He was a mighty good nigger, Jim was.

Source: Mark Twain, *Adventures of Huckleberry Finn* (New York: Charles L. Webster, 1885), p. 201.

Huckleberry Finn solidified Twain's reputation as a major American writer. After its publication, he became more popular than ever on the lecture circuit, entertaining audiences with his caustic humor in both the United States and abroad. Twain published several more popular books after *Huckleberry Finn*, including *A Connecticut Yankee in King Arthur's Court* (1889), *Pudd'nhead Wilson* (1894), and *Tom Sawyer Abroad* (1894). None of these books, however, generated as much discussion or controversy as Twain's novel about the abused boy and the runaway slave drifting down the Mississippi River aboard a raft.

Discussion of and debate over *Adventures of Huckleberry Finn* and its author's place in American literary history continued long after Twain's death in 1910. In 1920, Van Wyck Brooks published the first major critical study of Twain's work, *The Ordeal of Mark Twain* (revised in 1933), to which Bernard DeVoto responded in 1932 with *Mark Twain's America.* A decade later, DeVoto followed with *Mark Twain at Work* (1942). Both Brooks and DeVoto treated Twain as a major American writer. During the middle of the twentieth century, two of the era's most influential literary figures, Lionel Trilling and T. S. Eliot, praised *Huckleberry Finn* as Twain's masterpiece and one of America's greatest novels. Trilling included an essay on *Huckleberry Finn* in his book *The Liberal Imagination* (1950) with the title "The Greatness of *Huckleberry Finn*."

Despite such distinguished praise, Twain's most famous novel has always had its detractors. The final chapters of the novel—in which Huckleberry Finn meets Tom Sawyer on the Arkansas farm of Tom's aunt and uncle—have troubled both critics and readers alike. In *Green Hills of Africa* (1935), Ernest Hemingway wrote,

> All modern American literature comes from one book by Mark Twain called *Huckleberry Finn*. If you read it you must stop where the Nigger Jim is stolen from the boys. That is the real end. The rest is just cheating. But it's the best book we've had. All American writing comes from that. There was nothing before. There has been nothing as good since.

The final chapters, built upon the unlikely coincidence of Jim's becoming a captive on the farm of Tom Sawyer's aunt and uncle just as Tom is about to visit the farm, feature farcical comedy and an implausible plan, designed by Tom, to free Jim. At the end of the novel, Twain provides a deus ex machina resolution to the two main problems of the novel that troubles some readers. Tom Sawyer announces that Jim was set free in his owner's will, and Jim reveals that Huck's father, Pap, is dead.

A zealous critique of *Adventures of Huckleberry Finn* by African American educators and critics began in

1957, when the National Association for the Advancement of Colored People determined that Twain's novel was racially offensive. This argument centers on Twain's use of the word "nigger," which appears more than two hundred times in the novel, as well as his characterization of Jim. Huck consistently uses "nigger" to describe Jim and other slaves. In some episodes, Jim appears shrewd and asserts his manhood by demanding respect from Huck; in others—particularly in the final chapters—Jim appears passive, subservient, and unintelligent—a stereotype of the bumbling plantation slave. This racial critique of *Huckleberry Finn* has continued into the twenty-first century. Some American high schools have banned *Huckleberry Finn* from the classroom and library for its treatment of slavery and race.

Significance

Despite the criticisms that it has endured, *Adventures of Huckleberry Finn* remains one of the most widely read and studied American novels. More than fifteen million copies of the book, in countless editions, have been sold around the world. It is included in literary anthologies and widely covered in American high school and college literature courses. Although *Huckleberry Finn* has always generated criticism, it has also achieved the status of classic American novel. Twain is credited with grappling honestly with America's most serious moral issues, slavery and race, and with bringing to the American novel, through Huck's voice, the rhythms of realistic American colloquial speech. Twain is considered the literary ancestor of Sherwood Anderson, Ernest Hemingway, William Faulkner, J. D. Salinger, and many other American writers who capture the American vernacular in their fiction.

In 1984, the one-hundredth anniversary of the publication of *Adventures of Huckleberry Finn* was duly noted and extensively celebrated by American literary scholars, libraries, and universities. In December, 1984, novelist Norman Mailer reviewed *Huckleberry Finn* in *The New York Times Book Review* as if it were an exciting new novel. The 1985 centennial of the first American edition of *Huckleberry Finn* was marked by the opening of a successful Broadway musical based on it, *Big River*, which won seven Tony Awards. A National Endowment for the Humanities-funded film adaptation of *Huckleberry Finn* was aired on public television in 1986. Moreover, American writers continue to write Huckleberry Finn books. In 1970, John Seelye published *The True Adventures of Huckleberry Finn*; a novel by Greg Matthews titled *The Further Adventures of Huckleberry Finn* appeared in 1983; and Nancy Rawles's *My Jim*, a novel narrated by Jim's wife, appeared in 2005. Saul Bellow's 1949 novel, *The Adventures of Augie March*, features a Huck Finn-like protagonist in Chicago during the Great Depression. These literary efforts testify to the endurance of Twain's 1884 masterpiece.

—*James Tackach*

Further Reading

Brooks, Van Wyck. *The Ordeal of Mark Twain*. Rev. ed. New York: E. P. Dutton, 1933. First published in 1920, this first important study of Mark Twain's writing was revised by Brooks after Bernard DeVoto published *Mark Twain's America* in 1932.

Chadwick-Joshua, Jocelyn. *The Jim Dilemma: Reading Race in "Huckleberry Finn."* Jackson: University Press of Mississippi, 1998. A black scholar's defense of *Huckleberry Finn* as an antiracist satire that presents Jim as a strong and vital force in the novel.

Doyno, Victor. *Writing Huck Finn: Twain's Creative Process*. Philadelphia: University of Pennsylvania Press, 1993. Detailed discussion of Twain's writing process that examines every phase of his famous novel's creation.

Kaplan, Justin. *Born to Trouble: One Hundred Years of "Huckleberry Finn."* Washington, D.C.: Library of Congress, 1985. Centennial anniversary pamphlet by the author of the Pulitzer Prize-winning biography *Mr. Clemens and Mark Twain* (1966). Discusses the ongoing controversies surrounding Twain's novel.

Leonard, James S., Thomas A. Tenney, and Thadious M. Davis, eds. *Satire or Evasion? Black Perspectives on "Huckleberry Finn."* Durham, N.C.: Duke University Press, 1992. Collection of essays on *Huckleberry Finn* by African American scholars who examine the novel from a variety of perspectives.

Rasmussen, R. Kent. *Critical Companion to Mark Twain: A Literary Reference to His Life and Work.* New York: Facts On File, 2007. Greatly expanded edition of the author's *Mark Twain A to Z* (1995), with more than forty thousand words of material on *Huckleberry Finn*, including a detailed synopsis and a new critique of the novel.

Sattelmeyer, Robert, and J. Donald Crowley, ed. *One Hundred Years of "Huckleberry Finn": The Boy, His Book, and American Culture*. Columbia: University of Missouri Press, 1985. Another centennial anniversary consideration of *Huckleberry Finn* with twenty-four essays about the novel's place in American culture.

Twain, Mark. *Adventures of Huckleberry Finn.* Edited

by Thomas Cooley. 3d ed. New York: W. W. Norton, 1999. This edition of the Norton Critical Edition of *Huckleberry Finn* is the first to use an authoritative text prepared by the editors of the Mark Twain Project. However, the project itself later published an even more authoritative text in 2001, after drawing on a previously unavailable portion of Twain's original manuscript. The Norton edition also contains Kemble's original illustrations, early reviews, critical essays, a bibliography, and a chronology.

SEE ALSO: 1807-1850: Rise of the Knickerbocker School; 1819-1820: Irving's *Sketch Book* Transforms American Literature; Dec., 1849: Dostoevski Is Exiled to Siberia; 1851: Melville Publishes *Moby Dick*; Oct. 1-Dec. 15, 1856: Flaubert Publishes *Madame Bovary*; 1880's: Brahmin School of American Literature Flourishes; July, 1881-1883: Stevenson Publishes *Treasure Island*; Dec., 1887: Conan Doyle Introduces Sherlock Holmes.

RELATED ARTICLES in *Great Lives from History: The Nineteenth Century, 1801-1900:* Horatio Alger; Stephen Crane; Joel Chandler Harris; Henry James; Sarah Orne Jewett; Abby Sage Richardson; Mark Twain.

December 6, 1884
BRITISH PARLIAMENT PASSES THE FRANCHISE ACT OF 1884

The Franchise Act of 1884 was the third in a series of nineteenth century legislative reforms expanding the control of the people of Great Britain over their government. It extended the vote—already gained by much of the urban male populace—to agricultural and other workers, increasing the total number of British voters by almost 70 percent.

ALSO KNOWN AS: Third Reform Act
LOCALE: London, England
CATEGORIES: Laws, acts, and legal history; government and politics; civil rights and liberties; social issues and reform

KEY FIGURES

William Ewart Gladstone (1809-1898), Liberal prime minister of Great Britain, 1880-1885

Charles Stewart Parnell (1846-1891), leader of the Irish Nationalists in Parliament

Third Marquis of Salisbury (Robert Cecil; 1830-1903), Conservative leader of the opposition in the House of Lords

George Otto Trevelyan (1838-1928), radical parliamentary advocate of franchise reform

Joseph Chamberlain (1836-1914), radical Liberal, president of the Board of Trade, and head of the Birmingham Union

Second Baronet Dilke (Sir Charles Wentworth; 1843-1911), radical member of Parliament and president of the local government board

First Earl of Iddesleigh (Sir Stafford Henry Northcote; 1818-1887), Conservative leader of the opposition in the House of Commons

Eighth Duke of Devonshire (Spencer Compton Cavendish, Marquis of Hartington; 1833-1908), British secretary of state for war, 1882-1885

SUMMARY OF EVENT

Great Britain's Franchise Act of 1884 was passed by Parliament on December 6, 1884. Together with the Redistribution Act of 1885, the act represented the third legislative reform during the nineteenth century to contribute to converting the British government from an oligarchy of landed interests to a largely democratic system. The Reform Act of 1832 had given the vote to middle-class householders in the towns; the Reform Act of 1867 had extended the franchise effectively to all householders in the towns. The rural counties, however, still chose their representatives in Parliament under a system requiring property qualifications. One needed property worth twelve pounds in annual rental fees or freehold ownership of five pounds in order to vote. This meant that in rural counties, agricultural laborers had no vote, and in suburban and industrial county areas, the lower middle classes—particularly factory workers and miners—also had no vote. If a worker moved outside town limits, he would often lose his vote, and town limits mostly remained those established in medieval times. There was also a need to redistribute electoral districts since the Reform Acts of 1832 and 1867 had not really brought districts into line with population growth.

The movement for further reform was begun in 1874 by a radical member of Parliament, Sir George Otto Trevelyan. Each year he introduced a motion to extend the democratic borough franchise to the counties, but each year his motion failed because of opposition from Tory and Whig landlords who preferred to leave their agricultural laborers without a vote. In the election campaign of 1880, the Liberal Party did pledge itself to franchise reform. When they took office, however, William Ewart Gladstone, the prime minister, argued to his cabinet that franchise reform would better come when another election was approaching, and his colleagues agreed. In particular, Gladstone was fearful of the effect of franchise reform on Ireland, which was even then in virtual revolt against British landlords and eager to achieve home rule. Charles Stewart Parnell, the leader of the Irish in Parliament, already commanded enough votes to make life difficult for any administration seeking major legislation; Gladstone feared, and Parnell believed, that franchise reform would give the Parnellites an effective lock on any government.

There were others, however, who believed that franchise reform should be high on the government's agenda. Joseph Chamberlain, president of the Board of Trade in Gladstone's cabinet and also organizer and leader of the Birmingham Union, a liberal caucus that was the most effective political organization in England at that time, instigated agitation for reform of the franchise in 1883. Chamberlain and his associate, the second Baronet Dilke, also a minister in Gladstone's cabinet, held mass meetings, heavily attended by workingmen who advocated franchise reform. Gladstone continued to hesitate because he feared Irish complications and because the minister of war, the eighth duke of Devonshire, opposed reform.

Joseph Chamberlain. (Library of Congress)

Finally, in February of 1884, Gladstone decided that the time for franchise reform had arrived; another general election was in any case only a year away. Accordingly, the government introduced a moderate and fairly simple bill into Parliament. The prime minister proposed to extend all the borough voting qualifications of the Reform Act of 1867 to the counties. The proposal, however, did not include any redistribution of seats, nor did it do away with special property, ancient right, or other dual votes.

Fierce battles had marked the passage of the earlier reform bills, but this time little opposition to the government's proposal developed in Parliament, in the press, or generally throughout the country. The leaders of the opposition—the third marquis of Salisbury in the House of Lords and the first earl of Iddesleigh in the House of Commons—did not object in principle to the bill. Both the Liberals and the Conservatives had drawn considerable support from the workers after passage of the Reform Act of 1867, and neither party dared to take up undemocratic positions in public.

Arguments arose, however, over the side issues of redistribution of seats, dual votes, and minority representation—issues with which those on the Right who secretly opposed franchise reform hoped to kill the measure. Oddly, in this they had allies on the Left. Radicals sought to end all dual voting privileges enjoyed by those who had university degrees, had special ancient rights, or owned property in both town and county. Gladstone defended these property votes, and no amendments were carried against dual voting. Proportional representation and woman suffrage amendments were also decisively beaten.

There was also strong but unsuccessful opposition to applying English electoral standards in Ireland. An amendment along these lines had the secret sympathy of many Liberals who feared that reform would add to the power of the Irish Nationalists led by Parnell. Gladstone, however, would not alter the principle of his bill despite his dislike of Parnell's tactics. Parnell and the Irish Nationalists favored the bill but stayed quiet, confident that their power would be secure whether the bill passed or not.

The chief objection raised by the Conservatives was the need for an extensive redistribution of seats to accompany the Franchise Bill. It was on this issue of redistribution that Salisbury induced the House of Lords to block the Franchise Bill until a redistribution bill was introduced into the House of Commons. This action by the Lords caused an immediate revival of Radical agitation. Chamberlain openly castigated class privilege, as he and John Morley, another Radical leader, saw a chance to destroy the power of the House of Lords. Their agitation against the Lords' prerogatives almost resulted in a serious constitutional crisis, but neither Gladstone nor Salisbury wanted this to happen. Through the intervention of Queen Victoria, the two party leaders met and worked out an agreement. Gladstone agreed to introduce a redistribution bill, and Salisbury agreed to let the Franchise Bill repass the House of Commons and then the Lords. The final passage took place on December 6, 1884. Some radicals were upset by this arrangement, but Chamberlain acquiesced and the agitation against the House of Lords ceased.

Gladstone Informs the Queen of the Coming Franchise Act

On January 4, 1884, Prime Minister William Ewart Gladstone wrote the following letter to Queen Victoria, informing her of the cabinet meeting in which it was decided to introduce a third reform act in Parliament that year.

Mr Gladstone submits his humble duty to Your Majesty, and humbly reports that the Cabinet met this day to consider some leading points of Parliamentary business for the approaching Session.

They advise that the first great measure of the year should be a Bill for extending to the Counties the occupation franchise, and also the lodger franchise, now enjoyed in Boroughs, and for rendering it uniform as far as may be in town and country, and throughout the Three Kingdoms.

Certain limited franchises of a miscellaneous kind ought, as they conceive, to drop with the present holders: but they propose to have the whole substance of the property franchises, now subsisting in Counties, unaltered, only making provision against spurious votes by restraining subdivision and rent-charges.

The safe working of the household franchise in Boroughs has removed, in the judgement of Your Majesty's Advisers, all, even the most shadowy grounds for apprehension from the enfranchisement of what may be considered as even a safe class of the population.

The reasons formerly urged for combining redistribution of seats with the franchise lose nearly all their force in view of a large though not absolute assimilation; while the reasons against it subsist in still fuller force than heretofore, and the Cabinet conceive the severance of the two measures to be recommended in the highest degree by public reasons.

Significance

The Redistribution Bill was taken up shortly after passage of the Franchise Act. It was by agreement what the Tories had desired, and it passed as the Redistribution Act in June, 1885. The act was actually more radical and democratic than the Liberals had desired: Although districts were not yet all equal, the Redistribution Act accepted for the first time a population basis in legislative representation. It also abolished dual member constituencies, a practice that had enabled the Liberals to appeal to both radicals and liberals by teaming radical and liberal candidates in a single constituency. All boroughs having fewer than fifteen thousand voters lost their seats, making it possible to shift some 136 seats to more populous areas.

The Franchise Act of 1884 combined with the Redistribution Act of 1885 made Great Britain basically a democracy, at least for men. Women, and men who were not householders, had to wait until the twentieth century to win the vote. The act added 1.7 million voters to the 2.5 million already eligible to vote. It was the largest single enfranchisement in Great Britain during the nineteenth century, and it paved the way for universal adult suffrage in the twentieth century.

—*James H. Steinel, updated by Nancy M. Gordon*

Further Reading

Jenkins, T. A. *Gladstone, Whiggery, and the Liberal Party, 1874-1886*. Oxford, England: Clarendon Press, 1988. Explains the complex party issues that affected the 1884 reform.

Jones, Andrew. *The Politics of Reform, 1884*. Cambridge, England: Cambridge University Press, 1972. The entire book is devoted to the reform of 1884, in voluminous detail.

Matthew, H. C. G., ed. *The Gladstone Diaries*. Vol. 9. Oxford, England: Clarendon Press, 1990. Deals with the years 1883 through 1886.

Parry, Jonathan. *The Rise and Fall of Liberal Government in Victorian Britain*. New Haven, Conn.: Yale University Press, 1993. The last section is devoted to the 1884 reform.

Partridge, Michael. *Gladstone*. New York: Routledge, 2003. A reassessment of Gladstone's life and political career. Describes how Gladstone tried but failed to resolve his great obsession—the Irish question.

Shannon, Richard. *Gladstone*. Vol 2. Chapel Hill: University of North Carolina Press, 1999. A comprehensive biography by an expert on Victorian history. The second volume covers Gladstone's career from 1865 through 1898.

Southgate, Donald. *The Passing of the Whigs, 1832-1886*. London: Macmillan, 1962. Chronicles the gradual transformation of the Whigs into the Liberal Party.

SEE ALSO: 1824: British Parliament Repeals the Combination Acts; June 4, 1832: British Parliament Passes the Reform Act of 1832; Sept. 9, 1835: British Parliament Passes Municipal Corporations Act; Aug. 28, 1857: British Parliament Passes the Matrimonial Causes Act; July 26, 1858: Rothschild Is First Jewish Member of British Parliament; June, 1866-1871: Fenian Risings for Irish Independence; Aug., 1867: British Parliament Passes the Reform Act of 1867; Dec. 3, 1868-Feb. 20, 1874: Gladstone Becomes Prime Minister of Britain; May 2, 1882: Kilmainham Treaty Makes Concessions to Irish Nationalists; Aug. 3, 1892: Hardie Becomes Parliament's First Labour Member; Feb. 27, 1900: British Labour Party Is Formed.

RELATED ARTICLES in *Great Lives from History: The Nineteenth Century, 1801-1900:* Joseph Chamberlain; William Ewart Gladstone; Charles Stewart Parnell; Third Marquis of Salisbury; Queen Victoria.

1885
INDIAN NATIONAL CONGRESS IS FOUNDED

The first political association of English-educated and middle-class Indian professionals, the Indian National Congress was organized to impel the British government to investigate the social, political, and economic conditions of Indians and enact required reforms in British India. The loyalist and moderate association was later transformed into an effective vehicle of nationalist struggle that led to Indian independence in 1947.

LOCALE: Bombay (now Mumbai), India
CATEGORIES: Organizations and institutions; social issues and reform; government and politics

KEY FIGURES

Allan Octavian Hume (1829-1912), secretary to the government of India, 1870-1879, and general secretary of the Indian National Congress, 1885-1906

Womesh Chandra Bonnerjee (1844-1906), barrister, president of the congress, 1885

Surendranath Banerjea (1848-1925), civil servant, 1871-1874, and founder of the Indian Association, 1875

First Marquis of Ripon (George Frederick Samuel Robinson; 1827-1909), viceroy of India, 1880-1884

Frederick Temple Hamilton-Temple-Blackwood (1826-1902), first marquis of Dufferin and Ava, and viceroy of India, 1884-1888

SUMMARY OF EVENT

The nineteenth century constituted a new era for British India under the aegis of the British imperial culture that itself was a product of the European Enlightenment. The Enlightenment had wrought profound changes in the life and thinking of the people in the West. Consequently, the latter half of the nineteenth century saw a generation of Englishmen (those attending the Imperial Services College) influenced by the utilitarian philosophy of Jeremy Bentham (1748-1832) and John Stuart Mill (1806-1873). The two thinkers had believed that all men and women would be potentially similar if liberated from the strangleholds of tradition by a combination of good government, law, and political economy. This utilitarian attitude joined with the reforming enterprise of the Clapham (a prosperous suburb of London) Sect and the Free Traders in sponsoring the modernization of India.

Since 1835, English education, together with the missionary evangelical enterprise, introduced Western ideas and aroused among the urban Indians a critical attitude toward their own religious, social, and political lives.

BRITISH INDIA AT THE END OF THE NINETEENTH CENTURY

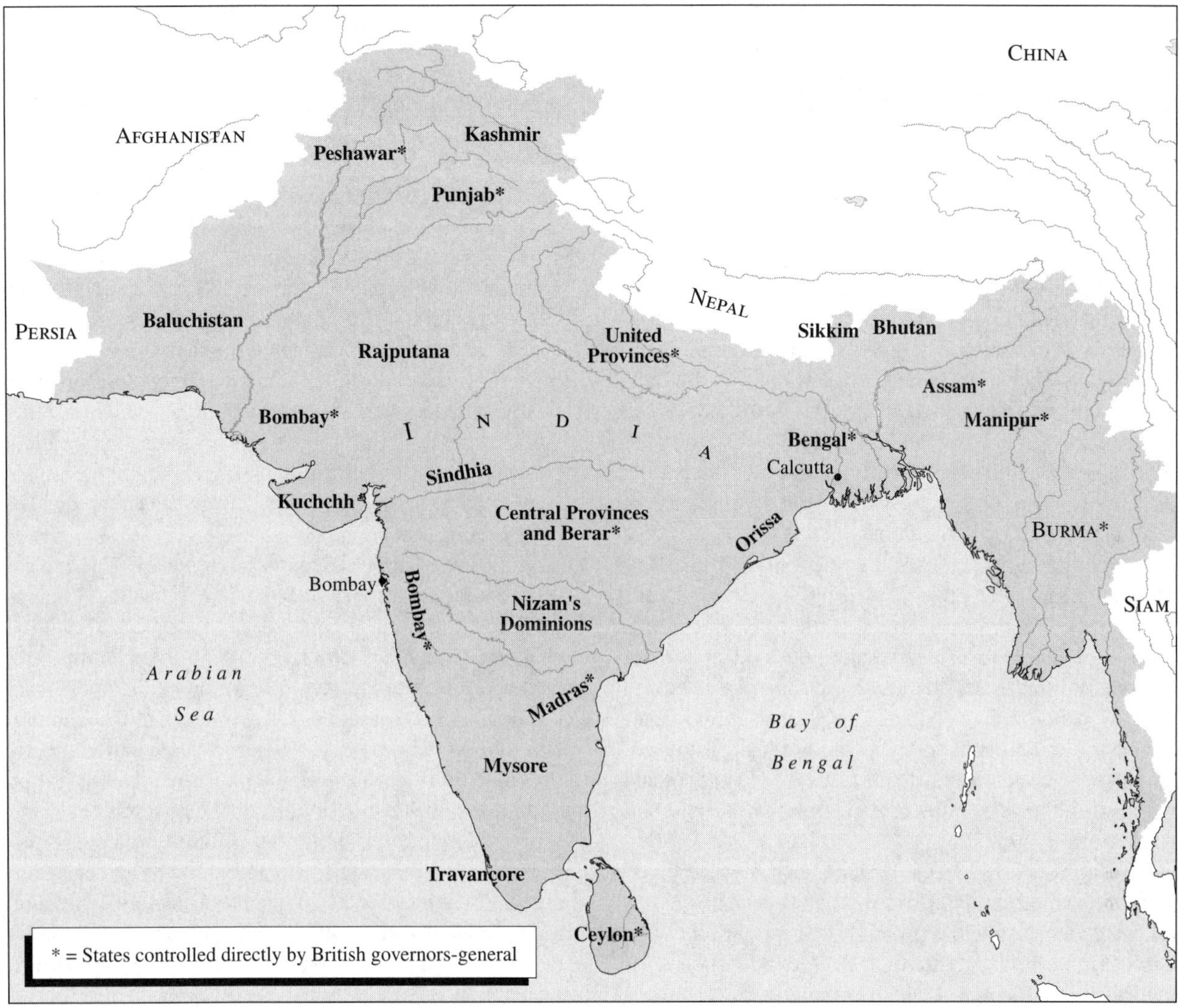

This attitude was discernible first in Calcutta, the busiest center of mercantile, missionary, and metropolitan activities of the empire. However, Western ideas and education also brought home to those affected by it the "foreignness" of the Christian rulers, leading to an intensification of Indians becoming aware of their native differences.

Also, the process of Westernization split Indians into two factions: the modernists, comprising the English-educated reformers of the Brahmo Samaj (founded in 1828) and of the Young Bengal movement (started at the Hindu College, during the late 1820's) and the traditionalists, comprising the (similarly) Western-educated upholders of Indian culture of the Dharma Sabha (1830) of Bhabanicharan Banerjee (1787-1848) and the Tatwabodhini Sabha (1839) of Debendranath Tagore (1817-1905).

Side by side with these groups there flourished also a compact but caring community of non-official but professional Englishmen nicknamed "interlopers" by the British East India Company government, who, by their social and political critiques, provided Indian reformers a practical example of constitutional agitation. A milestone was reached with the formation of the Landholders' Society on March 19, 1838, the very first political association of Indians. The society functioned as the mouthpiece for public grievances mainly because the landlords were recognized by Indian society, especially in Bengal, as the natural leaders of the people. In 1843 this society merged with the Bengal British India Society, forming a broader membership base, including some Britons but mostly members of the Western-educated bourgeoisie. In 1851 the British India Society metamorphosed into the British Indian Association, with a membership made up entirely of Indians. The new group promoted government efficiency and the welfare of the common people by legislative means, all in the common interests of Great Britain and India.

In its attempt to become an all-India body, however, the British Indian Association attracted a large number of landlords as members. The 1850's also witnessed an escalating racial hostility between the British and the Indians, which culminated in the Sepoy Mutiny of 1857. The post-Mutiny period saw feudal landlords supporting the British Empire of India and the English-educated middle class questioning the legitimacy of the continuance of foreign domination in the name of such Western values as individual rights and national freedom. In 1866, Rajnarayan Basu (1826-1899), an English-educated religious and social reformer, founded a society for the promotion of nationalism among the educated natives of Bengal. Furthermore, the middle-class-dominated Indian Association, founded in 1875 by an erstwhile member of the Indian civil service, Surendranath Banerjea, sought to achieve "the unification of the Indian races and peoples on the basis of a common political interest and aspirations."

During the early 1880's, Indian nationalism received support from the government, which had been headed by a liberal viceroy, the first marquis of Ripon. Following, however, the defeat of the Ilbert Bill of 1883 (named after Courtney Ilbert, a legal member of the viceroy's council), which sought to empower Indian judges in cases involving Europeans, the Indian intelligentsia and political leaders became acutely aware of the need for an all-India platform. On April 2, 1883, in the middle of the Ilbert Bill controversy, Surendranath Banerjea was imprisoned on a charge of contempt of court when he ran a leader in the *Bengalee* accusing a justice of the Calcutta High Court of sacrilege for using a Hindu idol on the witness stand. This event became a cause célèbre serving to dramatize the growing breach between the European community and the native educated elites of Calcutta.

In December, 1883, Banerjea would organize the Indian National Conference in Calcutta, a gathering that included Hindus and Muslims from more than twenty urban areas of India. Next year, a number of Calcutta lawyers, with some Muslims, formed the Indian Union to provide a base for political activities. Another association, the Madras Mahajana Sabha (Great People's Forum of Madras), was formed in the south. In 1885, the Bombay Presidency Association was founded. The three presidency associations appointed a delegation to sail for England to work with the pro-liberal candidates in Great Britain's general election (November 24 to December 18). This overture failed, bringing disillusionment to the Indians who had placed their trust in British liberalism.

The struggle for political participation in government gathered further momentum by the initiative of Allan Octavian Hume, a retired civil servant living in India. Hume was extremely critical of the ineptitude of the bureaucracy and was consequently demoted and forced to take an early retirement; thereafter, he devoted himself to working for India's regeneration. His mission in India had two goals: to help Indians acquire their legitimate rights and to help them acknowledge the advantages of the British connection.

Following Ripon's departure, Hume struggled to organize a national party of Indians. He contacted Sarvajanik Sabha Poona (People's Forum of Poona) and the political leaders of other important Indian cities. He also had received indirect, albeit cautious support from the new viceroy, Frederick Temple Hamilton-Temple-Blackwood, who possibly believed that a national body of Indian politicians could function as a loyal opposition and a safety valve, and could help the government monitor public opinion. In May, 1885, Hume circulated a private memorandum to a few individuals whom he considered the "the inner circle" of the proposed Indian national union, notifying them of a planned conference at Poona during the week of December 25-31. Hume left for England on July 14 to inform liberal leaders of the conference and to lobby among the British politicians and journalists for an Indian party.

Hume returned to India on December 2 and busily prepared for the Poona conference. Five other conferences, however, including the second national conference convened by the Indian Association, were planned for Calcutta during December 25-31. Also, Poona had been suffering through a cholera epidemic, so Hume had to change the date and venue for the national union conference. Also, at the suggestion of an influential newspaper editor of Calcutta, Hume preferred the Americanized term "congress" over "union," which had been suggested by a Calcutta journalist. The conference of the nascent congress was scheduled for Bombay on December 28. Calcutta lawyer Womesh Chandra Bonnerjee was elected the congress's president, and attendees included seventy-two delegates representing the three presidencies and other major provinces, together with thirty friends and sympathizers.

The congress was not initially a political party. Instead, it was an association for promoting "personal intimacy and friendship"; eradicating "all possible race, creed, or provincial prejudices amongst all lovers of country"; suggesting parliamentary inquiry into Indian affairs; and pooling "matured opinions of the educated classes in India on some of the more important and pressing of the social questions of the day."

SIGNIFICANCE

Although the Indian National Congress was not really an all-India body reflecting national aspirations, its activities and membership expanded in the course of the next half-century. Indian resentment against forced participation in World War I on behalf of the British had united Hindus and Muslims in their demand for self-government, a demand that culminated with a mass movement for independence in the 1920s and 1930s under the leadership of Mohandas K. Gandhi (1869-1948).

—*Narasingha P. Sil*

FURTHER READING

Andrews, Charles F., and Girija K. Mookerjee. *The Rise and Growth of Congress in India, 1832-1920*. 2d ed. Meerut: Meenakshi Prakashan, 1967. A reliable near-contemporary account.

McCully, Bruce T. *English Education and the Origins of Indian Nationalism*. 1940. Reprint. Gloucester, Mass.: Peter Smith, 1966. An insightful and rigorous analysis of the origins and evolution of Indian nationalism but most illuminating on the Indian National Congress (INC) in particular.

Mehrotra, S. R. *The Emergence of the Indian National Congress*. New York: Barnes & Noble Books, 1971. Standard history and a magisterial account.

Wedderburn, William. *Allan Octavian Hume 'Father of the Indian National Congress' 1829-1912: A Biography*. Edited by Edward C. Moulton. New York: Oxford University Press, 2002. Biography of the organizer of the INC by a colleague with an introduction by a noted scholar.

Yasin, Madhavi. *Emergence of Nationalism, Congress and Separatism*. Delhi, India: Raj, 1996. A comprehensive history of the INC with a useful and detailed bibliography.

SEE ALSO: Apr. 10, 1802: Lambton Begins Trigonometrical Survey of India; Dec. 4, 1829: British Abolish Suttee in India; Apr., 1848-Mar., 1849: Second Anglo-Sikh War; May 10, 1857-July 8, 1858: Sepoy Mutiny Against British Rule; Jan. 25, 1884: Indian Legislative Council Enacts the Ilbert Bill.

RELATED ARTICLES in *Great Lives from History: The Nineteenth Century, 1801-1900:* Sir Sayyid Ahmad Khan; Annie Besant; John Laird Mair Lawrence; Dadabhai Naoroji; Mahadev Govind Ranade; Rammohan Ray; Iswar Chandra Vidyasagar; Vivekananda.

March 19, 1885
SECOND RIEL REBELLION BEGINS

The last gasp of Native Canadian resistance to white expansion into western Canada, Louis Riel's second rebellion was crushed by the Canadian government, opening the way to settlement of the Canadian prairies by Euro-Canadians.

ALSO KNOWN AS: Second Metis rebellion
LOCALE: Saskatchewan
CATEGORIES: Indigenous people's rights; expansion and land acquisition; wars, uprisings, and civil unrest

KEY FIGURES

Louis Riel (1844-1885), leader of the Metis
Gabriel Dumont (1837-1906), Riel's adjutant general
Poundmaker (1842-1886), Cree chief who joined in rebellion
Big Bear (Mistahimaskwa; 1825-1888), Cree chief who sought peace
Leif Crozier (1846-1901), Royal Canadian Mounted Police officer
Sir John Alexander Macdonald (1815-1891), prime minister of Canada, 1867-1873, 1878-1891
Frederick D. Middleton (1825-1898), British soldier who quelled the rebellion

SUMMARY OF EVENT

In 1869-1870, Louis Riel led a rebellion in Manitoba against a provincial administrator sent out from Canada's newly formed dominion government in Ottawa. Believing that the lieutenant governor, William McDougall, represented only the English speakers of Manitoba, Riel and his largely French-speaking supporters blocked his entry and set up their own government. After some negotiations, the situation was resolved peacefully, and Manitoba was admitted into the Canadian confederation as a province in which both French and English were official languages.

As part of the settlement, Riel agreed amicably to go into exile in the United States. A complicated man, Riel belonged to the ethnic group known as the Metis, who took their name from a French word for mixture because they were part Native Canadian and part French. Although they spoke French and were part of francophonic culture, they also had good relations with Native Canadian groups, such as the Cree.

By 1885, Riel had become the most controversial figure in Canadian public life. He had run for parliament from Manitoba and won but had been expelled by that legislative body's pro-British majority because they saw his earlier rebellion as having been an act of treason against the Crown. Riel often had been accused of mental instability and spent extended periods of time in a hospital and a mental asylum. During the 1870's, his religious views, which had previously been conventionally Roman Catholic, veered in a maverick direction. He was starting to believe that a North American pope was needed. He proposed that idea to a French bishop of Montreal, who refused to have anything to do with the idea. Riel left Canada and moved to Montana, where he married an American woman and seemed to forsake his Canadian political ambitions. However, his absence from the Canadian political scene came to a dramatic end in 1883, when he returned to the Canadian prairies, this time to Saskatchewan, to help the struggling Metis cause.

In July, 1884, Riel arrived in the Metis stronghold of Batoche. He tried to engage in peaceful pro-Metis political activity, but his past and his controversial reputation shadowed that effort. On March 19, 1885, he decided to take the path of direct, violent action when he seized control of the main Roman Catholic Church in Batoche and mobilized his supporters into military formation, organizing an army led by a capable general, Gabriel Dumont. Riel declared himself governor in opposition to the constituted authorities.

The core of Riel's new supporters were no longer French Catholics and English-speaking frontier whites (who found Riel much too pro-Native Canadian and too eccentric), but Native Canadians. Riel found two crucial allies among the chiefs of the Cree peoples of the plains. These men had very different natures, despite their common ethnic origins. Poundmaker was a determined and vigorous warrior. He was convinced that the only way the native peoples could resist the onslaught of white settlers was through military force. Poundmaker saw that the time to take action was drawing to a close because the white settlers were rapidly gaining control of the prairie through the efficiency of the Royal Canadian Mounted Police (RCMP) and technological advances, most particularly the Canadian Pacific Railway.

Big Bear, whose Cree name was Mistahimaskwa, was of a more moderate persuasion than Poundmaker. He favored negotiations with Euro-Americans in order to safeguard his people's best interests. Although Big Bear never fully accepted the violent agenda advocated by Riel and Poundmaker, he did not stand in the way when some of his more extreme followers attacked the villagers of Frog Lake. The leadership skills of Big Bear and Poundmaker formed the backbone of the rebellion. Riel supplied the vision; they supplied the practical leadership.

Even before the so-called Frog Lake Massacre, the rebellion had begun in earnest. After Riel declared his provisional government on March 19, the RCMP reacted quickly. Led by Superintendent Leif Crozier, they engaged the combined Metis and Indian forces at the village of Duck Lake. After the police were forced to retreat, the Canadian prime minister, Sir John Alexander Macdonald, sent in Canadian troops. Aided by the logistical support provided by the railroad, more than five thousand troops went to Saskatchewan under the command of General Frederick D. Middleton.

By that time, many of Big Bear's troops had joined Riel and Poundmaker in the rebellion. To government authorities, it seemed as if the entire prairie was in rebellion. However, many Native Canadian peoples, especially the populous Blackfoot, remained neutral throughout the conflict. On April 24, Middleton's troops engaged Dumont's troops in formal battle. The confrontation ended in a stalemate, and Middleton's advance was stymied.

Middleton gathered additional troops. By early May, he was approaching Riel's headquarters at Batoche. Middleton devised an effective strategy of having his headquarters remain in a fortified camp south of Batoche while his troops sortied out during the daytime and attempted to wear down the resistance of the Metis. After enduring several daytime charges, the Metis were worn down by attrition. On May 15, Riel surrendered himself and Batoche to Middleton. Dumont fled south to Montana.

Poundmaker's resistance against the government was more effective. It took until May 26 for him to surrender his troops to Middleton at Battleford. Big Bear was never apprehended by the government. After evading capture for more than a month, he voluntarily surrendered to the RCMP at Fort Carlton in early July. Canadian historians later came to see Big Bear as the most farsighted figure on either side, the only leader who possessed a sound vision of how the prairies could be a place where English speakers, French speakers, and native peoples could all enjoy autonomy and self-determination.

In mid-July, Riel's trial for treason began. Although most French Canadians had turned against Riel because of his religious unorthodoxy and his penchant for violence, now that he was being prosecuted by the English-speaking Macdonald and his government, they again became his fervent supporters. Riel's lawyers advised him to plead insanity, but Riel decided to speak in his own defense. His explanations of his actions to the jury were lucid, but there was no hope that the jury, composed largely of English speakers, would be moved by his words. After the jury found him guilty, it was up to Macdonald to decide whether to seek the death penalty. Macdonald considered several factors in making the decision but finally concluded that only by executing Riel could the government satisfy the English speakers in Ontario. Despite further medical appeals claiming that Riel was insane, he was hanged on November 16 in Regina.

SIGNIFICANCE

Louis Riel's execution made him a national martyr. Whatever the complexities and ambiguities of his life, he has ever since remained a metaphor for unexamined possibilities in the Canadian national soul. Big Bear and Poundmaker were given lenient sentences of only a few years in jail. However, both men died before the 1880's came to a close, and the potential for political resistance on the part of the Native Canadian peoples of the prairies was foreclosed. With the opening of the railroad, the prairie provinces quickly became flooded by white settlers, and by the beginning of the twentieth century the provinces were firmly part of the Canadian body politic.

The Second Riel Rebellion was certainly one of the most dramatic events in nineteenth century Canadian history. Riel's failure, for better or for worse, helped bring into being the Canada that represented the opposite of so much for which he had hoped and struggled.

—*Nicholas Birns*

FURTHER READING

Beal, Bob, and Rod Macleod. *Prairie Fire: The 1885 North-West Rebellion*. Edmonton: Hurtig, 1984. Emphasizes the Native Canadian perspective.

Bowsfield, Hartfield. *Louis Riel: The Rebel and the Hero*. Toronto: Oxford University Press, 1971. A good introductory book.

Flanagan, Thomas. *Riel and the Rebellion*. Toronto: University of Toronto Press, 2000. Revisionist perspective on the Second Riel Rebellion that examines Riel's actions from the point of view of the Canadian government.

Friesen, John W. *The Riel/Real Story*. Ottawa: Borealis Press, 1996. Biography of Louis Riel that examines his importance in creating and shaping Metis culture.

Riel, Louis. *The Collected Writings of Louis Riel*. Edited by George F. G. Stanley. Edmonton: University of Alberta Press, 1985. Collection of Riel's surviving writings that demonstrate he was a thinker as well as a political leader.

Siggins, Maggie. *Riel: A Life of Revolution*. Toronto: HarperCollins, 1994. Readable and lively narrative account of Riel's extraordinary life.

Stanley, George F. G. *The Birth of Western Canada: History of the Riel Rebellions*. Toronto: University of Toronto Press, 1960. Argues that Riel's rebellions were the defining events in western Canadian history.

SEE ALSO: June 1, 1815-Aug., 1817: Red River Raids; July 1, 1867: British North America Act; Oct. 11, 1869-July 15, 1870: First Riel Rebellion; May 23, 1873: Canada Forms the North-West Mounted Police; Sept., 1878: Macdonald Returns as Canada's Prime Minister; July 11, 1896: Laurier Becomes the First French Canadian Prime Minister.

RELATED ARTICLES in *Great Lives from History: The Nineteenth Century, 1801-1900:* Sir John Alexander Macdonald; Louis Riel.

1886
RISE OF THE SYMBOLIST MOVEMENT

Symbolism, a revolutionary literary and artistic movement, stressed the creative importance of constructing an abstract reality as opposed to relying on the direct observation of the physical world for inspiration.

LOCALE: Europe, primarily France
CATEGORIES: Literature; art; theater

KEY FIGURES

Charles Baudelaire (1821-1867), French poet who was a forerunner of the Symbolist movement
Arthur Schopenhauer (1788-1860), German philosopher noted for "pessimist" thought
Jean Moréas (Yannis Papadiamantopoulos; 1856-1910), Greek-born French Symbolist poet
Joris-Karl Huysmans (1848-1907), French Symbolist novelist
Maurice Maeterlinck (1862-1949), Belgian Symbolist poet, dramatist, and essayist

SUMMARY OF EVENT

The Symbolist aesthetic was born out of a revolt against the conventions of the day. Whether through poetry, fiction, drama, criticism, or painting, the Symbolists wished to liberate themselves from the norm, from common, everyday reality. Out of this grandiose approach to creativity, Symbolists expressed themselves in very personal ways. The inner life of the mind and the spirit guided them in each of their creative endeavors. For them, reality could not be quantified or neatly unraveled. Furthermore, the late nineteenth century saw a general intellectual trend away from materialism and scientific rationalism.

Taking inspiration from philosopher Arthur Schopenhauer, the Symbolists saw art as a refuge from the torment of the world. Schopenhauer was a pessimist, and he envisioned art to be one of the few legitimate escapes from the everyday world. In 1886, poet Jean Moréas would write what would become the manifesto for the Symbolist movement. In the manifesto, he stated that Romanticism had indeed "tolled the bell of rebellion," but that it had since become "replete with common sense." Common sense was considered by the Symbolists a negative state of affairs.

Moréas wrote that the Symbolists frowned on "plain meanings, declamations, false sentimentality and matter-of-fact description." For him, a Symbolist strives "to clothe the idea in sensuous form." He openly criticized Parnassian poetry, the drama of realism, and the novels of naturalism for being too descriptive, too oriented toward the surfaces of life, and not directed enough to the life of inner experience. Moréas also had suggested that to use the term "symbolist" instead of the term "decadent" to describe the movement held more validity.

Poet Charles Baudelaire's "Manifeste du symbolisme" (pb. September 18, 1886, in *Le Figaro*) would be identified as an important document of Symbolism as well. Already in 1857, however, Baudelaire had published the first edition of his controversial *Les Fleurs du mal* (rev. 1861, 1868; *Flowers of Evil*, 1931). Because of erotic themes in his work, Baudelaire is often described as a decadent poet. The French government, who had found parts of *Flowers of Evil* to be obscene, suppressed six of the poems from the collection and prosecuted Baudelaire for offending public morals.

Employing a language that was rich in dark and erotic metaphors, some of the Symbolist authors became linked with the Decadent movement. Sensation was central to the creative process. The various sensory impulses that became cornerstones of the movement also had been central to poets such as Paul Verlaine (1844-1896) and Arthur Rimbaud (1854-1891). Symbolist poets broke out of the formal constraints of verse writing and found the writing of prose poems and *vers libre* (free verse) to be liberating. The concept of mere precision was jettisoned, and the ideas that came from the inner life of the poet became paramount. First and foremost, Symbolism valued individualism and everything exotic that flowed from the mind. For the poets, the very sound of words became of prime importance. The mystical, the bizarre, and almost anything else that would lead to a more intense experience were cherished.

Because Symbolists were strong individuals, the movement was no more than a loose organization. Symbolists, however, collectively turned their backs on naturalism or anything that claimed to directly represent the world. Symbolists employed nuance and suggestion in their work. Although the movement started with the French poets of the late nineteenth century, the Symbolist influence spread to the theater and to painting. The visual artists of Symbolism wished their works to evoke an emotional response, but they hoped to do so without presuming to capture a visual "reality." Some of the most powerful visual art of the movement was created by artists such as Paul Gauguin (1848-1903), Edvard Munch (1863-1944), Gustave Moreau (1826-1898), and Odilon Redon (1840-1916).

The idea of capturing reality, as was attempted by the realists and naturalists, was not crucial for the Symbolists. In fact, the Symbolists detested realism and naturalism. Symbolist thought can be considered a darker, more gothic, outgrowth of Romanticism. Baudelaire first introduced the "dark" work of the American poet and short-story writer Edgar Allan Poe to the French with his brilliant translations. From the Symbolist perspective, because truth lurks in the shadows and can be hinted atonly through suggestion, metaphor added weight to meaning. Sentimentality and directness were loathed.

While the Symbolist movement first took root in France, it spread to other parts of Europe, with Maurice Maeterlinck of Belgium, Munch of Norway, and Aleksander Blok (1880-1921) of Russia. The true Symbolist made a personal statement with each of his or her artistic endeavors. While there are a number of important Symbolist poets, there are only a select few novelists and dramatists who wrote memorable Symbolist works. Joris-Karl Huysmans wrote the most important Symbolist novel in *À rebours* (1884; *Against the Grain*, 1922). In this character study, also claimed as a decadent work, Huysmans describes various aesthetic experiments that are carried out by a rather bored aristocrat.

Belgian Symbolist dramatist Maeterlinck successfully avoided employing any traditional dramatic constructions. For the Symbolist dramatist, characterization was supposed to be less focused, and any action that does take place primarily should be expressed through symbols. Symbolism does not rely on external action. Suggestive language would serve as the link between the spiritual realm and the natural world.

SIGNIFICANCE

With the death of Stéphane Mallarmé (1842-1898) in 1898, the French Symbolist movement lost one of its most brilliant practitioners. By the early twentieth century, Symbolism as a movement was in decline, but its influence reached far into the future. Such literary giants as William Butler Yeats, T. S. Eliot, Eugene O'Neill, James Joyce, and Anton Chekhov took inspiration from the work of the Symbolists.

Symbolism's rise marked what would become the ultimate break with the classical humanism that began during the Renaissance in Europe. Instead of the tradition of narrative and obviousness, the Symbolists would evoke imagery and imagination, but they would do so in a way that legitimated, and liberated, the symbolic realm of the writer and artist. The Symbolist author and philosopher Rémy de Gourmont (1858-1915) wrote that for the Symbolist, life is one of "individualism in literature, liberty in art."

—*Jeffry Jensen*

FURTHER READING

Balakian, Anna. *The Symbolist Movement: A Critical Appraisal*. New York: Random House, 1967. A critical guide that comes close to being the definitive statement on the movement.

Betz, Anna. "The Symbolist Movement in France." *Romance Quarterly* 45 (Summer, 1998): 131-132. A concise, informative overview of the movement.

Block, Haskell M. *Mallarmé and the Symbolist Drama*. Detroit: Wayne State University Press, 1963. A critical look at one of the major Symbolist poets and how he influenced the world of theater.

Kearns, James. *Symbolist Landscapes: The Place of Painting in the Poetry and Criticism of Mallarmé and His Circle*. London: Modern Humanities Research Association, 1989. An examination of how crucial a role the visual realm played for the Symbolist poets.

Mathews, Patricia. *Passionate Discontent: Creativity, Gender, and French Symbolist Art*. Chicago: University of Chicago Press, 1999. An important study of the various components that make up the Symbolist aesthetic, including spirituality, sexuality, and madness.

Mathieu, Pierre-Louis. *The Symbolist Generation, 1870-1910*. Translated by Michael Taylor. New York: Rizzoli, 1990. An extraordinary examination of the artists associated with the Symbolist movement. Includes many illustrations as well as a general bibliography and a bio-bibliography.

Peyre, Henri. *What Is Symbolism?* Translated by Emmett Parker. Tuscaloosa: University of Alabama Press, 1980. A focused study of the Symbolist movement.

Porter, Laurence M. "Decadence and the *Fin-de-Siècle* Novel." In *The French Novel from 1800 to the Present*, edited by Timothy Unwin. New York: Cambridge University Press, 1997. An overview of the Decadent movement in France.

Symons, Arthur. *The Symbolist Movement in Literature*. Reprint. New York: AMS Press, 1980. A landmark study of the Symbolist movement, still considered the most critical work on Symbolism. Originally published in 1899.

SEE ALSO: 1801: Emergence of the Primitives; 1812-1815: Brothers Grimm Publish Fairy Tales; 1819: Schopenhauer Publishes *The World as Will and Idea*; 1836: Transcendental Movement Arises in New England; 1855: Courbet Establishes Realist Art Movement; c. 1865: Naturalist Movement Begins; 1870's: Aesthetic Movement Arises; c. 1884-1924: Decadent Movement Flourishes; 1893: Munch Paints *The Scream*.

RELATED ARTICLES in *Great Lives from History: The Nineteenth Century, 1801-1900:* Charles Baudelaire; Paul Gauguin; Edgar Allan Poe; Odilon Redon; Arthur Rimbaud; Arthur Schopenhauer.

January, 1886-1889

FRENCH RIGHT WING REVIVES DURING BOULANGER CRISIS

Boulanger, the French minister of war, became the focus of an antirepublican nationalist movement. The Boulanger crisis represented the resurgence of the right wing as a potent political force in late nineteenth century France.

LOCALE: France
CATEGORY: Government and politics

KEY FIGURES

Georges Boulanger (1837-1891), French minister of war, 1886-1887, and political agitator
Charles-Louis de Saulces de Freycinet (1828-1923), premier of France, 1886
Georges Clemenceau (1841-1929), French leader of the Radical Republicans
Paul Déroulède (1846-1914), French organizer of the League of Patriots
Victor-Henri Rochefort (Marquis de Rochefort-Luçay; 1830-1913), French republican journalist and politician

SUMMARY OF EVENT

The great depression of the 1870's and 1880's increased social and political divisions within France and led to the deterioration of the moderate center that had controlled the French Chamber of Deputies since the inception of the Third Republic in 1875. Following a serious setback in the elections of 1885, moderate republicans had to win support from the radical republicans to form a stable cabinet. Accordingly, Charles-Louis de Saulces de Freycinet, the new premier, agreed to accept General Georges Boulanger, a protégé of the radical republican leader Georges Clemenceau, as minister of war. Boulanger assumed his new post in January of 1886.

Boulanger's military promotions had until then been more the result of luck and courage than of any intellectual or organizational ability. After he was installed as minister of war, however, he began to attract attention. Boulanger cultivated support from the Left by expressing sympathy with striking coal miners in Decazeville and pressing for reforms designed to reduce the harsh discipline that prevailed within the army, while simultaneously pleasing militant nationalists by publicly stating his intention to recapture Alsace-Lorraine (lost in the Franco-Prussian War of 1870-1871). The fact that Boulanger seemed willing to plunge France into a war with Germany for which it was unprepared was unimportant. Many nationalists believed that France at last had a champion who had the courage to confront Otto von Bismarck and avenge the humiliating defeat of 1870-1871.

Boulanger's bellicose and irresponsible attitude combined with his growing popularity to encourage various right-wing leaders, such as the journalist Victor-Henri Rochefort and Paul Déroulède (a founder of the militantly nationalist League of Patriots organization), to think that they had found a man who could overthrow the republic and restore the monarchy in France. For his part, Boulanger became seduced by the flattery and machinations of these antirepublicans and decided to make a play for political power. Financed by a wealthy royalist widow, he ran as a candidate for the Chamber of Deputies from several districts in France. (At the time, French electoral law allowed a candidate to run simultaneously from as many districts as he wished.) His campaign was accompanied by some violence, as his supporters fought their political enemies in the streets. They also engaged in anti-Semitic and nationalistic rhetoric.

As ominous as it was, Boulanger's campaign was a success: He was elected in several departments. His political base proved to be surprisingly wide, including not only wealthy royalists of various types but also a large number of ordinary voters who normally voted for leftist candidates. Because he was still in the army, Boulanger was ineligible to serve in the Chamber of Deputies. Nev-

Georges Boulanger in 1887. (Hulton Archive/Getty Images)

ertheless, his success frightened many republican leaders, including Freycinet, and he was given command of the Thirteenth Army Corps in Clermont-Ferrand as a ruse to remove him from the political limelight of Paris. Shortly thereafter, he was officially removed from his position in the government.

Boulanger returned to Paris three times in the next year, against orders and in disguise. As a result, he was expelled from the army. Boulanger was now free to run for, and serve in, the Chamber of Deputies. He put himself up as a candidate from Paris in an 1889 by-election and won a resounding victory. His right-wing supporters believed that this victory represented a virtual plebiscite and that the time was right for Boulanger to make his move and seize power. In January of 1889, thousands of his supporters marched through the streets of the French capital shouting Boulanger's name and demanding that he launch a coup d'état. However, the general refused to act, afraid that the army would not support such an unprecedented move. Boulanger's failure of nerve at this critical moment lost him support, and his movement, known as Boulangism, rapidly lost its momentum. Republican moderates, with the support of the radical republicans, launched a counterattack, prosecuting him for treason, and Boulanger was ultimately forced to flee the country. He committed suicide on the grave of his mistress in England in 1891.

SIGNIFICANCE

The Boulanger crisis represented a severe test of the young Third Republic of France. It demonstrated that royalists and authoritarians were still a potentially significant force in French politics. The republic survived the test, but it was not the stronger for it, since many perceived that it had survived through no fault of its own. Republican politicians thus became aware of the precarious hold that democracy had on the nation. Nevertheless, the Third French Republic would strenghten and would survive all internal pressures in the coming decades, until the invasion of the country by the Third Reich of Adolf Hitler finally brought the republic to an end.

—Harold A. Schofield,
updated by Christopher E. Guthrie

FURTHER READING

Burns, Michael. *Rural Society and French Politics: Boulangism and the Dreyfus Affair.* Princeton, N.J.: Princeton University Press, 1984. An excellent case study of the reasons why French rural dwellers were attracted to right-wing movements such as Boulangism.

Fortescue, William. *The Third Republic in France, 1870-1940: Conflicts and Continuities.* London: Routledge, 2000. Detailed history of the Third Republic, including such crises as the Boulanger crisis and the Dreyfus affair.

Irvine, William. *The Boulanger Affair Reconsidered: Royalism, Boulangism, and the Origins of the Radical Right in France.* New York: Oxford University Press, 1989. This noted authority on conservative political movements in late nineteenth century France argues that the Boulanger crisis marked the beginning of the resurgence of the right wing in French politics.

Lehning, James R. *To Be a Citizen: The Political Culture of the Early French Third Republic.* Ithaca, N.Y.: Cornell University Press, 2001. A history of the early years of the republic, in which the French government worked to implement political reforms and to resist a return to authoritarianism.

Magraw, Roger. *France, 1815-1914: The Bourgeois Cen-*

tury. New York: Oxford University Press, 1986. Presents an excellent overview of the Boulanger crisis without, however, providing much analysis.

Mayeur, Jean-Marie, and Madeleine Rebérioux. *The Third Republic from Its Origins to the Great War, 1871-1914*. Translated by J. R. Foster. New York: Cambridge University Press, 1987. An English translation of a classic French text, this work draws heavily on the work of Jacques Julliard, the foremost French historian of the Boulanger crisis.

Nord, Philip G. *Paris Shopkeepers and the Politics of Resentment*. Princeton, N.J.: Princeton University Press, 1986. Although concerned with a number of other important issues, the author provides a very subtle and perceptive analysis of why so many members of the French lower middle class were attracted to Boulanger.

Seager, Frederick. *The Boulanger Affair: Political Crossroads of France, 1886-1889*. Ithaca, N.Y.: Cornell University Press, 1969. This book now appears a bit dated in comparison to the works by Burns and Irvine, but it nevertheless provides a very thorough account of the Boulanger crisis and its long-range impact on French politics.

Wright, Gordon. *France in Modern Times*. 5th ed. New York: W. W. Norton, 1995. The author emphasizes the ideological overtones of Boulangism but unfortunately downplays its social aspects.

SEE ALSO: Dec. 2, 1852: Louis Napoleon Bonaparte Becomes Emperor of France; July 19, 1870-Jan. 28, 1871: Franco-Prussian War; Feb. 13, 1871-1875: Third French Republic Is Established; Jan. 4, 1894: Franco-Russian Alliance; Oct., 1894-July, 1906: Dreyfus Affair.

RELATED ARTICLES in *Great Lives from History: The Nineteenth Century, 1801-1900:* Otto von Bismarck; Napoleon III.

January 29, 1886
BENZ PATENTS THE FIRST PRACTICAL AUTOMOBILE

Taking advantage of many previous inventions, Carl Benz succeeded in designing and building the world's first practical vehicle powered by an internal combustion engine and not confined to railway tracks. His name is still associated with many of the most important innovations of the automotive industry.

LOCALE: Mannheim, Baden, German Empire (now in Germany)

CATEGORIES: Inventions; science and technology; transportation

KEY FIGURES

Carl Benz (1844-1929), German mechanical engineer and inventor

Siegfried Marcus (1831-1898), Austrian engineer and inventor

Gottlieb Daimler (1834-1900), German inventor and businessman

Nikolaus August Otto (1832-1891), German inventor

John Wesley Carhart (1834-1914), American inventor and minister

Étienne Lenoir (1822-1900), Belgian inventor

Nicolas-Joseph Cugnot (1725-1804), French inventor

SUMMARY OF EVENT

With the growth of railroads during the early nineteenth century, many people naturally thought about the possibility of inventing a self-propelled road vehicle that would provide the flexible mobility of the horse-drawn carriage. Numerous engineers and amateur inventors devoted their time and talents to the realization of this dream. Although there are contradictory claims, most historians agree that Carl Benz's innovative automobile was the first that was truly functional.

Before Benz, a few inventors developed self-propelled vehicles that utilized steam engines. In 1769, Nicolas-Joseph Cugnot constructed a large steam-driven three-wheeled vehicle that traveled only a few yards before overturning; the discouraged Cugnot decided to pursue other projects. In 1801, Richard Thevithick's steam-powered passenger coach actually carried passengers successfully, but it was too heavy and slow to be of any practical use. Thevithick soon discovered that steam engines operated very effectively on locomotives confined to rails, and within two decades railroads were being used for commercial purposes. In 1872, John Wesley Carhart demonstrated an improved steam-powered automobile in Racine, Wisconsin, but like his predecessors, he was unable to overcome the problems of size and weight that steam engines presented when attached to automobiles operating on open roads.

Seeking an alternative to the steam engine, Étienne Lenoir in 1860 built an internal combustion engine that used coal gas and operated in a two-stroke piston cycle. It was a small and reliable engine that proved to be useful in small workshops. By 1867, Nikolaus August Otto had significantly improved on Lenoir's design, and ten years later he obtained a patent for a more powerful four-stroke engine. The Otto engine would become the standard design for modern automobiles. Austrian Siegfried Marcus would later claim that he had built a vehicle powered by a four-stroke engine in 1875, but the only reliable evidence suggests that he probably did not build a vehicle until 1889.

Carl Benz, the son of a railroad mechanic, began thinking about a "horseless carriage" during his high school years in Karlsruhe, Baden. He later wrote: "My favorite idea was to get the locomotive to run on the road. I wanted to release it from the fixity of its path." While studying mechanical engineering at the Technical College of Karlsruhe during the early 1860's, his science teacher, Ferdinand Redtenbacher, introduced the eager youth to the recently invented Lenoir gas engine. In 1871, after gaining experience in engineering firms, Benz set up a small workshop in Mannheim for making mechanical tools. His business faced chronic difficulties, and on several occasions he escaped bankruptcy only because of the assistance of his long-suffering wife, Bertha Ringer Benz.

About 1877, as the first step in building an automobile, Benz concentrated on improving the internal combustion engine. Because Otto still had a patent on the four-stroke engine, Benz had no choice but to work with the two-stroke design. After successfully building a two-stroke engine in 1879, Benz was finally able to attract interest from investors. In 1883, he established the Benz and Compagnie Rheinische Gasmotorenfabrik (Benz and Company Rhenish Gas-Powered Engine Factory) in Mannheim. Borrowing from the experiments of Austrian Julian Hook, Benz had decided to build an engine that used gasoline. The challenging project required three innovations: a carburetor to mix the fuel with air, an electrical system to ignite the explosion in the cylinder, and a radiator to cool the engine.

By 1884, Benz had developed a satisfactory single-cylinder motor. He then began working to overcome the many engineering problems associated with designing a functional chassis. He decided to copy the design of the pedal tricycle, which did not require the complicated steering arrangement of a four-wheeled vehicle. He used large wire-spoked wheels and mounted the rear axle on metal springs. The small engine was set horizontally in order easily to connect the engine to the drive wheels by side chains. A large flywheel kept the power running smoothly. The transmission was based on the belt-and-pulley arrangement that Benz had often seen in factories.

By the spring of 1885, Benz had an automobile ready for testing. In the first trial, he drove around the factory yard. On the second trial, the car crashed into a brick wall (the world's first automobile accident), but the damages were quickly repaired. By that summer, Benz had made numerous improvements to the vehicle and was able to drive it more than one-half mile at a speed of about seven and one-half miles per hour. In July, local newspapers for the first time described the new invention. On January 29, 1886, Benz obtained a patent on his automobile. Later that year, he was delighted to learn that Otto was losing his patent for the four-cycle engine, and Benz quickly adapted the more powerful engine for his automobile.

Benz was not the only person seriously attempting to develop a functional automobile at the time. During the early 1880's, Gottlieb Daimler of Württemberg, a talented engineer who had worked for Otto, was busy inventing a vertical single-cylinder engine that ran at a lower speed than did Benz's engine. In 1885, Daimler built the world's first motorcycle, and his son drove the bulky machine for two miles. Later that year, Daimler learned of Benz's automobile when he happened to see a Benz car in Paris, France. In 1886, he and his assistant, Wilhelm Maybach, fitted a one-horsepower engine onto the world's first four-wheeled motor vehicle, which reached the impressive speed of eleven miles per hour. For the remainder of their lives, Benz and Daimler remained bitter rivals, and each of them claimed to be the originator of the motorcar.

In 1887, Benz demonstrated his invention at the Paris Exposition, but it did not attract a great deal of attention. Nevertheless, that same year the company sold its first car to Émile Roger, owner of a mechanical workshop in Paris, France. In the summer of 1888, Bertha Benz drove one of her husband's cars from Mannheim to Pforzheim and back (fifty miles) with her two sons. By 1893, Benz's company was building four-wheeled vehicles that were commercially successful. By the end of the century, the company had sold almost five hundred cars and, stimulated by numerous competitors, it constantly worked on technical improvements. In 1926, the company merged with the Mercedes (Daimler) organization to become Daimler-Benz, one of the premier manufacturers of all time.

SIGNIFICANCE

Although crude and small by modern standards, Benz's first automobile represented a major technological breakthrough. If Benz had not completed his automobile in 1885, it should be noted that Daimler and others at the time were busy designing and building similar vehicles that were also powered by internal combustion engines. It would be a mistake, however, to minimize Benz's many contributions. His innovative designs for a carburetor, cooling system, and transmission provided models for many of the standard features of later automobiles.

Until the end of the nineteenth century, automobiles were so undependable and expensive that relatively few people purchased or used them. During the first two decades of the twentieth century, however, continuing technological improvements made them cheaper, more efficient, and more reliable. By the time of Benz's death in 1929, it had become almost impossible for affluent persons in the industrialized world to imagine daily life without the conveniences and hazards afforded by the automobile.

—*Thomas Tandy Lewis*

FURTHER READING

Bankston, John. *Karl Benz and the Single Cylinder Engine.* Hockessin, Del.: Mitchell Lane, 2005. Forty-eight-page book written primarily for young readers; emphasizes the difficulties and competition involved in Benz's work.

Diesel, Eugene. *From Engines to Autos.* Chicago: H. Regency, 1960. A standard treatment of the early history of automobiles.

Eckermann, Eric. *World History of the Automobile.* New York: Society of Automotive Engineers, 2001. Describes development of the automobile from its roots in animal-drawn conveyances to modern advances, including the early vehicles of Benz.

Feldman, Anthony, and Peter Ford. *Scientists and Inventors.* New York: Facts On File, 1979. Useful essays about Benz, Daimler, and other individuals from the ancient Greeks until the 1960's, with many provocative photographs.

Glancey, Jonathan. *The Car: The Illustrated History of the Automobile.* London: Carlton Books, 2003. Primarily noteworthy for its many fine illustrations.

Nixon, St. John C. *The Invention of the Automobile.* London: Country Life, 1936. A standard account of the pioneering works of Benz and Daimler.

Roberts, Peter. *The History of the Automobile.* New York: Exeter Books, 1984. Useful as a general introduction to the topic.

Singer, Charles, et al. *A History of Technology.* 4 vols. New York: Oxford University Press, 1958. A dependable work that includes an interesting summary of the development of automobiles.

Williams, Brian. *Karl Benz.* New York: Wayland, 1991. A forty-five-page account that is factually accurate with many illustrations, useful for high school students as well as adult readers.

SEE ALSO: Sept. 20, 1811: Krupp Works Open at Essen; June 15, 1844: Goodyear Patents Vulcanized Rubber; 1850: First U.S. Petroleum Refinery Is Built; 1860: Lenoir Patents the Internal Combustion Engine; Jan. 10, 1870: Standard Oil Company Is Incorporated; May, 1876: Otto Invents a Practical Internal Combustion Engine; Dec. 7, 1888: Dunlop Patents the Pneumatic Tire; Feb., 1892: Diesel Patents the Diesel Engine.

RELATED ARTICLES in *Great Lives from History: The Nineteenth Century, 1801-1900:* Carl Benz; Gottlieb Daimler; Étienne Lenoir; Nikolaus August Otto.

May 8, 1886
PEMBERTON INTRODUCES COCA-COLA

Originally touted as a medicine, Coca-Cola was soon advertised as a carbonated soft drink. Its remarkable commercial growth illustrates and parallels the triumph of American capitalism in the last quarter of the nineteenth century.

LOCALE: Atlanta, Georgia
CATEGORIES: Inventions; business and labor; trade and commerce

KEY FIGURES

John Stith Pemberton (1831-1888), pharmacist and inventor of Coca-Cola
Frank M. Robinson (fl. late nineteenth century), Pemberton's partner, who named Coca-Cola
Asa G. Candler (1851-1929), marketed Coca-Cola
Joseph B. Whitehead (1864-1906), and
Benjamin Franklin Thomas (fl. late nineteenth century), developers of the Coca-Cola bottling industry

SUMMARY OF EVENT

Between 1880 and 1910, the population of the United States grew from 50 million to 91 million people, nearly doubling in three decades. This growth corresponded to the transformation of the United States from an agrarian society to an urbanized society as mills and factories were built throughout the United States. The development of American capitalism in this era resulted in the growth of the advertising industry, which allowed companies to promote their products. At the same time, the railroads were expanding throughout the United States, allowing corporations to create national markets for their products.

In the new, hectic and stressful urban environment, a market for patent medicines thrived. Patent medicines were not medicines that had been patented. Rather, they were secret formulas and unproved remedies that were advertised and sold directly to the public. Often containing alcohol or other drugs and touted as healthful "elixirs," these medicines were inexpensive to produce and highly profitable. The medical profession had not kept pace with the Industrial Revolution, and patent medicines filled the void. The newspaper industry thrived from the advertising revenues generated by these tonics and preparations, with their promises of curing a broad variety of ills.

Coca-Cola was invented in this era by an Atlanta pharmacist, Dr. John Pemberton. Prior to inventing Coca-Cola, Pemberton had developed a wine called French Wine Coca, a drink that included ingredients from kola nuts and coca leaves. However, in November, 1885, when Fulton County, Georgia, voted to "go dry" by prohibiting alcoholic drinks, Pemberton began to experiment with his drink to find a way to sell it under the new law. He removed the wine and began experimenting the various combinations of oils, sugar, and citric acid. On May 8, 1886, his "temperance drink" was introduced to Atlanta consumers when he took a jug of his syrup to Jacob's Pharmacy, where it was sold as a soda-fountain drink by combining carbonated water with Pemberton's new syrup. First marketed as a nerve tonic, Coca-Cola was later promoted as a remedy for indigestion. In its first year, about nine glasses of Coca-Cola were sold daily. The cost to produce the drink was between a half cent and one-and-a-half cents; the drink sold for a nickel.

Pemberton's partner, Frank M. Robinson, was responsible for the name Coca-Cola. The name described the key ingredients of the drink with an alliterative ring. Originally, Coca-Cola contained cocaine, which came from the leaves of the coca plant; a second key ingredient was caffeine, which came from extracts of kola nuts. During the early part of the twentieth century, the Coca-Cola company removed all traces of cocaine from the drink; however, caffeine remains a major ingredient today. In June, 1887, the ornate handwriting used in the drink's logo was introduced.

Coca-Cola was not the first carbonated drink. Ten years earlier, Charles Hires had begun to market Hires Root Beer, made from a solid concentrate of sixteen wild roots and berries. In 1885, Charles Alderton had created Dr. Pepper as a cherry soda-fountain drink. What made Coca-Cola different was the marketing of the product, which over time resulted in Coca-Cola becoming the most recognized name in the world and an emblem of the "good life" in America.

Coca-Cola was originally sold in soda fountains, which were social centers within drugstores in the 1870's and 1880's. These soda fountains were most popular in the South, especially in Atlanta. At first, Robinson promoted Coca-Cola both as a medicine which could cure headaches and depression and as a soda-fountain drink. The first advertisement for Coca-Cola appeared in the *Atlanta Journal* in May, 1886. The ad described Coca-Cola as "Delicious! Refreshing! Exhilarating! Invigo-

Early advertisement for Coca-Cola. (Library of Congress)

rating!" Other media used to market Coca-Cola in its first year included oilcloth signs, streetcar signs, posters, and thousands of coupons for free sample drinks. The first point-of-purchase advertising was placed on the awning of Jacob's Pharmacy. It had red lettering on a white background saying "Drink Coca-Cola, 5 cents." Within a year, similar signs appeared at fourteen soda fountains in Atlanta. At the same time, thousands of posters were being distributed and signs appeared on every streetcar in Atlanta.

In 1887, the Coca-Cola Company was incorporated with Atlanta businessman Asa Candler as one of the partners. Over the course of the next three years, Pemberton sold the company to Candler for approximately twenty-three hundred dollars. Candler became the company's first president and was the first person to bring a real vision to the business. Within a few years he was sole proprietor, specializing in marketing. He transformed Coca-Cola from an insignificant tonic into a hugely profitable business by using brilliant and innovative advertising techniques.

Pemberton continued to promote Coca-Cola as a fountain drink and a medicine. He asserted that the best physicians recommended it for mental and physical exhaustion, headache, fatigue, and mental depression. Sales of the syrup used to make the drink grew rapidly. In 1889, 2,171 gallons of syrup (which pproduced 61,000 drinks) were sold. In 1890, 8,855 gallons were sold. By 1895, sales totaled 76,244 gallons. The key to this meteoric growth was Candler's ingenious marketing: The attractive Coca-Cola logo could be found in point-of-purchase signs, calendars, clocks, fans, urns, scales, cabinets, cases, bookmarks, glass plates, and newspaper ads. Early ads primarily targeted businessmen, but by 1895 advertising had shifted to the masses with ads that simply stated "Drink Coca-Cola, Delicious and Refreshing."

Candler also marketed his product by having the company's employees and sales representatives distribute complimentary coupons for Coca-Cola. Coupons were mailed directly to potential customers and placed in magazines. The company gave soda fountains free syrup to cover the costs of the free drinks. It is estimated that between 1894 and 1913 one in nine Americans had received a free Coca-Cola, for a total of 8,500,000 free drinks. By 1895, Candler was announcing to his shareholders that Coca-Cola was served in every state in the United States.

In the second half of the decade, Coca-Cola expanded along with the nation, as branch offices and syrup factories were opened in Dallas (1894), Chicago (1895), Los Angeles (1895), and Philadelphia (1897). The popularity of Coca-Cola resulted in the company's building a three-story headquarters, constructed in 1898—the first facility devoted exclusively to the manufacture of Coca-Cola syrup and the management of the business. Large-scale bottling of Coca-Cola began in 1899, when Candler signed an exclusive contract with Benjamin F. Thomas and Joseph B. Whitehead of Chattanooga, Tennessee, to open the first bottling plant there. In that year, Coca-Cola sold an estimated thirty-six million drinks. The second bottling plant opened in Atlanta in 1900. Within twenty years, there were more than one thousand bottling plants, 95 percent of which were locally owned and operated.

SIGNIFICANCE

The growth of the Coca-Cola Company mirrors the development of American capitalism in the last quarter of the nineteenth century. The developers of this most famous and profitable soft drink company identified a market in the nation's growing urban population, offering a brief respite for persons subjected to the new, fast pace of life. The company developed innovative advertising techniques that were instrumental in developing product recognition and acceptance in American society. These techniques were soon used by other companies. Coca-Cola also capitalized on new technologies that allowed it to bottle and distribute its product. Finally, the company took advantage of America's emerging interstate transportation system, the railroads, to market and distribute its product nationwide. Its success during the nineteenth century continued in the twentieth century: Coca-Cola became an international product recognized and available throughout the world.

—*William V. Moore*

FURTHER READING

Allen, Frederick L. *Secret Formula: How Brilliant Marketing and Relentless Salesmanship Made Coca-Cola the Best Known Product in the World.* New York: HarperCollins, 1995. A comprehensive history of Coca-Cola from its inception to the modern era by an award-winning reporter.

Hays, Constance L. *The Real Thing: Truth and Power of the Coca-Cola Company.* New York: Random House, 2004. A investigative study of Coca-Cola in the modern era of global businesses.

Pendergrast, Mark. *For God, Country, and Coca-Cola: The Definitive History of the Great American Soft Drink and the Company That Makes It.* 2d ed. New York: Basic Books, 2000. A detailed history of Coca-Cola as a metaphor for the growth of modern capitalism.

Witzel, Gyuel Young, and Michael Karl Witzel. *The Sparkling Story of Coca-Cola.* Stillwater, Minn.: Voyager Press, 2002. A history of Coca-Cola that includes text, vintage photographs, and information on collectibles.

SEE ALSO: 1869: First Modern Department Store Opens in Paris; Aug., 1872: Ward Launches a Mail-Order Business; May 1-Oct. 30, 1893: Chicago World's Fair; 1894-1895: Kellogg's Corn Flakes Launch the Dry Cereal Industry; 1896: Brooks Brothers Introduces Button-Down Shirts.

RELATED ARTICLE in *Great Lives from History: The Nineteenth Century, 1801-1900:* Lydia E. Pinkham.

June, 1886-September 9, 1893
IRISH HOME RULE DEBATE DOMINATES BRITISH POLITICS

The long-festering issue of Irish home rule intruded upon British politics as a major factor during the 1880's. The controversy would soon split the Liberal Party, engender a period of Conservative Party dominance during the late nineteenth and early twentieth centuries, and exacerbate the deep fissures in Ireland between Protestants and Catholics over unionism versus nationalism.

LOCALE: London, England
CATEGORY: Government and politics

KEY FIGURES

William Ewart Gladstone (1809-1898), Liberal prime minister of Great Britain, 1868-1874, 1880-1885, 1886, 1892-1894

Charles Stewart Parnell (1846-1891), leader of the Irish Nationalist Party

Third Marquis of Salisbury (Robert Cecil; 1830-1903), Conservative prime minister of Great Britain, 1885-1886, 1886-1892, 1895-1902

Marquis of Hartington (Spencer Compton Cavendish; 1833-1908), coleader of the Liberal Unionist Party and eighth duke of Devonshire, 1891-1908

Joseph Chamberlain (1836-1914), coleader of the Liberal Unionist Party

Katherine O'Shea (1845-1921), lover and eventually wife of Parnell

Lord Randolph Churchill (1849-1895), British Conservative member of Parliament

SUMMARY OF EVENT

Of the political events of the 1880's, few held more significant portent for the future of the United Kingdom of Great Britain and Ireland than did the conversion of the Liberal Party leader, William Ewart Gladstone, to the idea of Irish home rule. Home rule would undo the Act of Union of 1800 between Great Britain and Ireland, and the issue caused a difference of opinion among Liberals. Nevertheless, on January 27, 1886, six weeks after Gladstone's son announced his father's change of heart, the Liberals won the general elections. Gladstone became prime minister for the third time, displacing the Conservative government of the third Marquis of Salisbury.

Acting in concert with his former adversary Irish Nationalist leader and member of Parliament Charles Stewart Parnell, Gladstone proposed the Irish Home Rule Bill, which was defeated by only thirty votes in the House of Commons in June of 1886. The difference between victory and success for the bill lay in the ninety-three votes of Liberal Party defectors who refused to support their own premier. The defectors were led by the member from Birmingham, Joseph Chamberlain, and by the Marquis of Hartington (later the eighth duke of Devonshire). Members of this new faction called themselves Liberal Unionists.

In spite of this setback and the fall of the third Gladstone ministry in July of 1886, the momentum for home rule was increasing, and it seemed only a matter of time before the Liberals and Irish Nationalists would be in position to make another attempt with more likelihood of success. There had even been some hope that the Conservatives might decide to "steal a march" on the Liberals and combine with the Irish Nationalists to draft a home rule bill of their own. Subsequent events, however, were to complicate both these possibilities.

Salisbury's second government was to remain in power until 1892. Salisbury was adamantly opposed to Irish home rule, but even had he been inclined to compromise on the issue, he would have been limited by the open flirtation of the charismatic Lord Randolph Churchill with the Ulster Protestants. The Protestants feared that home rule would place the Irish Roman Catholic majority in a position to persecute and dispossess them. Churchill, who was known to covet the Tory Party leadership and not known for his scruples, had on occasion deliberately aroused that fear with inflammatory speeches during tours of Ulster. By playing the so-called Orange card, Churchill gained a level of political capital that could not be ignored. Protestants in northeastern Ireland were sufficiently roused to provide formidable and vociferous opposition to even the most moderate of home rule schemes. With Churchill breathing down his neck, Salisbury was not encouraged to take the risk of alienating influential party colleagues by pursuing too radical a course.

Lord Salisbury. (R. S. Peale/J. A. Hill)

This situation was further altered when singular and traumatic revelations brought both Parnell's leadership of his party and Gladstone's alliance with the Irish Nationalists into question. Throughout 1887, *The Times* of London serialized alleged exposes written by Richard Pigott that accused Parnell and his associates of having been involved in a series of terrorist killings during the Irish Land War era (1879-1881) and of conspiring in the assassinations of Lord Frederick Cavendish and Thomas Henry Burke. These men, respectively the chief secretary and undersecretary of Ireland, had been killed in Phoenix Park, Dublin, on May 6, 1882.

The articles were soon published in book form as *Parnellism and Crime* (1888), and they created a sensation. This scandal, however, fell apart when Pigott confessed to having lied and forged letters to incriminate the Parnellites. The writer fled to Spain and committed suicide there, and a special investigative commission of three high-court judges, meeting over the course of a year, completely exonerated the Irish Nationalist leader and his colleagues. From December 8 to 19, 1889, Gladstone and Parnell met at Hawarden, England, to iron out the details of a future home rule proposal and to formulate a strategy through which opposition could more effectively be overcome.

No sooner had Parnell's exoneration and return to power been effected, however, than another scandal broke. On December 24, Captain Willliam Henry O'Shea, a former supporter, named Parnell as a co-respondent in a divorce suit filed against his wife, Katherine O'Shea (popularly known as Kitty), on the grounds of adultery. This allegation was indeed confirmed by the court on November 17, 1890, and Kitty married Parnell on June 25, 1891. The scandal caused a backlash in Ireland, from the Vatican, and—most important for Gladstone, whose

IRELAND AT THE END OF THE NINETEENTH CENTURY

party relied on their support—from English Nonconformist Christians. The Liberal leader was forced to break with Parnell and to mail a letter urging his resignation as Nationalist Party leader. Parnell fought back grimly, even after the Nationalist Party itself voted him out of the leadership in Dublin on December 6, 1890.

With the Irish Nationalists split and Gladstone eager to distance himself from Parnellism, the issue of home rule was temporarily eclipsed. Parnell stubbornly went on campaigning on behalf of sympathetic candidates and refused to acknowledge defeat, despite rapidly deteriorating health. He died suddenly at Brighton, England, on October 6, 1891, and thus became a tragic and heroic figure, a martyr to the Irish Nationalist cause.

These setbacks and the split in the Irish Nationalist Party notwithstanding, Gladstone retained home rule as a major platform in the Liberal Party program. In August of 1892, the Liberals were returned to power, and Gladstone—now eighty-three years of age—formed his fourth ministry. On February 13, 1893, he again submitted a home rule bill. After months of acrimonious debate and of Protestant marches and rioting in Belfast, the House of Commons approved the bill over Tory and Liberal Unionist opposition on September 2, 1893. However, on September 9 in the House of Lords, Cavendish, now the eighth duke of Devonshire, successfully rallied support to kill the measure.

SIGNIFICANCE

The defeat of Gladstone's second bill was followed by a lengthy period of inaction. The Liberals lost power in 1895 and did not regain it until 1906. By that time, the Liberal Party and the Irish Nationalist Party were both under new, less aggressive leadership, and the home rule question waned until it was revived in the 1910's. By then, attitudes had become more radical, and the leaders of both parties would find that time and events had passed them by: They were supplanted by more revolutionary leaders, and home rule was superseded by the issue of complete Irish independence.

—*Raymond Pierre Hylton*

FURTHER READING

Boyce, D. George, and Alan O'Day, eds. *Ireland in Transition, 1867-1921*. New York: Routledge, 2004. Collection of diverse essays on an unusually broad theme; the most pertinent are James Loughlin's essay on nationality and loyalty and Alan O'Day's work on leadership.

Callanan, Frank. *T. M. Healey*. Cork, Ireland: Cork University Press, 1996. Offers the chance to explore the time and its issues through the eyes of a key Irish political figure and a steadfast opponent of Parnell.

Kee, Robert. *The Laurel and the Ivy: The Story of Charles Stewart Parnell and Irish Nationalism*. London: Hamish Hamilton, 1997. Well-written, sympathetic biography of the personage who was easily the most tragic and controversial among those involved in home rule.

Loughlin, James. *Gladstone, Home Rule, and the Ulster Question, 1882-1893*. Dublin: Gill & Macmillan, 1986. Iconoclastic work, in that the author sees the issue as more complex than the traditional nationalist vs. unionist struggle and views Gladstone as the central figure.

Mansergh, Nicholas. *The Irish Question, 1840-1921*. Buffalo, N.Y.: University of Toronto Press, 1975. Extremely thorough and involved account of eighty years of Anglo-Irish government and politics.

O'Day, Alan. *Parnell and the First Home Rule Episode, 1884-1887*. Dublin: Gill & Macmillan, 1986. Considers home rule a set piece of late Victorian politics whose impact is difficult to measure.

Peatling, G. K. *British Public Opinion and Irish Self-Government, 1865-1925: From Unionism to Liberal Commonwealth*. Dublin: Irish Academic Press, 2001. Expounds upon the ideological and intellectual evolution (or lack thereof) of British attitudes—mainly at more elevated levels. Touches only lightly on the masses.

Shannon, Catherine B. *Arthur J. Balfour and Ireland, 1874-1922*. Washington, D.C.: Catholic University of America Press, 1988. Renders a Tory (unionist) perspective from the point of view of one of that party's most accomplished functionaries.

SEE ALSO: Mar., 1842: *Commonwealth v. Hunt*; June, 1866-1871: Fenian Risings for Irish Independence; Dec. 3, 1868-Feb. 20, 1874: Gladstone Becomes Prime Minister of Britain; Sept.-Nov., 1880: Irish Tenant Farmers Stage First "Boycott"; May 2, 1882: Kilmainham Treaty Makes Concessions to Irish Nationalists.

RELATED ARTICLES in *Great Lives from History: The Nineteenth Century, 1801-1900:* Joseph Chamberlain; William Ewart Gladstone; Charles Stewart Parnell; Third Marquis of Salisbury.

October 28, 1886
STATUE OF LIBERTY IS DEDICATED

Conceived by historian French Édouard de Laboulaye and French sculptor Frédéric-Auguste Bartholdi as a centennial gift from France to the United States, the Statue of Liberty was meant to honor the two nations' joint commitment to liberty. Funding difficulties in France and widespread apathy in America nearly destroyed Bartholdi's dream, but the statue was built. It has come to be one of the most-recognized world monuments.

LOCALE: Bedloe's Island (now Liberty Island), New York, New York
CATEGORIES: Architecture; immigration; diplomacy and international relations

KEY FIGURES

Frédéric-Auguste Bartholdi (1834-1904), French sculptor
Édouard de Laboulaye (1811-1883), French historian
Gustave Eiffel (1832-1923), French engineer
Richard Morris Hunt (1828-1895), American architect
Joseph Pulitzer (1847-1911), American publisher
Emma Lazarus (1849-1887), American poet
Grover Cleveland (1837-1908), president of the United States, 1885-1889, 1893-1897

SUMMARY OF EVENT

The Statue of Liberty was dedicated in a ceremony highlighted by a two-hour parade and a flotilla in New York Harbor, with French and American flags lining the parade route and whistles, bands, and guns echoing across the city. Evoking painter Eugène Delacroix's famous painting, *Liberty Leading the People* (1830), the statue's designer, French sculptor Frédéric-Auguste Bartholdi, called the statue *Liberty Enlightening the World*. In a light rain and fog, just after the curtain was dropped by Bartholdi before a crowd estimated in the thousands, U.S. president Grover Cleveland reminded onlookers that the Statue of Liberty had made America its home.

Although conceived as a gift commemorating America's centennial celebration, the statue was being unveiled a full ten years after the centennial, in part because many of New York's most influential citizens, almost all of them in attendance that day, had given no support to the project. The statue's genesis was twenty years earlier, in 1865, at a dinner party hosted by historian Édouard de Laboulaye. Laboulaye had written a three-volume set of books about the United States, so the diners began discussing America's democracy, leading Bartholdi to envision a statue of Delacroix's liberty painting as a monument to the joint commitment to democracy shared by France and the United States. The

Assembly of the Statue of Liberty in Manhattan before it was erected on Beloe's Island. Frédéric-Auguste Bartholdi, the sculptor who designed the statue, appears in the inset photo. (Library of Congress)

1880's

POEM FOR THE STATUE OF LIBERTY

American poet and scholar Emma Lazarus penned the poem "The New Colossus" in 1883 for an art exhibition that had been part of a fund-raising effort for the Statue of Liberty's final construction. Written in memory of Jewish immigrants from Russia, the poem, which won an award at the exhibition and then was soon forgotten, would be inscribed on a bronze plaque in 1903 and placed on the statue's second floor. In 1945, the plaque—and the poem—was moved to the statue's main entrance as an embracing gesture to Lazarus and her work.

Not like the brazen giant of Greek fame,
With conquering limbs astride from land to land;
Here at our sea-washed, sunset gates shall stand
A mighty woman with a torch, whose flame
Is the imprisoned lightning, and her name
Mother of Exiles. From her beacon-hand
Glows world-wide welcome; her mild eyes command
The air-bridged harbor that twin cities frame.
"Keep, ancient lands, your storied pomp!" cries she
With silent lips. "Give me your tired, your poor,
Your huddled masses yearning to breathe free,
The wretched refuse of your teeming shore.
Send these, the homeless, tempest-tost to me,
I lift my lamp beside the golden door!"

Source: National Park Service, Statue of Liberty National Monument.

centennial of America's independence was just a decade away, so some at the party suggested that a gift to America honoring its independence would be a gesture worthy of France.

With his imagination set in motion by the conversation, Bartholdi traveled to New York and came home imagining a colossal statue, as big as the pyramids and sphinxes he had admired in Egypt, that would sit on a harbor island south of the city and offer a welcome to immigrants arriving in the United States. For Bartholdi, who had grown up seeing such monumental sculptures in France, the Statue of Liberty would have to be a work for the ages. The scope he envisioned was almost inconceivable, but the problem was not his ambition; it was the cost. Even with several successful fund-raising efforts in France, he and his supporters needed more than five years to collect the necessary funds for the statue.

Bartholdi secured the services of Gustave Eiffel to build an iron framework to support the copper skin of the sculpture. Eiffel was an architect and engineer who had built a number of brilliant iron bridges throughout France and would later build the Parisian tower that bears his name. By 1881, the first rivets were driven.

Across the Atlantic, things looked much bleaker. America had been expected to build the statue's pedestal and foundation and provide for its upkeep, but even after Bartholdi toured the country with clay models of the statue and displayed the thirty-foot arm and torch at the Centennial Exhibition in Philadelphia, Americans were so apathetic about the project that the money Bartholdi had hoped America would provide seemed out of reach. Newspapers mocked the idea and wealthy Americans refused to give even a token gift to the campaign. Even Congress failed initially to provide any funding.

Bartholdi's friends in the United States set about trying to raise the money through small fund-raisers. At one event, an 1883 art auction in New York City, a young poet named Emma Lazarus, who was active in Jewish causes and sympathetic to the plight of America's immigrants, read a Petrarchan sonnet she had written for the occasion. The poem, entitled "The New Colossus," offered an immigrant's view of America, a vision of Liberty as the hope of the masses and champion of the oppressed.

Still, the money came slowly. Then, in 1884, Joseph Pulitzer, the midwestern journalist and publisher of the *New York World*, heard about the campaign. Pulitzer, a Hungarian immigrant who had arrived in the United States in 1864, had made a fortune in journalism and saw in the statue the possibility of swaying public opinion toward his paper by leading the efforts to raise money for the pedestal. With his considerable wealth and prestige behind the project, more than 100,000 donors came forward to provide the money, virtually one dollar at a time. Within five months, the necessary funding was raised and Richard Morris Hunt, the premier architect in America at that time, was commissioned to build the pedestal.

The statue was completed in France in July of 1884, dismantled into 350 individual pieces, packed in 214 crates, and shipped to New York on board the French frigate *Isere*. Liberty was reassembled on its new pedestal during a four-month period, and, on October 28, 1886, the statue was dedicated in front of thousands of spectators. At the ceremony, no one read, or even mentioned, "The New Colossus." Emma Lazarus died the following year at the age of thirty-eight. In 1903, with no ceremony or even a public announcement, a plaque was affixed to the pedestal. Engraved on the plaque was "The New Colossus."

SIGNIFICANCE

The Statue of Liberty has become a worldwide symbol of freedom. Rising 151 feet, the statue stands on an eighty-nine-foot pedestal rising out of the sixty-five-foot-high paved promenade that was once Fort Wood. Smaller versions of the statue have been built across Europe, including a thirty-six-foot bronze replica on the Seine River in Paris, a gift to the French from the Paris American Colony in 1889. Perhaps most inspirational, however, is a thirty-three-foot Styrofoam statue inspired by Liberty that was built by protesting Chinese students in Tiananmen Square in Beijing in the spring of 1989, a statue the students called "Goddess of Democracy."

The Statue of Liberty acquired an enhanced emotional power as a symbol of freedom when, in 1890, President Benjamin Harrison ordered the first federal immigration station built on nearby Ellis Island. When the station opened on January 1, 1892, a fifteen-year-old Irish girl named Annie Moore became the first of more than twelve million immigrants to be processed over the next sixty-two years. Celebrating her birthday that day, the girl was given a ten-dollar coin by immigration officials with the image of Liberty stamped on its face. After that day, more than three generations of immigrants coming to America by ship would be welcomed to the nation's shores by Liberty's unforgettable image.

In 1965, President Lyndon Johnson declared Ellis Island part of the Statue of Liberty National Monument. In 1984, the statue underwent an $87 million restoration, and on July 5, 1986, it reopened in a worldwide celebration of the statue's centennial.

—*Devon Boan*

FURTHER READING

Coan, Peter M. *The Ellis Island Interviews*. New York: Facts On File, 1998. A compilation of interviews with immigrants arriving at nearby Ellis Island between 1892 and 1924, along with a brief biographical account of their experiences after getting settled. The Statue of Liberty makes an appearance in a number of accounts, including comedian Bob Hope's explanation of the statue's role in his theme song, "Thanks for the Memory."

Gordh, George. "Emma Lazarus: A Poet of Exile and Freedom." *Christian Century* 103 (November 19, 1986): 1033-1036. A careful reading of Lazarus's poetry, which the author finds imbued with a religious sensibility. "The New Colossus" is discussed at length.

Grigsby, Darcy Grimaldo. "Geometry/Labor = Volume/Mass?" *October* 106 (2003): 3-34. Examines the importance of geometric design and empty space in Eiffel's work on the Statue of Liberty, Eiffel Tower, and other projects. Appropriate for both specialists and nonspecialists.

Kaplan, Peter B., and Lee Iacocca. *Liberty for All*. Wilmington, Del.: Miller, 2004. A celebration of the statue's history and 1986 renovation through Kaplan's three hundred close-up and behind-the-scenes photographs and Iacocca's lively accounts from his perspective as head of the Statue of Liberty-Ellis Island Foundation.

Moreno, Barry. *The Statue of Liberty*. Charleston, S.C.: Arcadia, 2004. A brief and sometimes romanticized history of the statue written by a historian with the Ellis Island Museum.

_______. *The Statue of Liberty Encyclopedia*. New York: Simon & Schuster, 2000. A comprehensive reference work, well researched and well documented, and beautifully illustrated with photographs, paintings, drawings, posters, cartoons, and other documents. Extensively cross-referenced and includes an extraordinary number of fascinating but little-known details about the statue's design and history.

SEE ALSO: July 4, 1848: Ground Is Broken for the Washington Monument; May 10-Nov. 10, 1876: Philadelphia Hosts the Centennial Exposition; 1883-1885: World's First Skyscraper Is Built; May 24, 1883: Brooklyn Bridge Opens; Mar. 31, 1889: Eiffel Tower Is Dedicated.

RELATED ARTICLES in *Great Lives from History: The Nineteenth Century, 1801-1900:* Grover Cleveland; Eugène Delacroix; Gustave Eiffel; Emma Lazarus; Joseph Pulitzer.

December 8, 1886
AMERICAN FEDERATION OF LABOR IS FOUNDED

The American Federation of Labor—the first effective attempt to organize workers in skilled trades at a national level—became one of the most famous and influential labor unions in the United States.

ALSO KNOWN AS: AFL
LOCALE: Columbus, Ohio
CATEGORIES: Organizations and institutions; business and labor

KEY FIGURES

Terence V. Powderly (1849-1924), grand master workman of the Knights of Labor during the organization of the AFL

Samuel Gompers (1850-1924), first president of the AFL

William H. Foster (fl. late nineteenth century), secretary of the Federation of Organized Trades and Labor Unions of the United States and Canada

Adolf Strasser (1843-1939), president of the Cigarmakers' International Union and a founder of the AFL

Peter J. McGuire (1852-1906), first secretary of the AFL

SUMMARY OF EVENT

All indices of industrial production in the United States in the closing decades of the nineteenth century revealed a tremendous rate of growth. Stimulated by the arrival of millions of immigrants, the U.S. population spiraled from fifty million in 1880 to seventy-six million by 1900. With great strides in scientific and technological development, new industries burgeoned with the production of electric lighting equipment, telephones, street railways, adding machines, and typewriters.

Older industries consolidated, resulting in the concentration of ownership and control resting increasingly in the hands of relatively few. Trusts, pools, mergers, monopolies, "gentlemen's agreements," and other instruments of consolidation became widespread in the coal-mining, railroad, iron and steel, slaughtering and meatpacking, and oil industries. Intimately associated with this development were such captains of industry as J. P. Morgan, James. Jerome Hill, and Jay Gould in railroads; Andrew Carnegie in steel; and John D. Rockefeller in oil.

As industries changed and factories grew in size, workers found themselves increasingly distanced from management and from the control of their work. Unorganized workers and even members of many early labor unions were not effective counterweights to these aggregations of wealth and power. Seemingly powerless to press their claims for higher wages, shorter hours, or safe working conditions, various American labor leaders began to think of combining the existing trade unions into a national federation like the British Trades Union Congress (TUC). Like the TUC, this new federation would be able to lobby for legislation, both in Washington, D.C., and in the state capitals. Also like the TUC, it would be composed primarily of craft unions and would allow its constituent members complete autonomy in the operation of their local organizations. These union leaders contended that the first national workers' organization, the Noble Order of the Knights of Labor, founded by Philadelphia garment cutter Uriah Stephens in 1869, was unsuited to advance the material interests of skilled workers.

From its initial membership of only nine men, the Noble Order of the Knights of Labor had grown rapidly into a national organization, but it faced wide opposition from many segments of society. In response to opposition from the clergy and to avoid being linked with alleged terrorist organizations such as the Molly Maguires, the organization formally abandoned much of its ritualistic secrecy at its 1881 general assembly. Terence V. Powderly, the newly elected master workman, as the Knights called their chief officer, predicted that the new open policies would attract many new members.

For union organizers in the skilled trades, however, the policies of the Knights of Labor were impractical. The Knights of Labor promoted the equality of all workers, skilled and unskilled, black and white, male and female. This mixing of occupations in locals, along with the Knights' idealistic involvement in political action and reformist movements, were, the skilled-trade organizers believed, not merely unrealistic but also detrimental to the securing of such immediate bread-and-butter goals as improvements in wages and working conditions.

The Knights of Labor believed in organizing workers in assemblies; that is, all the workers in a particular factory or geographic location would be members together. Many craft workers, who believed that their unique skills made them more valuable employees than ordinary laborers, preferred to organize by trade; that is, shoemakers would be in one union and garment cutters in another. At first the Knights of Labor did not oppose the formation of craft unions, as the leadership believed that workers could benefit from both types of organization. Thus, many members of the Knights of Labor were also active in local trade unions. This spirit of cooperation changed dramatically during the 1880's.

Meeting in Pittsburgh in November, 1881, the national trade unions formed the Federation of Organized Trades and Labor Unions of the United States and Canada. The federation grew slowly, hindered at first by the economic recession of 1883-1885 and then by defeats in a number of labor disputes. As economic conditions improved, however, membership soared. However, it was also during these years that the rift between the federation and the Knights of Labor widened, primarily because the leadership of the Knights of Labor opposed striking to secure the eight-hour day. Powderly adamantly opposed the use of a work stoppage to advance workers' causes. Rather than striking, the Knights promoted the use of boycotts to pressure manufacturers into raising wages or improving working conditions. The federation, at its 1884 convention, had adopted a resolution asserting that after May 1, 1886, eight hours should constitute a working day. Appealing to trade unionists, many of the rank-and-file members of the Knights of Labor, and radical socialists, the eight-hour agitation mounted as May, 1886, approached and workers anticipated a nationwide strike to secure this goal.

May, 1886, was a momentous month for the American labor movement. On May 4 in Chicago's Haymarket Square, police attempted to disperse a group of workers demonstrating for labor causes when a dynamite bomb was thrown into the crowd. The blast killed seven police officers. In the resulting melee with the crowd, known since as the Haymarket Riot, the police shot and killed a number of demonstrators. More than one hundred people were injured. This bloodshed precipitated a wave of antiradicalism that almost fatally damaged the eight-hour movement.

Samuel Gompers. (Library of Congress)

A special meeting of the federation convened in Philadelphia. Called by William H. Foster, the federation's secretary, and by officers of the national unions, including Adolf Strasser of the Cigarmakers' International Union, its purpose was "to protect our respective organizations from the malicious work of an element [in the Knights of Labor] who openly boast that trade unions must be destroyed." The delegates drafted a "treaty" for presentation to the Knights of Labor, who, according to this proposal, should not, except with the consent of the federation, organize trades in which there were unions, and should not intervene in strikes involving federation members.

The Knights of Labor rejected the "treaty" in October, 1886. The trade unions then convened another meeting on December 8 for the purpose of drawing "the bonds of unity much closer together between all the trade unions of America" by means of "an American federation or alliance of all national and international trades unions." At that convention the American Federation of Labor (AFL) was born. Samuel Gompers of the Cigarmakers' International Union was elected the AFL's president, a post he held almost continuously until his death in 1924. Peter J. McGuire was its first secretary.

Significance

With the birth of the American Federation of Labor, skilled workers gained their own, forceful voice on the national stage. This meant that such skilled labor had greatly increased power, both in the market and in politics, but it also meant that the wedge between skilled and unskilled labor was formalized and strenghtened. By eschewing utopianism and promoting practical objectives, however, the AFL was able to survive the disastrous strikes of the early 1890's. It emerged from that decade's great depression in 1897 with 265,000 members and uncontested dominance in the American labor movement.

—*William M. Tuttle,*
updated by Nancy Farm Mannikko

Further Reading

Buhle, Paul. *Taking Care of Business: Samuel Gompers, George Meany, Lane Kirkland, and the Tragedy of American Labor*. New York: Monthly Review Press, 1999. A radical attack on Gompers and other American labor leaders. Buhle charges that labor leaders allied with corporate executives and government officials instead of representing the best interests of workers.

Fink, Leon. *In Search of the Working Class: Essays in American Labor History and Political Culture*. Urbana: University of Illinois Press, 1994. Historical work that provides a good overview of the labor movement.

Foner, Philip S. *Women and the American Labor Movement: From the First Trade Unions to the Present*. New York: Free Press, 1979. Thorough examination of the roles women played in the growth of unions both in the skilled trades and in factories.

Gompers, Samuel. *The Samuel Gompers Papers*. 9 vols. to date. Urbana: University of Illinois Press, 1986-2003. Serious readers in labor history will enjoy reading Gompers's own thoughts on the rise of organized labor.

Greene, Julie. *Pure and Simple Politics: The American Federation of Labor and Political Activism, 1881-1917*. New York: Cambridge University Press, 1998. A study of the AFL under Gompers's leadership, examining the organization's political participation during the Progressive Era.

Laurie, Bruce. *Artisans into Workers: Labor in Nineteenth Century America*. New York: Hill and Wang, 1989. Accessible analysis of the transformation of work in America.

Meltzer, Milton. *Bread and Roses: The Struggle of American Labor, 1865-1915*. New York: Facts On File, 1991. Definitive history of the labor movement in the United States.

Voss, Kim. *The Making of American Exceptionalism: The Knights of Labor and Class Formation in the Nineteenth Century*. Ithaca, N.Y.: Cornell University Press, 1993. Fascinating study of the Knights of Labor.

Yellowitz, Irwin. *Industrialization and the American Labor Movement, 1850-1900*. Port Washington, N.Y.: Kennikat Press, 1977. Examines the relationships between the growth of industry and the growth of organized labor.

See also: Dec. 4, 1867: National Grange Is Formed; June 2, 1868: Great Britain's First Trades Union Congress Forms; Sept.-Nov., 1880: Irish Tenant Farmers Stage First "Boycott"; May 15, 1891: Papal Encyclical on Labor; May 11-July 11, 1894: Pullman Strike.

Related articles in *Great Lives from History: The Nineteenth Century, 1801-1900:* Andrew Carnegie; Samuel Gompers; James Jerome Hill; J. P. Morgan; John D. Rockefeller.

February 4, 1887
INTERSTATE COMMERCE ACT

When the U.S. Congress passed the Interstate Commerce Act, it made the railroad industry the first industry to be subject to federal regulation in the United States. The act created the Interstate Commerce Commission to enforce its regulations.

LOCALE: Washington, D.C.
CATEGORIES: Laws, acts, and legal history; trade and commerce; transportation; government and politics

KEY FIGURES

Grover Cleveland (1837-1908), president of the United States, 1885-1889, 1893-1897
Shelby Moore Cullom (1829-1914), senator from Illinois
John Henninger Reagan (1818-1905), congressman from Texas
Thomas M. Cooley (1824-1898), first chairman of the Interstate Commerce Commission
Simon Sterne (1839-1901), chairman of the New York Board of Trade and Transportation
F. B. Thurber (fl. late nineteenth century), wholesale grocer in New York who lobbied for regulatory legislation

SUMMARY OF EVENT

By the 1880's, the United States had experienced more than fifty years of railroad expansion. Transcontinental railroad lines tied the nation together, while spurring the growth of industry and agriculture through the rapid transportation of both raw materials and finished goods. During much of this time, government had served as a willing partner to the rapid growth of the railroads. Both national and state governments had provided land for the railroad right-of-way, as well as other subsidies to underwrite the cost of this vital form of transportation. By the end of the Civil War (1861-1865), however, many people in the United States had begun to have second thoughts about the railroads.

Although almost no one doubted the need for railroads, many criticized the business practices of the railroad companies. Consumers suffered when railroad companies experienced either too much or too little competition. In regions where one company dominated, that company often took advantage of its monopoly of the market and charged its customers exorbitant fees for necessary services. Where competition was intense, the railroads too often resorted to unfair practices in order to attract and retain the business of large-volume shippers. They reduced rates in some areas to meet competition and raised rates in noncompetitive areas to compensate. They also engaged in such practices as offering rebates or kickbacks to large-volume shippers at the expense of the average consumer. The railroads entered into agreements, often referred to as "pools," among themselves to fix rates at a level higher than the free market permitted. They charged more for a short haul in order to offer special long-haul rates to large shippers.

The railroads also were guilty of watering their stock, or overcapitalizing issues, to bilk investors. These and other practices worked to the advantage of the railroads and a few favored customers. As a result of railroad manipulation of freight charges, it often cost small farmers more to ship their grain than they would receive in payment for it, while large mill owners would receive a discount on the shipment of the finished flour. The unethical business practices thus worked to the detriment of the ordinary shippers, farmers, and the public.

The states responded first to the demands for railroad reform. Many states passed laws that compelled railroads to offer standard rates for all, and many states set up regulatory boards to supervise the practices of the railroad companies. The states, however, could not supervise interstate operations. Farmers shipping grain from the Dakotas to Minnesota mills or cattle from Texas to Chicago slaughterhouses were not protected by individual state regulations. In addition, the state regulatory laws and boards often created more problems than they solved. Finally, the railroads resisted attempts at state regulation and fought enforcement in the courts. In October, 1886, the Supreme Court in *Wabash, St. Louis, and Pacific Railway v. Illinois* held that a state could not regulate commerce that went beyond its boundaries. This meant that any regulation of interstate commerce would have to come from the federal government.

Numerous groups and individuals had long pressed for national legislation to reform the railroads. Organizations of producers, shippers, and merchants demanded an end to practices by which railroad companies took advantage of the need for rail transportation. F. B. Thurber, a New York wholesale grocer, and Simon Sterne, chairman of New York's Board of Trade and Transportation, became active lobbyists. Some of the loudest demands for some system of national regulation began to come from the railroad companies themselves, particularly in the East, where competition was ruthless. Financiers such as Jay Gould recognized that without some reforms, public outrage could lead to harsh regulations in the future.

John Henninger Reagan, a congressman from Texas and the chairman of the House Committee on Commerce, during the 1870's and early 1880's introduced many bills in Congress that would outlaw specific practices, such as pools, rebates, and price discrimination between long and short hauls. Reagan's approach to the problem was an attempt to clean up the competition among the railroads on the assumption that fair competition was economically healthy for the entire nation. The proposed bills described what would constitute illegal practices but contained no provisions for investigation or regulation. Reagan's attempts to regulate the railroads met with little success until the first administration of President Grover Cleveland.

Cleveland, a Democrat, strongly opposed the growth of government but opposed the idea of government favors to business even more. Following the Supreme Court decision in *Wabash, St. Louis, and Pacific Railway v. Illinois*, Cleveland urged Congress to take action to regulate the railroads. This time, Congress seemed ready to pass regulatory legislation. Reagan once again introduced a bill in the House of Representatives, while in the Senate, Shelby Moore Cullom of Illinois proposed a more far-reaching solution.

Cullom's approach, which emerged from extensive committee hearings, embodied a regulatory commission with broad powers to investigate and to bring into court railroad companies whose rates or practices were unfair. Cullom proposed that the federal government take positive action in laying down precisely what constituted unfair tactics and rates. The Reagan and Cullom bills went to a joint committee of the House and the Senate. President Cleveland exerted some influence in favor of Cullom's proposals. From the joint committee emerged the Interstate Commerce Act, which was passed on February 4, 1887.

The act followed Reagan's suggestions and prohibited specific abuses, such as long- and short-haul discrimination. It also created the Interstate Commerce Commission (ICC). Under the provisions of the act, the commission would comprise five members whose duty it was to investigate and expose unfair rates and practices among interstate carriers. Congress empowered the commission to take unrepentant railroads into court. After decades of encouraging and subsidizing the railroads, the government had begun to regulate them.

SIGNIFICANCE

The jubilation of railroad reformers in the wake of the Interstate Commerce Act's passage was short-lived. The courts and the ICC itself seemed determined to frustrate substantive reform. The commission, whose first chairman was Thomas M. Cooley, a professor of law at the University of Michigan, often dealt with the railroads in an extremely conservative manner, and the Supreme Court weakened the commission's powers. Cooley believed in a strict interpretation of the Constitution and was reluctant to expand the power of the federal government. When the railroads chose to dispute the rulings of the ICC, they generally won in court. Of the sixteen cases involving railroads and the ICC that were heard by the Supreme Court between 1887 and 1911, the railroads won fifteen. In the process, the Supreme Court destroyed the commission's power to act against fixing rates, pooling, and long- and short-haul discrimination. Government regulation had been established in theory, but not yet in practice. The Interstate Commerce Act was significant chiefly as a precedent for the genuine economic reform that followed in later years.

—*Emory M. Thomas,*
updated by Nancy Farm Mannikko

FURTHER READING

Cullom, Shelby Moore. *Fifty Years of Public Service: Personal Recollections of Shelby M. Cullom.* New York: Da Capo Press, 1969. A memoir by a politician who lived through some of the most volatile times in U.S. history.

Jeffers, H. Paul. *An Honest President: The Life and Presidencies of Grover Cleveland.* New York: William Morrow, 2000. Jeffers portrays Cleveland as a staunch reformer, a man of high moral character and courage who restored dignity to the presidency.

Jones, Alan R. *The Constitutional Conservatism of Thomas McIntyre Cooley: A Study in the History of Ideas.* New York: Garland, 1987. An intellectual history that helps clarify why the ICC accomplished little of substance with Cooley as its chairman.

Neilson, James W. *Shelby M. Cullom: Prairie State Republican.* Urbana: University of Illinois Press, 1962. Biography of one of the prime movers behind the Interstate Commerce Act and its regulatory features.

Reagan, John H. *Memoirs, with Special Reference to Secession and the Civil War.* Edited by Walter Flavius McCaleb. New York: AMS Press, 1978. Originally published in 1906, Reagan's memoirs provide fascinating glimpses into the history of the Confederacy and Gilded Age politics in the United States.

Stone, Richard D. *The Interstate Commerce Commission and the Railroad Industry: A History of Regulatory Policy*. New York: Praeger, 1991. Good, detailed history of the ICC and the growth of both railroads and regulations.

Welch, Richard E. *The Presidencies of Grover Cleveland*. Lawrence: University Press of Kansas, 1988. A thorough examination of the Cleveland presidencies.

SEE ALSO: Feb. 25, 1863-June 3, 1864: Congress Passes the National Bank Acts; Dec. 4, 1867: National Grange Is Formed; Jan. 10, 1870: Standard Oil Company Is Incorporated; Jan. 16, 1883: Pendleton Act Reforms the Federal Civil Service; July 20, 1890: Harrison Signs the Sherman Antitrust Act; July 4-5, 1892: Birth of the People's Party; May 11-July 11, 1894: Pullman Strike; July 24, 1897: Congress Passes Dingley Tariff Act.

RELATED ARTICLE in *Great Lives from History: The Nineteenth Century, 1801-1900:* Grover Cleveland.

February 8, 1887
GENERAL ALLOTMENT ACT ERODES INDIAN TRIBAL UNITY

The General Allotment Act instituted a federal policy of alloting land to individual Native Americans. The act weakened the allegiance of American Indians to their tribes and ultimately resulted in the dissolution of some tribal nations and the assimilation of some Indians into mainstream American society.

ALSO KNOWN AS: Dawes Act
LOCALE: Washington, D.C.
CATEGORIES: Indigenous people's rights; laws, acts, and legal history; government and politics; expansion and land acquisition

KEY FIGURES

Henry Laurens Dawes (1816-1903), U.S. senator from Massachusetts
L. Q. C. Lamar (1825-1893), U.S. secretary of the interior, 1885-1888, and later associate justice of the U.S. Supreme Court, 1888-1893
Lyman Abbott (1835-1922), editor of the *Christian Union*
Carl Schurz (1829-1906), reform-minded secretary of the interior, 1877-1881
Herbert Welsh (1851-1941), secretary of the Indian Rights Association
Henry Moore Teller (1830-1914), U.S. secretary of the interior, 1882-1885, and senator from Colorado
Lewis Henry Morgan (1818-1881), anthropologist

SUMMARY OF EVENT

When the General Allotment Act became law on February 8, 1887, proponents hailed it as the Indian Emancipation Act and Secretary of the Interior L. Q. C. Lamar called it "the most important measure of legislation ever enacted in this country affecting our Indian affairs." The law dealt primarily with Native American ownership of land. It authorized the president of the United States, through the Office of Indian Affairs in the Department of the Interior, to allot the lands on reservations to individual Native Americans, so that they would hold the land in severalty instead of the tribe's owning the land communally. Each head of a household would receive a quarter-section of land (160 acres), single persons over eighteen years of age and orphans would receive eighty acres, and other persons would receive forty acres. In 1891, an amendment to the law equalized the allotments to provide eighty acres for each individual, regardless of age or family status.

Under the law, the U.S. government would hold these land allotments in trust for twenty-five years, during which time a Native American could not sell or otherwise dispose of his or her land. At the end of that period, he or she would receive full title to it. After dividing reservation land into allotments, the federal government could sell the surplus land (often a considerable portion of the reservation) to willing purchasers, most of whom would be Euro-Americans. The money from such sales would go to a fund to benefit Native American education.

The General Allotment Act also provided for Native American citizenship. Native Americans who received allotments in severalty or who took up residence apart from their tribe and adopted what Euro-Americans considered "civilized ways" became citizens of the United States and subject to the laws of the state or territory in which they lived. In 1924, Congress passed the Indian Citizenship Act, granting full citizenship to nearly all

AMERICAN INDIAN RESERVATIONS IN 1883

Native Americans who were not already citizens, and measures during the late 1940's extended such status to Arizona and New Mexico Native Americans that the 1924 law had missed.

Two groups of Euro-Americans especially welcomed the General Allotment Act. Land-hungry settlers who had long cast covetous eyes on the reservation lands—which, to Euro-American thinking, were going to waste because of the lack of productive agricultural practices by Native Americans, whom they considered to be hunters and gatherers—were now able to acquire the lands left over from the allotment process. No doubt, the less scrupulous among the settlers also looked forward to the day when individual Native Americans would receive full title to their land and be able to sell, lease, or otherwise dispose of it. Then pressure, legitimate or not, would likely induce the new owners to part with the acreage.

A second group of Euro-Americans, however, was more influential in securing passage of the General Allotment Act. These were the humanitarian reformers of the day, who considered private ownership of land in severalty, U.S. citizenship, education, and consistent codification of laws to be indispensable means for the acculturation of the Native Americans and their eventual assimilation into the mainstream of U.S. society. As ministers from the several Christian denominations, educators, civil servants, politicians, and even a few military personnel, these philanthropists exerted a clout beyond their numbers. Calling themselves the Friends of the Indian, these reformers had been meeting annually since 1869 at the Catskills resort of Lake Mohonk to discuss ways to bring the tribal peoples to what the conveners deemed to be civilization.

Federal politicians had long considered private ownership of land essential to the civilizing process. Thomas Jefferson and the like-minded policymakers of his time had strongly advocated it, and in 1838 the commissioner of Indian Affairs gave voice to a widespread view when he said, "Unless some system is marked out by which there shall be a separate allotment of land to each individual . . . you will look in vain for any general casting off of savagism. Common property and civilization cannot coexist."

It was not until the post-Civil War years, when increasing Euro-American pressures on the Native Americans created crisis after crisis, that humanitarians and philanthropists began a concerted drive for "Indian reform." Land in severalty would be the most important factor in breaking up tribalism. The reform groups that were organized—the Board of Indian Commissioners (1869), the Women's National Indian Association (1879), the Indian Rights Association (1882), the Lake Mohonk Conference of Friends of the Indian (1883), and the National Indian Defense Association (1885), to name the most important—all strongly espoused allotment in severalty. Nor were they satisfied with the piecemeal legislation that affected one tribe at a time; the panacea they sought was a general allotment law. Although supporters argued over the speed of implementing allotment, such proponents as Carl Schurz, Herbert Welsh, and the Reverend Lyman Abbott fought energetically for such legislation. They finally won to their cause Senator Henry Laurens Dawes, chairman of the Senate Committee on Indian Affairs, who successfully shepherded through Congress the measure that bears his name.

Only a few Euro-American voices cried out against the proposal. Congressman Russell Errett of Pennsylvania and a few others protested that the bill was a thinly disguised means of getting at the valuable tribal lands. Senator Henry Moore Teller of Colorado argued that the Native Americans did not want to own land in severalty and were not prepared to assume the responsibilities that went with private property and citizenship. He denied the contention of the reformers that private ownership of land would lead to civilization. Albert Meacham, editor of *The Council Fire*, maintained that there was little enthusiasm for severalty among traditionalist Native Americans, and anthropologist Lewis Henry Morgan thought that allotment would result in massive poverty. Presbyterian missionaries apparently were disunited on the subject of allotment, and their views fell by the wayside as the juggernaut of reform plunged ahead.

Significance

"February 8, 1887," one optimistic spokesman of the Board of Indian Commissioners commented, "may be called the Indian emancipation day." Although much sincere Christian goodwill motivated passage of the General Allotment Act, it turned out to be a disaster for Native Americans. The sponsors of the General Allotment Act had assumed an unrealistically romantic view of the Native American. People who had had firsthand experience with tribal peoples attempted to prove to the reformers that the "noble savage" had never existed. In 1891, Congress allowed Native Americans to lease their allotments if they were not able to farm for themselves.

Native American response to allotment has largely gone unrecorded. The Cherokee, Creek, Chickasaw, Choctaw, Seminole, Sac, Fox, and a few other tribes in Indian Territory, as well as the Seneca in New York, contended that they already mostly owned land individually and won exclusion from the act's operation. By 1906, however, Congress extended allotment to them as well. Most of the complaints came after the act's passage, when Native Americans lost land and found farming difficult under its provisions.

The allotments and the leasing moved faster and with less careful discrimination than Dawes and other promoters had intended. Instead of being a measure that turned Native Americans into self-supporting farmers, the act, through the rapid alienation of the Native Americans' lands, meant the loss of the land base on which the tribal peoples' hope for future prosperity depended. Tribal peoples held claim to about 150 million acres of land in 1887. The General Allotment Act eventually diverted two-thirds of that acreage out of Native American ownership, down to about forty-eight million acres by 1934. Not until that year, with the passage of the Indian Reorganization Act (the Wheeler-Howard Act, also known as the "Indian New Deal"), did the federal government repeal the General Allotment Act and encourage communal forms of ownership again, but by that time much of the former reservation land was gone as surplus sales, leases, or sales by the individual allottees.

—*Francis P. Prucha, updated by Thomas L. Altherr*

Further Reading

Coleman, Michael C. "Problematic Panacea: Presbyterian Missionaries and the Allotment of Indian Lands in the Late Nineteenth Century." *Pacific Historical Review* 54, no. 2 (1985): 143-159. Shows that the Presbyterians were not united about allotment of tribal lands.

Gibson, Arrell Morgan. "The Centennial Legacy of the General Allotment Act." *Chronicles of Oklahoma* 65, no. 3 (1987): 228-251. Examines the long-range effects of the General Allotment Act on Native Americans.

Greenwald, Emily. *Reconfiguring the Reservation: The Nez Perces, Jicarilla Apaches, and the Dawes Act.*

Albuquerque: University of New Mexico Press, 2002. Detailed study of the passage of the General Allotment Act and of its influence on two specific Native American tribes.

Hoxie, Frederick E. *A Final Promise: The Campaign to Assimilate the Indians, 1880-1920*. Lincoln: University of Nebraska Press, 1984. Examines the story of the General Allotment Act in the context of larger assimilationist programs toward Native Americans.

Mintz, Steven, ed. *Native American Voices*. St. James, N.Y.: Brandywine Press, 1995. Contains part of the General Allotment Act and a complaint by a Cherokee farmer in 1906.

Prucha, Francis Paul, ed. *Americanizing the American Indians: Writings of the "Friends of the Indian," 1880-1900*. Lincoln: University of Nebraska Press, 1973. Section 2 provides a representative sampling of primary source writings about the General Allotment Act.

Washburn, Wilcomb E. *The Assault on Indian Tribalism: The General Allotment Law (Dawes Act) of 1887*. Philadelphia: J. B. Lippincott, 1975. A concise summary of the attitudes that produced the act and its repercussions for Native Americans; contains the full text of the original law.

SEE ALSO: Apr. 24, 1820: Congress Passes Land Act of 1820; May 28, 1830: Congress Passes Indian Removal Act; Mar. 18, 1831, and Mar. 3, 1832: Cherokee Cases; Sept. 4, 1841: Congress Passes Preemption Act of 1841; Dec. 31, 1853: Gadsden Purchase Completes the U.S.-Mexican Border; May 20, 1862: Lincoln Signs the Homestead Act; July 2, 1862: Lincoln Signs the Morrill Land Grant Act; Mar. 30, 1867: Russia Sells Alaska to the United States; Oct. 21, 1867: Medicine Lodge Creek Treaty; Mar. 3, 1871: Grant Signs Indian Appropriation Act.

RELATED ARTICLES in *Great Lives from History: The Nineteenth Century, 1801-1900:* Lewis Henry Morgan; Carl Schurz.

March 13, 1887
AMERICAN PROTECTIVE ASSOCIATION IS FORMED

The American Protective Association was the largest anti-Roman Catholic, anti-immigrant, nativist group organized in the United States during the nineteenth century. Attracting native-born Protestants who feared the growing influence of Catholicism in the United States, the politically influential organization began to wane at the end of the century.

LOCALE: Clinton, Iowa
CATEGORIES: Immigration; religion and theology; organizations and institutions

KEY FIGURE

Henry F. Bowers (1835-1911), founder and leader of the American Protective Association

SUMMARY OF EVENT

The immigration of many Roman Catholics to the United States during the mid-nineteenth century resulted in conservative, native-born Protestants perceiving a growing threat to their way of life. Some Americans feared a "papal plot" (referring to the Catholic faith) to take over the United States; others simply felt that their values, economic position, and political dominance were threatened.

Before the U.S. Civil War (1861-1865), Protestants had organized nativist, anti-Catholic parties in order to oppose the new immigrants. Historians frequently refer to these groups collectively as the Know-Nothings because members would deny the existence of these groups if questioned about them. One Know-Nothing organization, the Order of the Star-Spangled Banner, founded the American Party in 1854. Its platform was dominated by nativism and anti-Catholicism. While it won a number of elections in the mid-1850's, it was eventually absorbed into the Republican Party.

Catholic immigration grew even more in the post-Civil War era. Approximately 25 million immigrants came to the United States between the end of the Civil War and 1917, when the United States entered World War I. These immigrants, many of whom were Catholic or Jewish, came primarily from southern and eastern Europe. This resulted in a new Protestant nativism in the last part of the nineteenth century as those Americans feared the growing economic, political, and social power of the Catholic immigrants. The anti-Catholic sentiment was part of a larger anti-immigrant nativism during an era when immigrants from Asia as well as poorer areas of Europe were entering the United States.

Short-lived nativist newspaper published in Boston in 1852. (Library of Congress)

1880's

After the Civil War era, the Republican Party continued to raise the question of Catholic political power. One major issue was keeping public schools free from ecclesiastical influence. In addition, the party advocated longer residence for immigrants before they could secure citizenship and the right to vote. In 1880, the Republican Party election platform supported a constitutional amendment that specified that no governmental authority could allow any public property, revenues, or loans to be used for the support of any school or other institution under the control of any religious sect.

While there were various anti-Catholic movements active in the 1860's and 1870's, the largest anti-Catholic group was formally organized on March 13, 1887, in Clinton, Iowa. There, a group of seven men, in response to the defeat of a municipal slate of labor union candidates by Irish voters, founded the American Protective Association (APA) to combat the growing political power of Catholics. Henry F. Bowers, a lawyer, copied many aspects of the rituals of the fraternal Masons (Bowers was a Mason as well). The APA was a secret organization with elaborate rituals and costumes. Members were required to take an oath, swearing never to vote for a Catholic, never to employ a Catholic if a Protestant was available, and never to go on strike with a Catholic.

The APA's 1894 program stated that the organization would defend true Americanism against the subjects of an un-American ecclesiastical institution by fighting for a free public school system, for immigration restrictions, and for a slower, more rigid system of naturalization. In particular, the APA called for a change in the laws so that immigrants could not be naturalized or allowed to vote unless they spoke English and had lived in the United States continuously for seven years minimum. The APA repeatedly denounced the Catholic pope and the Roman

Catholic Church for trying, according to the APA, to subvert American institutions.

APA leaders protested a perceived attempt by Catholics—by "Romanish" priests—to make whole communities "foreign" in language and religion. The APA also believed Romanism concentrated Catholic immigrants in large American cities to gain complete control of those cities, that Jesuits were controlling national government leaders, and that Romanism was influencing the U.S. Army and Navy. The APA claimed that while only one-eighth of the population was Catholic, half of public officeholders were Catholic.

To attract followers the APA used bogus former priests and former nuns on a lecture circuit, claiming to have escaped "captivity" in monasteries. The APA also distributed forged documents to show the Protestant population that there was a papal plot or conspiracy. For example, one forged document was a papal bull that called for the massacre of Protestants in 1893. The APA also developed a press in 1893, and it has been estimated that in 1894, the group published approximately seventy weeklies. These publications were designed for a local audience and normally had a limited circulation of no more than one thousand each.

Unlike the Know-Nothing movement before the Civil War, which created the American Party, the APA did not start its own political party. Rather, it targeted the Republican Party, promoting candidates at the local level and getting involved in primary elections and local party activities. The APA's greatest political success was, consequently, at the local level, especially in municipalities in the Midwest. Here, local campaigns frequently focused on issues such as Catholic influence in local schools or Catholic domination over municipal patronage. Some of the cities where the APA had its greatest influence were Omaha, Kansas City, Toledo, Louisville, Duluth, Saginaw, and Rockford. It also had an impact in Detroit, St. Louis, Denver, Buffalo, and Rochester.

In terms of states, the APA's greatest appeal was to residents in mountain and Pacific states, which had, more recently, been settled and were growing rapidly. These were areas where social tensions were greatest as a result of the influx of a large number of newcomers. The region where the APA was weakest was the South, which experienced little in-migration in the post-Civil War era. The APA had a number of supporters within the business community as well, but various later studies have indicated that the APA's membership was somewhat more working-class, native-born Protestant than it was middle-class, native-born Protestant.

SIGNIFICANCE

Although the American Protective Association claimed a membership of 2.5 million at its peak in 1894, historians have estimated that its actual dues-paying membership was closer to 100,000. By 1895 the APA's membership had begun to decline and its political influence began to wane.

In 1896, the APA had opposed William McKinley's nomination as the Republican Party's presidential candidate because some of his close friends and supporters were Catholic. The APA spread false rumors that McKinley was a member of the Roman Catholic Church, that his secretary and campaign managers were Catholic, and that he had two children in a convent. McKinley's subsequent election further illustrates that the APA's influence in national politics had been declining. Although the APA continued to exist for at least five more years, it ceased to have significant political influence. By the beginning of the twentieth century, the APA was, for all practical purposes, defunct.

—*William V. Moore*

FURTHER READING

Daniels, Roger. *The Golden Door: American Immigration Policy and Immigrants Since 1882*. New York: Hill and Wang, 2004. An examination of the U.S. government's policy on immigration, beginning in 1882.

Kinzer, Donald L. *Episode in Anti-Catholicism: The American Protective Association*. Seattle: University of Washington Press, 1964. The definitive history of the American Protective Association and its anti-Catholicism.

Knobel, Dale T. *American for the Americans: The Nativist Movement in the United States*. New York: Twayne, 1995. Examines a variety of nativist movements from the 1820's through the 1920's, including the American Protective Association.

Lipset, Seymour Martin, and Earl Raab. *The Politics of Unreason: Right-Wing Extremism in America, 1790-1970*. New York: Harper & Row, 1970. An analysis of right-wing movements in the United States within the framework of status issues and politics.

Wacker, Grant. *Religion in Nineteenth Century America*. New York: Oxford University Press, 2000. A historical narrative that discusses the rapid growth of evangelical Protestantism and its competition for dominance over religions such as Catholicism and Judaism.

SEE ALSO: 1840's-1850's: American Era of "Old" Immigration; May 6-July 5, 1844: Anti-Irish Riots Erupt in Philadelphia; 1845-1854: Great Irish Famine; 1871-1877: Kulturkampf Against the Catholic Church in Germany; 1892: America's "New" Immigration Era Begins; Jan. 1, 1892: Ellis Island Immigration Depot Opens; May 4, 1892: Anti-Japanese Yellow Peril Campaign Begins.

RELATED ARTICLES in *Great Lives from History: The Nineteenth Century, 1801-1900:* James Gibbons; William McKinley; Pius IX.

May, 1887
GOODWIN DEVELOPS CELLULOID FILM

Hannibal Williston Goodwin's development of flexible celluloid film facilitated the expansion of motion-picture lengths and eventually made possible the development of the feature-length film as a distinct art form.

LOCALE: Newark, New Jersey

CATEGORIES: Inventions; science and technology; motion pictures; photography

KEY FIGURES

Hannibal Williston Goodwin (1822-1900), American theologian and amateur inventor

Henry M. Reichenbach (fl. late nineteenth century), American inventor

William Dickson (1860-1935), American inventor

August Lumière (1862-1954), French inventor and filmmaker

Louis Lumière (1864-1948), French inventor and filmmaker

Georges Méliès (1861-1938), French filmmaker

Edwin S. Porter (1870?-1941), American filmmaker

James Williamson (1855-1933), Scottish filmmaker

Thomas Alva Edison (1847-1931), American inventor and entrepreneur

Louis Le Prince (1842-1890), French photographer and inventor

SUMMARY OF EVENT

In May of 1887, Hannibal Williston Goodwin, rector of the House of Prayer Episcopal Church in Newark, New Jersey, filed for a patent for "a photographic pellicle and process of producing same . . . in connection with roller cameras." His patent was granted thirteen years later, after a long court fight with the Eastman Kodak Company over who was the first to develop the concept of celluloid film strips. By then, motion pictures had been invented, and the advent of continuous film rolls allowed the burgeoning technology of film to evolve, as "one-reelers" would become common before 1910, and feature films would develop in the decade after that.

Goodwin, a devoted preacher, became interested in photography as a means of producing illustrations for religious talks and sermons. Various technologies were used to produce illusions of motion during the nineteenth century, including the phenakistoscope, invented by Joseph Plateau, and George Horner's zoetrope. One of the best-known photographers of motion was Eadweard Muybridge, who photographed horses in motion with a series of cameras and presented the results in a machine he called the zoöpraxiscope. Like the phenakistoscope and the zoetrope, however, the zoöpraxiscope used drawings rather than photographs to create its illusions. (As a result of the latter device's method of producing a motion effect, a photographed horse would have looked stunted on the screen, so a hand-drawn, unnaturally elongated horse was used. When projected, the elongated horse looked "normal" to the human eye.)

Most photographic technologies before 1887 were limited by the need to use heavy and fragile glass plates coated with chemical emulsions to register images. Furthermore, prints could not be economically produced from these media, so the images created could not circulated on a mass scale. Indeed, the primary form of projection at the time, the magic lantern show (essentially a slide projector), was associated with the skills of a particular showman in staging a unique and entertaining spectacle. The notion of standardized projection, in which every audience everywhere in the country saw exactly the same images in the same way, was unheard-of.

Celluloid is the name of a class of chemical compounds created from nitrocellulose, a plant material, and camphor, dyes, and other agents. There is some evidence that celluloid was developed in response to the need for a new material to replace ivory in billiard balls. By the late nineteenth century, celluloid was used for a variety of everyday items including collars and cuffs, toys, and pen nibs. As a result of its extreme flammability and instability over time, celluloid was replaced in most applications in the twentieth century by more stable plastics, such as acetates and polyethylenes.

As early as 1885, Eastman Kodak Company was manufacturing flexible photographic film, consisting of chemical emulsion coated on paper. Although this film registered images effectively, it was not transparent and could not be used to make multiple prints. Perhaps because he lived in Newark, New Jersey, the site of a major celluloid manufacturing company, Goodwin conceived the idea to use celluloid strips as the base for chemical emulsions to record images. By May, 1887, he had refined the process of creating the strips enough to file for a patent.

At the same time, Henry M. Reichenbach, an employee of the well-known and well-funded Eastman Kodak Company, was working on a celluloid-based version of Kodak's coated-paper film rolls; whether he knew of Goodwin's work or conceived the idea independently is not known. In any case, the courts ruled in 1913 that he had infringed on Goodwin's patent. By 1889, however, Eastman Kodak was manufacturing and marketing strips and rolls of film that could record several minutes of action at a time.

Thomas Alva Edison's associate William Dickson used film manufactured by Eastman Kodak to produce the first fully functional motion-picture camera, the kinetograph, in 1891. However, Edison was not initially interested in the projection of film, so he created a peep-show device, the kinetoscope, with which to view moving images derived from the kinetograph's photographs. Because he did not see a large financial potential in motion pictures, Edison failed to file for European patents, thus opening the way for multiple Europeans to complete their own work on photographing and reproducing movement.

One of these Europeans was Louis Le Prince, the son of a French army officer and student of chemistry. Having worked as a still photographer, Le Prince moved to Great Britain and became an employee of an engineering firm before moving to New York and managing a chain of theaters. Intrigued by the process of motion photography, he invented a very complex sixteen-lens camera, as well as a much simpler single-lens machine with a projector. As early as 1888, he used his invention and Eastman Kodak's paper film to photograph family scenes at his home, which survive today in limited copies of the original paper prints.

There is evidence that Le Prince intended to rent premises and publicly show his films, but after boarding a train in Dijon, France, after a visit with his brother, he disappeared on the way to Paris. Despite an extensive search and tremendous publicity, no sign of him was found; He is now believed to have disembarked and drowned en route. Therefore, though he was the first person known to create actual motion pictures on continuous strips of film, Le Prince's influence on motion picture development was minimal.

Eastman Kodak's film became commercially available in 1889, and it was used by the various pioneers of motion picture. Louis Lumière and his brother Auguste Lumière patented the cinematograph, a machine that could record images, develop them, and project the results. They showed their films in Paris to enthusiastic audiences in late 1895, though these entertainments consisted mostly

THE CHAOTIC WORLD OF EARLY CINEMA

One of the most important features of celluloid film proved to be the ease with which it could be cut at precise points into pieces that could be spliced together with equal precision. The editing together of discrete pieces of film became one of the most important narrative techniques of the mature art of cinema. Even before such editing was widespread, however, the juxtaposition of different images prevalent at the earliest cinematic exhibitions—an effect described in the following excerpt from Punch *magazine—foreshadowed the editing techniques that would be developed later.*

There's a rattling, and a shattering, and there are sparks, and there are showers of quivering snow-flakes always falling, and amidst these appear children fighting in bed, a house on fire, with inmates saved by the arrival of fire engines, which, at some interval, are followed by warships pitching about at sea, sailors running up riggings and disappearing into space, trains at full speed coming directly at you, and never getting there, but jumping out of the picture into outer darkness where the audience is, and then, the train having vanished, all the country round takes it into its head to follow as hard as ever it can, rocks, mountains, trees, towns, gateways, castles, rivers, landscapes, bridges, platforms, telegraph-poles, all whirling and squirling and racing against one another, as if to see which will get to the audience first, and then, suddenly . . . all disappear into space!! Phew! We breathe again!!

Source: Punch, August 6, 1898.

of scenes of everyday life, such as a train arriving at a station and workers leaving a factory.

Georges Méliès, a stage magician, asked the Lumières for permission to use their device to create his own movies. When they refused, he invented a motion-picture camera of his own and began experimenting with filming techniques that would create magical effects similar to those of his stage show. Méliès is often called one of the inventors of special effects. His fantastic films often involved multiple, lavish sets and costumes, and they were much longer than the earliest Lumière and Edison films. Scottish filmmaker James Williamson also created some of the earliest multishot films, utilizing techniques such as shot/reverse-shot and other forms of editing in films including *Attack on a China Mission* (1900) and *Fire!* (1901).

Another early director, Edison employee Edwin S. Porter, also helped develop narrative films. Like Williamson, one of his most successful early multishot films was based on the established genre of firefighters riding to the rescue, which had already been the subject of magic lantern shows for decades. Indeed, Porter's *Life of an American Fireman* (1903) was an adaptation of a magic lantern show. Later in the decade, the film reel became a standard length, and single-reel films were made by such early directors as D. W. Griffith (1875-1948) at Biograph (the American Mutoscope and Biograph Company). Griffith would be one of the directors to develop the first so-called feature-length films in 1914-1916.

Significance

Although Goodwin died in a car accident in 1900 before he could realize any substantial financial rewards from his invention, the development of flexible, translucent film in continuous strips and rolls was key to the invention and development of the cinema. Without the ability to record several minutes' worth of action at a time, film could not have progressed past a novelty entertainment and into a narrative medium. Furthermore, celluloid helped enable films to be projected to a roomful of people at one time. This, along with the ability to strike many prints from a single negative, made the economics of film production and presentation worthwhile for artists and businessmen to pursue. Without Goodwin's invention, a tremendously influential art form might never have lasted long enough to attract further innovation and interest from the public. Even though Goodwin is not as well known as many early film pioneers, his contribution was vitally necessary for film to exist today as a major cultural form.

—*Vicki A. Sanders*

Further Reading

Cook, David A. "Origins." *A History of Narrative Film*. 2d ed. New York: W. W. Norton, 1990. The first chapter of this standard history of film art is devoted to early technical and artistic developments.

Johnson, Allen, and Dumas Malone, eds. *Dictionary of American Biography*. Vol. 4. New York: Charles Scribner's Sons, 1960. Includes a short but fairly thorough encapsulation of Goodwin's life and career.

Phillips, Ray. *Edison's Kinetoscope and Its Films: A History to 1896*. Westport, Conn.: Greenwood Press, 1997. Thorough treatment of the peep-show films (all of which are listed, with many described) made by Edison's film company.

Rawlence, Christopher. *The Missing Reel: The Untold Story of the Lost Inventor of Moving Pictures*. New York: Atheneum, 1990. A dramatic and somewhat sensationalized narrative of Louis Le Prince's life and mysterious disappearance.

See also: 1839: Daguerre and Niépce Invent Daguerreotype Photography; Dec. 24, 1877: Edison Patents the Cylinder Phonograph; 1878: Muybridge Photographs a Galloping Horse; Oct. 21, 1879: Edison Demonstrates the Incandescent Lamp; Dec. 28, 1895: First Commercial Projection of Motion Pictures; Feb., 1900: Kodak Introduces Brownie Cameras.

Related article in *Great Lives from History: The Nineteenth Century, 1801-1900:* Thomas Alva Edison.

December, 1887
CONAN DOYLE INTRODUCES SHERLOCK HOLMES

The publication of the first Sherlock Holmes story by Arthur Conan Doyle helped launch the popular form of detective fiction and introduced a literary character instantly recognized around the world to this day.

LOCALE: London, England
CATEGORY: Literature

KEY FIGURES

Sir Arthur Conan Doyle (1859-1930), British novelist and short-story writer
Joseph Bell (1837-1911), British doctor and medical-school instructor
G. T. Bettany (1850-1891), British editor

SUMMARY OF EVENT

In 1886, a young medical doctor and fledgling writer named Arthur Conan Doyle had a short novel, or novella, entitled *A Study in Scarlet* (1887 serial, 1888 book) accepted for publication by Ward, Lock & Company. The story, which appeared in *Beeton's Christmas Annual* in December, 1887, featured a tall, hawk-nosed "consulting detective" named Sherlock Holmes and was narrated by Holmes's friend Dr. John Watson. Holmes was modeled on Dr. Joseph Bell, who was one of Conan Doyle's professors at the University of Edinburgh's medical school. Bell possessed an uncanny ability to discover a person's trade or life circumstances simply by quickly observing the person's appearance. Holmes demonstrated the same skill in *A Study in Scarlet* and subsequent stories. Although Conan Doyle aspired to write more "serious" literature, the success of his Holmes stories would define his reputation for the rest of his life.

A Study in Scarlet centers on the murder of an American in London amid several puzzling clues. Holmes is consulted by the police and eventually helps to solve a mystery with roots in a Mormon community in Utah. In narrating the story, Watson recounts how he met Holmes for the first time and how they came to share lodgings together. Many of Holmes's defining characteristics are described in this story, which is told with earnestness peppered with occasional moments of humor. From the earlier, American writer Edgar Allan Poe, Conan Doyle borrowed the essential device of an armchair detective who solves mysteries by reviewing facts that others have "seen but not observed." Conan Doyle admired Poe's work, and he even had Holmes explicitly mention Poe's fictional detective, C. Auguste Dupin, albeit disparagingly.

Conan Doyle wrote *A Study in Scarlet* in 1886 during the long intervals between patients. The manuscript was rejected by several publishers before its acceptance by G. T. Bettany, chief editor of Ward, Lock & Company. Bettany could offer Conan Doyle only twenty-five pounds for the copyright, and the story would not be published for a year. Conan Doyle said he would have preferred to receive royalties on the sales of the story, but ultimately accepted the offer. (Later Conan Doyle would

Actor William Gillette (1855-1937) in Charles Frohman's production of an original Sherlock Holmes play in 1900. Many actors, including Gillette, have made careers of portraying Arthur Conan Doyle's famous detective. (Library of Congress)

purchase back his rights to the story for five thousand pounds.) The 1887 *Beeton's Christmas Annual* containing *A Study in Scarlet* sold out, although probably not because of Conan Doyle's story. *A Study in Scarlet* received little notice from critics at the time. Later, however, the story would become immensely popular, being republished innumerable times and in dozens of languages.

At less than one hundred pages, *A Study in Scarlet* was particularly well suited for publication in the periodicals such as *Beeton's Christmas Annual* that were popular at the time. One such periodical in America—*Lippincott's*—commissioned Conan Doyle to write a second Holmes story in 1890. The result was a second novella, *The Sign of the Four* (1890; later pb. as *The Sign of Four*), which, like *A Study in Scarlet*, had Holmes solving a mystery with distant roots—this time in India. Also like its predecessor, *The Sign of the Four* did not garner much critical interest.

"MR. SHERLOCK HOLMES"

In the first chapter of A Study in Scarlet, *Dr. John Watson, recently returned to England from army service in Afghanistan, finds himself in need of a roommate. By chance, he meets an old acquaintance who knows of someone looking for a roommate. The friend takes Watson to a school laboratory where the man is working, and Watson has his first meeting with Sherlock Holmes.*

There was only one student in the room, who was bending over a distant table absorbed in his work. At the sound of our steps he glanced round and sprang to his feet with a cry of pleasure. "I've found it! I've found it," he shouted to my companion, running towards us with a test-tube in his hand. "I have found a reagent which is precipitated by hæmoglobin, and by nothing else." Had he discovered a gold mine, greater delight could not have shone on his features.

"Dr. Watson, Mr. Sherlock Holmes," said Stamford, introducing us.

"How are you?" he said cordially, gripping my hand with a strength for which I should hardly have given him credit. "You have been in Afghanistan, I perceive."

"How on earth did you know that?" I asked in astonishment.

"Never mind," said he, chuckling to himself. "The question now is about hæmoglobin. No doubt you see the significance of this discovery of mine?"

"It is interesting, chemically, no doubt," I answered, "but practically—"

"Why, man, it is the most practical medico-legal discovery for years. Don't you see that it gives us an infallible test for blood stains?"

Source: Sir Arthur Conan Doyle, *Sherlock Holmes: The Complete Novels and Stories* (New York: Bantam Books, 1986), vol. 1, pp. 6-7.

What finally launched Sherlock Holmes into the public consciousness (and Conan Doyle into a measure of prosperity and fame) was the publication of a series of short stories (rather than novellas) featuring Holmes. Still considering his Holmes stories to be a poor showcase for his literary skills, Conan Doyle nevertheless realized that they could provide him with the funding and access to support him in his more "serious" work of writing historical novels. The first of his Holmes short stories, "A Scandal in Bohemia," appeared in the *Strand* magazine in 1891. It was immensely popular, and subsequent issues of the periodical containing more Holmes stories were anticipated eagerly by the public. Conan Doyle produced an initial series of six stories, after which he agreed to write another six—at a somewhat higher price.

The popularity of the Holmes stories had its good and bad points for Conan Doyle. Although they did bring him the income and notice that he desired, he felt that Holmes was crowding out his other literary opportunities. He told his friends that he was tiring of the character and that he would "murder" Holmes. This he did in "The Final Problem" (1893), his twenty-third Holmes short story for the *Strand*. Public outrage followed the unexpected demise of Holmes. The editors of the *Strand* were frantic to return the popular stories to its pages. Conan Doyle stood his ground, refusing even the pleadings of his own mother that he resurrect Holmes—for a time.

Now free to pursue his other literary ambitions, Conan Doyle gradually learned that the public was less interested in him than it was in Holmes. Thus, after an eight-year hiatus, Holmes returned in print in another short novel, *The Hound of the Baskervilles* (1901-1902 serial, 1902 book). The story was instantly successful. Although it was supposed to take place prior to Holmes's death in "The Final Problem," most readers suspected that Conan Doyle would now have to find a way to resurrect Holmes for future stories. Bowing to public pressure, Conan Doyle did just this in "The Adventure of the Empty House," the first of a new series of short stories that appeared in the *Strand* starting in 1903.

In all, Conan Doyle would write fifty-six short stories and four novellas featuring Holmes. The final story, "The Retired Colourman," appeared in the *Strand* in 1927. Conan Doyle died three years later.

SIGNIFICANCE

Conan Doyle's canon of Sherlock Holmes literature practically represents a genre unto itself. Today all of the Holmes stories remain in print by numerous publishers and in various languages. They have also been made into hundreds of plays, films, and radio programs. The Holmes stories have inspired subsequent mystery writers to create such characters as Agatha Christie's Hercule Poirot. Others have created new Holmes tales using the characters developed by Conan Doyle. The character of Sherlock Holmes has become an icon for detection and intelligence, and even his trademark deerstalker cap and magnifying glass have become universal symbols for mysteries. The figure of Holmes—even simply his easily recognizable silhouette—is regularly used in signs, print advertising, cartoons, and other formats.

The popularity of the Holmes stories in Conan Doyle's time owed much to his rich but accessible writing style, engaging plots, and clever puzzles, as well as to the colorful characters who developed throughout the course of the stories. The stories' enduring popularity to this day must partly be due to their nostalgia value, emblematic as they are of Victorian London. Perhaps also contributing to their popularity is the unambiguous depiction of good and evil in the figures of almost melodramatically noble heroes and despicable villains. Such order and clarity can be comforting, particularly when coupled with the familiar and enduring friendship of Holmes and Watson.

—Steve D. Boilard

FURTHER READING

Baring-Gould, William S., ed. *The Annotated Sherlock Holmes*. New York: Clarkson N. Potter, 1967. Definitive two-volume set of all Conan Doyle's Holmes stories, extensively annotated and illustrated, with various essays, bibliographies, and other features.

Chabon, Michael. "Inventing Sherlock Holmes." *New York Review of Books* 52, nos. 2-3 (February 10-24, 2005). Nominally a review of the Klinger volumes, this two-part essay provides a solid general overview of the Holmes phenomenon. By a Pulitzer-Prize winning author who has written a novella featuring Sherlock Holmes.

Klinger, Leslie S., ed. *The New Annotated Sherlock Holmes*. New York: W. W. Norton, 2004. Generally follows the format of the Baring-Gould volumes, with extensive annotations, illustrations, and related essays. Like the Baring-Gould volumes, appears as a two-volume set, and includes all sixty Holmes stories by Conan Doyle. What distinguishes this set is a fuller discussion of the various inconsistencies, vagaries, contradictions, and speculations about the details in the Holmes stories. Also includes more developed "theories" to resolve these issues.

Millett, Larry. *Sherlock Holmes and the Red Demon*. New York: Viking Press, 1996. A good example of the post-Conan Doyle works that use the Holmes and Watson characters and that attempt to replicate the narrative form of Watson recounting the tale.

Stashower, Daniel. *Teller of Tales: The Life of Arthur Conan Doyle*. New York: Henry Holt, 1999. Detailed biography of Conan Doyle, with considerable focus on his writing of the Holmes stories.

SEE ALSO: 1814: Scott Publishes *Waverley*; 1819-1820: Irving's *Sketch Book* Transforms American Literature; Dec., 1849: Dostoevski Is Exiled to Siberia; Mar., 1852-Sept., 1853: Dickens Publishes *Bleak House*; Oct. 1-Dec. 15, 1856: Flaubert Publishes *Madame Bovary*; c. 1865: Naturalist Movement Begins; July, 1881-1883: Stevenson Publishes *Treasure Island*; Dec., 1884-Feb., 1885: Twain Publishes *Adventures of Huckleberry Finn*.

RELATED ARTICLES in *Great Lives from History: The Nineteenth Century, 1801-1900:* Sir Arthur Conan Doyle; Edgar Allan Poe.

1888
RODIN EXHIBITS *THE THINKER*

For a creation of bronze doors called The Gates of Hell, *Auguste Rodin sculpted several individual and group figures for the design. Many of these figures were later developed as independent sculptures.* The Thinker, *one of these individual pieces, was modeled during the early 1880's and displayed for the first time in public in Copenhagen, Denmark. It has became one of the most famous sculptures of all time.*

ALSO KNOWN AS: *The Poet*; *The Thinker-Poet*
LOCALE: Copenhagen, Denmark; Paris, France
CATEGORIES: Art; architecture

KEY FIGURES

Auguste Rodin (1840-1917), French sculptor and artist
Edmond Turquet (1836-1914), French undersecretary of state for fine arts, 1879-1881
Henri Charles-Estienne Dujardin-Beaumetz (1852-1913), French undersecretary of state for fine arts, 1905-1912

SUMMARY OF EVENT

Auguste Rodin began his art studies at the age of fourteen in Paris at the School of Decorative Arts, where he received practical rather than academic training in drawing and sculptural ornamental design. In 1863 he began work in Paris for the architectural sculptor Albert-Ernest Carrier-Belleuse (1824-1887) and then worked in Brussels from 1870 to 1877.

Aspiring to be a sculptor, Rodin visited Italy from 1875 to 1876 to study the sculptures of Michelangelo, Donatello, and other Renaissance artists. In 1877 in Brussels, Rodin's exhibition of a male nude, *The Age of Bronze*, elicited both praise and condemnation from critics. By 1880 his popularity had spread, and he gained the admiration and support of France's undersecretary of state for fine arts, Edmond Turquet, whose influence helped establish Rodin as an artist.

On August 16, 1880, the French government commissioned Rodin to create a large bronze portal with sculpted reliefs for the proposed Museum of Decorative Arts in Paris. He was given a studio by the government and an initial sum of 8,000 francs (increased to 30,000 francs in 1888) for the project. Rodin would work on this project intermittently for the next twenty years.

Rodin's design of *The Gates of Hell* was initially inspired by Dante Alighieri's *Divine Comedy*, a fourteenth century epic poem about a man's journey through the three realms of the afterlife. Rodin did hundreds of preparatory sketches, most of which related to episodes from the poem's first part, the *Inferno*. Rodin's usual method was to work from his sketches to create models (in plaster, ceramic, clay, or wax) that could then be transposed into marble or bronze. One advantage of his method was that his models, existing as separate pieces, could later be developed into sculptures that could be recast—and reduced or enlarged—from the originals multiple times. Several of the figures for the doors, which originally derive from Dante's characters, form the basis of some of his most famous independent sculptures, such as *The Kiss* (Paolo and Francesca from *Inferno* 5), *The Three Shadows* (the three Florentines from *Inferno* 16), *The Old Courtesan* and *The Crouching Woman* (Thaïs from *Inferno* 18), and *Ugolino and Sons* (Ugolino from *Inferno* 33).

The most famous figure associated with *The Gates of Hell* is *The Thinker*. Although several of Rodin's drawings depict a muscular male nude in a seated pose, one of the first drawings (c. 1880) represents Dante with his guide, Virgil, standing behind him. During his visit to Florence, Rodin might have seen the "Sasso di Dante" (Dante's Rock) upon which Dante is believed to have sat as he meditated on his vision of the afterlife. In line with the tradition that a seated figure holding his chin represented contemplation, philosophy, or creativity, Rodin's initial clay model of this figure represents Dante as the poet contemplating his vision. The figure, designed to protrude beyond the lintel of the panel at the top of the doors, indicated his connection to, yet detachment from, the vision that surrounds him.

Although the original inspiration for the portal was the *Divine Comedy*, its design evolved over time to take on new shapes and meanings. Rodin did not have a fixed design at the outset for the doors' five rectangular grids. By 1884, he had stopped illustrating specific characters from Dante's poem and abandoned a narrative orientation for a holistic approach to representing hell by means of multiple figures in unequal proportions and in a variety of poses. The figures would be arranged in a tumultuous, disjunctive manner. Rodin's initial inspiration was gradually transformed into a modern depiction of hell, chaos, and the pain and suffering of human existence, as evidenced by the writhing figures in fluid motion.

The creative evolution of Rodin's plan for the doors was paralleled by the evolution of the design and mean-

Auguste Rodin's The Thinker. (The Granger Collection, New York)

ing of *The Thinker*. Rodin cast the clay model of his Dante-figure-in-bronze for a client in 1884 and titled it *The Thinker* for the first time. Once removed from its context as part of *The Gates of Hell*, the figure could assume a variety of new meanings. When a new casting was made for its initial public exhibition in 1888 in Copenhagen, Rodin named it *The Poet*; ensuing castings were called *The Thinker-Poet* (1889) and, finally, *The Thinker* (1896). The original version that represented a nude Dante with his famous cap was changed by 1888 to a bare-headed figure, with the neck and left shoulder reworked for a rougher appearance; its meaning was no longer tied to one poet but represented all thinkers and artists.

The sculpture was enlarged beginning in 1902 for its 1904 exhibition in a Paris salon. It was hailed as a new Hercules or a modern common-man philosopher but also reviled as an enormous brute and a gorilla. Despite the controversy, the government acquired the bronze for public display. On April 21, 1906, Henri Charles-Estienne Dujardin-Beaumetz, the undersecretary of state for fine arts, unveiled *The Thinker* in front of the Pantheon. Reflecting Rodin's thinking at the time, Dujardin-Beaumetz referred to the figure as an anonymous thinker, one who represented French workers of all types. The sculpture's final shape and meaning had become universalized. It was divested of historical or personalized reference and had become a multivalent symbol for all creators, artists, and workers.

In 1922 *The Thinker* was relocated to the garden of the Rodin Museum in Paris, where it remains. There exist eighteen castings, which are displayed in museums worldwide. Because the French government never built the museum for which it commissioned the doors, *The Gates of Hell* were cast in bronze only posthumously in 1925, but their fame would be eclipsed by *The Thinker*, which already had established Rodin's reputation worldwide.

SIGNIFICANCE

The Thinker and *The Gates of Hell* are central pieces in any study of Rodin's art, methodology, and influence. His unique creative process—changing, improvising, designing several versions of one piece, and being inspired by the work-in-progress itself—is clearly demonstrated in these masterpieces. With the dissemination of his works to more than seventy museums, Rodin is known for his wide variety of works, the multiple interpretations that his works allow, and the changes he brought to the world of sculpture. Sculptures that combine rough and polished stone or that lack finish on their bases, sculptures of body parts, sculpted fragments, and so forth no longer generate controversy but are now acknowledged as art as well.

By 1900, Rodin was considered the most important sculptor of his time and thought to be the only modern sculptor on a par with Michelangelo. Almost single-handedly, Rodin raised the discussion of and interest in sculpture to the level that painting, for example, had so long enjoyed. Subsequent sculptors imitated or reacted against Rodin, but he was the benchmark. *The Thinker*, in particular, has been studied, photographed, copied, and imitated in art, film, cartoons, and even advertisements, making it the most recognizable sculpture of the twentieth century and perhaps of all time.

—*Marsha Daigle-Williamson*

FURTHER READING

Butler, Ruth, ed. *Rodin in Perspective*. Englewood Cliffs, N.J.: Prentice-Hall, 1980. A chronological presentation (from 1877 to 1967) of more than seventy reviews of Rodin's work by international critics and artists, including the dedication speech in 1906 for *The Thinker*. Brief biographies of all the reviewers; a few black-and-white photos.

_______. *Rodin: The Shape of Genius*. New Haven, Conn.: Yale University Press, 1993. Most important biography of Rodin, according to scholars of his work. More than two hundred black-and-white illustrations, a multilingual bibliography, and an index.

Curtis, Penelope. *Sculpture, 1900-1945: After Rodin*. New York: Oxford University Press, 1999. Trends in modern sculpture, with Rodin as the referential pivot point. Illustrations, annotated bibliography, art and history time lines from 1880, and index.

Elson, Albert Edward, et al. *Rodin's Art: The Rodin Collection of the Iris & B. Gerald Cantor Center for the Visual Arts at Stanford University*. New York: Oxford University Press, 2003. In-depth commentary on the largest collection of Rodin's works in the United States. Extended essay on *The Gates of Hell*, with a section on the history of *The Thinker*. Includes nearly six hundred illustrations, a multilingual bibliography, and an index.

Kolinsky, Dorothy. *The Artist and the Camera: Degas to Picasso*. New Haven, Conn.: Yale University Press, 1999. Rodin's use of, and objections to, photography in relation to sculpture; one of fourteen artists discussed. Illustrations, index.

Vernata, Kirk, et al. *Rodin: A Magnificent Obsession*. New York: Merrell, 2001. Four essays by different authors on Rodin's career and major works, with the third devoted to *The Gates of Hell*. More than 150 illustrations and an index.

SEE ALSO: 1803-1812: Elgin Ships Parthenon Marbles to England; Oct. 28, 1886: Statue of Liberty Is Dedicated.

RELATED ARTICLES in *Great Lives from History: The Nineteenth Century, 1801-1900:* Honoré de Balzac; Antonio Canova; Victor Hugo; Auguste Rodin; Augustus Saint-Gaudens.

1888-1906
RAMÓN Y CAJAL SHOWS HOW NEURONS WORK IN THE NERVOUS SYSTEM

Ramón y Cajal showed that nerve cells operate as the discrete entities that transmit impulses unidirectionally in the nervous system through specific points of contact. His neuron doctrine influenced histologists, physiologists, surgeons, pathologists, neurosurgeons, psychiatrists, psychologists, and educational theorists.

LOCALE: Madrid, Spain
CATEGORIES: Biology; health and medicine; science and technology

KEY FIGURES

Santiago Ramón y Cajal (1852-1934), Spanish histologist, physician, and winner of the 1906 Nobel Prize in Physiology or Medicine
Camillo Golgi (1843-1926), Italian anatomist and physician
Rudolf Albert von Kölliker (1817-1905), Swiss embryologist and histologist
Paul Ehrlich (1854-1915), German chemist

SUMMARY OF EVENT

During the late nineteenth century, a controversy existed among brain scientists as to the nature of impulse transmission through the nervous system. The more popular school of thought began in 1872, when the gray matter of the cerebrum (brain) was described as a diffuse nerve net with fusion of dendrites (fine processes). Such notables as Theodor Meynert and Camillo Golgi agreed with this "reticular theory."

According to reticular theory, the proper impulses were directed somehow out from this network of fused fibers to the appropriate muscles and organs, much like the streams flowing out from a lake being directed to specific locations. A. H. Forel showed that retrograde degeneration was confined to the damaged cells, and Wilhelm His showed that in embryos the nerve cells behave as centers giving origin to fiber outgrowths. At the time, the physical evidence was inadequate for determining which theory was more correct. No one had been able to see, with any clarity, the nerve fiber endings. Yet, Santiago Ramón y Cajal was able to provide the irrefutable evidence that resolved the issue eventually.

Ramón y Cajal's legacy was born of the microscope, an instrument he first became familiar with in 1877 while studying in Madrid. He soon became expert in histology, the field of biology devoted to the study of tissues. In the process, he made innovations in the staining techniques of the time. Tissue staining is a technique of applying dyes or other chemicals to the material studied so that particular structures or features are seen more easily.

While at the University of Barcelona in 1888, Ramón y Cajal made a major finding while working with bird and small mammal embryos. He studied those specimens because embryonic nerve cells have fewer interconnections and are not covered with myelin, a fatty layer of insulation that covers the axons, or long processes, of most adult neurons, allowing individual cells to stand out. He also modified the chrome silver staining technique invented by Golgi. Focusing on the cerebellum of the brain, Ramón y Cajal discovered basket cells and mossy fibers. He found that the long processes (axons) of the nerve cells terminate in proximity, not continuity, with other cells or dendrites. This suggested that the nervous system works by contact, and thus Ramón y Cajal developed his "law of transmission by contact." For the first time, it was proposed that the cells were the important components of the nervous system, as opposed to the fibers, which previously were believed to be a continuous network that transmitted impulses in the system. The popular notion was that the cells played a relatively minor, supportive role. Ramón y Cajal's evidence of definitely limited conduction paths in the gray matter would be substantiated by later investigations of the retina, spinal cord, and other brain regions. Yet, the reticular theory proponents would not be defeated so easily.

After giving a presentation to the German Anatomical Society in Berlin in 1889, Ramón y Cajal won the support of Rudolf Albert von Kölliker, then editor of a scientific journal. Kölliker helped to promote the theories of Ramón y Cajal throughout Europe.

In 1890, Ramón y Cajal turned to a different set of studies that would support his theory. He demonstrated that developing nerve cells send out axon "growth cones" that later sprout dendrites and make connections, supporting the theory of His and Kölliker. There was an alternate theory favored by the "reticular" advocates stating that developing nerves arise from the fusion of a row of cells.

In 1891, Ramón y Cajal returned to studying the cerebrum, a subject of some investigations several years past. He published a well-received book of his results. Wilhelm Waldeyer coined the term "neuron"; Ramón y Cajal's ideas became known as the "neuron theory." In 1892, Ramón y Cajal proposed his neurotropic theory to explain how the growth cone of the developing neuron is directed to its proper target. For the next few years, he would work on the retinas of various animals and on the hippocampus. The consistency of the results, with respect to his neuron theory, was unequivocal.

In 1896, Ramón y Cajal learned of Paul Ehrlich's methylene blue technique for staining tissues. This was a nontoxic substance and thus could be applied to living animals. Ramón y Cajal repeated many of his findings on living specimens using this technique to refute the criticism from such reticularists as Golgi that his results were an anomaly of his previous methods on dead tissues. Again, the results were irrefutable: Nerve cells existed as distinct units, making only the barest contact with other nerve cells in the system. Detractors of the neuron theory persisted. They objected on the grounds that Ramón y Cajal had not shown that neuron fibrils (internal structures) were not continuous, as they had claimed in support of the reticular theory.

The beginning of the twentieth century found Ramón y Cajal in Paris to receive the Moscow Prize of the Thirteenth Medical Congress. Not only did he receive the prestigious award, with its monetary bonus, but also the congress awarded Madrid the venue for the next congress to be held in 1903. This brought great praise and adulation to him at home. He was appointed director of the new National Institute of Hygiene, where he promptly persuaded the authorities to establish a laboratory of biological research. The government finally was supporting science in Spain.

By 1903, Ramón y Cajal had perfected yet another staining technique—reduced silver nitrate—which made the tissue transparent, allowing him to discover details about the internal structures of the nerve cells, including fibrils. He published twenty-two papers that year on fibrillar discontinuity, consistent with his neuron doctrine. Dozens of other scientists confirmed his work. For all intents, the debate over reticular versus neuron was won, but some die-hard reticular advocates persisted, even into the 1950's.

The recognition of Ramón y Cajal's theories reached a pinnacle in 1906, when he was awarded the Nobel Prize in Physiology or Medicine. Somewhat ironically, he shared the prize with Golgi, whose staining technique had made many of Ramón y Cajal's early findings possible, but who was still an advocate of the reticular hypothesis and a severe critic of Ramón y Cajal, so much so that he embarrassingly used his Nobel lecture to attempt a critique of Ramón y Cajal's methods and results. History would forgive Golgi his myopia and would establish

Ramón y Cajal as a scientist of tremendous impact on modern neuroscience.

SIGNIFICANCE

The neuron doctrine of Santiago Ramón y Cajal had an impact on many different fields within biology and medicine. The knowledge of the actual functional structure of the brain—being made of discrete, contacting units that transmit impulses in one direction—gave a better physical basis for understanding many nervous or mental disorders. Treatment now could be approached with a more accurate perspective on the possible deficiencies in the disorders. A modern understanding of impulse transmission through the nervous system, from sensory neurons to central nervous system and then to muscle, is directly reflective of Ramón y Cajal's theory. The "black box" that had existed between the reception of a stimulus event and the control of a motor response, while still not completely revealed, was at least partly illuminated by this work.

Possible mechanisms of learning and memory were developed with the framework established by the neuron doctrine. The foundation for the concept of the final common pathway of Sir Charles Scott Sherrington, the principle of reflex activity that is adhered to still, was laid by Ramón y Cajal and his microscope.

The concepts of neural inhibition, summation, and facilitation that are accepted now are possible only within the context of the neuron doctrine. English physiologists were led to their work on the synapse, the site of neuron-to-neuron communication, by Ramón y Cajal's studies, and this knowledge of the synapse has had a great impact on medicine such as in drug therapy and in the treatment of neurological disorders.

Ivan Petrovich Pavlov's famous treatise on conditioning was molded, at least in part, by the neuron doctrine, as was the work of Walter Bradford Cannon on the physiological aspects of emotion. Ramón y Cajal's work could be said to have had an impact on education because his neuron doctrine has influenced subsequent theories on mechanisms for learning.

In the course of developing his neuron doctrine, Ramón y Cajal made a number of advances and innovations in histological staining techniques, many of which are still the techniques of choice. The work conducted on regeneration in the nervous system has played a seminal role in nerve damage therapy.

It is possible that had it not been Ramón y Cajal, someone else would eventually have discovered the truth about the structure of the nervous system and the nature of impulse transmission. Nevertheless, this man of meager means and modest beginnings had the inspiration and fortitude to pioneer the murky waters of the time, to bring science out of the ignorance of complacency. His work had a domino, rippling effect on the direction of science, such that the rate of progress in the field of neuroscience has been phenomenal. If Ramón y Cajal had not paved the way, scientists may have been stumbling along into untold dead-ends for many years.

—*Harold J. Grau*

FURTHER READING

Bullock, Theodore Holmes, Richard Orkand, and Alan Grinnell. *Introduction to Nervous Systems*. San Francisco, Calif.: W. H. Freeman, 1977. Although this book is written for college and medical students, portions of it are accessible to the general reader. In particular, the introduction gives a good overview of the field of neuroscience. Ramón y Cajal's work is evidenced in nearly every chapter. A special section of chapter 3 gives a chronology of the debate over the structure of the brain. Includes illustrations, a glossary, a reference section, and an index.

Cannon, Dorothy F. *Explorer of the Human Brain: The Life of Santiago Ramón y Cajal: 1852-1934*. New York: Henry Schuman, 1949. This biography's narrative often includes the history of Spain during the periods discussed, putting the reader in a better perspective to appreciate Ramón y Cajal's life. Numerous references and footnotes introduce the reader to the many other scientists who influenced and were influenced by Ramón y Cajal. Includes a bibliography and an index.

Carola, Robert, John P. Harley, and Charles R. Noback. *Human Anatomy and Physiology*. 2d ed. New York: McGraw-Hill, 1992. An introductory college-level book. Includes many colorful diagrams and illustrations that will help the reader learn more about the structures and concepts of the nervous system and nerve cells. Full-color photomicrographs also are included. Includes an index, an extensive glossary, and appendices.

Fincher, Jack. *The Brain: Mystery of Matter and Mind*. Washington, D.C.: U.S. News Books, 1981. Written especially for the general public in a very nontechnical style. Includes several references to Ramón y Cajal and a brief description of the reticular versus neuron debate. Colorful illustrations and photographs, with a section in chapter 3 that covers the details about the neuron. Other chapters cover memory and learning, emotional aspects of the brain, language processing, and medical advances. Glossary and index.

Finger, Stanley. *Minds Behind the Brain: A History of the Pioneers and Their Discoveries*. New York: Oxford University Press, 2000. A collection exploring the history of neuroscience. Includes the chapter "Santiago Ramón y Cajal: From Nerve Nets to Neuron Doctrine."

Ramón y Cajal, Santiago. *Texture of the Nervous System of Man and the Vertebrates*. Edited and translated by Pedro Pasik and Tauba Pasik. New York: Springer, 1999. An annotated translation of Ramón y Cajal's 1899 work on the nervous system.

Williams, Harley. *Don Quixote of the Microscope: An Interpretation of the Spanish Savant, Santiago Ramón y Cajal, 1852-1934*. London: Jonathan Cape, 1954. A biography of Ramón y Cajal written in a very literary style, at times a bit overly dramatic and prosaic. Provides a different perspective. A brief reference list is included.

SEE ALSO: 1838-1839: Schwann and Virchow Develop Cell Theory; 1897-1901: Abel and Takamine Isolate Adrenaline.

RELATED ARTICLES in *Great Lives from History: The Nineteenth Century, 1801-1900:* Claude Bernard; Hermann von Helmholtz.

March 13, 1888
RHODES AMALGAMATES KIMBERLEY DIAMONDFIELDS

The discovery of one of the world's richest diamondfields in 1867 began the transformation of South Africa from an obscure outpost of the British Empire to an industrial power, and Cecil Rhodes used his successful amalgamation of the diamondfields to maximize their profits, while giving him the wealth he needed to play a powerful role in the expansion of British imperial influence in Southern Africa.

LOCALE: Kimberley, South Africa

CATEGORIES: Earth science; trade and commerce; expansion and land acquisition

KEY FIGURES

Cecil Rhodes (1853-1902), English businessman who became an influential imperialist

Barney Barnato (1852-1897), British financier who became Rhodes's main competitor

Alfred Beit (1853-1906), German financier

Charles Dunell Rudd (1844-1916), English entrepreneur who became Rhodes's partner

SUMMARY OF EVENT

Before the discovery of diamonds near South Africa's Orange River in 1867, Southern Africa was primarily an isolated farming region of little interest to Europe. The discovery of diamonds, and the later discovery of gold in the Transvaal, created a rush of people to the area that led to serious conflicts among the region's African, Afrikaner (Boer), and English communities. The struggle for control of the production of diamonds and the wealth and power that the diamonds created became important factors in the political development of Southern Africa. No one person was more important in these developments than Cecil Rhodes.

In 1871, a large source of diamonds was found at Colesberg kopje on the Vooruitzicht farm of Johannes Nicholas De Beers and Diederik Arnoldrus De Beers near the Vaal River in Griqualand West, an autonomous area near the Afrikaner-ruled Orange Free State and the British-ruled Cape Colony. This site would soon become famous as the "Big Hole" of the Kimberley diamondfield. Another valuable site one mile away became the De Beers Mine. Two smaller mines, Dutoitspan and Bultfontein, were also developed nearby. The large influx of people to this site created the city of New Rush, which was quickly renamed Kimberley after the British secretary of state for the colonies.

One of the young men who flocked to the new diamondfields was Cecil Rhodes, a young Englishman who had come to South Africa to improve his health at his brother's cotton farm in the Natal. Rhodes had a long-range dream of expanding the British Empire throughout the world. To play a role in achieving this dream, he knew that he needed wealth and power, and diamonds could provide both. He was nineteen when he followed his brother to the diamondfields in 1872.

Rhodes began by overseeing African laborers on 31-by-31-foot claims at Kimberley. However, he was a

Deep underground diamond miners at Kimberley around the turn of the twentieth century. (Library of Congress)

gifted businessman and was eager to try new business opportunities. He always worked with able partners, and an important partner of his from the beginning was Charles Dunell Rudd. One of the most profitable early businesses at the diamondfields was pumping water from the pits. Rhodes and Rudd ran a pumping service and accepted mine claims in payment for their service. They targeted the De Beers Mine for ownership. Even in the first years, Rhodes knew that all the little mines should be amalgamated. As he and Rudd increased their stakes in the mines, they formed De Beers Mining Ltd. in 1880. Having a partner also gave Rhodes the opportunity to return to England to attend Oxford University, where his dreams of imperial Great Britain were strengthened.

The diamond market was then, and always has been, volatile. Diamonds are expensive luxury items with limited demand, so oversupplies can easily lower their prices. Several individuals at Kimberley realized that the amalgamation of mine ownership would be necessary to effectively control diamond production. As events played out, it became clear that amalgamation would be a contest between Rhodes and Barney Barnato, another English immigrant. With help of partners such as his German financial adviser, Alfred Beit, and Rudd, Rhodes focused on controlling the De Beers Mine, and they succeeded in 1887.

Meanwhile, Barnato and his partners were consolidating their ownership of the Kimberley Mine in the Kimberley Central Mine Company. Rhodes made his first move on the Kimberley Mine in 1887 by trying to buy the part of the mine that was not already owned by Barnato, with financial support from the Rothschild banking house. Rhodes sold his claims to Barnato in return for 20 percent ownership in Barnato's Kimberley Central Mine Company. He then began a campaign to buy up shares of Barnato's company. On March 13, 1888, he formed the joint De Beers Consolidated Mining Company Ltd. By 1889, he had brought the Bultfontein and Dutoitspan Mines into his company, giving him effective control of the diamond production at Kimberley.

Rhodes now controlled 95 percent of the world's diamond production. He significantly reduced the labor force to cut back production to keep diamond prices at a profitable level. He offset the dislocations caused by his labor cuts by providing needed social services to the people of Kimberley. He also established a system of selling diamonds through a single syndicate to gain additional control of the market. Rhodes now had firm control of both diamond production and the city of Kimberley. Meanwhile, he also gained a profitable share of the new gold mines opening on the Transvaal's Witwatersrand.

Meanwhile, Rhodes was also building a wide political base along with his wealth. Griqualand West became part of the Cape Colony in 1880, and Rhodes was elected to the Cape assembly the following year as the representative of a rural district. He would serve in the assembly until his death. From 1890 to 1895, he was prime minister of the Cape Colony. He used his political power base to pass numerous laws that promoted the interest of mining and industry. He also used his wealth and political power to promote the colonization of what became the modern nations of Zimbabwe and Zambia.

SIGNIFICANCE

Cecil Rhodes was a dominant figure in the development of the Southern Africa region during the late nineteenth century and very early twentieth century. The amalgamation of the Kimberley diamond companies provided him with great wealth. Many men grew wealthy from South Africa's diamond and goldfields, but Rhodes used his wealth to help set the social and political agenda for the region. He was instrumental in institutionalizing the relationship between Europeans and Africans that would lead to South Africa's apartheid policies during the mid-twentieth century.

Rhodes was also deeply involved in the conflict between Afrikaner and English communities that led to the South African War and later to the creation of the Union of South Africa. Moreover, he played an important role in bringing Southern Rhodesia (now Zimbabwe), Northern Rhodesia (Zambia), Bechuanaland (Botswana), and Nyasaland (Malawi) under British rule. It is unlikely that he could have done any of these things, had he not been successful in amalgamating Kimberley's diamondfields.

—*Gary A. Campbell*

FURTHER READING

Kanfer, Stefan. *The Last Empire: De Beers, Diamonds, and the World*. New York: Noonday Press, 1993. Interesting history of De Beers, about half of which covers the Kimberley diamond discoveries and Rhodes's campaign to amalgamate the mines.

Leasor, James. *Rhodes and Barnato: The Premier and the Prancer*. London: Leo Cooper, 1997. Dual biography that examines the interaction between the two key figures in the Kimberley diamond companies' amalgamation.

Rotberg, Robert I. *The Founder: Cecil Rhodes and the Pursuit of Power*. New York: Oxford University Press, 1988. Biography of Cecil Rhodes by a leading historian of Africa who is well qualified to put Rhodes in a broad historical perspective.

Thomas, Anthony. *Rhodes: Race for Africa*. New York: Thomas Dunne Books, 1997. Study of Cecil Rhodes's imperialist schemes. Chapter 5 covers his diamond industry activities.

Worger, William H. *South Africa's City of Diamonds: Mine Workers and Monopoly Capitalism in Kimberley, 1867-1895*. New Haven, Conn.: Yale University Press, 1987. Fine scholarly study of the diamondfields during the period in which Rhodes was actively involved. Pays particular attention to the role of African mine workers.

SEE ALSO: Jan. 22-Aug., 1879: Zulu War; Dec. 16, 1880-Mar. 6, 1881: First Boer War; June 21, 1884: Gold Is Discovered in the Transvaal; Oct., 1893-October, 1897: British Subdue African Resistance in Rhodesia; Dec. 29, 1895-Jan. 2, 1896: Jameson Raid; Oct. 11, 1899-May 31, 1902: South African War.

RELATED ARTICLES in *Great Lives from History: The Nineteenth Century, 1801-1900:* Joseph Chamberlain; Lobengula; Cecil Rhodes.

December 7, 1888
DUNLOP PATENTS THE PNEUMATIC TIRE

The pneumatic tire designed by John Boyd Dunlop led to a revolution in transportation. It allowed bicycles, automobiles, and other land conveyances to travel with fewer shocks and vibrations from the road, decreasing wear and tear on the vehicles and increasing the comfort of their passengers.

LOCALE: Belfast, Ireland
CATEGORIES: Science and technology; transportation

KEY FIGURES

John Boyd Dunlop (1840-1921), Scottish veterinarian and inventor
Harvey Du Cros (1846-1918), first director of the Dunlop Rubber Company
Robert W. Edlin (1862-1923), Irish manufacturer
André Michelin (1853-1931), French industrialist
Édouard Michelin (1859-1940), French industrialist
Robert W. Thomson (1822-1873), British inventor

SUMMARY OF EVENT

John Boyd Dunlop, a Scottish veterinarian, invented the first popular air-filled bicycle tire, patented in 1888. Unknown to him, Robert W. Thomson had patented a similar idea in 1845, but it did not become popular. Dunlop's tires, built on the rims of actual cycle wheels, were encased in rubberized cloth wrapped between wheel spokes. These "mummy tires," which rapidly became popular, were not very user-friendly. Thus, they were modified repeatedly by engineers and inventors at the Dunlop Rubber Company and elsewhere. Ultimately, they led to manufacture of the tires used on all modern motor vehicles.

Dunlop was born the son of a tenant farmer on February 5, 1840, at Dreghorn, Scotland. He attended elementary and high school nearby and studied veterinary medicine at the Royal Dick Veterinary College (now part of Edinburgh University). At the age of nineteen, Dunlop began practice in Edinburgh. He moved to Belfast in 1867 and built up the most extensive veterinary practice in Ireland. Unhappy with rough Irish roads and uncomfortable travel on solid rubber carriage or bicycle wheels, he thought for twenty years about designing tires that would overcome the vibration inherent in the solid tires then in use.

In 1887, Dunlop developed the first practical air-filled tire. The project began after Dunlop's young son asked him to make a device to allow his solid-tired tricycle to run faster and more smoothly on the cobbled Dublin streets so he could outrace larger playmates in bicycle races. Dunlop set to work on the project. In his first experiment, Dunlop built around the periphery of a wooden disk a "pre-tire" made of a rubber inner tube covered with rubber-coated canvas. The pre-tire was inflated with air and then compared with a solid tire on a tricycle wheel by bowling each tire across Dunlop's cobbled yard. The solid-tired wheel rolled a short way along the paved yard and fell over. The pre-tire rolled across the entire yard.

Next, Dunlop made two prototype tires he called "pneumatic tires" to fit over the solid tires on the tricycle. The tires, constructed on wooden rims, had canvas covers over inflated rubber inner tubes and were covered with rubber sheeting, which was tacked in place around the rim edges. These pneumatic tires were slipped over the solid tires on the tricycle and bound in place. The modified tricycle was tried on the night of February 28, 1888. It worked well, and its tires were undamaged by the rough test road.

Dunlop was well aware that he had created something that would be desired by many people besides his son. He continued to make and test prototype tires, and he patented the pneumatic tire on December 7, 1888. Dunlop equipped a bicycle with pneumatic tires, built on the wire-spoke rims of the cycle's wheels. The way in which rubberized cloth was wrapped around each wheel and between the spokes led to the tires being called "mummy tires." The special wheels used were made by Belfast's Edlin and Company, owned by Robert W. Edlin. Exhaustive testing showed that they survived three thousand miles of cycling. Dunlop followed up his first patent with two others on March 8, 1889, including one for an improved tire valve.

Dunlop's mummy tires began to find their way onto racing cycles after a June, 1889, Belfast meet in which they were used by racer William Hume. Deemed only a fair race contestant, Hume won all the races he entered, defeating much stronger riders. His performance, or rather the performance of Dunlop's tires, excited the public so much that Edlin's company quickly sold fifty bicycles equipped with mummy tires.

The commercial development of Dunlop's tire began on November 18, 1889, with the founding of a small Dublin company first named the Pneumatic Tyre and Booth's Cycle Agency Limited. It was renamed several

John Boyd Dunlop testing one of his pneumatic tires. (Hulton Archive/Getty Images)

times before it became the Dunlop Rubber Company in 1900. The company was controlled by Harvey Du Cros, a paper manufacturer and avid cyclist who bought Dunlop's patents. Dunlop agreed to work for Du Cros at first, but in 1894, he quit the company and retired to Dublin to manufacture bicycle frames and tires. He died there on October 24, 1921.

From its founding, Du Cros's company had trials and tribulations because of legal battles with Thomson's estate, which claimed that the 1845 patent was being infringed. However, the company was able to survive, because the tires it manufactured had such important advantages over solid tires. Pneumatic tires nearly eliminated vibration, so riders were no longer as fatigued after long cycle trips. The tires minimized jarring, so cycles themselves lasted much longer than those having solid tires. The lack of jarring also made it feasible to use lighter cycle frames, which enabled cyclists go faster with less effort.

Despite these advantages, mummy tires were crudely designed and had to be fitted to wheels in a complex fashion that was beyond the skills of most cycle owners, so they were impossible for the owner to change. In addition, because of the questions about the validity of Dunlop's patent, numerous countries—including France—refused to accept it. Thus, many companies set to work attempting to create a pneumatic tire with increased commercial viability.

SIGNIFICANCE

Dunlop's invention arrived at a propitious moment. By the late 1880's, cycling and cycle racing had become popular pastimes enjoyed by thousands of Europeans and watched by tens of thousands of others. However, riding a bicycle was uncomfortable and fatiguing, posing a significant problem for many Europeans who cycled for enjoyment or for transportation to and from work every day. The pneumatic tire therefore rendered more appealing a means of transportation and a leisure-time pursuit that had already been gaining popularity even with significant disadvantages.

As time passed, more user-friendly bicycle tires were developed and were sold over-the-counter for customers to put on themselves. These included tires designed by Charles K. Welch, who joined the Dunlop Rubber Company. Welch's tire fit into the wheel rim and was held to it by wires. This made it fairly easy to put on and take off. Moreover, Welch's work gave the Dunlop Rubber Company an incontestably valid patent on an attractive tire. Others developed still better tires. For example, William E. Bartlett invented a tire made entirely of rubber, which was held in place on the wheel by turning it over the rim edge after inflation.

At about the same time in France, André and Édouard Michelin became very well established in the cycle tire field. Their tires won races all over continental Europe, including a 750-mile race in 1891 from Paris to Brest and back. Soon after this race, the Michelin brothers announced that they would have pneumatic tires ready for use on automobiles by the late 1890's; they did. In due time, others designed better pneumatic tires for both cycles and cars. Some leaders in the industry included the Goodyear, Goodrich, and Firestone companies. None of these companies or their refinements to the pneumatic tire would have come to pass as readily without the pioneering work of John Boyd Dunlop—or the relatively unappreciated earlier work of Robert W. Thomson.

—*Sanford S. Singer*

FURTHER READING

Fitzpatrick, Jim. *The Bicycle in Wartime: An Illustrated History*. Washington, D.C.: Brassey's, 1998. An interesting description of use of bicycle tires in wartime, from the experimental years, through the Boer War, to the 1990's. Many illustrations.

French, Michael J. *The U.S. Tire Industry: A History*. Boston: Twayne, 1992. A nice description of the development of tires and the U.S. tire industry, with illustrations.

Lottman, Herbert R. *The Michelin Men: Driving an Empire*. London: I. B. Tauris, 2003. A solid, well-indexed history of the Michelin brothers, their tires, their company, and the tire industry. Contains a solid bibliography, an index, and good illustrations.

Mcmillan, James. *The Dunlop Story: The Life, Death, and Rebirth of a Multi-National*. London: Weidenfeld & Nicolson, 1989. A solid, well-indexed history of the Dunlop Rubber Company and its successes, trials, and tribulations beginning with invention of the pneumatic bicycle tire by John Boyd Dunlop.

Tomkins, Eric. *The History of the Pneumatic Tyre*. London: Eastland Press, 1981. Describes the history of the pneumatic tire, from Thomson's and Dunlop's inventions through the 1970's. Well illustrated, and indexed. Explores bicycle, automobile, and war machine tires, and contains a number of interesting bibliographic references.

SEE ALSO: June 15, 1844: Goodyear Patents Vulcanized Rubber; 1860: Lenoir Patents the Internal Combustion Engine; May, 1876: Otto Invents a Practical Internal Combustion Engine; Jan. 29, 1886: Benz Patents the First Practical Automobile; Feb., 1892: Diesel Patents the Diesel Engine.

RELATED ARTICLES in *Great Lives from History: The Nineteenth Century, 1801-1900:* Carl Benz; Gottlieb Daimler; Rudolf Diesel; Étienne Lenoir; Nikolaus August Otto.

1889
GREAT BRITAIN STRENGTHENS ITS ROYAL NAVY

By strengthening its Royal Navy, Great Britain committed itself to creating a naval force strong enough to face any possible combination of opponents. In the process, it unwittingly started a European armaments race that raised international tensions.

ALSO KNOWN AS: Naval Defense Act of 1889
LOCALE: Great Britain
CATEGORIES: Military history; diplomacy and international relations

KEY FIGURES

George Francis Hamilton (1845-1927), first lord of the Admiralty, 1885-1892
Charles William de la Poer Beresford (1846-1919), fourth sea lord at the British Admiralty
Third Marquis of Salisbury (Robert Cecil; 1830-1903), British prime minister, 1886-1892
William Thomas Stead (1849-1912), editor of the *Pall Mall Gazette*

SUMMARY OF EVENT

Great Britain's extensive foreign trade, its widely dispersed empire, and the security of its home islands were safeguarded by the Royal Navy, whose adequacy nine teenth century Britons took largely for granted. During the 1880's, however, advocates of British sea power mounted a campaign in which they exposed the weakness of the Royal Navy. Significantly, the campaign coincided with the emergence of imperialism as a popular movement in Great Britain and with the collision of Britain and its chief imperial rivals, France and Russia, in geographic areas vital to British interests.

After Admiral Horatio Nelson's defeat of the combined French and Spanish fleets at Trafalgar in 1805, Great Britain enjoyed a long period of world naval supremacy during which, in a literal fashion, "Britannia ruled the waves." The expansion of the British Empire during the nineteenth century made the Royal Navy more vital than ever to the nation's interests, but a spirit of complacency and long years of relative peace hindered naval growth and the development and implementation of new technology. This situation changed in midcentury with the shift from wooden sailing ships to ironclad steamships. The first French ironclad was laid down in 1858, and the British responded three years later. Britain's competition with France was eased by the Franco-Prussian War of 1870, which left France weakened and its navy neglected. Since there was no German navy at the time, the Russians were relatively weak, and the United States remained largely uninvolved in European affairs, Great Britain seemed to enjoy the benefits of maritime supremacy without corresponding naval expenditures.

This complacency came to an end in 1884 with the realization that the French, who had been engaged in an ambitious naval rebuilding drive, possessed a navy almost equal to that of Britain in modern, first-class battleships. To meet this new challenge, Prime Minister William Ewart Gladstone's government allocated an additional 3.1 million pounds on warships and 2.4 million pounds for naval ordnance and coaling stations.

The situation seemed temporarily resolved, but even greater agitation for an even stronger British Royal Navy soon arose. The following circumstances explain why this should have been so. Anglo-French conflict centered on the Mediterranean, where the establishment of a French protectorate over Tunis in 1881 altered the balance of regional power. The British occupation of Egypt the next year, to protect the Suez Canal, caused a further deterioration of relations. Russia, too, entertained a historic and no less menacing ambition to be a Mediterranean power.

At the same time, Russian advances in Central Asia threatened India and nearly led to war with Britain in 1885. When Britain reached agreement with Turkey in 1887 for provisional evacuation of Egypt, the accord was wrecked, not by France alone, but also by Russia, foreshadowing the alliance of the two powers from which the British had most to fear. The international situation had deteriorated to the point that German chancellor Otto von Bismarck considered it necessary to caution the powers concerned about the threat of war.

Great Britain had hitherto felt reasonably secure by virtue of possessing a navy whose fleet was larger by one-third than that of France, the only other considerable naval power in the world. British numerical superiority in ships, however, was deceptive. Every few years, new ships were designed with improved armor. Possessing more effective armament, such ships rendered existing vessels obsolete and made it possible for foreign powers to put their fleets on an equal footing with that of Britain. After 1878, the French program of naval construction gradually narrowed Britain's numerical advantage in vessels. Moreover, the French were much quicker than the British in adopting innovations in guns and armor, which were the real determinants of naval power.

In view of rising international tensions and the danger of a war in which sea power would play an important and perhaps decisive role, British naval propagandists were able to argue effectively that the existing Royal Navy was inadequate and had to be strengthened. The first salvos were fired in "The Truth About the Navy," a series of articles published late in 1884 in the *Pall Mall Gazette*, whose editor, William Thomas Stead, was an influential naval propagandist. These articles were immediately reinforced by an outcry from the press and the public, and in Parliament by Lord George Francis Hamilton, first lord of the Admiralty, ably assisted by his fourth sea lord, Captain Lord Charles William de la Poer Beresford, who had taken part in the Nile expedition in 1884-1885. A modest program of naval expansion and improvement followed, but it was not sustained.

In 1888, agitation for strengthening the Royal Navy received a fresh impetus when French naval activity at Toulon raised fears that France was planning an attack on the Italian fleet. Because the British Mediterranean squadron was inferior to that of the French in both size and quality, a French defeat of the Italian fleet would have seriously weakened the British position in the Mediterranean. The clamor of a thoroughly frightened British public prompted Prime Minister Salisbury to propose legislation to strengthen the navy. The Naval Defense Act was passed in 1889.

SIGNIFICANCE

The 1889 act was a triumph for advocates of a larger navy. At the cost of 21.5 million pounds sterling, the act laid down a building program more ambitious by far than anything hitherto attempted. It called for eight first-class battleships larger than any then in use in the Royal Navy, two second-class battleships, nine large and twenty-nine small cruisers, four gunboats, and eighteen torpedo boats. The act was also significant in establishing the principle that the British fleet had to be equivalent to at least the combined strength of the two next strongest navies in Europe, which were those of France and Russia at that time. This principle, known as the "two-power standard," afterward dominated naval thinking. It was applied, however, only to battleships and first-class cruisers.

By committing itself to the two-power standard, Great Britain precipitated, however unwittingly, the naval arms race which helped to poison the relations of the European powers and bring on World War I only twenty-five years later. In 1891, the French announced a shipbuilding program no less ambitious than that of the British, while Russian naval expenditure increased by 65

PRINCIPAL NAVIES OF THE WORLD AT THE END OF THE NINETEENTH CENTURY

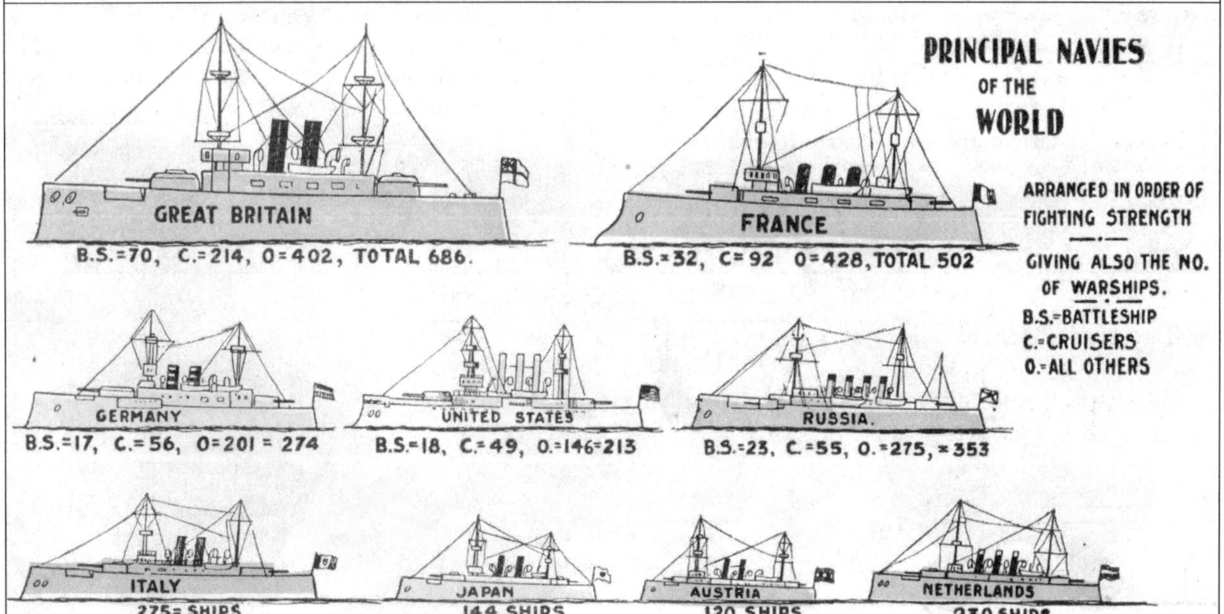

Source: Premier Publishing Co., 1902.

percent between 1889 and 1893. By that time, the combined naval budgets of France and Russia exceeded that of Great Britain. By then, the specter of a Franco-Russian alliance had materialized and had produced another navy scare in 1893, followed by another British building program. The competition for bigger and more powerful navies was becoming a headlong race that no one could win.

—*James M. Haas, updated by Michael Witkoski*

FURTHER READING

Clowes, William Laird. *The Royal Navy: A History from the Earliest Times to 1900.* 7 vols. London: Chatham, 1997. First published in 1897, this massive book remains a very readable history of British naval history through the end of the nineteenth century.

Herman, Arthur. *To Rule the Waves: How the British Navy Shaped the Modern World.* New York: HarperCollins, 2004. Well-written and engaging history of the Royal Navy whose underlying theme is that the British Empire provided a foundation for the modern world, and the empire's own foundation was the Royal Navy.

Hill, J. R., and Bryan Ranft, eds. *The Oxford Illustrated History of the Royal Navy.* New York: Oxford University Press, 2002. Collection of essays on each major period in British naval history, including the late nineteenth century. Equally useful to both students and scholars.

Keegan, John. *The Price of Admiralty: The Evolution of Naval Warfare.* New York: Viking, 1988. This book's section on the World War I Battle of Jutland contains a brief but revealing review of developments in naval design and strategy in the years leading up to the war. An outstanding military historian, Keegan places the events of the time into proper perspective from both a military and a political point of view.

Kennedy, Paul M. *The Rise and Fall of British Naval Mastery.* New York: Charles Scribner's Sons, 1976. Contains an informative discussion of the supposed danger in which the British felt themselves during the 1880's and how this led to the decision to adopt the "two-power" naval standard.

Massie, Robert. *Dreadnought.* New York: Random House, 1991. Although this volume has the post-1900 naval arms race as its major focus, it gives an informative review of the earlier British decision to expand and modernize its fleet.

Padfield, Peter. *The Great Naval Race.* New York: David McKay, 1974. As with the Massie work, this book concentrates on the years immediately preceding World War I but does place that contest in the context of earlier British actions, most notably the Naval Defense Act of 1889.

Stokesbury, James L. *Navy and Empire.* New York: William Morrow, 1983. Thorough review of Great Britain's dependence upon naval supremacy for its imperial position. This volume has an informative discussion of the Royal Navy's strategic thoughts during the last two decades of the nineteenth century.

SEE ALSO: Oct. 21, 1805: Battle of Trafalgar; Mar. 9, 1862: Battle of the *Monitor* and the *Virginia*; Jan. 4, 1894: Franco-Russian Alliance.

RELATED ARTICLES in *Great Lives from History: The Nineteenth Century, 1801-1900:* Otto von Bismarck; William Ewart Gladstone.

February 11, 1889
JAPAN ADOPTS A NEW CONSTITUTION

Japan's 1889 constitution was a major departure for the empire. It not only spelled out the responsibilities of the new Meiji government—largely patterned after European parliaments—but also placed substantial limitations on imperial power and granted many unprecedented civil liberties to common subjects.

ALSO KNOWN AS: Meiji Constitution
LOCALE: Tokyo, Japan
CATEGORIES: Government and politics; civil rights and liberties; laws, acts, and legal history

KEY FIGURES

Mutsuhito (1852-1912), emperor of Japan as Meiji, r. 1867-1912

Tokugawa Yoshinobu (1837-1913), last shogun of Japan, r. 1867

Kido Takayoshi (Kōin Kido; 1833-1877), Japanese statesman and one of the Three Heroes of the Meiji Restoration

Itō Hirobumi (1841-1909), Japanese interior minister, 1878-1882, prime minister, 1885-1888, 1892-1896, 1898, 1900-1901, and primary architect of the constitution

Hermann Roesler (1834-1894), German constitutional adviser to the Japanese government, 1887-1893

SUMMARY OF EVENT

Japan began its history as a modern nation with the fall of the Tokugawa government in 1868. While the emperor was the nominal sovereign, real political power lay with the shoguns, military dictators who supposedly ruled in the emperor's name. The family of Tokugawa shoguns ruled Japan in peace and isolation for some two and one-half centuries. However, during the 1850's, Americans and Europeans opened the island country to the outside world, demanding economic concessions and one-sided treaty agreements. The last shogun, Tokugawa Yoshinobu, was unable to prevent either these incursions by foreigners or the growing dissent of disgruntled samurai who wanted to restore real political power to the imperial throne. Yoshinobu resigned in a relatively bloodless coup, and the young Mutsuhito became the Meiji Emperor, taking as his dynasty's name the term Meiji, or "enlightened rule."

The new Meiji government's first goal was to fend off growing encroachment by Westerners. To do so, it decided to modernize all aspects of the Japanese economy, politics, and social life. While the Meiji Restoration eliminated many of the social inequalities and institutional impediments that limited progress, much work still needed to be done. After decades of improvisation and ad hoc governance, many political leaders and influential private citizens became convinced of the need for a representative government and a formal constitution. The question remained, however, as to precisely what kind of government it should be. There were two schools of thought.

The position advocated by the *genro* (the "original elder statesmen," or oligarchs of the Meiji revolution) was one of gradualism. They saw the need for changes, but believed those changes should occur slowly. Kido Takayoshi, who traveled to the United States and Europe as a member of the Meiji government's first goodwill mission in 1871, concluded that the West had become so powerful not only because of advances in science and technology but also because of its constitutionalism and parliamentary systems. He believed that Japan would not be accepted as an equal player on the world's stage until it demonstrated that it, too, was a country of rational laws, led by rational men. The Japanese people would also rise to the coming challenge of rapid industrialization—and be prepared for the sacrifices many would be required to make—if they felt they had a vested interest in their government. Representative government would provide them with that interest.

Members of the various factions of the Freedom and People's Rights Movement (*Jiyu Minken Undo*) could not have agreed more. They demanded suffrage for the common people and the immediate election of a national assembly. In contrast to the slow deliberations of the *genro*, some even drafted their own constitutions, which were far more liberal than anything suggested by the Meiji leadership. However, internal strife, theoretical disagreements, fluctuations in the economy, and preemptive political moves and police tactics by the government stifled radical attempts at reform. Nonetheless, public pressure mounted nationwide and from many quarters of Japanese society. In 1881, the emperor issued a rescript saying that Japan would have a constitution and parliament by 1890. He sent one of his most trusted confidants, Interior Minister Itō Hirobumi, to Germany and Austria to study constitutional law.

One of the major hindrances in writing a constitution for Japan was the conflict between representative democracy and the *kokutai* (the "national polity" or "national essence" of Japan). The notion of the *kokutai* entailed a belief in the divinity of the Japanese emperor and his natural position as leader of the state and head priest of the Shinto religion. All Japanese people were thought to be literal children of the imperial line, with the current emperor being directly descended from the original Sun Goddess. This so-called family concept of the state was as much a moral statement about filial piety, obedience, and loyalty to the government as anything else. As a result, it was unclear what the emperor's role would be in a constitutional government.

Itō returned in 1884 and became the primary writer of the new constitution. Starting in 1885, he secretly led a small group of colleagues—including the influential German law professor Hermann Roesler—in drafting a constitution, which they presented to the emperor three years later, in 1888. Itō was affected by what he saw in Germany—a country that, like Japan, was trying to forge a state from a group of semiautonomous regions. Germany's solution was to place authority in a strong executive branch led by Emperor William I and Chancellor Otto von Bismarck.

In Itō's constitution, known as the Meiji Constitution, the emperor was given sole authority to declare war, make peace, or establish treaties with foreign countries. He was the commander in chief of the armed forces, determined when the Diet—the new Japanese bicameral parliament—would meet, and could dissolve its lower house. The constitution reified the notion of the *kokutai*, explicitly saying that the empire of Japan would be reigned over by a line of emperors "unbroken for ages eternal." The constitution was even promulgated on an auspicious day—February 11, 1889, a national holiday celebrating the moment when the quasi-historical Emperor Jimmu supposedly declared Japan a country twenty-five hundred years earlier.

For all the powers assigned to the emperor by the new constitution, there were significant restrictions placed upon him as well. These restrictions and safeguards were

Emperor Mutsuhito opening the first session of Japan's new parliament. (Francis R. Niglutsch)

simply unheard-of in Japanese society, although in actual practice, all of them could sometimes fail. The emperor could do nothing without the advice and consent of the cabinet ministers. Only the Diet was empowered to initiate and approve legislation. In theory, it also controlled the budget. An independent judiciary was established, with judges holding lifetime appointments. Japanese citizens were—again, in theory—granted all the civil liberties of Western nations, including freedom of speech, freedom of religion, freedom of movement, freedom from unreasonable searches and seizures, habeas corpus, and due process of law. None of these rights had existed in Tokugawa times.

SIGNIFICANCE

It is often said that in spite of all its advances, the Meiji Constitution was the legal basis of the emperor system that ultimately led to Japan's defeat in World War II. By placing ultimate political authority and cultural legitimacy in the imperial court, the document prevented the Diet and the judiciary from providing effective checks and balances upon the emperor. Such a system was ripe for manipulation by powerful political elites or outside forces, such as the Japanese Imperial Army. Regardless of the validity of these assertions, it is certainly true that in the 1930's the internal contradictions between the idea of the *kokutai* and the idea of democracy became all too apparent.

The Meiji Constitution remained in effect until its replacement by a new constitution on May 3, 1947. Although this new constitution was, in essence, written by Japan's post-World War II American occupiers, in many ways it was actually an extension of the Meiji Constitution—a clarification of its principles and a completion of its undertaking. The status of the emperor was settled, powers were cleanly separated, and protections were added to guarantee in practice the individual civil liberties that had already been granted in theory. It could thus be argued that the almost immediate success of the post-World War II government was due in large part to the traditions established by the Meiji Constitution during the nineteenth century.

—James Stanlaw

FURTHER READING

Beckman, George. *The Making of the Meiji Constitution: The Oligarchs and the Constitutional Development of Japan, 1868-1891.* Reprint. Westport, Conn.: Greenwood Press, 1975. Classic study in English of Japan's constitution; includes the complete text of the document.

Beer, Lawrence, and John Maki. *From Imperial Myth to Democracy: Japan's Two Constitutions, 1889-2002.* Boulder: University Press of Colorado, 2002. A comparison of the strengths, weaknesses, and controversies surrounding both the Meiji Constitution and the current constitution adopted after World War II.

Gluck, Carol. *Japan's Modern Myths: Ideology in the Late Meiji Period.* Princeton, N.J.: Princeton University Press, 1985. An examination of Meiji period symbols and discourse; chapter 2 gives an enlightening and detailed description of the constitutional ceremony held in February, 1889.

Jansen, Marius. *The Making of Modern Japan.* Cambridge, Mass.: Harvard University Press, 2000. Excellent single-volume history of Japan's evolution into a modern nation, by one of America's most eminent Japanese historians. Jansen gives a very good discussion of the imperial restoration and the debate over the adoption of the constitution.

Keene, Donald. *Emperor of Japan: Meiji and His World.* New York: Columbia University Press, 2002. An exhaustive biography of Mutsuhito by an American authority on Japanese literature; the role of Itō Hirobumi and his relationship with the emperor shows, on a personal level, some of the issues that were confronting the new leaders of the Meiji state.

SEE ALSO: Mar. 31, 1854: Perry Opens Japan to Western Trade; Jan. 3, 1868: Japan's Meiji Restoration; Apr. 6, 1868: Promulgation of Japan's Charter Oath; Jan. 18, 1871: German States Unite Within German Empire; July 8, 1894-Jan. 1, 1896: Kabo Reforms Begin Modernization of Korean Government.

RELATED ARTICLES in *Great Lives from History: The Nineteenth Century, 1801-1900:* Mutsuhito; Matthew C. Perry; Saigō Takamori.

March 31, 1889
EIFFEL TOWER IS DEDICATED

The Eiffel Tower, built for the World's Fair held in Paris in 1889, introduced innovative techniques for the construction of extra-tall structures and has become the premier symbol of city of Paris.

LOCALE: Paris, France
CATEGORIES: Engineering; architecture; radio and television

KEY FIGURES

Gustave Eiffel (1832-1923), French civil engineer
Maurice Koechlin (1856-1946), French structural engineer
Emile Nouguier (fl. late nineteenth century), French structural engineer
Charles Léon Stephen Sauvestre (1874-1919), French architect

SUMMARY OF EVENT

Gustave Eiffel, who was born in Dijon, France, in 1832, studied at the École Central des Arts et Manufactures. He was interested in metal construction, although he received a degree in chemical engineering. His work was mainly in the field of civil engineering and construction. In 1866 he had founded a construction company, and in 1885 he designed the internal wrought-iron pylon used in Frédéric Auguste Bartholdi's Statue of Liberty, which now stands in New York Harbor. Eiffel supervised the construction of an iron railway bridge near Bordeaux, France, and helped design the movable dome of the Observatory at Nice.

Eiffel's greatest project was built for the Exposition Universelle of 1889, the World's Fair that was held in Paris to celebrate the one-hundredth anniversary of the French Revolution (1789). The exposition was held on the Champs de Mars, an open area that served as a royal parade ground before the French Revolution and the site of the Festival of the Federation, a celebration that had been held one year after the start of the French Revolution.

A worldwide design competition had been held to select the centerpiece of the Exposition Universelle. Eiffel's design for a huge, free-standing, steel-truss tower was chosen unanimously from the seven hundred proposals submitted. Eiffel was assisted in preparing the design by two engineers, Maurice Koechlin and Emile Nouguier. Charles Léon Stephen Sauvestre, the architect who had designed the Palais des Colonies (Palace of the Colonies) building for the Exposition Universelle, was added to the tower design team to improve its appearance and make it more acceptable to art-conscious Parisians.

Eiffel previously had designed a steel-arch bridge 525 feet (160 meters) in length, which spanned the Douro River in Portugal. He adopted the same open-frame design for the tower. However, Eiffel acknowledged that his inspiration for the design came both from his own work and from other sources. Among them was the Centennial Tower that had been proposed by the American civil engineering firm of Clarke, Reeves & Co. for construction at the U.S. Centennial Exposition in Philadelphia in 1876. This tower, designed to be 1,000 feet (305 meters) tall, was different from Eiffel's design in that it would have incorporated a 30-foot- (9-meter-) diameter central tube running all the way to the top. The tower, however, was never built, but a 290-foot (88-meter) Centennial Tower was featured at the exposition.

Construction of the Eiffel Tower began in January, 1887, at a site along the Seine River, along what is now named the Avenue Gustave Eiffel. The tower, which was completed in March, 1889, was built to celebrate the science and engineering achievements of the era. It was a marvel of nineteenth century engineering. About three hundred steelworkers participated in its construction, but there had been just one fatal accident on the site.

The structure of the Eiffel Tower was an extension of the open structure of the wrought-iron bridge pylons Eiffel had used in earlier projects. The design is quite simple and consists of four large, curved, lattice-girder piers that taper as they rise and join near the top. These piers, which are joined together at two levels by connecting girders, rise from a large, square base stretching 410 feet (125 meters) on one side. The tower contains more than eighteen thousand individual pieces of steel, held together by about 2.5 million rivets, and weighs about seven thousand tons. As built, the tower stands at 984 feet (300 meters) in height. Including the radio and television transmission antennas that were added to the structure in the twentieth century, the tower stands 1,052 feet (321 meters) in height.

The Eiffel Tower was the tallest artificial structure in the world for more than forty years, from its construction in 1889 until the Chrysler Building was built in New York City in 1930. At the start of the twenty-first century, the Eiffel Tower remained the tallest structure in France. Construction of the tower cost approximately 7.8

million French francs, equivalent to about $1.5 million in U.S. currency. The prince of Wales, later King Edward VII of Great Britain, presided at the opening ceremony on March 31, 1889.

Although a noteworthy achievement in engineering, the Eiffel Tower was not universally acclaimed. Many influential Parisians were appalled by the structure. A petition signed by three hundred influential Parisians condemned the construction of the tower. The petition, which had been presented to the city government, reads,

> We, the writers, painters, sculptors, architects and lovers of the beauty of Paris, do protest with all our vigor and all our indignation, in the name of French taste and endangered French art and history, against the useless and monstrous Eiffel Tower.

Other groups also opposed the construction. Environmentalists, for example, feared that the tower would interfere with the flight of birds over the city. The tower, however, was popular with visitors to the Exposition Universelle: 1,968,287 people visited the tower during the exposition.

Eiffel, who had been the leading European authority on the interaction between wind and frame structures, wrote *La résistance de l'air et l'aviation, expériences effectuées au laboratoire du Champs-de-Mars* (1910; *The Resistance of Air and Aviation Experiments Conducted at the Champs-de-Mars Laboratory*, 1913). In this work, he discusses how he had based the distinctive shape of the Eiffel Tower on simple principles of physics and aerodynamics, developing new techniques for the design of very tall structures. On September 18, 1884, he registered a patent for "a new configuration allowing the construction of metal supports and pylons capable of exceeding a height of 300 meters."

Eiffel's company designed the tower so that the maximum bending or twisting force, called a torque, generated by wind hitting the tower is balanced by the torque that results from the weight of the tower. Eiffel calculated the curvature of the piers so that forces resulting from the combination of weight and wind would be directed down the pier at each point of force. This design led to the construction of a tower that resists the wind while also requiring the lightest possible structure, so light that the tower has roughly the same weight as the air that would fill a volume just large enough to contain the structure. The tower's open-frame structure minimizes the effect of the wind. On days with high, gusting winds, the tower is closed to the public, but the motion is small. The record sway of the tower was about 6 inches (15 centimeters), recorded in 1971.

Eiffel's insights into the design of tall structures revolutionized architectural design, ushering in an era in which massive structures were designed and built around the world. The skyscrapers erected since 1960, such as the World Trade Center towers in New York City, are (and were) similar in structure to Eiffel's tower.

SIGNIFICANCE

Since the time of its opening the Eiffel Tower has attracted more than 200 million visitors, with 6,157,042 visitors in 2002 alone. The tower was not intended to be a

The Eiffel Tower and buildings of the Exposition Universelle in 1889. (Library of Congress)

permanent structure. Eiffel's twenty-year lease on the site expired in 1909, and the tower was almost torn down. Eiffel had argued that the height of the tower made it uniquely suited as a location for studies of aerodynamics and for communications antennas, such as those for what had been newly developing radio telegraphy. Since 1918, French radio has broadcast its signal from the tower, and French television located its broadcast antenna on the tower in 1957.

People interested in sharing the tower's fame have performed unusual stunts on or near the tower. In 1923, one person rode a bicycle down from the first level. In 1954, the tower was climbed by a mountaineer, and, in 1984, two Englishmen parachuted from the tower. In 1989, the tower's centennial was celebrated with a musical performance and an eighty-nine-minute fireworks show.

The most widely recognized symbol of the city of Paris, the tower also has become a focal point for political demonstrations and protests. After the German army overran France in World War II, the Germans displayed a sign on the tower that read "*Deutschland Siegt auf Allen Fronten*" (Germany is victorious on all fronts). In 1958, just a few months before Fidel Castro came to power in Cuba, his revolutionaries hung their flag from the first level of the tower, attracting worldwide attention to their cause. In 1979, Greenpeace, an international environmental organization, hung a banner from the tower that read "Save the Seal." On Christmas Eve, 1994, terrorists hijacked an Air France jet departing from Algiers for Paris; the hijackers were planing to crash the plane into the Eiffel Tower, but French authorities thwarted the effort.

—*George J. Flynn*

FURTHER READING

Harriss, Joseph. *Tallest Tower: Eiffel and the Belle Epoque*. Bloomington, Ind.: Unlimited, 2004. An updated reissue of the definitive history of the Eiffel Tower, written by an international journalist, which describes the tower's design and construction and places its opening in historical context. Well illustrated and with a detailed bibliography.

Harvie, David I. *Eiffel: The Genius Who Reinvented Himself*. Stroud, England: Sutton, 2004. A comprehensive survey of Eiffel's life and his major contributions to engineering, architecture, and aeronautics; includes a discussion of the world's tallest buildings following the September 11, 2001, destruction of the World Trade Center's twin towers. The bibliography identifies major Web sites devoted to Eiffel.

Hervé, Lucien. *The Eiffel Tower*. New York: Princeton Architectural Press, 2003. The focus of this 96-page book is Hervé's photographs of the Eiffel Tower, but the introduction, written by architectural historian Barry Bergdoll, describes the controversial history of the tower.

Loyrette, Henri. *Gustave Eiffel*. New York: Rizzoli, 1985. An easily readable, well-illustrated, 223-page examination of the career of Eiffel, emphasizing the significance of his achievements. Includes a chapter on the tower.

Thompson, William. "'The Symbol of Paris': Writing the Eiffel Tower." *French Review* 73 (2000): 1130-1140. Examines symbolic interpretations of the Eiffel Tower, from writers such as Charles Garnier, Guy de Maupassant, Jean Cocteau, and Roland Barthes.

SEE ALSO: July 4, 1848: Ground Is Broken for the Washington Monument; 1855: Bessemer Patents Improved Steel-Processing Method; 1883-1885: World's First Skyscraper Is Built; May 24, 1883: Brooklyn Bridge Opens; Nov. 3, 1883: Gaudí Begins Barcelona's Templo Expiatorio de la Sagrada Família; Oct. 28, 1886: Statue of Liberty Is Dedicated.

RELATED ARTICLES in *Great Lives from History: The Nineteenth Century, 1801-1900:* Sir Henry Bessemer; Isambard Kingdom Brunel; Marc Isambard Brunel; James Buchanan Eads; Gustave Eiffel; John Augustus Roebling; Louis Sullivan; Thomas Telford.

May 31, 1889
JOHNSTOWN FLOOD

This flood was one of the most devastating in U.S. history, killing more than twenty-two hundred people. Caused by mismanagement of an artificial lake, the flood was also the first major disaster responded to by Clara Barton's American Red Cross. It thus represents both a high and a low point in nineteenth century American history.

LOCALE: Johnstown, Pennsylvania
CATEGORIES: Disasters; environment and ecology

KEY FIGURES

Benjamin F. Ruff (d. 1887), American real estate broker and founder of the South Fork Fishing and Hunting Club
Colonel Elias J. Unger (1830-1896), second president and director of the club
Andrew Carnegie (1835-1919), American industrialist and prominent club member
Clara Barton (1821-1912), American Red Cross organizer

SUMMARY OF EVENT

A floodplain city in Pennsylvania, Johnstown lies below the confluence of the Little Conemaugh and Stony Creek Rivers, at the base of the steep and narrow Conemaugh River Gap, through which drain many square miles of mountain watershed. Annual floods were taken in stride by Johnstown's residents, but in 1889, a confluence of natural and human events resulted in a much more devastating flood. The disastrous flood of 1889 killed more than 2,200 people and destroyed 1,600 homes and 280 businesses.

Rapidly melting snow and heavy rain over several days gathered in the South Fork Fishing and Hunting Club's Lake Conemaugh, where the pressure caused the badly maintained dam to burst and send twenty tons of water rushing down the fourteen-mile Conemaugh River Gap. The water scraped the dirt down to bare rock and swept away trees, houses, people, steel plants, railroad tracks, cars, and locomotives. It boomeranged off the arched stone bridge in Johnstown, creating a tidal wave that returned to strike the city following the initial deluge.

Neglect and parsimony by the South Fork Club's owners and bad judgments by its engineer and director were compounded by complacency on the part of those living downstream from the dam. The first recorded flood in the Conemaugh River Gap occurred in 1808, and floods were a fact of life for all those living in the valley. They occurred not only in the spring but also after heavy rain. Over the years, as timber was cut off the mountainsides and the river channel was narrowed to accommodate buildings, the floods grew worse. From 1881 to 1888, seven floods were recorded, three of them serious. Each year, there were rumors that the dam would break. However, the ten thousand residents of Johnstown and some twenty thousand others living in the valley were accustomed to gathering in the upper stories of their homes until the waters receded, then cleaning up and resuming their business.

Lake Conemaugh was an artificial lake originally built to augment the summer water levels in Pennsylvania's canal system. Its construction took longer and cost much more than was planned, and six months after the dam was completed in 1852, the Pennsylvania Railroad started operations between Pittsburgh and Philadelphia. The railroad was a faster, more convenient, and more reliable mode of transportation than were canal boats. The canal system was put up for sale, and in 1857 it was purchased by the railroad for $7.5 million. Five years later, during a heavy June rain, the dam broke. Little damage was caused, however, because a watchman opened the release valves before the level of the lake rose too high.

The reservoir, then only about ten feet deep, was abandoned until it was purchased for $2,500 by Congressman John Reilly in 1875. Four years later, he sold it at a loss of $500 to Benjamin F. Ruff, a real estate broker. Reilly recouped some of his loss by removing and selling off five cast-iron sluice pipes, installed when the dam was built and controlled from a nearby wooden tower that had been destroyed by fire in 1865. Four years after purchasing the property, Ruff formed the South Fork Fishing and Hunting Club and prevailed upon fifteen prominent and wealthy Pittsburgh men to buy shares in it. The charter members—including Andrew Carnegie, coke king Henry Clay Frick, banker Andrew Mellon, and Pennsylvania Railroad division head Robert Pitcairn—named Ruff as the club's president.

Ruff immediately boarded up and filled with debris the stone culverts through which the sluice pipes had run and created a lake one mile by two miles in size that normally contained twenty million tons of water and was seventy feet deep. He stocked the lake with fish. Club

Receding flood waters in central Johnstown. (Library of Congress)

members built cottages on its shore and drove carriages across the dam, which had been lowered several feet to accommodate them. When Ruff died in 1887, Colonel Elias J. Unger, a retired Pittsburgh hotel owner, was named club president and manager and moved to the lake. The melting snow of April and the heavy rains of May, 1889, raised the water level in the lake, causing some concern, but Unger's first thought was to prevent the fish from escaping.

By May 31, the rivers were rising at a rate of more than one foot per hour. Men arriving for their 7:00 A.M. shift at the Cambria Mills were told to go home. At 10:00 A.M., schools were dismissed. At 11:00 A.M., a log boom up Stony Creek burst, sweeping away two bridges in Johnstown. Meanwhile, John G. Parke, Jr., the young, new South Fork Club resident engineer, observed the floating debris and the rising level of the lake with some concern. Colonel Unger finally ordered the spillway cleared of debris, but it was too late: Water was flowing over the top of the dam, leaks were observed at its base, and at 3:10 P.M., the dam collapsed outward.

Trees and farm buildings were the first to go. As the forty- to sixty-foot-deep torrent crashed downward, creating mountainous backwashes each time it hit a twist in the valley, it began to claim lives. It engulfed railroad tracks, equipment, and stone bridges, as well as the village of Mineral Point. It swept onward, over railroad cars, houses, human corpses, and the village of Woodvale and its woolen mill. One out of three Woodvale inhabitants drowned. The torrent next flowed over the Gautier barbed wire works before bursting into Johnstown just fifty-seven minutes after it had left the lake.

People did not see the floodwaters coming, but they heard them. They felt the wind and saw the dark spray that preceded the deluge. The water bounced off the side of the mountain, washed back two miles upstream, and returned to Johnstown with renewed ferocity. The arched stone Pennsylvania Railroad bridge held, protected by a curve in the river. Against it, the river piled all its debris, which by now included many human bodies, as well as living persons struggling to survive in the floodwaters. As the debris piled up to a forty-acre area, stoves in smashed but partly intact buildings set those buildings on fire. Rescuers worked through the night but were unable to save all the victims.

As Saturday dawned, those still alive searched the mud and debris and the few buildings still standing, finding bodies and body parts, both human and animal. Roads were impassable, the railroad had been destroyed, no telegraph or telephone lines were working, and there was no drinking water and little food. Soon, however, rafts were built, and people on the hillsides opened their homes to survivors. Farmers brought food, water, and clothing. A temporary hospital and a morgue were set up, a police force was organized, and survivors were asked to register at a temporary post office.

On Sunday, the first train came through, bringing newspaper reporters, volunteers, doctors, nurses, work crews, police, firefighters, supplies, tents, and coffins. Two days later, Clara Barton and her newly organized American Red Cross volunteers arrived for a five-month stay to set up and operate a tent city. The disaster represented a baptism of fire for the organization. At her departure, Barton would be presented with a diamond locket, and upon her return to Washington, D.C., she would be feted by President Benjamin Harrison.

By the end of June, sightseers rode the railroad to picnic and buy souvenirs of the flood, including the books about the disaster that had already been published. Contributions, eventually totaling more than $3.7 million, poured in. Typhoid broke out, killing an additional forty people. Blame was placed on the members of the South Fork Fishing and Hunting Club, but they stayed away and remained silent. The exception was Andrew Carnegie, who with his wife visited that summer and were prevailed upon to build a new library in Johnstown. Unger also returned and lived out the remainder of his life above the old lake site. Suits were brought against the club, but there was nothing to award.

Although careful descriptions were made of all the unidentified bodies before they were buried, one-third of the bodies found were never identified. Hundreds of victims were never even found. It was months before there was any realistic count of the dead and missing, and an exact count was never made. It is estimated that one out of nine residents was killed by the flood. Two bodies were found as late as 1906. However, Johnstown was rebuilt on its original site.

SIGNIFICANCE

The story of the Johnstown flood is a significant part of history, not only because of the tremendous loss of life and the dramatic way in which it was lost but also because it exemplifies enduring facets of the human experience. On one hand, the Johnstown story is one of greed and unwillingness to take responsibility; on the other hand, it reveals the generosity of strangers and the indomitability of the human spirit. The South Fork Fishing and Hunting Club has been resurrected as a historical organization and charges ten dollars per year for membership. The breached dam stands, grass-covered and diminished, at the end of a dry field. It may be viewed from a museum operated by the National Park Service. In the city itself, where the arched stone bridge still spans the now-quiet river, museums and the Chamber of Commerce tell the story of Johnstown's major tourist attraction.

—*Erika E. Pilver*

FURTHER READING

Burton, David H. *Clara Barton: In the Service of Humanity*. Westport, Conn.: Greenwood Press, 1995. Sympathetic yet critical biography of the woman who helped minister to the victims of the Johnstown Flood.

Degen, Paula, and Carl Degen. *The Johnstown Flood of 1889: The Tragedy of the Conemaugh*. Philadelphia: Eastern Acorn Press, 1984. An illustrated period photographic text, showing firsthand the devastation caused by the flood.

McCullough, David. *The Johnstown Flood*. New York: Simon & Schuster, 1968. The definitive account of the flood, written by a well-known historian.

National Park Service. Johnstown Flood National Memorial. http://www.nps.gov/jofl. Accessed February 28, 2006. The official Web site of the national memorial dedicated to the victims of the Johnstown Flood. Includes information on the history of the flood and its impact on the environment and community.

Walker, James Herbert. *The Johnstown Horror!!! Or, Valley of Death*. Philadelphia: H. J. Smith, 1889. This is the definitive history written at the time, although according to McCullough, it contains many errors.

SEE ALSO: Aug. 22, 1864: International Red Cross Is Launched; Oct. 8-10, 1871: Great Chicago Fire; Sept. 8, 1900: Galveston Hurricane.

RELATED ARTICLES in *Great Lives from History: The Nineteenth Century, 1801-1900:* Clara Barton; Andrew Carnegie; Benjamin Harrison.

September 18, 1889
ADDAMS OPENS CHICAGO'S HULL-HOUSE

Hull-House represented an attempt on behalf of middle-class American women to address the needs of Chicago's inner city, many of whose residents were poor immigrants.

LOCALE: Chicago, Illinois
CATEGORIES: Social issues and reform; organizations and institutions; women's issues

KEY FIGURES

Jane Addams (1860-1935) and
Ellen Gates Starr (1859-1940), social reformers who cofounded Hull-House
Alice Hamilton (1869-1970), physician who labored under the auspices of Hull-House
Florence Kelley (1859-1932), early resident of Hull-House
Julia C. Lathrop (1858-1932), early resident of Hull-House

SUMMARY OF EVENT

While traveling in Europe in 1888, Jane Addams and Ellen Gates Starr, close friends who had been classmates at Rockford College in Illinois, pledged to live together in a poor urban neighborhood upon their return to the United States. This decision was prompted in large part by their struggle to find meaning in a world that greatly limited opportunities for women. During the last quarter of the nineteenth century, many of the first generation of college-educated U.S. women rejected women's traditional role as mothers and wives but generally were denied careers in business, law, the ministry, and medicine.

The daughter of a wealthy mill owner and banker, Addams graduated from college in 1881, then dropped out of medical school, spent two years touring Europe with her stepmother, experienced several bouts of depression, and led a rather aimless life. After attending a gory bullfight in Madrid in the spring of 1888, she was appalled and ashamed by her lack of disgust with the carnage and resolved to become involved in the lives of suffering people. While returning to the United States, she investigated several reform efforts in London, most notably Toynbee Hall, a social settlement established in 1884.

Starr had been forced to leave Rockford College after one year because of limited family finances. She then taught a variety of subjects at a fashionable school for girls in Chicago. Like Addams, she was troubled by a sense of futility and searched for direction, a quest that eventually took her from Unitarianism to Episcopalianism to Roman Catholicism.

With Toynbee Hall as their model, Addams and Starr rented an apartment in Chicago in January, 1889, and sought to clarify their goals, raise money for their endeavor, and locate a suitable house. They visited society matrons, leaders of Chicago charities, and clergy. They received pledges of support from the Chicago Women's Club, the Chicago chapter of the Association of Collegiate Alumnae, the head of the Chicago Ethical Society, and the city's most popular minister, Frank Gunsaulus. The directors of the Armour Mission, a nondenominational institution founded in 1886 that sponsored many facilities for the city's poor residents, were especially helpful. Dozens of speeches to clubs, mission boards, and Sunday school classes won Addams and Starr many generous offers of financial support and made them celebrities in the city even before they opened their house.

On September 18, 1889, Addams and Starr moved into the second floor of the old Hull Mansion, built in 1856 on South Halsted Street on Chicago's West Side. It was surrounded by factories and tenements populated primarily by indigent immigrants. By Addams's own description, the area had inexpressibly dirty streets, inadequate schools, poor street lighting, miserable paving, unenforced sanitary legislation, and "stables foul beyond description."

Addams and Starr had originally intended simply to live in an impoverished neighborhood and develop cordial relationships with the residents. Their initial plan was simply to be a presence in the community, both to learn from and to teach their urban neighbors. They hoped that other young, directionless, college-educated women would live with them and find a purpose by interacting with Chicago's poor. However, Hull-House quickly evolved into an institution that furnished a variety of programs and services to those living on the West Side.

Convinced that the influence of the neighborhood's more than two hundred saloons, numerous dance halls, and widespread delinquency could be reduced only by wholesome entertainment and activities, Addams and Starr started clubs for girls and boys, a lending library, music programs, and a social science club. Hull-House also provided hot lunches, child care, classes in English, and lectures on art and philosophy. They hung reproductions of great European art in the house, and Starr patiently explained the meaning of these pictures to onlookers. Although their neighbors initially were skeptical, two thousand neighborhood residents soon were visiting the settlement each week.

A gifted group of women, including Julia C. Lathrop, Florence Kelley, and Alice Hamilton, soon joined the Hull-House founders. To improve the urban environment, these women campaigned for more effective garbage collection, cleaner streets, public baths, parks, playgrounds, and better schools. By means of their experiences, discussion, debates, publications, and reform activities, they advanced both the theory and practice of social welfare in the United States.

Hull-House was not the first settlement house in the United States. That honor belonged to the Neighborhood Guild (later called the University Settlement), founded by Stanton Coit on New York's Lower East Side in 1886. Several months before Hull-House opened its doors, two of Coit's associates established College Settlement, also in New York. The roots of these early social settlements were complex. They lay in British Christian socialism, the Social Gospel movement in the United States (an effort of many Protestants to apply biblical social teachings to urban, industrial, economic, and political life), the humanitarian desire to help newly arrived immigrants adjust to life in the United States and the poor to escape indigence, concern for social control, and the rise of sociology as an academic discipline.

Settlement houses were part of a larger crusade aimed at improving working and living conditions in U.S. cities, which included hundreds of institutional churches, civic organizations, and reform agencies. As more and more people moved into congested urban areas, settlement workers strove to replace the long-standing view of cities as dens of iniquity that should be abolished with a vision of cities as centers of commerce and culture that

Hull-House. (University of Illinois at Chicago, University Library, Jane Addams Memorial Collection)

could be reformed through better housing, sanitation, transportation, employment opportunities, and recreation, and by creation of a sense of community.

Hull-House and other settlements also sprang, in part, from the broader quest of U.S. women to improve themselves and their society. This campaign gave birth to the Women's Christian Temperance Union, the Social Purity League, the General Federation of Women's Clubs, and numerous other reform and philanthropic organizations. Moreover, settlements both reflected and contributed to the growing belief that poverty was not simply a result of individual flaws and failures but sprang from larger institutional and social forces that society must seek to change.

SIGNIFICANCE

For a variety of reasons, including the remarkable residents and visitors it attracted, the many facilities it developed, and Addams's zealous efforts to publicize its philosophy and programs, Hull-House became the nation's showcase settlement and the prototype for the four hundred other settlements founded during the next two decades. By 1906, only the University of Chicago had more buildings and programs in Chicago than Hull-House. Those associated with the settlement made it a center for urban research and social reform. Journalists, scholars, and welfare workers flocked to Hull-House to study its success and advance its aims.

In 1895, Addams and others issued *Hull House Maps and Papers*, a detailed survey of the conditions of the nineteen different nationalities who lived in close proximity to the settlement, which stimulated further research on Chicago and other cities. Much of the settlement's fame, however, stemmed from the national reputation Addams achieved as a result of her many books, articles, and lectures, and her participation in various reform crusades. By the early twentieth century, Addams was considered by many to be the leading lady of the United States. She was widely regarded as a sage and a saint, a rare exemplar of both practicality and spirituality.

—*Gary Scott Smith*

FURTHER READING

Addams, Jane. *The Jane Addams Reader*. Edited by Jean Bethke Elshtain. New York: Basic Books, 2002. Selection of writings by Jane Addams, the cofounder of Hull-House.

_______. *Twenty Years at Hull House*. Edited by Victoria Bissell Brown. Boston: Bedford/St. Martin's, 1999. Scholarly edition, with additional autobiographical materials, of a book that Addams first published in 1911. Provides a detailed account of the establishment, operation, and philosophy of Hull-House.

Bryan, Mary Linn McCree, and Allen Davis. *One Hundred Years at Hull-House*. Indianapolis: Indiana University Press, 1990. Collection of primary sources about Hull-House, including numerous photographs.

Carson, Mina. *Settlement Folk: Social Thought and the American Settlement Movement, 1885-1930*. Chicago: University of Chicago Press, 1990. Extensively documented examination of the contribution of U.S. settlement-house workers to the development of social welfare. Provides a historical and ideological context for the work of Hull-House.

_______. *Spearheads for Reform: The Social Settlements and the Progressive Movement, 1890-1914*. New York: Oxford University Press, 1967. Overview of the origin, guiding principles, activities, and accomplishments of American social settlements during their early years.

Deegan, Mary Jo. *Race, Hull-House, and the University of Chicago: A New Conscience Against Ancient Evils*. Westport, Conn.: Praeger, 2002. Study of Hull-House between 1892 an 1960, with special attention to its place within the wider context of racial and ethnic issues.

Glowacki, Peggy, and Julia Hendry. *Hull-House*. Charleston, S.C.: Arcadia, 2004. Well-illustrated study of Hull House, which is discussed in the context of its surrounding community.

Levine, Daniel. *Jane Addams and the Liberal Tradition*. Westport, Conn.: Greenwood Press, 1980. Useful discussion of the background, context, daily operations, institutional growth, and community influence of Hull-House.

SEE ALSO: 1820's-1850's: Social Reform Movement; 1864: Hill Launches Housing Reform in London; July, 1865: Booth Establishes the Salvation Army; 1892: America's "New" Immigration Era Begins.

October, 1889-April, 1890
FIRST PAN-AMERICAN CONGRESS

Although this meeting of representatives from Western Hemisphere nations did not resolve many substantive issues, it set a precedent for inter-American cooperation that laid the groundwork for creation of the Organization of American States.

LOCALE: Washington, D.C.
CATEGORIES: Diplomacy and international relations; organizations and institutions

KEY FIGURES

Thomas Francis Bayard (1828-1898), secretary of state under President Grover Cleveland
James G. Blaine (1830-1893), secretary of state when the congress opened, and architect of United States-Latin American relations
Grover Cleveland (1837-1908), president of the United States, 1885-1889, 1893-1897
Carlos Calvo (1824-1906), Argentine lawyer who championed the sovereignty of Latin American republics
Andrew Carnegie (1835-1919), industrialist who was a member of the U.S. delegation
Roque Saénz Peña (1851-1914), head of the Argentine delegation to the congress and president of Argentina
Emilio C. Varas (fl. late nineteenth century), head of the Chilean delegation

SUMMARY OF EVENT

The first Pan-American Congress took place in Washington, D.C., between October, 1889, and April, 1890. The first inter-American meeting to be held in the United States, it was called by President Grover Cleveland through invitations sent out by his secretary of state, Thomas Francis Bayard. Delegates came from all the independent nations of Latin America except Santo Domingo (later the Dominican Republic). When they arrived in Washington, they were met by James G. Blaine, who had succeeded Bayard as secretary of state and who had long advocated holding a congress of this nature.

The pan-American ideal included the promotion of closer political, social, and economic bonds among the independent nations of the Western Hemisphere. It had its roots in a meeting called in Panama by Simón Bolívar in 1826 that had been attended by delegations from Central America, Colombia, Peru, and Mexico. The American representatives did not arrive before the end of the conference on July 15, 1826. Bolívar's conference was a failure, but it established a precedent for inter-American cooperation that would follow a "good neighbor" policy advocated by Henry Clay during the 1820's. Subsequent conferences in Lima, Peru, in 1847-1848, in Santiago, Chile, in 1856, and again in Lima in 1865, however, did not include delegations from the United States and reflected the fear on the part of many Latin American nations of U.S. expansionism.

By the early 1880's, the United States had recovered from the physical wounds of its Civil War (1861-1865), and its financiers and industrialists were eager to compete for foreign markets. The country's leaders started to concern themselves with Latin America, which appeared to offer plentiful opportunities for trade and investment. There also was a revival of interest in Central America as a site for a projected canal that would link the Atlantic and Pacific Oceans. In March, 1881, Blaine, who was then secretary of state under President James A. Garfield, stated that one of the major aims of the Garfield administration would be the conservation "of such friendly relations with American countries as would lead to a large increase in the export trade of the United States."

Successful trade, however, demands peace and stable governments, and wars and civil disorders were endemic in Latin America. Blaine, who also had a vision of U.S. leadership of American nations, made it his personal mission to bring peace and stability to Latin America. On November 29, 1881, in the midst of the War of the Pacific (1879-1883), which was being fought between Chile and a Bolivian-Peruvian alliance, Blaine issued invitations to the Latin American countries to send delegates to a Washington conference in 1882. His announced purpose for the meeting was to find a means of preventing open warfare among American nations. Blaine expected that peace not only would be beneficial to trade but also would lead to a pan-American alliance and give the United States an advantage in securing the rights for an isthmian canal in Panama. Blaine intended his Latin American policy to blend harmoniously pan-Americanism and the Monroe Doctrine. However, many Latin American leaders were less confident that those two doctrines were compatible. Chile, fearful that the meeting would impose an unfavorable settlement in its war, refused to participate, and the meeting was postponed. It was finally held in 1889.

The invitation that the U.S. government sent out for

its 1889 Washington meeting stated that the conference would deal only with matters of arbitration and trade and would be consultative in nature, rather than policy making. It set the goals of finding peaceful solutions to the problems of the Latin American nations and of considering "questions relating to the improvement of business intercourse and means of direct communication between said countries." It also attempted to "secure more extensive markets for the products of each of the said countries."

As a way of demonstrating the economic capabilities of the United States, Blaine arranged for members of the Latin American delegations to be given a six-week railroad tour of the country's industrial centers. Delegates traveled to Buffalo, Detroit, Chicago, Pittsburgh, Baltimore, and New York. The American interest in opening markets was quickly understood by Latin American delegations to mean increased U.S. business, as U.S. imports of agricultural goods from Latin America then exceeded its industrial exports to the region.

The actual discussions at the first Pan-American Congress, as the gathering came to be called, lasted thirteen weeks. Nevertheless, nothing was accomplished on the proposal to establish obligatory arbitration on disputes between among American states. The head of the Chilean delegation, Emilio C. Varas, believed that the proposal was the first step in the creation of a permanent court of arbitration, which he feared would be dominated by the United States, and he led the opposition by refusing to discuss the resolution or vote on it. Also defeated was the proposal of the United States to create a customs union in order to attain "trade reciprocity approaching a large scale free trade system."

By the same token, the U.S. delegation rejected a Latin American resolution that would establish, as a basic principle of American international law, that "the nation neither requires nor recognizes any obligations or responsibilities of aliens beyond these established by the U.S. Constitution and laws for the native born in the same conditions." The Latin American proposal stemmed from the fact that foreign investors in the area, in cases of conflict, resorted to appeals to their own countries, which often maintained higher standards of protection for individuals. The Latin American delegates, however, believed that this constituted a clear violation of the principle of national sovereignty. They adopted the position of Argentine lawyer Carlos Calvo, who had vigorously defended what he called "indefeasible sovereignty."

Additional areas of interest included port dues, patents and trademarks, extradition, and banking. There were also disagreements. Roque Saénz Peña, the head of the Argentine delegation, wanted to maintain an independent policy that did not defer to the United States. One difficult point was a proposal for international arbitration. Chile, which was especially sensitive to its territorial gains in the War of the Pacific, objected to compulsory arbitration. Secretary Blaine finally attempted to write a compromise statement, but it was never ratified.

SIGNIFICANCE

Despite the congress's obvious failings, considerable progress was made in discussing social and cultural matters. The delegates discussed the standardization of sanitary regulations, the building of an intercontinental railroad, and the adoption of uniform weights and measures. Furthermore, the congress agreed to the establishment of the International Bureau of American Republics, and the precedent was set for meetings that have been held from time to time ever since. The congress also created the structure for the Pan-American Union which, housed in a magnificent building donated by Andrew Carnegie, industrialist and a member of the United States delegation, would eventually become the Organization of American States.

—*Maurice T. Dominguez, updated by James A. Baer*

FURTHER READING

Bemis, Samuel Flagg. *The American Secretaries of State and Their Diplomacy*. Vol. 8. New York: Cooper Square Press, 1963. Includes an essay written by Joseph B. Lockey for the original 1928 edition. Chapter 5 discusses Blaine's participation in the Pan-American Congress.

Crapol, Edward P. *James G. Blaine: Architect of Empire*. Wilmington, Del.: Scholarly Resources, 2000. Biography of the U.S. secretary of state that examines Blaine's relations with Latin America and his attempts to upgrade the merchant marine and U.S. Navy. Crapol argues that Blaine hoped to establish U.S. hegemony in the Western Hemisphere.

Healy, David. *James G. Blaine and Latin America*. Columbia: University of Missouri Press, 2001. Examination of U.S. relations with Latin America during Blaine's tenure as secretary of state. Healy contends that Latin America was crucial to Blaine's foreign policy and his vision of America as a world leader.

Langley, Lester D. *America and the Americas: The United States in the Western Hemisphere*. Athens: University of Georgia Press, 1989. Provides an overview of relations between the United States and Latin America, denoting the changes in emphasis over time, including the Monroe Doctrine and the Cold War.

Mecham, J. Lloyd. *A Survey of United States-Latin American Relations*. Boston: Houghton Mifflin, 1965. Chapter 4 treats the concept of pan-Americanism, dividing it into two phases: 1826-1889, during which the United States was excluded; and 1889 to mid-1960's, in which there was hemispheric cooperation.

Pascoe, Elaine. *Neighbors at Odds: U.S. Policy in Latin America*. New York: Franklin Watts, 1990. Reviews relations between the United States and its Latin American neighbors, from the Monroe Doctrine through the Cold War, placing the Pan-American Congress within the framework of gunboat and dollar diplomacy.

SEE ALSO: Mar., 1813-Dec. 9, 1824: Bolívar's Military Campaigns; c. 1820-1860: *Costumbrismo* Movement; Dec. 2, 1823: President Monroe Articulates the Monroe Doctrine.

RELATED ARTICLES in *Great Lives from History: The Nineteenth Century, 1801-1900:* James G. Blaine; Símón Bolívar; Andrew Carnegie; Grover Cleveland.

November, 1889-January, 1894
DAHOMEY-FRENCH WARS

France's growing demand for economic, diplomatic, and military expansion along the coast of West Africa led to a series of wars with the Dahomey kingdom. The Dahomeans put up one of the stiffest resistances to European incursions of any sub-Saharan African people, but the wars eventually led to a complete French conquest, the exile of Dahomey's king, and the establishment of a French protectorate.

LOCALE: Dahomey (now Republic of Benin)
CATEGORIES: Wars, uprisings, and civil unrest; colonization

KEY FIGURES

Behanzin (d. 1906), king of Dahomey, r. 1889-1894
Alfred A. Dodds (fl. late nineteenth century), commander of French forces in Dahomey
Glele (d. 1889), king of Dahomey, r. 1858-1889

SUMMARY OF EVENT

After the establishment of its Third Republic in 1871, France sought overseas economic growth. In 1879, it began expanding its empire in Africa. The French started by advancing inland from Dakar, their coastal trading outpost in Senegal. They declared a protectorate over Tunisia, expanded into the Congo Basin, and sent an army into the Sudan, thus creating the basis of an empire in Africa that would eventually encompass most of West and Northwest Africa, large parts of equatorial Africa, and the island of Madagascar.

Along the coast of Dahomey, in West Africa's Gulf of Guinea, French merchants wanted to trade without interference from the ruler of the Dahomey kingdom, Glele. France wanted to protect its palm-oil trade by establishing protectorates and signing agreements especially at Cotonou, a trading town strategically located on a large sandbar between an intercoastal lagoon and the Atlantic Ocean. The French claimed to have signed treaties with the rulers of Dahomey in 1868 and 1878, giving them a protectorate over Cotonou. However, it is unclear whether King Glele knew of the existence of the treaties, as they were signed by local Dahomean officials. Nevertheless, the French used the disputed documents to claim control of Cotonou.

The French initiated the first Dahomey-French war. In November, 1889, Dr. Jean Bayol, the French lieutenant governor of Senegal, was sent to the capital of Dahomey, Abomey, to reassert French claims to Cotonou and the nearby town of Porto Novo, over which France had already claimed a protectorate. Meanwhile in Paris, the French foreign ministry portrayed Dahomey as a barbaric society to generate popular support for its invasion.

When the French delegation arrived at Abomey, King Glele was ill, so his son Prince Kondo carried on negotiations. Kondo would not accept France's offer of compensation for Cotonou and would not cede any territory to the French. Bayol then asserted what he called "protectorate rights."

After King Glele died at the end of the year, Kondo succeeded him, using the regnal name of Behanzin. Determined to resist French aggression, King Behanzin sent troops toward the coast as the French moved troops to Porto Novo and Cotonou. In February, 1890, Bayol arrested Cotonou's Dahomean officials and took control of the town in the name of France. Behanzin then sent part of his army toward Porto Novo and Cotonou. On March 4, the Dahomeans attacked Cotonou in two columns of three thousand troops, including one thousand of their famed female soldiers. The French met their charge with cannon and machine-gun fire. Nevertheless, the women's unit breached the French lines and engaged in hand-to-hand combat. Despite their bravery, the Dahomeans were repelled. They suffered losses of 127 dead inside French lines and several hundred dead beyond the lines. French losses were only 8 killed and 26 wounded. Although this first Dahomey-French war ended with the French in control of the coast, the French position was not yet secure. Behanzin still commanded fourteen thousand troops, including two thousand elite female soldiers.

Both sides sought negotiations. Several French delegations went to Abomey. On October 3, 1890, Behanzin signed what was called an "arrangement." It conceded the French control of Porto Novo and the right to remain and trade in Cotonou, but the latter town was to remain under Dahomean sovereignty, and Behanzin was to be paid twenty thousand francs annually. However, because of the growing expansionist mood in Paris and the French desire to link Dahomey with French possessions to the north, the "arrangement" did not result in peace.

Afterward, the French continued to fortify their positions, while Dahomey bought modern weapons from German merchants. French emissaries who visited Abomey were more interested in intelligence gathering than negotiations. Meanwhile, the French assumed that their presence in Cotonou meant they owned the town, while Behanzin believed that he still held jurisdiction. In March, 1892, the Dahomean army raided several villages twenty-five miles north of Porto Novo. The French saw this as an invasion of their protectorate and sent a gunboat up the Weme River. About eighteen miles north of Porto Novo the gunboat exchanged fire with Dahomean troops.

This incident precipitated the second Dahomey-French war. Although Behanzin claimed the gunboat had violated his territory, the French parliament declared war. The French Ministry of the Marine appointed Colonel Alfred A. Dodds, the commander of troops in Senegal and a veteran of France's Indochina wars, as commander in chief. The French estimated that the Dahomean army had twelve thousand soldiers armed with four thousand rapid-fire weapons and six thousand old-fashioned muskets. They also realized that Behanzin was preparing defensive positions. On May 28, Dodds arrived in Porto Novo and ordered the coast blockaded to prevent Dahomey from receiving additional arms. He saw only one course of action: a march on Abomey, some seventy miles to the north.

Dispersed along the coast, the Dahomean army did not know where the French would strike. On August 17, Dodds left Porto Novo and moved north along the left bank of the Weme River. His force consisted of 76 officers and 2,088 regular troops, including 930 African soldiers from Senegal. They were organized into five companies of French Marines and four companies of Foreign Legionnaires from Algeria. They placed five gunboats and two hundred supply canoes on the river. Over the course of their first fifteen miles up the river, they faced little resistance and built defensive fortifications to protect their supplies.

Meanwhile, as Behanzin received information on the French troop movements, he ordered his forces eastward to await the enemy. The first major battle in this war occurred at Dogba, halfway between Porto Novo and Abomey. The French units formed a square on an elevated hill beside the Weme. As they had done in the major battle of 1890, the Dahomeans attempted a swift frontal assault, attacking at dawn on September 19. The charging troops encountered a heavy artillery barrage and machine-gun fire. Female Dahomean sharpshooters fired from trees and killed one French officer before the French return fire put them out of action. The Dahomean attack was finally stopped fifty yards from the French line, and then French gunboats rained fire on the retreating Dahomeans. The battle at Dogba was a disaster for Dahomey.

The French then continued north, fighting from village to village. Their aim was to cross the Weme River and head northwest to Abomey. French losses mounted but were insignificant compared to those of the Dahomeans, whose heavy losses included many women soldiers. The French marched in a defensive square formation, prepared for an attack from any direction. Progress was slow as they had to clear defensive fortifications. With fighting almost every day, it took the French another month to reach Abomey.

With the military situation looking grim, King Behanzin sent a peace mission to Dodds. The French commander mistrusted the king, thinking he was stalling for time while preparing his defense of Abomey. Finally, the battles of November 2-4 at Cana, a sacred city near the capital, broke Dahomey's power. The remaining women's units were in the center of the battle. The French killed many of them with a powerful bayonet charge. Dahomey suffered four thousand dead and eight thousand wounded.

The fighting stopped after Dodds agreed to negotiations. Behanzin was willing to surrender his coastal possession but wanted to maintain an inland kingdom. Now promoted to general, Dodds proposed the creation of a French protectorate, the surrender of Dahomean weapons, and an indemnity of 15 million francs to be paid by Dahomey. Behanzin officially accepted these terms but surrendered only a few weapons and paid no indemnity. Believing Behanzin merely to be stalling, Dodds prepared his final assault. On November 16, he marched on Abomey, where the French encountered an unexpected sight: The capital was burning. Behanzin had evacuated the city and set it on fire. The remaining Dahomean troops and the king had disappeared. Dodds returned to Porto Novo. French casualties were 81 dead and 436 wounded, and the wars were still not over.

The French began what they called a "pacification" campaign to secure the countryside. By January, 1893, all major Dahomean towns were occupied. Nevertheless Behanzin would not surrender. He hoped to maintain some type of autonomy on the Abomey Plateau. With some northern regions still not under control, Dodds considered another campaign. In April, 1893, he left for Paris to consult with the government. He returned in August with a mandate for the total destruction of Dahomean power.

Thus began the third war. After landing on the coast, Dodds headed north with three thousand soldiers. Behanzin could not mount significant opposition, and many Dahomean officials surrendered. Behanzin could not be located, as he had help from the local population. The French were frustrated. In January, 1894, Dodds ordered the burning of areas suspected of aiding the king. Realizing that holding out any longer would cause needless devastation and suffering, Behanzin finally surrendered. The French made his brother Agoli-Agbo a figurehead ruler. They exiled Behanzin to the island of Martinique in the West Indies and later to Algeria, where he died in 1906. The entire kingdom was under French control.

SIGNIFICANCE

During the decades leading up to the Dahomey-French wars, the French and the Dahomeans were on a collision course. France was expanding trade on the West African coast, while Dahomey was determined to protect its territory. The French eventually destroyed the kingdom of Dahomey, which had been founded during the seventeenth century. The kingdom and the region around it eventually became a colony with the name of Dahomey within French West Africa, and its political system and economy were subordinated to the interests of France. The wars represented a high point of French imperialism and low point for the people of Dahomey, who became colonial subjects. In 1960, Dahomey finally regained its independence. In 1975, it changed its name to the Republic of Benin, after the Bight of Benin in the Gulf of Guinea. (It is not related to the Benin Kingdom in neighboring Nigeria.)

—*Thomas C. Maroukis*

FURTHER READING

Alpern, S. B. *Amazons of Black Sparta: The Women Warriors of Dahomey*. New York: New York University Press, 1998. Popular history of female soldiers of Dahomey, from their role as palace guards to regular infantry in the Dahomey-French war.

Bay, Edna. *Wives of the Leopard: Gender, Politics and Culture in the Kingdom of Dahomey*. Charlottesville: University Press of Virginia, 1998. Well-researched study focusing on Dahomey's political evolution and the political and military role of women.

Edgerson, Robert. *Warrior Women: The Amazons of Dahomey and the Nature of War*. Boulder, Colo.: Westview Press, 2000. Analysis of the role of the elite female soldiers in the Dahomean army.

Manning, Patrick. *Francophone Sub-Saharan Africa: 1880-1985*. New York: Cambridge University Press, 1985. Excellent survey of the political, economic, and cultural history of French colonialism in Africa.

SEE ALSO: May 4, 1805-1830: Exploration of West Africa; June 14-July 5, 1830: France Conquers Algeria; July, 1859: Last Slave Ship Docks at Mobile; Jan. 22-Aug., 1879: Zulu War; Nov. 15, 1884-Feb. 26, 1885: Berlin Conference Lays Groundwork for the Partition of Africa; Oct., 1893-October, 1897: British Subdue African Resistance in Rhodesia; July 10-Nov. 3, 1898: Fashoda Incident Pits France vs. Britain.

RELATED ARTICLES in *Great Lives from History: The Nineteenth Century, 1801-1900:* Sir Richard Francis Burton; Louis Faidherbe; George Washington Williams.

1890's
RISE OF TIN PAN ALLEY MUSIC

"Tin Pan Alley" was the nickname given to a section of New York City's Twenty-eighth Street, where many of the largest popular-music publishing companies were located. The name was inspired by the chaotic sounds of pianos playing simultaneously throughout the "alley." Tin Pan Alley popularized music, and its success opened the door to what has become a multibillion-dollar music industry.

LOCALE: New York, New York
CATEGORIES: Music; business and labor

KEY FIGURES

Thomas B. Harms (fl. late nineteenth century), founder of the Harms music publishing company
Isadore Witmark (1871-1941), founder of the Witmark & Sons music publishing company
Charles K. Harris (1867-1930), New York songwriter and later a music publisher
Monroe Rosenfeld (1861-1918), journalist and occasional songwriter

SUMMARY OF EVENT

Before the emergence of the popular music industry during the late nineteenth century, the market for songs and sheet music was limited to professional musicians and those wealthy enough to afford music lessons. At the time, music publishing firms viewed individual sheet music as a side business and focused their attention on items such as hymn books, lesson books for music students, and sheet music for orchestras. The composers who worked for these companies were expected to be music scholars with academic connections.

The larger firms maintained vast catalogs of classical standards and religious music, and songs were not advertised or marketed. Sheet music, which averaged fifty to seventy-five cents per copy, could be purchased only at a music or instrument store.

These realities changed in the years following the U.S. Civil War (1861-1865), when Americans began to have more leisure time. Minstrel shows and early vaudeville performances brought music to the masses, and pianos had begun to appear in more private homes. In 1887, twenty-five thousand pianos had been sold, driving the demand for sheet music, both for the classics and for songs heard on stage.

A new type of publisher emerged in response, a publisher that would focus on popular songs only. Many of these companies established their offices in the buildings on or near New York City's Twenty-eighth Street, between Broadway and Sixth Avenue, in an area that would come to be known as Tin Pan Alley. Two of the most famous and successful publishing companies were Harms, Inc., founded in 1881 by Thomas B. Harms; and M. Witmark & Sons, founded in 1885 by Isadore Witmark. Harms is notable for having been one of the first to see the potential in publishing the music from a successful Broadway play, while Witmark is famed for publishing songs based on newspaper headlines.

In the days before phonographs and phonograph records, the amount of sheet music sold determined the popularity of a song; songs also were popularized by vaudeville performers and in the theater. These new publishers responded quickly to trends in music and frequently imitated the success of their competitors. Songs were often topical in nature, referencing and responding to current events. Charles K. Harris's "After the Ball" (1892) is considered the first Tin Pan Alley song. Its sheet music sold more than six million copies.

To meet the needs of new consumers, the Tin Pan Alley music publishers hired songwriters and placed them under contract that gave the publishers exclusive rights to the music the composers created. For the most part, publishers either bought the songs outright or paid to have them written. Fifteen to twenty-five dollars per song was the going rate, and royalty payments to composers, while not unheard-of, were rare. Amateurs also trying their hand at songwriting submitted thousands of unsolicited manuscripts to Tin Pan Alley publishers.

The publishers also realized that songs moderately popular on their own could become hits with the right marketing. Sheet music became more than just words and notes on a staff; presentation became part of the package, as elaborate illustrations were commissioned for the sheet music covers. Sometimes the cover illustration was of the subject of the song, and sometimes the cover showed the performer who made the song popular. No longer was sheet music sold exclusively in music stores at fifty cents per copy; it was now available at stores such as Woolworth's and Macy's at one-fifth the price of music stores.

Each year, before the vaudeville season began, performers and their agents made the pilgrimage to Tin Pan Alley to audition fresh material for their acts. Performers and other interested parties could stop by the publishing offices to have the new music performed for them, either by the composer or by an in-house pianist. Marketing people, known as "pluggers" or "contact men," were responsible for getting the new songs into the music stores and concert halls and for persuading popular performers to play or sing a particular song. A big name performer could even commission music written specifically for him or her. Traditionally, performers would pay for their own sheet music; now, they received it for free because every performance offered a chance for publicity.

As the industry grew, the larger publishing houses began targeting and swallowing up the smaller houses. Publishers were no longer musicians or even necessarily music lovers; they were salesmen. Some of the top songwriters became embittered by their lack of royalties and became publishers themselves. The Music Publisher's Association of the United States was formed in 1895 to protect publishers' copyrights. One of the reforms initiated by the association was the extension of the music copyright to forty years, with the option to renew for another twenty years.

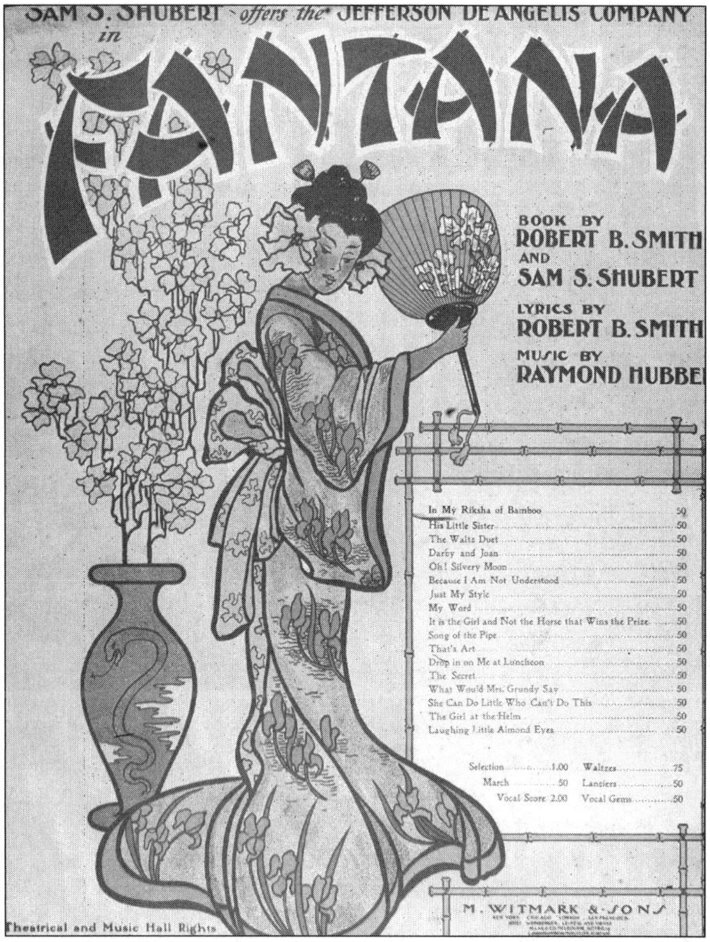

Sheet music for the 1900 production of the musical Fantana *in New York City's Lyric Theatre.* (Hulton Archive/Getty Images)

The phrase "Tin Pan Alley" did not come into popular use until it was used in an article about the music publishing companies that appeared in the *New York Herald Tribune* during the early twentieth century. The author of the article, Monroe Rosenfeld, was also an occasional songwriter and is said to have coined the phrase at the office of his publisher, Harry von Tilzer. While the two men met, they heard the sound of piano keys from the surrounding offices, and Rosenfeld noted the resemblance to the sound of tin pans being banged together. Eventually, the phrase "Tin Pan Alley" became a generic term that referred to any music-publishing firm.

SIGNIFICANCE

The demand for songs and sheet music increased in the final years of the century, as two new inventions, the player piano and the gramophone, revolutionized the way people could hear music. While pianos limited the appeal of sheet music to those who knew how to play an instrument, anyone could operate a player piano or a phonograph. Sheet music had been the only media available for music distribution, but by the late 1890's, publishers could distribute their songs also through player piano rolls and gramophone records.

The industry continued to grow after the beginning of the twentieth century. Legendary composers such as Irving Berlin, George Gershwin, Cole Porter, and George M. Cohan all got their starts with Tin Pan Alley publishers. At the time, it was highly desirable to have a song recorded or performed by as many artists as possible.

Gramophones would soon give way to phonographs, and radios would appear in private homes. Sources differ on when the Tin Pan Alley age officially ended. The date of its demise ranges from from 1920 to the end of the 1950's, when the birth of rock and roll effectively killed Tin Pan Alley. Performances became more important than songs themselves, and music was no longer marketed toward adults but to their teenage children.

—*P. S. Ramsey*

FURTHER READING

Ewen, David. *The Life and Death of Tin Pan Alley: The Golden Age of American Popular Music*. New York: Funk & Wagnalls, 1964. A classic and still-useful overview of the Tin Pan Alley publishers.

Furia, Philip. *The Poets of Tin Pan Alley: A History of America's Great Lyricists*. New York: Oxford University Press, 1990. Focuses on the songwriters who composed the music that made Tin Pan Alley famous.

Hischak, Thomas S. *The Tin Pan Alley Song Encyclopedia*. Westport, Conn.: Greenwood Press, 2002. Encyclopedic reference covering the most popular songs that emerged from the Tin Pan Alley era, including commentary and information about the composers.

Jasen, David A. *Tin Pan Alley: An Encyclopedia of the Golden Age of American Song*. New York: Routledge, 2003. Encyclopedic reference covering the Tin Pan Alley era, from the 1880's to the 1950's,

Tawa, Nicholas E. *The Way to Tin Pan Alley: American Popular Song, 1866-1910*. New York: Schirmer Books/Macmillan, 1990. An overview of the birth of popular song, which set the stage for the evolution of Tin Pan Alley.

SEE ALSO: Feb. 6, 1843: First Minstrel Shows; 1899: Joplin Popularizes Ragtime Music and Dance.

RELATED ARTICLE in *Great Lives from History: The Nineteenth Century, 1801-1900:* Scott Joplin.

1890
MISSISSIPPI CONSTITUTION DISFRANCHISES BLACK VOTERS

In 1890, Mississippi adopted a new state constitution. The explicit purpose of the new document was to prevent as many African American Mississippians as possible from voting, a goal accomplished through poll taxes, literacy tests, and other measures aimed to accomplish racial discrimination without violating the letter of the Fifteenth Amendment.

ALSO KNOWN AS: Mississippi Constitution of 1890
LOCALE: Jackson, Mississippi
CATEGORIES: Government and politics; laws, acts, and legal history; civil rights and liberties; social issues and reform

KEY FIGURES

Solomon S. Calhoon (1838-1908), lawyer, jurist, and president of the 1890 state constitutional convention

James George (1826-1897), U.S. senator from Mississippi and delegate to the 1890 state constitutional convention

Isaiah T. Montgomery (1847-1923), African American entrepreneur who was a delegate to the 1890 state constitutional convention

John M. Stone (1830-1900), governor of Mississippi, 1876-1882, 1890-1896

Edward C. Walthall (1831-1898), U.S. senator from Mississippi

SUMMARY OF EVENT

In the years following Reconstruction, Mississippi and South Carolina had the largest black populations in the United States. In 1890, fifty-seven of every hundred Mississippians were black. The Fifteenth Amendment to the U.S. Constitution (ratified in 1870) provided that no state could deny the right to vote on account of race; thus, Mississippi had a large black electorate. During the early 1870's, Mississippi voters elected hundreds of black officeholders, including members of Congress, state legislators, sheriffs, county clerks, and justices of the peace. During the mid-1870's, white Democrats launched a counteroffensive, using threats, violence, and fraud to neutralize the African American vote. After 1875, very few black men held office in Mississippi.

By the late 1880's, many politicians in Mississippi were calling for a convention to write a new constitution for the state. They complained that although only a small number of African Americans were voting, this small number could prove decisive in close elections. Many white leaders feared that black votes could decide close elections and worked toward a new constitution with provisions that effectively would disfranchise black voters. It would be difficult to draft such provisions, however, without running afoul of the Fifteenth Amendment.

The state's two senators illustrated the divisions of opinion that were so widespread among white Mississippians. Senator Edward C. Walthall argued against a constitutional convention, warning that it would only excite political passions for no good purpose. He felt certain there was no way to eliminate black political participation without violating the Fifteenth Amendment and that, if Mississippi made such an attempt, the U.S. government would show new interest in enforcing African American voting rights. On the other hand, Senator James George attacked the old constitution, claiming that it had been drafted by carpetbaggers and ignorant former slaves. George urged that the "best citizens" should now take the opportunity to draft a new state constitution. He warned that black voting could revive unless the state took measures to reduce the black electorate by provisions of the state's highest law.

A bill calling a constitutional convention passed both houses of the state legislature in 1888, but Governor Robert Lowry vetoed it, warning that it was better to accept the state's existing problems than to run the risk of creating new ones by tampering with the state's constitution. Two years later, a similar bill passed both houses of the legislature, and the new governor, John M. Stone, signed the law. Election of delegates was set for July 29, 1890. The voters would elect 134 delegates, 14 of them from the state at large, and the rest apportioned among the counties.

The state's weak Republican Party decided not to field a slate of candidates for at-large delegates. In heavily black Bolivar County, Republicans did offer a local delegate slate with one black and one white candidate. In Jasper County, the white Republican candidate for delegate, F. M. B. "Marsh" Cook, was assassinated while riding alone on a country road. In two black-majority counties, the Democrats allowed white conservative Republicans onto their candidate slates. In several counties, Democrats split into two factions and offered the voters a choice of two Democratic tickets. As it turned out, the constitutional convention was made up almost exclusively of white Democrats. The membership included only three Republicans, three delegates elected as independents, and one member of an agrarian third party. Only one of the 134 delegates was black: Isaiah T. Montgomery of Bolivar County.

Delegates elected the conservative lawyer Solomon S. Calhoon as president of the convention and immediately set about their work. Convention members had no shortage of ideas on how to limit the suffrage almost exclusively to whites without violating the Fifteenth Amendment. Some suggested that voters must own land, which few African Americans in Mississippi did. Others favored educational tests, since African Americans, only a generation removed from slavery, had had fewer educational opportunities than whites and therefore were often illiterate.

As finally devised, the Mississippi plan for disfranchisement had a number of parts, the most important of which were a literacy test and a poll tax. Under the literacy test, the would-be voter must either be able to read or to explain a part of the state constitution when it was read to him. This latter provision, the so-called "understand-

VOTING QUALIFICATIONS IN MISSISSIPPI'S CONSTITUTION

Article 12 of the Mississippi Constitution of 1890 established the qualifications to vote within the state. The sections reproduced below were explicitly designed to disfranchise African American voters.

SECTION 241. Every male inhabitant of this State, except idiots, insane persons and Indians not taxed, who is a citizen of the United States, twenty-one years old and upwards, who has resided in this State two years, and one year in the election district, or in the incorporated city or town, in which he offers to vote, and who is duly registered as provided in this article, and who has never been convicted of bribery, burglary, theft, arson, obtaining money or goods under false pretenses, perjury, forgery, embezzlement or bigamy, and who has paid, on or before the first day of February of the year in which he shall offer to vote, all taxes which may have been legally required of him, and which he has had an opportunity of paying according to law, for the two preceding years, and who shall produce to the officers holding the election satisfactory evidence that he has paid said taxes, is declared to be a qualified elector; but any minister of the gospel in charge of an organized church shall be entitled to vote after six months residence in the election district, if otherwise qualified.

SECTION 243. A uniform poll tax of two dollars, to be used in aid of the common schools, and for no other purpose, is hereby imposed on every male inhabitant of this State between the ages of twenty-one and sixty years, except persons who are deaf and dumb or blind, or who are maimed by loss of hand or foot; said tax to be a lien only upon taxable property. The board of supervisors of any county may, for the purpose of aiding the common schools in that county, increase the poll tax in said county, but in no case shall the entire poll tax exceed in any one year three dollars on each poll. No criminal proceedings shall be allowed to enforce the collection of the poll tax.

SECTION 244. On and after the first day of January, A.D., 1892, every elector shall, in addition to the foregoing qualifications, be able to read any section of the constitution of this State; or he shall be able to understand the same when read to him, or give a reasonable interpretation thereof. A new registration shall be made before the next ensuing election after January the first, A.D., 1892.

ing clause," was included as a loophole for illiterate whites. Delegates knew that voting registrars could give easy questions to white applicants and exceedingly difficult ones to African Americans. The poll tax provision stated that a person must pay a poll tax of at least two dollars per year, for at least two years in succession, in order to qualify to vote. The voter would have to pay these taxes well in advance of the election and keep the receipt. The tax was quite burdensome in a state where tenant farmers often earned less than fifty dollars in cash per year. Because Mississippi's African Americans were often tenant farmers, poorer than their white counterparts, it was thought they would give up the right to vote rather than pay this new tax.

In a notable speech, the black Republican delegate, Isaiah T. Montgomery, announced that he would vote for these new suffrage provisions. He noted that race relations in the state had grown tense and that black political participation in the state had often led whites to react violently. His hope now, Montgomery explained, was that black disfranchisement would improve race relations and as the years passed, perhaps more African Americans would be permitted to vote. The new constitution passed the convention with only eight dissenting votes; it was not submitted to the voters for their ratification.

SIGNIFICANCE

The new suffrage provisions went into effect just before the 1892 elections. The new voter registration requirements disfranchised the great majority of African Americans in the state; it also resulted in the disfranchisement of about fifty-two thousand whites. The new registration resulted in a list of seventy thousand white voters and only nine thousand African American voters. The predominantly black state Republican Party had won 26 percent of the vote for its presidential candidate in 1888; after the new registration, in 1892, the Republican standard-bearer won less than 3 percent.

Under its 1890 constitution. Mississippi had an almost exclusively white electorate for three-quarters of a century. This constitution served as a model for other southern states, which eagerly copied the literacy test, the understanding clause, and the poll tax into their state constitutions. Only after passage of new laws by the U.S. Congress in 1964 and 1965 would African American voters again make their strength felt in southern elections.

—*Stephen Cresswell*

FURTHER READING

Cresswell, Stephen. *Multiparty Politics in Mississippi, 1877-1902*. Jackson: University Press of Mississippi, 1995. Chapter 4 discusses the drafting of the 1890 constitution and its role in limiting the success of the Republican and Populist parties.

Green, Robert P., Jr., ed. *Equal Protection and the African American Constitutional Experience: A Documentary History*. Westport, Conn.: Greenwood Press, 2000. Includes the Mississippi Constitution of 1890, as well as many other relevant contemporary primary source documents.

Kirwan, Albert D. *Revolt of the Rednecks: Mississippi Politics, 1876-1925*. Lexington: University Press of Kentucky, 1951. Although dated, this remains the basic political history for the period before, during, and after the state's 1890 constitutional convention.

Kousser, J. Morgan. *The Shaping of Southern Politics: Suffrage Restriction and the Establishment of the One-Party South, 1880-1910*. New Haven, Conn.: Yale University Press, 1974. Detailed explanation of how new constitutions in Mississippi and other southern states led to a homogeneous electorate, essentially a small clique of middle-class whites.

McLemore, Richard Aubrey, ed. *A History of Mississippi*. Hattiesburg: University and College Press of Mississippi, 1973. Chapter 22, written by former governor James P. Coleman, provides a narrative history of the 1890 constitutional convention.

Stone, James H. "A Note on Voter Registration Under the Mississippi Understanding Clause, 1892." *Journal of Southern History* 38 (1972): 293-296. Argues that the understanding clause was not a grossly unfair instrument of racial discrimination, as is often charged. Lays the blame for disfranchisement chiefly on the poll tax.

SEE ALSO: Jan. 1, 1863: Lincoln Issues the Emancipation Proclamation; Dec. 8, 1863-Apr. 24, 1877: Reconstruction of the South; Mar. 3, 1865: Congress Creates the Freedmen's Bureau; Nov. 24, 1865: Mississippi Enacts First Post-Civil War Black Code; Dec. 6, 1865: Thirteenth Amendment Is Ratified; Apr. 9, 1866: Civil Rights Act of 1866; July 9, 1868: Fourteenth Amendment Is Ratified; Oct. 15, 1883: Civil Rights Cases; May 18, 1896: *Plessy v. Ferguson*.

RELATED ARTICLE in *Great Lives from History: The Nineteenth Century, 1801-1900:* Booker T. Washington.